T5:

D1149426

Learning Resource

LEARNING RESOURCE CENTRE ASFC

'Magnificent . . . This book is a definitive biography of a performing artist . . . It gives one not just an enormous admiration for the genius of Nureyev, but also a renewed respect and love for the art of dance'
Spectator

'A major accomplishment, the definitive biography of a major artist. It is a big book in every respect – in its reach, in its scrupulous composition, in its detailed analysis, but particularly in its generosity of spirit. Kavanagh makes no attempt to whitewash the monstrous Nureyev. By the end we have encountered a most difficult man, but a man whose unique gifts raised him far above us all' Brian Friel, *Observer*

'Kavanagh is the ideal biographer for Rudolf Nureyev . . . She writes about dancing itself so vividly, without technical fuss, that the reader imagines actually seeing it' Richard Sennett, *Literary Review*

'A meticulously researched and judiciously argued study which, as a record of Nureyev's career, will surely never be bettered' *Daily Mail*

'An engrossing study, sympathetic but clear-eyed . . . Kavanagh writes with authority, clarity and eloquence . . . true and honourable' Clement Crisp, *Financial Times*

'Impressive . . . reveals the narcissistic Russian ballet legend to be the prototype of modern celebrity' *Evening Standard*

'An exemplary modern biography, an "official" biography that is also a tell-all biography, of great significance as a prism through which to view the social, sexual, cultural and political history of the second half of the twentieth century, as well as being highly entertaining'
London Review of Books

'A magnificent example of the old school of biography – a warts-and-all portrait of a flawed but intensely lovable human being who ranks as one of the great performing artists of the last century'
Rupert Christiansen, *Spectator*

'Kavanagh writes thrillingly . . . with flair and abundance'
John Carey, *Sunday Times*

'An exemplary piece of work . . . keeps the reader turning its pages
even if sometimes in a trance of fascinated horror' *Irish Times*

'Julie Kavanagh's knowledge of her subject and her expertise in ballet
work together to evoke Nureyev's every step' *Vogue*

'Kavanagh reveals Nureyev's character, warts and all, as she charts his
rise from rags to riches in minute but gripping detail' *Tatler*

'It's unlikely that we'll need another study of Rudolf Nureyev after
Julie Kavanagh's' *Daily Telegraph*

'Kavanagh's definitive biography draws for the first time on private
papers, diaries and home movie footage, to create a portrait of this
extraordinary and troubled man . . . a fascinating read' *Daily Mail*

'Kavanagh tells the story of Nureyev's impoverished background,
defection to the west and international superstardom with great verve'
Independent

'Readable and revealing, a must for all ballet fans' *Saga Magazine*

'Superbly researched' *The New York Times*

'A rigorous and insightful look at a vital era of dance' *Time Out New York*

'The definitive biography of ballet's greatest star whose ego was as
supersized as his talent . . . A luxurious winter read, full of Russian
theatrics' Tina Brown, *American Spectator*

'A varied and vivid portrait . . . [Kavanagh] proves a lively guide.
She presents the intense minutes leading up to Nureyev's defection
with energy and descriptive power' *The Washington Post*

'Julie Kavanagh distills the fabulous spirit of Nureyev, the ballet world's
first pop icon' *Vanity Fair*

Rudolf Nureyev

THE LIFE

Julie Kavanagh

Date Rec. 6|4|11
Price £14.99
792.8
Dewey No. 792.8 KAV NUR B/C
2WL
Barcode T536023

PENGUIN BOOKS

PENGUIN BOOKS

Published by the Penguin Group
Penguin Books Ltd, 80 Strand, London WC2R 0RL, England
Penguin Group (USA), Inc., 375 Hudson Street, New York, New York 10014, USA
Penguin Group (Canada), 90 Eglinton Avenue East, Suite 700, Toronto, Ontario, Canada M4P 2Y3
(a division of Pearson Penguin Canada Inc.)
Penguin Ireland, 25 St Stephen's Green, Dublin 2, Ireland (a division of Penguin Books Ltd)
Penguin Group (Australia), 250 Camberwell Road, Camberwell, Victoria 3124, Australia
(a division of Pearson Australia Group Pty Ltd)
Penguin Books India Pvt Ltd, 11 Community Centre, Panchsheel Park, New Delhi – 110 017, India
Penguin Group (NZ), 67 Apollo Drive, Rosedale, North Shore 0632, New Zealand
(a division of Pearson New Zealand Ltd)
Penguin Books (South Africa) (Pty) Ltd, 24 Sturdee Avenue,
Rosebank, Johannesburg 2196, South Africa

Penguin Books Ltd, Registered Offices: 80 Strand, London WC2R 0RL, England

www.penguin.com

First published by Fig Tree 2007
Published in Penguin Books 2008

2

Copyright © Julie Kavanagh, 2007

The moral right of the author has been asserted

All rights reserved
Without limiting the rights under copyright
reserved above, no part of this publication may be
reproduced, stored in or introduced into a retrieval system,
or transmitted, in any form or by any means (electronic, mechanical,
photocopying, recording or otherwise), without the prior
written permission of both the copyright owner and
the above publisher of this book

Printed in Great Britain by Clays Ltd, St Ives plc

A CIP catalogue record for this book is available from the British Library

ISBN: 978-0-141-02969-6

www.greenpenguin.co.uk

Mixed Sources
Product group from well-managed
forests and other controlled sources
www.fsc.org Cert no. SA-COC-1592
© 1996 Forest Stewardship Council

Penguin Books is committed to a sustainable future
for our business, our readers and our planet.
The book in your hands is made from paper
certified by the Forest Stewardship Council.

To Ross for everything

623

CONTENTS

NUREYEV

1   A VAGABOND SOUL

Early one morning when six-year-old Rosa Kolesnikova woke up, she remembered first of all that she was on the train, and then she noticed the three Nureyev girls sitting on the bunk opposite. The toddler was whimpering, and her eight-year-old sister was trying to comfort her. She saw to her annoyance that her friend Lilia, who was also six, had taken her toy and was clutching it. Their mother was nowhere to be seen. Something was going on. In the corridor people were rushing back and forth talking excitedly, but no one would say what was happening. Later she noticed that next door there were sheets curtaining off the Nureyev compartment and doctors in white coats were going in and out. *Tyotya*-Farida must be ill. Throughout the morning, making some excuse, she and the other children jostled to see if they could peek through a crack in the screen of sheets, but her mother would call them back and try to distract them. 'Look, Lake Baikal! Lake Baikal! Isn't it beautiful?' she cried.

It was a cold, clear morning, and the lake, a sunlit ocean of ice, seemed to merge with the far-off white mountain ridges of Khamar Daban. For most of the day the train travelled along the southwestern shore beneath sheer cliffs and steep woods, offering sudden dazzling views of Baikal as it threaded through the tunnels. With its legend of the vengeful Old Man Baikal, who hurled a huge rock at his runaway daughter, the lake was a wonder for children: its size alone was breathtaking – four hundred miles long and one mile deep in the middle. By late afternoon, however, its fascination had worn off, and everyone was glad to get to the Mongolian city of Ulan-Ude, where the train stopped for several hours.

Almost all the passengers went into town to shop in the trading arcades and the poplar-lined main street, Leninskaya Ulitsa. When they returned, one or two of the women came up to the children with a large box and told them to look inside. There they saw a tiny baby swaddled tightly: 'We bought him in Ulan-Ude,' they said, laughing. 'It's a little Tatar brother for the Nureyev girls!' Rosa found this hard to believe. It didn't make sense that a Tatar child would be for sale in a place full of people who looked so foreign, with their big foreheads and slanting eyes. Besides, before they arrived, she had heard the adults talking about a new baby on the train. Rosa had a six-month-old brother of her own, but even so she was full of envy of the Nureyev sisters and tremendously excited. 'We were all in ecstasies, and in the carriage there was such jubilation! It was like a holiday, with everyone happy and wanting to share in the celebration.'

Word of the event spread quickly, and for the rest of the day people crowded into the carriage to see the new arrival: Rudolf Nureyev's first audience. His birth, he would later say, was the most romantic event of his life, symbolic of his future statelessness and nomadic existence. It was to be a life lived mostly en route to places, navigated by what he called his 'vagabond soul'. To Rosa he was never Rudolf or even Rudik, its diminutive, but *Malchik kotoriy rodilsay v poezde* said in one breath as a name: the-boy-who-was-born-on-a-train.

The order for the soldiers' families to leave had come suddenly. Almost full term in her pregnancy, Farida Nureyeva knew she was taking a risk by travelling at this stage, but she had had no choice. For the last two months, Farida and Ekaterina, Rosa's mother, had regularly gone together to the authorities to find out when they were going to be permitted to join their husbands, who were serving in the Red Army's Far Eastern Division. One delay had followed another until at last, at the beginning of March 1938, the wives were told that a military train would be leaving that night.

The children were asleep by the time the trucks arrived, and after waking them and bundling them in blankets, Farida left the barracks of Alkino, her home for the past nine months, and started for the station in Ufa, about forty kilometres away, where the train was waiting. There were two carriages set aside for the women and children, and a special wagon for their luggage. The compartments opened straight on to the corridor without the privacy of doors, but they were clean and quite comfortable, with an unoccupied single row of bunks on the opposite side, which all the children on the train immediately converted into a play area. 'It was the best of times! There was such a spirit of adventure and excitement.' Most of the wives were young, already friends, and delighted to be going to their husbands, whom they hadn't seen for several months. They were all very kind and solicitous towards Farida, making sure she had everything she needed, and each day one of the two doctors on board would come and check up on her.

The train travelled at varying speeds, sometimes racketing along, sometimes stopping for hours while waiting to be hooked up to another engine. At stations there was usually a straggle of *babushki* selling little piles of wares – spring onions, pickled gherkins, curds, smoked fish – but the women rarely bought anything, as the soldiers appointed to take care of them brought them provisions as well as hot water for tea and for washing. The children would have liked to get out and run along the platform, but their mothers were reluctant to let them go: they never knew when the train was going to leave. After nearly two weeks of travelling, everyone was growing restless. 'Is the Far East far?' became the children's endless refrain. 'That's why the day the little boy was born stuck in the memory. Given all the monotony, expectation and boredom, you couldn't forget such an event in a lifetime.'

Rudolf Nureyev was 'shaken out of the womb' as the train ran alongside Lake Baikal around midday on 17 March 1938. Farida was euphoric. Not only was the baby born safely, but at last she had the son her husband longed for. When the train stopped in Ulan-Ude, she asked one of the women to accompany her eldest daughter, also called Rosa, a solemn, responsible girl, to send a telegram to her husband, Hamet, with the news, even though she felt sure he wouldn't believe it. Once before, when her second daughter, Lilia, was born, Farida had sent word that she had given birth to a boy – 'She lied because she longed to make him happy,' Rudolf wrote in his memoir. It is far more likely, however, that as Hamet's work kept him away for long periods, her motive was to persuade him to return to their village. If so, it worked. 'Overjoyed, Father came home on leave as soon as he could and found out that the "boy" was Lida [Lilia]. He was speechless and utterly miserable.'

By 1938 Farida had been married to Hamet for nearly nine years, although they had spent much of that time apart. When they first met, in the city of Kazan in the late twenties, he was still a student, studying Tatar philology and the new ideology of Communism at the academy there. He was not then the rigid army officer he later became, but a debonair young man full of ambition and ideals. A studio portrait of Hamet at twenty-five, dressed in pinstripe trousers, dress shirt and bow tie, shows him sitting at a café table with an equally handsome friend, cigarette in hand; they look like a pair of Parisian *flâneurs*. Two years younger than Hamet and also of slight build, Farida herself was extremely attractive, with long sleek black hair parted in the middle, and dark round eyes. She rarely laughed, but had a quiet sense of humour that showed in her wry, closed smile: 'It came from inside as in a Rembrandt picture.' Although she had no education, she was bright and, like Hamet, self-confident and proud, giving relatives the impression that they both considered themselves a touch above their families.

The couple could not have chosen a more romantic place for their courtship than Kazan, with its elegant arcades and parks, and its skyline of minarets. There was a summer theatre, a bandstand and chairs, the beautiful fountain encircled with birch trees in the Lyadskoy Gardens, and the limestone-white kremlin on the hill from which one could look down at the boats far below on the Kazanka River. They both retained their nostalgia for the city, and years later would sing such Kazakh duets together as the 'Tower of Kazan', a plaintive ballad about the Tatar queen who chose to jump to her death from its upper terrace rather than forsake her birthplace. Before the revolution, Kazan had ninety-one houses of worship – monasteries, mosques and cathedrals – but by 1928, when Hamet and Farida were living there, many had been demolished by the Bolsheviks or were being used as administrative and storage buildings. Although brought up as Muslims – Hamet's father was a mullah – both were now party members, having been more than willing to exchange their religious beliefs for faith in the Communist regime. For them, as Rudolf said, the revolution was 'a miracle', opening up the possibility of educating themselves and sending their children to university, an opportunity previously undreamed of by peasant families.

Tugulbay, where Farida was born in 1905, was a large, relatively wealthy Tatar village near Kazan. Most households had a cow, but her parents, the Agilivulyevni, were poor, as there were four daughters and only one son to work the land. Farida's brother, Valiula, was fifteen years older than she, and when their mother and father died during the typhus epidemic, he took her and her three sisters – Gafia, Gandalip and Sharide – to live with his family in the city. Valiula's second wife, who was much younger than her husband, resented the sudden arrival of the four girls and loaded them with domestic chores. He, on the other hand, was kind and caring, and did everything he could to make them happy. Valiula had a phonograph and encouraged his sisters to sing and dance, and he sent them to school. Farida received an elementary education, learning to read and write in Arabic (but not in Russian), and left with no special qualifications. At first she worked for her sister-in-law as a nanny, but there was a good deal of conflict between them. Then, in the early twenties, during the period of NEP – the

New Economic Policy, which encouraged private enterprise – Valiula opened a bakery-restaurant near the Kirov Gardens, where all the sisters helped out. They loved being there: it meant that they were never hungry, and sometimes there were so many relatives sitting at the tables that there was no room for customers. Farida became an excellent cook, producing *kabartmi* (fried round cakes) from salty dough, and mastering the technique of making *pelmeni*, a type of dumpling, which remained her speciality. She was, her family claims, 'very good at attracting customers', and would stand at the stall outside the restaurant singing out her wares to passersby. One of them might well have been twenty-five-year-old Hamet Nureyev, who claimed to have fallen in love with Farida 'because of her good looks and sweet musical voice'.

In his Bashkirian village of Asanova, Hamet was known as Nuriakhamet Nuriakhametovich Fasliyev, the son of Nuriakhamet Fasliyevich Fasliyev. Saying he 'wanted to be different', he chose to use the shortened 'Hamet' and to combine his patronym with his surname when he left for the city. As children he and his brother, Nurislam, attended the local madrassa until 1917, when the Bolsheviks closed it down, at which point fourteen-year-old Hamet went to the village school for the next four years. His father, although no longer permitted to hold services, and forced to work in the fields, continued to be thought of as the mullah by the locals, most of whom still observed Muslim traditions and festivals.

With their two sons and three daughters – Saima, Fatima and Jamila – the Fasliyevs lived in a long narrow wooden *isba* at the edge of the village, the largest house in Asanova. It was a comfortable existence, with animals in the barns and rows of vegetables growing in the backyard. Across the dusty road was the Karmazan River, where the children spent so much of their time, swimming and fishing all summer in the bend where the water was deep and clean, and skating when it iced over in the winter months. During these long dark evenings the family gathered for music sessions, singing folk songs and dancing to Hamet's accompaniment on the accordion or harmonica. Sometimes, on a fine day, he sat on a bench outside the house and played for the local children, who sat cross-legged or danced around him.

In contrast to their neighbours, many of whom were illiterate, the Fasliyevs were one of the most educated families in the village. The siblings were encouraged to work hard, which Hamet did obsessively: 'Studying was his passion.' In 1921, when the famine years began, the school was shut down and the sole priority became the search for food. Asanova's mortality rate rose by the day; some villagers were forced to exist on *libeda*, a kind of gruel made from grass. Hamet had no choice but to join the workers in the fields until conditions improved. By 1925 he was working as an *isbach* in charge of the village club, organizing lectures on political issues, stocking the small library with propagandist literature, and arranging social evenings with dances and films. All the same he was restless. At twenty-two, he knew there was nothing but a peasant's life for him in Asanova, which to this day remains a backward village of primitive shacks. He felt he had to escape; young people were migrating to the cities to work, and Hamet wanted to be one of them. Kazan, the Tatar capital, a centre of science, culture, industry and commerce, was the obvious place to go. Deciding that military life was where his future lay, Hamet joined Kazan's cavalry school as a private in charge of horses; but either too impatient or too proud to work his way up through the ranks, he left after two years to continue his studies, enrolling at the Tatar Academy.

Farida, who met him at this time, had set her heart on going to the teachers' training college on the wide boulevard of Gruzinskaya Street, and when she married Hamet in May 1929 he promised her that after his course was completed it would be her turn to study. By the end of that year, however, Farida was pregnant, and by the following summer they had left Kazan for good. It had begun to look as if the promise the city had offered them had failed. Following the arrest in 1928 of Sultan Galiev, a prominent supporter of Muslim Communism appointed by Stalin, a number of other leaders of the republic – teachers, intellectuals and writers – were being prosecuted. Tatar autonomy was under threat and, uneasy about the outcome, Hamet decided to take his new wife back to his village. Stalin had just announced a radical switch from individual peasant farming to mass collectivization, and seeing in the changes an opportunity for self-advancement, Hamet volunteered himself as a senior worker in the Karmazan *kolkhoz*, Asanova's state farm.

It is not possible, as Robert Conquest has written in *The Harvest of Sorrow*, to separate collectivization from the savage policy of *dekulakization*, which took place at the same time. Those who had worked hard through NEP and managed to buy a horse or a cow were now branded *kulaks*, an enemy class that Stalin set out to liquidate (sixty-three per cent of these peasant families were either shot, imprisoned or deported). In Asanova, a poor village, there were no arrests, although locals still remember one rich landowner – 'The last capitalist!' according to eighty-five-year-old Hamza Usman Ula – in the Bayor forest who had hired paid workers and suddenly disappeared. Ula, a 'Son of Stalin', as he still calls himself, remembers Hamet's return and his attempts to persuade people of the benefits of collectivization. For many peasants it was abhorrent to have to hand over land, animals and equipment to the state. Their only resistance was violence, and throughout the country hundreds of murders and terrorist acts took place, many people choosing to destroy their livestock and crops rather than enter the *kolkhoz*. Even though few Asanova inhabitants were party members, Hamet, who along with two fellow villagers had been appointed proselytizers, found that he faced no serious opposition: 'People liked him,' Ula said. 'He was smart and he knew how to talk to people.'

By the autumn of 1930 Farida was pregnant again: her studying days were over before they had even begun. Hamet, however, was determined to continue. After working for eighteen months in a regional insurance office to earn enough money to support the family, he enrolled at the highest Communist *kolkhoz* school in the city of Ufa, about sixty kilometres away, for a three-year course in agriculture, eventually taking charge of his group. As Hamet's work often took him to other villages in the area, Farida was left to bring up their children alone. He was away one dreadful day when the new baby, Lilia, developed meningitis, and she lost her hearing because Farida was unable to get her to a doctor in time. 'It was March or April and the roads were mud. How could she have walked ten kilometres from Asanova to Kushnarenkova with two small girls?' remarks Lilia's daughter, Alfia. 'It was Hamet's fault,' she told me. 'She never forgave him for it.' As if acknowledging his culpability, Hamet was always especially tender towards Lilia, his favourite daughter, whom he would never punish. He was a good man who loved his wife and children, but his family was never his priority. Driven to succeed, he was becoming increasingly involved in local politics, and from 1935 to 1937 he worked as a political instructor for a party department in the Nurimanovsky region.

Over the next two years the Terror intensified. Along with the mass repression, and the murders and arrests of leading writers and scholars, Stalin and the NKVD struck at the best cadres of the Red Army, destroying tens of thousands of loyal commanders and commissars. These enormous losses were Hamet's gain. Profiting from the decimation of the military high command, he was among a second wave of recruits with the most basic military training to be appointed as *politruks,* a type of thought police employed by battalions to instil ideological orthodoxy in the men. A staunch Communist, competent worker and extremely popular leader, Hamet was ideal for the job. He could even draw on his religious upbringing. 'We were like priests,' a former *politruk* explains. 'The goals were the same. You had to communicate and inspire, take care of people's spirits.' Hamet began by working in an artillery unit, and within a year was promoted to senior *politruk* and sent to the Soviet-Manchurian border. Badly affected by the purges, the Special Army of the Far East was now increasing its numbers to deal with the recent deterioration of relations between Russia and Japan.

The greatest number of the new gulags were in the Russian Far East. It was there that 'enemies of the nation' were sent, herded by the hundreds into the infamous Stolypin penal wagons bound for Vladivostok. Following the very track along which Rudolf was born were the shaven-headed women of car number 7, stricken with dysentery, scurvy and malnutrition and rationed to a mug of water a day, whom Eugenia Ginzburg describes so powerfully in *Journey into the Whirlwind*. Their destination was a prison camp, to which they were marched by brutal guards in ranks of five, whereas Farida and the Ufa women and children ended their journey at Razdolnoye, a small town near the Chinese border, where they were met by a jubilant group of soldiers – the husbands and fathers who were waiting on the platform to welcome them.

Not far from the station up a main highway was a military settlement where the Nureyevs were billeted, sharing with several other families a long, single-storey building, which for some reason was known as 'Under the Roofs of Paris', after the film (and eponymous song) *Sous les toits de Paris*. The children loved Razdolnoye, which had a park where they could sleep out in hammocks on hot nights, an open-air cinema, and special activities organized for them by the army. Several families had portable phonographs ('pettiphones', they were called), and in summer with all the windows opened wide, in every corner of the camp the latest popular tunes were played – probably the first music the infant Rudik heard. It was a comfortable, cocooned existence, with only an occasional hint of the horrors taking place around them. 'Another musician or singer would be arrested and then we'd have to stop playing his records.' That summer in Vladivostok, where Farida once took the girls as a treat to shop for dolls, the poet Osip Mandelstam lay in a transit camp half demented and dying of starvation.

The hostilities between Russia and Japan were just beginning. In July, Hamet left his family for two months to join his battalion in defending a hill above Lake Khasan. This successful rout of the Japanese was directed by Marshal Vasily Blyukher, commander-in-chief of the Far Eastern Front, who immediately afterwards was mystifyingly arrested and shot on Stalin's orders. These were dangerously unpredictable times. Although Hamet remained with his artillery regiment for another year, he spent much of his time working on ways to get a transfer. 'He wanted the family to go to Moscow. He wanted that for Lilia.'

In Razdolnoye there was a kindergarten where Lilia was able to participate in games and communicate with the children in a sign language of sorts, but there was no school in the region that would accept children with disabilities; the only specialized institution for the deaf was in Moscow. Farida later told Rudolf that it had been her dream to educate her children in the capital – 'She wanted us to go to better schools and eventually to university' – and she was ecstatic when Hamet's request was granted. 'My mother wished that we had a Russian education. She even forbade my father to speak Tatar with us. That way it happened that, although paternally and maternally being Tatars, we spoke exclusively Russian.'

In August 1939 the family, this time accompanied by their father, set off once again on the long rail journey through the Urals and on to Moscow. Hamet began work immediately as a *politruk* in the artillery school on Horoshevskoye Street, opposite which they had settled into a small second-floor room. Over the next two years – the most stable period of Rudolf's early childhood – the baby would be lulled to sleep by the sound of trains rattling along the track beyond the back fence. As Hamet's work was so close to home, the soldiers became part of the family, playing with the children and sometimes smuggling the sisters under their coats into the local cinema. But such well-being was short-lived. In June 1941, when Hitler invaded Russia, Hamet was sent to the Western Front, and the military families were ordered to evacuate the city immediately. His division went on to help mount one of the most spectacularly successful counter-attacks in history: the defence of Moscow, for which, despite his lack of military experience, Hamet was decorated for bravery.

Although told to leave Moscow with only essentials, by turning a metal washtub into a makeshift trunk Farida even managed to fit in their samovar. She and the children were billeted in the village of

Shuchye, at the foot of the Ural Mountains, where they were given the most basic accommodation, sharing a room in a primitive *isba* with an old Russian couple who still clung to their Orthodox beliefs. Rudolf's first memories were of being gently shaken awake at dawn by the man or his wife, and led to kneel in front of an icon of the Virgin, kept constantly lit by an oil lamp: 'The peasants there gave me potatoes when I prayed with them, sweet, frozen potatoes. My poor mother suffered when she saw me . . . Brought up as a Muslim she had to watch her son praying to an icon in order to get something to eat.'

These were the years Rudolf called his 'potato period', a time defined by hunger, cold and loneliness. The winter of 1941 was one of the coldest on record, with snow piled up in dirty mountains on either side of the village lane, a 'narrow, frightening path' on which he played with no companions, games or toys. Almost everything had been left behind in Moscow, and except for a set of coloured pencils and paper animals Farida had bought to comfort him after he burned himself on their Primus stove, Rudolf had no possessions he could call his own – a deprivation he never forgot.

In 1942 Hamet, now serving as commissar of a mine battalion, arranged for the family to move into his brother Nurislam's apartment in Ufa. This small industrial town, the capital of Bashkiria, was just beginning to expand as factories (producing mostly arms and military equipment) were being moved there from Moscow and Leningrad as a safety precaution during the war. Today the city sprawls from the old centre along six-lane Stalinist boulevards as far as what used to be the town of Chernikovsk and incorporating Glumilino, the village in between. When the Nureyev family arrived it was rare to see a car in Ufa, and only the main roads were paved with asphalt; Sverdlova Street, where they lived first, was a muddy half-cobbled lane with single- or two-storey *isbas* backing on to a yard, characteristic of the old quarters of many Russian towns.

Although picturesque from the outside with their lacy, pastel blue wooden shutters, these little log cabins made grim dwellings: dark and cramped. Their second-floor 'apartment' was a room nine metres square, but at least they had it to themselves, as Nurislam was away at the front and his family was living elsewhere. Soon, though, Farida was able to find more spacious accommodation around the corner on Zentsova Street, where they also had more light as there were two windows facing the street and two more overlooking the yard. Remembering the kitchen and outside lavatory shared with eight other families, Rudolf was appalled in retrospect by the conditions in which he spent his childhood: 'Six people and a dog, all in one room. At night I could never stretch out completely and during the day I pretended for hours to read something, but I couldn't with everybody watching me.' On the other hand, communal habitation was the life most people knew, and it had its compensations. 'These days you don't know the name of your neighbour, but before we used to live as one family. If somebody needed something they would come and ask; if there was sorrow in one family it was sorrow for all families; if a letter arrived from the war it would be joy for the whole house.'

Everyone had approximately the same amount of money except for the Nureyevs: 'When the family first moved in they had nothing. Just an old wooden bed with a cloth on top and one blanket. Some of the neighbours tried to help and made a mattress for them by stuffing fabric with straw.' Farida was a fanatical housekeeper all the same, so fastidious that despite prizing every morsel of food, she would still cut off the outside of the bread and discard it, aware from her own experience of the unsanitary conditions of bakeries. Later they acquired a table made of planks that became the focal point of their life. For Rudolf, though, there was nothing cosily familial about these days, but only hardship and constant hunger:

> I remember those endless six-month-long winters in Ufa without light and almost no food. I remember, too, Mother trudging off in the snow to bring back a few pounds of potatoes on which we were to live for a week . . . When Mother had gone off on one of her exhausting trips in search of something to eat . . . my sisters and I would crawl into bed and try to sleep. We had sold everything we possessed and everything we could possibly exchange for food: my father's civilian clothes, his belts, his braces, his boots.

It was to Asanova that Farida made regular excursions on foot, a gruelling trek of sixty kilometres, but worth every step, as the Fasliyevs were generous with their crops and livestock, and would either share what they had or exchange food for army coupons. Setting off at around five in the morning, she would tow an empty sled behind her, hoping to have a sack full of provisions for the journey home – mostly potatoes but often flour, milk, eggs and once even a goose. The landscape, especially in winter, was drearily monotonous, its endless horizon broken occasionally by hamlets of brightly painted *isbi* surrounded by picket fences. When she reached the Podimalovsky Forest, notorious for its bandits, she would wait at the edge for a group of people to arrive, then cross it with them, as it was far too dangerous to pass through alone. At nightfall once, in a wood near the village, Farida noticed what she thought at first were fireflies all around, then realized they were the yellow-blue eyes of animals moving slowly towards her: she was encircled by wolves. Grabbing the blanket she had brought along to stop the potatoes from freezing, Farida set it alight, scaring the creatures away.

Arriving at last at the track that leads to Asanova, she counted the telegraph poles to see how much longer the journey would take – there were twenty per kilometre – and as she approached the family house would see the eager faces of her nieces and nephews waiting at the window. 'Farida-*apa* is here! *Ura!*' they would cry, running out to greet her. In summer Rudolf and his sisters often accompanied Farida – the only holiday they ever had. Madim, Hamet's mother, would prepare the house for their arrival, sluicing the floors so that they were cool and fresh, and ensuring that there was always plenty to eat, even meat for shashliks. The children slept on the big veranda or in the barns scented with sweet drying grass, and spent whole days on the river until they were gypsy-brown, swimming and throwing bread to net little fish they brought back for supper.

By 1943 Rudik, age five, was old enough to go to kindergarten, which meant that Farida could get a job. She had been ashamed when her son, whom she had carried on her back to school as he had no shoes, had been teased by the other children and called *bomsch*, the Tatar word for 'beggar'. She began working in the local factory that produced ice cream and *kefir* (a yoghurt drink), but was obliged to race back during her lunch break to provide a midday meal for her family, still dressed in her uniform of blue smock, white headscarf and rubber boots. (The factory floor was awash with water, causing the arthritis from which she suffered for the rest of her life.) The only perk was having access to ice cream wafers, which she and a couple of the other women occasionally managed to smuggle through the bars of the windows to their children. 'If their supervisor had caught them they would have got five years in prison,' said Federat Musin, who remembers standing waiting under the window with Rudik.

Farida was prepared to take the risk since they were still desperately short of food. 'Before the end of the war we really had *nothing* to eat,' Rudolf remembered. He once fainted from hunger at school, and to earn extra roubles, he collected old newspapers or used bottles, which he washed and sold back to the shop. When Hamet sent the family European chocolate from the front, Farida ground it into cocoa to sell at the market. Life was a bitter struggle, but Farida was determined that the children would have the best she could give them. 'In great poverty still you create a sense of luxury. Mother said I was very sensitive as a child. She never wanted me to see unpleasant things. She saw that I reacted badly to something ugly.'

For a New Year's Eve treat Farida bought a single ticket for the ballet, hoping to find a way to smuggle her whole family inside. At the entrance to Ufa's red-brick opera house, all five found themselves pushed through the doors by an impatient, elbowing crowd, and in the confusion were driven right into the auditorium. Even before the overture began, Rudolf was mesmerized; the wonder of the theatre's crystal chandeliers, stuccoed interior, classical murals and velvet curtains patterned with coloured dancing lights transported him at once from the grey world he knew. 'And then the gods came dancing.' *Song of the Cranes*, a three-act work based on a popular national tale about a bird-woman pursued by a hunter, is Bashkiria's *Swan Lake*. The star that night was Zaituna Nazretdinova, Ufa's own prima ballerina, her feminine, folksy movements in spectacular contrast to those of the charismatic leader of the hunters, who ends his solo by draining a bottle and flinging it off the stage. The drama seemed to speak directly to the seven-year-old, who felt utterly possessed and somehow 'called'. 'I knew. That's it, that's my life, that will be my function. I wanted to be *everything* onstage.'

By May 1945 the war in Europe was over and Russian soldiers began returning home. Full of excitement, Farida and the children went to meet the first train from the front, scanning the faces of the uniformed men in the crowd, but Hamet was not among them. They went back to the station again and again, feeling more despondent each time, until at last a letter arrived from Hamet saying that he was staying in Germany and would soon be sending for them. He was then working as a deputy commander helping to repatriate Soviet citizens – a welcome respite, however anticlimactic, from the action in which he had been involved. His rifle division had formed part of the Second Belorussian Front, which advanced across the Oder River, marching through Poland to the frontier, and helped to bring about Russia's victory over Germany. (For his 'battle merits' throughout these military operations, Hamet received two medals.)

As *politruk* of a battalion he was expected to be a leader. 'You ran in front of the soldiers shouting, "For Stalin! The Motherland!" secretly praying to God as the bombs crashed round you.' Loved by his soldiers, he not only inspired them to fight more bravely but acted as a confidant, listening to their problems and needs. His easy camaraderie shines out in a photograph in which he sits in a field surrounded by smiling comrades, one of whom, no more than a teenager, is playing the accordion. In another picture the boy is accompanying a comically stiff group of waltzing uniformed men, an event that Hamet, a keen amateur photographer, is likely to have captured himself on film as well as choreographed, as he made it part of his job to arrange *samodeyatelnost* – singing and dancing groups.

It was allowing himself to become too close to his men that led to Hamet becoming involved in a party in Poland that got out of hand. Brought up as a Muslim, he was unlikely to have been drunk himself, but was nevertheless held responsible and given a strict reprimand. This, combined with the offence – foreshadowing his son's future behaviour in Paris in 1961 – of 'communicating with foreigners' (socializing with Polish soldiers), led to his demotion from the rank of major. In August 1946, having worked for a year as a senior instructor in the political department of a 'capturing brigade' of the army, Hamet discovered that he was being retired. A character report cited, 'He has a general education, but not a special military one, which badly affects his work. In addition, his knowledge of Russian is poor.' Hamet's sudden discharge following his demotion was a humiliating blow, completely negating the medals he had won. It was a disillusioned and bitter man who returned to Ufa that summer to a family to whom he was virtually a stranger.

Except for a postcard he received from the front – 'My dear son Rudik! I'm saying hello to everybody, Rosa, Razida, Lilia, and Mama. I'm alive and healthy, Your father, Nureyev' – Rudolf had had no contact with Hamet, and held no childhood memories of him. His first impression was of 'a severe, very powerful man with a strong chin and a heavy jaw-line – an unknown force that rarely smiled, rarely spoke and who scared me'. Surrounded from birth by females, Rudolf had had no man in his life until then: both his grandfathers were dead, his uncle was at war, and so were most of the men in the neighbourhood. Suddenly he found himself supplanted in the household as the only male, and subjected to a whole new set of curfews and rules.

It was hard for Rudolf to obey and respect a man who had allowed his family to go hungry, and there was something comical as well as intimidating about his father's punctilious military manner. Every evening when he came back from his job as a security guard in a factory, Hamet took off his cap with his left hand and raked his hair with his right, staring straight ahead and never smiling. The ritual was always the same. On the other hand, Rudolf, like his sisters, felt awkwardly in awe of Hamet and wasn't able to look him directly in the eye. When the children addressed him they would use the formal *vy* rather than *ty* (the equivalents of the French *vous* and *tu*), which clearly hurt him. 'I told him it was because we hadn't seen him for eight years,' said Razida.

With his immense pride in having a son, Hamet came back from the war 'wanting to find a pal'. On their first outing together he took Rudolf shooting, hoping to impress him with the Belgian gun that had been given to him as a present by his Red Army superiors. 'He was so proud of it and would lend it to nobody,' remarked a fellow hunter. When Rudolf started lagging behind, Hamet decided to go on ahead and told his son to wait for him with the gear. Never having been alone in the forest, Rudolf was terrified. 'Suddenly I saw a woodpecker who scared me and ducks flying in and out . . . I started to say, "Papa, Papa, Mama, Mama."' Hamet laughed when he came back and heard all the wailing – the eight-year-old clearly needed toughening up – but Farida was furious when she learned about the incident. She could never forget her experience with the wolves.

Hamet's idea of male bonding was the traditional Bashkirian one of hunting and sitting around a campfire telling stories, all of which Rudolf found 'very uncomfortable'. Razida was more interested than her brother in hearing about Hamet's experiences in the war. He was not a man of many words – an army officer in Russia's political climate at the time was obliged to be taciturn – but occasionally a tale would emerge about how he had carried a hand grenade across the river Oder or how a German tank had targeted him, circling round and round. Given his gift for communicating with his comrades, it was distressing for Hamet to discover that he was not able to relate to his son. He began taking his nephew Rais hunting instead. What he could not know was that dance, already a fixation for Rudolf, would cause a far greater rift between them.

At kindergarten Rudolf, like most children, had learned folk dancing, immediately showing the kind of energy and spirit demanded by Bashkirian dance, and shining enough to be chosen as one of the soloists in school performances. 'From early years I knew how to be onstage and how to command it,' he said. Some concerts took place in Ufa's hospitals, where Rudolf and his little troupe were sent to entertain the wounded soldiers – an experience vividly rendered in Colum McCann's Nureyev novel, *Dancer*:

In the spaces between the beds the children performed . . . they sank to their knees and then they rose and shouted and clapped their hands . . . Just when we thought they were finished, a small blond boy stepped out of the line. He was about five or six years old. He extended his leg, placed his hands firmly on his hips and hitched his thumbs at his back . . . the soldiers in their beds propped themselves up. Those by the windows shaded their eyes to watch. The boy went to the floor for a squatting dance . . . When he finished the ward was full of applause. Someone offered the boy a cube of sugar. He blushed and slipped it into the top of his sock . . . By the time he finishes so many cubes of sugar are stuffed lumpily inside his socks that the patients laugh about his legs being diseased. He is given vegetable scraps and bread that the soldiers have set aside, and he crams them into a small paper bag to bring home.

It was when Rudolf moved to School Number Two, about a year before his father's return, that his real potential was spotted. A soloist from the theatre who came to give a course in dancing saw Rudolf and arranged a sailor's hornpipe especially for him, saying that he should go to the House of Teachers, a social club outside Ufa, where one of the classes was taught by a woman said to have been 'from the circle around Diaghilev', and who was, as Rudolf later remarked, '*almost* a real ballet teacher'.

Anna Ivanovna Udeltsova's studio on the outskirts of Ufa was a large hall with no mirrors, a barre made from a row of cinema chairs, and a stage at one end. It was there that Rudolf auditioned for her, performing a Ukranian *gopek* with emphatic arm movements, side kicks and big jumps, followed by a *lezghinka*, a Caucasian showstopper in which men, wearing supple boots, traditionally dance on pointe, with turned-in legs and fisted hands. Building up to a climax of turns and multiple falls on to the knee, the eight-year-old Rudolf stunned Udeltsova, who told him in her strange falsetto voice that he had a duty to himself to learn classical ballet, and must work toward joining the students of the Maryinsky Theatre in St Petersburg.

She began giving him ballet lessons twice a week, which immediately became the centre of his existence. 'Class was extraordinary ritual. All unpleasant things vanished.' Taking Rudolf under her wing, Udeltsova tidied him up, getting him to wash his hands and damp down his tousled hair before starting at the barre, and was soon casting him as the lead in her concerts. Even at this stage there was a feminine softness to his movements, leading a few parents to comment that it was only his costume that distinguished him as a boy. Nevertheless he was warmly praised for his talent, and sometimes given chocolates by a doting *babushka*. Often Udeltsova paired him with a ten-year-old girl called Valya, although neither felt comfortable about their dancing together.

> At school boys and girls studied separately so we were ashamed to be seen mixing with each other but, Rudolf so loved dancing that he was happy to do anything Anna Ivanovna wanted. We stayed behind sometimes to work on our duet but never spoke to each other and would leave the House of Teachers in silence, going our separate ways.

All the same, they were often teased about being 'a couple' by the other girls, who resented their special treatment. They would lie in wait for Rudolf before class, hiding behind snowdrifts until they saw him coming, then pelt him with snowballs and roll him in the snow while shrieking with laughter. 'Anna Ivanovna knew what was going on and scolded the girls, but it happened again and again.' Converting her students' behaviour into dance, Udeltsova invented a duet in which Rudolf and Valya exchanged a ball and a skipping rope, which diverted them from their gaucheness, and in another piece re-created the scene in the yard by encircling Rudolf with mischievous girls from whom he had to escape. For this piece, 'Dance of the Clogs', Udeltsova had somehow found authentic wooden clogs for the whole group. 'She was so inspired with ideas for ballets and so much in love with Rudolf that she made all his costumes herself.' For an arcadian shepherd's dance, Udeltsova kitted Rudolf out in breeches, a fitted jacket, and an eighteenth-century-style wig, and in the romantic 'Winter Fairy Tale', her homage to *The Nutcracker*, he played a prince who chose Valya, the prettiest snowflake, as a partner. In the end he was left alone onstage, opening his eyes and realizing it had all been a beautiful vision – the feeling Rudolf himself experienced each time he returned to his everyday Ufa life.

At first Rudolf had loved 'real school', and because of his unusually retentive memory, was one of its top pupils. 'I don't remember him being a brat like the other boys. He was outstanding for his obedience. If he had to go somewhere, participate in something, he would always ask permission in advance.' Geography, literature and physics were his favourite subjects, and he enjoyed the English lessons given by a woman who had studied at Cambridge, but once Rudolf had fallen under the spell of dancing, his school grades began to deteriorate and he became pensive and withdrawn.

There were days when he would sit . . . looking attentively at the teacher but he was in his inside world, dreaming about something. It seemed peculiar to the others and while he was sitting like that one boy would punch him from the side and when Rudolf would answer him he would receive a punch from the other side. While he would answer the second, a third would push his shoulder.

To the pupils Rudolf was 'somehow different . . . like a white crow', according to a classmate, and yet, however much they teased him for his eccentricity, he never conformed. During gym, when the members of the class were told to hold out their arms to the side, he curved his into a classical second port de bras. Much of his free time was spent listening to the family's 'terrible little radio', which was always turned on. He used to long for someone important to die because then nothing but the great nineteenth-century composers – Beethoven, Tchaikovsky, and Schumann – were played as a tribute around the clock. Almost every day he climbed the hill above the city and sat alone for hours watching the trains come and go. The sound of their wheels – the first lessons in rhythm, instilled in him from birth – gave him a subliminal thrill he later learned to exploit.*

He did not mix easily with children of his age, although he liked a boy in the yard called Konstantin 'Kostya' Slovohotov who always defended him. It was Kostya who put a stop to the girls ambushing him with snowballs at the House of Teachers. 'He was a big authority for us and the girls didn't dare try anything when he was with Rudolf,' Valya remembers. 'Many times Kostya came like a bodyguard to watch Rudolf dance. He would sit and watch the lesson and then the two would leave together.'

Kostya himself well remembers how unadventurous Rudolf was compared to the rest of the gang from the yard. Once they persuaded him to come on a fishing trip, which involved going part of the way by jumping on to a moving train. It wasn't hard, as trains always slowed down at a certain point on the track, but all of a sudden Rudolf turned on his heels and ran home. On another occasion a few of the boys decided to swim across the wide Belaya River, but Rudolf remained on the bank. Two girls dived in and tried to follow them but then got into difficulties in the fast current. Rudolf cried out to the boys to help, but he made no attempt to rescue them himself: 'He was jumping like a

---

* At the Kirov before creating a new role, he would often go and sit at Leningrad station 'until I could feel the movement become part of me and I part of the train'.

monkey and screaming on the side.' Rudolf already knew his destiny: he was not taking any risks.

He began seeking out the company of girls 'because he didn't like to fight', said Azalia Cuchimova, whom Rudolf often visited, lured mainly by the music they would listen to on the family's record player (her mother was a member of the opera chorus). He was also tender towards Clara Bikchova, who lived across the yard, and when he appeared her sisters would call, 'Clara, Clara, your fiancé's here.' But he grew closest of all to his eldest sister, Rosa, then studying to be a kindergarten teacher at Ufa's training college. A pretty girl with short curly hair, her father's black brows and mother's large shining eyes, Rosa was more intelligent than many of her contemporaries, and was considered the family intellectual. She called Rudolf *chertenok* (little son of the devil), but at home she was the only one who encouraged his passion. She herself was studying dance and piano as part of her course, and talked to Rudolf about ballet history, took him to lectures, and sometimes brought back costumes to please him: 'That to me was heaven. I would spread them out on the bed and gaze at them – gaze at them so intensely that I could feel myself actually inside them. I would fondle them for hours, smooth them and smell them. There is no other word to describe it – I was like a dope addict.'

Determined to make a man of his son, Hamet gave Rudolf a special position in the family. 'He did everything that my father thought a boy should do,' says Razida. 'Bring water, cut wood, bring firewood, dig for potatoes, fetch the bread.' This gave him a sense of superiority that never left him. Later, at the Kirov, he was the only dancer who refused to take his turn watering the studio floor (a daily drill carried out as a precaution against slipping), which he considered beneath him. His lifelong willingness to let women martyr themselves for him was also something passed on by his father, who shared the traditional Tatar view that a woman's duty is to serve a man. 'At home she must work harder than her husband and when he is relaxing she must still carry on.' When Farida was preparing a meal one day, she asked Rudolf to go out and buy something she needed, but at that moment Hamet came in and exploded: 'What's the matter with you? There are three women in the house and you're sending our son on these errands!'

Years later Rudolf would claim that his father had been physically violent towards his mother, but other family members find this hard to believe. Dressed in his Red Army uniform, which he continued to wear long after the war was over, Hamet might have looked threatening, scaring the children in the yard – 'He would come out glaring and we'd stop still like rabbits' – but Razida swears that he was never cruel. 'He was hot-tempered, but not for long, and I never saw him being aggressive to my mother.' 'Hamet was an army man with an army character but he could be soft and kind,' says Rudolf's cousin Amina, who came to live with the family when her mother, Hamet's sister Jamila, died. There were already six members of the Nureyev family living in a room sixteen metres square, the children sardined on one mattress on the floor, their parents separated by only a curtain. Amina insists that Hamet and Farida's marriage was a happy one, describing how in the evenings they would often sing duets together or go for walks with Palma, Hamet's chocolate brown hunting dog. 'The atmosphere was so calm, so peaceful. In the morning before he left for work Hamet would kneel down by us sleeping children and touch each of us in turn to say "goodbye."'

And yet, throughout his life Rudolf was adamant that he hated his father – 'a Stalinist', he called him, which he was, but so was his mother and almost every Russian at that time. There was only one real reason for his contempt: Hamet refused to tolerate his dancing. The extent to which ballet was interfering with his schooling was already clear from Rudolf's increasingly poor grades. Wanting him to train as an engineer or a doctor, Hamet saw his hopes for his son, and everything for which he and Farida had worked, being dashed. As Rudolf would not listen to reason, Hamet decided to seek the help of his son's class tutor, Taisiam Ilchinova.

> His father twice visited me at school. He asked me to use all the influence I had with Rudik. 'The boy is a future head of the family. Dancing cannot feed properly.' That was what made him upset . . . I knew Hamet-*agai* and he is not such an angry or blind person . . . [but] I am guilty because I did not talk to Rudik about that. I realised the uselessness of such attempts.

Rudolf, as Ilchinova realized, was '*very* stubborn'. The only influence he cared about then was that of Udeltsova, his ballet teacher, a highly cultivated woman who every summer would stay with relatives in Leningrad in order to catch up with what was new in the arts. She had begun introducing Rudolf to literature and music as well as talking to him about dancers she had seen from as far afield as Japan and India. 'She told me about Diaghilev, Massine and *The Legend of Joseph*; and how they all hated to dance barefoot . . . and how she worked with the young Balanchivadze [George Balanchine] who has always preferred girls with long legs.' And having watched the great Anna Pavlova perform, Udeltsova was able to convey how the ballerina had used her own electrifying personality to blind an audience to technical flaws – exactly what Rudolf himself went on to do. 'This conception thrilled me. The art of hiding art: surely this was the key to greatness in an artist.'

Like many Russians, Udeltsova was instinctively prejudiced against Tatars, a word synonymous in her mind not with Byronic hot-bloodedness but with dirt and savagery. She regarded Rudolf as a 'little Tatar boy, an urchin, untamed', and took it upon herself to educate him in St Petersburg etiquette and culture. After the revolution her husband, an officer of the tsar's army, had been banished to a Siberian labour camp and exiled to Ufa on his release. There remained a shadow of scandal about the couple, probably the reason why Udeltsova was never employed by the theatre. When she was reprimanded by the administration of the House of Teachers for making an exception of Rudolf by giving him free lessons, she was indignant enough to decide to close her studio altogether. She reassured her 'dear boy' that she was not abandoning him but would be sending him to a friend, also from St Petersburg, who had studied at the Imperial Ballet School and danced at the Maryinsky.

Tall and bohemian with dark skin, a gypsy scarf worn low over her forehead, and a voice made deep and gravelly by the cheap *papirosy* she chain-smoked, Elena Konstantinovna Voitovich now worked as ballet mistress at the Ufa theatre and gave classes in her spare time at the Pioneers Palace, the state social club for children. Intent on creating a serious approach in her young pupils, she could be extremely severe (even if they saw her in the street they would be expected to drop into a deep 'reverence'), but she had her favourites, and Rudolf was one.

She forgave him anything. He was a touchy boy and sometimes if she spoke harshly to him he'd walk away from the barre and go up to the window and just stand there in silence. Elena Konstantinovna would call him back, but he'd ignore her. So she would go up and tenderly say, 'Hey, Rudolf, It's O.K. Come on . . . Why don't you come back?' And only then would he join us again. It was curious for us to see that Elena Konstantinovna, who was so strict with all of us, would allow him to get away with such behaviour. When we were given presents after our *Elka* [New Year] performances we noticed that she would arrange for Rudolf to be given the best one. We weren't offended as we knew he was poor and that she was trying to help him.

At this stage Voitovich would have seen the ten-year-old Nureyev as gifted with not a great deal more than supple limbs, instinctive musicality and a strikingly compelling presence. Classical technique never came easily to Rudolf; he did not have natural turnout, and his proportions were far from ideal. All his life he wished for longer legs. But what struck everyone at the time was his intense commitment to dance. 'He took it so seriously, like a professional,' remarks one Pioneers classmate. 'Next to him the rest of us were just children.' 'He was so completely focused on what he was doing that he really impressed and inspired me,' admitted Natalia Akimova, who never forgot how he partnered her in a polonaise, standing in preparation beside her, his chin tilted imperiously. 'Then suddenly he let out a huge sniff – he always had a cold – but carried on looking so superior.'

As a dancer Voitovich had had a strong technique with a powerful jump, and was able to demonstrate very precisely what she wanted. She was also likely to have passed on to Rudolf tips on elevation as well as the rudiments of the Vaganova method, which she had learned in St Petersburg.* 'Elena Konstantinovna taught him to be professional, to do things cleanly and well,' said Ufa's veteran ballerina Zaituna Nazretdinova, who was regularly coached by her. When Voitovich choreographed *The Fairy Doll*, a special duet for Rudolf and pretty thirteen-year-old Sveta Baisheva, she explained the basic etiquette of partnering, showing them how to greet each other and how to move in unison. 'And she told us that the stage was a very special place. "Stage is an X-ray," she said. "The audience can see who you really are."'

In an interview he gave in the West in the 1960s, Rudolf claimed that his Ufa apprenticeship actually damaged him as a dancer. 'I am the wrong shape, the wrong size. When I started to dance I lacked the proper training so that I deformed both my body and my muscles.' Pictures taken of him at the barre in an Ufa studio show muscle-bound legs more characteristic of an athlete than a dancer, but whether this was Rudolf's natural physique or a result of early teaching is hard to assess. Voitovich was without question a responsible teacher who

* Named after the famous pedagogue whose system defines twentieth-century Russian ballet, Vaganova teaching works the whole body in harmony, emphasizing the expressive use of the eyes, head, arms, and shoulders while strengthening the legs and feet.

provided Rudolf with a sound classical base, but at the same time her exercises were designed more to develop than to elongate the leg muscles. 'That comes from modern methods in ballet and was something Rudolf would have learned later. Elena Konstantinovna was preserving the old classical traditions of everything being very clear and pure, but she didn't pay much attention to really lengthening the movements to their maximum.'

Yet Voitovich, as one of her pupils remarked, 'wasn't only giving us ballet classes, she was developing us spiritually'. A recently widowed St Petersburg intellectual, she began inviting Rudolf to tea at her home nearby, where she lived with her aged mother, who had once been a lady-in-waiting at the tsar's court and was always beautifully dressed and coiffed. Although they had only one small room in a communal apartment, it was full of elegant furniture and had a special, sweetly scented atmosphere that her pupils still remember. 'Elena Konstantinovna set a very high and special example. She believed in teaching boys to be gentlemen because she said that it showed when they danced.' While her mother served tea in traditional style, with little pots of jam, Voitovich held Rudolf fascinated by talking of her youth. She described how she and the other children at the Imperial Ballet School had been dressed in fur-lined capes and transported in carriages through the White Nights to performances at the Maryinsky Theatre. She illustrated her stories with photographs she kept in an old album. She, together with Udeltsova and another St Petersburg exile, Irina Alexandrovna Voronina, a pianist at the Pioneer Palace and concertmaster for the Ufa Ballet, formed a triumvirate of female mentors, with Voronina soon to become Rudolf's most dedicated champion of all.

A stout motherly figure with a kind, doughy face, Irina Alexandrovna was, an Ufa dancer commented, 'a one-person orchestra' who could make a solo piano piece sound like a symphony. In winter it was so cold in the studio that she wore gloves and yet still played beautifully. During rehearsals, she would sit on the piano stool with a cigarette in the corner of her mouth, unable to resist calling out corrections to the pupils. Rudolf's musicality immediately caught her attention and, intent on developing it, she began teaching him simple tunes on the piano at her home. 'She adored Rudolf and would have shared every last thing she owned with him.'

With music becoming almost as much of a passion as dance, Rudolf went to his father one day and begged him to buy a piano. Hamet was sympathetic. He loved music, too, but a piano was out of the question.

How could they possibly afford it? And even if they could, where was there space to put it? He offered to get his son an accordion, telling him that he could make himself popular at parties by entertaining his friends. 'You can't carry [a piano] on your shoulders.' Rudolf refused. 'Even then I knew this is ugly music.' But although he never played the instrument, towards the end of his life in an extraordinary fantasy motivated partly by wishful thinking, partly by the wish to concoct a good story, he told an audience of fund-raisers in San Francisco that Hamet had indeed bought him an accordion, 'so that I could go from bar to bar and get money'. He described how he had played it with expertise, and how after watching him waltz around the room with it as if it were a partner, his father had exclaimed, 'You can dance, my boy! I'm going to take you to Leningrad so that you can study at the Kirov!' Everyone in the room believed the story.

As far as Rudolf was concerned, Hamet was his enemy, forcing him to become underhanded and deceitful, in his endless struggle to overcome the obstacles standing between him and his passion for dancing. He liked to think that his mother was on his side, but Farida was just as concerned that dance was a precarious career for a man. 'Rosa, my only ally, had now gone to Leningrad. I became more and more distressed and secretive.' As an excuse to leave the house in order to go to class, he would volunteer to get bread or kerosene, often forgetting the errand itself and having to run back for the empty canister, which he had left in a corner of the studio. He claims that his father beat him every time he caught him, but Albert Aslanov, who had known Rudolf since their kindergarten days, takes a different view.

I never saw him beating Rudolf or swearing at him. He used to get Rudolf to roll the foil shots he needed for hunting and I would often help him till we were almost dead. Sometimes Rudolf didn't finish the job and Hamet-*abiy* could get quite angry and give him a clip on the arse, but all the fathers did that. It wasn't serious.

Albert's own father was far more tolerant about his dancing, his attitude being that it was better than being on the street. The boys in their yard were frequently in trouble – two grew up to be pickpockets – and everyone was involved in stealing from the vegetable gardens. 'Rudolf was our lookout,' says Federat Musin. 'He'd watch by the hole we'd made in the fence. We weren't often caught because we never went to the same place twice, but once we were shot at with salt pellets.' This gang of adolescents was 'a little like a wolf pack'; membership was compulsory, although Rudolf avoided doing anything – ski-jumping off *isba* roofs, for example – that might endanger his dancing. 'He wasn't mad about doing things with us,' remembers Kostya. 'It was always something a bit on the side for him. He preferred to be at the Pioneers.' Rudolf was never mocked for his interest in ballet – on the contrary, he was able to persuade a few of the boys from the yard to join his class – because the gang rule was never to pick on anybody: 'We were all for one and one for all.' He also made sure that he was active enough not to be considered an outsider. On a summer evening if he saw a ball game taking place in the yard, he would put down the kerosene can he was carrying and join in. The boys played *lapta,* a Russian version of cricket, or football, using a homemade ball stuffed with hay.

> When it got destroyed, it would be someone else's turn to cover and sew it for the next day. Because there were no showers at home, after a match we'd go our usual shortcut – twelve or fifteen of us – to cool off in the river. Everyone's underwear was full of holes so we'd strip off and dive in. There were no girls around. We all knew how to swim and would stay in the water until our lips were blue.

Even in winter Rudolf loved the river, and often ran down the hill after school with the other boys to watch the icebreaker in action. Once it crashed into some shanty dwellings by the shore, and they saw whole houses floating downriver with their inhabitants clinging to the corrugated iron roofs. But his favourite activity was the trips to the Rodina cinema, a building with a classical façade, even grander than the opera house, where one could see American 'trophy' movies that had been captured by the Soviets at the end of the war. It was in Ufa that Rudolf first saw Charlie Chaplin, a lifelong inspiration, influencing his own approach to physical comedy. To screenwriter Jean-Claude Carrière he later described other Western films he saw in Ufa.

> I remember those of Deanna Durbin, especially the one in which she appeared to wear more than a thousand skirts. She was very famous in Russia. Among the first films I saw was *Lady Hamilton* [*That Hamilton Woman*], with Vivien Leigh, *Waterloo Bridge* of Mervyn Le Roy and a film which I think was called *Ballerina*. A lot of them were in their original version with subtitles. For us, as for all the kids in the world at the end of the Forties, the cinema was a real passion.

The real catalyst was *Tarzan, the Ape Man*, a film Joseph Brodsky once said was more important to freethinking in Russia than *A Day in the Life of Ivan Denisovich*. 'This was the first movie in which we saw natural life. And long hair. And that marvellous cry of Tarzan which . . . hung over every Russian city. We were so eager to imitate Tarzan. That's what started it all.' In Ufa it was almost impossible to get tickets, and the gang half carried Kostya, 'stepping on people's heads' to get to the front of the crowd. *Tarzan* was the event of the year for them all, although Albert Aslanov refutes any deeper significance. 'It was about such great adventures, and we were boys. We had no feeling that we weren't free at that point: we had all the freedom we needed.' Except for Rudolf.

At home he felt like a prisoner. Hamet often fell asleep after supper, and Rudolf seized the chance to run out to folk-dancing classes that were held for workers two evenings a week. By now, though, Hamet was surely turning a blind eye, as Rudolf managed to stay out long enough to join the amateur troupe's night tours of neighbouring villages. Their performances – 'as wildly improvised and as primitive as when the theatre first began in Russia' – played to an audience sitting on rough benches surrounded by hanging kerosene lamps. The stage was a wooden platform balanced between two parked lorries, and a backdrop was made out of red-and-blue floral cotton – 'the kind you find in every Tatar *isba* on cushions, beds, and in the alcoves, a fabric that makes you warm just to think about it'. The experience remained so indelible that Rudolf re-created it in 1966 as a scene in the second act of his own production of *Don Quixote*. The village attitudes and traditions of Russian folk dance from the Ukraine, Moldavia and the Cossack steppes were a crucial influence on Rudolf, their power to ignite an audience clearly the force behind his own dynamism onstage. Full of aggression, Bashkirian dance envisages the male as hunter, with motifs like stalking with a bow and galloping hooves symbolized by movement. People still remember the command Rudolf showed during the hunting scene of the Kirov's *Sleeping Beauty*: he would find his own way of excelling at his father's favourite pastime.

There were times when Hamet was almost resigned to the idea of his son making a career of dance. When Rudolf discovered that a group of local children were to be sent to Leningrad to audition for the Kirov school, Hamet went with him to the theatre to find out more. 'He had all the goodwill,' Rudolf admitted later. They asked a cashier about the registration procedure, only to discover that the party had already left. 'It took me days to climb out of a state of black despair. For a long time after this incident my father seemed embarrassed whenever he laid eyes on me.' The reason became clear to Rudolf years later: Hamet simply didn't have the necessary two hundred roubles to buy a train ticket from Ufa to Leningrad.

As he progressed through his teens, Rudolf hardly involved himself in the usual adolescent pursuits – 'He could think of nothing else besides dancing' – although he once went with Kostya to a dance hall. 'Just to watch.' He gave no inkling of nascent homosexual tendencies, and his friends don't remember him paying much attention to girls except perhaps to Sveta, his shapely Pioneer partner, whom he made a point of sitting next to during breaks, even though he knew she was not interested in him. According to Sveta, 'He always dressed very poorly with holes in his socks, and a black velvet jacket which looked terribly old the first time I saw it, and he wore it for years after that.'

By now he was growing away from Kostya and the yard gang, spending almost all his time in the company of Albert, also a dedicated pupil of Voitovich. The pair were both so smitten with dance that during lessons they drew doodles of ballerinas' legs on their exercise books. Albert was the editor of the *Stengazeta*, the school's newspaper, to which Rudolf contributed, staying up one night to draw a picture of the scientist and poet Mikhail Lomonosov. They went often to Ufa's elegant art gallery, the Nesterov, named after the nineteenth-century artist who had spent his early life in the city. The two boys collected postcards of paintings by favourite artists – Ilya Repin and Valentin Serov among them – and talked of the day they would go to Moscow to see even finer examples of their work.

On 5 March 1953 Stalin died. His statue, eight metres high, was next to the opera house, and all around the block the grieving people of Ufa stood in line to place flowers at his feet. In Moscow, where Sergey Prokofiev died on the same day, the streets were blocked off, traffic was at a standstill, and all the florists' shops had been emptied. 'Nowhere could one buy even a few flowers to place on the coffin of the great Russian composer,' writes the soprano Galina Vishnevskaya. 'In newspapers, there was no room for an obituary. Everything was Stalin's – even the ashes of Prokofiev, whom he had persecuted.'

For Rudolf, who turned fifteen two weeks later, the only major event that year was the opening of a ballet studio attached to the local theatre. Now at last he had the chance to train as a professional.

'Before, we had just Voitovich and not a proper school.' Ufa was proud of its opera house, the centre of cultural life and always packed with people. The great basso Feodor Chaliapin had made his debut there, and since 1941, when a group of Ufa students graduated from the Kirov's ballet school, the Vaganova Academy, and formed the nucleus of a company, the ballet had maintained a direct link with Leningrad. Among the male soloists, several had been taught by Alexander Pushkin, who was to be the most important influence on the early careers of both Rudolf and Mikhail Baryshnikov a decade later. But whereas Baryshnikov had had the consistency of training in Latvia from the age of twelve at a Vaganova-style vocational school (where the academic programme was affiliated), Rudolf had been forced to snatch classes at a social club whenever he could. Even after his academic studies entered a more flexible phase at the School of Working Youth, he was still having to adopt his old ruse of running errands in order to escape to the studio. 'He would come with a big shopping bag as if he was going to buy bread.' And because he couldn't leave the house before Hamet had set off for work, he frequently arrived late, infuriating his new teacher.

As Voitovich taught only company members, Rudolf's first classes were taught by Zaituna Bakhtiyarova, a petite, impeccably chic woman who immediately took exception to his dishevelled appearance. 'He would arrive looking tousled and wearing a T-shirt that wasn't very clean. He had nothing bright or white.' If Rudolf answered her back when she upbraided him for being late, Bakhtiyarova would call him a hooligan and threaten to send him to the Matrosov, a colony for delinquents. But as she told one pupil, 'I criticize only those I think have a future.' And yet however offensive he found her remarks, nothing could have deterred Rudolf: he was obsessed. While other students took one class a day, he took three, and in between worked on steps with Albert and Pamira Sulamenova, another ex-Pioneer colleague whom he liked very much. 'He was more interested in what he couldn't do well than in what came easily to him.' They would work on difficult lifts together, and although Rudolf often grumbled to Pamira that she was too heavy, she felt completely safe in his hands and loved watching him work. 'He stood out because he had some kind of flame. He lived in his dancing. Whatever he did he did with joy.'

Rudolf was soon cast in walk-on roles for ten roubles a performance, and by introducing himself as 'an artist from the Ufa Opera' to workers' collectives, he was able to supplement his income by giving dance lessons for two hundred roubles a month. He was now earning as much as Hamet, who was forced to concede that his son's career could at least provide him with a respectable wage. And his sister Rosa, on her return to Ufa, had 'succeeded in persuading our parents to allow Rudolf to continue his beloved profession'. His life now revolved around the theatre; when he was not involved in classes, rehearsals, and performances, he was going to see every ballet and opera in the repertory.

That summer he went with the Ufa Ballet on a month-long trip to Ryazan, in the extreme west of Russia, and roomed with Albert, who was also employed as an extra. Although they earned very little, surviving on suppers of tea and fish-paste sandwiches, they managed to save enough of their salary to buy presents for their families. 'Rudik sent his mother money to buy shoes for his sisters. He was so kind.' As their days were free, they took the trolleybus after breakfast to a river to sunbathe and swim, a period during which he and Albert grew very close: 'Our dreams were the same.' If Rudolf's teenage fantasies contained caches of erotic excitement or shame, he kept them secret; Albert's discovery of his friend's homosexuality years later took him completely by surprise. 'He never acted at all strangely. I knew that some people from the theatre were gay and I kept away from them. Rudolf did the same.'

While on this tour, Albert and Rudolf also took the bus to Moscow, arriving in the middle of August when all the theatres and concert halls were closed. They decided to explore the city on foot, criss-crossing Red Square from GUM, the vast, glass-covered state department store, to the Kremlin, discovering behind its high walls the golden-domed cathedrals filled with treasures, marvelling at Saint Basil's, dominating the south end, and spending an entire afternoon at the Tretyakov Gallery. On their last evening they took the metro – just for the experience of the ride – and somehow got separated, meeting only the next morning at a prearranged rendezvous by the Gorky monument at Belorussia station. Albert had checked into a cheap hotel, but Rudolf had walked all night, unable to stop feasting on the sights and cosmopolitan atmosphere of the city. 'Never had I encountered so many races on the streets, so many different types of human beings.' Ufa was a world away.

By the autumn of 1953 Rudolf had started dancing with the corps de ballet and was taking class with the company's ballet master as well as with Voitovich. While colleagues remember him being well prepared – 'No one looked down on him for not having been professionally schooled' – he himself felt that by comparison he had had 'absolutely no classical training'. At the same time he found that he could quite easily reproduce qualities he observed in the other dancers. His main model was Halyaf Safiulin, an ex-Pushkin pupil and the husband and partner of Zaituna Nazretdinova – the co-stars of the company. Although past his prime and beginning to develop a paunch, Safiulin was still an impressive virtuoso, capable of executing triple cabrioles, multiple pirouettes, and huge jumps with cat-soft landings. But it was his charisma as a performer that most impressed Rudolf, who would try to emulate the challenging tilt of Safiulin's head and the way he compensated for his short stature by making every movement seem longer and higher than usual. A colleague at the time noted, 'Later when I saw videos of Rudolf in the West I noticed some of Safiulin's spirit and plastique.'

The lofty manner that had made Rudolf unpopular with some of the students in his Pioneers class became even more pronounced now that he was dancing with the company; already he was showing signs of the temperament for which he became infamous. 'If he didn't like the look of his costume he would fling it back at someone in anger. "What are you worried about?" they'd laugh. "You're in the back row; nobody's going to see you."' One day he was summoned to the office of the director, who told him that he had received eleven marks for bad behaviour; but instead of dismissing him he invited Rudolf to become a full member of the company. 'At my age, given the high standard of the classes and of the company in general I should have been thrilled . . . And in fact I was. But all I could think of was Leningrad. So I refused.'

The pianist Irina Voronina, well connected in the musical establishment, had been campaigning on Rudolf's behalf, persuading local luminaries to send letters to the Bashkirian Ministry of Culture recommending him for a scholarship to the Vaganova Academy. When a visiting minister sought Zaituna Nazretdinova's opinion, she insisted that Rudolf should be allowed to go, even though privately she considered him not much more than a capable beginner. 'He wasn't outstanding. The main thing was his desire to dance.' It was around this time, in the early spring of 1955, that Rudolf discovered that the republic was choosing dancers to take part in a major event – a celebration of a decade of Bashkirian Literature and Art, to be held in Moscow in the late spring of 1955. He was not asked to audition, but during a rehearsal of *Song of the Cranes*, one of the pieces chosen for the festival, the director asked if there was anybody who could take the place of a performer who had failed to show up. Rudolf immediately stepped forward: not only did he have a photographic memory for steps, but he had already danced the whole ballet in his head. The role of the herald, a Bashkirian Cossack, who performed a solo while waving a beribboned pole, would have provided Rudolf with a brief moment in which to shine, but once in Moscow, during the first day's rehearsal, he injured his foot too badly to go on.

Determined to make the most of his time, he threw himself into rediscovering the city, delighted this time to be able to attend performances – sometimes as many as three a day – since the students had been given free passes to all the theatres. Noticing that his friend Pamira felt intimidated by the bustle and unfamiliarity of the metropolis, Rudolf took her in hand, glad of a chance to show off his knowledge. All the same it was frustrating not to be dancing: the *Dekada* was to have been his first chance to show what he could do. Moscow that week was packed with teachers, dancers and directors from all over the Soviet Union, there for the purpose of recruiting new talent. 'Finally something came and clicked in my mind that nobody's going to come and take me by hand and show me anything. I had to do it all myself.'

On a warm May evening, Alik Bikchurin, an Ufa-born student then studying at the Vaganova Academy, was alone in front of Moscow's Hotel Evropeiskaya, idly kicking a tin can lid along the street, when a slim young man caught it with his foot and said with a wry smile, 'Provincial depression?' Alik took no notice, but the young man went on, 'Hello! I'm Rudik Nureyev from our Opera Theatre. I saw your *Giselle* pas de deux in the Tchaikovsky Hall. You were good. Listen, I hear that Balticheva and Kumisnikov are here with you. Can you introduce me to them?' Taking no chance of a refusal, Rudolf made a similar approach to another Vaganova student from Ufa, Eldus Habirov, who, like Alik, did indeed speak to the two teachers on his behalf. Abdurahman Kumisnikov and his wife, Naima Baltacheyeva, had just left Ufa to teach in Leningrad when Rudolf started classes, and were now among the city's most prominent dance personalities. The following day, in their hotel room, where Rudolf used the iron bedstead as a barre, the dancer auditioned for them. Impressed more by his 'craziness for ballet' than his natural abilities, they accepted him, telling him to come to the Vaganova school that September.

Meanwhile Irina Voronina, in Moscow as the Ufa Ballet's accompanist, had through contacts of her own arranged for Rudolf to audition for the Bolshoi's dance academy. Once again, he was offered a place for the following term, but as the Moscow school had neither a residential college nor a scholarship system for students from other states, Rudolf turned it down. Back in Ufa, he came up to Pamira and a group of students sitting on a sofa after class one day and said, 'That's it. I'm going to study in Leningrad!' Pamira immediately burst into tears. 'I was so surprised and I don't know why, but I became sad. I still can't understand why I cried so much. Maybe because I also wanted to study, maybe it was because it was a pity that he was leaving.'

On the day his son left for Leningrad, Hamet also broke down. 'It was terrible . . . I'd never seen him cry before.' But nobody could have held Rudolf back now. On a day in mid-August he found himself taking the route he had followed so often in his mind while sitting on the hill of Salavat listening to the sound of trains, 'Calling you, beckoning you to go somewhere.' Crossing over the Belaya River past the chicken-shack houses that shook with the vibration of each locomotive, Rudolf left Ufa behind him at last.

HOLLYWOOD STORY

Before he knew where he was going to spend his first night in Leningrad, Rudolf went immediately to the Vaganova Academy, on Ulitsa Rossi, one of the most elegant streets in the city. Tall, neo-classical buildings, painted buttery yellow and white, form a perspective of calculated symmetry from Lomonsov Square to the Pushkin Theatre, which corresponds to its contours and colours like a reflection. 'Do you know,' the choreographer Fyodor Lopokhov once pointed out, 'when you walk down this street to the theatre, the columns of the buildings literally start to dance?' Carlo Rossi, the designer of 'Theatre Street', was the son of an Italian ballerina, and his strict linearity is reflected in the Kirov school's own aesthetic of sublime classical precision. 'The architecture in Moscow has no order, it has no style,' Rudolf once said. 'In Leningrad you see beauty all the time. Like in Italy. Even if a man is sweeping the streets he sees beauty all around him.'

As he entered through the double wooden doors past framed sepia photographs of great Soviet dance teachers, Rudolf half expected to see the wraiths of Pavlova, Karsavina and Nijinsky, who had all begun their careers there. Instead he encountered cleaners and painters: the school was being renovated in preparation for the new term. Having sought out the director, he grandiloquently announced himself: 'I am Rudolf Nureyev, artist from the Ufa Opera. I would like to study here.' He was too early, Comrade Shelkov told him; he must come back a week later and be assessed.

With the prospect of an unexpected holiday ahead of him, Rudolf went to call on Anna Udeltsova, his Ufa ballet teacher, who was in Leningrad for the summer. Her psychiatrist daughter lived in a large apartment on Ogorodnikov Prospekt, and although there appeared to be more relatives than rooms, the family gave Rudolf a space to himself – a child's bed with a chair at one end to support his feet. He enjoyed being spoiled and well fed, and he appreciated the sombre grandeur of his surroundings; Udeltsova's sister had been married to a prosperous Moscow merchant, and there were still signs of past wealth

in the tsarist furniture and European paintings they had managed to
save. Rudolf learned how, during the revolution, Elena Ivanovna had
concealed her jewellery under her dress: 'Wherever she went her husband would follow her with a pistol and never let her out of his sight.'
The family had remained devoutly religious, and in almost every corner
was an ancient icon. 'Rudolf loved the atmosphere, although he never
went to church with us, and was far from being a believer himself.'
What delighted him most was the fact that there was a piano in the
apartment; Udeltsova's daughter began giving him rudimentary lessons, and he kept himself physically in shape by practising ballet steps in
the big kitchen under Anna Ivanovna's watchful eye.

After dinner she took him for walks along the Griboyedov Canal
and Fontanka River, reminiscing about dancers she had seen and life
before the revolution. Most of that week, however, Rudolf spent
alone, sightseeing from morning until nightfall. Nothing, not even the
majesty of Moscow's Red Square and the hidden enchantments of
the Kremlin, had prepared him for the beauty of Leningrad, a vision
made real by Peter the Great, who ordered a metropolis to rise where
nothing existed before but marshland and the sound of seabirds. Its
magical appearance, like a sudden set change, is perpetuated by the
theatricality of the city itself – the stucco façades washed with confec-
tionery colours of pale blue, pink and yellow; the glinting of gold on
spires, domes and eagles; the bridges with their Art Nouveau intricacies of wrought iron; the exquisite Italianate mouldings and cherubim
that even the most dilapidated buildings display on crumbling walls.
At the Hermitage Museum, housed in Rastrelli's Winter Palace, a
work of art in itself, Rudolf made his first discovery of the French
Impressionists and Italian Renaissance painting – 'a revelation to me'.
Avid for more, he took a train to the outskirts of Leningrad to visit
Peterhof, Russia's Versailles, set in the most ravishing park he had ever
seen; and he fell in love with the English landscape gardens of
Pavlovsk, the palace south of the city that Catherine the Great had
built for her son.

On 25 August Rudolf returned to the ballet school, where he joined
an assessment class given by Vera Kostrovitskaya, in his view the best
woman teacher in Russia, who had further developed and edited the
Vaganova system of dance. With her large eyes and beaky nose she
looked just like Pavlova, and Rudolf could feel her watching him intently
as he danced. When he finished the final *enchaînement*, she walked up to
him and announced in the full hearing of everyone: 'Well, boy, you will
either become something very unusual or you will be a great failure!',

later repeating her prediction to a group of students. 'He is a very talented boy. He will either be a great dancer or go back to Siberia.' He was accepted, but Rudolf knew exactly what she meant: his spontaneous, individual style came straight from the heart but lacked clarity and inner control. 'I would have to work and work and work – more than anyone else in the school.'

On his first day, 7 September 1955, the pale seventeen-year-old, wearing a thin sweater tightly cinched with a large belt to emphasize his slim waist, and carrying his belongings in a bag no bigger than a briefcase, was shown his living quarters – a large, light dormitory shared with nineteen other students whom Rudolf decided to ignore. 'He didn't say hello, or how are you. He didn't look at us at all, he went straight to bed.' In the morning, hating the idea of eating a communal breakfast with the *malchiki*, Rudolf kept his head hidden under the covers half an hour after everyone else had got up. These were long days, ending sometimes as late as seven o'clock, with academic lessons worked into the timetable around classical and character dancing. His first ballet classes came as a dismaying anticlimax. He had heard so much in Ufa about the genius of Alexander Pushkin, who had taught Halyaf Safiulin and the first wave of male Bashkirian soloists in Leningrad, and who was now in charge of the eighth grade. 'They said, "Pushkin is there and he is the only one to take classes from."' To his distress, however, Rudolf learned that he had been assigned to the sixth-grade class of Valentin Ivanovich Shelkov, a squat Soviet bureaucrat, whom he had met on his first day in Leningrad. Although a Pushkin pupil himself, Shelkov had absorbed nothing of the maestro's skill at tactfully guiding rather than driving the students, and his officious manner turned even the most lyrical exercises into military drill.

Compensating for his shortcomings as a teacher, Shelkov deliberately allocated the most gifted pupils to his own class – the reason for Rudolf's presence – but nothing this unusual boy did could please him. 'Shelkov was slighting me a lot. He would say to [Nikita] Dolgushin, Sasha Minz and others: "You are a good boy!" and to me he would say, "You are a provincial fool!" It was very offensive.' It was also hypocritical. Shelkov himself came from a town far beyond the Ural Mountains, and although it was he who had been responsible for obtaining a full grant for Rudolf's tuition from the Bashkirian Ministry of Culture, he was motivated by self-interest rather than altruism: he enjoyed nothing more than collecting honorary titles from different regions. Sly and as slippery as his name suggests – *shelk* is the Russian word for 'silk' – the teacher was 'an absolute Soviet product'. Rudolf referred to him as 'Arakcheyev' (a ruthless and ingratiating politician during the reign of Aleksander the First). When he wasn't taunting Rudolf about his lowly roots, he was reminding him that he was only there on his and the state's charity.

Academic subjects were just as demoralizing. During his last years in Ufa his schooling had dwindled to workers' evening classes, where he received nothing like the education his Leningrad colleagues had had. He was completely lost during lectures in maths and science, and had a poor grasp of the grammar and spelling of the Russian language, which had never been spoken well at home. One of the pupils, a petite blonde named Marina Vasilieva, used to help him with punctuation during dictation lessons, tapping her shoulder once to indicate a comma, twice for a semicolon, and so on. When the girl sitting between them blocked his view, Rudolf would hiss at her, 'Inna Skidelskaya, move to the side, *scom!*' Gradually, with subjects that interested him, he found himself able to appreciate the exceptionally high academic standards at the school. One of the music teachers was Shostakovich's sister, the art teacher was a curator at the Hermitage, and literature was taught at university level by a large Leningrad balletomane who always wore floor-length skirts. 'She read in English perfectly and talked to us of Dumas and Goethe. It came pouring from her.'

But only the solitary heroes and extreme emotions of Dostoyevsky interested Rudolf at that time. As he later admitted, 'I've always tended to reject everything in life which doesn't enrich or directly concern my single dominating passion.' His immediate priority was to absorb all he could from arts that would nourish his dancing, and the results in his first-year report card reflect this. He scored two 5s, the highest mark, for history of music and history of ballet; acting skills, classical and character dance each scored 4, as did geometry, French, chemistry and physics; but he got 3s, the lowest grade, for literature, history and geography.

'When Rudolf arrived in Leningrad, there was only one thing on his mind: to improve his dancing,' said Sergiu Stefanschi, a lively, round-faced Romanian, whose bed was next to Rudolf's:

> We started talking and found that we understood each other, as we were both beginners and the other pupils were so much more advanced. He knew I was having extra coaching classes and he would come back to the residence and say, 'Well, what did you do? *Tell* me.' And I would. It was like a business talk. After 11.30 when we were supposed to be in bed, he'd say, 'Let's practise pirouettes.' We'd wait

until the *babushka* had done her rounds – we hated her, she was an *aparatchik* like Shelkov – and then we'd start partnering each other and dancing. I was crazy about dance and he was crazy about dance. We didn't talk about other things.

Sergiu could see from Rudolf's clothes – his trousers were inches above his ankles – that he came from an underprivileged background. When teased, Rudolf, easily provoked, would retaliate in fury, calling Sergiu 'a rich bourgeois'. 'To make him mad when he wanted to dance, I'd pull the blanket over my head and say, "Leave me alone, Bashkirian pig." The next thing, Rudik would become like a crazed animal, biting and wrestling me to the ground.'

Such outbursts only increased Sergiu's awe of the young rebel: 'I used to follow behind Rudik a little bit. I was his echo.' Described by one colleague as 'more adventurously curious than the rest of us', Sergiu eagerly colluded in the kind of partnership that Rudolf had had in Ufa with Albert Aslanov – twin apostles of culture and beauty. 'For us, everything belonged to art, drama, music . . . We had this hunger all the time.' They went to concerts at the Philharmonic Hall; saw Shakespeare performed at the Gorky Theatre; and, to study different acting techniques, even sat through mediocre propagandist plays at the Pushkin Theatre, staged by an artistic director who had 'sold his soul to the devil'.

Every other night they went to the ballet. 'You had to be on a list, but we'd find a way to get in; sometimes we'd use a false name.' Later the *babushki* who sat in the corridors of the Kirov Theatre knitting or darning the ballerinas' pointe shoes got to know them and would let them past. The following morning they would often discuss the performance with Marietta Frangopoulo, curator of the school museum. The door was always open, and Frangopoulo, a motherly woman of Greek descent who transformed her solid figure with chic European clothes and Art Deco jewellery, sat surrounded by her gallery of ballet photographs and cabinets of memorabilia. 'She was our goddess. She was so erudite and had seen everybody dance.' It was Frangopoulo who instilled in Rudolf a lifelong veneration of Balanchine, whose classmate she had been. 'Privately, never in front of the class', she shared her memories of the teenage Georgi Balanchivadze's first attempts at choreography, but having been incarcerated in a prison camp during the terrors, Frangopoulo was still wary of talking about an artist whose name until Stalin's death a few years earlier could only be whispered.

By now Rudolf had discovered a little shop opposite Kazan Cathedral on Nevsky Prospekt that sold sheet music. There was a piano in the corner on which customers could try out a piece before buying it, or else the manager, an excellent pianist herself, would play it or put on a record. Rudolf took an instant liking to Elizaveta Pazhi, a small, plump, merry woman with tight curls of blondish grey hair. She was such good company – kind, cultured, full of humour – that he took to hanging around the shop until it closed and walking her to the tram stop carrying her bags. Enchanted by this eager young student with his radiant smile and worn Gogolian overcoat, Elizaveta Mikhailovna took pity on him and promised to find him a piano teacher willing to give him lessons free of charge. Her close friend Marina Savva, a concert pianist at the Maly Opera Theatre, was another warm, intelligent, childless woman in her fifties. She and her husband, a violinist in the orchestra, welcomed Rudolf into their home, and within four weeks, thanks to Marina Petrovna's gentle persistence, Rudolf had progressed from picking out tunes from *Sleeping Beauty* with one finger to playing an elegy by Rachmaninov.

He began to read scores for pleasure, and would play a game with his classmate Marina, hiding the name on the cover and making her guess the identity of the composer from the notes. He stored his growing collection of music under his mattress and guarded it fiercely. 'Has anyone touched anything?' he grilled Sergiu when he returned to the dormitory. Shelkov had come down hard on Sergiu for his nocturnal truancy with the warning, 'If you follow that Rudolf Nureyev, you're not going to stay in this school,' and more often now, Rudolf went out alone. Considering it an important part of his education to attend as many performances as he could, he was determined to see a newly updated version of *Taras Bulba*, a three-act ballet based on a Gogol short story, but when he returned to school around midnight, he discovered that his mattress had been removed and his meal tickets confiscated. He spent the rest of the night on a window ledge, and the next morning went to Ogorodnikov Prospekt to have breakfast with Anna Udeltsova's family, missing his first lesson. His absence and subsequent insolence to the teacher who had insisted on an explanation were reported, and he found himself summoned to Shelkov's office and violently upbraided. Demanding the name of Rudolf's friends, Shelkov had snatched his address book out of his hand, causing him to run back to the residence 'like a wild man', outraged by this invasion of privacy. 'That bastard!' he cried to Sergiu. 'He's a fascist. *Why* can't he be human?'

About a week later Rudolf went to the artistic director of the school, Nicolai Ivanovsky, and without complaining directly about Shelkov, told him, 'You know, I am seventeen now. If I stay in Shelkov's class for another three years, after I graduate they will take me straight into the army. Could I move up to Pushkin's class?'* A delicate, Proustian character who wore elegant suits and patent-leather pumps, Ivanovsky was a lecturer in historical dance and one of the most cultivated and popular teachers in the school. 'There had never been a request like it,' said a former student, Marina Vivien. 'No one had asked to change his teacher before, but Ivanovsky was a generous, intelligent man. He must have seen Nureyev's talent and did not allow Shelkov to do what he wanted, which was to expel the boy. He overruled Valentin Ivanovich, and Pushkin took the pupil of his pupil.'

From the moment Rudolf entered the attic studio where sunlight from huge, rounded windows slanted across the floor, he regarded Pushkin's classes as 'two holy hours'. A serene, almost hieratic man, the maestro was soft-spoken and direct, not given to elaborate verbal instructions, although pupils learned to tell if anything displeased him by the blush that slowly crept up from his neck. 'His colour would change but never his voice.' With his suit jacket hung over the back of a chair, and wearing his customary white shirt and tie, the balding forty-eight-year-old Pushkin would demonstrate elementary but wonderfully danceable combinations in which each movement seemed to flow organically into the next. No matter that he was half marking or that his back was slumped, he could convey exactly the rubato phrasing and harmonious coordination of the whole body that he had learned from his own teacher Vladimir Ponomarev. 'He was working in a great tradition; hand to hand from one master to another,' said Mikhail Baryshnikov, who has always claimed that he owes his career to Pushkin.

Many pupils new to his class found nothing special about Pushkin's method, not realizing that simplicity was his secret – the key to grasping the inner logic and natural transitions of steps. For Rudolf, having gone through the motions of Shelkov's cold configurations, every Pushkin class felt as intoxicating as a performance: 'kind of irresistible. Very tasty, very delicious.' Believing in giving a newcomer a chance to settle down and understand the rudiments of what he was doing, Pushkin hardly looked in Rudolf's direction for the first few weeks, but

* In his autobiography Rudolf describes this as a conversation he had with Shelkov, not Ivanovsky – possibly because it made a more dramatic anecdote.

even ignored as he was, he knew from the first lesson that he had made the right decision. Years later he told a friend that if he hadn't moved to Pushkin's class, he would have given up dancing 'because Shelkov repressed everything in me'.

Outside school, Rudolf had grown very close to Elizaveta Pazhi, who regularly brought him home for meals after she had closed her shop. Her husband, Veniamin Mikhailovich, was an engineer, a quiet, bearded man with a private passion for the verse of the Silver Age, which he would read to Rudolf when dinner was over. There was something enticingly taboo about discovering these nineteenth-century Russian symbolists who were not standard authors at school but derided as émigrés and considered decorative and superficial. Rudolf's favourites were the tuneful, accessible Konstantin Balmont and Valery Bryusov, whose style is more erudite and ornate. Cosmopolitanism is what they all have in common, and this, along with their technical virtuosity, musicality and attitude to art as a form of divine revelation, were qualities with which the young dancer passionately identified.

Rudolf made sure that he never missed these evenings, and both Pazhis grew to dote on him, but he began noticing how much Elizaveta Mikhailovna depended on his visits to the shop, how upset she would become if he failed to arrive. He saw 'even something Dostoyevskian' in the intensity of her feelings, which were beginning to be stifling. 'Maybe Lilen'ka fell a little bit in love with Rudik. She was so charmed by him.' He found himself missing the company of friends of his own age, and wrote a postcard to his Ufa soulmate Albert. 'In honour of our friendship. It's been twelve years since we've known each other,' as well as several 'tender' letters to Pamira (destroyed by her family when she married). In them Rudolf described performances he had seen, his walks in Leningrad and the museums he had visited. She remembers one long letter just about the Hermitage. 'In another he told me of his passion for the music of Prokofiev. I could tell that he was quite lonely.'

During a short break that autumn, Rudolf decided to spend a few days in Ufa. At home on Zentsova Street he found conditions as cramped as ever, although the family's quality of life had improved. Hamet had been promoted to chief of security at his factory, and Rosa was now independent, working as a kindergarten teacher in a small Bashkirian town. Lilia's new husband had joined the family, but they were both bringing in a salary. Lilia had a job as a seamstress and Fanel, who was also deaf, was a porter and odd-job man. Only Razida was still studying. She had wanted to major in geology but, this time, it was Farida who talked her out of an unsuitable career ('climbing over hills' was not something that would provide enough of a wage, she insisted). Razida's decision to enrol instead at Ufa's technical institute had her father's full support: 'He said that it must be my calling. He knew how from an early age I'd been a tomboy and always liked mechanical toys.'

When Rudolf suddenly appeared at the apartment, he was welcomed with delight by Farida, who had not expected to see him home so soon, although Hamet appeared as impassive as ever. 'Father didn't like to show his emotions. He kept good and bad inside of him. His attitude to Rudolf getting to Leningrad was, "So he went there. It's good. We'll see what will come from it."' In fact Hamet had mellowed considerably since Rudolf last saw him, and was far more at ease with himself. He knew that he was well respected at work, and although his position at the factory was a mindless occupation, he had recently developed a passion for horticulture. He read voraciously on the subject and, drawing on his agricultural studies, had created a small garden outside old Ufa, where he grew vegetables and fruit, including more than twenty different varieties of apples.

Everyone was expected to help with the vegetable plot on Sundays, but Rudolf managed to escape, instead visiting Alik Bikchurin, the *Dekada* go-between, who had returned home after completing his Leningrad training: 'The whole family was digging potatoes, but Rudolf wanted to talk about dance.' He spent as much time as he could with Albert, who had recently become a member of the Ufa ballet company, and together they went to call on their pianist friend Irina Voronina, whom Rudolf greatly missed. 'He played one piece that was a surprise for all of us,' Albert says, '"You play better than the ones who have studied for a year," Irina Alexandrovna told him.'

Back in Leningrad, Rudolf continued to be regarded by colleagues as an alien being, living a different existence and interested only in museums, theatres, the Philharmonic Hall, art books and musical scores. 'He seemed like some kind of fanatic to everyone,' said Alexander 'Sasha' Minz. 'No one knew what to make of him. And so they stayed away from him.' Already he was infamous. A young researcher at the theatre museum across the courtyard heard from his supervisor, the critic Vera Krasovskaya, that 'in Pushkin's class there had appeared a pupil – a Tatar who only eats horsemeat [a Bashkirian speciality] – with fantastic abilities, but who would have a hard fate because of his bad character.' Fellow pupils could not believe how, even in Pushkin's class, Rudolf frequently ignored the master and went his own way. As Sergiu recalled:

> Pushkin would set an adagio at the barre, but Rudik would often not follow it and do only what he wanted. The others would finish and he would hold his leg for thirty-two counts at the front, thirty-two counts at the side. 'Why don't you do what Alexander Ivanovich set?' I'd ask him. 'Don't be stupid,' he'd say. 'I'm not strong like the other boys. I need to build up muscles.'

Pushkin never reprimanded Rudolf; it was his policy to teach dancers to recognize their gifts and limitations – to give them what Baryshnikov calls 'the idea of self-education':

> In his class you could see boys, even in their teens, moving individually in the way that patterns of speech separate one person from another. With dance it's the same thing: you have to find that individuality, that internal understanding of phrasing. Pushkin was teaching boys to make their own decisions: creating *thinking* dancers.

Time after time Rudolf would return to an empty studio and practise the step with which he had been struggling until he could do it perfectly. Frustration was the most frequent cause of his outbursts, and only Pushkin was able to calm him. Other teachers would appeal to him in despair, saying, '"Sasha, please do something!" And Alexander Ivanovich would go and tell him, "Rudik, one can't behave like this. Try some pirouettes . . . that will calm you down." Then Rudik would grow quiet and continue the rehearsal.' He was often at his worst in pas de deux classes – 'a real torture for him' as he did not yet have the strength and coordination required for partnering, and few of the girls wanted to dance with him as he was thin, not particularly attractive at that time, and had such a high opinion of himself. One of the lightest, Marina Vasilieva, often found herself coupled with him. On one occasion, after struggling unsuccessfully to carry out a shoulder lift, Rudolf thrust her to the floor, picked up his towel, and stormed off. 'Kostrovitskaya was furious and told him to stay away. He often swore a lot during lessons, and we tried not to react. Later he struggled to contain himself, especially when girls were around. He was wilder at the beginning. Little by little he improved.'

Technically Rudolf was improving so rapidly that colleagues could see his progress from one day to the next. Nevertheless, Pushkin decided not to include him in the students' concert, considering that he was still not ready. Desperately disappointed, Rudolf begged his teacher to let him perform for him the dynamic male solo from the *Diana and Acteon* duet, on which he had been working alone, hoping it would help to change his mind. This is a variation in heroic Soviet style, which the Kirov star Vakhtang Chaboukiani had rechoreographed in the 1930s to display his virtuosity and dynamism. And in the studio that evening, as Pushkin watched Rudolf attack the final climactic diagonal of spinning leaps, fast *chaînés*, and dramatic lunges, his body arched and head flung back, it was impossible not to think of him as a reincarnation of the young Chaboukiani himself. The matter was settled: Pushkin agreed to let Rudolf perform, and throughout 1956 Rudolf continued dancing the lead in various solos and pas de deux for student concerts.

In January of that year Hamet sent a note to the school asking permission for Rudolf to have a short break in Ufa: 'If it's possible, please make the holiday time longer.' Since Rudolf's last trip home, relations with his father had improved substantially. A few weeks later Rudolf took the trouble to find a birthday card with a picture of a dog much like Hamet's Palma, in which his inscription shows a new eagerness to please: 'I hope you grow the garden you want to grow and have a very good rest and go hunting this summer.' Hamet had deliberately addressed the request to Rudolf's tutor, Yevgenia Leontieva, a calm, sweet-natured woman, who would probably have agreed to it had she not been obliged to seek the authority of Shelkov, who scrawled 'To be refused' across the note. 'Director never forgave me,' said Rudolf. 'At any given moment, he needled me.'

'Every day there was news of another "outrage" Rudolf had committed. Some way he had dressed, something he had said, something he liked.' And nothing Shelkov did could make Rudolf conform. He refused to become a member of Komsomol, the junior organization of the Communist Party, to which most of his colleagues belonged, and he disregarded countless school rules. Pupils were supposed to have a special case in which to carry their dance togs; Rudolf always piled his in his arms and threw them on his bed at the end of the day. Shelkov was fanatical about observing old Imperial School traditions: collars must be white and buttoned to the neck, pupils must stop and bow when passing a member of the staff in the corridor. Once, when Rudolf walked past him without making the traditional obeisance, the director called him back and, taking hold of the dancer's hair, forced his head down over and over again, shouting, '*Bow! Bow! Bow!*' 'Shelkov was very sadistic. We all used to think that he was gay,' said Egon Bischoff, Rudolf's contemporary, who believes that suppressed guilt about a physical attraction towards the young Tatar may explain the pathological severity of Shelkov's behaviour – a possibility that other students have confirmed. 'Shelkov used to love to call him into his office for long talks about sex,' said Alexander Minz. 'He took a kind of sadistic pleasure in doing that.'

By the spring of 1957 Rudolf had moved out of the dormitory and into a small, high-ceilinged room he shared with Sergiu Stefanschi and three other boys: Egon Bischoff from East Germany, Leo Ahonen from Finland and Grigore Vintila from Romania. As a student from Bashkiria, Rudolf was considered as foreign as the Eastern Europeans – 'I was intruder. Outsider from province.' Their new room was on the ground floor, and during the White Nights of early summer when the main doors had been locked 'with big jail keys', they would often climb out of the window and into Rossi Street. 'We loved to dance outdoors', says Sergiu, describing a euphoric *manège* of *grands jetés en tournant* that Rudolf performed round the Alexander Column in the vast, empty expanse of Palace Square.

Across the corridor was a little communal kitchen they shared with the female students, but Rudolf never bought food or cooked for himself as the others did: he ate his meals in the canteen because they were free. Nor did he gather around the girls' gramophone and listen to the Bill Haley records that Leo had brought to Leningrad – 'Rudolf wasn't interested, he preferred the Philharmonic Hall.' Often, instead of going to a single performance at the Kirov like the others, Rudolf would be more selective, perhaps seeing just one act, and then leaving to catch the second half of a concert. Already at school he was the hyperactive 'wind machine' he remained throughout his life. 'When we played, he worked. The only important thing to him was to study classical ballet. He knew how little time he had to get to where he should be and burned candles at both ends. Whatever he'd learned that day he liked to chew over later that night. He was always practising in the room. It was his homework.' Out late at performances virtually every night, Rudolf was in a different time zone from the others. As on his first morning, he would stay buried under his heavy blanket, refus-ing to get up for breakfast, and before leaving for class paused only to drink tea straight from the nozzle of a battered kettle in the kitchen. 'Sleep was more important to him than food.' The five never talked to each other about the lives they had left behind. Grigore Vintila had been brought up in a Romanian orphanage and 'felt so alone, like Rudolf did', yet neither knew about the other's background. The only time anyone was aware that Rudolf had a family was when his sister Rosa turned up at the school one day and asked if Rudik was around. When he came back to the room later and found his sister sitting on his bed, he made his irritation quite clear. 'He didn't like that kind of surprise.'

To his room-mates Rudolf was a figure of such authority that he seemed to be much older. 'When he said it was time to sleep, everyone slept,' says Leo, who once wrote a letter to his idol, reminding him of their dormitory days:

> Your mind was already at least ten years more developed than the rest of us . . . Each one of us had stupid, childish opinions about everything. But when you finally voiced your opinion, we all accepted it and the case was closed . . . I had come from the 'West', and saw things differently from others. I always thought it was such a shame that so many people thought you were a 'problem' at the school . . . When you were resting your legs in bed (next to mine), your arms were working, searching for that ultimate port de bras.

'We thought him incredible,' agrees Grigore, recalling how he once woke Rudolf up in the middle of the night to ask his help with a tricky sequence of steps: 'There we were in our pyjamas, with no music, rehearsing in the corridor.' Even lying in bed, Rudolf would be practising the castanets for a role. 'We didn't mind: we respected him for doing it. He didn't want to fake it.' And although regional Russian dancing was not taught at school, Rudolf made a point of keeping up his own traditions. Humming folk tunes he remembered from home, he used to persuade one of his classmates to improvise on the piano during breaks while he 'danced like crazy'. By drawing on Bashkirian dance's unique combination of fire and Oriental plastique, he knew that he could make the famous classical roles his own.

When Rudolf's behaviour was at its coarsest, he still managed to retain their esteem. There was a night when Rudolf came back to the room in a bad temper made worse by seeing Egon sitting on the bed next to his own eating a plate of fried potatoes he had just cooked. 'What are you doing?' he demanded. 'Can't you see? I'm eating.' '*What* are you eating?' insisted Rudolf, who suddenly leaned across and spat on Egon's plate. 'Are you crazy?' cried Grigore, leaping to Egon's defence, only to watch Rudolf, his fury rising, take off his shoe and fling it at the ceiling, breaking the lamp and extinguishing the light. In seconds the three were rolling on the floor, fighting in the dark, but then they all saw the ludicrousness of the situation and collapsed in laughter.

In the right mood Rudolf could be delightful company. Leo Ahonen's hobby was photography, and one night they all mugged for his camera, taking turns holding a blanket against the wall as a backdrop. Rudolf, who always loved being photographed, mimicked Chaboukiani in his bare-chested *Corsaire* pose, flexed his biceps, Mr Universe-style, and, with a pair of boys hiding behind him, formed a six-armed mythical creature. In another sequence Egon, looking like Noël Coward with his striped dressing gown and fake cigarette, lay on the bed draped across Rudolf's knees. As Egon flashed his long bare legs for one shot, Rudolf gazed into his eyes and cupped his cheeks in a mock movie clinch that looks more suggestive than it actually was. 'The pictures are only *acting* camp. They were really very innocent.' Three decades later, in reply to a friend's enquiry about one of the photographs, which he still kept in his wallet, Rudolf said, 'This was our view of the West.' (It may well have been a view inspired by a sapphic German film he had seen in Russia called *Peter*. 'To us it was a great sensation, because you saw women smoking and looking tenderly at each other.')

All four insist that there was none of the usual adolescent sex talk in their dormitory. 'Maybe they put something in the water, like in the army. Ninety per cent of our thoughts were about ballet.' Most of the students knew that Ekaterina Square in front of the Pushkin Theatre was a nocturnal cruising ground for *gomiki*, but this was a subject that Rudolf had no interest in discussing. One evening, as Sergiu cut across the garden on his way back to school, he saw a man lecherously open his coat and expose himself. 'And this was at a period when they would put you in prison for something like that.' In the ballet world, where it was well known that Chaboukiani, among others, was a practising homosexual, a certain licence existed. In 1957, when the dancer returned to the Kirov to appear in *Othello*, he cast his lover as Iago, and few in the audience failed to notice the homoerotic charge onstage as the Moor crawled like a snake towards an Iago who held him captive with one foot pressing on his ribcage. 'I felt a man behind leaning over me,' recalled Sergiu. 'He was very, very attractive and very excited. At the interval he invited me for a drink.'

Sergiu was one of several students who experimented with same-gender sex at school, allowing himself to be seduced in an empty dressing room by Alexander Minz, then in the process of discovering his own predilections. Rudolf's colleagues are convinced that if he felt an attraction towards any of the boys, he did nothing about it: 'He was too busy sponging up information.' Even Grigore Vintila, with his matinée-idol looks, sensed no special attention from Rudolf, who, if anything, appeared to take a greater interest in girls than the others did. Leo remembers his liking for a soloist in the Finnish National Ballet, when it toured Leningrad. 'She wasn't special as a dancer, so he obviously noticed a pretty face.' And like almost everyone at school, he was mesmerized by a Cuban girl, as alluring as a young Gina Lollobrigida, who was to become his first and only teenage sweetheart.

Trained in Havana by Fernando Alonso, husband of the famous ballerina Alicia Alonso, Menia Martinez suddenly appeared at the school one day like a rainbow in a leaden Leningrad sky. It was the middle of winter, yet she wore the thinnest of summer clothes – wild fifties outfits such as zebra-patterned stove-pipes, boat-necked tops, open-toed stilettos, and huge hoop earrings. She was as glamorous as a pop star to the girls in her dormitory, who begged her to do their makeup, tell them stories about life in Cuba, and sing Latin American songs in her husky voice. 'She used to sit on a bench in our kitchen with an upended washbowl between her legs and beat it like a tom-tom drum.'

Although the pupils were thrilled by this 'exotic bird', several of the teachers were shocked: 'Such a *thing* was not supposed to enter this traditional institution,' said Ursula Collein, an East German student who became her friend.

> I hope Menia never knew this, but we heard her being compared to a prostitute. We all liked her enormously, even though she didn't share our hardworking Prussian ways – if she didn't feel like it some days, she just wouldn't get up – but she was such a winning personality that no one could be critical of her for long.

No one except Shelkov. One day he summoned Menia into his office and lectured her about the school's regime on dress and makeup. Glaring at her long, heavily mascaraed eyelashes, he asked sarcastically if they were her own. Menia, who knew only a few words of Russian and was completely unfazed by the director, laughed coquettishly. '*Nyet. Magazin* [a shop].'

For all Menia's frivolity, her thoughts were largely grounded in politics. 'She was a serious Communist and very marked by her family and upbringing.' Her father had worked in the diplomatic service and was now a teacher renowned for his progressive ideas. Her older sister was married to a leading Communist newspaper editor who, like many other middle-class intellectuals in Cuba, was soon to be among the most influential leaders of the Revolution. Menia herself became an almost emblematic figure in Leningrad, a beautiful embodiment of the outside world – 'such an extraordinary event in our grey lives' – and Spanish people who had emigrated to Russia with their families during the civil war often came to the school to talk to her.

Soon after her arrival at the end of 1955, Menia's teacher Naima Balticheva (who had auditioned Rudolf in Moscow during the *Dekada*) told her about 'a fantastic dancer who's a little crazy and sloppy, and needs to get into shape'. At the time Menia was considering the idea of training as a teacher herself, and asked Pushkin if he would give her permission to watch his classes. 'Then slowly I started coming because of Rudolf – already people thought I was his girlfriend.' Menia loved the wild spirit of Rudolf's dancing while he in turn loved the moody recitals of Afro-Cuban song and dance that she gave at school concerts in the House of Culture. How luscious she looked with her bare feet, flounced skirt, and white bra showing through a tight, transparent black top; her eyes half closed and shapely hips swaying to the rhythm; and how well she could hold the stage alone. 'He once said to me afterwards, "I want to have the same emotion when I dance as you have when you sing."'

But, dismissing Rudolf as 'just another stupid boy', Menia was not romantically drawn to him at that time. She had been involved with a married man before she left Cuba, a leading cultural figure, and she preferred older men. 'It all started with her father, a lot of interesting friends of his would come to the house,' says Bella Kurgina, her closest friend in Leningrad, who used to share the 'thousands of chocolates' that Menia received from her admirers. 'You just had to look in those huge eyes to fall in love.' It was around the beginning of 1957 that she and Rudolf began to grow attached. They found that they were soulmates. The same things made them laugh – Rudolf often made fun of Shelkov, standing stiffly in a Stalin-like pose and pointing to an offensive scrap of litter in the corridor – and they loved listening to music and talking about books they had read. 'I was astonished. Where did he get that culture, that sensibility? How was it possible, this country boy with peasant parents?'

Menia never discussed politics with Rudolf – he was simply not interested – even though this period, the lead-up to Castro's overthrow of Fulgencio Batista, was the most turbulent in Cuban history. But she spoke about her family and encouraged him to do the same. It was the first time Rudolf had opened up about his life to anyone at school. He described the remarkable stoicism of his mother, and told Menia how his father had tried to talk him into playing the accordion instead of the piano. She spoke at length about her 'Leningrad parents', the couple who had practically adopted her. Estelle Volkenstein taught Spanish at Leningrad University and had participated in the civil war. When she heard of the arrival of a Cuban girl, she immediately contacted Menia, offering to act as her interpreter and to teach her Russian. Her husband, Mikhail Mikhailovich, a theoretician, was one of the brightest figures in Leningrad, an exceptionally cultivated, broad-minded man. 'Conversation with the Volkensteins was at its most elevated – about art, about books, about philosophy – and one of the things that most impressed Rudolf about Menia was that she could be a friend of this very brilliant pair.'

He was soon taken up by them, too; invited to concerts and to dinners at their house (a photograph from that period shows him sitting gazing up at Mikhail Mikhailovich, hanging on his words). It was through the Volkensteins that he and Menia were able to get tickets to see Glenn Gould during his 1957 Soviet tour. Recognizing a fellow maverick who breathed his own personality into his work, Rudolf was immensely impressed. 'You get a most weird and, to most critics, upsetting version by Glenn Gould,' he told the New York critic Walter Terry twenty years later. 'But my God! What a titanic talent! Such a talent and inborn sense of dynamism.'

Rudolf's friendship with Menia and his fervour for Gould only fanned his curiosity about the world outside: 'Western art, Western choreography, people . . . he wanted to travel and see. Travel and see.' He would study photographs of Margot Fonteyn and other Royal Ballet artists in a calendar, as well as in copies of the *Dancing Times*, which an English friend of Menia's regularly sent to her. 'He wanted to dance with all those stars. He had already decided to leave.' As indeed he had. Leo had two passports then, as the original was due to expire; Rudolf knew this, and one day he took his roommate aside and pleaded to be given the passport Leo was going to discard. 'He said, "We can change the pictures. It will be all right if the two of us keep this quiet," but I was too afraid – I thought we would both end up in prison in Siberia. Yet I knew at that moment that he was going to defect one day. It came as no surprise to me when he did.'

For a student performance in June 1957, Rudolf danced the *Diana and Acteon* pas de deux with the outstandingly gifted Alla Sizova, a performance that attracted no particular attention from the fans or critics but marked the beginning of an intense collaboration with Pushkin: 'I could not lose a second of that time. I had to hear everything. I had to extort knowledge from him. I was preparing my steps on my own a lot then, in the evening. I would bring him to the studio and ask, "How shall I do this movement. Like this? Or like this?"' By now his only rival at school was a remarkable pupil in the parallel class of Boris Shavrov, already being compared to Nijinsky because of his extraordinary jumps. Yuri Soloviev was the great hope for the future, and had an adoring following among the teachers and students: 'He was our type of dancer, whereas we couldn't really learn from Rudolf at that time,' says Leo. 'Yuri was a dancer's dancer – the kind that Misha Baryshnikov became: a ballet textbook – as exact as the Law of Vaganova. *Perfect.*' Sergiu, who was less of a Soloviev fan, remembers how pleased Rudolf looked when he told him that he found Yuri's angelic but expressionless face 'boring, plain boring'. It was hard not to be jealous of the fact that Soloviev was the school favourite, and yet his sweet nature made disliking him impossible. Besides, Rudolf himself admired Soloviev enormously. The dancer's extraordinary elevation and academic purity were the very qualities that he was working so hard to attain. In London years later, he would tell gushing fans, 'You think I'm good? You want to see Soloviev!'

Among the male dancers in Leningrad there was no one else whom Rudolf revered. Konstantin Sergeyev was at the end of his career as a *danseur noble*, and the principals who succeeded him, such as the virile, athletic Askold Makarov and Boris Bregvadze, were fundamentally character dancers. The glory of the Kirov was in its ballerinas – it was a period almost as rich as the golden age of Olga Spessivtseva and Pavlova. Among the veterans there was the inspirational Natalia Dudinskaya as well as Alla Shelest, both of whose performances Rudolf never missed. Young stars included Irina Kolpakova, Alla Osipenko and Ninel Kurgapkina, and among the new names emerging from the school were Alla Sizova and Natalia Makarova.

Male dancing was very rough in Russia at the time: they did not believe in lyrical passages, they did not believe that man could execute woman's steps, and that's what I was doing. They could not believe it, they could not be emotional; they could not really find that negative feeling which men are never permitted there; it was always positive.

Had Rudolf's idol, Vakhtang Chaboukiani, still been in the company and in his prime, Rudolf might well have developed into a very different dancer, but as he saw no role model among the men, he began consciously to assimilate technical skills from the ballerinas. These included distinctively feminine qualities such as split extensions, high attitudes, soft, expressive arms, and – his most audacious plagiarism of all – the use of a high *relevé* that looked almost as if he were on pointe. In Leonid Yakobson's *Spartacus*, which premièred in 1956, Rudolf would have seen ballerinas dancing not in pointe shoes but in sandals on three-quarter pointes – a departure that was considered anarchic by traditionalists. By adopting this innovation himself, and by introducing a high *retiré* position of the foot in pirouettes (which he later told Mikhail Baryshnikov he had taken from pictures he had seen of Western dancers), Rudolf discovered that he could make his legs appear much longer than they actually were. 'This sense that he created of really lifting himself up with everything stretched gave a very Western look to his dancing,' says Baryshnikov. 'At that time it really was unheard of to do those things. Russian male dancers were sturdy, thick, very much influenced by the bravura dancing of Chaboukiani. Guys were *big*.' 'There was no female style among the boys in the school,' agrees Margarita Alfimova. 'Rudolf was learning from all of us and danced with lovely plastique. And he enjoyed dancing the female parts, which none of the other men would have been able to do.'

With his acute visual memory Rudolf knew the ballerinas' repertory as well as his own. When Baryshnikov arrived at the school a decade later, people were still talking about the way he used to seize an opportunity to show the girls how the Petipa variations should be performed. As Baryshnikov recalled:

Before class, when everybody was standing and warming up, he would do Kitri's variation from the first act [of *Don Quixote*] full out, which made a few people kind of uncomfortable. But full out and really good . . . and with the panache . . . It was not being a queen . . . to him it was just another dance, not being a man dancing a woman's role.

In character classes with Igor Belsky, who, as a performer, had been one of Russia's most dynamic exponents of the genre, Rudolf was also attempting to break barriers.

Often pupils think that national dancing takes second place to ballet, but I had the impression that Rudolf *really* wanted to learn. It was very important for him. He was trying to bring folk dance closer to pure classical form. For example, a *tendu* in character dancing doesn't have to be turned out, but Rudolf was really forcing his turnout. In Spanish classes while everyone else did a pas de chat that was half measure, Rudolf did his full out. He was maximalist: that's why often he could be aggressive with people – he was afraid to lose time.

Even Pushkin, who made a point of steering his students early in their careers in one direction or another – 'this one towards the romantic-lyrical route, that one towards the virtuoso' – found himself nonplussed by Rudolf's cross-pollination of styles. 'He used to say, "I don't know who the devil you are! Are you a character dancer? A classical dancer? Or a Romantic dancer?" It was because I was good at all of that.' But Pushkin gave him freedom, freedom not only to mould himself but to choose the roles he wanted to study. The teacher had encouraged Rudolf to stay on at school for another year in order to consolidate the progress he had made, the result of which amazed colleagues who had graduated before him. One of those, Anatoly Nikiforov, remembers:

He changed so much in 1958. He got three times more from Pushkin's coaching than he had in all the previous years. When I saw Alexander Ivanovich in Rossi Street one day I congratulated him for doing such a great job with Rudolf, and he replied, 'He's a talent!' which was very unusual. He hardly ever praised people.

Rudolf himself knew his worth by now. At a 1958 New Year's Eve party attended by Pushkin, Vera Kostrovitskaya, and many of the students, he made a toast in honour of a girl who had failed to get into the Kirov but won a place in a small company in Siberia. 'Raising his glass to Inna Skidelskaya, he said, "Here's to getting Inna away from Novosibirsk," and turning to her mother, he added, "You have my promise that I'll help to get her back." "How do you expect to do that?" smiled Inna's mother. "Just you wait," Rudolf told her. "Soon the whole world is going to know about me!"'

In February, March and April that year, Rudolf danced the male lead in student performances of the great classical ballets – the first he had given in full costume and in front of an audience on the Kirov stage. Sergiu Stefanschi still remembers his *Nutcracker* solo:

> It was technically strong and already you could see the difference between him and the Kirov dancers. Rudolf didn't have the control of the upper body Soloviev had, and the way he moved his hands, his head and his torso was not so well-trained, but he had much more freedom than the others and he covered more space. He *flew*!

It was this extraordinary unconfined quality that stunned a Moscow audience in April during a national ballet-school contest – one of the most impressive gatherings of young talent in the history of twentieth-century dance. Other performers included the Bolshoi school's star pupils Vladimir Vasiliev and Ekaterina Maximova; Leningrad's Yuri Soloviev partnering the eighteen-year-old Natalia Makarova. Rudolf appeared with Alla Sizova, stealing the show on the second night with their duet from *Le Corsaire* (which they immediately repeated as an encore). Pale, composed Sizova – a paradigm of Kirov clarity – was the perfect foil to the blazing Nureyev. As a film of a subsequent performance in Moscow records, Rudolf's technique and placing at that time were very crude. 'Bursting out of proper form', as one critic put it, his arms and feet flap, his shoulders are raised, but those who saw him for themselves insist that the camera caught nothing of his power onstage, nor conveyed the wild pleasure that dancing gave him.

Even Vasiliev was dazzled. Also one of a new breed of Soviet males determined to transcend the role of partner and explore ways of synthesizing different dance genres, he was an amazing virtuoso, accustomed to executing at least a dozen pirouettes at a time. That night he watched the Leningrad contender making only a few revolutions as he turned (Rudolf, as Baryshnikov puts it, 'was never a multiple pirouette man like Vasiliev or Soloviev'), but it was the position of his feet in *relevé* that held Vasiliev transfixed. 'I thought, God! This guy is really dancing on pointe. It was so beautiful.' From then on Vasiliev began sacrificing the number of turns executed on a low demi-pointe and copying Rudolf's high *relevé*: 'It was a totally different aesthetic: more beautiful and cleaner.' Not having an ideal *premier danseur* physique himself, he noticed how the position of Rudolf's feet had given a more streamlined look to his legs. 'It helped Vasiliev tremendously,' said Baryshnikov. 'It stretched him – because of Rudolf, and nobody else.'

As a result of Rudolf's success, the Bolshoi immediately offered him a contract as a soloist, allowing him to bypass the traditional first rung of corps de ballet. Moscow's second company, the Stanislavsky, went one better by promising to make him a *premier danseur,* but its provincial standards and heavy touring schedule offered no temptation. Besides, there were still two months before his graduation in Leningrad, and he wanted to see what the Kirov had in store for him. 'So I patiently went back. Completed studies.'

In many ways Rudolf was better suited at that time to the Bolshoi's broad bravado style, which has always lacked the Kirov's refinement. (If the Leningrad school is reflected in the architectural precision and harmony of its city, the Bolshoi has similarly absorbed the characteristics of clamorous, exciting, haphazard Moscow.) 'In Moscow they did not teach the same way,' Balanchine has written. 'They had more running around on the stage naked, like show-offs, flexing their muscles. In Moscow there was much more acrobatics. Not the Imperial style at all. And that made sense – after all, the tsar lived in our city. Petersburg is Versailles.' Alexandra Danilova concurred. 'Moscow style – well, they always sort of seek the gallery approval. I think the Leningrad style is much more dignified. They just dance. There is no playing with the public. There is good taste . . . Something very royal about Leningrad dancer. Quietness and royalty.'

On the other hand, the Bolshoi still had the legendary Galina Ulanova (Prokofiev's inspiration for *Romeo and Juliet*), who was, in Rudolf's view 'the first ballerina of the world', combining the finesse and lyricism of her Kirov training with a Stanislavskian understanding of the internal meaning of her roles. But she was exceptional. Totally immersed in her performance – the personification of the Russian soul – Ulanova, he felt, was 'perennially uncorrupted', whereas lesser dancers had succumbed to the company's status as a national tourist attraction. 'At school we couldn't help feeling a sense of superiority at the sophistication of the Kirov dancers,' remarked Sergiu Stefanschi. '"Look how they move! Look how they do mime!" Rudolf said to me once, "Not making a big noise."' Even the Moscow balletomanes were less educated and easier to please than their Leningrad counterparts. Rudolf's mind was already made up: he may have been a born Bolshoi dancer, but it was the Kirov to which he aspired. 'At the Kirov, everything is best, writers, creators . . . Bolshoi practically never created anything . . . everything was simply borrowed . . . As a result they had Goleizovsky, they had Lopokhov, and we have Balanchine.'

On 19 June 1958 Galina Palshina, a 'usually very restrained' Kirov fan, wrote in her diary after the students' graduation performance:

> Stunning impression! First jump in *Corsaire* strong and soft. Armen's variation with torches [Khatchaturian's *Gayane*] with furious, vertical turns. It must be that tomorrow Nureyev will wake up famous and the whole city will know his name. At the end of the performance he came out excited, happy, embarrassed. His hair was falling over his eyes. He had a suitcase with no handle which was opening all the time and a modest bouquet of flowers in his hands.

Two or three days later, walking down the corridor, Natalia Dudinskaya, the Kirov's prima ballerina, saw Rudolf sitting morosely on the stairs. 'Rudik – what's the matter?' she exclaimed. 'The performance went so well.' The ballerina had been keeping an eye on the student ever since Pushkin had called her into the studio one evening to watch him perform the *Diana and Acteon* variations, which she herself had danced with Chaboukiani. 'I'd been surprised by how that boy, not even in the graduate class, could sense and feel the poses.' However, Rudolf did not confess his dilemma. He had received a letter of 'written gratitude' from the administration, and been told that he would be officially accepted in the Kirov at a salary of eighteen hundred roubles a month. But this was as a corps de ballet member, and with the Bolshoi demanding to know if he would be accepting his soloist contract, the time had come for him to make up his mind. Not even Nijinsky had started his Imperial Ballet career as a soloist, but Rudolf had been counting on setting a precedent, bragging to his classmates, 'You will see, you will see!' Sitting down beside him, Dudinskaya said, 'I hear you're going to dance in Moscow. Don't be foolish! Don't choose the Bolshoi – stay here, and we'll dance together.'

The idea, as Rudolf immediately realized, 'was fabulous!' Although in the final stage of her career, Dudinskaya and her partner, Konstantin Sergeyev, were regarded as national treasures: 'We had the Bronze Horseman, the Hermitage, the Russian Museum – and Dudinskaya and Sergeyev.' Rudolf had worshipped her from the moment he arrived in Leningrad, not only watching all her performances but studying the way she rehearsed other dancers. 'That was when I understood that I have to take everything available from all possible teachers.' For the company's prima ballerina to pick as her new partner a boy straight out of school was as much of an event as when

Mathilda Kschessinskaya — star of the Imperial Ballet and one-time mistress of Tsar Nicholas — chose the twenty-one-year-old Nijinsky to dance with her. 'Sounds like Hollywood story, doesn't it?' Rudolf later told film director Lindsay Anderson. 'I was waiting for something like that to happen.'*

Also in the audience at the graduation concert, sitting with a pounding heart in case Rudolf burned himself out, was a vivacious young physics student, Liuba Romankova, dancer-slim with large brown eyes, who had been introduced to Rudolf during an interval by their mutual friend Elizaveta Pazhi. Anxious for her protégé to meet people of his own age outside school, Elizaveta Mikhailovna asked Liuba if she would invite Rudolf for a meal — like many Leningrad families, the Romankovs kept open house on Sundays. 'Our cultural life took place at home. But it wasn't like a salon — it was a kitchen culture with people gathered round a table eating and talking.' A few weeks later, noting the promising omen of an address named after his favourite composer, Rudolf went along to 63 Tchaikovsky Street, a once-grand building with vaulted ceilings, peeling, panelled walls decorated with white Wedgwood-style cupid mouldings, and a sweeping wrought-iron staircase. The Romankovs' second-floor apartment, warmed by floor-to-ceiling wood-burning stoves, was crammed with relatives, three generations of whom were sitting at a large polished table surrounded by books, photographs and family clutter. Rudolf was immediately made to feel at home. 'Our mother and father were superb. They always treated our friends as their own.' At around three in the afternoon lunch was served — typical Sunday fare such as cabbage soup, blinis, cucumbers with dill, garlicky meatballs, boiled potatoes served straight from the saucepan, and sweet Georgian wine.

When people started getting up from the table at around seven, Liuba and her twin brother, Leonid, also a student at the Polytechnic Institute, invited Rudolf to stay and talk. As attractive as his sister, though much less outgoing, Leonid was tall and gentle, 'with a most delicate, refined mind and a generous heart'. (Years later Rudolf confessed to a mutual acquaintance that Leonid was probably his first love, although he hadn't realized it at the time.) Studying the subject they loved, playing all kinds of sports and attending the latest exhibitions, films, concerts and plays, they were the *Shestidesyatniki* — the children

---

* Dudinskaya gives a different version in Radik Kudoyarov's documentary *The Myth of Rudolf*, claiming, 'I didn't ask him — he asked *me*.'

of Khrushchev's thaw. 'It was an intoxicating time for young people in Russia. Our whole lives were ahead of us and the possibilities seemed endless.' Liuba and Leonid found the shy, taciturn Rudolf completely unlike anyone they had ever known. They noticed from the start how he didn't share their interest in politics – 'Not for anything would he allow himself to be drawn into a political debate . . . The only world he inhabited was that of the performing arts.'

That night they talked about literature and the new painting no longer banned from exhibition in Russia – Picasso, the French Impressionists and their favourite artist, the sensuous fauvist Kees van Dongen – chronicler of Rotterdam's red-light district and the Paris beau monde. Keen Anglophiles, then studying English with a private tutor, they immediately infected Rudolf with their enthusiasm to learn the language himself. Other passions – jazz being one – were of less interest to him: 'He was too immersed in classical music. His world of the arts was that of the nineteenth, not the twentieth century.' Nor did they share his fervour for Dostoyevsky – 'not popular with our group' – preferring the new writing they had discovered in the journal *Inostrannaya Literatura* (Foreign Literature), such as John Osborne's *Look Back in Anger* and work by such Americans as Hemingway, Faulkner, Kerouac and Steinbeck. They did not stop talking until the early hours of the following day.

Captivated by these two young people with their fresh perspective on life and learning, Rudolf suddenly saw his own horizon expanding from the narrow ballet world he knew, and as he left the house and walked back to Rossi Street, he felt euphoric.

He prolonged his sense of well-being on a Crimean holiday at the school *dacha*, where he kept himself apart from the other students – 'We never knew where he was' – and spent his time taking mud baths or lying on the beach. Then calamity struck. Returning to Leningrad, he was summoned to the director's office and given the following letter.

To Nureyev Rudolf Hamitovich
    The administration of the Kirov Theatre informs you that by the order of the Ministry of Culture of the Soviet Socialist Federation Republic you are being sent to the Ministry of Culture of Bashkirian Soviet Socialist Republic and you should apply there about your future work.

[signed] Temporary Director I. Glotov

The Ufa Ballet demanded his return as repayment to the Republic of Bashkir for its grant, and the Kirov administration agreed to let him go. Margarita Alfimova remembers seeing Rudolf running out of the room, 'crying and shouting'. Pushkin then arrived to calm him down, and he went back to the rehearsal. 'This was the first time I saw him in tears,' said Alla Sizova. 'He wept real tears and said, "I can't go back home. I can't leave the Kirov. I know there is nothing better in ballet than this theatre."'

Glotov had written back to the Bashkirian minister of culture, telling him that Nureyev would be returning 'to be at your disposal'. Rudolf, however, had no intention of complying. Almost immediately he caught a plane to Moscow and headed straight to the Ministry of Culture, where he was shown into the office of an assistant bureaucrat who told him that there was nothing to be done. He had to fulfil his duty to the state. But surely, Rudolf argued, an exception should be made when no fewer than three major companies had offered to make him their leading dancer. 'I said they were making a big mistake. I was being my own impresario.' There was nothing to be done, the woman repeated implacably. 'You'll be *damned*!' spat Rudolf as he stormed out of the room (later learning to his satisfaction that the day after their meeting she had been inexplicably dismissed). 'I cried on the pavement, and afterwards I went to the Bolshoi, and they took me. They said, "Go and collect your belongings and you'll start working in September."'

Back in Leningrad, where he began preparing to pack and bid goodbye to his friends, he found a note telling him to go immediately to the company office. There Boris Fenster, the Kirov's chief choreographer and artistic director, a kindly, avuncular man in his early forties, astonished him by saying wryly, 'Why are you making such a fool of yourself? Unpack your things and stay here with us.' Pushkin had successfully petitioned on Rudolf's behalf. He would not only be joining the company as a soloist but making his debut in a principal role by partnering Dudinskaya in *Laurentia* in November 1958.

Since graduating, Rudolf had been living in a workers' hostel, sleeping in a room with seven others, on bunk beds nailed to the wall like shelves. Now, however, he heard that the theatre would be allocating him a room of his own in an apartment in Ordinarnaya Street in the Petrograd quarter, a quiet, prestigious part of town. Such luxury was a dream to most Leningraders accustomed to communal living, but learning that he was expected to share the apartment with Alla Sizova, Rudolf was furious. Confronting Ninel Kurgapkina, one of his

favourite ballerinas, he exclaimed, 'Have you heard? They're giving me
a flat! With Sizova! They think by doing so I'll eventually marry her!
Never!!!'

Although so ideal together onstage, friends claim that they 'hated
each other in life', Rudolf once going so far as dismissing Sizova as 'just
a *Yivreka* [a Jewess]!' a remark that was not only crass but untrue.*
Most of his antagonism was rooted in lack of respect for her as a
performer; he found her emotionally cold and felt that she was
complaisant about her natural talent.† In the end, neither dancer
moved into the apartment. Rudolf preferred to stay in his 'cupboard',
which was near the theatre – Ordinarnaya Street was a forty-minute
bus ride from the centre – and where he did not have to arrange daily
chores like washing, cleaning, cooking, shopping; Sizova continued to
live with Natalia Kamkova, her teacher, while her parents moved into
her room. Rosa Nureyeva, who was longing for the chance to join her
brother in Leningrad, soon arrived to take over Rudolf's.

Most of November was spent preparing *Laurentia*, which Chaboukiani,
inspired by Dudinskaya's virtuoso brilliance, had made especially for
her. A Spanish tale with a suitably Soviet message, the ballet tells of a
heroine and her fiancé who lead a peasant uprising against a despotic
comendador. In it Chaboukiani created a new idiom for the male
dancer, giving it emotional power by blending bravura classical dancing with folk elements that he had imported from his native Georgia.
This was exactly the fusion that Rudolf had already been exploring in
character classes at school.

On the night of 20 November expectations in the theatre were at
fever pitch. 'Many of us remembered the brilliant creator of Frondoso,'
said Faina Rokhind, a Chaboukiani fan who was bereft when the dancer
left Leningrad. 'I was amazed that Rudolf didn't copy Chaboukiani,
who had always been the leader and soul of this ballet. Instead, he
brought elements of his own temperament and made the character
seem much more of a loner.' Friends in the audience sat holding their
breath, and for a second during a pirouette, in which Rudolf supported
his partner with one hand, they thought he was going to let her fall.

---

* Rudolf's habit of using anti-Semitic asides as obscenities, although common enough in
Russia, was a practice for which he would be seriously condemned in the West.
† Technique came so easily to Sizova that she hardly needed to work; Rudolf would set her
challenges when they danced together, getting her to substitute a sequence of Italian double
fouettés instead of the usual sixteen singles in her *Don Quixote* variation.

'But Dudinskaya was such a technician that she held herself up.' Before their entrance, the ballerina had told Rudolf to think only of himself, Laurentia was her most popular role and he should not concern himself with her. Intuiting this, one critic would write, 'In his duets with N. M. Dudinskaya, Nureyev dances too much on his own, forgetting that it is to Laurentia that his fits of passion should be directed, to her and her alone.' But for most of the audience, Rudolf's performance was thrilling – like 'an eruption of Vesuvius' – though some purists complained that his boiling bravura 'disturbed the subtle choreography'. Others were uncomfortable about the disparity between the dancers' ages – Dudinskaya was twenty-five years older than the twenty-one-year-old Nureyev. 'She was a prima ballerina on the decline; it was a privilege for *her* to dance with him,' remarked dance writer Igor Stupnikov, who remembered sitting in a box silently urging her to complete a notorious series of diagonal turns. 'A friend sitting beside me whispered, "At this moment, she has no enemies in the world."'

Rudolf gave Dudinskaya a new lease of life – as he would later do with Margot Fonteyn – but he would always acknowledge his debt to her. 'It was not just Pushkin who influenced my outlook on dance. Dudinskaya gave me the *idea* of classicism: musicality, attack, sense of time suspended.' From her he absorbed qualities that cannot be taught, such as stage magic and the power 'to sparkle, to make performance'. She was steeping him in an ideal, as the dance writer Elizabeth Kaye has noted. 'This was the nineteenth-century ideal of classicism.'

When his teacher Anna Udeltsova heard that they were screening a news item on Rudolf's *Laurentia* in Ufa, she rushed to the cinema, where she watched the 'inimitably delicate dashing Spaniard' as if spellbound. Immediately writing a letter to Rosa in Leningrad, she suggested that they should both start making scrapbooks of Rudolf's newspaper photographs and clippings. 'Previously, when I spoke about his talent, people used to mock me and said that I was probably carried away by him . . . [but] now the whole world can witness what was clear to me then, so let God give him good health and strong nerves.'

Offstage Rudolf's life was just as exhilarating. By now his friendship with Menia Martinez had developed into a romance; friends noticed how happy and excited they were in each other's company, always tender and demonstrative. 'It was the first experience for both of them to be in love. Although Rudolf was always a little self-mocking – he was very proud and didn't like to be seen to be sentimental – he was obviously very pleased that such a fabulous, sexy girl would give him her love.'

He also felt confident and stable in the company of the Romankov twins – the *Sportivniks*, as he and Menia called them because they were sports crazy. Having been nervous at first about joining in conversations that would expose his provincialism, Rudolf was now unintimidated by his intellectual friends, 'although it was obviously much easier for Rudik with our sports-oriented crowd'. On weekends he often joined them in Gorskaya, on the Gulf of Finland, where Liuba's volleyball team-mate had a *dacha*. Rock and roll was just catching on in Russia, and one night they held a contest in which the winner was the couple whose partner left her footprints on the ceiling. Rudolf enjoyed showing a couple of jocks who had mocked his slight physique how to lift a girl high above their heads, but he never took part in any activities that might cause him injury, choosing instead to sit alone on the beach watching the young madcaps at play. 'He was both with us and at the same time not with us.'

Early one evening as the sun was beginning to set, Rudolf walked away from the group and down towards the water. He had discovered an almost pantheistic fascination for nature, for the sea in particular, which would grow more intense throughout his life. He was gone so long that when he failed to return to the *dacha*, Liuba went in search of him. She had no romantic interest in Rudolf but felt a certain responsibility for him, and always made sure that he was not being left out. When she arrived at the edge of the shore, she found him staring out over the horizon. 'Rudik, what are you doing? Everyone's looking for you!' 'Ssh!' he whispered. 'Look how beautiful it all is.' As the enormous red ball of a sun slowly sank behind the gulf, the two stood watching until it disappeared and the sky began to darken. 'We turned away and, without saying a word, plodded back to the *dacha*.'

In April 1959, just before Rudolf was due to partner Dudinskaya in *Laurentia* for the second time, he tore a ligament in his leg so badly that he was hospitalized and declared unfit to dance for two years. When Pushkin visited the ward and saw his pupil lying on his bed in black despair, he invited Rudolf to move in with him and his wife. Since the Moscow contest when Rudolf's sudden success had brought home to the dance world how great a teacher Pushkin actually was, the two had grown closer than ever. And now, from the moment that Rudolf was taken into Pushkin's home, he became more of a son than a pupil.

'There, thanks to Pushkin's and his wife's vigilant care, and the doctor's daily visits, after twenty days I was able to go to class.'

Pushkin and his wife, Xenia Jurgenson, a forty-two-year-old Kirov coryphée coming to the end of her career, lived in a typical Soviet communal apartment opposite the school in Rossi Street. They shared a bathroom with their neighbours, and their room – twenty-five square metres – was unbearably hot in summer, as a chimney from the canteen below passed along one wall, but more than compensating for the discomfort was the cultivated atmosphere they had created around them. 'Here, in the Pushkins' household, Rudolf found not only the traditions of St Petersburg but also a home environment and ballet university all rolled into one.' The couple, who had no children of their own, were renowned for their kindness to young people – when the father of one of the students died, it was the Pushkins who nursed him through his period of mourning. And three times a year – on Alexander Ivanovich's birthday, after final exams, and on New Year's Eve – they would invite the whole class for a meal. Xenia considered the care of her husband's pupils an integral part of her duty to him; she darned their socks and shopped at the market for fresh vegetables and the best cuts of meat, which she cooked superbly. 'That's what impressed the boys so much: her taste and style – the trouble she went to for them. Alexander Ivanovich taught and Xenia Josifovna cared.'

She was also a born teacher in her way, drawing out youngsters by getting them to talk about themselves, and giving them advice, lending them books, and encouraging them to analyse what they had read – 'unobtrusively, never showing up their ignorance'. When shy young Galina Baranchukova arrived in Leningrad from Siberia, it was Xenia who took her under her wing, teaching her how to dress, how to shop:

> She set a wonderful example, saying how you should always buy things that were good even though they are expensive – there is no use in having cheap bad things – and teaching Alexander Ivanovich's pupils how to be gentlemen. When Xenia Josifovna came into the room after cooking in the kitchen, she would say to the boys who were sitting waiting for their dinner, 'So who is going to give me his chair?'

A tall, attractive Baltic blonde, Xenia looked half the age of her husband (who was ten years older), and was as earthy and extroverted as he was spiritual and mild. One day, soon after Rudolf had moved into the Rossi Street apartment, all three went to Tchaikovsky Street for one of the Romankovs' Sunday dinners, joining the usual group with Elizaveta and Veniamin Pazhi among the older guests. As the meal was coming to an end, Xenia, who was sitting beside Rudolf, reached across the table for a banana, which she slowly and suggestively began to peel. Just as she was about to put it in her mouth, she whispered something laughingly to Rudolf who, clearly embarrassed, snapped back one word in reply. Liudmila Romankova, the twins' mother, who heard what he had said, was shocked: '*Doura!*' (fool) was not a term that a young man should apply to an older woman. She waited until everyone had left, and when she and her daughter were alone together, said, 'I do believe that Xenia is having an intimate relationship with Rudik.' 'Mama!' protested Liuba. 'How could you *think* such a thing?' In her eyes Xenia was 'an old woman'. But then, over the next few weeks as she observed them together, she began to realize that her mother must be right.

3   XENIA AND MENIA

When Xenia fell in love with Pushkin she was a student at the Vaganova Academy and he was her pas de deux teacher. As relationships between pupils and staff were forbidden, they met in secret outside school – 'She was always running to a room somewhere to see him' – and as soon as Xenia graduated, they married. It was 1937: 'Ksusha', as Pushkin called her, was twenty and he was exactly ten years older. After a quiet wedding, they spent their honeymoon in the Ukraine – an eye-catching couple with their tanned, athletic bodies and stylish clothes. Pushkin sported a little skullcap to disguise his thinning hair, and dressed whimsically in pyjama-striped silk shirts or an all-white ensemble of flannels and shirt. As the daughter of a St Petersburg couturier, Xenia was even more fashion conscious: she might wear jaunty white ankle socks with character shoes, a bow tied round her head, or jewellery with her two-piece swimsuit, the white beads of her necklace highlighting her dazzling smile. Her vivacity and sense of fun affected everyone around her. That summer, she and her 'Sashinka' played like teenagers, lying in the shallows or practising lifts from their pas de deux classes. Barefoot on the beach, the teacher held his lovely young wife high above his head as she arched her back, her wavy blonde hair falling in a Rita Hayworth mane.

Xenia's first job in Leningrad was as a dancer with the Maly Theatre, but with Pushkin's help she was able to join the corps de ballet of the Kirov the following year. She had a good jump and was given the occasional key role, such as one of the two 'big swans' in *Swan Lake*, but being unusually tall for a ballerina, she did not progress beyond the next rank of coryphée. Nevertheless she took her work seriously, spending days in the studio preparing for a new role, often under Pushkin's guidance. At home their roles reversed, and it was Xenia, a formidably strong character, who was in charge. As Pushkin's closest friend, Dimitri Filatov, remembered:

> He was a very modest man, she was a motor. Xenia Josifovna was very supportive; she tried to help him, to protect him, as there were people

who took advantage of his soft, kind nature and he would be hurt quite often. Alexander Ivanovich was a teacher from God, but he was never rewarded because he was so shy: if you want medals and prizes, you have to push.

Pushkin's diffidence could exasperate Xenia at times – she resented the fact that colleagues in the theatre had been given decent apartments while they were still living in one room. He would not even appeal to Konstantin Sergeyev, artistic director of the Kirov Ballet during the early fifties, who, with his first wife, the dancer Feya Balabina, had been among their closest friends. But then Xenia herself refused to exploit the Sergeyev connection – 'She didn't want to put herself in the position of begging; she was too independent and saw it as going against her honour.'

It was Xenia, rather than the unworldly Pushkin, who minded about their inappropriate living quarters; her husband's thoughts were totally absorbed by his profession. 'Alexander Ivanovich worked *too* hard. He worked with his soul – never half power. He really loved his pupils; even when they were onstage, he'd be there in the audience, helping with his eyes.' Theirs was a good marriage, and they showed each other great affection, but after twenty years of conversations that invariably reverted to dance, Xenia 'wanted to hear something else'. As the granddaughter of Pyotr Jurgenson, Tchaikovsky's music publisher, she came from a wealthy family, and considered herself among Leningrad's intelligentsia. Her husband's parents, on the other hand, were simple people, and he had had only a basic education. When Liudmila Romankova went to the Philharmonic Hall with Pushkin one night, Xenia asked her afterwards, 'Was Alexander Ivanovich a very dull companion for you? He only knows ballet.'

In 1959 she gave up her career, but not by choice. 'It was very painful for her to stop; she felt she was still able to perform and had a great desire to do so, but Kirov dancers of her level were obliged to leave at a certain age.' This forced retirement affected Xenia bitterly – 'she never again came backstage to see us' – and with Alexander Ivanovich at school all day, and at the theatre most nights, she felt lethargic and isolated. Then Rudolf arrived. 'He was such an excitement in her life. After that, she had no other interests: Rudolf became her project,' says Liuba.

Determined to broaden his education by giving him only the best, Xenia cooked him delicious meals, guided his reading, took him to the theatre and concerts, and introduced him to their circle of friends –

'intelligent people with fascinating professions and a passion for the arts' – such as Pavel Vult, a professor of psychology, and Arno Gofren, an eminent surgeon with a scholar's knowledge of the architecture of St Petersburg. Every meal at the Pushkins' was a lesson in the finer points of etiquette: even when Xenia served just a snack, there would be a white linen cloth, candles, bone china and crystal glasses on the table. Rudolf had already been exposed through Anna Udeltsova and others to the niceties of St Petersburg manners, but it was clear that he still had a lot to learn. One evening, sitting with Xenia beside him as usual, he listened to a couple of guests praising a performance by the dancer Askold Makarov, who was also there. Unable to contain himself, Rudolf suddenly burst out with, 'When *I* leap, I leap right over Askold Anatolievich!' 'Puppy! You're such a puppy!' Xenia laughed, breaking the embarrassed silence by making everyone see the funny side.

With Rudolf, as with all her husband's pupils, Xenia played the role of both mother and coquette. Although no longer the beauty Pushkin had married, she had a good figure and liked to make an impact, continuing to dress modishly in clothes made specially for her. As Dimitri Filatov recalled:

She knew how to be attractive and how to make eyes at people. Alexander Ivanovich wasn't jealous, he understood. In their world it was normal for ballerinas to have admirers. They loved each other and had stayed together for a long time. Alexander Ivanovich knew that Xenia wouldn't do anything serious; he was sure she would behave properly.

In a clip of home-movie footage taken during dinner at the Pushkins' apartment, Xenia's deference towards her husband is clearly apparent. On her right sits a good-looking youth to whom she pays a lot of attention, but when the group stands up to make a toast, it's towards Pushkin that she instinctively turns first to clink glasses. With Rudolf's arrival, however, everything changed, and Xenia became fixated in a way she had never been before. 'She fell totally in love with Rudik and wanted to fill her soul with this feeling,' Liuba says.

Xenia was more than ready for a romantic escapade. All Pushkin's emotion was invested in his pupils, he was rarely at home, and when he returned late at night, he was always tired. 'She told Rudolf that Alexander Ivanovich no longer made love to her,' said Menia Martinez.

'And he was afraid, because he knew that she wanted him, and he had so much respect for Pushkin.'

To Rudolf, the strong-willed, sophisticated Xenia with her dancer's body and flirtatious ways was an irresistible force. However much he recoiled from the implications of what was taking place – the betrayal of a man he loved who had invited him into his home – he found himself in her thrall: she was a woman of 'enormous sexual appetite and great sensuality', he a twenty-one-year-old virgin who 'wanted to know'.

A close friend believes that Pushkin had no idea of his wife's transgression. 'He loved Rudik as a son and he thought that Xenia Josifovna shared his attitude.' If he did know, it may have been the reason he went out of his way to try to matchmake Rudolf with a Vaganova school contemporary, Gabriella Komleva: 'He wanted us to be together, and often invited me to Rossi Street, but nothing came of it.' Or he may have viewed Xenia's seduction as just another facet of his pupil's education, a timely initiation into the art of love. (Rudolf told Menia that the first time Xenia made love to him she'd said, 'I want you to know about this part of life . . . And also, I want you to feel like a man.') It caused no apparent rift in the marriage; the couple continued to work together as partners in Rudolf's development. Xenia was one of very few people from whom Rudolf would accept notes on his dancing. His contemporary Nikita Dolgushin remembers how he would watch her demonstrate original variations from rarely performed ballets, 'her husband correcting her when she couldn't remember a forgotten step'. Often after dinner Rudolf would stand – boots off, legs in position – in front of their antique oval mirror, practising his port de bras.

Xenia began coming to the school to watch classes, rehearsals and examinations. She had great authority with Pushkin and his boys, and would criticize and advise in a manner that was much more direct than her husband's. 'If one of the pupils couldn't do some complicated combination, she'd say, "Hey, how can you not do such a thing? It's simple! Try!"' One afternoon, after taking Rudolf to task for bungling a double pirouette in arabesque, she presumed when he didn't come home for dinner that she must have offended him. Eventually, just before midnight, he turned up. 'Rudik, where have you been?' cried Xenia with a mixture of exasperation and relief. 'Getting your two turns in arabesque,' came Rudolf's gruff reply.

To allow Rudolf to devote the maximum amount of time to his work, Xenia instigated a rigid schedule, persuading him to renounce

any aspects of his life which did not relate to the theatre. He obedi-
ently followed her regime, keen to avoid any dispute; he knew how
emotional and temperamental she could be – anything could make her
explode. Overseeing whom he saw as attentively as what he read, she
tried to dissuade him from going out at night, although from time to
time, feeling 'overfed with her care', he managed to slip away. He was
anxious to keep in touch with Elizaveta Pazhi, whom Xenia rarely
invited for dinner as she resented their closeness. 'She tried to create a
real wall between them.' She was also 'very against' Menia Martinez,
whom Rudolf was able to meet only when Liuba and Leonid covered
for him. 'He would tell the Pushkins that he was seeing us.' Although
never jealous of Liuba, because she posed no threat, Xenia became
'like a lioness' if she found out that Rudolf had been with the beautiful
young Cuban.

Xenia and Menia had virtually no contact with each other. It was
impossible for the twenty-year-old student to consider a woman twice
her age (and one she saw as 'large and looking like a man') as a rival.
'When Rudik told me he had been to bed with her, I thought: *What!*
With that monster!' With Menia herself, Rudolf was so affectionately
tactile that friends presumed theirs was a physical relationship, too.
'When Estelle Volkenstein asked me, I told her, "No, it's not what I
want, but I love him."' Even when the opportunity was there, Rudolf
did not attempt to take things further, telling Menia – 'the only virgin
in Leningrad' – that he respected her for holding back. 'It's good,
Menia. Good not to.' Once after dinner with Nikita Dolgushin and his
wife-to-be, a rehearsal pianist eighteen years his senior, they decided
to spend the night at the couple's apartment as it was too late to travel
home. 'They thought our situation was the same as theirs and put us in
a room with a single bed. We couldn't stop giggling because we were
so squashed and had to hold each other so as not to fall out, and then
we were giggling even more, thinking that they were thinking we were
making love.'

By the early spring of 1959, Menia's course was over, and the time
had come for her to return to Cuba. On the day she was due to leave,
Rudolf had a rehearsal scheduled with Dudinskaya to prepare for their
next performance of *Laurentia*. When he failed to appear, the ballerina
feared the worst: 'She was so nervous that Rudolf had eloped with
me.' But Rudolf was not among the group of friends at the station who
had gathered to see Menia off, and while she was glad to be returning
home, as she hadn't seen her family in years, Menia boarded the Red
Star to Moscow feeling badly let down. The train had barely pulled out

of the station when the door to her compartment slid open and there stood a beaming Rudolf, who announced, 'I'm coming with you!'

Throughout the journey they talked almost without a break: 'About how we were going to stay in contact, how we could be together. Rudolf was very emotional – it wasn't like before.' In Liuba's opinion, it had always been Menia who was the more committed of the two. 'She couldn't take her eyes off him. She was *totally* in love and dreamed that he would marry her. I had a lot of sympathy for Menia and tried to push Rudolf into proposing to her. "Oh, I know," he said, when I told him he should make a commitment to her. "But it would spoil my biography."'

Now, however, realizing that he was about to lose Menia, Rudolf began talking seriously about their future. In the middle of the night, stirred by the romantic atmosphere and rhythm of the train, he came down into her bunk and began to make love to her. 'But at that moment, I had no desire for him. I was stupid . . . A little girl.'

They spent their second night together in Moscow in a communal apartment near the Kremlin owned by Menia's friend Bella Kurgina, who was amazed to see Rudolf standing behind Menia at her front door. The two girls were as close as sisters, and Menia confided that he had proposed to her, adding excitedly, 'If we're together we can conquer the whole world!' Bella, who had never warmed to Rudolf – 'I found him very closed and uninteresting' – was concerned. 'I felt he was using her as a way to get out of Russia without a scandal, and yet I could see it was complicated – that he was genuinely attracted to her, and that there was great sympathy and feeling there.' The room where Bella lived with her husband and mother-in-law was only fifteen square metres; Menia slept on a camp bed with Rudolf beside her on the floor. 'Most of the night he was kneeling, kissing her hand and being so loving. From the way he behaved with Menia I could never have imagined that he would turn out to be homosexual.'

The following morning Rudolf insisted on going to the airport to see Menia off. When she was told that she would have to pay for the excess weight of her luggage – crammed with books and records – Rudolf reached for his wallet. 'It's not a problem,' he said protectively. When her flight was called, and the time came for him to say a final farewell, he had tears in his eyes and would not let her go. 'He thought he would never see me again.'

Rudolf went back to work. Since his triumph in *Laurentia* the previous autumn, he had resigned himself to accepting the frustrating regime of the Kirov, under which principal artists must wait, study and rehearse for performances that are few and far between. He had appeared onstage only twice in three months, on both occasions – 1 3 and 2 5 March 1959 – joining a quartet of cavaliers in *Raymonda* and acting, according to one observer, 'as if he'd been sentenced to hard labour'. The dance calls for perfect synchronization among the ensemble, but conformity was not in Rudolf's nature. 'It seemed to me that he was trying to jump higher, to make more pirouettes, irrespective of the other three.' In April his second performance of *Laurentia* came in for more criticism than praise. Neither he nor Dudinskaya was in top form, and fans detected an element of disrespect towards her. 'Everything seemed to disturb him that night, and we sensed he was thinking: I'm so young and pretty, but here I am dancing with an old lady. It was never put in words, but the audience understood, and everybody said, "This Tatar boy is so tough." '

Almost immediately Rudolf began preparing for his debut with the virtuoso ballerina Ninel Kurgapkina in *Gayane*. Nearly a decade older than he, and renowned for her spitfire temper, Kurgapkina proved more than a match for the brazen young star. First rehearsals took the form of a contest of wills until Rudolf realized he had met a fellow fanatic, and converted his initial combativeness into compliance and respect. Without protest, he repeated at least a dozen times a lift in which, crossing the stage, he carried Kurgapkina balanced on one hand above his head – until he had won her confidence. 'He was a little bit afraid of me, but he liked my attitude to work and life. I was obsessive in rehearsals but a normal person outside.' It was not long before the pair really had fun dancing together. Kurgapkina's 'amazing quality of earthiness and energy' excited him, and he admired her autonomy (during supported pirouettes she turned herself, and if ever he was over-attentive, she would snap, 'Don't mess!'). 'He saw real professionalism in Kurgapkina. She gave him a lot of advice and he listened to her, whereas there was nobody among the men that he took any notice of.'

In *Gayane*, a showy Soviet propaganda piece set on a collective farm, Rudolf performed the part of Armen, a hot-blooded worker-hero in the mould of *Laurentia*'s Frondoso. At his debut performance the verdict among the fans was that his rendering of the famous variation with flaming torches had been much better at his graduation performance. 'Surprisingly, the role did not suit his individuality, he's still very green. It was adequate but there was no courage,' noted his young fan Galina Palshinas in her diary. But by the next performance two weeks later, she had changed her mind. 'Everything went perfectly – I wanted to cover his path with flowers! If he had Diaghilev behind him he would be world famous tomorrow!'

Within the Kirov company itself there was no such enthusiasm for Rudolf's dancing. 'I didn't like his crazy technique onstage,' said Alla Osipenko, one of the new stars. 'I valued different aesthetics – the kind of good breeding [Nikita] Dolgushin had. At that time Rudolf was just a boy, he wasn't shaped. Pushkin gave him a base, but everything he became took place in the West. I was an admirer only later when I saw tapes of him.' The attitude of his male contemporaries was much the same. 'As an artist he didn't really reveal himself here' (Boris Bregvadze). 'He stunned Europe, but here nobody thought he was very special' (Serge Vikulov). 'We didn't appreciate what he was doing, because he based himself very much on ballet in the Western world which in those days we didn't know much about' (Vadim Desnitsky). Others found something distinctly disturbing about Rudolf's dancing. 'You didn't like it, but you couldn't stop watching it.'

Well aware of his own worth, Rudolf cared nothing about the opinion of 'the Salieris', except that he believed that within the company there were cabals of 'lifelong enemies' who actively wanted to get rid of him. When he learned that he wasn't among the dancers being called to Moscow for selection in the Seventh Communist World Youth Festival, to be held in Vienna, he suspected discrimination, and wanted to know why. He had refused to become a member of Komsomol, the youth wing of the Communist Party – 'I didn't want any group of people to decide my fate' – but had this made him too much an object of suspicion to be allowed to travel to the West? Or perhaps it was his impetuous dash with Menia to Moscow that had led the authorities to believe he might leave with her for good. When his mother told him that she had been 'grilled' about whether or not he was likely to defect, he decided to appeal to the unbiased Boris Fenster to plead his case. Not long afterwards, his name was added to the list of those going to Vienna.

That summer's trip to Vienna not only consolidated Rudolf's partnership with Ninel Kurgapkina, it marked the beginning of a lasting friendship. He had found a soulmate – 'Ninel had balls under her, so to speak,' remarks Baryshnikov. 'He liked that' – and one who similarly refused to toe the party line. On the long bus journey from Moscow, when the Komsomol representative instructed everyone to join in with a song, the pair remained silent; when everyone else was quiet, they sang out loud. The convoy stopped in Budapest for a short break, but half an hour later, when the dancers had settled back into their seats, there was no sign of Rudolf. 'This time he even ran away from me,' said Ninel. With some agitation the Komsomol official began searching the other buses while the group waited with increasing impatience. Eventually Rudolf appeared, to be greeted with wails of protest. 'How do I know when I'll be in Budapest again?' he declared. 'I wanted to see the opera house.'

When, on 25 July, the Russian convoy of forty buses arrived in Vienna, it was met by a crowd of émigrés who started trying to throw books through the windows of the buses. These were copies of *Dr Zhivago* (banned in the Soviet Union), every one of which was immediately confiscated. With their placards and protest songs the demonstrators made their presence strongly felt throughout the week, but failed to mar the sense of celebration and solidarity. The cafés, restaurants and dance halls of Vienna, 'the gayest, most beautiful and hospitable city' Rudolf had ever seen, were teeming with cosmopolitan young people – dancers, sportsmen, musicians – who had come from as far afield as the Americas and Australia. On one of their free evenings Rudolf suddenly said to Ninel, 'Let's run away and go dancing!' She changed into her favourite taffeta dress, which made a *schish, schish* sound as she moved, and looked simply stunning. As they took to the floor and started to jive, they created a kind of vacuum as everyone moved to the sides to watch. 'Nobody in the company ever found out. It was our secret.'

It was during a march past by the Cuban delegation that Rudolf suddenly spotted Menia Martinez: 'He was so happy to see me. He came to our hotel, to our classes, and spent so much time with me that my friends were saying, "Menia, this must be love."' She remembers Rudolf talking so openly about freedom that she feared for him. 'Ninel Kurgapkina came and begged me to tell him to stay with the Russians.' Although Rudolf insisted years later that defection was not on his mind at the time – 'Not then' – the urgency with which he kept proposing to Menia in Vienna suggests that he was at least keeping the option open: 'He was much more insistent, saying, "We have to do it here." But Rudik at that moment was not very important for me.'

With her emotions now invested in the political upheavals of Castro's new Cuba, Menia was no longer the doting young girl whom Rudolf had known in Leningrad; he found her 'cold', and told her, 'Now I think I love you more than you do me.' After watching her perform in a revealing costume, he could hardly contain his jealousy. 'It's not good for you to dress like that,' he remarked sulkily. Thinking that her attitude might change if he could find a way of going to Havana, Rudolf asked Menia to introduce him to Alberto Alonso, co-founder with his famous sister-in-law, Alicia, of the country's national ballet company. 'He was hoping for an invitation.'*

As Vienna was the first place where Rudolf had made any contact with the West, he was determined to exploit every opportunity the festival provided. 'I felt that, should I ever stay in the West, nobody would rush up to me to put me on a plate and hand me around like a cake. I understood that I would have to fight for myself.' With a multilingual Bulgarian colleague accompanying him as translator, he went out of his way to meet the French choreographer Roland Petit, whose *Cyrano de Bergerac*, performed that week, he had found 'so very new and strange'. Petit had specifically asked not to be disturbed, but found himself impressed by the 'young Cossack's curiosity and smiling eyes, recalling many years later his shy words of praise in English, and parting remark, "I see you again."'

During the ballet competition itself, staged in the Stadthalle, Vienna's largest concert hall, before an audience of seventeen thousand, it was once again Rudolf's performance in the showpiece *Corsaire* duet with Alla Sizova that created a sensation. They were the only couple to receive the highest score, but when Rudolf discovered that Natalia Makarova, Yuri Soloviev and the newly married Vladimir Vasiliev and Ekaterina Maximova were also to be given gold medals, he was far from pleased. To make his point, he refused to appear at the final ceremony, telling Sizova, who had to accept the prize and diploma for them both, 'I don't need that equality.' His behaviour offended his peers, but Rudolf didn't care. He was deliberately distancing himself from the Russian contenders.

In late August the Kirov arrived in Bulgaria to help mark the fifteenth anniversary of the country's liberation by Soviet troops. The members of the company were just waking up when their train pulled into the station and they heard a commotion outside. A welcoming party of fans, alerted to the 'Unique Phenomenon' of the young Rudolf by an article in the local press, were standing on the platform chanting 'Nu-re-yev! Nu-re-yev!' and passing crates of peaches to the dancers

---

* According to Alicia Alonso, they very much wanted Rudolf for their company, and approached the Kirov only to be told, 'It's not possible. He's not ready.'

through the window. 'It was events like this that made me aware of Rudik's incredible popularity and fame,' remarks Ninel Kurgapkina. On the way back to Moscow, the train stopped for forty minutes in Kiev, just time enough, Rudolf believed, to make a short expedition. He wanted to see the work of Mikhail Vrubel, the Russian painter who, together with Valentine Serov, Diaghilev had admired more than any other. To Rudolf he was a kindred spirit, 'a lonely figure in Russian art', who had broken with St Petersburg academic traditions and become a pioneer of modernism. On view in Saint Cyril Cathedral were the frescoes Vrubel had restored (chosen by Diaghilev to illustrate an issue of the magazine he founded and edited, *The World of Art*), together with four icons. Accompanied by an acquaintance from the orchestra, he took a taxi both ways, but by the time they got back to the station, the Kirov group had left.

> I told my friend that I was ready to bet he would find the entire orchestra waiting for him in Leningrad, laughing and joking about his missing the train, while my own absence would be construed in a completely different light by the company. It all happened just as I said . . . All the dancers had been unanimous in their conviction that this 'insubordination' would put an end to my career.

All it did, in fact, was cause comment: 'Have you heard? Rudik's defected . . . to *Kiev*!' quipped one dancer, while Boris Fenster was said to have remarked, 'One day he's going to stay behind somewhere for good.'

On returning to Leningrad, the company dispersed for the summer. Rudolf spent the first half of his holiday with his family, arriving with presents he had bought on tour: a mountain-goat fur coat for Farida, open-toed stilettos for his sisters. 'We had never seen such things in Ufa!' Walking past the Hotel Bashkiri, he spotted Pamira, who ran up to greet him. 'We talked for a bit, then I explained that I had tickets for a movie and was already late meeting my friends. He just stood and watched me go, probably not expecting that I would leave so soon.' Rudolf's schoolteacher Taisiam Ilchinova did not recognize him when he called out to her in the street – 'He'd grown up so much, become so handsome' – but they stood and chatted for quite a while. Others were equally amazed by the change in Rudolf. When Alik Bikchurin asked him how the 'feeble boy' he remembered could have turned into such an impressive young athlete, Rudolf replied, 'Exercise and food! Class, sports and dinners in the house of Alexander Ivanovich Pushkin.'

He had grown a whole head taller than Albert Aslanov, with whom he spent a good deal of his time; one night they walked until sunrise with Albert doing most of the listening as Rudolf held forth.

> He told me that on the journey to Ufa he had practised in the train with everyone in the carriage watching him. 'Well, so you haven't changed that much, my friend, you always needed nothing but ballet!' He laughed and then he started talking passionately about Vienna: the theatre, the architecture, the culture and the atmosphere.

They went several times together to see *A Flight with a Soul*, the film featuring Rudolf's 1958 *Corsaire* duet, which was showing locally. 'I was really impressed. I said, "I remember that you wanted to jump like Yasha Livshiz [a Bashkirian principal], but now you're doing it better. I've never seen *chaînés* like those!"' At the theatre where Rudolf took class while he was in Ufa, his ex-colleagues were also amazed by the huge improvement in his technique. 'Some already knew about his success, because they had friends in Leningrad,' said Sveta Baisheva, his partner from Pioneer days. 'He was just beautiful, and people looked on him very differently now.'

From Ufa, Rudolf went to spend a few days by the Black Sea. He had asked his Vaganova ex-classmate Marina Vasilieva where she was going for her holiday, adding vaguely, 'Maybe I'll come to see you.' Her mother, of whom he was very fond, ran a students' summer *dacha* situated on a long deserted beach backed by distant hills. Marina was sunbathing one day when she heard Rudolf calling her name. He didn't stay there long, but joined in all the fun, posing for photographs by performing showpiece duets with Marina in the sand. When he returned to Leningrad, Xenia was among a group of fans waiting for him at the station – she never failed to come and meet him – but spotting a favourite of his, a young girl who attended every one of his performances, he brushed straight past her. 'And that was my great mistake. Since that time, Xenia Josifovna changed her attitude to me one hundred per cent.'

Petite and pretty, with a round face and large plaintive eyes, Tamara Zakrzhevskaya was a student of literature and philology at Leningrad University, and also had an encyclopaedic knowledge of ballet. Their growing attachment was already resented by Xenia, who could feel her influence on Rudolf ebbing away.

> She got very jealous when she felt anyone coming too close to him; she thought he belonged to her. She was a very kind woman but a tough one, who gave you no possibility of escape. 'You must only think about tomorrow's classes,' she used to tell him. She was like a dictator. She had to know everything, to control everything – not just everyday routine but also his private life. To be Xenia's friend you needed to dance her dance and not everybody could do that.

Attempts to resist her hold brought out the worst in Rudolf. When Alla Sizova went into the studio one day, she saw him with Xenia and overheard him being 'very unpleasant'. As Sizova came closer to ask him something, he whipped round, hissing, 'This is not for your ears – get out!' 'The situation with Xenia was very uncomfortable for Rudik,' remarked Liuba. 'He couldn't push her away because she loved him and did everything for him.' And he couldn't do without her. Not only did Xenia take care of day-to-day practicalities, she was much more adept than Pushkin at helping him deal with theatre politics. Encouraging him, as Baryshnikov put it, 'not to pay attention to the assholes', she gave him the confidence to be himself.

> Rudolf was pushed around because he didn't play normal games. His way of dealing with people was totally unorthodox. He was a wild man compared with the standards of Leningrad behaviour: he said exactly what he thought. Xenia had a very rational approach to things. She sorted out his problems, told him how to behave, and calmed him down.

Although their liaison was no secret in the theatre, no one gossiped about it out of respect for Pushkin, who 'gave the impression that it was taking place in someone else's family'. Nevertheless the teacher's undiminished devotion to Rudolf struck fellow pupils as extraordinary; they looked on in disbelief as Alexander Ivanovich brought a tub of water into the studio one day to make him a footbath. 'It's not difficult for me to do and he needs to save his feet,' he felt obliged to explain. Quietly, patiently, always loyal, Pushkin allowed Rudolf the independence and liberty he craved. 'In Russia he met a wall, but Alexander Ivanovich encouraged and inspired him to do something new.' Like Chaboukiani collaborating with his teacher Vladimir

Ponomarev to change the old order of things, together they reworked the famous male variations to make the dancer appear more brilliant, introducing in *La Bayadère*, for example, a coda of *doubles assemblés* circling the stage, which is still performed today. 'It was a real example of how much a teacher could give his pupil and how a pupil could develop the teacher,' said Oleg Vinogradov.

Around this time, other mentors besides the Pushkins began to exert their influence, particularly Sergei Sorokin, a well-known balletomane and collector. 'Seriozha', as his friends called him, worked in the House of Books on Nevsky Prospekt, which specialized in foreign literature and art and dance books during a period when books were rarer than nylon stockings. Speaking several languages and able, due to Polish connections, to travel without restrictions, he seemed to know everyone in the ballet world, and would speak to Rudolf about Balanchine, Agnes de Mille, Frederick Ashton and Margot Fonteyn – all of whom he claimed to have met. When artists from visiting companies were in town, they would come to the shop or to one of his tea parties. 'Seriozha knew everything about everybody, but people adored him because he was very discreet.' His elegantly furnished apartment was 'a choreographic Hermitage', crowded with dancer figurines, postcards, documents, photographs and Western ballet magazines – an archive so comprehensive that it is now housed in the Vaganova school museum. 'It was here, in Leningrad, that Rudolf's passion for collecting first began,' said Vadim Kiselev, a young curator and ballet fan who lived next door. His room on Sozhusa Pechatnikov Street also housed a trove of antiques, art books, Meissen figurines, old English prints, tapestry screens and – his most prized possession of all – an eighteenth-century harpsichord that mesmerized Rudolf each time he came to visit.

Rudolf was still a student when Kiselev, who worked opposite the school at the State Museum of Theatre and Musical Art, first spotted him throwing snowballs in the adjoining yard. 'Even then I could see the beautiful catlike plasticity of his movements.' Encouraged by his tutor, Vera Krasovskaya, to befriend Rudolf, he invited him to view the collection. As they stood together in the beautiful, gold-panelled room, looking at engravings of Taglioni and Camargo, Rudolf made various comments such as, 'Oh – so already they knew how to do cabrioles!' and asked the kind of questions that would interest only a connoisseur. He was particularly fascinated to learn about early photography, wondering aloud how Nijinsky could have held his poses for the length of time the exposures required.

Five years older than Rudolf, with wavy blond hair and Cupid's-bow lips, Kiselev was 'an exotic' by Leningrad standards, one of a coterie of homosexual friends that also included Sorokin.* He says that they, together with Marietta Frangopoulo, the curator of the Vaganova school museum, were already aware of Rudolf's true orientation. 'We understood that his volatility came about partly as a result of this. Marietta used to talk to him about it, she would tell him that he shouldn't be ashamed.' One night Kiselev, who 'just fell in love with him and that's it', invited Rudolf to his apartment. With seduction in mind, he had bought a bottle of Armenian cognac and two hundred grams of caviar, which he served on bone china to impress Rudolf. But the evening did not go according to plan. His delicate sensibilities already affronted by the young Tatar's gross table manners, Kiselev then found his advances rudely repelled. They parted 'almost enemies', and had no further contact until Rudolf turned up at the museum one day, saying, 'I think I offended you.' He apologized, and while continuing to flirt with Kiselev (addressing him as 'Adonis'), resumed an acquaintance free of sexual ties.

Sorokin was also smitten with Rudolf, but much more timid about expressing his interest. An amateur dancer in a Palace of Culture troupe, and uninhibitedly camp, he was known as *Zub za zub*, 'a tooth for a tooth', because of his prominent, criss-crossed teeth. 'Rudolf felt pity for Seriozha because he was as ugly as Quasimodo, and he appreciated his kindness.' Lavish with his gifts of gloves and expensive scarves, Sorokin would take Rudolf on long walks around Leningrad, pointing out places of special interest and beauty. A Platonic figure, he often drew his young protégé into intellectual debates. Among subjects they discussed was Tchaikovsky's death, Rudolf being convinced that the composer had commited suicide to save his family from the shame of his homosexuality. But although his endorsement of this theory suggests that male love was starting to occupy Rudolf's mind, he was not yet willing to consider it as an option for himself. (Years later he told a lover in London that when he had found himself attracted to a boy on a Leningrad bus he had felt so ashamed that he got off at the next stop.)

He spent the early autumn of 1959 preparing for his debut in *La Bayadère* with Dudinskaya. Her original partner had been Vakhtang Chaboukiani, who had virtually rechoreographed the role of Solor as a showpiece for himself. Now a director of Tblisi Ballet, the

---

* By bizarre coincidence both men met violent early deaths; in each case their murders were a direct result of their homosexuality.

fifty-year-old Chaboukiani was on a visit to Leningrad when he suddenly appeared in one of the Kirov studios to watch Dudinskaya
rehearsing with the young Nureyev. Up until this point, the back-
grounds of these two male stars were almost identical. Born with the
same wild determination to achieve his goal, Chaboukiani also came
from a poor family in the south. He had set his heart on studying in
Leningrad where he arrived late in his teens, and within three years,
had caught up and covered the entire syllabus. 'They both gave themselves to dance with soul, with passion,' says Vera Krasovskaya.
'Chaboukiani and Nureyev were the type of performers who with
their appearance onstage changed its whole spirit.' The opportunity,
therefore, to show off in front of his idol would have been a thrilling
experience for Rudolf, had it not been for the fact that the veteran star
hardly paid him any attention. 'He was looking at him with only half an
eye, and later we heard that he had said, "That boy is too big for his
boots."' Dudinskaya was also said to be displeased with Rudolf's
attitude during rehearsals, and it was around this time that he received
a letter from a fan-turned-friend warning him that he was getting a
reputation for being impossible.

When he was in Moscow for the 1958 student competition, Rudolf
had forged a close rapport with Silva Lon, known as the 'ninth pillar of
the Bolshoi'* because of her unbending support of the company.
Responding to Silva's comment, he replied: 'I don't know what people
are saying, but I myself don't feel above it all because there is no
reason. I don't provoke Vakhtang . . . we don't have any contact, but
his courtiers [at the Kirov] have decided to keep me in the corps de
ballet.' Then came word that Dudinskaya was not going to perform
with Rudolf as scheduled. His fans 'knew for sure that Rudik had
offended Natalia Mikhailovna', but the ballerina insists that she cancelled because of a leg injury. 'It was such a pity for me, I really wanted
to dance it with him.' Olga Moiseyeva, a ballerina of Kurgapkina's
generation, was at home one afternoon when she received a telephone
call from the company office, telling her to get to the theatre as quickly
as she could: she was dancing *La Bayadère* with Nureyev in a few hours'
time. 'No, I'm not . . . I've never so much as shaken his hand,' she
protested. But dance together they did, 'and it was perfect'. Unlike
the peasant heroes Rudolf had danced to date, *La Bayadère*'s Solor is
an Indian warrior of royal caste whose nobility Rudolf conveyed
with extraordinary eloquence; never had his Oriental sinuosity and

* The theatre's classical façade has eight pillars.

ballerina borrowings been seen to greater effect, elongating his line and refining it with astonishing beauty and lightness.

In the audience that night were Hamet and Farida, watching entranced as their son flew across the stage 'like a god of wind'. 'It was then,' says Razida, 'that our father realized Rudolf had made the right choice.' However provincial his parents may have appeared amid Leningrad's cultural elite, Rudolf was eager to introduce them to his circle. Worlds apart, and with nothing but Rudolf in common, the Nureyevs and the Pushkins formed a bond of sorts; Alexander Ivanovich congratulated Hamet on his gifted son, while Xenia went out of her way to befriend Farida, keeping in touch with her over the years with letters and postcards.

At Rudolf's suggestion, his friend Tamara accompanied his mother to another *Bayadère* performance, but Farida could hardly concentrate on what was taking place onstage, so agitated was she that the fur coat Rudolf had given her would be stolen. The minute the curtain fell she rushed off to the cloakroom to find out.

> She was a dear little thing. She spoke Russian badly and would converse with Rudik exclusively in Tatar. I even learned one phrase by heart, so often did I hear it spoken. *Akcha bar?* (Got any money?), which is what Rudik would ask every time I saw them together. *Iok* (No) would come the reply, and without a word Rudik would reach into his pocket for money.

Back at work, still full of pride over his son, Hamet told factory colleagues of Rudolf's plans to move the family to Leningrad. (When news came the following summer that the dancer had been picked to perform at a private gathering before the Soviet premier and the Central Committee of the Communist Party, the usually taciturn Hamet could hardly contain his excitement: success of this kind in the family was beyond even the utopian dreams of his youth.)

With the most important debut of his career coming up – that of Albrecht in *Giselle* – Rudolf, who was determined to revitalize every aspect of the role, began thinking of ways to enhance his appearance. His interest in costume had begun at school when he would beg his room-mate Leo Ahonen to bring back Western tights from Finland (being nylon, they fitted much better than Russian ones, which were made of silk and wrinkled at the knees). 'He wanted them so badly that he used to pay me in instalments.' Once in the Kirov, Rudolf turned for advice to its leading designer, Simon Virsaladze, who started teaching him about colour and the texture of materials, as well as helping him contrive ways of disguising his physical disadvantages. 'Rudolf understood very early that with his middle height and short legs he had to do something to overcome this and to improve his line.' Virsaladze, who saw himself as a descendant of Diaghilev's designers, with a similar mission to inject his work with contemporary resonance while maintaining a reverence for the past, began to work with the dancer in the redesigning of his costumes, much as Alexandre Benois had done with Nijinsky.

With Virsaladze among them, a small group of intelligent and artistic homosexuals now surrounded Rudolf, each eager to contribute to his development. 'He very much wanted to get rid of his Tatar cheekbones,' remarked Vadim Kiselev, who demonstrated ways of using makeup to shade the face, and suggested that he try out different wigs because he would look more beautiful with a smaller head. 'Small head, big cock!' Rudolf joked provocatively. Through an acquaintance in the Paris Opéra Ballet, Sergei Sorokin imported a dance belt that enabled Rudolf to wear tights with a short jacket, Western-style, just in time for his *Giselle*. Walking into the Kirov's costume department one day, the dancer held out a sample of grey material and a pair of white tights, instructing a wardrobe mistress to dye the tights exactly the same shade; Virsaladze, a 'genius with colour', had encouraged him to aim for a more subtle combination of tones than the traditional Albrecht outfit. When the woman refused, telling him that she was not authorized to alter anything, he exploded, reducing her to tears. 'We never saw such impudence in the old stars,' she complained. But Rudolf got his way. 'Naturally people would say, "Why is this permission given just for Rudik",' commented Sergiu Stefanschi. 'And they resented it when he came onstage looking so beautiful. But the rest of us, we loved it. And the public adored him.'

On 12 December 1959 the Kirov Theatre was packed to capacity with people jostling for standing room. 'Everyone, let me tell you, knew something was happening, something new and wonderful.' Audiences were accustomed to seeing Albrecht played in Sergeyev's image: a nobleman who dallied with the pretty peasant girl Giselle, and when tragedy struck, signalled his emotions in exaggerated, old-fashioned passages of mime. But from Rudolf's first entrance – 'like a hooligan boy' with a ragged, rebel mop of hair – Kirov traditions were instantly overturned: what people saw instead was a thrilling embodiment of modern youth, 'a sparkling, beautiful, healthy young man', whose acting was natural and sincere. Rudolf's Albrecht was no urbane womanizer from a more elevated world, but a recklessly romantic kindred spirit who loses his head to love with all the ardour and impulsiveness that come with first experience. Even more remarkable was the way he adapted the role to fit his own abilities, making the drama speak through his own spontaneous style – and even through his technical limitations.

In the second act he introduced an innovation that 'had not been inserted without a struggle'. When the French star Michel Renault performed Albrecht to Yvette Chauviré's Giselle in Russia he substituted a long series of *entrechat six* beats for the usual *brisée* sequence.[*] Struck by how effective this was, Rudolf decided to borrow the idea, having first convinced his coach, Yuri Grigorovich, 'that they were a logical and natural part of my interpretation'. They certainly were. 'What we saw was not an exhausted dancer but the character of Albrecht who has to dance until he almost drops dead,' remarked Faina Rokhind. And because Rudolf was now featuring, rather than attempting to hide, his growing loss of control, critics found they could excuse his 'blurring of correct form', as he had made it completely integral to his performance.

This rawness was strikingly at odds with the academic clarity of Rudolf's Giselle – the elegant, airy Irina Kolpakova, so slender and exquisitely proportioned that she was often likened to a porcelain figurine. She, too, was young and inexperienced, but while some found her cold by comparison with Rudolf, others noticed a new freedom, 'as if he had awakened something in her'. To Vera Krasovskaya 'the two came together to complement one another perfectly'; yet the ballerina herself admits that she was not then sufficiently receptive to Rudolf's radical approach.

It was very strange for me, strange for everybody. It was a period in the Kirov when we tried to keep to tradition in order to help the audience understand the time and the place. Rudik had strength and energy, and his acting was fresh and new, but I wasn't really ready to see that. I was a very traditional ballerina at that time. I wasn't at all excited when I heard that I was cast opposite Rudik; I wanted my husband [Vladilen Semyonov] to partner me. I needed a prince, not a little boy saying love words.

* Renault was also the first male dancer Rudolf saw wear a short jacket.

There were others who felt similarly, that by depriving the hero of his breeding Rudolf's interpretation went too far beyond the bounds of convention. The feminine quality in his dancing, so alien to Soviet males, also divided people: the great ballerina Alla Shelest, his next Giselle, loved the 'tenderness that breathed from his Albrecht', but for his contemporary Serge Vikulov, this touch of androgyny was risible: 'With Kolpakova and Nureyev we had a girl and another girl as the boy: you couldn't believe in their love.'

Rudolf did, in fact, unbalance the ballet that night, but not in the way Vikulov implied. When he danced Albrecht the character ceased to be a supporting role, because all eyes were on him. Even during the heroine's key moment – the famous mad scene at the end of Act 1 – he diverted the audience's attention to himself simply by doing nothing. Instead of reacting with standard horror to Giselle's crazed despair, Rudolf concealed his feelings 'behind a mask of inertia', proving the power of stillness and stage presence over mimetic noise. Olga Moiseyeva asked him later, 'Rudik, why didn't you do something? She's *dying.*' 'I know,' he replied. 'I decided to do nothing because I felt nothing.'* 'With him there was no faking onstage, and as a result, the emotional impact was staggering.'

Faina Rokhind watched Rudolf through her opera glasses from the third circle, thinking of the great Russian dancers she had seen: Ulanova; Dudinskaya; her idol, Chaboukiani; and of legends such as Pavlova and Nijinsky. 'And I told myself "the name of Nureyev will be among them." For me that performance was a shock which affected the rest of my life. When I saw *Laurentia* I knew Rudolf was going to be a great dancer. When I saw *Giselle* I knew he was going to be a genius.' As the curtain came down the applause was so tumultuous that it seemed as though the vast crystal chandelier would come crashing to the ground. 'This was possibly Rudik's greatest performance the whole time he was in Leningrad,' writes Tamara.

The number of Nureyev fans grew with each performance. 'Soon a wonderful thing began to happen. It was like a fever, a madness.' Girls would pick armfuls of lilacs from the Field of Mars and wear huge skirts in order to smuggle the flowers inside the theatre, where they

---

* The passivity of Rudolf's Kirov performance was almost certainly following the example of Nijinsky, who 'stood pensive and bit his nails' during Karsavina's mad scene. As she wrote in her memoirs, 'I was sadly taken aback when I found that I danced, mimed, went off my head and died of a broken heart without any response from Nijinsky.'

were banned. Next, balletomanes with seats in the 'blind box' nearest the stage went into action, using ropes to lower the bouquets to a group waiting beneath. The completion of the final grand pas de deux was the signal. 'Then suddenly, from everywhere, the stage would be strewn with flowers for Rudolf.'

Complicity among the fans turned to jealousy at any sign of favoritism (one went as far as informing on another to the Komsomol Committee). Inevitably the girls to whom Rudolf paid attention were those who had something to offer him. Silva Lon, who worked at the state theatre booking agency in Moscow, would arrange tickets for him and somewhere to stay when he was in town. She often gave him books, and in return he sent her photographs of himself, and letters in which he confided thoughts on his performances. He was closest of all to Tamara, whom he would quiz whenever they met about what she had learned at the university that day. Her tutors had given him permission to attend lectures with her, and afterwards the pair would have long discussions, particularly about the Silver Age poets of the 1920s and 1930s. He absolutely devoured a slim volume of Balmont's verse she acquired for him from the faculty library, telling her that he had taken lines from 'Sin miedo' ['Without fear'] as his motto: 'It's about me,' he said pointing to the following passage: 'If you are a poet and wish to be powerful and to live forever in the memory of men, strike them to the heart with the melodious creations of your imagination, temper your thought upon the flame of passion.'

Increasingly solipsistic, Rudolf found he was moved most by literature that reminded him of himself. When he managed to get hold of a copy of Inostrannaya Literatura containing J. D. Salinger's Catcher in the Rye, he was captivated by the sensitive outcast Holden Caulfield, that fellow champion of youthful rebellion, and had just finished reading it when Tamara called at the Pushkins' apartment to see him. Pointing at the magazine, he exclaimed, 'No sleep for you tonight! You won't be able to put this down!' Xenia, who was also in the room, overheard him, and said that she would love to read it, too. Rudolf's reaction left both women speechless: 'What do you need it for, Xenia Josifovna? . . . Tamara can have thirty new thoughts in the time it takes you to come up with one!' With those words he disappeared out the door. Xenia was visibly shattered – her humiliation made worse by the fact that his young friend had witnessed it – but, incapable of blaming Rudolf, she directed her resentment at Tamara, who found that she was no longer welcome at Rossi Street. With a guilty sense of collusion, the pair went out of their way to avoid Xenia. Whenever they attended a concert together, Xenia would invariably be waiting outside the Philharmonic Hall to take Rudolf home. 'Xana!' he would exclaim under his breath, as they rushed towards another exit.

It's hard to know whether it was the shame Rudolf felt about the nature of his relationship with Xenia that accounted for his brutal behaviour towards her or the shame he felt he was expected to show – when they were alone together, things may have been quite different. Whatever the case, Xenia was unable to break free. 'She was completely obsessed by him,' remarked one friend. 'She wanted to live his life, and she enjoyed sharing his fame.' 'For the rest of her life there was only one person for her,' said another. 'I think she made up some kind of fairy tale for herself in her mind, building up the situation into romantic love.'

Their 'odd ménage' may have been even more complex. Years later Rudolf confided to friends that while he was living with the Pushkins he had made Xenia pregnant, 'But she didn't want to let the baby live.' Again, in 1992, only months before he died, he confessed to his Vaganova schoolmate Egon Bischoff about his involvement, adding: 'What would you say if I told you I might have had a child by her?' Pushkin, he said, never knew about the pregnancy or its termination. 'I was quite shocked,' said Bischoff. 'I hadn't thought the relationship would go that far.'

For Xenia to have undergone an illegal abortion would seem to have been the ultimate degradation, but in fact the procedure at that time was fairly matter-of-fact. 'Everybody did it,' said one friend of Rudolf's. 'I did it six times. It was only a question of paying.' More controversial is whether or not Rudolf's claim is true: there were two other women whom he said he made pregnant before he defected, and three more in the West. Fathering a child – and specifically a son – was a lasting ambition for Rudolf: it was a way of duplicating himself. But did it amount to more than a fantasy? Ninel Kurgapkina, whom Rudolf also claimed to have impregnated in Russia, dismisses the suggestion with a burst of laughter. '*Erunda* [bullshit]! It was Xenia,' she insists.

There was, actually, an infatuation of sorts between the two dancers. 'But not like those liaisons fraught with jealousy,' said Xenia's young friend Alla Bor. 'It was very open. Ninel was very pretty and very playful, and Rudik was always around her, laughing and having fun.' The ballerina Alla Osipenko agrees. 'He was always so bright and alert and smiling that we naturally assumed he was in love.' Outsiders assumed the flirtation was physical, but the two were determined to keep people guessing. Rudolf told some friends that he did have an affair with Ninel, and others that he wanted to but didn't. Ninel joked to a dancer acquaintance that she had 'practically to rape Rudolf', but now insists that they were no more than friends. 'A lot of people thought we were lovers, but we weren't. We had a romance, but we didn't make love. If he hadn't defected, maybe we could have had some sort of relationship. We were very, very close and I was good-looking then. Even when I met him years later, he said, "What a shame that we didn't."'

During an end-of-the-year tour of Egypt, they had a lot of fun together in Africa, 'which meant that we slept very little'. On New Year's Eve the whole company attended a banquet where a famous Egyptian belly-dancer provided the entertainment. When dinner was over, she sidled seductively up to the Kirov table and invited everyone to dance. Only Rudolf rose from his chair and followed her on to the floor. With his eyes fixed on the *ghazi*'s shimmering low-slung skirt, he began imitating her hip movements, contrasting voluptuous gyrations with rapid convulsions, spins and shimmies, building up to a climax of such intensity that he appeared to be locked in a kind of trance.

It was during this tour of the Middle East that a young man approached Rudolf in the hotel foyer one night and tried to start a conversation with him. 'Do you speak English?' '*Nyet.*' '*Parlez-vous français?*' '*Nyet.*' '*Sprechen Sie Deutsch?*' '*Nyet.*' '*Parla italiano?*' '*Nyet.*' For Rudolf the encounter was shaming, not because of its possible homosexual intent – and certainly not because of the company ban on contact with strangers – but because it made him seem provincial. 'So as soon as I went back to Russia I found a teacher straightaway to learn English.' When his sister Rosa asked why, he explained that 'he didn't want to be deaf and dumb when he was abroad'.

Back in Leningrad, Rudolf's disregard for rules became more brazen than ever: one scandal followed another, as if he were deliberately refuelling his growing reputation as a *monstre sacré*, indulging what Kenneth Tynan once called 'the athletics of personality'. He had several clashes with Mikhail Mikhailovich Mikhailov, a company *répétiteur* known for his old-school ways and civilized demeanour. ('You could spot him in the street because of his upright carriage.') Mikhailov was meticulous about retaining the traditions of Russian pantomime because he didn't want to lose the flavour of the Imperial Theatre. To Rudolf, however, this was an old-fashioned, posturing approach, more suited to opera than ballet. 'He and Nureyev came from two different worlds,' says Igor Stupnikov. 'It was a collision of pre- and post-revolution.' As Mikhailov's speciality was the coaching of character roles, it was under his eye that Rudolf prepared for his first *Don Quixote*, a robustly comic four-act ballet, with Ninel Kurgapkina cast opposite him. After giving much time and thought to his new role (the playful lover from volume 2 of the Cervantes novel), Rudolf had developed a particular effect he wanted to achieve – a more distinct colouring of the classical steps with a Spanish idiom. Instead of running onstage to perform his variation, he decided to come out slowly and deliberately, like a toreador approaching a bull. Dismayed by Rudolf's deviation from the correct tempo, Mikhailov stopped him and ordered him to do it again. The dancer quietly repeated his entrance, only this time it was even slower. 'Rudik,' Kurgapkina whispered, 'do it quickly just for Mikhailov, and then you can perform it onstage the way you want to do it.' 'Why should I?' he demanded. 'Why should I fake it for him if I'm going to do it my way on the stage?' Exclaiming that he refused to work under such conditions, 'Pihal Pihalovich', as Rudolf would now refer to him – *pihal* means 'fuck' – left the studio. 'At that time no one could argue with Rudik.'

His debut in *Don Quixote* acquired more notoriety still, as Rudolf was prepared to sabotage a performance simply to make his point. The first acts passed without incident, but during the last interval, which dragged on from twenty minutes to nearly an hour, it became obvious that something was wrong. In his dressing room, surrounded by flowers, the dancer sat with his legs casually propped up on a table, as both Sergeyev and Mikhailov remonstrated with him. He was refusing to go onstage in the fourth-act costume of short baggy trousers because these 'lampshades', as he called them, foreshortened the line of the leg. 'Why should I?' he argued. 'In the West, they've been dancing in tights for years.' As a dishevelled Xenia – 'terribly upset, on the verge of tears' – went rushing out into the auditorium to find Tamara in the hope that she could persuade him to change his mind, Rudolf's dresser stood by patiently, holding the offending breeches in his hands. 'Replace me with anyone you want. I'm not going onstage in them. They're ugly. Only without trousers,' he remarked implacably.

Finally Rudolf got his way and appeared onstage to a chorus of gasps. He looked naked! He was bound to be dismissed, just as Nijinsky had been fifty years earlier for daring in the presence of the dowager empress to wear 'an indecent and improper costume' of Renaissance-style tights without the traditional covering of a pair of trunks. It was, in fact, a replay of the scandal of 1911, but whereas Nijinsky, after his triumphant debut in *Giselle*, had been summoned to the director's office the next day and dismissed, Rudolf not only went unpunished but won the admiration of his male colleagues for having scored a pioneering victory. 'After that night, no man could tolerate those trousers. We were entering a new era and . . . Nureyev was a beacon of the future.'

The critics, on the other hand, were shocked by the arrogance underlying his *Don Quixote*. 'Why on earth does Nureyev – sporting his "trendy" haircut – feel he has to stalk the stage with such an air of imperturbable disinterest?' wrote Vera Krasovskaya. 'He should learn not to play so fecklessly with his own talent.' Valeria Chistyakova also deplored the visible indifference he showed onstage. 'This is unforgivable behaviour . . . and implies disrespect not only for one's own talent but also for one's audience.' Their comments were justifiable enough. Unchallenged by the lack of dances for the male lead, Rudolf made no attempt to hide his boredom as he sat onstage, smiling and nodding to a friend whom he had spotted in the orchestra. The audience, however, showed no sign of displeasure; when the final curtain came down, the theatre exploded, flowers cascaded around the dancers, and a large group of Americans – the entire cast of *My Fair Lady*, then touring Russia – 'went crazy'.

Afterwards the star of the production, Lola Fisher, was taken round to meet Rudolf by Liuba, who had been helping a student friend show her the sights. As they arrived at the stage door, 'an exultant Rudik' appeared with his arms full of flowers and, pushing past the mob of autograph hunters, headed straight towards them.

Lola began telling him what a wonderful impression he'd made on her. There wasn't any need for translation, for even if Rudik hadn't known any English, her shining eyes and the expression on her face spoke for themselves. At that point, Rudik did something that provoked a storm of indignation among his female fans. He presented all the flowers he'd been given to Lola, as if in recognition of her own talent.

Such tactlessness caused intense resentment among Rudolf's most fanatical admirers, who overnight turned hostile, shouting abuse as he walked down the street and telephoning him at all hours, 'making life unbearable for the Pushkin household'. It was rumoured they were going to throw birch twigs instead of flowers onstage – 'the equivalent of a public slap in the face' – but this never happened. Only a note attached to a small bunch of violets appeared among the bouquets one night with the words, 'An ass will always be an ass, even if you cover him with flowers!'

Yet notwithstanding his undiplomatic behaviour towards his fans, Rudolf realized it would be unwise to accept Lola Fisher's invitation to supper that night. Instead, while Xenia stood watchfully by, waiting to drive him home, he agreed to a less conspicuous meeting the following day. As Rudolf walked into the restaurant of the Grand Hotel Europa to meet Lola and her actor colleagues for breakfast, the entire company stood up to applaud – his first Western ovation.

A month later, when Rudolf was cast opposite Alla Shelest for two performances of *Giselle*, the Leningrad balletomanes were concerned not that he would eclipse her – no one could do that; her own stage personality was transfixing – but that he was too inexperienced to be paired with a dancer 'whose name is sacred'. One of her fans took it upon herself to visit the ballerina in order to dissuade her from dancing with him, but she had hardly begun to make her case before Shelest silenced her: 'What are you saying, Natasha? Nureyev is an epoch in ballet.'

Shelest had liked and admired him from their first rehearsal, noting his 'unusual inner liveliness', his instant reactions and sensitivity to every nuance of meaning. 'It was not necessary to explain to him why you did it that way and no other.' They formed a deep bond of sympathy and mutual respect. 'It was Shelest,' remarks Vadim Kiselev, 'who gave Rudolf a taste for changing himself. She taught him how from five per cent you can achieve a hundred.' Although a woman steeped in culture, Shelest was a dowdy figure offstage, plain-faced and plump, yet when she began to dance, something remarkable took place: she could hypnotize the audience into seeing her as a beauty. Noticing that Rudolf's impetuous, 'hooligan-boy' interpretation negated the fact that Albrecht is an aristocrat, she spent hours in the studio helping him to concentrate and moderate his interpretation. But on the evening of 30 June even Rudolf's most doting followers were apprehensive. 'I was very wary,' remembers Faina Rokhind. 'But what a marvellous performance they gave! Shelest allowed Rudik a lot of freedom; he had become so much more independent in the role.' 'There were many worries because he was dancing with Shelest,' Galina Palshina wrote in her journal, 'but everything went well. He was made for this role, for this ballet . . . I was so excited I couldn't sleep.'

Later that summer Rudolf had just packed his bags to go on holiday when he was told that he and Ninel Kurgapkina had been chosen to dance before Nikita Khrushchev at a gathering of high-ranking politicians with Russia's artistic and intellectual elite (clearly the scandal of his opening night and ill-advised rendezvous with foreigners had not been held against him). On a beautiful day in June 1960 he and Ninel were driven to a *dacha* outside Moscow owned by Nikolai Bulganin, the former Soviet premier. In idyllic wooded surroundings an extravagant Sunday picnic was taking place; guests could go swimming, fishing or boating, and there was even a fair with shooting booths. 'It was very gay and absolutely informal,' recalled Rudolf, who did not recognize any of the government officials except for Khrushchev; his wife, Nina Petrovna; and Marshal Kliment Voroshilov, one of the few friends of Stalin to have survived the purges. As the Soviet premier and his entourage sat eating their dinner at a table just in front of them, Rudolf and Kurgapkina danced the adagio from *Don Quixote* (the stage was too small and makeshift to accommodate anything more virtuosic). Another artist appearing that day was the pianist Sviatoslav Richter, playing Rachmaninov's *Preludes* with a passionate intensity Rudolf felt he 'could understand'.

When dusk fell the requisite speechmaking began, and Shostakovich was given the honour of making the return toast. Then, as the party's vodka-mellowed mood drifted into sentimentality, Voroshilov stood up and gave an impromptu recital of melancholic Ukrainian folk songs in a beautiful bass voice, soon accompanied by Khrushchev: 'They both knew every word of every folk song.' When the dancers returned and described the occasion to their friends, Ninel was almost speechless at the grandeur of it all: the champagne cooling in ponds and streams – 'You just had to reach down and pick up a bottle' – the buffet tables all over the garden covered with starched white cloths and laden with cornucopias of food. 'I can't express it even – it was like going to the White House: it was such a beautiful place with so much wealth on show.' Rudolf, on the other hand, was deeply cynical. 'Now finally I understand what Communism is,' he told Tamara on his return.

For his holiday that summer Rudolf wanted to go to the Black Sea, and had written to his parents suggesting that they join him. The letter Hamet sent back in reply declining his offer was affectionate enough, but it brought the unsettling news that Farida's declining health would not allow her to make the journey. Hamet urged his son to come instead to Ufa to see the family, but Rudolf had set his mind on going to Sochi, a subtropical resort with an arts-festival atmosphere in August much like those in Edinburgh or Saratoga Springs. Many young people came from Moscow and Leningrad to attend concerts and see Chaboukiani's Georgian Group as well as the Novosibirsk Ballet. Giving a recital one evening was the famous pianist Yakov Flier, who had performed with the twenty-three-year-old Texan pianist Van Cliburn in the first Tchaikovsky Competition the previous year. Rudolf, who was in Moscow at the time, had managed to get tickets for the dress rehearsal – '[Cliburn] played full out and we were in heaven!' – but on this occasion, he was in no mood to pay homage to a fellow artist. When Van Cliburn was spotted in one of the boxes and the whole audience rose to their feet to applaud him, only Rudolf remained seated. 'His face grew very dark as he looked from the audience to Cliburn and back,' said Faina Rokhind, who was there. 'I could read in his eyes what he was thinking: this is the kind of glory that I must get! He looked at what was going on and he wanted it so much.'

His mood had not improved when he wrote to Tamara complaining about his holiday:

> I have sold my voucher for the hostel. The Sh.K. Sanatorium is terrible, and I live in Dudko's apartment [a teacher in the Georgian theatre] where I have almost a separate room. It is far from the sea, and the water in the sea is dirty. It rains night and day and when it stops we go and swim. It was so nice in the Crimea and I will go back there if Xenia answers.
>
> I've been to see the Georgian Ballet's *Gorda* – rubbish, and I was surprised that the Moscow and Leningrad fans came specially for such shit. There is no Vakhtang [Chaboukiani]. He will appear only on the 1 2th in *Othello*. How can I trust the audience after that, and especially the fans? Their love can't come from any aesthetic perception . . . When it's good, it should be good for everybody.
>
> In general my hopes for the Caucasus haven't been satisfied and I will not return to Sochi [although] I live in Dudko's house in a very pleasant family . . . That's all for now. I'll wait for an answer.
>
> Rudik

The letter he wrote from Sochi to Xenia has not survived, but the fact that he wanted to return to the Crimea to stay with her suggests that tensions between them had eased. She had become less possessive, confident that there was no one at the time with whom he was seriously involved, and unaware that Rudolf was still hoping to visit

Menia. ('There is no invitation for the competition in Cuba,' he wrote to Silva Lon the following spring.) She knew that Tamara – her only rival for Rudolf's time and attention – was no more to him than a confidante. And Xenia had also made peace with herself. Resigned to the fact that Rudolf would never reciprocate the passion she felt for him, she was more able now to accept her role of taking care of him, finding she could identify with the married woman in Pushkin's *Eugene Onegin,* who 'sighed after another' but was able to find contentment of sorts by submerging herself in daily domesticity. In one of her letters to Rudolf sent soon after his defection, she says, 'I became so used to looking after you,' and quotes a couplet from the poem:

> Habit to us is given from above:
> It's a substitute for happiness.

'From the first minute I met you I understood your complicated nature,' she told him. 'I was trying to save you from anything that could destroy your equilibrium.' And certainly her influence on Rudolf was as profound as it was long lasting. As Liuba pointed out in a memoir, Rudolf's habit of attaching himself to someone else's life in the West, feeling completely at home there and expecting to be taken care of, 'sprang from Xenia'; just as when he began to choreograph he remembered her dictum that ballets should be based on literary classics – 'Don't use the primitive tales for ballet, choose only immortal works – Shakespeare, Byron, Homer,' she used to say, which he went on to do by making *Romeo and Juliet*, *Manfred*, *Washington Square* and *The Tempest*.

Yet in another respect, 'Xenia wasn't good for him,' says Liuba, who sees a parallel between Rudolf and the poet Alexander Blok, whose first sexual experience was with a woman twice his age. Her name was also Xenia – Xenia Mikhailovna Sadovskaya. In the summer of 1897, sixteen-year-old Sasha Blok spent a holiday at Bad Nauhein in Germany, where he astonished his mother and aunt by having an affair with a tall, enchantingly elegant widow. But while Xenia Mikhailovna remained in love with her schoolboy to the end of her life, for Blok the experience had a harmful long-term effect. 'My first infatuation, if I am not mistaken, was accompanied by a sweet feeling of revulsion for the sexual act,' he wrote, looking back on their affair when he revisited the spa town twelve years later.* Blok developed a dualistic view of women

---

* He titled the cycle of lyrics he dedicated to her *Twelve Years Later.*

as being either prostitutes or saints, and Rudolf, believes Liuba, 'also suffered from this double life. If a very young man has a relationship with an older woman, after the initial passion is over he begins to have other feelings. Rudik associated sex with shame, and women with the dark side of his nature: it's the reason he began to look for pleasure in other places.'

4   BLOOD BROTHERS

Teja Kremke was a seventeen-year-old East German boy with an erotic presence as visible as a heat haze. A student at the Vaganova school, he had shiny chestnut hair, pale skin, full lips and intense grey-blue eyes – extraordinary eyes whose seductive glint through long black lashes was there even when he was a child. It was Teja whom Rudolf later described as his 'first crush', but in the summer of 1960, with the prospect of a long tour of the GDR immediately ahead, the boy's main appeal was what he could tell Rudolf about the world outside.

East Berlin, where Teja grew up, had few luxuries, with food and clothing in short supply, but the arts were thriving, and there was no physical barrier between the two German states as yet. He and his sister would take the U-bahn across the border two or three times a week – 'We were part of a crowd that met in theatres and concert halls rather than cafés' – and Teja could talk about anything from recent developments in Western dance to Brecht's Berliner Ensemble or the latest Hollywood movies. 'Rudolf got a lot of information from him. Teja was very smart.'

The student's first letters home reveal an outlook that is both mature in its perceptions and surprisingly naïve. 'I would never have dreamed I would be introduced to great people like Sergeyev and Dudinskaya,' he wrote in January 1960, soon after arriving in Leningrad to begin his course. 'It's a weird feeling to talk to these people. They behave in a very modest way and one feels so small and insignificant next to them.' To Teja, who had seen every Nureyev performance since his arrival, Rudolf was almost as much of a deity as the fabled Kirov stars, and he could hardly believe it when the dancer volunteered to coach him and his partner from Berlin in their Sunday practice sessions. 'He would help us with pas de deux,' said Ute Mitreuter, another German student, 'showing Teja where to hold me or how to prepare for a lift. Rudolf was a fanatic, Teja was a fanatic, and so was I.'

Rudolf admired and encouraged the young students' drive. Although Teja was not especially gifted, he was determined to absorb everything he could from his surroundings. 'The Russian guys took all that for granted,' said Baryshnikov. 'Teja was a good scholar and very practical: he was studying for his future.' He had brought an 8-mm home-movie camera to Leningrad, and had begun making a record of classes, productions and roles, often filming in secret from the wings or the orchestra pit.* As Rudolf's tour of East Germany was to coincide with the appearance in Leningrad of the American Ballet Theatre, he asked Teja to film whatever he could of the performances. In return he agreed to deliver, through a contact in Leipzig, a present of three pairs of ballet shoes to Teja's girlfriend.

Rudolf was dismayed to be missing the ABT season for a second time. Three weeks earlier he had cut short his holiday in Ufa to see the company in Moscow, but Pushkin had urged him to return home. 'My teacher say to me, "Ah, don't stay there. I've got tickets for every performance in front row when they are in Leningrad. Tomorrow is my birthday. Come here!" So I abandoned Moscow.' Before he left the city, however, Rudolf went to a Bolshoi performance of *Swan Lake*, where he spotted the Danish star Erik Bruhn sitting in the audience with his two American partners, Maria Tallchief and Lupe Serrano. Having observed in photographs of Bruhn dancing exactly the streamlined purity he aspired to himself, he longed to go up and talk to the dancer.

> I prepared whatever little phrases I had for him. And I thought, What do I say to Maria Tallchief? I have nothing to say to her but everything for him. When I start to move towards them, fans, they just took me. They said, 'Don't you dare, because they will never let you out of Russia. Your career will be finished if you speak to them.'

It was Bruhn's schooling that Rudolf was 'desperate' to deconstruct and absorb. In addition there was the fact that the ABT repertory included *Theme and Variations* by Balanchine, the choreographer whose work he longed to dance more than any other in the world. 'I made that so clear that the authorities sent me to Germany to dance. They didn't want me to be influenced by Western styles.'

Not only was Rudolf convinced that his absence from Leningrad was deliberately timed, but when the tour began, he discovered that

* By the time he finished his studies, he had shot the exercises in Vaganova's famous tract on ballet using Baryshnikov as a model, and taken the photographs for an illustrated history of the Kirov with a text by Marietta Frangopoulo. (Rudolf is conspicuously absent from this book, which was published six years after his defection.)

he and Ninel Kurgapkina had been 'cheated' by the Kirov management, which had presented the tour as a special privilege (claiming
they were to replace an indisposed Ulanova), whereas in fact they
had been booked as just another turn on a variety-show bill. 'There
were clowns, jugglers . . . and us.' Feeling cold and cramped on a bus
travelling thousands of kilometres across East Germany and dancing in
seedy theatres and army camps for unenthusiastic audiences left
Rudolf grimly determined to vent his fury on the authorities as soon as
he returned. It was the influential Konstantin Sergeyev whom both
dancers blamed for their 'punishment'. Only recently, Rudolf had
publicly humiliated Sergeyev for correcting a pupil while Pushkin was
teaching class. 'There is a teacher here,' Rudolf exploded. 'You can
leave right away and shut the door behind you!'

Another motive, Ninel believes, was jealousy:

> Konstantin Mikhailovich would help people to rise up, but as soon as
> they became outstanding and threatened his and Dudinskaya's posi-
> tion, he would try to push them back down again. In our case this was
> impossible. I had a strong character and was very independent, and
> Rudolf was the same. That was something that made us close. We were
> very good at being alone against the world.

Determined to make the most of their travels, she and Rudolf went
to the National Gallery in Dresden, where he bought a book on the
collection and one on Rembrandt, which he planned to get Teja to
translate for him on his return. In East Berlin, the last stop on the tour,
Rudolf made contact with his former room-mate Egon Bischoff, now
a soloist and ballet master at the State Theatre. One night they went
out with Egon's jolly wife, Gisela, to Die Möwe, a popular artists'
haunt, where they drank a lot, reminisced, and danced so wildly that
the pearls on Gisela's necklace flew off and bounced around like
hailstones. Earlier in the day they had driven around the city, and
Rudolf, 'in a *lustig* [happy] mood', had insisted on being taken to see
the frontier. 'It was still open. If he'd wanted to go at this time he could
have.' Which Rudolf knew. 'I could go to West Germany very easily
and just go to embassy and ask, Please, I would like to stay in your
country.' At the beginning of the tour he had stuffed his suitcases with
cookies, sugar, sausages and tea, so that he didn't have to spend a single
kopek of his meagre salary on food. 'This money was meant for two
things: defection to the West. Or if it doesn't work, to buy piano.
Because you couldn't buy a piano in Russia.' He had complained a lot

to Egon about his exile – 'They have insulted me,' he said – and he even admitted that he was thinking of defecting. 'My friend said, "Don't be a *fool*. They'll make publicity about you staying in the West and they will send you back to Russia. They've done that to everybody." So I bought a piano.'

For Rudolf a decade later (as it had for Christopher Isherwood and his expatriate friends in the 1920s), Berlin meant boys, and Egon would be hard pressed to persuade him to forgo the clubs for a kitchen supper cooked by Gisela. But in the autumn of 1960 the city still had a certain prelapsarian charm – mostly the result of a single interlude that stayed in his memory for a long time. It was after taking class at the Staatsoper one day that he lingered to talk to a good-looking dancer who had caught his eye. Heinz Mannigel was two years older than Rudolf, with similarly sensuous features and a way of setting the simplest movements on fire. Spanish dancing was his speciality and, once again, Rudolf was determined to extract as much knowledge from another dancer as he could. They made a deal: Heinz would teach him authentic flamenco and the basics of German expressionism, while in return Rudolf would give him classes in the Pushkin method. 'Rudolf gave me the logic of classical ballet, and I showed him how to get crazy things out of yourself that you can't speak. I was a young wild boy and tried to get him to be like an animal – which was how I understood dance to be.' It was the dynamics of German interpretative dance that especially interested Rudolf, the principle of tension, and the primitive, powerfully rhythmic way with which pioneers like Mary Wigman and Gret Palucca had expressed themselves. 'He was curious about everything, and I never heard him be at all negative about the situation he was in; he just loved to dance.'

Wanting Heinz to see how electrifying he himself could be onstage even in a pastiche Spanish role, Rudolf invited him to watch a performance of *Don Quixote*. They drove to a Russian army camp on the outskirts of the city, and when Heinz was forbidden entry, Rudolf in retaliation refused to dance until his friend was admitted. Then, inspired by his new command of flamenco, he danced the whole variation three times before the curtain went up. Despite his rapport with Ninel, which had been deepened by the hardships of the tour, Rudolf didn't introduce the young German to her or even mention him, although he had invited Heinz to several other shows that week.

The two Kirov dancers were supposed to report their whereabouts each day to a Komsomol representative, a rule Rudolf completely ignored. He and Heinz went together to the Komische Oper to see Walter Felsenstein's spoof of Leoš Janáček's *The Cunning Little Vixen*, and walked for hours around the city visiting churches and museums. In the Pergamon Museum, Rudolf's knowledge of Greek antiquities surprised Heinz. 'It was he who explained things to me.' Eager to impress Rudolf, Heinz decided to take him on a trip to the West. 'We got on to a subway train and I told Rudolf where we were going. "No, please, Heinz," he said, looking really frightened. "I can't. I'll get into big trouble." I didn't understand, but I accepted it. We got off at the next station and went back.'

As Heinz had no money, and Rudolf was saving up for his piano,* they didn't eat out but would buy supper to take back to Heinz's small room off Unter den Linden. Even though the opportunity was there – 'I remember we drank a great deal at this time' – Rudolf did not attempt any kind of pass: if he was attracted to Heinz, his desire was subliminal. 'You feel if someone is homosexual, and I really believe that Rudolf wasn't at this point; he didn't walk like one or behave like one. We just had a very, very warm feeling towards each other.' They were both examples of what Heinz calls '*Verwahrlost* in the soul [lost souls]' – both strays from a poor, tough childhood with none of the privileges bestowed on their contemporaries. 'We were street kids with ambition, two friends who found in each other something that went extremely deep.' Rudolf evidently felt this, too, as when the time came to leave, he kissed Heinz on the lips with such ardour that Heinz was amazed and yet at the same time understood. 'We had become so close and really loved each other. It was a really beautiful kiss which to this day I don't regret.'

Wanting to keep in touch with Heinz on his return to Leningrad, Rudolf wrote him an affectionately nostalgic letter recalling their time together, and when he received a present of a nylon shirt – to him, a Western status symbol – he reciprocated by sending Heinz gifts of chocolates and green coffee beans, a Russian speciality. In January he found out that Heinz had married a girl two weeks after meeting her, but the news hardly registered, as his relationship with Teja was beginning to reach a new level of intensity.

The turning point was the student's eighteenth-birthday party, after which they began to meet frequently, mostly at the Rossi Street apartment. As one of Pushkin's pupils, Teja naturally was invited there for

* He was able to leave Egon Bischoff eight hundred Deutschmarks with which to buy one for him.

meals and educated in the nuances of life outside school. From the beginning Xenia was instinctively drawn to this beautiful youth, while Alexander Ivanovich, whom Teja worshipped, soon became a father figure for him, too. With Teja by his side, Rudolf would listen to records and talk until late into the night. The Kremkes were a musical family (Teja's sister, Ute, was a professional pianist, and he himself played the piano and the accordion), although it was only under Rudolf's guidance that he developed a real feeling for music, especially Bach.

It was rare that their conversations touched on subjects outside music and dance. Before his arrival Teja had spent a month in Moscow improving his schoolboy Russian and being indoctrinated in the ideology of the brotherland, but, like Rudolf, he had no interest in contemporary politics and hated the constraints of Communism. One evening they were talking in the Vaganova student kitchen while Ute Mitreuter was brewing coffee. 'Teja was telling Rudolf that he should go to the West – "There you'll be the greatest dancer in the world," he said. "But if you stay here you'll be known only to the Russians." "Yes of course I know that," answered Rudolf. "It's how Nijinsky became a legend. And I'm going to be the next one."'

Yet for all their freedom of spirit, their characters were completely at odds, with Teja's Teutonic pragmatism running counter to Rudolf's extreme impetuosity. There were many clashes. Slava Santto, a young friend of the Pushkins, watched them play chess together one night: 'Teja did everything very accurately, thinking slowly and carefully about his next position. But when Teja started to win the game, it was too much for Rudolf. All of a sudden he swept the chessboard and everything else on to the floor, then flew out of the room. Teja stayed exactly where he was: very calm, with no expression on his face.' Teja had more money than the other students, more money even than members of the staff, and set himself up as a kind of middleman, trading clothes, records and medicines from the West. This mercenary quality irritated Rudolf – 'That's Teja,' he once scoffed to a friend. 'Either buying or selling.' But he was quick to use it to his own advantage, persuading him to bring back from one trip something he had coveted desperately since he was a child.

It was when Teja hadn't appeared at the school one day that a concerned Ute Mitreuter went to his room and found him sitting on the floor setting up a network of rails of an electric train set. 'He was waiting to surprise Rudolf. And I remember thinking, My God, he cares only about him – how could he not go to class? For us this was very serious. It seemed so strange, this concern for Rudolf. It was as if he really loved him.' Ute Kremke had also been taken aback by the intensity of Teja's commitment to Rudolf. 'Rudik is my blood brother,' he told her, admitting that they had cut themselves to mingle their blood. 'But why? What do you mean?' she asked in amazement, not knowing about the American Indian ritual, and thinking, His feelings are too strong. Teja only smiled.

Their growing intimacy was a secret too risky to reveal to anyone – even to Ute Mitreuter, to whom Teja had always confided his sexual history in the past. 'Teja talked to me about all the things he did with girls. There were many of them who were mad about him – I heard he was a very good lover – and that's why I didn't think there was anything more than a friendship between him and Rudolf. It was only later that I knew it was a love affair.'

Teja had left a school sweetheart behind in Germany, a dancer with heavy-browed, lovely eyes like his, and although she had recently defected with her parents to West Germany, they wrote to each other regularly. 'Mietze' (Anne Enders) always believed that Teja was faithful to her while he was in Leningrad, whereas in fact he had established a reputation as the school philanderer from his first day. Arriving at his new lodgings, he found the common room being painted by a young *rabochaya*, who, while not at all pretty, had something in her coarse manner and fleshy, gleaming body that stirred him. He began chatting in his charmingly insinuating way until he had talked her into letting him ravish her on the grand piano, making sure her head was thrown back over the side so he didn't have to see her face. Even more sexually precocious than the young Sasha Blok, Teja was only twelve when he was seduced while on holiday with his family by a thirty-five-year-old woman – an encounter that left him with a far-from-conventional sexual outlook. (In the mid-sixties he would persuade his adoring Indonesian child-wife to live in a *ménage à trois* with a beautiful Aryan youth with whom he was having an affair.) 'Teja was always open to new experience. There was a perverse strain in his character. Something other people didn't find normal was very exciting to him.'

When, soon after Rudolf's defection, Teja was interrogated about their friendship by the Stasi, East Germany's secret police, he claimed that it was Rudolf who had tried to seduce him, but as Teja was the one with homosexual experience – at school in Berlin he had been caught in the shower with a boy – it is far more likely that the opposite was true. (Rudolf would one day tell a mutual friend that it was Teja who first taught him 'the art of male love'.) When Konstantin Russu, another student from East Germany, went to the Vaganova shower room one day, he found that Rudolf and Teja had locked themselves in and were refusing to open the door. It only confirmed what he had suspected for some time: often, when he came back in the evening to the room he shared with Teja, he had seen the Kirov star climbing out of the ground-floor window and running down Rossi Street. With only the two students sharing, it was easy for Rudolf and Teja to be alone when Konstantin was at class – 'They could just close the door if they wanted to.'

Yet more and more, Rudolf longed for a place of his own. 'It became a fixation for him. Somewhere, anywhere, but it had to be private with enough space for the piano he badly coveted.' He decided that he would try to exchange the room in the Ordinarnaya Street apartment (which the Kirov had given him and Alla Sizova to share) for two smaller rooms – one for himself and one somewhere else for his sister Rosa, with whom he didn't want to live. Having managed to obtain the special permit allowing her to remain in Leningrad, she was living in considerable style by Russian standards, leading what Sizova describes as 'a very free life with a lot of people coming and going'. Rudolf knew that she would hate the idea of giving all this up, and as he couldn't face breaking the news himself, he persuaded Tamara to do it for him.

Rosa was lying on a couch when Tamara arrived to see her, but as soon as she realized the implications of what was being said, she suddenly jumped up and began shouting, '*You* want the room. You will get nothing! It's mine. I live here . . . *And* I'm pregnant!' She became so hysterical that Alla's parents, who were in the room next door, came rushing in to investigate. Later, when Tamara told Rudolf what had happened, she saw his cheeks burn with shame as he forbade her ever to mention the subject again. The drama only heightened his growing sense of detachment from Rosa, his childhood ally, who no longer fitted into his world and was now alienating his Leningrad friends. They found her 'strange, closed, introverted', and so different from Rudolf that it was hard to believe they were siblings. As Leonid Romankov put it, 'Rosa was of this world; Rudolf came from the stars.' Tamara had vowed that she would no longer speak to her, and Xenia had disapproved of her from the start. 'Xenia Josifovna was from a good family, very intelligent, with wonderful manners; Rosa was the absolute opposite.'

Rudolf resigned himself to remaining with the Pushkins. However stifling Xenia could be, no one looked after him better, while the solicitous devotion of Alexander Ivanovich was boundless. Slava Santto arrived at the apartment one evening to find Pushkin confined to the tiny kitchen. 'Ssssh! Please don't go in,' he whispered. 'Rudik is there. He's listening to music.' Sure enough, Rudolf was lying on the floor listening to a recording of Bach. Another advantage of staying in Rossi Street was the fact that Teja was always welcome there, Xenia having adopted him as a new protégé, shaping his thoughts and tastes. By now a deep bond had developed among them all: 'It was a liaison à quatre. They were kind of bound together.'

It was nearly always Xenia who took charge of a situation, lighting it up with her vivacity, but Pushkin would often join in their more frivolous moments, playing up to Teja's camera during country weekends and allowing himself to be photographed side by side with Xenia in their large mahogany bed. Teja's daughter, Jurico, remembers seeing a photograph of her father with Rudolf and Pushkin in the bed, which may have led to the innuendos she heard from her mother about 'sex games' at the Pushkins' apartment (the kind of speculation Rudolf himself perpetuated when he shocked a friend by saying that he had slept with Pushkin as well as Xenia: 'Both of them enjoyed it!'). But if Pushkin was indeed drawn to his own sex – and several people believe that 'Alexander Ivanovich was the other way' – it was not a compulsion he was known to act on. In an album put together after their death by friends of the Pushkins, there is a photograph of Pushkin sitting on a beach beside a tanned, smiling Sergeyev. Like everyone else sunbathing around them, they are both naked. Yet whereas Sergeyev, standing with Pushkin in another picture taken at the water's edge, projects an unmistakable homoerotic charge, his magnificent physique on full display except for a slip of a towel around his loins, Alexander Ivanovich, with his shapeless trunks, skullcap and thin limbs, seems strangely out of place: in contrast to his earthy wife, there was something spiritual, almost ascetic about him.

Whether or not the Pushkins were aware of Rudolf's physical liaison with Teja can never be known (it was certainly not discussed with other members of their circle), but the importance Teja was assuming in Rudolf's life was something Xenia would soon start to resent. Far more unsettling, had they been aware of it, was Teja's constant goading of Rudolf to leave Russia. 'He'd say, "Go! Get out! At the first opportunity you have. Don't stay here or no one will hear of you!"' A decade later, afraid that Teja would have the same malign influence on Mikhail Baryshnikov, who had taken Rudolf's place in Pushkin's affections, the teacher, making some excuse, would usher his young charge into another room if Teja happened to drop in, keeping him hidden there until Teja had left. 'Alexander Ivanovich was a very, very Soviet man,' remarks Slava Santto. 'I know what it was like at that time: what was possible for Rudolf to speak about with comrades of his own age, and what was impossible for the Pushkins to understand.'

Little did the Pushkins know when they posed for Teja's movie camera during a weekend on the Finnish Gulf that they were, in fact, colluding in an extraordinary prophetic enactment of Rudolf's defection. This fleeting narrative begins with Rudolf walking up the steps of the Neva embankment and stopping to look back, as if taking leave of the city and his friends. There are smiling close-ups of Xenia, Teja and Alexander Ivanovich before we see Rudolf standing alone on a snow-covered platform as a train pulls in. While sunlight glints on rails and rotating wheels, a wintry Russian landscape rushes by, mixed with images of Teja and Xenia. Sitting pensively by the window is Rudolf, whose thoughts are visualized as the film flashes back to moments from his performances on the Kirov stage – the third-act pas de deux from *Swan Lake*, a triumphant curtain call – before focusing on Xenia dancing towards the camera with Slava Santto, and lingering on Teja, who provocatively holds the gaze of the lens.

Then, in a potent image of solitary flight, the footage ends with a long shot of Rudolf silhouetted with a sledge in a snowy landscape, finally skating off into the sunset. 'Teja predicted Rudolf's future,' says his friend Vladimir Fedianin. 'I think he had a gift of foresight. He knew that Rudolf would stay in the West or he'd turn into nothing but dust.'

Earlier in the winter of 1960 Janine Ringuet, a twenty-year-old assistant impresario who worked for a Parisian organization specializing in artistic exchanges between France and the Soviet Union, came to Leningrad for several weeks to observe the Kirov Ballet. It was seven years after the death of Stalin, and relations between the two countries were just beginning to open up. The Bolshoi had been to Paris with great success in 1958, but at that time almost nothing was known about the Kirov. Janine, who spoke fluent Russian and had been to almost every performance, was standing in the company office a few days before returning home, when she noticed a programme announcing a performance of *Don Quixote*, a ballet she hadn't seen. 'Oh no – that's of no interest to you,' she was told. 'It's old and we haven't worked on it recently.' But preferring to go to the ballet than stay in her hotel room, she insisted on going.

It's true that the ballet was dated, but I saw a young dancer who was absolutely wonderful and I couldn't understand why they hadn't shown him to me before. I was very impulsive and the next morning sent a telegram to my director saying, 'Last night I had the opportunity to see the best male dancer in the world. His name is Rudolf Nureyev.' A few hours later I received a cable back, basically telling me that I was too young and inexperienced to understand such things. However, when I returned to Paris and they saw how serious I was, they realized that it would be a great mistake not to engage this dancer for the Paris tour.

After consulting Ekaterina Furtseva, the minister of culture, who confirmed, 'Yes, he's amazing, but there have been some problems,' the French impresario Georges Soria insisted not only that Rudolf must join the tour, but also that Sergeyev and Dudinskaya must relinquish their roles to younger members of the company and travel only as 'artistic advisers'. 'We tried to indicate that they were glories of the past who should remain that way. Understandably they were very angry – this was a big blow to them – but they had no choice.' It was a decision with which Rudolf wholeheartedly concurred – at least as far as Sergeyev was concerned. He himself had said as much when he came up to Sergeyev and Dudinskaya after a performance and remarked, 'Natalia Mihailovna, you were wonderful and must dance for many more years, but for Konstantin Mikhailovich it is time to go.'

Rudolf left no one in any doubt about his contempt for Sergeyev's dancing. His own *Giselle*, as one critic put it, 'doesn't so much depart from Sergeyev's traditions as openly challenge them'. 'He didn't like his style,' confirms Irina Kolpakova. 'I always went to see performances of *Giselle* when Dudinskaya and Sergeyev appeared, but Rudik never did. He wasn't interested.' When, at the start of 1961, the Kirov star was reappointed director following Boris Fenster's sudden death, Rudolf greeted the news with dismay. Sergeyev's policy as a leader was as conservative as his approach to the repertory – the reason the choreographer Leonid Yakobson had successfully campaigned to have him removed from the job in the mid-fifties. Whereas the forward-looking Fenster had always supported Nureyev, Sergeyev posed a genuine obstacle to any kind of change. Consequently, when Rudolf learned that his name had been added to the list of dancers bound for Paris, he was amazed: 'Strangely enough I owe [this chance] entirely to someone who had always seemed most strongly opposed to me.' Only much later did he find out his champion was not Sergeyev but Janine Ringuet, who was completely unknown to him. Nor could he have foreseen that the director would unexpectedly become an ally when an opportunity presented itself for political manoeuvring.

Yuri Grigorovich, a thirty-four-year-old choreographer whose first work, *The Stone Flower*, had been greeted as a revolutionary departure from the formulaic dramatic ballets that prevailed, was planning his next full-length piece, and saw in Rudolf's Eastern plastique and romantic presence exactly the qualities he wanted for his hero. Grigorovich had rehearsed Rudolf in *Giselle*, and since then had become an admirer and champion of his, finding his innovative dancing close in spirit to what he was attempting with choreography. In *The Legend of Love*, based on a Turkish play about a stonecutter loved by two sisters, he planned to eliminate dated mime sequences and tell his story through classical dance tinged with national colour. Unusually for its time, the ballet was conceived as a collaboration in the Ballets Russes tradition with music specially written (by Arif Melikov, an Azerbaijani composer), and decor by Simon Virsaladze, the designer who had already done so much to stimulate Rudolf's interest in changing his appearance onstage.

For the lead role of Ferhad, Rudolf contributed many of his own ideas, helping Grigorovich reinvent the typical macho Soviet lead. The dancer's main inspiration was *Apollo*, Balanchine's extraordinarily limpid masterpiece to Stravinsky's score, which Alicia Alonso's company had brought to Russia three years earlier. Rudolf had left Leningrad without permission in order to see the company perform the ballet in Moscow, resulting in a salary deduction and official reprimand on his return, but he had no regrets. 'I was agog . . . I thought, How strange, how weird, how wonderful!' Conveying his excitement to Grigorovich, Rudolf would try to reconstruct specific steps he remembered from the ballet. 'It came back to me . . . and in a general way I said, well, he did this move and that move, and that one.' And with Grigorovich incorporating his own unusual images drawn from Persian miniatures, the process of collaboration was a stimulating time for them both. 'They were literally walking on air, unable to hide their mutual pleasure,' said dancer Nikita Dolgushin.

Beginning with Ferhad's first flying entry, Grigorovich created his hero as a revelation of Rudolf himself. Enacting the dancer's own belief in the equal status of the male lead, Ferhad doesn't shadow and support his lover like a stock ballet partner, but in a lyrical pas de deux imitates the youthful heroine's light gazelle leaps and fluttery hands in a mirror image of her. As Virsaladze was sitting in the studio one afternoon watching Rudolf and his partner rehearse this duet, he turned to Grigorovich and said, 'I don't think that we'll ever see anything like this again.' But as the final run-through of *Legend of Love* was taking place onstage, Rudolf began gathering up his things to leave; the rehearsal had run overtime, and the dancer was due to work on his first performance with Alla Shelest of *Laurentia*. 'Rudik, where are you going? I haven't yet said we're finished.' 'Yuri Nikolaivich, I'm off to rehearse some proper dances!' Rudolf replied, defiantly walking away. Grigorovich was enraged, and shouted after him that if he left now there would be no coming back. Rudolf ignored him. Vera Krasovskaya, who was sitting in the empty theatre, watched it all happen, and when it became clear that Grigorovich intended to carry out his threat, begged Virsaladze, his mentor and close friend, to intervene. According to Krasovskaya, he tried but failed. Two days later the choreographer denounced Rudolf in an official letter of complaint to the Kirov's administrative director, Georgi Korkin.

> On 18 February at 13.30 during the stage rehearsal of the ballet *The Legend of Love*, I suggested to the performer of the role of Ferhad, the dancer R. Nureyev, to begin the work. He not only refused to do so, but even used improper language.
>
> As this is not the first time that R. Nureyev has behaved so unceremoniously at work and I have been unsuccessful in attempting to explain to him that such behaviour is inadmissible, I have to ask you to protect the work in performance from escapades of this kind, which are giving a pernicious example to the whole company.
>
> Choreographer Y. Grigorovich
20 February 1961

However, for Rudolf, a near-contemporary like Grigorovich with only one other ballet to his name was not someone of great importance. Besides, working on the ballet had fired ambitions of his own to choreograph, and lately he had been discussing with Nikita Dolgushin the possibility of collaborating on a piece to a Bach score. 'We knew that Balanchine had staged *Concerto Barocco* to this music. And although we had never seen it, it was inspiring just to think what it could be like: we imagined it to be unique, elegant and graceful.' To Rudolf, Balanchine was omnipotent, the supreme creator. Nevertheless, a month later when *The Legend of Love* was complete and Rudolf saw it performed onstage for the first time with Alexander Gribov as Ferhad, he regretted his behaviour, considering the role to be the biggest lost opportunity of his career.

Western critics find it hard to understand the appeal of *Legend of Love* (dismissed by Arlene Croce as conventional Soviet kitsch), but in Russia it was regarded as a triumph, 'a dissertation on the art of choreography'. Hoping that Sergeyev might be persuaded to break the impasse over the ballet, Rudolf went to see him to plead his case. He knew that the director was jealous of Grigorovich and might welcome the chance to exert his own power. Sure enough, Sergeyev not only gave Rudolf his word that he would be cast in the role of Ferhad the following season but, eager to take credit for promoting the dancer, promised him two important debuts: *The Sleeping Beauty* and *Swan Lake*. 'The score is 2–0. We win!' Rudolf announced triumphantly to Tamara as soon as he heard the news.

By now the pair had become almost inseparable; Rudolf trusted Tamara enough to confide in her, not his innermost feelings but thoughts about roles or intrigues at the theatre, confident that he could count on her loyalty. Tamara, whose existence was 'completely filled by Rudolf', found that she had fallen in love. She lived for their long walks together, sometimes lasting five or six hours, and during the White Nights, often until the morning. Their favourite route was along the Fontanka Canal to Nevsky Prospekt, on to the Field of Mars and along the Neva, past the Bronze Horseman into St Isaac's Square and back down Nevsky to Rossi Street. One day Rudolf admitted that after a rehearsal he had walked with a friend until very late. 'Where? With whom?' she asked suspiciously. 'I walked with Teja,' he said, describing the direction they had taken, the special circuit Tamara thought of as their own.

It was only that spring that Rudolf had allowed Tamara to meet his young German friend (neither Liuba nor Leonid ever heard him mention Teja's name), but sensing a rival for Rudolf's affection, she disliked him from the start. The feeling was mutual: when Teja referred to Tamara he often called her 'the Black Cat'. True to his nature, Rudolf began using them both for his own ends. He loved being photographed, and during walks with Tamara would choose locations for her to shoot him with her little camera, leaning against the railings of the Fontanka Embankment, in front of the Kirov Theatre, the Russian Museum, the Summer Gardens . . . From his first acquaintance with Teja, when he had asked the student to film the American Ballet Theatre in his absence, he had profited from the use of his home-movie camera and projector, returning again and again to Teja's lodgings to watch the footage. He became as excited by Balanchine's *Theme and Variations*, a contemporary homage to Petipa, as he was by his first sight of Erik Bruhn's dancing. Although Tamara had been able to make out no more than 'a tiny man jumping' in extracts from *Swan Lake* and *Don Quixote*, Rudolf was transfixed by Bruhn's lean, elegant line. 'On the 8-mm film I saw what he can do with his legs. I wanted to learn that, how he does that.'

As a study aid Rudolf asked Teja to film his own performances, and together they watched and discussed the results. Teja had a very good eye and was one of the few people from whom Rudolf would accept corrections on his technique. 'They were comrades for each other, they learned from each other.' In this footage it is surprising to see how technically unpolished Rudolf still was at this point, awkwardly bent over the ballerina, his landings heavy, his turns corkscrewing down to a flat supporting foot. He was then being urged by the critics to refine his dancing, to strive for clarity in every step and work towards making his movements flow imperceptibly together. One suggested casting him more often in ensemble roles such as the Cavaliers' Quartet in *Raymonda*, so that he would be forced to model his movements on Kirov paragons such as the academically faultless Yuri Soloviev. But not only was compulsory uniformity contemptible to Rudolf, he was then deliberately 'washing away the classical rules', allowing innovation to take precedence over finesse. He could see his influence affecting his contemporaries, not the other way round. 'A lot of us liked and tried to copy his new ways,' admits former Kirov soloist Vadim Desnitsky. Even the grudging Serge Vikulov had begun to imitate Rudolf's coda of *doubles assemblés* in *La Bayadère*, while Boris Bregvadze, who particularly admired Rudolf's speedy *chaînés* – 'We did them fast, but his were even faster, and then he stopped dead' – was adopting a feature Rudolf had added to *Corsaire*, when instead of walking across the stage towards his partner, he performed a sequence of steps, then ran in a circle towards her. 'It has stayed to this day.'

Kirov ballerinas were now vying to dance with Rudolf – 'They felt that his energy, his input, would rub off on them too,' Bregvadze says. Alla Shelest believed that together they could create a legendary partnership. Their performance of *Laurentia* in February had been just as thrilling as their *Giselle*. Noticeably more mature and self-confident than he had been with Dudinskaya, Rudolf still presented a version of the hero completely different from any before him, re-creating Frondoso in his own image – 'more freedom-loving, more selfish and passionately in love'. His debuts that season, by contrast, were uneven. It was generally agreed that his two performances of the Prince in *The Nutcracker* two weeks earlier had been a disappointment.

'I saw a lot of technical errors,' says Faina Rokhind. 'And he danced without any emotion, as if he thought the part was not prestigious enough for him.' His Prince Désiré in *The Sleeping Beauty* in March, on the other hand, was a remarkable success: 'It was as if he was born to play this; his elegance was completely natural,' says a Kirov contemporary who has never seen a better Désiré onstage before or since. Having taken note of Sergei Sorokin's comment that *désiré* in French means 'desired' ('It's good,' he said, smiling. 'I like that!'), Rudolf projected a powerful physical allure most apparent in the hunting scene, where beplumed and bedecked in lace and satin, he stalked the stage with real aristocratic command. His Prince Siegfried in *Swan Lake* at the beginning of April reverted, in the view of his fans, to being 'very bad, not interesting, rough dancing', wrote Galina Palshina. 'And how we were waiting for this performance, which happened *after* his *Sleeping Beauty*!'

Rudolf always considered the famous classical works to be ballerinas' ballets, with the prince employed as no more than a foil and *porteur*. 'Petipa didn't want to make men dance. *At all*,' he said. 'Just walk or stand like statue onstage.' His lack of conviction in the Petipa repertory was tangible (though not in *The Sleeping Beauty*, possibly because, as his teacher Igor Belsky pointed out, 'He really felt the ballet's history'). His failure in *Swan Lake* may also have been due to the fact that he was not given sufficient rehearsal time; he was then beginning to prepare his repertory (*The Sleeping Beauty*, *La Bayadère*, *Don Quixote*, *Giselle* and *Taras Bulba*) for the Kirov's forthcoming tour to the West.

It was hard for Rudolf to accept that his dream of seeing Europe was about to be realized. He knew how dancers could be dropped from foreign excursions at any time and for any reason. Ninel Kurgapkina believes to this day that she was prevented from going abroad as a result of having been informed on while in East Germany for wearing trousers that were considered immodest. Alla Shelest's name was on the list, then suddenly removed – probably as a result of the French impresario's insistence on younger dancers. In the middle of rehearsing Rudolf and Alla Sizova in the Blue Bird pas de deux for Paris, Shelest, remembering that she would not be accompanying them, began to cry. Immediately understanding the reason, Rudolf came over to comfort her, and when she declined his offer to go back with him to the Pushkins, insisted on escorting her home. 'We scarcely said a word on the way, but nevertheless I felt his warm sympathy towards me the entire time.'

Considering the atmosphere of uncertainty surrounding the tour, it's extraordinary that Rudolf allowed himself to jeopardize his chances only days before he was due to leave. He had been summoned with the other dancers for a routine preparatory session at Smolniy, an administrative centre next door to Leningrad's famous blue-and-white baroque cathedral, and after being lectured on the 'modern international situation' and instructed on how they should behave abroad, Rudolf and a colleague were taken to a separate room. There, heading the special committee responsible for vetoing dancers for the tour, was Vitaly Strizhevsky, who was officially deputy to the administrative director but in reality worked for the KGB, something most people were aware of. Why, he demanded, had neither of them joined the Komsomol? 'Because I've far more important things to do with my time than waste it on that kind of rubbish!' exclaimed Rudolf impulsively. According to Dolgushin, 'It was exactly the kind of crazy thing he couldn't resist saying.'

It was clear Nureyev had to leave. As Baryshnikov said, 'He would have died in Russia . . . they would kill him or he would kill himself. There was only one way.' 'In Russia,' Rudolf later told a friend, 'I did not belong to myself. I had a feeling that I had a big talent which people would recognize anywhere.' This talent had already been spotted, and the news dispatched to the West by Yuri Slonimsky, whose June 1960 article on Russian ballet in the *Atlantic Monthly* singled out Rudolf alone among the younger generation of Kirov dancers. Recounting how the Kirov Theatre had been 'literally besieged' for his 12 December 1959 performance of *Giselle* the critic described Rudolf's Albrecht as 'unlike anyone's we have ever seen', instantly recognizing the revolutionary impact of his dancing. 'In a word, new people are interpreting even the deepest past in a new way. They are viewing this past in the light of modern techniques.' But after two and a half years of performing the Kirov's limited repertory, Rudolf had begun to feel that he had absorbed as much as he could from Russia, and longed for the chance to amplify his knowledge and refine his technique. He was already leagues ahead of his compatriots. Balanchine's *Theme and Variations* had been poorly received by Russian audiences unaccustomed to the severity of abstract work, but Rudolf had recognized it immediately as 'the most beautiful ballet'. He vowed he would learn it, just as he promised himself that one day he would study Erik Bruhn's method of dance. As critics and fans had commented recently, Rudolf's dancing could be hectic and rough-edged, whereas he noticed that Bruhn, the ideal *danseur noble*, embodied the very qualities of purity, ease and understatement that he knew he lacked. 'Whether as friend, lover or enemy,' he told himself, 'I have to go to that camp and learn it all.'

Rudolf's defection was 'prepared inside', but nevertheless, he still felt that he needed to gauge the reaction of his friends. During a long walk with Leonid a few days before his departure, Rudolf asked him, 'What would you think if I stayed in the West?' The question shocked Leonid profoundly, but keeping his answer deliberately oblique, he replied, 'Do you know what nostalgia means?' He wanted to remind Rudolf of the lifestyle he loved and would be leaving behind – Leningrad's 'kitchen culture', where a gathering of friends around a table had come to mean more to him than his family. Sensing his unease, Rudolf tried to make light of what he had said as no more than a hypothetical possibility, and made Leonid promise not to say a word about their conversation to anyone.

Rudolf, it was true, felt entirely at ease in his close circle – a milieu far removed from the theatre's world of rumour and scandal. And yet for an artist, a society dependent on friends can also be constricting. Rudolf felt increasingly trapped by circumstances at home. Now that Xenia could see how much of a hold Teja had on him, she had reverted to being jealous and contentious, going out of her way to cause trouble between them. 'They have quarrelled – Xana is the reason,' Elizaveta Pazhi told a friend. Xenia would never stop loving Rudolf – 'There was only one person until her death, he was like a god for her' – but at the same time she found herself involuntarily attracted to Teja. If Rudolf sensed the growing sexual chemistry between them he would have felt the kind of distaste and disenchantment experienced by Chinko Rafique, taken up by the Pushkins a decade later:

> I got very disillusioned and almost didn't want to dance. It was a feeling that there was a very harsh and sordid reality behind these people about whom I had such illusions. Xenia was predatory. She was sexually predatory, and I do think, looking back, that Pushkin really suffered a lot. I think he experienced enormous humiliation because of that. There was a lot of hurt. You could feel it. I think for Pushkin it was a very unhappy situation, and he had to close his eyes and really make his own private peace with himself for having to handle Xenia's excesses.

Liuba has always believed that Rudolf's involvement with Xenia was a key reason why he 'escaped to the West'. Ninel Kurgapkina also agrees that it was a situation from which he badly wanted to extricate himself. 'He was not very proud when he talked of Xenia. He didn't feel good thinking about her.' But even more of an incentive to leave Russia was the realization that he would never be free to follow his true sexual instincts while he was there. 'I did not have the possibility of choosing my friends according to my taste. It was as if someone battered me morally. I was very unhappy.' By now people within the Kirov were beginning to find out about Rudolf's homosexuality, 'although', says Gabriella Komleva, 'it was clear that he hadn't quite sorted himself out: it was a little of this, a little of that'.

In fact he was far more consistent in his choice of male love than Teja, who had already begun his pursuit of the Indonesian student whom he later married. Konstantin Russu remembers Rudolf bursting in on one occasion and making a jealous scene. 'Teja often had someone, or maybe he just told Rudolf that he had someone else,' said Ute Mitreuter. 'He could be very manipulative with people.' In the Stasi statement Teja was forced to write about his relationship with Rudolf, he said that in April, when the school went on a trip to Moscow, he had decided to sever the link between them.

After I had come back, he often tried to meet me in the dormitory or at school, but I avoided him. One week after my return he ran into me in the street and confronted me about why I had broken off our friendship. For me there were many reasons . . . During the last couple of days before our separating he had tried to start an abnormal relationship with me . . . It had become completely clear that because of this there would always be a distance between the two of us.

But Teja, Ute remarks, 'was writing and laughing', meaning that his story was concocted to appease his interrogaters. There was never any lasting rift, and Chinko Rafique, who was one of the few people to whom both young men talked in retrospect about their affair, confirms that theirs was 'a very deep passion'. For Rudolf, it was the rapture of a first infatuation, the highs and lows all the more intense for being illicit. For Teja, however, who remained in love with Rudolf much longer, their involvement – or rather, its consequences – would mark the rest of his life.

With Teja laid low by a painful abscess on his calf, Rudolf went for his last long walk in Leningrad with Tamara. It was early May, and the White Nights were just beginning, their pearly light making the familiar landmarks of the city recede like a stage set behind a screen. As they strolled along the streets until the early hours, Rudolf spoke of his concern about how the French audiences would receive him. 'Paris to us was the capital of the world so it was going to be like a big audition for him.' When Tamara heard that the Pushkins would be at the airport to see him off later that morning, she wanted to say goodbye there and then (Xenia was still ostracizing her, looking straight over her head whenever they met), but Rudolf insisted that she come.

Arriving at Pulkova airport after a night of virtually no sleep, he saw Xenia and Alexander Ivanovich sitting on a bench on the opposite side of the hall from Tamara. Then he saw Rosa making her way towards him with her new daughter in her arms, and his shame about the baby's illegitimacy made him very cruel. 'You shouldn't have come,' he hissed. 'Go home at once!' It was humiliating for his sister to be turned away under everyone's gaze, but Rudolf was implacable: there could be no gossip. It was the reason he had instructed Teja not to be there. There had been rumours that a member of the company was going to be sent back from the airport, and it was only when he saw a dancer being led away from the group, ostensibly for having the incorrect documents, that Rudolf felt able to relax. When Leonid Romankov arrived, he found Rudolf, jauntily dressed for his destination in a black Basque beret, 'very excited, and full of jokes'. His mood was catching. As the friends stood together at the barrier after finally waving him off, Xenia suddenly turned to Tamara and said, 'Alexander Ivanovich is going to work. Why don't you and I go to the Sever Café together?' Taken completely by surprise, Tamara agreed, and headed off with her to Nevsky Prospekt. Ordering a celebratory selection of *blinichkis* followed by profiteroles and coffee, the pair chatted like schoolgirls, exchanging stories about Rudolf and trying to imagine the impact he would have on the West. It was the beginning of a new bond that mutual dependence would soon deepen into real friendship.

5 SIX STEPS EXACTLY

At a backstage reception following the Kirov's gala opening at the Palais Garnier on 16 May 1961, the guests divided into two formations: the Russians on one side of the elegant Foyer de la Danse, the French on the other. Three Parisian dancers were chatting together when they noticed a young man edging little by little away from his group and coming towards them. Like all the Russian men in their strangely cut, old-fashioned suits, he appeared 'dressed but not dressed', but what singled him out was his intelligent, animated expression. 'Look, this one is completely different,' said Pierre Lacotte. 'You can see from the way he's looking around that he's interested in everything: he's talking with his eyes.' Like an inquisitive wild creature, Rudolf inched even closer. 'Now we were sure he would come to us.' 'Do you speak French?' Pierre asked. 'No, English,' he replied. Then, turning to the two women, he smiled and said, 'I recognize you.'

Tall, slim Claire Motte, newly appointed *danseuse étoile*, had performed on several occasions in Russia, and during the first days of the Kirov tour, she, along with fellow *étoiles* Claude Bessy and Attilio Labis, had been the only Paris Opéra dancers either to watch or take part in the Russians' classes. To Rudolf their eagerness to compare techniques and teaching methods had immediately established them as kindred spirits; he had nothing but contempt for their indifferent colleagues rehearsing in studios next door.

Although he himself had not appeared onstage that evening, he had been dazzling as Prince Désiré in the dress rehearsal of *The Sleeping Beauty* seen by the two ballerinas the previous day. Also present was the young dance critic René Sirvin, who would write ecstatically of 'a young aerial phenomenon of a stupefying virtuosity and lightness'. Sirvin's article, headlined: *'Les Ballets de Leningrad ont leur homme de l'espace'* * (The Leningrad ballet has its spaceman), was published in *L'Aurore* on 17 May, the day after the Kirov's opening, with the prom-

---

* The Soviets' mastery of space was a topical issue: Yuri Gagarin had just orbited the earth for the first time in history on 12 April.

ise that the twenty-two-year-old Nureyev would appear again as the
Prince that evening. In fact, he did not dance any of the scheduled
performances of *The Sleeping Beauty*, even though Rudolf claimed that
Ekaterina Furtseva, the Russian minister of culture, had specifically
asked for him to be given the opening night. He described how
Furtseva had entered the room and come straight towards him at a
welcoming reception held at the Hotel Moderne.

> Without saying hello to the company or to Sergeyev or anybody. And
> she said, 'This country waits for you to dance here.' She glanced at
> Sergeyev, who *rushed* in. 'And you make sure he dance first night and
> you send him to Cannes Film Festival to dance.' She wanted to make
> sure I go to Cannes and present myself. Sergeyev said, 'Yes, yes,
> yes . . .' So. He didn't give me first night of *Sleeping Beauty*. He gave
> me dress rehearsal. At that time, like in all Latin countries, dress
> rehearsal was *the* performance. Because all the press came. It didn't
> matter who dance first night. So – his plan failed.

Once again Rudolf suspected Sergeyev of jealousy, though Alla
Osipenko saw it differently. She suggests that by casting Irina
Kolpakova and her husband, Vladilen Semyonov (who received only
politely appreciative reviews), the director was vindicating himself to
the French impresarios. 'It was so that Sergeyev and Dudinskaya could
say, "You see, we gave the première to the young dancers and they
didn't have any success." If Nureyev had appeared, he would have been
a sensation.' Whatever the reason, the snub had made Rudolf even
more determined to do exactly as he pleased. While the company was
being shown the sights of Paris on supervised tours, he had already
gone his own way, jumping off the charter bus and running down the
street in order to explore the city alone. And now he even felt grateful
that Sergeyev had unwittingly provided him with an unexpected
opportunity. 'He gave me chance to go to Salle Pleyel and hear for the
first time Bach cantatas and sonatas with Yehudi Menuhin. Was
extraordinary thing.' It was after this performance, on 16 May, that he
joined the company in the Foyer de Danse.

Charmed by such an unusual, beautiful young man, the French
friends, who had planned to have supper together at Claude Bessy's
apartment, invited Rudolf to accompany them. 'I'd love to,' he said.
'But I'll never get permission.' 'At least we could try,' suggested Claire
Motte. 'We're not doing anything suspicious, we only want to talk
about dance.' In a delegation of three they went over to ask permission

of Sergeyev and Dudinskaya. 'They were both very embarrassed: "As you know it's not permitted," Sergeyev told them. "The dancers have to work so hard and should get to bed early. But," he added, relenting, "perhaps if you take another Kirov member with you we can make an exception." When Rudolf heard the good news, he was amazed: the dancers were forbidden to do anything independently of the group. Rudolf told them that he would bring the boy with whom he shared his hotel room: "He's called Yuri Soloviev." Having just seen Soloviev in the Blue Bird pas de deux with Alla Sizova, the French dancers were delighted to have the chance to meet the performer responsible for the evening's "*coup de tonnerre*". "For me it was Soloviev who was the Kirov's most impressive dancer," Claude Bessy remarks. "His quality of jump was incredible – lighter than a cat's. But Nureyev was the one who wanted to make contact with us."'

Claude lived on the rue de la Rochefoucauld, within walking distance of the Opéra, and en route, while Soloviev looked ill at ease and hardly said a word, '*comme un figurant*' (like a film extra), Rudolf talked enough for them both. He had been struck by the electric charge of Paris – 'like a perpetual party' – finding the French *flâneurs* especially intriguing. Why, he demanded, did everyone seem to be walking without any sense of purpose? My God, Pierre thought, this one has a lot of opinions about everything – a view shared by Claude, whose elegant apartment drew a barrage of comments from Rudolf from the minute he arrived. 'It was his first contact with a style of life completely different from the one he knew. For him it was all too chic, and he was very critical.'

But while Claude found Rudolf haughty and disagreeable, Claire and Pierre were soon won over by his evident delight at being in their company, and by his hunger to learn. 'I would like to talk to you about the past,' he told them. 'To find out all the things you know that maybe we don't any more.' With Pierre, who was fluent in English,[*] acting as translator, they went on to talk 'about *everything*. About Paris, about architecture and painting, about how ballet had started here with Louis Quatorze and Versailles . . . Rudolf already knew it all.'

---

[*] 'I wanted to learn both English and French,' Rudolf once told the journalist Lynn Barber. 'There was an old lady in Leningrad who spoke French and she said, "Yes, I will teach you. The only thing is that you will have to carry the bucket of dirt every morning" – there were no toilets. And I thought, No, I was too grand. I was a dancer . . . So of course I never learned French. But now I tell young people, "If you want to achieve something, you want to learn something, you have to carry the buckets of dirt."'

After 'a fantastic time' together, Claire and Pierre drove the two Russian dancers back to the dismal Hotel Moderne, dropping them, at Rudolf's request, on the corner of the place de la République rather than at the entrance. 'Because they observe us.' Rudolf was so reluctant to leave his new friends that when they presented him with a box of chocolates as a memento of the evening, he took two and asked to leave the rest behind. 'That way, I can take two tomorrow and two the next day.' 'Rudolf,' Pierre said with a laugh, 'are you afraid we won't see each other?' 'Yes, of course.' 'Well,' he said, 'you must trust us. Take the chocolates now and I guarantee that we'll see each other tomorrow.' 'But how? What can we do?' 'I'll come and watch you in class and afterwards, I won't speak to you, but we'll meet for a drink. Do you know that little bar at the back of the Opéra on the rue Auber? I'll see you there. I promise.'

The principals' class had already started when Pierre came into the studio. Dudinskaya, who was teaching it, welcomed him warmly and invited him to sit down. Immediately spotting Rudolf and Soloviev, Pierre also recognized Alla Sizova and Irina Kolpakova. 'But Rudolf stood out from them all: even at the barre he had such presence.' When the dancers moved to the centre, Rudolf began to show off, glancing out of the corner of his eye to make sure that Pierre was watching. 'He wanted to give me a performance, and he danced like an animal. Technically, it was superb: I realized then that he was absolutely exceptional.'

When class was over Pierre deliberately avoided any contact with Rudolf but went straight to the Café Pampam to wait for him. 'He arrived with a big smile and immediately asked me what I'd thought. "Rudolf, if you dance like this at your first performance it will be a triumph!" "That's what I want more than anything," he replied. "Nijinsky and all the great dancers made their names in Paris. But, tell me frankly, did you notice anything wrong? What can I fix?"' Having learned that Pierre, an independent choreographer and director, was not only a product of the Paris Opéra school and company but had also been a pupil of the Maryinsky ballerina Lubov Egorova, who had worked with Cecchetti, Rudolf resolved to absorb as much from him as he could.

With time on his hands, being between companies and recuperating from an injury, Pierre was more than willing to oblige; over the next couple of days they went to Sainte-Chapelle and Notre Dame, to *Ben Hur* (which Rudolf loathed) and to *West Side Story* (which moved him to tears). As they came out into the street, in a burst of euphoria he launched into an impersonation of the Jets, cha-cha-chaing along the Champs-Élysées.

When Pierre took Rudolf to his apartment on the avenue Wagram, he immediately made himself at home, 'like a cat on a cushion'. On one occasion he curled up and fell asleep there, but not for long – he couldn't afford to waste a second, and was constantly asking questions. Pierre's passion was for ballets of the Romantic era on which, through a series of meticulously researched restorations, he went on to become France's leading authority. Discovering that Pierre had danced *Le Spectre de la rose* at the Paris Opéra, Rudolf begged to learn it (the Spectre was one of the legendary Nijinsky roles, which he was determined to inherit). Having studied the famous photographs of Nijinsky with his petal-covered head framed by tendril-like, Art Nouveau arms, Rudolf already had his own clear idea of the style, and when Pierre attempted to elongate the exaggerated curve of his port de bras, gave a cry of protest, 'Don't kill my inspiration!'

They continued to work together in Claire Motte's studio, with Pierre also demonstrating steps he knew from ballets by Balanchine. What had begun as a creative alliance soon evolved into a friendship. 'He was so happy and charming, and said to me, "You're like a member of my family now."' Over the coming weeks Rudolf would reveal tantalizing details about his life in Russia, describing his difficult childhood, telling Pierre about Menia, his Cuban girlfriend, and talking often of Pushkin. But he never confided anything of a truly private nature. 'He was very discreet at that time. I didn't even know that he was homosexual. All that concerned him then was to visit, to know, to learn.' Nor at any point did Rudolf speak out against the Soviet system, although he did protest bitterly about the lack of opportunity in the Kirov, saying that he had often felt that he was suffocating.

A document in Rudolf's KGB file claims that Pierre was the main perpetrator of a plan to persuade Rudolf to stay in France. Pierre, however, insists that neither one ever mentioned the idea of defection. On the contrary, Pierre spoke of plans to come to London to see Rudolf's *Giselle*, and promised to visit him in Leningrad. 'Rudolf would complain, "They're against me all the time. I can't say or do what I think." But I'd tell him, "Listen, as a dancer you need that discipline. Remember that you're here in Paris and dance like a god."'

The day of Rudolf's debut, 19 May, arrived. Act 3 of *La Bayadère*, 'The Kingdom of the Shades', was shown in a mixed programme, which included the Cossack scene from *Taras Bulba*, a showpiece of Soviet machismo, in which Rudolf also appeared. The audience, most of whom had never seen *La Bayadère*, one of the great Russian classics, was entranced from the moment the curtain rose. Their first impression of the long, single file of corps de ballet dancers embodying Petipa's vision of bliss as they hypnotically repeat the slow arabesque sequence that seems to last for ever, was of a poetic beauty and purity beyond belief. After a pas de trois for three principal Shades, Rudolf suddenly appeared. Pierre felt nervous, 'because although he'd been so wonderful in class, with the emotion of a performance you never know what might happen. But the way he ran on without music made people start to whisper . . . Because he was like a tiger.'

To make a spectacular impact, Rudolf had decided to dance his trademark solo from *Le Corsaire*.* Pouncing on the first beat in a ballerina-high attitude, he began his now-famous diagonal of *sauts de basques*, launching into the air and sitting there, his legs tucked under him like a buddha, then sinking into a deep predatory lunge as if tensed to attack. At the dress rehearsal, René Sirvin had watched Rudolf stop the orchestra and shout abuse at the conductor – either for objecting to inserting a passage from another ballet into the score or for failing to play at the speed Rudolf wanted. (The tempo itself had to hover as he strove for that miraculous moment of levitation basketball players call 'hang time'.) Finding that the Kirov's elaborate, old-fashioned costume restricted his elevation, Rudolf had simplified the design, changing the colour to an ultramarine blue, and accentuating the preening arch of his torso with a *décolleté* neckline and white sash, his Tatar cheekbones with a plumed turban – 'How he shone!' remembers his partner, Olga

---

* 'Sergeyev suggested I should put in another solo, but he did not say which,' he told John Percival (*Nureyev: Aspect of the Dancer*). 'On the first night I danced my *Corsaire* solo and had a big success. But then I took Solor's solo from an earlier act of the ballet [the variation from the wedding scene].' There is some controversy over Rudolf's claim. Both Irina Kolpakova and Olga Moiseyeva, his partner that night, believe he could only have danced the Act 2 *La Bayadère* solo. 'This is absurd. It would be impossible to dance the *Corsaire* variation in *Bayadère*,' insists Kolpakova. But why, as Percival asks, 'would Rudolf have made this up'? In an interview with documentary director John Bridcut, Pierre Lacotte confirms that Rudolf did indeed dance his *Corsaire* solo that night. 'It was from another ballet – from *Corsaire*, which we'd never seen either. When he told me that afterwards, I said, "My God, I never heard such a thing!"' The critic Olivier Merlin wrote in his review, 'It's the solo of Solor the Warrior which won a deafening ovation at the première for the young Soviet artist. He had, in effect, arranged his own variation and executed a feat never seen before at the height of a spiral turn, a *double tour en l'air* incorporating a *grand saut du chat*, with one leg tucked under him' (*Le Monde*, 24 May 1961).

Moiseyeva. The West had never seen anyone like Rudolf – the paragon of animals – with his mix of hauteur and savage intensity, his '*façon féline*', created by the upward stretch and lightness of his line. 'Maybe his legs were not as long as they should have been,' Baryshnikov would later say, 'but it was like a touch of earth there, with that man's butt and overdeveloped calf. It was very masculine and at the same time [had] a touch of the feminine . . . That gave him a sort of sexuality nobody around had at that time. It was so exotic.'

The furore that followed the end of the solo was deafening. 'People *screamed*,' says Pierre. 'I've seen hundreds of Rudolf's performances, and never did he dance like that. Never!' There had not been a comparable ballet event in Paris since the first appearance of Nijinsky in *La Saison Russe* more than fifty years earlier – a debut that, by coincidence, fell on the same day of the same month. '*C'était déjà le Nijinski de l'Oiseau de feu*,' wrote Olivier Merlin in *Le Monde*, but octogenarian Lubov Egorova, who had been partnered by Nijinsky at the Maryinsky, vowed that Rudolf had something even greater than his predecessor. 'He is taller, longer, slenderer, which makes him appear lighter . . . And he has the same presence [as Nijinsky].' To those who had seen 'the soaring angel' for themselves, Rudolf's arrival was a second coming, and to those who had not, it was just as much of a wonder. 'He opened the eyes of the West to Russian ballet,' Irina Kolpakova remarked. 'Through him, people in the West fell wildly in love with our art all over again.'

Right after the performance Rudolf joined his French friends, who were waiting to take him out for a celebratory dinner:

> In the back of the car was a young girl whom I had never seen before: very pale, quite tiny, and looking no more than sixteen . . . She was introduced to me as Clara Saint . . . Clara hardly spoke at all during the evening. She had lovely straight dark hair with reddish lights in it, which she had a habit of lightly tossing in a soft, almost childlike way. She would shake her head and smile, always silent. I liked her enormously from the first moment I saw her.

Rudolf did not remember that he had encountered twenty-year-old Clara a few days earlier when Claire Motte had taken her backstage to meet the Kirov dancers. The only one who spoke to them was Rudolf. Having spent her early childhood in Buenos Aires, she had moved to Paris with her Chilean mother at the age of five, when her parents separated. Her father, who still lived in Argentina, was a wealthy industrialist, and Clara was the heiress to the family fortune. Attractive, intelligent and worldly, she moved in the society of dancers, artists and fashion designers, yet retained a quality of gentleness and understated style to which Rudolf had instinctively responded. Her fiancé was Vincent Malraux, the younger son of André Malraux, the French minister of culture. A 'very spectacular' philosophy student, Vincent was tall and beautiful with black eyes and great charm and humour, but he did not share Clara's love of ballet. Taking advantage of the fact that he and his brother were away for a few days in the South of France, she went to the Kirov with Claire as often as she could.

Before inviting everyone back for supper at her mother's house on the Quai d'Orsay, Clara took the three of them to see her new apartment on the rue de Rivoli. Although it was still in the process of being redecorated, Rudolf was clearly awed by its size and stunning views of the Jardin des Tuileries; he seemed relieved to discover that they would be eating in Clara's mother's kitchen. Exhilarated by the success of his performance and stimulated by the company of his French friends, Rudolf was more loquacious than ever before, surprising Clara with the range of his knowledge:

> I told him he must have had a wonderful education because he knew our music and spoke of French Impressionism and pointillism . . . But he said, 'I learned everything by myself. In Leningrad I go all the time to the Hermitage: I need it like food.' He was so happy that night, telling us about many things that he wanted to do. He never mentioned the idea of leaving Russia, but he said, 'I dream of being free to come here when I want.'

Eager to show Clara his favourite Kirov ballet, he offered to take her to Grigorovich's *The Stone Flower*, in which he was not performing. The night of its premiere, 23 May, almost every eye in the audience was focused on the VIP box in which the young couple sat side by side. A few boxes away were the Kirov officials, one of whom took Rudolf aside during an interval and upbraided him for associating with foreigners. Rudolf mentioned nothing to Clara about the reprimand, or the subsequent ban on their friendship. They spent the rest of the evening having supper together at a bistro on the boulevard St-Michel.

Most of the following day Clara waited at home for Vincent to return. She had lent her Alfa Romeo to the Malraux brothers for the long Pentecost weekend, and when they still hadn't appeared by midnight, she realized that something must have happened. Deciding to telephone their parents despite the late hour, she spoke to their mother, Madeleine, who said, 'You mean you don't know? Then it's better that you come to see us straight away.' Clara learned as soon as she arrived that both Vincent and his brother, Gauthier, were dead, killed while driving at high speed on the perilous corniche of the Côte d'Or.

The next few days passed in a blur for Clara. Given Valium injections by her doctor, she remembers almost nothing about Vincent's funeral or about the occasion, more than a week later, when, feeling like a sleepwalker, she went to the Palais des Sports (the huge arena in the southern suburbs to which the Kirov had just transferred), for Rudolf's Paris debut in *Swan Lake*. Some people were 'a little shocked' to see her already out on the town, but the ballet helped her to forget, and over the next two weeks she allowed herself to be swept up by the activities of the three friends:

> We started to see him before class, after class . . . Claire would say, 'Come and have lunch with us! What are you doing later?' We took him *everywhere*: to Versailles, to Béjart's *Bolero*, to the Crazy Horse Saloon . . . He could hardly believe all those naked girls and was laughing so much! He wanted to buy an electric train so we went to Le Nain Bleu – a toyshop where he stayed for two hours, absolutely mesmerized while we were very bored. He wanted to see an English bookshop, so we took him to Galignani on the rue de Rivoli. He'd never seen a shop with so many shelves of books – he thought it was a library and didn't realize that you could actually *buy* the books. Every day was a new experience, and he was so amused and excited about it all – kissing us and saying, 'I'm so happy!'

They noticed the way that, like a child, Rudolf wanted everything at once, ordering tea, a hot chocolate and a Coca-Cola all at the same time. Claire, who was the big sister of the group, chided Rudolf by saying, 'You're very spoiled! Have tea now and something else later.' 'Then he didn't talk to us for two minutes.' 'I'm not spoiled at all,' Rudolf murmured. 'You can't imagine how poor I was as a child.'

The greed was all part of his craving for new experiences. But while Rudolf was devouring every aspect of Western civilization, his Kirov colleagues spent most of their free time shopping, going to no more than one or two shows during their month in Paris. They were interested in seeing a rival *Sleeping Beauty*, which had just opened at the Théâtre des Champs-Élysées, performed by the Grand Ballet du

Marquis de Cuevas – a company that was soon to acquire special significance for Rudolf. This opulent production – staging it had been Georges de Cuevas's last extravagance before his death three months earlier – had been mounted at a cost of 150 million francs, forcing the marquis to sell his collections and Quai Voltaire apartment, but it failed to impress the Russians. 'It was small-scale, dainty dancing. Nothing like the Kirov,' said Gabriella Komleva. 'Strange costumes with huge Folies-Bergères feathers, more like music hall', according to Irina Kolpakova. Rudolf was equally critical, finding the elaborate designs distracting, the dancers lacking homogeneous schooling and emotional depth. All the same, when Pierre announced that they were taking him to dinner to meet the new director, Raymundo de Larrain, he was eager to discuss the two versions.

As it was Larrain who had designed the rococo *Sleeping Beauty*, Rudolf was somewhat surprised to discover that his apartment on the rue des Saints-Pères, while extremely grand with its velvet-covered walls and eighteenth-century antiques, was decorated with impeccable restraint. Larrain himself was equally refined – an urbane, amusing character with an aristocratic manner that verged at times on the supercilious.*

Retaliating against Larrain's criticism of the Kirov's old-fashioned repertory, Rudolf began mocking the de Cuevas company. 'How long will you be performing *Sleeping Beauty*?' he challenged Raymundo. 'For a *month*? That's not ballet, it's a musical run!' Pierre remembers Rudolf illustrating his contempt for the lavish designs by grabbing a crystal vase and balancing it on his head, 'Look! A costume by Raymundo de Larrain!' 'The boy is a *mujik*!' Raymundo muttered to Pierre. Yet despite their differences, Rudolf left under the impression that they had managed to part good friends.

In Rudolf's account of the evening, it was Soloviev who had accompanied him, but Pierre has no recollection of the dancer being there. Increasingly disdainful of company rules, Rudolf had long since ceased to get permission for his outings, or to take a chaperone along. He was given another of several warnings not to see friends described by the KGB as 'politically suspicious people . . . from artistic Bohemia'.

* According to Hugo Vickers, editor of *Alexis: The Memoirs of the Baron de Redé*, Raymundo de Larrain's claim to be Cuevas's nephew was apocryphal. 'Larrain was in fact a Chilean gigolo, and one of de Cuevas's boyfriends . . . a nervous creature, with a long nose, and even longer manicured fingers.'

'Then we'll have to stop,' Pierre remarked when Rudolf told him, but Rudolf reacted with dismay. 'How can you say such a thing? Are you a good friend or not?' 'Because it's for you,' protested Pierre. 'You have to be careful. We don't want you to be punished.' 'But I want to spend my time with the three of you. We have a wonderful friendship. I'm not going to pay any attention to them.'

Realizing that Rudolf's 'absolutely intolerable' conduct was not going to change, Vitaly Strizhevsky, the Kirov's assistant director and KGB emissary, reported him to the Communist Party's Central Committee. On 3 June, Sergeyev and Georgi Korkin, the Kirov's administrative director, received an order from the CCCPSU's Commission on Travel to send Nureyev back before the end of the tour 'with all the necessary precautionary measures', following this up with a reminder dispatched from Moscow three days later. Instead of acting on its instructions the two Kirov directors and the Soviet ambassador decided to make a case for Rudolf to stay. How would they explain the sudden absence of the star largely responsible for the success of the tour? Nureyev was the dancer everybody wanted to see. His impact in Paris was so dramatic that even the Leningrad paper *Soviet Culture* had commented on it. Lately, too, he had been more cooperative, joining a propaganda photo session – an entente cordiale between French and Russian Communists – as he, Sergeyev, and a trio of Kirov ballerinas posed with French journalists and the dancer Michel Renault in the editorial offices of the Communist paper *l'Humanité*. It was Nureyev, more than any other Kirov member, who was bringing glory to the Soviet state: earlier that week he had been awarded the Nijinsky Prize by Serge Lifar, who declared that for dance historians there would be three *époques*: '*l'époque Nijinski, l'époque Lifar et l'époque Noureev.*'

Unaware that his fate lay in such delicate balance, Rudolf capriciously reverted to form: his reception in Paris had made him feel invincible. One night, as he began his Act 3 variation in *Swan Lake*, he slipped and fell, but instead of continuing to dance, he gestured for the orchestra to stop, and left the stage. His three friends were horrified, as Pierre recalls:

> We waited and waited in silence. When finally he came back and sig-nalled to the conductor, 'Go!' I thought, My God, you'd better dance well otherwise people will whistle at you. In France we hate that kind of thing. After the performance we said, 'Rudolf, you took a big risk. Please don't do that again. It's better to put your resin on before the

performance. If you keep that up, you'll be in big trouble.' 'Yeah, but I danced well.'

It was true. He had danced superbly, bringing to the role of Prince Siegfried an authority and finesse that his Leningrad interpretation had lacked. Nevertheless the KGB's vigilance over Rudolf was tightening by the day. 'Look, there's someone behind us!' he exclaimed to Pierre when they were out together one evening. Pierre laughed. 'Are you dreaming?' 'You don't believe me? I know for sure. We're being followed by people from the Russian embassy.' Pierre turned around to look but could see no one. 'Of course,' said Rudolf. 'Because now they're hiding themselves.'

A couple of Rudolf's colleagues had warned him that he was being trailed. 'It was uncomfortable to tell him,' says Olga Moiseyeva. 'But we thought it would be fine, because although he would stay out late with his foreign friends, he would still dance beautifully the next day.' Others, staying in a different hotel, were delighted that the KGB were all sitting in the Moderne waiting for Rudolf, leaving them free to go shopping and walk the streets of Paris unaccompanied. 'We even went to a nightclub!'

During an evening on which the whole company were invited by the French impresarios to the '*spectacle des girls emplumées*' at the Lido, Rudolf, feeling bored, turned round to Janine Ringuet sitting behind him.

'You know that there are people who want me to stay in France?' I didn't understand. 'What do you mean, Rudolf?' 'If I left the company, what would you say?' He must have seen the expression on my face – if something like that were to happen it would be terrible for the work we were doing – because he said, 'Don't worry, I was just joking! I know perfectly well that I have to stay with the Kirov.'

Several of the dancers were being encouraged to inform on one another. When one ballerina heard from another, a KGB mole, that Rudolf had been telling his French friends things he wasn't supposed to – 'that he was suppressed in the theatre and they didn't let him do what he should be doing' – she reported the conversation to the secretary of the Komsomol organization, even though she herself admits, 'We were all complaining.'

Yuri Soloviev was constantly interrogated about his room-mate's comings and goings. 'One day he came to me and said, "Oh Rudka, they made me open your bags. I looked for your plane ticket."' But although Soloviev tried to protect Rudolf, warning him to be careful, he was growing tired of the pressure and disrupted nights (Rudolf rarely came back before two or three in the morning), and he asked to be moved. This immediately fuelled a number of rumours, one being that Soloviev had been set up by the authorities to try to seduce Rudolf in order to prove his homosexuality. A more likely version, confirmed by Soloviev himself, was that it was Rudolf who had made advances. Laughing scornfully at the suggestion, their colleague Sasha Shavrov, Soloviev's closest friend, insists, 'If Rudolf had tried anything like that, Yuri would just have hit him in the face in Russian tradition.' But this, according to Alla Osipenko, is exactly what happened. 'Yuri told me that when Rudik made a pass at him, he smashed his face.'* Mikhail Baryshnikov, who knew Soloviev well, maintains that the idea that he may have turned informer is ridiculous. 'Rudolf liked Yuri. He admired his dancing, and always said that he was a decent man.' Yet one story persists. Among the dancers questioned in Leningrad after Rudolf's defection, only Soloviev insisted that the act had been preplanned. When word got back to Tamara, she went to see Soloviev herself to ask him for an explanation. The reason he gave was that, unlike every-one else in the company, Rudolf had not been spending his money on Western luxuries: he must have known that he was going to stay.

Foreign tours provided the Russian dancers with their only chance to supplement their income, an opportunity to acquire items whose black market value at home was equivalent to a month's rent. (One dancer who brought back forty nylon shirts from Paris was caught and punished by never being taken abroad again.) Rudolf did, in fact, buy a few Western clothes and trinkets for his family as well as a selection of musical scores for Pushkin, but everything he acquired for himself – with the exception of the train set, which may well have been a pres-ent for Teja – was accessories for his dancing: tights, leg warmers,

---

* This is confirmed by a remark his wife, Tatiana Legat, made to Diane Solway. Soloviev, she said, had been 'so startled by Rudik's advance that he had slapped him across the face and avoided him for the rest of his stay in Paris'. Soloviev himself told a mutual friend, Terence Benton, 'Rudolf was always trying to get into my bed. So I said, "If you don't stop, I'll report you."' When Benton questioned Rudolf, he laughed and said, 'Yes, it's absolutely true. He reported me.' But this possibility is discounted by a theatre character report, written after Rudolf's defection, which states quite clearly that 'during the time Nureyev was in the Kirov there were no signals of immoral behaviour'.

ballet shoes, makeup. For his London debut in *Giselle* he was given a wig, 'blonde, like Marilyn Monroe', by his French friends, who took him to Perruque Bertrand, the best wigmaker in Paris, when he complained that the Kirov's were 'horrible'. The designer Simon Virsaladze was pleasantly surprised one day when Rudolf asked if he would accompany him to a Lycra factory to help him choose costume fabrics for *The Legend of Love* (in which he was counting on making his debut the following season). 'That's the first time in my life I've ever had a dancer ask me to do that!' Virsaladze exclaimed to Alla Osipenko. 'He spent almost his entire tour allowance at that factory. Alla, that boy's really on the ball.'

The *Legend of Love* fabric, like the *Giselle* wig, are evidence enough that Rudolf was not planning to defect in Paris. And yet the possibility continued to preoccupy him – it was just courage to carry it out that he lacked. Passing the place de la Madeleine's Romanesque temple, he decided to go inside. Although he was not a believer, he had always loved the atmosphere and aesthetics of churches – 'Mass is good show' – and the Madeleine's interior with its softly coloured marble, rich murals and gilt Corinthian columns was breathtaking. On this occasion, however, he had come to pray: 'I went to Mary, and I said: "Make it so that I stay without me doing it, you know, let it happen . . . that it will just happen . . . arrange so that I will stay."'

Shortly before he was due to leave, Tamara kept calling Rudolf's hotel room through most of the night. 'Finally he answered. "Rudik, where have you been?" "I was walking. Looking at Paris." "So, how is it?" "OK but I want to get to London . . . The audiences here are stupid."' On the afternoon of 14 June, two days before the Kirov's departure, Rudolf went alone to La Librairie-Galerie de la Danse, the ballet world's Shakespeare and Co., on the place Dauphine, having heard that it was exhibiting work by Bakst and Benois. Immediately recognizing Rudolf, and delighted by his visit, its owner, the dance writer Gilberte Cournand, said she would like to show him an extraordinary book that was in the process of being rebound. As the workshop was around the corner, she took Rudolf there herself, leaving him to browse through the book. After ten minutes Sergeyev came into the gallery with Dudinskaya. Neither of the three mentioned Rudolf, but Mme Cournand was convinced that they hadn't come by chance. 'They must have followed him. Like policemen.'

Rudolf would always believe that Sergeyev and Dudinskaya wanted somehow to prevent him from completing the tour. 'They devised

plan to send me back. So they would be asked to dance in London.'[*]
He had heard that Sergeyev's influence on Leningrad's Communist
Party was so profound that he had once been able to instigate the exile
of Chaboukiani, his greatest rival, to Georgia. 'Whisked away . . .
Things like that. They had extraordinary power. *Political* power.' But
Rudolf was completely wrong in suspecting Sergeyev of holding him
back. An apolitical, profoundly religious man, who Baryshnikov says
'deep down hated Soviets so much', the director was doing all he
could to protect the young rebel. That day, 14 June, he and Korkin had
received their third directive from Moscow, which this time was
'incontestable'. With a background in variety theatre, Korkin was a
very different character from the highly cultured Sergeyev, being far
more worldly and authoritarian, but the two were united in their
contempt for Soviet bureaucrats, 'all anti-intellectual, anti-Semitic,
anti-Western and anti-art'. Once again they insisted 'categorically'
that they would not continue the tour without Rudolf, but by now the
matter was out of their hands.

On 15 June Korkin sent for Nicolai Tarasov, a stagehand, and Sergei
Melnikov, head of lighting, telling them that they would be flying back
the next day to Moscow along with Natasha, the French translator, and
Alexander Grosinsky, the administrator in charge of transport.
'Nureyev will be coming too,' said Korkin, 'but he doesn't know about
it yet.' That night was the company's farewell performance in Paris.
Rudolf was dancing *Swan Lake* with Alla Osipenko, who had been
attracting acclaim as effusive as Rudolf's (for Olivier Merlin, their
names were 'joined with those of Karsavina and Nijinsky in the land of
the sylphs'). Renowned for her ravishing long legs and neoclassical
line, Osipenko already had a large following in Paris, having appeared
there while touring with the Stanislavsky and Nemirovich-Danchenko
Ballet in 1956.

That night, as she and Rudolf left the artists' entrance of the Palais
des Sports, they spotted their friends and fans waiting on each side of

---

* When it was known to the London critics that the couple would not be dancing, a letter
was sent to Korkin at the Royal Opera House, where the Kirov was already installed, asking
if he could schedule their appearance in a performance of *Giselle*. The request, Clement
Crisp recalls, was sincere enough. 'In view of their age, etc. I think the evening would have
been a disappointment, although the year before Nadia Nerina had danced *Giselle* at the
Kirov with Sergeyev, and told me that he was sensationally good as a partner . . . Maybe
their appearance here could have been a triumph. We shall never know. Because the answer
was "*Nyet*."'

the fenced corridor. Strizhevsky, who – following established KGB practice – was always a few paces behind, heard the dancers' plans to join a large group for a farewell supper, and refused his permission. Assigned to escort Rudolf back to Moscow the following morning, he was taking no chances. Realizing what was happening, some of the fans set up a chant of: 'Let them go! Let them go!' Turning to Strizhevsky, Alla said, 'Vitaly Dmitrievich, if you don't let us go, there's going to be a scandal!' Far from being a typical KGB roughneck, Strizhevsky was a well-educated man with a good sense of humour. 'He understood everything about the Soviet system, but it was all in his eyes, he never talked about it.' Like many men, he had a soft spot for Osipenko, with her fiery temper and *femme fatale* ways. Besides, as she reminded him, it was their last night in Paris, and also the eve of her birthday. Reluctantly he agreed to let them go. 'But if Nureyev doesn't come back to his room,' he told her, '*you* will be responsible.'

They went in different cars, Rudolf with his friends, Alla with hers. A maverick in her own way, she, too, had been mixing with 'undesirable' company, spending time with French friends and expatriate Russians, several of whom (including the choreographer Léonide Massine), had been trying to persuade her to stay in France. More imprudently still, she was having an illicit affair with a married man, a principal in the Paris Opéra Ballet: 'X and I were having a wonderful romance in Paris. We would escape together to a room he'd rented in a little hotel outside the city. I don't know why the KGB didn't follow me. With Rudolf, they seemed to want to provoke him, to catch him.'

At the restaurant that night the French dancer asked Alla if she had received her bouquet of birthday flowers, in which he had hidden a surprise present. 'Strizhevsky had asked me who the flowers were from, and I realized then that he must have confiscated the gift – X was very upset about it.' In the middle of dinner a waiter came over to the table and told the ballerina that she was wanted on the telephone. It was her mother calling to wish her a happy birthday. She had tried Alla's hotel first, and been given the number of the restaurant: the dancers' outing may have been authorized, but they were still under surveillance. As Alla left the table, Rudolf called out, 'Ask your mother to call Alexander Ivanovich and tell him about our success. Tell him it was a performance of *genius*!'

It was long after midnight when she and the French dancer got up to leave. 'Rudik,' she said playfully, 'I hope you're going back to your hotel to bed!' 'Of course, Alla, where else would I go? I have to finish packing. And, Alla, are *you* going home to bed?' 'We wished each other good night and parted in laughter, knowing that neither of us had any intention of turning in for the night.' While she and her lover drove out of the city to their hotel on the Seine, Rudolf and Clara stayed on at the restaurant long after everyone else had gone home.

'Then he said we should have a last walk together,' Clara says. 'He wanted to see the Seine and the illuminations one more time.' It was a warm June night, and Paris had never looked more beautiful, 'so we walked and walked and walked.' Crossing the Pont Neuf, they stopped to sit on a bench, still deep in conversation. It was one of the rare times they had been alone together, and to Clara, their friendship had become very special. She spoke a little about Vincent Malraux, but Rudolf was not very interested in hearing about her life. 'He was very narcissistic.' To her he revealed nothing close to his heart, never mentioning Teja, and concealing his Pushkin ménage by claiming to live in Leningrad with a girl from the Kirov – Alla Sizova. 'With a *girl*!' Clara exclaimed in surprise. 'Yes,' he replied. 'Two rooms.'

If Rudolf had been a *coup de foudre* for Clara, his own attraction to her was all part of the romance of Paris: he had fallen in love with the city itself. He spoke that night of how much he would miss Paris, although he was looking forward to England, the English style of ballet, and especially English audiences, which he believed would be more discerning than the French. Finally, at around six in the morning, they found a taxi, and Clara dropped Rudolf off at his hotel. 'It was not a sad farewell because we were coming to London in a few days to see him.' While Rudolf went upstairs to pack, Clara took the taxi on to the Quai d'Orsay and went to bed.

Olga Moiseyeva could see as soon as Rudolf came into her room to check the time of their departure that he had been up all night. 'You're so late!' she exclaimed. 'I know. We were walking . . . I'll go and get my things.' They sat next to each other on the familiar blue bus that had ferried the Kirov group, with the exception of Rudolf, around Paris. 'In the bus they gather all the tickets.' When they arrived at Le Bourget, then the city's international airport, he recognized among a dozen or so people standing by the bar the friends he had asked to come and say goodbye. He was not expecting Clara, whom he had just left, or Claire, who was on tour in Malaga, but he saw Pierre talking to Sergeyev and Dudinskaya, as well as Claire's Paris Opéra partner, Jean-Pierre Bonnefous – '*jeune, beau et blond*' – and Olivier Merlin, whose adulatory articles had pleased him. He went over to join them all for a last drink, and stayed on chatting until he saw the company start to head towards the departure gate. As Rudolf joined the queue he was taken to one side and told that he would not be going with the others to London.* Instead, he would be boarding a plane to Moscow in two hours' time, as he was needed for an important concert at the Kremlin. 'Khrushchev wants to see you dance.'

Rudolf's first reaction was one of disbelief: how could the dancer who had brought such phenomenal success to the Kirov Ballet have no place on the London plane? 'Corps de ballet have place; carpenter have place, but I have no place.' But when Korkin went on to tell him that he was also being sent back because his mother was ill, Rudolf was certain that he was being duped. It was not true – he had talked to her the night before and she had been fine. And if she really had suddenly fallen ill, why stop in Moscow first for a concert? Then he remembered a conversation he had had before leaving Leningrad, and his French friends watched him 'go white like enamel'. 'Bad news from home' was the 'terrible trick' played on Valery Panov, the Maly Theatre dancer who had been recalled to Russia two years earlier while on a tour of the United States, and victimized ever since.

Early in May, Rudolf had gone to talk to Panov to find out what had really happened to him in America and after. Everyone in the Kirov had been warned to learn from Panov's example, but the exact nature of his misdemeanours was never made clear – either to them or to him. Waiting until the dancer had finished his rehearsal, Rudolf listened intently to his story. What had made him appear a potential traitor, Panov realized in retrospect, was acting 'like an adolescent in love' with the variety, pace and abundance of 'mighty, magical' America; what had finally indicted him was the 16-mm camera bought with his advance wages, which was viewed by the KGB as payment for espionage. Sent home in disgrace, Panov found himself a scapegoat – 'a warning to others to beef up fear of the enemy' – and barred from any further trips abroad.

Rudolf, whose own transgressions on tour had been far more reckless, knew exactly what lay in store: 'No foreign travel ever again . . . I would be consigned to complete obscurity.' Sobbing, almost fainting, he told Korkin that he was going to kill himself, because this banishment

---

* In his autobiography Rudolf claims that it is a 'smiling Sergeyev' who tells him: 'Rudi, you won't be coming with us now. You'll join us in London in a couple of days' (he had always mistakenly believed that Sergeyev 'was instrument. He's the one.'). Pierre Lacotte also recalls seeing Sergeyev 'suddenly call Rudolf and talk to him', but all the accounts of the episode in Rudolf's KGB file cite Korkin as the administrator responsible for breaking the news of his recall.

would have terrible consequences for his life. People began rushing up to see what was the matter. 'It will be all right,' promised Janine Ringuet. 'Our organization is strong enough to help you. We can speak to Mme. Furtseva . . .' But Rudolf hardly heard a word. 'I am a dead man!' he told her, 'crying and crying like a child'. Seeing Olga Moiseyeva and Alla Osipenko coming towards him, he held up four fingers crossed like bars to show them that this was the equivalent of being sent off to prison. 'We all understood what it implied. Everybody was very upset – Dudinskaya and Sergeyev too. People knew that if he went back to Russia it would be really bad for him.'

Most of the ballerinas – even those who had always been openly against me – started to cry . . . They all begged me to go back without any fuss, promising that the first thing they would do upon their arrival in London would be to go to the Soviet Embassy en masse. They would explain my attitude, convince them that there was nothing political in my way of life, that I was simply an artist . . . [who] needed to be left alone and understood. 'They' will understand, you'll see, and fly you straight back to London. Go to Moscow. Don't do anything foolish . . . You'll commit yourself for ever if you do . . . But I knew better . . . I thought to myself: This is the end.

'Go and get me a taxi,' he called to Jean-Pierre Bonnefous, one of the French dancers standing at the bar. But the eighteen-year-old was too afraid, 'No, no, no. I can't.' 'I say, all right . . . OK, well, go and call my girlfriend.' With her Malraux connections, Clara might well be able to help. It was now nearly nine a.m. and the Moscow flight was due to leave at 12.25, which meant a wait of three and half hours. As soon as the Kirov had left for London, Strizhevsky suggested that they sit in the Aeroflot lounge, but Rudolf absolutely refused.

'Don't touch me. If you touch me I will start screaming.' So they let me stay on spot. I thought if they get me into separate room for Soviet pilots or something there would be no control . . . or nurses who were dying to inject me with things . . . 'If you move me one inch I will start screaming.'

Escorting him instead to Soucoupes Volantes, the bar in the main lobby, Strizhevsky, accompanied by Romanov, another KGB guard, offered him a drink. 'Nureyev did not want a coffee: he was too nervous.' Rudolf was desperate. His French friends were still standing around, clearly at a loss what to do. No one was taking any action, and time was running out. Olivier Merlin had parked his eight-cylinder Norton right by the exit and thought of suggesting to Rudolf that they make a speedy escape together, but this was a fantasy: not only was the dancer hemmed in by his two custodians, as in a film, but there was a third KGB guard blocking the way. Trofimkino was a man Rudolf already knew well by sight – 'During our whole Paris season he had spied on every gesture of mine.'

Clara had not been asleep long when she was awakened by a telephone call from Jean-Pierre Bonnefous. He breathlessly explained what had happened, and asked her to come right away to Le Bourget. Quickly dressing and tying a silk scarf over her tousled hair, she rushed out to find a taxi and arrived at the airport in just over half an hour. Bonnefous immediately came over to greet her, pointing out where Rudolf was sitting. 'He looked very small wedged in between the two men and so sad. He wasn't crying, just very pale.' 'What can we do?' she asked Bonnefous. 'I don't know. It's very difficult to speak to him.' She decided to try. 'I went up to the Russians and said in French, "*Est-ce que je peux dire au revoir à mon ami?*"' They nodded. 'I kissed him and whispered, "So, you're not going to London?" "No, I'm going to Moscow, but all my luggage is on the other plane." "Is it terrible for you?" "Yes." Then, very, very quietly, he said, "I want to stay here." "Are you sure?" "Yes. Please, please, do something."' At that moment Strizhevsky called out to Rudolf to return to their table. 'I said, "Au revoir, au revoir!" and kissed him again.'

Going straight up to the French group who were 'white and very worried-looking', Clara told them what Rudolf had said. No one, not even Pierre, was willing to get involved: the dancers wanted to be able to perform in Russia, the impresarios to maintain their good relations with the Soviets.* 'Don't take any risks!' Georges Soria warned: 'You don't know these people – it could be very dangerous for you.' But Clara, who had nothing to lose, knew she had to act on Rudolf's behalf, even if it meant doing it alone.

---

* Earlier, when Rudolf begged him to help, Pierre went with an interpreter to try to reason with Sergeyev, who had been very friendly at Le Bourget, inviting the French dancers to have coffee with him and Dudinskaya. 'I said, "If Rudolf is being punished because he went out with us in Paris, I can assure you – I could even sign a letter – that he never said anything against you, and we never talked about politics. I take the responsibility for everything, but I don't want him to be punished."' Implacably Sergeyev replied, 'He's not being punished. His mother is ill, he's going to Moscow, and after that, he'll come back.'

It was almost ten o'clock; she didn't have much time. Seeing a POLICE DE L'AÉROPORT sign, she went upstairs and on the second floor found Le Bourget's chief of border control, Gregory Alexinsky,* sitting in a small office with his deputy commissaire, Jagaud-Lachaume. 'You know, there's a problem downstairs,' she said, explaining about the Russian dancer being held against his will. 'Where is he?' asked Alexinsky. 'At the bar. Waiting for the next plane.' 'Are you sure he wants to stay?' 'Yes. I'm completely sure – I've just talked to him.' 'And are you sure he's a dancer?' 'Yes. He was dancing at the Palais des Sports yesterday evening. He's from the Kirov company. Why?' 'Because if he were a scientist it could be very dangerous.' 'Well, he's not. He's a very great dancer. If you go over there now you can see him. What can you do to help?' 'We can do nothing. It's against the law for us to go to him, he has to come to us.' 'But that's impossible. He has two men guarding him.' 'Well, of course we can go downstairs and stand by the bar, but he has to come to us. He has to say, "*Je veux l'asile politique*" and then we can take care of everything. Can you go and tell him that?' 'I'll try.'

She went back to the table where the KGB men were sitting drinking cognacs. 'I forgot to say something to Rudolf,' she said, smiling at Strizhevsky, who once again nodded his assent – the girl was clearly infatuated with Nureyev and reluctant to let him go. Whispering very quickly, she said to Rudolf, 'You see the two men there at the bar? They're French policemen. You have to go to them and say that you want to stay.' 'Then we made a big play of saying goodbye, and I left him, went to the bar, and ordered a coffee.'

Valery Panov had been given a similar opportunity to defect at the airport in New York by FBI agents who suspected that his recall to Russia foreshadowed trouble for him. They had allowed him through passport control, then detained his escorts by scrutinizing their documents. But whereas Panov had 'inched away from the FBI men in pathetic fear', Rudolf realized that this was his only chance. 'So I decide right there and then that I'm not going back. This was goodbye time.' He jumped up from his chair and rushed towards the bar, but Strizhevsky came after him, and asked him what was wrong. 'Nureyev was silent. And then he said, "I've made up my mind." He didn't say what that was, but repeated that his decision was firm, final and he wasn't going to change it.' Then Rudolf walked slowly – 'six steps

---

* Researching her Nureyev biography, Diane Solway discovered that the commissioner was in fact a White Russian by birth, but fearing that the Soviets would suspect a conspiracy, he decided not to reveal his nationality.

exactly' – directly up to the two French commissars. 'No jumping, no running, no screaming, no hysteria. Quietly I say: "I would like to stay in your country."'

Immediately two KGB men grabbed hold of him, with Trofimkino running up to help. There was a tussle – 'They were pushing and pulling Rudolf' – until finally, one of the French policemen cried out, '*Ah non! Ne le touchez pas – nous sommes en France.*' Knowing they were powerless to take Rudolf by force, the Russians rushed to a public telephone to call the embassy. Meanwhile Alexinsky and Jagaud-Lachaume took Rudolf up to the commissariat with Clara (who heard cries of '*Vous êtes folle!*' as she passed the French group) following behind. Asked by the police if he would like anything to drink, Rudolf replied, ashen-faced, 'A cognac.'

After contacting the embassy, Strizhevsky and Romanov also went upstairs in search of the dancer. 'We were insisting on being allowed to see Nureyev, but the French tried to deny the fact he was there.' Shortly afterwards, in a great fluster, the USSR's general consul, Mikhail Klementov, arrived. 'I must speak to him,' he cried, bursting into the room. 'Nureyev is a Soviet citizen,' Rudolf heard him say to the inspectors. 'You must hand him over to me.' 'This is France, Monsieur, and Monsieur Nureyev has placed himself under our protection,' came the reply. Klementov began talking to Rudolf in Russian, a monologue lasting about twenty minutes, to which the dancer repeatedly answered, '*Nyet!*' Janine Ringuet, who had picked up Rudolf's trench coat, beret and camera in the hall and was waiting outside the office to hand them over to the police, heard him plead in Russian, 'Leave me alone, leave me alone.' 'He was completely wild and mad.' But just as eyewitnesses in the terminal building have recalled increasingly melodramatic images of Rudolf in distress – 'He literally fell down!' . . . 'He took a paper knife out of his pocket' . . . 'He was banging his head against a wall!' . . . 'Osipenko said – she *swore* – that she saw me jumping through barriers. And on the runway!' – there are several versions of what went on upstairs. Rudolf himself described a nurse 'screaming' that he was mad and must be given an injection to sedate him; Grosinsky has claimed that the Russian consul, incensed by Rudolf's refusal to change his mind, suddenly slapped his face. 'It's not true,' says Clara. 'I was in the office the entire time.'

Strizhevsky was then given a chance to talk to Rudolf. Adopting a reasonable tone, he said, 'You're making a mistake. You're completely wrong about your recall to Moscow. You know that the decision to stay in France is a betrayal of your motherland – a shame for a Soviet man.'

Strizhevsky was determined to do everything he could to sway him, knowing that he, too, was about to be disgraced. Nureyev's defection could have been stopped, the Central Committee would inevitably conclude; his own lack of vigilance made it possible 'for the betrayer to succeed with his goal'. (In his defence, Strizhevsky would later insist that he was unable to prevent the escape because of 'the violence' of the French police; there were not two but *six* plainclothesmen involved, he claimed, five of whom tried to tie his hands and hold him down, 'while Nureyev went away with the sixth'.) Thinking that if he offered to take Rudolf straight to rejoin the Kirov this might weaken the dancer's resolve, Strizhevsky promised that he would personally escort him to London on the next flight. 'He didn't believe any of it. He said, "I want to stay here and have political exile."'

Then Sergei Melnikov, one of the Kirov technicians about to board the delayed Moscow flight, asked to be allowed to talk to him. To his question, 'Why do you want to stay?' Rudolf replied, 'Because they don't let me live the way I want to. I have been under surveillance ever since I went to Vienna. Here, as well, people like S—— G—— and K—— are watching me.* The dancer, he says, began to cry, saying that he understood he was a traitor and 'a lost person,' but that he had made his decision and would definitely not return to Russia. 'It's not something I planned, but I was hoping it would happen like this,' he would later confide to a friend, also telling René Sirvin that he had gone to the Madeleine to pray for some kind of sign, or gesture, 'and realized this was it'. As Melnikov moved across to give Rudolf a farewell embrace, one of the French policemen pushed him aside, escorted him out and shut the door.

Once all the Russians had left, the police began asking Rudolf a number of formal questions, including where he intended to live in Paris. A hotel would be too dangerous, they said, because the Russians would try to get him back – not necessarily by force, but by persuasion. 'Is there someone who can take care of you? And do you have money?' Clara answered on his behalf, guaranteeing to get Rudolf a room. 'You know, he's a great artist. In a few days he'll be dancing – you'll see.' Alexinsky told her to beware on her own account: 'You may have problems. They're going to follow you in order to find him, so don't see him for a few days.' Leaving Rudolf in their care, she again kissed him goodbye, promising to call as soon as she had found somewhere for him to stay. 'Don't worry, I have a lot of friends.' The two

* Kirov dancers employed by the KGB: 'They were a team,' said Alla Osipenko.

commissars then explained to Rudolf that, according to the rules, he must spend forty-five minutes in a room alone to reflect, away from all pressure, on the decision he had taken.

> The room, they told me, had two doors. Should I decide to go back to Russia, one door would lead me discreetly back into the hall from where I could board the Tupolev. Should I decide to stay in France, the other door led into their own private office . . . By now I was locked in, safely alone, inside that small room . . . Four white walls and two doors. Two exits to two different lives.

But Rudolf was not 'locked in.' For the first time ever he was free to choose for himself: 'For me this was already a return to dignity.' He knew perfectly well that his flight would not only sever ties with the people he loved, it would lay them open to the very intimidation that he himself was escaping: 'the systematic wearing down of the individual until his behaviour exactly mirrors that of everyone else around him'. And yet there was no other way. 'I was saving my life,' he told a friend, by which he meant his life as a dancer, the only life that mattered to him. 'If I'd gone back, Sergeyev would have thrown me out of the company, and perhaps sent me back to Ufa. No one would ever have heard another word about me . . . I would have been squeezed off the stage eventually. So I jumped to this side where I felt I still would be able to dance.' Even though his immediate future was frighteningly bleak – 'this would be utter solitude' – at least there was the prospect of being able to develop as an artist – 'to learn, to see, to grow.' He got up and opened the door of the inspectors' office.

At 3.30, while the police took Rudolf out by a side entrance and drove him to the Ministry of the Interior to formalize his exile, Clara acted as a decoy. As she came into the lobby a crowd of about forty photographers and journalists surged towards her. 'I was a star for one day: they had no one to photograph so they photographed me.' Forced into an impromptu press conference, she ignored questions of his whereabouts and answered others as obligingly as she could. 'No, we are not engaged. He's not married, but there was nothing serious between us,' she told the correspondent from the *Daily Mail*. 'It didn't appear to me that he was thinking of choosing freedom before this morning,' she remarked to a reporter from *France-Soir*. 'Nor that he was having "*une liaison sentimentale*" in Paris; he was a boy who worked a lot.'

With a cavalcade of photographers on motorbikes following her taxi, Clara returned to the Quai d'Orsay. Her first call was to her friend Jean-Loup Puznat, who gladly agreed to let Rudolf stay in his large empty apartment overlooking the Jardin du Luxembourg. Then she spoke to Raymundo de Larrain, who was 'very excited' and said, 'Tell Nureyev not to worry about work. I'll take him in the company tomorrow.' Immediately Raymundo volunteered to arrange a special performance in the dancer's honour, but Clara explained that the French police had told Rudolf to lie low for the first week. From her window she could already see two men who looked like cartoon KGB 'gorillas' sitting in a car. 'They were waiting for me to lead them to him.'

At about five that afternoon, Rudolf was taken to the apartment on rue Guynemer. When Clara telephoned to say that she was not able to come to see him yet, 'because they're all around', he had only one question: where he was going to take class. 'I can't go a week without my exercises.' 'Listen,' she told him, 'do your class in the apartment for the next few days, because for the moment you can't go anywhere.'

By now the Kirov had checked into London's Strand Palace Hotel near the Opera House – the hotel frequented to this day by visiting Russian ballet companies. Alla Osipenko was immediately surrounded by reporters, who asked if she was aware that her partner had sought refuge in Paris (she knew nothing until Simon Virsaladze met her in the corridor 'with huge eyes' and confirmed the story, which he had heard on the radio). At the London impresario's welcoming party, a birthday cake was produced for Alla – 'but none of us felt in the mood to celebrate.' Among the guests who came up to congratulate her was an English diplomat who had lived in Moscow, a balletomane well known to the company, who gave her a present and invited her to dine with him later at the Savoy. True to character, she accepted, even though the Soviet Embassy had just issued a new order forbidding the dancers to mix with foreigners. When she returned to the hotel that night, a KGB agent was waiting to admonish her, and at a meeting the following day she was denounced in front of the whole company. One 'brave girl' stood up in her defence: 'Alla Osipenko is a great ballerina,' declared Galina Kekisheva. 'Surely she is entitled to have fans and presents.' But to no avail. Not only was Alla locked in her room after the performance every night, but for the next six years she was excluded from any tour to the West.

Sergeyev and Korkin were also in trouble, branded by the Central Committee as 'undisciplined men' whose failure to obey orders in time had led to Nureyev's escape. On returning to Leningrad, Korkin was replaced by a hard-line party bureaucrat – the type who 'could be in charge of a mine one day and of an orchestra the next'; Sergeyev was issued with 'a severe reprimand'. But their immediate ordeal was having to mount the London season without the Kirov's main star. 'Rudik's defection was a horror for us,' says Dudinskaya, claiming that Sergeyev had decided to cast Rudolf in all four London premières – 'which shows that he had won the recognition of Konstantin Mikhailovich' – and had only three days in which to prepare four new soloists in the roles. 'We were all helping him . . . We didn't eat; we didn't sleep . . . It was a tragedy that Rudik left us. He had no reason; everything was open for him – and that's the truth.'

Still in a state of shock, Rudolf spent his first hours alone in the apartment feeling strangely detached and tranquil: it was as if he had lived through it all before. 'I had already danced in my mind everywhere . . . I had already read that script, I wrote it myself, and now it was all happening according to it.' He slept deeply that night and was not even surprised to wake up in a room he did not know. 'I had travelled a lot. I danced in Austria, Cairo, Beirut, Damascus, Bulgaria and the East. An artist often changes towns and decor. I opened the shutters and looked out at the view of the Luxembourg. Everything was marvellously calm and peaceful.' By the time Clara could join him, however, Rudolf was 'going crazy', and over the next few days he became seriously depressed. He had started to fret about the Soviets' retaliation against his family and friends, especially Pushkin, who as his mentor was certain to be suspected of having influenced him. And without Pushkin's support, without the discipline of the Kirov, how could he hope to preserve the purity of his schooling? 'I have to work, I have to work,' he wailed. Clara had bought him a toothbrush, pyjamas and a few shirts, 'white cotton, very simple, very nice', as Rudolf had virtually nothing – less than fifty francs in his pocket, and only the clothes he was wearing. 'But he was very difficult. Jean-Loup's apartment was built in the 1930s and Rudolf never stopped complaining about all the marble. "I'm so cold," he kept saying. "I'm bored." . . . He didn't like the colour of the shirts, and I thought, My God!' He demanded to have woollen knee supports, but it was Sunday and the pharmacies were either closed or didn't sell them. 'My friends were laughing: "How oversensitive he is."' He told them, 'I am not oversensitive. I am a dancer.'

The world's press had cast Clara as the heroine of a Cold War thriller. 'DANCE TO FREEDOM: girl sees Russians chase her friend' was the headline on the front page of the *Daily Express,* which reported that Nureyev had 'skipped to freedom to the delight of a red-haired girl'. 'Everyone called it a Romeo and Juliet story, but I say, "*Pas du tout.*" I think for Rudolf, I was like a key to open things easily. It was nice for him to say, "I want this" . . . and then – *voilà!*' Knowing that the only way to make Rudolf happy was to get him back onstage, Clara promised she would ask Raymundo to come and see him at once to talk about starting work.

While there was no question of Rudolf joining the Paris Opéra Ballet (a certain end to French–Soviet cultural relations), his presence in the de Cuevas company would not only be a scoop, it could also be its salvation. De Cuevas's widow, a Rockefeller heiress who didn't share her aesthete husband's passion for ballet, had made it known through her lawyer that the company could no longer depend on her backing. Troubled by creditors and half-empty houses, Raymundo realized at once that the new Russian star was the answer to his problems. Promising to make Rudolf a '*super-vedette*', he offered him a six-year contract, but Rudolf, who had already mapped out his immediate future, said this was too long. 'I accept only three months because I was determined to go to Balanchine. And also to go and study in Denmark with the teacher of Erik Bruhn, whom I considered the best dancer in the world.' 'He was like those instinctive predators who know precisely where to land and take their prey,' remarks Ghislaine Thesmar, then a young soloist in the de Cuevas company. 'He knew exactly what he could take from that situation and for how long.'

Rudolf had gladly accepted Raymundo's invitation to move into his own apartment, but was still proving impossible to please. 'Right away he was difficult,' says Jacqueline de Ribes, Raymundo's mistress and patroness. 'I want this, I need that . . . And already he had ideas about everything – staging, costumes. "*Il est interprète, pas créateur!*" Raymundo complained to me. They were always fighting, and yet they were friends at the same time.' The drawbacks of having Rudolf as a house guest were turning out to be far greater than Raymundo had anticipated – not least because in sheltering 'the betrayer' he was putting his own safety at risk. He had begun receiving threats by letter and telephone, and so had the Vicomtesse de Ribes, who returned home one day to find graffiti scrawled on the walls of her house, and 'people outside screaming at me'. Rudolf was so terrified the first time he left the apartment that he crouched on his hands and knees in the back of Claire Motte's car. 'I didn't know the source of fear, from where it will come. The danger. Fear was really that Russians will come and get you. And that came in a *lot* of nightmares . . . It took a long time.'

His fears were justified* since 1961 was the year before the KGB reassessed its policy of 'wet affairs' – the liquidation of major traitors. Only recently its laboratory had manufactured a weapon that fired a jet of poison gas, causing death (undiagnosable to pathologists) by cardiac arrest. The Thirteenth Department assassin who used the spray gun to kill two victims – leading Ukrainian émigrés – defected later that summer, and it was not until the following autumn that the widespread publicity generated by his trial led the Politburo to abandon assassination as a normal strategy outside the Soviet bloc. Even so, in November 1962, a campaign for dealing with defectors specified 'special action' against Nureyev 'aimed at lessening his professional skills'. The KGB dissident Vasili Mitrokhin, a former Soviet foreign-intelligence officer who for more than ten years secretly copied and smuggled out highly classified information from the archives, happened to be a passionate Kirov fan, who felt 'a sense of personal outrage' when he read about the plan compiled by the First and Second Chief Directorates to maim Rudolf. 'Subsequent FCD directives discussed schemes . . . to break one or both of Nureyev's legs.' It was this particular example of 'greater aggression' almost more than any other that strengthened Mitrokhin's resentment against his country's neo-Stalinist regime.

To protect Rudolf, Larrain hired two private detectives to accompany him wherever he went. 'This meant that I lived under constant surveillance, permitting only classes, rehearsals, lunch next door to the theatre, then straight back to the apartment.' He had started work on *The Sleeping Beauty* in a small rented studio near the Salle Pleyel, at first alone, then with the ballerina Nina Vyroubova, another émigrée, who was also considered to be in danger. At two o'clock every afternoon bodyguards would arrive at her home, escort her to the Plaza-Athénée Hotel, where, crossing the grand entrance, she would make her way to

---

* A *New York Post* article published on 17 March 1975 claimed that Anatol Golytsyn, a former KGB major who had defected to the United States in the early 1960s, told CIA agents that Khrushchev had talked about 'eliminating Rudolf Nureyev'.

a service exit in the kitchens. Outside, a taxi would be waiting to take her to the rehearsal. 'I was trembling all the time.'

The daughter of White Russian émigrés, Vyroubova had been brought up in Paris, where she was taught by ex-Maryinsky prima ballerinas Vera Trefilova and Olga Preobrazhenska, and became an *étoile* at the Opéra – a great Romantic ballerina whose limpid, feminine qualities were exotically coloured by her Slavic features and temperament. 'I am French in spirit but Russian at heart,' she always said. For the last three years Vyroubova had been under contract to the de Cuevas company, but having just turned forty she was approaching the end of her career. She was delighted to have the opportunity to be partnered by the young man whose debut had moved her to tears. After watching '*le triomphe de Rudy*' in *La Bayadère*, hardly able to breathe in case she broke the charm, she had gone backstage to congratulate him. At the time she found him affable and shyly grateful, but she faced a very different character on the day of their first rehearsal. 'He was extremely difficult,' says Vyroubova, describing how Rudolf had rebuffed her attempt to establish a rapport by saying coldly, 'You speak Russian, I speak Russian. That's all.'* However, Vyroubova's distinctive artistry soon won Rudolf over, as did her natural warmth. 'I was very tender with him. For me, he was a little brother.'

The marquise's fortune had enabled de Cuevas to engage several outstanding dancers, another being the American ballerina Rosella Hightower, who soon became Rudolf's favourite partner. In his view, though, their talents were wasted on a company that lacked a solid tradition. Aware that the choreography of the de Cuevas *Sleeping Beauty* was as eclectic as its style (it was begun by Bronislava Nijinska and completed by Robert Helpmann), Rudolf made up his mind to dance the Kirov version, 'hardly changed from Marius Petipa's original work'. '*Grand Dieu!* Rudik, darling, we don't have time,' protested Vyroubova. 'I would learn it with pleasure, but don't forget you have other ballerinas to partner.' Rudolf knew very well that his demands were impossible, 'but being a Tatar and so young, he was offended that a woman could be right'. Finally they reached a compromise: alternating in the roles of Prince Désiré and the Blue Bird, Rudolf would

---

* Rudolf's *froideur* could have been an attempt to disguise the awkwardness he felt in the presence of educated White Russians. When Clara once took him to Dominique's, an Old World Russian restaurant, he had insisted that she order his meal for him rather than address the elegant, white-haired waiters himself. She did not understand at first, and then realized that he must have been ashamed of his provincial accent.

perform his own variations in the Petipa choreography – 'exactly the way I had danced them a month before' – but the ballet would remain as choreographed.

He often found himself wondering in those first weeks whether he had not made a terrible mistake in leaving Russia. Having fought while he was there to revitalize the old roles and stamp them with his own interpretation, he had now become determined to do everything he could to preserve Kirov traditions. 'He felt very fragile at first, and wanted to hang on to all his knowledge and habits,' said Ghislaine Thesmar, who watched with fascination as Rudolf took a solitary class in the theatre foyer each day. 'To begin with, he was doing pure Pushkin dancing. On his own, to keep in shape.' She, like Rosella High-tower, stood and marvelled at the integrity of his training, which centred on his exaggeratedly turned-out fifth position – 'Pushkin's sign of the cross' – the sacred source of dance technique.

It was to Pushkin that Rudolf's thoughts returned again and again. When Sergei Melnikov had asked him at Le Bourget if he feared for his mother, father and friends, Rudolf had replied, 'Not for anyone except Alexander Ivanovich.' To a journalist's identical question a couple of weeks later, he had much the same reply: 'I am far more worried for my dance teacher in Leningrad. I have lived with him for several years; he is my best friend . . . certainly, he will be questioned. To him I have promised to return.'

On 15 June, the eve of Rudolf's defection, the Royal Ballet had appeared for the first time in Leningrad, their season deliberately timed to coincide with the Kirov's run at Covent Garden. Russian balletomanes had long anticipated the visit, the highlight of the year, which would give them the chance to see Margot Fonteyn (dancing two of her signature roles, in *The Sleeping Beauty* and *Ondine*), as well as *La Fille mal gardée*, a recent masterpiece by Frederick Ashton – 'each of these names a legend'. But at the second performance, on 16 June, the only talk among the fans was of Rudolf's defection, news of which flashed through the theatre as if telecast. Before the curtain went up, Tamara had been sitting on a velvet sofa outside the dress circle doing some last-minute revision for an exam the next day when Sergei Sorokin came up and told her as gently as he could that he had heard on the BBC World Service that Rudolf had asked for political asylum in France. She was confused. 'Rudik's never understood anything about politics in his life.' Sorokin began to explain, 'But I was no longer listening. He had decided to remain in the West. For ever. But why?'

Forgetting all about the ballet and her exam, she rushed to a pay phone and rang the Pushkins. No one answered, so she called the Pazhis. 'Tamara, dear, is it really true?' began Elizaveta Mikhailovna before bursting into tears. Heading straight for Vosstaniya Street, Tamara spent the rest of the evening with the Pazhis, 'talking, weeping, going through various theories', all the time aware that there was nothing they could do. They kept trying the Pushkins without success. Knowing that Alexander Ivanovich suffered from high blood pressure, they were 'afraid that someone would tell him suddenly and he would go into shock'. It was only the following morning that Tamara finally reached him: 'I already know' was all he said.

'Immediately the KGB began interrogating Alexander Ivanovich and destroying him,' said his pupil Nicolai Kovmir. 'At once he became ten years older.' Pushkin didn't even have the support of Xenia, who at the time was on holiday at their *dacha* in Estonia. On the morning of 17 June she received a deliberately cryptic telegram from Tamara: 'Mahmoudka [their nickname for Rudolf] in trouble. Fly home.' She returned at once, and that evening was seen by Slava Santto at the Kirov Theatre 'looking like an Egyptian mummy with no expression on her face'. He started to talk about Rudolf, but Xenia fiercely silenced him: 'Don't speak now!'

Liuba, who had been away in the country until the evening of Sunday 18 June, ran up the stairs of the Tchaikovsky Street apartment, hearing a persistently ringing phone. It was a friend who had been trying all weekend to reach her. 'Liubka, the Voice [the Voice of America] has announced that Rudik is staying in Paris.' For a long time afterwards she stood by the telephone, its receiver still dangling, 'thinking with anguish that for us Rudik was dead. He had gone to another world for ever.'

As far as his friends were concerned, Rudolf had done the unthinkable. The first Russian artist to defect, he was, as Arlene Croce has written, 'Mikhail Gorbachev's advance man'. But although his act was regarded as so damaging to Soviet propaganda that it was blacked out of the national press, politics were never Rudolf's motive: there was only the compulsion to dance. The one member of Rudolf's circle not in the least disturbed by the news was Teja. '*Molodetz!*' (Good for you!) he exclaimed; as his sister remarks, 'He had prepared this flight.' Concerned about Rudolf's safety, he decided to write and warn him not to think of returning. 'Soviet security is dealing with your case, and if you come back, you'll be arrested instantly.' As he had no idea where to find Rudolf, he sent the letter to a balletomane acquaintance in Hamburg asking him to forward it to Paris.

In Ufa, Farida and Hamet didn't hear what had happened for several days. Knowing that no one in their neighbourhood had a telephone, Rosa sent her parents a cable from Leningrad asking them to call her immediately. Although Farida was obviously distraught, her main concern was that her son had enough money. For the patriotic Hamet, though, the disgrace was almost too much to bear. Characteristically he did not express his feelings, but the shock caused such an extreme physical change in him that even the factory party leaders took pity. 'They didn't throw him out of the Party or dismiss him from his job, but they constantly interrogated him,' said a colleague. 'He never discussed his son with us, but we could see his distress – he became much older, much thinner and much more closed. He was afraid to say a single word.'

Paris, meanwhile, was going 'crazy, crazy, crazy for Rudolf'. There were posters everywhere announcing his first performance, and queues for tickets stretching past the Théâtre des Champs-Élysées as far as the place de l'Alma. At Rudolf's first press conference, on 22 June, he sat casually on the steps of *The Sleeping Beauty*'s stage set, facing a blitzkrieg of flashbulbs, and calmly admitted that he had been wanting to leave the USSR for some time but had made the decision only on the spur of the moment because he was being sent back to Moscow. He remained just as poised when individual reporters cornered him for 'exclusive' interviews, fielding personal questions by saying contemptuously, 'In Russia we are just not accustomed to people putting their noses into one's private life. Only the secret police does this.' To Patrick Thevenon, a close friend of Clara's, he was more confiding:

> In Leningrad it was very hard. There were two schools at the Kirov, those of the traditionalists who, with Sergeyev, wanted absolutely nothing changed, not a costume, not a wig, and then the others who would like very much to modernize the dance a little. Naturally I was one of the 'moderns', and I was very badly thought of by the directors. They didn't want me to dance very often and they held back roles . . . I will never return to my country, but I truly believe that I will never be happy in yours.

Rudolf's first appearance with the de Cuevas company on 23 June (the same night that the Kirov opened with *The Sleeping Beauty* in London), was more of a political event than a performance. There were police cars outside the Champs-Élysées theatre, a legion of photographers and news cameramen in the foyer, plainclothes inspectors mixing with the public and three bodyguards posted outside Rudolf's dressing room, refusing to open the door even to friends. Slipping into the auditorium among a young, fashionable crowd, Clara managed to remain unnoticed, despite the fact that US press agents were offering a million dollars for paparazzi images 'which took her by surprise'. Inspired by the tangible sense of anticipation, Nina Vyroubova, performing Aurora's Rose Adagio, held her balance as never before. At the first entry of Prince Désiré in Act 2, the static in the air was almost crackling, and after Rudolf's first variation, the audience called him back five times. Vyroubova, in turn, received four curtain calls, and by the end of their duet both Russians had tears in their eyes as they stood taking their bows, Rudolf resplendent in his pale blue costume, his hand resting on his heart. But all the emotion suddenly became too much, and in his dressing room between acts he broke down. *France-Soir* headlined its ecstatic review the following day '*Noureiev* [sic] *a pleuré en voyant Paris à ses pieds.*'

Yet despite the final ovation, with more than two dozen curtain calls, there were cognoscenti in the audience who were disappointed by Rudolf. 'I'm not very impressed,' whispered choreographer Jerome Robbins to Pierre Bergé, Yves Saint Laurent's partner. Nor, for that matter, was Harold C. Schonberg of the *New York Times*, who noted that Nureyev was 'not the most finished of artists'.* But it was precisely Rudolf's rawness – his 'exposed, vulnerable quality' – that so overwhelmed ballerina Violette Verdy that night. To her he seemed not so much wild as uncorrupted: 'He had conceived the part of the prince as a man in search of an ideal, with the wonder of discovering it – and with that extraordinary sense of being mesmerized by what he was looking for, and being mesmerized by what he was finding . . . You could see the purity right away in his dedication and total involvement.'

A week later, minutes before he was due to appear onstage, this time in the role of the Blue Bird, the Soviet Embassy delivered three envelopes to Rudolf's dressing room: from his mother, his father, and Pushkin.

---

* Few people noticed that in the coda, without any warning, Rudolf abandoned Petipa's choreography and substituted his showy *Taras Bulba* variation in order to make a more climactic end. Nina Vyroubova was not amused, and rebuked Rudolf by saying, '*C'est un crime de lèse-majesté!*'

The letter from Pushkin was shattering. The one man who really knew me well didn't seem able to understand me. He wrote that Paris was a city of decadence whose rottenness would only corrupt me, that I would lose not only my dancing technique but all my moral integrity if I stayed in Europe. The only thing left for me to do was to come home immediately, for no one in Russia would ever understand my action.

My father's short letter was to say that he couldn't bring himself to believe that a son of his could betray his fatherland and that for what I had done there was no excuse.

Come home, begged my mother's telegram, come home.

Devastated, yet determined not to give in to emotional blackmail deliberately timed by the Soviets to sabotage his performance, Rudolf resolved to go out onstage and let the dance obliterate his thoughts. He had been impatient to show the West 'the real Maryinsky Blue Bird', suspecting that he would make a far greater impression here than in Russia, where his interpretation had been widely criticized. ('The duet is a tender invocation of love, but Nureyev savagely tore into its fine cloth,' Vera Krasovskaya had written.) But Rudolf had just made his entrance towards the end of the second act, when a cacophony of booing and whistling broke out. A gang of about forty or fifty Communists planted in the audience had been waiting for this moment to stage their demonstration. 'À Moscou! Traître!' cried one voice. 'À Budapest!' echoed another, their jeers counterpointed by cheers of 'Bravo! Vive la liberté! Vive Noureev!' from fans in the balcony. There was virtually a riot as stink bombs were let off in the auditorium, tomatoes, banana skins, and coins thrown onstage. Rudolf could hardly hear the music, yet kept on dancing, feeling a strange sense of detachment and serenity. The destructive behaviour of the Communists had made him feel surer of himself. For the first time, he told René Sirvin, he knew that he was right to have cut himself off from the USSR – 'avec son régime de salauds'.

There would be satisfaction, too, in discovering that his least successful role in Russia was suddenly to become his signature piece. Before, no one had understood that he was trying to counter the standard portrayal of the Blue Bird 'softly moving his arms and body as if poised for some gracious but meaningless flight'. What had appeared to Leningrad's critics as 'slipshod and improvised' was, in fact, Rudolf's deliberate attempt to convey a sense of urgency and idealism – 'to show a bird . . . tense with a strong desire to really fly away'. But now, buoyed up by a feeling of peace and lightness, he knew that the audience was seeing not just a great dancer imitating the weightlessness of a bird, but a symbolic tour de force: 'Nureyev choosing freedom right there before our eyes.'

To reward Rudolf for his success and allow him to unwind, Raymundo and Clara suggested that they should all go to the South of France for the weekend. They flew to Nice and stayed at La Reserve, a terracotta pink villa-hotel in Beaulieu-sur-Mer, with its own private beach and port. Rudolf could hardly believe the affluence of Riviera life – the yachts, floodlit casinos and fast cars – but what excited him most was the Picasso museum at Antibes, the Matisse interior of the little white chapel at Vence, and swimming off the rocks of Cap d'Antibes. Falling in love with the Côte d'Azur – 'We said, "Even in winter it's like this"' – he gazed at the hills above Monte Carlo and told his friends that he was going to own a house there one day.

The rest of July 1961 passed uneventfully in hot, empty Paris with Rudolf teaching himself French from an *Assimil* book he carried with him, and attending almost everything, from a Gustave Moreau exhibition at the Louvre to a visiting Mexican ballet company and a French version of John Ford's Jacobean melodrama *'Tis Pity She's a Whore*. Directed by Luchino Visconti, it starred the exquisite young 'fiancés of Europe', Alain Delon and Romy Schneider, both making their theatre debuts. 'Delon couldn't act onstage, but who cared?' says Peter Eyre. 'The audience was full of queens – just staring at him. He was so beautiful.' Mostly, though, Rudolf went out of his way to extend his knowledge of the cinema, seeing a show devoted to the work of silent-movie pioneer and visual sorcerer Georges Méliès, as well as several films starring the romantic idol of the forties and fifties, Gérard Philipe. Philipe's sanctification had been ensured by his recent death, and in his soulful beauty and complex liaisons on screen (most famously in *Le Diable au corps* and *Le Rouge et le noir*), Rudolf saw a reflection of himself.

He also went several times to a studio in the place Clichy to watch Violette Verdy in class. Raymundo had recently introduced them, and they had bonded at once, each equally impressed by the other. Having seen Rudolf dance both roles in the de Cuevas *Sleeping Beauty*, Violette had been mesmerized by his plasticity. 'He wasn't just using his body in a square manner, as an ordinary dancer would. He was using it *poetically* – as an instrument of poetic exploration.' Then contracted to the New York City Ballet, she was not performing in Paris at the time, but Rudolf was fascinated to see her work with her mentor and coach Viktor Gsovsky, who had been a pupil of the Imperial ballerina Eugenie Sokolova. When class was over Rudolf would wait for Verdy, eager to discuss Gsovsky's Old Russian methods and idiosyncratic phrasing of exercises. 'Rudolf was still testing his own ground then, and he had a little more time to talk with everyone. He was absolutely darling to me . . . very open and curious and interested in *anything* good.'

Increasingly infatuated with Paris – 'its people, its freedom, its *flâneries*' – Rudolf now walked around without protection, even though, as KGB secret records show, his safety was still seriously under threat. When he was not alone he was usually with Clara, whose culture and chic he continued to identify with the allure of the city. 'Our relationship was about all the things we did there together.' One day, sensing that she was becoming too attached – 'He was twenty-three, I was twenty-one, it was a very romantic feeling' – Rudolf showed her a photograph he kept in his wallet of his friend. 'It was a boy. Rudolf told me that he lived in Cuba and danced with Alicia Alonso's company. Of course I knew what he was trying to say: I was young but not completely innocent.'

Compulsively evasive, Rudolf had conflated Menia with Teja, who recently had been much on his mind. One night, feeling especially lonely, Rudolf called him at his mother's apartment in Berlin, knowing he would be at home during the school holidays. His sister, Ute, remembers two or three telephone calls from Rudolf that week, one lasting around forty-five minutes. 'He said to Teja, "Come to me, I am alone. We can be together here, and both make our careers in the West."' Six months later, wanting to protect his family by dissociating them from his defector friend, Teja would claim to the Stasi that these calls had caused 'big arguments' with his mother, who demanded to know who was contacting him from the West. 'I calmed her down by telling her that it was only someone from the Kirov Ballet who was in Paris at the time.' In fact Johanna Kremke knew all about her son's friendship with the famous Nureyev, whom he often mentioned in his letters. Their only conflict was over Teja's intention to join him. 'He had to choose: his best friend or his mother.' A powerful character determined not to relinquish control over her children – especially after their father had moved out and distanced himself from their lives – Teja's mother insisted that he must first get his diploma in Leningrad. 'Wait until you've graduated – it's only two more years. *Then* you can go.' Although 'really disconcerted', Teja agreed, and accompanied his mother and sister on a holiday by the Baltic.

The end of July was Collections Week in Paris, and while shooting couture for *Harper's Bazaar*, New York photographer Richard Avedon arranged a sitting with the young Russian star. There had been intense competition between America's two leading fashion magazines for a world exclusive: *Vogue* had Irving Penn standing by, but *Harper's Bazaar* won because of Avedon's connection with Raymundo. Penn's Nureyev photograph appeared a month later in the October issue of *Vogue*. In May, Avedon had shot a double portrait of the director and Jacqueline de Ribes as a mirror image of each other – 'a study in narcissism' – which had led to Raymundo asking him as a favour to take publicity pictures of Rudolf. 'I said I would do them on condition that Nureyev posed for the magazine.' At thirty-eight, Avedon had already photographed many of the artistic deities of the century – Jean Cocteau, Marilyn Monroe, Igor Stravinsky, Pablo Picasso, Alfred Hitchcock, Leonard Bernstein, Brigitte Bardot, Mae West, T. S. Eliot, Ezra Pound – while he himself was almost as celebrated as his subjects, and was the inspiration for the 1956 film *Funny Face*, in which, as fashion photographer Dick Avery, he is played by Fred Astaire.

Accompanied by Clara, who did not stay long, Rudolf went to a hired dance studio a few doors down from the Hotel San Régis, where the photographer and his team were waiting. The first stage of an Avedon session was always a well-practised ritual of social interaction: drawn into a charmed state of intimacy and relaxation, the sitter provided glimpses of the authentic private self the portraits would lay bare. Completely at ease from the start, Rudolf amazed Avedon with his intelligence and sense of wonder.

'He was so open, and wanted to communicate, to connect. He said he'd read *Catcher in the Rye*, which I found stunning.' The admiration was mutual. In brilliant, boyish Dick Avedon, with his 'Holden Caulfield vocabulary', Rudolf found a kindred soul with the same passion for art in all its forms, and the same endlessly voracious appetite to learn. 'I felt that I was meeting my first Occidental friend.'

In homage to Rudolf's glamour and beauty, Avedon focused as much on the dancer's face and naked torso as on the shapes he made in space, capturing myriad expressions – challenging, wry, off guard and giggling, languidly sensual with rumpled hair and half-closed eyes. After several hours Avedon told Rudolf that he would like to photograph him in the nude. 'Your body at this moment should be recorded. Every muscle. Because it's the body of the greatest dancer in the world.' Rudolf needed little persuasion. Like many in his profession, he was not prudish, regarding his sexuality as just another manifestation of his physical prowess. 'Who better to do it than me?' Avedon told him, and Rudolf agreed. He felt in complete accord with this fellow artist – the most theatrical of photographers, all of whose 'occasions are perform-ances; all his subjects, actors, all his images, scenes'. Stripping off his remaining practice clothes, Rudolf began to collaborate with Avedon on a series of flying poses that were breathtakingly abandoned while still discreet. Then, without any prompting, he stopped moving, faced the camera, and stared into the lens.

> As I went on photographing, he slowly raised his arms, and as his arms went up, so did his penis. It was as if he was dancing with every part of himself. His whole body was responding to a kind of wonder at him-self. I thought this was the most beyond-words moment – too beauti-ful to be believed. A narcissistic orgy of some kind. An orgy of one.

The next morning, full of remorse, and remembering the words of Pushkin's letter – that Paris was a city of decadence that would corrupt his moral integrity – Rudolf decided to call on Avedon and beg him to destroy the final frames. 'He just walked in the door and said, "I've left Russia – that in itself is a scandal. Now I'm doing exactly what they expect of me."' Convincing Rudolf that he must safeguard the pictures – 'Because when you're an old man, you'll want to look at the miracle you were' – Avedon summoned an assistant who went into the darkroom and returned with an envelope he handed to Rudolf. The dancer then moved in very close and lifted up Avedon's glasses. 'Look at me,' he whispered, 'and tell me these are all the negatives.' Avedon stared back, his eyes bloodshot with exhaustion after working through the night in the developing room, and repeated, 'These are all the negatives. But don't destroy them.' Satisfied, Rudolf left the studio.

There was an unfinished roll left in Avedon's camera. Thirty-seven years later, wanting to feature the dancer as an erotic icon of the decade, he used one of the few remaining full-length, full-frontal Nureyev nudes in his book *The Sixties*. Rudolf would occasion-ally feign hostility towards Avedon, once preposterously claiming that he had sold one of the nudes to the CIA, 'who used it in an antihomosexuality booklet'.* In fact his rancour amounted to no more than a caprice; not only did he eagerly return for several subsequent Avedon sessions over the years, but he admitted when seeing the pictures for the first time, 'I knew that he had understood me.' Revealing the same sensitivity to movement that the photographer admired in Fragonard, the frames translate Rudolf's sexuality into images of perfect control, yet keep 'the nervous edge of it alive always, not simply a pose'; while the explicit nudes are the '*terrible et merveilleux miroir*' that Cocteau described to Avedon in a telegram of thanks: evidence of vulnerability as much as superhuman virility – the exposure of having entered a new life with no possessions, 'almost as naked as when I was born'.

It was around this time that Rudolf, determined to contact Balanchine and 'not daring' to do it himself, asked Olivier Merlin to write on his behalf. Not only was the critic his most effusive champion, but Rudolf knew that Merlin and Balanchine were on very good terms. (In 1947, when, as guest ballet master at the Paris Opéra after Lifar's dismissal, Balanchine found himself caught up in a political nightmare of plots and counterplots, it was Merlin who went out of his way to support the unwelcome intruder.) In a letter dated 6 August, Merlin tells Balanchine that 'Noureev' is anxious to come to America, and has expressed a desire to perform with the New York City Ballet. He gives details of the dancer's present contract, and says that he will be in New York in September, when the de Cuevas company was due to break for its holiday.

Arriving two weeks later, Balanchine's reply is friendly but firm. While he is obviously eager to meet his young compatriot, he makes it clear that Rudolf will not be able to dance with the company in September as there won't be time for him to learn the repertory; nor, he adds, will he consider presenting the dancer's own ballets.

This is what I suggest. When Noureev is here in September he can come and see all our performances, talk with me, and decide for

---

* A nude shot, either pirated from the studio or copied from one of the prints that Rudolf took away with him, did appear in the late sixties in the magazine of a US gay rights organization. A New York dance critic also spotted a grainy Avedon nude of Nureyev blown up as a life-size poster – 'like a copy of a copy of a copy' – at the entrance to a male porn film house on Broadway during the 1970s.

himself if he likes our ballets, our style of dancing, our music, our small stage, and meet the people he would work with in a relaxed atmosphere.

As you know our company is not made for Guest Artists. We haven't anything that shows only one dancer. If Noureev comes to us, I want to include him as a permanent member of our company, and this is why I propose to him that when he visits us in September, he can observe us, and make up his own mind as to whether or not we would be able to work happily together . . . Would you also tell Noureev that we do not sign long contracts . . . In this way people are never bound for any long periods of time, so they are always free to plan their future.

The choreographer's response came as a disappointment to Rudolf, who told Avedon the next time they were in touch that Balanchine had invited him to join the company but not as a star. 'Do you think if he *sees* me dance he'd make an exception?' Rudolf asked. He resolved to wait for an opportunity.

Later that month he and Raymundo went back to the Riviera, this time taking two days to drive through France, bronzed and windswept in their open-top white Chevrolet. Raymundo had decided to educate Rudolf in *savoir-vivre*, dressing him in designer suits and shirts – he had never seen cufflinks before – and taking him to the finest restaurants en route. With his striking resemblance to Jean Cocteau, Raymundo was not at all the *'petit voyou'* (pretty boy) type that Rudolf found appealing, and yet the dancer told several friends that Raymundo had been the first man to seduce him. 'Absolutely not,' insists Jacqueline de Ribes, who was closer to the director than anyone else at the time, but she says that Rudolf did confide to him during their trip that he was a homosexual. 'He said he'd left Russia because it made his life too difficult there.' An American expatriate named James Douglas, who knew both young men well, is just as sceptical. 'Raymundo was too feminine, too scrawny and bizarre. But they'd have had a great time together as he was very amusing and outrageous.'

Raymundo was indeed an entertaining travelling companion, although he could be maddeningly unpredictable and highly strung: 'Everything was a drama.' He, in turn, however, became increasingly disenchanted by Rudolf's 'insupportable' behaviour, particularly his lack of gratitude. 'He was very spoiled and took everything for

granted – all the time playing the big big star with the big big story.'
They had been invited to stay in the South of France with Commandant Paul-Louis Weiller,* a wealthy financier and patron of the arts.
Among his twenty-four properties (including the Villa Trianon at
Versailles), was La Reine Jeanne, which he had built in the commune
of Bormes-les-Mimosas in the early thirties. It was there each summer
that the commandant assembled his carefully chosen court – the reason Greta Garbo called him Paul-Louis XIV – the usual group comprising *grands bourgeois* mixed with Saint-Germain *jeunesse*, European
monarchs both crowned and uncrowned, international politicians,
financiers, economists, writers, stars of the silent movies and the
Nouvelle Vague, as well as the latest society beauties. Name, talent,
intelligence and grace were the criteria of selection – 'It was a combination of *les nouveaux riches et les nouveaux pauvres*.'

After passing through the great entrance gates, Rudolf and Raymundo
drove on a long private road through dense pine forest, finally reaching
a sumptuous Provençal-style villa built on a cliff above a long sandy
beach. Having just left one world for another, Rudolf was now entering
a third – a paradisical enclave devoted to pleasure, once described by
Lady Diana Cooper as the 'Babylon of beauty, shame, flesh and hedo-
nism'. Jacqueline de Ribes was already there to greet them, a little contemptuous of their flashy convertible. 'I was amused that Rudolf could
be so easily impressed.' To begin with, they were the only guests, wonderfully treated by Weiller who was always especially charming in the
presence of stars. As a *mondaine* star herself, fêted by the press for
her elegance and high style, the Vicomtesse was given the best suite.
'Rudolf's was second best and Raymundo's third.' The first newcomer to
appear was an attractive young starlet featured in that week's *Paris-Match*
but, finding her uninteresting, Rudolf made no attempt to talk to her:
'He wasn't friendly with anybody – possibly because he spoke very bad
English. Let's face it, he was not brought up for our world. He was like
a refugee then – *très sauvage et soviétique*. He didn't understand about
kindness or politeness – how to say the right words at the right time.'

After a few days, quietly observing and making the occasional
remark, Rudolf began to feel 'like a prisoner in a golden cage'. The
commandant was possessive about his guests and disapproved of

*Awarded the Legion of Honour for bravery as a reconnaisance pilot in the First World War,
Weiller was a pioneer in the aircraft industry, eventually creating the airline that became
Air France.

anyone leaving the property – even to go shopping in St Tropez. But although it meant he would miss the arrival of his idol Charlie Chaplin, Rudolf suddenly insisted that he was unable to stay any longer.

At almost exactly the same time, Teja and his family had cut short their Baltic break after hearing rumours from other tourists of Russian tanks in East Berlin. They had been camping 'outside civilization' with no radio, and returned home to the shock of finding that, like everyone else in the city, they were prisoners. 'In July, Teja was free to go,' said Ute Kremke, 'in August there was the Wall.'

Rudolf's family and Russian friends were all experiencing the repercussions of his defection. Within only a few days, after questioning his English teacher, Georgi Mikhailovich, the KGB had called on Liuba at her Physics Institute, demanding to know whether the dancer had mentioned anything to them about staying in the West. Unaware of Rudolf's conversation with her brother, she was able to deny it with conviction. Leonid did not betray Rudolf's secret, but nevertheless received no promotion for the next ten years. Tamara had been immediately expelled from the university with the explanation that being a teacher implied trust. Spending most of the summer depressed and apathetic, she lay around the house just 'thinking, remembering'. As she had no telephone, she would visit the Pushkins every day in case they had received any news. The three were together when Rudolf's luggage was returned, and with strangely ambiguous feelings, they went through it. 'When we came across the *Legend of Love* costume, we knew one thing for sure: Rudik wasn't planning to defect.'

Pushkin was convinced that he could have persuaded Rudolf to be more circumspect in Paris if only someone had put them in touch at an early stage of the tour. 'He blamed Sergeyev very much for not doing this,' said his old friend Dimitri Filatov. Now they were asking Alexander Ivanovich to go to Paris to bring the dancer back, but it was too late: his weak heart would never withstand the journey. He and Xenia were under enough strain, not only relentlessly interrogated but dropped by the majority of their friends, who would cross the street to avoid greeting them. And because they were both regarded as mentors to the traitor, parents were forbidding their sons to visit the Pushkins' home. Miraculously, though, Alexander Ivanovich was saved from the humiliation he dreaded most – dismissal from his job. This was entirely due to the intervention of someone Rudolf had always considered an enemy: Valentin Shelkov. Out of loyalty to his ex-teacher, the director had managed to convince his superiors that

Pushkin should be allowed to stay. 'With all my antipathy for this man, I respect him for that,' Baryshnikov had said.[*]

In return Pushkin was obliged on several occasions to go to Moscow to report to the Ministry of Culture and condemn his pupil's behaviour. 'He knew Rudik would understand that his denunciations weren't sincere.' Belonging to the generation that survived the Terror, he was 'very spooked by it all', Baryshnikov says. 'Alexander Ivanovich was a product of the Soviet regime, and totally suppressed.' Even with close friends, Pushkin rarely talked about Rudolf or his interrogations. 'But Xenia Josifovna told us what had gone on, and with *lots* of humour,' said Dimitri Filatov. With no career of her own, Xenia had nothing to lose. Unintimidated by the authorities and desperate to make contact with Rudolf, she sent him one telegram after another, all of which were returned to her, marked address unknown.

In Ufa the KGB was hounding Rudolf's family, which had also received death threats. But while Hamet was angry enough to feel compelled to reject Rudolf, Farida was unflinchingly supportive from the start. When instructed to 'deny' her son at a party meeting, she threw her membership card on to the table and walked out. And, infuriated by a remark made at one of many interviews at the KGB house on Lenin Street – 'If you miss him so much, tell him to come back' – she retaliated by saying defiantly, 'It's only because you want to send him past me in a van with barred windows.' But when the KGB provided her with a European phone number and ordered her to call her son, even knowing that their conversation would be monitored, she was hardly able to hide her delight, so grateful was she for the chance to speak to him.

By late August Rudolf had rejoined the de Cuevas dancers in the Normandy resort of Deauville, which still retained much of its social cachet from the twenties and thirties. The marquis had been on excellent terms with Monsieur André, the owner of the casino, and it was a company tradition to perform there during the summer season.

Rudolf was staying in the Normandy, the most elegant hotel in town, half-timbered like a regional manor house, and overlooking the sea. When the telephone rang in his room one day he was amazed to hear

[*] Ninette de Valois always maintained that Rudolf had been unfairly critical of Shelkov – 'a nice old boy', in her opinion (Letter to Nigel Gosling, 10 October 1962).

his mother's voice. 'I mean, what do they know about Deauville – they never *heard* of Deauville!' Primed by the KGB, Farida immediately launched in with, 'Oh your country, your mama, your papa and all this . . . ', only to be interrupted by Rudolf. She had forgotten to ask him one important question. Was he happy? '*Ty schastliv?*' she asked. Yes, he was, he told her. 'End of discussion. Sometimes you have to remind . . . That my duty is not only to be eternal son, but also life *have* to belong to me. She gave me birth. And I'm on my own. I have to make my life. . . . I have duty . . . more important . . . in front of my talent.'

People who had already served their purpose in advancing that talent inevitably became dispensable. People like Clara, who was immersed in a world that was no longer of such interest to Rudolf. She had followed him to Deauville but, discouraged by his egotism and relentless demands, was beginning to withdraw her affection. 'I admired his application to work: it was never enough – again and again. . . . With partners, do it again. And he was always right. But in life . . . impossible: too tiring and too demoralizing.' A photograph taken earlier that summer in a chalet garden in Geneva shows a tactile accord between the couple as Rudolf, wearing nothing but tight swimming trunks, cajoles Clara to pose for the camera, his arm around her shoulders. Dressed with characteristic chic and modesty, her dress covering her knees, her classic pumps pressed together, she leans on Rudolf's thigh and shyly hides her face against his neck. She admits that she was incredibly infatuated with the dancer, finding him funny, intelligent and seductive, but all the same she was not prepared to sacrifice her own life. 'I was still really moved by him, but after a while, you're ready to say, "Oh, please!" That happened to me.' 'Clara helped him to get the freedom and after that, well . . . Rudi is Rudi,' said Pierre Bergé. 'He was not a gentleman, and he knew very well how to manipulate people. Clara couldn't accept that.'

As things turned out, all Rudolf's attention had transferred to someone else who had arrived in Deauville that week – a woman directly connected to the two people he wanted more than any others to meet: the thirty-six-year-old Maria Tallchief, America's most celebrated prima ballerina, had been not only wife and muse to George Balanchine but was also the partner of Erik Bruhn. (It was their Black Swan variation, performed during the American Ballet Theatre's Leningrad season, that Rudolf had watched in Teja's footage over and over again.) Experiencing difficulties in her subsequent marriage, and

deciding to travel to Europe for a break, Maria had come to France
with her three-year-old daughter, Elise, to pay a surprise visit to her
sister, the ballerina Marjorie Tallchief. An *étoile* with the Paris Opéra
Ballet, where her husband, George Skibine, was joint *étoile* and director, Marjorie had seen Rudolf's performance of the Blue Bird and
immediately written to Maria about 'this sensational boy'. As the
Skibines had already left on a company tour of South America when
Maria arrived, she decided to take Elise and her Swiss nanny to the
seaside for a few days, and booked rooms at Deauville's Normandy.
On her first afternoon while exploring the town, she spotted Rudolf's
photograph on a de Cuevas poster and, when she returned to the
hotel, immediately recognized him standing in the lobby.

> Before I could catch my breath, he came rushing over. He introduced
> himself by reaching out for my hand and shaking it. 'I am very
> glad . . . to meet you, Miss Tallchief. . . . I am very familiar with
> your career.'
>   I smiled and said, 'Thank you,' trying to be polite, and turned away.
> But he wasn't going to let me go.

This was exactly the kind of fateful moment that Rudolf had seized
before. A chance to enact his belief that in life you have to control
destiny and make your own luck. 'Please,' he ventured. 'I have
proposal. . . . Tonight please come see me dance.' Maria shook her
head, telling him that she had only just arrived. 'Tomorrow, perhaps.'
But no, it had to be that night. She looked at the young dancer staring
intently at her, so alluring and so boyish, and stared back. 'I couldn't
help it. I couldn't take my eyes off him.' 'OK,' she said. 'Tonight.'
    Deauville's casino stage, where Rudolf danced the *Don Quixote* duet
with Rosella Hightower, was tiny, but Maria found his performance
thrilling all the same, never having seen *chaîné* turns done at such
speed. 'I remember thinking that Rudy was a phenomenon. Unique.'
After the show they went out for a drink, and Rudolf listened
fascinated to every word she spoke about Balanchine, admitting that
he wanted to go to America to work with the choreographer, but not
mentioning the fact that they had already been in contact. 'He kept
talking about a home movie that a friend had taken of my performances with Erik in Russia.' One reason he had defected, Rudolf told
her, was to learn to dance like Bruhn, and he was determined to go to
Denmark to study with Bruhn's teacher, the Russian-born Vera
Volkova, a childhood friend of Pushkin's. About to make her debut

with the Royal Danish Ballet with Bruhn as her partner, Maria offered to take him with her to Copenhagen to meet them both.

The two dancers saw each other every day in Deauville, starting with company class in the morning. With her steely technique, Maria embodied the power, speed and amplitude of American neoclassical style, being, in the legendary critic Edwin Denby's view, 'the most audacious and the most correctly brilliant of allegro classicists'. Immensely impressed, Rudolf tried to persuade her to give him a private lesson in Balanchine technique, but she refused, explaining that there *was* no specific Balanchine class – 'One day he would do this, another day that.' And, just as awestruck by him, she 'wasn't about to tell Rudolf Nureyev how to point his toes'.

When the company dispersed for the summer break, Rudolf asked Maria to accompany him to Frankfurt, where he was booked to dance *Le Spectre de la rose* and extracts from *Giselle* for German television. As she had time to spare before going to Copenhagen, she agreed. Leaving Elise with her nanny in Deauville, and giving Rudolf a few driving lessons en route, Maria drove through Germany and France to the Skibines' house in Sèvres, narrowly missing the two dancers themselves.

His mood darkened when they flew to Frankfurt and he discovered that there had been a misunderstanding: he was expected to dance *Le Spectre de la rose* without being taught the choreography. Apart from the few poses he had learned from Pierre Lacotte in Paris, he was forced to improvise the rest – a travesty of the real thing, with Rudolf, absurdly girly wearing a headband of roses, swooning in the chair vacated by the Young Girl Gisela Deege, adding a lot of frilly business when his arms drooped above his head, and inserting an incongruously virile *manège* of *chaînés* and barrelling jumps. But what strikes one most is the deterioration in his classical placing, the lack of rigorous, daily Kirov training resulting in a performance as shoddy as those he would give while paying 'Homage to Diaghilev' thirty years later. His interpretation of Albrecht opposite Irene Skorik is more refined, though with his strawlike wig and baggy tights he looks lumpenly Soviet – still light years away from the romantic Nureyev who would enrapture the West in *Giselle*.

An atmosphere of mutual antagonism developed between the dancer and the programme's director, Russian-born Vaslav Orlikowsky, who had made his name as a choreographer in Germany but found he had no authority over Rudolf. 'Nothing impresses him but his own perfection,' he complained to a journalist, citing how the dancer had repeatedly asked him to delay the final take because he wanted more rehearsal time.

Compounding the tension on the set was the fact that Rudolf badly missed home. Orlikowsky comments on the way he sat by the river embankment staring at the factory buildings opposite, as if reminded of the Neva, and spent most of his day listening to music, playing a Scriabin symphony 'sometimes three, five, ten times in a row'. Then largely unknown in the West, Scriabin was Rudolf's favourite composer, and a figure of cultish idolatry in Russia. Like the Silver Age poets Rudolf also loved, Scriabin believed in art as a superior form of knowledge, a means of elevating man's spirit and providing a transcendental passage to divinity. Rudolf did not have the religious faith to aspire to Scriabin's fusion of a 'superindividualistic I' with God – for him, solipsism was an end in itself. Nevertheless, *Symphony No. 3* (*The Divine Poem*), with its insurgent hero striving for the victory of freedom, seemed to narrate his own story, articulating in its slow movement all the vicissitudes of doubt and anxiety he himself was going through.

With his heavy case of records that accompanied him everywhere, Rudolf reminded Maria of the young Balanchine – 'music was his whole life'. He told her how envious he was of her musical training (she was a first-rate pianist), and said that he wanted to be a conductor one day. Although their conversation rarely strayed from 'ballet, Balanchine and Erik', as they walked together or sat at night by the river holding hands, Maria found herself growing '*very* fond' of this beautiful, romantic youth – 'a real *Russkie malchik*'. Tall and long-limbed, with dark, exotic looks inherited from her father, an American Indian of the Osage tribe, she, too, was striking, but what interested Rudolf was her knowledge and experience. He also liked the fact that he could be direct with her, and made no attempt to hide his homosexuality, openly flirting with boys they passed in the street. Once, while walking back late to their hotel, they were approached by an American serviceman who made a pass at Rudolf: 'Now whether Rudy had made some kind of eye contact or advance, I don't know. But when I said, "How dare you!" he suddenly took out a knife – a switchblade. Rudy grabbed my arm, and we ran down the street to get away.'

Rudolf also told Maria – 'he even boasted' – that he was attracted to women, recounting the story of his affair with Xenia. This time she was shocked. 'But Rudy, this was the wife of your beloved teacher. Why did you do it?' 'Because she wanted to,' he replied. One evening she came back to the room they shared to find Rudolf in her bed. Giving herself time to compose her thoughts, she pretended not to notice. 'And then Rudy said – it was so cute! – "Maria . . . you don't see me?"' Rudolf had no qualms about carrying out his invitation; as one dance historian aptly put it, 'Whatever it takes, he will go the whole way. There is nothing he will not dare to fulfil his destiny.' And while Maria, now aware of an unfaithful side to Rudolf, had resolved not to get involved, she 'wasn't going to shy away from a little excitement either'.

It had been years since she had had so much fun. Every night they hit the town like teenagers, going to the movies, and to nightclubs, where she taught Rudolf the twist. Accustomed to intimacy with an older woman, he showed no sign of flagging in the physical side of their liaison – 'On the contrary,' Maria laughs – although she did notice that he had not been exaggerating when he said that he was obsessed with Erik Bruhn: 'He couldn't drop the subject, and repeated over and over how much he admired him.'

As it happened, she herself was infatuated with Bruhn – 'probably in love'. During the 1959–60 New York City Ballet season they had formed a near-perfect partnership onstage, but Bruhn, recoiling from Maria's emotional demands and distressed by an increasing lack of rapport with Balanchine, had decided to return to Denmark. In the early summer of 1960 the two stars were reunited on the American Ballet Theatre's six-month Eastern bloc tour, but tensions ran high. Desperately missing her baby daughter, and unable to dance with Erik, who had cancelled his performances because of an injury, Maria was left 'utterly forsaken'. By the time they got to Moscow, with Erik in perfect form, she was consoled somewhat by the rhapsodic response to their Black Swan duet, but could not fail to see that he spent most of his time trying to avoid her. In Tbilisi she became 'very demanding, very aggressive', and as the tour reached its close, Erik decided to put an end to the situation by severing all contact. 'I simply couldn't handle it and told her that I no longer wanted to dance with her, talk to her, or ever see her again.'

By the following spring he had recanted, and during the Ballet Theatre's Broadway season they performed the Black Swan duet again, as well as collaborating closely on *Miss Julie*, Birgit Cullberg's choreographed version of Strindberg's play. A few months later, having heard of their success in the ballet, the new director of the Royal Danish Ballet persuaded Erik to invite Maria to dance it with him in Copenhagen. As this would make her the first American ever to be a guest with the Danish company, she had decided to accept, and it was while out walking in Frankfurt with Rudolf one afternoon that she stopped to call Erik collect from a pay phone to give him her answer.

Erik's first reaction on hearing that she planned to come to Denmark was to make sure that she agreed to the condition he had outlined in his letter: that they would not see each other outside the theatre. 'But of course,' said Maria dismissively, telling him that she was in Germany, and making him guess the identity of her companion. When Erik refused to believe that she was standing in the street with 'her wonderful Russian dancer', Maria handed the receiver to Rudolf.

For a few seconds he found it almost impossible to speak. Erik Bruhn was the one dancer he regarded as his peer – even Pushkin had described him as a revelation. Teja alone had been disparaging. 'Bruhn is cold,' he remarked when they watched the film together, prompting Rudolf's now-famous oxymoron, 'Yes, he's so cold he's like ice; you touch it and it burns you.' Soon regaining his composure, Rudolf told Bruhn how much he wanted to come to Denmark, and, watching him, Maria noticed the way his eyes had become bright, his expression rapt as if realizing he now had the world before him.

When they arrived in Copenhagen, Elise and her nanny were already there, staying at the Langeline, a small boarding-house near the theatre, where Maria had made reservations for them all. Hearing that he would be sleeping in a separate room, and that there would be 'no more anything', Rudolf grinned amicably and looked at his watch: 'So . . . How long it last?' Late that afternoon they went across the square to the Hôtel d'Angleterre, where Maria ordered 'Red Specials' (champagne with berry juice) and called from the bar to invite Erik to join them.

It was an unusually warm late-summer day, and when Erik came into the bar he was surprised to see that the young man sitting beside Maria was wearing a sweater. As his eyes grew accustomed to the gloom he noted that Rudolf, exactly ten years his junior, was extremely good-looking with 'a certain style . . . a kind of class', while Rudolf, slyly studying Bruhn in turn, was struck by the classic beauty of his noble, Nordic face, whose perfect proportions had been undiscernible in Teja's grainy images. Although neither dancer looked the other in the eye, Maria could see that they were attracted to each other. They began by talking about Rudolf's immediate plans as, in halting English, he said that he wanted to dance with a leading European or American company but was not sure how to go about it. To make conversation, and give Erik an idea of the intensity of his admiration, Rudolf mentioned how he had spotted the two dancers at the Bolshoi on their first night in Moscow. 'He knew who he was looking for and he saw us there,' Erik told his biographer, John Gruen, while

Rudolf confirmed, 'I was dying to speak to those dancers . . . but I didn't dare, because I was warned that I would be expelled from school . . . So I radiated words through my eyes – by just looking at them.'

The awkwardness between Erik and Maria, which they tried to cover with a lot of forced conviviality, was obvious even to Rudolf. 'Of course, I could see that Rudi could see that there was something up,' said Erik. '[He] mentioned much later that he had hated the sound of my laugh. Anyway, it was all I could do to get through that hour we spent together.' Eager to leave, Erik offered to pay the bill, but Maria insisted on paying her share, adding Rudolf's contribution from a supply of cash that he had asked her to safeguard. As Rudolf seemed mystified by the expression 'going Dutch', Erik explained that in America people often split the bill. 'But we're not in America,' shrugged Rudolf, no wiser.

Over the next few days he saw Erik in company class every morning, when they would exchange a few words. After barre, when the dancers divided into two groups, Rudolf automatically went to the centre of the first group, while Erik chose as usual to be at the back of the second group. Although this meant they were able to watch each other, Rudolf was troubled by the fact that Erik was not given pride of place by his colleagues, and asked, 'Why do the Danish people not respect you?' In fact it was he whom the other dancers held in low esteem. Shocked at the way Rudolf thrust himself to the front or stopped the whole class if the tempo was too fast for him, they failed to understand why the great Erik Bruhn was hanging out with this Russian boy whose dancing they found so impetuous and rough-edged. Their training, formulated in the mid-nineteenth century by choreographer and ballet master August Bournonville, had taught them to be meticulously controlled and to disdain what Bournonville described as 'the obvious lascivious tendency' of Russian virtuoso dancing. To the young Danes, Rudolf was 'a dirty dancer. Not clean . . . sort of messy.'

Erik, on the other hand, while aware that Rudolf was still raw, was able to appreciate his tremendous force and vitality. Capable himself of dazzling pyrotechnics, he had always been more open-minded than his insular compatriots. After he graduated in 1947, feeling that Denmark had sealed itself off from advances in world ballet, he joined London's Metropolitan Ballet to encounter 'different lives, different bodies, different thinking', and six months later accepted an offer from the American Ballet Theatre. 'It was certainly not that I was ungrateful to the Danish Ballet, but somehow the unknown attracted me more than the known.'

For some time before Rudolf's arrival, Erik, lacking the stimulus of competition, had felt that he had reached a dead end. 'Seeing Rudik move was an enormous inspiration . . . It was through watching him that I could free myself and try to discover that looseness of his.' One afternoon when he and Maria were warming up onstage, he asked Rudolf to give them both a Russian barre. Halfway through, however, Erik suddenly announced, 'I am so sorry but this is so different for my muscles that I have to leave.' Like all Danish dancers, he was accustomed to a short, fast barre. Most of the exercises concentrate on the feet, ankles and calves in order to achieve the brilliance and lightness of Danish technique, but make little use of *plié* and *fondu* – the deep, sinking knee bends that both launch and cushion the Russian leap. (The Bournonville jump, which gives the impression that the dancers hardly touch the floor, is much bouncier than Russian elevation. Since attempting to improve his *plié* during training in America, Erik had been plagued by knee trouble, and he feared that if he continued with the heavy adagio exercises he would not be able to perform that night.

Although Rudolf knew the reason for Erik's departure, he felt slighted all the same. 'At beginning I came to him with compliments, took my heart on my knees. And he stamped on it.' He was 'like a starry-eyed boy' in the presence of his idol, and wanted to be with him all the time. 'Rudy used to sit in Erik's dressing room and just stare at him,' said Maria. 'He would look at how he made up, how he tied his tie. . . .' While flattering at first, this adoration had begun to irritate Erik, who had always valued his independence. Glen Tetley, who was touring Copenhagen at the time with the American Ballet Theatre, remembers Erik remarking over a drink one evening, 'Maria's here pursuing me, and so is this Russian boy I'm supposed to be meeting. Well, he can wait!' Ordering another round, he stayed at the bar chatting and laughing with Tetley and dancer Scott Douglas, his singular, 'rather sinister Mephistophelian' guffaw ringing out across the room. Suddenly they heard a cry from the seating area: 'We saw this wild-eyed Tatar face, totally incensed that we were monopolizing Erik. Rudolf stormed off, and Erik groaned and said, "I'd better go and find him." Scott and I followed behind, and were given a very cold greeting by Rudolf, who was waiting outside. Then he and Erik went off somewhere together.'

The next morning when Maria went to collect Rudolf for class, he was not in his room. 'I went to the theatre to wait for him, and eventually he came rushing in very late with Erik. I could tell they'd spent the night together.' Until this point all three dancers had tried hard to establish a constructive, uncomplicated friendship, and in the studio, where they often practised together, had developed an exceptional rapport. 'It was marvellous,' said Maria. 'We criticized, we helped each other. Rudolf was especially good in helping me with elevation.' As a result, they had become inseparable, forming such a close *Jules et Jim* threesome that when Maria, relishing her Jeanne Moreau role, was invited to the American ambassador's wedding, she was not sure which of the two to bring. But the moment Erik and Rudolf began their affair, moving in together at a downtown hotel, the situation changed completely. 'The men were becoming emotionally involved, and because of it Erik was pushing me away, which I found upsetting. I valued our artistic collaboration, and derived a great deal of inspiration from it. I didn't want it to end.'

Each day became a battle for attention. When Erik, whom Rudolf had asked to watch his private class with Vera Volkova, discovered that Maria was already sitting in the studio, he immediately left, causing offence all round. On another occasion, when Rudolf told Maria that he and Erik wanted to have lunch alone, she created a major scene, threatening to leave Copenhagen unless they included her. Then there was an evening at Erik's house when Rudolf thought that he was paying too much attention to Maria. Announcing that he was going back to the hotel, Rudolf went out into the hall and ordered a taxi, surprising the other two with his command of English. 'The period in Copenhagen was a puzzling time,' Maria wrote in her memoir. 'For all his bravado, Rudolf was easy to get along with. He wasn't devious. Erik, on the other hand, was very manipulative, and I could never understand what he was after. Being between them, I could never quite tell who was in control.' 'In retrospect,' Erik remarked to John Gruen, 'I can see that it was not an easy time for her, and it wasn't an easy time for me. It was certainly a confusing time for Rudik.'

Professionally, too, it was a period of great uncertainty for Rudolf, as he did not know what he was going to do next. He badly wanted to leave the de Cuevas company where he felt he was treated 'as a freak, or a curiosity', but when his holidays were over at the end of September that was all he had to go back to. 'It must have been horrible for him watching Erik and me rehearse for our performances. We were busy having a great success, and he was feeling very sad and very left out. Only studying with Volkova gave him a purpose.' Twice a day Rudolf had private lessons with Volkova, an original personality with an amusing way of mixing up her English colloquialisms and using onomatopoeia and vivid images to get the effect she wanted. 'You must *svoooosch* your foot!' she might remark before an *assemblé*, or say of a misplaced working leg in attitude, 'You are hugging one of zose red English pillar-boxes. You must hug ze *gasworks!*' As a pupil of Vaganova and Nicolai Legat, Volkova had been the first exponent of the Kirov method in the West, and was deeply revered at the Royal Danish Ballet, where she had taught for the last decade. When she arrived, the company was set in amber, its dancers, although extremely gifted and beautifully schooled, badly lacked range as they had no experience of any style other than their overprotected, Romantic Bournonville tradition. 'She brought her Russian training and somehow combined this in a wonderful way for us because we could still keep our heritage,' says ballerina Kirsten Simone.

Rudolf, however, was unsettled by reverting to Kirov-based teaching at this stage – it was not what he had come to Copenhagen to learn. 'I couldn't understand why I was there. It was very strange.' He had hoped that Volkova would help him fuse the dynamism of Russian ballet with the lightness and precision of the Royal Danish system, but in fact discovered that he knew far more about Vaganova training than she did. When Volkova studied in St Petersburg, Agrippina Vaganova was just starting to formulate her teaching method and only later, mostly under the influence of Fokine's poetic choreography, evolved the liquid, quintessentially Russian way of harmonizing the whole body in motion. 'What [Volkova] had was base of school. It was beginning of alphabet. . . . Just first letter.'

Erik, who felt indebted to Volkova, resented the way that Rudolf, as he watched her general class, would repeatedly say, 'That's wrong . . . it's not Russian!' and tried to explain that there was more than one way of approaching a step. But Rudolf was equally equivocal about pure Danish style, finding it 'quite dull. Very dry, very small, rather empty.' Although he liked the speed, complexity, and wit of the *enchaînements*, he noted the paucity of adagio movement and of virtuoso pirouettes, and saw steps he 'didn't have any desire to dance'. What he admired was the prominence Bournonville gave to the male dancer. In his duets a couple will often perform the same variations side by side, so that instead of being just a foil and partner to the ballerina, the man can eclipse the woman with his strength and virtuosity. Particularly brilliant at nurturing young male stars (Peter Martins would be among them), Vera Volkova had done much to give Danish dancing a more forceful and contemporary edge, but to Rudolf her influence was not evident enough. 'I did every day the same class. It was given by different teachers – the same class, the same steps, the same combinations.'

This obsessive preoccupation with classroom technique was what had driven Erik to leave Copenhagen in order to forge his own identity, and since then he had never ceased trying to push against the boundaries of his art. 'I want so much to go beyond everything that is supposed to be correct,' he told Rudolf. 'To feel I am dancing and not working.' Returning from America, Erik had attempted to teach his colleagues how to revitalize and 'play' with their classical base without losing its essential purity, but in Rudolf's view he alone had succeeded. 'When Erik dances – that not so Bournonville, he has understanding. . . . He make it alive.' For him every glimpse of Bruhn in class or onstage was a tutorial, an opportunity to study male dancing at its zenith.

He learned from Vera Volkova, too, but mostly outside the studio, in her own home. Reminding him of his childhood mentors Voitovich and Udeltsova, Volkova was a White Russian, the daughter of a hussar officer, who had been brought up in an elegant house on the Neva. At the outbreak of the First World War she and her sister were sent to Odessa with their French governess, but then they were on their own. Surviving on dried mushrooms strung into necklaces, they reached Moscow, where they lived with other refugees on the station platform until finally being reunited with their mother in Petrograd. By 1929 Volkova was dancing with GATOB, the state ballet organization, which became the Kirov, and while on tour in Vladivostok she defected. She had intended to join the Ballets Russes but, hearing of Diaghilev's death, decided to settle in Shanghai, where she danced in the company formed by the Russian émigré George Goncharov and taught at his school. (Among Volkova's first pupils was Peggy Hookham, a gifted thirteen-year-old, who would soon make her London debut as Margot Fonteyn.)

Volkova loved to reminisce about her youth, and Rudolf enjoyed listening, but it was her life in the West that held him in thrall. In 1937 she moved to London with her husband, an English painter and architect, opening a studio in West Street, which throughout the war attracted all the leading English dance figures and any visiting foreign star. Frederick Ashton, whom Volkova eased into shape after military service, considered her to be his most inspiring teacher since Nijinska, while Fonteyn, who had modelled her own style of dressing on

Volkova's ballerina chic, was as much in awe as she had been as a girl. When Volkova began teaching the Sadler's Wells company and school, she was largely responsible for establishing the technical and artistic standards that led the company to international fame, a vital influence on shaping Fonteyn's signature role of Aurora and on Ashton's postwar masterpiece *Symphonic Variations*. Although Ninette de Valois had offered Volkova a permanent position as resident ballet mistress, it was on condition that she close her West Street studio, which she refused to do. (As a result the offer was withdrawn, and the company was forbidden to attend her classes.) In 1950 Volkova decided to accept an invitation to be artistic adviser to the Royal Danish Ballet, 'to the lasting shame of the English who had her and let her go'.

Yet even in Copenhagen, Volkova continued to be a pivotal force, staying in close touch with Fonteyn, and commissioning Ashton to create a new ballet for the Danes: his 1955 *Romeo and Juliet*. One evening over dinner at her house with Rudolf, Erik and Maria, the friends were discussing Rudolf's future – 'We all loved Rudy and were worried by how low his spirits had fallen' – when Volkova came up with the idea of recommending him to the Royal Ballet.

As it happened, at exactly the same time Margot Fonteyn had been trying to make contact with Rudolf. President of the Royal Academy of Dancing and responsible for attracting stars for its annual fund-raising matinée, she was looking for a replacement for Galina Ulanova, and had been told by her co-organizer, Colette Clark, that the young Kirov defector would be the perfect choice. The daughter of the renowned art historian Sir Kenneth Clark, Colette was a passionate balletomane, quick-minded and unusually perceptive about dance. Her twin brother, Colin, had recently married Violette Verdy, and had been just as electrified by Rudolf's Paris performances.

Wanting another opinion, Fonteyn decided to consult her friends Nigel and Maude Gosling, who had also seen him onstage. Better known under their joint pseudonym of Alexander Bland (the *Observer*'s ballet critic), the couple had gone to Paris in June to get a preview of the Kirov company before its London season, and during a performance of *The Sleeping Beauty* had 'just sat up' at the entrance of the Prince. 'Even his walk made him different from everyone else.' Although uncertain of his name (names in Kirov playbills rarely corresponded with those of the performers onstage), the Goslings went back to London and told almost everyone they knew – including David Webster, general administrator of the Royal Opera House – about the extraordinary young Russian. 'You must try and get this boy,' they urged. 'He's floating around Paris and he's marvellous.' But by this time Rudolf had defected, which made it impossible. Webster told them not to have anything to do with him. 'We're due in Moscow and Leningrad in a few weeks' time. If we touch him, if we even mention his name, the Russians won't have us.'

He was not the only member of the English dance establishment to regard Rudolf as a political hazard. The eminent critic Arnold Haskell, in a letter published in August's *Dancing Times*, sounded off about 'The Sorry Affair' of Nureyev's defection, which, he said, not only showed lamentable disloyalty to the organization which had schooled him but threatened all future cultural exchanges between Russia and the West. In a counterblast in the following issue, headed 'A Sorry Affair Indeed!' Nigel Gosling defended Rudolf's right to freedom, and was seconded in another letter from critic James Monahan.* No stranger to political scandal herself, Fonteyn was unfazed by the controversial issues surrounding Nureyev and, having been convinced of his uniqueness, was now determined to include him in her gala. With Colette Clark assigned to make the initial approach, there followed two weeks of thwarted attempts to track Rudolf down, until, hearing that he was in Copenhagen, she happened to call Vera Volkova on a night when he was with her. Negotiations began, with Vera and Colette passing numerous messages between the two stars. Nureyev could not come to London that month to discuss the gala, Fonteyn was first told, because he did not have enough money for the fare. This was not a ploy. According to impresario Paul Szilard, who knew the details of his contract with de Cuevas, Rudolf's salary was 'a joke'. The Goslings were consulted again, and as a result the *Observer* agreed to provide the dancer with a ticket in return for an exclusive interview.

Responding to Rudolf's next concern – that his visit would be seized on by the press ('They follow me everywhere . . . it's terrible.') – Fonteyn gave her assurance that his trip would be kept secret even from the Royal Ballet. Rudolf then agreed in principle to perform at

---

*Although the correspondence was brought to a close by the editor, the debate went on for months, with Haskell hounding Gosling in private with his views on the Nureyev affair:

My Dear Nigel,
No personal feelings of course . . . [but] I believe that there are many circumstances where opting out is selfish in the extreme and in no sense a heroic gesture. I believe in the owing of a certain loyalty to one's country . . . I can wax very indignant about the whole Pasternak business but I do not think it illiberal to believe that Nureyev has done the wrong thing.

the matinée in December, but only as Fonteyn's partner. Ever since he was a student, it had been his dream to dance with Margot Fonteyn. Even in photographs he could tell that she embodied the kind of under-stated classicism he admired – elegant, immaculate and yet warmed by a lyric beauty. Fonteyn, however, who had formed no such positive image of Rudolf, resented being dictated to by a dancer half her age. 'I thought, well, I've never seen this boy . . . why should he insist that I dance with him?' Word came back to Rudolf that Fonteyn would be happy to welcome him to London as her guest, but that they could not dance together: she already had a partner. 'Rudy was so upset,' recalls Maria. 'When he showed me the telegram he had tears in his eyes. And I said, "*Believe* me, Rudy, once Margot sees you she'll never want to dance with anyone else."'

7 : JAZZ, LONDON

It was seven o'clock in the evening when Maude and Nigel Gosling arrived at the Panamanian Embassy in London, a large Georgian terraced house in Thurloe Place, where Margot Fonteyn, the ambassador's wife, had invited Rudolf to stay. 'Margot had rung us that first day and said, "You're the only ones who've ever seen this boy. Will you look after him? I've got three seats for you to bring him to my *Giselle*."'* With the performance due to start at 7.30 and still no sign of the dancer by 7.05, the couple was sitting in the formal drawing room wondering what to do when the door opened and a tousled youth appeared wearing stove-pipe trousers and a sports shirt. 'I'm sorry. I was asleep,' he said, adding by way of explanation, 'I was supposed to be met but they miss me.'

Rudolf's flight had arrived early, and after waiting three hours at the airport for Fonteyn's chauffeur, who had failed to find him, he made his own way to the embassy. 'I looked too scruffy for the chauffeur,' he later told the journalist Elizabeth Kaye. 'He was used to Duchess of Roxborough or something. He came twice to airport and would not recognize me.' When Rudolf arrived at the embassy, he was greeted by Colette Clark, whom Margot had entrusted to settle him in and to discuss plans for the next few days. But exhausted by his journey, and clearly put out at being welcomed by someone other than his hostess, Rudolf was 'terribly squashing' towards any attempt at conversation,

---

* Confronted by various conflicting accounts of Rudolf's first night in London, I decided to base my narrative on Alexander Bland's 1961 *Observer* profile, as well as on my own conversations with Maude Gosling – if only because this version seemed to me to be the most plausible. Rudolf cannot have gone that night to the Ballet Rambert's *Giselle*, as his *Autobiography* claims: it was not in repertory in September. Margot Fonteyn, in her vivid description of their initial meeting, may well have confused the occasion in her mind with a subsequent London visit, as Maude is convinced that the ballerina had left for the theatre by the time Rudolf arrived. Colette Clark's memory of the day is also unclear, but in a letter of consolation to Maude after Rudolf's death in January 1993, she wrote, 'I was the first person to greet him on English soil (because he missed the car at the airport & so arrived late & Margot had to leave for another engagement!!).'

dismissing Colette's first nervous question, 'Is it a surprise to be here?' by looking out of the window and replying superciliously, 'What surprises me are these houses which are all exactly the same.' By the time the Goslings arrived, however, his mood had improved. Bowing courteously, he calmly disappeared, only to return five minutes later, appropriately dressed, much to their relief, in a well-cut dark suit. 'I am ready,' he said with a grin. They arrived at the theatre just as the curtain went up.

Accustomed to a more ostentatious setting, Rudolf was disappointed by the Royal Opera House, its striped crimson interior and pink-shaded wall lights reminding him of a Parisian café or boulevard theatre. 'Maryinsky is better proportions, built better. Stage is wide and big and deep with incredible effects . . . this beautiful blue velvet, ivory, gold and silver – make you nostalgic.' Also something of an anticlimax was Fonteyn's Giselle, a role in which her interpretation had left many people, Clive Barnes among them, 'stonily unmoved':

> Her flashing smile search-lighting out over the auditorium, has never, to my mind, succeeded in subjugating the ballerina to the peasant girl Giselle. Her acting seems like a contrived mask, carefully thought out yet somehow lacking in warmth and humanity. . . . Her mad scene is a masterpiece of artifice . . . and in the second act her exquisite dancing, for all its marvellously individual quality, never spells out love.

Aware that Fonteyn had not been seen at her best, Maude tried to deflect any criticism by saying pointedly to Rudolf, 'We all love Margot. She's been our ballerina for years, and we adore her.' He remained silent, his only comment being, 'She uses her eyes well.' When they asked what he had thought of the opera house, he replied with equal tact, 'I like. I like to dance here.'

As Margot had a dinner engagement after the performance, the Goslings had decided to take him to a small bistro near their house in Kensington. There was not much conversation that evening, but no awkwardness either. 'We were just very comfortable together,' recalled Maude, a poised, slender ex-dancer whose South African upbringing was still faintly detectable in the inflection of her voice. In her gentle, balding husband, Rudolf immediately recognized the serenity and innate distinction he had loved in Pushkin. Only Nigel, he would later say, was able to put his thoughts into words, and this almost psychic link between them was there even on their first outing.

When they arrived at the restaurant, Rudolf had asked to go to the men's room. To show him the way, Nigel followed him into the basement, sensing as they continued down a 'rather alarming' dark corridor the Russian's sudden frisson of primal fear: 'I became aware of this very natural instinct he had that there could be a kind of trap . . . I realized there was this strange mixture [in him] . . . of almost animal sense, overlaid by extremely social sophistication.'

After dinner they took him round the corner to their house in Victoria Road, which, unlike Thurloe Place (it had escaped bombing during the war), was an assortment of old and new architecture. Rudolf approved. 'I would like a house like this,' he said, looking around the second-floor living room with its high windows, house-plants, comfortable chairs and clutter. Above the framed photographs, invitations, bronzes and china on the mantelpiece was a fragmented Roy de Maistre abstract, and from ceiling to floor on each side were shelves of art albums, sepia Gallimard paperbacks and leather-bound classics. Rudolf was astonished by such an abundance of books in a private home. 'He was so young and so interested in everything,' said Maude. 'You couldn't feed him enough.' Before he left he asked if he could use the Goslings' telephone to call Copenhagen. When Erik answered, they heard Rudolf say, 'I'm safe. I'm with friends.'

Instinctively Rudolf knew that he had found his English family – another husband and wife to dote on him, but with a difference. Sweetly undogmatic, and content with her supporting role, fifty-three-year-old Maude was Xenia's opposite, while Nigel had the sophistication and scholarly mind Alexander Ivanovich, with his peasant roots and basic schooling, could never claim. 'He could talk dancing to me,' said Maude, 'but he could talk everything else to Nigel. Which is what he preferred.'

Educated at Eton and Cambridge, Nigel Gosling came from a family of country gentry on both sides (his grandmother was the daughter of the Duke of Buccleuch; his father, a major in the Scots Guards, descending from a family whose banking firm had been established in the seventeenth century). It was a traditional upbringing, with the four Gosling brothers engaged in squirely pursuits of 'hunting and shooting almost every day, and dancing most nights', yet, even as a schoolboy, Nigel loved anything that broke with convention and was almost exclusively preoccupied with the arts. The diary he kept as an undergraduate shows a writer in the making, with glimpses of the mix of urbanity and lightness that defined his criticism. 'I am suffering at the moment from my *sangfroid habituel*, which I must have caught off somebody. It always goes to my throat.' By the age of twenty-nine he had written his first novel, *Thicker than Water* (published by Longmans, Green & Co. in 1938), a sentimental education of two young men that draws on his own experiences at public school and in Europe, where he spent a year after university.

Fluent in French and German, and well read in the literature of both, Nigel had planned on a career in the Foreign Office, but changed his mind after living in Berlin, where he became obsessed by European culture. On his return to London he took lessons in art technique with Roy de Maistre, whose studio, a converted café in Pimlico, was a salon to such luminaries as Douglas Cooper, Henry Moore and Graham Sutherland. Although de Maistre was an accomplished painter himself, his real gift lay in encouraging young men of talent to make the best of themselves. When Nigel arrived, he had begun nurturing Francis Bacon, then a wild Irish youth designing furniture, into one of the greatest artists of the age. De Maistre's young lover at the time was fellow Australian Patrick White, who has always claimed that it was his mentor, de Maistre, who helped him to discover his talent and voice as a novelist. Nigel, though a skilled watercolourist, knew he would 'only ever be a Sunday painter', and was not as conspicuously influenced by the teacher as were his two other protégés. Nevertheless the Pimlico studio was his entrée into London's art world, and its ambiance undoubtedly left an imprint. Just as de Maistre was a modernist who affected Edwardian manners, so Nigel 'seemed to belong to an earlier age yet [to be] fully in touch with the culture of his day'.

It was because of its decor by twentieth-century masters such as Picasso, Bérard and Derain that Nigel discovered ballet. He bought a season ticket for the summer appearances of Colonel de Basil's Russian company at Covent Garden and, wanting to extend his knowledge of dance, contacted Marie Rambert to find out if she gave tuition to amateurs. She would consider it, Rambert told him, if he rounded up a sufficient number of pupils to make a class. So, in 1938, together with half a dozen acquaintances including an old Etonian and a couple of girls who worked in the Foreign Office, Nigel began to study ballet once a week. The teacher Rambert provided was Maude.

At this time Maude Lloyd and Pearl Argyle were the two beauties of Ballet Rambert, regarded by their colleagues as the Garbo and Dietrich of the company. Frederick Ashton made Maude a reflection of the exquisite Pearl in *The Lady of Shalott* and, inspired by her responsiveness, grace and femininity, cast her in ballets about the *jeunesse dorée* at play, such as *Les Masques* and *Valentine's Eve*. It was Antony Tudor, though, who adopted Maude as his muse, basing aspects of his masterpiece, *Lilac Garden*, on dynamics in the deep friendship that had formed between himself, Maude and the dancer Hugh Laing, his life-long partner.

When Nigel met Maude, ballet was her life, but gradually, over the period of a year, he drew her into his world, inviting her to tennis parties and weekends at Hassobury, the Goslings' enormous mock-Gothic estate in Essex. It was a slow, gentle courtship, even though Maude regarded Nigel then as no more than 'a friend who was always with us'. By now, he, too, had become part of her sphere, and they spent that summer together with Tudor and Hugh Laing in the hills of the South of France, having borrowed a beautiful old farmhouse and an open-top car. 'It was the most wonderful holiday, and I think that's when we fell from friendship into love.'

The couple was honeymooning in the Haute Savoie when war broke out. A pacifist who felt incapable of killing, Nigel became a conscientious objector. Their son, Nicholas, was born in 1943, and when Nigel was sent abroad in charge of Red Cross camps throughout Europe Maude lived in the country with the baby, moving back to London only in the late forties, when Nigel wanted to find full-time work. He was standing at a bus stop on his way to see a publisher when he met a friend from Eton, David Astor, then the editor of the *Observer*. Described variously by his staff as 'a Renaissance patron', 'everybody's spiritual father' and 'the last great actor-manager', Astor liked to surround himself with colleagues who had had some bearing on his life. (His literary editor, Terence Kilmartin, the translator of Proust, had helped to rescue him in France during the war.) Hearing that Nigel, whom he had known since they were children, was on his way to an interview, he immediately offered him a job. 'But I'm not a journalist,' Nigel protested. 'No,' replied Astor. 'But you're a writer, and that's what I want.'

In 1950, when Nigel took up his new post as a staff reporter and editor on the arts pages, the *Observer* was a bastion of English liberalism peopled by intellectual writers including Kenneth Tynan, George Orwell and Arthur Koestler. The dance critic then was the brilliant and irrepressible Richard Buckle, whom Nigel edited until Buckle left in 1955, when Nigel himself took over the column. As he was already reviewing art under his own name, he decided to use a pseudonymn – 'After Beatrix Potter's Pigling Bland – hopelessly volatile and very fond of song and dance – just like us.' The short, spirited and accessible chronicles of Alexander Bland, combining Maude's technical insights with his own scholarship and wit, grew into a highly respected double act that lasted more than twenty years. To Rudolf, though, who considered that he knew more about dance than any critic, it was only Nigel's art reviews that he took seriously. Nigel's mastery of the subject and general breadth of learning were a source he never ceased to tap. Even that first night Maude remembers him saying, 'Tell me about Freud. What window did he open?'

The next morning the Goslings arrived at Thurloe Place for Nigel to conduct his *Observer* interview and for them all to discuss what Rudolf should dance at the gala. Maude's suggestion that he should appear with Margot in *Le Spectre de la rose* was laughed off by the ballerina, who said, 'Don't be silly, Maude, I'd look like his mother!' But by now Rudolf seemed reconciled to the idea of performing without Fonteyn, and in the end it was decided that he should dance a Petipa showpiece duet with a partner of his choice, and that Frederick Ashton should be asked to choreograph a special solo for him: 'It seemed the obvious thing to do.' Then it was Margot's turn to take Rudolf in hand. Having caught a defensive glint in his eye, she had decided that she liked the young Russian only 'nine-tenths', and was delighted to see his face suddenly light up with a laugh at a flippant remark she had made. Her relief was matched by his own. 'First impression and strongest – it stay for ever, was that such a *big* lady and *big* name was tremendously simple. And warm.'

Deriving obvious pleasure from putting his secret identity to the test,* Margot took him to the Royal Ballet's Baron's Court studios, where she introduced him to her colleagues as Zygmunt Jasman, the real name of a leading Polish dancer due to appear in the gala. (For some time to come, 'Jazz' would remain her pet name for Rudolf as well as his own alias – 'Jazz, London' was how he signed a letter to a Hungarian friend in order to protect them both from surveillance.) Aligned along the barre he saw several faces he recognized from dance magazines: lovely, Lithuanian-born Svetlana Beriosova; the young principal David Blair, who had just succeeded Michael Somes as Fonteyn's partner; and Blair's soloist wife, Maryon Lane. Rudolf was curious about local competition and one of his first questions to

---

* Fonteyn had always relished a plot. Two years earlier she had helped her husband and a ragtag band of Cuban Communists launch an abortive revolution in Panama (described in the press as one of 'the funnier fiascos of recent history').

Margot had been, 'How good is Brian Shaw?' (the leading English virtuoso throughout the forties and fifties). And to everyone's surprise, he even knew the name of an astonishingly gifted newcomer: eighteen-year-old Anthony Dowell.

If he had failed to impress the Danes in class, he dazzled the English dancers from the moment he walked into the room. 'We were completely thrown – just by his presence,' says Georgina Parkinson, then a fast-rising ballerina, while another, Monica Mason, remembers how everyone just stared at him. 'He already looked special. Before he'd even done a step.' By the end of class, having witnessed a series of thrilling technical feats, there were few who had not deduced that the stranger in their midst was the Kirov's errant young star.

Over the next few days, when Margot had rehearsals Rudolf went sightseeing alone, looking at London from the top deck of a bus, not particularly impressed by what he saw. 'I expected different thing: very picturisky [*sic*]. Dickens times. I thought it would be older.' He went to the Tower of London, to the National Gallery, walked in Hyde Park and along the King's Road, which, as Margot remarked, he 'scented' as soon as he arrived. Although still a village with its greengrocers, newsagents, fishmongers and old-fashioned ladies' outfitters, it had a couple of fifties bohemian coffee bars, and was then 'just *beginning* to be cruisy'.

While in Chelsea, Rudolf went to Margaretta Terrace to see Violette Verdy, who had settled briefly into Colin Clark's house before rejoining the New York City Ballet in the autumn. He was anxious to renew contact with the ballerina who, as one of Balanchine's current muses, could prove a vital link. Not only that, but he wanted her to dance with him in the gala. When Colette had written to invite her at the end of August (offering the lure of Nureyev as a possible partner), Verdy had declined, as she was due to dance in America at that time. Rudolf hoped to persuade her to change her plans.

The ballerina would not be swayed, but the visit proved satisfying for Rudolf nonetheless. Violette was always enchanting company – effervescent and intelligent, with the eloquence of a writer – and she had assembled a small group of like-minded people for him to meet. Among them was the Bolshoi-trained Hungarian principal Zsuzsa Kun, who remembered seeing Rudolf limbering up in a Moscow studio: 'a boy at the barre dressed all in black with fantastic placing, and this arrogant face'. They spoke in Russian about 'dancers, choreographers, companies, salaries, hopes and aspirations'. In reply to Kun's question about his own immediate future, Rudolf said, 'Yes I have plans but not certain what they are yet. One thing I know for sure: I want to dance with Margot Fonteyn. She's a *lady*. An aristocrat.'

Having made contact over a few days with three of the people who were to prove of most lasting importance in his life, Rudolf then returned to the fourth. Erik was at home in Copenhagen, waiting to appear with the Bolshoi in Moscow, but had just received a letter from the Russian Embassy postponing his engagement. They both knew the reason. '[Rudik] was staying with me at the house. [It was] obvious that they were having him followed, and that we had been seen together.' When Erik heard from a freelance ballerina, the Bulgarian-born Sonia Arova, that Anton Dolin was assembling a troupe of international stars for a short season, he decided to join her in Paris where she was then living. Soon due to rehearse there himself with de Cuevas, Rudolf accompanied Erik by train, glad not to be travelling alone, as he still dreaded abduction by the Soviets. Erik remembered him crossing from one border to another, standing 'absolutely pale and petrified waiting to be grabbed'.

Sonia Arova was at the Gare du Nord to meet them, eager to discover the identity of Erik's companion (he had asked her to book a double room at a cheap hotel near her rue Lecluse apartment, but deliberately avoided mentioning Rudolf's name on the telephone). She instantly recognized the Russian star, and greeted him warmly, noticing at the same time how he did not return her smile. 'All Rudi did was eye me in a very strange manner.' Sonia had been Erik's first love. When they danced together after the war in London's Metropolitan Ballet, and later with the American Ballet Theatre, they were engaged to be married though they had never been lovers.* 'Erik is strange also, like me, about an emotional attachment,' Sonia once said. 'Sex is sex. It's not interesting. One has to have much more. The intellectual side, the sensitivity . . . the beauty and the purity.' For Erik, however, this New York period was also one of sexual discovery; he had several encounters with male dancers, most of them casual, until in 1959 he began a serious affair with corps de ballet dancer Ray Barra and brought his relationship with Sonia to an end. Over the years they had managed to remain friends, and had even recently recaptured some of

* During the course of interviews for a possible biography, Sonia Arova told the writer Anna-Marie Welch: 'We never slept together because we were so young when we met and incredibly innocent. Our sex drive was sublimated by our love for this art form.'

the closeness of their early years. This was the first time that Erik had openly acknowledged to Sonia his love for a man, an admission that she now felt able to take in her stride. 'I was actually very helpful towards their relationship, which is why Rudolf felt he could trust me.'

Sharing Eastern European roots as well as a bond with Erik, Rudolf soon grew fond of Sonia, a dancer with the intense dedication and self-sufficiency he admired. And while her marked resemblance to Maria Tallchief had troubled him at first, her easy, platonic rapport with Erik made a friendship of three possible, even enjoyable. It was Paris itself with all its memories that unnerved him: he carried a switchblade in his pocket, and would suddenly stop in his tracks, convinced that they were being followed. It was only in Sonia's apartment that he really relaxed, soothed by the affectionate hospitality of her mother, whose heavy wintry cooking reminded him of home.

Every day the three dancers took class together in a studio on place Clichy, and afterwards, when Erik and Sonia began rehearsing Bournonville's famous duet from *Flower Festival at Genzano*, Rudolf sat and watched. Mesmerized by Erik's nobility and refinement, he was determined to analyse how the dancer was able to achieve a sense of such effortlessness with no gesture superfluous, no movement overinflated. Part of the illusion came from the buoyancy of the Danish style, as well as its use of stage space. More than any other choreographer, Bournonville loved transition steps that were delicate and fleeting, a fast *pas de bourrée* leading unexpectedly into a soaring jump, a *chassé* used instead of a *glissade* because it's freer and lighter. Rudolf studied the dancers silently and intently, offering no advice, but when they started to rehearse Petipa's *Don Quixote* pas de deux he began to take charge. He wanted Erik to adopt the slow matador walk that he had patented in Leningrad; predatorily circling the stage before adopting a starting position, and signalling for the music to begin. It was his way of building up what Fonteyn called 'that amazing tension', alerting the audience to the fact they were about to see something spectacular. Erik and Sonia were not impressed. They tried explaining to Rudolf that Western dancers did not break the atmosphere in this way, that by the time the ballerina had finished her variation her partner must be there, ready to start. 'We didn't wait for him to walk onstage and take his preparation as if to say, "Now I'm going to perform a trick."'

A decade earlier, when Erik had been disenchanted with Danish conformism, he might have been more receptive to Rudolf's innovations, but that year he had written a book with the American critic

Lillian Moore on Bournonville's *Études chorégraphiques*[*] and rediscovered his appreciation of the master's technique. He knew that it was precisely this Russian focus on bravura that had affronted the choreographer when he visited St Petersburg in 1875 and was shown *Don Quixote* by Petipa himself. Although the two maestros admired each other, Bournonville had found it impossible to suppress his view during their conversations that ballet should not be a show. The duet not only was difficult, it *looked* difficult, he said, whereas true artistry disguised the mechanism of technique. 'The appearance of ease,' he wrote, 'is achieved only by the chosen few.' Erik, of course, being the archetype.

As much as Rudolf aspired to the suave grace of Erik's classicism, he was not inclined to relinquish his own ideas. Preparations to steps, which Danish dancers had been trained to conceal, he believed should be made part of the performance (a prime example being his soft-footed run around the stage in *Corsaire*, which was just as rousing as the solo that followed it). 'The art of dancing is not to make a difficult step look easy,' he believed, 'but to make an easy step look interesting.' The incompatibility of their two schools kept surfacing: the Danes preferred pirouettes with the working foot wrapped ankle low; Rudolf had invented the ultra-high *retiré*. Bournonville technique for me separates the upper from the lower body with torso and arms held still in perfect *bras bas* so as not to distract attention from intricately beating feet; the Vaganova style works the body in harmony. 'One step. You do that step by whole body . . . nobody understand well enough in the West. It's not technique. The use of the back, arms, neck, shoulders, all ports de bras – it's all Vaganova.'

More mature, and at a stage in his career when he could accept the validity of different approaches, Erik was also the more controlled of the two, but nevertheless there were constant arguments, Rudolf's rages being intensified by his frustration at having tried – and failed – to reproduce Erik's flawless execution. The conflict continued outside the studio. There was one night when Rudolf came to rue Lécluse in a panic, telling Sonia that they had had a fight, and that Erik had walked out. Taking Rudolf with her, Sonia began to search all the places she thought Erik might be until, eventually, they found him. 'That was the only time I have ever seen Rudi so humble.' And yet for all the

[*] The book would be published in February 1962, but the first of four extracts, 'Ballon and the Bournonville Style', appeared in *Dancing Times* in November 1961.

turbulence during this period, Erik described himself as having a kind of epiphany in Paris:

> In the very beginning when he first arrived in Denmark, because of Maria and my situation I was very tense and uptight and was not very open to seeing anything . . . It was not until we were in Paris actually . . . that I really had a chance to sit back and look at him. I had been looking but not actually seeing anything and suddenly I saw!

What he could now appreciate was Rudolf's remarkable candour and impetuosity, which were in such contrast to his own veiled, inscrutable self. 'He just responded to that very powerful thing in Rudolf, who could suddenly open everything and let you see his soul,' said Glen Tetley. On their return to Copenhagen, Erik asked Rudolf to move in with him.

Number 16 Violveg, a two-storey house hidden behind a hedge, was where Erik had lived since he was a child. About ten kilometres from the city, it was in the pleasant garden suburb of Gentofte, whose streets have flower names, and which has a lake nearby. Erik's mother lived there, too, but unlike Sonia's comforting '*Mamushka*', Ellen Bruhn was a hard, possessive character who made her resentment of Rudolf's arrival quite clear. 'These two people had what seemed to be a violent reaction to each other,' Erik recalled. The maternal figure in his life had always been his aunt Minna, a loving woman who took care of him and his four sisters while their mother went out to work. Fru Bruhn, who ran a hairdressing salon, was the family breadwinner, as the children's father, an ineffectual man who gambled and drank, had long since moved out of their home. In this overwhelmingly female environment Erik was doted on and constantly in demand – an emotionally draining situation now intensified by Rudolf's own dependence on him. 'When I came from Paris . . . my family – especially my mother – wanted *all of me*, and there just was not enough of me,' he later wrote to Rudolf, explaining his distant moods. But Erik was all Rudolf had. 'He combined the teacher, lover, mother and father. He was Rudolf's family now. He no longer had any roots.'

On 13 September a telegram arrived at Rossi Street congratulating Alexander Ivanovich on his birthday. The Pushkins were overcome with relief. They had been convinced that the Soviets would kill Rudolf in the West – 'It could be a car accident, it could be something else' – and they never knew if the rumours they kept hearing were true. One

Rudik as a toddler with his mother, Farida.

Rudik's father, Hamet, *right,* photographed with a student friend in Kazan.

Hamet's own photograph, *below*; a highly popular leader, he arranged singing and dancing groups for his Red Army comrades.

A summer vacation, *above,* for the Nureyev children and their cousins in Asanova. In the group shot below, Rudik is in the front row, *second from left,* with his sister Razida on his right. Their cousin Amina is in the second row, *far left,* next to Rosa Nureyeva. Rudik's third sister, Lilia, is in the second row, *far right*.

The teenage Rudik displaying his innate,
unconfined elevation in an Ufa ballet studio.

Two of Rudik's first mentors with their pupils.
Elena Voitovich, *left,* the tall, bohemian ballet mistress
at the Ufa Theatre, and motherly Irina Alexandrovna,
the theatre's piano accompanist.

Rudik, *left*, with an Ufa yard gang friend.

Posing outside the Nureyevs' *isba* on Zentsova Street.

Alexander Ivanovich Pushkin teaching his class of male students at the Vaganova Academy.

Alexander and Xenia Pushkin on their honeymoon in the Ukraine.

The Pushkins photographed in their Rossi Street bed by Teja Kremke, mid-1960s.

Marietta Frangopoulo, curator of the Vaganova Academy museum. To her pupils she was 'a goddess . . . so erudite and had seen everybody dance'.

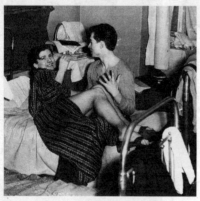

Clowning for Leo Ahonen's camera
in the Vaganova dormitory, 1957.

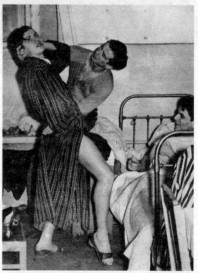

Rehearsing in a Vaganova studio with Alla Sizova, *c.* 1958.

The portrait of himself which Teja gave to Xenia.

The Cuban dancer Menia Martinez, Rudik's Leningrad sweetheart
and fellow student at the Vaganova Academy.

Left: Dancing the solo from *Le Corsaire* during an April 1958 national ballet school contest in Moscow; the Bolshoi immediately offered him a soloist contract.

Above: Tamara Zakrzhevskaya, a Leningrad fan who became one of Rudik's closest friends.

Below: The Romankov family, with the twins, Rudik's life-long friends, Leonid and Liuba.

With the legendary Kirov ballerina
Natalia Dudinskaya, performing *Laurentia*.

Soaring above the Kirov stage as
Frondoso in *Laurentia*, April 1959.

As Albrecht with his first Giselle, the delicate Irina Kolpakova.

With idol Alla Shelest in the Act 1 pas de deux from *Giselle*.

'Sit down on suitcase for a minute. It is old Russian superstition. Will work.'

day someone rang to tell the couple that Rudolf had been captured, taken to Moscow and incarcerated in a mental hospital. In a terrible state, Xenia begged Tamara to go there immediately and search them all. Teja described the atmosphere:

> In the theatres, in the schools, as well as in the dormitories of the ballet school there was a lot of talking. Someone said he had gone to England, another said to Paris, yet another said he was dead or that he was about to join the Kirov troupe in America to return together with them. Another one said they had already sentenced him to death.

And, in a sense, they had. Rudolf was to be tried *in absentia* for state treason, the maximum sentence for which was execution. Determined to do whatever they could to halt the procedure, and at a huge cost to themselves, his parents sent three telegrams in succession to the chief prosecutor and chairman of the Leningrad court, paying in addition sixty roubles in advance for an answer: 'We are asking you to suspend the trial of Nureyev Rudolf Hamitovich until he returns. We are applying to the government so that we can help him to come back, but we believe that the process of the trial will hinder his return.'

Rosa followed this up with her own telegram from Leningrad, making the same request, and adding, 'We believe that he will return if we help him.' As it happened, Rudolf's court case had been delayed because key witnesses were away on the Kirov tour of the United States until 10 December. Meanwhile the KGB opened its file on the traitor, number 50888, comprising his confiscated passport, details of items seized from Ordinarnaya Street, including his piano, Western press clippings attached to a Russian translation, and depositions recorded in preparation for the trial.

Among the testimony by Kirov colleagues is a surprisingly hostile account by Alla Osipenko, clearly made to atone for her own misdemeanours in Paris. 'He was not respected by the company,' she said. 'People resented him for being rude and too self-regarding.' Speaking out in Rudolf's defence, Rosa outlines her brother's difficult background in Ufa, and suggests that the physical strain he put himself under was the main cause of his volatility. 'By nature, he was a kind, honest and loving son.' Alexander Ivanovich explains how Rudolf came to live in their home, and mentions the 'special understanding' that he and his wife were able to provide. He admits that the dancer could be ill-mannered and highly strung, but insists that he never heard him express anti-Soviet sentiments. 'His act was carried out in a fit of passion because of the pressure he was under.' Xenia also stresses that art alone was paramount to Rudolf, and agrees that he could be extremely difficult. He had no friends, she says, claiming that her own attitude to him was 'the same as with any of my husband's students: I took care of him'. Knowing they were under KGB scrutiny, she confesses that a week after Rudolf's birthday telegram they had received a telephone call from him. Telling Xenia that he was in Copenhagen and planned to go to London soon, he seemed particularly interested in knowing which dancers had been chosen for the company's tour of the United States. To her question 'When are you going to come back?' he did not make a definite reply. Then, with characteristic impulsiveness, Xenia volunteers her own suspicion: 'I understand there's something keeping him there.'

Her intuition was right. By now 'a totally reciprocal deep passion' existed between Rudolf and Erik, their emotional intimacy coexisting with an extraordinary artistic interchange. This began each day at the barre. Home-movie footage shows them working together in a studio, both dressed in black. Erik raises one arm into an arabesque position, Rudolf, facing him, does the same. They study themselves in the mirror, not with vanity but with the self-critical scrutiny of dancers. Then they change sides. Still facing each other, they move in close, their heads almost touching as they begin a *fondu en arabesque* exercise. A faintly homoerotic undertone now emerges, which also plays on the idea of gender reversal, as they partner each other. Rudolf supports Erik's leg on his shoulder effecting a *grand rond de jambe* as he promenades around holding Erik's hand and forcing the arch of his back. Rudolf studies the effect in the mirror. Erik then does the same for him. Still at the barre, they try out a *Don Quixote* matador stance known in the bullfight as the *quiebro*: feet immobile, the body twisted and extended into the curve adopted by the matador before he plants the sword – upper torso sensually arched, head inclined, eyes half closed. Rudolf's crescent is less exaggerated than Erik's, but also more arrogant and commanding. Erik watched how Rudolf took the same steps and made them his own. 'It was like speaking the same language, using the same words, but expressing oneself with a different accent and intonation.'

In the centre they take turns to set exercises: Rudolf leading a Pushkin-inspired, controlled *adage*, Erik a *grand élévation* sequence followed by a series of *entrechat six*. Here the difference in their schooling – and in their ages – is unmistakable. Erik executes the *petite batterie* with his arms placed and perfectly relaxed, Danish-style, whereas

Rudolf is more agile in a Petipa diagonal of beaten *cabrioles en arabesque*, which Erik struggles through. Having begun working separately, neither wanting to influence the other, they slowly start to experiment, one trying the other's way of doing things. 'That's how we began to take from each other. We got so that we hardly talked at all: we knew and understood each other just from a gesture of the hands.' Stirred by the lyrical ardour in Rudolf, which he himself lacked, Erik had begun inflecting his movements with more force and passion, while Rudolf, never ceasing to marvel at Erik's attention to detail, was working towards achieving classical calm and perfection for himself. They were Apollo and Dionysus who had found their opposite and were feeding off each other. And this was more than a metaphor: each, in his way, had apotheosized himself. 'When you listen to Bach you hear a part of God . . . When you watch me dance you see a part of God,' Rudolf once said, while for Erik, too, the artist was semidivine, capable of attaining what he described as 'something *total* – a sense of total being.' 'There have been certain moments on the stage – four or five times – when I have suddenly felt a feeling of "I am!" A moment that feels as though it's for ever. An indescribable feeling of being everywhere and nowhere.'

Here Erik is almost quoting the Romantic mystics (echoing Coleridge's 'The Great Eternal I Am' in the *Biographia Literaria,* as well as Scriabin's resounding 'I am,' the orgasmic climax to the *Poème de l'extase*[*]). Rudolf, too, describing the sense of exultation he felt after a performance of *Corsaire*, said, 'Not "I did it!" But "I AM!" Sense of exultation; you become somebody else. You become IT . . . You yourself are thrilled. And it passes on. The thrill of BEING.' And yet it was not Erik but Rudolf who was the self-appointed 'Romantic kind of dancer', the solipsist and embodiment of the physical gusto Hazlitt called 'animal spirits'; Erik, by contrast, was self-effacing. 'The question of to be or not to be haunted Erik all his life,' said his close friend Susse Wold, to whom he once confided an out-of-body experience he had had as a child. 'He had climbed an apple tree, and was sitting on a branch listening to his mother calling for him, but felt that somehow he wasn't there. He could see himself, and yet he was *gone*.' Erik, who had tried various kinds of Buddhism, always returned to the way of Zen – its doctrine being the dissolving of the ego into the universe, the total extinction of the self.

---

[*] 'I am God' declarations in Scriabin's Swiss Notebook of 1905 are truncated into a single 'I am' (Faubion Bowers, *The New Scriabin*).

At an October 1961 London performance of international stars, Rudolf's influence on Erik was never more apparent: his whole manner was suddenly more theatrical as he walked onstage with deliberate, big cat steps, or made a standard pirouette more thrilling by giving it 'a whiplike quality'. His performance was the only highlight of the evening; everything else being 'a travesty and a parody of ballet', as Colin Clark wrote in a colourful account to Violette Verdy:

On Tuesday we went to see Anton Dolin Presents . . . AAARGH!! Celly [Colette] who is normally pretty reserved, actually booed she was so disgusted (which much surprised *The Observer* critic who was sitting in front of us). Nina Vyroubova – terribly out of practice, lazy and slack, Sonia Arova – better but again not taking any trouble, Lycette Darsonval – 70, need I say more. She managed to make it look a real feat to get out at all . . . Michel Renault, 60 . . . and Anton Dolin who gave his own inimitable performance of Bolero for the 7,200,001th time at the age of 63 . . . Then suddenly, divinely, Erik Bruhn. Quite marvellous, and getting a really fed-up audience back to life by *dancing*, yes actually dancing – the first person so far to do so . . . We saw him afterwards and he is so sweet and modest and shy. Celly tells me he is only happy in a deadbeat group where no one expects anything, as he is so neurotic and nervous. But he certainly is a really very great dancer . . . Poor Celly was beside herself to see the art she loves so much debased to such a level and no wonder. I am glad to say the audience agreed, and only clapped for Erik Bruhn. Him they gave a thunderous applause.

The Royal Ballet's director, Ninette de Valois, was also there that evening and, after the performance, invited Erik to guest with the company in November – a stroke of fate, it seemed to him and Rudolf, as this coincided with the date of Fonteyn's gala. In the meantime Rudolf was due to join the de Cuevas tour of Israel, an experience that proved far more enjoyable than he had anticipated, as the landscape with its small clustered villages and half-old, half-new towns felt curiously familiar. 'I had very good time. I swim and I have performances. It was perfect. It was sun. Reminded me of south of Russia: the construction of Tel Aviv and the people – very alive. Warm.'

With his partner, Rosella Hightower, and a couple of other dancers he rented a car to explore what he described as 'places of Christ and Biblia' – biblical scenes – driving from Haifa to Jerusalem, with Rudolf occasionally taking the wheel. Although 'just bumping about', he loved the sensation of being in a car, as he felt safe there, and unafraid. Rosella was amazed to see how much more relaxed he was than in Paris, 'where he was always hiding': 'No matter where we went, he'd want to get out to see and to talk. He was anxious to know everything. As a race, the Israelis are so friendly and clannish that they must have felt to him like family. He was very much at home.'

Many of the people he met were Russian émigrés, and a number of English-speaking fans also befriended him. 'They find me . . . invite to house to make parties.' One was a wealthy young woman who worshipped Rudolf, and followed him throughout the tour. Rosella remembers Rudolf being extremely rude to her, treating her as if she hardly existed, but nevertheless he was clearly thriving on all the attention. 'Whether it was the girls or the boys – he'd just disappear in the evenings. He was discovering a new angle on the way he thought he could live and having one helluva good time.'

The cruising had begun.* To the company's amazement – and Raymundo's fury – Rudolf would pick up 'n'importe quoi' on the Tel Aviv beach and bring him back to his dressing room. 'We were horrified,' said Ghislaine Thesmar. 'There was a bunch of good-looking boys in the company, but Rudolf didn't concern himself with them. What he discovered on those beaches was the freedom of anonymity; partners you never saw again. It was a choice.' And it was another difference between Rudolf and Erik.

In London at the end of October Rudolf's first rehearsals with Frederick Ashton took place behind closed doors. The choreographer had agreed to create a special solo, but only grudgingly, as he had never seen Nureyev perform. More important to Ashton even than working with dancers he knew was his choice of music, and in this case the score had already been decided by Rudolf: Scriabin's Poème tragique. For some time he had been wanting to dance to this short prelude, but not because he felt himself to be a tragic figure. 'Not at all. Not because of name. I used [sic] like that piece very much.' He had loved it in Russia, and a year earlier had seen it performed by the Bolshoi in a new ballet by Kasyan Goleizovsky, the most prominent innovator in Soviet ballet, who often used Scriabin's music. Although written in 1903, a turning

---

* The late Vadim Kiselev, not always a reliable source, insisted that Rudolf's predilection for 'the accidental people' started in Leningrad. 'Of course it started here. He was very attracted to young Russians, blond, good bodies, and he had all kinds of contacts. He wasn't very careful, but you can't blame him for that. If he'd had a permanent romance with someone it would have been a great scandal.'

point for the composer who then went on to experiment with agitated rhythms and unusual tonality, the *Poème tragique* for Piano, *op. 34 in B flat*, was still under the influence of Liszt and Chopin, two of Ashton's favourite composers.

Dancer and choreographer spent their first hours in the studio taking each other's measure. To Ashton, who felt overawed by the young Russian's heritage—'a more wonderful schooling than I ever had' – Rudolf seemed reticent, ill at ease, and unconvinced by his authority. Struck by the dancer's physical magnificence and more than a little frightened by his feral power, Ashton admitted being 'perfectly willing to accept what he wanted to do' and in the end put in too many ingredients – much as Rudolf himself did when he went on to make his own work. The kind of choreography that Rudolf had seen evoked by Scriabin's music was rhythm made visible in flowing, plastic, sometimes acrobatic movements, an impressionistic effect that transposed itself into the solo with Rudolf 'darting round . . . dipping and weaving, turning in screws'. He had been allowed, he told Nigel Gosling, to follow his ideas 'pretty freely'. And yet, although Nigel agreed that there was 'not much of Ashton' in the solo, the choreographer had, in fact, drawn extensively on inspiration of his own.

Seeing at once that Rudolf possessed the same overwhelming emotional impact – 'an impact of personality' – as the two muses of his youth, Anna Pavlova and Isadora Duncan, Ashton decided to infuse the dance with memories of their performances.* In homage to Pavlova's erotically charged *Bacchanale* (lasting, like the Scriabin piece, only a few minutes), as well as Isadora's dramatic entrance with a cloak to Chopin's *Funeral March*, Ashton soon had Rudolf 'bounding passionately round the big rehearsal room . . . flourishing a borrowed white sheet'. His free and open gestures, expressing a sense of liberation with a hand defiantly raised, were based on Isadora's *Marche Slave*, which represented a peasant rising from slavery to freedom. 'Reeking of revolution', the music of Scriabin perfectly served this atmosphere of revolt against destiny, and spoke, too, of Rudolf's flight. And behind this sense of upsurge towards otherworldliness was a powerful erotic impetus that not only substantiated Rudolf's view of creativity as 'very

---

* Although Scriabin deplored Isadora's old-fashioned choice of music, he acknowledged that her liberated dance language, with its expression of symbolic gestures, was close in spirit to 'the plastic magic of rhythms' that he admired in choreography.

much akin to sex, sexual drive or sexual appetite if you wish', but also emphasized the 'enormous sexual impulse' Ashton wanted to exploit: 'a kind of animalism, a violence, a sort of tremendous physical intensity'.* Like the music, the dance verged on the histrionic, and as Ashton said, was 'so charged with things that we really had to eliminate quite a lot because it was too exhausting to get through'.

Margot and Colette, who had never seen Rudolf dance, watched the final rehearsal alarmed by the strain and violence of his exertions. He was 'nervous, intense and repeating every step with all his might until he almost knocked himself out with the effort'. Colin Clark, who joined them at the Theatre Royal, Drury Lane, also described the sight as 'really pretty frightening', as Rudolf, leaping as high as he possibly could, would land each time with a crash on the slippery raked stage. That evening over dinner at the embassy with her husband and the Clark twins, Margot urged Rudolf to try to relax more in order to finish the dance as well as he began it. 'But Nureyev declared that this was cheating, and if in Russia he couldn't finish, he just stopped and walked off. This really panicked Margot and Celly.'

As the curtain went up for the gala matinée at Drury Lane, a crack of applause broke out from the house, 'palpitating with a lust for something new'. Standing at the centre of an empty stage was a lone figure wrapped in a scarlet cloak. He struggled to release himself from its folds, then hurtled towards the footlights – a living symbol of Soviet repression set free. Long-haired, wild-eyed, and half naked in grey-streaked tights, a red-and-white sash striped across his chest, Rudolf seemed to the English audience to be a primordial force of nature. The shock produced by his savage intensity was compared by Alexander Bland to that of seeing a predator let loose in a drawing room. Other critics felt that the dance too obviously exploited Rudolf's own story, its 'mixture of sobs and spins . . . an unrelated *obligato* of anguished hair-tearing' seeming to Clive Barnes little more than a parody of a Soviet-style solo. But everyone agreed that the piece made thrilling theatre, that in a matter of minutes Ashton had captured the very essence of Rudolf's persona: 'rebellious, charismatic, sensational and yet a figure of great poise and dignity'.

---

* John Lanchbery, who orchestrated the *Poème tragique* for the gala, delighted Rudolf by telling him of a theory he had heard, that the theme stated fortissimo on five trumpets in unison at the climax of the *Poème de l'extase* represented the composer in a state of erection. 'The story goes that Scriabin used to excite himself with pornography while composing.'

Over almost before it had begun, the solo ended with the dancer sliding to the floor, his despairing arms reaching up towards the gods as the lights grew dim. Cecil Beaton described the immediate aftermath:

> The audience was for a moment stunned. Then, recovering, it produced its storm of lightning and thunder applause. The boy responded with charm, dignity and superb Russian pride. This 23-year-old creature from the woods was now, beatnik hair and all, a Russian emperor imperviously accepting the acclaim of his people.

It was the grandeur and sweep of Rudolf's front-of-curtain bow – 'not so much what he danced, actually' – that made Ninette de Valois decide there and then that she wanted him for her company. 'All I thought was, He's doing that at Covent Garden as soon as I can possibly organize it.' His performance after the interval had been technically erratic and uncontrolled. Partnering Rosella Hightower in the Black Swan pas de deux,* and looking oddly epicene in his Parisian blond wig, Rudolf had fought his way through the virtuoso steps, landing badly and throwing both himself and Rosella off balance. 'Rudi didn't believe in covering up his difficulties,' remarked Violette Verdy. 'It was part of his barbaric quality. He was in the raw. But the way he *burned* the stage with his intensity was completely unique.' The audience thought so, too, responding to the point of delirium, and demanding that Rudolf repeat his solo as an encore.

After the performance the stage door area of Drury Lane was a scene of 'terrifying mob passions' as the two dancers tried to make their way to Fonteyn's car. The whole theatre seemed to be waiting in the street to see him, and surged forward, screaming and straining to touch Rudolf. (Rosella's costume, carried over her arm, was ripped in the mêlée.) It was London's first taste of Rudimania. Erik, who had stood in the wings with Sonia listening to the 'hyena baying' and realizing that something incredible had just happened, found himself thinking, Where does that leave me?

Fonteyn was thinking the same thing. Despite having been coached in *Le Spectre de la rose* by Karsavina, who had created the role, her appearance in the gala had made no impact, described by one critic as 'a nostalgic shadow of past glories', and dismissed by Rudolf as

---

* A last-minute substitute for the *Don Quixote* duet advertised in the programme 'because we'd had much more success with it in Israel'.

'unfortunate'. She looked tired, her technique was in decline, her best years seemed to be over. During the Royal Ballet's tour of Russia that summer, hampered by a foot injury and nervous of appearing on the Kirov stage, she had given what she regarded as her worst performance ever of Aurora, her signature role. 'Fonteyn didn't have any success here,' said Tamara, remembering the ballerina's low arabesque line and feeble attempts at pirouettes. Although still the company figurehead, she had been made guest artist in 1959 quite against her wishes, and had been expected to retire at the same time as her partner Michael Somes. Even Ashton appeared to have lost interest in her since *Ondine*, his last 'Fonteyn-sonata', and was now building his work on the Royal Ballet's young dancers. Yet here was the twenty-three-year-old Russian star pleading to dance with her, and de Valois, who wanted Nureyev to dance Albrecht in *Giselle* the following season, urging her to accept. She asked to be allowed to think it over.

At the post-gala cocktail party at the Duchess of Roxborough's Bayswater flat, Rudolf, the guest of honour, handled all the compliments and questions with poise, deflecting Ambassador Arias's curiosity about why he had been spending so much time in Copenhagen by replying darkly, 'Is story better not told.' But he had been startled when Cecil Beaton came up and impetuously kissed him on the cheek and forehead, savouring the vellum-soft smoothness of the dancer's skin. The photographer had been moved to tears when he discussed Rudolf's performance with Ashton, recognizing the dancer as 'something almost perfect in the taste of today'. This kind of ecstatic acclaim, though hardly new to Rudolf, was intoxicating all the same, giving him exactly what he needed: world confirmation of his talent. As the last guests were leaving, feeling too elated to retire for the night, and yielding to the pull of the prowl, he asked to be dropped in the King's Road.

For those who had seen him dance, Rudolf's impact reverberated for days. There was some degree of uncertainty about his true aptitude, which could not be judged from a fragmentary gala programme; to Beaton he was a 'genius', to Colette a genius 'in fits & starts – in flashes . . . Sometimes he dances very wildly & undisciplinedly & other times like an angel, but he has this fantastic star personality & charm & looks & he will always be The Star wherever he is . . . In the end Everybody male & female fell in love with him including, I think, Margot!'

Richard Buckle was one of several critics to comment on Rudolf's rough edges, and the jarring lack of elasticity in his landings, but he followed up his original review of the matinée with an article titled 'More About the Man from Leningrad', a select anthology of responses:

Lady Juliet Duff (in a letter). Nureyev's ballon may not yet be developed, but he has *magic* just as Nijinsky had. Have not been so stirred since I first saw Nijinsky and Karsavina dance the *Spectre*. I so *long* to see the new boy in that. Dying to know what Karsavina thought of him. Please find out and tell me.

Mme Tamara Karsavina (on the telephone). I agree with you about his landing badly, but he has a remarkable technique. Certain steps he does better than Nijinsky, but he is without Nijinsky's gift for pausing in the air. On the other hand, he has not got Nijinsky's overdeveloped thighs, which makes for better line. Erik Bruhn is certainly a wonderful dancer, but he lacks Nureyev's nerve . . . I certainly felt a thrill.

Frederick Ashton (on the telephone). He has a marvellous engine inside him, like a Rolls-Royce. You could feel his power when he started up at rehearsals . . . Chaboukiani was the most *exciting* dancer I ever saw; and Nureyev has some of his fire; but more grace. There is a strangeness about him. I feel he's a mixture of a Tatar, a faun and a kind of lost urchin. He's the Rimbaud of the Steppes.

Meanwhile Margot had made an overnight decision to dance with Nureyev. A refusal, she felt, would put her at risk of becoming 'an absolutely back number, a nothing', as he was clearly going to be the sensation of the year. She had reached this conclusion after a discussion with her husband, who had every reason to encourage her to prolong her stage career. As a glamorous Cambridge undergraduate, Roberto 'Tito' Arias, the tanned, sleek-haired son of Panama's ex-president, had been eighteen-year-old Margot's first love but had disappeared from her life, breaking her heart, until the Royal Ballet's 1953 New York season, when he turned up at the Met: a chubby, bespectacled delegate to the UN. By this time Margot Fonteyn, *prima ballerina assoluta* and belle of New York, was ballet's greatest star, and Tito was determined to make her his wife. Although married already, with three small children, he began courting her with diamonds, mink and El Morocco suppers until, two years later, she finally relented – swayed less by his indulgence of her 'one-track tastes . . . Dior, the Mediterranean, Cartier's and the best' than the sense of well-being she felt in Tito's company (she was part South American, after all).

During her subsequent years as Panamanian ambassadress, Margot, now a Dame of the British Empire, had brought tremendous prestige to the embassy as well as undoubted respectability to her husband. Politically and socially ambitious, counting senators and movie stars among his friends, Tito was also a philanderer and gambler with a shady entrepreneurial side said to involve gun-running and brothel-keeping. He loved money, and when his own ran out, he spent his wife's. Her retirement would clearly change all this, limiting not only his profligacy but the freedom of his double life. As Maude put it, 'Tito always wanted her to carry on, because then he could carry on with his girls.' The following day Ninette de Valois received a call from Margot to say that she could go ahead and announce the Fonteyn–Nureyev partnership in *Giselle*.

Immediately after the gala Rudolf rejoined the de Cuevas tour in Hamburg, learning to his dismay that the company was not performing at the Staatsoper but at a cabaret theatre on the Reeperbahn, the city's 'sin centre'. (Three months earlier a group of teenage Liverpudlians, also making their Hamburg debut, had been equally dejected to find themselves booked to appear not in the famous Kaiserkeller nightclub but in a cramped basement strip club. It was in Hamburg that the Beatles learned to make a show, experiment with stimulants and style their hair into the mushroom mop adopted by the *Exis* – the young existentialists.) But aware neither of the city's youth culture nor its extremely clandestine homosexual club life, Rudolf hated Hamburg on sight. Its neon-lit garishness, and the overtness of its sexual trade, with prostitutes outlined in the pink-lit windows of Herbertstrasse, upset him 'a lot'. And just as disturbing was the discovery that he had to share his role of Prince Désiré with Serge Golovine, who had been cast in the first act. He had been spending much of his time 'nearly desperate' in his room when he received a call one morning to say that he had a visitor. It was a friend of Teja's: Axel Mowitz.

Having heard that the twenty-three-year-old, a graduate of Hamburg University, was unusually beautiful, Rudolf invited him straight up to the room. When Axel first saw the dancer he was sitting on the bed wearing a small towel and smiling provocatively. 'It was clear that he was offering me the possibility.' But not only was Axel unattracted to someone his own age – 'my contacts then were fifteen or sixteen years old' – he also felt overwhelmed by Rudolf's stardom. 'I was impotent with awe.' They decided to go out for breakfast and, finding much in common, spent the day together. Talking incessantly (in English, which Axel spoke fluently), they discussed European dance criticism as well as aesthetics, philosophy and the work of Brecht, Axel's major subject, on which Rudolf held his own. Also passionate about dance, Axel was a friend of the ballet historian Cyril Beaumont and a regular customer at his London bookshop.

He took Rudolf to Hamburg's own ballet bookshop and, wanting to show him the picturesque side of the city, gave him a tour of the Alster Lakes. As they walked along the western shore, with its exclusive nineteenth-century villas, watching the boating activity on the water, Rudolf suddenly stopped in astonishment at the sight of a red flag. 'It's a sign for danger,' Axel explained, which made the dancer burst out laughing. 'He was still feeling the shock of his departure from Russia.' Recapturing his delicate interlude with Heinz Mannigel in East Berlin, Rudolf spent the rest of the week with the young German, in whose company he felt completely at ease. When they spoke of their mutual friend it was only glancingly, and rather condescendingly on Rudolf's part. 'Teja had become a light thing for Rudolf: his obsession was Erik Bruhn.'

At around lunchtime on the day Rudolf was due to perform *The Sleeping Beauty*, a stagehand lowering the scenery pulled the wrong lever and the fire-protecting sprinklers went into action. For twenty minutes as a mechanism prevented the water from being turned off, the crew and dancers grabbed buckets and set to work mopping up and rescuing what they could. Raymundo was in tears as he inspected the damage to his filmy sets, but Rudolf, who despised the costumes and decor anyway, viewed the scene with *schadenfreude*: 'At that moment I was not sorry' – particularly because the cancellation of that evening's performance meant that he could fly to Munich for the première of Erik's *Swan Lake* with Sonia Arova.

When Rudolf returned to Hamburg he was accompanied by Erik, whom he introduced to Axel as 'my dear friend'. The student had prepared an elaborate lunch for the three of them, but sensed that Bruhn felt uneasy about the situation – 'He could see how excited I was to be with Rudolf.' Axel, in turn, was in no doubt about the dancers' mutual passion – 'You only had to be with them to feel it. They made a very beautiful couple.' Nevertheless he was dismayed when Rudolf said to him as they were leaving, 'Erik doesn't have a ticket for tonight – could you give him yours?' 'I'd been to every performance and felt deeply depressed by this suggestion. But after Erik arrived, he didn't have any more time for me.'

*

Italy was the next stage of the tour, where Rudolf was delighted to be partnering guest star Yvette Chauviré, who was as much of a national heroine in France as Edith Piaf and was acclaimed all over the world. During her 1958 tour of Russia with the Paris Opéra Ballet, Rudolf had been in the audience on the night she was called to encore her Dying Swan solo three times: 'Satisfaction for us.' When they were first introduced in a Paris studio he had kissed the ballerina's hand with profound respect, and over lunch as they sat together, spoken in a very serious tone – '*Moitié anglais, moitié français*' – of the impact her performance had made on him.

The essence of Parisian allure, with her long slender limbs, languorous femininity and swan neck, Chauviré in fact embodied three different schools, as she had acquired lightness from the Italians as well as strength and lyricism from the Russians. It was her rare ability to fuse classical clarity of line with Romantic feeling that had made her one of the great Giselles of all time. She noticed the way Rudolf was always watching her, but having been slightly intimidated at first, he felt as soon as they began to rehearse that they had 'danced all life'. Chauviré felt the same, and the next time she performed the role sent Rudolf a card saying, 'Giselle without you is not Giselle.'

Between performances Rudolf flew back and forth to Cannes to rehearse with Erik, Sonia and Rosella. The dancers had decided to form an experimental group along the lines of a musical quartet, providing a programme of dance without the 'orchestration' of elaborate decors or productions. Having just retired from the stage, Rosella had opened a dance school in Cannes with an enormous studio – 'like they have in Bolshoi' – where the friends rehearsed from early afternoon until late into the night. Although the work was immensely strenuous, they were all glad of the opportunity to do exactly what they wanted without interference or interruption – Rudolf and Erik being especially delighted to have the chance to choreograph. In a small theatre in Haifa, Rudolf had already experimented on Rosella – 'grabbing me whenever he could' – to try out his own version of *The Nutcracker* pas de deux, which he had previously worked out on paper. Refining this for their programme, he also added the *Don Quixote* pas de deux and *Dances from Raymonda* – all three being extracts from Petipa ballets he would later stage in their entirety.

Erik's contribution was a lighthearted *Fantaisie* about four young people meeting in a park, as well as plotless dances to Bach's *Toccata and Fugue*, one section of which showed him and Rudolf re-creating the simultaneous practice work they had done in Copenhagen (and

gave a male twist to the traditional Danish duet in which the ballerina
and her partner dance identical choreography together). But as they
worked on the Bach piece, the two men argued constantly, Rudolf
criticizing Erik for what he regarded as his cavalier treatment of the
music. Erik's model was Bournonville, whose choreography goes on
and off the beat, whereas Rudolf, who regarded Bach as sacred,
believed that the steps should be set 'squarely to the music without
varying.' 'It always ended up as a big battle,' said Rosella. 'Being the
eldest, I found myself taking over and organizing things: "Rudi, if you
do this part, Erik can do that. . . . Stop *arguing!*"'

The couple's working relationship had become increasingly diabolical, 'as if each existed to be a challenge to the other, and to fill the other
with despair'. Intently studying Erik's approach to a role, Rudolf once
announced in Rosella's hearing, '*I'm* going to dance that, and I'm going
to dance it even better.' And if rehearsals were discordant, what took
place afterwards was 'absolute pandemonium'. Not always the glacial
figure he looked, Erik had a furious temper that was probably genetic
(his sister Else was the victim of a deeply neurotic personality, and he
remembered 'long and violent quarrels' between his parents). His
anger was lurking, mean and caustic, whereas Rudolf's tended to be
more melodramatic and physical. 'But once the Dane had had his
whisky, and the Russian his vodka, it didn't take much to set them off,'
recalled Rosella. She would hear the next morning from Sonia, who
shared their seafront apartment, how the pair had run through the
rooms chasing each other with knives 'as if wanting to end everything'.

The prospect of rejoining the de Cuevas tour did little to improve
Rudolf's mood. He had told Yvette Chauviré, 'I will *not* go to Venice
for this *Sleeping Beauty*,' and although he arrived as expected, he was
not even appeased by the city itself, snow-covered for the first time in
years, its stucco façades and wrought-iron work all the more exquisite
for being outlined in white. 'I couldn't stand it despite all that beauty.'
His hotel was cheap, uncomfortable and so poorly heated that he felt
warmer outdoors. He was wearing his Russian fur hat when Ghislaine
Thesmar met him crossing a bridge, and dismissed her comment on
the snow by saying, 'Of course it snows. *I'm* here.'

With the Venice performances taking place during the festive
season, Rudolf felt more foolishly like a Christmas tree than ever in his
spun-sugar wig and tiara. Desperate to retain the purity of his Kirov
schooling as well as his memories of its own *Sleeping Beauty* production, he had never attempted to understand the decorative aesthetic
of the de Cuevas company. Raymundo, whose heightened sense of

invention and imagination came from having worked with the surrealist painter Leonor Fini, had set out to create a private company with an atmosphere all its own – certainly nothing like that of the Paris Opéra – designing strange, dreamlike decors, costumes in the newest fabrics and exaggerated, Kabuki-white makeup. 'Raymundo was *so* aesthetic, he loved working with things like transparent nylon. He was never going to put the prince in velvet,' said Jacqueline de Ribes, who had been adored by the marquis for being what he considered the only aristocrat in Paris with a sense of fantasy. In this sophisticated European milieu, Leningrad's maverick and modernist, insisting on wearing his own blond wig for *Don Quixote* and finding Raymundo's ideas completely crazy, seemed exceedingly Soviet and old-fashioned. He was, they believed, a great artist, but not a man of taste. 'It was too soon for Rudolf to be caught up in such phantasmagoric tra-la-la,' said Violette Verdy. 'He wasn't used to such extravaganza.' To make his point, Rudolf appeared onstage on his last night in Venice wearing his own black velvet costume. He had nothing to lose; his contract was at an end. And, by now, this was as much of a relief to his colleagues as to himself. 'The atmosphere in the company was chilly too. I parted from it without many tears.'

8   A CELESTIAL ACCIDENT

Towards the end of December Rudolf received a letter from Teja, forwarded to him by Axel Mowitz.

Sweet Rudik,

Much time has passed since we last saw each other. I wanted to write to you long ago, but where could I find you? I'm sending this letter to a friend who will probably be able to trace you.

Here in Leningrad a lot of people talk about you, but who can I trust? One says you are in England; one says you are crazy; one says you are in Paris . . . Well – you know what sometimes they can say here. I, myself, think that you are now very devastated; you don't know what to do. My advice is: don't be afraid of truth. We all think that you'll come back to us soon. What is the Kirov Theatre without you? When I'm there and walk around during the intervals, we often recall your dancing. Do you remember how we always worried before the performance? . . . There is no such worrying now. When I go and visit Pushkin, we often remember you. He and Xenia can't believe that you've forgotten them. He has become much older recently. Why am I writing all this to you? I feel that you want to come back home, but are afraid. Why should you be afraid? We all know why you did it – don't think that nobody here understands you. We all know that you aren't very guilty and we would take that into account. Of course, your situation in the theatre wasn't easy: the arguments you had about costumes, and when people disagreed with your innovations. But in art you always have to fight for the new – don't give up so quickly. Our profession is linked to troubles, as Pushkin says in his novel *The Captain's Daughter* . . . Think about everything that I've written to you and don't be afraid . . .

We're having winter in Leningrad. Everything is covered with snow like in a fairy tale, with the Neva freezing up. Everything stays as it always was . . . I don't know what else to say to you. I hope you'll be

able to read my writing; two years here isn't enough to learn Russian.
Everybody is waiting for you here. Come!

> Many regards, I kiss you, your friend, Teja

However affectionate and understanding its tone, this letter, as Teja
would later tell Rudolf, was 'all lies'. Earlier in December he had been
contacted by a member of the East German secret police and told that
an agent would be travelling to Leningrad to speak to him. The reason
was the letter he had written Rudolf that summer which had been
intercepted by the KGB and passed on to the Stasi. 'As the KGB has
invested a lot of work into persuading the dancer to return, the
informer was asked to talk to Kremke to prevent further warnings,
otherwise all their efforts would be in vain.'

On 13 December Teja met the Stasi agent in his hotel room. To
the first question, asking if he knew why he was there, Teja, clearly
very nervous, replied that it was probably because of the dancer who
had stayed behind in Paris. 'About the warning, he said nothing, of
course.' Told to disclose everything he knew about Nureyev, he began
talking with considerable confusion about how they had become
friends. And then he was asked if he wanted to say anything about the
letter.

> It was obvious that Kremke had expected this question, and he became
> extremely agitated, immediately admitting having written the letter
> and asking how he could put things right. He agreed that he had been
> in the wrong, and said that if he could help in any way, he would.
> Kremke kept saying that he was ready to make amends. He agreed to
> write a report concerning his relationship with the dancer, and to
> write another letter trying to convince the dancer that he had acted
> wrongly, and trying to influence him to return.

That night Teja was more terrified than he had ever been in his life.
He was only eighteen, and felt completely on his own. He couldn't
even call his mother, as the agent had ordered him 'in sharp tones' not
to talk to anyone about their conversation. 'Kremke assured me that
he would stay silent.' The Stasi's aim was to frighten the boy, pointing
out how he had made himself a focus for Western secret services, and
warning that if he were rash enough to attempt to caution the traitor
again, he would be found out and made to bear the consequences.
(Threats included being sent to work in a factory and forbidden to

continue his dance studies.) Panicking about any evidence that might incriminate him further, Teja tore several pages out of his diary dated from 20 to 24 July, destroying a record of Rudolf's calls, and took a box of films, photographs and personal papers to leave in the safe-keeping of his student girlfriend. And then he sat down to write.

In a three-page statement mixing truth with fiction, Teja describes how his acquaintance with the Kirov star had brought him special perks – 'I was often able to go to the theatre with a real ticket instead of just a pass for the upper circle' – and says that he felt sorry for Rudolf, who had no friends apart from the Pushkins, Tamara and himself. They often fought, and he had to put up with a lot of abusive behaviour, but when the dancer made it clear through 'various little overtures' that he wanted to take the relationship a stage further, Teja decided to bring it to an end. 'Then, eventually, he asked me to make peace and also apologized for his behaviour, saying that he would never again approach me in an abnormal way.' Fearing that their Berlin telephone may have been tapped, Teja decided to confess that Rudolf had asked him to join him in Paris but insists that at the time he had thought it best to 'forget about everything' and sever all contact.

Quite often at Mrs Pushkin's house we talked of him coming back to his senses. But as Mrs Pushkin was unable to provide any news, I got scared that something might happen to the great talent Nureyev, and with my letter I tried to get in touch with him again . . . I wanted to remind him about me and tell him about everything I had heard. That way I hoped to start a correspondence between the two of us . . . Had I written a letter telling about myself, how and where I was, he would never have answered it . . . I wanted to make him think about the situation he was in . . . [but I] fully recognize that I had committed an offence as well as a breach of trust. Knowing Rudolf, I regarded this to be the only possible way to make him eventually reconsider everything. With this I have written the entire truth . . .

[signed] Teja Kremke,
Leningrad, Dec. 13, 1961

Also that evening, Teja wrote the letter to Rudolf according to Stasi directions, and the following day, exactly on time, returned to the hotel. Appearing far more relaxed this time, he admitted that he had been corresponding with a girl in Germany (which the Stasi already knew).* The agent appeared satisfied with the new letter, 'written in a very persuasive tone', but made a note in his report that it was imperative to continue their investigation of the student: 'Find out about his connections in West Berlin; whether he is involved in any enemy activities; whether he can be used as an informer.'

Two days later, on 15 December, Xenia wrote her own letter to Rudolf. Like Teja's it contains reassurances of his friends' continuing devotion, nostalgic descriptions of snow-draped Leningrad, 'so beautiful that it is hard to describe this winter landscape in words', as well as theatre gossip and references to their beloved Pushkin (whom she disguises as 'The Elder'). But if it was also written to order – and with the approach of Rudolf's first Christmas and New Year away from home, the KGB knew that the dancer would be more than usually receptive to attempts to lure him back – Xenia nevertheless used the opportunity to unleash an extraordinary outpouring of emotion, bludgeoning Rudolf with the extent of 'worrying and suffering' she had endured since last hearing from him in September.

> I've been waiting all this time . . . you could have just spat on a piece of paper and sent it to me in an envelope. But . . . zero attention. Well, God bless you. I just so badly wanted to get a few letters from you, but there was always something preventing you from writing letters. I don't know how to be angry with you, but I believe there will come a time when you will write to me. Oh! If you could know how I worry about you. I got so used to taking care of you . . . You can't imagine what I felt when I heard that you are alive and well . . . Now I can despise the dirty little souls [the KGB] with reason. I hate your Kotochko [Sergeyev], even though we used to be friends with him . . .

> I've heard about your success and, of course, I've read about it. I will wait for news from you impatiently. Pull yourself together – write to me.
>   I think about you all the time. Kissing you. Hugs, Your X.J.

Rosa also wrote to Rudolf on 15 December, wishing him a happy New Year and telling him how much he meant to the family. 'You can't

---

* They also had a record of the night he and his current girlfriend had spent together in the Europa Hotel.

imagine what a celebration we have when we find out something
about you. That you're alive, healthy, and dancing well.' Knowing how
much Rudolf worshipped the Bolshoi's Galina Ulanova – 'I cannot talk
about her like the others. I cannot describe her. When I say her name I
see her dance' – she tells him about a recent conversation she had with
the ballerina. Charmingly simple and forthcoming, Ulanova said how
sorry she was that things happened the way they did for Rudolf, and
asked Rosa to call her if she heard any news. But among the assurances
of sympathy and understanding are asides deliberately put there to
unsettle him, like the emphasis on the strain he is inflicting on their
'poor Mama', who is planning to leave Ufa and join Rosa in Leningrad
until her son comes home. They are all so worried about his life and
future, and are just waiting and dreaming about his return. They miss
his performances – 'adoring you and being proud of your success' –
but feel sure they will see him again soon. 'Come, Rudinka! Everything
will be fixed somehow . . . So *come*. Make us happy.'

On New Year's Eve, knowing that his mother and sister would be
together at Ordinarnaya Street, Rudolf telephoned them. Describing
the company's two-month tour across Europe and his recent schedule
in London, Paris and Copenhagen, he tried to get across the extent to
which he was able to enrich his dance knowledge, assimilating new
influences while preserving and adapting his Russian schooling. But
instead of being impressed, they were deeply concerned, immediately
writing a joint letter warning him repeatedly not to overwork. 'Or as
Mother says, it won't be long before you end up on a rubbish heap.
Colourful? Yes, Mother knows. Listen to her.' Rudolf had told them
that his circumstances in the West were not bad, that he was able to
find elements in other methods of dance that he could accept, but just
as Rosa had listened intently to her neighbour Alla Sizova's descriptions of the Kirov's recent American tour, trying and failing to picture
the world now surrounding Rudolf, she 'heard but didn't understand'
what her brother was trying to say.

Rudolf also called Rossi Street that night to wish the Pushkins a
happy New Year. He told Xenia that he had left the de Cuevas company
and was now in Copenhagen, doing exactly what he had always
planned: studying with Erik Bruhn. He described the situation at le
Bourget that had forced him to stay in the West – something Pushkin's
'abrupt letter' arriving the night of his debut had not taken
into account. 'Tell Alexander Ivanovich that if he's got nothing
better to say – and Tamara hasn't either – they shouldn't write at

all.'* Desperate to reassure him of their love and support, Xenia responded immediately. 'Don't be angry with Pupik,' she wrote. 'He didn't know the whole adventure. He is an honest man and a good man.' Tamara, alone and unhappy on New Year's Eve, sent her own pledge of fidelity to her 'Rudenka':

> Nothing has changed for me. My attitude is the same. It's just that now I have a feeling of longing – desperate longing – and endless questions: Where is he now? What's happening to him?

News that Rudolf was safe was 'like a sedative' to Xenia, who turned Russian Christmas on 7 January into a special celebration in his honour. As a memoir and billet-doux, Teja and the Pushkins made a film of themselves at Rossi Street, completing their *ménage à quatre* of old by playfully seating an outsize teddy bear in Rudolf's usual chair. Candlelit and wonderfully evocative of old St Petersburg, it begins with a close-up of tea from an antique silver pot and milk from a silver jug being poured into bone china cups, and closes in on Alexander Ivanovich spooning jam into his tea. He eats a piece of cake, delicately, fastidiously, while Xenia, wearing a ravishing rose-printed satin dress, takes a pear from the fruit bowl, holds it to the light and sensuously peels it. Pushkin pours champagne into crystal glasses and gives one to Xenia, who, as usual, makes the first toast to him. Then Teja, dressed in a jazzy black-and-white sweater, toasts Alexander Ivanovich, and both Xenia and Teja turn towards a picture on the wall: her favourite study of Rudolf in a pose from *La Bayadère*. Pushkin raises his glass to it, and so does Xenia with a special smile.

---

* Immediately after the defection, Tamara, like Pushkin, had written to Rudolf, leaving her unsealed envelope with the teacher, who gave it and his own to the KGB agent who arrived at the school the next day to collect them. Not knowing what to say, she had sent a few lines by the nineteenth-century patriotic poet Nikolay Nekrasov, whose work often contains real depth of feeling beneath its pamphleteering façade:

> Alas! The wife will be consoled,
> And friend forgets the dearest friend.
> . . . In all the world I only saw
> Tears, that are saintly and sincere –
> The tears of mothers are the ones!
> They can't forget their poor sons.

(From 'Harking to Horrors of War', translated by Alexander Storozhuk.)

In another, more intimate scene, Xenia is sitting in her bedroom, applying her makeup while Teja stands behind her, slowly and attentively brushing her hair. Since Rudolf's defection they had become much closer, each taking comfort from the other as a way of extending their ties with Rudolf. 'Xenia transferred all her desires to Teja when Rudik left – they were seen together everywhere.' Watching this Turgenev moment of tender rapport between the radiant older woman and beautiful boy feels like spying until we realize that, with the hand-held camera, Pushkin must be there, too. So is Rudolf. As if reassuring him of this, Xenia picks up his framed photograph on her dressing-table and places it lovingly in front of her with the candles and perfume bottles forming a little shrine.

Ending with footage of Rudolf's Leningrad – the Kirov Theatre, Pushkin's studio, the Hermitage from across the Neva, the circular route of his favourite walk – the film, which eventually found its way to him, acted as a potent siren call. And just as affecting were the sentiments expressed in Rosa's latest letter. She tells him that she, their parents and the Pushkins have all come to the conclusion that his quest to learn new forms of dance in the West is a dangerous mistake. 'I'm afraid that you will lose yourself . . . Rudik, be careful! Those years in school and at the theatre: this was great work.' Leningrad, she says, is where he belongs – the place where he became a man, where people understand him and where his heart is. 'This is where you can completely open yourself up in terms of creation.' Anticipating his fears of reprisal, she tells him of a Georgian defector who returned to the Soviet Union to face no more than a community court hearing. More enticing still was her promise that if Rudolf came back, the Kirov would accept him into the company in exactly the same position, provided that he is contrite and admits that he was in the wrong. Rosa then urges Rudolf to contact Russia's ambassador in London, one Soldatov, in order to arrange the practicalities of his return – a suggestion that would immediately have alerted him to the fact that this was a letter written to order as 'Soldatov' was hardly a name his sister would have known. His suspicions were confirmed a week or so later by the arrival of a second warning from Teja, sent at great personal risk, just over a month after his Stasi interrogation.

> I couldn't write for a long time. I hope you understood that. In Russia everybody knows where and from whom I get correspondence. You probably received one letter from me, but there was no truth in it. Others I sent you didn't get to you: they were caught by our

government people. In one I wrote a lot of things which you can't say in this country, but I implore you not to tell that to anybody.

Black Cat [Tamara] and others are collecting all your photographs, etc. They've set up court procedures here – but without you.

I envy you, because the atmosphere here is terrible. Impossible. If you want to come back – it shouldn't be now. But I don't think you want to do such a stupid thing. If you ever call me, talk to me very carefully. They are listening to everything that I say . . . Berlin is closed now. It's very hard for us to go to Western Europe. But that's not a problem. First of all I have to complete my studies, and then we'll see what will happen . . . I've heard a lot here about your success. Xenia and Alexander Ivanovich will be very happy if you send a picture through the person who will give you this letter, and I will pass it on . . . In Leningrad everything stays the same. Soloviev has broken his leg but probably you've been told all this on the phone. The most important thing is that the government departments are not done with you yet; they want to capture you. If you want to come back, think carefully – the circumstances are not good.

Obviously, it was now impossible for Rudolf, the West's 'new revelation', seriously to consider returning home. January was the month when Paris was vibrant with what the *New Yorker*'s Janet Flanner called 'the kind of collective balletomania that used to seize upon the Diaghilev crowds on a great first night here'. And Rudolf was its cause. At the Théâtre des Champs-Élysées on 12 January, the Cannes quartet gave the first of two 'peculiar, pinch-hit galas', performing without costumes on an empty stage, yet people went wild, throwing flowers and shredding their playbills into confetti: 'I think to this day that was the most excited audience I've ever been in,' exclaimed the music critic of the *Boston Globe*. Writing with a great deal more enthusiasm than knowledge, both he and Janet Flanner focused their reviews entirely on Rudolf, referring only in passing to the other members of the ensemble. 'Everybody was only interested in Nureyev,' recalled Sonia Arova. 'I thought [Erik] . . . needed to talk about it or else he was going to make himself ill.'*

Just before the second evening Erik injured a tendon so badly that there was no question of his going on. Without a moment's hesitation

---

* A more balanced and informed appraisal appeared in *Dance & Dancers* which paid tribute to the striking qualities of all four performers but was crushingly dismissive of the choreography in the programme itself.

Rudolf volunteered to take over his roles – even the Bournonville duet, which he had observed in Paris but never danced.

> In the Bach Fugue I danced all parts. I was without stopping . . . in *Raymonda* I did all his coda and his part, and after came my *Don Quixote*. I just felt warmed up and went out and danced better! I didn't know the [*Flower Festival*] choreography and just three minutes before they show me what to do. I just changed costume and I went on; it was quite a risk. I made up what I couldn't remember. I wasn't very wrong! I enjoyed that. It was my first Bournonville ballet.

The quartet was due to disperse the following morning, since despite having received several offers to tour the programme, each of the dancers had decided that they wanted the freedom to work on their own. 'It was strictly for the experiment,' Erik told an interviewer. 'We could make a lot of money in concert work, but it would leave us all exhausted, and the artistic effect in the long run could not be as satisfying as working in a ballet company.' Sonia had a freelance engagement in New York, and Erik had planned to travel with her, as he was expected to appear in a televised duet from *Flower Festival* with Maria Tallchief. With Erik hardly able to walk, this was clearly out of the question, and a situation Rudolf was again quick to turn to his advantage. Making sure that he was awake before seven, he went downstairs to the hotel lobby to meet Sonia, and as they were saying goodbye, he remarked as casually as possible, 'If you can arrange it so that I can take Erik's place, it would be nice.'

Here was the perfect opportunity to make his US debut, particularly since a previous attempt had fallen through. At a dinner of Raymundo's in Paris, he had met Paul Szilard, who offered to act for him in America, only to discover that as yet there was no interest in Nureyev there. Negotiations for an earlier television project had come to nothing, and Rudolf wasn't even able to take up Balanchine's invitation to see the New York City Ballet in September, as he was unable to get a visa in time. Now, though, with recommendations from both Sonia and Maria as well as a promise from Erik to act as coach, the NBC executives agreed to let the young Russian be flown in as a replacement, and they pulled strings to fix the necessary immigration papers within days.

The excitement Rudolf felt at the prospect of going to New York was somewhat dampened by the ordeal of getting there. This journey, the longest time he had ever spent in the air, gave him his first real experience of the phobia that would haunt him all his life. 'I am used to flying, but . . . the fear grows.' Buffeted by atrocious weather conditions – 'they said one plane had crashed' – his flight was diverted to Chicago for three hours before the pilot made another attempt to reach New York. As they circled for an hour Rudolf had convinced himself, 'Well, soon we drop!' but when at last they landed, he found his nerves soothed by the smoothness of the arrival itself. 'Very beautiful, no custom difficulties . . . No journalists, very quiet, like real vacation.' Determined to see Martha Graham and her company perform that night, he went straight to the theatre from the airport, but felt too jet-lagged and disoriented to watch the whole programme. 'I saw the first ballet, and she had to appear three ballets later, and I get dizzy and I left. But what I saw I liked very much.'

Erik had arranged for them both to stay with his agent, Christopher Allan, a New York publicist who was famous for his all-night parties. 'Opera singers partnered ballet dancers, people sang and acted out scenes, and everyone had a ball.' While Erik and Chris Allan settled in at his East Seventy-second Street apartment 'for some heavy-duty drinking', Rudolf would take a cab across town to City Center every evening to see the New York City Ballet perform. Waiting at the stage door with his ticket was Balanchine's assistant, Barbara Horgan, who remembers how 'smitten' she and her colleagues were by the idea that Rudolf Nureyev should even consider joining their company. 'It was a big, big deal to have him around. *Nothing* like Rudolf had ever happened in our world.'

Even Alexandra Danilova, one-time star of the Ballets Russes and Balanchine's early muse, was enthralled to meet Rudolf when they came across each other at the theatre. He recognized her immediately. At school he had been shown photographs in secret of the early, poetic duets which Balanchine had created for Danilova, his partner and ex-schoolmate, before they and several other dancers left Russia for a tour in the West. And although, since giving up her stage career, the ballerina, now a teacher, had fallen on hard times, her imperious carriage, showy jewellery, and large, heavily made-up eyes still projected an aura of old Maryinsky glamour.

I said, 'Ah, Nureyev!' And he said, 'Ah! Danilova!' Then I said, 'How do you do and how very exciting that you are here.' And I remember his first impression was, 'Oh, I don't like America. I don't like anything here.' And I said, 'Well, don't come to conclusions when you don't know. You are sort of under the Margot Fonteyn wing in London.

That's why. But we will see later when you come and dance.' And he
said, 'I don't want to dance in America. I don't like.' And so I said,
'Well, you will see it, how you will change.'

Intent on not appearing the wide-eyed émigré, Rudolf was adopting a deliberately misleading attitude. Having expected 'some monsters, building monsters', he had been delighted by New York, and was
even more taken by the dance he saw there, telling the Goslings when
he got back to London, 'I want to *feel* Balanchine. I want to *eat* it.' In
Russia he had been almost alone in appreciating the stark beauty of
Theme and Variations, which Teja had filmed in his absence, because he
understood at once that this was not a work devoid of feeling but a
'story of the body'. To him it represented exactly the kind of choreography he wanted to explore in the West: classical dancing, independent
of plot or design, which served the music so precisely that the timbre
of each instrument seemed visible in the steps.

Included in the repertory that week was *Apollo*, the only Balanchine
ballet Rudolf had seen staged in Russia; *Serenade*, the choreographer's
American debut, made in 1934 for students in his new school; and the
extraordinary *Agon*, in which Stravinsky's new twelve-tone style is
translated into a dance syntax distorted to new extremes of asymme-
try and expression. This was classicism made thrillingly new, just as the
performers themselves were not typical ballerinas but healthy, athletic, all-American girls, whose 'reach, get it, take it, go!' energy had a
force and reckless speed that exactly reflected the pulse and dynamism
of the city. Rudolf found the dancers technically stronger than his
Kirov colleagues, and admired their long, sleek bodies – especially the
extra pull through the thigh that he had always striven for himself.
Their breadth and clarity of movement was as inspiring as their musicality, its phrasing so clear and detailed that, to the critic Edwin
Denby, a crescendo and decrescendo could be detected within the
thrust of a move.

Just as exhilarating was the freedom of expression Rudolf saw in
other New York companies. He 'went gaga over' Jerome Robbins's
Opus Jazz, and was intrigued by Alvin Ailey's *Revelations*, a modern
interpretation of the meanings and ecstasies of black hymns. 'I love the
Americans,' he would say years later. 'They have the liberty to create.
They are not oppressed by the European past.' And yet, at the same
time, Rudolf felt a certain equivocation about the work he was seeing,
finding it too abstract, too collective: 'Everything tends to neglect or
to overpower the individual dancer.' It is telling that he was talking

here of Robbins, not Balanchine, because the impersonality of the New York City Ballet style, with its imperative to keep '*self* out of the picture' was something Rudolf would never fully comprehend.

When Erik joined the New York City Ballet in 1959, Balanchine, uneasy about the dancer's star status, had made a point of telling him that he was interested only in the performer, not the person. To help adapt himself to this new approach, Erik turned to the discipline of Zen. 'I was still stuck with what I was . . . [and] tried to think in terms of "to be" rather than "I am." It was not Erik doing this or that step; I had to become that step.' Rudolf, however, had the feeling that Balanchine wanted to get to know him: 'To be close . . . to see what kind of man I was.' They met for the first time together with Alexandra Danilova in the Russian Tea Room, where Balanchine, a courteous, patrician man, was extremely friendly. As Maria had already observed, he and Rudolf were strikingly alike in many ways; quite apart from their passion for music, both were born pedagogues with the same religious devotion to their profession and a fierce contempt for any half measures. 'Why relax? . . . What are you saving yourself for? Do!' Balanchine would urge a dancer, adding with a Marvellian relish for *carpe diem*, 'Now is the time! Relax is for the grave, dear.' (A near echo of Rudolf's own endorsement of the present: 'If you look back, you fall downstairs.') But although Balanchine's interests were much wider-ranging than Rudolf's at that time (itemized by his first biographer as 'Braque, Pushkin, Eisenhower, Stravinsky, Jack Benny, Piero della Francesca, science fiction, TV Westerns, French sauces, and American ice creams'), over dinner that night he seemed willing to confine the conversation to their homeland. As they reminisced about Russian literature and Tchaikovsky's adaptations of Pushkin, Rudolf discovered small differences of taste in their choice of operas – 'I loved *Pique Dame*, his preference was *Eugene Onegin*.' And when Balanchine began talking about the Kirov, which had toured New York in December, he became more aware of disparities between their artistic ideas.

In reply to Rudolf's question about his view of the company, Balanchine, with characteristic directness, said that he found the style lacking in attack and much too heavy. Russian dancers have a tendency to settle back on their heels, to sit in *plié* before a jump or pirouette, whereas he had evolved a technique that projected the weight forward and upward with the least amount of visible preparation before each step. 'Balanchine wanted linkage, the steps linked to one another, the dancing linked to the music,' his male star Edward Villella has written. 'Imperial grandeur and posturing – posing – were passé, no longer a vital part of twentieth-century dancing.' In developing a modern American style of classicism, Balanchine had drawn on the Bournonville method, which he studied while on tour with his company in Copenhagen by watching children's classes at the Royal Danish school. Rudolf had instantly spotted the Danish influence on the NYCB style, but although he envied the dancers' speed and brilliance, he nevertheless missed seeing the kind of smooth, legato work in which he had been trained. 'He doesn't seem to go in for adagio,' Rudolf remarked when Nigel Gosling debriefed him on his return.

Balanchine, however, could tell immediately that Rudolf had just left a Russian company that was fifty years behind the times. To him, as Arlene Croce has written, adagio and allegro technique were not polarized but complementary, 'each partaking of virtues once thought exclusive to the other: fullness of volume in allegro, crispness of accent in adagio'. After thirty years in the United States, inspired by its open spaces, energy, and popular culture, Balanchine had embraced the American scene so wholeheartedly that his patriotism was apparent even in the clothes he wore – his own elegant version of a Wild West dude's garb, with pearl-buttoned shirts and black string ties. For Rudolf, though, it was still too soon to 'put the "Russe" legend' completely behind him. The need to retain the purity of his Kirov schooling remained a sacred obligation, and he was not yet convinced that any other company in the world could give him the same quality of teaching and discipline. Not only that, but the letters he was receiving from home had taken effect, making him long to see his family and friends. When he mentioned that he was thinking of returning to Russia, Danilova pounded the table. 'You must not!' she cried. 'They'll throw you in jail . . . [then] what kind of a dancer will you be?' Rudolf just shrugged. 'I do what I must do. But I do not know now what that will be.'

His immediate priority was to perfect his Bournonville technique for the 19 January broadcast of the *Flower Festival* duet. The remaining days were spent in a studio rehearsing with Erik and Maria with none of the tensions of Copenhagen – 'We were too busy working.' The only setback was the order Rudolf received from the conservative sponsors of the *Bell Telephone Hour* to get his hair cut. As far as he was concerned, this was out of the question. When he appeared in his debut solo in London, it was his unusually long, flying hair – 'both an expression of his individuality and a harbinger of the rebel era to come' – that had contributed so dramatically to the impact he made. He now realized that the 'frightful yellow disintegrating wig' he had insisted on wearing for the pas de deux had been a mistake – 'Everyone was saying "pity about the wig"' – and he had seen for himself in the German TV extract from *Giselle* just how unattractive a bad wig could be. For his upcoming London performance he wanted to base his appearance on the famous portrait of Nijinsky looking like a great silent-movie star, his head tilted to show his swan neck, his long tousled hair – a wig he had deliberately 'ruffled up' – curling on to his collar. But to NBC Rudolf was forced to give way when word came back that another dancer would be found to replace him. 'Ordinarily he would never have consented,' said Maria. 'But he desperately wanted to appear on American television . . . so he let me take him to a barber. He gave the man directions for every snip.'

When Rudolf makes his entrance in the nine-minute television broadcast, we see that his hair is not exactly short, but so brilliantined against his head that it looks painted. His blue knee-breeches, white tights, and white shoes, designed to draw the eye to the choreography's clean, multiple beats, also emphasize the vast improvement in the finish of his own technique – the first really clear manifestation of Erik's influence. Rudolf has triumphantly mastered the elasticity of Danish style (the ballon he so noticeably lacked at the gala in November), as well as its clarity and crispness. By contrast, the Russian-trained Tallchief is conspicuously miscast as a Bournonville ballerina, being much too tall and expansive, her timing too languorous, her long feet lacking in precision, her flowing arms unnaturally coy in the foreshortened, Romantic lithograph poses. She admits that she felt ill at ease in the pas de deux (on pointe she is almost a head taller than Rudolf), but agrees that he was '*incredible*' in their performance. Transmitting the sheer joy of the *Flower Festival* dances – 'movement where your total being is involved' – his solos not only flaunt his new Danish correctness but fuse it with Russian height and breadth. His jumps are not just bouncy but huge, swinging and shaded with Vaganova *épaulement*, his landings softly plastic. In one of the most impressive film performances of his career, Rudolf made the nineteenth-century choreography seem newly minted and distinctively his own. As Alexander Bland remarked when he danced it later that year in London: 'This was not quite Danish, but it was something just as good.' With two thousand dollars in cash in his pocket, he left New York for London, knowing that he would be seen by millions of Americans – Balanchine among them.

As usual, back in London Rudolf went straight from the airport to a performance: the Ballet Rambert's *Giselle*, which was playing at a theatre in the suburbs. He was taken there by Colette Clark, as Margot, with whom he was again staying, had a social engagement that evening. Having arranged to meet for a late dinner at the Brompton Grill near the Panamanian Embassy, Margot invited Marie Rambert to join them, thinking that the dynamic, Polish-born director was someone bound to fascinate Rudolf. 'Rythmichka', as her Ballets Russes colleagues nicknamed her, had been Nijinsky's assistant during the creation of *Le Sacre du printemps* (employed by Diaghilev because of her training in Dalcroze's system of gymnastic rhythms), and in the 1920s founded the first English ballet company. Uniting tradition and experiment, the Ballet Rambert was considered 'the Tate to the Royal Ballet's National Gallery', its productions mounted with authenticity and impeccable period style. Asked by Nigel what he had thought of the company, Rudolf replied, 'I liked, yes, I liked,' and certainly he had been impressed by two of the dancers, telling Madame Rambert when they met, 'You have good hunt' (Hilarion the Huntsman, played by John Chesworth), and commenting on the neat feet and 'edible legs' of the Giselle, Lucette Aldous, whom he would choose twelve years later as his partner for his film of *Don Quixote*.

In Marie Rambert, a voraciously curious seventy-three-year-old, Rudolf had immediately spotted a kindred spirit – 'An extraordinary woman. Very large-minded. Such a life!' – although she for her part felt somewhat intimidated by him. 'Mim liked sweet, good, innocent people – not stars,' remarked Colette, who herself still felt ill at ease with Rudolf. Usually delightful company, quick minded, and perceptive about dance, Colette was extremely withdrawn that night, and remembers the dinner proving 'a total flop' as Rambert had decided to switch from speaking Russian to English, and Rudolf made it clear at that point that he was not interested in anyone except Fonteyn. 'He knew she was the important one.' Then, after what seemed an interminable length of time, Margot arrived – 'gorgeous and all sweetness and giggles' – and everyone relaxed.

While visiting the ballerina backstage after her performance in Monte Carlo earlier that winter, Rudolf had indirectly invited himself to the Panamanian Embassy for the duration of their *Giselle* rehearsals: 'He stood in my dressing room, looking like a little boy, and said, "Tell me. I must be in London long time . . . I cannot stay so long in hotel. What do you think I do?" ' He had clearly enjoyed the comforts of Thurloe Place, and, unintimidated by its formality, considered it 'not an embassy just a house'. On this second visit, however, it became apparent soon after his arrival that he was anxious about something, though reluctant to appear ungrateful to his hostess by revealing what it was. Finally he could contain himself no longer. 'I am like dying,' he told Margot. 'Four days I hear no music.' Distracted by its rhythms, she rarely played music at home, and for Rudolf this silence was strange and dispiriting. He was also finding it hard to accustom himself to traditional English cooking, although it was two weeks before he confessed to hating cold roast beef. Beef – preferably in the form of an entrecôte steak – had to be thick, blue and hot before he would eat it; when it arrived he would slice off a piece to see if it was rare enough, then test the temperature with his tongue – sometimes even his cheek. Only steak, he believed, could give him the extra stamina he needed onstage, and when Margot took him to meet her mother for the first time,* they heard him mutter disapprovingly when the food appeared, 'Chicken dinner, chicken performance.'

He was considerably more forthright in getting what he wanted during rehearsals. From the first day it became clear that Rudolf planned to make his Albrecht more important than Margot's Giselle – 'something of a jolt' to the company's *prima ballerina assoluta*, who had danced the role for twenty-five years and was accustomed to most of the limelight. But although radical to the English, the idea that the action of the ballet revolved not around the heroine but around her partner had been accepted in Russia since the thirties, when Leonid Lavrovsky conceived his Bolshoi production as a Pushkin-like drama of regeneration. (Shaken from his youthful philandering by the peasant girl's madness and death, Albrecht is transfigured by the tragedy into an acceptance of his betrayal and an awareness of a far more profound kind of love.) Margot's debut in the role at the age of sixteen had been opposite the almost comically self-promoting Robert Helpmann – 'If he was on the stage, no one was going to look at me, frankly' – an experience that had quickly taught her how to make her own presence

---

* Hilda Hookham, an archetypal stage mother, was known as BQ (Black Queen), a name most people in the ballet world associated with the fearsome protagonist of de Valois's ballet *Checkmate*, but which some say referred to her black-market activities during the war. 'If you wanted a pound of butter or a length of silk, you went to BQ – Queen of the Black Market.' Although she was hardly the comforting maternal type to whom Rudolf was drawn, he admired BQ's toughness, and the fact that she had devoted her life to her daughter's career. She was also unusually game for someone of her generation – 'You couldn't shock her; she'd just roll her black eyes,' according to Terence Benton – and once she had learned to cook steak to Rudolf's liking, he regularly stopped off for lunch at her rooftop studio a few paces from the company premises in Talgarth Road.

felt, and since then, she had come to expect her partners to defer to her way of doing things.

In London it was Frederick Ashton who acted as mediator, writing in the *Sunday Times*, 'This is a classical ballet where the two roles are of equal importance . . . there has been no loss of integrity on either side . . . There is harmony between the two protagonists.' And although the choreographer had revised the production with the help of Karsavina, he, too, had acquiesced in several changes and additions, including the *entrechat* sequence Rudolf had introduced at the Kirov, and a new ending in which Albrecht is left alone onstage as the curtain falls. 'It would have been absurd and lacking in imagination and tact to have attempted to squeeze Nureyev into a preconceived mould,' Ashton remarked. 'Fortunately for his future he is not above taking criticism . . . if he is convinced that it is better than what he has thought out for himself.'

The negotiating that had led to 'a fifty-fifty compromise' between the Kirov and Royal Ballet versions of *Giselle* was exactly the process of give-and-take through which the two stars achieved their own equilibrium. Each immediately sensing the other's intelligence, and realizing how much each could do for the other, they began to exchange ideas and experiment with different ways of doing steps, while discovering at the same time a deep mutual respect. 'She can accept me young and not experienced. Not just English politeness but real interest.' Visual proof of Margot's growing trust in her partner was witnessed by Nigel when he visited the studio one day and watched Rudolf hold the ballerina way above his head in a Soviet lift as she shrieked and giggled with delight, 'Put me down – it's much too high!' What had so impressed her was the intensity of Rudolf's involvement in his role, the extraordinary conviction that had also helped to win Ashton over: 'He is completely engaged in his part, and therefore the image is true.'

Once again Rudolf's model was Nijinsky – 'I study photographs of him whenever I can . . . I see in those photos that he is totally engulfed in his characterization. Incredible!' – but it was the teaching of Stanislavsky that had influenced them both. Although not part of the Vaganova school syllabus, the Stanislavsky method was second nature to Russian theatre people. 'It was there. We lived and breathed it,' says Rudolf's ex-classmate Gabriella Komleva. Guided by Diaghilev, Nijinsky had steeped himself in Romantic music, painting and literature in order to find the essence of the character, while Rudolf, who regarded Stanislavsky as 'one of the earliest of my teachers', alluded directly to the principle of 'Before Time' when he told Nigel, 'I could describe, for instance, exactly when I first met Giselle and how.'

The drama unfolding in the studio reached such an emotional pitch that onlookers felt they were watching a performance, not a rehearsal. 'I remember corps de ballet crying,' said Rudolf. 'Just standing there with their tears dripping.' In class, too, his level of commitment astonished the English dancers, especially Margot, who made a point of coming to watch and learn from him. 'Never had I seen each step practised with such exactitude and thoroughness. It was paradoxical that the young boy everyone thought so wild and spontaneous in his dancing cared desperately about technique.' Wanting to pass on his own knowledge to her – 'everything that I had learned about dancing at the Kirov' – he began teaching her Russian bravura skills. She was rehearsing *Swan Lake* at the time, and having more trouble than usual with the multiple *fouettés* of Act 3. 'Left arm is too back,' Rudolf remarked after watching her struggle through the sequence, suggesting that she also try the 'mechanic' of keeping both arms held out at the sides, and using the impetus of her shoulders to help her leg whip around. 'It did work and suddenly she could do those thirty-two *fouettés*!' David Blair, then the Royal Ballet's male lead, had, since Michael Somes's retirement the previous year, been cast opposite Margot in this and several other ballets. But although an excellent partner, handsome and virile, with a flamboyant technique and breezy charm, the thirty-year-old Blair had not brought out the best in her. Only too aware of this, Margot asked Rudolf if he would dance with her in *Swan Lake* later that season. To her surprise he did not agree immediately, telling her that he wanted to see the Royal Ballet's production before making up his mind.

With his London debut in *Giselle* just a couple of weeks away, Rudolf flew to Copenhagen to be reunited with Erik, and at the same time to take the opportunity to absorb further insights into the role. Regarded in the West as '*the* Albrecht', Erik had always maintained that age and experience had enabled him to give a more complete portrayal of the character – 'In a more mature state, one has more imagination as to what a youth would do.' And his conviction that 'without an idea behind it, the movement will not communicate' had sanctioned Rudolf's own belief that there must be a reason for each step and gesture. 'Without this it could have no truth – otherwise it is immediately seen by audience and everybody that it's wrong.' Burdened by family pressures, however, Erik was in no mood to lend his support.

'Forgive me if I did not help enough,' he wrote later. 'I hate to see you upset, it hurts you, and it hurts me.' It was he who needed stimulus from Rudolf, not the other way round; for more than two years, he had felt jaded and purposeless, no longer able to use his dancing as an escape. '[But] I have seen a little glimpse of beauty and of love and I believe in it, I know it exists. . . . You have given me more hope and more belief in every way and beauty too.'

As they walked together by the lake in Gentofte, each experienced a sense of completeness – 'that kind of hypnotic, physical, deeply erotic love' – neither had found before. And inevitably Rudolf's departure on the morning of 7 February left Erik feeling desolate. 'Now, as it is evening, I feel like I have a big empty hole inside me, which you fill up, when we are together . . . If you can, and will be able to wait for me, while I must be here, it will make my time here much easier. You are in my heart, on my mind and in every fibre of my body'.

He wrote again the following day.

My baby Rudik,

I do not know why I call you baby – you are not a 'baby' but not old either, still it sounds nice to me and it expresses something of me to you, which is good . . . I look at the telephone, wanting it to call me to hear your voice and to tell you that . . . to be with you this moment would mean more than anything, than this present world could offer me . . . You are the secret of my life, a secret that will show itself freely . . . a paradox but so true.

On 23 June Rudolf, having promised Margot that he would be back in time to see her *Swan Lake*, sat in Ninette de Valois's box to watch the performance. 'I suddenly see extraordinary thing . . . when Prince meets Odette they have a mime . . . they start gesticulating. It was a great shock to me.' He had been just as dismayed during a general rehearsal of *Giselle* to discover that the Royal Ballet retained the long mimed monologue by Berthe, the heroine's mother, which recounts in traditional gestures the Slavic legend of the Wilis – the pitiless ghosts of jilted girls who rise from their graves at midnight and dance any man they encounter to his death. Basically outlining the background to the plot of Act 2, this long sequence, though part of the original libretto and strangely chilling if well performed, not only interrupts the flow of the dance but virtually brings Act 1 to a halt. 'In some theatres in south of Russia we have also . . . I find it isn't necessary at all.' Like Odette's narration of the plight of the bewitched swan-maidens now bothering Rudolf, these passages had been omitted by the Kirov because they were of no interest to audiences, most of whom knew the story already. 'In the West they use old mime . . . In Russia they had it also, but they forget it after the big influence of Stanislavsky,' Rudolf told Clive Barnes who, in a long piece criticizing the Royal Ballet's *Giselle* the previous year, had already commented on the fact that the Russians and Danes had abandoned 'the stilted Maryinsky style of mime we guard so zealously'.

Western classical repertory had been based on notated scores smuggled out of Russia in 1918 by the Imperial Ballet's chief *régisseur*, Nicholas Sergeyev, a pupil of Petipa and Ivanov. He was an impoverished émigré living in 1930s Paris, 'a lonely little man with his great volumes', when de Valois invited him to London to mount the Maryinsky classics for her company. The music-based notation from which Sergeyev worked – in some cases just rough floor plans – give only an approximate idea of steps, leaving out important gestures and upper-body nuances, and, as a consequence, certain solos have become mechanical. Nevertheless the Royal Ballet's *Swan Lake* was as close as it is possible to get to the original production – a fault, not a virtue, as far as Rudolf was concerned. 'There had been a revolution in Russian dance since Sergeyev came to England to show that version.'

Though held in great esteem in the West, Nicholas Sergeyev had long been discredited in Russia. To dissidents such as Michel Fokine, who left the company to join Diaghilev's community of artists, the Sergeyev regime was stagnant, authoritarian and hostile to change. A brilliant choreographer whose ideas were as revolutionary and influential as those of the French theoretician Jean-Georges Noverre a century earlier, Fokine wanted to rid the art of its tired formulaic combinations, and in a famous letter to *The Times* outlined his principles for reform: freedom of choice for subject matter, music and costume; the expressive use of the whole body; and the elimination of set mime. At school in Leningrad, Rudolf had devoured Fokine's writings on dance, applauding these and other innovations (especially the promotion of the male dancer from *porteur* to the ballerina's equal). Consequently, when he saw *The Firebird* for the first time at Covent Garden, he could hardly believe that this was the work of the same man. 'Fokine said . . . he fight against pantomime [but] plenty silly pantomime all through the performance. I was horrified.'

Rudolf belonged to the generation that had not only benefited from Fokine's 'new ballet' (his Isadora-inspired, non-balletic plasticity was the foundation of Vaganova teaching) but was also familiar with more radical advances in choreography. Taking anti-classical experiments even further, Nijinsky's 1912 *L'Après-midi d'un faune* was truly archaic, its meaning compressed into austerely angular, ritualistic forms. This was modernism at its most uncompromising – 'a revolution in dance', as Rudolf said – as well as a complete denial of Imperial Ballet virtuosity and personality. At the same time, taught even from his Ufa days that Petipa was the 'king of ballets', Rudolf still regarded the Maryinsky classics as his true heritage. These were works he felt should be preserved but not embalmed – dancers' techniques and physiques having changed so dramatically over the century.

> For example, they had long tutu and long low arabesque . . . and they had pretty arms and just some headdress and jewellery and they didn't need to dance so much, to do so many steps. [Then] they became more slim and . . . dancing and choreography had to be changed – actually not choreography – but way of doing those steps to bring them more alive, and mime and everything clarified and renewed from generation to generation.

This was Diaghilev's attitude, too. Commissioning Nicholas Sergeyev to stage *The Sleeping Princess* for his company in 1921, the impresario lifted numbers from different Petipa ballets and ordered others to be rechoreographed while still preserving the master's basic style and steps. Rudolf admired Erik for taking similar liberties with the Bournonville repertory, making changes that communicate to a modern public. 'I simply draw from the original source, from where I feel the life is,' Erik explained. In the English classical repertory, however, Rudolf saw no such development. 'They terribly happy that they have that dead body – they think it will last for a long time, but it doesn't.'

He made up his mind that if he was going to appear in the Royal Ballet's *Swan Lake*, there would have to be significant improvements. And while he had been genuinely impressed by Margot's Odette/Odile, he was not prepared to stand to one side while she plaintively mimed her story. 'I came to her, and I said, "Well you were so beautiful and . . . you did mime so well, but I couldn't find place for myself. I can't do that performance. I'll destroy it."' Looking him straight in the eye, Margot replied amiably, 'Just you try.'

In conversations with Nigel Gosling, Rudolf could not be held back from airing his views on the classics:

'For me it's very funny. You have a kind of theatre like Old Vic or Stratford and you have very old and experienced players and I am sure they
don't go like they were playing in Shakespeare's time, quite modern in
construction and decor and everything and everybody accept it. And
when it comes to ballet you have that old version – it's dead . . .'

'What about period feeling in *Giselle*?'

'I don't care really. It have to be for me not in period but in spirit.'

The two were then spending a lot of time together at Victoria Road
carrying out the interviews for Rudolf's autobiography. While in
Paris, a week after meeting the Goslings, he had told the publishers
Opera Mundi that he would not allow them to go ahead with the book
they had commissioned unless 'that Englishman' was brought in to
rewrite it:

> I just really emptied myself totally. And when I read it I was *horrified*.
> And many things were misunderstood or made on purpose more
> clumsy. Then somebody from *Sunday Times* and he with his very anti-
> Soviet sentiments coloured into such venom . . . I practically fainted.
> And finally I met Nigel and he made it more palatable.

One sentence that had baffled him was, 'I leapt to freedom with a
knife in my hand,' and when the Goslings explained what this meant,
Rudolf muttered contemptuously, 'I did not leap anywhere – I
walked.' He hated the way the press had sensationalized his life, and
was determined to be taken seriously – as Nigel immediately understood. 'He wanted to work as a dancer and be judged as a dancer, an
artist for whom the present and the future were more important than
the past.'

They would sit together by the large drawing-room window, Rudolf
in a low, dusty pink velvet chair, Nigel perched on the window seat
with a tape recorder (which he had great difficulty operating). The
microphone's hurricane of interference combined with Rudolf's
thickly accented, idiosyncratic English makes some passages virtually
unintelligible. (His description of Hamburg's 'lakes and rivers' was
first heard by Nigel as 'Legs & Ringwort'.) Gradually Rudolf's solemn,
monosyllabic replies become more playful and insinuating. Asked if he
had any adventures on his first trip to London, he giggles, 'Well even if
I do have I don't say it. I intend to be abstract.' And he is, summarizing
events after Hamburg as 'pages of private life'. When things begin to

flag, Nigel reduced to asking, 'Do you like ships?' and sighing, 'Well, that's Hamburg,' the conversation moves to Cannes. With another adolescent giggle, Rudolf throws in a surprise aside, saying that he 'caught, probably, a tart' in a South of France bathhouse, adding enigmatically, 'I got caught I think too.' Nigel chuckles. 'You went there privately?' 'Yes. Between performances. For five days.' Still chuckling, and hardly missing a beat, he goes on to ask Rudolf about Rosella Hightower's Cannes studio.

Nigel's unshockability was to prove a vital part of their bond. His 'riotous' year in Isherwood's Berlin, like his apprenticeship in Roy de Maistre's studio, had given him insider access to the louche, alternative world of artists such as Francis Bacon, his 'beautiful pansy-shaped face, sometimes with too much lipstick'. And while completely at ease in homosexual company, he was detached enough to be gently satirical at times, depicting, for example, a camp and gushing ballet conversation in his novel. '"My dear, you simply must see Gilpinsky; he's divine." "Yes, I always say he's got the nicest bum in the ballet. And his *rez-de-chausées* are impeccable."'* It was this mixture of bawdiness and seriousness, of irreverence and kindness that made Nigel so immensely likeable; his friend Terence Kilmartin remarked that he was so innocent of the usual resentments, snobberies, aggressions and neuroses that 'one was tempted to regard him as a sort of saint.' To Rudolf he was like Francis of Assisi, his ability to find a language compatible with those around him being so all-embracing that he 'could even talk to the birds and the beasts'. 'Nigel was the only person who seemed to understand what he was trying to say,' remarked Maude, 'because . . . he doesn't like to open his ideas too much. They're inside him, but to externalize them is not easy for him.'

Their empathy was enhanced by the fact that Nigel understood what Rudolf was talking about. He had been an early champion of Balanchine (unlike the majority of English critics), and had even encountered Nicholas Sergeyev, whose classes he took for two years in London. Although intellectually Rudolf's superior, he created an atmosphere in which the dancer felt he could talk freely and on equal terms, making the process of writing a true collaboration. Conceding to Rudolf's greater knowledge of Russia and its artistic heritage, Nigel

---

* This is not, as it may seem, a joke at the expense of the English dancer John Gilpin (who would have been only seven years old at the time) but self-mockery of the hero, Richard Gilpin, who is trying to amuse the girl he is pursuing. *'Rez-de-chaussée'* (French for 'ground floor') in this instance is a nonsense pun on the sliding step, chassé.

gladly incorporated his changes and elisions. Chapters in a final draft, filed in a torn cardboard folder marked 'Nureyev His Corrections', display their workings side by side: Rudolf's emphatic, often misspelled scrawl three times the size of Nigel's exact, scholarly hand. They also colluded in fictionalizing certain incidents, one being the telephone call Vera Volkova received from London the previous autumn. Instead of it being Colette Clark who calls to enquire about the possibility of Rudolf participating in the RAD gala, a conversation is staged between the two stars themselves: 'I knew nobody in England. Who could it be? It was a small, composed voice – nothing imposing. But the name made me jump. "It's Margot Fonteyn here. Would you dance in my gala in London? It's to be in October, at Drury Lane."'

Ignoring the incorrect date (which should be November), Rudolf has crossed out one sentence so vigorously that his blue ballpoint has almost sliced through the flimsy carbon paper. He was 'sertanly not', as he wrote and underlined in the margin, startled by the mention of the famous ballerina's name. He had no intention of being portrayed as an *ingénu* when he was about to prove himself her peer.

It was 21 February 1962: the date everyone in London's ballet world had been waiting for – at least, those lucky enough to have tickets for this, the first Fonteyn/Nureyev *Giselle*. (Seventy thousand applications were turned down.) 'Not even the queen could get in,' bragged a clerk in the Opera House box office, while the ticket touts outside were demanding £25 for a 37s.6d seat. As the curtain rose on Act 1 there was a wave of excitement in the auditorium. When Rudolf appeared, the standees at the back of the orchestra 'moved as one body forward', but this was not the flamboyant star the London audience was expecting. 'He came on stealthily,' remembered Maude. 'He didn't come on and say, "Here I am. Look at me. He wasn't aware of the audience. He was right into his role."' In their combined *Observer* review the Goslings dwelled on the way Rudolf did not actively project emotion but drew the audience into the world they were creating onstage. '(This is Ulanova's style) . . . the true sign of a great artist greatly taught.'

The element of nobility missing in the first Kirov performances was unmistakable that night, not only in his general bearing and the mannered elegance of his hands, but expressed in occasional telling gestures, like the way he kept pulling down his rough jerkin as if ill at ease in his peasant disguise. And yet, unlike the 'playboy' of Erik's interpretation, or the 'complete cad' then standard in Russia, this was not a worldly aristocrat dallying with a pretty country girl but the same intense, infatuated youth of Rudolf's Russian debut. Even when Albrecht's guilt was disclosed, he seemed immature and impulsive rather than insincere, his betrayal motivated by no more than what the Alexander Bland review defined as post-adolescent instability. 'It is the James Dean charm of a boy who will always be in trouble and always forgiven.'

Responding to his ecstatic displays of love, Fonteyn seemed to recapture much of the youthful *esprit* she had been lacking for many years. 'The Giselle she gave that night with Nureyev was different,' wrote Clive Barnes. 'More rhapsodic, more intense.' Rudolf, too, was more engaged than before; no longer diverting attention to himself by capriciously adopting an inert mask during Giselle's Ophelia-like display of madness. (Even Erik – the paragon of dramatic restraint – had verged on the histrionic at this point, his performance described by Barnes as 'the real thing, stark and raving'.) But while still leaving it to the audience to imagine the full extent of his grief, Rudolf now disclosed his horror in 'one sudden glance'. To Tamara Karsavina, who was in the audience, this kind of naturalism was far too small-scale to register onstage.

> I wonder if it was not the present tendency of the Russian Ballet towards elimination of mime gestures out of dramatic scenes which may have influenced Nureyev to be sparing of gesture. It seems to me that he missed the great opportunity of expressing grief and contrition at Giselle's grave in emotional gestures; Nijinsky's acting of the scene was more poignant.

Certainly Rudolf's underplaying was at odds with the rhetorical bombast and semaphore mime favoured by the Royal Ballet, which, as Barnes pointed out, appeared to be taking part in an English melodrama while he was playing Chekhov. 'Here one would ultimately concede that everyone was out of step except Nureyev.' In the second act, a nocturnal reverie, there was no such disparity. On the contrary, the two dancers' symmetry of line was so remarkable that, as Ninette de Valois remarked, 'You couldn't believe they both hadn't sprung from the same school.' They seemed to hear the music in the same way, their instinct for filling out a phrase to their fingertips quite uncanny in its simultaneity. It was as if one were the other's shadow or mirrored reflection – 'two ends meeting together and making a whole'.

New elements introduced by Rudolf were also perfectly integrated; there was nothing gratuitously showy about the Russian lifts; they intensified the slow-motion, vaporous effects of the second act, making the incorporeal Giselle seem prevented from floating away only by the restraint of her partner's hands about her waist. Inspired by Rudolf, Margot had so totally immersed herself in the drama that the audience was hardly aware they were acting. Danced to the point of death by the vengeful wraiths, Rudolf lay in a state of collapse, his chest heaving with exhaustion, sweat polishing and highlighting the Slavic contours of his face. Gazing down at him for a long time as if transfixed by his beauty, Margot then half-swooned when he recovered, and he carried her forward, his face brushing against hers. At the climax, when she cradled his head in her arms, a quick intake of breath was heard throughout the house.

When the curtain came down there was no applause for what seemed a minute. No one could quite believe what they had just seen: the icon of English ballet paired with a boy half her age, not the usual courtly *danseur noble* but an independent force who, with his huge personality and loping runs, seemed thrillingly alien and yet in perfect accord with Fonteyn. 'My husband called it a celestial accident,' Maude said. 'To probe into its components is like trying to analyse a moonbeam.' And despite her 'practical, unmoonshiny qualities', de Valois agreed. 'Emotionally, technically, physically – in every way. They were just meant to meet on this earth and dance together.'

When the two stars took the first of twenty-three curtain calls together, 'all hell broke loose.' Pulling a red rose from the bouquet (sent by her husband), Margot gave it to Rudolf, who impulsively sank to one knee and covered her hand with kisses. This sudden gesture has become as legendary as their actual performance, the *Dancing Times* writing that it was the herald of a new era in ballet. Clive Barnes, with equal prescience, described it as the kind of act typical of a star capable of changing the public's attitude towards an art form: 'It has happened in opera with Maria Callas . . . possibly it happened with Nijinsky. A single personality who catches the public's imagination.'

To Margot it was only Rudolf's way of expressing his feelings without resorting to standard social phrases like 'Thank you for your help,' which seemed to strike him as stilted or false. Rudolf himself was bemused by the fuss. The tradition of what the French call *le baisemain* is alive to this day in Russia, where it remains a gesture of male esteem towards a woman (he had instinctively kissed Yvette Chauviré's hand on first meeting her). By the second performance, the dancers had clearly rehearsed and toned down the culminating moment of their curtain calls; this time it was Margot who curtsied low to Rudolf and presented her hand to be ceremoniously kissed. 'It is more effective than the impulsive prototype, but it was somehow right that the first performance should have just one unique flourish to it that was never to be repeated.'

The critics agreed that although Fonteyn had surpassed herself – 'brilliantly, wonderfully, surprisingly', as Clive Barnes said – it was Nureyev's night. They commented on how much more polished his technique had become, praising in particular his glittering series of *entrechats*. Interviewed on BBC radio, Karsavina spoke of his unusual ability to accelerate or decelerate his pirouettes in absolute accord with the rhythm, and also drew attention to the rare elegance of his line. The feminine aspects of his movements, the hallmark high *retirés* and attitudes 'tending upwards', as Karsavina put it, came as a complete surprise to Londoners accustomed to 'those sturdy and violently masculine' Soviet males. From the moment he walked slowly on to the stage in Act 2, his long cloak flowing behind him, an armful of white lilies held to frame his face, Rudolf was in his element – an embodiment of the Romantic image, 'all lilies and languors'. 'The entrance was so beautiful that people were practically in tears, some of them, before he started the dancing,' said Maude.

But if Rudolf had modelled his androgynous, poetic look on Nijinsky, their interpretation of the character could not have been more different. Drawing on Alexander Blok's lyrical drama *The Stranger*, Nijinsky's Albrecht was a hero in search of an unattainable feminine ideal; Giselle to him – for all Karsavina's resistance – was an abstract symbol, an alienated embodiment of his own spiritual discord. For Erik, too, these wraiths, the Wilis, were figments of Albrecht's mind – 'all the things we are afraid of, that we have tried to escape.' Rudolf, on the other hand, transformed Théophile Gautier's libretto into one of the great love stories. By portraying the doomed passion of a beautiful youth for an older woman, this Giselle and Albrecht aligned themselves with the more celebrated couples of nineteenth-century French literature – Stendhal's Mme de Renal and Julien, Benjamin Constant's Ellénore and Adolphe, Flaubert's Madame Bovary and Léon. The mutual tenderness and poignant contrast in age had been there in the Kirov performances with Alla Shelest, but now there was a difference: Rudolf understood the meaning of romantic love.

In the film of the Fonteyn–Nureyev *Giselle* made three months later, we see to an almost voyeuristic degree the extraordinary sensuality

Rudolf brought to the performance. The moment, for instance, when he tries to recapture the shape, feel, smell of Margot's hand, holding his own hands against his face with eyes closed and lips half-parted; or the erotic frisson, almost too subtle to catch, as she watches him lie panting on his back, his hand stroking down his chest and hovering for a fraction of a second above the swell in his 'so-white, so-tight' tights. 'What we were watching was a kind of seduction,' remarked the writer Brian Masters. 'She responded to his *advances* – which is what they were – with a tremendous quiver of excitement which we all felt in the theatre'.

In fact, all Rudolf was doing was inhabiting his role to the full, acting out the Stanislavskian principles of 'Emotion Memory' and the 'Dramatic I' with complete conviction. 'I was Albrecht, and Albrecht was in love with Giselle; on the stage I was seeing her with the eyes of a lover.' From that evening on, however, audiences would interpret the ardour they saw in Rudolf as the 'Real I', believing in a real-life, offstage romance. So would Margot, who sensed 'a strange attachment' forming between them, despite the fact that she knew he was 'desperately in love with someone else at the time'. Even Erik, who had stood in the wings watching their performance, found himself overwhelmed by a confusion of private emotions and professional rivalry. 'He stare. He stare . . . He just couldn't understand that kind of success and why it should be.' And instead of waiting for Rudolf, he fled from the theatre. 'I was running after him and fans were running after me. It was a mess.'

9 THE BEATNIK AND THE PRINCE

There was nobody missing that night, Saturday 10 March 1962. Word had spread quickly of the 'Dream Duo', whose *Giselle* – 'the success of the century' – had made a paragraph in *Time*. And even though Rudolf's US stage debut was taking place not in Manhattan but at the Brooklyn Academy of Music (BAM), it seemed as if the entire dance population of the city crossed the East River to see him. His sole appearance, lasting only ten minutes, was in the *Don Quixote* duet (included on a Chicago Opera Ballet mixed bill), but as one critic put it, '*Le tout New York* was there, Brooklyn or no Brooklyn.' Richard Avedon, who had taken a party of friends including Gloria Vanderbilt and Leonard Bernstein, sat at the very front of the auditorium. 'You looked around and saw the oldest dancers, the youngest dancers . . . and thought, "Oh my God, this is it!"' A few rows back, beside Alexandra Danilova, was Balanchine – the only person Rudolf had come to America to impress.

He entered with authority, performing the adagio with a quiet, self-effacing dignity, admirably attentive to his ballerina, Sonia Arova. The audience watched intently but impatiently, their excitement rising with the crescendoing drum roll of the climax: it was his solo they were waiting for. At last the dancer took up his starting position at the back of the stage, and with his first double cabriole came 'an audible sigh of relief and pleasure'. Avedon saw the conductor cross himself. 'As the baton went down, Nureyev went up. My memory of it is he simply rose; you never felt there was preparation for it.' The ovation that followed Rudolf's final flourish – 'a veritable Niagara roar' – modulated into an insistent rhythmic pounding until he repeated the variation, when it exploded into a tumult of whistling and shouting.

A number of dancers and celebrities came backstage afterwards to meet and congratulate the new star. But not Balanchine. Having no plans for the rest of the evening, Rudolf had gladly accepted Avedon's invitation to supper, but decided to go first to the opening-night party in the hope of seeing the choreographer there. On entering the room, he was instantly surrounded by admirers, several of them White Russian émigrés anxious to talk about the motherland. Rudolf ignored them. 'I like when I am in America to meet American people . . . I didn't stay for Russians to cry about Russia.' There was no sign of Balanchine. When Anatole Chujoy, the editor of *Dance News*, led him aside to conduct a short interview, he took the opportunity to address the choreographer indirectly. 'Mr Balanchine's ballets are a new field for me, very different from the field where I work now, and I should like to know it better. It would be perfect for me if Mr Balanchine would accept my working with the Royal Ballet part of the year and with the New York City Ballet part of the year.'

It was well after midnight when Rudolf took a taxi to Avedon's Park Avenue apartment. Most of the other guests had already gone home, but he found his host sitting in the kitchen talking to film director Sidney Lumet. 'When Rudi walked in, he said almost immediately, "Can you find out what he thought?"' Offering to make Rudolf scrambled eggs, Avedon said that he didn't know Balanchine well enough to call him himself, but would ask a mutual friend. 'It was left in the air.'

Balanchine, Rudolf had decided, was the only choreographer in the world who could use him to the full measure of his talent. His first collaboration with Ashton had been a disappointment; he found the Scriabin solo derivative – 'It wasn't his idea. It was the idea of Isadora Duncan' – and even trite. 'Run forward and throw yourself at the mercy of the West!' Certainly Ashton, inhibited by the fact that Rudolf knew more about classical schooling than he did, had been far too accommodating with him, admitting, 'He made very good suggestions which I promptly adopted.' Rudolf would soon learn to appreciate Ashton's genius – in his words, 'a magician of theatre, of dance' – but what he sought at this point was a master. He craved new roles, in particular the kind of repertory that Fokine had tailor-made for Nijinsky. The choreographer had interpreted the dancer's quiddity – his unconventional appearance and aura of strangely barbaric, *fin-de-siècle* perversity in early works like *Cléopâtre* and *Schéhérazade*; his androgynous Romanticism and expressive use of the whole body in *Chopiniana* and *Le Spectre de la rose*. 'It was a great fortune for him to have Fokine,' Rudolf told Margot. 'Who find way to have this jewel surrounded by setting.' And to Clive Barnes he made the same point. 'Fokine discovered those peculiar talents of Nijinsky and he creates the real Nijinsky, and discovers, sees his potential: because of Fokine, Nijinsky blossoms and blossoms to whatever he is.'

*

Women, not men, were Balanchine's inspiration. His muses, the ballerinas with whom he was in love, were as influential as Dora Maar and her predecessors were for Picasso. Talking softly of Fabergé and Van Cleef, and playing up his St Petersburg charm, Balanchine flirted constantly with the young women in the company, and for the most part ignored the men. 'We were all striving to be number one,' remarked his 'Prodigal Son', Edward Villella, 'but the men knew they could never be.' To Balanchine a woman's body was faster, more flexible and more musical than a man's. She was queen, he was consort, 'the accompaniment', 'only the second half'. And yet Rudolf was well aware of the glorious roles that Balanchine had made for male dancers: *Apollo* and *The Prodigal Son* (created on Diaghilev's orders for Serge Lifar), or the serpentine, acrobatic adagio in *Agon*, a duet of real equality.

Moreover, it was not only as a performer that Rudolf needed Balanchine. 'I wanted to learn everything I could from him – his choreography especially.' Again he envisaged the kind of collaboration Nijinsky had had with Fokine, whose great mind 'soaked . . . rubbed off' on the dancer, enabling him to build on his mentor's achievements while forging an extraordinarily innovative choreographic language of his own. And although not an intellectual, Balanchine was an artist of the magnitude of Mozart or Stravinsky, as well as what his friend W. H. Auden called 'something deeper, a man who understands everything'. His affiliation with Stravinsky was as monumental in the history of ballet as that of Tchaikovsky and Petipa a century before, Petipa being the master from whom Balanchine himself claimed descent. It was on the Russian classics that he modelled his own hierarchy of dancers – corps de ballet, female soloists and their cavaliers, principal couple – as well as basic structural devices that merge and separate ensembles in symmetrical lines and polyphonic patterns. In Balanchine's hands this nineteenth-century material is made completely new – filtered, accelerated, intensified, concentrated to embrace what Arlene Croce called 'physical and metaphysical, ethical, and aesthetic implications Marius Petipa never dreamed of'.

Having seen the original *Swan Lake* at the Maryinsky and remembering it lasting 'all night' with as much mime as dance, Balanchine distilled his own version into one act of only thirty-five minutes, while Petipa's *The Sleeping Beauty* was 'kind of foreshortened or telescoped' by him into *Theme and Variations*, the ballet that had so impressed Rudolf in Russia. Had Balanchine attempted to stage a full production of this classic (in his view a work of sheer genius, he told his amanuensis Solomon Volkov), he would not slavishly reproduce Petipa's work but would develop his own ideas, making additions and cuts where necessary, not abandoning the mime completely but making these sequences understandable to the public today.

> Ballet isn't a museum, where a painting can hang for a hundred or two hundred years. And even a painting needs to be cleaned once in a while. If it cracks, they restore it. But every museum has rooms where people don't stop, they just look in and say, 'Ah, it's boring in here, let's go on.' Ballet can't survive like that. If people are bored at the ballet, they'll stop buying tickets. And the theatre will simply disappear.

This, of course, was Rudolf's own view. 'The art must grow . . . Fokine modernized Petipa and Petipa modernized his predecessors. We can never stop . . . We must explore.' And it is why he had been so contemptuous of the Royal Ballet's 'dead body' of a repertory – their scrupulously faithful classical productions. But although in his opinion English ballet was 'not much more modern than what we have in Russia', this emphatically was not the case. On a mixed bill that season, for example, was Ashton's modern masterpiece *Scènes de ballet*, an abstract treatment of a Stravinsky score, excitingly innovative with its diverse tempi, shifting dynamics and contrapuntal rhythms, the music's tonal dissonance mirrored in an angular stylization of classical positions. Ashton's particular favourite among his ballets, it has what he called 'a cold, distant, uncompromising beauty', standing as a testimony of his personal extension of the classical style, its traditional idiom stamped with playful and poetic embellishments that make it quintessentially his own.

It is quite possible that Rudolf had not yet seen *Scènes de ballet* (Maude Gosling has no recollection of him talking about it), but it is equally possible that he saw it and dismissed it. Like *Theme and Variations*, it is an outright homage to *The Sleeping Beauty*, which had influenced Ashton much as it had Balanchine. *Beauty* was the Petipa ballet that, more than any other, epitomized the St Petersburg style. Balanchine had not only seen the original performed at the theatre for which it was created but had forged a living collaboration with Stravinsky – also a 'true Petersburger' – whose music repeatedly proclaims his lineage from Tchaikovsky. With no first-hand knowledge of this heritage, Ashton, in Rudolf's view, did not understand classical dance. 'He said, "Rudka, let me rehearse you, let me prepare you . . . you know in Russian school you learn it as it is not supposed to be," . . . and I said, "I have no courage, I just can't yet, let me do this year the way I learned from Pushkin, from Kirov, from Sergeyev . . . the way it was passed on."'

Balanchine, on the other hand, using his pure St Petersburg schooling as the basis for a continuous exploration of ballet, was exactly the teacher and mentor Rudolf sought; as Violette Verdy remarks, 'There was potentially a magical affinity between them.'

The following day, having heard nothing from Balanchine, Rudolf 'rather uncertainly' telephoned him. Although sounding very distant, the choreographer agreed that they should meet, suggesting Castellano, the bar and restaurant opposite New York City Ballet's old home on Fifty-fifth Street. When Rudolf arrived, he saw Balanchine sitting with his assistant, Barbara Horgan. 'The atmosphere was a bit constrained. I sensed he had not much enjoyed my performance.' Rudolf was right. As an audition piece for Balanchine he couldn't have picked anything worse. This 'old chestnut' duet represented exactly the nineteenth-century Soviet legacy he had been striving for years to eliminate – the virtuosic showpiece that always rouses the most applause. As for the excited fans themselves: 'Behind me were about twenty-five boys with red lips sitting and screaming, "God! Oh God!",' Balanchine told the writer Leon Harris. These were 'sensationalists' attracted by a superstar, the kind of audience Balanchine despised. To him they were reincarnations of the philistine Maryinsky balletomanes who would sit in the theatre smoking room discussing the scantily dressed figures of their favourites. This new public swooning at the young Russian's undeniable erotic force was in Balanchine's view a dismaying regression to the days when ballet was considered not an art but a form of titillation: 'Actually when you dance, there are no erotic impulses at all. Absolutely none! It's out of the question, completely! . . . The stage eliminates sex . . . It's pure technique.'

The change in Balanchine's manner was hard for Rudolf to understand. At the Russian Tea Room in January he had seemed so enthusiastic about the possibility of their working together. Finally, unable to contain himself any longer, Rudolf asked Balanchine outright if he would have him. 'Came out very bad.' 'You know I don't have pas de deux in my company, my ballets are very dry,' the choreographer told him. 'But I like them dry,' replied Rudolf. Which was true. Most Russians, not understanding the concept of abstraction, found the ballets lacking in 'soul'. ('It's not that he didn't care about the soul,' as Joan Acocella has written. 'He just thought that the soul was in the feet.') But while there is no doubting Rudolf's genuine appreciation of Balanchine's work, his grasp of the Balanchine aesthetic was almost nonexistent. It was the ballets themselves that the choreographer felt should draw the public, not the box-office appeal of a particular dancer. When Edward Villella, on tour in Russia in 1962, succumbed in desperation to the cries of 'Encore! Bis!' that followed twenty-two curtain calls, Balanchine snubbed him for days. Violette Verdy explains why:

> [Balanchine] does not compromise. He has a company which is very consistent in its policy – a sort of selflessness in which it's understood that everybody will dance at his best, but chiefly to serve the choreographer . . . As a dancer with Balanchine, it is your duty to show what extraordinary choreographic material we have in that company. A dancer cannot show himself off either at the expense of the ballet or of the rest of the company. Balanchine does not want to set that kind of example.

The Brooklyn performance had made it quite clear to Balanchine that Rudolf was already too much of a star to become part of the ensemble he had spent so long establishing. His presence would violently unbalance the proportions of the company, which in 1962 was a much more fragile institution than sixteen years later, when Mikhail Baryshnikov joined. 'It takes teamwork to win at polo or baseball. That's what we have and Rudi doesn't. He's a one-man show, "I, me, a beautiful man, alone." . . . Frankly, we don't need this.'

But frankly neither did Rudolf. He hadn't defected from Russia to be only 'small part of big machine', constantly chastised for failing to learn 'that the leading role is after all only part of the artistic whole'. The definition of New York City Ballet discipline – 'total cooperation – not to any individual ambition, but to the principle of a general humane alliance' – was the dictum of Communism. Balanchine's criticism of Rudolf was just a rephrasing of the Soviet charge against him of 'insubordination, nonassimilation and dangerous individualism'. How could someone with a mind as inquisitive as Rudolf's submit to a regime in which 'nothing was described or discussed'? He believed, just as Erik did, that only when a performer understands what he is doing does he become creative; that without an idea behind it, movement does not communicate. Balanchine did not want anyone analysing his part; his credo was 'Don't talk. Just do.' He would not have tolerated Rudolf's control of his own career, nor his crusade to raise the status of the male dancer. Balanchine dancers, as Villella has written, were all part of a preordained structure. 'No one was allowed to violate or disrupt it. Balanchine could clearly make his displeasure felt when some other dancer detracted from the Chosen ballerina. He chose who got the spotlight.'

It was for this reason that Erik had not remained a member of the New York City Ballet. 'Rudik always claimed . . . that I would do exactly what I wanted without regard to others,' Erik had said, and to Balanchine he was the epitome of the egocentric star. And although Erik had come to New York in 1959 at the choreographer's invitation, he was made to feel so ill at ease by Balanchine – 'the most destructive and negative relationship I have ever had' – that he left after spending less than three months there. 'He likes [Balanchine]. He admires him completely,' Rudolf told Nigel, 'but all those tricks he hates . . . And someone like Erik has something of their own to say. It's impossible.' Why, then, did Rudolf not see that the situation would be just as impossible for him? Balanchine, as Violette Verdy remarks, 'was the *only* one who could be a master for Rudi, but he was already becoming too much of a young master himself. Balanchine wasn't ready to make room for that . . . He didn't want someone polluting New York City Ballet with ideas other than his own.'

It was that evening at Castellano that Balanchine made his famous statement, 'When you are tired of playing at being a prince, come to me.' Barbara Horgan says that Balanchine was trying to explain to Rudolf that if he joined the New York City Ballet he would have to '*commit* to it,' in other words, give up the idea of dividing his time between London and New York.[*] Although NYCB dancers were not tied to formal contracts, there was an unwritten rule that if you danced between seasons with other companies, 'Mr Balanchine would not have you back.' He made exceptions, allowing Verdy, for example, to guest abroad. 'She probably gave him the impression that she really *wanted* to work with his company, really wanted a permanent repertory situation,' Horgan says. And Verdy was already a Balanchine dancer, whereas Rudolf would have to relearn how to dance. As a principal with the

---

[*] Danilova remembers Balanchine confirming this. 'The people always ask, "Why you didn't invite big star like Nureyev?" Mr B said, "All right. Presume I ask him. He will dance one ballet. Everybody will come in and see him. He goes, and people will say, 'He is gone. The ballet is nothing without him.'" And it shouldn't be like that. It would be different if he want to be *member* and learn all the parts like the others' (Quoted in David Daniel's interview for *Nureyev Observed*).

company, he would need to be taught several dozen new roles, roles that not only demanded knowledge of 'the higher mathematics of twentieth-century music' but were technically and stylistically completely different from anything he was used to. (Even Baryshnikov, in his first season with the New York City Ballet in 1978, was described by one critic as 'terrible'.)

Rudolf, as Balanchine was well aware, wanted to dance 'on circuit': his plan was to spend eight months of the year in London and two with Balanchine. 'Only two. Not long. Just for myself to learn the choreography.' This was deemed 'too selfish' by the choreographer, but from Rudolf's point of view it made sense. He could hardly think of giving up the partnership he had just established with Fonteyn, and however much he craved a modern repertory, he felt that it was more pressing to 'work up again' and perfect the classical roles he had learned in Russia.

> People don't seem to understand that I must first be seen in roles that I know – a prince in *Swan Lake*, a prince in *Sleeping Beauty*, a nobleman in *Giselle* – so that I can be seen to the best advantage. Once I have done this, I will not have to play at being a prince and can experiment with my career. Then to Balanchine.

But although in advising the dancer to go off and play his princes, Balanchine was telling him exactly what he wanted to hear, Rudolf still felt as if he had been spurned, telling the journalist Lynn Barber in 1990: 'So I go to Balanchine but he rejected me.' To study with Balanchine and with Erik Bruhn had been his two obsessions on arriving in the West; and the fact that the Erik goal had been so easily achieved made this seem even more of a failure – the first major setback of his career. Instead of examining the reasons, Rudolf looked for pretexts: 'There was some kind of black cat that ran between me and Balanchine for many years' . . . 'The rift, I think, began between us when an article about me appeared in a magazine. The writer who interviewed me put words into my mouth about why Balanchine didn't do ballets for men. I think Balanchine heard about that.'* 'The thing misfired. It was

---

* But the remark to which Rudolf is referring appeared nearly three years after his New York debut. In the *Sunday Times* of 27 December 1964, he is quoted as saying, 'I know at any rate that Balanchine – who is, after all, still the greatest modern choreographer – will never create a work for a man. He's never been interested in male dancers – he's tended to eliminate and even emasculate them.'

mishandled. I didn't really know how to go about it properly. He was probably annoyed by some idiotic letters he received about me. The press sent out stupid information. I think it was instigated by the de Cuevas company . . . they wanted a permanent contract. I said no. I will dance with you only for three months, because I want to go to Balanchine. So they sent bad publicity ahead' . . . 'I had some wrong people handling it.'

On the other hand Rudolf's intuition was right. There does appear to have been an element of conspiracy involved in the decision not to allow him to join the New York City Ballet – an obstructive force embodied in the towering figure of Lincoln Kirstein. Dance scholar, art critic, poet, patron, polemicist, Kirstein was not only a force in the cultural life of New York – 'the twentieth century's truest successor to Diaghilev' – but the man responsible for bringing Balanchine to the United States in 1933. The son of one of the owners of Boston's Filene's department store, he had, by providing financial support, helped make it possible for the choreographer's genius to evolve freely for thirty years. Although Balanchine alone formed the company aesthetic, created a school and honed sleek all-American girls into his modern muses, Kirstein, who had dedicated his life to the New York City Ballet and the School of American Ballet, was always there, a permanent spectator at rehearsals and performances, 'hustling, animating, inspiring, bullying, proselytising in the service of their great cause'.

Included in a lengthy, gossipy correspondence between Kirstein and the English ballet critic Richard Buckle is the following aside dated 18 April 1962: 'Master Nureyev is making peeeteeyous Russky noises about how I stopped Balanchine taking him. He wants six months with us and six with the Royal Ballet; think of our repertory and how much time he would give himself to learn it. No; Mrs K says defunutely: Nyet.'

Maria Tallchief was with Rudolf at City Center one night soon after his BAM debut when Kirstein came up to them in the lobby. Without any initial pleasantries he began furiously to berate Rudolf. 'Lincoln was outraged that he'd defected from Russia. It was very violent, and very shocking.' Enormously tall – in Christopher Isherwood's phrase, 'like Gulliver among the Lilliputians' – Kirstein not only looked physically threatening, with his glowering brows, hawk eyes and convict crop, but was known to be quite capable of losing control in public, once having got into a sudden fistfight with Lucian Freud on the way to the painter's favourite pub. The sheer force of his personality and intellectual intensity makes Maria certain that he helped sway Balanchine against taking Rudolf into the company: 'Absolutely. Lincoln was very vociferous.' Barbara Horgan disagrees: 'Absolutely not. He'd listen to Lincoln . . . but when it came to what happened onstage, Balanchine was the master. He did what he wanted to do.'

Kirstein, though, had always anticipated and seconded Balanchine's aims. It was by mutual agreement that there were to be no *Swan Lakes*, no *Giselles*, and no guest stars. For decades he had been railing in print against the star system, blasting at audiences seduced by the showstopping formulas of Russian ballet. Since his student days, Kirstein's 'life's breviary' had been Eliot's famous essay 'Tradition and the Individual Talent', which had helped form his own creed, that art is not the expression of personality but an escape from it. 'Hymns against the horror of unleashed egotism appear everywhere in the pages of Kirstein's anti-personal aesthetic,' his literary executor, Nicholas Jenkins, has written. As a prime example of 'picturesque, romantic, marketable narcissism', Rudolf was the natural target of his contempt. 'Rudi was so shaken. He couldn't believe it,' recalls Maria. He was even more taken aback a couple of weeks later when, in an article in the *New York Times*, he was lambasted again for leaving Russia – and, in effect, for being a star. Written by John Martin, then the most influential dance critic in America, the piece pours scorn on the frenzied reception at BAM – in Martin's phrase, 'an advanced manifestation of ephebolatry' (his pompous coinage for 'the cult of youth' – *ephebe* deriving from the ancient Greek word for 'early manhood'), which he saw seeping into all realms of art. 'It is a virus to which Mr Nureyev's resistance is weak; it has already seriously jeopardized and may actually have destroyed his career as an artist.'

Rudolf may not yet have known that John Martin was a confidant and ally of Lincoln Kirstein. In a letter of appreciation for what may have been financial support, Martin wrote to Kirstein, 'I wish I could tell you in words of one syllable as a parting gesture how deeply grateful I am to you for everything. But I know you don't want to hear it and I can't say it. I can say, however, that I love you very much.'

In the early years of New York City Ballet, Martin had, in fact, been actively hostile to the company (in a published diary he dedicated to the critic, Kirstein thanked him for this initial lack of support, explaining, 'Without your first notices and final confidence, we would never have been as stubborn, insistent or directed as we have been'). For the last decade, however, he had been New York City Ballet's prime champion. It was Martin whom Rudolf had met in Paris and quizzed 'to the point of unmannerliness' about Balanchine. Their conversation took place after a performance at le Palais des Sports – the occasion on which he had left the stage in the middle of his variation. Having described this 'shocking breach of theatrical responsibility' in his BAM review, Martin then linked it to the 'starry-eyed gullibility' he claimed had led to the downfall of an enormously gifted dancer:

> If he had had the sophistication to resist the blandishments of Paris . . . and behaved with more circumspection, he . . . would not have been picked up by the Soviet authorities to be sent back to Russia ahead of schedule. Day after day he was told by word of mouth and in print that he was the greatest dancer in the world and with his naïve wishful-mindedness he may well have believed it and blamed the Kirov for not having told him so . . . He has thrown himself to the lions.

Appearing after a unanimously positive press – one critic claiming that Rudolf had conquered New York 'as immediately and decisively as perhaps no other dancer has done since Margot Fonteyn' – Martin's attack was baffling, and not only to Rudolf. 'About John Martin's apparent antipathy to Rudy,' wrote a friend of Sonia Arova, 'everyone says in New York that he is influenced by political issues, so I don't think that it is too hard to understand.' Certainly, with his condemnation of Rudolf's 'appalling lack of discipline', his description of the defection as a 'tragic' mistake, Martin's tone is decidedly pro-Soviet. He had, in fact, been championing Russian ballet since 1956, when he spent two weeks in the Soviet Union – 'the two most fully lived weeks of my life'. In a long paean of praise published in the September issue of *Dance Magazine*, Martin called Leningrad the ballet capital of the world, and contrasted its great school and tradition with the lack of cultural background in American ballet, where 'they don't know anything except barre exercises.'

At the same time, without going into Stalinist history, he admitted in this essay that the Russian repertory was severely limited, explaining that its compulsory realism and ideologically acceptable themes were the result of a regime in which the arts had been controlled by nonartists, and cut off from all outside influences for more than forty years. The lack of finesse and subtlety in Soviet productions – 'the elements of Barnum and Bailey' and 'the last days of Pompeii' – he saw mirrored in the aesthetic coarseness and technical excesses of the dancing itself, especially that of the men, whose style he found blunt and unpolished. 'There is much refinement yet to be done,' he remarked, suggesting that the solution would be a cross-fertilization of the two dance cultures, 'which could well prove to be a revolution in the art as powerful as that caused by Fokine's insurgency in 1909'.

That, actually, was precisely the fusion Rudolf had already achieved. His awareness of the Soviet male's 'bulky and prosaic quality' (Martin's phrase), was what had led him to draw on the inspiration of Kirov ballerinas to refine his line and, on arriving in the West, immediately seek out the two exemplars of noble simplicity and purity of style from the Danish and English schools. Unchallenged by ballets like *Corsaire*, 'with its quaint complexities of plot and its lurid melodramatics' (Martin again), Rudolf had come to America to experience exactly what the critic had proposed Russians should do: get 'an eager eyeful of fresh aesthetic forms'. Why then denounce him for finding the Kirov old-fashioned, and for choosing to leave?

The reason was simple enough: Martin was protecting his own relations with the Soviets. Whatever his politics may have been, he was clearly exhilarated by the idea of acting as a kind of cultural bridge between Russia and the West, a position he would immediately forfeit were he to champion the young defector. Not only that, but at the time his piece appeared, negotiations were being carried out for New York City Ballet's first visit to Russia in which Martin himself was closely involved.

Arranged by the US Department of State in exchange for the Bolshoi's American season in September, this extended tour was due to take place that October – a particularly precarious time for diplomatic relations (in fact, the Moscow run in October coincided exactly with the Cuban missile crisis). The possibility of taking his company to Russia, where he had not been since 1924, had been on Balanchine's mind for several years. In a letter to Kirstein in 1955, Edwin Denby remarked: 'Moscow! mercy me, George would talk himself into jail. You'd want to send John Martin to take care of the official side.' It was not only that Martin had the connections (when he saw the Bolshoi for the first time in 1956, it was at a Kremlin state banquet in honour of Marshal Tito), he was indispensable to the company as a propagandist voice. As Kirstein himself later acknowledged, 'When you came with us to Russia in 1962 you sent back coverage justifying us on an international level as well as clarifying the return of Balanchine to Russia with its local effect. This was an historical service which no one else could have provided.'

With Rudolf as a member of the company, there could have been no question of a season in the Soviet Union. And yet, while Kirstein and

Martin almost certainly colluded in making sure the tour took place, as far as Balanchine was concerned this was not the issue. Much as he wanted to take his dancers to Russia, he also didn't want to make ballets for a male star. Having the New York City Ballet dominated by a brilliant young renegade would never have worked; Balanchine realized this immediately, but Rudolf was too bewitched by the choreographer's genius to admit it.

Back in London, Rudolf spent his first birthday in the West at Victoria Road with the Goslings, Erik, Margot and Frederick Ashton, 'very very happy' to be surrounded by the people he liked most. After dinner Nigel suggested they all go down to the basement, where he had set up a projector to watch a 1957 film about Martha Graham, *A Dancer's World*. 'Oh, I don't think Rudolf would be interested in that,' remarked Margot, to which Erik countered, 'Oh yes he would.' 'Erik was jealous of Margot,' his close friend Ray Barra says. 'He felt she was too much a part of Rudolf's life, and she didn't like him any more than he liked her.' As Maude recalls, Rudolf was tremendously excited by the film. 'He couldn't wait to meet Martha Graham and see more of her work.'

    This was the period when Erik had an almost total hold over Rudolf. For three months the two stars were in London, guesting with the Royal Ballet and living together in a rented flat in South Kensington. To the English dancers they made a stunningly glamorous couple – 'a Beatnik and a Prince', one critic called them – arriving for class every morning in Rudolf's new white Karmann-Ghia sports car (even though neither had a licence yet). As Erik's English was much better than Rudolf's, he found himself acting as go-between, often having to explain what Ninette de Valois had been trying to say to Rudolf. 'That became a bit tiring . . . I sometimes felt like a secretary.' The March issue of *Dancing Times* had featured Erik Bruhn as 'Personality of the Month', its photograph captioned 'And as for being the world's greatest male dancer – if he isn't, who is?' But the magazine had gone to press before Rudolf's *Giselle*, and since then, although Erik was making his debut with the Royal Ballet, Fleet Street had virtually ignored him. 'There was no sensation in the arrival of a modest and self-effacing Dane.' Guilty about the fact that his idol was being overlooked, and aware that the situation would worsen in May, when his autobiography was to be serialized in the *Observer*, Rudolf went out of his way to generate publicity for Erik. 'He was very considerate. That was enough for me. The rest I could not control.'

All the same, this was not a happy time for Erik. The partner he had been delegated was Nadia Nerina, a ballerina he had to 'learn to like'. Her triumph the previous year, guesting with the Bolshoi, had injected her dancing with real Russian aplomb – exploited wonderfully by Ashton in *La Fille mal gardée* – and after their scintillating performance in the *Don Quixote* duet in May, it looked as if Erik would prove the catalyst for Nerina that Nureyev had been for Fonteyn. Five weeks later, however, in their first *Swan Lake*, it was clear just how ill-matched they were. Nerina did not have the lyrical temperament for Odette and lacked an inner, musical rapport with Erik, that sixth sense that allows one dancer to intuit what the other is going to do. In the audience, Rudolf was distressed to see his idol dancing way below his usual standard, his low-key performance prompting one reviewer to remark that he seemed 'anxious to efface himself'. Why, Rudolf asked Sonia Arova, sitting beside him, did Erik not insist on another partner? 'It's Erik's fault,' he muttered. 'He won't put his foot down.'

When the two dancers began to prepare *Giselle*, Rudolf came to every rehearsal until Nerina, noticing the extent to which Erik was unsettled by his presence, refused to continue unless Rudolf left the studio. Somewhat sheepishly, he did, but remained outside the closed door, watching through the glass. Oppressed by Rudolf's burning insistence on analysing every gesture, Erik was losing confidence in himself, astounding his ballerina one day by confessing that he was not a classical dancer. He had reached this state of crisis before, while working under great pressure with Vera Volkova. 'It got to a point where I couldn't move . . . and it finally dawned on me that I was *thinking* too much.' Sonia, who was living in a flat nearby and often had dinner with the couple, tried to ease the tension, saying, 'You are two of the most fabulous dancers there are, and there shouldn't be this thing disturbing either one of you.' But to Erik it felt as if people had placed bets on which of the two was going to survive.

On 3 April he faced the ordeal of following Rudolf's *Giselle*. His debut in the ballet in 1955, partnering Alicia Markova, had been described by P. W. Manchester as 'The Matinée That Made History', launching him as an international star. For this performance he decided not to attempt to dazzle the London audience with a 'new' interpretation but to reveal the true spirit of Romanticism – *Giselle* being close in style, and of the same period, as the Bournonville ballets. 'It is a pleasure to see how simple, how chaste ballet can be and still go to your heart,' Edwin Denby wrote of the Danish interpretation of the Romantic genre, but the English critics, missing the wild rapture that Rudolf had brought to the role, remained unmoved. 'Bruhn is too reserved to give more than a hint of that romantic abandon and despair which are necessary in *Giselle* though no one can perform better than he does the exacting dances,' remarked Richard Buckle; while an unsigned review in *Dance & Dancers* avowed that the memory of Fonteyn and Nureyev had 'dimmed down' the Nerina/Bruhn performance – 'even though so much of what they did was excellent and perfectly right'.

The cool elusiveness of Erik's performance, the impression he gave of being (in Arlene Croce's phrase) 'inwardly rigid, absorbed in his own perfection', had the potency of an aphrodisiac for Rudolf – the paradoxical burn of ice. 'Eighty per cent of Erik's talent was secret, and Rudolf didn't have those secrets,' remarks the Danish actress Susse Wold. 'It was like an iceberg. You saw so much, and underneath was the world. Rudolf showed the whole iceberg; he turned it upside down and showed it all.' Betty Oliphant, another close friend, agrees. 'If you take two men: one very obviously sexy, and another who's extremely attractive and sends shivers down your spine, yet doesn't make you aware of him as a sexual object. That was Erik – a very, very understated artist, not this animal.' From the public's point of view, however, 'animal magnetism' was more alluring than glacial impassivity – and the box-office figures were there to prove it.

The constant comparisons between the two dancers were inevitably affecting their private lives, becoming the cause of many violent scenes. On one occasion, angry enough to be deliberately vicious, Erik accused Rudolf of defecting to the West in order to destroy his career. 'People would say that Rudolf was out to kill me and how could I put up with it? I never believed it. I only used it once against him . . . He got so upset and [was] crying and said who could be so evil . . . "Of course I don't believe it," I said. "I believe you."'

It is quite true that Rudolf's motive had never been to eclipse Erik – on the contrary, he needed him there as inspiration. As he himself admitted, watching a great dancer was a source of self-nourishment. 'I receive. I am no longer empty.' Even in Russia he had made up his mind to seek Erik out in order, vampirically, to feed himself – or, as he put it, to 'Go there and *suck*.' 'He was draining Erik,' Sonia said, 'absorbing everything that Erik had.' Sexually, too, Rudolf expected to be the recipient, and with just as voracious an appetite. 'He was very demanding sexually and very possessive, which sometimes got too much for Erik,' Ray Barra says. 'Possessive and yet still very promiscuous.'

In April, Rudolf received a postcard from a Hungarian dancer he had known in Leningrad, suggesting that they should try to see each other that summer. Rudolf replied immediately, describing his itinerary and adding, 'From 7–9 July I will be in Italy. In August we'll go to Greece for holidays. But if I would know where and when you would want to come, I will be able to come quickly.'

Viktor Rona, a tall, charismatic principal with the Budapest State Choreographic Institute, was two years older than Rudolf, and had admired him since 1959, when they both appeared at Vienna's international youth festival. He had seen the Kirov contestants perform only the pas de six from *Laurentia* but had been amazed by one dancer who stood out so conspicuously from the rest: 'Who is he? I asked myself.' The Budapest company maintained close links with Russian choreographers and ballet masters, and at the end of that year, Viktor arrived in Leningrad with his partner and school contemporary, Adèl Orosz, to study the classics under Pushkin's tutelage. On 12 December Viktor notes in his diary how they both rushed to the theatre after class to see 'new artists Kolpakova and Nureyev' in *Giselle*, and it was not long before Rudolf himself went out of his way to watch the young Hungarians dance. Alexander Ivanovich had told him that the couple knew the Lavrovsky version of *Giselle*, and Rudolf began coming to their rehearsals in order to learn the choreography himself. Sharing the same impassioned enthusiasm for dance, they worked late into the night, and then went across the road to the Pushkins' apartment where Xenia would be waiting with dinner. 'What had begun as a working relationship developed into true friendship,' says Adèl, who was born on the same day of the same year as Rudolf, and on 17 March shared a double celebration with him at Rossi Street. When the time came for the two dancers to leave, Rudolf and Alexander Ivanovich took them to the airport, where they parted in the hope of seeing each other again.

They kept in touch. When Rudolf made his London debut, he sent Rona a photograph of himself in the Ashton solo inscribed, 'To beloved Viktor, Wish you big happiness on the stage and also in life, Your great friend Rudik.' But it was Pushkin who regularly corresponded with the dancer, sending affectionate New Year's greetings from all three of them – 'Kiss you a thousand times' – and reminding him in one letter how much Rudolf wanted to appear in 'your *Giselle*'. In the winter of 1962 Viktor and Adèl came to London to film the *Gayane* duet for BBC's *Music in Camera* series (transmitted on 27 August), and were met by Rudolf at the airport. They were thrilled to discover that he was taking them to lunch with Margot Fonteyn, and he for his part seemed equally pleased to have news from home. In Leningrad, Rudolf and Viktor, a warm-hearted young man with lively eyes and black curly hair, had rarely, if ever, spent time alone together, but it was over the next few days that, according to Adèl, 'their deeper friendship started'.

A month or two later, following several letters from Viktor, a postcard arrived from Helsinki, where the dancer was on tour, suggesting that they should see each other either in Berlin, where he was filming *The Nutcracker*, or in Italy or France, where he planned to spend a two-week holiday: 'I will write you where and when I will be exactly. My best regards to Margot, Kisses, Viktor.'

As it happened, their next encounter was not a romantic tryst in Europe but a 'cloak-and-dagger' rendezvous at London airport at the end of the year. In the meantime Rudolf hoped that Viktor might be useful to him. The dancer was then preparing the part of Mercutio in Lavrovsky's *Romeo and Juliet* – a ballet Rudolf himself longed to perform in London. 'Margot also wants it,' he wrote, 'but everything depends on whether Lavrovsky will stage it.' Viktor was the obvious link, and he also had a direct connection with Pushkin. 'I'm trying to call Alexander Ivanovich but no success,' Rudolf told him. 'If you write him please give my telephone no. Fremantle 1603. He'll need only first three letters.'

So far Rudolf's only contact with his teacher had been through Xenia. Her many letters and cards (addressed 'c/o Mrs M. Fonteyn for Rudi, the Royal Ballet at Covent Garden, London') never mention Pushkin by name, but refer to him as 'The Elder', 'your professor' or 'our teacher' (in English). She had recently told Rudolf how upset and worried Alexander Ivanovich became when there was no news from him. 'And then he gets terribly irritated because all the time people get to him and tell him their fantasies and thoughts about you.' Xenia herself, forced to dissipate her emotional energy into her daily routine, had become as listless and confined as one of Chekhov's women. 'I have never had a diary in my life and now I am writing to you every day. I have nothing to write about day after day, my days are so much one like another,' she says, describing her walks to the market – even what she has for breakfast. Very occasionally a friend at the local library would discover an English article about Rudolf, unnoticed by the censor, which she would then translate for Xenia. 'It was so that she could still live with Rudik in her memory and mind – she missed him so much.' Refusing to abandon her hold on Rudolf entirely, Xenia scolds him for having danced too many pas de deux in succession. 'That's terrible – You are not thinking about your legs at all' – and warns him of potentially corrupting influences in the West. 'Everywhere are attractive and unattractive people who may ask you to go out for a beer or invite you to a club. And this is not good for a dancer. With your nerves you have to be especially careful. It is so easy to get under the influence of evil. Remember you must stay the same, as I know you – an honest, true person.'

Often she ends her letters by admonishing, 'Take care, be intelligent!' or 'You have to be serious and educate yourself. Don't waste your time on nothing.' In one she tells him about a Van Cliburn concert she watched on television, which reminded her of how sad she is that Rudolf no longer plays the piano. Using code names, she gives him snippets of news about his friends, such as 'your ex-love Ella' (Ninel Kurgapkina) or 'our beloved Bobik Sh' (Alla Shelest). The one person she never mentions is Teja. He was now involved with an Indonesian temple dancer studying at the Vaganova Academy. 'You know how I was always inspired by the East!' he told Rudolf in a letter of his own, explaining, 'After you left I missed you so much, I didn't know whether to be alone or get married.' Xenia had disliked Nureini on sight. 'She would say to Teja, "I'm inviting you but without your monkey."' To her the relationship was not only a threat to their own bond but also a betrayal of Rudolf. 'Everybody was supposed to wait for him,' said Tamara. 'Xenia Josifovna felt that if Rudik had loved you, then you should never become close to anyone else. You had to be free and waiting for him.'

They were all waiting in suspense for the outcome of Rudolf's trial, the date of which had been set for 2 April. The process, which was closed to the public, took place in Leningrad's Municipal Court, the panel consisting of a judge, a public prosecutor, a woman defence lawyer hired by the Pushkins, two jury members and a secretary. None of Rudolf's friends or relatives was called to give evidence, although Xenia, Alexander Ivanovich and Rosa had recorded their depositions several months earlier. Hamet and Farida, 'suffering from many problems', remained in Ufa, relying on their daughter Rosa and the Pushkins for information. Desperate to know what was happening inside the courtroom, Rosa and Tamara had gone together to the municipal hall, where they were able to watch the opening stages through a slightly open door until they were spotted and the door was kicked shut.

One by one the five witnesses were interrogated in a small room overlooking the Fontanka Canal: Rudolf's partner in Paris, Alla

Osipenko; the director Georgi Korkin – the only person to speak unequivocally in Rudolf's defence; the KGB's Vitaly Strizhevsky; and two members of the company's technical and administrative staff due to travel on the same flight to Moscow. As the trial progressed, the evidence appeared to be going in the dancer's favour, with everyone united in saying that the defection had not been premeditated. Even Strizhevsky was forced to admit, 'His things were on the plane to London, and he was preparing to fly there.' Making the point that Rudolf had not been seduced by the material temptations of capitalism, Korkin remarked how surprised he had been by his indifference to his clothes and appearance in Paris. 'All his attention was paid to buying costumes for the stage. There was nothing except art for him.' The director also implied that Nureyev's frustrations about the company were justified, as the young generation of Kirov dancers were being held back by Sergeyev and Dudinskaya, both equally unwilling to relinquish their roles. (He gave as an example the fact that the veteran stars had taken their costumes on tour even though they were under orders not to perform.) In fact the same charge had been made in a newspaper, which published a letter of complaint about their leadership signed by thirty-six Kirov members, including its leading ballerinas. Rudolf's lawyer, Irina Otlyagova, read this aloud to the court.

From beginning to end the proceedings lasted less than four hours. The final summing-up was given not by the judge but by the public prosecutor, who also pronounced the verdict: 'According to the tenets of article N64,' he said, 'Nureyev has been proved guilty.' Ronzin continued by saying that Nureyev's refusal to return from the West was a betrayal of the motherland, and that his defection, used by the bourgeois media for anti-Soviet slander, had caused considerable damage to the interests of the state. 'However, taking into consideration Nureyev's youth, his lack of experience, and his unbalanced character, together with the fact that our representatives mishandled his expulsion to Moscow, he will be given the minimum punishment of article N64.' Irina Otlyagova then intervened with the plea that article N43, which carries 'a lower than minimum punishment', be applied instead. The final verdict was that Rudolf was guilty according to article N64, but in view of his circumstances would be punished according to article N43: seven years' imprisonment.

As a penalty for high treason, this sentence was light – light enough for some to suppose that Rudolf would now return home. Farida tried for several days to reach him by telephone but was unable to get through. 'Maybe they're interfering with the connection over there,'

Rosa remarked when she wrote to Rudolf later that week. She made no mention of the trial or its outcome, but sent him a clipping of the published letter of complaint. 'It's possible to hope, I think, that your own episode happened as a result of the Sergeyev intrigue. This could justify you.' But Rudolf had no intention of coming home: he had just found out that the Royal Ballet was inviting him to become a full-time member of the company.

This news, though hardly surprising, was in fact a reversal of Ninette de Valois's policy of having no foreign guest artists on a long-term basis. Unwilling to topple a structure that had been meticulously built up over thirty years, she was just as determined as Balanchine to prevent her company from becoming a backup team for a star. In Nureyev's case, however, she was willing to break her own rules. 'When a dancer of genius appears, the company has to submit.' Rudolf was to become what Lord Drogheda, chairman of the Royal Opera House, would call 'a sort of permanent Guest Artist'; Erik, on the other hand, despite having been engaged long before Rudolf's arrival, and having danced more than twenty performances to Rudolf's three, would not be appearing the next season. As board-meeting minutes note, 'he was not playing to capacity.'

Hating the itinerant life of a guest star, and longing to be part of a company, Erik was devastated. He could not understand de Valois's decision, as he felt the Royal Ballet was absolutely right for him. Which, of course, it was. His technical control, meticulous footwork and reticent temperament were easily absorbed into the British style – a model of perfection to the young dancers. Anthony Dowell admits to identifying far more with what he calls 'Erik's withheld, aristocratic style' than with Rudolf's wild Russian panache. When Erik staged Bournonville's *Napoli* for the company, he cast the nineteen-year-old in his first featured role, and was just as formative an influence on the upcoming ballerinas. 'There was the most wonderful atmosphere in the company when Erik was with us,' recalls Georgina Parkinson. 'We gave ourselves completely to him; we were his students. We hadn't had contact with many people from the outside, and here was someone who really knew what he was talking about, and was so generous about passing it on.'

When Rudolf arrived shortly afterwards, the dancers felt blessed – it was even inspiring to watch the pair warm up together: they were like two star matadors performing *mano a mano* in the same ring – *Los Dos* – whose antithesis in styles could be summed up in Kenneth Tynan's description of El Litri and Ordóñez at the great final bullfight of the Valencian fair: 'When Reach was confronted with Grasp, Accident with Design, Romantic with Classic, *Sturm und Drang* with Age of Gold.' This was a time when, as Clive Barnes has written, 'artistry was almost of secondary importance to charisma', and the same thing was happening in bullfighting. The embodiment of the quality the Spanish call *tremendismo* was twenty-five-year-old El Cordobés, whose early career was strikingly similar to Rudolf's.*Tynan first saw this wild, tousle-haired youth in 1961, the year the matador began his domination of Spanish bullfighting, and was reminded of a trend he had already encountered under several other names: 'In France, the *blouson noir*; in Britain the mod; and in America the hipster.' Bringing something new into an old art form, El Cordobés was the first hip bullfighter – '*le Beatle des toreros*', *Paris-Match* called him – just as Rudolf was 'ballet's first pop star, the long-haired icon for the decade's spirit of rebellion and sexual freedom'. Applause for the young Cordoban was a 'collective madness', the kind of delirium last evoked in the fifties by Elvis Presley, and Rudimania was equally phenomenal. Replacing the typical dance audience, described by Richard Buckle as 'mad old maids in moth-eaten musquash [muskrat]' was a generation of 'squealing bobbysoxers', most of whom had never been to the Royal Opera House before. It is no accident that Ordóñez, abdicating to the new cult of personality, decided to retire in 1962. But while the anti-academic, anti-traditional El Cordobés was intentionally vulgarizing classical standards, burlesquing the techniques refined by his predecessors, Rudolf was doing the opposite. It was his intention to fuse sensationalism with Apollonian refinement, and by the following year, he had done it, achieving what Ninette de Valois considered to be an astonishingly correct and noble style. 'By the age of twenty-five his dancing was virtually perfect.'

In May, as Margot was on tour in Australia with a small group of dancers, Yvette Chauviré was brought in by the Royal Ballet as a partner for Rudolf in *The Sleeping Beauty* – a performance that did neither star much credit. Their *Giselle* twelve days later was even more of an anticlimax. Chauviré's portrayal was only a blurred outline of what it used to be, her sophisticated, intellectual manner far too remote to interact with Rudolf's boyish spontaneity. 'He was always impressed

---

* Born a year earlier than the dancer, Manuel Benítez Peres – El Cordobés – had also left a life of poverty in the provinces and headed north to the city 'as though being pulled'. In 1957, sharing the same fanatical drive, he anticipated Rudolf's own so-called leap to fame by jumping into the bullring at Las Ventas, which made him front-page news.

by the intensity of Yvette's concentration,' says Ghislaine Thesmar, 'but unlike Margot, who was so communicative with him, Yvette was completely in her bubble. She wouldn't let anyone in.'

In mid-June, taking advantage of Margot's absence to insist on his conditions, Rudolf agreed to appear in *Swan Lake*. His partner (making her Royal Ballet debut) was Sonia Arova, whom he had warned that if she mimed the traditional 'I-you-love' sequence in Act 1, he would walk off the stage. Notwithstanding her disapproval, he also introduced a long pause after her Black Swan variation in order to build up audience expectation for his own solo. This was *Swan Lake* with Siegfried as its focus – an immature, rebellious, Byronic Prince whose hectic, unleashed technique left some critics feeling that the young Russian was being overpraised.

The Prince in Act 1 was usually portrayed as a carefree youth, but Rudolf, clearly influenced by Erik, whose recent Siegfried at Covent Garden was a skulking, morose figure, made him complex and moody. 'The Prince was exceptional man. It does not happen just to everybody to see there are swans.' Yet, whereas like most Danes, Erik equated Romanticism with melancholy, Rudolf, wanting to emphasize the Russian spirit of *Swan Lake,* projected the kind of soulfulness that Russians call *dushevnyi.** To convey this in choreographic terms, he introduced a contemplative danced soliloquy in Act 1, the legato solo now standard in most productions of *Swan Lake*. At the time it caused an outcry, the rumpus even reaching New York, where Clive Barnes's *Spectator* review deriding Rudolf's lack of talent as a choreographer was picked up by the *New York Herald Tribune*. And yet this controversial solo, which everyone presumed was the 'Nureyev version' and 'entirely new', had in fact already been performed at the Kirov. Rudolf's contemporaries claim that he took the idea from Konstantin Sergeyev, whose Act 1 solo had used the same deep, sustained movements, and even the same music (the Andante sostenuto written for, but not used in, the pas de trois). Sergeyev, in turn, had the model of Chaboukiani, who often rechoreographed and expanded his own roles, so that in making his changes Rudolf was only continuing the Soviet tradition. The English critics, though, were appalled that a twenty-four-year-old boy, never having created a ballet before, had been allowed to sabotage what several generations had laboured to preserve.

* Balanchine would have argued that people confuse *dushevnyi* with *dukhovnyi* (spiritual). 'Tchaikovsky's music isn't soulful, it's spiritual' (Solomon Volkov, *Balanchine's Tchaikovsky*).

For Rudolf, however, it was hard to understand why the kind of radical transformations of the classics taking place in English theatre were not paralleled at the Royal Ballet. His autobiography, published in November 1962, contains several paragraphs on the subject, but reviewing the book for *Dance & Dancers,* Peter Williams makes a convincing counter-argument:

> What he has not taken into consideration is that ballet in England is still but a child starting to walk, and that when British ballet started but a little over thirty years ago we had no foundation, nothing to build upon. Ninette de Valois, Marie Rambert and a few others pursued the only course open to them which was to build up British ballet in the precious fragments from Russia which had been brought to these islands by Diaghilev. There was no other ballet tradition that made itself felt in this country . . . We are not yet old enough to start monkeying around with classical works and making them what is generally called 'alive'. We still have to guard our meagre heritage even though Nureyev's presence in London is the surest bet that a little refurbishing of the classics is imminent.

In his *American Glossary*, published in 1959, Lincoln Kirstein had already made the point that ballet in Britain showed little of the vitality and innovation present in contemporary art, drama or fiction. What was needed, he said, was a sense of outrage and energy: 'an Angry Young Man on his way to rouse the Sleeping Princess right out of Windsor Forest'. But while prophetically heralding the arrival of Nureyev, Kirstein, in slighting the Royal Ballet's 'self-satisfied parochialism' and 'sweet, moderate graciousness', badly underestimated Ninette de Valois. Along with her conventional qualities – the sound leadership, common sense and discipline inherited from her army-officer father – ran a bright thread of Celtic unpredictability. To Richard Buckle she was as capricious as an E. M. Forster heroine who might bolt off over the hills without a hat or gloves 'if the right breeze blew at the right time'. And it was 'this romantic spark, this moonshine, this "artistic nonsense"', that, as Buckle says, had led de Valois to conceive the almost impossible ambition of transforming half a dozen girl pupils into a national ballet. 'From the marriage of inspiration and discipline works of art are born.'

Having danced in the 1920s for Diaghilev, the single most important influence on her career, de Valois had heard all about the dangers of ossification and bureaucracy inherent in a state institution – the constrictions from which Rudolf had fled. And although she joined the company when, as she put it, 'the impact of the present was meeting the past,' working with the most innovative choreographers of the day, including Balanchine and Nijinska, she had also learned that it was tradition and a classical background that lay beneath the experiments of the Ballets Russes. In the same way it was the solid base that she established in her own company through the 'correctness of execution' and 'efficiency in administration' mocked by Kirstein that allowed her to take risks. 'It shows a great weakness if you daren't take in something new. You must be able to say: "For a moment we'll upset this applecart and see what happens."'

Since the late fifties de Valois had been longing for what she called a real virtuoso dancer, and when she first saw Rudolf, remarked, 'Exactly what we need, not only a virtuoso dancer but one with taste.' Her decision to have Rudolf in the Royal Ballet was, as her biographer says, 'a fighting point of view, the policy of an inspired general taking a calculated risk in order to improve a position'. Inevitably there would be casualties, her own leadership would be called into question, but she wanted her company – its choreographers and teachers as well as its dancers – to profit from as close a proximity as possible to Rudolf's rare and wonderful schooling. Calls to 'put her foot down' and prevent the young interloper from further undermining the Royal Ballet's heritage were shrugged off by de Valois, who was realistic about the fact that there *are* no definitive versions of the nineteenth-century classics.

> Nureyev's alterations have really meant very little to me . . . because I know the enormous changes we've made during the last fifteen years in ballets like *Giselle* and *The Sleeping Beauty* and *Swan Lake* without people noticing . . . We don't know how accurate his version is in comparison with what he either learned or saw in Leningrad. All I know is that in style and approach and musicality they are like everything I've ever seen over there . . . Thinking of the phrasing and the general style, he's carrying on the tradition of the Russians, that's quite obvious.

And yet, in taking Rudolf into her company, de Valois was ruled as much by her heart as by her head: quite simply she adored him. 'They really laughed together, and got on as equals.' There was, she believed, a special kinship between the Irish and the Russians, the same affinity and fascination that Sean O'Faoláin and Brian Friel share in their

allegiance to Chekhov. When she collaborated with Yeats (who brought
her to Dublin to stage his *Plays for Dancers*), it was his love of what she
called 'the moving thought, the progress and the "excitement"' of the
mind with which she could most identify. This, too, was the quality
she immediately recognized in Rudolf, whose mind, as she often said,
interested her just as much as his feet. 'He didn't run away from Russia
just because he wanted to get out . . . He wanted to know what was
going on in *his* world in other parts of the world.' The admiration was
mutual. Rudolf was delighted by de Valois's intelligence and wit, and by
the fact that she seemed instinctively to understand him. 'Essentially he
remains, and probably will remain, an outsider in our community. He
has his own creed. He will live by it and fulfil it in his own time in
his own way.'

Inevitably, though, Rudolf's solipsistic trajectory had left several
casualties in its wake. One was Alexander Ivanovich, who that summer
suffered a severe heart attack, 'undoubtedly brought on by the inner
tension of the previous months'. The guilt of knowing he had been the
catalyst of his teacher's illness had left Rudolf inconsolable. And then
there was Erik, who, according to Nadia Nerina, had left London
broken in spirit even before finishing the season. 'Rudi demoralized
him to such an extent that he had to go into a nursing home in
Denmark . . . He never did recover completely. One can date the
beginning of the sad decline of this superb dancer from the beginning
of his relationship with Nureyev.' Never having felt so bleakly culpable
and alone, Rudolf must have confided in Xenia, who wrote to console
him. 'I understand about melancholy feelings, but you must not let sad
emotions get to you. You must study and the only salvation to this –
work.'

On 5 July Rudolf was to dance *Swan Lake* with Margot for the first
time, at Italy's Nervi Festival (the idea being to give them a few experimental performances away from the London critics). Their two
rehearsals in London had not boded well, their arguments cut short
only because Rudolf began to giggle when Margot reminded him that
she had been dancing *Swan Lake* since 1938 – the year he was born. 'It
broke us both up completely.' In fact this had always been one of her
most dreaded ballets, its technical hurdles – particularly the thirty-
two *fouetté* sequence – never ceasing to terrify her. With a foot injury
seriously undermining her technique, she had danced her so-called
farewell performance in 1959. 'We all knew it was her last,' said
Georgina Parkinson. 'And she did her usual 23½ *fouettés*, and everybody cheered . . . and we all shed a suitable tear.' Three years later,

with her injury significantly improved, Margot had made a comeback in the role in February with David Blair, but it was an uninteresting performance, dismissed by *Dance & Dancers* as a 'Lack-lustre Lac'. On 17 June, in the audience at the London Palladium, she had watched Rudolf dance a scintillating Black Swan pas de deux with Nadia Nerina for the Sunday-night television broadcast, followed a few days later by the 'elemental and exciting' Nureyev-Arova *Swan Lake* at Covent Garden. She knew then that she had no choice: the time had come to drop her defences.

When their rehearsals recommenced in Italy, Margot, despite having broken their deadlock, sensed a major challenge. Who in the audience would look at her 'with this young lion leaping ten feet in the air and doing all these fantastic things'? Enormously competitive by nature, she also thrived on adventure and risk (the side that had made her a *faux*-guerrilla in her husband's abortive mini-revolution in Panama in 1959). Tapping into this, Rudolf taunted her one day by saying, 'So – you are Great Ballerina. Show me!' Suddenly she found herself virtually outdancing her partner, while he watched 'puzzled', asking himself how it was possible that she, 'without technique was doing technical things, and me, taught the best technique . . . not always there'? Only too aware of her stature – her name in world terms being far better known than that of Ulanova – Rudolf himself now 'felt a bit . . . Well, when I'm onstage beside her, who's going to look at me?' He had always found it extraordinary the way Margot, even without this new virtuosic confidence, could make her impact felt not through showy aplomb but through her soft, lyrical, English restraint and unforced line. There was no trace of sensationalism to her artistry, yet something so excitingly internalized that, even when standing motionless, she could draw all eyes towards her. 'She came onstage,' as Rudolf said, 'and she made light.'

The fact that they were both 'inspired – egged on, as it were – by the other one' gave an unbelievable charge to their Nervi performance, and at the same time they found that as soon as they went onstage, all aspects of self-interest and rivalry were forgotten. The state of total harmony they rediscovered in Italy was enhanced by the theatre's extraodinarily romantic open-air setting, the balmy Mediterranean night, the backdrop of the sea. Talking later about her performance, Margot said beatifically, 'I've found the perfect partner.' Rudolf felt the same: 'We become one body. One soul. We moved in one way. It was very complementary, every arm movement, every head movement. There were no more cultural gaps; age difference;

we've been absorbed in characterization. We became the part. And public was enthralled.'

Before returning to London, Rudolf went to Florence to watch Erik's *La Sylphide*, which the Danish ballet had invited him to perform on its tour of Italy. Bruhn's next engagement (with the Stuttgart Ballet) was consolation of sorts for his Royal Ballet disappointment, as he and Georgina Parkinson were to dance the première of John Cranko's new version of *Daphnis and Chloe*. The South African-born Cranko, having reached a point of stagnation in his career as resident choreographer of the Royal Ballet, had recently taken over as director at Stuttgart, and was already beginning to build it into a world-class company, inviting a roster of international dancers for a week-long festival in July. Erik was thrilled to be working with Cranko, as this was the first time he had been chosen by a leading choreographer to create a ballet. 'Tudor told me that Ashton should do something for me and Ashton told me that I should go and work with Balanchine . . . They kept passing me on to someone else.' But although the 15 July première was a great success, Erik had been 'horrified' by his follow-up performance (his self-expectations were always so high that, as Elizabeth Kaye once wrote, 'He could give an impeccable performance and come offstage feeling suicidal').

Augmenting his distress was the furore of publicity that accompanied Rudolf's unexpected arrival. Ray Barra, appearing as the lead in Cranko's *Prince of the Pagodas*, remembers how 'the photographers were wanting him, him, him, and this caused – oh, *lots* of friction'. Erik had always prized his anonymity, enjoying the fact that he could elbow his way through a crowd of waiting fans and be asked if Erik Bruhn was still backstage. 'If I have left the audience with some idea of the performance, I seldom have the strength or the intention to give them any more of that performance at the stage door. There is nothing left. The job is finished.' He could even, he claimed, pass his best friends in the street without being noticed. 'There was something ethereal about Erik. Transparent,' says the Danish dancer Ingrid Glindemann. Now, suddenly, he found himself actively seeking the spotlight, resenting the way 'no one knew of me and I was very lucky to be hanging on to Rudik'. Not only that, but he was expected to help journalists understand Rudolf's English – even to act as Rudolf's agent. 'He came to Stuttgart as a friend and then the press said, "Why is he not dancing in the gala?" '

Georgina Parkinson remembers how Rudolf volunteered to perform at the festival's closing gala. 'It was more than Erik could bear,' though it was, in fact, his own idea. He and Yvette Chauviré were scheduled to dance Victor Gsovsky's *Grand Pas Classique* together, but during one of their rehearsals Erik asked Rudolf to take over, blaming his indisposition on 'back trouble'. Naturally, Rudolf was delighted to have the chance to perform the duet he had so admired on Chauviré's tour of Russia, although she was more than a little displeased to find herself dancing with a partner with whom she had only an erratic rapport. Erik, meanwhile, had taken to his bed. 'I felt this tension growing, first of all within myself about *Daphnis*, and then the general bad atmosphere that pervaded when Rudolf and I were together . . . People were provoking us. Jokes were being made, and it just got to me . . . I coped with it the only way I knew how: I cancelled.'

Erik still had several performances left, but when Cranko, accompanied by Kenneth MacMillan, went to his room to see how genuinely sick he was, Erik threw them both out. (It was five years before he would have any further contact with Cranko.) That night, having bought a convertible from one of the dancers, and without saying a word to anyone, he left Stuttgart. When Rudolf awoke early the next morning he found only a brief note scrawled on a hotel envelope:

My dear Rudic,
Take care of yourself, words
Are decieving [*sic*] and always misunderstood –
So I will not say anything, but good Bye! Love Erik

Sick with dread, Rudolf immediately called Georgina Parkinson to ask if Erik was with her. Going straight to Rudolf's room, she found him desolate and frightened. 'He didn't have a passport, so I suggested that he get in touch with Margot because she had diplomatic contacts.' When Chauviré saw Rudolf later that day, she, too, was shocked by the extent of his anguish. '*Il était complètement bouleversé.* He *adored* Erik. And for him to leave like that . . . Why did he do that?'

In his book on the pathography of Strindberg and Van Gogh, Karl Jaspers titles one section 'Persecution and Flight', describing how the writer, seeking to free himself from unbearable pressures of his environment, would be overtaken by intense restlessness leading him to go 'instinctively on a trip, without any preconceived plan'. Strindberg was a schizophrenic. In Erik's case, with no later history of serious mental disorder, a diagnosis of the illness would be doubtful. Rudolf's arrival in Stuttgart had plunged him into such spiritual crisis that, as Georgina Parkinson remarked, 'he completely withdrew, and wasn't available to any of us'. Self-retreat, combined with a mistrust of joking, suspected conniving by 'so-called friends', and the violent stomach disorders from which he suffered, can be indications of the schizophrenic process, although friends close to Erik, including the young doctor Lennart Pasborg, insist that he was not psychologically disturbed.

> He was certainly very melancholic, and a person with a very strange sensitivity to what I can only call something transcendent. He had seen this, felt this, been in contact with it . . . This made him a loner – a need to go deep inside himself; trying to get in contact with this . . . He suffered from not being able to reproduce it when he wanted . . . This inner struggle that may have accounted for the ulcer.

To Susse Wold the dark moods and recurrent dreams and nightmares were no more than manifestations of Erik's nationality. 'There was a reason Shakespeare made Hamlet a Dane.' But she also attributes his escapes from reality (and there were many) to a mystical, rather than pathological, side. 'Erik had a hard time being in the here and now . . . He would disappear like he'd disappeared in the apple tree when he was a child.'

It was not until the end of that week that Rudolf finally tracked down Erik, who had taken three times longer than he should have to drive to Copenhagen because of agonizing spasms in his back. During the course of their emotional telephone conversation, Erik told him that he never again wanted to be with people who would 'play off' their relationship. 'I said to him . . . that I am the only one who could say get out and I could not explain myself.'

By now it was the end of July and they both badly needed a holiday. Rudolf persuaded Erik to come to Monte Carlo, where he was hoping to buy a house. The town was full of dancers that summer, and one night they met Anna Pavlova's partner Edward Caton, then giving classes at the ballet school. Born in St Petersburg and taught by Vaganova herself, he held them fascinated with his stories and insights. 'He could explain Pavlova and show them, with his big feet and big shoes, the grand manner of a *danseur noble*.'

Borrowing a Monegasque friend's beach tent, they spent long relaxing days in the sun, were photographed together in a pedal boat, seemingly at peace with the world. Only a week or so later, however, Rudolf again found himself caught up in a deeply neurotic, Strindbergian situation. He had moved into the Bruhns' house in Gentofte, where the atmosphere was overshadowed by the recent death of Erik's beloved aunt Minna and the serious illness of his mother. Visibly in pain that seemed to worsen by the day, Ellen Bruhn virtually ignored Rudolf. 'A gruesome person' in the opinion of many, she had always had a profoundly destructive relationship with Erik, whose own feelings towards her were so complex that he would use his 1967 production of *Swan Lake* to explore the Oedipal intensity of the Prince's relationship with his mother. Also staying with them was Sonia Arova, whom Erik was to partner in a centennial gala at the Tivoli Gardens. As his mother was making it quite clear that she did not want Rudolf in the house, Sonia advised Erik, who felt unhappily divided in his loyalties, that he should show her more consideration and make Rudolf move to a hotel. 'Plus Rudi and Erik were having tremendous fights.' Rudolf did leave, but not for long; profiting from Sonia's departure for Paris, he immediately moved back into the house.

On an evening when Erik and Rudolf were having dinner with Vera Volkova, one of Erik's sisters telephoned to say that their mother had just been taken by ambulance to the hospital. Erik left immediately, but by the time he arrived, Ellen Bruhn was dead. He had not been forewarned of this, but was taken directly into the ward. 'I saw that she was lying there covered up with a sheet. I was told that she had died only a short while before.' He went straight back to the house, where he called Volkova to tell her what had happened. 'Rudik immediately got on the phone and said he would come home right away.' 'Rudi was the one who reacted spontaneously on this,' Susse Wold says. 'And his reaction helped Erik to release his feelings. If someone is able just to hold you . . . without words . . . to take you in their arms and just be there. That is what he did.' Although scheduled to fly to New York the next day, Rudolf told Erik that he would stay on for a few more days so that he didn't have to be alone in the house. His devotion touched Erik deeply. 'He could have run away, but he didn't.'

Rudolf was in New York rehearsing another *Bell Telephone Hour TV* appearance (*Le Corsaire* duet with Lupe Serrano), when a letter from Erik arrived.

My dear Rudic,
    I wonder how you are . . . I feel very lonely here in the house, I keep thinking of my mother and then my aunt too. They meant so much to me, and in some way, they are both very much alive to me. I

have been thinking of you too, yes us both, the future. Are we really happy together, or is it pretentious of me to believe that some happiness should exist where we can overcome and forget a bit of ourselves, our egotism and desires. There have been tensions, fights, problems of overcoming ourselves between us, only desperate fights or sudden deaths seem to calm us, but only for a day or two and then it seems we are back to the same again like the rest of the world. I kept on believing all the time, but now, it seems to me unrealistic to believe in something good, at least in this life. I need to be calmed too. I have my difficult periods with myself, then I go my own way alone, to get rid of them. I need help at those moments, but spiritually, not physically. You talk every so often about your body, but Rudik, it is your mind, without mind or heart, you would not feel your body at all. You can get calm by exhausting your body, but I can't ask myself to come to you only for physical reasons, then it is just another body which you can get anywhere. Maybe as you said that next year, we will be together more but what will be next year? We failed to be together, failed to believe that there is a future while and when we were together. With all my heart and love which still is in my heart I wish you to find some happiness wherever you are. Erik.

The letter's valedictory tone came as a tremendous shock to Rudolf. When they had parted in Copenhagen, it had felt as if they had never been so close, and although they had not been in touch since, this was only because Rudolf had been engulfed by work – something another dancer should understand. He wrote back immediately, desperate to convince Erik of his belief in their love and future, but his letter crossed with a second from Erik, this time written in a manic mood swing 'of joy and warmth':

When you had to leave I thought and felt like something died in me, like I would never see you again. I have only you left in my life, the only person alive I love and who is alive to me. It was depressing to think we were going such separate ways in our work that we were always on the move . . . with so many indifferent people around us . . . I don't feel like going out because people ask and feel sorry for me . . . So many sad things have happened to me this year, yet . . . I forget that something wonderful and beautiful happened when I met you. I shall be grateful in spite of everything else and I will be happy to see you any time here for a moment I will treasure, be assured you are my life and I love you deeply.

A third immediately followed, dated 20 September:

My dearest, my darling, got your letter just now. Can you forgive me? . . . I cannot think exactly how I wrote that first letter only my conditions were so bad. I hope you will understand and forgive. I saw death around me all the time, I was lost, had no-one near me to help or to feel any life. I have hardly slept since you left . . . I drive so much around so not to be here alone in the house but Rudic my love, I do feel better and it's because of you and your letter, assuring me of a love I need so badly and also to give, and I did not hear from you it seemed like years. Oh my darling, please don't worry. As long as we love we will make and work for a happy future together.

At the beginning of October, Rudolf went to Chicago to dance in Chicago Opera Ballet's productions of *The Merry Widow* and *Prince Igor*, breaking off rehearsals to fly back to New York, where Erik was stopping briefly en route to Australia. After spending a 'wonderful' recuperative two days together, they parted again – this time for two months.

It was the Opera Ballet's Ruth Page, dancer, director and choreographer, who had pulled off the coup of getting Rudolf to make his American debut with her company at BAM in Manhattan in 1962. A warm, vivacious woman with a great sense of style, she was a close friend of Margot, who, during the Nervi festival, had encouraged her to get to know Rudolf better. Ruth's husband was Tom Fisher, an ebullient, wealthy lawyer as cosmopolitan and hospitable as she. Their circle extended far beyond the world of ballet to include actors, directors, couturiers, poets and publishers, whom they often entertained at their large penthouse apartment on Lakeshore Drive. It was there they had invited Rudolf to stay during his Chicago performances – though with some misgivings, having received a letter from Christopher Allan warning that the dancer's long-distance telephone bills would be huge. 'I know he wants to pay for them, but sometimes he gets vague about details.' As things turned out, however, Rudolf could not have been an easier house guest: 'As long as he got a steak, plenty of tea, a little whiskey, a massage, a game of chess (which he played with my husband), and a telephone call to Erik in Australia, he was very undemanding.'

At the theatre it was a different story. When Ruth showed him the costume he was expected to wear as the Tatar chieftain, he went straight to the window to throw it into the river – 'I grabbed it just in time' – and when another was produced that pleased him, he ordered it to be cut to bare his midriff. Chicago Opera's *Prince Igor* was a fine production, which retained the original Roerich designs and had a cast headed by the Bulgarian bass Boris Christoff and a chorus singing in Russian. Nevertheless, having discovered that the Bolshoi would be in town at the same time, Rudolf told Ruth 'how very good Igor will have to be', and insisted on making improvements. She had strong ideas of her own about Fokine's dances, having performed the Polovtsian girl with Adolph Bolm (who created the leading male role), but was willing all the same to let the choreography be 'fancied up' for Rudolf. True to form, he did much as he pleased, substituting more spectacular steps, and introducing breaks between his leaps to catch his breath. 'I don't think Fokine would have approved of that,' she commented. 'Anyway, it was a thrilling performance.'

Waiting for Rudolf in London were two letters from Erik, the first describing his arrival in Australia, where he had been met at the airport by a large turnout of journalists. 'Even TV was there,' he remarked, adding provocatively, 'I felt almost like a "star".' The second, written a week later, expresses his delight that Rudolf had timed his own letter for the opening night in Sydney. 'I can hardly believe that I am holding something you touched and I read & read again your words . . . I pray that you will have enough strength to be alone for all this time.' Within days, however, Erik had retreated again, and was torturing Rudolf by refusing to take his calls. Suffering from the continuing shock of losing his mother, he was convinced that he had in some way 'helped the illness that precipitated her death'.[*] Longing for absolution, he turned for support to Sonia, his partner throughout the tour, whom he knew his mother had liked and trusted. 'For the two months we were there, we talked every night till 5 a.m. It all had to come out.' It was Sonia who answered the telephone when Rudolf called, and when he begged to be put through to Erik would tell him gently, 'No, Rudi, Erik can't talk to you tonight.' Sonia and Rudolf would then discuss the situation at length – 'London to Australia!'

Inevitably Erik's unattainability only fanned Rudolf's frenzy; the more ardour he displayed, the more distant Erik grew. This obsessive love was beginning to overshadow Rudolf's dancing. He called it

---

[*] At Sonia Arova's suggestion Erik arranged for his mother to undergo an autopsy on his return. 'This . . . finally put him at rest' (Transcript of John Gruen's interview for his biography *Erik Bruhn*).

'the Curse' – and he vowed never again to commit himself with such intensity. 'Better to have stone in place of heart!' he exclaimed in despair one day to Margot. Familiar herself with the torments of an unstable relationship, she was already becoming Rudolf's salvation – not as the woman in love adored by the public but as the defuser and conduit of his passion.

On 3 November 1962 Rudolf and Margot made their debut in the grand pas de deux from *Le Corsaire*, which, although only a gala fragment, was even more astonishing than their *Giselle*. The thrill of the conceit lay in the match of a barely clothed, semi-barbaric Tatar with England's *prima ballerina assoluta* – as incongruous together, or so it seemed, as in the well-known photograph of them offstage: he in a gondolier-striped T-shirt, sandals and pornographically tight shorts; she in Dior, white gloves and pearls.

Once again Rudolf had thrown out the costume designed for him, replacing it with his own, Bakst-inspired ensemble of filmy harem pants, a silver-mesh bolero, and a thin band encircling his flying hair. Looking like an escaped slave from *Schéhérazade*, masculine in the power of his leaps, feminine in his pulled-up placing and the Oriental delicacy of his arms, he invoked the sexual mystique and lurid theatricality of the legendary Ballets Russes seasons while making the role entirely his own. From his first unleashed run onstage, Rudolf's personality, as Alexandra Danilova said, 'just pours'. Working every sinew to flaunt the beauty of his body, he is god both of earth and air, using the elasticity of gravity-drawn *fondus* to rebound in space and sit there, for several seconds, *en tailleur*. His final pose at Margot's feet enacts the duality in his own nature of arrogance and humility: as he commands the audience to look at her, he is at the same time exulting in the miracle of himself, his imperious profile and grand St Petersburg *épaulement* angled to perfection. 'I had animal power, yes, but there was a finesse. I am not a brutal force. There's a subtlety.'

The heart-bursting, percussive impact of a bravura showpiece, though 'bang-on Nureyev territory', was quite new to Covent Garden. Rudolf had taught Margot a simplified version of the role originally created by Dudinskaya, but she struggled with it at first, and at the première was gently written off as miscast. Within three performances, however, she had mastered the technical hazards and was able to deliver all the razzmatazz while retaining the calm integrity of her line. 'I never saw her so liberated,' Ninette de Valois remarked. 'The confidence it gave her was incredible. It was a development of somebody who suddenly had about ten years taken off her.'

Waiting in the wings for her entrance, the ballerina admitted that she found it so exhilarating to watch Rudolf that she lost all nervousness for herself. She claimed that it was her belief that the audience was looking at him, not her, that had allowed her to relax, and 'really dance for the first time'. And yet this was not self-gratifying exhibitionism on Rudolf's part, but a true partnership. He had to *share* a stage with Margot, a star with a real presence of her own. They borrowed from each other, and if Rudolf had 'brought her out', she, in turn, 'brought him up'. 'For him,' as Violette Verdy says, 'it was the beginning of a taming of sorts – without losing the primitive thing, but learning how to show it in a more artistic way.' Comparing film footage of Rudolf's *Corsaires*, one sees how the ruffian edge of his 1958 student performance has been refined; the foreshortened puppet arms and raised shoulders giving way to expansive, expressive port de bras, the hectic hit-and-miss poses now flawlessly photogenic and controlled.

Margot's revelation that she, with her immense prestige, took Rudolf seriously as an artist had helped to neutralize the shock of his initial notoriety. 'We have to remember what Rudolf looked like back then on a staid British stage,' says writer and photographer Keith Money. 'The bare midriff and all that glitzy Soviet campery were to some the absolute height of bad taste.' Most people, however, were transported by the sight of this exquisite youth yearning up towards Margot as the curtain fell, his fingers splayed, his back arched and pelvis thrust forward – 'like a great Moslem whore'. And it was not only his passion and animality that were so stirring, but the speculation their union prompted about the ballerina's own sexual depths. It made Verdy think of the King Kong legend – a 'scene of seduction and cruelty . . . like the whole thing really was a bedroom . . . and you were watching through the keyhole'.

Tito Arias was in the audience on the first night, and amid all the shouting and cheering – an unprecedented tumult that, as predicted, lasted twice as long as the duet itself – could be heard his mocking sibilant cries of '*Sexy* pants!' Rudolf had always suspected that Margot's husband made fun of him behind his back, and he resented Tito's superciliousness – 'that jokey superiority'. The antipathy was mutual. To Tito, Rudolf was a threat – not in a sexually competitive sense but because he felt that the dancer, 'a sort of urchin opportunist', jeopardized the Establishment role he expected Margot to play. 'Tito saw life

in chess moves,' says Money. 'For one's wife to be all over the newspapers performing with a renegade Soviet dance beatnik was a "wrong
move". Pawn damaging Queen's territory.'

In fact, although she was considered to be the apotheosis of restraint
and respectability, Margot's South American origins and Eastern
upbringing made her as intrinsically un-English as her Tatar partner.
The two dancers' styles were as complementary as they were disparate;
their physical expressiveness and purity of line showing just how much
of the Russian school each had inherited. Theirs was an equality of
talents, a similar way of looking at things: 'It's as though we work on
parallel lines,' Margot once said. 'We have the same attitude towards
what we're trying to do.' Even their differences harmonized onstage,
blending into an effect much like the neo-Impressionists' 'simultaneous
contrast', in which diverse colours seen from a distance recompose in
the eye of the spectator to produce new shades, themselves enhanced
by reaction with the others. And evidence of this mutual intensification
creating a mirage of shimmering luminosity was there for all to see in
their performance of *Les Sylphides* three nights later.

Margot, who had never made much of an impact in *Les Sylphides*, said
that it was Rudolf who revealed to her a whole new way of looking at
the ballet. She began to time the take-off of her jumps to land in unison
with his, and he taught her the fluid, slow-breathing phrasing that is the
mainspring of the Vaganova system. She followed everything he
showed her, and together they became one body, one movement, their
lines a natural extension of each other, their fingertips simultaneously
marking out the arc of a phrase. There were many discussions and
try-outs behind this appearance of spontaneous symmetry, but Margot
herself had noticed that 'something quite special' happened when they
danced together, something they had not consciously worked to
achieve. 'It's odd . . . yet there in the photos both heads will be tilted
to exactly the same angle, both in perfect geometric relationship to
each other.'

While of the same Romantic period of style and setting as *Giselle*, *Les
Sylphides* does not have the joint passion of the earlier ballet; there are
moments of euphoria generated by sheer rapture of movement, but its
overall mood is elegiac and impersonal. In total contrast was the storm
of emotion taking place in the studio where Rudolf and Margot had
begun to work with Frederick Ashton on *Marguerite and Armand*, the
ballet he was creating especially for them. The choreographer had
thought of adapting Alexandre Dumas fils' *La Dame aux camélias* for
Margot after seeing Vivien Leigh in an English version of the play in

1961. Margot seemed to Ashton to be the epitome of Marguerite Gautier, from the chime of their names to the way each embodied opposites of great sophistication and great simplicity, but having found the existing score to be too long and elaborate, and nothing else suitable, he dropped the idea. Then, one evening in the spring of 1962 he heard Liszt's *Piano Sonata in B Minor* played on the radio, and envisaged the whole ballet – the music's circular structure and single encapsulation of the sonata form suggesting to him how the narrative could be speeded up and told in flashback, 'pared down to nothing'.

Added to this was the fact that by now, as Margot said, Rudolf had 'burst headlong into our world'. Contained in Liszt's masterpiece were all the extremes in the dancer's own nature of demonic intensity, flamboyance and violence, combined with heartbreaking lyricism and tenderness. Rudolf himself was almost a reincarnation of Liszt, whose Romantic beauty and charisma as a performer had inspired the same kind of idolatrous worship in audiences a century earlier – the reason Ken Russell's 1975 film *Lisztomania* starred a rock singer (Roger Daltrey) in the lead. Similarities abound, from their vagabond lives to their shared passion for Byron and Bach – even their love for the exoticism of Turkey. Eyewitness accounts of the two artists are interchangeable at times, 'the divine soul' shining from the face of Liszt at the piano closely anticipating a fan's description of Rudolf: 'He was transfigured when he danced. I'd never seen such unearthly beauty. He seemed unreal; not of this world – like an archangel.'

Ashton's choice of music appeared almost predestined when he then discovered that the model for Marguerite, Marie Duplessis, the most remarkable young courtesan in Paris, had had an affair with the composer. It was reading about their brief but ecstatic attachment that made Ashton wonder whether Liszt's recollection of Mariette, as he called her, could have inspired this very sonata. 'It may not have been, possibly not in the least. But you see, it *could* have been.'

Certainly for Rudolf it was the Lisztian pursuit and transmission of passion that drove his performance of Armand. The character, as he said, 'Was sitting already in me'; while for Margot the real Marguerite, with her long black hair and fragile ballerina shoulders, was a woman to whom she felt strangely linked. In the love duets she abandoned herself as never before in a display of recklessness that amazed even Rudolf, 'Margot throw herself – God knows where – and I have to wrestle.'

In the play the heroine is so dominant that she overshadows her young lover, but Ashton's ballet was created for Rudolf as much as for

Margot, the change of inflection endorsed by the title. Far from resenting the division of this famous diva vehicle (played definitively by Sarah Bernhardt onstage and on screen by Greta Garbo), Margot was enormously stimulated by Rudolf's demand of an equal share in every stage moment. 'He brought her to a higher pitch of approach,' Ashton said. 'He came at a period when she had lost Michael [Somes] and it was all rather run of the mill. Suddenly this enormous impulse came, and she just *responded* to him.'

Michael Somes had been Margot's partner for fourteen years, and presumed that when he retired, she would follow suit. They were supposed to have danced for the last time together at the gala in which *Corsaire* was performed, but Somes found to his distress that he had been taken off the programme without even a telephone call of warning. True, Ashton had cast him in the new ballet as Armand's father, but it was in a walk-on character role, whose function was to provide a cold and static contrast to the emotional furore (a situation some suggested could be intentionally allegorical, showing Somes, 'a symbol of duty and morality', frowning on his former partner's new rhapsodic freedom). Somes certainly did disapprove of Rudolf's inflammable, thrusting nature, which was so alien to his own disciplined, conventional approach. He felt, too, that people's memory of his partnership with Margot had been wiped out by the young Russian, who made him seem as ploddingly predictable as a shire horse.

And yet, in Rudolf's account, Somes is no stiff, reproving outsider but a collaborator who was intimately involved with the ballet's creation. Even the passionate duets, Rudolf claimed, were '*Totally* improvised by four of us – we had like kind of orgasm.' So intoxicating were the first rehearsals that Somes, usually an exacting and pedantic *répétiteur*, was unable to pin down and rehearse the choreography. This began to infuriate Rudolf:

> Nobody remembered not one step and we had to start all over again from beginning. Each time came something else. It was *very* unsettling to me. That's why I was all the time speaking of Balanchine saying *he* would give you language exactly and exact steps. And that way I don't have to delve into myself and dig out of me something. I wanted from Fred to give something definite. So I had quite a few tantrums.

In addition to the 'hellish tensions' in the studio, Ashton often had to wait for his two stars to finish other rehearsals, only to find that when at last they were able to start work, Rudolf 'would sit down every two minutes'. He was having treatment for a dislocated ankle-bone, which, while not sufficiently severe to prevent him from filming *Les Sylphides* on 19 November, was reason enough for him to cancel the rest of the year's performances and to announce that he was going to Australia for a rest. The première of *Marguerite and Armand,* scheduled for 13 December, was postponed until March.

Rudolf was desperate to join Erik, who was also finding their separation 'almost impossible to bear'. But having sent a telegram to say that he would soon be coming, Rudolf then cancelled his flight. Word had spread about his arrival in Sydney, and Erik, fearing a repetition of the Stuttgart situation, when 'all the publicity started and many questions and gossips', seemed to have changed his mind about wanting Rudolf there: 'I hurt you on the phone like many times before. You ask to tell you OK to come, to be with me [but] I am looking for someone who would come anyway regardless. I wish this someone to be you and you only. When I give you "no reasons to come" that's the time to come to help me and love me.'

Concerned that he might have gone too far this time in testing Rudolf's love and loyalty, Erik sent a telegram – MISSING YOU PRAYING YOU WILL COME ALL LOVE E – as a result of which the trip was rescheduled for December.

Rudolf's injury was genuine enough (Erik refers to it in a letter dated 21 November), but the press implied that his 'foot condition' was, in fact, a convenient way of getting out of an embarrassing double booking. Having 'definitely agreed' to perform in Chicago with the American Ballet Theatre over the Christmas period, the dancer was also billed to appear at that time in *Sleeping Beauty* at Covent Garden. This was due entirely to lack of communication between the press office and the management (committee meeting notes confirm that de Valois had known about the Chicago engagement at least six weeks earlier). However, the affair only exacerbated Rudolf's reputation for wildness; indeed, *Time* magazine quoted a Covent Garden official saying: 'I'd rather deal with ten Callases than one Nureyev.'

Rudolf's absence in Australia meant that he would also be letting Margot down, her annual gala taking place as usual in December. Before he left he promised that he would teach her the duet from *Gayane,* suggesting as her partner his young Hungarian friend Viktor Rona. The idea that Margot Fonteyn would invite a completely unknown foreigner to dance with her was so unlikely that when the ecstatic Viktor first broke the news to his colleagues in Budapest, not one of them believed him. He hardly believed it himself, especially when he arrived at London airport to find the ballerina waiting to meet him together with a large press corps. Although responsible for giving the twenty-seven-year-old the greatest break of his career, Rudolf kept out of sight, aware that publicity about their friendship could jeopardize Viktor's position in Hungary. However, the two young men were briefly reunited in the airport car park, where they just had time to run through the *Gayane* dance before Rudolf's Sydney flight was called.

Seriously frightened, not only by the prospect of being twenty hours in the air, but also by the possibility of abduction by the Soviets, Rudolf travelled under an assumed name, and had obtained permission to stay aboard the aircraft at all scheduled stops.* He had also been filled with anxiety by Erik's latest cable which warned, EMBASSY INFORMED RADIO NEWSPAPERS TODAY BE PREPARED AT ARRIVAL FOR MUCH PRESS. As it happened, however, Rudolf arrived at Mascot airport to find only one person waiting for him, a smiling Australian in his mid-thirties, who, as he stepped forward to greet Rudolf, handed him a note.

My dearest dearest Rudic,

I am so happy you are here. I am waiting for you in a car. The man who is giving you this letter you can trust. He will get you through as easily as possible . . . No matter what the world knows or thinks, my darling, you are here and I am waiting for you.

A few days earlier Erik had summoned the company publicist, Noel Pelly, and, swearing him to secrecy, asked him to try to persuade the head of customs and immigration to allow Rudolf to leave by an entrance off-limits to the press and general public. Apart from being ambushed outside the terminal by an enterprising reporter and

---

* The Hollywood-style episode Rudolf related to Keith Money of an attempted snatch at Cairo airport is more likely to have been an account of thoughts that had run through Rudolf's mind rather than an incident that actually took place. This saga, 'which, somehow, never reached the ears of the press' – and that certainly would have required the collusion of the Egyptian airport authorities – involved a pair of KGB agents who searched the plane for the dancer while the other passengers were waiting in a transit hut. As Rudolf hid in one of the lavatories, the 'two goons' were diverted by a quick-thinking flight attendant who had remained on board. Money says that it was the vividness of Rudolf's 'replay of *himself*' that convinced him at the time that the story was true (Keith Money, *Fonteyn and Nureyev*).

photographer from the *Sydney Daily Telegraph*, everything went according to plan: Erik was indeed sitting in a car parked nearby, and they drove immediately to his apartment overlooking Double Bay. 'Rudolf couldn't wait for us to get there,' recalled Pelly. 'It was as if this was Mecca.'

Euphoric at being reunited, the two dancers spent their first days at the beach and going for long walks, both grateful that they could be out together without Rudolf constantly being recognized. At the theatre, where the new director was Peggy van Praagh, a teacher friend from Rudolf's de Cuevas period, he was made to feel completely at home, and although he was receiving physiotherapy for his ankle, he did not let the injury trouble him. He took company class each day with Erik, and even demanded taxing Danish footwork – 'You give me knitting!' he would say to the Volkova-trained ballet master Ray Powell. Impressed by the vitality of the Australian dancers, Rudolf regularly watched performances from the wings, often calling out directions. 'He loved our company,' says Powell. 'He was watching and planning for the future, and thinking about what could be *done*. It wasn't long before we were learning *Raymonda* and *Don Q.*'

Sonia Arova, who was Erik's partner on the tour as well as a constant companion, remembered Rudolf's visit growing increasingly strained as the weeks went by. 'You could feel the tension. Erik was trying to pull away . . . he began to realize that, as far as his career went, he had to do something drastic.' In his letters, however, Erik gives quite the opposite impression. More in love with Rudolf every day, he pledges his determination that they should have a future together 'even if I have to just follow you around'. He finds himself drawing strength from working with Rudolf, now his own 'dancing ideal', telling him, 'You have been my inspiration and also sometimes my frustration because in you I see everything I want to be able to do.' Rudolf's departure for America left him desolate and directionless. On Christmas Day, preferring to be on his own rather than 'crying inside' with friends, he retraced the steps of their last walk along the harbour. Hearing no word from Rudolf over the coming week, and hardly able to sleep, he sank even lower, overcome by a sense of doom that made him afraid to be with people and afraid to be alone. 'I hope it stops because it makes me feel like I could break down . . . Oh darling I miss you so or am I going crazy?'

The last thing Rudolf wanted to accept was the knowledge that Erik was at breaking point; he was having problems enough of his own. Unimpressed by the standards and style of the American Ballet

Theatre, which had engaged him for three performances in December 1962, he found himself frequently at war with its artistic director, Lucia Chase, and furious that bungled advance publicity (in the *Chicago Tribune* he was billed as 'Rudolph Douglas') had led to a week of dismal houses. A bad cold forcing him to cancel one performance hardly improved his 'crabby mood', but at least by this time Erik was able to rally himself to lend strength and support: 'My dearest beautiful monster . . . Don't get upset over silly burocracies [*sic*] or people. Sit down and relax when they choose not to understand you . . . just keep looking at them till they do better for you.'

Rudolf's ABT debut should have been a landmark for him – the opportunity at last to dance not only his first Balanchine work but the one that had so impressed him in Russia. He was even to appear with the same ballerina, the Chilean-born Lupe Serrano, renowned for her powerful technique. Erik himself had taught Rudolf the role, a modern incarnation of a Petipa prince, intended to be danced at breakneck speed. But having found the St Petersburg adagio element lacking in Balanchine's work, Rudolf took it upon himself to reinstate it, performing the variations with such exaggerated rubato that Serrano says, 'It was not Balanchine as I knew it.' The taxing sequence of *tours en l'air* interspersed with pirouettes became so weighted down that it was a struggle for Rudolf to stay in control. Even the devoted Maude Gosling commented, when shown amateur film footage of *Theme and Variations*, that Rudolf was 'all over the place'.

After a few days with Erik in New York, Rudolf returned to London followed by a flurry of letters. The Australian Ballet's plea to Erik to return in the spring, together with the offer he had received from Balanchine to rejoin the New York City Ballet six months later, meant that they would be spending another year dancing on opposite sides of the world. In the view of Susse Wold, this situation suited Erik better than he would admit. 'If you're emotionally afraid, and uncertain of committing, it's much easier to love from a distance. You don't have the day-to-day routine.' Certainly the troubadour style of Erik's letters – 'dreaming that my dreams, or our dreams will be true one day soon . . . I am under a magic spell . . . I am thirsty and hungry for you in every way' – express a language of longing too conventional at times to be convincingly real. Rudolf's own side of the correspondence is harder to judge, as only two notes have come to light (suggesting that Erik alone honoured the pact they had made to destroy each other's letters). Undated, unfinished and unmailed, they

were found among a batch of Erik's correspondence Rudolf kept in a
suitcase of miscellaneous papers at the Goslings' house. One contains
the following lines:

> My dearest and only one Human in the world I spoke with you only in
> morning and I still can't not to think about you. I am completely lost
> and alone and no satisfaction at all I am sertanly [illeg] from life just
> what I deserve. Our situation probably . . . difficult and for you it is
> not easy to [illeg]. I still hope that it exsist the way to be together and
> even to work. I need very much to see you, to feel, to look . . .
> You are the esense the focuse off all my world take my life if you
> want you so dear to me I don't [know?] what to offer to you else. I get
> into very strange mood I don't now why may be because of your sade
> voice or music or after performance [illeg] I probably dreaming
> always.

Rudolf must have mentioned the letter in a telephone call, as Erik's
reply, dated 17 January 1963, asks him to send everything he writes –
'however mad or hysterical'.

> We have nothing to hide from each other . . . Darling I love you, not
> only you as an ideal or an exciting idea but I love you for all you are and
> what you are . . . I am glad we are not like most 'normal' people who
> are neither strong nor weak. We have got something even more beau-
> tiful coming, and perhaps also something of great suffering ahead, but
> please darling let us share that and all to come together. Let us face it
> together, let us not be alone . . . I have found you, I hope you have
> found me too.

They were kindred spirits in solitude, but although Rudolf would
often sink into Russian *dushevnyi*, it was a Romantic kind of melancholy, not the dark, suicidal lack of motivation from which Erik
suffered. Erik was in this mood – wanting 'just to take some pills and
no more think, no more dreams' – when Rudolf telephoned on the
night of 26 January. Their contact brought Erik a few minutes of
comfort, but then all the doubts returned:

> Each day I write, or I read your letters full of love and also suffering
> and suddenly, it seemed like that is our future, our life together, sitting
> always, writing about our love, our longing and suffering, putting
> everything we feel so strongly for and about down on paper . . . to

reach the other, on the other side of the world. We haven't been able to
spend much time together lately and in the future it seems we will
have even less time. The only time we really were a long time together
was in London last year, but I don't think either of us were happy all
the time. No excuse can be made, not even my bad foot, my aunt's
death, or even later my mother's death, no excuse either for whatever
other ambitions we might have had too. We had little consideration for
each other at that time, and later too. We thought perhaps as we
worked so hard and we did, and for selfish reasons which are most
natural to us. Perhaps we thought that happiness was something we
deserved . . . but neither of us deserved it, and now we sit in each
part of the world and suffer from it, and our love and our desperate
dreams of meeting for a few hectic days, now and then, so we can
forget in each other's arms our aching feet and muscles, so we can
forget the sound of the audience, our responsibilities and our own
expectation to stay on top and ahead, our craving and hungry ambitions for life in this society. Yes my darling, we do work very hard for it
and we deserve everything we get, because we worked for it, but my
dearest we do not deserve happiness . . . I can see myself or
you, . . . forever sitting so far apart writing down all our love without
having it near us, it is unnatural our love cannot grow that way, only
our dreams about love and happiness will grow . . . Oh my darling,
there is nothing untrue or unreal about my love and desire for you, it is
so big, it is destroying me because there is only paper to release it on.
If we need distraction, we might as well go out in the street and pick
up a few hours of love, but I am afraid that is too late for me, because I
do know how much I love you and nothing can compensate or replace
it, that's my big suffering. Darling, help me find a way, I cannot do it
alone I am not that strong, and could we make it if we were together?
Or should all our ambitions for everything else as well make us
unhappy. My darling how to say I love you any more, you know I do
please help love, Erik.

Within a matter of days, however, having surfaced from his despair,
Erik continues as if this 'long and honest letter' had never been written, counting the hours until they meet and believing in a future
together – even the unlikely prospect of working with Balanchine at
the same time. Arriving in London on 6 February, he moved into
Rudolf's rented apartment, impatient to see 'all the new things' in his
Royal Ballet repertory.

*

Rudolf's ambition to collaborate with contemporary Western choreographers had been one of the main reasons for his leaving Russia, and yet, in London, he found himself dancing the same roles as before – a situation Ninette de Valois acknowledged when she admitted, 'We were after his past and he was after our present.' In January, as the conniving Etiocles in John Cranko's 1959 *Antigone*, he had his first opportunity to try a new style, revealing a stark angularity and air of menace that had not been seen before. The ballet itself amounted to little, its combination of American and Greek modern dance dismissed by Edwin Denby as 'pompous and . . . delivered with a BBC accent'. To Rudolf, however, it was the experience that counted. 'It is more important that you work, work and something good comes out. You try . . . mistakes, bad, old-fashioned or something like that. But work onstage really provides knowledge and develop art.'

Two weeks later, he was back in the role of the Prince, dancing *Swan Lake* with Margot for the first time in London. Mary Clarke's review described the 'cold wave of disapproval' felt in sections of the house when Odette danced her introductory passage with Siegfried instead of miming it. But if Margot had capitulated to Rudolf over the question of mime, her own mark on him had never been more apparent. What the audience was seeing was a complete transformation – 'a new Nureyev, an English Nureyev' as Richard Buckle called him. 'A beautifully behaved modest and controlled Nureyev, giving simply and splendidly a well-thought-out, carefully rehearsed performance. For who could show temperament or be other than on their best behaviour in Fonteyn's presence?'

Turning an *enchaînement* into a musical phrase was a Fonteyn speciality: her quick, light connecting steps were a highlight of her performance – 'an expression of spirit, some burst of joy', as Violette Verdy put it. And it was seeing Rudolf begin to join steps together in a continuous line rather than tackling each one separately that made Margot realize the extent of her influence. It did not stop there. With her vertical carriage and squarely angled limbs, she may have lacked the plastique, breadth and voluptuousness of Russian-trained ballerinas, but it was in this orderly restriction that her artistry lay. A great actress probably without knowing it, she could give meaning to a glance or the smallest gesture – the reason that both Peggy Ashcroft and Irene Worth made a point of going to watch her performances. Her Odette, in the words of Robert Greskovic, was 'a little symphony of shifts and shades', and it was to this that Rudolf responded, her every nuance evoking an instinctive response from him. Understanding between the two dancers reached its peak in *Swan Lake*; as Alexander Bland remarked, 'They seemed aware of each other even when their backs were turned . . . When their eyes met, a message passed.'

A year earlier Clive Barnes had commented on the need to find a way of taming Rudolf without breaking him – 'He cannot be allowed to ride roughshod over everything' – and it was Margot who, like a horse whisperer, had achieved this. 'She'd just go over and sort of pat him,' said Maude. 'Almost like patting a racehorse.' Pushkin had had the same power over him, a power made possible, Margot believed, by the difference in their ages and professional experience. 'Had I been younger, I would have found it extremely difficult to accommodate to Rudolf's very fixed ideas and his, shall we say, *outspoken* way of expressing them. Quite simply, we were so far apart that we *could* come together.'

Margot as the target of Rudolf's abuse was hard for outsiders to accept; in terms of ballet protocol, it was shocking for a young person to insult a senior. Royal Ballet colleagues attributed her tolerance either to the masochism of a woman in love – 'That's when you put up with *anything*' – or to her recognition that, like the comedown after the rush of a drug, the exhilaration of dancing with Rudolf inevitably had unpleasant side effects. 'We could see that she didn't mind,' says the ballerina Anya Sainsbury. 'Having found someone who gave her so much, she could laugh it off.'

There was also the fact that Margot was surprisingly submissive in her relationships with men. As a young dancer in the Vic Wells company she had spent eight years in thrall to Constant Lambert, the brilliant conductor and composer – 'a kind of Diaghilev to her' – who opened her eyes to Proust, paintings and the world outside the ballet. Along with Lambert's immense culture went a roistering, wayward side, and Margot had taught herself to ignore his 'bouts of whoring', just as she later refused to acknowledge that her husband was unfaithful to her. With Tito, however, who had none of Lambert's erudition, her meekness was harder to understand, and Rudolf often wondered if she could be playing some kind of role. But Margot, as Keith Money has written, was 'two distinct people'. Shoring up the vulnerable femininity was a steely stoicism – the quality Rudolf particularly admired in her. 'He was always saying that she had the mind of a man,' remarks Maude Gosling. 'It was the reason he respected her so much.' Because Margot was fundamentally as tough as he was, Rudolf's taunts and tantrums rarely bothered her, and if they did, she would simply leave the room.

Rudolf's *izyuminka* – which he translated as 'what you call "charisma" – abnormal drive, nervosity, which are accepted onstage but in real life are rejected' – was also tolerated by de Valois. 'It was only fair that we had to put up with it . . . We must accept in him the quality of stardom – the inner fire . . . which surmounts the usual standards of critics.' Brought up to do exactly what was expected of them, the other dancers could hardly believe their disciplinarian director's acquiescence towards Rudolf. They watched in amazement as he ripped off his wig and snarled his contempt for the bulky costumes Philip Prowse had designed for Kenneth MacMillan's ballet, *Diversions*. 'He was so badly behaved,' recalls Georgina Parkinson. 'But he was obviously insecure. This was his first foray into contemporary dance, and he wasn't used to Kenneth's acrobatic lifts.' Hardly in top form himself, MacMillan was ill at ease with Rudolf – 'He hated the whole thing of him being such a star' – and produced an unexceptional, plotless work, which nevertheless was a baptism of sorts. For the first time, as Clive Barnes remarked, Rudolf was performing *with* the Royal Ballet rather than having the company provide a decorative setting *for* him. And yet, although he had clearly mastered the new technique, he still appeared an outsider, dancing with what Barnes called 'a mixture of romantic ardour and sulky heroism that needed a lot of toning down'.

In *Marguerite and Armand* a month later, there was no question of Rudolf having to subjugate his individuality; the ballet actually exploits what Ashton called the impact of personality – the stage presence of his stars. The choreography for Armand not only incorporates Nureyev-patented steps, it absorbs his personal style, blending the feline plastique of *Corsaire* with Albrecht's romantic intensity. By now Rudolf had realized that even without Balanchine's decisiveness in rehearsals Ashton was a 'kind of genius'. He may not have demonstrated or articulated the actual steps he wanted, but a mysterious process of osmosis took place. 'You have extrasensory perception and feel that.' At the same time, determined to retain the choreography, Rudolf decided to take charge of rehearsals himself. 'I start to observe what we did. Try to remember . . . Then I start to do tortuous, step by step, movement by movement creating those passions.'

Hardly surprisingly, the process resulted in a number of eruptions. And while Ashton 'gave as good as I got, my dear!', he could not endure Rudolf's rough treatment of Margot, even though he could clearly see that she didn't mind. 'It was only me with that natural exaggerated sense of courtesy, I suppose you could call it. I was brought up to believe that a ballerina is a sacred object.' This was a period when Margot was no longer Ashton's sole muse, but all the same he felt hurt and undermined to see her completely under Rudolf's sway. In the past, if they disagreed over a point, she had always deferred to him – '"You're always right in the end!" she'd say' – whereas now it was Rudolf who inevitably had the final word. Quite justifiably, 'Fred felt that he was stealing her away,' says Maude.

Emotions reached their height at the dress rehearsal, which even de Valois recalled as 'really awful'. Watched by about fifty photographers, Rudolf ripped the collars off two shirts, flung a riding crop at the stage manager, partnered Margot 'abominably', and 'with extraordinary passion' tore Armand's jacket into small pieces. Clutching publicist Bill Beresford's arm, de Valois finally could stand it no more, and strode up the ramp on to the stage.

I told him, 'Rudi, this can't go on. I'm not making you another shirt. What's worrying you?' What he had on was a gentleman's dress suit – white tie and tails. But he kept saying, 'I don't like it. It makes me look like a waiter.' And I couldn't imagine what he meant until I remembered that in the Soviet Union, the only people who wear tails are waiters! And you see, this conflicted with his vision of nobility.

But there was more to it than that. The designer of *Marguerite and Armand* was Cecil Beaton, whose main inspiration for the costumes was the 1937 film *Camille*. And while Garbo's ravishing, bare-shouldered ballgowns perfectly suited Margot and offset the play of *épaulement* in Ashton's choreography, the buttoned-up formality of Robert Taylor's outfits – however authentically *en lion* – was completely at odds with Rudolf's own carefully careless Byronic style. Having seen *Camille* in Leningrad, he well remembered how ludicrously overdressed Taylor looks at times, and he also resented the way the long jacket foreshortened the line of his leg. Rudolf's 'rehearsal outburst' was staged specifically for Beaton, though he knew, too, of course, that subsequent newspaper reports of the 'Fiery Russian' ripping off his collar would only heighten the atmosphere of thrilled expectation surrounding *Marguerite and Armand*.

No Royal Ballet première had ever been so eagerly anticipated as the charity gala on 12 March 1963. It had been a risk submitting a

nineteenth-century penny-novel melodrama to a public just waking
up to a new era of kitchen-sink reality (even Ashton admitted his story
was 'old hat'). But to Peter Brook, reviewing the ballet for the
Observer, the dancers' depth of conviction not only brought dramatic
credibility to their roles, it breathed life into the genre itself, making
'the most artificial of forms suddenly seem human and simple'. There
was certainly nothing conventionally 'balletic' about Margot's display
of anguish, the kind of raw, visceral emotion said to have defined Sarah
Bernhardt's[*] portrayal of Marguerite.[†] It was a starkness that derived
from the novel, not the play, which is as trite, sentimental and far
removed from the original as the 1966 film of *Marguerite and Armand* is
from the stage version of the ballet.[‡] Ashton wanted a kind of jarring
effect from his dancers, their primal lack of inhibition countering the
billet-doux sweetness of what had gone before. Keith Money still
remembers the bluntness of the closing image: 'When at last he let
her hand fall away, she let it thump of its own weight on to the stage.
Audibly. It was simply gut-wrenching, and so final. I'd never experienced quite that sort of theatrical involvement before – of being
absolutely *wrung out*.'

The first-night audience (which included the Queen Mother
and Princess Margaret) gave *Marguerite and Armand* a tumultuous ovation. ROYALS AND SUBJECTS DELIGHTED 21 CURTAIN CALLS . . . a
euphoric Ashton cabled a friend. The critics, however, were more
circumspect, the consensus being that the ballet would be expendable
without its two stars. But then, as Richard Buckle volunteered, 'What
is *Le Spectre de la rose* without Karsavina and Nijinsky?'

Rudolf's next debut in an Ashton ballet two weeks later required him to
suppress every trace of exhibitionism and submit completely to an
ensemble. Created in 1946, *Symphonic Variations* is the choreographer's

---

[*] So real and 'germ-laden' was the atmosphere Bernhardt created during her death scene
that when critic James Agate's old family doctor saw a performance at the Manchester
Hippodrome he kept commenting on the criminal folly of allowing a tubercular patient
to receive visitors, repeating, 'Everything she touches is infected' (Gerda Taranow, *Sarah
Bernhardt*).

[†] It was the element missing from the portrayal by Sylvie Guillem, despite the fact that
she identified with Marguerite's distress to the point of crying genuine tears during her
performance.

[‡] Rudolf was dismayed by the misty-edged fastidiousness of director Pierre Jourdan's
camera, telling Elizabeth Kaye, 'I hated that . . . And all the Vaseline on the lens – oh gosh!
I gave him hard time.'

manifesto, its lyrical purity and understatement a paradigm of native style. This was exactly the kind of twentieth-century classicism that Rudolf admired – the English equivalent of Balanchine's reminting of the language of Petipa: idiosyncratic, contemporary, yet true to tradition. Only too aware of the expectations surrounding this near-sacred piece of work, Rudolf found the rehearsals an ordeal: struggling to master the slow, sustained lifts, the play of Ashton's musicality from literal exactness to a complete departure from the beat, the anomaly of dancing collectively. Like a sextet of musicians, the cast of six was required by the choreographer to form a unit. 'They're all equal . . . it's not a display piece . . . you've got to be together with the other two boys, and that was a problem for Nureyev. It all has to be dovetailed, and nobody can shine out. They can, of course, if they have radiance.'

Ashton was alluding here to Margot, the inspiration and 'unintentional star' of *Symphonic Variations*. Its qualities were her qualities, those around which the company's style had been formed, and it was she who, as he said, 'gave the clue' to the ballet, an exultant expression of the religious faith he had rediscovered during the war. Standing hypnotically still at the side of the stage, she appeared to be in a state of grace, in that state of suspension during which the Carmelite mystics believed visions could occur.* 'A deep, almost mystical, ecstasy' emanated from Rudolf, too, deriving in part from the extraordinary potency of his willed restraint. Several critics commented that *Symphonic Variations* had never been more highly charged, nor Margot more intensely luminous. 'Something of this emotional dimension . . . seemed to transfer itself to Fonteyn,' wrote one. 'She adds a certain rapt quality. The impassive delicacy has thawed into positive serenity.' But Ashton did not want Margot's pure, undemonstrative lyricism augmented in any way, any more than he wanted a rapturous private exchange between two of his 'perfect sextet of instrumentalists'. After that one performance on 1 April 1963, Ashton never cast Rudolf in the ballet again.†

---

* Ashton had been reading Saint John of the Cross, whose doctrine on quiet was a major source for the ballet's motif of stasis. 'The soul waits in inward peace and quietness and rest.'

† Rudolf did, however, cast himself. On tour later that year with Margot and a small group he attempted one more performance (about which Ashton would undoubtedly have heard, as Alexander Grant, his closest friend and confidant, also danced it that night). 'It nearly killed Rudolf,' recalls the third male soloist, Ronald Hynd. 'He took himself straight out again, and [American Ballet Theatre's] Royes Fernandez took over.'

The next hurdle was the uncertainty over his participation in the Royal Ballet's spring and summer tour of the United States. Since its landmark debut in 1949, the company had been represented there by the powerful impresario Sol Hurok, whose Russian performers included both the Kirov and Bolshoi companies. Hurok had also been responsible for sending several of his American clients on tours to the USSR, among them Igor Stravinsky and the pianist Van Cliburn. The aftermath of the Cuban missile crisis had led to an important change in East–West cultural relations, one Hurok was in no mind to disrupt by promoting a Soviet defector. 'Of course I understood,' Rudolf would later comment. 'He was afraid that he might lose all the lucrative Russian engagements and Russian artists.' Used to having total casting control over the dance companies he presented, Hurok, however, met outright resistance from Ninette de Valois, who told him, in effect, 'No Nureyev, no Royal Ballet!' As a result, the impresario travelled to Moscow in February to explain his predicament to the Russian minister of culture, Ekaterina Furtseva. Their subsequent conversation was described in the KGB report as 'unpleasant'. In the end, according to the conductor and pianist Vladimir Ashkenazy, who made his own decision to leave Russia in July, it was Khrushchev himself who intervened, giving the impresario his personal agreement that he could take Nureyev to America without forfeiting his Soviet business.

Negotiations for Rudolf's participation on tour had also involved a hasty trip to Moscow the same week by the head of the Royal Opera House, Sir David Webster. The Russians had recently finalized a cultural exchange agreement with the British government and were now threatening to cancel the Bolshoi's Covent Garden season scheduled for July. While supporting de Valois's insistence on including Rudolf, Webster was determined to 'play him slowly', a decision that, as he remarked in a letter to Lord Drogheda, was as much out of concern for diplomacy at home as abroad. 'In ballet as it is not in a way in opera, THE COMPANY is the thing,' he wrote, warning of the dangers of stirring up jealousy among the dancers. As a result, the Royal Ballet opened its season at the Metropolitan Opera House on 17 April, 1963, with no casts advertised in advance and no star billing, the dancers' names being listed in alphabetical order. At the traditional opening performance of *Sleeping Beauty*, Margot's partner was David Blair.

Predictably, though, it was Rudolf everyone wanted to see. Absence of publicity due to a prolonged newspaper strike meant that the Royal Ballet had never before played to so many empty seats. Even Margot's

performances were not sold out, but an underground excitement
began to spread about the 'new Nijinsky's' debut in *Giselle* the following week. On the evening of 25 April, for an act and a half the audience took a cool, 'show-me' attitude – until Rudolf's solo. Then they
went wild, and at the end of the ballet stood and screamed – 'yes,
screamed', said the *Herald Tribune*'s Walter Terry – for half an hour
before flocking to the stage door for a final glimpse of the star.

After the adulation of the New York public, the critical reaction
came as a shock to Rudolf, who felt he had been 'pounded'. His performance in *Marguerite and Armand* was dismissed as histrionic, the
ballet itself considered 'old-fashioned and danceless'. Even the enthusiastic reviewers were, like the audience, disappointingly impressed by
his virtuosity alone (his *Giselle* solo was described in the *New Yorker* as
'one of the miracles of the current ballet season', and it was only Terry
who commented on the poetic eloquence of his interpretation). The
most startling divergence of opinion took place in the *Saturday Review*,
whose regular critic, Irving Kolodin, the music columnist, responded
positively, only to be followed in the next issue by John Martin,
recently retired from the *Times*, who wrote a long article Rudolf
described as 'slashing me to shreds'.

Citing the Kaufman-Hart play *The Man Who Came to Dinner* as an
example of how a guest can take over a household, Martin warned in
his article that Rudolf was a disintegrating force in the Royal Ballet, a
concern David Webster had already voiced: 'While Nureyev could be
an asset . . . he equally might start its dissolution.' Martin continued
with a number of valid, even prophetic remarks: Nureyev is an artist
who knows his place – 'front and centre' . . . he is always essentially
in competition with the ballerina . . . he makes the other male
dancers seem inferior for all the wrong reasons . . . he tinkers with
the classics 'to give himself all the plums' . . . The Royal Ballet is
simply his vehicle of the moment – 'sooner or later he can be confi-
dently expected to depart for pastures that seem greener'. But what
undermined these points, turning a considered appraisal into a
destructive private vendetta, was the pervading tone of ugly sarcasm –
the descriptions of Rudolf's Blue Bird in 'Boris Karloff makeup'; of
Albrecht '*en travesti*'; and most ludicrous of all, the crass dismissal of
the Fonteyn–Nureyev partnership: 'She has gone, as it were, to the
grand ball with a gigolo.'

Once again, though, Martin's attempt to discredit the 'international
glamour boy' had absolutely no effect. Glamour, youth and personality were the era's defining attributes, its archetypes America's young

president and his wife. For Jackie Kennedy, these Fonteyn–Nureyev performances were among the most powerful artistic experiences of her life, making up, she said, for having missed seeing Nijinsky and Chaliapin. Having applauded throughout the forty-odd curtain calls for *Marguerite and Armand* until her hands were 'black-and-blue pulp', the first lady wanted to make her customary visit backstage, but found herself blocked by Hurok, who was 'fearful of the political repercussions'. Undeterred, she invited Rudolf, Margot, and a few of their Royal Ballet colleagues to a post-performance supper in her suite at the Carlyle, but gave up when she received a message that Nureyev was not available.* Defying the furious Hurok, Mrs Kennedy, who was accustomed to getting her own way, then ordered a private plane a few days later to bring the dancers to tea at the White House.

Since her husband's inauguration, borrowing paintings and objets d'art from galleries and museums, tracking down and reclaiming priceless period furniture, Jackie Kennedy had transformed a characterless official residence into a national showplace. Justifiably proud of her achievements, she led Rudolf, Margot, Ashton, Michael Somes and the conductor John Lanchbery around the state rooms, pointing out treasures, just as she had done the previous year when she gave her famous televised tour to the nation. After tea she took the group into the Cabinet Room, where she left them, saying that she would go and find out if her husband was free – an opportunity Rudolf immediately seized to see what it felt like to sit in the president's chair (the old North Carolina porch rocker). Good-naturedly accepting the fact that the White House was becoming 'a sort of eating-place for artists', Jack Kennedy received his wife's visitors with his customary easy charm, although he would have been the first to admit a lack of enthusiasm for 'all that cultural jazz'. Rudolf, on the other hand, immediately appreciated Jackie's knowledge of and passion for the arts, for antiques and for excellence in general, and it was this encounter that marked the beginning of their lifelong friendship.

It was all heady stuff. While moving in high-powered circles and being celebrated as the icon of the age, Rudolf was developing a taste for his own potent mixes of American cocktails – port and ginger ale, 'then brandy, then rum, then Negroni'. Arriving at a post-performance

---

* Greta Garbo had more success. Although not a ballet lover, she was keen to see this new version of *Camille*, and when she met Rudolf afterwards they bonded immediately, recognizing in each other what Cecil Beaton called 'the same untamed quality of genius, of not fitting' (Diane Solway, *Nureyev: His Life*).

reception in Toronto in early June, he immediately drank three whisky-and-ginger-ales, and cleared the floor to do the twist with Margot. By three a.m., having managed to escape the clutches of a socialite in a white sylphide dress and matching satin shoes, he was in a mood for carousing, oblivious to the fact that Toronto then was 'a very, very Waspy, uptight city which rolled up its sidewalks at ten o'clock'. Pointed down Yonge Street in the direction of his hotel, he was seen performing a series of *grands jetés* at the intersection with Queen Street, tapping the roofs of cars that had slowed down to watch him. One was a police car. Intending to caution Rudolf, who instinctively lashed out as if to 'give us a good kick on the shins', the inspectors then arrested him for jaywalking. The 'very emotional fellow' was driven off in handcuffs to the station, where he was released only after the company's general manager, the tall, courteous Michael Wood, had been roused from his bed, and managed to convince Toronto's 'wonderful, understanding policemen' that no harm had been intended.

In Los Angeles, Rudolf stayed high up in the hills with publicist Rupert Allan (the brother of Erik's friend Christopher), whose partner was the film producer Frank McCarthy. Surrounded by trees, their house was dark and not particularly comfortable, but they made a great effort to entertain him, inviting a number of movie stars to a party in his honour. He was thrilled to meet Bette Davis, the only woman he included in his personal pantheon of screen idols (Montgomery Clift and Erich von Stroheim were among the men), and he told the actress how much he had admired *All About Eve*, which he had seen in Russia. When he and Fred Astaire were introduced to each other as the greatest dancers of their time, Rudolf found it hard to respond with appropriate enthusiasm, Astaire then being completely unknown to him. 'I found the man affable and charming, but it was impossible for me to see in him a person of legend . . . we just smiled politely and had nothing really to say.'* Natalie Wood, on the other hand, he recognized immediately from *West Side Story*. The child of Russian émigrés, born Natalia Nikolaevna Zakharenko, she was exactly the same age as Rudolf, and when at last the food was served, they took their plates into a corner where they talked excitedly in Russian. One of the guests imagined they were saying to each other, '"So . . . they think we are just behaving like a couple of peasants? We'll show them!" and watched

* 'It was only little by little that my admiration for him was aroused and developed,' he told ex-Vaganova colleague Egon Bischoff. '[But then] I was bowled over by this man, and tried to see every film he'd ever made.'

their growing abandon as they started eating their chicken legs with their fingers . . . crunching the bones and chucking the debris on the carpet.'

Cecil Beaton, who was in Hollywood working on designs for the film of *My Fair Lady*, approached Rudolf cautiously that evening, their last encounter having been the tempestuous dress rehearsal at Covent Garden. But instead of being cold and disdainful, the mildly drunk Rudolf was surprisingly affectionate. 'We hugged and kissed and . . . it was all very agreeable and an amusing comedy,' said Beaton, who then found himself listening to a string of grievances. People were being very mean to him, Rudolf told him; he was not going to leave, but they would have to pay him properly. He said he was going to continue dancing for television in New York, but grumbled about having to pay most of what he earned in US taxes. Later, noticing that the dancer had disappeared from the party, Beaton went upstairs, where he found Rudolf alone in his room, sitting on the edge of his bed, dangling a loose shoe.

'What are you doing here? Are you sad?'

'Yes and very lonely – this awful house – you suffer so. Maybe I have five days in Paris with my friend, but we have been travelling a month without meeting; and when you love you are apt to be sad and there's no hope for us. We can't work together. It is *always* travelling for me; always on the road – without a window . . . Nobody understands me, perhaps Margot a little from time to time, and Freddy's nice, but he offers me nothing, and they hate me. But I don't care.'

Rudolf must also have confided his discontent to the Hollywood designer Jean Louis[*] and his wife, as the ebullient Maggie Louis immediately wrote Rudolf a letter 'full of exciting new schemes'. They had talked to one of the heads of Universal Pictures about the idea of his doing a film part that had nothing to do with dance, and they volunteered to raise the finances, should he want to start a ballet company of his own 'or in partnership with Margot or Eric [*sic*] or anyone else you chose'. When the tour ended, they invited Rudolf to join them at their Malibu beach house – 'You do know how much we love you . . . even though our friendship is so new – ' but Rudolf wanted

* Whose best-known creation was the sequins-and-skin dress that Marilyn Monroe had worn the previous summer to deliver her breathless rendition of 'Happy Birthday' to President Kennedy.

to see Erik, who was waiting for him in Paris. On his last day in America, having spent ten hours in a Brooklyn TV studio filming the *Diana and Acteon* duet with Svetlana Beriosova, he rushed straight to Idlewild Airport as soon as the last take was finished, and caught a 9.30 flight that night.

After a few days together in the city, the two dancers drove down to the South of France in Erik's convertible, Rudolf looking 'more St Tropez than the Tropezians' in a striped jersey and beret. People in the port recognized him immediately and followed the car shouting his name. 'No one even noticed the equally great but less sensational Danish star.' The remark is that of Ruth Page, who spent the summers in a converted Provençal olive-oil mill two villas away from Brigitte Bardot. Rudolf had planned to stay overnight with the Fishers and practise in Ruth's studio, but the sea had flooded the floor, and there was no available bed, so they left, heading for Monte Carlo, as Rudolf was impatient to see the house that friends had just bought on his behalf.

Marika Besobrasova, a White Russian who ran Monte Carlo's internationally renowned dance school, had met Rudolf in July 1961 when she and her husband, Roger-Felix Médecin, travelled to Geneva to see him perform with the de Cuevas company. Spotting the dancer walking with a heavy bag outside the theatre, Marika called out to him, offering him a lift. Although startled to hear his name spoken in a Russian accent, Rudolf recognized Roger, a Monegasque lawyer whom he had once seen in a Paris café with Pierre Lacotte, and agreed to go with them into town. When they spoke Russian, Marika was curious to know why Rudolf used the same language she did – 'the *old* words, not Soviet speak'. 'I was never a Communist!' he told her sharply. However, when they began discussing ballet in depth, and he saw how receptive Marika was to his profound knowledge of St Petersburg schooling, Rudolf lowered his defences. He also felt comfortable with Roger, who had grown up with the children of the Ballets Russes de Monte Carlo dancers and so was close to the ballet world without being professionally involved. The couple helped him buy a Bell & Howell movie camera 'for my dancing', and when they parted, gave Rudolf their telephone number, urging him to come to stay with them in Monte Carlo. Not long afterwards the phone rang late one night, and they heard a voice saying, 'You remember me? You invite me.' They collected Rudolf from Nice airport and took him home to their apartment, beginning what was to be a lifelong friendship.

Roger-Felix's skills as a notary and Marika's sisterly devotion made them the ideal people to find him a property in the South of France. Within weeks of arriving in the West, he had discovered a passion for the Mediterranean – 'A sort of celestial privilege – for me who came from a cold, icy country, with a sun high and hardly tepid' – and the moment he felt he was earning sufficient and consistent money, 'began also to look for my sea'. Anywhere on the coast would cost a fortune, Marika told him, but for $69,000 they had found him somewhere in the hills, with distant views of the Bay of Monaco: Villa Arcadie. Built into the rocks of Mount Agel, the roughcast stone house stands in a large wild and wooded garden about a kilometre above the small shuttered town of La Turbie. Rudolf was delighted with it. 'Outside, mountains, sky and not a human being in sight; inside big white spaces.' Its empty white stucco rooms divided by wrought-iron gates would remind one friend of a Greek chapel; and later, when Rudolf had added a Gothic arch, candelabra and heavy, medieval leather-covered furniture, another would compare the interior to the set of *Camelot*. To the Fishers, however, who drove down a week or so later to see Rudolf's new property, it seemed illogically palatial. '*What* does he want with a grand villa like that? A capitalist at heart!'

This was true enough. Within weeks of defecting, Rudolf had made up his mind to demand the highest fees possible, believing that money was what 'decides one's worth' in the West. It had never been an issue in Leningrad, where, ever since his student days, his food and lodgings had been free – provided either by the Vaganova Academy or by the Pushkins. When he defected in Paris he owned nothing apart from the clothes he was wearing and basic essentials bought for him by Clara and Raymundo. His salary with de Cuevas, combined with German and American television fees, had been large enough to buy Villa Arcadie, but now, as 'permanent guest star' with the Royal Ballet, Rudolf's expectations were much higher. Having dinner after a performance with ballerina Nadia Nerina, Rudolf turned to her husband, Charles Gordon, a wealthy financier, and said, 'Charlik, Erik say you help me. I am poor man – no money. I want to make money. Tax free!' The ballerina's agent was Sandor Gorlinsky, a Hungarian émigré who had made himself as eminent as Sol Hurok by managing such stars as Maria Callas and Tito Gobbi. Contacting Gorlinsky on Rudolf's behalf, Gordon suggested forming an offshore investment company in Luxembourg, which would be 'owned by Rudolf' and have the sole right to receive fees paid to him without deductions. Until now Rudolf had been using his New York bank account to deposit his income, 'not necessarily money earned in the US,' and the Internal Revenue Service had begun hounding him for $30,642.70 in back taxes. He and Margot had also been advised to avoid massive tax demands by staying out of England until the end of the fiscal year the following April. (In September, David Webster warned the board that the pair's Covent Garden appearances would be limited because of the income tax regulations about residence.)

Most people assumed that Rudolf's villa had been bought in order to take advantage of tax benefits offered to Monte Carlo residents, but although overlooking the principality of Monaco it is, in fact, situated in the French Alpes Maritimes.* Arcadie was Rudolf's first attempt to put down roots in the West; he loved its beauty and isolation – 'Sometime I go there and not come back' – and created a calm, lyrical atmosphere with light flowing through the rooms, a log fire and music constantly playing.† He had only just moved in when Maude and Nigel, who were staying at a hotel nearby, wound their way up the hairpin bends one evening to visit him. When they arrived, Rudolf was there alone, grilling a chop over the open flame with rosemary from the garden, but immediately exclaimed, 'Come and see my view!' Taking Maude by the hand, he helped steer them in the dark to the front of the house. Even though it was a moonless night, the panorama was breathtaking, stretching from the shadowy ruins of a Doric colonnade below all the way down to the lights of the Corniche and the distant coast of Italy.

But Rudolf had little time to spend at his new house that summer, as he and Margot were heading a small troupe of Royal Ballet dancers on a world tour. Earlier, he and Erik had discussed the idea of forming another quartet of stars, this time with Margot and the Italian ballerina Carla Fracci, whom the two men would alternately partner. But Margot wanted neither to share Rudolf with Fracci nor to dance with Erik, and so the plan was dropped. Nevertheless Rudolf was determined that Erik should accompany him, and asked the Australian tour manager, Joan Thring, if he could be included. No was the answer

---

* In 1966 he did buy a Monaco property with tax relief in mind. Lotus Bleu, on the boulevard du Jardin Exotique, is a one-bedroom, fourth-floor apartment with two terraces and good views, but Rudolf spent no more than two nights there. 'And it didn't change anything for him,' Marika says. 'Because he had asked for political protection from France.'

† When the Scottish-American soprano Mary Garden (Debussy's first Mélisande) lived in Beaulieu-sur-Mer, she would give recitals at Arcadie, which was originally a barn and has wonderful acoustics.

she came back with – 'We can't really afford it.' A day or so later Rudolf came up to Joan and handed her a clutch of unused air tickets, which he presumed could be exchanged: 'I had to tell him they were useless, and they were flung at me. I was screamed at. *Punched*. I didn't know when I took this on that I was going to be beaten up every day.'

This initial encounter set a pattern of mock S&M, with Joan, a tall, chic former model, her waist-long hair coiled into a large bun, frequently playing the role of dominatrix. ('You crack good whip!', Rudolf would eventually compliment her at the end of the tour.) To keep the peace it was decided to take Erik as far as Greece, their first stop, where he could mount duets from *Flower Festival at Genzano* and *La Sylphide*. However, the truce between Rudolf and Joan did not last long. On the plane to Athens he asked her if she had booked him a room with a double bed, and at her reply, 'Not specifically,' spat out a Russian expletive and stalked back to his seat. Deciding 'If I let this pass, I'm ruined,' she marched up to where Rudolf and Erik were sitting, and demanded to know the meaning of the word. The noun *pizdá* (cunt) is one of the four cornerstone obscenities known in Russian as *mat* – underground street words that have far more impact than their English four-letter equivalents, and are never used in a woman's hearing.* When Erik asked Joan what had caused the outburst, she explained, relishing Rudolf's evident embarrassment. 'He was shrivelling by that time. *Shrivelling.*'

Margot was *pizdá*, too (sometimes negligibly softened to *pizdushka*) – frequently, on this tour. Ballet master Ronald Hynd had watched several times in disapproving silence as Rudolf carried her off into the wings and thumped her down to the floor, but seeing her rush out of the door one day following a particularly 'nasty scene', he was concerned, and asked if she was all right. 'Oh, I'm not scared of him,' she said nonchalantly. Certainly Margot knew better than anyone how to handle Rudolf, evidence of which is captured in the journal and photographs of Keith Money, who was with the dancers in Athens. He was taking pictures of the ballerina in practice clothes on the stage of the open-air Herod Atticus amphitheatre when a very tanned Rudolf appeared, wearing

* In a 'Letter from Moscow' published in the *New Yorker* (15 September 2003), Victor Erofeyev writes definitively about *mat*, deriving from the Russian word for 'mother', a component of the key phrase *yob tvoyu mat* (fuck your mother), which until recent times was taken so seriously that the bloody brawls it incited often ended in murder.

casual clothes and a mutinous expression. Hearing him announce that he 'probably' would not dance that evening, Margot frowned, but carried on rhythmically darning her pointe shoe as she began what Keith calls 'a fine little pavane of applied reason – and reasonableness'.

'Well, that's for you to decide' . . . Stitch, stitch . . . 'I suppose I can do one or two extra solos.' R stared at her, at this. She was not reacting correctly! . . .

'But I expect they won't be satisfied with *that*,' she said, after a longish pause. 'Perhaps we'd better just give the money back?'

'Huh?'

'Give the money back. If you're not dancing.'

At this R became interested in the stonework . . . 'I see,' he said rather distantly, and then strolled off through one of the arches . . .*

Keith Money's 'odyssey' of photographing Margot (resulting in a quartet of books) began with an image taken from a television screen of the 1962 Fonteyn–Nureyev *Giselle*. He was working in London as a professional illustrator when he was asked to contribute sketches of *Marguerite and Armand* for a commemorative album and decided to try his hand at dance photography. As the 'new boy' at press calls, positioning himself to one side, he discovered his métier – ballet reportage that appeared snatched from the wings: spontaneous, sweat-soaked and slightly off-limits. To begin with he found that Rudolf, who had picked up on Margot's 'genuine phobia' about cameras, and learned from her how to terrorize photographers, would turn a photo session into a tiger shoot – 'You might get the beast, but then again, the beast might get you.' Gradually, though, he relaxed his guard, noticing the degree to which Margot had come to trust the young New Zealander. With his wide-ranging interests, wit and discretion, Keith soon found himself fulfilling the functions of a cavalier, escorting the ballerina to official receptions. After Greece, however, once Erik had left, Margot and Rudolf again became inseparable.

'In many ways they were very bad for each other,' says Annette Page, one of the Royal Ballet principals on tour, and the wife of Ronald Hynd: 'Margot had always been so serious and professional, but she changed entirely when Rudolf was around. They were never on time, and we'd sit in the bus waiting to go to rehearsal until finally they would roll up giggling and joking like a couple of children.'

* Needless to say, 'Russia's Number One capitalist' danced that night.

There was none of the team spirit of the previous year, when Margot toured Australia with David Blair, and the dancers felt that they were there only as a road-show backup for Fonteyn and Nureyev. When Annette and Royes Fernandez followed a dazzling performance of the *Don Quixote* duet by repeating the coda, they were furiously upbraided by both stars for slowing down the programme. 'We only did it because the audience wouldn't stop clapping,' Annette said. The next night, however, Margot and Rudolf danced the Black Swan pas de deux, and they, too, performed an encore. Behaving like 'a big diva', Rudolf would change the repertory on a whim, and the only company member besides Margot who was prepared to challenge him was Robert Helpmann (her first partner), who, as someone once said, had the presence and personality to outface the devil himself. The writer Francis King, then living in Japan, witnessed the following exchange:

'Tonight I dance *Corsaire.*'

'No, it's *Swan Lake* tonight,' Helpmann corrected him.

'No, tonight *Corsaire.*'

'Dance what you like, Ducky. The orchestra will be playing *Swan Lake.*'

Everyone on tour that summer had observed how flirtatiously tactile Margot and Rudolf were with each other – 'always hugging and kissing'. Having bidden the two stars good night in the hotel lift, Alexander Grant met them again in the lift the following morning. 'Margot had an *enormous* love-bite on her neck. It was very very obvious, and she hadn't done anything to cover it up.' On another night there was a rooftop party at which everyone, according to Annette, 'got fairly sloshed, including (unusually) Margot, who was lounging on a mattress with Rudolf'. The next morning, as the dancers were once again sitting in the bus waiting to leave, 'BQ', who travelled everywhere with her daughter, was heard to remark, 'I don't know what's got into Margot. She was sick this morning.' When at last the pair appeared, Margot, who was wearing dark glasses, sat in the back of one of the cars, 'very quiet and rather slumped'. En route to class they passed some beautiful ruins at the water's edge and decided to stop for a quick dip. Revived by the sea, her hair hanging loose, Margot, as Ashton often said, was like an ondine when she swam. But when she came up to the surface this time her face was white. Since last seeing Tito she had been wearing his ring above her wedding band, and being too big for her, it had slipped off. Everyone began diving down to the seabed to help her find it, but they eventually gave up and returned to the cars. Margot – 'a devastated heap' – sat next to Ronald, who longed to put a comforting arm round her. 'But you didn't do that with Margot.' 'She was unbelievably upset,' says Annette. 'We did sort of wonder then if she had betrayed Tito. But it was all supposition.'

From then on the mood of the tour 'disintegrated – certainly darkened'. Margot, who had damaged her calf muscle, was dancing with difficulty, and 'always ringing up and wanting' her husband. It was troubling for others to see the degree to which she was bound to a man whom, as Joan Thring says, 'everyone took for granted was a shit'. But her feelings for Tito had come full circle, and she had reverted to 'the formerly love-sick girl' of the 1930s. The metamorphosis of the glamorous Latin American undergraduate into a paunchy married man who hunted her down some twenty years later in a stifling and vulgar courtship had left Margot emotionally numb. She came to realize, however, that Tito was the only person with whom she felt 'just fundamentally complete', and now, as her biographer Meredith Daneman says, it was in his 'very elusiveness that his true romantic power lay'. Tito had promised to be with her for the whole of the tour, but at the beginning decided that he would have a better time if he stayed in Monte Carlo. Annette, who shared a dressing room with Margot, remembers her continuing to hope that he would change his mind. 'She'd say, "Well, maybe he'll come *next* week," but was always being disappointed.' It was Margot's idea to include Ashton's *Scènes d'Amour* in the programme, and in Greece she asked Ronald Hynd to partner her. This short, plaintive duet, created as a gala item for Fonteyn and Somes in 1959, depicts the passionate leavetaking of a young girl and her lover on the eve of his departure for the Crusades. Holding his cloak as he walks away until it slips from her fingers, she is left alone – 'desperately unhappy, desperately in love, and losing her lover to goodness knows what'. Annette, who had never seen Margot dance the role more movingly, told her she had been 'just incredible'. 'Well, it's the story of my life,' she said, smiling. 'Saying goodbye to Tito.'

Rudolf, on the other hand, was in his element on tour, walking off into the night after dinner, when he and Helpmann could be spotted 'competing with each other on the waterfront'. He was particularly happy to be back in Israel, charmed as much as before by its 'south of Russia' ambiance, its climate and people. He had renewed contact with friends he made in the summer of '61, and struck up a new

encounter with a swarthy young man called Dani to whom he sent
gifts of cuff links and a sweater.* Erik, meanwhile, who had heard
nothing from Rudolf for several weeks and wasn't tempted to what he
called 'fill the time with anyone', was finding their separation unen-
durable. 'Erik was basically very very fastidious and chaste,' remarked
Glen Tetley. 'But Rudolf was lusty and wanted to experiment. He
wanted a game. It was all a big, wonderful game.'

From California and Hawaii, the final stages of their trip, Rudolf
returned to London in October and the reality of living alone in furnished accommodation. Now, as Margot noted, there was something
tragic in the sight of him 'diminishing in perspective down a desolate
street after the uproar of laughter and gaiety over supper'. On an
evening he spent with Svetlana Beriosova and her friends, he went
back to his flat and began a letter to Erik, its tone of bleak nihilism
almost an imitation of Erik's own:

> My very very dearest Erik, it is so sad that the world is such a cruel
> machine, and it seems the only [solution?] is to try to [illegible] for
> some time before it . . . destroy you. I feel incredibly sad, and have
> feeling that I can't explane, I need you every second, I feel that we are
> so alone in this world, very offen I have feeling that I am on edge of
> madness and whant to scream.† I whant to cover you with my hands
> and body and not to [illeg] to anybody my very dear and very much
> beloved one. Missing you enormous It's very hard without you. Today
> [November 17] I danced on TV *Diana and Acteon* with Svetlana and
> it was not specialy bad, but after show I had dinner with people of
> Svetlana and sadenly all my inside been so distorted and I felt empti-
> ness and uselesness of everething and I was missing you so impossibly
> hard, I was screaming inside and tearing all of myself to pieces.

Rudolf, influenced by Erik, was now drinking to a serious degree.
Walking past the Brompton Road taxi stand in the early hours of the
morning, the English actor Peter Eyre saw a young man lying curled
up in the luggage compartment of an empty cab. 'It was Nureyev. He
was very drunk and quietly whimpering.' Eyre waited until the driver

---

* Dani's letter of thanks was written from jail. 'I have got much time for thinking here, and
I'm thinking about the wonderful time we had had and we could have had' (Rudolf Nureyev
Archive).
† This echoed a remark in Erik's last letter, 'Sometimes I can scream to forget my loneliness.'

returned and, although Rudolf's flat was only around the corner in Ennismore Gardens, begged him to take 'the most famous dancer in the world' to his front door. When Tennessee Williams met Rudolf the previous summer he recognized him as someone condemned to be lonely – like himself, and like his own Stranger in a snakeskin jacket from *Orpheus Descending* – 'both sort of hunted creatures'.* They were having dinner at the Pimlico house of Maria St Just, the playwright's great friend, and on this occasion it was Williams who was helplessly drunk. Agreeing to 'take him out for a while', Rudolf drove Williams to Ennismore Gardens, where they talked for a long time. 'I discovered,' Williams said, 'that he was deeply devoted to Russia and very depressed that he was unable to return there.'

Rudolf's debut in *Petrushka* on 24 October 1963 conveyed much of his own character as the archetypal outsider and rebel. Fokine had built the role of the fairground puppet around the fragile spirit of Nijinsky (who six years later would be certified insane), one that, as Alexander Bland wrote, is 'virtually impossible for any rational performer to imitate'. Rudolf had worn a similar red wig and exactly copied Nijinsky's twisted, flaked-paint makeup. 'But it just didn't go with me. My mouth is not that small so, if you extend those lines it becomes really gigantic. I had an eternal smile.' *Petrushka* was also physically built round its short, stocky creator, who had an astonishing ability to combine bravura dancing with the heavy, swinging, soulless motions of a sawdust-filled doll. Nijinsky could make himself ugly and stooping, whereas Rudolf's *danseur noble* stature – what novelist Colum McCann calls 'the Michelangelo of him' – was always discernible. It was an interpretation that, as one critic wrote, had 'too much blood and no sawdust'.

If *Petrushka* proved disappointing, Rudolf's next Royal Ballet venture was a triumph. As soon as he joined the company, Ninette de Valois, seeing how Rudolf's gifts extended far beyond those of a performer, had told him that if he was interested in trying his hand at choreography, he had only to ask for a group of dancers. 'He *teaches*

---

* It was to 'Snakeskin' that Williams gave one of his favourite lines, 'Nobody ever gets to know *no body*. We're all of us sentenced to solitary confinement inside our own skins, for life!' On a night when Rudolf went out with Williams in the United States years later, he wore a snakeskin jacket. 'It made me think of Nijinsky and how when he danced *L'Après-midi d'un faune* he dressed himself like an animal' (Quoted in David Daniel's interviews for *Nureyev Observed*).

dance most perfectly – a sign in the right direction,' she wrote to Nigel Gosling in October 1962. What Rudolf most wanted at that time, however, was not to create new work himself but to preserve his Russian heritage by staging the classics. He had first asked if he could mount *La Bayadère* – 'the *whole* of *Bayadère*' – for the school, but not surprisingly, an unknown Russian classic with spectacular crowd scenes was considered too ambitious for a student performance. Ashton, who had taken over from de Valois as director in September, suggested that the company should perform only the abstract 'white' scene from Act 3. Even this, though, according to Assistant General Administrator John Tooley, provoked tremendous opposition from 'the old diehards', who were outraged that a temperamental, untried twenty-five-year-old could be entrusted with the role of producer. When Michael Somes refused to fit *Bayadère* into the schedule, using as his excuse the upcoming tour of America, Ashton, 'although very much in the hands of Michael, was bold enough to insist'. 'I said, "I'm sorry, but you've *got* to get it in" . . . The company needed something at that time; we had a marvellous corps de ballet, and so I *fought* for it . . . and we got it. And he staged it beautifully.'

Rudolf had been preparing for this for years.

At the Kirov Theatre I was all eyes and nothing else. I just looked at every step, at every member of the company moving whether to the right or to the left, which way they would make a bow or which way they would take off their hat, what they had in their hands, how they carried their partner, how they behaved, where the servants are, where the rich people were and who are the nobility and how they all behaved in relation to the other. I was very aware of all this and I took mental notes of everything . . . I loved those productions which I saw. So they stayed in my memory. And they became rather useful.

From Leningrad, Xenia sent him detailed notation of the Kirov version, which a young friend had transcribed from company archives, using a system of little pin men on musical staves. When Karsavina came for dinner at the Goslings one night, Rudolf questioned her in Russian about the ballet (it was her last performance at the Maryinsky, in May 1918). 'She was holding on to our mantelpiece and showing him some of the steps.' A link between the Maryinsky traditionalists and innovators like Fokine and Diaghilev, Karsavina was a guiding light to Rudolf, who intended to create a reconstruction of the Petipa original revitalized with touches of his own.* In the famous 'scarf duet' (when a length of chiffon, held taut or softly festooned by the couple, becomes part of the dance itself), Rudolf adapted the male role to allow him to mirror the ballerina's movements – his favourite choreographic device.

Initially, he had doubts about casting Margot in the lead – 'She's not what you would call a robust ballerina in the Soviet style' – but he should have known by now that she was always at her greatest when challenged. Goaded by Rudolf to 'pull up [your] socks. Compete with me,' she did exactly that, executing Nureyev-style marvels such as a thrillingly fast diagonal of *chaînés* that overturned his and everyone else's vision of her. 'We didn't think it was the sort of body that could go much further,' said Georgina Parkinson. 'And then she suddenly loosened up. She pushed the frame out.'

It was Maude who suggested which three ballerinas Rudolf should use for the demanding Shades solos. 'He needed to be told because he hardly knew the dancers, really.' Not only that, but in his view, the company itself was 'mediocre', redeemed only by Margot's presence. 'Suddenly everything was *perfect*. And nobody saw that Royal Ballet was really nothing. She *dazzled* everybody . . . When you see her onstage this confidence, this brilliance – it is a light reflected from everybody.'

Coaching each of the soloists individually, Rudolf cast Merle Park, renowned for her fleetness and daredevilry, in the fast dance. He made her move in a way that completely contradicted her Royal Ballet training – 'our arabesque arm had always been in front of the nose' – but she loved the element of novelty and risk, and responded by combining her own *terre-à-terre* precision with wafting Russian port de bras and astonishing suppleness in the torso. Monica Mason, a dancer with great strength, danced the waltzing-cabriole solo, which Rudolf made even slower than the Kirov version to showcase Mason's big jump. 'He wanted it done like a man's variation.' He encouraged her to exploit hidden reserves of power and to create theatrical tension by making the audience aware of the effort involved. For her, working with Rudolf was a revelation – 'the beginning of understanding

---

* Rudolf's main change was a new coda borrowed from another part of the ballet. 'I don't feel this was a very great crime, because it was still in the style of Petipa with actual Petipa steps and choreography.' But on his instructions, Margot had made up a diagonal bit of 'business' for Nikiya's variation with fast, overlapping footwork and a rippling torso, while Rudolf's solo is flavoured with his own improvised flurry of Bournonville-inspired steps.

something about the art'. As she recalls, 'I'd never been taught anything so precisely, so absolutely exactly. He described everything with such nuance . . . and he could demonstrate it so that you could *see* . . . But he didn't just leave you with a picture of him doing it. He then described to you how you would feel doing it.'

Rudolf gave Lynn Seymour the variation she calls 'the slow stoppy one which doesn't have any wow factor to it', telling her, 'It's because I know you'll make something of it.' Recognizing a fellow maverick with a fierce dance intelligence of her own, Rudolf was particularly sensitive in his approach. 'He was very clever the way he asked for things. It wasn't "Do this, do that" or anything very specific, it was just a gift he had for drawing out the individual. With me, it was an elegance, a calmness and serenity.'

The young ballerinas understudying the trio of Shades – Antoinette Sibley, Deanne Bergsma and Georgina Parkinson – were also outstandingly talented, ambitious and eager to learn. 'We gave ourselves to the whole experience,' says Parkinson. 'Rudolf was very warm with people who wanted what he did. He took the blinkers away and opened our eyes.' Anxious to instill in every member of the cast his belief that 'plastique is what makes magic onstage', he taught the corps de ballet the essence of St Petersburg schooling. 'All of the body must dance . . . You must dance the turn of a head. You must dance the lifting or the lowering or the placing of the arms. There can be no mannerisms but there must be total body feeling in total body movement'.

But having tried at first 'to force' the dancers into his own tradition, Rudolf admitted that he was wrong. 'They naturally take from me what is good for them.' The result was a wonderful fusion of Russian breadth, fluidity, and risk with the precision of what Arlene Croce called 'good old British Cecchetti technique'.

It was *La Bayadère* that instigated the golden era of the Royal Ballet, and at the same time marked the true integration of Rudolf into the company. The dancers it excluded, of course, were the Royal Ballet men. There was one male role, the lead, and this was danced only by Rudolf for the first season. He was well aware that he was considered a threat – or, as he put it, '"Cuckooshka" because I threw all out of nest' – particularly by the established principals. 'Kingpin at the time' was David Blair, who had all the technical swagger for *Bayadère* but was a *demi-caractère* dancer, not a classicist, and so was overlooked to the advantage of tall, dark Donald MacLeary – the ultimate cavalier. Gracious, attentive and self-effacing, MacLeary was a dancer in the mould of Michael Somes, embodying the kind of traditional qualities

that Rudolf disdained. Christopher Gable, on the other hand, the third
cast Solor, was his only serious rival. Pretty yet rugged, he had a
contemporary glamour and naturalism quite new to ballet, and one
which, as Keith Money points out, had 'absolutely paved the way for
Rudolf'.

In 1961, Christopher became a sort of Cliff Richard of the Provinces
with the touring company . . . and he brought all that right into
London, when Ashton's *Two Pigeons* first opened. He had a huge effect
on the public. He made them receptive to the whole 'pop star' bit, not
least the slightly long, unruly hair. They *loved* it! . . . Anyway, post
Pigeons, apparently out of nowhere, along comes Rudolf, who neatly
scoops up this juicily pre-softened audience. It was tragic for Christopher, really.

Although Gable was highly jealous of Rudolf, he also welcomed him
as a role model. The young Russian's 'very floaty, romantic arms' were
lyrical in a way no English dancer would have dared to be at the time,
the tradition being wooden, reserved and 'male with a capital M'. But
Rudolf also found himself disconcerted by Gable's allure and popularity, the pair often acting, Keith Money says, like two adolescent rivals
in a school playground. He vividly remembers a day in a rehearsal
room when Rudolf was trying to get the attention of Gable, who was
sitting on the floor with his head down. 'Eventually he positioned
himself virtually on top of Christopher and began doing *pirouettes à la
seconde* above his head, just skimming his hair. And *still* Christopher
wouldn't look up!' Ashton's *Daphnis and Chloe* was revived that season,
with the boyishly tousled Gable in his element as the modern-dressed
young lover. The stage rehearsal was in progress when Rudolf suddenly appeared in practice clothes, held on to a ledge of scenery, and
started to warm up. Marching straight up to him, the stage manager
asked him to leave, and would have been punched had some dancers
not intervened and physically dragged Rudolf into the wings. 'It was
very tense and nasty,' Ronald Hynd recalls. 'And it upset a lot of us.'

The 15th of January saw the first cast change in *Bayadère*'s 'frighteningly exacting' lead roles. Donald MacLeary's partner was the exquisitely graceful Svetlana Beriosova, but both were so ill at ease that they
'made rather a hash of it', according to Annette Page. When it was
the turn of Gable and Page a week later, they decided to 'throw caution to the winds and send it up slightly'. Exaggerating her arms in
mock-Soviet style, and taking liberties with the timing, Page danced

dazzlingly, but although Gable's explosive run on to the stage created what the *Dancing Times* called 'the authentic frisson', nothing else quite matched the potential implied in his entrance. Not only that, but both he and MacLeary had omitted the 'diabolical' *doubles assemblés en tournant* in the second variation, which are so integral to Solor's role that, 'to duck them seems rather like a tenor omitting the traditional top C . . . at the conclusion of Manrico's *Di quella pira*'.

Rudolf, as de Valois often said, altered the status of male dancers overnight by setting an unprecedented standard to which they could aspire. 'As Gable showed,' wrote Peter Williams, 'one can dance as well – if not better than any British dancer ever has danced – and still miss the mark.' Knowing that the public now expected a much higher level of technical proficiency, Gable's generation had no choice but to deliver it. They eventually got the measure of 'those double-double things', but whereas Gable 'always *looked* centred, even if he wasn't', Rudolf attacked them with far greater force and risk. Ease, not strain, is classical ballet's defining characteristic, but Rudolf's aim was to make an audience sweat by recklessly leaving himself open to failure. 'He comes on to the stage as if into an arena,' Violette Verdy said. 'Is he going to be eaten by the lion or not? That is the feeling of danger we get from seeing him perform.'

In fact, although rightly lauded for revolutionizing male dancing, Rudolf, as Hynd says, 'didn't really bother much with the boys'. It was the ballerinas who were blessed with his hands-on attention, finding themselves cast against type to increase their range. Of course Rudolf's greatest 'donation', as he put it, was to Margot, to whom, in her forties, he gave not only a Russian technique but almost an entire Maryinsky repertory. As one critic remarked at the time, 'If he were to fly away tomorrow, he has already now achieved enough to ensure that British ballet will be forever in his debt.' *La Bayadère* profoundly affected not only the dancers but native dance itself; *Monotones*, Ashton's ultimate distillation of native classicism, was made, as Arlene Croce says, 'in what must have been a moment of direct inspiration'. The calm, slow, sustained monotony of the Shade corps' entrance has the very qualities that Croce sees embedded in the Ashton ballet: 'Royal Ballet virtues' such as 'chaste and flowing arabesques' . . . 'limpid contrapposto harmonies' . . . 'strict *épaulement*'. And for an audience it is the same 'uncompromising experiment in concentration' that *Monotones* is; with no set, character or drama, the ballet had, in Alexander Bland's words, 'a stern severity' previously unmatched by anything in the Royal Ballet repertory. 'He has given us a glimpse of the spare simplicity which forms one often unnoticed side of the Russian temperament. "I love thy severe harmony," wrote the poet Pushkin of his adored home city, and he might well have been talking of *La Bayadère*. It is a little chip of Leningrad.'

It was during the *Bayadère* performances in November that Rudolf received a letter from Teja, now dancing at the Staatsoper in Berlin. He had married Nureini, his Indonesian girlfriend, and they were expecting their first child in January. As her father had forbidden them to meet, they had hastily arranged a secret wedding – 'an exciting Romeo and Juliet story' for her, but for Teja, according to his sister, no more than 'a project'. Having decided to extend his training to include a teaching course, he planned to return to the Vaganova Academy for a further two years. In the meantime, he suggested that Nureini, who still had her Indonesian citizenship and, unlike him, was free to travel, could bring Rudolf his pictures and films. [Those] 'I tried to send you were seized . . . I wanted to see you so much, but you know that they have closed the way for me.'*

Rudolf also had a plaintive letter that winter from Viktor Rona, written on the first anniversary of their London meeting. 'I am already not interesting for you. I do not understand why, but that's life. You will see how much I adore you. Perhaps we will not meet again in our lives – I don't know – but all the time I'm with you I wish you success and I thank you for your help!!! . . . I kiss you strongly.' Viktor was right. Only Erik counted, and even he was not fulfilling Rudolf's expectations. 'When I came to the West,' Rudolf told Maude, 'I thought Erik would be a guide for me. He was my god. But then I found that I was much stronger in spirit than he was.'

---

* It was Teja who was the Soviets' prisoner now. He still hoped they might be reunited, telling Rudolf that after he completed his studies in Leningrad, 'Then it is not long until you. I am even sure about this.' But Rudolf never again contacted Teja, who, for the rest of his life, was not permitted to travel beyond the Iron Curtain (not even to stage his own ballets, which were performed by companies as far afield as Japan). His family was punished, too: his daughter, Jurico, born with ideal ballerina physique, was refused permission to study at the state academy on account of her father's association with a traitor, his sister's telephone was tapped, his nephew exiled to Siberia for army service. Becoming a depressive and a heavy drinker, Teja met an early death in 1979, drowning under mysterious circumstances. His second wife, Jutta, also a dancer, who inherited his archive of films and photographs, knew all about his dangerous liaison with the Russian star, but not even Rudolf's closest friends in the West had heard any mention of Teja's name. 'Teja always remembered,' says Jutta. 'But he was behind the Wall, and Rudolf was in another world.'

It was Margot who was now his prime inspiration, her English restraint and simple, seamless dancing helping him to reach the pinnacle of his art. 'Forging as a dancer happened at Covent Garden,' he acknowledged; 'Becoming of a dancer happened here.' To Margot, he even applied the same term with which he had once described Erik: 'Sometimes, like in *Swan Lake*,' he said, 'she has coolness which burns.' But she also had the very qualities Erik lacked: strength and stability. In Violette Verdy's remark, 'Margot was Home,' her smiling, undevious nature and common sense leading him to discover a more humane and restful aspect of himself. 'I really felt that he created through her a whole family of women – the sisters and the mother he had lost.' Unlike Erik, Margot was never mournfully introspective, believing that it was work one took seriously, not oneself. 'She was very cheerful and concerned for me. That I am too grim and gruff and miserable . . . She made great effort to shake me out of my miseries.' With Margot he could open up and be himself – 'There was no condescension, no English politeness. It was wonderful' – and he loved the fact she shared his own '*carnivorous*' approach to knowledge: 'She ate everything . . . Volkova, Ashton . . . Roland Petit . . . comes young boy; me. Twenty-three. Tells her *Giselle* is not so good . . . She embrace, she indulge, she doesn't *shrink* from it.'

Contrary to her gracious image, Margot also had a sense of humour as profane at times as Rudolf's – the result of her bohemian years with Constant Lambert. She was as unfazed by his foul language as she was by his errant libido, instructing a friend while on tour, 'Go next door and find out what the boy is doing. And be careful to knock!' Margot herself had a stable of picturesque, predominantly homosexual young admirers (at least one of whom she 'kissed properly'), while the description in her memoirs of a soft-eyed soldier who had enchanted her, his battle dress hung with hand grenades and a knife, is a frank admission of what Freud called *Schaulust* – sexual pleasure in looking. The picture that emerges from Meredith Daneman's biography of Margot is of a woman with a warm, liberal, 'completely natural' outlook towards sex.

One Sunday in early December Rudolf was crossing the King's Road when he was knocked over by a scooter, injuring his foot. To be near the Royal Ballet premises, he moved in with Margot at her mother's studio house in Baron's Court, where she had been living since Arias's London ambassadorship came to an end. Now increasingly involved in Panamanian politics, Tito was not there 'ninety per cent of the time', and Erik was also away for several months, dancing for Balanchine in New York – the consequence of which led a number of journalists 'to make copy out of the fact that Nureyev was staying at Dame Margot's apartment while recovering'. Colette Clark was one of many friends and colleagues who believed they had cause. Visiting Margot in her dressing room after a performance, she had been very surprised to find Tito there, whom she had not seen for well over a year. 'Heavens, Tito, what are you doing here, my boy?' And he said, 'When I read in the newspaper he moved into the flat, I think it's time I move back.' Margot, meanwhile, was 'frantically' powdering her nose in the mirror. 'For the first time ever she was not beaming and smiling at Tito . . . She was *livid*.'

To Colette the episode spoke for itself. 'She was definitely in love with Rudolf. You could see it shining out of her and in the way she couldn't stop talking about him.' Certainly the tremendous change in the ballerina's stage personality, the way – as Nadia Nerina put it – she had 'somehow become very feminine and relaxed, and swayed and swooned', seemed confirmation enough to many people that the two dancers were having an affair. There are just as many, however, who remain convinced that the Fonteyn–Nureyev relationship was platonic – like Joan Thring, who since the world tour ended had been working 'twenty-four hours' a day for Rudolf as a full-time personal assistant, and who makes the point that the couple were rarely alone. 'I've tried and tried to believe it could have happened, but I cannot see *where*, or *when*. Most nights the three of us would have dinner in my house in Earl's Court, and sometimes Rudolf would throw plates at us because he'd want to go and find a boy. Margot was like me, she treated him as a child most of the time.'*

When Norfolk neighbours Frederick Ashton and Keith Money discussed the matter, each was as 'adamantly certain' as the other that nothing ever took place, and when questioned in his eighties, Ashton had not changed his mind. 'I don't think that he awakened in her any sexual thing . . . I don't think that at all. You always love the person you dance with *for that moment*, and something must emanate from you that communicates itself to the audience. Like I *loved* Karsavina when I danced with her; and Karsavina must have loved Nijinsky.'

Rudolf was, of course, as Margot well knew, passionately in love with Erik. But this would not be the first time he had a triangular liaison with a man and an older woman – in fact, in the case of Tallchief

* Margot did indeed consider Rudolf 'very mature artistically, but immature emotionally' (*Dance Magazine*, January 1964).

and Bruhn it was as if coition were a compulsory first step towards absorbing the Balanchine and Bournonville styles. When asked directly, Rudolf would tell some people that he had not made love to Margot ('No. I missed the bus,' was his reply to Colette), and others that he had – even claiming, as he did about Xenia and a number of other women, to have made her pregnant. In the nineties, talking graphically about heterosexuality to his straight assistant, Rudolf said, 'Perhaps I should have married Margot. But I had many women, and it was like your aquatic salad.* Bang-bang-bang . . . Hammering away for hours and hours' – a remark that in itself could be taken as strong evidence for the Case Against, Margot having been praised by more than one admirer for the dexterity of her pelvic floor muscles ('She can activate me of her own accord,' Constant Lambert told a friend).†

Margot's response when asked at the time if she and Rudolf were lovers was dismissive: 'That's all I need.' Her marriage was complicated enough. It was to spare Tito from retrospective jealousy that she prolonged what amounted to a conspiracy of silence about her relationship with Lambert, whom she barely mentions in her autobiography. And yet, by all accounts, Rudolf was never a threat to Tito – certainly not enough to instigate his sudden return to London. '*Very* un-Tito,' remarks Keith Money. 'I can see Colette making jokey remarks to Tito in the dressing room, and if Margot was livid it was because Colette was getting into areas where she might risk annoying Tito on his "fleeting visit". The idea of Tito "moving back in" *anywhere*, is ridiculous. He simply never stayed in the same place more than forty-eight hours.'

Joan Thring agrees. 'Tito would never have said "time to come back". He didn't give a damn. It didn't occur to him that they would sleep together, and it wasn't a threat to him anyway. Nothing was a threat to Tito Arias.'

Whatever Tito's reason for coming back, his presence at Baron's Court promptly sent Rudolf back to his own flat where, in answer to press speculation, he had himself photographed drinking whisky, 'listening to Mozart,' and relaxing with his bandaged leg propped up.

---

* 'Aquatic,' Simon 'Blue' Robinson explains in his book, *A Year with Rudolf Nureyev*, means 'sloppy'. 'He reckoned I always put too much dressing on the salad.'

† Also making an affair unlikely is a remark of Rudolf's to Nigel Gosling when they were considering collaborating on a ballet based on Strauss's *Rosenkavalier*. Margot, he said, 'might be shocked' by the part of the Marschallin, an older woman who commits adultery with a young boy.

'I returned here as I always like to be alone,' he is quoted as saying. That night he went to the opening of *The Comedy of Errors* at the Aldwych Theatre where Margot arrived late with Tito, and where Rudolf sat with Alfie Lynch, one of London's new breed of working-class actors. 'Very cockney, very bright and full of joie de vivre,' according to director Anthony Page. Lynch was then having a fling with Rudolf, and the pair left together after the play.

If Rudolf and Margot were not lovers, the conclusion must surely be Colette Clark's: 'Well, then they were *jolly nearly.*' And yet Ashton's theory is equally valid. The reckless ardour that convinced every onlooker that they were playing out their own story happened only when they danced together. Margot, as Keith says, allowed herself to be 'in love' with Rudolf on the stage: 'That seems plausible to me . . . the more so because I believe that, deep down, that's where she thought the *real* world was, anyway.' Rudolf maintained as much himself: 'Margot always said that for her, real life comes when she's onstage. I absolutely agree. We functioned between those snatches of real life onstage. We only lived when we danced.'

It was the same kind of intensity that Balanchine's muse Suzanne Farrell described when trying to explain their own unconsummated bond − 'extremely physical and extremely gratifying in that kind of way [but] more passionate and more loving and more *more* than most relationships'. 'A love affair without scars', one 'consummated on the stage' was also how Erik described his partnership with Carla Fracci, but he was too insular a dancer, 'too absorbed in his own perfection', as Arlene Croce says, to transmit physical passion. 'He remains Erik Bruhn, possibly the only major male star in ballet who can't walk towards a woman and appear to love her.'

Together in Copenhagen in the New Year, taking classes with Vera Volkova, Rudolf and Erik were able to recapture some of the productive intimacy of their first months together. Yvette Chauviré was staying at Gentofte, too, relieved, after the dramas she had witnessed in Stuttgart, that there were 'no tensions' between them. She was there to rehearse *Giselle* with Erik, who was making his Paris Opéra debut in February. (Rudolf himself would have danced the ballet in Paris with Chauviré had not the management cancelled his performance to prevent difficulties with the Soviets.) Wary of stealing Erik's thunder, Rudolf flew out for the second night, avoided the press, and told Erik that he wanted to see no one but him. When they went to Maxim's for a late dinner, however, it was the usual story: 'Everybody knew who he was and nobody knew who I was,' Erik commented. It seemed strange to Erik that Rudolf had made no comment about *Giselle*, which, with Volkova's help, he and Chauviré had radically reappraised. Finally Rudolf told him that he had planned to include the ballet in the repertory of his Australian tour with Margot that spring, but, having seen their Paris version, felt he could not dance it again. 'I told him . . . he should rethink and rework his interpretation of the role, and I believe that's what he did.'*

Rudolf badly wanted to reinstate their original positions of master and disciple, but the balance had irrevocably tilted. Remembering how, in the beginning, his obsessive idolatry had seemed to drive Erik away, he noted with surprise the extent to which Erik's passion had increased as his own desperation had abated. ('In those days,' commented Richard Buckle, 'I guess, he had not read Proust.') Now it was Erik wanting to telephone him all the time – 'and believe me, it's not money that's holding me back' – even wanting to follow him to Australia. Also, the tone of recent letters had been dismayingly self-abasing:

> How wonderful of you to call me just after so much work, excitement and strain for you, and still you find time and desire to call me and think of me . . . This is the most wonderful thing to me, that in spite or because of everything, you are involved in that I have a place I hope, no one else will take in your life. [30 November 1963] . . . I hope you have a moment for me now and then in the midst of all your work and activity. [22 March 1964]

Rudolf was indeed extremely occupied, choreographing a new polonaise and mazurka for the Royal Ballet's *Swan Lake* and mounting assorted Russian variations. Leningrad's maverick of three years earlier was now its greatest traditionalist and proselytizer, declaring, 'Soviet ballet is the best!' He reacted furiously when he saw that Christopher Gable and Anya Linden, whom he was coaching in *The Flames of Paris* duet, had added an extra-spectacular lift: 'What you do change – eh?'

---

* On 23 October Rudolf presented a significantly revised interpretation of Act 2 – 'Gone were all the fireworks!' – making effects with Bruhn-like restraint and masterly control. 'Nureyev,' wrote the critic Fernau Hall, 'somehow managed to make the turns slow and elegiac, canted slightly forward, and expressing growing exhaustion as well as his tender feelings for Giselle. Only a dancer with complete command of the technique of the step could so alter its style and impact, in harmony with the dramatic situation' (*Ballet Today*, December 1964).

'But Rudi,' Anya protested, 'it's just for a gala . . .'

'*Disappear!*'

He trusted '*nobody* from the West' – not even Ashton – to rehearse him in the classics. 'Big handicap I was protecting my school; trying to keep my style undiluted. I'd tell Fred, "Not *this* year . . . But next year." . . . And I was evading every year . . . Finally he lost interest and got cold hands. And that's the birth of Anthony Dowell.'

For his new ballet, a one-act version of Shakespeare's *Midsummer Night's Dream*, Ashton had cast the twenty-two-year-old Dowell as Oberon. A flawless product of English schooling, he was, the choreographer believed, better suited than Rudolf to his vision of the ballet. 'My approach is much more lyrical; softer, understated, understressed – the antithesis of his in a way.' In fact it had been Erik who first exploited Dowell's potential, and Rudolf who claimed to have brought it to the attention of Ninette de Valois. Sitting next to her during a performance, he said, 'Madam, *there* is your first truly classical dancer.' Ashton's *Dream* not only gave Dowell his first leading role, it launched his partnership with Antoinette Sibley, their perfectly matched proportions and reciprocal musicality allowing them to move together as one body. Although it was a lost opportunity for Rudolf to have been passed over for Oberon – a part for which he was virtually typecast – *The Dream* is still imbued with his presence. The climactic reconciliation between Oberon and Titania, a danced conversation that subsides into a mirrored, moving image of each other, sublimely enacts Rudolf's insistence on male equality; his declaration that a pas de deux must be a dialogue ('How can there be conversation if one partner is dumb?'). In addition, Rudolf's *Swan Lake* solo is the model for Oberon's adagio control, whose cantilena phrasing was taken by Dowell to a zenith no other male dancer has ever reached. As Alastair Macaulay has written: 'It was Dowell who went beyond Nureyev in making a male dancer's line poetic . . . But Dowell would not have happened had it not been for Nureyev.'

'Anthony seemed right and would do exactly what I wanted,' Ashton said, whereas Rudolf had the 'sort of superior attitude' that had always displeased him (the story of how Ashton was unable to work with the young Margot until she had 'really *conceded*' to him is well known). Rudolf's arrogance was, as he later acknowledged, misjudged in many cases, one being his response to Ashton's offer to cast him in *La Fille mal gardée*. With its clean yet virtuosic variations drawing on both Bournonville and Russian techniques, the role of Colas would have been a wonderful showcase for Rudolf, its charm and humour also revealing an unknown side to him. However, well aware that, after the interval, Lise's lover spends much of his time hidden behind a drying hayrick, Rudolf could not resist asking, 'What happens to me in the second act?' Ashton said, 'So I told him, "If you feel like that, that's all right, but I'm not going to change it. The second act remains as it is." So we dropped the matter.'

Resenting the unfavourable comparisons with Balanchine, the constant challenges which 'stopped [his] flow,' 'Fred,' in the words of a friend, 'got so rubbed up the wrong way by Rudolf.' After *Marguerite and Armand*, Ashton never created another major role for the dancer.

Kenneth MacMillan was also 'never very comfortable' with Rudolf, and made only a quirky little gala solo and three minor pieces for him. One was a pas de trois in a ballet based on a Shakespeare sonnet, and premièred on the same anniversary programme as *The Dream*.* Danced to an ineffective commissioned score by Peter Tranchell, and prefaced with loudspeakered quotations, *Images of Love* was an endless-seeming suite of divertissements in semi-abstract style, the most original item of which was sonnet no. 144: 'Two loves I have of comfort and despair.' This closely intertwined *ménage à trois* among a witch-wigged Lynn Seymour (the 'bad angel'), Christopher Gable (the 'better angel') and Rudolf (the authorial character) was, as one critic put it, 'a very kinky modern interpretation of the situation hinted at by Shakespeare'. Interesting psychologically rather than choreographically, it was not only an attempt to explore ambivalent sexuality in dance, but also the aspect of professional rivalry. MacMillan, as Keith Money points out, had been clever at spotting Rudolf's rather 'guarded insecurity' about the success of the Seymour–Gable partnership (significantly, the pair was the only alternative cast for *Marguerite and Armand*). And this, augmented by the intense rivalry between the two young men, provided a charged subtext to which only insiders were privy. As Money recalls:

> The Comfort and Despair was extraordinary, and years ahead of its time. Quite electrifying. Christopher coming out of the shadows and just floating beside Rudolf into that second jump, matching him to the

---

* Only in Robert Helpmann's fast-moving distillation of *Hamlet* did Rudolf have the starring role, one which, to the critic of *Ballet Today*, was his most impressive achievement to date. 'He was particularly good in his exchanges with Ophelia [Lynn Seymour], whom he flung to the ground with terrifying but anguished brutality' (*Ballet Today*, May–June 1964).

millimetre; it was a flawless mirror image: the two Crown Princes. The third jump travelled downstage, straight at the audience, and you couldn't mistake the parity on display. It must have been very unnerving for Rudolf. Christopher was clearly the stronger, just then, and nobody could drag their eyes away from him; there was a sort of golden glow about him . . . like something out of a Lord Leighton painting.

One Royal Ballet dancer, sitting in on rehearsals, was just as struck by the element of competition between them:

A point evident from day one was that Christopher had worked very often with Kenneth and knew how to deal with his creativity, and Rudolf was at a complete loss. This threw Rudolf, as Christopher was always three steps ahead of him. Christopher was charming and always very sweet, but Rudolf was not coping and swearing his usual Fuck and Shit. However, as it progressed there evolved something very sexual in the atmosphere. It was like Rudolf was provoking Christopher. For me, Lynn faded from the trio . . . There were just these two beautiful fascinating men vying for something. Control, creative expression, power over each other. The pas de trois had become a pas de deux, and a very erotic one.

In April and May, Rudolf and Margot spent a month together guesting with the Australian Ballet, but while he was elated to be dancing every night, the element of competition was taking its toll on Margot, who was exhausted by the end of the tour. Rudolf, she noticed, seemed to have lost his natural spontaneity onstage, and now needed a kick-start of excitement before every performance: 'He did it by getting angry.' Onlookers were amazed by the ease with which she was able to subdue him – 'She'd just walk up to him and say, "That's enough" ' – but they also saw that the ballerina herself was clearly under strain. 'She was so worried about Tito, about being *away* from him,' recalls Noel Pelly. Margot had counted on being reunited with Tito in Miami in time for her birthday, but he was running as a candidate for Panama's National Assembly, and told her that it would be impossible for him to leave the campaign. Resigned, she consoled herself with the thought of their spending time together at their new house in Panama – a quiet, 'heavenly place', with a lawn sloping down to the beach – but instead, when she arrived, she found Tito oblivious to everything but the outcome of the election. Feeling lost amid all the political excitement, she left soon afterwards for Europe and yet more performances.

Defeat was not in Margot's nature – 'Somehow, against the odds, she'd keep paddling along, steadily' – but she made herself face the fact that her marriage was over. Knowing she would be in Rome for several days with Rudolf, she asked Tito to meet her there so that they could discuss the subject of divorce. Once again, though, he never turned up. While she went back to the hotel every few hours to call Panama and try to track her husband down, Rudolf, Joan says, would go sightseeing. 'He really didn't care – it wasn't his problem. He kept out of it. We both did. The only one who really got involved was Keith. She did cling to him a lot at that time.'

From Rome, they went straight to Bath, where the two dancers were due to perform a new MacMillan duet at Yehudi Menuhin's annual music festival. They had all arranged to meet for dinner with the choreographer and his designer, Barry Kay, but Margot, in a strange state of agitation, wanted to be alone with Keith. 'We walked all over town for hours and hours: she was reviewing her whole life. I thought how is this day ever going to end . . . She was almost hysterical, and kept talking about a friend of theirs who had been shot. "It couldn't happen again! It couldn't happen again!" she kept saying.'

It was about ten o'clock by the time they arrived at the new, fashionable Hole in the Wall restaurant, and not long afterwards a waiter came up to Margot and whispered something. Everyone at the table became aware of the sudden change in atmosphere, especially Rudolf, who was acting like an animal sensing danger. 'The nostrils were twitching.' The press was waiting outside, and the moment they stepped through the door there was a volley of flashbulbs, followed by running feet and car doors slamming – 'hardly the behaviour of society photographers'. Back at the Francis Hotel, Diana Menuhin was waiting at the entrance, 'looking anxious but not saying why'. Seeing the paparazzi trying to snap the two stars by each other's side, Joan instructed Rudolf to go up to his room. 'For once he did as he was told.' By now she had heard what had happened. Newly elected as a deputy, Tito was being driven through a suburb of Panama City in mid-afternoon when a political associate pulled up alongside at an intersection, leaped from his car and fired point-blank at him. One of the four bullets had lodged next to his spine, and it was not yet known whether he would live.

Deciding that Margot might be calmer if she were surrounded by their 'cosy little group' from dinner, Joan began telling her what had happened, but refusing to listen, Margot let out a scream and flew down a corridor. As Keith said, 'It must have been horrifically spooky for her. She had almost prefigured it earlier in the day.' Someone sent for Rudolf, who came downstairs to find the ballerina crumpled in an armchair in an empty ballroom. As he took her into his arms, Joan called Tito's brother in Panama for more news. By now the would-be assassin had surrendered to the National Guard. It was Alfredo Jimeinez,[*] who, it was said, had been enraged by the fact that he had not been chosen as Arias's second-in-command, entrusted to serve in his absence. 'No, no you've got it wrong. He's our best friend,' Margot protested when Joan told her, but she was greatly relieved to hear that Tito was out of danger, and said that she would stay in Bath for the opening the following night.

In the morning there was an encampment of press outside the hotel, complete with Movietone cameras on ladders. But instead of making a quick getaway with her chauffeur positioned nearby, Margot chose to walk with Keith to the rehearsal, followed 'at a diplomatic distance' by Rudolf and Joan, a rush of newsmen surging after them. Although as bemused as everyone else by the way she appeared to be 'her usual giggly self', Rudolf was trying hard to concentrate on their new ballet; from his perspective, as Keith remarks, 'all that twenty-four hours was simply "crazy private lives – why mess up *important* things?"' He had been extremely diligent in learning MacMillan's *Divertimento* (a piece especially choreographed for the occasion, accompanied by Menuhin playing Bartók's sonata for solo violin onstage), finding the sinuous movements interestingly new. The critics thought otherwise, Clive Barnes commenting that the duet could have been an addendum to *Images of Love* without anyone being the wiser. Leaving Rudolf to perform *La Sylphide* with an under-rehearsed Lynn Seymour, Margot flew to Panama.

Her first sight of Tito flat on his back on a narrow table like a sheet-covered corpse was shocking beyond measure, although in fact

---

[*] It is now well known that Jimeinez had discovered that Tito was having an affair with his wife, a story Rudolf relished, later enacting the part of the gunman trembling with rage. 'You know why he was shot? Because he was cheating on Margot. She was going to divorce him, and his friends . . . shot him. They missed because they had such fury' (Simon Robinson, *A Year with Nureyev*). Margot, according to Joan Thring, never let herself believe the truth. 'Her head was in a bag all through that marriage. She used to attack ambassadors at dinner parties and say, "Why haven't you arrested the man who shot Tito?" They had a law allowing crimes of passion, that's why.'

his condition had significantly improved. He had regained his ability to speak, and though he was paralysed, the doctors now believed that it might be only temporary. Despite intense Arias family resistance, Margot began arranging for him to be transferred for rehabilitation treatment to England's famous Stoke Mandeville Hospital. By 17 June, she was back in London, dancing in the Royal Ballet's summer season at Drury Lane and rehearsing Rudolf's new production of *Raymonda*.

The two had already danced a scaled-down version of Act 3 for the world tour, but Rudolf was anxious to stage the complete ballet while he still remembered the steps. With Ashton unwilling to commission 'a costly old warhorse – even if it *is* Petipa' – Rudolf resigned himself to mounting the ballet for the Royal Ballet Touring Company in time for July's Spoleto Festival. It was to be the most expensive production Gian Carlo Menotti's festival ever incurred, and – still unknown to Rudolf – the Covent Garden administration had placed restrictions on the design budget. It was only when he arrived in Italy that he saw Beni Montresor's sets for the first time. He was appalled. Having jettisoned most of Petipa's impenetrable medieval libretto, he found that the designer, himself intent on stripping away the 'tinsel' of traditional ballet, had provided a set consisting of virtually nothing but gauze scrims. As Rudolf remarked, he would not have gone to the trouble of 'filleting out the trash' if he had known the extent to which Montresor had already removed the period details. With the choreography unremittingly exposed, the audience's attention would now be focused entirely on the dancers, and as the young 'second company' was clearly being stretched beyond its capabilities, this meant that the ballet's success depended principally on Margot – 'the star in an avowed star vehicle'.

Like Arlene Croce, Rudolf held the view that the main reason for mounting a full-length version of *Raymonda* was its large and glorious ballerina role; and according to Keith, he began to realize the weight he was making her carry. 'The whole enterprise now has overtones of Sadler's Wells hoping to woo New York with the *Sleeping Beauty* of '49' – perhaps the most testing performance of Margot's career. On the day of the final rehearsal the ballerina was in her dressing room putting on her makeup when Joan came in to tell her that she had booked a flight for her immediate return to England: Tito had had a relapse.

As Margot was being hustled away in a car to the Rome airport with her mother, Rudolf was arranging to prepare her understudy for the première. He was lucky to have Doreen Wells as a standby, an attractive, technically feisty dancer, although film footage of their rehearsals shows her either ignoring or simply not seeing the Dudinskaya-inspired inflections in his demonstrations. He did what he could with his cast, but when Ashton arrived in Spoleto, he was shocked by the standard of dancing. Rudolf was now beside himself with suppressed nerves, and when Joan happened to walk backstage during a rehearsal break, he hurled a stray pointe shoe at her head. 'It thudded into one of the new gauze flats with surprising force, about four feet off target . . . Joan just blinked and scarcely broke stride, and said, "Stop it!" as if she were admonishing a slightly fractious child.'

Things came together for the première and subsequent four performances, however, as Noël Coward recorded in his diary: 'He was fine. She perfectly efficient and the ballet well danced but not enthralling.' Rudolf, however, was not happy – as he made clear when he arrived late for a party at Gian Carlo Menotti's villa and found that not only did he have to queue for the buffet but that most of the food had been eaten. Paul Taylor, whose troupe was performing at the festival on alternate nights, watched what happened next: 'What he did – which . . . was just what people wanted – was pick up a wineglass and throw it on the floor and walk out. And it was the talk of the town for a while.'*

And then Margot returned. By now, despite the suitcases she had left in Spoleto, no one had expected her, but she had arrived in time for the final performance and promised to continue with the tour to Lebanon. Having miraculously survived a fever of 108 degrees, Tito had been pulled back from the brink of death. It would take a long time for Margot to accept the fact that her husband would probably be a quadriplegic for life, but, practical as ever, she had taken stock of their alarmingly depleted finances and told herself, 'No performance, no pay.' Blanking out her interminable hospital vigil, the bottles, ugly gadgets, feeding and breathing tubes, she came onstage and danced so

---

* Mythologized as the incident in which Rudolf declared, 'Nureyev does not serve himself,' this story has several versions. In one a plate of spaghetti is hurled at the wall; in another (also from Paul Taylor) Rudolf 'generously gives everybody an extra performance by smashing several wineglasses against the wall'. Rudolf's own explanation was that he had agreed to come to Menotti's party 'Only if I can sit down – because I was exhausted after being in the theatre all day long . . . So I did not serve myself, that was all. I did not want to stand in a queue. I was tired' ('The Lynn Barber Interview: A Dance to Defy Time' *Independent on Sunday*, 19 August 1990).

dazzlingly that to those who had seen previous performances, it seemed another, quite different ballet. 'Such was the irradiance Fonteyn's personality threw over the whole stage and anyone on it,' wrote the critic of *Ballet Today*. Noël Coward had stayed on another day to see the Fonteyn–Nureyev matinée, and described it as 'one of the *great* moments' of his theatrical life. After their thirty-two curtain calls, Coward took the two stars out to dinner and drove to Rome afterwards with Margot sleeping all the way on his shoulder (Rudolf having decided to hop into a Ferrari with some friends). Earlier that day Keith Money noticed that for the first time in two weeks Rudolf had allowed himself 'a tiny smile'.

SACRED V. PROFANE,
EAST V. WEST

In Leningrad early one evening in October 1964, Nigel and Maude Gosling were in their room at the Astoria Hotel waiting for Xenia. Rudolf had bought a fur coat for his mother, asking Maude to wear it through customs and Xenia to collect it from his English friends. It was a dangerous mission. Russian visitors were forbidden in the bedrooms of tourist hotels, where there was usually a watchful *dezumaya* sitting by the lift on every floor. When Xenia arrived, Maude recalls, she looked terrified.

> The first thing she did was put a finger to her lips and wouldn't speak until she had taken a pillow from the bed and put it over the telephone. Nigel had learned a few words of Russian, and she spoke a few in French, so between them they managed, but we could see that she was in a great hurry to put the coat on and leave.

'Oh! Oh!' Xenia had cried when the fur proved to be much longer than the large loose raincoat she had worn to hide it, but Maude fetched a needle and thread, and together they sat on the bed turning up the hem. 'Then we said, "This is for you." ' Rudolf had sent Pushkin a large art book, but Xenia shook her head, refusing to take it. Going over to the window, she opened the curtain and pointed across the square to St Isaac's Cathedral, gesturing, 'Meet me there.' Before she left, Xenia took off her headscarf and tied it round her legs 'to bunch up the coat', and as she went out of the door, she crossed herself.

The Goslings were going to a performance at the Kirov that night, but duly sat on a bench in the light drizzle outside the cathedral waiting for her to reappear. After half an hour they gave up, took the album back to their room, and rushed to the theatre. At the first interval they were spotted by Pushkin, who came up to them and said immediately, 'You weren't there.' The couple, it turned out, had missed Xenia, who was at the back of the cathedral exterior while they had been at the front. Pointing to eleven o'clock on his watch, he said that his wife would be waiting in the same place. This time the three met and quickly exchanged presents: Nigel handing over a leather briefcase with the art book inside, Xenia giving them a pink bag – 'Ah, Xana's shopping bag!' Rudolf would exclaim when he saw it – which contained a box of chocolates and some sheet music. (Pushkin had borrowed a score Rudolf had asked for and had spent several nights copying it out by hand.) The Goslings' last sight of Xenia was her '*running*' from St Isaac's with the briefcase.

The following day at the Vaganova Academy they were introduced to Pushkin, who had to pretend that he was meeting them for the first time. After watching his 'Class of Perfection', they were shown around the school museum by Marietta Frangopoulo. There were no photographs of Rudolf, and she never mentioned his name but plied them with questions about Tamara Karsavina, a close friend of the Goslings. '"*Why* doesn't she come and see us" she kept asking. And we couldn't say that Tamara had told us she would *never* go back. It would break her heart, she said.' At a performance in the Maly Theatre, a Russian woman with a little girl stopped them in the foyer and introduced herself as Rudolf's sister Rosa. 'She was very thick-set, but you could see the likeness.' A day or so later a frightened-looking Rosa appeared at the door of their hotel room, this time without her daughter, three-year-old Gouzel. She had come to deliver an enormous glass jar of caviar for Rudolf, and honey 'for his chest'.*

From Leningrad the Goslings flew directly to Vienna, where they were going to join Rudolf. Despite vigorous 'tactics of obstruction' by the Soviet cultural attaché, the dancer was about to stage his first production of *Swan Lake* for the Staatsoper. His arrival on 3 1 August had been kept secret from the press, and, with Vienna only a short distance from the border of Soviet-controlled Hungary, he had been offered the protection of a bodyguard even though, according to the police report, Rudolf 'felt neither threatened nor persecuted and needed no escort'.† It was also noted that when publicizing the production, the dancer had 'cleverly avoided' any controversy, telling one interviewer,

---

* Rosa had telephoned Rudolf in London and 'screamed blue murder at him' for thinking that their mother could be seen in Ufa wearing a Western fur coat.

† It was Joan Thring who had 'slightly exaggerated' the danger to the authorities – and with reason: she remembered what had happened in Sydney in April 1954 when Evdokia Petrova, wife of the Soviet defector-spy Vladimir Petrov, had been frog-marched on to a BOAC plane by KGB apparatchiks and 'escorted' back to Moscow.

'Politics do not exist for me. But it simply was time for me to leave. I wanted independence.'

It was a need for independence as well as what Rudolf called his 'instinct for self-preservation' that had brought him to Vienna. 'Already,' he confided to his biographer John Percival, 'I didn't trust the Royal Ballet to make my whole career for me.' At the beginning of April he had received a letter from Jean Louis's wife, Maggie, who, concerned about his low spirits the previous summer, had been strenuously campaigning on his behalf. Now, having secured the necessary funds, she was writing to offer him the chance of forming a company and school of his own based in Los Angeles.

Rudolf, however, who viewed the venture as 'pure dilettantism', never returned the enclosed letter of agreement. Although dissatisfied with the lack of opportunities in London, he knew that he could not do without the discipline and stability of an established company. The Royal Ballet provided him with a framework – in Ashton's words, 'A beautiful stone must have the right setting.' And yet Rudolf's dilemma continued to be 'how to become truly incorporated in the company and how to progress as an artist at the same time'. Once again, he decided that it was no use waiting for other people to create chances for him. 'That's why I took the initiative myself and revived the classical ballets that formed my own particular training.'

Having mounted two Russian classics, he intended *Swan Lake* to be next, but the Royal Ballet already had its own new production. Not only that, but Ashton was unconvinced of Rudolf's ability to handle a full-length classic. (He had not wanted to commission the skeletal *Raymonda* for the main company, explaining to the board that the dancer had 'left no dramatic element in the ballet'.) It was, he avowed in a 1967 article on Petipa written almost as an open letter to Rudolf, 'impertinent' to tamper with the mime as with any other aspect of a nineteenth-century classic. 'Things can be old-fashioned and dated, but many masterpieces are dated in the right way . . . I do not like to see hotch potches of Petipa's work with another choreographer imposing his own, often trite, ideas.'

Curatorship of the classics is, as Arlene Croce has written, 'a questionable business'. The record is fragmentary, and the master scores are based on the incomplete notation of Nicholas Sergeyev, who may not have worked from rehearsals conducted by Petipa, and who was unmusical to a degree de Valois described as bordering on eccentricity. Rudolf would have argued, too, that limitations in the classics were often dictated by circumstances. The reason, for example, that there is 'nothing for Siegfried to do' in *Swan Lake* was that Petipa's *premier danseur*, Pavel Gerdt, was over fifty when he created the part, and way past his technical prime. 'So there were no chances for any other dancers . . . Since today you cannot put on the classics without giving opportunities for the male dancers, to talk about reviving these classics just as they were then is so much nonsense.'

Creating a credible character out of a hero who 'sits on his ass for thirty-five minutes' during Act 1, and spends the rest of the ballet doing little more than partnering Odette/Odile, was, Rudolf insisted, quite impossible. His *Swan Lake* would present a consistent, subjective view of Siegfried, who is, after all, the perpetrator of the action, with its focus not on the Swan Queen but on Rudolf himself.

He began planning a new production of the ballet while he was in Spoleto, where the designer Nico Georgiadis – 'a massively built Greek with a face akin to a pharaoh' – was spending the summer painting.* Together they went on several walks – 'small Grand Tours' – around the famous Italian villas, Georgiadis, who had studied architecture in his native Athens and at Columbia University, answering Rudolf's constant questions about their interiors as well as exteriors. While Georgiadis shared Rudolf's view that tradition must be reappraised in contemporary terms, he was surprised to find when they began working together that the dancer was 'terribly terribly uptight about classicism', resisting any ideas that he considered too avant-garde. 'If you wanted to find other ways of doing things he'd seen in Russia he would feel very uneasy. In those days he imagined one would do a kind of nineteenth-century painted set.'

And yet, as Georgiadis points out, the concept for *Swan Lake* was entirely Rudolf's own – a concept that the dancer well knew was 'too radical a departure' for Covent Garden. Recently, however, he had been approached by the director of the Vienna Opera Ballet, who was offering him 'a free hand as choreographer to produce what he chooses whenever he wishes'. Aurel Milloss, a highly cultured man whose ambition to focus international interest on his company had brought Massine and Balanchine to stage works in Vienna in 1963, agreed to commission a new production of *Swan Lake* – 'not only in the original form but with a more creative input'. This was no great risk. With only three full-length ballets in their repertory and no

---

* Having seen Georgiadis's designs for Cranko's *Daphnis and Chloe* and Kenneth MacMillan's *The Invitation*, Rudolf had wanted him for *Raymonda*, but the designer declined the commission because of the insubstantial fee he was offered.

classical heritage to protect, the Austrians were more than ready for
their own *Swan Lake* – even a revisionist version as self-promoting as
Rudolf's.

Aware that he still had much to learn about production – particularly
the bridging of scenes – Rudolf was grateful to be able to use the
Vienna experience as a period of apprenticeship: literally, as John
Percival put it, 'to teach himself the job'. On the other hand, counter-
balancing the freedom of approach, unlimited time and financial independence was the difficulty of working with a company almost wholly
unschooled in the St Petersburg style. Rudolf intended his production
to pay homage to Petipa's assistant and modest shadow, Lev Ivanov,
who created the lyrical 'white acts' of *Swan Lake*, now considered to be
the essence of Russian choreography. The Vienna company had been
exposed in the past to the Maryinsky style, through its ballet masters
and through visiting stars such as Pavlova and Ulanova, but the influence was not enough to instill in the dancers' movement the kind of
adagio plastique that Rudolf was demanding.

Then there were 'other unpleasant things'. Governed by union
rules and cushioned by lifelong civil-servant contracts, the dancers, as
far as Rudolf was concerned, were 'ugly, fat and lazy' – and never
more so than when they insisted on having 'rest breaks' in the middle
of rehearsals. Establishing a precedent he never relinquished, Rudolf
disregarded company hierarchy and gave leading roles to the young
and promising. One corps de ballet dancer who interested him was
Michael Birkmeyer, whom he approached after class to ask where he
was from. 'He could tell I had been trained differently' – or, as Rudolf
put it, 'Not so bad.' The third generation of male dancers going back to
the mid-1800s, twenty-three-year-old Michael was the son of Toni
Birkmeyer, who had been a soloist and ballet master at the opera. His
father sent him to study in Paris with Viktor Gsovsky, where his fellow
students included Violette Verdy and such rising Paris Opéra stars as
Noëlla Pontois. When Michael returned to Vienna, however, he felt
like an outcast, relegated to the back row of the corps, even though he
was now technically far more advanced than his colleagues. 'I'm thinking about leaving the company,' he admitted to Rudolf, who told him
decisively, 'You will not. You will dance in my *Swan Lake*.' The next day
Michael saw his name listed for the pas de cinq (a Nureyev innovation
replacing the pas de trois, which is traditionally danced by the most
talented soloists). Used as the guinea pig to try out steps by Rudolf,
and also by Erik, who attended all the early rehearsals, Birkmeyer
began to understand for the first time that there is more to dance than

technique: 'I was not fast in picking things up, and was always thinking about what step came next, terrified that Rudolf would scream at me. But he and Erik taught me that you should never dance without a story in your mind: that's where art begins.'[*]

Initially intended to be a Nureyev–Bruhn collaboration, which Erik then planned to stage for the National Ballet of Canada, *Swan Lake* began as a synthesis of two models: the 1953 Bourmeister version which had greatly impressed Erik when he saw it performed by the Stanislavsky Ballet; and John Cranko's elegiac Stuttgart production in which Rudolf had danced in May 1964. Both had made the Prince central to the ballet, and changed the usual happy ending by omitting the reuniting of the lovers, instead having Siegfried die alone in a torrent of waves. 'He lost,' Rudolf said. 'This was tragic – and tragic in a way that official Soviet art could not understand.' In fact, though, as Vera Krasovskaya points out, 'the banal optimism' of the St Petersburg production must also have disturbed Ivanov, who instinctively discerned the music's deep melancholy, particularly in the final act. Drawing his movements from the 'broken sighs of Tchaikovsky's phrases', Ivanov invested classical form with a psychological profundity way ahead of its time. It was this element that the Vienna *Swan Lake*, originating as it did in Freud's home city, would take much further.

To Rudolf the Romantic ballet heroes were all versions of Erik – 'they already have in them that character. That brooding, Danish character' – and this troubled Siegfried, whom Clive Barnes would describe as 'a manic-depressive . . . a Hamlet who faces no longer any alternative question, but who is just longing not to be', was more Bruhn-like than any other. The ballet itself, dramatizing the unattainability of ideal love, seemed to allude to their own story, the White Swan being, in Erik's words, 'a spirit of love who makes him aware . . . they can never be together'. In a letter [dated 5 March 1964] . . . he tells Rudolf, 'It is the right thing to accept that love can exist as a spiritual and ideal love and still be a happy one providing we forget or try to forget our hunger and thirst.' The two extremes, he believed, could not be combined, and Siegfried's fatal flaw was the conviction that he had found 'both the pure love and the sexual in one and the same person'.

Rudolf, by his own admission, 'loyal and disloyal, good and bad', also viewed Siegfried's dilemma as his own, his 'existential and artistic

---

[*] When Rudolf left Vienna, Birkmeyer was promoted to demi-soloist and began appearing in the role of the Prince. He was appointed principal dancer in 1972.

problem' being, in Horst Koegler's words, 'the conflict between soul and body, between Odette and Odile – or, if you want, between East and West, between the Kirov's purity of tradition, and the more degenerate pleasures of the Western ballet world'. This division of self was also one of sexual orientation, experienced to a degree by Rudolf and Erik, and by no one more acutely than Tchaikovsky himself.

Hinting at the idea of a homosexual hero – and anticipating by a decade John Neumeier's more explicit treatment* – Rudolf shows the Prince recoiling from his mother's attempts to persuade him to get married, waltzing impassively with each of the six Prospective Fiancées as if in a world of his own. Earlier, during Act 1's festive mazurka, when everyone other than himself onstage is coupled, the Prince stands to one side as if enacting Tchaikovsky's own account of his extreme loneliness. 'It is true that my damned pederasty does form an unbridgeable abyss between me and most people. It imparts to my character an aloofness, a fear of people . . . qualities which make me grow more and more unsociable.'

In this context Rudolf's addition of a slow, contemplative solo for Siegfried is completely justified. The drawn-out *développés*, sinking *fondus*, and arms that droop like Nijinsky's above his head not only speak of sadness and solitude but provide a perfectly judged transition of mood from the celebrations at court to the mysterious lakeside world of the swan maidens. Erik, who had always been sceptical about Rudolf's interpolation in the Royal Ballet production, quickly changed his mind. 'Suddenly he got excited. He saw that it worked and it did portray the mood of the Prince – brooding, melancholy . . . and makes him unique.' Their influence on each other went deep; the steps themselves, which Rudolf had borrowed almost unchanged from a Pushkin *adage*, were now fine-tuned with Bruhn-like streamlined control. As rehearsals progressed, however, the extent to which Rudolf was turning the ballet into a four-act showcase for himself began to rankle. Erik refused to condone what he considered to be severe lapses of judgement (the worst being the bouncy virtuoso solo Rudolf gave himself in Act 2, completely destroying Ivanov's mood of lyricism). As Horst Koegler would later point out, Rudolf was badly in need of an artistic mentor – 'a sort of Diaghilev, whom he is able to trust and who

---

* The hero of this 1976 version was Ludwig II of Bavaria, obsessed by imagery of the swan and tormented by his homosexuality. Like Siegfried, Ludwig himself died by drowning in a lake.

is able to shape and mould his wild flowing talents and direct them towards an artistically desirable aim'. Older and more experienced, Erik could have fulfilled this role – 'the *only* one over here who can tell me things I don't already know' – but he was too combustible and too emotionally involved. The pair fought constantly, until Erik could take no more. 'You do what you want,' he told Rudolf. 'I'm leaving.' Later that month, director Celia Franca was told that Erik would prefer to stage *Swan Lake* in Toronto 'alone without Nureyev'.*

When Margot, whom Rudolf wanted as his partner, arrived in Vienna not long before the première, she, too, was far from happy to be associated with a classic she barely recognized – one the *Dancing Times* would review as 'The Ballet Called Siegfried'. Even Odette's first appearance was different, with the ballerina now expected to impersonate the mechanical swan that traditionally glides across the lake (an ungainly process that involved arching out of what Robert Greskovic has described as 'a belly flop position with her torso, arms and legs curving up from her abdomen which is resting on what might well be a skateboard'). More crucially, with Odette perceived as an abstract image of purity, the Fonteyn–Nureyev *Swan Lake* was no longer the great love story of before, when conventional movements of partnering had seemed more like forms of embrace. Now, confusingly, it was Odile, the Black Swan, who had become the main recipient of Siegfried's tenderness.

In order to lessen the emotional disparity between the Petipa and the Ivanov acts, Rudolf decided to exchange the brashly percussive music associated with Odile for the more melodic oboe piece composed as part of the original Moscow score. But while a softer, more swanlike temptress vindicates the hero for being duped by her, the sexual excitement Odile embodies is lost – and with it the glinting, diamantine hardness of one of Margot's greatest interpretations. Not surprisingly 'a terrible row' ensued, followed by a telephone call to Joan Thring

---

* Toronto Ballet's *Swan Lake*, which premièred on 27 March 1967, also included a lyrical and 'murderously difficult' new solo in Act 1 to establish the brooding, introspective character of the Prince. But although Rudolf claimed that Erik had stolen 'everything' from his production, this was not, of course, the case. The Bruhn version conflated the ballet into two acts, and, exploring his own dark bond with his mother, transformed Rothbart into a woman. 'I called her the Black Queen. I wanted to equate the Prince's relationship to Von Rothbart with that of his mother, the Queen. Well, everybody, including Rudik, got very upset over this major alteration, because the whole ballet was now seen in Freudian terms' (John Gruen, *Erik Bruhn*).

telling her to come immediately to the theatre: 'Margot had walked out, and they were sure there was not going to be a performance.'

By the time Maude and Nigel arrived from Leningrad, the dress rehearsal was in progress, and Rudolf was going out of his way to accommodate his ballerina. Aware that she had not yet mastered the new variation, Margot asked if she could perform it once again, but the orchestra refused: they had agreed to one complete run-through only. Walking downstage to the orchestra pit, Rudolf announced that if Dame Margot did not get what she wanted, he would abandon the production. 'Go then,' came the reply. The dancer had not endeared himself to the renowned Vienna Philharmonic, either with his demands that the tempo be slowed down, or by ordering the director of music to 'Go back to [his] Glockenspiel!' It was only after the *Intendant* himself was brought in that the musicians reluctantly agreed to play.

Mounting the ballet, Rudolf claimed, had put more demands on him 'as a lawyer than a dancer', and yet the first night proved such a triumph that the Staatsoper immediately began negotiations for his return. Curtain calls for Margot and Rudolf throughout the ballet totalled a record eighty-nine, and even after they had returned to London the production continued to be a box-office success. Rudolf would later admit that there was much about the production that could be improved, but his main goal had been achieved. 'Here in Central Europe where the classics are often petrified mummies,' wrote Linda Zamponi, 'Nureyev's attempt to bring a classic up to date was blessed. Blessed too is the disturbance and controversy he brings to our stages.'*

In London, however, when dancing the Royal Ballet version, the Vienna experience was having an adverse effect on its two stars.

---

* A corps de ballet member coming to the end of her career, Zamponi had begun to write about dance. She was to review all of Rudolf's Vienna productions for *Dance Magazine*, and was one of several pet critics whom he went out of his way to befriend. Not only did she fill the role of amanuensis – articulating in print what he had been trying to achieve – but being well educated, speaking perfect English, and having access to several apartments in Vienna, she could be extremely useful to him. 'Rudolf used her as a private secretary,' says company manager Traude Klockl. 'She would do things like drive him to and from the airport because she really worshipped him.' But, inconveniently for Rudolf, Zamponi had also fallen in love. 'Moody,' she writes in one of her letters. 'You might prefer to sleep with boys, but *it is the female that puts its mark on your art*. Why do you close yourself up towards me? Don't you realise I'll always be there for you? . . . How can one compromise and live among MIDGETS – after knowing you?'

Reviewing their 'Turgid Lake' at Covent Garden, Peter Williams described the way in which Rudolf appeared to be dancing alone, completely unconcerned about the fate of Odette – a lapse he attributed to the fact that both dancers were having to 'unlearn' the Nureyev version. There could have been something else diverting Rudolf's attention. Erik was then in Canada mounting a full-length production of Bournonville's *La Sylphide*, and although Rudolf was not scheduled to appear in it, he was becoming increasingly attracted by the idea of portraying its hero. Like Siegfried and Albrecht, James is an unfaithful Romantic mystic who falls obsessively in love with a supernatural woman. With his troubled, tense features, Erik played him as a man haunted by a fearful intuition, but Rudolf believed that a more passionate, youthfully impulsive approach would help absolve the hero of his betrayal. Notwithstanding the fact that Erik was recognized to be the definitive interpreter, Rudolf was determined to make James a signature role of his own. And just as he had travelled to Florence to see Erik's performance in 1962, he now used a period of convalescence from a tonsillectomy to fly to Toronto to 'glean as much as he could'.

To Erik, the perfect Sylph was Carla Fracci, once called 'a modern incarnation of Marie Taglioni', who created the role in the first version choreographed by her father, Filippo Taglioni. The pair had already danced the pas de deux for an American television broadcast in 1962, but as Fracci was not free to come to Toronto, at Rudolf's suggestion Erik had asked the Royal Ballet's Lynn Seymour, herself a Canadian, to be his partner. With her light, noiseless jump and round, seemingly boneless arms, Seymour had the plump contours of a dancer in a Chalon lithograph, which Rudolf, who had partnered her in the *La Sylphide* duet at the Bath Festival, thought 'old-fashioned and nice'. Erik, however, was dismayed by what he saw. Far from representing a chaste, inaccessible ideal, Seymour belonged more to the earth than the air; sensuous, ribald, tangibly real, she was, in Arlene Croce's phrase, 'the Magnani of dance actresses'. 'Erik didn't like me at all, but there was no point getting upset. Fortunately, Rudolf was there to make me feel a bit better about it.'

When they did 'go around as a three', the atmosphere, Seymour recalls, was turbulent and uncomfortable – no more so than on the night she was left standing alone in sub-zero temperatures outside one of Toronto's most exclusive restaurants. Looking wonderfully striking in a fur coat and cashmere turtleneck, Rudolf had lost his temper when the manager refused to seat them because he was not wearing a tie. Grabbing the man by his shirt and crushing his nose into the fur collar, he had shouted, 'Feel! If the coat isn't worthy of your restaurant then nothing is!' before storming into the street and flinging fistfuls of snow at the window. Appalled by his behaviour, Erik went off on his own, walking in the opposite direction from Rudolf, who, a few minutes later, trudged back through the slush to fetch Lynn. Returning to their hotel, they passed an empty parking lot pristine with fresh snow. 'Do you know how to make snow angels?' Rudolf suddenly said, letting himself fall backward in a cruciform and fanning his outstretched arms like wings. Lynn fell down next to him, and they began to play like children, tumbling over each other, singing, laughing and throwing snowballs into the sky.

Over the next days the existing affection and trust between them deepened. 'We've become very very good friends,' Lynn wrote to her mother. 'A sort of fan club for each other.' 'She is *fabulous*,' Rudolf told a television reporter. 'She educate herself as I believe Canada didn't help her.' They had much in common. Both late starters, 'aware that we had a lot of time to make up and it would always be like that', they had each struggled to master wilful, unconventional bodies, and combined their cerebral autodidactic approach to dance with an affectingly visceral exposure of themselves. 'What you give to the public is more than they realize . . . it's like in the Colosseum,' said Seymour – a view Rudolf echoed. 'Every time you dance,' he said, 'it must be sprayed with your blood.'

With Erik hardly paying any attention to his ballerina, Rudolf, who had learned most of *La Sylphide* by watching the rehearsals, took it upon himself to coach her. 'I didn't agree with everything he told me. I thought that dancing should look effortless, and didn't approve of the fact he made it look hard work. I had my principles.' Seymour noticed how Rudolf was becoming increasingly restless, making obvious the extent to which he longed to be dancing in the ballet himself. Consequently neither she nor anyone else was particularly surprised when, having performed the opening night, Erik 'developed a bad knee'. 'We all knew that he was "pulling an Erik",' said one of the soloists. "Faking an injury to give Rudolf a chance." ' The Canadian ballet's Earl Kraul took over the following night, and when Celia Franca and Betty Oliphant were discussing who else in the company could replace Erik, he interrupted them by saying slyly, 'What about Rudik? He knows it.' Sure enough, despite having had only two days to rehearse the whole ballet – 'something like learning *Hamlet* in a weekend' – and despite an injury resulting from a fall on the ice, Rudolf wrapped up his 'half broken foot' and gave a performance of astonishing authority. For the Canadians it was 'a profoundly exciting theatrical coup', but for Erik the immensity of Rudolf's success was unsettling. Having watched the performance from the wings 'looking very wistful', according to Oliphant, he went backstage, where he was spotted 'mysteriously walking with a perfect gait in spite of a reported leg injury'. Elbowing his way through the mob of admirers surging outside Rudolf's dressing-room door, he suddenly turned nasty, threatening to smash the camera of one of the photographers. Rudolf, meanwhile, was in an excellent humour. Although tired and still husky voiced from his tonsil operation, he relaxed in his dressing gown, obligingly answering the reporters' questions. His reply to whether or not he had done 'an emergency good turn for his friend' made the reason for his appearance even more equivocal: 'I tell you how it was. Mr Bruhn from the beginning he asked me because it is tremendous strain to produce and dance at the same time. And he said, If you could come and do first performance. And I said I will of course. I would pay my fares and everything and just come and dance.'

The next day Erik's knee had 'miraculously recovered'. Partnering Lois Smith, making her debut in the title role, he gave the performance of his life, scoring twenty-five curtain calls to Rudolf's nineteen, and proving himself 'the still undisputed master of the Bournonville style'. In his perceptive appraisal of the two versions, the *Globe and Mail*'s Ralph Hicklin, while admiring Erik's restraint, admitted that he found Rudolf's showier, more yearningly romantic James more affecting. 'There was established between Nureyev and Seymour a passion – always with decorum – that is lacking in the cooler interpretation of Bruhn . . . his is a cool approach to the melodramatic narrative of *La Sylphide*, an approach that allows the dance to speak for itself.'

Dancing with Seymour, Rudolf said, made him aware that he was dancing with a woman; just watching her move affected him like an aphrodisiac – or, as he quirkily put it, 'Heaven descends into your lap.' Offstage, too, he found her physically arousing – 'He used to love my skin' – and the sexy complicity between them is tangible in rushes from a documentary made at the time. Wearing a funny little boater perched on top of her Mary Quant crop, she edges her way into the crowded dressing room, snuggles up to Rudolf, and kisses him so languorously on the lips that he takes a second or two to recover . . . She picks up a whisky glass. Empty. Rudolf slaps her rump with a chuckle, and as she is stroking his hair, looks her up and down. With her way-out clothes, round face and large, heavily mascaraed eyes,

'Liluchka' (his diminutive for her) must have reminded him of Menia Martinez, an equally original personality. 'He adored her,' Georgina Parkinson says, 'especially her maverick side. She was fat . . . nonconformist . . . He was really tender with her.' Seymour recalls, 'He told me later on that he *did* try to make a move on me. I didn't realize it – which shows how naïve I was. Thank God. Because it really would have disturbed me. If Margot's relationship was anything like the one Rudolf and I had, that's all you ever needed. It's really sacred as opposed to profane love.'

Also relished by Rudolf was what Seymour describes as her 'sort of Russian thing'. She had been trained in Canada by Russian teachers, and the lift and yield of her upper body, her expansive, floating port de bras, and the way her arms, legs and head moved seamlessly together in one single line were Vaganova hallmarks. To Kenneth MacMillan she shared 'the same liquid quality' that Galina Ulanova had, the quality that had made Lynn his muse. The flow of Seymour's dancing had influenced his choreography from the beginning, but in *Romeo and Juliet*, the ballet he was now creating on her, the steps seemed to grow out of her body 'as if she had drawn them on the air'.

Prokofiev's *Romeo and Juliet* was a work Rudolf had coveted for years. Through Viktor Rona, he had tried courting its original choreographer, Leonid Lavrovsky, who, in November 1963, did in fact agree to produce his ballet at Covent Garden, but withdrew a year later when he discovered that he would not be free. Instead Ashton, who had earlier created his own *Romeo and Juliet* for the Danes, decided to commission a new three-act work from the company's resident choreographer. MacMillan was more than ready for a challenge on this scale. He chose Nico Georgiadis as his designer and took as his inspiration Franco Zeffirelli's tearaway, anti-Romantic Old Vic production of 1960, with Judi Dench and John Stride. 'Kenneth was determined that his ballet, full of slashing vigour, should overflow with the same vital accent on youth.' As Romeo to Seymour's Juliet, he cast not Rudolf (whose satirical, catlike qualities he felt would make him an ideal Mercutio) but the 'cockney kid' Christopher Gable.

This came as no great surprise. Not only had the choreographer already created a masterly balcony scene on Seymour and Gable for Canadian television, but he was someone who felt comfortable collaborating with a small coterie of friends. Because Lynn and Christopher were dancers he liked and trusted, he encouraged them to contribute their own ideas, and as the work took shape, the three became inseparable, 'living every moment of the ballet – "our ballet".' From Lynn's point of view, much as she loved Rudolf, she was grateful to be part-nered by Gable, a dancer with whom she felt fearless. 'We were able to take death-defying risks, each knowing almost intuitively what the other was going to do.' Her Juliet had been conceived by MacMillan to be the driving power behind the action – 'a modern free spirit who knew exactly what she wanted and would risk all to get it' – which in itself ruled out what she calls a 'dangerous' Romeo. The perfect foil to her reckless intensity, Gable only had to be himself: wholesomely handsome, gentle and level-headed. He, together with the puppy-plump Seymour, seemed exactly the kind of King's Road teenagers that Zeffirelli would later pick for his 1968 film: fifteen-year-old Olivia Hussey and sixteen-year-old Leonard Whiting from Palmers Green. In *Vogue*'s description: 'Neither dancer fills a balletic cliché. They simply break hearts.'

Romeo certainly did break hearts – those of its three creators. Not long before the first night, David Webster called a meeting at his house in Weymouth Street and announced that he wanted a first-night cast change. Using as an example the way that Lavrovsky's Juliet at Covent Garden in 1956 had been Ulanova, 'succeeded by other fine dancers', he said that the première must be danced by the company's prima ballerina in her famous partnership with Nureyev – 'a decree against which there was no appeal'. MacMillan was shocked into speechless-ness. 'He knew that he would have to admit Fonteyn and Nureyev, but not for the opening,' said John Tooley, who witnessed it all. 'That hit him only that dreadful morning at Webster's house. It was, in my view, a *huge* mistake.'

Why then did Ashton, as artistic director, not challenge Webster's decision? He may have felt threatened to a degree by the fast rise of his younger rival, but he had always supported MacMillan (encouraging him to choreograph a new *Romeo and Juliet* when he could just have revived his own version). It was a practicality about theatre manage-ment that seems to have held sway: Margot needed a new ballet for the American tour and, as Ashton told the board in September the previ-ous year, MacMillan's *Romeo and Juliet* would be ideal. He did, how-ever, genuinely believe that this was not just a Fonteyn–Nureyev vehicle, but a work expansive and important enough to shed lustre on each of its five different casts. As he said to Lynn and Christopher, '*Everyone's* going to be a success in this ballet. No one can fail.' But as Lynn remarked, 'Fred's comfort was cold comfort, really, but at least he said *something* to us: everyone else carried on as if it just wasn't happening. The only ones who showed concern were Margot and Rudolf. They were both very sweet about it – absolutely divine. But it was out of their hands.'*

With the choreographer at breaking point, it fell to Lynn to teach the role to Margot, which, quite apart from the emotional strain, proved extremely difficult. Moulded on her own idiosyncratic line – not classically perfect but something that 'melts and flows and extends itself in heroic sweeps of movement' – the steps simply would not curve into the same oblique shapes on Margot's symmetrical physique. More crucially Margot's Romantic interpretation made a mockery of the ballet's new realism – MacMillan's version of Zeffirelli's Italian *verismo*. Certain moments were designed to be 'almost revolting, not pretty', such as Seymour's retching after taking the poison, an action so violent that it pulled her up on pointe; or the way her body became a loose, heavy corpse falling into positions too mockingly distorted to fit in any dance lexicon. Margot, Lynn said, 'instinctively made adjustments'. Instead of daring to sit frozen on the edge of the bed throughout Prokofiev's long, turbulent passage of music, she expressed her inner turmoil in a flurry of dance. Nor did she choose to die in a manner that was jarringly unballetic. Her Juliet, one critic wrote, was among her 'most refined, most perfect portrayals', but to MacMillan it was an act of sabotage.

'We were trying to honour Kenneth's vision', Lynn explains. 'But Margot and Rudolf were both putting an old concept on to the new production.' A case in point was the balcony scene, for which the three collaborators had very consciously devised a series of spinning, reeling steps, all slightly aslant, to create a sense of continuous flow. Teaching

---

* In her biography of Margot, Meredith Daneman points out how the episode preyed on the ballerina's conscience almost to the end of her life. At a private dinner given after a fundraising gala for her, she was overheard asking Lynn Seymour to forgive her. 'Lynn, with customary largesse, was conducting herself as if there was nothing to forgive.' And Seymour was right. Keith Money was present at a lunch with Margot and Sol Hurok in New York in January 1965, when Margot tried hard to persuade the impresario to open with Seymour and Gable. 'Margot wanted to do the ballet in her own time,' says Keith Money. 'To ease into the NY season in the second or third week. Less pressure; less strain . . . When we left the lunch, I really thought she might have won her case.' In the event, Hurok phoned London within the hour, and said, 'Fonteyn or else . . . ' The rest is history except that nobody gets it right. It's a better story to see a powerful diva cutting a swathe through weak-kneed management, and 'grabbing' the ballet for herself. In fact, Margot, behind the scenes, was possibly Lynn's biggest advocate. She did everything, at the time, to *un*-grab; *and*, she *adored* Lynn.

Rudolf his role, Gable was distraught to see him break the duet up with an explosion of 'double something or others round the stage'. This was partly because, as Gable says, he felt it did not focus enough on Romeo, and wanted to give the audience a thrill. On the other hand, to Rudolf there was nothing contrived or old-fashioned about expressing a surge of excitement with a spontaneous virtuoso *manège*. Less justifiable was his deletion of any lift – the 'pendulum' one for example, where Juliet hangs suspended down his back – that he felt would sap his energy from his solo. In the end, too dejected to fight to maintain the integrity of his conception, MacMillan let the stars make their changes, and continued to regard the Seymour–Gable cast as his template.

Certainly Rudolf's Romeo was anything but the 'nice, normal fellow' envisaged by the choreographer. Combining the poetry of Gielgud with the raw impulsiveness of Olivier, he was electrifying from the moment he first appeared. Enveloped in a black cape and slowly stalking his way down the staircase, his absorption in the character was so complete that, even when he was not moving, his body seemed to speak the text. He made his costume part of the performance, too, allowing his cape to slip meltingly to the ground as he stood beneath the balcony, his back to the audience – 'so still you can almost hear his heart beating'. And an image associated for some reason with Rudolf alone was the sight of his shirt billowing to bursting point as he danced for Juliet – a dazzling intensification of his own speed, energy, power and ecstasy.

Margot, too, had little in common with MacMillan's headstrong heroine. Seymour's Juliet, shaping her own destiny rather than waiting for events to take their course, had a character close to Rudolf's own, whereas Margot's was shyly submissive.* On the balcony, while Lynn projected what Alastair Macaulay calls 'this great whoosh of sexual need', Margot was at her most 'moonlit', an arm drifting romantically up towards the stars. But if her duet with Romeo was bashful and decorous, there is a moment towards the end more erotically charged even than the climax of their *Corsaire*. Kneeling at Margot's feet, Rudolf spreads his fingers and gathers up the hem of her dress to kiss it, hungrily, as if the fabric itself were erogenous. Shuddering, Margot pushes him away with instinctive modesty, and runs to the corner only

* Her own model was Galina Ulanova – the only other person, Rudolf said, who was vulnerable on the stage. From Ulanova she learned the art of longevity, how to transform herself, even without makeup or costume, into a radiant fourteen-year-old.

to return a second later, her resistance in vain. As she succumbs, Rudolf lifts her by the thighs until she is lying horizontally above him, pushing her up and lowering her down, again, rhythmically, up and down, as the chiffon of his shirt and her fleshy dress flow into each other like fluids. By the end the audience is left in little doubt that this union has been consummated long before the bedroom scene.

As the final curtain came down there was a thunderous roar lasting almost forty minutes. Margot and Rudolf may not have been Mac-Millan's 'darling, terrible children', but most people weren't aware of the choreographer's vision for the ballet and were swept away by the impact of their performance. Among the dancers, however, the feeling of antipathy was 'company-wide'. The injustice of 'that *Romeo and Juliet* business was like a turning point for us all', Annette Page says, adding:

> When Christopher and Lynn danced the full call in the big studio it was the first time we'd actually seen anything of the pas de deux. They were so wonderful that everyone had a lump in their throat. Then two days later Margot and Rudolf took over. Neither really knew the choreography and Rudolf [still in pain from his Toronto ankle injury] marked most of it. I looked around and saw that almost everyone had a look of frozen horror on their faces.

What might have seemed to outsiders a minor matter of casting precedence was devastating for the members of the company, who were shocked by the clear power that the star duo could exercise. It was mainly this that drove MacMillan to leave the Royal Ballet for Berlin, where he became director in 1966, taking the 'shattered' Seymour with him. Later that year Gable gave up dancing altogether to pursue an acting career.

The New York première presented a double blow. After seeing all five casts, the *Financial Times*'s Andrew Porter spoke for many when he wrote that it was hard not to take Seymour and Gable's performance as the definitive reading. Predictably, though, despite the London crit-ics' enthusiasm for MacMillan's original cast, Sol Hurok insisted on a Fonteyn–Nureyev first night and Ashton supported him, telling MacMillan that for an international success he must have the two stars. Not giving the public a chance to get to know other young principals was damaging to the company, but Hurok had gauged the mood of his city: Fonteyn and Nureyev, the most famous partnership in world ballet, were now 'the symbols of the Royal Ballet in New York'.

This time no attempt was made to share the spotlight: Rudolf had it virtually to himself. In addition to the double-page spread of Irving Penn photographs in *Vogue* and the long profile by Clive Barnes in the *New York Times*, there was 'the extreme rarity' of a cover story in both *Time* and *Newsweek*. The Royal Ballet's ebullient Australian press officer, Bill Beresford, had been 'aglow' at having duped the American correspondents into believing that each had an exclusive on the star, and yet it was mostly due to Rudolf's adroit two-timing that the ploy came off. (When Barnes met him for a late lunch in South Kensington, the dancer had refused anything to eat and sat toying with a Negroni before confessing that this was his second business lunch of the day.)

To all appearances *Newsweek* had the scoop, its photograph of the 'New Nijinsky' in a Romeo pose far more alluring than the unrecognizable, blurry foetal face in *Time*'s Sidney Nolan portrait. And while *Newsweek*'s Hubert Saal had spent a long night on the town with Rudolf, wooing the 'New Nijinsky' with caviar at the Connaught (so much that the hotel's supply ran out) and nightclubbing until 4.30 a.m., without equivalent access *Time* was reduced to padding its piece with digressions about the history of dance. And yet, *Time* had been granted a glimpse inside Rudolf's apartment. The gilt-bound volumes of Balzac and Schiller incongruously scattered about the living room among model trains and such other toys as a football game, a yo-yo and a gun that shot table-tennis balls were indeed 'effects that mark the mystery of the man'.

On 16 May Rudolf and Margot danced together on the *Ed Sullivan Show*, an appearance that made such an impact that they were invited back by popular demand the following week. It was no accident that dance in the United States and all over the world began to explode at just this time, the excitement of their extraordinary celebrity turning an elitist art form into mass entertainment. The Fonteyn–Nureyev curtain calls – 'almost an encore, of the ballet they had danced' – became an essential ritual for the fans. Far more demonstrative than their English counterparts, the Americans would scream their applause and shred their programmes into confetti, sending it raining down onstage like a ticker-tape homage. The emotional impact could be overwhelming; one New Yorker named Marilyn LaVine, whose discovery of Rudolf on this tour was literally life changing, said that she was transported into a 'state of bliss'. La Vine's description of losing all sense of self and merging into a collective unconscious – 'unified on a spiritual level, understanding the inexplicable – like a truth, like being part of a truth' – echoes Nietzsche's on hearing the music of Wagner. ('Each person not only united, reconciled and blended with another,' Nietzsche wrote, 'but altogether fused.')

For the majority of fans, however, the experience was more mundane. The mid-sixties saw the development of the groupie, of whom five thousand had keened and howled at JFK airport the previous year when the Beatles arrived to conquer the States. The summer of '65 belonged to the Rolling Stones, who needed police protection to escape the hundreds of screaming girls outside the theatre. Meanwhile at the Met mounted police were brought in to prevent Rudolf from being mobbed – a phenomenon in itself, as never before had a dance audience demonstrated the kind of group hysteria usually reserved for rock stars. The Stones' biographer Philip Norman must have been thinking of Rudolf when he compared Mick Jagger 'to a male ballet dancer with his conflicting and colliding sexuality: the swan's neck and smeared harlot eyes allied to an overstuffed and straining cod-piece'. In many ways the two were mirror images of each other. To Cecil Beaton, Jagger was simultaneously 'archangel and satyr . . . sexy, yet completely sexless', while Violette Verdy, almost paraphrasing him, called Rudolf 'totally profane and totally sacred . . . He creates another type of sex altogether.' The erotic ambiguity both stars projected was so potently and disturbingly physical that it affected even the most conventional. As David Daniel put it, 'In the sixties there were straight boys who would sleep with Rudolf who never looked at a boy before or since.'

Sensing 'a British renaissance', the owner of Arthur, New York's first high-fashion discothèque, had timed its launch on 5 May to coincide with the Royal Ballet's arrival in town, and with the opening of the first New York Vidal Sassoon hairdressing salon on Madison Avenue – the powerhouse of sixties chic. Sybil Burton had modelled Arthur on London's Ad Lib, whose rousing music and anything-goes atmosphere had made it the favourite hangout of the Beatles and other glamorous young revellers. The first-night mob mixed 'celebrity investors and the most marvellous looking girls' with Sybil's film, theatre, and ballet friends. 'People like Steve Sondheim and Lenny Bernstein put in a thousand dollars each, and someone had invited every model from an agency. Tiger Morse was there in a dress that lit up.' The 'dowdy little Welsh mouse', in Shelley Winters's phrase, who had recently lost her husband to Elizabeth Taylor was hardly recognizable that night.

Platinum blonde and beautifully elegant in an outfit of pink silk and ostrich feathers, she frugged for the cameras with Rudolf, who was dancing 'like a poker' in a tweed sports jacket. Later, one of the models, 'a pert young girl' called Susan, took him in hand. 'He can't dance a damn step, I was trying to teach him,' she said affectionately. *Journal American*'s gossip columnist Dorothy Kilgallen watched the pair writhe together under blue and red spotlights, then voyeuristically followed them to a dark corner near the telephones 'where they could cuddle and neck in comfort, if not exactly privacy'.[*]

A week or so later, at Andy Warhol's silver-sprayed Factory on East Forty-seventh Street, Rudolf was dancing in the arms of architect Philip Johnson's boyfriend David Whitney, 'a young kid who worked at the Castelli Gallery'. The occasion was the 'Fifty Most Beautiful People' party, but as guests included Tennessee Williams, Allen Ginsberg and William Burroughs, the rule of entry seems to have veered from an aesthetic elite to the usual Warhol imperative that everybody be somebody. This was the party 'when the stars went out and the superstars came in', according to Gerard Malanga, poet, experimental film-maker and founding member of the Warhol entourage. Indelibly described by Factory groupie Mary Woronov as 'dressed in black leather with a Boxex camera in one hand and a bullwhip in the other', Malanga was referring to people like himself, pioneers of artistic far-outness, 'for whom life was a twenty-four-hour stage'. It was certainly true, as he said, that more people were staring at underground superstar Edie Sedgwick, 'looking beautiful and laughing a lot with the Rolling Stone drummer Brian Jones', than at Judy Garland, whose vaudevillian entrance from the Factory's goods lift on the shoulders of five young men nobody except Warhol seemed to notice. He looked on as, too inebriated to walk unsupported, she was picked up again by her cavaliers, who carried her over to a couch,

---

* The Royal Ballet's Alexander Grant, who was also at Arthur's, was taken aback by how possessive of Rudolf Robert Kennedy was that night. The two dancers had been standing talking close together against a wall when the senator came up and said, 'Hey! What's going on between you two? Break this up!' 'It was very strange, because it was only *kind* of jokey, and I thought, "Why should he care?"' In Rudolf's own account, told to Gore Vidal, 'Nothing happen.' But if he was indeed the object of Kennedy's 'homosexual impulses' (Gore Vidal, *Palimpsest*), he did not seem inclined to take things further. When they went out to dinner in a group after his appearance with Margot on the *Ed Sullivan Show* on 16 May, Maria Tallchief was surprised when Rudolf made 'a big point' of taking her home. 'It was very unlike him. But then it occurred to me that he was leaving the field clear for Bobby and Margot.'

from which she suddenly sprang up and yelled out, 'Rudy!' 'She staggered forward with her arms out towards Nureyev, who yelled back, "Judy!" and walked towards her, and it was stagger/step/Rudy!/Judy! Back and forth until she fell around his neck.'

Asked two decades later about the '65 season's fan mania and celebrity 'madhouse', Rudolf said that he remembered only the pictures. 'You didn't have the chance to enjoy it all. It was such a struggle to get in the car and get away.' Just one famous face had impressed him – an encounter lasting no more than a few seconds that had taken place outside his dressing room before his New York debut in *Giselle*. 'A strange lady pass by my door and stared at me. She had a velvet beret.' With her oval head, melancholy eyes and smooth hair looped Russian ballerina-style over her ears, she looked strangely familiar. Then he remembered. Marietta Frangopoulo had kept a framed photograph on her desk of Olga Spessivtseva, the only Maryinsky dancer of whom Balanchine had spoken with awe; whose supernatural lightness and tormented soul had made her possibly the greatest-ever interpreter of Giselle. For twenty-two years Spessivtseva had been incarcerated in an American mental institution, rescued only recently by her friend the dancer Anton Dolin, who had moved her to a rest home in upstate New York. It was Dolin who had brought 'the Sleeping Ballerina' backstage to meet Margot. Although she was frail, her raven hair now completely white, her manner and composure were still those of a grande dame. For a few seconds she and Rudolf looked at each other without saying anything. 'And then she went away.'

Rudolf was desperately missing Russia. He had taken David Richardson, a young New York City Ballet dancer whom he was pursuing, to the Jean and Maggie Louis party at El Morocco, luminous with Hollywood stars, when suddenly he ran out into the street. Richardson followed him, and they walked together for about twenty blocks while Rudolf reminisced. 'He talked and talked about his country; his mother. I was surprised – I had no idea that he had this soft and sad side. I tried to ask questions, but it was making me feel I wasn't smart enough. "You're a kid," he said. "You're not a Russian – there's no way you can understand."'

Back in London in October, the Finnish dancer Leo Ahonen, one of the four foreigners who had shared his Vaganova room, paid Rudolf a visit on his way to Amsterdam, where Leo was taking up a new position as principal dancer and ballet master. 'He let me stay in his apartment. For two weeks I sleep on couch.' Eager to impress an old schoolmate, Rudolf took him to the Scotch in Mason's Yard, the rival 'jumping night place' to the Ad Lib, where Leo was indeed wide-eyed at the password rule of entry, the 'live fish and very very rich people'. Touchingly protective, Rudolf never left his side. 'I was in his armpit – he always liked to keep me close.' Later they walked down Jermyn Street window-shopping for Michael Fish shirts and Indian dressing gowns. Leo saw that Rudolf 'had everything' – a ten-thousand-dollar Mercedes-Benz, a brick of brand-new pound notes next to his bed – yet felt that he was not happy in the West. Rudolf seemed to envy Leo for having a wife and children, and when they began talking about Russia and Pushkin, he became distraught. Defensively responding to Leo's assumption that he had lost touch with their teacher, Rudolf glowered. 'I talk with Alexander Ivanovich all the time!' 'But he had to go into a little alley and cry for a while. He couldn't help it. Probably I hit him right at the head.'

In fact Rudolf rarely if ever spoke to Pushkin. If the teacher happened to pick up the receiver when he called, he would say nothing and pass it immediately to Xenia. 'Everything went through her,' said a mutual friend. 'It was Xenia who did all the talking and keeping up.' Aware that his first responsibility was towards his pupils, Pushkin was naturally afraid that any contact with Rudolf would jeopardize his position at the school. But it would have been far too emotional for him to speak to Rudolf, from whose loss he never recovered. 'Alexander Ivanovich was deeply hurt that his star pupil had chosen to go. And he never fully understood his reasons.'* Having heard all kinds of rumours about Rudolf – 'I was drunkard, I was neurotic' – Pushkin genuinely believed in the corrupting influence of the West. When he was shown a newspaper photograph of the long-haired dancer leaving a London club, he had laughed dryly. 'Look at our girl! What is he doing in the West anyway? *What* does he think he's doing?'

Pushkin's detachment can only have been increased by the fact that he now had another outstanding protégé, one who was himself already a legend at the Vaganova school. In September 1965 Pushkin had come home one evening in a state of elation, telling Xenia that he had just accepted an extraordinarily gifted pupil. 'What, better than Rudik?' she asked cynically. 'Completely different,' he replied, 'but no less

* It was only after Rudolf had sent his teacher the film of *Romeo and Juliet* (Joanne Woodward had helped him to have a 16-mm print made) that he received a letter from Pushkin, with his blessing. 'Now he say that I had done well in the West' (Quoted by Jean Battey Lewis, *Washington Post*, 9 June 1974).

talented.' Still looking like a child at seventeen, with wide-open blue
eyes and a small, compact physique, Mikhail Baryshnikov was a time
bomb of power and precision, able to perform unimaginable technical
feats – not as a display of acrobatics but as a thrilling extension of classical form. Even at his most virtuosic, every movement – every linking
step – would be executed with such sublime and flawless artistry that
Clive Barnes, watching the student in class during a visit to Russia,
described him in his diary as the most perfect dancer he had ever seen.
There can be no doubt that Rudolf knew about Pushkin's phenomenal
new pupil: there was, as Baryshnikov says, 'quite a lot of traffic
between London and Leningrad'. Sleeping on the sofa where Rudolf
himself had spent so many nights, 'Mishenka' was now 'their pride'.
And while, in Xenia's eyes, he would always be the 'Little Prince' to
Rudolf's 'Big Prince', to Alexander Ivanovich he was something
Rudolf could never be: an embodiment of the classical ideal.

Retaining his St Petersburg schooling was still Rudolf's greatest
concern. In his continuous search for a strong and inspiring teacher, he
had recently sought the help of the Russian-born Valentina Pereyaslavec, who had been Vaganova's assistant in Leningrad and was now on
the staff of the American Ballet Theatre school. They had got to know
each other when she was invited to teach the Royal Ballet Company
for three months in 1963 and 1965, her main goal having been to 'give
something a little extra in the arms, *épaulement*, arms, arms,
arms . . . to make every step fluid [as] in the corps de ballet in
Bayadère'. A tiny, spirited disciplinarian, Madame Pereyaslavec shared
several of Pushkin's qualities. She, too, was a teacher of few words
who did not believe in correcting or analysing but whose steps were
instructive in themselves – combinations that, even at the barre, were
as beguiling as miniature ballets. More to the point, like Alexander
Ivanovich, she could be trusted to tell Rudolf the truth. 'He don't like
you come after he dance and tell, "You is wonderful. You is beautiful."
This is not important for him. He always tell me, "Why are you so
quiet? Tell me what you don't like." And . . . he listen . . . I say, "You
like me tell you what little bother my eye?" And he say, "Tell me." And
I tell him.'

Frankness was also what he had come to expect from the Joffrey
School's teacher and choreographer Hector Zaraspe, an eccentric
Argentinian who from their first class had been the one in control.
Refusing to prepare for a pirouette from fourth position, Rudolf had
argued, 'I'm sorry. We take from second in Russia.' 'I'm sorry,' coun-
tered Zaraspe. 'We are in America – from fourth position.' 'He loved

that,' Zaraspe says. 'He loved when the teacher demand.' But neither teacher would ever be a mentor to Rudolf, able to provide the kind of spiritual and intellectual guidance lavished on him at Rossi Street, with its nightly discussions about classical style, costumes, past productions – they were too much in awe. 'He so inspire me to teach,' Pereyaslavec says, 'and he always use his schooling, what he learned at home.' 'He is my touchstone,' adds Zaraspe. 'I teach his way, his movement, his expression.' But both knew Rudolf only as an artist, not as a friend. Like Zaraspe, who 'try never to move in closer', Pereyaslavec deliberately withheld her affection. 'Because I don't want bother him . . . I don't want be friendly too much.'

Rudolf had never been more alone. At the end of October Erik wrote to him from Chicago, lamenting the distance between them. 'It seems like a terribly long time since I saw you felt you and looked at you . . . Sometimes I feel like maybe it was just a dream that we knew each other . . . but I do wish and pray for you that you are all right and happy somehow.'

Nor did he see much of Margot, all of whose free time was spent in Stoke Mandeville Hospital with her husband. When Tito came off the critical list, she had taken a room at a mediocre hotel in Aylesbury, and after a performance would catch a train with a bag of sandwiches for supper, and sleep there until six the next morning so that she could feed Tito his breakfast. With a single bed and an unheated communal bathroom at the end of the hall, it was such a grim existence for a prima ballerina that anyone who witnessed it could hardly believe the extent of Margot's self-abnegation. Their manservant, Buenaventura Medina, was one: 'Everyone thought that when he became paralysed she would just pay someone to take good care of him and that's that. But she said, "No, I'm going to show the world that I can dance *and* I can take good care of my husband." And she did it – right up to the end.'

To the Arias family Margot's sense of responsibility towards Tito was that of a true Latin American wife, but some sceptics found her 'volte-face from prospective divorcée to wifely martyr' hypocritical, or at least, an act of some kind. 'Tito didn't want her there, so what was the point?' says Joan Thring. 'The whole situation irritated Rudolf, as it did me.' Margot, however, was not playing a role – she had what she wanted: Tito by her side on whom to lavish love and devotion, an end to suffering the pain of his roving and a sense of duty as unconditional as her dance vocation. But where did Rudolf fit in?

More often than not he would have dinner on his own. He liked La Popote in Walton Street, where the food was mediocre but the waiters exceptionally pretty; or the Casserole on King's Road, which had in its basement the added attraction of Le Gigolo, one of London's first gay clubs. Rudolf was having his usual steak at La Popote one night when his eye was drawn to a young man who had just walked in. Somewhere in his early thirties, with thick black hair, he had the classically handsome looks of a Jean Marais or a dark Erik Bruhn. Rudolf stared at him without smiling, but seeing a waiter with a menu on his way to take the young man's order, he called him over and pencilled something on the back. It was just one word: 'Hello.'

Keith Baxter knew whom the message was from. He was an actor who had come close to making a film of the Bible with Rudolf, to be directed by a quartet of well-known names including Orson Welles.*

That night at La Popote, two years later, Keith – showing no sign of interest in Rudolf – began talking to a critic at an adjoining table. Sitting in a corner across the room were Francis Bacon and a companion in a Merchant Navy uniform, so drunk that he had slumped across the table. Rudolf paid his bill and ordered another coffee at the same time. When he saw the young man ask for his own bill, he immediately stood up and left. As Keith got into his car, there was a flash of headlights from a Mercedes parked opposite. Rudolf pulled out, waited to be followed, and they drove in convoy to Belgravia.

The apartment was comfortable but ordinary and anonymous. As Rudolf went into the kitchen to get them a drink, Keith sat down. Minutes passed. He was taking off his shoes when the door opened and Rudolf appeared carrying two glasses of vodka. He was naked. 'I had no time to touch my drink. He lay on his stomach on the rug. It was all quite mechanical. When it was finished, he got up and went into another room. I waited to see if he would return, but he did not appear. It seemed a pity to waste the Stolichnaya, so I drank mine, then his.'

Putting on one shoe (which was the only thing he had taken off), Keith went into the kitchen with the glasses, preparing to leave. As he

---

* In the film, which was never made, Welles wanted Rudolf for the role of the Angel of God who wrestles at Peniel with Jacob (to be played by Keith Baxter), a sequence to be shot against the rays of the sun. 'How much speak?' asked Rudolf. Welles explained it was an important part, but silent, and added that he wanted Rudolf to be naked. 'Agreed. But no speak? You want me to make with muscles only?'

was picking up his car keys, Rudolf suddenly appeared. 'No keys. You stay,' he said.

> I did not want to stay. I don't know how much he understood, but I told him he should hire a robot. Also, he had been dancing that day, and his body had a staleness to it. 'You stay,' he said, holding my keys behind him. When he grinned he was irresistible; the scar on his top lip made him look like a street urchin. I went into the bathroom and ran a bath. He was watching me with wide eyes. I made him climb in, and I washed him. He was laughing and splashing me, but he found it very arousing, and so did I. I dried him and put a towel on the bed, and as he lay on it I rubbed baby lotion into his skin. His body had the musculature of an athlete, and only his dancer's feet were slightly misshapen. I turned him over. His back of course was beautiful, and he was justly proud of it.

The sky was lightening by the time Keith left for home. Rudolf had not asked what he did for a living and he had not told him – not even mentioning the Welles connection. 'I really had no plan to see him again.' They exchanged numbers, and a few days later Rudolf called him.

Arriving at the apartment, Keith was glad to find two youngsters there – an attractive girl and her equally attractive husband. Nellie Liddell worked as a model booker at Nev's agency and Tony, a Bermondsey cockney, was a painter. The couple were fans, whom Rudolf had literally picked up one night outside the stage door. They had been walking down Floral Street after watching a performance when the star's convertible, followed by a running, squealing horde, drew up beside them. 'Get in,' he said. 'We go to eat.' They went to La Popote, where they spent most of the evening just looking at one another – not just because of the language obstacle, but because the couple were extraordinarily striking. Nellie, who was petite enough to have been a dancer, wore miniskirts not much wider than a belt with black Anello & Davide boots, or mannish trouser suits long before Yves Saint Laurent's 'smokings'. Tony had long raven black hair past his shoulders, clothes that were as eyecatching as his wife's, and the same androgynous sixties beauty. Being with Rudolf that night, they said, 'was like meeting a soul person'.

As Tony and Nellie lived in nearby Victoria and were such good playmates, he began seeing a lot of them. They would go to the movies or dancing at the Ad Lib, and occasionally Tony would borrow something of Rudolf's to wear. ' "Bitch!" he used to say, because I looked much better in it. But he never tried to make a pass – he knew Nell and I were an item.' In a sense they were London's version of Leningrad's Romankov twins, young and fun yet able to provide Rudolf with the homely kitchen culture he so missed. Even when they moved much farther away to council housing in Clapham, Rudolf still made the effort to go to see them. 'He'd come round for a meal and we'd sit on the floor and 'ave a laugh. Maybe because we'd had the same poor upbringing, we could all relate to each other. I think for him we must've been like his sisters or whatever he was missing.' If they went to a restaurant, Tony insisted on paying for the three of them. 'But I've got lots of money,' Rudolf would argue. 'I didn't care. I wasn't going to sponge off of him.' He told the couple they could use his flat in Monaco at any time, but they couldn't afford the fare. They were neither sycophantic nor impressed by his grand admirers; in fact they were in his dressing room one evening with Lee Radziwill, when he asked Tony to escort the princess to the stage door. 'If she found her way here, she can find her way back,' Tony said conclusively. The pair had nothing to offer Rudolf except their friendship, a simple, touching bond that lasted, they noticed, 'until he became aware of what money was'.

On that first evening with Keith, Rudolf left the three of them to take a telephone call in another room. It was Farida, calling from Leningrad. Out of politeness Keith asked whether Tony painted land-scapes or portraits. ''ouses,' he said. He was a painter and decorator. Nellie looked hard at Keith: 'Haven't I just seen you on the telly?' He had appeared that week in a detective drama, and when Rudolf came back more than an hour later, Nellie told him that Keith was an actor. 'He was surprised I hadn't told him myself.' The four went on to La Popote for dinner, but having first wanted the Liddells with him for support, Rudolf soon began seeing Keith alone, clearly appreciating his intelligence and sense of fun. Keith recalls: 'I took him to *Les Enfants du paradis*, and he was enthralled. But he liked the Bond films and the "Carry On" films too. I tried to get him to come to Twickenham to watch Wales play England, but he would have nothing to do with it.'

As they were rowing on the Serpentine one afternoon, their boat was bumped by another with four men in it, all rowdy and shouting. Rudolf was frightened and wanted to leave. It was beginning to rain, with no taxis in sight, so they walked to Hyde Park Corner, and Keith took him into Apsley House. Once the home of the Duke of

Wellington, it has in the entrance a colossal white marble nude of Napoleon – Wellington's trophy – with a staircase winding round it. Keith started climbing it, followed by Rudolf, who suddenly stopped and, with a huge grin, pointed to the massive curves of the emperor's buttocks. 'Look! Is me!' he exclaimed, prompting Keith's nickname for him, 'Modestivich', which he thought very funny.

While between homes, Rudolf stayed in Keith's Thameside apartment in Westminster, astounding the cleaning woman with the strange items of washing – the jockstraps and tights – with which he festooned the bathroom. They would listen to music, drink Stolichnaya – two bottles one night. 'Rudolf got very sad when he was drunk – that typical Russian melancholy.' And they spent a lot of time in bed. Keith was determined to teach his 'very apt pupil' that lovemaking could last more than five minutes, although sexually he found Rudolf extremely unsophisticated, interested only in following the particular pattern that satisfied him:

> With me, at any rate – he was ferociously passive, so that sex was energetic and exciting but I always felt there was a part of him that was challenging me to subdue him, and then, abandoning himself to surrender, he found fulfilment. It was as if there was some inner loneliness, some sense of rejection that he could never overcome, and he provoked this frenzied eroticism to hide from it for a little while. I didn't analyse it at the time; it was just terrific, and exhausting. But, looking back, I wondered what need was expressing itself in him that he had to be treated with such savagery. Afterwards, tugging one of my arms over him, he fell asleep quickly and deeply like a child. Once he woke me in the middle of the night talking animatedly in his sleep in Russian, and kicking.

Keith knew all about Erik, who posed no threat. 'Rudolf would say, "Is such pity I cannot be in love with you, Keith. You're not in love with me, and I'm not in love with you." And we would laugh.' The more Keith saw of Rudolf, however, the more he was made aware of how lonely Rudolf was. 'Because his English was still so rudimentary, he had no small talk and couldn't gossip or exchange ideas easily, so that the usual dancer camaraderie was denied him.' When they were with other people, Keith noticed the way Rudolf would use his natural hauteur to mask the fact that he did not understand much of what was being said and seemed nervous of revealing his lack of manners: 'He would look to see which knife and fork I was using. In those days he seemed secure only onstage or when we were alone. Onstage and in bed he was classless. I felt that he was desperate for company of his own age.'

In the spring of 1966 Rudolf returned to Vienna. He had asked Lynn Seymour to come from Berlin to dance his *Swan Lake* with him; and he also wanted to exploit the workshop appeal of the company by choreographing something of his own. *Tancredi*, which premièred at the State Opera on 18 May 1966, took its name from the score, Hans Werner Henze's *Tancred und Cantylene*. This was a shorter, revised version of a piece written in 1952 with a new libretto by Peter Csobadi. Henze would have welcomed a collaboration with Rudolf but says that the dancer made 'not a single attempt' to get in touch.* This seems oddly uncharacteristic. What Rudolf originally had in mind was a Balanchine-style work – 'perhaps to Stravinsky's music, without a story and very classical'. Since Henze was Europe's most eminent contemporary composer, it seems that Rudolf would have seized the chance to try out his own version of the kind of music–ballet partnership that Balanchine had had with Stravinsky. The music's twelve-tone austerity prompted movements that were plainly derived from Balanchine's Stravinsky- and Webern-based ballets – in fact Michael Birkmeyer remembers Rudolf setting out in one sequence 'to beat Balanchine'. Using as his model a grouping of the Three Muses in *Apollo*, 'He was trying to go one better,' Birkmeyer says. 'But it all ended up with him and the girls stuck together in a clump. He just burst out laughing, and said, "Sorry, Mr B!"'

The protagonist of *Tancredi* was virtually the same as Rudolf's Siegfried – 'the outsider, the neurotic male'. Forced to choose between a chaste Odette-type ideal and a blatantly seductive 'second female image', Tancredi was torn to the point that his personality literally split in half. The ballet then became an enactment of mental schizophrenia, 'a tone poem of the subconscious', with Barry Kay's dark, membranous, vein-streaked setting providing a visualization of the human

---

* On 29 July 1964, Henze wrote to say he was sorry they had just missed each other, but talks of an earlier encounter with romantic memories. 'My dearest Rudolf . . . Please write to me soon, and let me know where you are and where I can meet you. For me it was a rencontre of splendour and beauty: to listen to your voice, seeing your eyes and to absorb a sense of energy and elegance who support a soul which must be deep – and far away – as all Asia! For you I hear music. All my love, Hans.'

brain. Like Rudolf's *Swan Lake*, *Tancredi* was an exploration of Erik's bipolar psyche as well as the abiding love–lust conflict within himself. If anything, though, it was even more self-revelatory, its hero a man who was no longer able to love his ideal 'because he loves nobody as much as himself'.

Preempting the charge of self-interest, Rudolf told John Percival that when he began *Tancredi* he 'divided up the music carefully to give equal opportunity to my cast as well as myself'. Nevertheless the fact remains that eight of the other male roles were reflections of the hero, not characters in their own right, and there was hardly a moment when he himself was not onstage. While praising Rudolf's stunningly dramatic performance, even the partisan Linda Zamponi was forced to admit that the ballet perplexed critics and audiences alike. It was also disappointing choreographically. With steps as feverish as the scenario – acrobatic runs, dives, a human trampoline, strobe jerks – there was no sign of a personal or original style. Michael Birkmeyer agrees. 'There *was* no style. Rudolf realized very fast that this was not his way of choreographing things, and he went on to do productions where he knew what he was doing.'

In order to prepare himself for the job of staging the ballet *Don Quixote*, Rudolf decided to spend his summer reading Cervantes's novel, an experience the writer Martin Amis has compared to 'an indefinite visit from your most impossible senior relative, with all his pranks, dirty habits, unstoppable reminiscences and terrible cronies'. Rudolf himself hated Petipa's Don 'quite a lot', although at this point he knew only the ballet's unfunny, befuddled clown. 'There is so much there,' he said, 'but in a ballet you can only skim the surface. I tried to put in a lot of things I felt about the book, like impressions of the Callot lithographs, but you daren't put too much comment in. It really is largely a lot of dances and great zest and comic spirit.'

Certainly no one could claim this Petipa work to be a masterpiece. Like other nineteenth-century versions, it focuses on a pair of child-hood sweethearts from volume 2 of the novel and banishes Don Quixote and Sancho Panza, his roly-poly sidekick, to no more than walk-on roles. With Petipa having considerably reworked the ballet within a space of two years, it was difficult to determine the original choreography, so Rudolf decided to base his production on the Kirov one he knew. Although he could reconstruct most of the parts from memory, he was also able to draw on a rough, pirated film sent by the Pushkins* with the help of a Canadian dancer then studying in Leningrad. Anna Marie Holmes, who also smuggled out the full score, claims that Rudolf's production hardly departed from the film. 'It was when there was a gap because of a reel being changed that he made up his own stuff.'

Wanting his *Don Quixote* to be even more robustly comic than the Kirov's, Rudolf decided to commission John Lanchbery to inject the Minkus score with a lighter-hearted tone. He also set out to restore authenticity to the Spanish dances, which he believed were just as vital to the ballet's success as the thrust and flavour of Cervantes's words in their original language. He began by asking his teacher Hector Zaraspe, an ex-Antonio dancer, to show him dances like the jota, fandango and seguedilla – 'where the accents go, the expression, the positions of the body'. And he also tried hard to enlist the help of Heinz Mannigel, the young dancer who had shown him the spirit of real flamenco during the tour of East Germany in 1959.

Having himself defected to the West, Heinz was now dancing in Hamburg, and had come across Marika Besobrasova at a ballet summer school in Cologne. Impressed by her teaching, he and his dancer wife decided to audition for the International Ballet Festival which she was staging in mid-July as part of Monte Carlo's centennial celebrations. 'There Rudik was in Marika's class with Erik Bruhn. "My God," he said. "Heinz: it's *you*!" He invited me to come to his house and drove me around in his old Volvo.' Heinz had little Russian and even less English, so few words were exchanged – 'it was more feelings between us . . . looks, smiles' – but both must have wondered if they could recapture their rapport of seven years earlier. On this occasion, though, Rudolf had a very definite idea in mind. In December he would be premièring a first draft of his *Don Quixote* in Vienna,† but he had intended all along to stage the ballet on the Australian company (a plan that did not come about until 1970). Not only did the dancers

---

* Baryshnikov and Xenia's friend Alla Bor remember the efforts at Rossi Street to aid Rudolf's 'factory of productions'. Both Alexander Ivanovich and Xenia would handwrite each part, movement by movement, some described in Russian, some in French. On one occasion, unsure of a detail, Xenia went specially to see the ballet itself in order to transcribe it accurately.

† The Vienna production which premièred in December fell flat. Although Rudolf himself danced with electrifying commitment, his Kitri (Ulli Wuhrer) had none of the charm or heel-kicking spitfire quality of a Ninel Kurgapkina. Nevertheless, Horst Koegler, writing for *Dance & Dancers* (February 1967), recognized the ballet's potential. 'What a roaring finale this must be, if danced with the right swing – which unfortunately it wasn't.'

have the energy and panache to reanimate this 'old warhorse', but he felt that Heinz's fire and expertise in flamenco could inject it with the ardour verging on dementia that had made such an impact on Petipa.[*] Instead of asking Heinz for his assistance, however, Rudolf made him a strangely unrealistic offer. 'Come to Australia!' he urged. 'You will choreograph *Don Quixote*, and I will be your guest star.' Heinz says:

> I just thought, this is much too much for me. I was a dancer. I'd taken a teacher's course in East Germany, but I'd never made a ballet. He was very insistent. He really believed in my work, and kept saying, 'Heinz, you should do it. It would be a very good thing for you. And I'll be there too!' But I never thought about big opportunities: I was only twenty-five . . . my wife wouldn't have wanted to go to Australia – I just thought about being happy.

Erik was at La Turbie, too, that day, reserved but not at all hostile towards Heinz. Having spent the last three months in Rome dancing, teaching, and producing new works, he had arrived in the South of France in a state of near-collapse. He was spending six weeks in Cannes with a dancer friend, but after a few days the strain began to show and he became violently ill with his recurring stomach problem. He had only just recovered when Rudolf arrived, and feeling that he had no emotion to spare, refused to stay with him at La Turbie. Distraught that Erik would not agree even to come to the house for dinner, Rudolf turned up one evening at the Cannes apartment of Arlette Castanier, a close friend of Erik. They began drinking, and Erik, who had a supper engagement with the director of the Harkness Ballet, went out soon afterwards, leaving Rudolf with Arlette. 'You do what you want with this drunk *mujik*,' he told her, 'but don't let him drive back.' By now in a woozily amorous mood, Rudolf lunged at Arlette and began trying to kiss her. 'A wonderful girl with a wonderful heart', she understood he was 'needing comfort', and gently humoured him while plying him with coffee until he was sober enough to go home. The following day a huge bouquet of roses arrived for her, and Erik went to stay at La Turbie. A snippet of 8-mm footage taken by Arlette in their garden captures Rudolf's unleashed euphoria as, watched by Erik – wearing an expression of affectionate resignation – he performs his own, Russified take-off on Isadora Duncan.

---

[*] The choreographer had been amazed by the passionate intensity of performers and spectators when he witnessed Spanish national dancing during a tour of Andalusia in the 1840s.

Rudolf's high spirits did not last long. He had asked Heinz to appear as Hilarion to his Albrecht as he and Margot were to dance *Giselle* in the festival. 'I told him that I couldn't, that I wasn't good enough. But saying no to him again clearly made him angry.' Rudolf remained angry. Several French dancer friends who were in Monte Carlo were shocked by his brutishness during rehearsals with Margot. 'He was *impossible*' (Rosella Hightower); 'He was calling her "an old cow" in front of the young kids' (Ghislaine Thesmar); '*Il était odieux!*' (Yvette Chauviré). Instead of shrugging things off as usual, Margot was in despair, quietly crying as she waited for her entrance. 'But she dried her eyes and went onstage,' said Pierre Lacotte, who had been standing beside her in the wings.

In fact there was nothing new about Rudolf's behaviour. It was Margot's circumstances that had changed. With her domestic life in perpetual crisis, she badly needed the escape of her world onstage. Unhappily, though, she was now entering the bleakest phase of her career, a period when the Royal Opera House had begun systematically to reduce the number of her performances. This was part of a new policy to promote the younger ballerinas, but it was one that Margot's admirers, particularly the protective Keith Money, viewed as 'quite evil towards her'.

> Those were awful days, because it was just so completely, utterly, discreditably *shoddy*. And as a result Rudolf got quite perplexed and scared, not knowing how to hedge his bets safely in terms of the management. He distanced himself from Margot rather obviously, like scuttling off as soon as the curtain calls ended. None of the usual 'Are you going to get some food?' Just slipped out of the theatre and away. I'm sure this attitude hurt Margot, even if she could work out the political dimension of it.

For some time, John Tooley says, Rudolf had been making it very clear that he did not want to confine himself to partnering Margot. The extraordinary resurgence in her that he had instigated had waned, and she was finding it a strain to keep up with him. Much of his aggression towards her in Monte Carlo had been, in Marika Besobrasova's view, 'a big kick for the energy'. She was becoming untidy and too reliant on his support, when more and more he expected a ballerina to be autonomous. If he felt that his stamina was being deflected from his variations, he would retaliate (as he would do during a December performance in Vienna, when he almost dropped Ulli Wuhrer 'not once, not twice, but three separate times'). Carla Fracci, a ballerina he had dismissed at first as 'lazy', says that being partnered by Rudolf required a completely different discipline. 'You have to learn to stand on your own legs, to find the strength to help him, make preparation *he* needed.' They had performed together during Erik's brief tenure as director at the Rome Opera Ballet, but Fracci, the diva of Italian ballet, had no intention of tolerating the kind of abuse that Margot accepted. 'She was excusing him because he was young, but I had the nerve to say "Enough! You are *viziato* – spoiled – by Margot!"'

Although she and Erik were now consolidating what would become their famous partnership, Fracci was someone with whom Rudolf badly wanted to forge a link of his own. Not only a wonderful dancer with the serene beauty of a quattrocento Madonna combined with the glamour of a movie star, she was also the wife of director Giuseppe 'Beppe' Menegatti, a powerful force in the Italian arts. From Fracci's point of view, although she idolized Erik – her 'friend, partner and master' – she knew that working with Rudolf would significantly extend her resources as an artist: the one gave her confidence and security – 'He *presented* me' – the other strengthened her technique. Her March 1966 performances with the two dancers in Rome (Rudolf partnering her in *La Sylphide*,* Erik in his own Balcony Scene from *Romeo and Juliet*) were considered by Vittoria Ottolenghi, Italy's preeminent ballet critic and historian, to be Fracci's 'most beautiful and magical'. Understandably this short run was a huge theatrical event, with fans sleeping in the street waiting for tickets and the auditorium teeming with such celebrities as Elizabeth Taylor and Richard Burton. At that time, Menegatti says, there was great rivalry between the Rome Opera House and La Scala – 'One theatre jump on reputation of the other' – a situation the couple took advantage of when the administration of La Scala came to Rome to see a performance. 'We push, we push for Rudolf to do a production in Milan.'

The invitation could not have come at a better time. Vaslav Orlikovsky, with whom Rudolf had clashed over the filming of *Le Spectre de la rose* in 1961, was now director of the Staatsoper in Vienna and had no intention of staging any further Nureyev productions after

---

* Adapting himself to Fracci's Sylphide – 'coquette, terribly sweet, and brainless' – Rudolf had toned down the high-Romantic element. According to Freda Pit writing in *The Dancing Times*, his 'virtually immaculate' James was now much closer to Erik's, although he still brought enough glamour to justify 'the folly of the happy free creature of the woods preferring the love of a mortal to the delights of a superhuman world'.

Don Quixote (an Aurel Milloss commission). It was Rudolf's idea to mount *Sleeping Beauty* at La Scala; it was the ballet that had helped form both Balanchine and Ashton as choreographers, and one he believed could be equally educational for him. 'When you know these ballets, you know what is what in choreography. Only to that point can you do something of your own. Petipa teaches. This is this. That is that. He is the basis of all ballets.' The experience of having tried and failed to create an original work of his own had tempered his audacious attitude towards the classics – 'It is my duty to be truthful to Petipa' – and for the La Scala production he planned no radical departures or even cuts. *Sleeping Beauty* was, he said, 'the *Parsifal* of ballet . . . very long and very lush', and he wanted his own version to have all the resonance of grand opera.

Although often perceived as a *féerie* ballet – the reason Rudolf had so hated the Folies-Bergères frivolity of the de Cuevas version – the lavish original was criticized at the time for being too serious. Rudolf felt it was significant that the tsar and all his court had attended the *répétition générale* as this not only endorsed the actual link between the imperial household and the Maryinsky Theatre but was reflected in the ballet's own opulence and majesty – what Alexander Bland called 'the peculiar Russian furs-and-diamonds glitter so marvellously conveyed in the score'. Nico Georgiadis was the obvious choice for designer, although he had not been particularly pleased with his decor for the Vienna *Swan Lake*. 'It was the first time I'd done something classical, and I felt that it was all much too constricted.' Nevertheless the broodingly atmospheric, darkly burnished sets had been a step in the direction of the 1965 MacMillan *Romeo and Juliet* – a visual feast with exactly the architectural splendour, rich textures and Byzantine colours that Rudolf had in mind for his *Beauty*. He described to Georgiadis a lavish earlier Kirov production he remembered, and they agreed on an imperial Russian approach, the designer noticing how 'suddenly, Rudolf's own inherent Russian baroque/Russian expressionism came out'. Rudolf was full of suggestions; one, inspired by a black-and-white film he had seen of *Peter the Great*, was to begin the ballet with a baronial dinner, the Prologue's colours similarly grey, silver and black. It was also his idea to make the production more than usually architectural, with a long table stretched diagonally across the stage, and a great central staircase conveying the sense of monumental structures beyond the confines of the proscenium – 'great gardens, a great empire'.

Inevitably it was hard for the dancers to compete with these sumptuous mass effects, but this in itself was deliberate. If the look of Rudolf's

Sleeping Beauty was an ultra-masculine Romanov opulence, the quality of movement he wanted was Margot-inspired English reticence. Having cruelly mimicked the ballerina's distinctive low-legged, squarely placed arabesque in Monte Carlo two months earlier, he now described it to the dancers as something of incomparable integrity, using it to demonstrate the kind of moderate, restrained classicism he wanted to see. 'He worked so much with us,' said Fracci, 'but he was very demanding, very tough, I must say. There was one time when he slapped a girl, which caused a big scandal.' For Carla he did not need to invoke the image of Margot's dancing – it was already her lodestar. As a student she had appeared as a page in a Fonteyn performance of *Sleeping Beauty* at La Scala, and, from the moment of Aurora's first joyous entrance, discovered her real vocation. Margot, as Menegatti says, was 'the inside push for Carla', and remained her 'idol for ever'. Nevertheless, as an exceptionally pliant dancer she found it hard to restrict her line to the ninety-degree angles and 'poses like still pictures' that Rudolf was demanding. Consequently their battle of wills continued.[*]

Undeniably Aurora's ballet, *Sleeping Beauty* could not be colonized by Rudolf as a showcase for himself. He did, however, make Act 2, the Hunting Scene, revolve around the Prince – and with cause: Désiré, as Arlene Croce has pointed out, is a fantasy version of the Sun King. Rudolf had read the new English edition of Saint-Simon's memoirs and drawn inspiration for the Prince from descriptions of the louche, sumptuous life at Louis's hunting lodge. With the same hypnotic presence, ruthless streak and vast appetite for life and beauty, Rudolf made a dazzling reincarnation of Louis XIV, always the cynosure, almost by divine right.

The court dances in this act are, as one critic noted, 'mere breathing pauses for our hero'. Despite Rudolf's vow of fidelity to Petipa, he was never going to stage a nineteenth-century classic without providing more dance opportunities for the Prince. Following Konstantin Sergeyev's example, he added an extra solo, then went one better by appropriating Tchaikovsky's musical entr'acte for himself.[†] A passage

---

[*] Insisting on no trace of flamboyance, Rudolf had told Fracci he wanted her to do only two pirouettes in the grand pas de deux. In particularly good form one night, she was spinning into her third turn ready to finish on the music, when Rudolf suddenly brought her to a halt just as she was facing him. Staring into her eyes, he very deliberately turned her back in a counterclockwise direction so that everyone in the audience knew there had been a blunder.
[†] Nico Georgiadis told Nigel Gosling (1 July 1981, diary entry) that Fracci 'failed to turn up for a rehearsal during which he was to arrange the Act 2 Entr'acte solo for her. After waiting for half an hour, he said, "Well, I will grab it for myself." And he did.'

usually reserved for the first violinist, spotlighted in the orchestra pit, this became an opportunity for a five-minute dance described by Alexander Bland as 'certainly more Nureyev than Petipa in style'. Dense with favourite fiddly Bournonville steps, it twists and turns back on itself as if trying to express indecision and introversion but looking only awkwardly improvised. Carla Fracci remembers Rudolf hurriedly choreographing it after one of their rehearsals. It was the evening when Erik had just arrived. Rudolf had asked his opinion a couple of times, 'but I don't think Erik said too much'. (Once again Erik's silence was heavy with censure.) With Désiré now consigned to the 'sad dynasty to which belong the princes Siegfried, Albrecht and Hamlet', this was one too many of Rudolf's soulful soliloquies. All the same Rudolf was proud of his La Scala *Sleeping Beauty*, a production he would always consider his most successful. He told Nigel Gosling how disappointed he was that no one from the Royal Ballet made the effort to see it. In fact, the opera house's John Tooley did see one performance in Milan: 'When we had dinner afterwards, Rudolf asked me if he had overdone it, and I told him *absolutely* you have.'

Learning that the National Ballet of Cuba was due to appear at the Théâtre des Champs-Élysées in November 1966, Rudolf went to Paris, hoping that Menia Martinez would be with them. At the general rehearsal, trying not to be recognized, he sat far back in a side balcony seat, but once he had spotted Menia onstage, he asked the company *régisseur* to deliver a note to her during a break. Rumours that Nureyev was in the auditorium had already filtered backstage, and it was with great excitement that Menia read the message Rudolf had scrawled on a scrap of paper: 'When you've finished, go to the Hotel des Ambassadeurs. I'll be waiting for you.' The subterfuge had not escaped the notice of director Alicia Alonso, who, supported by her husband, Fernando, forbade Menia to leave. As a member of the National Ballet she was a representative of her country. Nureyev had betrayed the motherland, he was known to be a friend of Jacqueline Kennedy.* If she met him she would not only compromise the company but put her own political standing in jeopardy. (This in itself was considerable. When Fidel Castro and Nikita Khrushchev met in New York for the first time, in September 1960, it was Menia who was

---

* One of the conspiracy theories surrounding John Kennedy's assassination had involved Fidel Castro.

chosen to be their translator.) Menia refused to be deterred. 'I don't care,' she told the couple. 'Even if you fire me, I'm going. He was my best friend.' The impasse was finally broken by a colleague who had 'influence on the Alonsos', and who volunteered to chaperone her.

It was only a short walk from the theatre to the hotel, where Rudolf was standing outside. Seeing Menia's male companion, he raised an ironic eyebrow. 'Cuban KGB?' 'No,' she said firmly. 'This is my friend.' Her colleague left them, and they fell into each other's arms. They were still 'grasping each other' when dance critic Claude Baignères passed by: 'I saw Rudolf take the girl to the hotel. They looked as if they were going to stay there for three days without leaving!' In fact they left soon afterwards to go for dinner, and as they were walking towards a taxi stand, noticed that they were being followed by a photographer. 'No pictures! No pictures!' snarled Rudolf, throwing his jacket over Menia's head and saying to her softly, 'I don't want them to hurt you.' Under her coat she was still wearing her rehearsal clothes, but despite her protests, Rudolf insisted on taking her to Maxim's. It was important to him that she be made aware of his enormous change in stature. He introduced her to Brigitte Bardot, and later they went on to Régine's nightclub.

As if anxious to justify himself, Rudolf began to explain almost immediately why he had stayed in the West, recounting every detail of the Le Bourget trap. He had hoped to stay in Paris, he said, but the French had not wanted him because of their cultural alliance with Russia, which was why he had gone to England. He told her how much he had learned from Margot – 'she was like a mother to him, he said' – and what a great revelation working with Erik Bruhn had been. 'But you're Nureyev and you come from Pushkin,' Menia protested. 'Yes – but I'm so much cleaner now.' She was 'surprised, yes – very surprised, no' – to hear from Rudolf of his long affair with Erik. 'Erik Bruhn was a very big personality, and I understood that Rudik would have wanted him to be a passage of his life.' Rudolf told her about their problems, saying that it had been so hard being constantly apart that Erik had finally decided to end things. 'It's finished,' he said, breaking down. 'He's the love of my life, but it's finished.' There had been no dramatic breakup, he told her, and they would always stay good friends. 'But now,' Rudolf said, 'now I am alone.'

At that moment I could have gone to bed with him: It was so wonderful to see him again. He told me that there was something about me that he'd never found in anybody else, and he start to cry again, saying, 'I love you . . . Please, Menia, stay with me. I want you to stay with me.' I realized then why the Alonsos hadn't wanted me to go.[*]

Rudolf was flying to Vienna first thing in the morning – the company was waiting for him to teach them *Don Quixote* – but this made him all the more insistent that Menia should accompany him: Vienna was exactly where he had proposed to her eight years earlier. 'But why now?' she wanted to know. 'I always thought you asked me only to leave Russia.' 'Well, I'm on the other side, and I'm still asking,' he replied quietly.

Her first thought was that with the Cuban première scheduled for the following day she could not let her company down, but longer-term considerations made the idea of elopement seem even more 'impossible'. She planned, as soon as she could, to return to Russia to dance with the Kirov or the Bolshoi. 'I wanted to prepare *Giselle* there – in Cuba only Alicia Alonso danced *Giselle*. And for me it was very important to have this freedom – to open the door of my life as a dancer.' Rudolf, more than anyone, could understand her obsession with 'only dance, dance, dance', and consequently kept contradicting himself. 'He was saying, "*Come* . . . please come!" And then "No, I can see that you can't."' Finally the answer Menia gave him was just as equivocal. 'I told him not yes, not no, but *pattamo* [because].'

It was after five in the morning by the time they left Régine's and Rudolf dropped Menia back at her hotel. As she lay in bed, her thoughts still racing, she felt very sad, wondering if she had made a mistake. But instead of being impressed by Rudolf's enormous celebrity, it had made her 'a little afraid,' and she knew without any hesitation that she did not want to spend the rest of her life just following him around. 'A few days later, I think it's good that I say *pattamo*.'

For Rudolf this had been an episode he would not repeat. Never again would he try so fervently to recapture an encounter from his past, which, however sweetly nostalgic, had only served to augment his belief that one should never look back. Taking the taxi on to the Hotel des Ambassadeurs, he went inside – not to sleep but to collect his luggage: he had another plane to catch, a new ballet to stage.

---

[*] Eight male corps de ballet dancers defected in Paris at the end of the season, not, according to Menia, for political reasons, but because they were all homosexual, 'and Alicia Alonso was not *d'accord* with this.'

12   WILD THING

As in the old romances, where the virtuous beauty is offset by a sorceress – Una by Duessa, the primeval female bringing forth destruction and death – Menia had a dangerous counterpart. A wild child of the decade – *Tatler*'s Girl of '65 – Talitha Pol was 'a total, complete transfixer of men'. To her friend Christopher Gibbs, a fellow *enfant terrible*, she was as lethal as Wedekind's Lulu, a ravishing young woman who 'had elevated flirting into an art form'.

> Talitha was a difficult person for anyone to be in love with as she had several strings to her bow – young and sexy; lecherous and old; doting aristocrat; dim pretty boy . . . all of whom she kept expertly wound up. She was very seductive and very touching, and at the same time, a little bit aware of how to put these qualities to work.

When they met for the first time at a party in early 1965 Rudolf had been totally captivated. Born in Indonesia, Talitha had alabaster-white skin and high cheekbones and eyes much like his own. Although he did not find her particularly intelligent, she was intuitive and sympathetic, and they instantly seemed to recognize something in each other. Her family had been living in Bali when the Japanese arrived in 1943, and interned them in appalling conditions. Talitha learned to feed herself by stealing, and retained horrific memories of the prison camp. Her mother, who never recovered from their ordeal, died in 1948, and Willem Pol, a Dutch painter, moved to England, where he soon remarried. The daughter of Augustus and Dorelia John, Poppet Pol had all the sophisticated flamboyance of her parents, and Talitha's upbringing changed almost overnight into a bohemian idyll. In a mirrored dress from Lebanon, or a Berber wedding gown with shawl and King's Road canvas boots, Talitha created what *Vogue* called 'her own inimitable fantasies' as one of London's first hippies. (When Rudolf took her as his guest to a royal gala he had to ask Joan Thring to lend her something suitable to wear.)

What had so impressed him, Gibbs says, was the way Talitha had triumphed over her background. 'She was sparkling and delicious, yet vulnerable and damaged at the same time.' And although what he was actually seeing was an exquisite, androgynous reflection of himself, Rudolf had never felt so erotically stirred by a woman, telling several friends that he wanted to marry Talitha. She was just as enthralled by him. When Claus von Bülow, Rudolf's Belgravia neighbour, invited them both to dinner, she made him promise to seat them next to each other. For some reason Rudolf was unable to come that evening, and instead von Bülow invited the son of his business associate J. Paul Getty. The die was cast: J. Paul junior fell in love as soon as he saw Talitha, the woman who 'would all but ruin his life'. By December 1966 she had become Mrs Paul Getty, her wedding dress a white mink-trimmed miniskirt. The couple began dividing their time between Rome and Marrakesh, where they had bought a nineteenth-century palace in the ancient walled city, soon becoming friends of Yves Saint Laurent and his partner, Pierre Bergé, who had themselves just acquired a house in the medina. Saint Laurent's immediate rapport with Talitha had seemed inevitable to Bergé – as inevitable as the 'very, very close bond' he had observed between her and Rudolf: 'People like Talitha, Rudolf and Yves have the same flair – the same perception of life, more or less the same behaviour. It's a decadence, a mix of Burne-Jones and Rossetti. For these people the rest of the world is square.'

They were all together in Paris in June 1967 at a performance of Roland Petit's *Notre Dame de Paris*, for which Saint Laurent had designed the costumes. Rudolf was particularly interested in the ballet as it starred Claire Motte, one of his first friends in the West, who was now married to Mario Bois, a tall, good-looking director of a music publishing house.[*] After the performance, joined by the Gettys, they all went for dinner at a restaurant Bois describes as '*chic avant d'être à la mode*'. Talitha was looking particularly stunning that night, dressed in a sumptuous fantasy cloak and matching hat, which, later in the evening, Rudolf removed and imperiously placed on his own head. 'You want it? I'll give it to you,' she said, laughing. It was five a.m. when the group finally left the restaurant, and although everyone was fairly drunk, Claire and Mario drove Rudolf in their battered *quatre-chevaux* to the Ritz. The place Vendôme was totally deserted, and Rudolf, still wearing Talitha's toque and somewhat dishevelled, started to dance – *tours en l'air* followed by little burlesques. One was

[*] BMB, Bureau de Musique de Mario Bois, is responsible for the contracts of Nureyev productions.

a self-caricature mocking his continuing infatuation with the married Talitha: an impersonation of the tragicomic Petrushka competing with his rival for the attentions of the Ballerina.

With his fascination for Talitha combined with an innate passion for exotica, Rudolf would have been charmed by the sybaritic ambiance the Gettys had created at Le Palais Da Zahir (the Pleasure Palace). In gardens lit by camphor flares against a backdrop of the Atlas Mountains, dancing street boys balanced trays weighted with mint tea and candles; guests either dined outside on antique rugs among roses wound with mint, or in high-beamed rooms where huge fires of olive logs blazed at either end. Was it, then, his animal-like sense of potential danger that kept him away? With hallucinogens at their most fashionable by 1967, Da Zahir had become a mecca for the 'hippie deluxe' set Cecil Beaton called 'the druggists' – Mick Jagger and Marianne Faithfull, Chrissie Gibbs, Robert Fraser, Brian Jones and Anita Pallenberg. At a 1968 New Year's Eve party, amid the haze of *kif* smoke exhaled from hookahs, Paul McCartney and John Lennon were spotted flat on their backs. 'They couldn't get off the floor, let alone talk.' Following the example of Talitha – 'the daring one' – Paul junior had started experimenting with increasingly perilous drugs, and together they floated off on the hippie trail around the East. Although claiming to be still very smitten, Rudolf refused to discuss Talitha's heroin addiction – 'He preferred to ignore bad things about people he liked.' And yet, with a growing aversion to any kind of drug, he had instinctively distanced himself, and unlike the susceptible Yves Saint Laurent, who was now 'tripping regularly', managed to resist Talitha's siren call.*

More enticing to Rudolf at that time was the discovery of a grand lifestyle. In 1967, while waiting to find somewhere permanent to settle, he was invited to stay in 'two of the prettiest houses in England' – the town and country homes of Prince and Princess Radziwill. Like her older sister, Jackie Kennedy, Lee Radziwill was one of Rudolf's most passionate admirers. Both sisters had inherited the Bouviers' extravagance and daunting sense of entitlement – what Truman Capote called the sense of the right to luxury. Their determined, socially ambitious mother had brought up her daughters to believe that wealth

---

* Arriving for a lunch at her London house, a beautiful Thamesside property once owned by Rossetti, Rudolf was told by the butler that Mrs Getty had been unavoidably detained but wished the meal to proceed without her. Only later did the painter Michael Wishart, who had been another guest, learn that that morning Talitha had been rushed to the hospital, unconscious from a heroin overdose. By June 1971 she was dead.

and position ranked far above romance. Lee's second husband was described by Janet Bouvier as a European version of her father. Nineteen years her senior, Stanislas 'Stas' Radziwill, a Polish aristocrat, had an Old World prestige that was irresistible to Lee. Forming a partnership with a well-known London property magnate, he had made enough money to provide her with an Edwardian roster of staff, as well as everything Lee needed to dress and live well. He loved spoiling her, and overprotected her like a child-wife, 'like Nora in *A Doll's House*', says her friend, actress Leslie Caron. 'I had the feeling that she wanted to try out her wings and be independent in the same way.'

Ever since she was a young girl, escaping the domestic tensions at home, Lee had let herself be swept up into a world of illusion and mystery: 'The music, the painting, the *atmosphere* I'm most drawn to is always the nineteenth century. It was wild, romantic, soaring, out of control – oceans booming, horses galloping. Not in the least cold and pretty like the eighteenth century. I love all the dramatic composers, Debussy, Scriabin, Mahler, Ravel, and painters like David and Delacroix. They had such power and vitality, and such warmth.' It was only natural, therefore, that she would be drawn to Rudolf, and early in March 1966, she had telephoned Joan Thring to say that she knew his birthday was approaching and wondered if she could give him a party. 'After that,' Joan says, 'she never let go.'

To begin with, Lee admits, Rudolf was deeply suspicious of her motives – 'like a very alert animal: on guard and afraid of being caught or trapped'. He responded 'quite warmly' when she began coming to watch him in class and rehearsals, but it was seeing 'the way we lived, the way I did things' that finally lured him. Lee's flair was remarkable – 'not safe, good taste', as decorator Nicholas Haslam put it, but something more theatrical. At Turville Grange, a rambling Queen Anne house set in fifty acres of Thames Valley countryside, the dining-room walls were the work of stage designer Lila de Nobili, who had set portraits of the Radziwills' two children into Sicilian kerchiefs painted over in 'faded Russian-y blues'. De Nobili's protégé was Renzo Mongiardino, who, in partnership with Lee, had transformed rooms in both Radziwill homes. His decorating style, a fusion of decadence with classicism, was 'eighty per cent Lila' combined with the aura of the Genoese palazzo where he grew up, its fragrant, flower-filled rooms and sunlight filtering through the half-closed curtains the inspiration behind Lee's own interiors. The way in which Mongiardino could light a room and his architectural skill impressed Rudolf enough to use him as the designer of his next production. More crucial, though, were his interiors, which were paramount in forming Rudolf's own taste in decor. He loved the 'blaze of Turquerie' Mongiardino had produced in Lee's London drawing room, but what he really coveted was the dining room with its walls covered in antique Cordoba leather – originally a Mongiardino set for Zeffirelli's *Taming of the Shrew*. 'It was heavy and dark, and Rudolf adored it. He'd never heard of Renzo before he came to my house, but he was always so curious and receptive, and he had an extraordinary eye.'

Finding that they shared a passion for beautiful objects and opulent fabrics – 'Eastern things particularly' – he and Lee would go midnight window-shopping after performances.* 'The next day we'd go back.' Lee herself was 'a fantasy girl', whom many found a more intriguing personality than the relatively conventional Jackie. She had a *dégagé* quality, a much more nonchalant elegance, and, as Cecil Beaton often pointed out, was also 'infinitely more beautiful' than her more photogenic sister. Rudolf found her bright as well as beautiful. 'After all,' he said, 'she's not just a socialite. She attracts people of substance.' He was adept at sharing himself equally between the two competitive sisters, photographed shopping on Fifth Avenue with Jackie, dancing with Lee in Monte Carlo, but there was a time when he was very much closer to Lee – a bond she says her sister greatly envied.

Aware that Rudolf was becoming a major part of her life – 'to care about, to protect' – Lee had invited him to live in their three-storey house in Victoria until he found somewhere of his own: 'I felt that he wanted desperately to live in a home. We were able to give him that, although our hours were quite different. He came home late and slept late, and would want lunch about four o'clock. Always a blue steak.'

Although Rudolf rarely saw Stas Radziwill, who left early for his office, it was in the country that Lee made sure she had Rudolf pretty much to herself. Their rapport was quite different from the 'very emotional friendship' she had established with Capote – 'Rudolf was much more passionate, much more masculine' – and yet she vows that she never had any delusions about Rudolf's sexuality. He had confided to her his 'tremendous love' for Erik,† and she had already made up her

---

* As a remarkable token of her affection, Lee bought Rudolf a Russian double-headed eagle of solid gold studded with diamonds and rubies, which he kept hidden in a secret alcove of his enormous fireplace at La Turbie.

† Rudolf told Lee that he had 'torn up all their correspondence', leading her to believe that it was his own letters that he had wanted destroyed (as was the case). 'Having a very suspicious nature, he thought Erik might use the letters against him somehow. Maybe he was ashamed of showing such passion. He thought it would reveal a great weakness, and it was a side he didn't want to share with the public.'

mind that he was 'ninety-nine and a half per cent homosexual'. If a woman set her heart on Rudolf, she would, Lee says, 'have to take the initiative' (as she had done when, at the age of nineteen, she had proposed to her first husband). And there are those who are convinced – 'in the way that you just *do* know' – that Lee succeeded in getting Rudolf into bed. (A weekend guest at Turville Grange watching the pair stroll off into a meadow at sunset concluded 'from their body language' that they were lovers.) But while Rudolf told Maude Gosling that he had made Lee pregnant – 'And what do you think she did? She destroyed my baby' – Lee insists this is untrue.* She does, however, admit to having been completely besotted by Rudolf. 'I *only* ever wanted him to myself. Always.'

Marlene Dietrich felt much the same. She was crazy about Rudolf – 'That Boy', as she called him – once copying his picture with tracing paper and bringing it to him to sign. She also kept several other inscribed photographs of Rudolf, on one of which he had written, 'To very dear Marlene with anough [*sic*] admiration.' According to Nico Georgiadis, though, Rudolf was not a Dietrich fan: 'He found her false in the Sternberg films – he didn't understand the stylization.' They met at the Goslings' house the evening that Kenneth Tynan brought her as his guest, Rudolf 'wondering who this old showgirl was'. Living close to Rudolf's flat in Eaton Terrace, Dietrich would sometimes drop by unannounced or come on her own to the ballet. On one occasion Rudolf had asked Joan Thring to arrange tickets for Dietrich and a few friends whom he planned to meet after the performance at the Caprice. When Joan arrived at the restaurant she saw Dietrich sitting alone at a corner table, waiting 'to have a tête-à-tête with Rudolf'. 'I'm sorry, but you're not,' she said firmly, ushering the star to the larger table, where Sean Connery and his wife, Diane Cilento, were sitting. When Rudolf appeared shortly afterwards, he found Dietrich 'attacking' Connery for no reason other than the fact that 'she had a terrible dislike of tall people'. After dinner they went on to a party in Chelsea, but having been cornered by a gushing April Ashley, a well-known transsexual, Dietrich insisted that Rudolf drive her home. 'If

---

* Two decades later Rudolf was still making the same claim. When Ninel Kurgapkina showed him photographs of Misha Baryshnikov with his children, asking Rudolf why he had not had any of his own, he replied, 'Because women are fools. The first – Xenia – was afraid; the second – an American woman – was also afraid. They thought I would not pay attention to the child.'

I'm not back in twenty minutes, you come and get me,' he instructed Joan, fearing that Dietrich 'might chain him to the bed'.

More and more Rudolf found himself regarding women as dangerous predators. He had even cast Margot as some kind of succubus. 'Maybe . . . it's that Margot has gained very much from this dancing with me, and me much, much less, until now I am sitting alone on the floor, tired and exhausted. Maybe it's that she has taken from me because she wishes to be the one to survive.'

Women, he had decided, were 'silly, but stronger than sailors. They just want to drink you dry and leave you to die of weakness.' He hated being hunted down by obsessive fans who followed him wherever he went – one being Roberta Lazzarini, who admits that she 'was everywhere'. In Vienna she threw flowers onstage after a performance of *Tancredi*, and she remembers 'the shock and the look of absolute loathing on his face' when he glanced up and recognized her. Typically, though, Rudolf would use a character flaw to feed his dancing, and he drew on his new misogyny to define the personalities of his next two roles.

He had finished a performance at the Palais des Sports in Paris in December 1965 when an elderly Frenchwoman, who had been waiting in the corridor outside his dressing room for the last of the admirers to leave, came inside. Without introducing herself, she asked him in English if he had heard of a ballet by Jean Cocteau called *Le Jeune homme et la mort*. Still removing his makeup, Rudolf looked at her in the mirror.

'Yes, Babilée created it.'
'Would you like to dance in a film version of it?'
'I wouldn't know . . . I have danced nothing but classical ballets.'
'Would you like me to talk about it to Roland Petit?'
'If you wish. He must create a ballet for me at Covent Garden.'

Denise Tual was a cinematographer, director and producer* who had been sent by Roland Petit, the choreographer of the role Jean Babilée

* The wife of surrealist Roland Tual, she had made documentaries on Luis Buñuel (her previous husband, Pierre Batcheff, had starred in Buñuel's *Un chien andalou*) and on the filming of Fellini's *La Dolce Vita*. Working with Stravinsky and Cocteau, Tual was responsible for reviving the stage production of *Oedipus Rex*.

made famous in 1946. When Rudolf travelled with the Kirov to Vienna for the 1959 youth festival, he had gone out of his way to make contact with Petit, whose sexy, vaudevillian style he found so new and strange. The ballet he saw was *Cyrano de Bergerac*, its Antoni Clavé-esque sets and Saint Laurent costumes typical of the kind of modern Parisian chic reflected in Petit's work. Of most interest to Rudolf now, though, was the choreographer's flair for showcasing personality: Babilée had become a cult figure after *Jeune homme*, and it was Petit's *Carmen*, transforming Zizi Jeanmaire into 'a sort of asexual fury' – her long black curls nail-scissored into the celebrated spiky gamine crop – which had made her a star throughout the world.

A month later Petit and Jeanmaire were renting a house for the summer in St Tropez, and Rudolf was expected to stop off with Erik on their way to La Turbie. They waited, Tual says, one day, two days . . . 'The third day a sportscar, blue and yellow, erupted into the garden and stopped at the edge of the swimming pool. Around the pool were a group of friends, among them a young journalist. Rudolf saw him and, cursing, flung his keys on the ground.'

It was a critic who was 'quite naughty', Zizi recalls, and Rudolf, furious at being forced to confront him, got straight back into the car. Erik began trying to reason with him, but Tual had to spirit the journalist away for a drive in the countryside before Rudolf would join the party. By the evening the two dancers had disappeared. In their absence a Monte Carlo garage called with a convoluted story about a 'borrowed' car, incorrect papers and a police summons for speeding on the Corniche, and when they returned the next day, Petit and Tual both felt that the atmosphere was hardly propitious for discussing the film project. In the end it was Rudolf who brought it up: he wanted to do *Jeune homme*, he said, but it must happen quickly, sometime in September, the only gap in his schedule. He had not seen the 1951 film of Jean Babilée's performance, but he knew that the ballet had made his career: 'That idea alone excited him,' Tual says.

Rudolf first heard about Babilée from Marika Besobrasova, who had been talking about a dancer with a technique so phenomenal that he could do a double *manège* of *jetés entrelacés*, and four more *entrechat* beats than Nijinsky. '*Who* is doing this?' Rudolf demanded, and Marika explained. It was in 1940, at the time of the German invasion of France that she received a call from Babilée's father, a well-known Parisian eye specialist, begging her to take care of Jean. He was then seventeen and a star pupil at the Opéra school, but he was half Jewish (born Jean Gutmann), and his father wanted Marika to take the boy into her Monte Carlo home 'to save him from Hitler'. Marika formed her own company in Cannes with Babilée as her leading dancer, and when the war was over and the company disbanded, Babilée joined Les Ballets des Champs-Élysées in Paris, the troupe Diaghilev's colleague Boris Kochno had just cofounded with the young Roland Petit. It was Kochno who commissioned Cocteau to write a new ballet, telling him that he must have a new *Spectre de la rose* for Jean Babilée.

Apart from being a work for only two dancers, the story of *Le Jeune homme et la mort* has nothing to do with the earlier ballet but is, like Cocteau's *Orphée*, a story in the Eros and Thanatos tradition in which death is personified by a beautiful woman. It begins with a young artist in his atelier lying, impatiently waiting, on a rumpled single bed. 'Enter the young girl who is the cause of his distress. He throws himself at her. She repulses him; he begs her; she insults him, scorns him and departs. He hangs himself.'

Keen to get away from 'the style of Petipa – ballerinas in tutus, carried aloft by male dancers', Cocteau wanted the choreography to consist mainly of everyday movements electrified with emotion. Completely original – 'like a wild boy', an 'angel-thug' – Babilée was incomparable at this, investing everything he did with meaning. Just the action of looking at his watch became an expression of violent internal revolt. He was the first contemporary classical dancer and, even in his seventies, would be an inspiration to Baryshnikov, who admired the way he could combine aerial lightness with a sinking, Grahamesque earthbound quality. Rudolf, however, intimidated by the idea of attempting a new genre, was not receptive to Babilée's influence, and when, out of admiration, the older dancer offered to coach him in the role, Rudolf refused his help. 'He had complexes about being in a modern situation for the first time,' says Tual. 'This was a turning point for him.'

Rudolf demanded to be alone with Petit and Jeanmaire during rehearsals, and when filming began, shut himself in his dressing room. He had stipulated in his contract that he would be responsible for his own makeup, dismissing any attempts to persuade him how much more subtle it needs to be for the screen. When he emerged, Tual says, he looked terrible, 'The eyes outlined in blue, the wings of the nose red, the eyebrows so arched they make him look like a doll. Realizing this, Rudolf is furious and demands a makeup artist.' [*] Eventually

---

[*] According to Keith Money, who has a photograph of him as *La Sylphide*'s James in Athens, Rudolf had begun doing 'horrendously disfiguring eyebrow makeup – great smears like

Rudolf became less guarded, allowing the rehearsal process to be filmed and photographed.

As he subsequently did for other interpreters of *Jeune homme,* Petit adapted the role to bring out Rudolf's own qualities and beauty; as one writer put it, 'We get the perfume of him.' There are close-ups of his tiger crouch, and movements that are far more classical than they were in the original. The frenzied solo of erotic frustration is now much longer, and where Babilée violently swings and flings a chair, Rudolf partners it like a ballerina. The outcome, Babilée has complained, is not the same ballet, which is true: the film, which jettisons Cocteau's rooftop scene, is not a literal version of the stage production but a newly conceived work for the camera. It is, however, not correct to say that in Rudolf's interpretation 'Cocteau is no longer there.' Babilée's character was *un homme fatal,* so 'infernal' that he frightened his new wife, Nathalie Philippart, dancing the part of La Mort. 'She used to say, "You're crazy – you're going to kill me!" because I would grab her with such . . . *verité.* If you don't reach that point it's not *le Jeune homme.*' Rudolf, on the other hand, drawing on his own early experience, makes the character more of an innocent – an intense, highly strung youth of ambiguous sexuality who is in the thrall of a strong-willed older woman. As Jeanmaire says of her role, 'She seduce him during that ballet.' The way he is both helplessly drawn and repelled by La Mort's advances introduces undercurrents of misogyny and homosexuality to the ballet that are intrinsically Cocteauesque.

Jeanmaire's own conception is also entirely different from that of the first stage versions: Philippart had danced with no emotion – 'I was *hors-lyric*'; the proud, unattainable Claire Sombart had cruelly rebuffed her clinging lover; whereas Zizi's character resembles La Mort of *Orphée,* who involuntarily falls in love with her victim. 'Beware of the sirens,' the hero is warned in Cocteau's film, to which he replies, 'It is I who charm *them.*' Zizi admits that she herself had 'great feeling for Rudolf. I loved him very much – my God, he was attractive.' Far from being a starkly glacial *belle dame sans merci,* she

---

black bananas' – as early as 1963. Becoming self-conscious about the thinness of his hair, he had also begun teasing and lacquering it with hair spray – the result, combined with his vivid turquoise-shadowed eyes, comes as something of a shock in the first close-up of his Vienna *Swan Lake* film. 'With the coiffed hair he looked like a cross between June Allyson and Doris Day,' remarks Money. 'I discussed it with Margot who said, "I simply *daren't mention it.*"'

dances like a sexually responsive vamp, striking Casino de Paris poses, and caressing herself with the tips of her long manicured nails.

When *Jeune homme* was created, it was Cocteau who 'did everything', Babilée claims, whereas the film, with its slick veneer of Hollywood glamour, is pure Petit.* Instead of a softly flowing dress, Zizi wears a tunic as revealing as her *Carmen* corset in order to vaunt the famous legs, while Rudolf's sexuality is magnified by the camera's homoerotic relish of his naked torso and taut, denim-skinned thighs and buttocks. In fact, though, Rudolf's look – the teased hair, the lips outlined and glossed – is totally in tune with Tom Wolfe's sixties – the 'Bangs manes bouffants beehives Beatle caps butter faces brush-on lashes decal eyes.' It is, as Baryshnikov says, 'a high camp beauty parlour' *Jeune homme*, and it was instigated by Petit, who has always adored artifice. 'The diamonds, the eyelashes, the makeup – everything is fake but everything seems sumptuous, everything fostering dreams . . . It's the supreme art of eye shadow. It's magic.' He admits encouraging the dancer to enhance his beauty, reminding him to touch up his lipstick before they shot the next take. When Rudolf asked, 'Am I good on the screen?' Petit would assure him that he took the light like Marilyn Monroe. 'I would tell him how photogenic he was. And he was so happy.'

Paradise Lost, Petit's first ballet for both Rudolf and Margot, would go even further in merging ballet with sex and high fashion, bringing to the Royal Opera House stage 'the world of nightclubs, a touch of sadism, flashing lights, pop and op art'. Even at the age of eighteen, when he staged his wartime recitals in Paris with dancer Janine Charret, Petit had shown a Diaghilevian flair for attracting the era's most modish painters and musicians. Members of Cocteau's circle, including Christian 'Bébé' Bérard, Marie Laurencin, Henri Sauguet and composer Georges Auric, were among his first collaborators, and following the success of les Ballets des Champs-Élysées, Petit, then twenty-one, was idolized by the Parisian artistic elite. Christian Dior, who frequented the same restaurants on the avenue Montaigne, introduced his young assistant Yves Saint Laurent to the choreographer. This was the start of a working relationship that would continue over thirty years, Petit and the designer each seeking to promote the overlap between art and fashion. In 1965 Andy Warhol began exhibiting in Paris, and no one was considered more '*dans*

---

* Petit told Baryshnikov, when they came to work together in the 1975 version of *Jeune homme*, that he wanted it to be *his* version. 'Roland, who was in perpetual conflict with Babilée, didn't want me even to look at any of the earlier films.'

le coup' than the artist and his coterie (in particular his suave manager, Fred Hughes, viewed as a new Proustian – 'un Swann "Pop"'). The following autumn Saint Laurent's Rive Gauche line came out. It was a hommage to Warhol, its baby-doll dresses emblazoned with the pop art images of red lips and comic-book faces. Exactly the look that Petit had in mind for his new ballet.

Paradise Lost was based on a poem by French writer Jean Cau, the first line of which is, 'Every paradise is found in order to be lost.' But although its starting point was the Fall, Petit changed the story and made another version of *Jeune homme*. It's a vignette of an ardent youth at the mercy of an emasculating woman – and Margot's character, Cau writes, is '*le même que celui de la mort*'. The designer Petit chose was the New Realist painter Martial Rayss, whose use of neon, plastic, photographs and fluorescent colours was Warholesque in the extreme. They had recently worked together on a ballet with Petit's long-term collaborator Marius Constant, the composer of *Paradise Lost*. Margot and Petit also had a history of their own, in his words, 'A big flirt with lots of tenderness and love games.' And after the war, feeling at a stale point in her career, she had taken a break in Paris, where the choreographer had just formed his own company and was offering to create a new work for her. An egotistical parable of a young man (Petit) who succeeds in making a woman out of a pure white cat, *Les Demoiselles de la nuit* caused quite a stir, Margot's short, cutaway tutu as provocative then as the white vinyl miniskirt Petit would dress her in for *Paradise Lost*.

Before they began work Margot had warned the choreographer, still a close friend, not to allow '*le joli moujik*' to get the upper hand. Apart from an initial squabble, however, Rudolf could not have been more accommodating. He found the quirkiness of the movements great fun, amiably carrying out a series of slow somersaults while conventionally supporting Margot in a rotating arabesque. As in all Petit's work, the style of *Paradise Lost* was acrobatic and eclectic, the flexed foot borrowed from Balanchine, the angularities from Martha Graham. Most of the steps were designed, as were Margot's miniskirt and the straining codpiece of Rudolf's white tights, to lead the eye to the crotch – 'the erogenous zone of the sixties', in Mary Quant's view. ('The way girls model clothes, the way they sit, sprawl or stand is all doing the same thing.') Petit's trademark, 'body sculptures à deux', was never put to better use, with Margot and Rudolf appearing as twin halves, their clean-cut positions of exact anatomical geometry both an endorsement of male equality and a refashioning of the Fonteyn–

Nureyev synchronization – one body perfectly complementing the other.

Although five male dancers made up the snake of temptation, and a large corps de ballet represented life outside Eden, they counted for little; what the audience watched were the two stars – individually and in the ballet's revelatory extension of their partnership. They both responded superbly to the unclassical idiom, Margot looked stunning, despite her cruelly young guise as a King's Road dollybird. Never to be forgotten by anyone who saw it was the ballet's *coup de théâtre*, a passage in which Rudolf ran lopingly around the stage, continued at full tilt up a ramp, and then – in a pop art update of Nijinsky's spectacular leap through the window in *Le Spectre de la rose* – dived head first through a gap in the Warholesque lips.

One member of the audience who found this moment 'absolutely fantastic' was Mick Jagger. The plushy red lips on the backcloth were a version of Jagger's own – the 'two peculiarly gross and extraordinary red lips' famously extolled by Tom Wolfe.[*] (Five years later, much the same design would be used as the logo of the Rolling Stones' record label.) Jagger's stage performance has always been essentially an act of making love to himself, and in Rudolf he recognized an idealized physical reflection – 'It was like seeing himself there on the stage,' his girlfriend Marianne Faithfull remarked. They had the same chicken-breast-white skin, hairless torso, and androgynous appeal, as if (as Violette Verdy said of Rudolf) they had created another type of sex altogether – 'a kind of dancing *creature* . . . something wild and very beautiful'. Both made the concept of the star into a twentieth-century god, celebrity of a kind that, as Faithfull once remarked, cannot be understood by comparisons in the modern world. 'You must go back to Louis XIV, the Sun King, or to the gilded boy despots of ancient Rome and Egypt.'

Each curious to meet the other, Rudolf and Jagger arranged to have lunch one day at a restaurant in the King's Road, an encounter that, far from being momentous – what Lincoln Kirstein might have called a twinning 'of Harmodius and Aristogiton, Damon and Pythias' – proved 'dead boring'. The pair had very little to say to each other, and, according to Joan Thring, who had been 'dragged along' as the driver, 'just grunted every so often'. Rudolf also remembered the occasion as

---

[*] 'This boy has extraordinary lips . . . They hang off his face like giblets . . . the lips start spreading into the most languid, most confidential, the wettest, most labial, most concupiscent grin imaginable. Nirvana!'

uneventful. 'I didn't smoke, I didn't take dope: we didn't have much in common.' Not even an esteem that was mutual.

Always responsive to the intricacies of new movements and rhythms, from ballet to Balinese lion dancing, Jagger, friends claim, 'hugely admired – possibly even desired Rudolf'. 'He was always saying how much he wished he could have been Nureyev.' Rudolf, on the other hand, never having seen Jagger onstage, knew nothing of his hypnotic power as a performer. His large record collection included only two albums that weren't classical (one by Edith Piaf and one by Marlene Dietrich, who had given it to him), and he dismissed any form of pop or jazz as background music – 'I wouldn't sit and listen.'

By contrast, Rudolf was smitten by Peter O'Toole, one of the New Aristocracy – actors, photographers, pop stars, interior decorators, models, hairdressers, even villains – whose celebrity and/or youth cut across the class divide. David Bailey commemorates them in his *Box of Pinups*, in which Rudolf appears among a gallery of thirty-six contemporary icons. Having seen his portrayals of Lawrence of Arabia and Hamlet – 'which totally burned' – Rudolf was so in awe that he did his best to match O'Toole's excesses. He recalled that O'Toole once drank until five in the morning and 'then woke me and said: "Buy me a taxi." Of course my day was ruined.' *Dazzled* by Rudolf in turn, O'Toole often took him on the town, twisting one night away with a couple of hostesses from Al Burnett's club, their inseparableness prompting the rumour that reached John Gielgud in February 1964: 'Peter O'Toole and Nureyev are shacking up in Hong Kong or somewhere during *Lord Jim*.' At this point, though, Rudolf needed no encouragement to drink – 'a little habit I picked up in the West'. O'Toole's ex-wife, the actress Siân Phillips, remembers seeing Rudolf arrive at a smart Belgravia dinner and make straight for the drinks cart. 'Picking up a smallish bottle of plum brandy . . . [he] drained the lot in what seemed like seconds while we all watched in silence.' Rudolf's classic drunken behaviour that night, of dancing on the table, throwing up violently, curling up to sleep, was sympathetically interrupted by O'Toole. 'Come on, munch,' he barked, and seizing him by the legs, began to bump him down the thickly carpeted stairs, before making their way into the street. Once settled into a taxi Rudolf became 'angelic', Siân recalled, 'wanting to kiss us all'. But despite the White Nights, Rudolf never lost sight of what Verdy calls 'his real business – the sweat, the toil, the going back to the first position every morning. The getting up early no matter what time he's gone to bed the night before.'

Now as much of a trend-setter as Twiggy or the Beatles, Rudolf could be seen in striped bathing trunks on the cover of *Men in Vogue*, or in a white canvas raincoat for a feature on Courrèges – the embodiment of swinging London fashion. His was not the foppish eighteenth-century look adopted by pretty-boy pop stars Brian Jones and Jim Morrison, with their lacy cuffs, velvet pants, flowing scarves, and floppy-brimmed hats, but the spruce English mod. The collarless suits and trousers tucked into space boots derived from Pierre Cardin, who, anticipating the 'peacock revolution', had extended his ready-to-wear strategy to men's fashion. Rudolf, wearing his boots thigh-high with a matching ponyskin jacket, and suits buttoned tight to emphasize his tiny waist, made the style completely his own. 'When Russian student caps take the suburbs as well as the King's Road by storm, you know who launched that craze,' wrote the *Daily Express*. Rudolf's 'natty "Nuri" way' of hanging his leather jacket from his finger was even copied by Jagger. According to Philip Norman, 'He too began to experiment, slipping off his Cecil Gee Italian jacket and dangling it on his forefinger.'

Rudolf's sixties superstardom was a phenomenon that no longer exists in ballet. In London the crowd after a Fonteyn–Nureyev performance jostling elbow to elbow along the length of upper Floral Street was the equivalent of today's celebrity-mad horde crushed behind the barriers at an Oscar ceremony in Hollywood. As far as Rudolf's fans were concerned, the performance began at least two hours before the curtain went up, with drinks in the Nag's Head pub, the exchange of photographs and ballet gossip. The thrill of the ballet itself could be prolonged by at least half an hour of curtain calls, and the strewing of the stage with daffodils. Then followed what Roberta Lazzarini calls 'the fearful ritual of the stage door':

> His car would draw up – that was the first excitement – and there was more pushing and shoving and the old stage doorman would say, 'Mr Nureyev will sign tonight.' Then he went into a sort of a booth, usually in a magnificent fur hat, and signed. And we were thrilled, we'd really had our money's worth then. I don't know why, because he rarely even looked up.

During the first New York tour, in '63, Rudolf wouldn't stop at all to give autographs. 'You couldn't get near him, he'd just bolt. He thought they were following him, and they probably were.' Robert Gable, 'the oldest living Rudi fan,' hadn't known how to pronounce

Nureyev's name in 1961, but had cut his picture from *Paris-Match*, struck by 'the greatest face I'd ever seen'. By 1967 Rudolf in New York was lingering at the stage door and making the acquaintance of a few of his admirers. When Gable came up to him at a bar across the street from the Met, he stood up and very formally shook his hand. Gable told him he had painted his portrait from an Avedon photograph. 'Bring it to theatre,' Rudolf said, which Gable did, thrilled to find himself invited into the star's dressing room. 'I told him it was his if he wanted it, and never saw it again.'

It was Hurok's policy not to release casting details in advance, but through Bob Gable and others who had graduated from the stage door, fans were able to get advance information as to when Rudolf would be dancing. Tickets would go on sale at ten on a Sunday morning, but a phantom queue of those in the know would already have formed four days earlier. Someone would have been delegated 'head of queue', responsible for gathering signatures, and people would add their names to a list, be given a number, and check in at the theatre every twelve hours. (On Saturday this changed to every hour.) Gable's friend's brother had a car he could sleep in; others brought sleeping bags and bedded down in the subway tunnels, 'like London during the Blitz'. By Sunday morning there would be more than a thousand people waiting for the box office to open.

Compared with the London queue, which was orderly and polite, New York's equivalent was camp, expert and extremely belligerent. The first time Marilyn La Vine went to buy a ticket for a Nureyev performance she had set her alarm for six a.m. to be at the Met several hours before the box office opened. 'But when I arrived the queue was already round the block with people who'd spent the night on the street. I was *screamed* at: "You can't get on this queue – we have numbers." There was this whole other society I didn't know about – a hierarchy with secrets and group rules, and people who lorded over and manipulated the other fans.'

Other New York diehards were the Perry sisters; Rose Curcio, known as Rose Curtain-Call; Nancy Sifton; Bonnie Prandato, who got herself a job at Sotheby's with a view to being transferred to London so that she could be near Rudolf; Helene Britton, an unofficial, unpaid girl Friday – 'the only one who could touch his costume, wash his tights, sew his shoe elastics'; Arks (Anne Rosemary Kathleen Smith), who met Bonnie in the queue and became her closest friend, their perpetual topic of conversation '*Rudolf*, of course.' 'You couldn't talk to those Nureyev people about anyone else,' said Baryshnikov's lieutenant, the late Charles France – 'they didn't want to know.'

As the only available photographs, released through Hurok's office, had been taken at London press calls, there was an enormous market among the New York fans for more candid shots. Shooting from the first stage box with his quiet Leica and telephoto lens, David Daniel made enough money selling his black-market photographs of Rudolf during the Royal Ballet's six-week season to live in Europe for the rest of the year. Arks, Bob Gable and Luis Peres also took good photographs, while Lucia Wayne, a tiny, chain-smoking New York character who always dressed in black to be less conspicuous, would film Rudolf's perform-ances from the fifth ring.* Marilyn La Vine paid one hundred dollars for a silent amateur cassette of Rudolf's *Bayadère*. 'You felt fortunate if Toby, manager of the Ballet Shop, chose to sell you a copy. The film was so dark the action could hardly be seen, but it was all we had. It was priceless.'

In May '67, while Margot and Rudolf were dancing at the Met, across Lincoln Center plaza at the New York State Theater Erik and Carla Fracci were guesting with the American Ballet Theatre – the ballet calendar's most memorable events of the year. But if few of the Rudolf regulars were interested in seeing Erik – 'He simply didn't have that life force' – to Fracci's husband, Beppe Menegatti, just watching the four stars take class together was a profound artistic experience.

'It was as if those four dancers were naked in the soul. It was not an exposition of bravura; of what or who were better, but an exposition of *faiblesse*, of where they are weak. They discuss very simple things: where has to go the finger and the thumb in a port de bras . . . Things Margot had been shown by Karsavina she was now showing to Carla.'

The previous spring Arlene Croce had commented on 'the first fraying threads' of Erik's technique, but what distressed her more were his new stage mannerisms. 'Here he was, lifting and extending monumental palms in an apparent parody of *danseur-noble* deportment . . . a wish to appear grand and important in a way even the dullest member of the audience would not miss.' This was, of course, Rudolf's influence. And in the '67 season, by choosing roles now associated with the younger dancer, Erik seemed perversely to have gone out of his way to

* The Lucia Wayne Collection of 8-mm films is now held in the Jerome Robbins Dance Division of the New York Public Library at Lincoln Center.

invite direct comparisons. His Albrecht, though elegant in the extreme, did not, in the view of Winthrop Sergeant, have 'quite the uninhibited boyishness of Mr Nureyev's'. Likewise, memories of Rudolf's Romeo made Erik's restrained, unattainable character seem merely blank and unengaged. Fracci herself admits that Erik was a 'little bit absent' when they first danced *Romeo and Juliet*'s Balcony Scene (the Bruhn version). 'I had to *pull* him, get him to *react*!'

But if Erik had at last established a legendary partnership of his own, his hold on Rudolf had never felt less sure.

> My dearest Rudic,
>   I am suddenly awake in the middle of this terrible night, and feel very strangely that I know something about you, that I did not know before, or understand . . . Suddenly I see very clearly why you cannot be alone. I had hoped and believed you were able to wait for me, till I could come to London. I would have believed you loved me, like I do and still do with all my heart and soul. If your secret is, that it is impossible for you to be alone, that there must be someone with you, then perhaps this letter is already too late . . . This night I saw you, before I woke up, your life, as it has been before you met me, and I saw it continue without me, with others . . . It was a dream, but not a good one . . . If your nature is . . . that you are even afraid of staying one or two nights alone . . . then you don't really know true love. I would like to believe you do and if you are not with someone else already . . . then you can give me all the strengths, all my belief and hope back, by writing or calling me to tell that you are able and strong enough in your love to wait for me. If I do not hear from you, I shall understand. My love for you will remain the same always and any way . . . God bless you and give you strength when you should need it the most.

The letter is undated, and it can never be known whether Erik received a reply, but its gentle, valedictory tone suggests that he is finally letting Rudolf go. It was not only the emotional strain he could no longer endure, but physically, needing time to recover between performances, he could not keep up with Rudolf's pace. 'Erik was almost too old at that time,' Kirsten Simone says. 'The legs, the strength all begin to go . . . You help someone to become clean, but then your own dancing begins to go.' Needing to talk about his suffering Erik arrived one night at Carla Fracci's Broadway apartment. 'He was very upset. He told me, "I love him but I don't have the strength to be with him." Maybe this is when Erik started to understand that it was impossible to go on. He was happy to stay home and be together, but Rudolf needed to go out, to see people . . . He was like a bird in a cage. He felt the need to escape his prison.' Fracci's account was an echo of Holly Golightly's in *Breakfast at Tiffany's*: 'You can't give your heart to a wild thing. The more you do, the stronger they get. Until they're strong enough to run into the woods. Or fly into a tree. Then a taller tree. Then the sky . . . If you let yourself love a wild thing, you'll end up looking at the sky.'

Life for Rudolf had never been so much fun. Among the fans crowding his dressing room one night was a forty-two-year-old shapely blonde actress who had brought along her trophy boyfriend – a faun-eyed youth of quite astounding beauty. Monique van Vooren had invited Rudolf to dance with her at the opening of Arthur, and since then they had met several times for lunch at the Russian Tea Room. More interesting than the European jet-set type she appeared to personify, she was, as Bob Colacello has said, the kind of 'hypersophisticated, hyperdramatic, hyperhysterical' character who exists only in Fellini movies. Her eccentricity made Rudolf laugh, he liked the parties she took him to, and then, of course, there was the boy connection: Monique was renowned for her very young, very attractive lovers. Her current escort was Rusty Underkoffer, a twenty-three-year-old from Georgia who had come to New York 'to be a movie star'. The first thing he had to do, Monique told him, was change his name. So Rusty became Hiram Keller and joined Lee Strasberg's acting classes at Carnegie Hall, soon finding, however, that he 'just couldn't get into it'. Through the agent she shared with Sybil Burton, Monique got Hiram a job waiting tables at Arthur (which he also quit almost immediately), and when Rudolf met him in the late spring of '67 he was 'kind of aimless'.

After the performance Monique had planned to take Hiram to the Copacabana to hear Diana Ross and, realizing Rudolf would enjoy this, too, told Hiram to go back and ask if he would like to join them.

> I wait and wait and wait. Hiram doesn't appear. I go again to the dressing room and everybody's gone. I go to the Copacabana – no Rudolf, no Hiram. I know Rudolf is leaving for Boston the next day, so

I call the Navarro where he's staying. There's a Do Not Disturb message on the phone. I'm beside myself: Rudolf had taken Hiram.

The boy had been impossible to resist. Not only stunning-looking – an exotic, even more ravishing mirror image of Rudolf himself – he was also obligingly bisexual. Rudolf, he told Diane Solway, 'expected me to be his boyfriend, and I thought, "Why not?"' But what had been an easy conquest proved in the event to be extremely disappointing. As Monique put it, 'They had both been expecting Superman, and it just didn't happen.' Things got worse. Hiram became increasingly bored sitting around waiting for Rudolf, and resented his supporting role. 'Rudi had a hard time being with people who were as attractive as he was. He always had to be the one.' Rudolf, in turn, complained that Hiram spent all his time in the hotel room running up enormous telephone bills, and that 'After the sex there wasn't anything else.'

A couple of days later, when Rudolf was back in New York, Monique went to the Russian Tea Room knowing that he would probably be having lunch there. Spotting him at his usual table, she marched up to confront him, angry and pale from not having slept for two nights. 'Rudolf, how could you do that? You could have anybody in the world: why did you take my friend?' 'Don't be stupid, bitch. Sit down; have soup. He's not interesting at all. He'll be back at your house tonight.'

Sure enough, 'Hiram came home. And I forgave him.' But all along the boy had never amounted to much more than bait for Rudolf. It was Rudolf with 'his pale skin, his Slavic bones, his awesome body, his terrifying anger', who had bewitched Monique, and her fantasies eventually found expression in a bodice-ripping *roman-à-clef* that she later published. Its hero is a Russian defector, the beautiful Vladimir, 'the most spectacular ballet dancer since Nijinsky', who dresses in black Nehru suits with knee-high leather boots – 'a sexual magnet to both men and women':

> Suddenly the urge to fling herself at this young man erupted from the most profound depths of Mariela's being. She moved towards him, and before she could take a breath, Vladimir had crushed her in his arms . . . Clasping her waist, he picked her up and, kicking the door open with his boot, carried her into the bedroom . . . Obsessed, he ripped open the bodice of her negligée . . . His hungry hands caressed her hair, her eyes, her shoulders . . . He unhooked the filmy net brassiere. The luscious breasts spilled out.

And so on . . . But although the publication of *Night Sanctuary* abruptly ended their friendship, this was well over a decade away, and for now Rudolf was happy to humour the almost comically vampish Monique, sensing, no doubt, that she could prove more useful to him than any other female admirer.

San Francisco, where the Royal Ballet performed for a week in July, provided Rudolf with another stage-door adventure. In 1967 came the Summer of Love, when Flower Power was at its height, its anti-materialistic, anti-political ideals the inspiration behind the Beatles' 'All You Need Is Love', and the making of an instant hit by a British group called the Flower Pot Men: 'Let's Go to San Francisco'. Its epicentre was the Haight, a neighbourhood of large, rundown Victorian houses in the vicinity of Haight and Ashbury Streets, which had been colonized by the 'peaceniks' – hippies, beat poets, ecologists and youth culture icons such as Janis Joplin and the Grateful Dead. The older dancers, Leslie Edwards among them, dismissed the hippies as 'scruffy and irksome', but Margot was fascinated – 'I can't take my eyes off those people,' she told Rudolf – and he was just as intrigued. 'All I hear is Haight Ashbury,' he remarked to Alexander Grant, who was sharing his dressing room. 'I told Rudolf I was going to walk around there after the performance was over,' said Grant. 'And I have always felt a bit guilty about putting the idea into his head.'

As Margot and Rudolf were leaving the theatre, a figure with a biblical beard stepped out of the crowd and asked if they would like to come to 'a freak-out'. Hesitating only because they had planned to join a group for dinner at Trader Vic's, Margot nevertheless took down the address. Rudolf, in the meantime, had been approached by a flirtatious blond youth in tight jeans and knee-high boots who told him – 'audacious, but what the hell – that I would like to make love with him'. Rudolf beamed, 'Well, come with me,' and, taking Margot by the arm, he led the way down the aisle of parting fans to a waiting white limousine. As the three settled themselves side by side in the backseat, Margot looking particularly svelte in a calf-length white mink coat, Rudolf introduced her to his new acquaintance: Robert Hutchinson. 'Being the most gracious of women, she said, "It's wonderful to meet you," although she had no doubts at all about what was happening.' Telling Robert that they were thinking of going to a hippie party in the Haight Ashbury area after dinner, Margot asked if he knew the way. 'Sure I do,' he said. 'I've already had dinner, so why don't I meet you later outside the restaurant and show you how to get there?'

It was well after midnight when they took the Cadillac to a typical Victorian house in Ashbury Street. With other 'escapades of pleasure' in mind, Rudolf had been far from eager to go, but Margot persuaded him to give it a try 'just for twenty minutes'. They walked up several flights of stairs to where music was playing, but there was no sign of any Happening. 'It wasn't a hippie party at all. There were no zonked-out people on the floor, but it was awkward because we didn't know *anyone*.' Somebody took Margot's coat, adding it to a pile in a bedroom, and the new arrivals were asked what they would like to drink. Could they have tea? Margot and Rudolf both asked, but there was no tea, coffee, wine 'or any of the usual things'. Hearing a girl being sent to buy a 'half lid [of marijuana]' Margot said quickly, 'For heaven's sake don't get it for us; we don't smoke.' The three were just sitting down when a man ran up the stairs, shouting, 'It's a raid! The police are here!' Everyone seemed to be heading for the kitchen, and as Rudolf had been one of the first to flee, Robert stayed behind to make sure Margot had her coat and knew where to go. At the kitchen door he was stopped by the police. 'Whose apartment is this?' 'I don't know.' 'Where are your friends?' It was clear by now that everyone else had climbed out of the kitchen window via the fire escape and was hiding on the roof; Margot had folded her mink inside out and was sitting with it on her knees, Rudolf, in a double-breasted jacket, tight pants and cowboy boots, was hiding some distance away, stretched out flat behind a chimney. When he was confronted by the police, he made no attempt to resist, 'but didn't look too happy about it', allowing himself to be herded with the others back down to the living room. As no one would confess to ownership of the apartment, the police told them they were trespassing. 'You're going to be taken to the precinct, fingerprinted and booked.'

A group of about sixteen sat waiting for at least two hours for the paddy wagon to arrive. A few people there worked in the entertainment business; their bearded host was a philosophy graduate from Trinity College, Dublin. There was little conversation. Rudolf was silent and sulky; a girl who had fallen from the fire escape on to the pavement was crying loudly, and Margot, fearing that she might have broken her back, had asked for an ambulance to be called. Searching the apartment, the police had discovered marijuana ciga-rettes, a smoking pipe, and several reefer butts scattered on the front steps – evidence enough for them now all to be arrested on a narcotics charge. At around three a.m., as Margot and Rudolf were walking out into the street, there was a volley of flashbulbs and floodlights blazed on the house. 'All of a sudden we realized that they knew who we were. The police were making a real issue of it, and had alerted the press.' As they climbed into the Black Maria, Rudolf, retaining his 'proud, tight look', remarked dryly to Robert, 'Now you know what it costs to go to bed with me.' Seeing how tearful and frightened the boy was, Margot was more consoling. 'Don't worry,' she said softly, 'I've been in jail before [in Panama]. It will be just fine.' He put his head in her lap, she patted his cheek, and away they went.

There was another gaggle of press waiting at Park Police Station. The two stars were the next day's lead story, their pictures – taking up most of the front page of the *San Francisco Examiner* – flippantly captioned, THE END OF THE TRIP IS A RIDE; BALLET GREATS MAKE A NEW AND DIFFERENT SCENE. For the Movietone news footage, which caught them waiting to be put in the cells, Rudolf gave one of his sexiest performances. Staring at the lens with utter contempt, he modulates his glare with shades of hauteur, irony and flirtatiousness, signalled by a barely perceptible wink. He and Robert then found themselves locked up in an enormous concrete room with an open lavatory in the corner and a narrow concrete bench rimming the four walls. It was 'a free-for-all of all types', most either drunkenly slumped or snoring, no one giving the newcomers a glance. 'So Rudolf and I had some time to get acquainted. We walked around talking, and at eight o'clock they came and yanked him out.' As Rudolf left, he told Robert to call him later at the St Francis Hotel, adding meaningfully, 'I'll see you there this afternoon.' Vernon Clarke, the Royal Ballet manager, had arranged for the two stars to be released on bail of $330 each (later, charges of disturbing the peace and being on premises where marijuana was found were dropped on the grounds of insufficient evidence). After calling his attorney, Robert was let out two hours later. 'He couldn't believe I was involved; he said, "It's *world* news!"' That evening hippies in their thousands flocked to the opera house to stage a love-in. Wearing their tie-dyed robes, beads and flowers in their hair, they had come to pay tribute to the new patrons of counterculture and freedom – to ballet's 'dope stars'.

The US tour ended on 6 August 1967, and on 11 August Rudolf flew to Stockholm, where Erik, recently appointed director of the Royal Swedish Ballet, had asked him to mount a new production of *The Nutcracker* (intended as a tryout for Rudolf's staging for the Royal

Ballet). It had taken three years for Göran Gentele, the general director of the Royal Opera House, to persuade Erik to accept the post, and in that time he and his wife had become the dancer's close friends. He had been unwilling to be tied down for a long period, Marit Grusen, Gentele's widow, recalls, 'But my husband made it very easy for him so that he could take time off to perform elsewhere.' The other reason for Erik's procrastination had been his dismay at the standard of the company – 'I felt they didn't know *how* to dance.' Following Balanchine's example, Erik decided to make the school his starting point, and had brought over Betty Oliphant from the National Ballet of Canada to revolutionize the training. When Rudolf arrived, Erik was away performing in Oslo, but he met Betty after what had clearly been a particularly trying rehearsal, greeted her warmly, then continued contemptuously, 'It's like pouring water into a bucket with a hole in it.'

But if Rudolf was 'raging some days about fat ballerinas, sloppy dancing', he was patient and encouraging with students from the school. In Kirov style he had decided to use a lot of children – not just to gambol around in Act 1's party scene but to perform in Petipa rows like a mini-corps de ballet. He also picked out a twelve-year-old star-in-embryo, Anneli Alhanko, casting her in an Act 3 pas de trois with her future partner Per-Arthur Segerström* (five years later the pair were dancing *The Nutcracker*'s leading roles). Having all fallen in love with the glamorous Russian star, the Swedish students were shocked when the ballet was put together and they saw how differently he behaved with the company. 'We discovered that he was not the guy we thought he was,' Anneli says. Erik returned to a full-blown scandal: Rudolf had been accused of trying to strangle one of the dancers. He continued, however, to give his full support, aware that Rudolf '*had* to be rough because the company was just too lethargic.' Erik also gave him carte blanche with the production. With little of the original Ivanov choreography surviving, apart from that of the grand pas de deux (whose authorship is itself disputed), Rudolf was free to come up with a fresh and individual adaptation. All the same Erik had his doubts about Rudolf's abilities as a choreographer, telling the Genteles, 'It will be fine as long as he keeps to what he remembers from the Kirov.'

As a springboard, Rudolf did intend to use the Vassily Vainonen

* It was Rudolf, Segerström says, who first taught him the meaning of 'aplomb'. He had a particular gift for working with children and, as Lynn Seymour observed after watching him work with the Royal Ballet schoolchildren for the London version, could make 'little knobbly boys all feel like princes'.

version in which he danced as a student,[*] a production that had solved the problematic lack of a star ballerina role by having the child heroine Clara mature into Act 3's fairy-tale princess. But although he keeps Vainonen's solo for the Prince in Act 2, the rest of the choreography is entirely his own. His main intention, naturally, was to create a more challenging opportunity for the male dancer, which he does by combining the role of Drosselmeyer with that of the Nutcracker/Prince. The faintly sinister avuncular figure of Act 1 is now compellingly charismatic, cloaked like a sorcerer as he entertains the children, then magically transformed into the ballet's dream hero. The interest the elderly Drosselmeyer shows in the Stalbaum family's little girl, always disconcerting, now takes on far more sinister implications, his metamorphosis into Clara's handsome young consort a virtual enactment of a paedophiliac fantasy. And this was Rudolf's intention: not to make a sparkling Christmas ballet for children but something more Freudian and forbidden. Discarding the trivial Dumas version on which the ballet is based, he went back to the original source – E. T. A. Hoffmann's much darker *Nussknacker und Mauskönig*. Clara becomes not just an observer of the ballet's action but an active, Alice-like participant in a terrifyingly surreal world. The toy soldiers' opponents are no longer the traditional 'dear little furry mice, but horrible bald-stomached rats'; and when Clara's relatives reappear before her, they have mutated into unrecognizable batlike distortions (a scene Rudolf kept altering 'to make it more Hoffmannlike; more weird').

Rudolf had cast the company star, Gerd Andersson, as Clara but chose to work out the choreography on the Royal Ballet's Merle Park – his partner for the London production. They had already danced together earlier in the year in *Sleeping Beauty* and *Romeo and Juliet*, but Rudolf had had his eye on her for some time before that. He had asked the ballerina to appear abroad with him as a guest artist in *Giselle*, but Ashton had refused his permission, grumbling, 'I'm not here as an agent to provide Nureyev with dancers.' Until this point she had been viewed by the Royal Ballet as a soubrette, 'but almost the next day my name was up on the board for *Giselle*'. As things turned out, Merle was unable to dance any major role because she was

* Rudolf's first attempt at production was his re-creation of the Vainonen duet in 1961, while on tour in Haifa with the de Cuevas Ballet. Rosella Hightower 'lent herself for experiment', and they danced it together on BBC television, and for the concert group they formed with Erik and Sonia Arova in Cannes and Paris in January 1962.

pregnant. After giving birth to a son in September 1966, she was back onstage six weeks later, determined to be taken seriously as a classical dancer. During the '67 New York season she made her debut as Giselle, a performance hailed by Clive Barnes in the *New York Times* as 'dramatically in the true line of succession from Ulanova's'. She had not, however, established a partnership with anyone (her Albrecht, Anthony Dowell, had seemed to Barnes 'more like a kid brother'), and so was overjoyed when Rudolf invited her to spend five weeks working with him in Stockholm. She had always felt they had a special rapport, and with her marriage to dance critic James Monahan on the verge of collapse, this was just the break and excitement she needed. Bringing her parents from Southern Rhodesia to England to look after the baby, Merle moved into Stockholm's Palace Hotel on the waterfront, where, as one of her Royal Ballet colleagues put it, 'she just fell into Rudolf's lap'. They had, Merle recalls, 'a *fantastic* time'. 'Rudolf thought her a giggle,' Joan Thring says. 'He was very flirtatious with her, and she was definitely after him a lot.'*

When they began working on *The Nutcracker,* Rudolf did not confide his ideas about the ballet, but Merle would challenge anything she actively disliked. 'She has the right temperament for me,' Rudolf conceded. 'She will argue, and that is good.' Merle showed the same kind of spirit as a dancer, with a recklessness Rudolf exploited to the full. To begin with, though, he wanted her to portray a young girl's delicate transition into adulthood, and their first duet is choreographed entirely from Clara's point of view. She is still dressed as a child when he first bows deeply before her – as heart-stoppingly glamorous as the Nureyev of *La Bayadère.* Her timid bob-curtsy is followed by swooning *bourrées* and dreamy air walks – an homage to Ashton, the master of the romantic pas de deux. But as they take each other's hand and move freely and easily side by side, Rudolf's inspiration is Fred Astaire and Ginger Rogers, whose equality as dance partners would be his ideal. As the music grows more bombastic, the virtuosity of the movements increases, with Clara lowered into

* Her husband evidently thought so, too. After spending a few days in Stockholm at the end of August, Monahan came back and told the New Zealand dancer Gail Thomas, their dangerously pretty twenty-two-year-old lodger (with whom he had begun an affair), 'There's something going on.' Rudolf would once again claim that his affair resulted in a pregnancy – a claim Merle emphatically denies. Her marriage to Monahan was dissolved two years later, and Gail, a Royal Ballet coryphée, subsequently became the critic's third wife.

Rudolf and Margot in the final pose from *Le Corsaire,*
which incongruously paired England's *prima ballerina assoluta*
with a barely clothed, semi-barbaric Tatar boy.

Rehearsing *Swan Lake* in the Royal Ballet studios at Baron's Court. Rudolf's insistence on tampering with this hallowed classic incurred the wrath of the dance press.

Below left: Rudolf and Margot's 1962 *Giselle* was a ground-breaking, stirring event that led their public to believe in a real-life, offstage romance.

Below right: Margot's mark on Rudolf had never been more apparent than in *Swan Lake*. What the audience saw was a complete transformation — 'a new Nureyev, an English Nureyev', as Richard Buckle put it.

Rehearsing one of the rhapsodic duets from *Marguerite and Armand,*
the 1963 ballet that Frederick Ashton created for the two stars,
and in which Margot abandoned herself as never before
to her young partner.

The final moments of Kenneth MacMillan's 1965 *Romeo and Juliet*,
the ballet that marked a turning point in their fellow dancers' acceptance
of the Fonteyn–Nureyev phenomenon.

Twin halves in Roland Petit's *Paradise Lost,* a 1967 Fonteyn–Nureyev vehicle that paid homage to the Pop-Art sixties, merging ballet with sex and high fashion.

Christopher Gable, *left,* with Rudolf in MacMillan's 1964 *Images of Love,* a highly charged, homoerotic duet that also brought out the aspect of professional rivalry which existed between the two male stars.

In a 1963 gala performance of *La Sylphide* by August Bournonville, the Danish choreographer whose light, clean style was a challenging new technique for Rudolf and one he was determined to absorb on first arriving in the West.

The seduction scene in the film of Roland Petit's *Le Jeune homme et la mort* in which Rudolf's co-star is the vampish Zizi Jeanmaire.

Rudolf surrounded by his Claras from his Royal Ballet *Nutcracker*. *From left:* Merle Park, Lesley Collier, Jennifer Penney and Antoinette Sibley.

Performing for the Dutch National Ballet with Benjamin Feliksdal, *right,*
in Rudi van Dantzig's *Monument for a Dead Boy,* 1968. This was Rudolf's
rite of passage into the alien world of modern dance.

A 1973 Royal Opera performance of Balanchine's *The Prodigal Son* –
not by any means a signature role but one in which Rudolf excelled.

A climactic fish dive from *The Sleeping Beauty* with National Ballet of Canada's youngest principal, Karen Kain, one of Rudolf's protégées and favourite partners.

The Royal Ballet's Ann Jenner with Rudolf in Jerome Robbins's *Dances at a Gathering*, the 1970 ballet in which Rudolf finally achieved his wish to be 'part of the company; on a par with all of them'.

Jerome Robbins, *back row, centre*, with the cast of *Dances at a Gathering*. *Clockwise from left:* Jonathan Kelly, Lynn Seymour, Michael Coleman, Robbins, David Wall, Monica Mason, Antoinette Sibley, Anthony Dowell and Ann Jenner. Rudolf is in the centre, with Laura O'Connor on his right.

Discussing Scriabin's score with Frederick Ashton, *left*, for *Poème tragique*, the explosive solo in which Rudolf made his London debut.

Watching Kenneth MacMillan demonstrate the kind of quirky, jazzy movements that defined the solo created to Bach's *Fantasia in C Minor* for a Royal Academy of Dance gala in 1963.

Rudolf and Rudi van Dantzig, *right,* in Amsterdam, 1968.

A dress rehearsal moment, *below,* while performing Paul Taylor's 1981 gala piece in New York, *From Sea to Shining Sea;* Rudolf flanked by Mikhail Baryshnikov and Taylor.

Rehearsing in a New York studio with Murray Louis, who sees Rudolf
as the pioneer in the breaking of barriers between ballet and modern dance.

scissor splits or flung high in a short outburst of ecstasy, only to be reined in with English decorum and restaint.

By Act 2 Clara has become a prima ballerina. The couple begins the grand pas de deux in a mirror image, balancing next to each other as their working legs rise slowly into a side-angled arabesque. Rudolf had always admired the beauty of Merle's legs – slim and turned in like Pavlova's, with the same highly arched insteps – and made the arabesque in its many variants the theme of the duet. She was a fast dancer with a command of music that allowed her to take extreme liberties with the tempo, but it was Rudolf who convinced her that 'you can't be fast until you've learned to do things slow'. In *The Nutcracker* her movements acquire a new control and subtlety of shading – unhurried, expansive, very Russian, in fact, with large rangy movements conveying a sense of the enormity of the stage. As the dancing gathers speed, Park comes into her own, impetuous and totally fearless. The most spectacular moment is when she is flung into space and rolls horizontally before being caught in a stage-skimming fish dive, a terrifying feat the pair performs twice, as if to defy belief. The final image is a recapitulation of the beginning, the Prince now standing in an open arabesque with his ballerina balanced on his hip, her elongated legs aligned to the side with his – the subtext: 'Your legs are beautiful, but so are mine.'

The traditional his-and-hers solos that follow are made into an equal contest of virtuosity: Park given Rudolf's favourite fast *pas de chats* and *ronds de jambe* as well as an almost impossibly difficult series of spins end-stopped with arabesques. His double *manège* of huge jumps is followed by the ballerina's conventional *fouettés* – not the repetitive clockwise spins but a kinetic equivalent of tongue-twisters – each turn complicated by a *développé* to the side and a *pas de bourrée*. The couple comes together holding hands for the section they nicknamed 'meowki' because of its multiple *pas de chats*. This is a speeded-up version of the stately tandem dancing of the beginning, which concludes with a competition, 'seeing who could *chaîne* faster' – and a playful ending during which Rudolf flashes repeatedly in front of Merle as if vying for the ballerina position of centre stage. (She wins, but only just.) Idiosyncratic, witty and perfectly constructed, this duet is Rudolf's most outstanding piece of original choreography, one he would perform as his favourite showpiece with different companies throughout the world.

When they began rehearsing with the company, Rudolf was astounded to see every dancer leave the studio on the stroke of four o'clock, regardless of whether or not they had finished a sequence. 'Just you wait, girl,' he jeered to Merle. 'It's going to come to England soon.' His contempt was directed at the union rules, although in fact there was a good reason for the exodus. The Royal Swedish Ballet school shared the company's studios, its classes and rehearsals taking place between four and seven o'clock, when the company then returned. If Rudolf was in charge, work would continue until midnight, 'which meant you *had* to go home at four to have some food, see your kids. But this he didn't like.' Rudolf, the Swedes felt, hardly set a good example himself. His itinerary for the autumn of '67 dictated a constant shunting among Vienna, Paris, London, Monte Carlo, Copenhagen and Milan, and each time he reappeared in Stockholm, he would expect to see the kind of standards that could be achieved only if he were there. 'We had a tough time with him coming in and screaming,' says Gerd Andersson. It was rare that he was on time for rehearsals, and at the start of the first stage call without orchestra he had kept everyone waiting as usual. When four o'clock came and he said, 'Now we take from beginning again,' the dancers, as a body of one, walked out.

In the auditorium Gösta Svalberg, who was head of the union, watched what happened next. 'Rudolf gets furious and goes down to the orchestra pit, to the conductor's pulpit, and with his boots he trashed this pulpit. He destroyed it completely.' Almost immediately afterwards Rudolf gave a television interview, his face still thunderous. Asked his view of the company's future, his reply was cold and measured:

> You have an excellent chance with such a great artist as Erik Bruhn, who is going to direct the company, but nothing will happen if theatre, society will not help him to break your routine, your lack of desire to work. Because to be dancer, it is sacrificial work. If you want to have double life, nurse your children, and just for physical fitness come and fiddle around and take place of somebody who *wants* to dance and *wants* to work – Nothing . . . Ever . . . Will . . . Happen . . . Here.[*]

---

[*] Having heard every word, Svalberg told the reporter that he would like to address Mr Nureyev's complaints. 'I used one of our ballerinas as an example of someone who had significantly grown as an artist after having had children.' Considering it important to back Svalberg, whom Betty Oliphant had chosen as the school's new director, Erik came up to him afterwards and thanked him for what he had said.

The dress rehearsal brought more problems. Rudolf had designed Clara's fleet solo with Park in mind, but Gerd Andersson, not accustomed to the intricate petit allegro at which English dancers excel, strained a calf muscle 'on the first little step'. Until this point Rudolf had been very deferential towards Andersson, but he lost his temper when she told him that she could not dance the first night. 'He got so angry. He was screaming, "I come here to dance with you and you get sick!" I *had* to quit. I was injured, I was overworked, but I really don't think he believed me.' The première, which took place on 17 November 1967 in the presence of King Gustav VI Adolf, had company principals rather than stars in the lead (Marianne Orlando, known more for her dramatic abilities than for her technique, and Caj Selling – 'not great but very blond and beautiful'). The local press, already hostile as a result of Rudolf's public condemnation of the Swedish Ballet, was grudging in its praise, the reviews ranging from tepid to downright scathing. 'I remember one so well,' says Anneli Alhanko. 'The headline was A PLAGUE OVER THE OPÉRA, and the critic hadn't liked the choreography or the setting. I felt very sad about it.' Another panned the production's heavy-handed attempts at humour and 'depressingly unimaginative' divertissements, while the most common complaint was Rudolf's insertion of small classroom steps into the grand pas de deux, which was thought to mar its flow and splendour.

Eager to get an idea of what London would be seeing, Frederick Ashton had come over for the première. He was impressed, though with reservations. 'He did some beautiful things . . . The Snowflake Scene . . . the Valse des Fleurs . . . I think the final pas de deux lacks grandeur and simplicity. It's a bit overcharged . . . When you're young, you're apt to overcharge because you want to impress. And so you put in everything. You enrich things too much.' Some problems of the scenario remained, such as Clara's lack of involvement with what is happening in the second act, and there were descriptively explicit passages of music that Rudolf, for some reason, chose to ignore. The choreography itself veered from the exceptional to passages that were downright absurd. (The ensemble of Snowflakes repeating the same steps as they exit up a ramp is a reversal of the Shades' entrance in *La Bayadère* – Rudolf's self-homage – but the ugly, rhythmic movements led one critic to compare the dancers to 'poultry going into a chicken coop'.) On the whole, though, with its seamless transitions and judicious use of male solos, this was Rudolf's most successful and 'most favourite' production, giving a flawed classic the star parts it had always lacked.

He himself did not dance at all in Sweden. He was supposed to return later in the season as a guest, but the outcry his television interview had caused meant that, as Gerd Andersson said, 'Erik simply couldn't invite him back.' Erik, too, had not liked the random scattering of small Bournonville steps through the choreography and tried to tell him that it was musically unresponsive. 'Then,' recalls Marit Grusen, 'Rudolf was like a son against his father.' She likens their relationship to a Strindberg marriage – 'explosive and passionate' – and says that Erik told them that he had no more energy for their battles. 'I can't be around him,' he said. 'I don't want to live like this any more.' At the same time there were many tender interludes, 'moments when Rudolf was like a little boy, and you saw a young man's devotion to a master. He had that fine side. He didn't have to be an *enfant terrible* all the time.'

Mostly, however, finding him 'a little boorish, not at all refined', the Genteles chose not to see much of Rudolf without Erik. On one occasion when he did come for dinner, he had asked Marit to invite a few dancers who had caught his eye. Hearing her hesitant 'Well, I don't know so much about this group that you like,' Rudolf interrupted, 'Don't worry. I bring my own salt and pepper.' He arrived at the house that night 'with *two* boys'. Marit also thought little of Rudolf's 'ungraceful' behaviour towards Lee Radziwill, who had accompanied Ashton to Stockholm, eager to see both him and the Mongiardino designs.* Lee, however, was learning to accept Rudolf on his own terms. 'Because of how he has to live – it's an economy of time. Some people might say that's not a real friendship, but he returns so much. It's there for your taking.'

They had a family Christmas together at the Radziwills' country house, idyllic even in winter with log fires and scented flowers in every room, festive meals in the candlelit, Turgenev-inspired dining room. Rudolf loved the atmosphere and rhythm of Turville Grange, his inspiration for an English home of his own – a large, country-style house secreted among woods and parklands, but within an hour's drive of central London.

Rudolf had bought number 6 Fife Road for forty-five thousand

---

* It has not been possible to ascertain why Ashton did not want the Mongiardino sets for the London production – or to get a real sense of what they were like. Nico Georgiadis, who was commissioned instead, was busy with a new staging of *Aïda,* so that the London première of *The Nutcracker,* intended for Christmas, was postponed until the end of February 1968.

pounds in November, having chosen it from a picture Joan Thring sent him while he was on tour. Leading to one of the gates of Richmond Park, Fife Road is the most exclusive street in East Sheen, a wealthy suburb of southwest London. When the Goslings went to inspect the property for him, they had thought it was too far out of town. 'But Rudolf liked it because it was wild and beautiful,' said Maude. Originally a farmhouse built in a cobbled courtyard overhung with trees, its split levels contained six bedrooms and four large reception rooms, with servants' quarters over the garages. The thirty-foot drawing room and master bedroom had huge windows looking over the garden and Sheen's wooded common. The kitchen, with a low-timbered ceiling, was the oldest part of the house, and there was a small cosy library, where Rudolf kept his albums of classical music piled up against the walls. Impatient to start decorating in Mongiardino style, Rudolf bumped into Georgiadis's assistant Martin Kramer in a London nightclub and said what sounded like, 'I have corps de ballet and I want you to organize it.' Puzzled, Kramer then realized that he was talking about Cordoba leather. 'He wanted me to figure out how to put it on his walls.'

Once Rudolf had moved in, however, he began to think he had made a huge mistake. He was accustomed to city life, but Fife Road, with its stockbroker mansions, is a sheltered backwater with no passing taxis, the nearest shop a car ride away, and rush-hour journeys to the Baron's Court studios or the opera house now nerve-rackingly protracted. His young cockney friends, Tony and Nellie, received a telephone call one day in November from Joan Thring. 'Thringy said to us, "Listen, Rudolf doesn't like it. You've got to come and tell him how wonderful it is."' Keith Baxter was also invited that day, and when he said he had already arranged to visit some actor friends, Joan told him to bring them along, too. 'She was so anxious for him to be happy there, and wanted to fill the house with people.' In the end just the three friends came for Sunday lunch and, as soon as they arrived, were shown round the house by Rudolf. 'The whole purpose of us being there was to browbeat him into liking it, so we all wandered around this vast place saying, "But it's incredible – absolutely brilliant!" which of course it was.'

Later in the afternoon Rudolf and Keith went for a long walk together in Richmond Park. The extraordinary 2,500-acre expanse of open land with free-roaming deer and vast, moorlike stretches of bracken was once royal shooting terrain, and the eighteenth-century hunting lodge built for George II is now the home of the Royal Ballet's

Junior School. The garden of number 6 leads directly on to playing fields, and to reach Bog Gate, an entrance through the park wall known to locals, one must walk for ten minutes through Sheen Common, an area of dense woodland, which Rudolf always said reminded him of Russia. But what on one day is a sun-dappled copse of silver birches filled with blackbird song can turn threatening on another, with rustlings in the undergrowth and paths suddenly ending in dark, cavernous bushes. 'Rudolf kept looking around when we were walking,' Keith recalls. 'He was still very nervous about being followed.'

For the past year Keith had been appearing in a production of *The Rivals*, and going out with Rudolf 'in a nonexclusive sense'. Hearing that he and Margot would be dancing together at the Paris Opéra, Keith remarked that he had never seen *Giselle*. 'But you must,' insisted Rudolf. 'Is my ballet!' They stayed at Margot's favourite hotel, the Trémoille, where they spent three or four days, their last time together as lovers.

One night Keith remembered going with Rudolf to a mixed gay and straight club – 'an absolute revelation of freedom' – after one of Pierre Bergé and Yves Saint Laurent's Sunday suppers at their place Vauban apartment. Everyone there, particularly Yves, was charmed by the handsome young actor, as *Chimes at Midnight* had recently been released and was a great *succès d'estime*. The same group was at Maxim's one evening when Aristotle Onassis sent a note to their table inviting them to join him and Maria Callas. Callas, Keith recalls, never took her eyes off Onassis. 'She was not the least bit interested in anyone else at the table – not Yves, nor Margot, nor Rudolf.' Clara Saint was with them on both occasions as, having been introduced to Bergé and Saint Laurent by Margot, she was now a good friend and colleague.* She had also become very close to Margot herself, who frequently stayed in the *chambre d'ami* of her large rue de Rivoli apartment. Clara's affection for Rudolf, on the other hand, had waned considerably: 'My story with Rudolf was a little bit short. Strong, but short. He had so much money, and yet he never invited me even for a coffee. If we had dinner together he would wait for me to pay. I found it not so pleasant to see him, and more pleasant to see him onstage.'

After Keith had gone back to London, Rudolf went to another evening on place Vauban, where Paris's chic intelligentsia was out in

---

* With most of her inheritance spent, and realizing that she would have to find a job, she had suggested to Bergé – 'I never would have thought of Clara working' – that she handle the press for the just-starting Rive Gauche ready-to-wear range.

force. Rudolf, however, was interested only in making the acquaintance of a stunning youth he had spotted. Like Helmut Berger, the actor Pierre Clementi* was a protégé of Luchino Visconti, and an idol of '*les années pop*'. He had the slightly feminine beauty of a corrupt angel, but he was not homosexual and made that quite clear. After Rudolf's advances became more insistent, there followed what Gilles Dufour, one of the guests, describes as 'a friendly fracas. It was physical pushing – but no drama. Just amusing.' Unperturbed, Rudolf then turned his attention to Gilles himself, the other decorative youngster in the room, a twenty-one-year-old trainee fashion designer known for his striking 'Tatar physique.' 'Rudolf liked me because I was looking a bit like him. He was very direct about picking people up – asking them to come with him or forget it. I was shy then, not free like I am now, and I was also dating girls at this time. I didn't want things to be that open, so . . . I didn't go.'

A few days later Gilles came with a friend to see Rudolf backstage, and was imperiously ignored. His interest now aroused, he contacted a mutual acquaintance in order to meet the dancer again, and this time, Rudolf's approach was entirely different. 'He asked me to come back with him to the Ritz and sleep – just sleep – because he had a performance that evening.' At five o'clock they walked to the Palais Garnier together and, as they were saying goodbye, Rudolf invited Gilles to London. 'He wanted me to spend some time with him at his house.'

Gilles came over the following weekend intending to see Rudolf's performance at Covent Garden. Because of ice and dense fog his plane was severely delayed, and by the time he got to Covent Garden, everyone had left. He took the cab on to Fife Road, where Rudolf was waiting for him at the door with slippers – 'He was very charming.' There was a baronial dinner party in progress, its guests – who included Roland Petit and the Goslings – all eyeing Gilles, he felt, 'as if I were Madame de Pompadour'. But it was his innocence that Rudolf liked – the reason he called Gilles 'the Child'. And like a child, he would trail after the dancer as he pursued his usual routine: class and rehearsal at Baron's Court on Saturday; a visit to the cinema; dinner in the King's Road; nocturnal window-shopping for antiques. The second London weekend followed much the same pattern, and by the third, despite the fact that the physical side of their liaison had not amounted

---

* Pierre Clementi was Fellini's first choice for the role of Ascylto in *Satyricon*, but as he demanded too much money the director cast Hiram Keller instead.

to much – 'sex was just mechanical. Rudolf had the most beautiful body but was not tactile at all' – Gilles found that he was falling in love. 'Rudolf could see that I was much too clinging. I was exhausting him. It was Sunday morning when he explained to me that he was not the right person for me to be with because the main thing in his life was dancing. He told me nicely, and said he'd like to have me as a friend. And then he left.'*

A year or two earlier Rudolf would have used Erik as the reason he could not commit himself, but now it was love itself that was the obstacle. He no longer wanted to be a victim of the kind of obsessive passion he had experienced in the first stages of their affair, the Romantic agony he called 'the Curse'. Although this had been, without question, the sustenance of his artistry – the motive force for his rhapsodic performances with Margot – Rudolf had come to believe that emotion of such intensity was destructive to his career. He would never, he decided, repeat the same mistake. 'I had to cut out all personal involvement. Do you read me? No personal involvement, that's been abolished. So it doesn't distract me from dancing.'

* Rudolf asked his cook-housekeeper to make breakfast for Gilles. 'My tears were dropping into the eggs.' (In 1995 he bought the silver egg cups at the Nureyev sale.)

13 TIME TO CRASH THE GATES

On 25 February 1968 Hamet Nureyev died from lung cancer, two days after turning sixty-five. Farida had been distraught to hear that there was nothing more the hospital could do and had taken him home, where she nursed him herself until the end. A telegram from Rosa broke the news to Rudolf, and later a photograph arrived. It showed his mother, vigilant, next to the bed on which his father's body was laid out – the custom in many Russian households, where the washed and dressed corpse is displayed until the day of burial. Some years later, while helping to clear out the library at Fife Road, the Goslings came across the picture and were shocked by the starkness of the image. 'It made my blood run cold,' Nigel remarked in a letter. 'How terrible for you to get that, poor Rudi. We shut it away.'

Rudolf did much the same with his emotions, and yet he can have felt little grief. It had been seven years since they last had any contact, and it was only Farida or one of his sisters who ever made the trip to Ufa's post office to telephone him.[*] If father and son did not make their peace, Hamet's anger had nevertheless abated with time. 'He became much softer towards Rudolf and what he did,' Razida says. The letter of denunciation he wrote in the aftermath of the defection is not something for which he should be held to account. As his granddaughter Alfia realized, 'He was afraid for the family. When Rudolf left he thought they might take our home away. He just wanted them to leave us alone.'

Alfia remembers the funeral being small, 'not fancy', the factory having provided an open lorry for the coffin and a little band of musicians. Colleagues helped to dig the grave, relatives and neighbours provided vodka and a couple of chickens for the *pirousa* broth. 'People liked my grandfather. Everybody said, "He is different."' In this, and other ways too, Rudolf was his father's son, both disgraced, in Soviet

---

[*] When the Nureyevs got a phone of their own Rudolf could sometimes hear his father coughing in the background but neither asked to speak to the other.

eyes, for mingling with foreigners, and both sharing the same passion to educate and improve themselves, to escape from the world into which they were born. Rudolf told most people that he hated his father, but there were also those to whom he admitted that he wished he had known him better.

There was no time to dwell on it as the London première of Rudolf's *Nutcracker* was a couple of days away. He had coached the young stars Antoinette Sibley and Anthony Dowell to perform the first night, and they were, as the critics acknowledged, 'just about ideal', as perfectly symmetrical in the parallel duet as the two wings of a bird. For Ninette de Valois, Rudolf's version was 'the best *Nutcracker* England ever had', although Ashton was less enthusiastic, complaining, 'The trouble is, he can't be simple. He feels he has to produce a step for every note of music.' A new solo the choreographer created for Rudolf in the March revival of *Birthday Offering* was nothing if not a caricature of this, giving John Percival the impression that Ashton had 'worked on the principle of trying to establish how many steps could possibly be fitted into one dance'.

Ashton's latest ballet, *Jazz Calendar*, which premièred in January, had also been made in a flippant frame of mind. Paired with Sibley, Rudolf performed Friday's Child, with its theme of 'loving and giving' reduced to Petit-style bumping and grinding – a send-up of *Paradise Lost*'s somersaults, floor slithering and mirror-image movements. The couple wore two-tone unitards designed by Derek Jarman, a Slade protégé of Nico Georgiadis. At their first costume fitting, the embarrassed twenty-six-year-old found himself being mercilessly put to the test by Rudolf, who met him completely naked, drying himself from a shower. Picking up the costume between two fingers and contemptuously dropping it, Rudolf then lectured the designer on the desirable texture and colour of tights. As Jarman had suggested a wig, Rudolf turned up at the next rehearsal with 'an awful black plastic number from Woolworth's', wearing it back to front to amuse his shrieking colleagues. It would have been no use appealing to Ashton to intervene; he had warned Jarman at the beginning of their collaboration: 'Nureyev you'll have to deal with yourself.' *Jazz Calendar*, moreover, with its in-jokes and stylistic parodies, was only 'a *little* ballet' in the choreographer's view – one Rudolf clearly shared. Nevertheless, against all expectations (and his doctor's orders), he performed the first night with a temperature of 102, providing what everyone agreed was one of the highlights of the evening.

In April the company heard that Ashton, much against his will, would be stepping down as director in 1970. Kenneth MacMillan's tenure with the Berlin ballet was coming to an end, and it was de Valois's wish that the younger choreographer should now take charge of the company. For Rudolf this was not good news. His current Royal Ballet contract, due for renewal in July 1970, was both generous and flexible. Paying a fee of £1,250 per performance and granting him long periods of absence, it promised to try to ensure that he appeared in at least one new production a year. Rudolf thought it unlikely that MacMillan would continue the arrangement. The rift that had occurred between them during the making of the 1965 *Romeo and Juliet* was soon to widen even further. Anxious to make amends by demonstrating his enthusiasm for the choreographer's work, Rudolf had flown to Berlin in November 1968 to see *Cain and Abel*, a new ballet, which MacMillan would be asked to restage in London early the following year. He had devised the role of Cain around the sensational jump and dramatic power of Frank Frey, a German dancer he wanted to keep in the Royal Ballet production, with Rudolf cast in the role of Abel. Having seen the ballet, Rudolf, needless to say, felt that he should be Cain. De Valois took his side – 'Frey's not even a star – he's just a beginner,' she protested, but MacMillan refused to mount the ballet without him. 'He was the only one,' said director Peter Wright. 'Kenneth never found anyone who matched Frank's extraordinary virility.' Deadlock was reached, and in the end MacMillan's feeble *Olympiad* (without Rudolf) was performed instead.

Aware of Rudolf's disappointment, Margot suggested that Roland Petit be invited to create another ballet for them both. Rudolf agreed, but with reservations. His last collaboration with Petit – at La Scala, Milan, in September – had not been a success. Still 'much obsessed and possessed' by Scriabin he had been excited by Petit's idea of using the composer's masterpiece, his *Poème de l'extase*. Instead of attempting to reflect Scriabin's expression of the sublime, however, the choreography had been banal in the extreme – 'a direct affront to the literary content of music', in one critic's opinion. Now Petit was proposing another challenging score: Schoenberg's symphonic poem based on the Pelléas and Mélisande legend. A one-act work was commissioned and scheduled for the spring (something new was needed for the American tour, and could also be included in the programme planned to celebrate Margot's thirty-fifth anniversary on the stage in March). Hearing about the new piece, MacMillan was furious. According to Maude Gosling, he assumed, unfairly, that it had all been Rudolf's plot, that his own ballet had been sabotaged in order to make way for a new Fonteyn–Nureyev vehicle. She had said, 'That wasn't true at all – Rudolf would *much* rather have done *Cain and Abel*. But from then on there was great coolness. Kenneth was coming to dinner with us all, but rang up at the last minute and cancelled. He never did anything for Rudolf after that. Rudolf had to *beg* to be given *Manon* [MacMillan's 1974 three-act work].'*

Rudolf's next course of action was quite clear: 'If Covent Garden can't provide you with work and incentive, you go and get it somewhere else. Get off your ass; go, telephone, organize, provoke, make performance somewhere else.' After all, winning the freedom to dance how, when and where he wished – 'everything everywhere, the new ballets and the old' – had been the main impetus behind his defection. 'Idea was not just, "Here I am, the best, the greatest." I came *to learn*.' The crucial difference now, seven years later, was that Rudolf was no longer inhibited by the fear of tainting his schooling. 'When I came to the West, I arrived with what I was taught by the Russians. It was hammered into our heads that Russian ballet dancing is the best – the ghosts of Diaghilev and Nijinsky were constantly hovering over us. We are the best!'

Veneration for his Vaganova training had been tangible in the exactness with which he would take even a simple preparation, 'his whole foot seeming to caress the floor', as Mary Clarke put it in 1966. With ballet rooted in these basic positions – the origins from which a dancer proceeds – it was as if Rudolf was clinging to them in the belief that losing even the slightest element of precision would be the beginning of losing everything. 'It has taken a very long time of observing and experiencing to live down whatever I saw or learned of the grandeur of the Kirov company which is very overpowering . . . it does take a long time to accept other forms of movement.'

In 1966 he had remarked that dancing *Giselle* or *Sleeping Beauty* was like singing Mozart, modern ballet being 'no more than Puccini'. Now, however, he felt that a dancer was as entitled as any musician to mix his repertoire, to combine old with new: 'You have Isaac Stern, Richter . . . able to play Mozart and Chopin, Prokofiev and Shostakovich . . . Stockhausen . . . Cage. You should be able to become that instrument on which diverse choreography could be

---

* In fact, though, in April 1972, almost as if in revenge, MacMillan made the lamentable *Sideshow*, a knockabout burlesque, for Lynn Seymour and Rudolf, who played a circus strongman.

played. And have the mental capacity to grasp the essence and technical ability to change yourself into a different idiom.'

Reunited with Egon Bischoff, his Vaganova contemporary who had become Staatsoper director in East Berlin, Rudolf criticized the lack of an antithesis in Russian ballet. 'There, modern school did not develop.' He had even become aware of flaws in the teaching method itself. When another schoolmate, his 'echo', Sergiu Stefanschi, visited him in his dressing room in Madrid, Rudolf immediately instructed him to take off his shoes and show him a *battement tendu*. 'Hah! I thought so!' he exclaimed as Sergiu curled his toes under while extending his foot to the side rather than keeping them straight as English dancers do. And again, when the young Chinko Rafique arrived from Leningrad to join the Royal Ballet in 1967, his Russian posture making him 'stand out a mile', Rudolf avuncularly took him aside. 'Forget your schooling,' he told him. 'You've got to dance like they dance.'

There were those, however, who considered that Rudolf's own style had become much too Westernized. Attilio Labis, the Paris Opéra star who studied in Leningrad with Pushkin in 1961, urged Rudolf never to forget that he was a *Russian* dancer. Dismissing the neatness and purity he had acquired in the West, Labis remarked, 'He did that to please Margot. It's academic, and classical dance is not academic; it's the expression of the body and of the soul.' Kirov ballerina Gabriella Komleva felt much the same: 'Maybe he spoke very nicely, but to us he had lost the song.' On the next occasion Sergiu Stefanschi saw Rudolf, after a performance in Paris, he decided to speak his mind. Rudolf had invited the dancer to join a large party for dinner, and although there were a number of celebrities present, including Jean Marais, Rudolf ignored them all and spoke in Russian to Sergiu:

He wanted to know what I thought of his performance. We fight a little bit. 'Rudolf,' I say, 'I think you lost a little bit of your *plié*. Before in Russia, you would do it and *go*, but now you're stopping . . . I miss that legato. What you had and what we did in Pushkin's class.' He start to get red . . . 'If I do a *glissade* and someone takes a picture of me, I want to be *perfect*.'

At this point, though, the end of the sixties, Rudolf was no longer demonstrating the flawlessness he had projected throughout most of the decade. Travelling relentlessly and working with different teachers, he had begun to lose the clarity of his arabesque line. Russian classes put great emphasis on the back, and without this constant practice, Rudolf's strength and suppleness were deteriorating. At the same time it can be no coincidence that 1968, the year that trained eyes began to notice a decline in Rudolf's technique, also marked the end of his love affair with Erik – his lodestar of purity and perfection.

On the other hand, technical decline was in itself a kind of liberation. For now Rudolf was able to accept the validity of the new – dance that 'does not depend on beautiful line, unearthly balance or sexual titillation', in choreographer Paul Taylor's words, but is 'abstracted to express, in aesthetic form, the drives, desires and reactions of alive human beings'. Its pioneer, Isadora Duncan, used modern dance as a means of greater emotional communication; Martha Graham, to explore psychological ideas and complex personal relationships. It is a language that, as Rudolf himself recognized, 'allows one to delve into one's inner being' and, unlike classical ballet, one that sanctions the solo form. 'Martha did all the ballets centred around herself. [Glen] Tetley did that for himself. And Taylor.' What would this unfamiliar idiom do for him? Rudolf wanted to know. 'With these new movements: will I be more expressive or less expressive?'

For a dancer who embodied freedom, bringing its 'large, magical aura' with him onstage, it was only natural that he would want to 'crash the gates' between ballet and modern dance, yet again crossing from a familiar world to an alien one. It was a period when there was still a great deal of hostility between the two genres, each being, in Rudolf's words, 'like a medieval fortress, with no exchange from the outside'. Although others before him had attempted a bridge, Rudolf, as choreographer Murray Louis acknowledges, deserves most of the credit for freeing the way for future dancers. 'He took the plunge, he took the largest gamble, he had the most to lose.'

Rudolf's first engagement with modern dance came about through a young Dutch choreographer whose work synthesized both forms of dance. Describing himself as 'a sort of bastard between classical ballet and modern', Rudi van Dantzig had been galvanized into making dance that reflected something of his own life and experience by seeing Martha Graham during her 1954 tour of Holland. Thirteen years later he was appointed co-director of the Dutch National Ballet, a company that greatly interested Rudolf because of its Balanchine repertory, then reputed to be the largest outside that of the New York City Ballet. Van Dantzig would not only continue to enrich DNB's Balanchine heritage, and improve out of recognition the standard of the nineteenth-century classics, but also foster new choreography, himself creating psychodramatic pieces of originality and everyday relevance.

Of particular note was his 1965 *Monument for a Dead Boy*, an adolescent's rite of passage, inspired by Dutch poet Hans Lodeizen, a young homosexual whose romantic self-absorption and contemporary outlook had great personal resonance for van Dantzig. Lodeizen died of leukaemia at the age of twenty-six, and it was the poet's early end, as well as the suicide of a brilliant young painter van Dantzig had met, that 'mingled in [his] head' when he heard the electronic music of Jan Boerman, leading to the creation of the ballet. Its central role was created by Toer van Schayk, van Dantzig's lover since 1956, a dancer and painter who designed this and many other works for the theatre. Gentle and kind-faced, van Schayk brought real subtlety and sensitivity to the part of the youth, a character he describes as 'someone who doesn't know how to cope with his life . . . Doesn't know himself; doesn't know his sexual predilections.'

Having been told about the Harkness Ballet's successful 1965 revival in New York – 'I have perfect system of information, spies everywhere' – Rudolf contacted van Dantzig when the Royal Ballet toured Amsterdam in July 1968. 'You did ballet that I heard good things about. I wonder if I can perform it,' Rudolf remarked when they met in his dressing room after a matinée. He had some time free in October, and asked how long it would take to learn the choreography. 'Two weeks, three at the most,' replied van Dantzig, prompting a scornful laugh from the star. 'Two, three days is all I can give you . . . Nothing more.' Believing nothing more would come of it, the choreographer was surprised to receive a follow-up telephone call a few days later when Rudolf suggested that they meet in Milan to discuss events further. After that things happened very quickly. Rudolf arrived in Amsterdam in late May – straight after the Royal Ballet's New York tour – and 'Dutch Rudi' was waiting at the airport to take him to his hotel. When he suggested a time to rehearse the following day, Rudolf was incredulous. 'What do you mean? Nothing tomorrow, now, at once!'

In the studio, however, there was no sign of urgency. As if wilfully playing for time, Rudolf began arranging different pairs of ballet shoes, towels and sweaters, tying on a headband, blowing his nose (on a hotel towel), before strolling over to the barre. While van Dantzig looked on he started a slow warm-up, stopping occasionally to change shoes or pull on an extra leotard. It was the first time Rudi had seen the dancer at work, so he was not bored, and yet Rudolf's total lack of communication made him feel 'like some immobile and mesmerized victim being slowly but surely eviscerated'.

Finally, after about an hour Rudolf, sweating profusely, announced that he was ready, and asked to hear the music. 'Noise,' was his only comment on hearing the tape of Boerman's strange electronic wind howling. 'Noise. Interesting.' When van Dantzig asked him to try marking time to it, he received a glance of startled incomprehension. The procrastination and offhandedness had been a cover. Later Rudolf admitted how thrown he had been on first hearing the score. 'I thought, "That's not music, there's nothing to grasp," but little by little you . . . realize the strong inner structure and it has even rhythm and there are a lot of landmarks.' Rudi was terrified himself. 'It all seemed so ridiculous, what was this man supposed to do with my weird movements?' He began to demonstrate, hearing his voice wavering as he explained what he wanted. But instead of the steps appearing to come naturally to Rudolf, he was inflecting each one with such exertion that to Rudi it seemed 'followed by an exclamation mark, as it were'.

'All right?'

'What was I supposed to answer: "No?"'

'The music is complicated and you still have to get used to my way of moving . . .'

'Good is good, not good is not good, please.'

Rudolf repeated the piece and this time seemed almost to be deliberately caricaturing it: they struggled on, with Rudolf moaning, puffing and panting over movements that were complex but should not have been that tiring. When someone came in to tell Rudi he had a phone call, he tore downstairs to his office, relieved to escape the stifling atmosphere in the studio. When he returned, Rudolf was going over the choreography, but stopped instantly when he realized that he had been seen. However, the short break had eased the tension, and by the end of the rehearsal, they were both laughing.

'And what happens tonight?'

'You'll want a rest, won't you?'

But no. Having worked only on the solos, Rudolf now intended to try out the duets. A couple of hours later they were back in the studio with Yvonne Vendrig, an unusually expressive dancer of no more than eighteen, whom Rudi was currently nurturing. Although in awe of the famous guest, Yvonne proved a fair match for him, not allowing herself to be intimidated when it became clear from the 'crashes, falls and stinging abuse' that Rudolf was finding the lifts in *Monument* more than usually arduous. Rudi tried to diffuse the situation by explaining the motivation behind their parts. 'They are fascinated by each other . . . both feeling their way towards each other, both afraid of going too far. The boy keeps withdrawing sooner than the girl; it is she who takes the initiative, over and over again.' 'She's a bitch,' Rudolf muttered audibly, making Rudi wish he had not subjected his protégée to such a disillusioning first experience of collaborating with a star. At the end of Vendrig's 'brave fight', she sat sobbing in a corner while Rudi comforted her; a curt 'bye', and Rudolf had left the studio.

About half an hour later Rudi knocked on Rudolf's dressing-room door, certain he would not find the dancer inside. 'It seemed most likely he would pack his bags and say: "This is no good for me; I've made a mistake." ' But there he was, sitting alone, like a sulky child, and immediately suggested that they should go out and eat. By now it was eleven o'clock, much too late to find a restaurant still serving food, but they stopped off at an oyster bar whose owner recognized Rudolf and volunteered to reopen the kitchen. Over dinner Rudolf for the first time expressed an interest in the content of *Monument*, rather than just the steps.

'Tell me what is the ballet about? He loves boys, no?'

'No, that's just it, he's a boy who's still unsure whether he's attracted to boys or girls. He's imprisoned in a number of nightmarish impressions and experiences.'

'A stupid boy, then.'

Uncertainty was an emotion so alien to Rudolf's nature that Rudi found it hard to understand why he had wanted to take on the role. His ballets were about ordinary people, not the kind of epic hero Rudolf had been brought up to be. 'The Soviet ballet was built around extraordinary individuals. He was like that as a person, too.' But Rudolf was there to learn a new language, and Rudi van Dantzig was his instructor of choice. At thirty-five he may have been too close in age for Rudolf to accept his authority, but he was unusually frank, a quality Rudolf respected. As Toer says, 'There were so many sycophants around him and here was someone very bluntly telling him what he thought.' Articulate, intelligent and attractive, with long tousled blond curls, Rudi was also a good companion, and as they left in the small hours, walking along canals so redolent of Leningrad, the two linked arms like old friends. Curious about 'human stories, about fathers and families', Rudi encouraged Rudolf to talk of his Ufa childhood and his years with Pushkin, and they would stop from time to time to look in the windows of antiques shops in Spiegelstraat. 'What can we do now?' Rudolf asked, pointedly. But even with Toer away, there was no question in Rudi's mind of taking things any further. 'I'm no saint, and it wasn't out of nobleness to Toer. But I was never really attracted to Rudolf, so I don't think I gave out any signals.' Instead, he told him where he could find the type of nightlife he seemed to be looking for. Amsterdam, with its radically tolerant social climate, had for more than a decade been the gay capital of Europe, its clubs being what interested Rudolf, not its easy access to recreational drugs. 'This was very soon after the San Francisco incident and he had an enormous fear of being caught.' Accompanying him as far as the Kerkstraat district, Rudi then bade him good night. 'I said, "I'm sorry, this is something you'll have to do on your own. It's not for me, that scene."'

When Toer van Schayk returned to Amsterdam Rudi suggested that he dance the role for Rudolf. Since creating it Toer had developed it greatly, to such a degree that, when he finished, Rudolf walked over to his bag, threw in his shoes and towels, and said, 'Why don't you let *him* do it then?' before striding out and slamming the door. Ignoring the outburst, Rudi went on with the rehearsal, and within two minutes Rudolf had returned. 'In my heart I felt for him . . . Over the years, when I knew him better, I would notice that whenever he entered a new environment or an unknown company, he would harbour suspicion and mistrust, as though everyone was conspiring against him: the inhabitants of the safe, protected nest against the unknown intruder.'

Earlier Rudolf had played up to the audience of dancers sitting on the sidelines, making faces, showing off 'in a sort of *commedia dell'arte* way', when differences of opinion arose between him and Rudi. Now, however, he ordered everyone to leave the studio, Toer alone staying, seated beside Rudi. Together they watched Rudolf demonstrate what he had learned in those two and a half days – both amazed that he had absorbed so much in so short a time. More confident now, Rudolf noticeably relaxed and even went so far as to ask Toer for help: 'We have to start from beginning,' he said. Toer did his best, but he could see that the movements were not really within Rudolf's scope. 'Not technically, but because he wasn't a modern dancer.' By the end of the fourth day, although he had mastered the steps, Rudolf's interpretation needed refining, and it was only with great reluctance that Rudi got him to agree to an extra series of rehearsals. 'He was a person to be onstage. Rehearsing was a drag for him. A loss of time.'

On his next visit to Amsterdam, Rudolf surprised Rudi and Toer by asking if he could stay with them. They lived in a narrow little seventeenth-century house, a converted grocery, in the Jordaan, the old artisans' quarter, the shop area now serving as a studio for Toer. At the top of a steep crooked staircase was a ladder up to the loft where they slept, with a tiny guest room beside it for Rudolf. In his ankle-length leather coat, harlequin boots, fur hat and flamboyant shawl – 'like the captain of some fairy-tale galleon' – he immediately seemed to fill the house to bursting point. But having imperiously announced on arrival that he drank only vodka, Stolichnaya vodka (resulting in Rudi cycling around town in search of a bottle), Rudolf in fact proved to be an 'astonishingly meek' house guest. Coming upstairs the first morning after preparing breakfast, Toer saw him in the process of making his bed, and laughingly pointed out their own bed still in complete disarray: 'Rudolf didn't understand that I meant he shouldn't bother. "Yes, yes, I know," he said. "I'll do that too."'

In the studio it was a different matter, Rudolf continuing to be difficult and often late for class. On the morning of the third day he arrived early because Rudi had moved the wake-up hand on his alarm clock forward by three-quarters of an hour. Realizing that he had been tricked, Rudolf was furious, 'You *fiddled* with my alarm!' he exploded. Then, grim-faced, he began his own daily routine at the barre: checking his port de bras, slowly arching his back. 'It was certainly effective; all eyes were on him.' When class began he kept to his own tempo, working exasperatingly slowly and ignoring everyone around him. It was as important for Rudolf to ground himself in his Russian roots as it was to demonstrate to his fellow dancers that in this manner – in the ritual of classical class – he was beyond compare. Now he felt in complete control, whereas once the rehearsal started there would be those struck, as Rudi was, by 'how awkward he could be, how uninventive.' Film footage taken at the time shows Rudolf straining to make an effect – 'to create a character of desperate anguish', his facial grimaces completely at odds with the delicately nuanced acting of his classical roles. When they first began collaborating, Rudolf had told his choreographer, 'You are the boss, get it out of me and tell me when it is wrong.' But when Rudi tried to get him to subdue his portrayal, to understand that his 'militant, sensual and extrovert' youth was quite the opposite of the hesitant antihero he had had in mind, Rudolf became 'rather snappy and sour and bitter'. While he badly wanted to do what was required of him, he could not bring himself to relinquish his own conception of himself, and in his debut performance on 25 December 1968 insisted on dancing *The Nutcracker* pas de deux on the same programme. 'This is what public expects from me,' he said defensively.

If Rudolf never completely mastered his first contemporary role, it was generally agreed, when he performed it exactly a year later with the Dutch National Ballet in London, that he gave it 'a pretty impressive shot'. In *Pelléas et Mélisande* for the Royal Ballet, however, not even the combined forces of Rudolf and Margot could prevent 'yawns of exasperation' from audience and critics alike. Summed up by Cecil Beaton as 'ugly . . . pullings across floor on bottoms', the ballet was unanimously dismissed as nothing short of a disaster, with 'Oh dear!' heading the *Dancing Times* review. The 'contemptible farrago' fared no better when premièred in New York, and only served to fuel the current backlash against the Fonteyn–Nureyev stronghold. Writing to Richard Buckle, Lincoln Kirstein described the two stars as the worst thing that ever happened to British ballet 'except for that Royal Charter', adding that their presence had demoralized the male dancers in the company and unbalanced the whole principle of *esprit de corps*.

At this particular time, though, Kirstein was mistaken. Pressured by assistant directors Michael Somes and Jack Hart (who, according to Keith Money, saw their principal task as '*getting rid of Margot*'), Ashton had become more determined than ever not 'to run a national company for the benefit of two people'. Peter Wright's new production of *Sleeping Beauty* coincided exactly with the twentieth anniversary of the ballet's historic New York première, Margot's crowning glory, but Wright insists there was never any question of mounting the role of Aurora on the company's *prima ballerina assoluta* – nor, indeed, that of the Prince on her famous partner. The first night, both in London and New York, was danced by Antoinette Sibley and Anthony Dowell, on whom Ashton's new 'Awakening' duet had been created. To Arlene Croce, Dowell was 'the finest classical stylist before the public', while to Beaton the dancer had 'discreetly become even more of a star to rival Nureyev'.

Having been responsible for pairing Margot with Rudolf, Ninette de Valois was only too aware of the box-office rewards of big-name casting. Ashton himself was unashamedly starstruck – the lush extrovertism of his Romantic style having been forged by such star personalities as Pavlova and Garbo. Left alone, it is more than likely that his theatrical pragmatism would have nurtured the phenomenon a good deal longer; instead, Money remembers, he became very agitated about Margot and Rudolf: 'He was made very unhappy by the constant bullying from Somes and Hart, who strove ceaselessly to set up Antoinette and Anthony as the replacement hot ticket. They worked on him in tandem, like synchronized trip-hammers.'

And to a degree they achieved their end. The Fonteyn–Nureyev blaze had dimmed considerably by the end of the decade; Sibley, Park and Beriosova were now each capable of filling the house, and Dowell and David Wall could provide their own English style of youth and glamour. Even so, no other Royal Ballet pairing would ever achieve the level of transcendence reached by Margot and Rudolf, that ineffable effect Clive Barnes struggled to define in his review of their New York *Swan Lake*: 'There are times when even the most devoted ballet fans wonder just what ballet can convey without the poetically vague, yet always imaginative specifics of words. And then you see a ballet by Balanchine or Ashton, a performance by Fonteyn and Nureyev, and you realize the challenging eloquence of silence.'

In his book *Fonteyn: The Making of a Legend*, Money quotes the Barnes piece in its entirety, believing that it illustrates '*exactly* why the management of the Royal Ballet felt threatened by finding themselves in the grip of forces which they simply couldn't control'.

Rudolf's companion in New York was Robert Hutchinson, the young architect arrested with him and Margot in the summer of '67. They were staying in the East Sixty-sixth Street home of Monique van Vooren, then in Europe, who had offered Rudolf the use of her apartment whenever he came to town. Decorated in Mae West–fifties Hollywood style with gold candelabra, a white carpet, tigerskin rugs and a mirror above the bed, it was the natural habitat of the 'va-va-voom' Monique, but a surprising setting for Rudolf to choose for himself. The white grand piano had no insides – 'It was just a shell, a kind of cocktail table' – and directly opposite the bedroom window was the Russian consulate. Day and night, armed soldiers were visible on the roof, and although Rudolf kept the curtains closed, he was always aware of their presence. 'When we went outside he'd say, "Don't look up! They want me. They want to punish me." He never stopped thinking he was going to be snatched and flown in a helicopter all the way back to Moscow.'

Rudolf had seen Robert on and off over the last two years, sometimes making a special detour to San Francisco to pay him a visit. 'He'd fly in, and I'd pick him up from the airport and whisk him home so we could have a night together.' Describing himself with a grin as 'one of the great homosexual studs of the nation' and going on to elaborate why, Robert had proved quite a catch. The success of his own career as a specialist in 'sculpturesque' architecture and interiors had given the young American more than usual self-esteem:

> Rudolf couldn't take advantage of me because I felt equally important. He didn't have to pay for me; and if I was with him and he misbehaved, I could walk away proudly – something that he both despised and loved. When he got angry I'd ignore him and drive off, leaving him standing on the street. He wouldn't see me for two days, and then he'd call up and it would be on again. I think he was pleased to find sexual contact with somebody who was presentable. When we went to see Marietta Tree or someone like that he knew I could converse with people because I was not just some little tramp he'd picked up and was going to say goodbye to.

If he was at ease in grand drawing rooms, Robert was also indispensable as an entrée to what he calls 'the dark side of life'. Since *Life* magazine's 1964 feature about San Francisco's burgeoning underground, the city had become a mecca for homosexuals from all over the United States. Bars and coffeehouses like the Head Hunters, Last Resort and Rendezvous were as welcomingly unclandestine as the city's bathhouses – no longer the seedy Turkish bathing establishments catering to 'the pansy men of the Nation', but modern, flourishing, gay-owned institutions. Encouraging Rudolf to cruise independently, Robert understood that anonymous sex in a dimly lit walk-in locker smelling of sweat and urinals was a necessary release for him – 'a blank moment of irresponsibility and escape from all the pressure'. He never resented Rudolf's promiscuity – 'because I was the same' – although he admits being infatuated with him for a time, happy enough to indulge Rudolf's cosy side by massaging his feet late at night – 'his big toes with their bunions'. All the same, he says he knew perfectly well that they could never have a long-term relationship: 'He was always here today, gone tomorrow. And although there was that temptation to go with him – and he kind of let it be known that I could – it would have meant being an assistant: answering phones, carrying luggage, seeing that other people were taken care of . . . I'd had a taste of that already and thought, No, I'm not the type.'

Not having a willing 'vagabond lover' meant finding someone new in every port of call. 'Is there anyone interesting in Atlanta?' Rudolf asked Monique. 'Let me find out from Hiram,' she replied. Son of a state supreme court justice, Rusty Underkoffer, as he was then, had been a habitué of Atlanta's Piedmont Park, a gay cruising zone, his 'partner in crime' one Ed Barnum, a successful real estate developer, who claimed to have lost an arm in the Korean war but in fact had been born with the disability. Hiram remembered that the previous spring when Ed paid him a visit in New York he had brought with him a friend from Atlanta, a twenty-one-year-old student. 'How do they look?' enquired Monique. 'One good-looking; one not so good.'

Wallace Potts was, in fact, quite stunning. Not girlishly pretty like Hiram, but handsome and muscular, with long shiny hair and an irresistible soft Southern drawl. Having just graduated from Georgia Tech as a physics major, he had been more interested in theatre and cinema than in what he was learning in college; in what was happening in New York's East Village and the hippie culture out west than in the Southern Gentlemen's fraternity culture. 'And as I was discovering hippiedom, I was discovering other aspects about myself. And I guess one of them is that I was gay – or half-gay, as a friend of mine used to say. Because I still had relations with girls.'

Having moved on from his 'drug period' to a phase of physical fitness, Wallace was walking from the gym one night to the waffle house on Peachtree Street when Ed Barnum pulled up in his Lincoln convertible and offered him a ride. Unaware that 'Atlanta's Sunset Boulevard' was the main gay pickup strip, Wallace nevertheless admits that by then he knew the score. Their assignation turned into an affair, and before long they were living together (though when Ed's intensity proved too suffocating, Wallace moved into one of his apartments). 'I was never in love with Ed, but he fascinated me. I was attracted by anyone with real passion.' Far from being an 'effeminate swishy queen', Ed was conventional-looking and extremely cultivated. He introduced Wallace, who had begun taking acting lessons, to all the theatre people he knew and took him on cultural trips to New York. In April 1968 they went to see the new Broadway production of the hippie musical *Hair*, in which Hiram was appearing as a 'member of the tribe'.* They met up with him in Monique's apartment, and it was as a result of this encounter that Rudolf was offered the use of Ed Barnum's guesthouse a year later when the Royal Ballet toured Atlanta.

In June, having arranged special clearance, Ed collected Rudolf and Margot in his open-top car directly from the plane – 'He did the grand number' – Wallace having stayed behind to finish painting the ceiling of the converted garage they were hurriedly redecorating. Watching Rudolf walk into the room was nothing less than 'awe at first sight' for Wallace, who had never seen the dancer perform and yet felt he already knew him. (An ex-girlfriend was a fan, and had papered her bedroom with Nureyev posters and photographs. 'So when I'd go over to her house, I'd be surrounded by him.') For Rudolf, the image of this paint-splattered youth poised on a ladder in blue jeans – an all-American incarnation of Cocteau's *jeune homme* – was an outright invitation. 'He moved *very* fast. After, I guess, "Hello, how are you?" we fell right into the sack.'

When Wallace saw Rudolf onstage that night, it was, he said, like having sex again. 'It was extraordinary – the wild animal we'd all heard of. I mean, you've never seen anything like it – especially in Atlanta.' Ed, who had taken Wallace out to dinner with the two stars – 'He was happy to use me as a toy' – then left town on business. 'He must have thought that would be it, that Rudolf would move on to the next one, and I would go back to my summer job as a waiter.' Within hours of taking Rudolf to the airport, however, Wallace got a telephone call from New Orleans asking him to come out to Los Angeles for a couple of days:

> So here I go from working tables in some joint in Atlanta to living in a bungalow that joined Jean and Maggie Louis's house in Malibu. It was a period when the rich and famous – even the conservatives in Hollywood – were having hippie parties, and at the party for Rudolf there was Jimmy Stewart and Burt Lancaster and Ryan O'Neal and Ursula Andress . . . all in hippie drag. I felt very outside my element,

---

* Monique had invested in *Hair* after someone defaulted, and as a return favour, Michael Butler had agreed to see Hiram. When he was performing in a show out of town, Monique had rehearsed him on the telephone, singing 'Lucy in the Sky with Diamonds', but after the audition Butler had called her and complained, 'That friend of yours can't sing and can't act.' 'Yes,' protested Monique, 'but he's so beautiful that everyone will be talking about him.' This proved true enough. It was Franco Zeffirelli's seeing Hiram in the chorus that led to him being given a lead role the following year in Fellini's *Satyricon*.

but Rudolf treated me just like one of them. He didn't tow me around; he always introduced me.

Margot was rather formal and offhand with Wallace at first, probably, as he says, because she assumed this was just another passing fling. 'Why get involved with someone who might be gone tomorrow?' She liked him enough, though, to take him to the zoo when Rudolf was rehearsing – 'I was wearing cut-off denims, a tank top and was actually barefoot, but she didn't bat an eye.' She also showed an interest in his subject. 'I remember we talked about the latest cosmological theories of the universe. She didn't know physics in depth, but she could hold a conversation.' Wallace had been equally impressed by Rudolf's awareness of things outside ballet, although he admits that, at this point, sex more than anything else was the bond between them. 'I was very . . . as they say in England "randy" – a word Rudolf also loved.' Wallace remained on the tour as far as San Francisco, by which time he had had enough: 'It was just that Rudolf was so difficult – screaming at the waiters when they brought him overcooked eggs.' The moment of decision came when Robert Hutchinson, 'innocently trying to impress Rudolf with pleasure, and not knowing his friend's capacity to perform', arranged a foursome in their hotel room:

> I don't know what Rudolf was trying to tell me at that point, whether he wanted an open relationship, or didn't want to be committed to me, but I was very uncomfortable with the idea of having sex with more than one person. I remember sitting in the window of the St Francis Hotel kind of sulking while three of them performed on the bed. And I couldn't do it.

Wallace went back to Atlanta, and Rudolf set about finding someone else. That summer, while staying at La Turbie, he pursued Charles Jude, a sixteen-year-old Vietnamese ballet student whom he would later describe as his favourite partner after Margot. Charles had been lying on the beach at Eze when someone came over to tell him that Rudolf Nureyev was looking for him. Much against his will – 'My father wanted his children to be involved in the arts' – he was studying dance at the Nice Conservatoire and had been taken by his teacher to see a Fonteyn–Nureyev performance of *Giselle*. He had found Rudolf 'good but not much more', and consequently when the star asked if he would like to have lunch with him, Charles shyly declined, saying that he wanted to be with his friends.

Rudolf had better luck with dancer Robert Denvers. They had met briefly in Portugal the previous summer when Robert, a member of Maurice Béjart's troupe, had felt 'some headlights' from him. But it was not until the Béjart company was in Paris in October 1969 that Rudolf, after watching Robert onstage, made it very clear at the post-performance party that he wanted to spend the night with him.

Well, I did, of course. If I have to find out that I'm gay . . . But it didn't work: I couldn't get turned on by a man. This was probably the first time ever that something didn't cook for Rudolf. But he was most endearing – like the big bear you hold – and I felt unbelievably at peace with him. It was *very* tender, *wonderful*, but there was nothing sexual. After one week he said, 'For Chrissake, Robert, we're like two dykes together. We have to stop this now.' From that moment I felt that I had become different to him, because somehow I had gone through the ritual of wanting it. I mean, I loved the man, but it had nothing to do with his dick.

Rudolf also sought out anonymous encounters. London's Jermyn Street Turkish Baths were nothing like the New York and San Franciscan 'tubs' with their buddy booths, glory holes and graffiti-emblazoned bondage and fisting rooms – 'daisy chains of fucking and sucking, exploding cocks, exaggerated genitalia'. It was old-fashioned and respectable, such action as there was being immensely discreet. Open all day and night, the baths were 'a bit of a melting pot', with anyone from members of the venerable White's Club around the corner dozing off an overindulgent lunch to rent boys from Piccadilly Circus with nowhere to sleep. One regular was Talitha's friend Christopher Gibbs, who says he often saw Rudolf there. A key player in the Getty-Stones-Marrakesh set dedicated to the quest of hedonistic oblivion, Gibbs once dropped acid at the baths, leaving 'completely out of my head'. But with his Mr Fish shirts, Blades jackets and Anello & Davide boots, he was more sixties dandy than dopehead, as well as being an antiquarian decorator of exceptional flair. His shop in Chelsea's Elystan Street was a fantasy chamber of treasures combining European history with echoes of the Orient – a Chinese screen from Hampton Court, a chaise longue from Napoleon's house on St Helena draped with a four-hundred-year-old carpet piece from Isfahan. Rudolf would often pass by to 'shop and flirt', the proprietor, who was exactly his age, being just as beguiling as his wares: witty and intelligent with the flop-haired charm of a slightly debauched English public-school boy.

Gibbs remembers one 'crazy night out at Sheen' with Talitha and Hiram, who had met in Rome during the filming of *Satyricon* (Fellini gave him only one direction: 'You are evil and you lay everything in sight') and were having an affair. After dinner and huge quantities of vodka, the mood turned amorous. 'Rudolf I think liked the idea of taking Hiram from Talitha, but instead started flirting with me.' The two ended up in Rudolf's canopied, carved-oak Jacobean bed. Abiding memories of that night? 'Gamy, wild and romantic . . . sombre and glittery . . . the act itself quite vigorous and stagy. We did it again on a few more occasions.'

In the middle of a more formal evening, Rudolf's housekeeper came into the dining room to report that two youths were waiting for him at the front door. 'Nice looking. They say they have an appointment with Mister Rudolf.' Jumping up to investigate, Rudolf was heard a few minutes later going upstairs with the new arrivals, leaving the guests around the table to continue their meal. They included Margot and the wheelchair-bound Tito, the Goslings, Joan Thring and Sandor Gorlinsky with his wife, Edith – '*la croqueuse de diamants*' as Rudolf called her. ('Every time I've been on tour, *she* acquires another diamond.') Suddenly Joan, unable to contain herself any longer, burst out laughing. 'That's just the way he is,' she said, slapping one hand on the other and flipping them both over. 'He tosses them like pancakes!' The group smiled politely. When the front door had slammed shut, Rudolf returned to the table still aglow from his pleasurable *amuse-bouche*. 'And was it nice?' Margot asked sweetly.

Even on sexually abstemious nights there was something Saturnalian about Rudolf's style of hospitality. Banquet-size dinners, beginning at midnight, would be held in the shadowy, Cordoba leather-walled dining room, from which emerged two life-size bronze candle-bearing arms – an homage to Cocteau's *Beauty and the Beast*. 'Twelve courses served on silver plate', reported Richard Buckle. 'Gargantuan throne, chairs of ebony, vast goblets of wine', echoed Cecil Beaton – both having dined there once with Vanessa Redgrave (Rudolf later complaining that she had wrecked the evening by being 'a totally humourless bore'). Beaton's opinion of Rudolf on this occasion was just as caustic: 'A vague host, without manners or responsibility, leaves everything to Joan Thring [*châtelaine*], who must suffer a lot.'

It was indeed Joan who took charge of Rudolf's entertaining, and 'just did it all' until she found Alice, a tiny, eccentric Cape Malay house-keeper, who wore a blonde wig and stilettos. She made no claim to cook but could, at least, make breakfast (startling Rudolf the first morning she came in to wake him without her heels, wig or teeth). Her sense of humour was equally unconventional, and not at all appreciated by her employer, whom she took great glee in caricaturing. Rudi van Dantzig remembers Alice wearing an embroidered dressing gown with a towel draped like a turban around her head, Rudolf 'coldly ignoring her act while she screeched and pointed and winked'. Nor did he approve of how, after a night spent dancing at the Hammersmith Palais, she would sometimes smuggle one of her partners back home. 'Well, what about what *you* bring into the house?' Joan retorted when Rudolf complained.

Hearing from Alice that Joan had asked to be given a list of everyone who visited the house, Rudolf told the Goslings that he was now con-vinced that Joan was working for the CIA. Finding her too controlling, he had begun looking for reasons to discredit her – not easy, given the parameters of her job. Chauffeur, cook, social secretary, unofficial man-ager and accountant, Joan would even – to please Rudolf – accompany him to dubious bars and go over and 'be nice to' anyone who took his fancy. So integral was she to his life that one demented fan, suspecting they were having an affair, took her revenge by telephoning and abusing Joan throughout the night and dumping rubbish on her doorstep. Although theirs had always been an explosive working relationship – 'We had our spats when I threatened to leave and *did* leave' – Rudolf had come to resent his dependence on Joan and decided one day to bring things categorically to an end. As Maude recalled:

He'd asked her to do something which she felt was unfair, which it probably was, and she said, 'I'm sick of you: I'm leaving,' and he said 'All right.' She still had the key to Fife Road and the next night walked in, saying, 'I've come back.' He just looked at her, 'No you haven't. You said you'd gone.' And everyone thought, of course, Rudolf would *never* manage, because she did everything for him. But he did.

And the reason he did was Claire, a French cook-housekeeper whom he had brought to London from his house in La Turbie. She had originally been living in Los Angeles, working for friends of Jean and Maggie Louis, when Rudolf persuaded her to return to France with him. Plump, motherly and very respectable, she adored '*le Patron*', always serving him first at dinner parties even though she had been told that this was not quite *comme il faut*. 'She was a real peasant, so Rudolf and she understood each other,' said Wallace Potts. 'She took everything in her stride, and Rudolf would put up with things from Claire that he wouldn't from anyone else.' Maude Gosling agrees. 'She was very strict, but Rudolf respected her so much, and she'd do anything for him. She was a darling. She'd even sew the elastics on his shoes.' Cooking French country cuisine – *petite marmite*, *ris de veau*, *île flottante* – Claire was able to tempt Rudolf to try more adventurous dishes than his usual blue steak. And although she spoke only 'baby's English' when she arrived, she was wonderfully good-natured about having to order every ingredient by telephone (the shops in East Sheen's main street being more than a fifteen-minute walk away).

When Rudi van Dantzig came to stay towards the end of 1969 he was amazed that Rudolf had chosen such an isolated place to live, remarking to Claire that he could never find a London cab-driver willing to bring him back at night. 'That's why he can't find anyone to run his house,' she replied. 'It's a voyage around the world each day.' Rudolf had invited his 'new discovery', as Ashton called him, to live at Fife Road for two months while he created his first work for the Royal Ballet. In case Rudi needed help and advice, Rudolf had introduced him to the Goslings, his 'parents in the West', with whom he often stayed if it was too late to get back to Fife Road. Their Kensington house had a self-contained apartment that was always available for Rudolf, and was filled with his own antiques, records and books. At Maude and Nigel's suggestion Rudi moved in, soon followed by Toer, who used one of the rooms as a studio to construct the set he was designing for the new ballet.

The commission, the first in the company's repertory created entirely as a showcase for Rudolf, was all his own doing. 'If I don't hunt down the choreographers myself, nothing happens.' Called *Ropes of Time* after a line in a poem, again by Hans Lodeizen, it was meant to 'communicate a little message for Rudolf – that there comes an end'. Rudolf had asked for an electronic score not only intending to 'dust-down' Royal Ballet audiences but wanting the English dancers to share an experience from which he had just benefited. 'They'll learn what listening *means*.' Apart from stipulating that he should have no understudy and that all the other figures be secondary, Rudolf had left the casting to Rudi (expressing surprise, all the same, that he did not intend to use Margot – 'Then success with the English is guaranteed').

Antoinette Sibley was chosen to be the driving force behind the protagonist at the height of his powers, and Monica Mason the ebbing current as his talent goes into decline.

The first week of rehearsals Rudolf was 'amenability itself'; just the fact of being on home territory gave him the confidence he had lacked in Amsterdam. He made it clear to everyone in the studio that he considered the ballet as much his enterprise as Rudi's and, while they were watching rehearsals, it was often he who took charge, clapping his hands to stop if he was dissatisfied or even demonstrating a step to the dancers. 'I was forced to say: "No, Rudolf, that's not the idea . . . I want it like *this*."' As far as Rudi was concerned, his choreography still did not come naturally to Rudolf. 'It is like somebody who speaks a different language and you can always hear the mother tongue underneath. I could always detect the classical training and the classical dancer that Rudolf was. It always came through and he never really, for me, grasped totally the modern side.'

It crossed Rudi's mind that Rudolf was sitting in on group rehearsals to keep track of how much time was left for him. 'Don't worry, Rudolf, you'll be in the action from beginning till end.' 'But surely,' countered Rudolf, 'not the way it was in *Monument*, where I only stood and watched.' There was a time – in early performances of *Giselle*, for instance – when Rudolf would make a passage of stillness as dramatic as even the most climactic outburst of dance, but now he felt impelled to be moving nonstop. 'If I don't have steps . . . I will collapse and I will not be able to recover my full strength at the end of the ballet.'* The first real difficulties came during rehearsals with Sibley. It was the fact that she was Dowell's partner – 'a special challenge to Rudolf' – that Rudi believed had made him tense and distant, deliberately allowing movements to go wrong. 'No, no, not at all,' Antoinette insists. 'It was me . . . *panicking*.' As a dancer motivated entirely by the music – 'music no later than Stravinsky, with tune and rhythm' – she had been shocked by Boerman's score, a jarring din that sounded to her as if milk bottles were being thrown at a mirror.

* Rudolf told a *Newsweek* reporter in May 1970, 'What I have done is develop a number of devices to preserve myself. I know, for example, that I dance best when I am on to my second wind. So before the actual performance I go through every move that I will make onstage . . . so that my body is near exhaustion. Then, when the body is under great stress it will move despite any mental block.'

That expression 'Does my head in' was made for this situation. I loved the idea of doing a modern ballet and *adored* Rudi van Dantzig, and so I was determined to find a way. I could see Rudolf and Monica lapping it up, which made me even more frustrated, but I just couldn't cope, I couldn't fight it any more. It had started sending me over the edge, and I went into a deep depression.

On her doctor's orders Antoinette flew off for a holiday by the sea, and Diana Vere, a young soloist Rudolf clearly enjoyed helping, took her place. He himself vanished on a number of occasions to perform with other companies, and, unable to proceed without the focal point of his ballet, Rudi was forced to insist on a second cast. Provocatively, Ashton chose Anthony Dowell, a deliberate slight as far as Rudolf was concerned. On his return he sullenly retaliated, marking rather than dancing the steps full out until in despair Rudi called for Dowell to take over. It was Rudolf who strode back into the centre. 'Is your name Anthony?' Rudi snapped like a tetchy schoolmaster.

I had never felt so distant from him as at that moment, and I felt dreadful having to put him in his place like that, in front of the whole group but, on the other hand, I knew it had to happen sometime. At the end of the afternoon I informed Ashton that Rudolf had departed with the announcement that I would not be seeing him at rehearsals any more. Ashton chuckled. 'He'll be back and otherwise you can just go on with Dowell.'

An attempt at a *rapprochement* was made by Maude, who invited the two to dinner at Victoria Road, but the mood was strained, and Rudi went downstairs early to bed. A little while later Rudolf knocked on the door, asking if they could talk. They decided to go for a walk in nearby Kensington Gardens, each speaking in turn of the pressures they felt they were under. The Royal Ballet, Rudolf said, still considered him a stranger, 'a barbaric intruder, a threat to their male principals'. But this of course was no longer the case: it was younger forces such as Dowell who were now threatening to overshadow him – the theme of *Ropes of Time*. The ballet illustrates the situation with a technical trial of strength between Rudolf and two young soloists (David Ashmole and Graham Fletcher) who step in after he has been dancing for twenty-five minutes and appear to outshine him. The idea was to show the star 'gradually giving up his battle to be the best', but naturally this was unthinkable for Rudolf. 'I shall do everything in my power to be better than they are,' he announced, to Rudi's dismay.

There were many more arguments, and it was always Rudolf who was the first to make amends, suggesting lunch, or a shopping trip to Portobello Road, by which time the whole atmosphere would have changed. 'Nothing stayed long with him. I could keep it up two weeks. He forgot it the next morning . . . he didn't have this sort of smouldering on that I have.' Nevertheless Rudi remained upset that Rudolf, having agreed in the studio not to overintensify his interpretation, would revert to doing it his own way onstage. 'He struggled, he really tried to do what I asked – what we wanted to do together – but in the end, he was thinking of his fans.'

The audience gave *Ropes of Time* a frenzied ovation, showering daffodils down on Rudolf, who 'took the tribute like a gladiator', but the critics were almost unanimously disparaging. Although the ballet was, they conceded, an adventurous new direction for an Establishment company to take, it had proved in the main a failure. The chief complaint was the unrelentingly tortured nature of Rudolf's dancing and emoting – 'so similar to the performances Nureyev gave in *Paradise Lost* and *Pelléas et Mélisande* that one suspects he imposes too much self will on his choreographers', wrote Mary Clarke, who was not alone in being bored.

The American reviews would be equally harsh, and, as if anticipating Arlene Croce's reproach that such experiments were 'the most wanton distortions of a great classical dancer's technique and style', Rudolf returned – albeit briefly – to his Russian heritage. He had been asked to mount his *Don Quixote* for the Australian Ballet, a company that, with Sadler's Wells veterans Peggy van Praagh and Robert Helpmann at the helm, combined precise English schooling with the Australian dancers' innate extroversion and vitality – the very qualities his original Viennese cast had lacked. 'He could see the Aussies really having the guts,' said Lucette Aldous, a tiny, racy antipodean then in the Royal Ballet, whom Helpmann – 'my Svengali' – wanted for the part of Kitri. The two went out to Fife Road to visit Rudolf, who, having seen Lucette sparkle in the Ballet Rambert's staging of the Bolshoi version, already had her in mind as his ballerina. 'He was so sweet and polite, and said, "Do you mind doing mine?"'

While essentially a vehicle for three stars, Rudolf's *Don Quixote* would also spotlight a trio of unknowns. Bypassing the company's *premier danseur* (Garth Welch), he 'zoomed right in' on late-starter Kelvin Coe, who although lacking the foundation of training was very good-looking with a soft, youthful quality, 'a bit like Anthony Dowell'. Rudolf gave Kelvin the Espada, the second male virtuoso role, and as his partner cast beautiful, sexy Marilyn Rowe whom, together with another outstandingly gifted corps de ballet dancer, Gailene Stock, he went out of his way to push. (Both were subsequently promoted 'purely because of Rudolf'.) 'He was on your tail the whole time,' recalled Gailene, who had been performing an *entrechat six* with great gusto 'hoping he wouldn't notice that it wasn't a true six,' when Rudolf, watching from the wings, exploded, 'This is *entrechat piss!*' 'No other guest artist ever took that much interest in the company. Even in ballets that weren't his.'

Between rehearsals one day Rudolf's Australian personal assistant, Roger Myers, came up to him looking unusually disturbed. He had been asked by the management to break the news to Rudolf that his 'teacher, friend, father figure, mentor from the Kirov' was dead. On the evening of 20 March 1970 Alexander Ivanovich had gone for his favourite walk over the Fontanka Bridge towards the Five Corners junction, where, like *Crime and Punishment*'s Marmeladov, who also frequented those streets, he was struck by a fatal heart attack and fell to the ground. 'He died instantly,' Dimitri Filatov said. 'But it was terrible, because he lay in the rain for so long.' The next morning, Baryshnikov, stopping off for breakfast at Rossi Street as usual, met a Vaganova teacher leaving the Pushkins' apartment. Startled by her 'upside down' face, he asked immediately what was wrong. 'She pointed behind her and didn't have to say anything. I just knew.' For Baryshnikov the shock was too much to bear. Battering his fists against the wall and door of the Pushkins' apartment, he smashed right through the glass partition; when a friend met him later in the day, both his hands were bandaged.

Rudolf's own response was complete incredulity – 'What? When? Where was he?' he demanded. And then he simply crumpled. 'The only thing I could do was to just take him in my arms and comfort him,' Myers recalled. 'I just held him in my arms and he cried.' But although it was cathartic to be able to mourn Alexander Ivanovich the way he could not his own father, Rudolf's grief was compounded by guilt and regret. It was not so much his sexual betrayal as the knowledge that his defection had quite literally broken his teacher's heart.

In May, Wallace Potts heard that Rudolf was in New York and had been trying to reach him. He was now living in Los Angeles, having been accepted at USC Film School after submitting 'what would now be called a pop video' – a visual realization of the Beatles song 'Maxwell's Silver Hammer'. He had driven out to California with a friend, Bronte 'Myron' Woodward, whom he had persuaded to try his hand at screenwriting. 'I told him he had as much talent as any of the people I'd met in Hollywood.' (Woodward wrote the screenplay of *Grease* in 1978.) Myron, who had taken Rudolf's call, had written down a number Wallace recognized as Monique's. When he called, Rudolf himself answered, saying immediately, 'Would you like to come to New York? I'm here in town.'

> I was in the middle of editing a film, but I had a Super 8 machine like a little rinkydink toy, which I could take with me. So this time we actually got along quite well, because I had something of my own to do. I remember sitting in his dressing room at the Met editing while he was onstage; I had these strips of film taped to his dressing-room wall.

When the week was up, Rudolf asked Wallace if he would like to join him for three months in Europe. Never having travelled outside the United States, he was tempted and hesitant at the same time. 'But since we had got on so well in New York, I thought, OK, well, let's give it a try.' After going back to California to finish his film, Wallace took the Royal Ballet charter plane from New York to London, and then flew on to meet Rudolf in Milan. Although it was a disappointing start – 'Milan is not the most glamorous place and it was very hot and humid' – they were driven through the French Alps to La Turbie, where they spent three days. 'Dear Folks, Have never seen anything like it!' Wallace exclaimed on a postcard home. Their chauffeur as far as Turin had been 'a crazy Greek girl', Lisa Sottilis, a friend of Rudolf's who had a jewellery business in Milan making Dalí-esque brooches out of twenty-four-carat gold. She was dark-skinned, striking and self-dramatizing – a Mediterranean version of Monique van Vooren, whom they also saw when they were in Belgium: 'By the time we got to London, I'd had it with the jet set. When Nigel and Maude came to dinner I was openly hostile to them. *So* sarcastic. Then I realized to my shame that they were not like Rudolf's fancy friends; that they were dear, decent people, intelligent and a lot of fun too.'

They were due to spend the second half of August in Paris. Hollywood producer Harry Saltzman was backing a multimillion-dollar feature film on Nijinsky, and had cast Rudolf in the title role opposite Paul Scofield as Diaghilev. Ever since he came to the West, people had been wanting to put Rudolf on the screen. One was Maggie Louis, who in a letter dated 20 May 1964, wrote that she and Loretta Young had been evangelizing about him to one of the founders of the Technicolor corporation:

He is *more* than interested. If we can find the right story he will finance & produce a film for you. He is a man of great taste so it won't be the usual Hollywood sequined junk. If you run across a story that interests you please let me know right away. Meantime Loretta & I will be reading everything in sight as a possible vehicle for you.

Also in 1964 Luchino Visconti gave a dinner at London's Savoy Hotel in Rudolf's honour, the purpose, according to French actor Jean-Claude Brialy, was to discuss his own venture on the life of Nijinsky. In Brialy's account, Rudolf discourteously stood up and left after about ten minutes, dropping a tiny piece of paper on the actor's plate as he passed. '*Je t'attends*,' it said, followed by a telephone number. A sexual assignation (which duly followed) was then more interesting to Rudolf than a film project, and there were other occasions on which he resorted to 'all kinds of hindering' to forestall the possibility of making a movie. The reason, he said, was Margot, who had convinced him that 'as with Moira Shearer and Robert Helpmann', it wouldn't do his dancing any good: 'I thought if you do film it's immediate success. It never came to my mind that it could be terrible flop . . . The film will be too enormous; that I will not be able – with this gigantic fame – to fit into Royal Ballet. I wanted to be part of the company; on a par with all of them; and I thought that would have been great threat to me as an artist.'

Older now, and less idealistic, Rudolf had reconciled himself to the idea of appearing in a film, but still insisted on the right to choose the director, the scriptwriter, 'stars – everything'. One of the names proposed by Saltzman was Herbert Ross, who 'raised money in no time', but Rudolf had more ambitious ideas. He wanted Franco Zeffirelli (in the summer of '65 they had met in Rome with the playwright Edward Albee and talked about making a film together); and he even considered Ingmar Bergman. ('Nobody delved into dark side of human psyche as Bergman.') But since the autumn of 1968 the project had been in the hands of Jerome Robbins, choreographer and director of *West Side Story*, who had approached writers of the stature of Harold Pinter, and spent a considerable amount of time developing strategies of his own. The 'really interpretive impressionistic film style' he envisaged may have been too uncommercial for Saltzman, producer of the Bond films, though Rudolf claims what 'killed the subject' was Robbins's insistence on taking nine months to film it. Then in London one evening Saltzman took Rudolf to meet Ken Russell over dinner and showed him the director's television documentaries. Rudolf already admired much of Russell's work, particularly his Debussy film, but did not like him personally. When Russell launched into a lecture on how he would have to commit totally to the project, cancelling his New York season and 'giving up everything for the picture', Rudolf, feeling that he was being patronized, decided to bring things to an end: 'I sent him away. Packing. Because I saw Isadora Duncan [*The Loves of Isadora*] . . . And he treated her . . . *ungallantly*. And I thought, well, that's not possible – what is he going to do with Nijinsky? So he was fired.'

Finally it was the turn of Tony Richardson. Oscar-winning director of *Tom Jones*, he was better known as a man of the theatre, an innovator, whose Royal Court production of John Osborne's *Look Back in Anger* had been the catalyst for a revolution on the British stage. With Paul Scofield secured for the Nijinsky venture, Richardson presented Edward Albee[*] with an outline of visual ideas on which to base a screenplay, and sought the advice of Lincoln Kirstein, who had collaborated with Romola Nijinsky on the biography of her husband. In a letter to Richard Buckle, Kirstein airs his views on Richardson's 'sort of half-assed proposal': 'I can't do much more than disapprove of Nureyev . . . Have you seen DRUGSTORE [MIDNIGHT] COWBOY in which Dustin Hoffman plays Ratso Rizzo? I think he would be the perfect Nijinsky; he is an actor, not a dancer; he is small and very intense and he doesn't look like Nureyev who doesn't look like Nijinsky.'

There is a sophisticated dance intelligence to Albee's script (the description, for example, of the Maryinsky's *prima ballerina assoluta*, Mathilda Kschessinskaya, doing a 'very old-fashioned, almost pre-Petipa variation'), but what is unmistakably Kirstein's imprint is its acknowledgement of the revolutionary importance of Nijinsky's choreography. 'Rudi liked it a lot,' Albee says,[†] and when they met in

[*] In 1973 Tony Richardson directed the film of Albee's Pulitzer-winning play *A Delicate Balance*, with Paul Scofield starring opposite Katharine Hepburn.
[†] To Christopher Hampton, who was brought in at a later point to write a more acceptable Nijinsky script, Rudolf said, disloyally, that the Albee version had been 'terrible', his reason

London they discovered they shared the same views about how the dancer should be portrayed on screen. The main premise, in Rudolf's opinion, was that Nijinsky's descent into madness was caused by the end of his affair with Diaghilev: 'What is interesting to me was their sort of abnormal relationship, which produced very interesting things. The result was very beautiful and everlasting. Then there is the normal relationship, which produced zero.'

In its frank depiction of the love between two men, Albee's script is way ahead of its time – and this was the problem. Suddenly, in the middle of June, the producers announced that they were pulling out: 'There was not enough money for the film.' Wallace wrote to tell his parents that their plans had changed. 'Contracts not signed, Tony Richardson, the director dismissed, and Saltzman the producer upset by the stock market decline, so the film may be off although a million dollars has already been sunk into it.'*

Nijinsky, as Albee and Rudolf imagined it, could have been extraordinary – not only the first mainstream movie about gay love but a chilling study of a disintegrating mind. In keeping with Rudolf's greatest achievements, it was intended to be a breaking through of barriers, a trajectory into the future, but Hollywood was not ready for it.

A week or two earlier, scouting for locations, Tony Richardson had gone to Leningrad with Renzo Mongiardino and Lee Radziwill. Through Xenia, Rudolf had asked Liuba Romankova, who could speak English, to entertain his friends, even though he must have known the possible consequences for her. As a scientist at Leningrad's Ioffe Physico-Technical Institute she was forbidden to make contact with foreigners without special consent. Violation of this rule could put her whole career in jeopardy, as the certain withdrawal of her 'certificate of secrecy' would render her unable to collaborate on projects with other research institutes. The only way to obtain permission was through the First Department, the company's KGB division, but a written request had to be sent to Moscow's Big House, where it could sit for 'more than a week, sometimes a month'. She decided to take

---

being that there was 'too much Diaghilev'. When they met in New York to discuss the project, Hampton promised Rudolf that Nijinsky would be on screen from beginning to end. Once again, however, nothing came of it.

* Exactly ten years later Herbert Ross directed his own Nijinsky film produced by his wife, Nora Kaye, with Alan Bates as Diaghilev and George de la Peña as Nijinsky – a venture considered to be a 'brave attempt at a gay love story, but not brave enough to work'.

the risk.* After leaving Lee a note at the Hotel Astoria, they met later in the lobby, together with the 'two handsome, very nice young men'. Over dinner in the Astoria restaurant, the visitors plied her with questions about the cultural life and sights of Leningrad while she, in turn, asked eagerly about Rudolf's life in the West.

Lee said to me that he is OK, that he is charming, amazing, wonderful, that he is a great dancer, that she loves him very much . . . She told me that Rudolf is cheerful, but at the end of any evening party he suddenly becomes sad and begins to gaze off into the distance and she feels that he is very far from the place he is. 'Damned Slavs!' she said. 'Just like my husband. When they are sitting and do not react to the surroundings I know that they are mentally in their homeland at that moment.'

The next evening Xenia joined the four of them for a performance at the Kirov and afterwards they all walked together along the Neva embankment, which was lit with the pearly fluorescence peculiar to Leningrad's White Nights. With no shops, neon signs or tall buildings, it was, Liuba could tell, a very special cityscape for the three foreigners. 'Lee was full of emotions, and there were tears in her eyes as she spoke of how she understands Rudik better now, how impossible it must be to forget this wonderful city and never be able to return.' Lee would later describe that time in Leningrad as one of the most memorable of her life, telling writer David Daniel, 'I know I never would have had the same feeling . . . had it not been for these charming friends of his. They showed such great love for him and concern over his well-being.' She could see how much Xenia, in particular, worshipped Rudolf from her hunger for details about his development in the West. 'She was concerned about his dancing in modern works, really anxious that it might destroy his knees and ruin him for classical ballet. She *begged* me to persuade him against that.' Once so extroverted and glamorous, Xenia had grown thin, frail and withdrawn, and seemed to the

---

* Sure enough, having spent the weekend with the foreigners, Liuba was summoned to the First Department on Monday, and interrogated by a KGB officer. 'He began to ask me about Lee's companions, about the topic of our talks, many different questions. But I repeated over and over again that we talked about ballet and about the arts generally. Then I was asked to write a statement. They were angry but could not do anything with me. I was not punished, but for many years I had no promotion and did not receive a permission to participate in any international conferences because I had become a "suspicious" person.'

ultra-chic American 'a vulnerable creature' who looked much older than her years, with noticeably bad teeth. Parting from her, Lee could sense 'Mme Pushkin's desperation, almost, to know about Rudolf and whether he had been corrupted'.

Rudolf, however, settling for the first time into a stable domestic relationship, had never been less degenerate. He hardly drank, having switched from vodka to white wine. 'He'd mellowed, and I'd adjusted,' says Wallace, who had found ways to deal with his lover's extreme demands, treating any outburst with indulgence and good humour. Maude Gosling remembered how they would play together like children, 'Wallace big and strong and galloping round the room with Rudolf on his back – both collapsing with laughter and falling on to the sofa'. They found they had similar cultural tastes, although Wallace admits that it was Rudolf who first educated him in world cinema and theatre, taking him to see everything from an Ingmar Bergman season to Chekhov and Noh plays. Expected to attend most Nureyev performances, he also began learning about ballet – 'I was like John Q. Public at first' – but sensed that it was a relief in a way for Rudolf not to have the kind of esoteric battles of the Erik years. And while Rudolf, he says, would always be 'really wired' after a performance, this was something Wallace knew exactly how to defuse: 'Half the time our sex was mechanical – more like a release for him – and he quite separated it from any feelings of tenderness or romance. Afterwards he used to read, and I would snuggle up until we fell asleep. He used to call me "Boo-boo" [after the TV bear] because he liked the sound of it.'

That summer each had an opportunity to meet the other's ex-lover. In July of the previous year, Rudolf had heard from Erik for the first time since they parted:

> Just a little note to say hello . . . It just occurred to me that this will be the first summer we are not in France together, it feels kind of sad but maybe it's the beginning of something new . . . I think of you very often and hope that I sometimes am a good thought to you too . . .
>
> With much love,
> Erik

Six months later a few more lines arrived: 'I am tired, bored, I could scream . . . so let us dance dance dance, bless you, as ever.' Erik was eager to establish a friendship without ties, but would this unfamiliar equilibrium withstand an encounter with Rudolf's new partner? Wallace admits how nervous they both were the night Erik came to Fife Road for dinner:

> I had heard all these stories about how much Erik drank, and how mean and vicious he could get. Well, I was so relieved when he came to the house that night. I really liked his wit and his sarcasm; I thought, Oh, thank God for some New York cynicism! We got along very well – in fact, at the time we had more to talk about than Rudolf and I had.

Ed Barnum was also in England in July. He had been 'quite hysterical' when Wallace first went on tour with Rudolf, threatening to shoot himself unless he returned immediately to Atlanta. 'I came back to find all my clothes in the street. Literally.' Ed, who always carried a gun in a holster – 'he had a lot of enemies' – was equally furious when Wallace and Myron Woodward moved to Los Angeles, even though they had never been more than soulmates. And when Myron's car careered into the woods across the street one day (someone had cut the brake lines), they both immediately assumed that Ed had somehow engineered the accident. But however apprehensive Rudolf might have been about a rendezvous with Wallace's volatile friend, he nevertheless offered to take him out to dinner. It was a shrewd move. In his note of thanks, Ed wrote, 'I'm convinced now that Beanie [Wallace's nickname] is happier with you than he's ever been – this makes me happy.'*

Towards the end of July the Kirov came to London for a six-week season at the Royal Festival Hall. In the six years since Yuri Grigorovich had left the company for the Bolshoi in 1964, its repertory had badly deteriorated, with *Giselle* the only complete ballet being shown on the tour. It was the Kirov stars – Alla Osipenko, Yuri Soloviev, Natalia Makarova – who carried the company, but no one generated more excitement than the new twenty-two-year-old Pushkin protégé, Mikhail Baryshnikov. No photograph of the dancer, or even a listing of

---

* Some years later Barnum was arrested on a murder charge. Having found a boy squatting in one of his apartments he claimed to have shot him in self-defence, and was released without charge. He himself met an early death following an arson attack on one of his properties. It was a Victorian house on a hill, 'not unlike the one in *Psycho*', recalls Wallace. 'Ed was in a second-storey bedroom with a boy, but when the trick jumped out the window, he went back and burned to death in the flames. It was real Southern Gothic stuff.'

his name, appeared in the programme, but word had spread quickly, and in response to public demand a solo was added – LeonidYakobson's *Vestris*, which had been created especially for him. (Baryshnikov had won the gold medal when he danced this at the 1969 Moscow competition; the legendary Maya Plisetskaya, one of the judges, had given him thirteen out of a maximum twelve points.) Rudolf, who had gone with Margot to several Baryshnikov performances, was determined to find a way of meeting him, and as Chinko Rafique was Misha's Vaganova contemporary and a mutual friend, Rudolf prevailed on him to act as go-between.

The idea of spending a day with Rudolf Nureyev – whatever the repercussions – was too momentous an opportunity to turn down. During the last couple of years Pushkin had spoken at length about his ex-pupil – 'mostly about his work, never about him as human being' – and granted this confidence to Misha alone. (The framed photograph next to the dinner table of Rudolf in *La Bayadère* would be missing if any other student were there.) Managing to evade the 'four goons tailing him', Misha was waiting for Chinko when he arrived early in the morning at the Strand Palace Hotel to drive him to East Sheen. Rudolf, Chinko recalls, was noticeably playing the 'grand seigneur' as he received the younger artist. Misha, by contrast, was 'like a little boy – impressed but determined not to show it'. As he was led round 'this big, beautiful English house', he was struck by how sparsely furnished it was, with no pictures on the walls, only books piled up on the floor. 'It was an interesting kind of emptiness . . . almost like nobody lives there, and at the same time it was him.' The atmosphere was warm, however, and he was made to feel very relaxed as they spoke in Russian about the school, the theatre, people they both knew, making 'jokes about this, jokes about that'.

They sat down to lunch with Wallace and Chinko. Misha stayed sober because he had a performance that night, and Rudolf 'got sort of emotional and drank this bottle of wine'. Later the two went outside and lay on the grass talking intently about different techniques. Misha, who had taken a few classes with the Royal Ballet, wanted Rudolf to explain why the barre practice had been so long. 'Because with Russian exercises, it's very short.You have to really warm up before the class [with the Kirov] because the barre is thirty minutes.' Rudolf then took him upstairs to a huge walk-in closet. Having sent Misha a few of his costumes when he first joined the Kirov, Rudolf was eager to show off his whole collection and to demonstrate the best way to construct a costume.

He was pointing things out . . . putting a few on me . . . because Erik was teaching him to build the costumes. You know, that you could lift the arm and nothing goes here . . . it's really the set and inner belt and all that kind of stuff which makes – sits around your torso so tight that it complements the line, and at the same time you could lift the arm very freely.

They were standing, talking in the master bedroom, when Chinko arrived to take Misha back into town. 'Rudolf being *wicked* as ever had pulled out all these gay magazines and strewn them across his enormous double bed. He was looking sideways at them interested to know if they would spark something in little Mikhail Baryshnikov.' Misha himself has no memory of this; only how touched he was when, on parting, Rudolf gave him an album of Michelangelo drawings and a scarf as a keepsake. He would later reciprocate by sending Rudolf a book from Russia with a note saying that he often remembered their meeting. It was to be another four years before the dancer would defect from the Kirov, but on 4 September, the penultimate day of the London season, it was announced that Natalia Makarova had decided to stay in the West. Rudolf's immediate response was complete dismay: 'Oh fuck!' he exclaimed to Nigel Gosling, who called to break the news, believing like Xenia that 'everyone will think he had something to do with her leaving', that now it was even less likely he would ever see his family again.

At the end of the summer Wallace went back to film school in Los Angeles, having narrowly missed being called up for military service in Vietnam. 'On the new classification for the draft I was number 210, and the lottery got up to 195 that year.' Being apart after three months of living together was harder for Wallace, who had never been in love before and was completely consumed by it. Rudolf himself certainly missed having his faithful 'dog there to jump in [his] lap', but his feelings for Wallace were those of tenderness and need rather than the torturing kind of intensity that he had had with Erik.

Rudolf once told me how in love he had been with Erik, how at that time he thought about him day and night to the point that this obsession was destructive not only to his career but also to their developing a sustainable personal relationship. He said that was why he didn't want to repeat the same mistake with me. But who knows, maybe he wasn't really in love with me and was only trying to give me a reason why he showed very little passion towards me.

Terrified that he would be forgotten, and unable to focus on his film editing, Wallace wrote Rudolf a letter.

I spend all my time missing you . . . Each week is getting worse – I'm sure everyone around me simply thinks of me as a silly lovesick boy or as a bore. I don't know what to do. I've been editing the Sharon Tate movie, which absorbs some intellectual interests . . . but my spiritual life is lacking. It's you – I don't know why I didn't see it at the time. I was just afraid that if I gave myself completely to you and you dropped me I would have no place to go. That's my ego talking, and as you can see from reading it's gradually giving in. I love you so much that I'm physically aching. I want to come running back to you, but I linger here in the hope of being able to work . . . I don't think I can bear to wait till December to be with you, I love you too much.

Rudolf, by contrast, had never felt more creatively fulfilled. For the past few weeks he had been working with Jerome Robbins, whose recent New York City Ballet masterpiece, *Dances at a Gathering*, an inspired plotless visualization of Chopin's piano pieces, was being restaged for the Royal Ballet in October. Known to the world as the king of Broadway, Robbins was, in Rudolf's view, 'so wonderful', his modern reimagining of classics from Shakespeare's *Romeo and Juliet* as *West Side Story*, to Nijinsky's *Afternoon of a Faun* making him one of the century's most innovative choreographers. (As far as Rudolf was concerned, this was next best to collaborating with Balanchine.) Robbins's personal reputation, on the other hand, was notoriously unsound, one dancer after another describing the 'mental outrage and physical anguish' they experienced during rehearsals. 'We'd all heard the rumours,' says Antoinette Sibley, 'but I can only say that there was no chair throwing with us. We all worshipped Jerry, and would have killed ourselves for him.'

What was hard, she says – 'because we were all top principals and pretty busy' – was Robbins's insistence on the dancers learning several other numbers as well as their own. For Rudolf this was ballet heaven. As a student in Leningrad he had taught himself *Sleeping Beauty*'s Fairy variations, and now hoped that Robbins would consider him for one of the girls' solos. 'He'd fallen in love with it and felt that he could do it better,' the choreographer said with a smile. Sibley, who had been paired with Rudolf in *Étude, op. 25, no. 5*, remembers how he had also 'absolutely set his heart' on another duet (*Waltz, op. 42*), which they had nicknamed the 'giggle dance'. 'Whenever Monica [Mason] and

Mick [Michael Coleman] rehearsed it, he'd be there pulling me up, saying, "Come on, we must do this."'

As with most Robbins ballets, the dancers did not know until a day or two before the première which specific role was theirs, but Robbins claimed Rudolf 'accepted that very well'. Extreme perfectionism and a refusal to compromise were qualities common to the two men, and, as Lynn Seymour remarked, 'they really, really admired each other'. She noticed, all the same, how 'terribly respectful and cautious' the two artists were at first, 'both of them treading carefully'. There were certainly weaknesses to be concealed on either side. Robbins, who had always felt that he did not belong in ballet and gave classes in order to learn more about the classical lexicon, would have been immediately aware that Rudolf's knowledge of the genre was far greater than his own. The choreographer, on the other hand, was demanding qualities for *Dances at a Gathering* that went against everything for which Rudolf stood. Like Balanchine, Robbins expected his dancers to serve his work, deploring the old-fashioned concept of the heroic, self-thrusting star. 'I don't want the audience to know who you are until you're off the stage,' he warned Rudolf. And whereas much of the thrill of a Nureyev performance came from the audience being made aware of the difficulties and risk involved, Robbins never wanted the mechanics on display. 'Jerry just wanted us to be natural,' Sibley says. 'No turning out, no standing in positions, no breaking of the flow.' In his diary Robbins confided, 'Rudi – is Rudi – an artist – an animal – & a cunt. A child & a smart cookie, he was plenty to handle.' But to Rudolf's Royal Ballet colleagues his compliance in this ballet was unprecedented. 'He felt very subservient to the great masters,' Lynn Seymour remarks, and Anthony Dowell agrees: 'The ego didn't get in the way when he knew something was good.'[*]

When the curtain rose Rudolf was alone onstage. Wearing calf-boots he began walking contemplatively until, as if compelled by the music, he swayed, and gently swung into a solo – *Mazurka, op. 63, no. 2*. He was one of ten young dancers who performed, either alone

---

[*] There was, however, one near-showdown between choreographer and star on the afternoon of the opening night. Rudolf was insisting on wearing light-coloured tights because, as designer Joe Eula put it, 'you could see the veins in his cock and the cheeks of his arse better with white.' Robbins, who was determined that he should wear the tights Eula had made for him ('the earth colour was the whole point – the guy *was* part of the earth'), went into the dancer's dressing room before curtain up. 'Whatever transpired, Mr Nureyev came out in the brown tights' (Greg Lawrence, *Dance with Demons*).

or in groups of shifting numbers, moving spontaneously in space and seemingly unaware of the audience. Described by Robbins as a ballet that celebrates 'love & being & togetherness', *Dances at a Gathering* had no story but was delicately brushed with touches of character and emotion, the changing of partners suggesting a community of friends or lovers. Folk gestures in the movements, like the fragments of tunes and rhythms in the music, invoked Poland, Chopin's homeland, but never appeared grafted on. In the words of Robbins's biographer Deborah Jowitt:

> There are heel-and-toe steps; feet stamping; heels clicking together; hands placed on hips; men dancing in a line, their arms across one another's shoulders . . . But these mingle with classical steps that have been eased to look natural and unposed. No man plants himself to spin, and women rise on to pointe as if such an act were the natural consequence of drawing breath. Women fall into men's arms and are spiralled up to sit on a shoulder without visible effort on either dancer's part.

Part of an ensemble and yet all having the chance to make their own impact, the dancers were, in Sibley's term, 'individual equals'. Rudolf, it was agreed, had never been better in a contemporary work. 'He conforms, but he is also the catalyst that brings an extra ounce of performance out of his colleagues,' commented the *Dancing Times*. This time, instead of feeling threatened by an element of competitiveness with Anthony Dowell, Rudolf clearly revelled in their duet's playful combat. For sheer deftness and academic clarity of line, Dowell was technically the better of the two, but Rudolf gave each movement a unique sense of weight described by one critic as 'a feeling of the muscularity of the dance and what sculptors call "mass"'. This quality was also shared by the role's creator, Edward Villella.

After some sixty minutes the dancers all came together onstage as if, having gone through the vicissitudes of their various relationships, they were returning to their roots. To Sibley it meant, 'We're all still alive, we're all still on the earth, which is the important thing – the earth.' Robbins wanted them to imagine that 'it's a place you're coming back to years later that you danced in once'. The gesture that symbolizes this – the most evocative in the ballet – took on additional meaning for London audiences watching Rudolf in the role. 'He knelt down,' said Maude Gosling, 'and when he put his hand on the ground it brought tears to your eyes because you knew exactly what he was feeling.'

Even though there are upbeat elements of Robbins's musical comedy work in *Dances at a Gathering*, it was a ballet that marked a departure for him, being not, as he put it, 'punch & sharp & dramatically or theatrically effective . . . [but] romantic, lyric, sensuous & delicate'. It was a rarity for Rudolf, too. For the first time he looked as if he really belonged to the Royal Ballet, triumphantly achieving his wish to be 'part of the company; on a par with all of them'. Robbins was delighted. On the night of the première, admitting that he found it difficult to express himself when they spoke together, he wrote Rudolf a note of gratitude:

Dear Rudi – *October* 20 1970

First of all I thank you very deeply for your huge contribution to 'Dances'. You achieved all I asked of you and more: understanding your place in the entire piece – and delivering your dances beautifully! Your modesty and enjoyment that is so evident in your performance is a remarkable and recognized part of the work you have done for me, the ballet, and mostly for yourself. I hope we will work together again and soon.

14 CAMERA FRONT, CAMERA SIDE

Rudolf's close affinity with the Royal Ballet did not last long. He spent the rest of the year working with other companies, including the Australian Ballet, with which he guested from December 1970 until March 1971 and danced sixty-eight of the company's seventy perform-ances while on an American tour. Then, without taking a break, he flew straight to Brussels to begin work with the choreographer Maurice Béjart. Since its creation in 1960, Béjart's Ballet of the Twentieth Century had been regarded as one of the world's most exciting contemporary troupes, its 'total-theatre concept of dance' performed by youngsters whose energy, athleticism and street fashion – 'the boys in their blue-jeans and long, sweat-matted hair' – attracting huge audiences new to ballet. To the dancers, Béjart, a philosophy graduate, was 'a genius – a marvellous theatre man'. And with his piercing, Mephistophelian features and hypnotic presence, he had the qualities of a cult leader, relating to each person in a way Robert Denvers describes as almost psychic. 'Working with Béjart meant becoming metaphysically involved. It was like being in the Actors Studio: he was pulling out of you as a performer what you are as a person. We were his family, a very tight-knit set.' The question was whether Rudolf, himself a guru to young dancers – 'the guru of classicism' – would submit to Béjart's method of mind control.

The two had met socially several times, one occasion in February 1969 being particularly memorable to the choreographer. 'Rudi was *very* depressed, and felt that what he was trying to do was not understood by people in Europe.' Their conversation preyed on Béjart's mind, and a few days later he wrote Rudolf a letter:

Rudi,
    Please, you are killing yourself and the other night I was really sorry because you deserve better than that life of yours.
    Go back to Russia, be yourself, a wonderful young boy made for work and creation, made to be happy . . . and you are not. Go back to Russia.

Rudi I have the feeling you are a real person . . . and believe me I have met very few . . . a real person! Your name, your fame, your money all this is nothing . . . Keep your purity of Russian boy and don't let them spoil you with their money and their publicity.

I don't know if I can help you, I just want to come to another human being and say 'you are great and strong, don't be scared and sad, go your way . . . but the real way and spit on that world of nonsense around you.'

I am not very clever to write in english, but I have to because when we meet it is allways in a situation where it is difficult to talk.

Courage. Je vous embrasse de tout mon coeur et le jour où vraiment vous avez besoin de moi, je ferai cette heure là, ce que je pourrai pour vous aider.

Ou alors quittez ces pays stupides et retournez chez vous, en Russie, vous pouvez les aider et c'est la seule chose importante, aider les gens qui le méritent.

Maurice

This was a bleak time in Béjart's own life: his diary entry before their 21 February meeting elliptically notes, '*Agitation. Vide. Paresse. Absence de Dieu. Quitter Paris, vite.*' And on 22 February he writes, 'Why seek to save others if I am not capable of saving myself?' And yet the choreographer did genuinely believe in the corrupting power of money and success – 'that world of nonsense' – which he saw engulfing Rudolf. To Denvers he was like a Lutheran priest preaching the necessity of 'suffering, sweat and work. He was the complete opposite of Roland Petit. Both were French, but one was hieratic and communistic, the other light and social, loving shopping and beauty, Yves St Laurent, parties, Folies-Bergères . . . Béjart had *absolutely* no patience with any of that.'

Nor had Béjart ever condoned the kind of glamour brought by big-name guest artists, although just recently things had changed. After a falling-out with Balanchine, the New York City Ballet's ballerina Suzanne Farrell had joined the Brussels company, and for the first time 'Béjart fell in love with stars.' To the New York dance intelligentsia Farrell's departure was incomprehensible. Why forfeit virtual ownership of leading roles in some three dozen Balanchine ballets and choose 'an alien and diseased repertory' whose main purpose was to provoke football-style frenzy from a mass audience? It was, in Joan Acocella's words, 'as if Farrell had run off with a biker'. And yet it was not long before a kind of osmosis took place. Accustomed to a young generation with 'come as you are' shreds of temperament and technique, Béjart could not fail to be influenced by one of the great classical artists of the age. Farrell herself, meanwhile, would eventually return to the New York City Ballet, having acquired what even Arlene Croce, the most strident Béjart-phobe of all, conceded to be a new, unaffected style. Now, clearly, was the moment for a Béjart/Nureyev collaboration, and although both choreographer and dancer were reluctant to make a direct approach, Rudolf urged Robert Denvers to intervene. 'Basically, I brokered it. I arranged for Rudolf to call me one afternoon when I knew that Béjart was going to be there in my apartment. I put him on the phone to Rudolf, and that's how the whole story started.'

True to form, Rudolf had enlisted more than one matchmaker. Trained in classical ballet, Italian dancer Paolo Bortoluzzi had joined Béjart's company at its inception, submitting to its rigid mandate – 'no other star than Béjart himself'. Lately, however, he had begun guesting with foreign ballet companies, achieving the duality of technique to which Rudolf himself aspired – the ability to dance a Petipa duet on the same programme with a modern piece. Exactly the same age, he and Rudolf became friends when they were performing at La Scala, Milan, and had subsequently met at each other's homes in Brussels and London. Having often discussed with Paolo the possibility of working with Béjart, Rudolf went out of his way to remind him to speak to the choreographer on his behalf. It worked, Béjart promising that he would create a pas de deux for the two of them 'if Nureyev will accept'.

An added attraction of the Ballet of the Twentieth Century was that Menia was now performing and teaching there. She and Rudolf had seen each other the year before, once again in Paris, where she was dancing Béjart's *Opus 5*. Having dyed her hair blonde, Menia was hardly recognizable except for the Vaganova imprint on her technique – the beautifully supple Russian back and wafting arms. After the performance they went to a restaurant with a group of Béjart dancers, one of whom was Menia's new husband, Jorge Lefebre. Also Cuban, and a choreographer of note, Lefebre had known Menia slightly in Havana, and fallen in love the previous summer, when he went back to mount a new piece for the National Ballet of Cuba and took her with him. The dark, Hispanic Lefebre was a handsome, macho figure, and Rudolf found him 'very *simpático*'. Lefebre was equally at ease, despite the fact that Menia had told him all about her 'history with Rudik'.*

Having absorbed a great deal from watching Pushkin at work, Menia was particularly gifted at teaching male dancers, and she taught the men's class every morning. 'She could charm the pants off you,' Denvers says. 'Seducing you to try out things you didn't know you were capable of. She's an excellent teacher and also very beautiful – which is rare.' The Béjart dancers noticed how close she and Rudolf were, but even so she stood firm in refusing his request to slow down the tempo of her class. For him, venturing once again into an unfamiliar world, it was comforting to have this link from home, and throughout the rehearsal period he asked Menia to be there in the studio. 'Always I was with him. He want that.'

For the new pas de deux Béjart had chosen Mahler's *Songs of a Wayfarer*, a work that attracted him by its '*very* personal' relevance for the composer, even though its subject – the despair of a spurned lover – has nothing to do with the ballet. Mortality is the main theme of Béjart's *Songs of a Wayfarer*, as omnipresent here as in his 1970 *Serait-ce la mort?* to Richard Strauss's *Four Last Songs*. It is another *Le Jeune homme et la mort*, with the Wayfarer led away at the end by the 'Man of Death', who is, at the same time, his reflection or other self. Shadowing him throughout, Bortoluzzi, who was slenderer and more elfin than Rudolf, moved sometimes contrapuntally, sometimes in unison, each executing a perfect *tour en l'air* to chime with a climactic note in the score. 'Rudolf, of course, wanted to dance better than Paolo,' says Denvers, who remembers him complaining that he had 'nothing to do', meaning that Béjart was not getting the best out of him. 'But what Béjart made him do was so different from anything he'd danced before, and I think he finally realized that, although he didn't have his double *assemblés* and cabrioles, the emotional impact of this pas de deux – something that was coming from deep inside him – allowed him to go in another direction, and to have much the same success.'

This was also a new direction for Béjart, who admits that the discipline and restraint Rudolf showed in rehearsal led him to create a work significantly different from the one he originally had in mind. '[Rudolf] understood that he had to dominate his instincts. Without this I might perhaps have conceived for him a more brilliant, more

---

* When Béjart's company came to London, Rudolf invited Menia, Jorge and Suzanne Farrell to Fife Road, where Margot, who had heard all about Menia, greeted her with special warmth. 'She was wonderful, and spoke with me and Jorge in Spanish.'

exterior role, but he helped me without realizing it, by his silent presence, to go further in my intentions to interiorize the ballet.'

Béjart's audience, however, was as riotous as ever. On 11 March 1971 a mob of 5,800 packed Brussels's vast sports arena of the Forêt National, spilling into gangways and, as soon as the twenty-minute piece was over, letting rip with a clamour that astonished even Rudolf:

> Public carried on and carried on and carried on. It was ridiculous, exaggerated . . . I thought the reason for that was acoustics. It was a dome and the more they screamed and yelled and clapped the more they get worked up, and excited. They heard themselves . . . they became the performers. We were the public . . . two of us were the witnesses and they were the performers. From three sides they were around us. A quite incredible experience.

Giving a more measured evaluation, Tania Bari, who danced with Rudolf on the same programme in *Rite of Spring*,* described his interpretation of *Wayfarer* as 'very, very interesting, but not Béjart. I saw it later with [Jorge] Donn and [Daniel] Lommel, and it spoke more to me. They moved like one body when they were together, whereas Nureyev and Bortoluzzi, the two stars, *always* were separate.' Rudolf himself would dance with both these performers as well as several others over the next twenty years; he had asked Béjart for a duet he could 'take everywhere', which is exactly what *Wayfarer* became: as much a signature role in Rudolf's later years as Albrecht had been in his youth.

So, had he found a choreographer at last? Béjart says that it was already too late for them to establish the kind of master–muse relationship that he then had with wild child Jorge Donn, the inspiration behind so many of his ballets. 'I took Donn when he was seventeen. When I met Rudolf he was already a star.' And although Rudolf was eager to perform existing works in the repertory, such as the full-length *Faust*, he was not prepared to adapt his schedule in order to give the requisite amount of time to learn it. 'Béjart and Rudolf never really got on,' Denvers says. 'There was a lot of respect on both sides, but they remained like two cats circling around each other.' In the end, far from being a Béjart disciple, Rudolf went out of his way to appropriate his role of mentor – certainly as far as Denvers was concerned.

> Rudolf took me away from Béjart. He said, 'You have to get out of there because otherwise you have no future. If you don't start to know

---

* A performance that was, Bari recalls, 'like a wild animal's. It was the contrary of what he was doing in the Mahler.'

about a classical repertory, when you finish with Béjart you can bring his tea or be his ballet master, but that's the end of the line.' He kind of pushed me . . . 'Why don't you go to Cranko, to Stuttgart?' . . . But I was not ready to leave Béjart. He organized something, but I didn't go to the audition, because Béjart said, 'Stay with me.' Rudolf was very annoyed, because he'd stuck his neck out and I'd let him down.

But Rudolf did not give up, and two years later, when he mounted his *Sleeping Beauty* for the National Ballet of Canada, he arranged for Denvers to be engaged as a soloist. The other dancer who left Béjart soon after *Wayfarer* was Paolo Bortoluzzi, although his friends insist, 'He knew – he didn't need Rudolf to tell him – that it was time to fly'. Paolo's encounter with Rudolf had been akin to a religious conversion. 'For the first time in my life,' he said, 'I felt in the presence of an incredible force that I had to grab hold of. He communicated to me an extraordinary sense of exultation.' The following year, determined to make an international name for himself, Bortoluzzi joined the American Ballet Theatre, plunging 'with a sort of drunkenness' into the classical repertory: *Giselle*, *Swan Lake*, *Sleeping Beauty* – the Nureyev roles.

In Brussels with Rudolf throughout this time was Wallace, his constant companion for the past four months. In November, Ruth Potts had handed her husband a letter telling him that it would 'blow [his] mind':

Dear Mama & Daddy,
    Well, I really don't know where to begin, so I'll tell you the current news first . . . Anyhow, I'm on my way back to Rudolf in London . . . I basically love to make films (to direct, to edit, to light, to act, etc.) but I miss Rudolf – I love him and I think he loves me . . . I hope all this isn't too much for you to fathom because I really love you and I hope this doesn't alienate us. Please bear with me . . . I know now that I can work and function in Rudolf's milieu with confidence which I didn't have last summer . . . Anyhow, I'm on my way to happiness. I don't know how you rate that . . . I know you put a lot of emphasis on happiness through working and I know Rudolf would not love me if I were following him around so I realize I have a lot of pressure from all sides.

Your son,
Beanie

Wanting to compensate for having abandoned his studies, Wallace had immediately started to make a short film at Fife Road: an exploration in dance of Einstein's theory of relativity, using three Royal Ballet members – David Drew, Vyvyan Lorrayne and Wayne Sleep. Rudolf then being on tour, he had dismantled the Jacobean four-poster and converted the master bedroom into a studio. 'I put up these Cartesian grids and had the dancers move like electrons against them.' Encouraged by Nigel Gosling, he had filled out an application to join the Royal College of Art's film division, but then everything had been put on hold: Rudolf was going to be out of the country for the next few months and expected Wallace to be with him. Having watched daily video footage of the *Wayfarer* rehearsals, Rudolf had rediscovered the value of film as an aid to improving his dancing, and on their last day in Brussels he bought a 16-mm Aeroflex camera so that Wallace could record his subsequent performances.

Their first stop was Buenos Aires, where Rudolf had been invited to mount *The Nutcracker*. It is a city which has always drawn great stars as guest dancers and choreographers (among them Diaghilev's Ballets Russes, Isadora, Pavlova, Massine, Nijinska and Balanchine). The fee being offered was certainly not the lure in Rudolf's case, as they were forced to travel like students, flying economy, Rudolf sleeping in one of the aisles. Wallace's letter to the Goslings described how 'wrecked' the two of them were on arrival, both having developed some kind of virus.

The ornate Teatro Colón is one of the world's most beautiful opera houses, but as Rudolf soon discovered, it held a company in chaos. 'The director refuses rehearsals and/or says they have to pay all the dancers,' Wallace wrote to his parents, adding that Rudolf was nevertheless enjoying a huge success – 'partly because of the production but mostly because of his halo!' Intending to film all three acts of the ballet from a box at the back of the orchestra, Wallace spent most of his time at the theatre familiarizing himself with the choreography, the entrances and exits. 'It was a process of trial and error. I tended to go in for close-ups, and generally Rudolf wanted to keep things wide to show the complete body at all times. But I was having to work with existing light, and had never shot dance before, so the result was almost useless.' After nearly a month in the city, 'feeling like a fifth wheel' and frustrated by not being able to resume his Einstein project, Wallace found himself a cheap hotel and went into hiding. 'I was unhappy; I had to think things out.' After a few days Rudolf, who had been searching for him, noticed

Wallace in the street. 'Rudolf said something like, "Oh, *there* you are. C'mon back."'

There was a professional as well as a private reason for Rudolf to initiate a *rapprochement*: in the last week he had been offered three performances of *Apollo*, the Balanchine work he loved more than any other, and he wanted Wallace to film him. The company's Balanchine heritage had been established during the American Ballet Caravan's 1941 tour of Latin America, the ballets continuing to be performed by the Teatro Colón although the choreographer, according to Balanchine's assistant Barbara Horgan, paid little attention to their legality or artistic integrity: 'That's just the way he was: out of sight, out of mind. And what Rudolf would do is contact companies that had *Apollo* in their repertory (legitimately and not legitimately) and offer his services . . . Who knows, Balanchine might have even enjoyed the fact that Nureyev was so anxious to dance this role. It certainly didn't hurt either's reputation.'

The oldest and most revered of Balanchine's extant works, *Apollo* is the ballet the choreographer himself considered pivotal to his career, the one in which he dared 'to not use all my ideas'. Diaghilev is said to have described it as 'pure classicism, such as we have not seen since Petipa's', but it was Balanchine's departure from tradition that created the masterpiece. The contemporary spin he puts on Apollo's very first gesture (the arms are raised in an academic fifth *en haut*, but with hands horizontally hinged) is, as Edward Villella exclaimed, 'Neoclassicism . . . exemplified by that *single* move!' To Rudolf, *Apollo* was the blueprint for all his beliefs about the need to regenerate tradition, but unlike Villella, who was nurtured in the role by the choreographer, he was forced to create every opportunity to perform it himself. 'Royal Ballet would not let me dance *Apollo*, so I went to Vienna and had them produce it for me . . . I did it at La Scala in Milan, and in Amsterdam. I came to London with the Dutch National Ballet and danced it at Sadler's Wells, and finally the Royal Ballet was forced to give me the role.' (Rudolf's Covent Garden debut in *Apollo* on 6 July 1971 is considered to be one of his finest performances in the West.)

Aware that he was '*dying* to do that ballet in New York', Alexandra Danilova, on whom Balanchine had created the role of Terpsichore, had, at Rudolf's prompting, tried to use her influence to get the choreographer's permission. When he refused, Danilova was hardly surprised. 'Nureyev is *anything* but Apollo . . . He is Adonis, he is David. Because, to me, Apollo should be tall and blond. That is my picture of Apollo.' The image, however, of a Hellenic ideal of manhood – the refined deity of the Apollo Belvedere statue – was not Balanchine's initial conception. His Apollo was 'a wild, half-human youth who acquires nobility through art'; his first interpreter, Serge Lifar, described by a contemporary reviewer as 'Etruscan' and 'archaic'. When the New York City Ballet's John Taras coached Rudolf in the role in Vienna, he, too, urged the dancer to bring out Apollo's initial primitiveness – something Rudolf hardly needed to be taught. The character's rite of passage from raw naïveté to artistic refinement and worldliness was a process he understood only too well. 'He becomes god by the end of the ballet through his research of space around him . . . he starts to measure himself, relate himself to the earth and to the surrounding . . . you can see that exploration of space brings despair to him, but then he takes control. In the end.'

After she had watched Rudolf's performance in London, Danilova admitted that she had been mistaken, that he was 'really extremely good in it – the best I saw after Lifar'. And yet she had been right in saying that Apollo is a role antithetical to everything Rudolf stood for; he was a Dionysus who, as a classical dancer, constantly strove to be what Stravinsky called 'the perfect expression of the Apollonian principle'. It was Erik, the quintessential classicist, who had been taught 'the meaning of every moment' of the role by Balanchine and who, in turn, had first taught it to Rudolf. Their difference as dancers was in itself a visualization of the Apollonian/Dionysian duality – the eternal conflict to which art owes its evolution. And it was precisely this sense of struggle in Rudolf's performance that, as Horst Koegler wrote of his Vienna debut, added a whole new dimension to the ballet: 'All his elementary powers and instincts steer him towards a free life, free from moral considerations, free from social obligations. But the gods have chosen him . . . and he has no choice but to accept their call . . . Apollo has finally conquered Dionysus, but it was a tragic victory, for it alienated him from his very nature.'

At the same time Rudolf had a natural affinity with Apollo – the golden youth with uncut hair whose other name, 'Phoebus', like 'Nur', means 'light'. The image of Balanchine's young god, a suspicious, awkward pupil imprisoned in winding sheets, is the Soviet Rudolf, who becomes free only when he starts to dance. It was also the young Balanchine. Asked by Villella the meaning of Apollo's opening and closing of hands, the choreographer explained, 'You know, I was in Soviet Union, awful place no colour, no paint. Lousy. No light. I went first time to London to Piccadilly Circus. Saw for first time flashing lights.' Apollo's growing sense of wonder and delight is marvellously depicted by Rudolf in the Buenos Aires footage, particularly the moment he hears the lute played for the first time. Listening so intently that you start to listen with him, he then registers the sound of the melody just with the expression in his eyes.

Having to formulate an interpretation almost entirely on his own meant, as Violette Verdy points out, that there was no possibility for him to explore a new facet of himself 'that only a Balanchine might have detected and wanted to play with'. Exactly the kind of thing, in fact, that Balanchine was doing with Villella, a kid from the streets of Queens, when he described one leg movement as the 'Soccer Step . . . Man kicking ball.' 'He was telling me to be myself in the role.' Rudolf, on the other hand, had no choice other than to be faithful to the choreography as it was taught to him by John Taras, Verdy says, and consequently his conception of Apollo was, 'strangely enough', one of the most classical she had ever seen. But that was later; Wallace's footage of Rudolf's 1972 Covent Garden portrayal shows movements that are much more sculpted, more recognizably Balanchinian. Rudolf's Buenos Aires Apollo, like his Vienna and Dutch National performances, was technically still a work in progress, and yet it was much closer in spirit to Balanchine's vision. 'I remember him being very unspoiled,' remarks Rudi van Dantzig. 'So different from the traditional picture of Apollo – more like a faun. He wanted to make a real transition, and that's what he did. It was very moving.'

In March, while Rudolf was in Buenos Aires, Monique van Vooren was in Ufa and Leningrad visiting his family. It was a return favour for the kindness he had shown when her fiancé – 'the beautiful Francesco, the man I adored' – was killed in a car crash. Monique had been staying in La Turbie when she heard the news, and Rudolf, gently supportive, insisted that she accompany him on his travels. They went to visit Jean and Maggie Louis in Malibu before driving up to San Francisco. 'He made me part of everything.' Knowing that Monique would soon be herself again (she was, Bob Colacello once said, always heartbroken but never missed a party), Rudolf had given her a Jean Louis dress as a present, an apt combination of funereal black crepe embroidered with mirrors. Before long she was back in the society pages, and a week or so after giving a dinner for Franco Rossellini, with Salvador Dalí and Princess Irene Galitzine among the guests, she was travelling by train from Moscow to Ufa.

Visiting Farida in her 'two humble rooms', Monique had been

amazed by the extent to which Rudolf's mother had absolutely no comprehension of his world or his fame. 'She wanted to know if he needed food. She told me how much he loved trains, and gave me a wooden toy to give to him, the toy he'd had as a child.' Rudolf had asked Monique to take his mother to Leningrad to join Rosa, and to call on Xenia, which she dutifully did. They all went to the ballet one evening along with Rudi van Dantzig, who happened to be in Leningrad at the time. Wearing gold hotpants and suspenders under a long sable coat Monique caused a sensation in the Kirov foyer. 'I didn't want to be seen with her,' Rudi recalls. 'I was there on business talking to teachers and dancers, and she looked so shocking with her green contact lenses and her bosoms hanging out.' When Monique went to check in her coat, Rudi's Dutch ballet master tried to prevent her from taking it off. 'The *babushka* was pulling it, and Ivan was closing it!' During the performance of *Sleeping Beauty*, Farida had wept because this was the ballet in which she had last seen her son dance, and wept again later when Monique took everyone back to her room at the Astoria and called Rudolf collect. 'I put his mother on the phone, and Rosa and Xenia and the dresser he had at the Kirov. There were tears and laughter and it took for ever and ever.' When Rudi van Dantzig next saw Rudolf he offered to show him the few minutes of home movie he had shot in Leningrad. Sitting huddled on a bench in the snow with her granddaughters and Rosa, Farida looks unsmilingly at the camera, pushing a strand of white hair under her scarf and wiping a drip from her nose with the back of her hand. But Rudolf never saw the footage, the reel having stuck just before his family appeared. 'It's meant to be like that,' he said gruffly to Rudi.

There were a number of other emissaries. When Rudolf heard that Marika Besobrasova was going to Russia, he asked her to buy four of anything she got for herself – 'bigger sizes and one small size (for my mother)'. She found herself travelling to Leningrad with thirty-three kilos of fur coats and evening gowns, Rudolf wishing, as she says, 'to show the Soviets his worth'. Farida was so proud of her black fur coat and matching hat that she had a studio portrait taken so that her son could see how well it fitted – 'just as if it was made for me.' Not wanting to return to Ufa, she was still staying in Rosa and Gouze's room in Ordinarnaya Street, where their cramped conditions were 'very bad', she said. In her letter of 4 September 1971 (transcribed by Alfia in an impeccably neat schoolgirl hand, as her grandmother could write only in Arabic), Farida confesses that she has been forced to sell some of

Rudolf's other gifts because her pension is so small – just twenty-five roubles a month: 'Forgive me, don't be offended, but what can I do – I have to live.'

It was hard for Rudolf when, a month or so later, Wallace's parents travelled to Europe. 'I could see how painful it was for him – the fact that my family was free to fly around the world to visit me and his wasn't. I wondered at the time if it was a good idea for my parents to come over for that very reason.' The Potts, who were themselves 'once removed from farmworkers', like Hamet and Farida, had also wanted their son to have the college education denied to them, and had been dismayed by his decision to follow a completely different course of his own. 'I cannot say that I approve of what you are doing, neither can I say that I condemn it,' wrote his father in his reply to Wallace's letter. Both were concerned that it was the glamour of Rudolf's existence that had attracted Wallace, but were equally at pains to reassure him that they loved him 'no matter what'. Their tolerance towards their son's homosexuality – 'Believe me, dear, we're not as naïve as you probably think' – was unusual enough for Middle America, and would have been unimaginable to Farida. But Rudolf was not asking for his mother's acceptance of his relationship with Wallace: he only wanted to be able to see her again. 'My life is coming to its end; not everybody lives long,' she had written in the September letter, a remark that had only served to heighten Rudolf's sense of loss. One Saturday after rehearsals he asked Glen Tetley to have lunch with him at Fife Road, where he talked at length about his desperate loneliness. 'It was coming deeply out of his Russian soul. The house was a huge echoing half-empty place made to be lived in by many people, and he clearly felt very isolated. There had been many times, he said, when he had felt close to suicide.'

Rudolf had first made contact with Tetley after seeing a Ballet Rambert performance of his *Pierrot Lunaire*, a work whose protagonist – 'an outsider . . . robbed of his innocence' – he acutely identified with at the time. It was Tetley's first venture as a choreographer, a ballet he had created on himself, and the one about which he felt most protective. 'I was intrigued by the idea of working with Rudolf, but felt it would not be Pierrot Lunaire but Rudolf Nureyev. So I said no. He was totally persistent and every time we met would say, "Give me a chance. I will do anything." He saw *Ziggurat* and all the ballets I did, but his heart was set on *Pierrot*.'

In November 1970, when Tetley was commissioned to create his first work for the Royal Ballet, he excluded Rudolf from the cast, still believing that he was 'too formed – not only as a principal artist but as a star'. An uncompromising work to a Stockhausen score, *Field Figures* used animal imagery and positions of display and submission to explore its theme of territorial instinct. Its style derived from Martha Graham, and as a Graham dancer as well as disciple, Tetley was much closer than either van Dantzig or Béjart to what Rudolf regarded as 'the source,' and the opportunity to work with him would be, in Nigel Gosling's words, his 'baptism of fire' in modern dance. After a year of Rudolf's relentless '*pleading*' to be allowed to appear in *Field Figures*, Tetley finally relented, pairing him with Monica Mason. But whereas his Royal Ballet colleagues had spent three months creating the ballet with Tetley – 'hours and hours just doing exercises and classes with him' – Rudolf had to do a crash course in Graham technique. The method of contraction and release combined with a spiritual element, 'the centring of concentration and personality on one's highest instincts', made even the simplest classroom exercises very different from anything Rudolf was used to. 'The movement had to be studied from the very beginning, like going back to school,' he said, and in Tetley's view, he immediately proved himself a star pupil. 'I have to say that he learned the choreography impeccably, just soaked up the movement and got right down to the basics of it. The floorwork and use of contraction and isolation of the body to the torso . . . he caught all of that. He was truly brilliant.'

Wanting once again to show that he had not abandoned his classical roots, Rudolf made his next priority the staging of Petipa's *Raymonda*, the first three-act Russian classic he had mounted in the West from memory. This time, instead of pursuing the almost abstract vein of his two earlier versions, he decided to go in the opposite direction and exploit what Alexander Bland called 'the other face of Romanticism, the warm-blooded sex-and-violence exoticism celebrated by men like Sir Walter Scott or Delacroix'. With its far-fetched plot, jousting warriors and surging crowd scenes, the ballet, and in particular its second act, is much like a Hollywood blockbuster (Danilova, who staged it with Balanchine for the Ballets Russes de Monte Carlo, described it as 'a little bit B picture'). But because of its wonderfully danceable Glazunov score and wealth of Petipa solos and ensembles, Rudolf was determined to make it work, now believing that a ravishingly extravagant production could entice a modern audience into accepting the 'inordinate silliness' of the story. Zurich's Municipal Theatre, which had commissioned *Raymonda*, was wealthier than most ballet companies and was allowing Rudolf to use Nico Georgiadis, the designer who had been too expensive for Spoleto, and who knew better than anyone else how to portray real opulence onstage.

Focusing on a young girl awaiting the return of her fiancé from the Crusades, *Raymonda* is the ballerina's ballet, requiring a performer of formidable technique and strength. This was the reason Rudolf had brought in the Stuttgart Ballet's Marcia Haydée, renowned as 'a trojan worker' and also as one of the world's great dance actresses. She and Rudolf had already appeared together in *Giselle* and *Swan Lake* with the Stuttgart Ballet at the end of 1968, even though director John Cranko had been ambivalent about having Rudolf as a guest. 'He realized his value but was appalled at times by his behaviour,' says Peter Wright, who was ballet master at the time. 'It was Marcia who liked dancing with Rudolf and got him invited back. She loved stars and always longed to be pushed to the limit.' Which is exactly what Rudolf did in Zurich, testing the ballerina's stamina by making her repeat sequences 'again and again and *again*'. His ideal in the role was Dudinskaya, whose phrasing and accenting of the choreography he never tired of describing. 'Without her, *Raymonda* is not possible. She's the only one who made [it] sparkle. The way she made steps important . . . the way she hold a pose, the intensity. It's what I took from her. Never to crawl into positions but to get there directly and completely.' And in Wallace's 16-mm footage we see Haydée herself really shine as, Aurora-like, she picks up roses and hops and paws the floor on pointe, her youthful lightness contrasted with a mellow, lusciously supple and fluent Russian quality.

As for Rudolf, although appropriating music from other places in the score to acquire extra solos – 'three more than Petipa and Glazunov planned for' – he had not made any significant changes. Even more surprising is the fact that he had given another male dancer the more sexually dynamic role. As Jean de Brienne, Rudolf is deliberately insipid at first, overworshipful towards his betrothed, who seems always to be pulling away from him. When Jean goes to war, an unexpected visitor arrives, the Saracen knight Abderakhman, who has heard of Raymonda's beauty and come to woo her. When she falls asleep that night it is he who takes Jean's place in her dreams – an alteration of the ballet's original dream sequence by Rudolf, who wanted a more contemporary Raymonda, a young girl with 1970s sexual awareness and fantasies. Renowned for her portrayal of women of passion – Cranko's Juliet, Tatiana, Katherine and Carmen – Haydée is superb at conveying the heroine's mounting excitement as she watches the Saracen's weird, primitive movements culminating in a wild Polovtsian dance. When he attempts to kidnap her, in contrast to Fonteyn's Chloe, who exuded real terror as she was carried high above her abductor's head, Haydée's Raymonda seems to relish the thrill of it all. At the crucial moment Jean arrives and slays Abderakhman in a hand-to-hand duel, standing victoriously astride him in thigh and bicep-baring battle dress like Charlton Heston's Ben Hur. Almost swooning at the change in her mild-mannered lover, Raymonda runs into his arms. Unlike Siegfried, forced to chose between Odette and Odile, the sacred and the profane, she has found erotic fulfilment with the person she loves – an experience Rudolf had only lately discovered for himself.

Raymonda's third act, a Hungarian-flavoured spectacle in honour of the couple's wedding celebrations, is often staged in isolation as the uplifting finale to a mixed programme – as Rudolf's own version had been since entering the repertory of the Royal Ballet Touring Company in 1966. Recently, though, the board of directors had conceded that there was 'something to be said' for commissioning the whole ballet, particularly as Margot wanted a new work for the next New York tour, and had proposed Rudolf's full-length production. At the board's suggestion Michael Somes and Peter Wright travelled to Zurich to see it, and met Rudolf after the performance at the famous Kronenhalle restaurant. Dining on his favourite combination of vodka, caviar and blinis and surrounded by genuine Matisses, Picassos and Braques, Rudolf was in good humour – until, that is, the two Royal Ballet delegates confronted him with the fact that they had not liked his ballet. 'There was a *huge* row, almost a physical fight between Somes and Rudolf,' recalls Wright. And at the meeting of the Ballet Subcommittee on 15 February 1972, the two remained implacable in delivering their report:

It had been hoped that they might find it suitable for inclusion at some later date into the Royal Ballet's repertory but, unfortunately, having seen the ballet, both Mr Wright and Mr Somes decided that it was not suitable. In spite of some fulsome Press praise for this production, they had found that it was no better than Nureyev's previous two attempts to make sense of the outdated story of the ballet. The Committee agreed with the opinion of Mr Wright and Mr Somes that *Raymonda* should not be brought into the Royal Ballet repertory.

Clearly Rudolf's suspicions of a Royal Ballet conspiracy 'to keep [him] out of the theatre' were not entirely unfounded, and made him more determined than ever to seek opportunities elsewhere. It was his prerogative, he felt, to 'go and choose brain', and with *Raymonda* perhaps reminding him of his 1963 sojourn in Spoleto, he decided to get in touch with Paul Taylor, whose ballet *Aureole* had so excited him there. He had told Taylor at the time how much he longed to appear in his work, but the choreographer had not believed him. 'Well, it's a remarkable thing for somebody like him to want to do. So I didn't think too much about it. And then every time I'd see him he'd bring it up again . . . I didn't take the initiative.' But in fact Taylor had forgotten that he was the first to make an approach, writing to Rudolf on 22 July 1964, exactly a year after their first encounter.

> Dear Nureyev,
>   Since I met you in Spoleto, I have been thinking of you and how much I would like to create a piece for you. Suddenly, and fortunately, it seems possible – if you are interested . . .

He had been offered the New York State Theater (the new home of the New York City Ballet) for two weeks in February 1965, but the deal fell through, and after that it was Rudolf who went out of his way to stay in contact. 'So, we became friends, but he said, "You are not serious and you won't be able to learn my way of dancing."' Finally, however, almost a decade later, Taylor 'did realize that this guy was really sincere about wanting to do it, and would go through the effort to get it right'. They worked together in March 1971 on a US television project, an abbreviated version of *Big Bertha*, and three months later Rudolf joined the Paul Taylor troupe's tour of Mexico. When he arrived at his hotel in Mexico City there was a notated version of *Aureole* waiting for him, inscribed, 'For my crazy Russian geek, with much love, Paul.'

Surprisingly for a choreographer whom Arlene Croce has described as 'a major Establishment figure with a style as individual as a thumbprint', Taylor has no school or technique of his own but works directly with his dancers – 'Everything happens in rehearsals.' With movements gravitating to the floor from the waist down and the upper body 'ethereal, uplifted, open', the choreography is much harder to master than it appears. 'I knew it would be difficult, but not that difficult – not just psychologically but technically,' Rudolf admitted, driving himself so mercilessly that Taylor kept telling him to stop and rest. He could see Rudolf struggling and failing 'to switch over; to drop ballet habits that were so ingrained', and yet he admired the dancer's fortitude, his willingness to take corrections, and the speed with which he picked up the steps. 'The style no one could learn quickly.'

For Rudolf, the experience had been chastening. 'I hadn't realized how far apart Paul and I are, how much I have to learn, the work I must put in to achieve his demands. You just can't put other clothes on, you have to know in your bones what he is asking of you.' This was a very different guest artist from the one who had worked with the Dutch National Ballet two years ago, his litany of demands – 'Can you get me tea? . . . See if masseur is in . . . Ask office to call London for me' – remembered to this day by Rudi van Dantzig. When he performed with Taylor, Rudolf could not have been more obliging. 'He did not come as a temperamental star. He came as a dancer, an instrument . . . In a close company like ours everyone pulls together, and he was no exception.'

And yet a month later in London, working with the Royal Ballet on a new Glen Tetley piece, Rudolf relapsed again, 'behaving appallingly', according to Tetley, even towards his adored Lynn Seymour. The ballerina had put on a lot of weight, and when it came to trying out a difficult lift across his shoulder, Rudolf 'just let her drop to the floor'. Named after its Luciano Berio score, *Laborintus*, a starkly modern piece about people walking into the inferno, featured five other Royal Ballet principals – and this, Tetley feels, was the root of the problem. 'Because, if a new work was being created, Rudolf thought it should focus on him.' Noticing, when he began his solo, that two dancers were still performing their duet behind him, Rudolf had stormed out, refusing to allow 'all that monkey business going on' to spoil his own entrance. Taking Rudolf aside, Tetley put an arm around him and begged him to be more trusting. 'I told him, Rudy, I don't want you to make an entrance, nineteenth-century style, for a solo variation . . . I have a transition across your entrance, and it's very exciting because you come out of darkness into light, instead of coming on with a battery of spotlights.'

A reason for Rudolf's insecurity was the fact that one of the two dancers was Margot's new partner, twenty-six-year-old David Wall. They had danced their first *Swan Lake* in 1969 when, in Keith Money's words, 'a rapturous reception immediately cemented a long-lasting and harmonious pairing'. Not only that, but Wall had recently established a close rapport with Merle Park, sanctioned by Ashton, who had just created a new pas de deux for them. An exceptionally handsome young man with red hair, a virile build and natural charm, Wall says that it was

seeing Rudolf perform in London for the first time in 1961 that had
changed his whole approach to his work. 'Not so much technically –
more his commitment, vitality, and understanding.' The two had
become friends, Wall claiming to 'really love the man', and Wallace
confirming, 'David was probably the only Royal Ballet male dancer that
Rudolf got along with well enough to have to dinner.' But despite
Rudolf's fondness for 'Ginger' Wall and his ballerina wife, Alfreda
Thorogood, he was not willing to invite direct comparison onstage
with a new star, an exemplar of flawless Royal Ballet placing, who also
happened to be nearly a decade his junior.*

London was where Rudolf felt he met with his harshest criticism,
and yet he still regarded it as home. Life with Wallace had evolved into
'a kind of marriage', providing the continuity and stability Rudolf
craved, even though he would not allow himself to be confined by it. 'I
used to fly to Paris from London for sex,' he once boasted. 'God, it was
great. The English were too prudish and reserved, but in Paris . . . !'
News that Rudolf was cruising the gay clubs on the rue Saint-Anne
would filter back to Wallace, who was nevertheless determined to
remain faithful. 'I was actually very conservative in our relationship. I
didn't screw around at all.' Described by Nigel Gosling as 'the least
mercenary and calculating person', Wallace was an unusual consort to
a star, ungrudging about the fact that he had no regular allowance and
was forced to ask Sandor Gorlinsky for money, whether it be to pay a
doctor's bill or a train fare. Mostly to please Rudolf, he was making
tremendous efforts to educate himself, learning Italian, improving his
French and reading a number of challenging texts. He had just
discovered Bertrand Russell's *History of Western Philosophy*, which he
found so stimulating that he could hardly put it down. They were
travelling together by rail to Zurich when Rudolf, 'thinking I was
spending more time with the book than with him, suddenly grabbed it
and threw it out the window'. Then, continues Wallace:

> We got in a real physical fight – a fistfight in the train. It just ended
> because we were both too exhausted to continue. Rudolf was very
> demanding and he wanted attention. I think he felt that he had so little

---

* Wall was soon to achieve Rudolf's greatest ambition: the acquisition of a classical repertory tailor-made to his talent. It was Kenneth MacMillan who was the first to exploit the
dancer's power as an actor, detecting a dark, debauched undercurrent to his naturally sunny
stage persona, and giving it full expression in *Mayerling* – the first Western three-act ballet
ever created for a man.

time on earth – just some strange feeling he had about his mortality . . . And when he was offstage he wanted attention . . . If I happened to be doing something at that time, he expected me to stop what I was doing and be with him, whether it was eating dinner or watching TV.

But Rudolf knew very well that Wallace longed to lead a more independent life, and would occasionally agree to release him. In October 1971 Wallace had toured England as a production assistant on Pier Paolo Pasolini's *Canterbury Tales*, and now, five months later, was in Italy, working on a spaghetti Western directed by Franco Rossellini. From an isolated location in the mountains, he kept trying and failing to reach Rudolf by telephone – either because of the two- to three-hour Italian delays, or because, when the call finally came through, there would be no answer at Fife Road. Badly missing Rudolf, and disturbed by his own lack of ambition, Wallace laid bare his feelings in a long confessional letter.

Went alone to see Mount Vesuvius after arriving in Naples. I've been in the worst state for the past 2 weeks. I'm so apathetic about everything; nothing excites me or interests me even. I don't even care about finishing my 16-mm film . . . I feel like a vegetable. When I think about doing something with myself or trying to become something I just get so depressed. I have a feeling I'm afraid to admit that I'm so in love with you I'm afraid of getting involved in my work or getting excited about anything in case it causes tension between us. I had sex with 2 different people when I first came here, but have not had the desire for over 4 weeks. Even when I think it may be exciting or rather that it should be exciting to have sex, when it comes down to going out & looking for it, it's such a let-down. I get excited thinking about you, but then I start missing you and then I get depressed that I'm so dependent on you.

This was the first time that Wallace had admitted to casual sexual encounters, although he did not tell Rudolf about the fling he had while in Rome with Hiram Keller. The pair 'used to pal around' with actor and songwriter Paul Jabarra, who had appeared with Hiram in the original cast of *Hair*. Wallace was a close friend of Paul's, never a lover, though Rudolf thought the contrary and had been so suspicious when they spoke on the telephone that Wallace immediately wrote a postcard to reassure him: 'You sounded a little bit apprehensive when

I said Paul was living here also. Well you shouldn't be. I love you, Boo-Boo! I should be the apprehensive one: 6 weeks with David Wall etc.' It failed to work, as Wallace then received a call from Rudolf saying that things would be over between them unless he came back immediately. 'So I got on a plane and went home.' In August they went together to La Turbie for a week, spending most of their time in Monte Carlo. 'Much livelier than the last year when it seemed like a retirement colony,' Wallace told his parents, mentioning the fact that 'the Burtons came on their yacht' and describing an open-air concert at the Palace of Monaco, where Mick Jagger had invited them the same night to Cannes to see Sviatoslav Richter give a solo recital. It was, as Wallace admitted, all too easy to 'fall back on being Mrs Rudolf Nureyev', and for the next three months, while touring Canada and North America, he did exactly that – devoting any film work from then on entirely to Rudolf.

It was Erik who had encouraged Rudolf to establish a link with the National Ballet of Canada, a company with which he had worked throughout the last decade as a dancer, choreographer and coach. Not only did it have one of the finest schools in the world (its director, Betty Oliphant, had been his choice to revitalize the Swedish academy), but the dancers' Russian and Cechetti-based training had produced an ensemble of unusual homogeneity and finesse. Needing a new production of *Sleeping Beauty*, its British founder, Celia Franca, had invited Rudolf to mount his version but had been 'dead against' having the dancer himself as the star. Her mission all along had been to develop an indigenous ballet, her company had just returned from its first European tour, and she was not about to let it become what one critic described as 'the parsley round the salmon of Rudolf Nureyev'. Sol Hurok, however, would not back an American tour without him, and so, in the summer of 1972, Rudolf joined the Canadians for six months. 'Our kids were young; they were extremely well-trained,' remarked Oliphant. 'They were too young to feel threatened.'

Sergiu Stefanschi, at that time a principal in Toronto, had talked excitedly to his colleagues about what Rudolf had been like in Russia – 'how extraordinary he was' – and on the day of his arrival the National Ballet's sixty-five dancers waited apprehensively in the studio for the 'living legend' to make his entrance. 'What we hadn't expected,' the company's star, Veronica Tennant, has written, 'was a *man* – who was not tall, oddly dressed in a woollen cap and tight leathers – a man – whose eyes twinkled . . . who made immediate, irrevocable contact with every person in the room'.

A *répétiteur* from La Scala had already taught the company the steps, Celia Franca had distributed the roles, and Rudolf was impatient to get to work. Tennant, the company's 'unofficial prima', was told that she and Nureyev would be rehearsing together, but when, after almost an hour, he still had not appeared, she decided to begin without him.

> I'd just got to the *pas de chat* section when Rudolf suddenly flew into the room and began dancing next to me. It was wonderful. Apparently he'd been late because of an intense argument with Celia Franca. He'd wanted to bring over his own ballerina – Marcia Haydée or Carla Fracci – and Celia had insisted that he dance with us.

Rudolf had capitulated, but battles over casting continued. While rehearsing the Prologue his eye was drawn to one of the Fairies, a real beauty, with modern, fashion-model looks, and he demanded to know why she was not learning Aurora. Twenty-year-old Karen Kain, the company's youngest principal, had been chosen by Franca to dance *Swan Lake* with Rudolf later in the tour, but was cast only in soloist roles in *Sleeping Beauty*. 'I had just recovered from a serious illness, and Celia felt my workload was enough. Rudolf, though, was determined that I would dance Aurora, and it became this contentious issue between them.' In the opening performances Kain was to appear in the Blue Bird pas de deux with Frank Augustyn, a tall, elegant soloist for whom Rudolf had equally ambitious plans. 'You, boy!' he would say, indicating that Augustyn should step in for him while he directed from the front. 'I thought I was there as Rudolf's body double, and it never occurred to me that I was being considered as the Prince.' The eighteen-year-old Augustyn remembers experiencing a strange combination of fear – 'because of the power of his presence' – and something infinitely more comforting:

> It was like jumping into a kangaroo's pouch. Rudolf knew exactly what he wanted to do and he was going to take us along with him. From the most arrogant to the shyest and most insecure dancer there – we all felt the same way. Something was happening that we'd never experienced before, and we knew it was going to be a wonderful ride.

But while the youngest members of the company were feeling 'as if a door was opening', the established men were lining up outside the director's office to complain. Rudolf had even bypassed his friend

Sergiu, who 'didn't feel sour', he insists, 'because I knew Rudolf preferred to pick someone just starting whom he could nourish'. Someone also, no doubt, who would not question his decisions. On the first day, spotting Sergiu resting on the studio floor, Rudolf had walked up to him and, speaking in Russian, come straight to the point: 'You know, Seryosha, you have to forget everything you remember about *Sleeping Beauty* because this is going to be completely different.' The two had been onstage together as pages in the Kirov production and 'knew every step the way it was'. Having been told of their ex-teacher Igor Belsky's outrage over his appropriation of the entr'acte music for his solo, Rudolf did not welcome the thought of any further cavilling from Sergiu. 'He just wanted to clear that up with me.'

As in his Milan version, Rudolf aimed to contrast a Margot-like simplicity of style with Nico Georgiadis's opulent designs. The latter came close to bankrupting the company. Originally estimated at $250,000, the budget ran over by $100,000, the production saved only when the chairman of the board mortgaged his house. No one in the company had ever seen extravagance like it, '*Pillars* were being thrown away because Rudolf said he had no room to dance.' The costumes were all made from the finest silks, brocades and satins; Veronica Tennant, whose third-act tutu was so encrusted with jewels that she could hardly raise her arms, remembers one argument between Georgiadis and the technical producer about the carving on the *back* of the throne.* But Rudolf insisted on his vision. 'There was no compromise,' recalled Oliphant. 'Rudi kept saying that if Nico Georgiadis didn't get his way, he was leaving.' In despair, Franca removed herself to the sidelines – or, as Rudolf put it, 'didn't get into my soup' – giving him sole charge of her company.

He took class with the dancers each morning and worked with them until nine or ten in the evening, his intention to inspire, Augustyn says, rather than conventionally teach. 'He wasn't there to show you how to do a pirouette. You had to know the ABC of dancing. I remember him in the studio in his boots, tight pants and toque, never actually doing a step.' What Rudolf did do was pass on everything he himself had learned about technique, artistry and stagecraft. 'Try to find impulse of movement,' he directed. 'It is that impulse that gives attack and interest.' . . . 'Dance boldly and full out. Hold back nothing! Timid is not interesting . . . Take the stage and command

---

*On his thirty-fifth birthday, in jokey retaliation, the dancers presented their gift to him onstage – a jewel-encrusted, fur-lined dance belt custom-made by the wardrobe master.

it! . . . Audiences come to theatre to see people obsessed by what they do!' Wanting to help Veronica Tennant with the perilously difficult Rose Adagio balances, he called Margot one night for advice. 'She suggested you try for strength of equilibrium in the shoulders rather than thinking about balancing from the toes,' he told the ballerina, and instructed all three Auroras, 'You have to give everything you've got on this piece because after that, *I* come.'

In the lead up to the opening night, the production, now lasting more than three hours, had run into overtime fees, and Franca, using Betty Oliphant as go-between (she and Rudolf having long before stopped speaking), pleaded for the pas de cinq to be cut. Rudolf remained implacable – 'Tell them to play the whole thing faster!' he scoffed – and, in the end, the intervals were shortened by about seven minutes. But for all the distress it caused, Rudolf's *Sleeping Beauty* brought the National Ballet returns beyond imagining. Broadcast soon after the première, the televised version won an Emmy Award and was seen by thirty-three million people when shown worldwide. To Frank Augustyn, they had 'reached the stars, the real pinnacle of ballet', and Veronica Tennant felt much the same. 'With Rudi, we came of age and we grew. Because to dance with him meant to be taught by him, to be cajoled and inspired to share in his example and vision of what was possible in dance.'

'*Sleeping Beauty* is so fantastic, so *elegantissimo*!' Wallace wrote to Nigel and Maude, sending them a copy of the tour itinerary. He had made his own record of the ballet using the new high-speed film stock, and had also begun cutting Act 2 of *Raymonda*. Life on the road was proving a lot of fun. They were travelling with a hired Moviola editing machine and viewer (nicknamed Johnnie and Janie because they had to ride like passengers in the backseat), and when they were in Montreal, Wallace had 'dragged' Rudolf to see Alice Cooper perform in a stadium before an audience of twelve thousand people. 'This was quite something as Rudolf *hated* rock music and would only let me play my records when he wasn't there.' They were both equally intrigued by America's burgeoning gay porn scene, and drove to New York City with the sole intention of seeing *The Boys in the Sand*, the first technically proficient hard-core gay feature film. This had opened at the end of December 1971 and proved an unprecedented commercial success, earning model-star Cal Culver celebrity status and launching the concept of 'porno chic' (popularized by *Deep Throat* a year later). Wallace's eight-page letter to the Goslings describes their astonishment at seeing men having sex on the big screen.

It's so surprising – there's a complete lack of censorship now . . .
There's not one 'thing' that they can't show and don't . . . *Screw*
magazine is so hysterical – they review all the porno films now, straight
or gay and like the old 4 star system, they rate the films by 4 phalluses.

Their next stop was Boston, where the choreographer José Limón
had arrived to teach Rudolf *The Moor's Pavane*,[*] his 1949 classic focusing on the four main characters from *Othello*. A pupil of American
modern-dance pioneer Doris Humphrey and a charismatic figure in
his own right, Limón could have been crucial to Rudolf's induction
into the genre, but, as usual, he did not allow himself enough time
to absorb the new style. Instead of internalizing the Moor's rage into
imploding, weighted movements he 'let his feelings come seething to
the surface', as one critic would write; his desperate, rolling eyes and
flared nostrils reminding another of a close-up from *Ivan the Terrible*.
There was no other opportunity to collaborate with Limón, who died
unexpectedly in December, but Rudolf considered *The Moor's Pavane*,
like *Songs of a Wayfarer*, to be a key work in his repertory, and was still
performing it two decades later.

The night before rehearsing with Limón, Rudolf had stayed up until
five a.m. talking to cinematographer Geoffrey Unsworth and designer
Barry Kay. His next major project was to make a feature film of *Don
Quixote*, and as his every experience of dance for the camera had fallen
short of his expectations, he was determined to take charge of this
venture from the start. Although disappointed by the unimaginative
way *Romeo and Juliet* and the BBC *Nutcracker* films had been shot, he was
not at all in favour of a radical approach to dance on film, complaining,
'The minute they get hold of you they start dancing with their cameras.
They forget about the artist.' Valentina Pereyaslavec, who was with
him in Vienna during the filming of *Swan Lake*, remembers his irritation:
'One day Rudolf say, "What camera is this?" And Rudolf point to corner.
And cameraman say, "This is camera for your jump." Rudolf say, "I don't
want this camera here because we must see *my* jump, not one you
invent with camera." . . . Rudolf control everything for movie. Light.
Camera. Camera front. Camera side. Everything.'

Even when working with someone as established as the English
feature film director Bryan Forbes, Rudolf had insisted that all the
cameras were in the wrong positions. Forbes, at the time, was shooting

---

[*] Rudolf had asked Hurok for a modern work to perform on tour, and planned to make his
debut in a tryout performance in Baltimore in October before premièring it in New York.

additional ballet sequences for the movie *I Am a Dancer*, which had begun as a television documentary by a young French director, Pierre Jourdan. EMI had brought in Forbes for the new footage and to blow up the 16 mm to the standard 35 mm. Admitting that this was his first venture into the closed world of the ballet, Forbes had five cameras in position at the London Coliseum at eight o'clock on a Sunday morning. Seven hours later Rudolf appeared. It was, in Wallace's view, a misunderstanding. 'Rudolf would *never* have agreed to dance at that time; I don't think any dancer would.' But Forbes was furious, and in no mood to accommodate Rudolf on technical issues. 'Why don't you put your feet in the rosin and start to dance and leave the filming to me!' he snapped. As far as he was concerned, the dancer was 'fairly contemptible as a person': Rudolf had apparently announced before filming that he would not perform unless he was paid in cash each day, and at one point, distracted by the sound of a camera shutter, he had spat in the face of the 'inoffensive stills photographer'. Things were much calmer during the shooting of an extract from Tetley's *Field Figures*, and Deanne Bergsma, Rudolf's partner in the duet, remembers Forbes becoming so excited that he grabbed the camera himself and began moving among the dancers. But having decided from the first screening in Paris that he 'despised the film', Rudolf made no attempt to hide his displeasure. At the June 1971 première he had stormed out of the theatre without so much as a word to Forbes, and was much quoted in the press saying that he would gladly pay to have the film destroyed.

He now became fanatically intent on taking sole charge of *Don Quixote*. This would not be the usual television-style multi-camera recording but a large-budget feature film, Rudolf wanting, as Wallace put it, 'to do for ballet what *Singing in the Rain* and Jerome Robbins's staging of the dance sequences in *West Side Story* did to advance the art of filming a musical'. Robert Helpmann, co-director of the Australian Ballet, the company Rudolf had chosen to perform with him, was also to co-direct the film – at least that was the idea. According to Lucette Aldous, cast once again as Kitri, it had been 'Bobby's absolute dream to get *Don Quixote* for the company so he could have that part'. Wanting to expand it for the film, Helpmann wrote to Rudolf in October outlining his idea for a silent pre-prologue featuring just the Don and his muse, Dulcinea. 'They are to indicate to the audience the other adventures of Don Quixote and to clarify the storyline.' Rudolf, however, had no intention of allowing the title role to be anything more than a cameo, and planned to launch directly into the action in the town square, thereby accelerating his own entrance. Uncharacteristically Helpmann gave way. Although just as forthright and egotistical as Rudolf, he had devoted all his energies recently to establishing the Australian Ballet internationally, and he knew it was not his name but Nureyev's that would guarantee their film's success.*

And Rudolf knew that Helpmann would be able to attract the best talent in the field. Leading the Old Vic company in the forties and fifties (appearing as Hamlet and in *The Taming of the Shrew* opposite Katharine Hepburn), Helpmann had been one of the great theatrical stars of his generation. Not only that, but his collaboration with Michael Powell and Emeric Pressburger on *The Red Shoes* had produced the definitive ballet movie, its influence extending from *Singing in the Rain* to the fight scenes in Martin Scorsese's *Raging Bull*. It was Helpmann's network of connections that had secured the appointment of Geoffrey Unsworth and cameraman Peter MacDonald – the team responsible for the visual brilliance of *Cabaret* and *2001: A Space Odyssey*. But there was to be no surreal or fantastical film-making in *Don Quixote*, both directors agreeing that the style should be 'real as real', with, for instance, genuine Melbourne market vendors employed as extras for the opening scene.

Allowing virtually no preparation time, Rudolf arrived on the set on a Sunday with principal photography due to begin on the Monday. 'We had a director for a day and a bit.' However, according to Wallace, Rudolf already had 'nearly the entire film mapped out in his head'. As he later told director Lindsay Anderson in their 1974 television interview, 'I set all the camera shots. Every frame, every second on the film is my responsibility, whether you like it or hate it. It's me.' He wanted most of the dance sequences to be filmed in one long wide shot, each carefully and classically composed. And instead of relying on the traditional variety of full-length, close-up and wide shots, there was to be extensive use of the crane – ideas that met with remarkably little opposition from the two experts. While Rudolf's relationship with Peter MacDonald was 'creatively adversarial', in Wallace's phrase, he was especially deferential towards Unsworth, 'the kind of soft-spoken,

---

* The two, in fact, got on remarkably well, much appreciating the other's wit and pornographic sense of humour. 'Privately is where they really connected,' says Aldous. And although as Sadler's Wells Ballet's first *danseur noble* Helpmann had epitomized the kind of old-fashioned cavalier and mime artist Rudolf scorned, as de Valois protégés and Margot's most famous partners they had much in common, doing more than any other male dancers of their time to popularize the art of ballet.

old-world personality that he had a lot of respect for'. The crew found him easy enough – 'provided you don't delude him' – but after a number of clashes, the first assistant director withdrew from the project, and Rudolf 'pushed' Wallace into his place. 'Just because of the time constraints they took me.' The shoot had to be completed in three weeks, and soon the pressure of the deadline combined with the extreme summer heat began to take its toll. The set had been constructed in an unused hangar at Essendon airport outside Melbourne, in which temperatures became so unbearable in the midday sun that the rubber paint on the floor was melting. There was no dressing room or canteen, and the dancers, who had been sitting around since seven o'clock each morning, were expected to be in peak form up to sixteen or seventeen hours later. It was midnight when Rudolf asked Gailene Stock to step in as one of the leading Dryads.

When he came to scoop me around the waist I wasn't ready, which made him really angry. He grabbed hold of the chain necklace I was wearing and started dragging me around, and because I was resisting, the metal was biting into my neck. When he said we had to do it again, I refused and the crew backed me up. We struck, and they made him apologize to me. 'I'm sorry,' he said, 'but you're still stupid.' By this time I'd had enough. I was leaving the company anyway, and as the filming was virtually over, I decided not to come back on set. *

'I'm amazed that nobody got killed,' says Wallace, laughing. 'It was chaotic – a nightmare. It's unheard of to make a feature film in three weeks.' Post-production work was just as rushed, as Rudolf was needed for the second lap of the Canadian tour, and he was determined to see the finished edit before he left. He had been furious when the producers of the *Sleeping Beauty* film cut several variations without his authority, Nigel Gosling witnessing the scene in a Chinese restaurant when his temper 'suddenly boiled up & he hit one culprit on the knuckles with his wooden chopsticks so hard that S. let out a yelp. A

---

* Stock got her revenge. Her expensive watch had disappeared while on set and she had reported its loss to the police, who telephoned her at home early the following morning. 'I was barely awake, and when they asked if there was anyone I suspected, I said, half-jokingly, "Rudolf Nureyev." I heard later that two policemen had turned up on set to question him.' Stock, who had applied to join the National Ballet of Canada, Rudolf's next port of call, also heard that when the director, Celia Franca, asked Rudolf if he knew her, he replied without a moment's hesitation, 'Take her.' 'Which I thought fantastic.'

few shits & fucks went with the blow, finally breaking into doubtless
unprintable Russian.' This time Rudolf literally moved the Australian
film editor into his house. Anthony Buckley would sit in front of a
Moviola machine in a corner of the master bedroom at Fife Road
cutting shots together while Rudolf was rehearsing, and at the end of
his day, or at night after his performance, they would work on the edit
together. Knowing that he was still concerned about 'what Bobby may
do to the film' in his absence, Buckley wrote a note to reassure him:

> London Monday night 1.30 a.m.
> Dear Rudolf,
>   Today was my last day on DQ. In the morning I fly home . . . The
> film is *exactly* as you left it and absolutely no alterations . . . The film is
> in the laboratory so no one can alter what we have done, and Bobbie
> goes to America on Wednesday so he won't be a problem either.[*]

For the time being the only problem was Wallace. The situation in
Australia had been awkward for him, having been allowed to work on
Don Quixote only through Rudolf's insistence. 'He really forced them
to take me. But that certainly didn't ingratiate me with the crew.' And
things were not any easier now they were home, and he was having
to watch Rudolf edit the film – exactly what he felt he should be
doing on his own. The only answer was to get away and, not wanting
an emotional scene, he wrote Rudolf a letter, leaving it by the front
door on his way to Heathrow.

> Rudolf,
>   I know this seems very secretive and premeditated . . . I have gone
> to Los Angeles. I suspect you think I'm returning to Myron, but in Los
> Angeles I know the film arrangements much better, and I thought I
> would find a cheap apartment and finish that goddamn Einstein film
> once and for all. I have to refilm my titles completely – they fucked
> up the whole film. I know you would think why I didn't want to do
> it here. Well it's taken 2 years so far here and with you too here
> editing . . . and your hectic ballet schedule I don't feel happy here
> working on something that you all may regard as a toy or self-indulgent.
> Anyhow, I won't write a self-pitying letter, just that I'm unsatisfied with

---

[*] According to John Percival, Rudolf was not at all happy with the sound that was added in
his absence. 'I shall know next time,' he said. 'It's not enough to lay your own eggs, you have
to hatch them, too.'

what I'm doing right now. I think once I finish that film it will help me spiritually. I think I will stay in Los Angeles until you arrive there, then if you are still interested in the Raymonda film we can work then. I thank you for asking if I wanted to work on it, but I think Don Quixote must take priority now. I will take Raymonda workprint with me but leave the negative here, & am taking that Borges book, too, and perhaps I can make a short film of one of his stories though I have a feeling LA is not one of his archetypal cities. I will call you when I have found an apartment. Dance well tonight, edit well,

Love,
Wallace

Rudolf was convinced that Wallace had gone for good. Onstage that night when he launched into his *Corsaire* solo 'like a raging tiger', Nigel Gosling, who had heard a rumour that Wallace had 'crept away', knew then for certain it was true. 'My professional half couldn't help thinking "If that's what it does to his dancing, I wish Wallace would leave him more often!"' But the jocular tone is misleading, as both Goslings had grown very close to Wallace and were deeply saddened by his sudden flight. 'I really love W & so does Maude. He will make a hole in our lives & it is the end of something so beautiful & good for R . . . But he is surviving fantastically. "I will dance harder & better, that's all," he says. And he will – but I fear for the next year alone.'

Rudolf spent the rest of January 1973 'terribly nervous and wrought up', worrying his friends with the crazy recklessness of his driving. When it was suggested that he should hire a chauffeur to take him to and from the Opera House now that Wallace was no longer there to do it, he contemptuously refused. 'That's so pompous,' he sniffed. With only one person in the house, Fife Road was not the tranquil refuge it appeared, the stairs and floorboards mysteriously creaking at night 'as if people were literally walking around'. (When Wallace's mother stayed there by herself she was so terrified that she moved her bed against the door as a barricade and slept with a police whistle around her neck.)*

Because they had been together so much as a foursome, the Goslings had feared that, with Wallace gone, Rudolf might keep his distance. 'But not a bit of it.' He began to use their house in Victoria Road as his sanctuary, the place he came to rest before a performance and to have supper afterwards. As Maude cooked in the tiny galley kitchen he would flop down on the sofa, pick up a newspaper, or watch an old film on television, and not talk. 'Then I'd say, "It's ready." And we'd go and sit down. Once Rudolf started to eat, he came to life again. He liked being here because he didn't have to make any effort with us.' The couple had been astonished to hear of the dancer's New York routine – 'invited out every night followed by a retinue, drinking etc' – because in London he rarely went to parties, kept calling for more soda water to dilute his white wine and chose to spend his one free evening with them. Only in their company could he be

---

*Rudolf's peace of mind was not improved by an anonymous letter that had just arrived warning that he would soon be receiving a letter bomb. Sure enough, a parcel was delivered but was found to contain nothing more than a number of photographs and a note. They were from someone Rudolf had come to call 'the Mad Irish Girl', a fan who, like many others, seriously believed him to be in love with her. She was the most bothersome because of her ability to locate Rudolf, and however often he changed the phone number she somehow always managed to find out the new one. The calls stopped abruptly when Scotland Yard, alerted to the bomb scare, paid the young woman a visit, 'and frightened the living daylights out of her'.

completely himself. 'Sometimes it hurt, even,' Nigel admitted in his diary, 'to see him switching [the charm] on for other people – & then off again for us!' It had taken five years before he had been anything more than polite and faintly affectionate with Maude, and there were times during this period when he had been so distant with Nigel that the writer wondered if Rudolf actually liked him. Now, however, a decade later, finally able to accept that these were the two people in the world who would never let him down, Rudolf had mellowed, becoming 'as gentle & caring & careful . . . as you could wish'.

The Goslings' own son, Nicholas, was a few years younger than Rudolf, and people often wondered what he must feel about his parents' intense devotion to the Russian star. But as Rudolf came into their lives at around the time that Nicholas went to Oxford and was starting to lead an independent life, he says he never felt threatened. 'I was an only child, and at the age when one wants to break away from one's mother and father, so if anything, it was rather useful to know that they had their own interests.' He did not share Maude and Nigel's passion for ballet, describing himself as 'a bemused bystander to all the mania', but he was crazy about films and after graduating worked for over a decade in cinema and television. It was Nicholas who initiated what Rudolf used to call 'Roxies', setting up his projector and screen in the living room after dinner, and showing two or three movies he had rented – 'usually classics of Western cinema and underground films'. It was at Victoria Road that Rudolf first saw *The Red Shoes*, as well as several Garbo movies that were new to him. 'And he had never seen the Eisenstein films,' said Maude. 'So you can imagine his excitement – he became a real film buff. Sometimes on a Sunday we'd go to two movies, one after the other.' When Wallace appeared, 'Roxies' became even more frequent. 'He and I got along really well,' says Nicholas. 'We had very similar aims.'

The Goslings were the hub of a small inner circle of London friends, among them Charles Murland, a company director who kept his gay life a secret from his City colleagues. Plump and cheerful, with red hair and a ruddy complexion – 'like a character out of Dickens' – he was a man of great taste and culture, who loved to surround himself with beautiful young men, especially dancers. His house in Trevor Place, Knightsbridge, was 'an all-party place' where the food and wine was always wonderful and where you could be sure to find the Royal Ballet's most decorative males, from David Wall and Wayne Eagling to the newest member of the corps de ballet. Treasurer of the Royal Ballet School and on the board of the Festival Ballet, Murland had hoped to be appointed a Royal Ballet governor, but both Lord Drogheda and John Tooley refused to have him, saying that he was 'too involved with the dancers'. In Rudolf's case this was certainly true, as being considerably well off, with a flexible work schedule, Charles was able to follow the star around the world, arranging chauffeurs or giving parties in whichever city they happened to be. 'That's what Rudolf got out of it,' said a mutual acquaintance. 'Convenience. And Charles got to be a friend of the god. He was always everywhere; he'd just book a plane and turn up.'

Like Charles Murland, Terence Benton and Paklusha Bicat were fans who had become friends of Rudolf and several other stars. They always reserved the same aisle seats in row F of the Royal Opera House orchestra stalls so they could go straight through the pass door back-stage before the curtain calls had finished. The granddaughter of a White Russian oil magnate, Paklusha was brought up in Paris, when her parents, the Chermoyeffs, fled the Revolution, taking with them the family jewels and documents as proof of their ownership of the vast Caucasian and Georgian oil fields. In 1958 when Terence Benton left Kansas for London – 'ignorant of life, tactless but veneered with good manners and a deeply nurtured Englishness' – a friend introduced him into the White Russian colony, and within a few months he had met Paklusha. Although married to André Bicat, an Anglo-French artist, and the mother of their three children, she fell in love, and Terence found himself part of the free, Bloomsbury-like bohemia of their family life in Oxfordshire. The couple soon discovered a mutual passion for music and ballet, and when the Bolshoi and Kirov began coming to London, they would throw parties for the dancers at their elegant Carlos Place apartment. Having 'known Margot for ever', they naturally longed to befriend Rudolf, and it was the ballerina who volunteered to bring them together. They met at a restaurant in Jermyn Street, Terry look-ing like Count Dracula with his black cape and slicked-back black hair, and Paklusha as round and serene as a *matryoshka* doll. She was the quintessential Russian earth mother, whose straightforward, unshock-able manner immediately won Rudolf over. 'She had a wonderful quality about her – the aura she exuded,' recalled Wallace. 'Paklusha could get along with anyone from a doorman to a duchess.'

Although they had not known each other long, Paklusha was the only person in whom Rudolf had confided at the time of his father's death. And on tour in March 1973, when he heard that Xenia had died, it was Paklusha who undertook to discover the cause. Rudolf had received a telegram from Margot (whom Baryshnikov had managed to contact), saying how sad she was for him, and Rudolf, 'in great agitation', had immediately called and asked Paklusha to find out more. He was unaware that a year and a half earlier Xenia had undergone surgery for stomach cancer. She had told only two or three of her closest friends and begged them to keep it a secret. 'I didn't know anything for months,' Baryshnikov says, 'maybe because she wanted to keep me away from another traumatic experience [after Pushkin's death].' She certainly did not want Misha or anyone else to see her when she was ill, telling Alla Bor that she felt ashamed she 'let it happen', that she was unable to will the cancer away. She would, in fact, have lived longer had the local hospital not given her a transfusion of the wrong blood type. 'She took a taxi home and was dead two hours later.' Since losing Alexander Ivanovich, Xenia had greatly changed, becoming reclusive and withdrawn, but nevertheless she and Rudolf had stayed in touch, their telephone calls his only source of Kirov news and gossip. 'Xenia was his last link with Leningrad,' noted Nigel in his diary. 'Now he will have nobody; he is really cut off. And she was quite young. Oh what bad luck.'

Thinking it a good idea to have someone living at Fife Road while Rudolf was away, the Goslings had arranged for Wallace's brother to house-sit. Tommy Potts, then studying in London, was glad to oblige, but Nigel could not help slightly resenting this amiable rather gauche young man for not being Wallace. The couple had been invited for dinner by Claire, the housekeeper, who was also missing Wallace's company and thought it highly unlikely that he would be back. 'Came away feeling low,' wrote Nigel. 'This is the saddest news: I am convinced R will never find anybody so nice.' The Gosling group – a private fan club of five – who met often in Rudolf's absence (on one occasion, over dinner at Daphne's in South Kensington, all signing a tablecloth to send off to him), set about trying to engineer a reunion. Terry Benton had managed to find out Wallace's address in Los Angeles, to which Nigel wrote, saying how distressed they had been by his sudden departure, and how much he was missed. 'I see Rudolf will be in LA at the end of the month so give him our love too,' Nigel added as a hopeful postscript, keeping a note of any progress in his diary.

Monday 26 February: Charles M reported that he had heard . . . W had visited R there . . . In any case, good news. '*Ça va mieux*' was the report.
Saturday 17 March: R's birthday; the first one since his arrival in the West that we have missed . . . He rang . . . sounded v cheerful, says

they are booked solid everywhere . . . what's more, had a 'terrific' time in LA with Wallace (who is joining him again briefly later). That is great news.

Wednesday 21 March: Niko [Georgiadis] rang & said he had talked to R . . . Wallace answered the phone . . . isn't that great. How I hope that continues.

Sunday 25 March: It seems he is with R again. O Frabjous day – calloo callay!

Wallace, who had spoken to Rudolf only once since leaving London, was living downtown near the Shrine Auditorium in a tiny apartment with no telephone, his 'total cutoff' a deliberate policy to allow him to work without interruption on his Einstein film. He had also been steeping himself in the short stories of Jorge Luis Borges, an author Rudolf had 'badgered' him to read, having become so inspired by *The Circular Ruins* that he had immediately written, in a single session, the synopsis for a film – 'an animated-pornographic film'. The new market for porn was proving irresistibly lucrative, he explained to his parents. 'Cinematically (& erotically) they are a pile of trash, but people pay $5 a head to see them.' Rudolf, who, according to Terry Benton, 'thought Wallace's pornographic film thing was a nonsense', did not hide his disappointment. 'I'm sure he had wanted his project for me to be a bit more serious,' Wallace told the Goslings, adding, 'I've been filming the "fuck" sequences out here since I have a film lab that will process it. Finally we went over it and [Rudolf] seemed placated if not amused.' Determined to make things work this time, Wallace joined Rudolf on the road, travelling first to Arizona, then overnight to Las Vegas. 'Allan Carr . . . "The King of Las Vegas" arranged a gigantic suite for us at the Tropicana Hotel and to see the Ann-Margret Show,' he went on. 'We arrived here in San Francisco Monday morning and Armen Bali as usual is going crazy preparing activities for us.'

They had been in Rudolf's dressing room on an earlier tour with Robert Hutchinson and his new partner when a note, written in Russian, was delivered. 'I am Armen Bali,' Rudolf read. 'I am Armenian. I have Armenian restaurant and tonight, after the performance I want to treat you Armenian way. Please, do not refuse.' Deciding that this sounded like more fun than the formal Royal Ballet reception at the Mark Hopkins Hotel, Rudolf sent Wallace down to the stage door. Armen Bali, a vivacious woman in her late forties, wearing large owl glasses, was waiting in the crowd outside with her daughter, Jeannette

Etheredge, when she heard a voice over the loudspeaker calling her name. Excitedly, the pair followed Wallace up the stairs and into the star's dressing room, where Rudolf was at that moment emerging from the shower, a towel around his hips and water still dripping down his body. Grinning and throwing open his arms, he cried, 'Well, greetings to the Armenian! Let's get acquainted!' And without a second's hesitation Armen threw herself into his wet embrace.

They sat down together and began talking as intently as if nobody else were in the room. 'Just instantly connected,' Jeannette recalls. 'Rudolf was a Tatar and my mother was Russian Armenian – both people who, under the Russians, didn't fare very well.' Brought up in Manchuria, to which her parents had escaped during the Turkish Armenian massacre, Armen had married a man from Tsingtao, north of Shanghai, where Jeannette was born. When war broke out, the family was interned in a Japanese POW camp, during which time Armen gave birth to a son. Suspected of being a spy because he spoke Japanese, her husband was beaten by his captors and was never able to readjust to normal life, but Armen was made more and more resilient by their experience. After spending two years in a United Nations relocation camp in the Philippines, the family emigrated to San Francisco, where Armen opened a restaurant. By the 1970s, Bali's, on the port, had become that city's Russian Tea Room, a favourite literary and showbusiness haunt. With carved wooden screens and brass light fixtures, its decor was as Middle Eastern as its cuisine, and later that night Rudolf sampled the dish for which Bali's was famous – rack of lamb marinated in pomegranate juice. He stayed talking to Armen until it was light outside, his undivided attention a result of having learned something of great interest to him. Situated opposite the restaurant was San Francisco's Customs and Immigration office, whose employees Armen had got to know well over the years as they often called on her to translate for them. It was this connection that led to contacts in the US State Department, contacts that had helped her to bring her parents, sisters and their children from Communist China to the West.

During a stopover in San Francisco a month or so later, Rudolf walked into Bali's wearing exactly the same outfit – a Nehru jacket and tight trousers. 'Do you remember me?' he asked with uncharacteristic meekness. 'After that,' Jeannette says, 'he became part of our family.' At Rudolf's invitation Armen travelled to London to stay with him, and every time the Royal Ballet toured San Francisco she would tell him to bring anyone he wanted to the restaurant. Often after a performance Rudolf would arrive with the entire company and order rack of lamb all round, Wallace helping out by waiting at tables. 'Pay? That never,' scoffs Armen. 'He didn't know how. He'd bring a hundred people and never even tip. What Rudolf gave you was himself.' And ever since the local press had reported the fact that 'Nureyev preferred dinner at Bali's', his frequent presence there had been amply reimbursed in publicity. 'I could not wish for more. The proof of what this sensational advertising did for many years to come served me beyond imagination.'

With Rudolf sharing equal billing, the National Ballet of Canada made its New York debut at the Met in April and May 1973. By now he had forged a partnership of his own with Karen Kain, who, although too tall for him, had invigorated his dancing with her youth and glamour. 'You make *me* dance taller,' he told her. He had come to prefer taller ballerinas as their waists were directly in front of his hands and he did not have to bend to support them. Their first *Swan Lake* in Montreal had been a revelation to them both, and since then Rudolf had been more determined than ever that Kain should dance Aurora. Despite Celia Franca's resistance, he began to rehearse her whenever he had spare time, goading her to push herself far beyond her limit. 'His belief in me was so much stronger than my own that I did things out of a kind of will to please him,' she says, remembering how Rudolf would give her tips on how to make her arms appear longer, her face rounder. '"Do like Margot — puff up hair!" he'd say.' Together they worked on creating different dance textures, helping Kain to arrive at a style of her own, her riskily distended phrases described by one critic as 'an unexpected blend of the fluid and the almost clenched'.

New York had fallen in love with Canada's beautiful new star, but intending the other ballerinas to grow from their Met experience, Rudolf went out of his way to provoke a sense of rivalry between them. 'With Karen he would stand in the wings and say things about me, and vice versa,' Veronica Tennant recalls with a laugh. 'He'd try to stir things up, but we'd tell each other what he'd said. "You Canadians — I can't make trouble!" he'd complain.' When Rudolf had first partnered Tennant in what she admits was then 'a scared-rabbit, neophyte performance', he seemed to be directing all his energies not at her but at his public. 'The audience knew it was hubris,' wrote one Philadelphia critic. 'But instead of punishing him for it they applauded, screamed, cheered.' By the time the company got to New York, however,

Tennant was dazzling audiences in her own right, and, wanting to reward her, Rudolf did not come out for his call after their pas de deux one night, leaving her to experience the acclaim alone: 'He was telling me that this was my moment. He was so pleased when we were all lifted to another realm of achievement. I'd never really listened to audiences before, to that roar you get at the Met, and thanks to Rudolf, I learned to understand that live theatre is a connective art, a dialogue and a moment never to be repeated.'

In July Rudolf was in Paris for twelve performances of *Swan Lake*, partnering his two favourite *étoiles*, Noëlla Pontois and Ghislaine Thesmar, as well as Natalia Makarova – the last an event that made world news. The two defectors, who had never danced together in Russia, had recently appeared in London in *Sleeping Beauty* and *Romeo and Juliet*, which 'went rather well', in Rudolf's view, although rehearsals had been tempestuous. Like most Russians, Makarova was an adagio ballerina by nature, melting one movement into another in a long, liquid line, her phrasing more luxuriantly legato than that of anyone else before her. To Rudolf, however, now accustomed to the sharply defined shapes and rhythms of Western ballerinas, such indulgent tempi were 'totally unmusical'. 'We are from different cultures now,' he shouted at her (in English) during one of their many altercations. 'You underestimate the West. They know more about our art than we do.'

Feeling 'older and wiser', he was determined to subjugate 'Fuck-arova' as he called her – 'much pleased with his own joke' – before committing himself to a regular partnership with the ballerina. What he failed to see, though, was that Makarova was at precisely the vulnerable stage he had been on his arrival in the West, clinging to her Kirov schooling as a way of maintaining control. Appearing 'isolated and inviolable', her Swan Queen was an expression of this – 'a drama about freedom', as Arlene Croce has written, 'the fate of a slave'. Makarova was one of the great Odette–Odiles of her time, her exquisite Kirov plastique forming the kind of inhumanly supple, 'swept-wing' swan shapes of which Ivanov could only have dreamed. 'She was the best I'd ever seen,' said Ghislaine Thesmar. 'But Rudolf hated all those feathers and flourishes we all took from the Russians. He used to tell me to "Stop being so baroque!"' A diplomat's daughter with innate elegance and refinement, Thesmar easily achieved 'the ladylike effect' Rudolf wanted, 'the clean lines and neat dignity of Margot'. So did Pontois, a delightfully feminine dancer with perfect proportions and an effortless technique – 'a petite plume', in Thesmar's

phrase. But Makarova had no intention of changing her style to please
Rudolf – or of substituting her usual Black Swan duet for the Nicholas
Sergeyev version he had danced with Margot.

It began to look as if the first night would never happen. The
production – a huge venture featuring forty-seven swans and seating
for more than six thousand people – was taking place on an open-air
stage in the courtyard of the Louvre in one of the worst summers on
record. As the public began filtering in, the dancers were refusing to
perform because of the wind and rain – all except Rudolf, that is, who
was very deliberately warming up onstage. 'He was showing that he
was ready to go on so the others had to do the same,' says Paris Opéra's
Hugues Gall, who had arranged the event and was himself helping
to mop the treacherously wet stage. Shivering under rugs and coats,
the audience, resolutely sticking it out, then witnessed what was
to become the most infamous Nureyev–Makarova moment. Having
reached the *pirouette-penchée* sequence in Act 3, the ballerina
performed the doubles a count later than Rudolf was expecting and,
moving too far away for him to support her, fell flat on her back – or,
as Rudolf put it, 'decided to be Sleeping Beauty at that moment'.
Ghislaine Thesmar was watching from the wings at the time. 'He was
so taken aback that Natasha dared do what *maybe* was not on the
musical count he wanted that he didn't react. He didn't make her fall,
she just went past him and he was taken by surprise. But her head went
choc parterre, and for one second she was stunned. You could see him
thinking, Oh my God . . . And then she stood up, took a preparation,
and they went on.'

Chilled and shaken, Makarova refused to dance the Variations and
Coda, which drove Rudolf into a fury: this, after all, was his big
moment. 'What about the people out there?' he demanded of Gall.
'They have paid their money. I want to dance. Fetch Pontois, announce
half hour delay'. Then, in full view of the audience, he stamped across
the stage in leg warmers and boots to Makarova's tent, where he began
violently haranguing her. The ballerina got her way, and after dancing
only three of her scheduled six performances, flew to Canada,
'announcing to the world' that she would never again dance with
'that man'.

The incident reverberated for weeks. Retaliating against her 'bitchy
remarks', Rudolf himself spoke out to the press, complaining that the
ballerina was immature and unmusical, and had decided to 'make a big
fuss' only because she had not received enough attention in Paris.
Mutual friends tried to intervene. Armen Bali and Paklusha told

Rudolf that Natasha was just waiting for 'an apology and a bunch of flowers'. Gorlinsky took his more established client's side and urged Makarova to write to Rudolf and apologize. Two weeks later in New York, Makarova had dinner with Erik, who sent Rudolf a letter saying that naturally they had talked about 'the slip-up', and that Natasha 'was very sad and sorry about the whole thing'. In the meantime Rudolf had told John Tooley that he *might* consider partnering Makarova again. 'But not yet. I danced with her too soon: I should have waited another year until she learned more about the West.'

In late August, Rudolf was with Wallace at La Turbie, where they spent most of their time by the coast, 'swimming at a private beach of a girl whose family owns half of the mountain'. Douce François was the niece of Arturo Lopez-Perez, a Chilean tycoon of incredible wealth who, before the war, had bought ten hectares of hillside stretching down to the sea. With her brilliant smile, high cheekbones and gamine dancer's frame, she had made an instant impression on Rudolf when they first met in 1969. She had travelled to London with the layout of a book of Raymundo de Larrain's Nureyev photographs. Because of legal wrangles the book project (with a text by Alexander Bland) came to nothing, but Douce, who was then Larrain's girlfriend, began 'spending more and more time with Rudolf and less and less with Raymundo'. Her house in Villefranche, a two-storey Mediterranean villa, was not grand, but it had a wonderful view of Cap Ferrat bay, where Rudolf loved to swim, diving off the rocks directly below the house.

Staying with him and Wallace at La Turbie were Marcia Haydée, Rudolf's Raymonda, and her young lover, the American dancer Richard Cragun, also a principal with the Stuttgart Ballet. Having declined the 'very overt advance' Rudolf made when he first guested with their company – 'I was one of the few babies he didn't bite' – Cragun presented an enticing challenge to Rudolf, who remained playfully insinuating whenever they were together. 'Something in his manner was always saying: I know you're Marcia's, but I'll flirt with you anyway.' And yet both dancers could see from Rudolf's behaviour towards Wallace just how solid their attachment was. 'It was what he *didn't* do, and *didn't* say . . . it was his quiet reflection – the way he looked at Wallace, or said his name . . . that made me think, Ah, there's something very serious here.' But also apparent to them was the difficult choice that Wallace was then having to make: whether to stay in Europe 'and tag along with Rudolf', or go back to Los Angeles and get on with his own life. 'It was very painful for them both,' says Cragun. 'Rudolf had found a really *good* fellow, and I sensed a sad situation of right person, wrong time.'

In London several months later, Nigel sensed much the same thing. 'Silence from Fife Rd for a week,' he noted on 13 December. 'This always makes me slightly uneasy: W is not basically content & inherently volatile. Hope everything is OK: R is the kind to clam up when in trouble.' The two had spent most of the autumn together in London, Rudolf dancing at Covent Garden and Wallace making his porno cartoon in an upstairs bedroom.* There had been wonderful moments, Wallace galloping around the house one night 'like Batman' in Rudolf's new sable coat,† but an underlying melancholy was always there. Over a late supper at Fife Road with the Goslings in December, Rudolf suddenly sighed and said, 'Oh, the time is getting so short!' By the beginning of February he had flown off to Toronto to tour America with the Canadians for six months, and Wallace, who had been engaged as a gofer on a new Mike Nichols film, left London for Hollywood a few weeks later.

Soon after their departure, Rudolf's domestic support – 'very important to him' – began to collapse. At Fife Road, Claire, who must have been at least seventy, was having health problems and suffering from *cafard* (which Nigel translated to Rudolf as 'longing for her cabbage patch back home'); while at La Turbie, Natalie, the cook-housekeeper found by Marika Besobrasova, had been diagnosed with cancer and was undergoing chemotherapy. A White Russian, she – like her husband, Serge Ivanov, who acted as chauffeur and shared the household duties – was 'very proper but not off-puttingly so', according to Wallace. 'Rudolf liked them a lot because they knew how

---

* Aptly called the Blue Room because of its blue carpet and paisley wallpaper. The animated figures used male movie stars' heads superimposed on to photographs of naked musclemen – 'like cut-out dolls fucking each other'. When Wallace came down to breakfast one morning he found a cut-out on the kitchen dresser. 'It must have blown out of the window and been put there by Claire. She didn't say a word about it. And when I mentioned it to Nigel and Maude, they said, "Don't give it another thought. Claire used to be a chambermaid at the George V – she's seen everything!"' After dinner at Fife Road, Wallace showed the Goslings the finished film on a viewer, the projectionist at the screening room he had hired having found it too 'distasteful' to continue running it. In Nigel's view, Wallace's cartoon was 'v original & has a real style but straight porn-homosexual. I fear using Brando's head will be the real stumbling block.'

† The coat was what Rudolf called 'quiet money' to compensate for having been excluded from Hurok's birthday gala in favour of Bolshoi dancers.

to keep their distance.' Trying to find a solution, Nigel had spoken to Gorlinsky, who was hardly much help – 'not really his job, anyway' – suggesting that Rudolf should let the Ivanovs go and replace them with a retired policeman and his wife. 'I told him it would have to be a retired policeman with a Russian wife – should we advertise?' joked Nigel, and, trying to downplay the 'chaos at home' to Rudolf, wrote saying, 'If you run across an Ideal Couple in Milwaukee, snap them up as I can see your present case needs covering.'

Meanwhile Nigel took things in hand himself. Since Joan Thring's departure, Rudolf had not employed a secretary to deal with his correspondence, and so Nigel had assumed the responsibility of sorting through black rubbish bags crammed with unopened fan mail, in case, Maude said, 'there were sad letters or a letter from someone who really should have an answer'. Throughout that spring it was he who arranged repairs for Rudolf's car, for the silver to be stored in Gorlinsky's safe and for new locks to be fitted in the house. There was one day in May when he drove out to Fife Road at nine a.m. to meet the locksmith, returned at midday to take Claire to the airport and went back again at eleven p.m. to check that a door was secure. Being on the telephone side of the bed, it was always Nigel who took the nocturnal calls from all over the world. 'Did I wake you up?' Rudolf would ask. 'Yes.' 'Good.' And they would have a long conversation, after which Rudolf would want to talk to Maude. 'So I'd have to say hello, then try to go back to sleep.' On 26 May the three a.m. call was from Paris: 'He wanted some costumes from Fife Road to take to Vienna. Managed to wake Tommy [Wallace's brother] & eventually decided to go out v early & pick them up, but his telephone went out of order so I couldn't fix for him to let us in. Rang Paklusha early & arranged for her to bring them. Maude didn't sleep much after all this.'

To outsiders it seemed as if the Goslings were putting themselves 'almost masochistically at [Rudolf's] disposal', but their close friend, Nigel's editor Tristram Holland, insists that this was not the case. 'It wasn't hugely onerous for them. Maude didn't work, and I suspect it was a bit of a focus in their lives – all of it was slightly good fun, Nigel getting in his Jaguar and rumbling off to Fife Road.' But there were times when Nigel in particular was deeply affected by problems in Rudolf's life. In mid-May, when the dancer injured his leg, resulting in the cancellation of the Washington season, Nigel was made so distraught by the news (one rumour had hinted at the possibility of a blood clot) that he hardly slept that night and got up to be physically sick. He may have seemed on the surface a model of English imperturbability, but friends say that he internalized his anxieties 'to an incredible degree'. He tried to make light of things ('Cluck cluck . . . here I go like an old hen'), but Rudolf's friendship was so important to him that anything threatening it became a major concern. In the letter he wrote Rudolf the day after the injury scare, he was also fretting about an article he had written. 'I am terrified by the idea that you might think I was being even the tiniest bit of a traitor and cashing in your trust in my discretion . . . It is so easy to destroy something by mistake.'

By late May Nigel's main worry was that the combination of domestic problems and dwindling work prospects – 'as the Royal B slowly (& perhaps naturally) squeezes him out' – would force Rudolf to leave London altogether. In fact, he could not have been more mistaken. For the past two years, since the *New Statesman and Nation* published its long attack on Kenneth MacMillan's directorship (beginning a campaign of perniciously personal criticism), Rudolf's name had been among those mentioned as MacMillan's likely successor. Even Lincoln Kirstein, once the dancer's most ferocious adversary, was backing him, as Erik discovered when they dined together in New York. 'He told me that MacMillan is being fired and you were going to be asked to direct the Royal Ballet. I hope so for them and you.' Kirstein's own letter to Richard Buckle dated 21 May confirmed this as much more than hearsay. 'I spent the whole night with John Tooley who is asking Nureyev to head the Royal Ballet; the company is demoralized; Kenneth is as impotent as Nixon . . . please don't talk about Nureyev, etc, until you hear it. I don't know whether he will accept.'

Tooley's offer was, in fact, conditional, requiring the star drastically to reduce his number of performances. To Rudolf this was unthinkable. He had always believed that the more often he appeared, the better he performed, and the huge success of his debuts that season in Ashton's *La Fille mal gardée* and MacMillan's *Manon* had convinced him that his best years were still to come.* He was born to be a performer, not a spectator, he later told the *Observer*'s Lynn Barber. 'When I don't dance, I can't bear to watch ANY ballet.' Nigel, believing that Rudolf had about thirty years of directing ahead of him

---

* The *Manon* duet had never been so excitingly performed, Rudolf and Merle Park making the two lovers insatiably sexy by continuing kissing long after the music had stopped. In the biggest climax he spun her two full revolutions while lifting her diagonally upwards, and then let go only to catch her a second before she hit the stage. 'We hammed it up! – which it needs,' Park says with a laugh. 'We're both peasants and we both know how to ham.'

but only three of dancing, told him that he would 'be crazy' to accept the position. But Rudolf anyway felt much too daunted then by the prospect of taking on a national company. 'It's too big. It directs itself . . . It would be terribly complicated – to take care of them, to be tied to them – it's another family.' The answer, he decided, was to create a small family of his own.

In June he launched his first 'Nureyev and Friends' venture at the Palais des Sports in Paris since his Béjart experience had proved that he had the drawing power to fill a massive space. This '*la première* "one-man show" *de la danse*' would introduce the work of choreographers little known to the French general public – Balanchine, Taylor, Limón, Bournonville – in a chamber recital of Rudolf's favourite repertory. Among the 'Friends' were Merle Park and two Opéra *étoiles*, Wilfride Piollet and her husband, Jean Guizerix, whom Rudolf had chosen for their ability to be equally at ease in classical and contemporary styles. The big surprise was the prominence Rudolf gave to a corps de ballet dancer to star with him in *Aureole*. Charles Jude was the student he had tried to befriend on the Monte Carlo beach in the summer of '69, and, five years later, during the Louvre Festival's open-air perfor- mances, he had suddenly spotted the twenty-one-year-old onstage among the Prince's friends. '*Ah, c'est vous!*' he had exclaimed aloud, and at the end of the performance, as he exited into the wings after his final call, Rudolf had given all the flowers in his arms to Charles.

For a young dancer who was then just one of the Opéra Comique extras brought in to swell the ranks of the festival's corps, Rudolf's attention was as embarrassing as it was flattering. And when Douce François, in the role of go-between, invited him to have breakfast with Rudolf at the Ritz the following morning, Charles, once again, felt disinclined to accept. 'I was so timid. But Douce was very kind to me and made me understand how lucky I was to have Rudolf's interest.' At Maxim's soon afterwards he joined a long table of people waiting for the star to take the *place d'honneur*, but when Rudolf swept into the restaurant, he reshuffled everyone around so that he could sit beside Charles. They 'talked à deux' throughout the evening, Rudolf tenderly feeding the dancer alternate forkfuls from his plate of beef Stroganoff. 'He wanted to know everything about me. I told him how my family had left Vietnam in '66 because of the war, and we talked about my work and his work, but I felt very uncomfortable because I could see the others – "*toute la clique Parisienne*" – were not at all happy.'

This was the group that dined with Rudolf almost every night, usually at Le Sept, the chic restaurant-discothéque in the rue Saint-Anne's gay quarter. Among Rudolf's clique was a very beautiful girl – 'one of the last courtesans in the corps de ballet'; a pianist from the Opéra, Elisabeth (Babette) Cooper, who, like Douce, often acted as a pander; and a photographer, Jacques Loyau. 'Present at all the great moments in dance', Jacques had got to know the dancer in London in the early sixties, when Rudolf had singled him out among the stage-door crowd and taken him to dinner. A man of culture with a louche flip side to match Rudolf's own, Jacques was not only an amiable accomplice in the public gardens and '*les bas fonds*' of Paris and London, he went out of his way to indulge Rudolf's obsession with boys. Letters would arrive advertising possible conquests such as, '*un joli et typiquement voyou anglais, en blouson noir, très gentil, il fait et se laisse faire absolument tout pour un prix forfaitaire de 100 Fs pour deux*'. In addition, Jacques had a studio on the rue Dauphine, which he claims to have kept uniquely for '*les parties fines, les orgies*', once presenting Rudolf with a harem of six youths, each so enticing that he could not decide which to take on first.

But it was Charles with whom Rudolf wanted to spend every one of his evenings during those two weeks in Paris. 'You and I are two of a kind,' he told him. 'We are both alienated from our own country.' And in the dancer's Eastern features and feline plastique, Rudolf saw the reflection of his younger self, for him the inevitable trigger of attraction. Now, a year later, during their *Aureole* performances, he had declared his feelings for the first time. 'I told him that I wasn't at all interested; I was living with someone then,' said Charles, remembering how 'very quickly' Rudolf was able to accept his heterosexuality, his attitude seemingly unchanged by rejection. They kept in touch by telephone, the older dancer urging the younger to read widely and educate himself by seeing as many films, plays and exhibitions as he could. 'He was very protective and always worrying about my future.' From time to time Rudolf would enquire half mockingly, 'Are you still with women?' perfectly aware that the only solution was to find a surrogate – '*un type asiatique*'[*] – which Jacques Loyau would be more than happy to provide.

Two weeks later in Milan, Rudolf was telephoned early one morning by Nigel informing him that Misha Baryshnikov had defected. The dancer had been on tour in Canada with a small troupe of Russians when he made his escape to a safe house, spending his first days of freedom with Sergiu Stefanschi and Karen Kain. Sounding not in the least surprised, Rudolf laughed and said, 'I was told he was intending it.' Next came a call from Armen Bali's daughter in San

---

[*] The boy had demanded four hundred francs for his services, which Rudolf refused to pay.

Francisco. 'There's somebody by the name of Baryshnikov in Canada who's looking for you,' said Jeannette, who had not yet read any of the press coverage about the Kirov's latest renegade. Sending a message for the dancer to call him and reverse the charges, Rudolf then heard from Misha himself, dismissing his polite enquiry of 'How are you?' with, 'OK. But the real question is, "How are *you?*"' They arranged to see each other in New York where, in July, Rudolf would be appearing with the Canadians at the Met, and Baryshnikov would make his American debut at the State Theater across the plaza.

It was Jeannette who accompanied Misha to Rudolf's first night, and hearing applause as they entered Lincoln Center, she turned round, thinking that 'someone like Jackie Kennedy' must just have walked in. She was wrong: the ovation was for Misha. 'Start smiling,' I told him. 'This is for *you.*' More alarmed than flattered by the crowd's attention – 'he hated the fact people knew who he was' – Misha insisted that they leave the theatre before the house lights went up. They met Rudolf backstage and then the three went to dinner at Monique van Vooren's apartment, joining several other people, including Rudolf's Vaganova contemporary Sasha Mintz. Jeannette was not alone that night in being struck by Rudolf's kindness towards Baryshnikov. 'He was telling him to see this movie and that play – he wanted everything to be good for Misha.' Above all, Rudolf was anxious to steer his fellow Pushkin pupil away from the mistakes he felt he had made. 'He told me not to write autobiography too soon, who the best teachers were, to stay with one company, not jump around.' In London Nigel had been similarly impressed by Rudolf's 'extraordinary lack of jealousy' towards his young rival. He had been 'relaxed and jokey' whenever he spoke of Misha, remarking on one occasion, 'I am getting better press in America this year. Maybe my goodbye before the invasion of Mars begins.'

This took place on 27 July, with the Baryshnikov–Makarova *Giselle*. And it presented Nureyev devotees with a dilemma: whether to attend the hottest ballet event in a decade or to be loyal and see Rudolf's *Sleeping Beauty*. Marilyn La Vine bought tickets for both, planning to watch only one act of *Giselle* so that she could still see the whole of Rudolf's performance. (The Prince does not appear until Act 2.) Giving her ticket stub to a friend – 'like handing her $2,000 in cash' – she ran across to the Met with a thumping heart, thinking, 'They won't let me in, the door will be closed . . . You've betrayed him.' But as she made her way to her usual seat she saw that the first row and front boxes usually filled by the 'regulars' were empty. 'And don't think

Rudolf wouldn't have noticed.' At the stage door afterwards, however, all the familiar faces were there.

> I remember this scene as if it just happened. When Rudolf came out there was a hush over the crowd, and what was unspoken filled the atmosphere with such an intense intimacy. As the fans parted to let him through, he paused. He never usually said anything to us, but this time he spoke to the group as if it were one person. 'New boy in town – huh?' We all started to clap and didn't stop, until finally, he said, 'I believe you, I believe you!' It was very, very touching.

When Paklusha telephoned Rudolf a couple of days later, he sounded depressed. He had been seeing Baryshnikov, Makarova and Mintz virtually every night, he told her, complaining that they had been 'ganging up against him'. 'Actually,' Nigel noted in his diary, 'I suspect that he is inevitably the Odd Man Out . . . the father figure of defectors.' But it was more than that. In the latest issue of the *New Yorker*, Arlene Croce, the doyenne of American dance critics, had described Baryshnikov as 'the greatest male dancer to have escaped Russia since Nijinsky got himself fired by the Imperial Ballet in 1911'. No mention of Rudolf. Croce's remark appeared in her review of 'Makarova's Miracle', the ballerina's staging for the American Ballet Theatre of *La Bayadère*'s Shades act – Rudolf's own first 'astounding success'. Next to dancing, his productions of the Petipa classics were his greatest achievement, and hearing that Baryshnikov had watched a rehearsal of *Sleeping Beauty*, Rudolf immediately wanted to know his opinion. Misha had hesitated. To him, Rudolf's version had seemed more English than Russian – 'a different ballet . . . more Ninette de Valois' than authentic Petipa. 'Well . . . I . . . I . . .', he found himself stammering as he tried to think of something positive to say.

Rudolf had also 'known instinctively' that Misha had not liked his dancing. For someone who had grown up in Russia with the infamous Nureyev as 'his lodestar, a fantasy figure', it was disconcerting to find that, in terms of pure technique, Rudolf's dancing was not nearly as accomplished as his own. He had 'a lot of faults and ups and downs', Baryshnikov told Joan Acocella, flaws he was able to cover with his extraordinary charisma. 'It was like – oh, burning. His eyes were burning – everything. He created that kind of an atmosphere around him, electrifying!!' But there was no 'internal logic' to Rudolf's phrasing, he said, 'no natural flow from beginning to the end'. 'He really was not interested in the cantilena of it. The joining steps.

Everything is about showmanship: 'Look at me, how I do this.' Watch my fifth position – it's clean, you know . . . and all those preparations, like: Ooooh!! Now I'll do something!'

Baryshnikov himself was a performer for whom preparations did not exist and the virtuoso steps were only transitions in an overarching dance picture. What Rudolf saw, however, was 'a very good technique' and nothing else – 'no spirit, no soul, no trembling of your feelings'. So it was distressing for him when Erik, the dancers' dancer and his own lodestar, had been completely overwhelmed by Baryshnikov's performances, telling his biographer, 'Misha may well be the most dynamic dancer of his time.'

Erik was then in New York to stage his production of *La Sylphide* for the Canadians, and although he had officially retired from the ballet stage in January 1972, he had agreed to make his debut as a character artist, performing the role of Madge the Witch. Initially Rudolf had wanted Erik to play Iago to his Othello in *The Moor's Pavane*, news that had sent Lincoln Kirstein into an ecstasy of anticipation: 'Erik told me I WILL KILL HIM KILL HIM KILL HIM!' he exclaimed to Richard Buckle, gossiping about this 'duel of the century'. But Erik, who had been operated on six months earlier for a stomach ulcer, did not want to push himself too hard, joking that his transposition into a hideous, toothless hag was type-casting enough – 'a perfect way to release everything that was evil inside of me'. (Rudolf later admitted that when Erik had lifted the Witch's stick above his head, there was a moment when he had literally feared for his life.) Professionally their battle of egos continued, Misha observing how 'each step one of them made was judged by the other', and yet the première on 9 August 1974 – the first time the two stars had appeared together onstage since 1962 – was so emotional for them both that when the curtain came down they had instinctively embraced.

For some time now Erik had been living with Constantin Patsalas, a Greek-born dancer and choreographer with the Canadian ballet, having at last found the domestic stability he craved. 'Constantin is very patient with me, so that is good,' he told Rudolf, remarking in the same letter how much he had liked Wallace. They went out several times as a foursome with no apparent awkwardness, although, from Rudolf's point of view, this was no wonder: it was Misha, not Constantin, who posed the threat. Coaching the dancer for his debut in *La Sylphide*, Erik had been 'amazed that a Russian, who had never before attempted Bournonville, could achieve such purity and authenticity of style', and Misha was no less admiring. Like Rudolf, he had seen Erik for the first time in Teja's 1961 footage, and been struck by exactly the qualities that had so excited Rudolf – the beautiful length of the Bruhn line, and the dancer's 'cold power' (Misha, by describing this as 'an incredible white heat', virtually echoed Rudolf's own famous oxymoron). Making no attempt to hide his jealousy, Rudolf would quip, 'So you're with Erik again! Maybe you two will get married,' but nevertheless he was determined that they should be friends, and invited Misha to stay with him when he next came to London.

They spent the second half of November together at Fife Road, driving off to morning class at Baron's Court, where Rudolf seemed to take great pleasure in introducing the young star to his Royal Ballet colleagues. They went to see the London Contemporary Dance Theatre, to 'some low-low travesty show featuring transvestites' and to supper with the Goslings. The couple's first impression was of a polite, clever, but still very childlike young man – 'much less complicated than R', remarked Nigel, 'which I fear may make him less interesting onstage'. But while Misha remembers 'just having a really good time', Rudolf claimed to have been disappointed by how taciturn the dancer was. 'He was dying to hear all about Russia, and couldn't believe that Misha hardly said a word. It was as if he thought the walls were listening.' Rudolf must have decided to liven things up, as it was very late one night when Misha arrived unexpectedly at Terry and Paklusha's flat. 'He just turned up on our doorstep, and said, "Can I stay with you? I was with Rudolf and he chased me all round the house. I can't get away from him, so I left." Rudolf thought it was going to be a seduction scene; it just wasn't, so Misha got a taxi to Carlos Place and stayed with us for the rest of the time.' (An entry in Nigel's diary dated 28 November reports, 'Misha apparently v upset by open homosexuality in Western ballet. He likes girls.')

Like Paklusha in London, Armen Bali had become 'Mother of the Defectors' in San Francisco, a role she felt to be destined in Rudolf's case. 'A fortune-teller once said, "You will have two children, but there will be someone else, too, perhaps someone like a son, perhaps a friend, and he will open the world to you."' As Rudolf indeed did, taking Armen with him on his travels – 'Breakfast in London, dinner in Rome, next day, Monte Carlo.' Speaking five languages and well read in the Russian classics, she was, as Misha says, exactly the kind of strong-willed, educated woman that Rudolf admired. 'Armen was exotic and very straightforward and loud and street-smart and made him feel at home.' She had, in addition, turned herself into a paragon of Russian motherhood – cooking him *pelmeni*, inventing a Bashkir salad (shredded and marinated raw beef with beets and new potatoes), washing his clothes, massaging his feet, and even scrubbing his back in the bath. 'When he was in bed at night I would recite Pushkin and talk and talk until he dropped off to sleep, and then I'd tuck him in and go back to my room.'

It had not been long before Rudolf set Armen to work on the project he had had in mind for her all along: to get his family out of Russia. With his signed letter of authorization, she had made contact the previous summer with the American consul general in Leningrad appealing for temporary exit visas for Farida and Rosa. Letters from the consulate and the embassy in Moscow were then sent to the relevant authorities in Ufa, the US State Department having requested to be informed of any progress. In June '74 Armen travelled to Russia, taking clothes and twenty-five thousand dollars to buy gifts while she was there;* the cash, taken from her own account, was intended to help not only the Nureyevs but a Russian singer she had known in Manchuria, who now lived in Leningrad. She met her friend and his two daughters in a park near her hotel, and was distributing the contents of her package when Rosa, who was also there, suddenly started shouting and snatching things out of Armen's hands. 'She thought I'd been spending Rudolf's money.'

Soon after Armen and Rudolf met she had written Rosa a letter saying how guilty she felt to be having 'all the joy' of her brother while Rosa herself was so far away. 'I said, "I wish for the day that you'll be able to enjoy the glory that he has and be proud of him."' But to Rosa this had seemed like gloating and, from the moment they met, she had made her resentment clear. Farida, too, had been cold and unwelcoming: 'I had tears in my eyes when I asked, "Do you miss him?" but it was absolutely like she was mute and dumb, with a heart made out of ice. She kept looking at Rosa, and said not a word except when I gave her my mother's ring and beads of coral – the Tatar national stone. Then she thanked me.'

It was almost as if she knew that Armen had hopes of casting herself in Farida's role, once having asked Rudolf to 'Please accept me as your

---

* Imported goods from Intourist shops – 'anything from car tyres to sweets' (Armen Bali) – were available only to foreigners, and parcels sent to Rudolf's family by Gorlinsky's office had recently been refused by the Russian authorities. Barclays Bank money orders had arrived (three hundred British pounds to Farida in Ufa, and another three hundred to Rosa in Leningrad) but the state took forty per cent and paid the remainder in roubles at the swindling 'official' exchange rate of 66 kopeks to the dollar.

mother.' ('No,' he had replied emphatically, 'you're not my mother, you're my friend.') Nevertheless the plan was for Farida to stay with Armen in San Francisco, and by the time of Armen's departure at the beginning of July all the necessary papers were in order and air tickets were being held by the US ambassador. A week later, though, Rudolf, in a state of fury, woke Nigel up at three in the morning.

> At the v last minute Rosa rings from Leningrad (she had wanted to come too – R didn't want her) to say the Collektiv had vetoed the trip. Apparently she had once been a Party member & been expelled. R exploded, said he would go to the Press, kick up a 'Panov' row etc. Said he would spill all at an interview with *Time* next day. Managed to dissuade him, & let it run for a few days.

Three weeks earlier the dancers Valery and Galina Panov, who for two years had been living in Leningrad under virtual house arrest, had finally been allowed to emigrate to Israel. In recent years a number of Jewish or half-Jewish Russians had been granted affidavits to come to the West on grounds of 'family reunification', and when this entitlement was withheld from the Panovs, the couple, with the help of influential foreign friends, were able to arouse spectacular support from abroad. Thousands of fellow performers, including some of the greatest names in theatre and dance, signed petitions and held demonstrations and all-night vigils to show solidarity, their outcry taking effect on 7 June, when the Panovs learned that they were free to leave. At no point had their English friend and chief activist, Patricia Barnes, Clive's wife, tried to enlist Rudolf in the campaign – 'It would have been an imposition: he had too much to lose.' But even though, after speaking to Valery sometime later, Rudolf had expressed regret at not having done anything to help, the international crusade to 'Free Russian Jewry' was not one to which he subscribed. On the contrary – 'I will fight with the Arabs!' he once declared during a heated debate on the subject, an issue that had sparked his most malign expressions of anti-Semitism. 'Sure it did,' said Wallace. 'He was very upset that Russian Jews were getting out, and his mother wasn't.'

While Rudolf was dancing in Paris in October, his spirits had sunk even lower. *Le Monde* had given him 'a disastrous notice', and Wallace had telephoned several times threatening to kill himself. 'It had got to the point where I couldn't live without him, and I couldn't live with him.' Rudolf told the Goslings that he was going to get Wallace on the first plane out of Los Angeles, but Nigel, who had received a letter from Wallace of similar bleakness, had already written to persuade him to return to Europe. 'It would make a lot of sense. We are all going through a tough patch (Rudolf too – he is in the most difficult part of his whole career obviously), and we need each other's support. Everybody asks after you. What could tempt you back?' A strong inducement was the fact that the Goslings themselves were to be in Paris at that time, and when Rudolf flew to New York for one night to launch Paul Taylor's season, he returned with Wallace in tow.

> W rang, quite cheerful & said we should all meet for dinner at 7pm: then later rang again, suicidal, to say R had walked out on him & he was going to drink himself to sleep if he didn't put himself out of the window. Wouldn't come out or let us go there. So we went & dined & found a message from R to meet them at the Club Sept as usual, around 9. We arrived late & found W red-eyed with crying & almost incapable of speaking: he cheered up slightly slowly. Next day we lunched together & he seemed better but that evening at a private dinner (about 10) he suddenly left the table & was found in the next room shouting into the street through the open window.

During the performance the following night, Rudolf had slipped and hurt his leg after the final *assemblé* turn, and when the Goslings saw him in his dressing room, his mood was ominously dark. 'Wallace seems better,' they volunteered, but Rudolf glowered; this relationship was proving an unnecessary drain on his energy. 'If he gives more trouble I will kick him out,' he said to Nigel, whose 'heart froze', as he remembered how sweetly solicitous Rudolf had been on the first night, feeding Wallace as if he were a child. 'It was the reaction of fury at falling etc., but it might happen again.'

The end of the year saw Rudolf presenting the first Nureyev and Friends venture in New York, his small ensemble this time including Louis Falco, a Limón protégé, and four members of Paul Taylor's company. The point, he said, was to introduce a Broadway audience prone to 'burst into screams' to modern, more challenging works. 'These are not spectacular ballets: these are ballets to contemplate. It's to the great credit of the public that they respond the way they do.' For this, and every subsequent season, the Uris Theatre was sold out for five weeks, though it was Rudolf's name, not his choice of repertory, that had filled the two thousand seats. To Alan Kriegsman of the *Washington Post*, Rudolf was turning himself into 'the ballet world's no. 1

missionary'. 'Nureyev is trading on his own box-office galvanism, but not for even remotely venal reasons. Nothing would have prevented his continuing in the conventional mould, guesting with one troupe and one partner after another, making ostentatious pas de deux a life work . . . He has chosen a far harder, more visionary, more courageous course of risk and adventure.'

Not everyone agreed. Asked once again by Rudolf to be Iago to his Othello, Erik had turned him down. 'I said to him, "Rudik, I cannot be one of your 'friends' on that programme, because there isn't one person on it who is a real friend."' And hearing of Rudolf's latest project, Ninette de Valois had been incensed by its 'egotistical vulgarity', complaining to Nigel, 'I am convinced that Nureyev's attitude is undergoing a sad change . . . He is not only dance mad but money mad.'

But ever since he arrived in the West, it had been Rudolf's belief that how much you were paid was a sign of how much you were worth. His Broadway scheme may have been motivated by what Kriegsman called 'Nureyev's own magnanimous artistic conscience', but it was also an inspired business idea involving minimum overheads, no scenery and only a handful of dancers and musicians. For the Palais des Sports season Rudolf had received five per cent of box-office takings in addition to his fee of $3,000 a performance, while his share of the Uris run was as high as $45,000 a week. Broadway is big business – the reason that Balanchine had finally allowed Rudolf to perform *Apollo* in New York, reckoning that the five per cent of the gross he demanded for the five-week run would rescue his school from what Barbara Horgan called a 'perilous' financial situation. 'I think it came out to about twenty-five thousand dollars, which was more money than you could possibly imagine in those days.'

Whether providing dance numbers for legendary hoofers or a troupe of elephants, Balanchine had relished his spell in commercial theatre – choreographing four Rodgers and Hart shows among many others – going on to spice his masterworks with a hint of low culture, and lavishing the money he had made on a Long Island house and ermine coat for his Hollywood-star wife, Vera Zorina. On the other hand, to the spartan de Valois (who even in old age was renowned for refusing the offer of an Opera House car in favour of taking the underground), the Broadway Nureyev was impossible to understand. She could no more see why he would want to surround himself with 'a senseless money-making gang of friends' than she could condone his crusade to bring minority-interest modern works to the masses.

She had never made a secret of her contempt for most modern choreographers – 'She loathes [Hans] van Manen too – & Tetley, it appears,' remarked Nigel – and she was furious that Anthony Dowell, 'a truly great & dedicated artist', had profaned himself by appearing with Rudolf in *Songs of a Wayfarer*. 'I would not enter into a discussion over the pretentious Béjart work,' she told Nigel, 'except to quote Nureyev, "We do everything up to conceiving on the floor." I hated seeing Dowell in it.'

It was, she believed, 'the hysterical effect of freedom' that had led to Rudolf's downfall, his multitude of talents driving him 'to lick the whole map as fast as he could' in order to explore them all. 'He never would stay anywhere more than five minutes, so no one could get very far with him. Which of course is very much the reaction of any Russian exile from being so boxed up.' It was upsetting to her that this lifestyle had taken its toll on Rudolf's classicism, once 'the most aristocratic style' she had ever seen, and she blamed Nigel for ignoring this in his reviews. Recent Alexander Bland pieces had, she complained, focused on Nureyev far more than on any other Royal Ballet artist, though in his letter of defence Nigel points out that he (or rather, they, 'for Maude reads – and often emends – every word I write') had inevitably written at length about Rudolf as he had featured prominently in three of the six current works. 'It is possible that we rate . . . Nureyev's performances differently,' he went on. 'Everybody has their own priorities and so ends up with different assessments.' But this infuri-ated de Valois even more. 'Do you really think this is a correct attitude from a critic? It is, to me, too subjective,' she snapped in the two-and-a-half-page polemic she wrote in reply. 'I ask more of Nureyev than you do . . . You say that Nureyev suffers from "nerves" in London. Of course. He is no fool & knows that most of the time he is ill-prepared . . . I would ask him not to learn Manon in 5 days & make a mess of it.'

De Valois was probably justified in accusing Nigel of being 'espe-cially indulgent' towards Rudolf. In his introduction to *Observer of the Dance* (the 1985 collection of Alexander Bland criticism), Rudolf describes Nigel as 'totally objective', 'completely without prejudice', and 'extraordinarily detached' – which is straining to prove a point. Nigel himself was only too aware of conflicting interests, questioning if he had been fair to Makarova in his review of *Song of the Earth* – 'knowing that I start with a personal prejudice against her'. His rela-tionship with Rudolf was, by his own admission, 'one of the most exciting and enjoyable bits of my life', his guru status increasingly more stimulating to him than his job as a critic. This is tangible in Nigel's letters, his description, for example, of a 'fabulous *pas magnétique*' in a pre-Petipa *Sleeping Beauty* with choreography by Espinosa, 'in which the Prince dances with Aurora while she is still asleep, *then* he kisses her . . . Could you use it sometime? It is annoying to think that you won't!' In recent months, however, he had been overstepping into Gorlinsky's territory by assuming a more impresarial role and steering Rudolf away from projects that he felt to be unwise.* With Charles Murland, who had been offered the chairmanship of London Festival Ballet, Nigel was also playing power games, advising Charles to think seriously about accepting the post as a way of 'maybe replacing Beryl Grey [the current director] with R'. Through Terry Benton, the archivist at the Opera House, with access to board minutes, Nigel received inside information denied to his fellow critics, and on 4 December 1974 wrote a confidential letter 'on a slightly delicate subject' to John Tooley:

> A few weeks ago Rudi Nureyev asked me if I knew where he could get a copy made of his ms piano score of *La Bayadère*, in case it got lost . . . [It] transpired that [the archives] already have a photograph record of the whole score, presumably made when the 'Shadows' episode was being arranged in Jack Lanchbery's day . . . I well understand Jack's zeal in snatching the opportunity but I am sure you will realise that [Rudolf] would be very upset if he knew about it. I am inclined to sympathise . . . Would you let me know if you agree? . . . 1977 will be the centenary of the première of *La Bayadère* in St Petersburg and, having seen the single ballet in Leningrad, I think it might be well worth while using the excuse for a (Rudi-Fred?) revival.

* A New York agent had recently sent Rudolf the first draft of a new Tennessee Williams play, *This Is (an Entertainment)*, to be directed by Frank Dunlop. He was being offered the dual role of a chauffeur who in Act 1 is having an affair with a countess, as well as the commanding general of a revolutionary army, who becomes the countess's lover in Act 2. Williams told the writer David Daniel that he had designed the two parts to 'bring out what he thought were the contradictory and complementary sides of Rudolf's sexual allure'. But finding it 'far too obscure and precious', Nigel sent Rudolf a letter outlining 'GOOD POINTS (e.g. a good author and director for a debut); BAD POINTS (the verbal style demands great speaking technique . . .); and GENERAL POINTS (I cannot see this being in any way a widely popular long-running money-making play).' The end result was that Rudolf turned it down.

In Marina Vaizey's review of *Observer of the Dance*, she claims, quite rightly, that Nigel was more ambitious for the arts he discussed than for himself, quoting his own definition of the critic as 'a modest figure with a diminutive power to help and a little more to hurt.' There can be no doubt, however, that at this point in Rudolf's career, both he and Maude were compromising their critical impartiality by doing far too much to help. As if aware of this, the Goslings had always been careful about maintaining a front, never going to see Rudolf backstage except when they were abroad – 'because nobody knew us'. And when their colleague Oleg Kerensky joined them at Fife Road one night for dinner, Nigel confessed to having been 'a bit alarmed' by the fact that Kerensky might detect just how intimately linked to Rudolf they were. 'We left all the adjectives to the other people,' Maude would insist, a claim also voiced by Nigel in a letter written to Rudolf in the spring of 1971:

> It suddenly came over me, during *Apollo*, how horrible it is that by your letting me be your friend you have stopped my pen from saying outright . . . just what a fantastic thrill I get from your dancing. I have to try to look cool and detached and all that and leave the superlatives to my colleagues. So I just wanted to put in a private word to say that I still get the same shiver down my spine when you walk on and the same tingle when you start to move . . . Not to mention that you have the most seductive bum in the business, but that is a different – but related – matter. Anyhow this is to say that after ten years I am turned on just exactly the same, damn it. I supposed it was around June 12th 1961 when you first walked across my eyeball (in the Hunting Scene in Sleeping B in Paris) . . . [and] this is a token to show I did not miss the anniversary . . . just accept it as a kind of chaste little love-bite.
>
> Loveski, N

Richard Buckle was not alone among London's dance critics in believing that Nigel was in love with Rudolf. 'Everybody knows that. He was a queen when he was young.' And yet despite Nigel's sojourn in Berlin, there is no evidence of youthful homosexuality in the early diaries or in his autobiographical novel, *Thicker Than Water* (about two young men competing for the love of a girl). In one of the three existing 1970s journals, Nigel admits to having been 'pleased of course' when Rudolf kissed him on the mouth for the first time while saying goodbye. 'Since then always à la Russe [on each cheek three times].'

But although mentioning the fact that he had briefly and inadvertently seen Rudolf naked when the dancer was sitting on the stairs with a towel around his loins, his matter-of-fact comment – 'It is big & solid like a club' – is hardly evidence of any lascivious feelings. 'Nigel was only writing in terms to which Rudolf would relate,' maintains Tristram Holland, referring to the 'anniversary' letter. 'He loved all that joshing – and it was exactly the same with Wallace.' Certainly, although genuinely mystified by Wallace's idiosyncratic treatment of Borges's *Circular Ruins*, Nigel would use this and other pornographic pursuits as an opportunity for fun. 'Now, Wallace,' he once wrote, 'the question is – what are the prospects of *Members Only* or *Mr Gooniverse* or whatever the name is of your film (what about *Coming Shortly?*).'

Throughout his life the friends Rudolf chose were always those who were in some way useful to him. And yet Alexander Bland's panegyrics – a veritable Nureyev industry – were not the reason he counted the Goslings as 'family'. Maude herself admitted that Rudolf rarely, if ever, read their criticism (if anyone raised an eyebrow about an especially favourable review, he would reply with just one word: 'Love'). It was Nigel's writing on art that he admired. A critic 'instinctively sympathetic to what was new', Nigel was among the first to champion British and American modernists from Henry Moore to Roy Lichtenstein and Mark Rothko. It was through the Goslings that Rudolf had met the avant-garde directors, writers and artists 'who excited me with their ideas', and it was at the Victoria Road 'Roxies' that he was introduced to the films of Jean Genet, Gregory Markopoulos, and Kenneth Anger, enabling him 'to catch up on some of those things that I had left Russia to find'.

It was also Nigel and Maude who had given Rudolf his first sight of Martha Graham on film, and taken him to a performance when she toured London with her company in 1963. Having vowed at the time that he 'had to see more', Rudolf was delighted when, more than a decade later, he learned that the choreographer had suggested creating a new ballet for him. The diva of modern dance, Martha Graham had formulated what Rudolf called 'the complete alphabet', an extraordinarily innovative language that her biographer Agnes de Mille compares to that of *Finnegans Wake*. While James Joyce never wrote another book in the same idiom, the Graham vocabulary was copied, adapted and developed by the leading choreographers of the next generation – 'the Children of Martha'. 'Merce [Cunningham] and Paul [Taylor] made what Martha was doing more palpable,' noted Rudolf. 'They translated Martha's language to our day.' Among the century's choreographers, only Balanchine had anything comparable to Graham's influence on dance. She brought to it not only a new method but new subject matter, reflecting, in Joan Acocella's words, 'the post-Freudian psyche – fear, wrath, sex – and, by wedding that subject to ancient myth, ennobled it'.

It was *Night Journey*, Graham's version of *Oedipus Rex*, that had 'hypnotized' Rudolf when he saw her dance in London. As Jocasta she had an intensity and forcefulness the like of which he had never encountered, 'an incredible command and focus of every movement'. When the Goslings took him backstage to meet the dancer he was still so struck by her performance that he simply stared at her without saying a word. With her long, Oriental-black hair, white skin, scarlet mouth and skeletal cheeks, Graham was in any case a startlingly inhibiting presence. And yet she had always been a lusty, highly sexed woman who, as Paul Taylor once remarked, seemed to view men, even homosexual men, as no more than 'giant dildos'. Considered shockingly explicit at its 1947 première, *Night Journey* depicted Jocasta expressing 'the cry from her vagina' on meeting Oedipus, her leg raised high as she surrendered herself to a violent contraction. Faced with the silent young Russian in her dressing room, Graham had assumed that 'he did not like my dance', but years later Rudolf told her that he had not said anything because he had been so moved. 'I'm not very good with words, so I just gave my admiration.'

The admiration was mutual. In New York he would go to watch Graham's company and school, and she would come to his performances, even heretically kissing his hand after a particularly exciting performance of *Corsaire*. In Rudolf she recognized the kind of 'brutality, even savagery' that had drawn her to her dancer lover and muse, Erick Hawkins, and even though Nureyev, the ballet star, stood for everything against which she had fought, he also embodied the very essence of her art – the intense passion, attack and ferocity. 'That was that,' recalled Rudolf. 'From there we had a comparlance.' This was inevitable, as the two had much in common, both creating ballets out of a necessity to perform, Graham's mythical works centring on a single woman – Medea, Joan of Arc, Clytemnestra, Hérodiade – all ultimately versions of herself, just as Rudolf used the classics to explore conflicting aspects of his personality. Each was as solipsistic as the other – 'enraptured selfishness' Graham's manager called it – and both had dedicated themselves totally and mercilessly to their art. The chasm between their two dance genres had by now sufficiently narrowed, Graham felt, for her to shatter the idol of her own making and invite not only Rudolf but Margot, too, to collaborate on her new ballet. More to the point, as Graham herself admitted, 'there were bills to be paid.' To help the company settle debts of $75,000 and to celebrate its fiftieth anniversary, the two stars agreed to give the première of the new piece at a fund-raising New York gala on 19 June 1975, and also offered to perform the pas de deux from *Swan Lake* as their own gift to Graham.

The subject and title of Graham's ballet was *Lucifer*, not the biblical devil but the principal angel fallen from grace, whose name means light. Rudolf had described Nijinsky as 'a lucifer – he brought light with him onstage. What Margot did' – and so was gratified by the concept, which, as Graham said, was almost type-casting for Nureyev. The five weeks they spent together proved to be equally stimulating for them both, the only time, Graham admitted, that she had allowed herself to live through another person. 'Rudolf is not a substitute for myself,' she told the *New York Times*'s Anna Kisselgoff, 'but working with him gives me a very definite identification.' Kisselgoff had hoped for Rudolf's own views on this historic alliance, but he had not wanted 'to gibber-jabber', wary of 'sounding like a monkey' by attempting to mimic Graham's famously verbose pronouncements.* It was her dance vocabulary he was after – 'Martha had movement and I was stealing it.'

Although Graham claimed to have taught Rudolf the basics herself, it was actually a member of her company, David Hatch Walker, who gave Rudolf his first private lessons. When his knee began to swell after only two classes ('because of her fourth position'), Graham, concerned lest he injure himself further, instructed him to 'Go directly to repertoire.' 'Martha wouldn't let me take class with the company. I would have felt more comfortable being behind someone copying the exercises and seeing what they do.' But the Graham movements – the '*bourrées* on the knees, jackknife turns, hinge falls' – were not something that a classical dancer, even one as assimilative as Rudolf, could pick up in a matter of weeks. Inspired by the Kundalini, the Hindu system of spiritual energy that motivates physical movement, not an arm or leg could be lifted until 'the life impulse' had risen to its highest level. What in classical ballet is a simple *retiré*, a drawing up of the leg, becomes in Graham terms an expression of 'inner being'. Aware that

---

* Art historian David Scrase vividly remembers Rudolf's parodying Graham in Margot's dressing room. 'He came in nude except for a plastic laundry bag, and "yearned and yearned" as Margot ticked him off.'

feelings could be communicated by the upper body – 'Arch the spine and you have emotion' – Graham concentrated on the torso, her hallmark contraction (the spasm of the diaphragm muscles used in coughing) driving the limbs by its percussive force, 'much as the thong of a whip moves because of the crack of the handle'.

Having spent most of his years as a dancer rigidly corseted in nineteenth-century-style costumes, Rudolf found Graham's pliantly eloquent torso as unnatural as he did her use of the floor, not to be resisted in a balletic defiance of gravity but succumbed to as if in quicksand – 'a descent and lowering in thighs and back . . . a melting and sliding, a communion with the ground and then a recovery and regalvanizing'. And even though Graham had made Margot's role of Night the Temptress more classically oriented than the others, the ballerina found a side fall so difficult to master that Graham offered to substitute something else. Rudolf was not impressed – 'Be comfortable,' he scoffed and, rising to a familiar Nureyev challenge, Margot made herself perform the step perfectly, dissolving into the floor 'like silk'. Rudolf, in turn, was determined to work until he got things right; as one member of the company observed, 'This was not a lark.' At first Graham had been intent on fusing their two styles, but Rudolf preferred to 'stick to her, then meld the two'. He began to suspect, however, that what he was doing was not 'really Graham', and he was right. The Martha Graham of 1975 offering to make things easy for her dancers rather than hurling philosophical edicts and mocking their lack of passion, was not the Circe-like figure of before. This was the Disco Graham with aspirations of her own to be a superstar – appearing beside Rudolf and Margot, for example, in a glossy magazine promotion for Blackgama minks – and whose style, according to Joan Acocella, bore 'not a shred of continuity' with that of her past.

In 1969, at the age of seventy-four, Graham had given her final performance, the subsequent deprivation of not dancing turning her into a bitter alcoholic, so self-destructive that she twice came close to death. In 1972, after her second collapse, she began to rehabilitate herself, and it was around this time that Ron Protas, a young photographer, came into the picture. Making himself indispensable to Graham, Protas encouraged her to make a complete break with her former life, a renaissance that required the elimination of the original Graham image from her company's performances. 'This was not just a new period in Graham's life. It really was a new life . . . One by one the veterans left, and Protas took their place as Graham's primary adviser.' Graham had made only four short pieces in the six years since she retired, and Protas got her working again, seeing an association with an international star as a way of capitalizing on her new phase. Graham, he told Rudolf, had become disillusioned with modern dance, which she felt had become as conservative and stagnant as ballet had been when she first began her revolution. Now was the moment for change; she wanted to begin fusing both genres, and would even consider ballets being performed by her company.

Lucifer premièred on 19 June, and the celebrity audience included ex-Graham pupils Woody Allen and Betty Ford, who had paid up to five thousand dollars for a ticket. As a result of spraining his ankle before he arrived in New York, Rudolf wore a bandage that seemed to cover more flesh than his costume, which consisted of a gold jockstrap designed by Halston. Studded with Tiffany jewels, it was as ornate as the joke one given to him by the Canadian dancers, and yet, as Arlene Croce wrote in her review, Rudolf did not appear ridiculous. 'The element of camp in his personality frees him for incongruous undertakings such as this.' Incandescently lit, his hair 'blown out like an angel by William Blake', he looked absolutely stunning as the ballet opened, the men surrounding him falling backwards as if blinded by his brilliance. The *Lucifer* choreography itself was considered to be not much more than a recapitulation of all Graham's other tortured-hero roles, Rudolf's interpretation described as 'a passable portrayal in a Graham work which is itself barely passable'. But the fifty-six-year-old Margot fared even less well with the critics. Clive Barnes decided to remain tactfully doubtful about her involvement. Rudolf himself had no delusions about the enterprise – 'a publicity stunt with me and Margot, Martha, Betty Ford, Woody Allen and Halston . . . It was all like an MGM promotion.' Nevertheless, this was just the beginning of an intermittent, decade-long association with Martha Graham, and his repertory eventually included her few master roles for men.

Rudolf had spent most of the summer in New York, where Wallace had been living and working and where wealthy acquaintances had offered him a room in their Upper East Side house. Elena Rostropovich, the cellist's daughter, lived on the top floor, and it was through her that Wallace had met the millionaire benefactor Howard Gillman, who had put up four-fifths of the money for a new film – a live-action porno venture called *More, More, More*. It was Rudolf who had arranged for Wallace to come to New York. 'He thought it would be more creative and stimulating than LA.' And never more so than now. The city had become a bohemia, a melting pot of the performing and graphic arts, where dance was no longer confined to proscenium stages but had spilled into galleries, lofts and churches. The performers themselves were more liberated than ever before, often not formally trained and required to perform only everyday movements without regard to grace or technical skill. 'Why do *grands battements* when you can push a mattress round the room and carry a pot of paint?' quipped the choreographer Murray Louis, who often saw Rudolf at these postmodern Happenings. 'All over Soho the Loft scene was opening up, and Rudolf went everywhere – he loved watching this stuff. It was like nothing he'd ever seen before, and people were so flattered that this giant took it seriously. That same freedom permeated everything. It was just a very wild, indulgent, careless, promiscuous period.'

The Golden Age of Promiscuity, the gay world called it, when, as Edmund White has written, 'life was radically different from anything before unless we go back to *The Satyricon* of Petronius'. A seasoned habitué of the infamous bathhouses – St Marks, the Club Baths and the Everard ('Ever Hard') – Rudolf took Wallace along with him to the Club Baths one night. With anonymous multiple encounters becoming 'the new reality' of urban gay life, Wallace knew that he would have to accommodate Rudolf if their relationship was going to work. 'I'd never been to the baths before, and as chance would have it, I was very successful and he wasn't. People recognized him and were intimidated. I'd say, "Well, Rudolf, he was fine with me!"' Soon a regular himself of New York's 'venereal boiler rooms', Wallace got hepatitis at exactly the time the Royal Ballet was in town, and every dancer in the company had to get a shot of gamma globulin, as the virus, which attacks the liver, can be life-threatening. The night before he was diagnosed, Wallace and Margot had eaten food from each other's plates, and she had flown straight to Panama the next day. 'We tried to track her down to warn her, and finally succeeded, but she paid no attention.' 'Gamma globulin gobbledygook,' Margot had laughed. 'I'm not going to worry about it!' The Goslings had not been quite so laissez-faire. 'Tell your Hepatite friend that we had our haemoglobbery shots and feel fine,' Nigel wrote on 31 July. 'How is he? He must be careful or he can wreck his liver for good, eg no alcohol at all for months.'

Rudolf and Wallace were then staying with Douce in Villefranche, where the atmosphere between the two men was increasingly tense. 'Sex was a problem. We were both very aware that I still might be infected, so that side of things was just a mess.' Rudolf kept complaining to Douce that Wallace did not understand him, and she remembers how he began ostentatiously 'to kind of flirt with people' in Wallace's presence. One was a youth their mutual friend Jimmy Douglas describes as 'someone very special', a fellow guest at a grand party on Cap d'Ail. With long hair, sleepy brown eyes, full lips and hippie-chic clothes, Patrice was a Rive Gauche icon – 'a kind of star', whom Rudolf had instantly homed in on. When Wallace went upstairs he was confronted with exactly the scene he had been expecting: 'Rudolf fucking with a Frenchman.'

> Well, I saw red with rage . . . I thought it was a cliché. But no. Well, actually, you don't see red, you see pink. Everything just went totally pink, and I remember when he came back downstairs, I picked him up – my adrenaline was really pumping – and threw him across the room. He crashed into the bar . . . glasses, bottles flying everywhere, and I left the party in a very dramatic sweep.

Unhurt but very groggy, Rudolf was dragged out of the house by Douce, who half carried him on her shoulder. Wallace, meanwhile, drove up into the hills:

> I wandered around there for a couple of days, and then I think we ran into each other at the Rocks – this cruising place in Nice, where I don't think anything much was said. Soon after that I went back to New York, and that was pretty well the end of our romantic relation- ship . . . I don't remember him being angry with me . . . I think he understood that I just couldn't live with him the way he needed – touring with him and not having a life of my own.

Feeling that he had become too fond of Wallace, Rudolf may also, as Terry Benton believes, have actively pushed him away. 'My view is that Rudolf was afraid. Maybe he was thinking, Here's Erik again – No thank you.' Rudolf himself, in answer to Lynn Barber's question about why he could not live with anyone, said, 'I'm too problematic, too independent . . . one *wants* to, but then it's too painful, it's too dangerous. One cannot share, a dancer cannot share life with anybody. No go.' And talking sometime later with Linda Maybarduk, a Canadian dancer who had become a friend, Rudolf insisted that he was entirely to blame for the breakup with Wallace. 'I expect people to be there for me, and when they need me I can't be there for them. Until I stop dancing I won't be able to have a permanent relationship again.'

And how much longer would that be? Since 1973 Rudolf had been dancing with a permanent tear in his leg muscle; he had destroyed his Achilles tendons by years of landing too heavily; he had heel spurs; the bones were chipped – so that even basic walking gave him pain. When he emerged from his dressing room, slowly limping in his clogs and full-length bathrobe, he looked more like a hospital patient than a ballet star, often making straight for the special chair put aside for him in the wings. He now employed a full-time physical therapist to accompany him on his travels. 'Without him I could not get on,' he told Nigel. 'I am at the end of my teeter [tether].' Luigi Pignotti was working in an exclusive health club in Milan when one afternoon he received a call asking him to go to the Hotel Continental to give Rudolf Nureyev a massage. He had not heard of the dancer, but the recommendation had come from the conductor Zubin Mehta, one of his clients, and, despite the suspicious 'slit, cat-eyed look' from Rudolf on their first meeting, the two men struck up an immediate, wordless rapport:

> I found Rudolf in very bad condition because he had a problem with his calf. Both calves were like wood. And on top of this he was a very nervous person, so the body all the time was very hard. I worked on each foot for twenty minutes. Rudolf was totally abandoned. He say he pay me double what I ask, and after I learned how stingy he was – I realized he must really have liked me. 'Come back tomorrow,' he said. And then he start to ask me how much salary I made a month. And before he left Milano he say, 'Do you want to work for me?'

Wanting Luigi to accompany him on the Canadian tour of the United States, Rudolf had instructed Sol Hurok to 'treat him well', which in monetary terms amounted to six hundred dollars a week with a thirty-dollar per diem. A fair deal, as Luigi would double as a bodyguard if necessary. Murray Louis recalled an incident in a New York saloon bar when 'someone got wise-arsed' with Rudolf. 'Luigi walked up to this guy and laid a hand on his shoulder and the guy crumpled – just from the strength of that arm.' The same power was required to penetrate Rudolf's muscles, now as gnarled and compacted as an ancient olive trunk, during the forty-five-minute massage he was given every afternoon. This was preceded by a two-hour siesta and followed by a scorching hot bath, while the rest of the time Luigi would shadow Rudolf, carrying a bulging shoulder bag stuffed with bandages. 'So,' Rudolf admitted, 'it's always bandages, heelpads for ever.'

When Glen Tetley took Rudolf backstage to meet Murray Louis, then touring London, he had watched entranced as the choreographer removed a bandage from his foot. 'In those few minutes we talked silently, we talked foot talk.' 'How do you do that?' Rudolf asked, and Louis promised to show him how he made the special bandage he used when the skin on his feet split. Rudolf had been wanting for some time to work with Louis, a descendant not of Martha Graham but (through his teacher Alwin Nikolais) of Mary Wigman, the 1920s German expressionist. Linking him with Paul Taylor and Merce Cunningham, Rudolf saw Louis as a choreographer 'for male dancers in particular. They invent strange movements and enrich [them] to incredible degree.' As Louis himself admits, his knowledge of ballet was nonexistent. He would say, 'The leg is up behind you' if he wanted an arabesque, but being exceptionally smart and fun to be with, he soon became as much of a soulmate as a collaborator. 'We're comfortable with each other,' Louis once remarked. 'We challenge each other.' Choreographing *Moments*, his first piece for Rudolf, Louis says that he spent most of their time teaching Rudolf to get his 'long heroic spine' to move fluently. 'The torso can't be supple when the legs are locked. But Rudolf's legs were trained to secure him all the time, so I had to choreograph the leg action to go with it. He learned that, but it didn't come naturally. He would bend his knees when it should have been an extension of the chest – not a knee movement.'

Moments, an all-male work, also involving four young soloists from the Scottish Ballet company, premièred on 19 September 1975, at a dance festival in Madrid, John Percival's review noting the emphasis on the upper part of the body, especially hands and arms. Quirky fractured lines – hands moving one way, arms another – combined with unexpected stops and starts of energy is stock-in-trade Murray Louis style. 'I never gave him anything that frustrated him, and if it was awkward I'd modify it.' Eliminating jumps and leaps, *Moments* was tailored for a mature male dancer, whose inevitable isolation from the four young men was made its subject matter, although the work ended with Rudolf being supported on their backs.

Suffering from arthritis exacerbated by a punishing whirl of foreign guest appearances, Margot had also been limping recently. In November 1975, when the two stars appeared together in *Fonteyn & Nureyev* in New York, one critic described Rudolf having 'to support Fonteyn way beyond the call of duty'. They were performing *Amazon Forest*, a 1975 Ashton duet originally made for Margot and David Wall, in which the movements had been specially designed to accommodate the last vestiges of her technique, the ballerina's raised leg immediately held in place by her partner. In *Marguerite and Armand*, however, Margot's arabesques were noticeably 'left dangling', and the programme itself was poorly presented with an inept orchestra and canned music for the Béjart and Louis works. Sympathetic about the financial drain of Tito's medical expenses, Rudolf tried to help by including Margot in his lucrative Broadway venture: 'Well, Royal Ballet doesn't hire us together.' And although he had gone through a phase of being 'a bit browned off' about her dancing with increasingly younger rival partners* (complaining to Nigel that she was 'trying to put me down'), their mutual respect had never wavered. '*Genuine* respect . . . The oneness of thoughts; the oneness of aim'. They were still each other's best critics – 'After every performance I went to her and checked and re-checked' – and Margot was the only person with whom Rudolf was openly affectionate. 'There was a physical closeness between them,' says Misha Baryshnikov, who remembers seeing them sitting drinking coffee and cuddling in the Opera House canteen. 'He adored her.' Margot had asked Rudolf once, 'When my time comes, will you push me off the stage?' And he had answered, 'Never.' For each there simply *was* no alternative: life was real only onstage.

At the end of the year Rudolf rejoined Martha Graham, this time performing *Lucifer* not with Margot but with Janet Eilber, on whom most of the choreography had been worked out. The company was celebrating two centuries of America's independence by performing dance dramas rooted in the American heritage: Graham's classic *Appalachian Spring* (with the composer, Aaron Copland, conducting); and the world première of *The Scarlet Letter*, based on Nathaniel Hawthorne's novel, viewed by Walter Terry as 'a work-in-progress but also as a work-of-promise'. To Clive Barnes, Rudolf's 'fierceness of belief' in the repertory that season made him closer than anyone else onstage to capturing the original spirit of Martha Graham. 'I don't claim to be an expert in modern dance,' Rudolf told *Newsweek*, 'but I improve with each performance. And I take back into classical dance a new awareness of myself.'

And just as he had learned how to pace himself with Graham technique – at first, he said, 'I was hammering away. I was plunging,

---

* Rudolf had enjoyed hearing that when Margot asked rising star Fernando Bujones to dance with her, he had come back and solemnly replied, 'I'm afraid my mother says you're too old for me.'

going crazy' – Rudolf had also found a teacher in New York who had made him realize that ballet class did not have to be strenuous. Poached from Denmark by Balanchine to teach at his school, Stanley Williams helped dancers not to waste their energy but to channel it directly where it should be. 'Working this way alleviated any injuries. He was like a healer, almost – all your aches and pains went away,' said Lynn Seymour, who maintains that 'the great Stanley Williams completely changed my life'. A slight, wiry man who spoke in a near-inaudible murmur, Williams had Pushkin's gift for teaching with a logic and simplicity that verged on genius. Pupils describe how he instilled the sparseness of Zen Buddhism into dance, reducing passages of movement down to an initial impulse. Edward Villella claims that studying exclusively with Williams for two months gave him an extra fifteen years of dancing, and Seymour also credits the teacher for giving her, a ballerina in her thirties, 'a technique for the first time ever'. She had been introduced to Williams by Rudolf, who 'had already hit the magic, and he knew what it would do for me. Stanley extended *everyone*'s careers.'

Watching Rudolf in class for the first time, Williams noticed his tendency to sit in preparations for too long, the teacher's own characteristically Danish approach being to disguise the difficulties of technique. 'Even the preparation for the next step is a movement . . . I don't use any flamboyant steps. I don't believe in showing off. I don't use strength unnecessarily.' It was Williams, Rudolf said, who made him understand the importance of linking one step with another – the cantilena effect that Baryshnikov found missing in his dancing – though to begin with Rudolf had found the classes much too fast.

> I used to work very slow: ten*du* and close *fifth* . . . and very often onstage I would lose balance because I didn't know how to stand on my feet. It's a system which confirms that technique comes from the feet . . . The deportment, proportion of the body, the movement of the arms . . . everything comes from the feet. In Russia you hold your arms and you get kind of stiff. It's Balanchine who invented and taught that. He used to tell Violette Verdy, 'You have to be like a bird on your toes. The toes and the feet have to become the most intelligent part of the body.'

To strengthen the metatarsals Williams would set innumerable *battement tendu* exercises, 'like a racing car that has an rpm from 0 to 5,000', says Robert Denvers, another disciple. 'You warmed up fast because of the differentiation in rhythm from the first *battement tendu* to the last, and after twenty minutes you were ready to do *doubles tours* and *entrechats six*.' He remembers Rudolf being mesmerized by the syncopation and the counterpointing of the steps, so different from the Russians' even, regular musicality. 'After the age of thirty-five you start to have problems with the huge jumps, and this acceleration in class made Rudolf's muscles feel great. He started working with more elasticity, more speed, more ease.'

But if Rudolf was now working more constructively in class, he was still determined to 'beat the hell out of myself', convinced that he danced his best on a second wind. The combination of what he called 'that awful confrontation of body and will' with his gruelling transatlantic schedule proved to be far too much for even Rudolf's constitution to endure. Having danced in Paris while ill with pneumonia and a temperature of 103, he flew straight to Los Angeles to appear with the American Ballet Theatre in his production of *Raymonda*. A doctor had stood by in the wings, and although Rudolf completed the performance, he had to be rushed to the hospital later that night – 17 February 1976. He did not return to the stage until late March, when he had never felt so lacking in stamina. 'I had some very rough moments. It was frightening.' Six weeks later, however, when the Royal Ballet was at the Met, he had drawn on superhuman reserves of strength to pull himself back into form, Anna Kisselgoff writing that 'The old Nureyev magic has returned . . . [He] is dancing better than he has in years.'

It was, as Merle Park said, Rudolf's 'forced rest' that had brought about this resurgence, and he was soon to have the longest break from dancing of his career. In September 1975 the movie director Ken Russell had sent Rudolf a script based on the life of the silent-screen star Rudolph Valentino, offering him the cameo role of Nijinsky (who is supposed to have taught Valentino the tango). Not long afterwards Russell and his wife, Shirley, the film's designer, had appeared in Amsterdam, where Rudolf was performing, and proposed the title role instead.* Rudi van Dantzig remembers how hesitant Rudolf had been about stepping into such an unknown medium, but what eventually made up his mind was the chance it would give him 'to quiet down'. 'I thought it would force me into a holiday. I don't like

---

* In a letter dated 22 January 1974, Sandor Gorlinsky tells Rudolf about an earlier feature film offer – an approach by Michael Powell, who wanted Rudolf to co-star with Omar Sharif in *Taj Mahal*, a project that never saw the light. 'It sounds a super film with some ballet, but not a ballet film, and it may open the road for some future prospects.'

holidays, without dancing . . . That would force me to rest the muscles.' And if Rudolf was now considered 'mature' as a dancer, in movie terms he was still young enough to play romantic leads. The role itself was extremely tempting. Valentino had been a dancer before he became an actor, his voice, like Rudolf's, was not known, and both were renowned for their exotic, androgynous allure. The quality that most interested Rudolf, however, was Valentino's way of moving. 'He would hold still and just turn his head or move his hand to indicate an emotion . . . In those days film actors were very jittery. Valentino was much slower, more sinuous in his movements.'

François Truffaut once remarked during an interview with David Daniel that he found it understandable that Rudolf had not yet starred in feature films because the primeval traits in his character made it almost impossible for him to play opposite other men. 'He would have to be filmed in nature with animals as partners.' (This was precisely how Dino De Laurentiis and John Huston, one of *The Bible*'s four directors, had pictured Rudolf in 1964 when they offered him the role of the snake in the Garden of Eden for their planned epic *The Bible*. 'He will slither down the tree,' Huston remarked. 'He will be a man-serpent, a kind of hybrid, homo-reptile.') Truffaut went on to tell Daniel that it was seeing Rudolf in the film of MacMillan's *Romeo and Juliet* that had given him the idea that a man could play the part of a near-animal. The result was the 1970 Truffaut classic *L'Enfant sauvage* (*The Wild Child*), based on an early nineteenth-century memoir about the efforts to assimilate a feral child into society, the film posing questions about what is intrinsically human in human nature. In the same year the director had made *Domicile conjugal* (*Bed and Board*), in which the image of Rudolf is crucial to the film, so potent that he virtually becomes another character. Jean-Pierre Léaud plays Truffaut's alter ego, Antoine Doinel, a young husband who has developed a passion for a Japanese girl who works with him. His pretty wife, Christine (Claude Jade), has a secret fantasy life of her own. When the couple are in bed he is reading *Les Femmes japonaises* and her book is Rudolf's *Autobiography*, and at a later point, when she is alone, she removes Antoine's photograph from a frame on their bedside table and reveals the hidden picture of her idol. This ability to arouse powerful erotic feelings was exactly what Rudolf and Valentino shared: 'He gave [the public] fantasies to take home with them. I suppose I give fantasy to people when I dance – and it's not just restricted to women.'

Rudolf was thought to be so key to the *Valentino* project that he had been allowed to sign his contract even before undergoing a screen test.

Prior to principal shooting, the plan was for him to have a fortnight's 'holiday' during which he would be available for costume fittings and coaching with lines. 'But then, this holiday shrank from two weeks to one week, then to four days, then to none. So I flew directly to Spain from New York – and that flying day was my only day off.' At least the Almería location was by the sea and the weather was hot – far too hot for the English, but Rudolf was 'rather happy', swimming for an hour early each morning before arriving on set. 'Everyone was amazed at my tenacity . . . not carrying on, and surviving it all.' And although he insisted on viewing every take on a videotape playback machine, he had relaxed the kind of obsessive control he maintained throughout the making of *Don Quixote*. On the whole Rudolf liked what he saw.* His beauty and charisma were relished by the camera and enhanced by his personal wardrobe – the djellabas, Spanish gaucho trousers, gangster-style pinstripes, and rolled-up shirtsleeves – every frame in which he appeared as magnetic as an authentic Valentino still. Unfortunately, however, he was no more able to adapt his Russian accent to Valentino's Italian American one than to modulate his powerful stage persona to the subtle requirements of the screen. And Russell did nothing to help, freely admitting that he did not know how to direct actors. Rudolf told friends that he felt 'abandoned'.

He had never much liked Ken Russell (the reason Rudolf claimed to have got him 'fired' from the Harry Saltzman *Nijinsky* project), but he admired the director's style, finding it 'full of invention and daring'. Combining a love of German expressionism with Hollywood slapstick, it frequently lapsed into the histrionic, but Rudolf felt this approach worked in some of the films; *Tommy*, he said, 'mirrored properly that bombastic epoch'. In a discussion with French screenwriter Jean-Claude Carrière, Rudolf remarked of Russell, 'The person is without doubt questionable, but he has a visual imagination that is unique.' And although he would fight the director over 'stupid' lines in the script, he was trusting enough to agree to scenes that others would regard as excessive or exploitative. The main problem was not having the guidance he badly needed. Russell, who was 'very keen on the girls', appeared interested only in his female star.

Better known as a singer with the pop group the Mamas and the Papas, Michelle Phillips had been cast as the beautiful Natacha

---

* Though when Lord Snowdon, commissioned to take photographs on set, sent one of his assistants with stills for Rudolf to approve, the dancer took one transparency and stabbed it right through with his ballpoint, scoffing, 'Eyes like elephant arseholes.'

Rambova, Valentino's second wife. Influenced by Bakst, Poiret and Erté, Rambova was a gifted Art Deco stage designer and had also been a ballet dancer – 'a very fascinating type', in Rudolf's view. 'Very temperamental, very cunning and intelligent'. Phillips, on the other hand, he found 'hard and empty', her lack of humour and lanky, fashion-model looks so unappealing that it made him physically recoil during their naked love scenes. 'I hope you understand that I have no interest in women,' Rudolf told her at their first meeting, and relations between them deteriorated to such a degree that there was an ugly exchange of blows one day, which brought filming to a halt. 'Just because you play cunt in film, doesn't mean you have to be cunt in life,' Rudolf infamously remarked to Phillips, who remembers their encounter as the most miserable working experience of her life.

Valentino's other leading actresses, by contrast, were charmed by him. With Felicity Kendal (cast as screenwriter June Mathis), whose parents had run a touring Shakespeare company in India, Rudolf had 'endless conversations' about *Romeo and Juliet*, which he was planning as his next production. Carol Kane, playing a kooky starlet, found him neither mean-spirited nor misogynistic but 'so mischievous, so game, willing to try and fail'; while Leslie Caron, cast as silver-screen star Alla Nazimova, proved most supportive of all – not only Rudolf's main ally throughout filming but becoming a friend for life. 'I was instantly touched by him, and by his tenderness. He was an extraordinarily intimate person.' Photographs taken the day Caron arrived on set for the first time capture their closeness, with Rudolf's head resting on her shoulder displaying the inevitable complicity of dancers. Trained at the Paris Conservatoire, Caron was a deliciously gamine sixteen-year-old in Roland Petit's Ballets des Champs-Élysées when Gene Kelly picked her to star with him in *An American in Paris*. An MGM contract and several box-office hits followed, among them *Daddy Long Legs* and *Gigi*, in which she appeared, respectively, opposite Fred Astaire, and Maurice Chevalier and Louis Jourdan. Rudolf, she says, was 'naïvely interested' in her Hollywood co-stars, particularly Astaire, and as if echoing her much-quoted declaration that she was not a ballet dancer but a hoofer, he used a tabletop dance in *Valentino* as an opportunity to improvise a convincingly dapper Astaire routine. To Caron, Rudolf had 'the makings of a great star', and he was just as enthusiastic about her. Her Nazimova, a deliberate send-up of the Yalta-born actress known as America's Eleonora Duse, made Rudolf laugh 'like mad. It is completely different image than what people think of . . . absolutely contrary to *Gigi*.'

'*Kenrussellisé à mort*' was the phrase a French reviewer coined to describe Caron's portrayal, one she agrees was pushed to its limit. 'The Fellini of the North', as she calls Russell, wanted everything to be overdramatized. 'He only behaved in superlatives at that point in his career.' It is not surprising, then, that the film's most effective scenes are those without dialogue. 'All my films are choreography,' Russell once said, and his directing technique draws considerably on his own early dance training. 'Most directors start from the text,' Caron has said. 'With Russell it's all visual.' In *Valentino* the star's prowess as a dancer is emphasized time and time again. Rambova's photograph of her lover posing as Nijinsky in *L'Après-midi d'un faune* is enacted by Rudolf, naked except for a thong of vine leaves and patterned paint, and showing what Arlene Croce called 'tantalizing' glimpses of authentic Faun *plastique*. The Valentino–Nijinsky tango lesson (one of several tango sequences) becomes a memorable pairing of Rudolf with Anthony Dowell, the former stepping aside to allow his young rival to end their session with a Nureyev-style blaze of balletic virtuosity.

As it happened, Rudolf had by no means abandoned dancing for the duration of *Valentino*. In addition to replacing an injured Dowell for a number of performances at Covent Garden, he often worked until late at night, either trying out ideas for *Romeo and Juliet* on a small group of dancers in the Donmar Studios, or learning *Pierrot Lunaire*, which Glen Tetley was finally allowing him to perform. After rising at four a.m. and filming at Elstree Studios all day (the studio had rented him a suite at Grosvenor House Hotel because Fife Road was too far away), he would be driven back into London and rehearse for several hours – amazing Tetley with his stamina. During the day he never took a lunch break but used the time to do his own training, surviving on sweet tea brought to him in a flask by Luigi. During a boxing sequence filmed inside Blackpool Tower, Rudolf, wearing cobwebby woollen leg warmers and watched by a handful of extras, used the rope of the ring to do an hour's barre practice to the accompaniment of Chopin Nocturnes crackling from a tape recorder.

Valentino was due to be released in the United States in July 1977 and in the United Kingdom three months later. Rudolf, according to Tristram Holland (who edited an Alexander Bland book on the film), 'expected it to be nothing other than excellent'. He had told Carrière that what Russell needed were *des couilles en fer* (iron balls) to maintain the violent statements of his style from start to finish. This, though, turned out to be the main problem. 'He gives you no respite, he needed to temper it,' comments Caron. 'John Ford used to say, "Let them rest," but Ken goes unrelentingly from one climax to another.' In Pauline Kael's opinion, however, nothing could have salvaged *Valentino*: 'There is no artistry left in Ken Russell's work. By now, his sensationalist reputation is based merely on his "going further" than anybody else . . . His films have become schoolboy Black Masses – a mixture of offensiveness and crude dumbness . . . Spitefulness is almost the sole emotion of *Valentino*.'

What had particularly nauseated Kael – more even than the sight of the star 'smeared in vomit and forced to soil himself' – was Rudolf looking as prematurely aged and effete as the duc de Chartres from Valentino's film *Monsieur Beaucaire*, 'a textbook example of a director's sadism towards his own star'. With the right director and photographed with care, he could, she believed, have been 'supremely entertaining' as a film actor. 'Seen up close . . . Nureyev has the seductive, moody insolence of an older, more cosmopolitan James Dean.' Opening on both sides of the Atlantic to unanimously bad reviews, *Valentino* proved a regrettable showcase for Rudolf's big-screen debut. And yet he had turned the experience to his advantage, widening his own directorial expertise by studying Russell's working methods. 'Process often more interesting than result.' The greatest benefit of *Valentino*, however, was allowing him, in Luigi's words, 'what he never have: a holiday for his body'. Rejoining the Royal Ballet on 18 November 1976, his hair still styled in a twenties crop, Rudolf over the next six months gave some of the greatest performances of his career.

His playmate on location had been Armen's daughter, Jeannette, who was then going through a divorce. 'You have to get away,' Rudolf had said, urging her to come to London and stay in his suite at Grosvenor House. 'So I did. And he couldn't have been nicer, keeping me with him and introducing me to everyone on the set.' The first night when shooting was over Rudolf was getting into the car when Jeannette said that she would see him later. 'I told him that some of the boys had asked me to go to the pub. And he looked at me and he said, "Bitch! I've been working on this movie for two months and nobody has ever invited me for a drink".' Rudolf enjoyed debriefing Jeannette on her adventures with the crew, and expected her to accompany him on his nocturnal cottaging expeditions in Hyde Park: 'I'd have to stand there waiting outside the public lavatories.' Until this trip she had always felt a little intimidated by Rudolf, though he had thought of her from the beginning as an ideal sister – fun and free-spirited in ways that Rosa, Razida and Lilia could never be. He also took an avuncular interest in her nine-year-old son, volunteering to babysit a number of times. 'I'd done some errands and was coming back through Chinatown when, all of a sudden, I see this sable coat walking down the street – it's Rudolf with Devin on his shoulders!' On another occasion she got home to find the pair watching a football game on TV, Rudolf drinking Heineken out of a bottle with his feet slung up on the coffee table. 'He was very eager that Devin should be a *guy*', says Jeannette, remembering how he rebuked her once for dressing her son as a butterfly for a children's party.

Their friendship had flourished on the understanding that there was no romantic expectation on her side – 'I've gotta say he didn't appeal to me as a man I could be sexually attracted to.' Consequently Jeannette couldn't have been more taken aback when, skinny-dipping with her in a lake en route to Santa Barbara, Rudolf casually asked her if she would like to have his baby.

> And I looked at him and said, '*Why?*' And he said, 'Because it would be nice to have a baby'. 'Well, what would I do: have this child and give it to you to raise?' And he said, 'Well, yes.' And I said, 'Well, no.' I was in my early twenties and this wasn't something in my game plan – I'd had my baby. And besides I was married then, and a good Catholic girl.

Rudolf (like Jean Marais before him) wanted a son by a woman who, in Cocteau's words, was 'willing to be used for that purpose only'. 'If he could have been an androgyne and made the son himself he would have been delighted,' says Ghislaine Thesmar. But there was someone else Rudolf had in mind as the perfect brood mare. Described by her actress friend Candice Bergen as 'the mother we all wanted to have and to be', Tessa Kennedy had five children, four of whom were boys. They had recently met when film director Milos Forman brought Rudolf to lunch at her house in Hyde Park Gardens. A successful interior designer, she was then married to her second husband, producer Elliott Kastner, her movie milieu being one reason she and Rudolf had bonded immediately. 'Elliott was a member of the academy, so we had all these films – films not even finished yet.' The other reason, she reckons, was her sons – 'I'd had all these boys, so he thought he'd be sure of having a son with me.'

But there were many other appealing sides to Tessa – not least her Slav roots and intriguingly colourful past. One of twin daughters of a

Yugoslav shipping family, her mother was a wealthy beauty known as the 'Pearl of Dubrovnik', and Tessa had acquired a romantic label of her own. In 1957, when, at the age of eighteen, the blonde, melting-eyed debutante eloped with journalist Dominick Elwes to Cuba, she was fêted by the press as an icon of young love – the 'Runaway Heiress'. Hunted by Interpol, she and Dominick, an irrepressible character of whom Kenneth Tynan (quoting Shakespeare) once said, 'He speaks holiday,' drove a pair of pastel-blue-and-pink Cadillacs, and hung out in bars with Ernest Hemingway and members of the Mob. Reality hit in Tessa's early twenties, when, while she and her husband were living in London with their three small sons, Dominick developed chronic depression. 'I thought one day the children would find him dead and they'd never get over that. Which is why I had to leave him.'* Having apprenticed herself to decorator David Mlinaric for five pounds a week, Tessa was running her own company within three years. Her spirit and energy were as invincible as Rudolf's; neither went to bed before the early hours, and if he did not share the taste for gambling Tessa had acquired in Havana, he loved her juxtaposition of male savvy and business acumen with feminine allure.

Being 'very married at the time', she, like Jeannette, was unwilling to conceive to order, but welcomed Rudolf's mentoring of her own boys. Knowing that Cary Elwes had ambitions to be a movie actor, Rudolf insisted that he first learn to speak the lines of Shakespeare, and when Damian decided to be an artist said, 'He's got to suffer. Tell him to read [Mario Praz's] *The Romantic Agony.*' 'Rudolf *adored* education. He used to say, "You can lose your country and all your possessions, but they can never take away your knowledge."' His desire for a child – and specifically for a son – was partly a reflection of his desire to have someone he could mould – 'though probably he would disappoint me in so many ways. If he doesn't live up to my expectations.' And it was partly a means of self-perpetuation; having felt 'a slight anxiety that it will soon be over', Rudolf now wanted, as Thesmar says, 'to clone himself'. He had passed his thirty-ninth birthday in March 1977, and was suddenly aware of 'warning bells', remembering his father's caution: 'You don't see men dancing after forty.' He told Rudi van Dantzig, who was concerned about the signs of distress Rudolf was then showing, 'I must expand my horizons . . . do other things.'

*

* Elwes did in fact commit suicide in September 1975.

He had put his faith in contemporary dancing as a way of extending his performing career, regarding this other vocabulary as an investment in his future. 'But by the time he worked with me he was a pretty old dog,' says Murray Louis. 'Misha came to this technique when he was much younger.' And this in itself was another cause of Rudolf's agitation. It was 'astounding' to van Dantzig that he should feel so threatened – 'was there no room in the world for two such talented people?' – but Baryshnikov's superiority as a contemporary dancer was too striking to ignore. His physique, gift for mimicry and exceptional coordination had allowed him to make the transition more naturally than Rudolf, whose achievements had come about only through tremendous effort and will. 'It's a different lightness and breakup in the body that Misha intuitively understands,' says Glen Tetley, while to Violette Verdy and others, Rudolf would never look anything other than a ballet dancer in modern roles. 'He adapted himself, but only up to a point. There was a look that was almost right. But at the core it was still the great Nureyev doing that thing . . . His identity was too established. He conjugated; he didn't disappear.'

And because Baryshnikov (in Jerome Robbins's words) 'could drop himself and become the character', he was a lot more popular with choreographers, who also found him much easier to work with. Tetley describes how Misha's 'playful quality' helped to create an open atmosphere – 'the ideal situation in which movement can happen.' And Murray Louis, remembering the way Rudolf would always 'mark' the steps rather than fully perform them, says, 'I let him get away with murder.' It was, however, the rehearsal aspect of dancing that Baryshnikov enjoyed most. 'I was bored when they start to perform . . . [Rudolf] was completely opposite. He wanted to do very fast, learn very fast and go.'

Rudolf was the first to acknowledge this. Congratulating Misha after seeing him in Twyla Tharp's *Push Comes to Shove*, the 1976 piece that brilliantly showcased his improvisational and comic talents, Rudolf remarked, 'You move so well . . . And I know, I know it takes a lot of time . . . And I don't have it!' But he was becoming increasingly resentful of the way the younger dancer was 'aping' him. *Theme and Variations*, the first Balanchine ballet he had vowed to learn, and had subsequently danced with the American Ballet Theatre a year after coming to the West, had returned to ABT's repertory in October 1974 at Baryshnikov's request. Rudolf had been the first male star after Babilée to perform Petit's *Le Jeune homme et la mort*; Misha had been the next. 'I went the same way in a way,' he admits. '[Rudolf] worked with Paul Taylor, I worked with Paul Taylor; he worked with Martha Graham, I worked with Martha Graham.'

And it did not stop with dancing. Rudolf had set out 'to create Russian ballet in the West', Misha immediately following suit by staging *The Nutcracker* and *Don Quixote*. Both stars had made their debuts as screen actors the same year, but whereas *Valentino* had been written off as a disaster, *The Turning Point*, despite its soap-opera script, had earned Baryshnikov an Oscar nomination for best supporting actor. 'I remember how jealous Rudolf was that Misha had been such a success,' says Tessa Kennedy. 'He always thought he was a much better actor.' Furious that Misha was now 'taking things away' from him – that is, opportunities to stage the classics – Rudolf had begun making jibes about him. 'There are no secrets in the ballet world,' remarked Charles France. 'So Misha would hear about things Rudolf was saying. But he looked on it with a sense of: well, if he has to do that – fine. I don't.'

Rudolf had instructed Gorlinsky to tell the Canadian ballet that under no circumstances did he ever want to appear in any season 'where they book him at the same time'. And yet the last thing he had to fear was that Baryshnikov would try to emulate his long crusades with foreign companies around the world. 'Rudolf was looking for gigs . . . I was not that hungry for work.' In fact, although he would never have admitted it, Rudolf was indebted to the New Boy. In May 1973, a year before Baryshnikov's defection, he had 'a terrible dream'. He was in a lift that kept going down and that he could not stop. 'Not hard to interpret,' he told Nigel, who in turn noted in his diary, 'Poor R. Maybe he won't go any higher but he has a long way to come down before others find him on their level.' The last three years, however, had seen Rudolf, galvanized by the element of competition, in exultant form. To a new generation of balletomanes who had missed the Fonteyn–Nureyev phenomenon of the sixties, there was 'a triumvirate of three equally great male dancers' – Rudolf, Baryshnikov and Dowell. To quote critic Alastair Macaulay: 'Nureyev was a key part of my life for that short period: 1975–7. I was twenty and twenty-one, and he was part of the end of my adolescence. He was my first Florimund, my first Siegfried, my first Colas, my first Oberon, my first Apollo, my first Prodigal, my first Jean de Brienne, my first Albrecht, my first Drosselmeyer, in my first *Dances at a Gathering*.'

Natalia Makarova had also re-inspired the classicist in Rudolf. In December 1976, with no special announcement, the two stars had

appeared at the Royal Opera House together in *Swan Lake*, as the ballerina's regular partner, Anthony Dowell, had been injured. Two months
later they were together again in Paris dancing *La Sylphide* at the Palais
des Sports – 'the happiest of reconciliations' – and in May Rudolf had
included Makarova among his 'Friends' in New York. Later that summer Rudolf would dance a mixed programme with Seymour, Fonteyn
and Makarova, the two Russians' *Corsaire* duet 'making even senior
critics feel that time had stopped and that Nureyev was still dancing as
he had with Fonteyn in *Corsaire* in 1962'. 'We had all right vibrations
this time around,' Makarova told a journalist. 'He is softer now. We are
getting to know each other.' As Murray Louis witnessed one night during a dinner in New York, the pair almost immediately, 'like two conspirators', had fallen into conversation in Russian. They discussed
fouetté technique and the difference between Russian and American
musicality, Rudolf explaining to Natasha how Broadway dancing had
restructured rhythmic phrasing, and how this had influenced Balanchine when he first arrived in America. He was holding her hand as they
were talking, and both their hands were resting on Louis's stomach.

> I felt like a mother with two children on her lap . . . I am sure if
> Baryshnikov were there, his hand would have also joined theirs and the
> three would have found their communion back to Kirov and back to
> the heart and soul of Russia, which none of them have ever left or ever
> will or can. No matter how long they live in the West, they will always
> be Russian. No matter how they insult and slander each other, they are
> a family and can never be separated.

16   THIS THING
OF DARKNESS

New York's 'Culture of the Night' was inaugurated in the spring of 1977, when Bianca Jagger made her legendary appearance on a white horse at the newly opened Studio 54. Wearing white with Manolo Blahnik stilettos, she was led by a near-naked youth whose black skin glittered with silver dust. For one defining moment Bianca's birthday party focused media attention on an unknown West 54th Street discothèque much as the Summer of Love had blazoned the name of Haight-Ashbury exactly a decade before. Owners Steve Rubell and Ian Schrager transformed an old off-Broadway theatre, staking out a huge parquet dance floor with strobe-lit tubular columns, leaving the original balconies as a seating area, and implementing a shamelessly partisan door policy. Ruled by whim as much as aesthetic principles, it granted entry to 'one big mix' of revellers from pretty preppy couples, visiting English aristocrats, models, fashion designers and pop celebrities, to, incongruously, such distinguished figures as concert pianist Vladimir Horowitz. Regulars included the Studio eccentrics – Disco Sally, a septuagenarian who loved to dance; a Jewish couple in Nazi uniform; a Harpo Marx character with HERPES VIRUS inscribed on his costume; and Rollerina, 'supposedly a prim Wall Streeter by day', whose signature rollerskates were worn with a ballgown and tiara. Friends of the owners, among whom were the core group of VIPs – Liza Minnelli, Andy Warhol and Truman Capote – were fenced into their own private sanctuary, though Capote preferred people-watching from the DJ's booth above the dance floor. 'Isn't it too bad that Proust didn't have something like this?' he exclaimed.

Rudolf had danced with Rollerina, spent the whole of one Friday night at the club, walking out into the sun with Capote the following morning, and yet Studio 54 was not really his scene. He enjoyed eyeing and propositioning the coquettish, mostly gay waiters bobbing about in nothing but silk baseball shorts and trainers. And it was a useful way of impressing potential conquests, sweeping them past the implacable Marc and his fellow bouncers on the door, and introducing them to the likes of Halston and Martha Graham. But Rudolf had never liked disco dancing or the drug and soft-core-sex culture that went with it. He had no intention of taking advantage of the 'best things' served in the VIP lounge – the Thai sticks, Quaaludes and cocaine (the club's motif was the man in the moon snorting 'snow' from a spoon) – any more than he would have joined the exhibitionists flaunting their naked genitalia on the dance floor or carrying out Kama Sutra antics on the balcony. 'You would look around and you'd see somebody's back,' said one observer. 'And then you'd see little toes twinkling behind their ears.'

Commenting on her visit to Studio 54, Lillian Carter, mother of former US president Jimmy Carter, said, 'I don't know if I was in heaven or hell. But it was *wonderful*!' To Rudolf, however, it was nothing. In the sulphurous backrooms of the downtown fetish bars, which he far preferred, the predators in their black leather or jockstraps, army boots and nipple clamps made Studio's bouncy waiters seem as innocuously teasing as Playboy bunnies. The Mineshaft on Washington Street was a seventies corroboration of Shakespeare's 'Hell is empty, / And all the devils are here!'* In almost total darkness, men pressed themselves to a wall pierced with crotch-high 'glory holes', or wandered into an amber-lit labyrinth of barren rooms, their walls and floors made of concrete blocks that could be hosed down daily. 'You'd glance in and see whips and chains, or somebody lying butt-up waiting to be fucked.'

Meanwhile, at the Anvil nearby on Tenth Avenue, the entertainment witnessed by Wallace one Sunday night was 'a guy whose act was to be fist-fucked on the bar. And that was in the *front* room.' Emerging at two a.m. into the meatpacking district was, he said, 'too Dante-esque', the pavements splattered like Jackson Pollock canvases with fresh blood, and 'huge, dangling, slabs of raw meat coming at you' as carcasses lurched along moving overhead hooks from the lorries to the warehouses. The nightly row of lorries was another sex destination for Rudolf, either there or parked further afield by the wharves at the Hudson end of Christopher Street. To Edmund White the immense expanse of rotting piers was like a vast ruined cathedral: 'We were isolated men at prayer, that man by the font (rainwater stagnant in the lid of a barrel), and this one in a side chapel (the damp vault), that pair of celebrants holding up a flame near the dome, those communicants telling beads or buttons pierced through denim.'

To Rudolf, however, sex was sex, and only dance warranted any

* Ferdinand's cry in *The Tempest* Act 1 Sc. 2.

form of consecration. 'Stage is a cathedral,' he once said, and morning class was his rite of purification, its daily articulation of first position his own genuflection and sign of the cross. 'There's almost a fanatical religious quality about it,' agrees Violette Verdy. 'Dance is Rudolf's great purifying, sacred touchstone. That is his faith.'

In March, Rudolf had made his New York debut as the 'always white, always pure, always innocent' *Pierrot Lunaire*, a role he had long coveted. His conversation with Margot for her *Magic of Dance* television series expresses his fascination with this *commedia dell'arte* figure, 'a kind of spiritual being', whom we first see suspended like an acrobat on Rouben Ter-Arutunian's scaffolding abstraction of Pierrot's tower.

> He's soaking in moonlight; getting drunk on moonbeams, being tickled by it. He's absolutely in delirium . . . His tower is his home and he protects it and caresses it with the joy of innocence . . . Later, Brighella and Columbine, they rob him of his tower . . . they take his personality, they take his dress, his hat, his jacket . . . and all his whiteness also disappears. So he loses his innocence. He dies many times, but he comes back to life.

Pierrot's spiritual degeneration was, Rudolf believed, akin to his own situation since arriving in the corrupting West – a view Ninette de Valois shared. 'There was an innocence about his dedication when he first came out of Russia that invested his performances with an unforgettable detachment and purity far removed from the screaming fanatics that surrounded him,' she wrote in her memoir, *Step by Step*, also published in 1977. 'But now he is their slave, and travels and dances where they bid.' This was the reason Glen Tetley had withheld his ballet from Rudolf, feeling that an international superstar could never portray Pierrot's qualities of innocence and insecurity. According to Flemming Flindt, the dancer and choreographer who was then artistic director of the Royal Danish Ballet, Rudolf 'went behind Glen's back' to ensure that he got the role. Discovering that Flindt had an open contract with Tetley to cast whomever he wanted in *Pierrot Lunaire*, Rudolf had invited the Dane and several of his dancers to be part of his 'Friends' season. 'In New York they hate Glen Tetley, and I managed to persuade him to stage *Pierrot* on Broadway with Rudolf. I said, "It's a good chance for you, Glen. They're not going to pan your ballet with Nureyev in it." And little by little he realized how good Rudolf was.'

Tetley, who had put a lot of autobiographical detail into the role, agrees that he soon began to see the extent to which Rudolf was responding to many of the same things. 'Pierrot is, above all, a dreamer, an outsider. It's why I had the idea of putting him up in space. Later, I realized the enormity in Rudolf of the loner: he'd left everything behind – his family, his country, his language.' Working with the dancer in London during the *Valentino* period, he found him in extraordinarily good physical shape, impressively strong in his upper body, but struggling to submerge his own personality into that of Pierrot. 'I had to work on him to *show* vulnerability,' recalls Tetley, who began by teaching Rudolf the principles of Oriental technique. 'You have to empty out everything inside you, to give over being you. You go into the deepest subconscious areas and remain suspended there.' In the New York performances Rudolf was '*wonderful*', he says – 'He was Ariel, he was pure' – but later the dancer began playing to the audience and 'doing things in a surface way' that disappointed Tetley. In his *Magic of Dance* Pierrot (filmed for TV in 1978), Rudolf is dismayingly winsome with wide-open eyes and mouth opening and shutting 'as if hungering for someone to kiss', having to feign virtues he was long past feeling.

This duplicity – the glimpse of worldliness beneath the Pierrot mask – is brilliantly captured in a portrait by the American realist painter Jamie Wyeth. Entitled *Nureyev – Purple Scarf* it shows Rudolf wearing full stage makeup with street clothes, something Wyeth says he was then in the habit of doing. His painted face is still that of Pierrot, and yet with its haunted expression is far more reminiscent of Dirk Bogarde's Von Aschenbach in the final scene of *Death in Venice*, whose white skin, kohl-lined eyes and lips ripe as strawberries are a desperate attempt to conceal age, decay and mortality. 'That was what totally intrigued me about Rudolf,' says Wyeth. 'The pathos, the split personality.' The artist had planned a whole series inspired by 'this mix of theatre and real life', but Rudolf forbade him to continue, so that it was only after the dancer's death that Wyeth was able to 'revisit' the painting. 'Which I did with a wonderful freedom.'

Watching Rudolf apply his Pierrot makeup was, Wyeth says, 'what triggered my thing', an obsession that resulted in more than thirty small-scale studies. When he had first approached the dancer three years earlier, Rudolf had refused to cooperate, and Wyeth had turned for help to Lincoln Kirstein – 'the only ballet person I knew'. A close friend of his father, the painter Andrew Wyeth, Kirstein had commissioned the sixteen-year-old Jamie to paint him in 1965. The result is such a masterly evocation of his patron's eagle profile and awe-inspiring presence that, in Kirstein's view, it immediately established Jamie as the finest American portrait painter since John Singer Sargent (a pronouncement he makes in his introduction to the catalogue of the first Wyeth exhibition, at New York's Knoedler Gallery in 1966). Encouraging the handsome prodigy to work in a room on the top floor of his Nineteenth Street town house, Kirstein was, as Jamie realized, 'completely beguiled' by him, and remained so over the next decades. But when asked to use his influence to persuade Rudolf to change his mind, Kirstein had flown into one of his rages. '*Why* are you interested in Nureyev?' he demanded. 'He's a star and nothing to do with dance.' After Kirstein had tried to sabotage the project, Jamie 'pursued it else-where', by which time Rudolf, presumably discovering the Kirstein connection for himself, had agreed to collaborate. 'That was in the back of his mind. He was very aware of these things: what people could do for him.' Certainly, in Rudolf's philosophy, there was 'always some reciprocal factor. You have to do this, and then you can do that. It's always tit for tat. Life *is* tit for tat.'

Jamie had suggested Warhol's Factory as a place to work (where the two artists had completed portraits of each other the year before), but Rudolf refused to sit for him there.* 'Something about Warhol bothered him. "He's so ugly," he said. "Why do I want to be there?"' So Jamie 'just bird-dogged him around', catching Rudolf in his hotel room, dressing room or ballet studio during the March '77 Nureyev and Friends season. 'To me a portrait is not so much the actual painting, but just spending the time with the person, travelling with him, watching him eat . . . It's really osmosis.' And it was also 'the act of recording'; Wyeth wanted to 'record this creature' with the kind of clinical exac-

---

* Rudolf had never given any credence to the cult of Andy Warhol. Although agreeing in 1972 to be featured in *Interview* magazine and photographed by Robert Mapplethorpe, he became so irritated by the vacuity of Warhol's questions that he cancelled the session. 'Following that Andy popped a Polaroid. And another. And another. Rudy [*sic*] demanded to see the results. The first, a beautiful portrait, he signed. The second, ditto. But the third, a close-up of dancedom's most famous crotch, provoked a sneer, a snarl and a smile as he flung the offending image to the ground. Andy, not one to be stopped, knelt to pick it up. Rudy, equally unstoppable, set a slippered foot down squarely on the photo. Quick-thinking Robert Mapplethorpe focused his Polaroid on that possessive foot. Rudy grabbed the camera, pulled out the undeveloped photo and crumpled it into a useless wad. "Don't you like your foot?" queried Robert. "My foot, yes . . . ", replied Rudy' (Andy Warhol's *Interview*, June 1972).

titude he had applied to dissecting bodies while studying anatomy at a Harlem hospital morgue. Employing calipers to get the proportions correct – 'tools of torture', Rudolf called them – he focused on the dancer's face and naked torso, using the background colour of his tan board for flesh, contrasted with white highlights and dark washes. Rudolf had not liked the first of the large portraits, *Profile in Fur*, so Jamie and his wife had taken it to Lincoln Kirstein for another opinion. 'There wasn't great approval,' Phyllis Wyeth noted in her diary, but an exchange she had with Kirstein that night provided exactly the kind of benefit to himself that Rudolf had foreseen:

> I then asked Lincoln why hadn't he ever had Nureyev dance for the New York City Ballet. He was full of excuses – they had no stars; they couldn't have him . . . Now that the American Ballet Theatre had Baryshnikov – Balanchine only had girl stars. But it ended up with Lincoln saying if he had his way he would have him tomorrow. I really think something may come of the conversation.

As indeed it did. An invitation soon followed for dinner at Kirstein's. 'It was just the four of us,' recalls Jamie, 'and Lincoln was *wonderful* to him.' Finding himself left 'quite cold' by Baryshnikov, Kirstein was to become so enamoured of Rudolf that he would go to see *Valentino* ten times. Also, knowing that the fee for the Nureyev *Apollo* had virtually saved the School of American Ballet, he began regarding Rudolf as 'the next heir apparent', hoping to persuade him to take charge of Balanchine's school. 'Finally,' remarks Jamie, 'Lincoln was able to see him for the remarkable creature that he was.'

Rudolf had first met Phyllis Wyeth, a tall, elegant blonde, at Elaine's restaurant, when he had been surprised to see her reaching under the table for the crutches she needed to walk. At the age of twenty-one her neck had been broken in a car accident, but she had never allowed her disability to interfere with her life. 'You have spirit and enthusiasm,' Rudolf told her admiringly that night, and he began inviting her to performances, getting his masseur, Luigi, to put a special chair in the wings. 'Last night I went to see Pierrot again,' her diary continues. 'I saw R warming up before his performance – he casts an eye & smile just to see if you are watching.' At Rudolf's suggestion, she joined him and Martha Graham at an Iranian Consulate party and, a night or so later, at a post-performance dinner at the Russian Tea Room with American Ballet Theatre principal dancers Natalia Makarova, Cynthia Gregory and Lucia Chase. Not being part of their world, she 'hadn't known what the hell they were all talking about', and admits she began to wonder why this great star was being so kind to her.

While Rudolf had genuinely warmed to Phyllis, telling Maude how tremendously brave and determined she was, he was also well aware that she could prove useful to him. 'One thing he wants is to get his money out of Europe and is looking for a farm to buy,' she noted at the time. Within weeks of meeting him, Phyllis was arriving at Rudolf's suite at the Pierre with photographs of possible properties in Virginia and Pennsylvania, where the Wyeths themselves had a farm. Late one night after a performance Rudolf had driven to Chadd's Ford to find Phyllis still waiting up to make him supper, and had felt immediately at home. Looking up at the collection of baskets hanging from the kitchen ceiling, he had remarked, 'This is for cheese, that's for potatoes, and that one's to sift wheat' – the only visitor, she says, who had ever commented on their use. 'They were like the ones he remembered from Russia.' The next morning Rudolf was already sitting in the dining room expecting to be served breakfast, but when he sent the toast back for the crusts to be cut off, Phyllis had exploded: 'Rudolf, if you stay here you cut off your *own* crusts!' She had passed the test – forthright enough to earn his respect ('I was never scared of him – whoever the hell he was'), and from that day on he would come into the kitchen in his clogs and make his own tea.

Chadd's Ford looks out across the valley of the Brandywine River with the railway tracks so close that each passing locomotive rattled the windows of the old house. 'I want farm with railroad through it; river and barns,' Rudolf had announced, describing, in effect, the Wyeths' own property. 'Phyllis was so crazy about him that I thought, "My God – she's going to give it to him!"' The more Rudolf went there the more he grew to love Chadd's Ford: riding with Phyllis in summer in her horse-drawn carriage along the riverbank, wearing one of her straw hats strewn with roses; or down a muddy track in winter, exclaiming, 'This is like road I took to *banya* once a week in Ufa!' One night when they were out in a big four-in-hand it started to snow, and the snowflakes settling on Rudolf's fur hat and coat made him look like a character from *Doctor Zhivago* – 'just fabulous, unbelievable – and of course he knew it'. If Phyllis was finally closer to Rudolf, Jamie, who nevertheless 'adored him', knew that he was there to work on his project. Rudolf was genuinely interested in the dynastic aspect of the artist's talent (Jamie's grandfather was the famous illustrator N. C. Wyeth), and enjoyed his encounters with the eccentric Andrew Wyeth, who appeared wearing a First World War uniform the first time they met.

Back in New York, it had not been long before Rudolf began taking control of the Wyeth sittings. 'I think Jamie has caught his interest as he has become opinionated on what is right or wrong,' wrote Phyllis. 'The right leg was turned out too much making everything stiff . . . that "James" must put on the neck & head right.' But if Jamie had been allowed nearly two hundred sessions in which to complete the Kirstein portrait, he had 'an incredibly difficult time' with the dancer, who was in town for only three weeks and had no time to pose.

Rudolf spent April 1977 in London working with the Festival Ballet on his new production of *Romeo and Juliet*, and in early May he returned to America to appear before Congress in Washington. The Helsinki Accords were due to be reviewed in Belgrade that summer, and in a letter to the *New York Times* on 31 March Rudolf had written a plea for freedom of movement and human rights to be observed.[*] 'I feel that I have created only goodwill for the country of my birth, and I urge the Soviet authorities to demonstrate their sincerity at Helsinki by allowing my family to visit me.' The Washington tribunal had come about as a result of Armen Bali's petitioning on his behalf, and she had paid for her lawyer 'to teach Rudolf how to talk', but nevertheless he dreaded the cross-examination. Conservatively dressed in a brown turtleneck sweater and blazer, he appeared extremely nervous and spoke in low, hesitant tones, his voice inaudible at times so that Representative Dante Fascell had to tell him he could not be heard. The hearing had created an enormous amount of publicity and was covered by all the television news channels – but to no avail. At the beginning of June, Armen received the following letter from the Bilateral Relations Office of Soviet Union Affairs: 'The White House and Department of State are following this matter closely, and our Embassy in Moscow and Consulate General in Leningrad are in touch with the family. We have made representations to the Soviet authorities in support of their exit visa applications, but unfortunately the Soviet Government has not relented to date.'[†]

---

[*] In August 1975, thirty-five nations, including the Soviet Union, met in Helsinki. Among the human-rights areas covered by this conference were those calling for greater freedom of travel, particularly for Russians wishing to visit, or be reunited with, relatives abroad.

[†] The plan was to create a Panov-type public clamour, and active committees, whose members included Beverly Sills, Edward Albee, Paul Taylor and Frederick Ashton, were established in New York, London, Vienna, Geneva and Paris, resulting in the collection of more than 56,000 signatures.

Launching that summer's Nureyev Festival at the London Coliseum, Rudolf's full-length *Romeo and Juliet* may have been choreographed in record time, but it was, in fact, a ballet he had been mentally preparing for years. In August 1973 Nigel had received a postcard from Wallace in La Turbie with the news that Rudolf had been reading Shakespeare's play and two books of criticism. Wanting to let himself 'be carried by MacMillan's choreography', Rudolf hadn't read the text when he first performed Romeo, but he had noted several titles – a 'formidable' list of books he now sent Nigel to track down. Many were out of print, but in a long letter Nigel included the notes he had made on two of them, *Not Wisely but Too Well*, by F. N. Dickey and *Shakespeare's Young Lovers* by E. E. Stoll ('A silly book debunking play'), as well as his own summary of the prose narratives, plays and poems in Olin H. Moore's *The Legend of Romeo and Juliet* – an account of the origins of the story before it reached Shakespeare. Dozens more pages arrived with quotations from famous Shakespearians, general notes on key themes and personal thoughts from the 'Useless Suggestions Dept'. But it was the long introduction to Nigel's own Penguin New Shakespeare edition of the play that proved fundamental in setting the tone of the ballet.

'The mutual passion of Juliet and Romeo is surrounded by the mature bawdry of the other characters,' writes T. J. B. Spencer. 'In this highly sexed world . . . the innocence of the lovers is emphasized.' Rudolf would follow this idea to the letter, making Juliet's Nurse a lusty young woman caught in a compromising clinch by her charge, and hinting at an adulterous complicity between Lady Capulet and Tybalt. 'Juliet's family is very libertine,' he told Nigel. 'I want her to see her father's hand on her mother's crotch, the boys pushing the girls against the wall.' More crucially it was Spencer's attention to the interplay of chance and choice, fate and character, that struck a chord, one quotation being emphatically underlined by Rudolf.

> Some consequence, yet hanging in the stars,
> Shall bitterly begin his fearful date
> With this night's revels.

The idea of an outside force controlling his future was unthinkable to Rudolf, whose mantra throughout life was 'You make your own luck.' He did, on the other hand, share the Elizabethan susceptibility to superstitions and auguries. 'I have dream, like premonition. I used to know what is going to happen next day – where the dangers are coming. I just knew; I couldn't prevent them. I used to kind of herald it in advance and say: well, that is going to happen.' To him fate was 'the central thing' in *Romeo and Juliet*, and he decided to emphasize this by beginning and ending the ballet with a group of sinister cloaked figures playing dice ('Gods playing with human distini [*sic*]' he scrawled in the margin of the typed scenario).

Almost all ballets of *Romeo and Juliet* are based on the libretto devised by its first choreographer, Leonid Lavrovsky. Thinking of ways to make his production different, Rudolf had initially wanted to use music from the period in which the story is set, but then reckoned that several hours of thirteenth- and fourteenth-century music might become 'very tiresome'. The solution came from reading the play, and deciding that, instead of omitting the scenes which narrate the cause of the tragic climax, he was going to tell the full story. 'For people who knew the play he wanted this to be a production that honoured the original. And he wanted to explain to those who didn't know the piece how it all came about.' Rudolf's determination to prove that he had understood every nuance of Shakespeare's imagery, including words 'that were stumbling blocks' for him, would make the ballet overliteral at times – nowhere more so than Act 3's person-ification of Death who, in reference to Juliet's avowal – 'I'll to my wedding bed, / And death, not Romeo, take my maidenhead!' – really does appear onstage to have his way with her. As a consequence, the young lovers' bedroom duet is completely superfluous, its des-perately acrobatic movements an attempt to compensate for its lack of emotion.

And yet it is Rudolf's approach to Shakespeare as a Russian that makes his *Romeo and Juliet* so fascinating – its Slavic pessimism one that (to use his own description of Innokenty Smoktunovsky's films of *Hamlet* and *Lear*) 'is definitely not cups of tea!' His 'bible' became a book by the Polish scholar Jan Kott – *Shakespeare, Our Contemporary* – which also views the plays through personal experience. Kott is, as Peter Brook remarks in his Preface, 'the only writer on Elizabethan matters who assumes without question that every one of his readers will at some point or other have been woken by the police in the middle of the night'. And to Rudolf, Russia's brutal social order was at one with the tyrannies of Elizabeth's England, Kott's 'cruel and true' portrait of Shakespeare convincing him that Verona of the Renaissance and Elizabethan London 'had in common sex and violence and were singularly close to another age: our own'.* His designer, Ezio Frigerio, and lighting designer, Jennifer Tipton, were told to construct a Verona 'that was dark, anguished, dangerous, full of shadows', so much so that the first-night audience could hardly distinguish one character from another.

It had made sense for Rudolf to create his *Romeo and Juliet* for the London Festival Ballet, a company with which he had established an easy rapport while staging his *Sleeping Beauty* in 1975. His first Juliet was Patricia Ruanne, whose talent he had spotted when she was 'a brand-new corps de ballet baby' dancing in his Spoleto *Raymonda*. 'There was a lot of affection there, a great tenderness,' says Frederic Jahn (then Werner), Pat's Australian boyfriend, whom Rudolf had got to know from his seasons with the Australian Ballet. The couple, now both principals with the Festival Ballet, together with two former Royal Ballet dancers, Nicholas Johnson and Elizabeth Anderton, had been happy to work late into the night after Rudolf returned from the set of *Valentino*. And although all four would be rewarded with leading roles (Johnson as Mercutio, Jahn as Tybalt and Anderton as the Nurse), at the time nobody was quite sure which character they would be playing. 'At first I did Paris, then Romeo, then Tybalt,' says Jahn. 'Betty filled in as Lady Capulet. Then everything changed around again.' This workshop atmosphere continued to a degree throughout the making of the ballet, with Rudolf encouraging an improvisatory, Stanislavskian approach. 'The death of Juliet was never choreographed,' Ruanne says. 'Rudolf would say, "Explore. Ad lib."' Nor would he allow the confrontation between Juliet and her parents to be rehearsed. '"Don't cook it," he said, because he wanted to create the kind of confusion you get in a family row, where everyone shouts and no one makes sense.'

Rudolf's choreographic style was just as experimental, as he intended to include the contemporary technique he had learned. Act 3's oddly stilted quadrille for Lord and Lady Capulet, Paris and Juliet is a nod to José Limón's *Moor's Pavane*, while the inspiration for Juliet's off-balance whirling in the love duets derived from a film about Turkish dervishes, and from the principle of the spiral he had learned from Martha Graham. Pat Ruanne, who had had no training in modern technique, recalls how she was constantly falling over. 'The centre of weight is not the same when you're on pointe. I watched and tried to imitate, but it was a hit-and-miss thing.'

---

* Recent theatre productions by Terry Hands (1973) and Trevor Nunn and Barry Kyle (1976) had also brought out the 'shocking violence' of the play.

Rudolf had not passed on to Ruanne any of his background research, but he did insist that she reread the play, 'and read it *my* way'. What he meant, of course, was a reinterpretation of the traditional romantic image of Juliet as 'a pretty, drifting little thing' – a departure she admits was difficult for her at first. 'I knew that I had to change my point of view and realize that she was the strength in the play . . . Because if Rudolf had had his way, Juliet would have been a boy.'

He had become fascinated with the Elizabethan tradition of boy actors playing women's roles, as well as by the image of the androgyne in art and literature – girlish boys like Michelangelo's Bacchus and Donatello's David; boyish girls like Botticelli's Flora, the master-mistress of the Sonnets. The multilayers of amorous disguise in *Twelfth Night* and *As You Like It*, where a boy dresses up as a girl, who disguises herself as a boy, was exactly the kind of ambiguity Rudolf wanted from Ruanne, a ballerina whose gamine delicacy belied her exceptional strength. 'I tried my best to be a counter-role. Because as a woman, basically, I know I'm playing a boy playing a girl. It's complicated . . . but it was a truly new approach.'

A compromise of sorts was the way Rudolf choreographically reverses the genders. In the lovers' first duet it is Juliet who takes the lead, Romeo always a step behind her, imitating her movements. Pat describes how she was made to share the load of partnering as if she were a man: 'Two men dance together in a very different way, there's an equal dispersal of strength, and of balance, a counterpoint. It's why today's Juliets find the pas de deux so difficult: you're pulling into play muscles you don't normally use; it's a question of strength in the arms and wrists. You *both* take the weight; you *both* carry the can.'

As a contrast to his 'tough-cookie Juliet', Rudolf envisaged Romeo as a much weaker, more indecisive person. 'He is bottled up, probably a virgin . . . Juliet releases his juices.' It was a notion influenced by the first *Romeo and Juliet* he had seen in the West – the 1961 version arranged for the Paris Opéra by the German dancer Peter van Dyk, whose 'gentle' Romeo he had liked and admired. When he danced the MacMillan ballet in which Romeo, as Rudolf remarked, is 'a winner from the start', he refused to convey any kind of passivity, but as the choreographer himself he faced a dilemma. 'I see it one way. Public will not want to see that way. Public will want *doubles assemblés*,' he complained to Ruanne. 'I felt that he had two *Romeo and Juliets* up his sleeve: one that he would dream to have done, and one that would bring the public in, the acceptable production.' Again Rudolf compromised, allowing Romeo a *manège* of spiralling turns as a climax to his most euphoric solo, but for much of the time 'almost making himself invisible'. Now, as Jahn comments, 'he knew the balance of the production depended on *all* of us'.

For Rudolf the ballet was intensely personal and a reflection of the literature he had read. To the critics, however, its plethora of quotations, dense narrative and relentless activity were excessive, and more than one of them expressed a longing for an occasional calm interlude of simple lyricism. Dancing twenty-five consecutive performances, Rudolf was not able to see the flaws, and although he would later make a number of changes, his *Romeo and Juliet* remains to this day something of a work in progress: 'when good', as James Monahan put it, 'very, very good, when bad, horrid'.

The Coliseum season included what Alastair Macaulay described as 'one extraordinary week' (4–9 July 1977) when Rudolf and Margot appeared in their last-ever *Marguerite and Armand*, and, performing the *Corsaire* duet with Natalia Makarova, he showed himself to be in sixties-style, 'heart-stoppingly exultant' form: 'Until and including that week, Nureyev was the greatest star I have ever seen . . . The real crash came in the seventh and final week . . . He was lurching forwards in arabesque every time . . . His spine had lost its strength. Nor did it ever recapture its former power. Within months, his whole lustre seemed to drain away.'

This was soon to happen, but not quite yet. But what became apparent over the next few months was a much greater disparity in the quality of Rudolf's performances, verging from 'uneven and uneasy' to 'suddenly brilliant and dazzling'. On 17 July he flew with the Festival Ballet to Australia, and over the next three months (in the Philippines, America and Canada), inspired some of the most exuberant reviews of his career. His return to Vienna in December was 'triumphant', his technique notably smoother than it had been two years before, his preparations 'less forced and separate' (evidence of Stanley Williams's influence). Martin Bernheimer remarking in the *Los Angeles Times* that Rudolf's career had entered its 'twilight zone', apologetically retracts this a week later, confessing that the star had 'made a liar' of him. In Venice, in March, partnering Elisabetta Terabust in *Giselle*, Rudolf's dancing 'seemed forced in the first act but found mysterious strength for the double cabrioles and *tours en l'air* of the second'. He was still capable of pulling off a consistently brilliant display in places where it really mattered. In April 1978, 'roaring back into New York' 'at his most thrilling old self', Rudolf added the *Corsaire* duet to his Nureyev and Friends programme to prove that he was 'still perfectly capable of wondrous things'.

While still in New York he appeared in a season of new modern ballets by Friends who had 'choreographed for *him*'. Dancing Murray Louis's work was in itself an elixir of longevity – 'like having a ball of energy inside your body'. *Vivace*, his ten-minute solo to a Bach fugue, made no real technical demands, its movements echoing the variants and developments of the musical phrases; while *Canarsie Venus*, to Cole Porter melodies, provided Rudolf with a rare comic role. He performed this delightfully, although he had been 'as corny as hell at first', Murray recalls. 'I did a lot to clean him up in terms of humour. He would purse his lips and deteriorate into cutesy. "Rudolf, don't be cute," I'd say, and he would *cringe*.' Toer van Schayk's *Faun* was also a lighthearted piece, a modern reworking of Debussy's *Afternoon of a Faun* music, in which Rudolf is a factory caretaker and his nymphs are two assembly-line girls. Sauntering onstage with a trolley of detergents and suggestively polishing a horizontal pole, he then swaggers and lolls about while taking his lunch break, jokily alluding to Nijinsky's famous pose by tilting his head back and sensuously feeding on a bunch of grapes. The piece was largely dismissed as 'a feeble try at humour', and the New York critics liked Rudi van Dantzig's latest Nureyev vehicle, *About a Dark House*, even less. A Kafka-esque, psychosexual melodrama, it cast Rudolf as an intruder at a macabre dinner party, held aloft, dragged about, and left in total isolation at the end, stripped virtually naked while still in the company of the formally dressed guests.

Learning the two new works in Amsterdam in March, Rudolf had insisted on adding to the programme *Four Schumann Pieces* by Hans van Manen, whom he much admired. But by not giving himself enough time to prepare all three, he often turned up tired and confused from one rehearsal to another, 'trying out steps from *Faun* during *Schumann Pieces* and rehearsing *Dark House* in the movement idiom of van Schayk'. Amateur film footage records this perfunctoriness, showing the dancer defining the steps so haphazardly that he hardly looks trained. In complete contrast, Rudi van Dantzig remembers their two weeks on Broadway as 'a spell of pure unsullied joy', his company and its guest star in peak form, Rudolf's behaviour as enchanting as that of 'a tame foal'. When they next worked together, however, Rudi was shocked by the change in his friend. It was at the end of the year in Vienna, where they collaborated on *Ulysses,* a showpiece for Rudolf commissioned by the Staatsoper, the whole experience, Rudi recalls, disintegrating into a miserable failure. 'We walked in the city a lot and he was very negative, torn to pieces. A total mess. I had absolutely the feeling that something awful was happening in his life. The Vienna Opera situation, the dancers he didn't like . . . but it was something else.'

Shortly after the 7 January 1979 première, the choreographer flew to New York to stay with Rudolf in his new apartment in the Dakota, minutes away from the Met. Infamous now as the site of John Lennon's murder in December 1980, it has the gloomy exterior of a Teutonic town hall, with high gables, dormers, balconies and balustrades, but its rooms are light and spacious with palatially high ceilings and views of Central Park. Rudolf could only just have moved in, as the apartment looked more like a warehouse, most of the furniture still in crates and a clutter of statues, paintings and huge rolls of Cordoba leather stacked against the walls. Van Dantzig had arrived there 'with a sinking feeling', knowing that his first task was to tell the dancer that he could no longer invite him to guest with their company. 'His artistry had deteriorated to such an extent that I did not feel I could defend why he should appear with the National Ballet . . . except for selfish reasons: the tours and publicity.' 'So, you mean you've sacked me!' sneered Rudolf. 'Am I too old, or what?' Certain that he had precipitated an end to their friendship, and embarrassed to be taking advantage of the star's hospitality, Rudi volunteered to find a hotel. 'Of course not,' insisted Rudolf. 'You stay here.'

He had invited Rudi to New York for a purpose, and the following morning pushed a thick wad of paper across the breakfast table, saying, 'Read this.' It was a script for another Nijinsky film, conceived this time by Jean-Claude Carrière (Luis Buñuel's collaborator on *The Discreet Charm of the Bourgeoisie* and *That Obscure Object of Desire*). Entitled *Nureyev's Nijinsky*, it would feature Rudolf (as himself) dancing extracts from the legendary roles and choreographing a ballet based on Nijinsky's life. What Rudolf proposed was a van Dantzig restaging of the 1913 ballet *Jeux* as Diaghilev had originally envisioned it – a flirtation during a tennis game between a man and two boys. In his memoirs Nijinsky claims that it was his mentor's dream to have two lovers at the same time. 'He often told me so, but I refused.' A ballet with a homosexual theme was, Rudolf enthused to Rudi, 'something right up your street'. But the film-makers immediately vetoed the idea. Their meeting in New York with Carrière's co-writer, John Heilpern, was 'all a bit bleak', Rudi recalls, and he sensed that Rudolf was in any case having second thoughts about the project. 'I hate it,' he had said of Heilpern's script, and the film's director, Anthony Page, witnessed the extent of Rudolf's antipathy when they all met in Paris to discuss the first draft: 'It was at Maxim's after a revival of *La Sylphide*. Heilpern had been to see it and hadn't said anything about the performance, which angered Rudolf. It was not far into dinner when he suddenly turned on John and said, "The script is shit. I wouldn't wipe my ass with it. It's too trivial to be even worth discussing."'

It was, Page says, 'too journalistic' for Rudolf, but its conclusion may also have been too autobiographical. The Nureyev of the story discovers that an old man who filmed Nijinsky's final recital in Switzerland (when all he did was repeat four simple arm movements over and over again) had in fact taken more footage of Nijinsky actually dancing on that occasion but had destroyed it in order to perpetuate the myth. A decade earlier, at the time of his final rupture with Erik, Rudolf believed that Nijinsky's insanity had been precipitated by the end of his affair with Diaghilev. Now his view had changed. Nijinsky's 'mind broke,' he said, 'because he could no longer dance' – an explanation more likely than any other for his own recent despair.

Rudolf's life was anyway imitating fiction. The script begins with a press conference at which he announces his 'Diaghilev Season': *Le Spectre de la rose*, *Petrushka* and *L'Après-midi d'un faune* – the same three ballets that he was soon to perform for Robert Joffrey's company in New York. Acting on Erik's advice, and not wanting to be seen 'jumping on dead man's bones', Rudolf had deliberately avoided the Nijinsky repertory (except for *Petrushka* and *Les Sylphides*), but now, as a fortieth-birthday present to himself, he decided that it was 'time to indulge, to be foolish if I wish'. It was, as he realized, one more experience to be gained from the West, the famous Ballets Russes works known in Leningrad only for their notoriety.

> The teachers used to talk about Diaghilev but in a hushed voice as though it was about a scandal. We learned about *Faune* from the gossip point of view . . . You must remember that Diaghilev is something which happened to you, not to us . . . Even today when he is officially accepted, people in Russia are still trying to relate to him. He was a bit unreal and exotic, like a rich uncle who turns up suddenly in America.

As far as Rudolf was concerned, dancing the Nijinsky roles – learning 'what he was about, how he moved, what goals he had, what discoveries he made' – was a way of bringing the history of his art to life. An eleven-minute distillation of ballet modernism, Nijinsky's *Faune* developed and crystallized the innovations made by Fokine: the turned-in leg positions from *Petrushka* and the two-dimensional, sideways-angled body from *Cléopâtre*.

The most ephemeral of the performing arts, ballet owes its survival to the baton-passing knowledge of veteran performers, and aware of this, Rudolf went out of his way to consult those closest to the source. He learned *Spectre* from Alexander Gavrilov, who took over from Nijinsky; he asked Baryshnikov to show him the version he had learned from André Eglevsky (taught by Fokine), and Margot to lend him the notes she had taken from Tamara Karsavina, who created the role of the young girl. For *Faune* he got Charles Jude to demonstrate the version he had learned from Nijinsky's replacement, Léonide Massine:

> We were all laughing at the rehearsals because Nijinsky's sister, Bronislava, had come over from America and set it. Then Lifar arrived and showed another version, then Nijinsky's widow came and tried to change that. I guess they arrived at some sort of compromise. Then I went to the Ballet Rambert who had learned it from Diaghilev's own dancers and worked with William Chappell and Elizabeth Schooling; even they each had different ideas. So in the end I had to make up my own mind.

Choreography, he said, was like an item of clothing – 'you have to try it on and move around and make it fit your own body'. Naturally the same went for costumes. Designer Rouben Ter-Arutunian had steeped himself 'in the atmosphere of Bakst' to arrive at his authentic designs, but to Rudolf the pink, petalled skull cap that Nijinsky wore as the Spectre looked 'like a skin disease'. He commissioned Toer van Schayk to come up with something more flattering, and soon adapted the original makeup – the red eyes and pointed Dr Spock ears – that Ter-Arutunian had overseen for *Faune*. 'There are two ways of going about a reconstruction. Either petal by petal, just as it was, or whether it suits you or not . . . You try to make the thing alive. You have to try to say it with your own tools.' It was far more important, Rudolf believed, to convey the *spirit* of the original. When Nijinsky's sixty-four-year-old daughter Kyra came to his San Francisco dressing room, a poignant figure wearing a little sequinned hat, her teeth stained with lipstick, Rudolf claimed that from the way she lifted her heavy arms to strike one of her father's *Spectre* poses, he could tell what power Nijinsky must have had, power that 'comes from inside'.*

Baryshnikov would argue that no contemporary dancer, himself included, has excelled in the Nijinsky roles. 'Those Diaghilev pieces didn't work on anybody: they're better than anybody who danced them.' Indeed Rudolf's Joffrey season made little impression – least of all *Le Spectre de la rose*, which looked dated and sentimental as Rudolf strained to prove his virtuosity instead of recapturing the Spectre's evanescent aura. He had more success in *Faune*, and Arlene Croce praised the 'creaturely warmth' that bonded the two dancers, as well as the power they showed in slow motion. Rudolf had closely studied the still photographs of *Faune* – but that led to the problem Croce saw as a 'pose to pose performance . . . too anchored in static opposi-tions'. For this production of *Petrushka*, wearing almost no makeup, he seemed to be relying on his own 'expressive, hollowed-out Slavic face'. But if Jerome Robbins 'could not lose Rudi', in other words see him in character, Croce was far more damning: 'He is a truly terrible Petrushka – waggling, flapping, hunching like a small boy in need of a bathroom . . . and his effortful bad acting is inflamed by pathos.'

And yet despite the critical hammering, Rudolf was much happier than he had been. Not only was he performing to full houses seven times a week for a month, he had received 'a gift from God': the chance to collaborate with Balanchine for the first time. He had been crushed the previous summer on learning that Baryshnikov had achieved his own dream of 'entering the ideal future of the Maryinsky Ballet' by becoming a member of the New York City Ballet. But although Baryshnikov had gone to Balanchine with the highest expec-tations, the choreographer, who was then seventy-four and suffering from heart problems, was not well enough to create any new ballets for him. What Rudolf had been offered was the title role in *Le Bourgeois gentilhomme*, a new version of a work Balanchine had created twice before (in 1932 and 1944). Using the score written by Richard Strauss

---

* There is a poignant letter to Rudolf from Kyra Nijinsky dated 24 August 1973, hoping that he, or one of his 'good jet-set friends', might be interested in buying a Marie Taglioni letter for fifteen hundred dollars. 'Forgive me,' she writes. 'I have to help myself to get somehow on my feet . . . I long to see my son and my grandchildren . . . and even my mother in her old age.' She also has Weber's score of *Le Spectre de la rose* to sell, and several 'gorgeous pictures' of her father. Signing herself, 'your friend in Christ, Kyra Nijinsky', she tells Rudolf about a small sketch she copied from a programme of him dancing in *La Sylphide*. 'I have [it] in my prayerbook.'

as incidental music for Molière's play, it was a ballet intended not for his own company but for the New York City Opera, who would be presenting it on a double bill with Purcell's *Dido and Aeneas*. 'Tell Rudolf if he wants to participate, that's fine,' Balanchine had said, a proposal Rudolf described as 'Nothing much. Very cryptic.' But even this was too good to be true. 'I'm not an optimist,' Rudolf told a journalist. 'So I said, "Keep me posted. I'll believe it when I'm there."' He was right to be sceptical. According to Susan Hendl, the ballet mistress on *Le Bourgeois gentilhomme*, the only reason the choreographer had agreed to take on the project was because the opera was in financial difficulty, and being a good friend of the NYCO's co-director Beverly Sills, Balanchine wanted to help out: 'Nureyev would sell tickets.'

When rehearsals began in February 1979 the choreographer, finding that he could not recall a single step from his earlier versions, had been forced to start over, though focusing once again on the young lovers, Cleonte (Rudolf) and Lucile (Patricia McBride), who succeed in outwitting her father, the credulous parvenu Monsieur Jourdain (Jean-Pierre Bonnefous). There had been surprisingly little advance publicity about Rudolf's arrival – 'no hype or hullabaloo like the other guy [Baryshnikov]' – but this had made it possible for Balanchine to accept him as a dancer, not a star. 'I think Balanchine was surprised at how easy it was to work with him,' remarked Patricia McBride. He seemed genuinely impressed by Rudolf's versatility, commenting on the adroit way he moved his head like an Oriental in the ballet's Turkish initiation ceremony, and congratulating him on taking the right amount of time to bow. 'Americans don't know how to bow,' Balanchine said, laughing and breaking into Russian. Balanchine had chosen Flemming Flindt for several of the works he mounted at the Paris Opéra, and Flindt remembered he would say, 'Here's a male variation: do what you think you do best.' Rudolf was given much the same freedom – Cleonte's solos becoming a compendium of signature Nureyev steps. Susie Hendl was struck by how almost comically curious they were about what each thought of the other. 'What's he saying about me?' Rudolf would ask over dinner. 'And then Mr B would ask exactly the same thing.'

It soon became apparent, however, that Balanchine's health was fast deteriorating (in May he would undergo a bypass operation), and he was often unable to finish a rehearsal, leaving Susie to take over. On the day Rudi van Dantzig watched a rehearsal, Balanchine seemed absentminded and uninspired.

He tried out some steps and asked Rudolf: 'How would you do this?' 'Does that feel right to you?' or: 'Don't make this too complicated, it should be simple, just a little joke, a little nothing,' then nosing around like a mouse and coming up with a few weird little moves. Rudolf copied the master, but the essence was gone. All that seemed natural and obvious with Balanchine gained an unnatural emphasis when Rudolf tried it out. Frighteningly little else happened at all; it saddened me, was this Rudolf's great dream?

It was at this point that Jerome Robbins told Rudolf that he should feel free to withdraw from the project, adding, 'If anything happens to George, it will be on your conscience.' But having finally achieved his ultimate wish, Rudolf had every intention of keeping the choreographer in good-enough health to see their collaboration through. 'Are you going to go home and lie down or something, have lunch?' he would ask, and when Balanchine refused to oblige, he began getting Luigi to bring borscht or chicken soup each day from the Russian Tea Room, even going as far as to feign stupidity, pretending to need extra time to work out the counts, in order to force Balanchine to rest. ('He learns so slowly,' Balanchine complained to Barbara Horgan.) Soon, though, the choreographer became much too ill to continue, and both Robbins and Peter Martins stepped in to contribute dances of their own. When Balanchine returned in time to complete the ballet, Rudolf's relief was palpable. 'All I can remember is Rudi's warmth, so warm and so funny,' said Patricia McBride.

And yet with only one classical *pas de sept* making it identifiably a Balanchine ballet, *Le Bourgois gentilhomme* (premièred on 8 April 1979) can only have disappointed Rudolf. Two-thirds mime, it is at times as farcical and old-fashioned as the creakiest sections of *Don Quixote* – in Arlene Croce's tactful phrase, 'one of those developments in [Balanchine's] career which lie outside his creative life'. She believed that by having Cleonte assume the disguises of those employed to make a gentleman out of Jourdain – the tailor and dancing and fencing instructors – Balanchine was making fun of 'the quick-change artist that Nureyev has become, hopping from company to company, from role to role'. Certainly Balanchine had a vengeful streak, as his biographer Robert Gottlieb confirms. 'This was a complicated man. He would find a way to get his point across, to say: "You're not such a star."' When Gelsey Kirkland saw Baryshnikov in *Prodigal Son* wearing his newly designed costume, an ugly loose overall, she found herself wondering 'if he had any idea that Balanchine was making a fool of him'.* The same thought occurs when Rudolf, with effortful brio, flings himself into the kind of nineteenth-century Russian solo that Balanchine deplored, the feather in his turban only emphasizing the ballet's grotesque caricature of the Nureyev of *Corsaire* and *Bayadère*.

Rudolf was not unaware of a subtext to *Gentilhomme*, but he told friends he suspected that by giving him what was essentially a character role Balanchine was telling him to retire. Richard Buckle was more direct. 'My advice to you is to give up dancing. You are getting past it,' he wrote to Rudolf in June. 'There are many more important things which only you can do. Don't listen to Nigel: he is a senile old fool.' It was advice Buckle claimed had never reached Rudolf because, 'believe it or not', he told Lincoln Kirstein, 'Nigel Gosling intercepted and suppressed my letter.' A month later Nigel received a Buckle admonishment of his own. 'You may think me manic, but I always say what I mean. I think Rudolf *should* retire. His *Spectre*, seen in New York, with open gasping mouth and terrified eyes and jump one foot from the ground was painful to watch. By all means repeat this. I am much too fond of him not to say what I think.'

For that summer's Nureyev Festival, Rudolf invited Margot, who had just turned sixty, to appear with him in two works from his Diaghilev season. But with the ballerina hardly able to rise on pointe in *Le Spectre de la rose* and Rudolf, who had broken a toe, also struggling with the up-and-down kneeling in *L'Après-midi d'un faune*, these were performances that brought to mind Misia Sert's description of the fading star Serge Lifar: the Spectre of a Faune and Afternoon of a Rose. William Chappell, who coached Rudolf in *Faune*, remembered how exhausted he had been throughout the rehearsal period. 'So I asked him, "Why do you overwork? You don't need to." And he said, "If I stopped dancing for a minute, I'd die." Very firmly, he said that. The trouble is his legs are turning into stone. He's torturing himself – he really will become immovable.'

*

* This was not impossible. Susie Hendl describes how Balanchine got his revenge after Edward Villella had broken an unspoken NYCB rule by performing an encore during the company's 1962 tour of Russia. 'A few days later he called Eddie to the wardrobe for a costume fitting. Eddie is rather small anyway and discovered that Mr B had cut him up in all different colours.' 'Good,' said Balanchine with mean, ferrety glee. 'You know it looks like you're dancing on your *knees*.'

Rudolf was now pursuing lovers almost half his age. 'He was always talking about my youth. He felt his own was being taken away from him.' One of a dozen students from the School of American Ballet used as extras in *Le Bourgeois gentilhomme*, twenty-three-year-old Robert Tracy was, as Murray Louis said, 'wonderful for Rudolf at that time – fun and fresh and vivacious'. Both were late for a rehearsal one day and started a conversation about Greece, where Rudolf had begun spending his summers, which led to the subject of classical literature. Robert had studied ancient Greek at university, and Rudolf was then drawn to the idea of *eromenos*, the ethos of boy worship by the Greek gods. Casting himself as Zeus, he saw Robert as 'his Ganymede' and, inviting him back to his hotel for tea, seduced him that afternoon. 'That's when everything started . . . He was the master and I was the apprentice.' (The dancer's role in the ballet as 'the lackey who carried the Moët & Chandon bottle' coincided neatly with that of Ganymede, Zeus's cupbearer, Rudolf describing to friends how Robert 'ran messages for him, as it were, and brought him drinks'.) They soon discovered a mutual obsession with Balanchine; Robert was in the process of taping conversations with the choreographer's muses for a book.* At Skidmore College he had been taught by Melissa Hayden, who although not a favourite Balanchine ballerina, was renowned in the company for her staying power, intelligence and exceptional artistry. 'It was Melissa who prepared me for Rudolf.' Then, in the spring of 1978, before winning a scholarship to Balanchine's school, Robert had danced with Chicago's Lyric Opera Ballet, whose director was Maria Tallchief. And yet, although he was not untalented as a dancer – Danilova used to call him 'the Fly Boy' because of his high jump – Robert saw his future not as a performer but as a dance historian. 'I was an academic. My hero was Lincoln Kirstein.' For Rudolf it was Robert's intelligence combined with his extreme youth that was the major part of his allure. Maude remembered their first conversation. 'Rudolf said, "Robert's interesting. He can talk about books and music and he listens to good music on the radio." Rudolf liked Robert because he had a brain, but I don't think he was ever in love with him. It wasn't like it was with Wallace. Not *at all*. He was just a young boy who was carried away with admiration for this star.'

Determined not to get involved again, Rudolf had warned Robert

---

* *Balanchine's Ballerinas: Conversations with the Muses* by Robert Tracy with Sharon DeLano was published by Linden Press/Simon & Schuster in 1983.

that 'there were going to be lots of boys around.' 'But there were lots in my life, too. I was wild . . . it meant I was free.' If Rudolf had an assignation planned, he would ask a friend to 'take Robert some place'. Gilles Dufour, then working in New York and also living in the Navarro Hotel on Central Park South, remembers how 'the poor guy was always coming to my room and waiting.' There was one point, Robert claims, when Rudolf wanted him to participate in a *Jeux*-style multiple coupling with two dancer brothers, Robert and Edmund La Fosse, although both insist that this was never offered to them as an option. Rudolf had enjoyed his brief fling with Edmund in the spring of 1976, after meeting him at a Royal Ballet party, and he had homed in on Robbie, a member of the American Ballet Theatre, when he guested in the company's *Swan Lake* in April 1978. Spotting the young dancer standing at the bar of Studio 54, Rudolf succeeded in sweeping him off that night to Pennsylvania to stay with the Wyeths. 'You don't say no to Rudolf: what he wants, he gets.' But if Robbie felt ill at ease at Chadd's Ford – 'I was aware that everyone knew what I was there for' – he became even more disenchanted by the star after a visit to his suite at the Pierre Hotel some months later. 'I should have charged him. It was like a call service.'

As Rudolf got older and his conquests younger, he frequently assumed the sexually active role, though, as the dominant partner, he was 'aggressive, never tender or gentle', Robert Tracy claims, and Robbie La Fosse agrees. Meeting Rudolf at the Dakota for what turned out to be their final encounter, he found him more exploitative than ever.

> I realized this man was not sensitive to me. He was not sensitive to the fact that I was young. Either that night or next morning I went into the kitchen and there was Robert Tracy, whom I knew from school. I couldn't figure things out. I didn't know what his situation was with Rudolf. We didn't say anything to each other, but I thought, This is awkward, and I left.

Robert was expected to disappear when Rudolf announced that his 'boyfriend from Paris' would be arriving. Rudolf had met Franck Raoul-Duval before a performance of *Romeo and Juliet* at the Palais des Sports in October 1977. The twenty-year-old had been taken to his dressing room by Paris Opéra dancers he had befriended when the company toured Russia earlier that year. He was in Moscow to study Russian, and had become so infatuated with ballet that on his return to Paris he started taking classes himself. He and Rudolf had struck up an immediate rapport, talking animatedly in Russian until it was time for the dancer to go onstage. Anticipating Rudolf's intentions, Franck had turned down an invitation for dinner. Rudolf instructed Douce to seek him out at his business college ('She didn't succeed because she'd got my name wrong'), but by this time Rudolf had begun to withdraw, suspecting that the boy, who also spoke perfect English, might be a KGB plant. After about a month of tentative encounters described by Franck as 'one step ahead, two steps back', they had dinner together at Douce's apartment, and that night began a relationship that was to last more than a year and a half:

> Rudolf was not good at talking about emotional things, but eventually he told me about Wallace, and said he had put too much pressure on him. He felt a bit guilty for having kept him on a leash, so to speak, and he knew that I would not follow him like a little dog . . . I was keeping my distance, but that suited him as he was always performing. 'Do your own thing; go your own way,' he'd say. 'And of course, finish your studies.'

In the spring of 1978 they saw each other again during the Dutch National Ballet's US tour. Franck endeared himself immediately to Rudi van Dantzig and his dancers. 'I think Rudolf was annoyed that he spent so much time hanging out with our young kids, but everyone liked him very much. He was so innocent, so unspoiled, and didn't seem at all aware of what Rudolf wanted of him.' In San Francisco Jeannette Etheredge and her brother met the couple at the airport, taking them right off to sail on the bay. 'Franck didn't say much, but he was very charming. He seemed very happy all the time.' In London they had stayed with Nigel and Maude. 'Franck used to love to come and talk to Nigel about books. He was such a cultured boy.' 'I will be able to form him,' Rudolf had told the Goslings, meaning not only culturally but socially, as Franck, by his own admission, 'was quite rough at the edges then'. Rudolf introduced him to Margot – 'her gentleness, her manners were overwhelming' – and took him on a summer cruise of the Greek islands on Stavros Niarchos's yacht. Flying from New York to Athens, Franck was picked up at the airport in one of Niarchos's helicopters, dropped off at a beach, and told to wait there until a dinghy arrived to transport him to *Atlantis II*. 'I sat there on the sand with my suitcase, jet-lagged from the flight, until I saw this huge white ship approaching. It was like a mirage.'

*

Rudolf had met Niarchos through Tessa Kennedy, who had decorated the Greek tycoon's house in Nassau so successfully that she had been given the *Atlantis II* commission. 'I was sent off in Stavros's jet to see [Adnan] Kashoggi's new yacht so that everything I did would outclass that.' Rudolf had been at the 21 Club in New York late one night in the spring of 1977 when Niarchos, who was there with a party of friends including Marie-Hélène de Rothschild and Jordan's Princess Firyal, said immediately, 'Tessa's coming on a cruise with us this summer: would you like to come too?' ('Stavros was always competing with Ari [Onassis] for publicity,' a friend remarks. 'And since Ari had [had] Callas, Stavros decided he'd have Nureyev.') Wanting to bring a couple of guests of his own choice, Rudolf had asked Tessa to arrange for Douce to be invited, and Wallace had 'fixed him up with a friend from Hollywood,' a handsome part-time hustler by the name of Victor Davis. It was soon made clear to Rudolf, however, that the inclusion of 'this blond nothing' on the trip was something of a social solecism. 'None of us could see the point of him. He didn't say a word.' The following summer Franck, on the other hand, was an infinitely more acceptable companion, liked by everyone from the formidable Marie-Hélène to Texan millionaires Oscar and Lynn Wyatt, who offered him a lift back to the States in their private Boeing.

Rudolf's immersion in the world of Greek shipping magnates was his first taste of what Princess Firyal calls '*big* money'. It was impossible not to be impressed by the wonders on board *Atlantis II* – the seventeenth-century olive-wood panelling, the collection of paintings by Delacroix, Degas and Toulouse-Lautrec – as much as by the 'James Bond stuff', the dining-room wall that rotated to reveal a huge screen or the swimming pool that rose up at night to become a dance floor.

Like many Russians, Rudolf was a capitalist by choice, but his tsarist appreciation of luxury was combined with a peasant's distrust of banks. (Vacuuming under his bed one morning, Monique van Vooren's maid pulled back the carpet to see what was causing the bump and found a thick wad of dollar bills.) Rudolf's agent, Sandor Gorlinsky, had taken care of things, depositing Rudolf's earnings in Swiss accounts in four different currencies and in numerous different names (among them 'Nine Muses' and 'Terpsichore Establishments'), the total in the mid-to-late seventies amounting to more than ten million dollars. He had introduced Rudolf to the Chicago lawyer Barry Weinstein, who from 1974 took care of his tax concerns, and in 1975 had helped establish the Ballet Promotion Foundation, a Liechtenstein

organization intended to act as a repository for the dancer's assets during his lifetime.*

For Rudolf, however, this was not enough, and he made it known
during the 1977 Palais des Sports season that 'he was upset with Sandor
because he was not making as much money as he should have been.'
He had already begun seeking financial advice from well-placed
friends, among them Jackie Onassis. 'The first real money he made
was under Jackie's influence,' says Armen Bali. 'She's the one who
made him buy gold just before gold went up by thousands.' Behind
Gorlinsky's back, the banker Charles Murland also offered investment
advice. His company, Minster Assets, had taken ailing British Midland
Airways into the black, and according to his close friend Geordano
Ponticelli, 'There was talk at one point of Charles taking over Rudolf's
financial matters.' Finally, though, it was Jacob Rothschild who won
Rudolf's unequivocal trust. A financial genius, he had amassed a personal fortune estimated at $1 billion and in five years increased the
funds of Rothschild Investment from $66 million to $231 million. He
was also the kind of man Rudolf most admired since his Renaissance-
style breadth of culture and love of ballet was combined with great
wit, urbanity, and personal charm. 'What Sandor did was perfectly
sensible and prudent,' comments Rothschild, 'but I don't think he'd
have claimed to have spectacular skills as an investor.' Taking matters in
hand himself, he wrote to Gorlinsky on 26 July 1978, including a list
of Rudolf's investments, which he recommended transferring from
Credit Suisse in Geneva to the Rothschild Bank in Zurich. 'I feel confident that we will be able to do better than Credit Suisse because we
will care more . . . If Rudi and you find that we do . . . I would hope
you would consider giving us a bit more, and having seen the performances at the Coliseum I feel that he will rightly earn huge amounts in
the future!'

In the summer of 1979, Rudolf made another tour of the Greek
islands with an entourage of Robert Tracy, Douce, Rudi van Dantzig,
and Toer van Schayk, this time on *Aspasia*, the yacht owned by Perry

---

* Wanting to capitalize further on tax benefits, Rudolf wrote to Prince Rainier of Monaco
on 8 October 1975, requesting Monegasque citizenship. He had been advised to make the
letter 'the most sentimental possible', mentioning the apartment he already owned in
Monte Carlo and emphasizing the fact he wanted to be 'in a country which is a country of
Arts' and would continue the great tradition started by Diaghilev and continued by Colonel
de Basil and the Marquis de Cuevas. A reply from the prince himself followed on
27 October, favouring Rudolf's request and inviting him to make the necessary application.

Embiricos. 'Reading Byron non-stop', and intent on re-creating his own Childe Harold journey as inspiration for a ballet, Rudolf persuaded his host, a fervent admirer since the mid-sixties, to end their two-week cruise on the south coast of Turkey. Rudolf, like Byron, who adored the lush textures and colours of Eastern clothes, had succumbed to Turkomania. He scoured the bazaars for antique fabrics, pelisses, caps and burnouses, and as if in imitation of Delacroix's portrait of the poet in his gold-and-crimson-velvet Albanian outfit, dressed in rich Turkish robes, his head imperiously turbaned. In Byron, as in Liszt, Rudolf recognized an alter ego, all three having experienced the same explosive kind of fame, peripatetic life and passion for the exotic. The erotic charge of the poet's Eastern tales, insinuating a dark subversiveness that aroused both mass adulation and secret fantasies, was exactly the impact of Rudolf's own *Corsaire*; even the description of Byron as 'a wild mountain colt' was a mirror image of the young Nureyev. But to Rudolf the most deeply felt link of all with Byron was the sense of alienation, 'the feeling of belonging to *no* country', their attraction to beautiful youths having forced each in his turn 'To seek abroad, the love denied at home.'[*]

The work Rudolf had in mind (for the Paris Opéra Ballet) was based on Byron's *Manfred*, a long poem that, more than any other, defines the cult of alienation at the heart of nineteenth-century Romanticism. Focusing on a reclusive magician figure living in his mountain eyrie and tormented by guilt, it presents an exaggeratedly diabolical version of Byron himself, a kind of atonement for the 'crimes' of his youth: his propensity for boys, and the incestuous relationship with his half-sister Augusta. Rudolf had dismissed the character of Manfred as 'a pompous bore', but had been persuaded by Mstislav Rostropovich that Tchaikovsky's *Manfred Symphony* would be 'a wonderful idea' for a ballet. The poem's dominant theme of sexual guilt and anguish had understandably resonated with Tchaikovsky, and his first movement conveyed the profound sense of brooding that seeped into his *Hamlet*. But finding himself unmotivated by a programme that was not his own idea, the composer had considered dispensing with the other movements and making a tone poem of the score.

Rudolf, too, had been unconvinced by *Manfred* as a subject for a full-length work. 'All that torment may be easy to demonstrate in five

[*] An entry in Hobhouse's diary dated 5 October 1809 confirms that 'Pederasty . . . is practised underhand by the Greeks, but openly carried on by the Turks.'

lines of poetry, but it is not easy to translate into dance.' Nevertheless he went on thinking and researching, and Nigel, who had begun the libretto, steered Rudolf towards Byron's letters and journals. 'I honestly think you will not get much from reading the poetry, most of which dates horribly . . . It's *him* who counts.' Rudolf admitted that he found the work itself more difficult than Shakespeare (giving up on *Childe Harold* after reading two-thirds), although he had been delighted by the wit and liveliness of *Don Juan,* and proclaimed Byron to be his 'most favourite English author'. Characteristically he had extended his research to the poet's contemporaries, becoming particularly interested in Shelley, whose work Nigel was then reading for him. Choreographer Antony Tudor, with whom the critic once discussed the two Romantic poets, had exclaimed, 'Ah, maybe something there for a ballet – Rudi and David [Wall],' but Nigel himself was doubtful, telling Rudolf, 'After reading [Shelley's] *Ariel* I don't find much material in their real life except their contrasting temperaments (Air and Fire). Obviously Shelley would be Petipa-ish to Byron's more modernish; probably Byron secretly respected Shelley's lofty idealism?'

It was, however, the copy of *The Romantic Agony* that Nigel gave him which provided Rudolf with the approach he was looking for. 'It became my "Bible" and I grabbed from it everything that fitted my ideas. So much so that at first I wanted to call the ballet *Romantic Agony.*' Reissued in 1970 with an introduction by Frank Kermode, Mario Praz's book is a classic of literary criticism with the same power attributed to Kott's *Shakespeare, Our Contemporary* 'to alter a reader's understanding of the history of his society, and perhaps of his own history'. Recounting European literature's scenes of cruelty and horror spiced with sensual pleasure, it seemed to throw light on Rudolf's own epoch, the defiant *mal-de-vivre* described by novelist Martin Amis as 'the heavy-gay, pre-AIDS sex-crypts of downtown Manhattan . . . the intent, aggressive, leathery, specialist sexuality of the seventies'. And in the Romantic theory that life imitates decadent art, that the best means of expressing passions is to experience them for oneself, Rudolf found substantiation of his own belief. 'As a creative artist you have to feel, you have to *know* how to be both. That's what people with talent have: the ability to know what it is to be the purest and the dirtiest.' This duality was what had excited him about Byron, just as Byron in turn had identified it in Robert Burns: 'What an antithetical mind!' he exclaimed of the Scottish poet's 'never-to-be-published' letters, 'Tenderness, roughness – delicacy, coarseness-sentiment, sensuality-soaring and grovelling, dirt and deity – all mixed up in that one compound of inspired clay!' These extreme contradictions between debauchery and the ideal were a motivating force for Rudolf, whether enacting Siegfried's moral dilemma in *Swan Lake*, the plight of his schizophrenic *Tancredi*, or the 'half dust, half deity' figure of Manfred himself.

In his preliminary notes Nigel had written, 'The music gives me the image of a procession of Goya's flagellating monks, perhaps with B dragging his foot and his guilt (dim figures) hanging on to him,' an idea that Rudolf took almost literally as his opening. To alternate with him in the title role he had chosen Jean Guizerix, a powerfully virile dancer with the technique and dramatic authority to sustain the ballet's one-hour duration. In rehearsals Guizerix had been puzzled by Rudolf's repeated cry of 'Laocoön! Laocoön!' thinking that it must be one of his Russian obscenities. In fact, what the choreographer wanted him to envisage was the Trojan priest of the Louvre's statue *Le Laocoön*, whose incredible suffering, expressed by his face and distended muscles, was to Rudolf the very expression of 'Romantic Agony'. His first solo combined sinuous movements to convey the sculpted serpents coiled across the priest's shoulders with a cumbersome motif alluding to Byron's lameness. Rudolf also drew on his and Guizerix's experience of modern dance by incorporating some effectively anguished Grahamesque contractions.

The ballet, however, was intended to showcase not only Manfred but 'the whole Byron', becoming a mingling of real characters with imaginary ones and visions. It is a technique Nigel compares to that of the Synthetic Cubists, who selected symbolic fragments of reality, 'using them as elements in a dominating structure'. But it is mystifying why, when he admits how much harder this is to follow in a ballet than in a painting, Nigel provided Rudolf with such a bafflingly complex libretto. Even Tudor, ballet's master of psychological nuance, would have been hard pressed to make a coherent scene of the following:

Byron and Augusta [his half sister]
Byron loves Mary [his cousin, Mary Chaworth, a youthful sweetheart]
Byron loves Edleston [the boy chorister with whom he was infatuated]
Byron loves Augusta
Byron with wife
(pas de trois – Byron, Edleston, Augusta – B dances with wife and

thinks of Edleston
Byron dances with Edleston and thinks of Augusta)

The second tableau is more lucid, if somewhat regressive with its nineteenth-century-style ensemble of mountain spirits. This time the 'real' figures are Shelley; his wife, Mary; and her stepsister, Claire Clairmont. Rudolf's idea is to try to re-create the atmosphere of personal and intellectual complicity between Byron and his three friends during the three months they spent together in Switzerland. The Shelleys were famously liberal in their attitude to love, and it is this close entanglement that Rudolf captures in an elaborately intertwining, canonic *pas de quatre*, which is the ballet's most inventive and successful choreography. The portrayal of *amitiés amoureuses* was enhanced by the casting. Shelley was performed by Charles Jude, newly married to Florence Clerc, who appeared as Astarte (Byron's 'Ideal Spirit'), sharing her role with Jean Guizerix's wife, Wilfride Piollet. Rudolf's special rapport with Charles, reflected in the libretto by Byron's mentoring of the younger poet, was expressed in *Wayfarer*-like duets, his erotic desire for the dancer betrayed by the fact that, as Nigel pointed out, there is nothing in the choreography to indicate that Shelley was not just another boyfriend.

From this point until the curtain falls there is a dizzying confusion of Byron's biography decipherable only to those familiar with its details. The stage becomes a blur of Greek soldiery; marauding pirates; visions of Corsaires; the reappearance of Byron's mother; Edleston; the Contessa; and Augusta/Astarte, who by the end of the ballet has come to represent the figure of death. 'Alas, alas,' wrote a French critic of the ballet's Paris première on 20 November 1979. 'One loses oneself in this confusion as much as in the amalgam of personages and situations, which are ill-defined and lacking any dramatic progression.'

Rudolf had to postpone his own debut in the piece as he had broken a metatarsal bone in his foot and was limping badly. The five-thousand-seat Palais des Sports remained half empty, and, when the star returned to the stage two weeks later, his lacklustre performances did little to create any new enthusiasm for the ballet. 'Not only did the relentlessly difficult choreography he had devised for himself leave him out of breath and preoccupied with technique, but his usual stage presence and charm were absent.'

To what extent, though, did *Manfred* reveal Rudolf as a choreographer? In notes marked 'Private' by Maude, who 'has seen them and agrees', Nigel gave Rudolf what was probably the most critical appraisal of his work. 'The great merit of the ballet lies in its pace and power, its ensemble patterns . . . [but] except for Byron's striking solos there are few exceptions to the twisting, swirling, arm-waving style. Some of the duets seem interchangeable, with movements arranged more to match the music than to make a dramatic point or identify a character.'

This was all true, but encumbered with its libretto, the ballet never stood a chance. To Ninette de Valois, Rudolf had 'a certain talent as a choreographer, but not very much', and he himself once admitted to Marika Besobrasova, 'I know I'm not a choreographer, but I have to do things' (meaning, provide a repertory for himself). Few would contest Rudolf's gift for orchestrating large numbers of dancers, either en masse or canonically in groups – 'I can move *hundreds*!' he once boasted – but the composition of innovative, dramatically telling movement did not come naturally. His ballets pay homage to the choreographers he valued most, particularly Bournonville, whose busy *petite batterie* and multiple *ronds de jambe* became, as Baryshnikov says, 'sort of his trademark'. Comparing the founders of English and American dance, Rudolf described Ashton as 'not a vocabulary giver', whereas Balanchine had provided him with the new language he craved on arrival in the West. What he never learned to apply to his own work, however, was Balanchine's 'lesson in simplicity'. Every Nureyev ballet is so overloaded with steps and ideas, so richly full, that Violette Verdy was reminded of 'all those threads in a kilim carpet'. Then director of the Paris Opéra, Verdy was well aware that the ballet she commissioned had not worked, but nevertheless continued to admire what she calls *Manfred*'s 'layers of recognition'. Most of the critics dismissed the ballet altogether, and Alastair Macaulay, in his review of the London première, drew attention to Rudolf's lack of skill in depicting his own persona in dance: 'It's baffling to see him chunter through steps that are both exposing and inconveniently rapid, like meaningless chatter, if one is used to thinking still of Nureyev in terms of a grand sweep of heroic temperament . . . Strange that the dancer who made his personality a major glory of recent theatre is working as a choreographer to cancel himself out.'

In fact this was far from the case. As an anthology of all the dance influences in Rudolf's career – Petipa, Bournonville, Balanchine, Ashton, MacMillan, Graham, Béjart, Tetley, with 'a few flashes of bravura variations reminiscent of *Le Corsaire*' – *Manfred* is an act of self-glorification, not obliteration. It was Rudolf's most autobiographical

ballet to date, as confessional and solipsistic as *Manfred* was for Byron
'the beginning, the middle and end of all his own poetry – the hero of
every tale – the chief object of every landscape'.

Working outside the Opéra in the more intimate setting of the Atelier
Berthier (where the scenery was constructed), both Jean Guizerix and
Charles Jude had the impression that the Paris Opéra company was '*la
troupe de Rudolf*' at that time, so strong was the solidarity and affection
between them all. Rudolf was already considering making Paris his
base. 'He really hates England,' Nigel noted in his diary on 14 March
1981. 'He feels rejected here, unlike in Paris where he is the grand
vedette.' He had recently bought an apartment on quai Voltaire, with
magnificent views of the Seine and the Palais du Louvre. Plans for
basic structural changes had been drawn up in January 1979 by
Douce's architect brother Pierre François, and Rudolf had appointed
Renzo Mongiardino's 'right hand', Emile Carcano, as his designer. It
was the opulently theatrical Mongiardino style Rudolf was after, and
having a few rolls of Cordoba leather left over from the decoration of
Fife Road and the Dakota, he asked Carcano to find an artisan to
reproduce it for the grand salon of the quai Voltaire. He had already
begun his serious collection of furniture, paintings, fabrics, kilims and
Ptolemaic maps, and the *sixième*'s antiques dealers and informed
friends tempted him daily with possible new acquisitions. 'Herewith
the Superbed,' wrote Nigel, enclosing a photograph of a six-foot
scroll-ended, Karelian birchwood chaise longue priced at £25,000. It
was Douce who took the practicalities in hand, arranging the installa-
tion of a new kitchen; the rewiring, heating and plumbing; as well as
making regular excursions to the flea market and country sales in
search of rarities: a copper bath, ancient parquet flooring, black-and-
white eighteenth-century stone floor tiles for the entrance hall.
'Douce was incredible,' says their mutual friend Leslie Caron. 'She
coordinated everything in that apartment from the door handles to the
last chandelier.'

Until now Rudolf had based himself at Douce's rue Murillo
apartment in the exclusive eighth *arrondissement*, moving Claire, his
housekeeper, into an upstairs room so that she could cook for him.
Doting on Rudolf, Douce insisted that he should have her own
bedroom, its French windows overlooking a pretty little garden with a
gate leading directly into the Parc Monceau. The apartment had been a
gift from her Chilean great-aunt Ana Santa Maria de Lopez-Perez, one
of the richest women in France, who had raised Douce in a huge *hôtel*

particulier on the avenue Wagram and wanted her to continue to live in the style to which she had become accustomed. Douce's mother, a beauty painted by Boldini, with huge eyes and a swan neck, had died when her daughter was ten days old. Her father had returned to their home in Santiago and 'Tatanita' had taken charge of the children, sending the boys to school in Switzerland and employing someone to look after the baby. Living with a formidable and aged aunt who always wore black was a dismal upbringing for a child, tempered only by Madeleine, Douce's nanny and governess. In her teens she found herself becoming '*la petite protégée*' of the Paris beau monde, drawn into the set surrounding her wealthy uncle, Arturo Lopez-Perez, a world once compared to 'a small eighteenth-century court'. 'I didn't need Rudolf as an entrée to society,' said Douce. 'Marie-Hélène de Rothschild was already receiving me like a goddaughter.' On the contrary, it was Rudolf who needed her. 'I didn't want him in my group. I thought he belonged to the stage. He didn't belong to the salon,' the Vicomtesse de Ribes dismissively remarked, and Rudolf was only too aware of the Proustian clannishness of Paris society. Gloria Venturi remembers how he held on to her hand like a frightened child when they arrived together at an exceptionally grand soireé, and Leslie Caron had also observed Rudolf's insecurity on such occasions. 'Rudolf never knew what fork to use, or how to dress. He didn't know the form, the terms of address . . . So he felt at ease with Douce because she knew all that and she knew *everybody*. It gave him the sense of having arrived.'

Douce took control of Rudolf's social life, and in return, he would occasionally reward her, once buying her a ravishing Marie Antoinette gown to wear to a ball. Being 'a little devil, an adventuress, and oodles of fun', she made any event sparkle, but in private Rudolf was disturbed about her increasing fixation on him, complaining to friends, 'Douce eats my air.' 'He became her everything,' remarks her confidante Yasemin Pirinccioglu. 'She was crazy for him like a child,' says Gilles Dufour. 'It was a passion but a childish passion.' Like Byron's Lady Caroline Lamb, Douce went out of her way to appeal to Rudolf's transgressive side, cropping her hair, dressing like a boy and, 'motivated by a kind of delirium', would even go cruising with him in the Bois de Boulogne. She was ferociously possessive, and 'got in between' other women, Leslie Caron among them, when she felt they were getting too close. 'She was so completely in love with him, and so jealous that I just didn't fight.' Rudolf's boys posed less of a threat. Franck, whom Douce described as 'not serious – a little breakfast', spent most weekends with Rudolf at rue Murillo as his own room was on campus outside the city. 'Douce was always trying to accommodate Rudolf. If I was in favour she'd be nice; if not, she'd ignore me.' On first meeting Robert, she had surprised him by saying, 'I must be careful of you,' but soon realized that this was someone she would have to accept.

For about six months the two boyfriends had been 'overlapping' and Rudolf relished the game of playing one off against the other, even to the point of having them both to stay with the Goslings at the same time. 'Robert was madly jealous,' Maude recalled. 'They were such different characters,' says Rudi van Dantzig. 'Franck seemed a bit embarrassed by the whole situation. There was not a trace or suggestion of anything sexual between them, whereas with Robert it was so obvious.' By the spring of '79 Rudolf, who had developed 'a fairly regular relationship' with Robert, began making it clear to Franck that he was letting him go. 'At forty you know how to handle things, and it pretty much evolved in a very natural manner. I told Rudolf, "You know where to find me. Whenever you need me, call me." For me it had always been much more emotional than physical, so staying friends wasn't going to be a problem.'

Having inherited his father's entrepreneurial skills, Franck had maintained his independence all along, showing signs of wanting to start up on his own. Robert, on the other hand, was prepared to devote himself entirely to Rudolf. 'He was good for Rudolf. He'd get things done,' says Charles Jude. He was indeed unusually efficient, supervising travel arrangements, restaurant reservations and Dakota dinner parties, tracking down scores in the Harvard library, and even taking on the role of unofficial press officer. 'I was the liaison between Rudolf and "Suzywoozy" [Aileen Mehle, who wrote the daily 'Suzy' gossip column in the *New York Post*].' And whereas Franck preferred to see Rudolf alone – 'I couldn't care less about the social side' – Robert was never happier than in the company of what Maude called 'Rudolf's rich ladies'. 'He would *disappear* in the function of harmonizing everyone with Nureyev,' remarked Violette Verdy. Robert was, as he well knew, 'Rudolf's slave', but admits that this was his own choice. Besides, as Rudolf pointed out, 'being slave means that you do something without pleasure', whereas Robert was enraptured by his new life. 'Those were the great years. I was twenty-five, dancing around the world, writing books, and loving being with Rudolf – I don't think things could have been any better.'

Their summer holiday in 1980 was another cruise of the Greek islands and the coast of Turkey on Perry Embiricos's yacht. Rudolf liked sailboats, and unlike the liner-size *Atlantis II*, *Aspasia* was a sloop that slept ten. The Goslings were on this trip, and Nigel noted any particularly memorable images of Rudolf: 'In a floppy straw hat, a jersey & a tiny jockstrap standing in the harbour to watch a boy do a high-dive, sensationally shocking the local inhabitants but quite unaware . . . R doing a barre on deck in the harbour after dark, watched by a dozen children on the jetty.' Their days were spent swimming in deserted wooded coves and following Rudolf on 'fantastic scrambles' to look at sites to build a house. He had decided that Turkey, with its dirt tracks and little wooden houses, 'smelt like home', telling the Goslings that the backyard of one tiny café – 'all flowering creepers & chickens & wooden sheds' – was just like his Bashkirian *isba*. He had been amazed at how many words – including his family's names – were the same in Tatar. '"Farida" is "Feride"; "Hamit" or "Hamitola" is very common; "Razida" is "Reshide"; "Gouzel" means "beautiful",' said his Turkish friend Yasemin Pirinccioglu. And he had been reminded of Ufa every time he saw people sitting on cushions on the floor; peasant women spinning from raw wool as they walked, or carrying water in two cauldrons hung on a stick across their shoulders – 'just like my mother used to do'.

Towards the end of the trip there was one emotionally fraught night when Rudolf seemed intent on reminding everyone of his transition from peasant boy to superstar. Instead of dining on the boat as they did most evenings, eating wild boar shot by the captain, the party went to a café on the water's edge, joined by the crew, a local priest, a schoolmaster and a policeman. When it transpired that there was nothing on the menu but greasy little fish and bread, Rudolf, who had spotted more enticing fare at the rival café, suddenly got up and walked off. As Nigel wrote in his diary: 'The meal concluded with considerable embarrassment. As we left for the boat we passed R sitting alone at his café eating his big fish. He started to say something but Embiricos, who had also drunk a lot by now, spat at him that it was unforgivable, shut himself up in his cabin & did not emerge until R had left 24 hours later . . . R said simply, "He wasn't looking after me properly."'

This was the solitary, misanthropic Byronic hero 'soaring beyond or sinking beneath the men with whom he felt condemn'd to breathe'. But it also showed a nihilistic side that was surfacing in Rudolf, a sense of the absurdity of social conventions. He had been gripped that holiday by Dostoyevsky's *Diary of a Writer* – 'he took it everywhere,' Nigel remembered, 'reading snatches on deck, in the cabin, on beaches, among the pine trees in the mountains' – and it had served to fuel his own increasing embitterment against the world, the belief that he, like the writer, had been given 'such a rough deal'.

Rudolf's lifelong conviction that no one could be trusted now included even his closest friends.* That spring, for the first time in thirty-two years, the Paris Opéra Ballet had been invited to perform in New York, but only on the condition that Rudolf appear with the company as guest star. General Director Hugues Gall had been in his office when a union representative arrived, accompanied by Charles Jude. 'Charles sat there telling me, "If you have Rudolf as guest, we won't dance." Ok, I said, I'll cancel the tour. The union members were doing their job, but Charles should have said he couldn't be part of this. After everything Rudolf had done for him, I thought he was a real pig.' Others, Jacques Loyau among them, also considered Charles '*un vrai traître*', but the dancer insists that he had no choice. 'I told Rudolf, "There are eight performances and you'd be doing seven of them. In my position at the Opéra I can't support the system of that."' Jean Guizerix was equally divided in his loyalties. 'Rudolf called me and said, '*Vous traître! Vous êtes dans quel camp?*' and I told him I was with the majority. It was the Paris Opéra, not Nureyev and Friends. But it was a very difficult moment for me.' And yet for Rudolf, their action only proved what he had come to accept: 'There's always the betrayal . . . betrayal – yes, like *The Moor's Pavane*.'

His next big project at the Met had also come to nothing. He was to have made his directorial debut in July collaborating with David Hockney and John Dexter on a revival of the Ballets Russes work *Parade*, but fell out with them both over what Clive Barnes would

* Compounding this was the 1987 UK edition of Monique van Vooren's *Night Sanctuary* (published in the United States in 1981), with its fictionalized version of Rudolf as its protagonist. Even the motive for Vladimir Volodin's defection was the same – a false claim made at the airport that the dancer must return to perform at the Kremlin. But whereas fifteen years earlier Rudolf might have been amused by Monique's audacity, in his current state of mind it was just another betrayal – especially as the actress admitted that she had written the novel for the 'six-figure advance'. 'I don't want to be poor' (*Women's Wear Daily*, 22 October 1981). He refused any further contact with her.

call the production's 'phoney thematic links'.* Then, at the end of November, came the really 'cruel blow'. Balanchine, who was mounting a Tchaikovsky Festival in 1981, had promised to include *Manfred* and invited Rudolf to come to New York to cast the ballet. This, as Nigel reported in his diary, was 'Fantastic news – even if the critics slaughter it,' especially as the company's most glamorous principal, Peter Martins, had volunteered to alternate with Rudolf.

> *28th [November].* In the morning the telephone rang & after much crackling & buzzing it turned out to be R ringing from Paris where he had just arrived. I asked whom he had picked for Manfred & heard him reply 'It didn't work out.' From the little I could hear, he seemed to say that 'Balanchine hadn't liked the ballet' . . . Presumably he had been watching the scraps of tiny 8-mm rehearsal film – not a very fair guide! To be fair I always thought it a weird choice – Manfred is the *opposite* of the NYCB in style, mood & content.

Barbara Horgan surmises that Rudolf 'must have "talked" a good ballet to Mr B' and consequently, Balanchine had offered to see the film. 'After all, what could he say: "I don't want to consider it"? Who knows, it could have been great!' But Balanchine, whose devotion to Tchaikovsky verged on the fanatical, had clearly decided that Rudolf's muddled *Manfred* had traduced a sacred score. All the same, to have let the project go as far as to suggest Rudolf should choose his cast was, as Nigel remarked, 'a sadistic way of dealing with it'. 'I remember him sitting in the car and sobbing like a little child,' says Robert Tracy. 'Balanchine had rejected him again.'†

A month later it was the Royal Ballet who were 'the biggest traitors'. He had been upset by the postponement of the new Hans van Manen ballet for him, complaining to Nigel that the administration was

---

* As all three works date from 1917–18, Dexter used a First World War theme to link them.
† Rudolf later seized an opportunity to restage *Manfred*. In the spring of 1981 he had approached Patricia Neary, the ex-New York City Ballet dancer who was now director of the Zurich Ballet – 'George Balanchine's European Company'. 'Why doesn't *your* company do *Manfred*?' Rudolf had urged, but knowing its history, Neary hesitated. 'Mr B didn't really want us to do it. We might have had an enormous fight, and he could have withdrawn his name' (*Ballet News*, May 1983). In the end she decided it was worth the risk; the Zurich Ballet had never succeeded in touring America (the Met had wanted 'no more second-rate companies tagging along with Rudolf' (Nigel Gosling, diary entry, 13 October 1981), and *Manfred*, Neary felt, could be the entrée they needed.

'Mickie Mousing him' — which Nigel understood to mean playing cat-and-mouse. Rudolf had made sure that Ninette de Valois knew about the situation, sending her a message saying, 'Lately there has been a separation, this will mean divorce — with custody of the children!' (his Royal Ballet productions of *La Bayadère* and *Raymonda*). He had also been upset by the London Festival Ballet's change of decision to produce *Manfred* in 1981, and, by voicing his resentment to its newly appointed director, John Field, had managed to antagonize '*both* companies within a month'. Through Gorlinsky, John Tooley had bluntly told Rudolf, 'No choreographer wants to do a ballet for you,' and this had immediately been borne out by a letter that arrived from Netherlands Dance Theatre's Jiří Kylián. Taking three pages to recount how, when he left Czechoslovakia for England in 1967, Rudolf's performances had been his 'inspiration for the years to come', the choreographer nonetheless remained implacable in his decision. 'It is strange that this love and respect I feel for you makes it impossible for us to work together. It sounds paradoxical, but it is true . . . I would feel totally unfree, and would have constantly a feeling of a student before a master, which is a totally wrong relationship between a dancer and a choreographer.'

By the beginning of 1981 Rudolf was seriously considering retiring, telling Nigel that he was thinking of asking Ashton to create a new ballet for him as a swansong. 'He saw me in, so it would be nice if he could see me out.' Several times over the coming weeks he mentioned giving up dancing, saying he 'had better cope with it', and wondering if he would 'crumble' as a result. Certainly the indecision appeared to be taking its toll. During dinner at Charles Murland's house in March,

---

Feeling he should clarify the ballet, Rudolf had prefixed each tableau with Byron quotations intended to be read aloud, and commissioned Nico Georgiadis to design costumes that would make it easier to distinguish the characters from one another. In the end, although there was little significant difference between the two versions, Rudolf considered Zurich's *Manfred* to have been a worthwhile undertaking. With eighty per cent of its dancers Balanchine trained, the company was able to give his choreography a satisfyingly sleek and speedy NYCB edge — which, if nothing else, was consolation for the Tchaikovsky Festival disappointment. It remained to get Balanchine's approval. Waiting until he had actually arrived in Switzerland in December, Pat Neary told Balanchine firmly that the ballet was now part of the Zurich repertory. With little option and good grace, Balanchine admitted that Patricia Neary had done an excellent job, and was even grudgingly positive about *Manfred* itself. 'Not bad, but too many steps' (*Ballet News*, May 1983).

Rudolf got violently drunk and abusive. Guests watched aghast as the scene crescendoed, the dancer smashing the glass of a picture frame and roaring, 'May you all burn in hell!' as he lurched out into the night.

Charles, who had immediately followed him and driven him back to Victoria Road, had been, Nigel wrote, 'wonderfully forgiving about the damage'. This was behaviour he had come to expect from Rudolf, who, soon after they had met in the early sixties, had flung the contents of his dressing table at him. But then Charles himself had a malevolent side, his personality marked by what a newspaper once described as 'an Ulsterman's predilection for not forgetting those who thwarted him'. With Rudolf, though, Charles was never anything other than indulgent, and however often 'hurt and stung', would continue cravenly putting himself at the dancer's disposal. 'Maybe I wish to be more helpful to you than you wish or need or closer than is tolerable for a loner like yourself. Anyhow, suffice it to say I would do anything for you . . . I love you – sort of!'

To Rudolf this constant eagerness to please was as stifling as Charles's omnipresence. He was always there – whether eavesdropping ('somewhat dubiously', in Nigel's view) on the Palais des Sports clash with Makarova, or going as far as to retrace Rudolf's steps in New York's sexual ghettos. 'How else did a London banker discover the West Side trucking scene? I can hardly believe he was looking for the *Queen Elizabeth*!' Charles loved ballet gossip and the glamour of dancers, but the art itself eluded him. 'He would often arrive at the Opera House, knock back two glasses of champagne, take his seat and be snoring quietly within three minutes, only to wake up with the applause.' There was a certain closeness between them ('Charles was like an overprotective older brother'), but it was the element of expediency that Rudolf valued most in Charles's friendship. Not only could he be relied on to take care of Maude and Nigel, he was impressively shrewd about money matters.

But by the summer of 1980 it became apparent that Charles himself was in severe financial difficulties, and the strain seemed to be telling on his health. In April 1980 Nigel had described him in a letter as 'slim and pale which means love, I guess – or maybe dieting which is just as bad', but by the following April, Charles was bedridden. The night of Friday the fourteenth was the grand celebration he had planned for his fiftieth birthday, but Charles was able to put in no more than a brief appearance. 'We all knew something was seriously wrong that night,' says Teddy Heywood. He was never ever ill.' Two weeks later Charles was admitted to hospital with infectious mononucleosis, pleurisy and pneumonia.

It was that spring of 1981 in California and New York that doctors were becoming aware of a startling increase in the number of cases of a rare lung infection: *pneumocystis carinii* pneumonia. At the same time a relatively benign skin cancer, Kaposi's sarcoma, common among the elderly, had started afflicting young men in a far more aggressive form. By June the general public was beginning to talk about a new 'plague' afflicting American homosexuals, although the disease did not yet have a name. Concerned about the rumours, Rudolf, who was then completing negotiations for the feature film *Exposed*,* refused to have the blood test that was required for insurance purposes. ('My doctor will send you a paper for the insurance company,' he told the director, James Toback.) Having previously been confined to medical journals, articles about 'gay cancer' were now appearing in mainstream newspapers and magazines, fanning panic in the backroom bars and bathhouses of New York and San Francisco with their message: 'Security lies only in celibacy.'

Rudolf had no intention of changing his sexual habits. It was the summer he had been 'inseparable' from Flaubert's travel notes and letters from Egypt, an account of the young writer's 1849 tour – a period saturated with immense vices. 'Speaking of bardashes . . .' Flaubert told his close friend Louis Bouilet, 'here it is quite accepted. One admits one's sodomy, and it is spoken of at table . . . It's at the

---

* Rudolf had much admired James Toback's 1978 cult thriller, *Fingers*, the movie that inspired Jacques Audiard's brilliant 2005 remake, *The Beat That My Heart Skipped*. The main character in *Fingers*, Harvey Keitel, an urban guerrilla and aspiring concert pianist obsessed by playing Bach, was yet another example of a man continually pulled in two by the warring sides of his nature. The hero of *Exposed* – musician with a handgun – seemed much of the same. Toback cast Rudolf in the role of a classical violinist involved in an international terrorist cell. With Keitel cast as the villain and Nastassia Kinski playing a Wisconsin girl turned fashion model, the leading actors were first rate, and just as propitious was the appointment of Henri Decae, one of Truffaut's collaborators, as cinematographer. The main problem proved to be the dialogue. Rudolf claimed that Toback would make up his lines in the taxi journey to the set each morning, the result sounding so stilted and pretentious that cinema audiences were bursting into laughter every time Rudolf spoke. He had begged 'the Maestro', as he called Decae, to make him look young and beautiful, but it is the ravishing twenty-two-year-old Kinski who dominates the screen, virtually eclipsing her middle-aged co-star. 'Rudolf hasn't seen even one take of the film and doesn't intend to,' Maude told Wallace. 'He has always said that, even while he was filming it.'

baths that such things take place . . . you skewer your lad in one of the rooms.' Rudolf had been tremendously excited by Flaubert's frankness. 'Those letters are fantastic – huh? Aren't they *great*?' he exclaimed during an interview with Elizabeth Kaye. It was not only the discovery of Flaubert's 'how you call it? – bawdy' side that delighted him, but the fact that the novelist's journey anticipated almost exactly the trip up the Nile that he had recently made with Douce. 'Suddenly you come across the same feelings, sentiments, the people, the colour of the country, the erotic side of it, still quite the same.' In *The Romantic Agony*, Mario Praz points out that Flaubert can scarcely have had any illusions as to the real significance of his longing to travel to 'the lecherous, blood-stained Orient'. 'It was a means of providing an outlet for the "*fond noir à contenter*" that troubled him.' This was something Rudolf understood all too well. 'Sex was very liberating for Flaubert. Well, for me, too, it's liberation . . . liberation,' he told a journalist in 1981, and, as if equating Flaubert's 'venereal souvenirs' with the current perilous sexual climate, his voice had faded 'ruefully' as he repeated the last word.

In July, Rosa's daughter, Gouzel, telephoned Rudolf to say that she was in the West. She had married an Ecuadorian geology student in Leningrad and once in Quito had immediately applied for a visa to the United States. As a past member of the Communist Party she was found to be ineligible, but a telegram to the American Embassy from the secretary of state in Washington, DC, had led to the granting of a waiver by the US Immigration and Naturalization Service. On 21 July Mrs Valarezo, 'niece of ballet artist Nureyev', an attractive nineteen-year-old with the family high cheekbones and almond eyes, flew to San Francisco, and on 12 August arrived in New York. The Goslings, who were then staying at the Dakota, had never seen Rudolf so nervous as he sat waiting to meet the relative he had last seen at Leningrad airport as a baby in Rosa's arms.

> We opened a bottle of champagne . . . A long chat. R was v reserved when she left. 'She must make up her mind what she is going to do.' After fixing her up financially, he is making it clear he can't/won't take her under his wing. (He was just off to Miami, Puerto Rico, Caracas, Verona, Stockholm, etc!) He says he doesn't mind what she does so long as she is put into some kind of school. 'Needlework, if necessary.' He thinks she will come to no good in NY. She is quiet, buttoned-up, probably obstinate. I can foresee some confrontations.

It was Nigel whom Rudolf was more concerned about. In the autumn of 1980 he had undergone an operation for a bladder complaint, and since then his health had been deteriorating rapidly. He was soon to be diagnosed with pancreatic cancer, and although neither he nor Maude ever mentioned the fact that it was terminal, Rudolf had instinctively feared the worst. 'This is not easy for me to say,' he had told Rudi van Dantzig when they last met, 'but if you want to see Nigel, you'll have to do it soon. He is dying of cancer.' By September 1981, when Rudolf and the Goslings were staying with Niarchos on his private island of Spetsopoula, it was clear that Nigel was in great pain, but the two men were aware of how little time was left, and spent most of the week collaborating on a new project. Rudolf was planning a ballet based on Strauss's *Rosenkavalier*, and Nigel had begun the libretto, discussing each scene as they sat together on the terrace, 'the incessant swing of waltzes on Rudolf's cassette player', or shouting to make each other heard over the roar of Niarchos's helicopter transporting Rudolf to and from his performances in Athens. Already thinking of the choreography, Rudolf had asked Tessa, who was joining them, to bring out a Chinese checker board so that he could plot the dancers' entrances and exits. Nothing came of it, as Strauss's son withheld his permission for the score to be used for a ballet, but another idea had presented itself that week. It was Nigel's remark that Niarchos was like Prospero – king of an island, 'a magic abode', and able to conjure almost anything at his will – that sparked the beginning of a new idea.

On 25 November 1981 Nigel noted in his diary that the Royal Opera House had 'surrendered to R's demands' by offering him several performances of *Swan Lake* and *La Bayadère*. Having learned not to expect anything from the Royal's administration 'except bucket of shit', Rudolf was determined not to appear other than cynical. It was 'another city, another place, another company', he shrugged to Barry Norman during a BBC *Omnibus* programme celebrating his return. Privately, though, despite the fact that he had recently dismissed the Royal Ballet to Nigel as 'company of boiled eggs', he was elated by the prospect of mounting his Kingdom of the Shades on a 'new crew'. With its glorious fusion of Kirov plasticity and Royal Ballet precision, *La Bayadère* was the work that, more than any other, revealed his imprint on English ballet. In the sixties it had made stars of its three soloists (Lynn Seymour, Merle Park and Monica Mason) and consecrated the corps dancers as the finest in the world. This time, he cast Bryony Brind, Ravenna Tucker and Fiona Chadwick as the leading

Shades, and, for the second performance, chose twenty-one-year-old
Brind as his surprise Nikiya. A soloist just beginning to perform principal roles, she was too tall for Rudolf, and yet her lyrical, Russian
quality of movement complemented him perfectly, their arms falling
naturally into Fonteyn/Nureyev-style painterly lines. With her swan
neck, russet gold hair and slender, swayback legs, Brind was a beautiful dancer with the fragile nerves of a thoroughbred filly. Colleagues
watched her blossom under Rudolf's guidance, his faith spurring her
into technical feats no English ballerina had ever attempted.

To the young male dancers, however, the arrival of this great star
had been something of an anticlimax. As they watched him for the first
time in class they saw 'an old man – and we really did think of him as
old' with virtually no muscle tone. 'But then this transformation took
place,' recalls Bruce Sansom. 'Rudolf had such control of his body that
he could forcibly mould himself into shape.' Sansom, along with
Stephen Beagley and Stephen Sherriff, was among the new generation
of gifted, good-looking youths whom Rudolf began singling out for
special attention. And having feared he would be 'cold-shouldered' by
the company as a whole, he had been greatly touched by their
response. 'They were marvellous, and kind of exuding love . . . I
don't know how long it will last, but it was there.*

This *rapprochement* had only intensified Rudolf's deep disappointment that he was not going to be appointed director when Norman
Morrice retired in 1986. His Royal Ballet comeback had coincided
exactly with the culmination of negotiations for the directorship of the
Paris Opéra Ballet, who were now offering him a definite contract.
'I had no doubt that Rudolf would bring enlightened and inspiring
direction to the Royal Ballet, but I feared that many of these benefits
would be eroded if he continued to dance,' says John Tooley. 'As
Rudolf intended to carry on performing, he declined the invitation.
Paris applied no restrictions, enabling him to direct and dance.'

Rudolf had been asked a decade earlier if he wanted to head the
Opéra Ballet. 'Yes, why not!' he told General Director Rolf Liebermann
of the Paris Opéra and Hugues Gall over dinner one night. 'But only
on condition that you fire at least fifty per cent of the dancers and I will

---

* When Antoinette Sibley made her comeback in the mid-eighties – a glorious Indian
summer conclusion to her career – it was Rudolf who insisted that she dance *La Bayadère* in
order to regain her confidence. 'He said, "If you can do that, you can do anything." But it was
utter faith to entrust it to me at forty-five – to give me back what he first gave me all those
years before. It was an act of a friend. An artist friend.'

bring fifty per cent from London.' It was, as Gall puts it, 'End of question.' Until, that is, the election of François Mitterrand in May 1981, when the problem of what to do with the Opéra came up again. Since Liebermann's departure in 1979 the theatre had suffered a crisis of identity with a succession of different directors, and what Minister of Culture Jack Lang now sought was a personality who could bring a new strength to ballet. Optimism was high at this point in French politics – a moment one observer defined as 'the ecstasy of socialism' – and it has been said that Lang wanted to rename his role minister 'of Culture, Beauty and Intelligence'. The idea of a star of the magnitude of Nureyev heading the Opéra was in tune with this mood, and discussions began in earnest. When the Soviets attempted 'une menace de veto', Lang took the matter to the presidential level. 'OK, Mitterrand agrees' was the verdict, but there were still Rudolf's conditions to be settled. He was insisting on foreign guest teachers, better studios, compulsory classes, a clause in his contract that enabled him to perform for another five years and one that committed him to reside in Paris for no more than six months a year. Having put all this to Lang's inspecteur générale de danse, Igor Eisner, Rudolf challengingly quoted from Verdi's Aïda as they parted, 'Ritorna vincitor! (Return when you have won!)'

By March 1982 this appointment looked definite – it was to be officially confirmed in February the following year – but Rudolf could not help having serious doubts about accepting. 'When I think about it, all of a sudden, it gives me a funny feeling in my – how do you call it? – spleen,' he told Nigel. 'The end of youth and all that!' And yet it was the logical next step. Baryshnikov was now director of the American Ballet Theatre; Erik was about to become director of the National Ballet of Canada; and for Rudolf to end up as director of the Paris Opéra Ballet in the city where he first arrived in the West had a compelling symmetry. Nigel tried to convince him: 'It sort of seems a good idea. You could make it the finest company in the world, just when NYCB and ABT and RB are fading . . . Exciting anyway – and I think it could make a useful switch in your dancing career; probably better two years too early than two years too late (I'm not thinking of a sudden total retirement of course, only a weeding out of roles).'

By now Nigel had started radiation treatments, and Rudolf, who (through Gorlinsky) had offered a specialist at his expense, was seeing him as often as he could. In February, having come to Victoria Road from Rome at 2.45 a.m., he sat up talking to Nigel until four, awoke

two hours later to catch an eight a.m. flight for Zurich, flew on to
Copenhagen, rehearsed, performed and returned on a private plane,
appearing again at the Goslings' around two, 'chatting very cheerfully
till four'. When Nigel was admitted to St Thomas's Hospital at the
beginning of March, Rudolf, in a panic, immediately got in touch with
Wallace. 'He wanted me to go to London and see what I could do for
Nigel and possibly bring him back to New York, because at that time
we thought American hospitals were better for treating cancer. But as
soon as I arrived, I could see that Nigel was too sick to make the
transatlantic trip.'

Instead Wallace persuaded the doctors to let him have Nigel's X-rays
and medical records, and drove to Heathrow late that night so they
could be couriered on the next morning's Concorde. Meeting the plane
at JFK airport was Niarchos's chauffeur, who then 'whipped them off to
the tip-top consultant in NY' who, it turned out, was no more able to
help than the London consultant, Nigel's cancer having metastasized
too far by this stage. Knowing the end was coming, and overwhelmed
by his friend's love and attention, he wrote to Rudolf for the last time –
'not exactly saying Thank you etc. (I'm too Britishly inhibited for
that)' – but reminding him of how blessed his life had been.

March 9th 1982:

    Rudi, mein lieblings schlagerisches little Pumpernickel! . . . I
wanted to write so often from the hospital but didn't quite feel up to it
– and then there was always that nice strong supportive voice from
Boston to keep me going . . . I have probably been softened up by all
that . . . & medicine, but I did find myself lying there & looking back
(which usually gives me a stiff neck) and thinking just what an incredibly lucky fellow I have always been . . . Spoilt & happy childhood, a
little tiny delicate pretty mother whom I adored, a good firm father
who took little interest & so let me get on with things as I liked. A
cushy kind of war, then a chance introduction to the career which
suited me exactly & then – well, you know the rest, that I should
somehow have acquired a family like Maude, Nicholas & you is quite
incredible. One of the things I like most about you is that you were a
Surprise Packet: the chance of you turning up from Ufa must have
been millions to one . . . – you are my something specially special as
you know. (Oddly the first para I ever wrote about you, when you
came over here as a boy, described you as 'extraordinarily extraordinary'.) If only I could put my clock back forty years, what mischief we
might have got up to together! There – I am getting sentimental: but

your ringing & thinking & caring has really helped fantastically . . . A few more Bayadères & I should have been OK . . . I know I have long passed my [illegible] so just send you the biggest & lovingest of hugs,

N.

P.S. Delacroix is *fantastic*! Echoes of Flaubert here & there. I am reading the letters, but the journal is the real thing. Can't get it in paperback here or I would send it to you.

Rudolf had said nothing about the letter, but a day or two later just dropped into their conversation the fact that he had started the Delacroix journals, the dancer's way – Nigel believed – of telling him that he had read his 'sentimental' farewell and yet Rudolf had been genuinely enthralled to discover another nineteenth-century soulmate. It was not only the Orientalism, literary intelligence and turbulent sensuality that linked them both to Byron, but their shared interest in evil: Delacroix had illustrated the poet's most satanic verses as well as the darkest scenes of *Faust*. Reading Mario Praz's chapter 'The Metamorphoses of Satan', Rudolf had become intrigued by the idea that he might be a descendant of Milton's Satan – that charismatic archangel whose ruined statue was the dancer's own image of his mature self, his splendour and heroic energy diminished, and yet still he stood out 'proudly eminent' above the rest.

At the beginning of the year he had asked Nigel to look out for a Fuseli painting of Satan, and when Fuseli's 'lost' masterpiece, illustrating a scene from *Paradise Lost* (*Satan Starting from the Touch of Ithuriel's Lance*), came up for auction at Sotheby's in 1988, Rudolf bought it for £770,000 – almost triple its estimate. He now considered himself to be, as Fiona MacCarthy wrote of Byron, 'a man grandly and fatally flawed, who had lived so intensely and sinned so outrageously that he, and he alone, was doomed to suffer the retribution of the gods'. Friends recall how obsessed he became with the concept of guilt. 'He was talking about it all the time,' said Nico Georgiadis. It was almost as if he had come to accept his fallen state and the homily being delivered in the popular press: 'God has put his foot down.' . . . 'You get what you deserve.'

In April, Nigel, confined to St Thomas's, was fretting about Rudolf, who had been calling almost daily from quai Voltaire. 'He doesn't sound too happy, he isn't sleeping, worrying, I think, about the Paris job.' What Nigel would never know was the extent to which Rudolf was then fearing for his own health. Thierry Fouquet, his newly appointed dance administrator, was with Rudolf when he received a phone call telling him that a young Canadian friend had just died with all the symptoms of the new disease. 'I could see that he was very worried. Worried for himself.' Rudolf now realized the importance of finding a discreet doctor in Paris, and at the end of January, Charles Murland had succeeded in doing just that. After a performance at the Opéra, he had met Michel Canesi, a fresh-faced young man who had recently opened his own practice after completing studies in dermatology and venereology. A group went on to dinner, and as Michel spoke good English, he and Charles spent most of the evening talking. Rudolf's name did not come up, but the next morning Charles telephoned the doctor to ask if he would come right away to quai Voltaire as Rudolf Nureyev wished to consult him on a medical matter. Excitedly cancelling a previous engagement, Michel went straight to the apartment, where Charles greeted him and took him into the bedroom to meet the star. 'It was sympathy at first sight,' he says, and as they were talking and laughing, he took a sample of Rudolf's blood. 'He was someone who was very active sexually, and wanted me to check for syphilis.' The test proved negative, and although there had been no mention of 'gay cancer', either on this occasion or the night before, it was a sign of extraordinary intuition on Charles's part to have singled out Michel Canesi. Then working in the department of sexually transmitted diseases at the Institut Vernes, he was one of a small community of Paris doctors who had begun preparing themselves for the onslaught of this new plague. 'We said, "It's in America, but it must come to Europe, so we must be ready." What we didn't know then was that we were at the beginning of something incredible.'

Until then antibiotics had made gay men invulnerable to what Edmund White calls the 'puritanical menace' of such venereal diseases as syphilis and gonorrhoea. But what was now being referred to as GRID (gay-related immune deficiency) responded to no medical treatment and spread itself in ways that were still not understood. Tessa Kennedy remembers having an intense conversation with Rudolf around this time. 'He was asking me in detail: did I know how it could be transmitted? I said, "Rudolf, you *must* be careful!" And he just looked at me without saying anything.'

On a night in mid-May when Rudolf arrived in London, Tessa had driven him directly to St Thomas's to see Nigel. 'I could see in the car how much he was dreading it. It *paralysed* him.' Maude, who was with them, explains why: 'Rudolf had never been in a hospital in his life before, ever. He's horrified of illness; doesn't like even to talk about it. He doesn't ever talk about his own injuries, and he *hates* to hear about other people being ill. He always sounds as if he's unsympathetic but it's really because he has a real horror of it.'

Compounding it all was the knowledge that this was probably the last time he would see Nigel. 'It's losing my father – *more* than that,' he had confided to Rudi van Dantzig. But Nigel was in 'unbelievable form', joking about the view of Big Ben outside his window – 'the best bedside clock anyone could ask for!' He had managed to make the visit almost enjoyable, and when Rudolf left with Maude for Victoria Road, he pleaded with her to bring Nigel home. 'But I said, "No, the doctors say he's better there." "Well, then, I can't go away." "Yes, you must," I told him. "It's your only holiday, and we don't know how long Nigel will live."' So Rudolf went off the next morning, leaving Maude in the care of Charles Murland – 'a rock for me to lean on'. On 21 May she spent all day and evening at Nigel's bedside, and around midnight was woken in her chair by a nurse, who told her that her husband had just died. 'Then Charles arrived. He'd said to people at the hospital that when it happened they were to call him – whatever the time.' She spent the rest of that night at Trevor Place, and Charles telephoned Rudolf with the news.

He was back in London in time for the funeral, the only one he had ever attended. It was held in Roehampton's ugly suburban crematorium, where one incineration was taking place after another. Tristram Holland remembers seeing Rudolf huddled in a big dark coat as they all waited outside the chapel for someone else's service to finish. 'Afterwards, we went back to Victoria Road, and he sort of hovered around the kitchen looking pale and withdrawn and obviously not knowing what to do with himself. Then I remember him sitting on the sofa, very quietly having lunch, as all the other mourners milled about. I guess it was about the first time he hadn't been the prime focus of attention in the house.'

One of the first things Rudolf asked Maude after Nigel died was if she would come and live with him. When she explained that she didn't want to leave home, that Victoria Road contained too many memories, he replied, 'Then I stay too.' ' That was it,' says Maude. 'He never went back to live at Fife Road.' It was an unconventional ménage. Claire moved in upstairs so that she could do the cooking and housekeeping, Maude's South African friend 'Tiny' did the shopping,* and

---

* Muriel Monkhouse – a staunch Red Cross volunteer – had come to England to be Maude's bridesmaid and never left, becoming a kind of companion-lodger. Rudolf was fond of her because she always videotaped films and programmes she thought would interest him.

Luigi slept in a little room next to Rudolf's on the ground floor. With clothes, books, videotapes and cassettes strewn across a threadbare carpet, Rudolf's own room looked like an undergraduate's. The only signs of its occupant's star status were an antique icon on one wall and a painting of Catherine the Great above the fireplace. But this was now Rudolf's London base, his massage table permanently extended; a small modern piano keyboard balancing on a cluttered table; his clothes, practice things and costumes crammed into a single cupboard and chest of drawers. He spent most of that summer at Victoria Road, performing every night at the Coliseum, and taking Maude with him.

> He would sit me quietly in a box with Sandor Gorlinsky, so that I wouldn't be alone. I remember once I went backstage because we were going out to supper afterwards, and one of the older dancers came up and flung his arms round me. Of course I burst into tears, and Rudolf just took my arm and whisked me into his dressing room to sit down while he took off his makeup – rescued me straightaway. And as soon as the season was finished he took me with him to New York – in Concorde, which I'd never been in before . . . He really got me through the most terrible year.

Until now Maude had always kept somewhat in the background. Nigel had been the one to take Rudolf's calls and write him letters, and Maude had done little more than scribble a few lines at the bottom. After his death, though, it was Maude alone who came to 'mean home' to Rudolf, their relationship more tender than any other. 'I can't tell you how much love he has given me,' she wrote to Gregory King. 'And how kind he is to me – so *gentle* – very few people know that side of his nature.'

Conjoined to the saint, though, was always the sinner. In September, Franco Zeffirelli invited the dancer to Positano to receive an award from the town. The director had spent the whole summer entertaining friends at his idyllic Mediterranean home (that week the guests included movie star Gregory Peck, the Hollywood producer Dyson Lovell and playwright Christopher Hampton). Built on a hill above the bay, Villa Treville is made up of three separate houses, one of which was where Diaghilev had stayed with Nijinsky, the Russian owner reputedly having had the villa's interior walls removed and the floor sprung so that the dancer would be able to practise. Rudolf had been irked to discover that it was not he but Peck and his wife who were in the 'Red House', but he appeared in high spirits nonetheless. Hampton remembers his mischievousness at the award ceremony, when, during the mayor's interminable speech in Italian, he had played with a tape measure he wore suspended from his belt, 'extending it to indicate the enormous size of his member'. After the presentation dinner, when Zeffirelli's motor launch brought them back to the villa, Rudolf remained behind on the rocks, 'making out, we all presumed'. The following evening their host took everyone to a restaurant in the town, where he had very deliberately separated Rudolf from a French boy he coveted, the lover of one of Zeffirelli's close friends. The boat then took the party back, and Rudolf, expecting 'more of the same', lurked behind. When Luigi arrived three-quarters of an hour later (instead of coming by sea, he had walked the long, circuitous route back), he found Rudolf in a rage. Not only had the rendezvous he planned been foiled, but the gates leading to the villa had been locked. 'He was like a *hurricane*. Whatever was in his way – pah! pah! *pah!* – he start to destroy.'

Villa Treville's terraced garden – an Eden of pines, cacti and cascades of bougainvillaea and plumbago – has a precipitous stone staircase leading down to the beach. Symmetrically placed at intervals were eight-foot-high pithoi – Ali Baba-style Cretan vases containing exotic shrubs – which Rudolf began pushing over, leaving behind a devastation of earth, uprooted plants and terracotta shards. Confronting Zeffirelli, who was enjoying a game of table tennis and not sufficiently apologetic, Rudolf picked up a wrought-iron chair and hurled it, 'narrowly missing Franco'. He then stormed into the main drawing room, grabbed a curtain rod and began using it to smash a collection of Majolica pottery displayed along one wall. Hearing the noise, Christopher Hampton rushed in, and Rudolf, pausing for a second, said with ironical, Jeeves-like civility, 'Oh, good evening.'[*]

No more was said. Rudolf went to his room and proceeded to fling various objects out of the window. At this point Zeffirelli arrived with an ex-footballer as reinforcement, and launched himself at Rudolf. Luigi joined in, trying to separate them, but in the fray was injured himself, his white suit now splattered with blood. 'Rudi,' I said, 'let's go. *Now.*' After grabbing their belongings, Luigi went into town to find

---

[*] Robert Tracy believes that Rudolf's fury had been rooted in the fact that Zeffirelli had chosen to cast Vasiliev instead of him in the film of *La Traviata*, a theory that Zeffirelli himself emphatically refutes.

the taxi-driver who had brought them from Rome, and Rudolf, wearing tight shorts and high-heeled boots, set off alone on the corniche. 'Come along, pony!' he called out to his bag on wheels, dragging it behind him as he walked.

Dyson Lovell has described how, when he unlocked the gate to let Rudolf in, the dancer, wanting to demonstrate his contempt for Zeffirelli's hospitality, had defecated on the stone steps. Luigi, however, insists that this is not true. 'Everybody tried to make more, more, more of this story. Come on – this is not Nureyev style.' But Hampton confirms that it happened – presumably before Luigi arrived. 'And I heard what Rudolf said about it.' Yet what was even more shocking about this notorious episode, Hampton says, was the way the dancer had demonically cursed Zeffirelli's house as he left, turning round and gesturing with his index and little fingers raised. 'This is what really upset Franco.'

'It may be that no successful man was ever more primitive or more extraordinarily refined,' Elizabeth Kaye has written. 'He was brutal and tender, spiritual and carnal. In the span of a few minutes, he could evoke Christ on the cross and Mephistopheles.' And once again Rudolf would use dance to explore these rival impulses in himself. With a ballet version of Shakespeare's *Tempest* now taking shape in his mind, he decided to make Ariel and Caliban represent conflicting sides of Prospero's nature, the pair first appearing from within the magician's cloak as if born out of his own body. Airborne and white-faced like Pierrot, Rudolf's Ariel somersaults and dances on wires above his master's head, while Caliban, his features lined with black, emerges faecally from between his legs. Impervious to Prospero's attempts to educate him, he remains 'a devil, a born devil . . . a thing of darkness', whereas Ariel is seen by Rudolf as embodying the magician's 'higher spirit, his better self restraining him'. When Prospero is about to strike his brother, Ariel appears just in time to snatch the staff from his hands, much as Ithuriel, the angelic guard in Rudolf's Fuseli painting, surprises Satan, his spear raised in fury, and prevents him from pursuing his evil schemes. 'The tempest', Rudolf told an interviewer, 'is not something which happens from outside so much as within. Prospero makes the tempest. He has this rage. He has to overcome something.' Asked to define the cause, Rudolf then gives what is clearly an analysis of his own state of mind. 'Well, . . . I think he's come to a dark forest. I think his age – he's kind of over forty . . . End of desire, whatever. It's an unpleasant time.'

Dedicated to Nigel and staged by the Royal Ballet, *The Tempest* was the first major work that Rudolf had attempted without his mentor's help, although he had 'quizzed' him on several aspects of it. He had seen and admired Tetley's 1979 ballet for Rambert, but decided that its Prospero was not prominent enough; he wanted to give this lonely, isolated figure the Romantic centrality of a Byron hero. The six weeks he spent working on the libretto at Victoria Road were surprisingly effortless, as *The Tempest*, a highly visual spectacle staged by an enchanter, is a far more suitable source for a ballet than *Manfred*. 'Spare, intense, concentrated to the point of being riddling', in Anne Barton's view, it compels from its audience the kind of imaginative response provoked by dance, both sharing the same 'aura of suggestion . . . a meaning at once irreducible and mysterious'. Barton continues:

> More perhaps than with any other work of Shakespeare's, this is a drama which the actors could walk through silently and still manage to convey much of its essential nature . . . Nor should one forget the omnipresent background of music, the sheer number of songs in the play, and the manner in which they draw to themselves and translate emotions which words alone seem inadequate to express . . . Even the comic scenes . . . [are] of an essentially non-verbal nature.

As with his *Romeo and Juliet*, wanting to explain what happened before the play began, Rudolf begins his one-act ballet with a prologue set in Milan before Prospero's deposition. As he stands alone and crowned, a phantasmagoria of events reels through his mind, a hallucinatory, flashback device that Rudolf borrows from Robert Helpmann's highly condensed *Hamlet*. Tchaikovsky's *Tempest* overture begins when Prospero is already in exile, but Rudolf, wanting ominous-sounding music that would suggest the duplicity of his courtiers, chose to preface it with the Fugue, Divertimento and Polonaise. 'First I didn't want to touch the Polonaise because Balanchine had choreographed [to] it in *Theme and Variations* . . . so I had to do something bigger and better.' It inspired him to attempt his most Balanchinian composition since the '64 *Raymonda*: the opening section becomes an abstraction of a story ballet with a mass of black-and-gold-clad dancers ebbing and flowing in artfully complex patterns. Then, all of a sudden, as the pillars of Nico Georgiadis's set collapse, the stage empties into a black void and Prospero, stripped of his finery like the protagonist of van Dantzig's *About a Dark House*, crouches in stunned shock on the island.

In a catalogue of Fuseli drawings he owned Rudolf had been struck by an image of Caliban, Stephano and Trinculo running hand in hand, with Ariel above them, and this image influenced his idea of the inseparability of Prospero, Ariel and Caliban. Dressed in gold, white and black, they entwine, tussle and tumble, their bulging codpieces and bondage overtones of leather straps giving their threesome a provocatively sexual edge. With Miranda the only significant female role, the prevailing dance style of *The Tempest* is sinewy and athletic, the Royal Ballet's new generation of young males performing with unprecedented machismo. Ninette de Valois was amazed, exclaiming to Maude in the interval, 'We have to get him back here! *Look* what he's done for those boys!' Rudi had cast the company stars Wayne Eagling and David Wall as Ariel and Caliban, and had worked out all the steps on himself – 'The usual Rudi sort of thing,' Eagling says. 'Lots of very fast knitting of the legs and feet.' And although Anthony Dowell was the first-night Prospero, his commanding presence, plastique and speed the defining qualities of the role, the ballet remains the 'concert of one' that Henry James saw as Shakespeare's indulgence in *The Tempest*. Its Prospero is the Prospero of the end of the play, the work serving as a kind of confessional in which Rudolf could admit his own failing powers.

By having several episodes take place onstage at once, Rudolf leaves room for long, reflective solos, which, far from complementing Prospero's great speeches are disappointingly lacking in invention. Twirling his long staff like a drum-majorette, he appears to be doing no more than marking time, while his use of the staff as a vaulting pole looks like a desperate attempt to recapture his legendary elevation. In poignant contrast to the sixties Nureyev, his cloak blazing behind him, we see him half-heartedly flicking, swishing and winding Prospero's cape around him like a shroud. But in defiance of anyone who might view *The Tempest* as his voluntary valediction to his profession, Rudolf makes the other dancers literally drag him off into the wings as he reaches back yearningly towards the stage. 'The whole thing is metaphor,' he acknowledged. 'The cloak is his metaphor for art, and finally he has to renounce it.'

Rudolf believed *The Tempest* was his best original work. Though dramatically far from clear, it is full of imaginative touches, such as Ariel appearing to land on Prospero's finger, and also strong on theatrical effects (the instantaneous scene changes from court to island, and island to storm-racked boat). 'We switch in a flash,' wrote David Dougill. 'From our island viewpoint of the tossing galleon to being right there in it, on deck amid tearing sails.' All that was conceived by me,' insisted Rudolf. 'Every single thing they attribute to Georgiadis in fact he fought against!' But Georgiadis himself remembered *The Tempest* as a particularly harmonious collaboration. 'We were very much on the same wavelength . . . It had very very good things, and I never understood why they dropped it.'

Watching the gala première on 2 December 1982 was Rosa, who had succeeded in getting a three-week visa to visit her daughter in London. Rudolf had asked Tessa Kennedy to sit beside her and to drive her after the performance to Fife Road, where he was hosting a party for the whole cast. 'I thought she might be worried that I was KGB,' says Tessa. 'So as soon as I saw her, I said, "I'm from Rudolf."' With neither able to speak the other's language there was little communication, though, oddly enough, Rosa's single comment about the Opera House – 'Like teahouse' – was exactly the same as her brother's to Nigel and Maude in 1962. Rudolf was excited that his relatives were managing to thwart the Soviets by getting to the West, since a reunion with his mother now seemed far more achievable. Having recently bought the farm he wanted in Virginia (a 415-acre property with a beautiful eighteenth-century house, three cottages and a barn), 'his big fantasy' was to bring his whole family from Russia to live there. 'He really was trying to do everything he could,' says Franck Raoul-Duval. 'He felt a debt towards them. He'd had all the glamour for twenty years while they had suffered as a result of his act.'

As Rosa's visa was soon to expire, the only way of legally keeping her in London was through marriage to a Westerner. Douce offered her brother Pierre. 'I said I wasn't opposed to the idea, but would have to ask Mengia, the woman I'd lived with for twenty years.' Persuaded by Douce, Mengia agreed, and the François siblings immediately boarded a plane for London, accompanied by Rudolf. Seeing that Pierre had no tie, he bought one at the duty-free shop – 'I feel as if it's my wedding!' – and, still in jovial spirits on the flight, ordered two bottles of champagne. At Fife Road, Rosa, 'looking like Rudolf in a skirt', was rolling *pelmeni* for a celebratory supper, and seemed pleased with the gift of lace handkerchiefs brought by her husband-to-be. Later that night, Douce and Pierre went off to stay with Maude, and arranged to meet at Richmond Register Office at nine the following morning. As it turned out, they arrived considerably later, having stopped their taxi en route and rushed into a jeweller's to buy two rings. A small gathering of guests waited for the ceremony to begin: Gouzel and her Ecuadorian husband, Sandor and Edith Gorlinsky,

Maude – but not Rudolf, who had decided not to attend. 'He thought he'd be recognized and the story would be leaked to the press,' says Pierre. The service took three times longer than usual, with the couple's vows translated from English into French and Russian. No wedding breakfast followed the ceremony; after a few photographs had been taken, the groom flew straight back to Paris.

Now that the plan had been successfully accomplished it was incomprehensible to Rosa why Rudolf chose to go on living with Maude instead of being with his own family in his big, beautiful house. As Maude explained:

> He told me – it seems unkind – that when his sister came to the West he didn't want to be near her because she drove him mad . . . He always had this weak chest – which was one of the things that Rosa kept fussing about. He must have had it when he was a child. After she'd rung him up here once, he came back into the room in an absolute rage. 'That bitch! Do you know what she said? That I should stop dancing because of my health.'

The prospect of Rosa applying her peasant remedies – the emollients of goose fat or honey rubbed into his bronchial chest – must have seemed absurd to Rudolf in the current climate of fear. That month's *Harper's & Queen* magazine, featuring a model cuddling a baby white rabbit and advertising 'Parties of the Year' and 'Christmas Food and Wine', also carried the jarring cover line, HERPES AND THE OTHER HORRORS. Titled 'Plague', Michael Pye's article described the two sexually transmitted diseases holding America 'in a grip of chastity and terror', reporting that of 634 known AIDS victims in September more than forty per cent had not survived. The subject of mortality had never seemed more pervasive. Balanchine was now terminally ill and confined to New York's Roosevelt Hospital with Creutzfeldt-Jakob disease. In January Rudolf went to the New York State Theatre to see the choreographer's sublime Mozart *Divertimento No. 15*, and to the hospital to bid him farewell. The designer Rouben Ter-Arutunian accompanied Rudolf, suggesting that they take caviar and Château d'Yquem (which so delighted the dying man that his eyes lit up and he reached out to embrace them). 'We talked Russian and French. It was very sad. I wanted to see if he would give a number of his ballets to the Kirov . . . but he was totally uninterested. He said, "When I die, everything should vanish. A new person should come and impose his own new things."' Rudolf must have stayed on alone, as when

Balanchine's doctor, William Hamilton, went into the room he found the dancer still there, kneeling by the bed, weeping.

Balanchine died at age seventy-nine on 30 April 1983, and on 3 May, the day of his funeral, the Zurich Ballet's *Manfred* opened in Washington. While noting that it was hardly the disaster the French and British reviews had implied, Anna Kisselgoff nevertheless found the ballet very old-fashioned, and Clive Barnes remarked on 'the little flashlights going on throughout the theatre while the audience attempted to catch up with the story'.

Charles Murland was now critically ill. He spent a few weeks that summer at the little house he owned in Malta, and when he returned to London it was in a wheelchair. After being admitted to a private clinic he was transferred to St Mary's Hospital, Paddington, where, as Maude informed Wallace, the doctors did every possible test and never revealed what they had found. Charles's own doctor, William Davidson, confirms that they suspected AIDS. 'It was very early days, but in medical minds the syndrome existed . . . Charles fitted the criteria.' What were becoming recognized as AIDS-related symptoms – Kaposi lesions and candidiasis, a fungal infection of the mouth – had brought doctors to St Mary's from all over the country. 'They were coming to look.' Charles himself was still telling friends that he had leukaemia, but Pat Ruanne was among those who were not convinced. She and Ric Jahn had been told not to touch anything, and given protective clothing to wear – helmets, gloves, suits and boots. 'It was hard to get a straight answer from the staff, but when I glanced at Charles's chart and saw he wasn't taking any medication, I thought, This has got to be It.' Monica Mason had seen Keith Money shortly after her visit, and told him of the hospital's draconian precautions. 'Then she stared at me wide-eyed, and said, "But surely this is AIDS!"'

Tessa Kennedy brought a Catholic priest with her to St Mary's together with about six of Charles's friends. 'It was Father Rooney's idea that we should hold hands in a circle around the bed, which wasn't easy in those big thick gloves. To Charles we must have looked like weird astronauts.' She had asked a nurse, 'Is this so he doesn't catch anything from us?' and been told, 'No, no. It's so you don't catch what *he* has.' But despite fear and ignorance about the contagion of AIDS in 1983 (Charles had been enclosed in a plastic bubble to be transported from one hospital to the other), virtually everyone the banker had known well, including his cleaning woman, had been to St Mary's to visit him. Everyone, that is, except Rudolf. He had heard how Charles had become so emaciated that he was barely recognizable.

Rudolf's own recent weight loss had become more apparent – 'his cheeks are very hollow now,' Maude had remarked in May. He would have to wait another year before a definitive AIDS test became available, but, according to Tessa, Rudolf had long been convinced that he, too, was 'one of the first'.

'He'll be a director,' declared Ninette de Valois. 'He'll know a good choreographer when he sees one, he'll know a good teacher, and above all things, he'll know a good dancer.' De Valois was right, of course, as right as she had been when she predicted the Fonteyn–Nureyev partnership, and yet this was no radical change in direction for Rudolf. Ever since coming to the West he had been regenerating every company he joined, enriching the classical repertory, and picking out potential principals – from the twelve-year-old Anneli Alhanko and Per-Arthur Segerström in Sweden to Michael Birkmeyer in Vienna, Karen Kain and Frank Augustyn in Canada. And this is not necessarily a gift bestowed on legendary dancers. Margot Fonteyn would agree only grudgingly to coach young colleagues; Baryshnikov, although he had been director of the American Ballet Theatre for four years, was no pedagogue. As a performer he was the perfect exponent of what he called 'the mystery and exultation and quietness of the St Petersburg school', but he was not able to pass this on. His maverick American partner Gelsey Kirkland complained that he was 'unable to explain either how or why he produced a step in the way he did . . . to articulate his approach either in Russian or in English'. Baryshnikov may have been Alexander Pushkin's greatest creation, but Rudolf was their teacher's rightful heir – the messiah of pure classicism, and a moulder and maker of stars.

In Paris Rudolf had already spotted a whole generation of dancers, all in their teens, whom he was determined to elevate into a pleiad of *étoiles*. Achieving this, however, meant having to overthrow one of the Opéra's most ancient traditions, '*la sacro-sainte hiérarchie*', which, as Ghislaine Thesmar explains, still functions to this day. From bottom to top, this hierarchy comprises *quadrilles*, *coryphées*, *sujets*, *premiers danseurs* and *étoiles*. 'From the moment you're taken into the company you're competing in front of a jury for a certain number of free places that come up every year. It's very simple, very primitive, but it works. The technical competition is what makes the strength of the Paris Opéra Ballet: you have to be the best.'

Although virtually every dancer dreads the *Concours de Promotion*, nobody wanted the system changed. 'Rudolf tried to put an end to it, but everyone in the company gave him total veto,' says Thesmar. 'He really couldn't touch that.' Within months he was handing in his letter of resignation over 'intolerable' opposition to his choice of casting, and threatening to withdraw his productions from the repertory. But although Rudolf never succeeded in ridding the Opéra of its harsh annual examination, he soon found ways of circumventing it. He began breaking rules by picking corps de ballet members to accompany him on his private tours, and using the company in Vienna as a workshop for Parisian *étoiles*. 'All those young dancers made their debuts in Vienna – and not one of them a soloist yet,' says Gerhard Brunner, former director of the State Opera Ballet. 'Rudolf was determined to promote them as speedily as possible.' 'If you were good, there was no question of waiting. With Rudolf you were given your chance,' Florence Clerc confirms. 'He *knew* the importance of time,' adds Sylvie Guillem, 'because dancers don't have the time.'

Rudolf considered the dancers to have been 'dulled' by the Opéra's past repertory, so his priority was 'to *force-feed*' them with a new vocabulary: 'a Bournonville course and a course of modern dance, preferably the Graham technique . . . When one has that one can tackle everything, from Cunningham to the postmoderns.' First, though, he wanted to fine-tune their classical style. Finding the men overly sporty and lacking polish, he wanted them to aspire to the feline plastique of his youth fused with Erik's long, elegant line. The women, he said, were 'too frontal' (meaning they had not grasped the concept of *épaulement*, the Russians' eloquence of the upper back), and 'too French'. Edwin Denby's description of the feminine flourishes of Parisian ballerinas during the company's 1950 season in Florence – 'a fluster of waist wriggles, wrist flicks, and . . . those little shakes, pecks and perks of the head that look so pretty around a Paris dinner table' – was precisely the kind of affectation that Rudolf was determined to eliminate. He wanted nothing gratuitously decorative or nonfunctional, but rather to forge innate French chic with what former *étoile* Elisabeth Platel calls '*du vrai style classique, du vrai Petipa pur*'.

To transform the Paris Opéra Ballet into *his* company, with its dancers exhibiting traits of his own schooling and experience, Rudolf needed to 'attack on all fronts'. An immediate stratagem was to insist on compulsory daily class, arranging the schedule so as to prevent anyone from taking class outside. 'I thought if they all go and listen to their private gods, it's paganism, you know? You want to hear only one source of truth . . . So . . . I bring in excellent teachers and entice the dancers from their own gurus to my gurus.' To improve the company's footwork and speed of execution, Stanley Williams was the first Nureyev guru to be approached, and when Williams declined to come ('Stanley was too private to survive in Paris'), Rudolf turned to someone he knew could pass on the same methods. Elizabeth Anderton, the Festival Ballet dancer who created the role of Juliet's Nurse, had become a teacher of exceptional panache, and Rudolf had helped to enrich her classes by feeding her 'bits of information from Stanley'. 'Betty would have incorporated a lot of what Rudolf believed into her work,' says Monica Mason. 'Rudolf picked up instantly on courage and energy, intelligence – people he could sweep up to be as hungry as he was. Betty has an extraordinary way of inspiring people – that genuine ability to take people to another place.'

He gave the role of ballet mistress to Claire Motte, his oldest friend in Paris, and brought in Yvette Chauviré to coach the principals. 'A fact that is very important with Rudolf is how faithful he was,' remarks Elisabeth Platel. But if this was an act of loyalty, it was also politically canny, as both women were exemplars of French schooling at its most refined, the veteran ballerina having become a virtual institution, 'La Chauviré Nationale'. As ballet master Rudolf appointed Bolshoi-trained Eugene 'Genia' Poliakov, who had been one of his most devoted fans in Russia. Then working in Florence as director and choreographer, he had refused the offer at first because his position in Italy was so good, but after several visits to Paris decided that working with Rudolf would be a greater challenge. A small, unassuming man with close-cropped, gingerish hair and a beard, Poliakov was the personification of the Russian intelligentsia, with a quality his Florentine colleagues describe as *garbo*, which in Italian means something beyond civilized. 'It's more like grace . . . . Everything Genia did was infused with this civilized grace.'

One of the new director's conditions before taking on the job was to demand the departure of the administrator, George Hirsch, an authoritarian figure with the kind of old-fashioned outlook Rudolf despised. He had been replaced by the young, bilingual Thierry Fouquet, who had spent the past months working closely with Rudolf in preparation for his arrival. Rudolf had chosen as his assistant Franck Raoul-Duval, who had just finished his military service in the Far East. 'Rudolf called me and said, "I need my people," but after a few months it felt as if the whole bureaucracy of the Paris Opéra was falling on me, and I knew it wasn't going to work. They seemed to think, "Rudolf alone is hard enough to cope with, but if he brings his own team it will be impossible."* Rudolf inherited Hirsch's personal assistant, Marie-Suzanne Soubie, whom Thierry Fouquet had thought of letting go until he was warned, 'Watch it!' (Her husband, Raymond Soubie, an eminent civil servant, had been former prime minister Raymond Barre's main adviser, and in 1987 would be appointed president of the Opéra.) A petite, elegant woman with a lovely heart-shaped face and dancer's physique, she was, Rudolf informed Maude, 'A real lady. Too much of a lady to be working at the Opéra.' After a couple of weeks Sandor Gorlinsky rang to tell her Rudolf was so pleased that he wanted her to be 'a little more present'. So indispensable, in fact, did Marie-Suzanne become that to the doting Douce François, Rudolf's personal assistant was to prove more threatening than any other relationship in his life.

The new director's most iconoclastic early move was to insist on the demolition of the Salle Lifar, the huge practice room in the Opéra's rotunda, named after Serge Lifar, an earlier redeemer of twentieth-century French ballet. Rudolf's idea was to divide the space into three separate studios, remarking, 'It's only when [these] are complete that one will be able to really work. I will have all the dancers together in front of me, and this situation will attract the foreign choreographers who are still reticent to come.' The salon at the top he christened Petipa, and the two underneath it Balanchine and Bournonville – the Trinity.† But although very few Lifar works had survived, and only vestiges remained of his training, Rudolf was strongly urged to drop Bournonville's name for that of Lifar who, to most of the senior staff, was still synonymous with Paris Opéra Ballet.‡ 'He wasn't happy,' recalls Marie-Suzanne, 'but he was forced to acquiesce.'

The last of Diaghilev's protégés, the beautiful, charismatic Serge Lifar had reigned over the Ballets Russes in the late twenties, and after the impresario's death in 1929, was invited to the Opéra, where he

---

* Wanting to keep his link with the dance world, Franck began a business making ballet shoes, which is now the internationally successful Sansha dance accessories company.

† When Robert Denvers became a director Rudolf advised him to schedule nothing but Petipa, Bournonville and Balanchine for the first couple of years, saying, 'If they've done that they're ready for everything. This should be your programming, and *then* you should do the moderns.'

‡ Yvette Chauviré, Lifar's muse, had created roles in more than a dozen of his works. Claude Bessy, the director of the Opéra school, continued to view him as 'my master, my spiritual father', while Claire Motte was another '*adoratrice*'.

became *étoile*, choreographer and director. 'Lifar was more than a star dancer,' Lynn Garafola writes. 'He was a celebrity . . . A force to be reckoned with in the corridors of power.' Intent on reviving the moribund French company, he sent its youngest members to study with Paris's great émigrée professors: Kschessinskaya, Preobrazhenska, Trefilova . . . their vastly improved technique also acquiring a lush Maryinsky lyricism. And by combining a number of much-needed new reforms with a touch of the innovative magic he had absorbed from Diaghilev, Lifar succeeded in restoring to the Paris Opéra Ballet the cachet it had not enjoyed since the Romantic era.

In 1961, during the Kirov's three-week season in Paris, Lifar had gone out of his way to befriend the young Russian he considered to be 'incontestably the star of the Leningrad company'. Awarding Rudolf the prestigious Nijinsky Prize, Lifar described him as the most influential male dancer to have emerged since Nijinsky and himself. There were undeniable resemblances. All three had strived to redress the imbalance between male and female dancing, and as history's greatest Albrechts, made this quintessential Romantic hero assume an importance equal to Giselle's. Photographs of Lifar at the grave, his arms full of lilies, his trailing black cloak an extension of his grief, were as formative to Rudolf's interpretation as those he had studied of Nijinsky. Lifar, too, had come late to dance – 'a diamond in the rough who willed himself to dazzle' – displaying the same kind of lithe, wild-animal grace and burning stage presence. Both had dared to challenge their own fate by moving to the West in search of opportunity – in fact, there was speculation at the time of Rudolf's defection that it was Lifar's example that had influenced him. (An article in the *Sunday Times* claimed that the older Russian was 'almost certainly – if unwittingly – involved in Nureyev's decision to seek asylum in France'.)

Two years later, however, in 1963, an astonishing attack on Rudolf appeared in the 9 April issue of *Izvestia*, translated and reprinted from *Paris-Jour* (2 April 1963). Signed by Lifar, it was titled 'He Loves No One and Betrays All'. 'He has become a star by sheer virtue of the fact that he is a traitor . . . his moral behaviour is unbalanced, hysterical and vain. His first attempts at choreography came to nothing and showed no imagination whatsoever. All he did was regurgitate what he had learned from Petipa and his tutor Pushkin.'

Invited to return to his homeland for the first time in forty-six years, Lifar, according to René Sirvin, had been 'bought by the Russians', and was, therefore, obliged to take this line. But to Rudolf a denunciation of such malevolence from someone who himself had been attacked as a traitor when the war ended was staggering hypocrisy. Lifar, he told Robert Tracy, had 'choreographed entrance for Hitler into Paris . . . . He showed Hitler Paris Opéra – took him around.' And indeed, although Lifar always denied being at the Palais Garnier the day Hitler made his tour, he did openly fraternize with high-ranking Nazis during the occupation, making a number of tours at Goebbels's request, and meeting the Führer in Berlin. (To Sirvin, Lifar boasted that Hitler had been 'so taken with [his] body' that he sent his private plane to fetch the dancer.) Summoned for trial when the Allies entered Paris, Lifar was banished from the Opéra for life, but several months later this verdict was revised, and the period of exclusion reduced to a year. In September 1947, cleared of all charges, Lifar was reinstated as the Opéra's *maître de ballet*, remaining in power until his retirement in 1958.

Taking up his own position in the autumn of '83, Rudolf had received a note of congratulations from Diaghilev's friend and secretary, Boris Kochno, but no such welcome came from Lifar. 'It's sad, because they could have talked a lot,' says Charles Jude, who has a photograph of the three of them in Paris. 'It was Rudolf's dream to have the same career as Lifar: to be director, star and choreographer, staying at the Opéra for thirty years, and creating all those ballets.' But Lifar had achieved Rudolf's dream before that: a personal repertory created for him by Balanchine. *Apollo*, the choreographer's earliest masterpiece, had been made specifically for the twenty-three-year-old youth from Kiev, transforming him into 'a glamorous deco god: sleek of limb, neoclassical in line, athletic in style.' What Rudolf could never forgive was that this had directly rebounded on him. Four decades later the memory of having been forced by Diaghilev to choreograph vehicles for a male star still rankled, Balanchine vowing, 'I never do that again.'

Rudolf could never bring himself to like Lifar, a character with an ego as massive as his own. There was also the fact that he had hardly any regard for Lifar's choreography, finding its theatrical, symbol-laden style 'kitsch, and "everything he didn't rate".' '*Suite en blanc* and *Icare* – those are very good ballets,' he told Charles Jude. 'All the rest are shit.' To Edwin Denby even the best works had 'a curious anti-musical and desperate pound', while Violette Verdy described them as 'not what Balanchine could be even on a bad day'. Despite having written several treatises defending the principles of classical ballet, Lifar was no craftsman. And because he had not been formed by a particular school as a child, his own dancing had always lacked precision and control. 'He didn't know how to do a true fifth position, his pirouettes were unfinished – everything was done for effect,' says Hélène Traïlene, then the Opéra's director of programming. 'Rudolf was the complete opposite of this.' If each star choreographed in order to promote and explore his own persona, the profound difference was that Lifar did not have the technical knowledge to bring out the best in his dancers. To Rudolf this deficiency as a classicist had negated a legacy of any lasting value in the Paris company. Not only that, but he believed that the three decades Lifar monopolized the repertory meant that 'the Opéra cut itself off from the rest of world creation and ignored it.' The malign presence of Lifar was 'everywhere', Rudolf told Gore Vidal. 'In rehearsal halls. Backstage. We name rooms after this one, after that one. *They* make me name Lifar Room. Always evil in that room . . . Bad ghost.' And it was the one ghost that Rudolf was determined to exorcise.

Rudolf's own ambition was 'not to be a new Lifar, but to permit other choreographers to come to the opera'. In the five years before he arrived, the repertory had become (in the hands of Violette Verdy and Rosella Hightower) considerably more international, with the restaging of key works by Balanchine, MacMillan and Cranko. There had also been programmes of contemporary choreography – though not at the Palais Garnier. Modern dance was seen to be 'the business of GRCOP' [Groupe de Recherche Chorégraphique de l'Opéra de Paris], a workshop organization run with foresight and great efficiency by Jacques Garnier. According to Jean Guizerix, Rudolf was jealous of Garnier's achievement, but if Rudolf was dismissive of this splinter group it was largely because he saw no need for it. 'I want it to be the company and not GRCOP who dance the works of Lucinda Childs or Karole Armitage.'

His vision of a repertory comprising 'fifty-fifty classical and contemporary work' was a lot more pioneering than it might seem. Until the arrival of Garnier's predecessor, the Alvin Ailey dancer Carolyn Carlson, who ran the Opéra's experimental troupe from 1974 to 1980, Paris audiences had little experience of modern dance. Martha Graham's only season in Paris in 1950 had been a disaster, closing on its 'second excruciating night'. (Exhausted by all the symbolism and metaphysics, the *Figaro* critic was left with a craving for frivolity – 'to see the French cancan or the ballet from *Faust*'.) Rudolf, however, was determined to educate the Palais Garnier audience to appreciate the avant-garde, which meant enticing the world's greatest innovators to Paris, among them Merce Cunningham, William Forsythe and theatre director Robert Wilson.

Recognizing that the Opéra must also represent the French tradition, he had already written to Béjart to ask him to remount 'notre *Faust*', and also to create a new piece, offering to put at the choreographer's disposal a number of dancers to perform experimental work, to be presented to the public or not. He had announced the revival of Roland Petit's *Phantom of the Opera*, but over the summer the two men had fallen out, and in retaliation, Petit had withdrawn all his ballets.[*] To Rudolf this was no great loss. Disliking the choreographer's recent work, he had taken to calling him 'Roland Pas de Pas', meaning 'no steps'. It wasn't that Rudolf did not think that Petit and Béjart should be seen at the Opéra, but as Thierry Fouquet said, 'He had many other more important things in mind to do first.' One journalist wrote, 'It does not seem that the French are much appreciated,' to which Rudolf replied that he had 'a boundless admiration for the French school of the nineteenth century'. His first programme in September was to be Pierre Lacotte's authentic revival of *Coppélia*, and he had asked Lacotte to bring to the Opéra the production he had recently mounted in Rome – a reconstruction of *Marco Spada*, a three-act French ballet not performed for more than a century. He had scheduled Balanchine's homage to Molière, *Le Bourgeois gentilhomme*, and he planned to introduce baroque dance to the Opéra 'because that's where it was invented' (the Paris Opéra Ballet was a direct descendant of the Académie Royale de la Danse, established by Louis XIV in 1671).

Rudolf's immediate concern, however, was to restore to France its own neglected genius – Marseilles-born Marius Petipa, the most influential choreographer of all time. Although it was not until he went to St Petersburg that Petipa created his masterpieces, he was intimately linked to the Paris Opéra by his family, teachers and partners.

---

* This 'accident of an evening' took place after the Ballet National de Marseilles's season at the Met in July 1983. Rudolf, guest-starring with Natalia Makarova, had arrived at the last minute, not leaving himself enough time to learn the part of Quasimodo. The performance itself was lamentable – 'Rudolf was improvising', says René Sirvin, aware that the dancer was making a mockery of the role. 'He didn't like being deformed.' Adding insult to injury, Rudolf then failed to bring Petit out onstage for a curtain call. ('It was actually Natasha who had forgotten,' says Jane Hermann. 'But Roland blamed it on Rudolf. He said he was hogging the bows, which was absolutely untrue.') Later, at Hermann's post-performance party, Rudolf, who was sitting next to Martha Graham, called out to Petit, telling him to come and say hello to her. 'Pissed off and sulking,' Petit refused. 'Finally Rudolf stands up. He says, "You fucking get over here or" . . . and Roland says, "If you talk to me like that I'm taking all my ballets away from Paris Opéra."'

Astoundingly, though, the Petipa classics – the mainstay of ballet companies throughout the world – were hardly known at the Palais Garnier. The reason for this was the French public's preference for short, innovative pieces rather than revivals spanning a whole evening. 'The Parisian audience like what is outré; what is special, exotic or novel; or, more often, what is shocking,' wrote Agnes de Mille, explaining the 'cold failure' of Graham's season. 'What is simply sound dramatically . . . or what is essentially intellectual, they find difficult to accept.'

This was borne out once again during the Sadler's Wells Ballet's ill-received appearance at the Opéra in September 1954, when it was critically regretted 'that the British programmes included classics rather than more recent works'. 'The French public want novelty at all costs,' remarked Rudolf. 'It's the unfortunate legacy of Diaghilev, who evolved among snobs and said each day to Cocteau, "*Étonne-moi!*"' (When Diaghilev, having kept the interest of his fashionable audiences with an exciting diet of experimentation, decided to return to nineteenth-century classicism, he chose London, not Paris, as his venue.) Knowing his audience, Lifar had selected what he called *Divertissements* from *Sleeping Beauty* (the first-act waltz and Awakening scene), but his rendering of the choreography was so inept that it made Edwin Denby 'cringe'. As far as Rudolf was concerned, Petipa had been 'treated very unjustly' by the Opéra, and his own inaugural production in November – a sumptuous new staging of *Raymonda* – would waste no time in putting this to rights.

Due to be interviewed a week after his arrival at the Palais Garnier, Rudolf was to be found not in his office – 'I don't even know where it is' – but in the studio rehearsing the dancers. In vivid orange boots, he was demonstrating the ballerina variations and highlighting details such as the little feminine circles of the wrist, while performing a taxing series of *entrechats*. The Parisians found themselves being pushed as never before. 'We were *armed* for this ballet,' says Elisabeth Platel, Rudolf's first-cast heroine, a long-legged, aristocratic dancer whose exceptional strength was tempered by a softly limpid style and intensity of absorption. Platel remembers how taken aback she and her fellow *étoiles* had been to find themselves in a studio with the corps de ballet – as inconceivable until then as it would have been for the Sun King's courtiers to mix with the city's *sans-culottes*. 'With Rudolf,' she says, 'we became a team.' And wanting *Raymonda* to be a showcase for '*everyone* in the company', he cast *étoiles* in secondary roles (Monique Loudières as Clémence, Claude de Vulpian as Henriette), brought Yvette Chauviré out of retirement to play Countess Sybille, and used the ballet to spotlight two of his stars-in-embryo. He had already given Laurent Hilaire the leading role of Frantz in *Coppélia*, and now he twinned him with fellow *sujet* Manuel Legris as the friends Bernard and Beranger – 'Ber-Ber!' Rudolf called them – flaunting their taut line and nimble footwork with a show-stopping duet. (Soon afterwards, brushing aside Claude de Vulpian's refusal to dance with a corps de ballet boy, he cast Legris as Jean de Brienne to the *étoile*'s Raymonda. Remembering everything he had absorbed from Dudinskaya, Shelest and Fonteyn, Rudolf wanted the nineteen-year-old to learn as much and as soon as he could by partnering *une femme d'un certain a^ge*.)

This version's main difference from the standard *Raymonda* was Rudolf's enhancement of the role of Abderakhman. Establishing once again the concept of an Odette–Odile duality, he added new solos that would bring out the Saracen's savage magnetism and explain Raymonda's attraction to him. 'Abderakhman is a sex symbol,' Rudolf remarked, meaning that he excites the heroine in a way that Jean does not. Working on the variations with Jean Guizerix, Rudolf demonstrated examples of Caucasian folk dancing, and tried to instil the kind of exotic, animal sensuality he himself had exuded in *Le Corsaire* and *La Bayadère* – a style of choreography that, as Guizerix says, is '*très Solor*'. (Charles Jude would have far preferred the role of Abderakhman to that of Jean, whose personality he describes as '*nul*'.)

Without exception the dancers remember the experience of working with Rudolf on *Raymonda* as an absolute joy; after the first rehearsal they had expressed their appreciation by applauding him. The Ministry of Culture's Igor Eisner was no less enthusiastic.

> Très cher Rudolf,
> You have just given us a great and vigorous ballet dignifying both the Opéra and the name of Petipa. Powerful enough for the French to learn at last to look at dance. The company has been marvellous: it already owes you a great deal.

Marie-Suzanne Soubie was not alone in thinking '*tout nouveau, tout beau*' – that it was all too good to last. For this albeit brief moment Rudolf was more content than ever before. 'I have finally found a nest where I can relax,' he admitted. 'I feel good here.' The cradle of classical ballet, Paris, he realized, was 'the best place in the world to have a company'. It was the company Balanchine had twice come

close to running.* Moreover, by a balletic divine right of succession
it was where Rudolf belonged (Petipa, a student of Auguste Vestris,
was replaced at the Maryinsky by Nicolai Legat, teacher of the young
Pushkin).

Rudolf's contract required him to reside six months a year in Paris,
but this was no hardship. He never tired of the view opposite 23 quai
Voltaire – the *bouquinistes'* stalls along the embankment, the Louvre
through regimented plane trees, its stone changing from grey to gold
depending on the light. And although his short journey to work was
always a rush, it was a constant source of pleasure – the avenue de
l'Opéra running in a wide straight line to the Palais Garnier, whose
ornate baroque façade, magnificent cupola, and winged golden statu-
ary provide one of the world's most exquisite architectural vistas.

At the end of an afternoon, he often spent time in Gilberte
Cournand's La Danse, a specialist bookshop and gallery on the rue de
Beaune, around the corner from quai Voltaire. As one of France's most
acute voices on ballet, the critic was not only excellent company but
had been delighting Rudolf since 1961 with her collection of dance
figurines, books, prints and costume designs. He also loved to roam
the *sixième*'s Carré Rive Gauche, the antiquarian quarter, each shop
like a salon in the Carnavalet Museum, with its display of ancient
ceramics, statues, plinths, chinoiserie, Aubusson rugs, Renaissance
tapestries, inlaid cabinets and ornate clocks. Antique collecting had
become Rudolf's 'next passion', and, aware of this, before closing for
the night some shop owners would put objects in their windows that
might tempt him. 'They knew that after a performance he used to
"*faire du lèche vitrine*".' He even began 'dancing for the furniture he
wanted to buy', asking Tessa Kennedy to arrange for the dealer to
come to the theatre to collect his money. 'He said, "Now I'll be
thinking of that wardrobe when I'm onstage – it will inspire me!"' The
pride of his collection was the nineteenth-century Russian furniture of

* In 1929, soon after Balanchine had been elected ballet master at the Opéra, he contracted
pneumonia, and Lifar was asked to take charge. 'When he came back, door was locked,'
said Rudolf. 'They wouldn't let him in.' Invited to be guest ballet master at the Opéra in
1947, Balanchine would have stayed on if it had been possible to divide his time between
Paris and New York. But, according to Bernard Taper, 'Balanchine found himself in the
midst of intrigue, plots and counterplots. Lifar adherents were constantly active on his
behalf.'

Karelian birch, the arched and ebonized *bibliothèque*, the chairs, tables, cabinet, bed and canopy, ormolu-mounted and upholstered in Caucasian kilims. 'I have only one dream. Always the same. That one day I can receive my mother here. It's her I am waiting for.'

But it was Rosa who was now with Rudolf, staying in his guest room overlooking the Seine. Her 'husband', Pierre François, had spotted her one day on quai de la Mégisserie, and was about to greet her, French fashion, with a kiss on each cheek, when Rosa instinctively recoiled as if fearing assault. Pierre suggested that she come home with him to meet his long-term partner, 'but Rosa was afraid that Mengia might hit her'. He managed to persuade her, and the three spent an awkward hour trying to make themselves understood, Pierre noting how 'the brutal change in her way of life, language, country, social level had given her an air of being almost drunk with it all.' They urged Rosa to visit them whenever she cared to, but he did not see her again. 'Only Rudolf interested her,' Pierre says, a situation her brother was already regretting.

> Very quickly Rosa took his affairs in hand and considered all people gravitating around him as rivals, swindlers or parasites. She filtered all the comings and goings and rebuked Rudolf on his way of life and his *fréquentations*. So Rudolf then put her in the studio upstairs, but as she continued to make his life impossible, he sent her to La Turbie with a monthly allowance on condition that she never came back to Paris.

Rudolf's niece Gouzel was also proving a problem. He had wanted to do the best for her when she arrived in Paris, taking her to shop at Saint Laurent, and subsidizing French lessons. He believed she was bright enough to go to the Sorbonne, but Gouzel had other ideas – as Maude witnessed one night at the quai Voltaire apartment: 'Gouzel kept saying, "*Nyet, nyet, nyet*," and finally, Rudolf turned to me and said, "Maude, isn't she wrong? I want her to go back and learn something – whether it's history of art or whatever, just so she has a knowledge of something. But she says it's boring and she won't do it."'

Rudolf had turned to several friends for help, asking Tessa to employ her in the interior design company she owned, and Jeannette to give her temporary work as a waitress in Tosca's, her fashionable San Francisco bar. 'But she was too lazy,' Jeannette recalls. 'Her uncle was famous; why should she make something of herself? Why not just live in the apartment he'd given her and enjoy her life?' Having left her husband, Gouzel was looking 'to meet men', asking Tessa if she knew of any bars to which she could go. 'I said I'd try to find out from my children.' Stories of this kind were filtering back to Rudolf, who told Gouzel angrily, 'You're *damaging* me.' In despair he telephoned Armen, who was then working in San Francisco's Immigration Department. 'Do anything,' Rudolf begged her. 'You've got to send them back!' 'But I told him, I can't start asking for your relatives to be deported just because you're disillusioned, because you made a mistake by bringing them in.' And yet she realized how upset Rudolf was to discover the unbreachable cultural gap that now existed between him and his family. 'When Rosa came she was a different person. He saw a different Rosa, a different Gouzel . . . Wild, not polished.' 'These people speak a different language,' he told Armen, laughing dryly. 'Do you know I'm absolutely convinced that we come from the wolves.'

Rudolf himself now knew everyone there was to know in Paris society. He had become a member of Guy and Marie-Hélène de Rothschild's court, spending several Christmases at Ferrières, their massive belle époque château on the upper Seine, and dining at the Hôtel Lambert, their seventeenth-century Paris town house. Not even kings could afford Ferrières – Wilhelm I of Prussia is said to have remarked, 'It could belong only to a Rothschild' – while the Hôtel Lambert, built on the Île Saint Louis by the architect of Versailles, and restored to its former glory by Marie-Hélène's friend Alexis de Rédé, had one of the most sumptuous domestic interiors in all Paris. To be invited to a Rothschild soirée was in itself an education in ancien-régime elegance, the kind of opulence unchanged from that Flaubert describes when Frédéric, the young hero of *L'Éducation sentimentale*, encounters *le beau monde* for the first time. He is enraptured by the great candelabra reflected in the mirrors, the footmen in gold braid, the buffet 'looking like the high altar of a cathedral' with its display of silver platters and iridescent cut glass.

Rudolf rarely refused an invitation to the Hôtel Lambert, particularly as he had grown extremely close to Marie-Hélène. A mix of American and European cultures, the wife of Guy de Rothschild was no beauty, but with her couture clothes and reddish-gold hair coiffed by Alexandre, she had great personal style. Her aesthetic sense and extraordinary attention to detail had found expression in the legendary costume balls she gave at Ferrières. The haute cuisine and great wines Rudolf had sampled with the Rothschilds began influencing the dinners he gave at quai Voltaire; a typical menu of quenelles with lobster accompanied by Montrachet or Roederer Cristal was far more extravagant than anything he had served before. Marie-Hélène was proving as formative to his taste as Lee Radziwill had been in his youth, and as a friend could be equally demanding. 'She expected complete loyalty. You had to *worship* her or not see her at all.' With Rudolf, however, it was Marie-Hélène who did the worshipping, her esteem so profound that she viewed him as quasi divine – 'an instrument in the hands of a higher being, come to earth not to give life meaning but to reveal its mystery . . . *Celui-là, il faudrait s'incliner réligieusement devant lui, et lui donner un autre nom: "l'inter-prêtre".*'

They were together at a grand dinner one night given by Princess Margot Aliatta; Rudolf sat on Marie-Hélène's right, and on her left was Jimmy Douglas, an urbane young American expatriate. Finding it a strain to keep Marie-Hélène amused – 'She was like Louise de Vilmorin, she took everything out of you' – Jimmy was glad when Rudolf persuaded him to leave. 'He kept telling me how bored he was, and wanted me to take him to le Trap, which was a low dive good for adventures.' Opening at midnight and signalling its existence on rue Jacob with an ice blue neon sign saying 'Bar', le Trap was much like any other gay cruising venue. 'Pinball machines. A garish jukebox. Just a touch too much red light.' Announcing, 'I know where to go,' Rudolf made straight for le Trap's 'stairway to paradise', disappearing for about an hour into a warren of little back rooms. Jimmy, meanwhile, sat waiting for him at the bar:

> I had fallen by chance on an extremely attractive boy and when Rudolf came down he showed that he would really like to meet him, so I introduced them. Rudolf was delighted. 'You're *wonderful*!' he said, and gave me a big kiss, sticking his tongue right into my mouth. He was doing it to be funny, but it turned out to be a very bad thing for me, because in a couple of days I came down with some terrible virus. For two months I ached all over and had fevers, and none of the doctors knew what it was. I feel it was definitely something Rudolf gave me; he was doing a lot of things up there in the dark. Many people I knew caught AIDS upstairs at le Trap.

At the Institute Verne, a clinic devoted mostly to gay men, patients with symptoms of the new disease were arriving in increasing numbers. 'It started with one, two, then ten, twenty . . . And very quickly we understood that we were going to be overwhelmed by this.' Rudolf's young doctor, Michel Canesi, worked there part-time and realized that he, like everyone else at the institute, was on the frontline. He kept in almost daily contact with a colleague at Claude-Bernard Hospital who was one of very few in their profession to take seriously '*la prétendue maladie d'homos*'. In June 1981, Willy Rozenbaum, a thirty-three-year-old specialist in infectious and tropical diseases, had received a patient, a ship steward, suffering from a rare strain of pneumonia. The doctor had just read in the weekly review of Atlanta's Centers for Disease Control its now famous account of five young homosexuals afflicted with this same *pneumocystis carinii* pneumonia, and as more information appeared over the year he became convinced that GRID was already present in France. By 1982, with no more than a few dozen cases in the country, the disease was still considered marginal, and Rozenbaum found himself struggling constantly against the incredulity and inertia of his colleagues. There was also considerable prejudice against the frequent presence of homosexuals at Claude-Bernard. Rozenbaum succeeded in finding a new post at La Pitié-Salpêtrière, and with several like-minded physicians formed a small group with the intention of working together to isolate the agent responsible for SIDA (*syndrome immunodéficitaire acquis*), as it became known in France.

One night at the beginning of February 1983, Canesi was having dinner with Rozenbaum and another dermatologist from the Institute Verne. 'Willy told us about a phone call he'd received that day from Luc Montagnier at the Pasteur Institute. He'd sent a sample of a lymph node from one of his patients, and Montagnier was calling to say that he thought he might have found something new.' A specialist in human retroviruses, Montagnier had begun to suspect that the AIDS virus existed not only in the blood but in the lymph nodes, a theory that Rozenbaum's biopsy (taken from a young male homosexual) had confirmed. 'Something's happened,' Montagnier told him. 'We've identified the activity of a retrovirus. We have to talk.' They began to collaborate, and four months later Rozenbaum sent another sample from a young gay male known as LAI (after his initials). LAI's lymph node was invaded by Kaposi's sarcoma cells, and when cultivated, the virus multiplied very quickly. 'It would become famous in fact, since this strain was to be used the world over.' By the end of 1983 the human retrovirus Montagnier had christened LAV (lymphadenopathy associated virus), and which his American co-discoverer, Robert Gallo, called HTLV-I was known to be the agent of AIDS.

It was shortly after this, at the beginning of 1984, that Michel Canesi sent Rudolf to see Rozenbaum. Although a test would not be commercialized for another year, the Pasteur Institute had developed a prototype from LAI's lymphocytes that detected the presence of antibodies specific to AIDS patients. Using the name 'Mr Potts' (Wallace's surname), and entrusting Marie-Suzanne Soubie with the task of driving him to La Pitié-Salpêtrière, Rudolf had his first consultation with Rozenbaum. A puckish man with tight curly brown hair and wire-rimmed glasses, Willy Rozenbaum believes '*le secret médical*' to be paramount, and therefore refuses to discuss his association with Rudolf, but the memoir he wrote about his pioneering work* reveals someone not only passionate about his vocation but exceptionally nonjudgemental. Marie-Suzanne remembers his intensity on that first occasion, as he impressed on her the need for total secrecy. 'He said, "This could be very serious: are you going to help him?" But I knew already that Rudolf needed someone who would have died rather than say anything.'

Rozenbaum called Canesi to tell him that the test was positive, and Canesi in turn broke the news to their patient. Hearing what he felt he already knew, Rudolf was concerned but not unduly so, particularly as it was thought at the time (wrongly) that AIDS developed in no more than ten per cent of *séropositif* patients. He found himself in what Rozenbaum describes as 'that strange state where people are at the same time in good health, perhaps soon [to be] sick, but "dangerous" because capable of transmitting the virus'. When Rock Hudson was diagnosed with AIDS a few months later, he sent anonymous letters to his three most recent sexual contacts suggesting that they have tests done 'to make sure you're ok'. Rudolf, however, had no regular partner and would have been hard pressed to track down his multiple casual encounters. He and Robert Tracy had split up in the summer of 1981, and although they had since got back together (Rudolf installing the young dancer as a kind of châtelaine in his Dakota apartment), the relationship was now, in Robert's words, 'The same – except no sex.'

The only people Rudolf told were two of his closest colleagues. At the beginning of February he had a dinner after an Opéra Comique performance with a small group including André Larquié, president of the Paris Opéra, who had helped to 'cook the arrival of Rudolf', and subsequently had become a good friend. 'At one point in the evening Rudolf

---

* *La vie est une maladie sexuellement transmissible constamment mortelle* (Paris: Éditions Stock, 1999).

turned to me and said, "I am sick. Please call my doctor. He knows and Marie-Suzanne knows – that's all."' Larquié understood instantly what he meant. 'We were very aware now of the problems of AIDS, and, of course, I knew the life of Rudolf.' The following day he called Canesi, who told him, 'Yes, Rudolf wanted you to know that he is *séropositif*, but he's well, so don't worry. If I see any changes, I will tell you.'

It had been only a matter of months since AIDS researchers confirmed that the virus transmitted itself through semen or blood, but ignorance about contagion – fear even of shaking the hand of a *sidaïque* – was to persist for years to come. This climate of anxiety also existed in the medical profession: Rozenbaum described a doctor who confessed to having burned his gloves, and asked if he should also burn the chair on which the patient had sat. Marie-Suzanne vows that at no point did she consider herself to be in danger – 'It just didn't enter my mind.' But Rudolf's dread was that other colleagues would feel differently. 'If I tell people, if the world knows that I am ill, dancers are afraid of me – they don't want to work with me.' Maude, in whom Rudolf confided the following year, understood this only too well. 'His professional life would have been finished. The press would never have left him alone. And he wouldn't have been able to travel. He wouldn't have been able to do anything. All he wanted to do was work. If he was going to die it would be onstage.'

In March, six weeks after his highly successful homage to Martha Graham, Rudolf mounted a homage to himself. It began with *Le Bourgeois gentilhomme*, for which he rechoreographed so many steps that, seeing a video of the performance, Susie Hendl found his role '*unrecognizable*'. In *The Tempest*[*] he introduced an additional soliloquy for Prospero, a long farewell to the island, and in *Marco Spada*, the three-act work which Pierre Lacotte had staged especially for him, Rudolf insisted on dancing so many bravura solos that he made complete nonsense of its already unfathomable plot. In the original production, Angela's bandit father was a role confined almost exclusively to mime (the ballet's main attraction was the choreographic duel fought by its two rival Italian ballerinas). Rudolf, however, kept flinging off his cape to launch into one swashbuckling display after another, so that anyone

---

[*] Shown on the same programme with Lifar's *Les Mirages*, *The Tempest* was loathed by the French, provoking a noisily hostile reception from sections of the first-night audience, and condemned as turgid and pretentious by critics. By comparison, wrote one, Lifar's forty-year-old ballet appeared to be the true creation of the evening. Not to John Percival. It was hard to understand, he countered, why an audience that rejected Nureyev's ballet should receive the dated, 'monumentally stupid' *Les Mirages* with such warmth.

unfamiliar with the story would have assumed Marco Spada was Angela's favourite suitor. 'The brigand chief's role is needlessly massive,' wrote Freda Pitt. 'Three or four solos should surely be sufficient for anyone . . . (he has six or seven).' Rudolf's Prince Désiré-style apparel certainly gave him the appearance of a *danseur noble*, but his flaccid technique soon exposed the fact that he was not up to the role. *Marco Spada* provided him with one of his most strenuous roles to date, its hero, who was part villain, part aristocrat, was yet another example of the kind of double personage to which he was drawn.

Francine Lancelot's *Bach Suite,* which premièred on 16 April 1984, was a far more seemly role for its forty-six-year-old exponent. Technically untaxing, it also indulged Rudolf's delight in the intricate little steps that clutter his choreography, which Olivier Merlin cites as '*gargouillades, ronds de jambe, petits battements sur le cou-de-pied* in the twittery manner of ballets from the court of Louis XIV'. The king, who danced every day for twenty years, had made the art he loved a male affair, and Rudolf saw himself shown to great advantage in this royal style. Aware that performing baroque dance – the very source of classical ballet – could only enrich his knowledge, he had asked its leading specialist, historian Francine Lancelot, to create a special solo for him. Presenting her with a very specific piece of music, Bach's No. 3 Partita for cello, Rudolf did not hold back with choreographic ideas of his own. 'In the saraband, for example, he practically executed movements à la Martha Graham. Some called this heresy, but it didn't shock me. Even in Rameau's time artists like Mlle Sallé or Noverre sought in their interpretation . . . to personalize their dance.'

Lessons at the Vaganova school in *danse française* had given Rudolf a basic grounding, but Lancelot had been astonished nonetheless by the ease with which he assimilated complex *enchaînements* with an instinctive grasp of authentic gestures. She remembered the stage fright he experienced before performing the twenty-minute solo – 'a great solitude on this immense stage accompanied only by the cellist' – and yet Rudolf had seldom felt more in his element. 'He had a passion for the baroque,' says his colleague Jean-Luc Choplin. 'He loved the symmetry; the intellectual construction of Bach's music; he collected drawings of dance costumes from this period. *Bach Suite* was a *big* pleasure for him.'

'From me to me' was a favourite Nureyev expression, and although his dancers were becoming increasingly disgruntled at seeing their director performing so often, Rudolf considered this to be a much deserved reward. 'I have been thrown brutally into a surreal universe,' he complained, referring to the Paris Opéra's invasive administration system. 'He just didn't understand it,' remarks Thierry Fouquet. 'He didn't understand the rules, the bureaucracy, and in particular, the union regulations which you *have* to take seriously in order to run a company as big as this.' Maude was aware of this, too. 'Rudolf hated meetings, he hated arguments.' On the other hand Rudolf's innate belief that no one was completely loyal made it possible for him to tolerate the Opéra's infamously Byzantine intrigues. And, of course, the Paris Opéra had to tolerate Rudolf. The dancers had never before been subjected to this kind of leadership – the foul language, the attacks of rage usually culminating with a Thermos flask of tea smashed against the mirror. 'I always thought of it as a way for Rudolf to control himself,' Jean-Luc Choplin says. 'Otherwise he might have been very violent against somebody.'

In May 1984 Rudolf did in fact physically assault a colleague, fracturing the jaw of a teacher who had infuriated him. It was a scandal that made newspaper headlines: *'Quand Noureev boxe.'* At eighteen, the handsome Michel Renault, a protégé of Lifar, had been the Opéra's youngest-ever *étoile*, and in 1957, when he and Yvette Chauviré toured the Soviet Union to great acclaim, he was seen by Rudolf in *Giselle*. According to Chauviré, it was not only Renault's short tunic and *entrechat* sequence that had so impressed the young dancer. 'As Michel ran around the stage his cape flew behind him. He did this for the first time in Russia, and it's where Rudolf got the idea from.' After their performance Rudolf had been chatting to his Moscow fan Silva Lon when they both spotted the French star. 'Silva went up to him and said, "I want to introduce you to *our* Albrecht." But Michel Renault ignored her and walked away.' Rudolf never forgot. His attitude to Renault, as with Lifar, was a mixture of admiration, personal grudge and genuine dislike. Not only was Renault a disagreeable character, famously pretentious and superior, but in Rudolf's opinion he had very little skill as a classical teacher. Watching a class one day, Rudolf kept stopping it to explain the way he wanted certain steps done. 'Michel had been teaching at the Opéra for twenty years and took it very badly,' recalls Fouquet. 'He was insolent with Rudolf, and Rudolf punched him.' Marie-Suzanne Soubie remembers her boss coming back to the office after the incident 'hanging his head like a little boy' as he told her what had happened. She just laughed. 'A *lot* of people would love to have done that!' Renault sued, and won, receiving 2,500 francs in compensation. 'If I'd known it would be that little,' quipped Rudolf, 'I'd have hit him a second time.'

Just as the Opéra's new director wanted his dancers to assimilate different methods of training, so he was determined to reinspire its veteran professors. Alexandre Kalioujny, a Lifar disciple, was one. 'Sasha had always been a very good teacher for the boys, but the moment he met Rudolf he became a master,' says Elisabeth Platel. She remembers that Rudolf had given Kalioujny books to read, and that they had animated discussions in Russian during class. 'Genia Poliakov would be there too – it was a trio – and the most amazing time for all of us. We were staying after class and trying different things. Rudolf wanted us to be every day new – to be open to learn.'*

Rudolf himself could now admit to having been wrong about certain things – even his signature high demi-pointe. 'I did that, but it was mistake. Very often onstage I would lose balance – just taking a bow I would stumble, because I didn't know how to stand on my feet.' He no longer believed that Kirov dancers knew best; the Russian slow, sustained way of working was something he had come to question. Robert Denvers, another guest teacher to be invited, says that Rudolf wanted hardly any adagio movements at the barre. 'He liked the almost Balanchinian beat. He had gone to the opposite end of the spectrum.' Rudolf intended the Parisians to benefit from his own evolution as a classicist. He was aware, for example, of a lack of flow to their dancing. 'They do each isolated gesture very well, but like successive exclamation marks. The phrase is too short. It's a series of affirmations more than a dialogue.' What was missing, Rudolf said, was 'a certain respiration' – the very quality that classes with Stanley Williams had helped instil in him. Having failed to lure the master himself to the Opéra, Rudolf was delighted when Ghislaine Thesmar, who had worked with both Williams and Balanchine, eventually agreed to become a full-time *répétiteuse*. Combining America's '*fantastic* teaching' with her traditional French base as well as her experience of performing in Russia, Thesmar could give the young dancers a balance of the 'three upbringings' that Rudolf prized.

---

* When Platel danced *Swan Lake* with the Royal Ballet she had wanted to perform the Bourmeister pas de deux, but Rudolf insisted that Merle Park should teach her the English (Nicholas Sergeyev) version. 'He said, you just have to learn – *learn, learn, learn*. And when you are older you will choose.'

He said, 'Try to remember everything you learned from outside and make a melting pot; come as if from the market with lots of different things to feed everybody.' He was eager to impart these influences from outside to the Paris Opéra dancers, saying if we had that en plus, it would be phenomenal. But the old French school resented it, thinking that it was rubbish. My own husband [Pierre Lacotte] thought that it was rubbish.

Rudolf met his most formidable opponent in Claude Bessy, who was in charge of the Opéra's École de Danse.* Not only a staunch upholder of the *Concours* examination and determined to perpetuate the name of Serge Lifar, she was 'like a tigress' when it came to protecting the integrity of her school. A former *étoile* with blonde hair, long legs and curvy lines, Bessy had the glamour of a movie star (in 1960 Gene Kelly created *Pas de Dieux*, a famously raunchy duet, for the two of them), but in late middle age her position of authority had turned her into a fearsome virago. 'We had a *lot* of fights,' she recalls. 'Rudolf told me, "I am the director, I decide," and I said, "Not at the school, you don't!"' Their disputes were often very minor, such as contesting the semantics of ballet vocabulary, which Bessy claims that Rudolf had Russified. 'But he was never prepared to give way. He was always very open about culture, about painting, but with dance he resisted like a stubborn child.' Jean-Luc Choplin agrees. 'There could be no compromise. Rudolf was a dictator, a tyrant, but it was always for the good of dance.'

Like the Kirov and the New York City Ballet, the Paris Opéra rarely, if ever, auditions dancers from outside; as Balanchine put it, 'We just take from the school.' And as the school inevitably forms the company style, Rudolf knew how vital it was to win Bessy over to his ideas. Wanting graduates to arrive 'fully informed, disciplined and capable of counting rhythms', he insisted that Balanchine's method should form part of the curriculum. 'This was not a popular idea then.' Of equal value, he said, was the Bournonville technique, and he suggested that Erik be invited to teach the students, an idea Bessy agreed was

* The *directrice* had taken against Rudolf the moment they first met in 1961. When they had dinner at her apartment with Claire Motte and Pierre Lacotte, she had been irritated by his opinionated ways, and her dislike was later compounded by the fact that the one de Cuevas star whom Rudolf completely eclipsed was her future husband, Serge Golovine. 'Overnight he looked dated,' says Robert Denvers.

excellent. But in the letter she wrote confirming her approval, she took the opportunity to remind Rudolf contemptuously that the Danish system owed its very existence to Louis XIV's Académie Royale de la Danse: 'I understand that you attach great importance to the Bournonville technique, but I'm astonished that you have remarked on this to me. If you came to see what we're teaching at the school you would realize that we practise these said *enchâinements* which, by their essence, are French.'

Rudolf was just as convinced that his own dancing was a vital method of instruction. 'It is by dancing with them in rehearsals or onstage that I can bring them the most.' Certainly, by being in class every day – whatever shape he was in – Rudolf could keep his eye on how the dancers were developing. 'That's how he really managed to change the look of the company.' Not only that, but Charles Jude is certain that Rudolf would not have been able to direct if he had stopped dancing. 'He needed to dance with us, to be with us, to show us things.' And Rudolf genuinely believed that what he had lost in technique he had gained in authority and inner power. 'I admit that those who know me from fifteen or twenty years ago could be disappointed. But if someone is seeing me for the first time in *Giselle*, for example, I can still bring to him something coming from the depths of myself, an idealization of a gesture, which he will not find in someone young, no matter how high he can jump.'

He was having dinner one night with Yvette Chauviré when he suddenly asked, 'Tell me, Yvette, why is it when we have finally gained all our knowledge that we have to stop?' 'It's just something you have to accept,' she replied. 'But *why*?' 'He was really unhappy, and I said, "Rudik *duchka, c'est comme ça*."'

Acquiescence was not in Rudolf's nature and, hearing derisive whistles while taking a curtain call, he had instinctively retaliated with an obscene *bras d'honneur*. This happened for the first time after his December '83 *Don Quixote*, in which he had presented what Gerard Mannoni described as a 'tragic approximation' of his former self. 'What a shame that the greatest dancer of our epoch has not known how to . . . turn a page of his career by devoting himself to character roles if he can't live without appearing onstage.' But like Margot, who admitted being 'bored to death' as she walked about as the queen in *Sleeping Beauty*, Rudolf knew that 'the only real pleasure is dancing'. Maude felt sure that part of him yearned for someone he respected to tell him to give up. 'If Margot had said, "Yes, you must stop," or perhaps if I had told him that he should, I think Rudolf would have stopped.

But actually, I don't think anybody has a right to tell somebody to get offstage and stop living, as it were.' In fact they were both doing just the reverse. On 21 June 1984 Margot wrote telling Maude how Rudolf had asked her in New York, 'Come on, tell me, is time to stop?' 'I said I couldn't possibly tell him to stop when he gives such wonderful performances. Please give him the excerpt from Joe's letter and say that is exactly why he shouldn't retire.' Ending her own letter with an emphatic, 'Hear! Hear!' Maude encloses the panegyric from Margot's Philadelphian friend. 'Rudolf brought his magnificent *Bach Suite*. He danced in a handsome baroque costume a solo that defied description; a complete exposition of the development of the classical tradition . . . It is miraculous the way he did this, and all within the confines of one composition for unaccompanied cello.'

Having always considered *Swan Lake* to be 'a kind of indicator whether I am on form', Rudolf's next move was to mount a new production at the Opéra. It was, he said, one of the most important ballets in which to display the company from top to bottom, but mostly it was a testing ground for himself: 'For me and my body *Swan Lake* is indispensable.' And if his 1964 version had been called '*The Ballet Called Siegfried*', this, two decades later, was '*The Ballet Called Rothbart*'. The malevolent storybook sorcerer who, in most productions, does little more than transfix Odette and introduce Odile was now to be given a real role. Rudolf said, 'The whole story of this ballet comes from this one man.'

Making a dual role for himself, Rudolf reintroduces to the first act the tutor, Wolfgang, transforming him in Siegfried's mind into the scheming Rothbart. In Act 1, he is both *metteur-en-scène* and mentor, his intense friendship with the young prince sanctioned by the philosophic concept of *Eros socraticus*: the love between an adult man and a boy. In their duet Siegfried imitates and follows his tutor, literally step by step, and it is Wolfgang who introduces him to an all-male alternative world. The usual Polonaise is performed here by sixteen young men, coupling and canonically grouping themselves as Siegfried watches from the side. When the dancers disappear, he and Rothbart are left alone, and the slow solo that follows – the now classic Nureyev interpolation – takes on a completely different dimension. In his first *Swan Lake* Rudolf intimates that the hero shares Tchaikovsky's struggle to overcome his unnatural tendencies, the adagio solo plaintively expressing a similar conflict within himself. This, by contrast, is a heterosexual Siegfried. Because of his love of women, he withdraws from Wolfgang's proselytising and exposure to an implicitly gay fraternity. (The point was effectively underlined when Charles Jude performed the role with his wife, Florence Clerc, as Odette.) A reluctant puppet, Siegfried is unable to free himself of his tutor's magnetic influence and still retains his independence by pursuing Odette. In revenge Wolfgang tricks Siegfried into being seduced by Odile, and so destroys the hero's chance of happiness with his beloved.

As a concept it is both brilliant and original, and Rudolf had also rethought the choreography of Act 1. In line with Ezio Frigerio's bare box of a set he planned a near-Balanchinian abstraction of the usual story ballet. There would be nothing but classical dance, its architectural patterns forming a cohesive link with the White Act that follows. Excited to begin work, he learned a few weeks before the first rehearsal that the company refused to be part of the production. French television had just broadcast Rudolf's Viennese version and the dancers did not like it, complaining there was too much of his own choreography. Since 1960 the Opéra had included in its repertory Vladimir Bourmeister's *Swan Lake*, which had been widely acclaimed when first seen in Paris four years earlier. Subordinating dance to character and dramatic action, it retained only the second act of the original Petipa–Ivanov production, making it, in Rudolf's view, 'an ersatz *Swan Lake*'. In Paris, however, as he was discovering, there was a lot of affection for the Bourmeister. 'After twenty-five years they grow accustomed to that production and consider it was born there. They didn't want my *Swan Lake* to supplant it.' By a unanimous decision ('minus six voices') the company voted against a continuation of rehearsals.

On Friday 9 November a meeting was called for the director to present his case. Sitting on the floor and leaning against walls of the studio were 150 dancers of the Paris Opéra Ballet, whom Rudolf was forced to confront 'like a guilty man in a courtroom'. Admitting that this was not easy for him, he began reading (in French) from a statement that Thierry Fouquet had helped him prepare. The idea was not only to break the deadlock over *Swan Lake* but to respond to a number of accumulated grievances. It was, Fouquet says, 'a big turning point for us all'. While conceding to contractual points in his favour (the agreement that he could dance for another three years and perform forty times each season), Rudolf reminded the dancers of significant improvements in their working conditions since his arrival: the new studios, the increase in number of performances and opportunities to dance on tour. Denying the accusation of contempt for French schooling, he avowed his great respect for Claude Bessy but at the same time stressed the importance of incorporating Balanchine and Bournonville methods in the syllabus. 'A school must not stay fixed and must keep itself alive by nourishment from exterior influences.' He also defended his dislike of the *Concours* examination, saying that only by allowing dancers to express themselves in major roles onstage could star talent be detected.

Then there was the question of his behaviour.

> You have also reproached me with being violent and insulting. If during rehearsals or in the heat of the moment I am excessive in my language or comportment, it is only through love of the absolute and my desire to communicate to the dancers my wish that they perform to the best of their abilities. I have an impulsive temperament which leads me to do things I regret. And if it concerns the Michel Renault affair or others I am the first to reproach myself . . . What counts in our arts are the results obtained in spite of the words I have used that could injure you and for which I ask your pardon.

But although such obsequiousness was difficult for Rudolf, what he resented most of all was having to defend his competence in mounting the classics when, as far as he was concerned, he had nothing to defend. As he told the dancers, 'It is in this domain that I have acquired my reputation . . . due to my experience in the Kirov or Covent Garden and other companies in which the classical repertoire has a more solid reputation than that of the Opéra de Paris.'

The conflict was eventually resolved by 'un gentleman agreement', a compromise dividing the season's twenty-five performances of *Swan Lake* into fifteen of Nureyev's and ten of the Bourmeister. As a solution it was, as Fouquet remarks, 'a bit silly', but it did allow the company to see that Rudolf's version was far preferable to the crudely literal Bourmeister with its Soviet-style happy ending. While serious flaws remain (the misplaced bravura solos for Siegfried in Act 2 and Rothbart in Act 3, and a perversely zany, Busby Berkeley distortion of the elegiac Act 4), there is more craftsmanship in this production than in anything else Rudolf ever did.

This time, with the exception of Charles Jude, Rudolf had been let down by even his new protégés, and yet he could not help admiring the dancers for standing up to him. 'Among the youngest there are strongly individual elements . . . They are attention-seekers and they create a spirit of competition which is excellent for a ballet company.' Elisabeth Platel agrees. 'We are Latin by temperament, we like to argue, and Rudolf was not disappointed when we were fighting with him.' Guests from outside, however, felt otherwise. The young English choreographer David Bintley, invited by Rudolf, says he spent the first week in an office drinking tea because nobody turned up for his rehearsals. 'It was the most frustrating time of my life. And when I did get to work with the dancers I found nothing but blank faces or terrible conceit. There was such unwillingness to any kind of change – they'd just shrug and walk away. I thought it must be because they didn't like me, but then I'd watch other rehearsals – Rudi van Dantzig's, for example – and it was exactly the same.'

Both choreographers left Paris without completing their ballets, van Dantzig writing to Rudolf to complain that he had 'felt cheated and not taken seriously at all'.* Lynn Seymour, who came to assist with rehearsals, was someone else who hated every minute of working at the Opéra. 'I found the men were slightly more receptive than the women, who were full of preconceived notions and refused to break any old habits. They're fabulous dancers, but they're brainwashed from pretty early on into a particular manner – the Parisian Allure, which makes me want to vomit.' Rudolf claimed there was little he could do: 'I can't be a policeman. There's no point putting them in straitjackets: they should become aware.' His frequent absences from Paris only exacerbated disciplinary problems. 'Dancers are very spoiled, greedy children, and when he left, it always created an emptiness,' Thesmar remarked, and Monique Loudières, interviewed in 1986, said much the same. 'He has no time when he performs to counsel people, and we need that because he's fantastic when he teaches.'

'Why don't you smile at your dancers when we meet them in the passage?' Maude once asked Rudolf. 'Because they don't smile at me,' he replied. 'I said, "That's because they're nervous, and if you smiled at them they'd eat out of your hand."' But communication was at an impasse. 'You reproach me with not talking to you, but I can tell you that you are not coming to talk to me,' he told the dancers during the *Swan Lake* meeting, and yet Rudolf did not make it easy for them. As Sylvie Guillem put it, 'He wanted to go towards people but at the same time he couldn't allow himself to do it because he was shy. Yet he didn't seem to be shy.' And when he was not being reticent, Rudolf was exploding, astounding Murray Louis by the force of his fury. 'I was in Paris watching rehearsals and saw him absolutely torture young people.' To 'go and repair' Rudolf relied on his two lieutenants: the

---

* When Rudi decided to return to Paris, Rudolf greeted him with a bear hug of gratitude, and *No Man's Land* was premièred at the Opéra on 16 April 1984.

diplomatic Claire Motte and Genia Poliakov, who was also wonderful at placating dancers Rudolf had upset. 'With Genia, nobody felt insulted. Everybody felt good.'

Poliakov was also able to bring out the best in Rudolf, considering him to be 'a lamb – very tender, very kind'. Soon to be diagnosed *séropositif* himself, Poliakov shared Rudolf's guilt about his corruption by the amoral West – what a friend describes as 'this bitterness Genia felt for sex without love' – but their real complicity was dance. Jean-Luc Choplin watched them at quai Voltaire animatedly 'speaking with their hands' as they studied old-fashioned laser discs of Russian ballets. 'Rudolf was so happy to have someone from his country with him in Paris, someone he could trust in terms of taste.' It was also 'a gentle' Rudolf that Marie-Suzanne Soubie saw, her serene, Maude-like manner enlivened by the same unshockability and sense of fun. At home she found herself repeating Rudolf's witticisms and remarks, leaving out definite articles, Russian-style, and adopting his favourite expletives. 'My daughter reprimanded me one day; she said, "*Maman, maintenant tu parles comme God!* [their nickname for him]".'

Marie-Suzanne claims that the five years she worked with Rudolf were the happiest of her life, but for Douce, this Paris Opéra period was '*terrible*. Absolutely terrible.' Playing one off against the other, Rudolf relished his role of manipulator, telling Douce, 'You must help my secretary,' and assuring Marie-Suzanne, 'Don't think you have to do what Douce asks.' Having been telephoned by Rudolf to say what time his flight arrived, Douce would drive to the airport, only to see 'Marie-Suzanne hiding in a telephone kiosk'. One day he arrived at the office saying, 'We're divorced. Douce was driving me and nagging so much that I left the car and walked.' It was anxiety to please that led Douce to make dramas out of trivialities. 'If Rudolf wanted osso buco for dinner and the butchers didn't have it, Douce would turn it into a tragedy,' recalls Gloria Venturi. 'A tragedy over a piece of meat!' Marie-Suzanne, on the other hand, was blessed with what one observer called 'a rare quality of *lightness*. Too many heavy people weighed down Rudolf's life, and Marie-Suzanne was light. She was fun.'

Attempting to 'dethrone Douce', Rudolf had asked Marie-Suzanne to arrange his dinner parties, but she refused, saying that it was not her role. 'I had a husband, a daughter . . . My life was with them, not with Rudolf.' And so, 'with no respect, thanks or praise', Douce continued to run quai Voltaire, poaching a cook-manservant, Manuel Ortega, from the Chilean Embassy, and volunteering her own services as '*une bonne à tout faire*'. She would invite guests such as Boris Kochno or director Patrice Chéreau, whose company Rudolf always enjoyed, and she often helped Manuel to prepare the food. Expected to note down her expenses in order to be reimbursed by Gorlinsky, Douce itemized everything from a box of tissues to a lemon, but presenting Rudolf with a bill to sign invariably triggered a row. 'How do I know the cost of a kilo of carrots?' he demanded one day. 'Come with me to the market, and you'll find out,' she said with a laugh, only to be warned, 'You are insulting me!' And yet Douce's loyalty never wavered. Whether driving to quai Voltaire every morning to wake Rudolf at nine and take him to class, or arranging for a pair of tights he had left behind to be flown to Seoul by a representative from Korean Airlines, she was, as Leslie Caron says, the best friend he could have had. 'She had this quality of energizing and supporting you and just being there.' But it was precisely Douce's omnipresence that Rudolf resented. 'You *strangle* me,' he would fume. 'The only place I don't see you is in my bath.' As Ghislaine Thesmar says, Rudolf expected his women to keep a certain distance, and Douce could never do that. 'She overdid things and lost his respect. She was running around like a little dog, doing things before he asked, so he just walked all over her. Douce was not very intelligent, but she had a big heart, existing entirely in order to care for other people. She needed to devote herself to someone; she couldn't live for herself. She was a waste of a great mother.'

It was in the spring of 1985 that Douce began to suspect that there was something she was not being told, 'something Soubie was hiding'. Then she received a telephone call from a friend telling her that Rudolf had been spotted at an AIDS institute. 'I said, "No, it's not possible – *I*, of all people, would know."' But she began noticing the way Rudolf was getting more and more tired, and one morning an envelope arrived returning a social security application she had made on his behalf. 'The letter said, "We are sorry we are unable to process this because it is not in Mr Nureyev's name." Rudolf had been using a different name at the institute, but he still wanted to get his medical reimbursements!' Now that she had written proof, Douce went to La Pitié and asked to see Willy Rozenbaum, but the hospital staff, assuming she was a journalist, threw her out. The more anxious Douce became about Rudolf's health, the more he detached himself, fending off her attempts to win his confidence with increasing outbursts of anger. Friends who were fond of them both begged him to be kinder, and Gloria Venturi urged Douce, 'For once in your life say something really tough. But she was too afraid. She was afraid he'd tell her to go away.' Margot was also concerned. On a visit to Paris she had been driven by Douce to the airport at 6.30 in the morning and wrote telling Maude about it. '[Douce] had not read an interview with Rudolf in which he said how lucky he was to have a friend who looked after everything for him . . . It cheered her up a bit, but I find her saddened.'

It was during this trip that Rudolf brought his twenty-year-old protégée to her Palais Garnier box to meet Margot. It had been a long time since the Paris Opéra Ballet had produced an international star, but Rudolf knew that Sylvie Guillem had that quality and wanted Margot's blessing. Until the age of eleven, when she decided she would rather be a dancer, Guillem had trained as a gymnast, an Olympic hopeful. At the Opéra's school she was 'this little girl – like nothing you've ever seen before', and in the company, as just another corps de ballet swan, she had dazzled Rudolf with her singularity. Like an example of futuristic architecture, the curve of her insteps converging in perfect linear perspective with the concave planes of her hyperextended legs, Guillem redefined the image of a ballerina. Not only did her extraordinary flexibility liberate the confinements of the human frame, but what she presents when she dances is a miracle of spatial harmony and abstract form. Possessing what Rudolf saw as '*un talent fou*', Guillem was, at the same time, completely lacking in maturity, turning into an angry child if she did not get her way. They clashed constantly, 'screaming at each other like wildcats', and in retrospect, Guillem wishes their encounter had come several years later. 'I was too young. I had to make my own mistakes. He couldn't talk. I couldn't talk. We just communicated by our instinct. So that was a bit wild, sometimes. Because he was not a very patient speaker and I was not a very patient listener, it couldn't work. We went directly to the point without all the talking before.'

Expecting her to absorb and follow everything he wanted to pass on, Rudolf complained that the ballerina was not attentive enough. 'Rudolf wanted to *keep* her, in a sense,' says Jean-Luc Choplin. 'To be really a Pygmalion to her. But Sylvie was too rebellious.' Despite her young age, she had strong ideas of her own, convinced that there was little Rudolf could teach her about dancing or interpretation. It was too late for him to impress her with his technical prowess, and when he performed she saw not the character he was portraying but Rudolf himself. What she did learn from his example, however, was how to conduct her life.

I learned a way of being. I saw someone fighting for everything, fighting for his opinions, fighting for other people, for something that was
true for him . . . So I saw that. I saw someone very strong, very lonely,
and learned a lot from his behaviour . . . I had admiration for him that
was not for the same reasons as the others. My admiration was from a
woman to a man. It was not the Director, the Choreographer. It was
just the man. Because he was an exceptional man.

It was the maverick in Sylvie that Rudolf loved, and to him she was
'an untamed young animal and *une femme provocante* at the same time'.
Tall, with green eyes – 'part Garbo, part gamine' – she was not
the feminine mirror image that had attracted him to women such as
Talitha – it was Sylvie's personality that matched his own. He said more
than once that he would like to have married her, telling one friend, 'I'd
switch back. I'd switch back for Sylvie.' To formalize his esteem,
Rudolf allowed the young ballerina to make Paris Opéra history by
promoting her twice in the space of a few days. On 22 December 1984,
after the corps de ballet's annual *Concours* examination, Guillem was
elected *première danseuse*, and on the twenty-ninth, after a performance
of the Nureyev *Swan Lake*, Rudolf came onstage to announce to the
audience that he was making her an *étoile*. 'That,' he told a *Paris-Match*
journalist, 'is my *raison d'être*.'

'Diaghilev Pygmalion' was the name of the character he invented
for himself in *Cinderella*, the ballet he was soon to create as a special
vehicle for Guillem. But it also encapsulated his bond with his other
teenage discoveries: Laurent Hilaire, Manuel Legris, Elisabeth Maurin
and Isabelle Guérin, known as the '*Chou-chou de Noureev*'. Rudolf
would take the coterie with him to perform galas abroad or New York
seasons of Nureyev and Friends, disregarding the missed Opéra
rehearsals or the growing resentment of the dancers he had left
behind. 'Going out with the boss implies certain favouritism,' says
Thierry Fouquet. 'Rudolf's group earned a lot of money and prestige.'
Inevitably there were casualties. The director's relegation of Patrick
Dupond, the most popular ballet star in France, to the position of
guest artist was seen to be 'a rare lapse in his otherwise sound business
sense'. To Rudolf, however, Dupond was a crowd-pleasing *demi-
caractère* dancer completely lacking in classical finesse. 'Patrick was *un
voyou, très mal élevé*,' says Hélène Traïlene. 'He had a special kind of
force, youthfulness and an aura that audiences loved. He would do
twelve pirouettes, but it was dirty dancing – *un peu style Lifar à son
époque*.' Hilaire and Legris, on the other hand, were near-clones of the

young Nureyev. As the Royal Ballet's Wayne Eagling observed, 'You can see Rudolf onstage through them: the way they walk, their mannerisms, the way they take a fifth position or present themselves. His legacy goes on through those people that he was teaching . . . You see a bit of Rudolf in all of them.'

Wanting the dancers to acquire the refinement of *le style anglais*, Rudolf planned an Ashton evening at the Opéra, but the choreographer refused to allow any of his ballets to be staged. The dismally received 1954 Sadler's Wells tour had left bitter memories. Ashton's work had been described by Parisian critics as 'somewhat unmusical', the movements of the shepherds in *Daphnis and Chloe* compared to 'Swedish gymnastic exercises', their costumes to 'tennis shirts with engineers' trousers'.* 'Freddie had a horror of the Paris Opéra,' says Alexander Grant. 'He thought the French were so snooty about English taste.' It's no coincidence that Ashton's reply to Rudolf – 'Maybe not this year . . . next year' – was an exact echo of Rudolf's own words to him. 'I'd tell Fred, "Not *this* year . . . But next year."' With the wisdom of hindsight, Rudolf now regretted the fact that he had not allowed Ashton to rehearse him in the classics when he first came to London: 'I spurned this relationship . . . This drove us apart.' But he did not realize the extent to which Ashton was a self-confessed 'old elephant. I never forget.' Rudolf begged Sylvie Guillem to visit the choreographer in the hope that he would allow the Opéra to stage his *Ondine*: '*Please* go and see Sir Fred . . . You go and smile.' 'With my little English, I try, I try,' recalled the ballerina, but the result was, in Rudolf's words, 'No going.'†

Antony Tudor was also proving difficult to woo. Rudolf had told the choreographer when he was in New York how much he would love to mount his masterpiece *Lilac Garden* at the Opéra, but the reclusive Tudor 'soft-pedalled [his] response'. To their mutual friend Maude, Tudor explained that he did not know the company, and was concerned that the dancers would not grasp the subtlety their roles required. '[Rudolf] should know well that my approach to ballet has nothing of the assembly line . . . for I have always approached and

---

* Rudolf suspected that Lifar, who had had no success in England or America, was behind it. 'The French dance critics were all great friends of his.'

† Alexander Grant was with Ashton when Rudolf came to ask if he could stage *La fille mal gardée*. 'Freddie didn't say anything, and Rudolf took that to mean he'd agreed. He announced it in the press, Freddie heard about this and went crazy. He prevented Rudolf from doing it and Rudolf had to get another version (by Joseph Lazzini).'

choreographed my works as though they were plays.' Promised a whole evening at the more intimate Opéra Comique, however, Tudor was eventually persuaded, telling Maude, 'The talk had gone on for so long that there comes a time. He is used to getting what he wants, and finally he may be in a work by the choreographer who eluded him. Till now.'*

Maude, who had danced in the original productions of two of the three ballets (*Lilac Garden* and *Dark Elegies*), went to Paris for the Tudor homage, staying at quai Voltaire. Rudolf would have liked her to come much more often, and said that her visits were never long enough. 'You bring light,' he told her. 'You make people calm.' But because he was so busy she saw very little of him, and felt a burden to the friends he had asked to take care of her – Douce most of all. 'In the evening she would fetch me and sit with me . . . She looked after me as much as she looked after Rudolf.' After a few days Maude would find herself longing to be back in Victoria Road, where she felt closer to Nigel, something Rudolf understood only too well. At a New Year's Eve dinner at quai Voltaire, while the other guests were chatting and waiting for the moment of midnight, he looked across at Maude and said quietly, 'We need Nigel here, don't we?' 'Nothing escaped him. He was so caring . . . He used to watch and at about half-past twelve, he'd say, "Maude, you're tired." Somebody told him that twelve o'clock was the latest he should ring me after Nigel died . . . At the time, I wasn't sleeping very well and would have loved him to ring me up at two in the morning. But he wouldn't because he'd been told that I couldn't get back to sleep.'

Now in her late seventies, her eyesight and hearing slowly deteriorating, Maude did not want Rudolf worrying about her when it was *he* who was causing concern. In a letter to Wallace written on 8 March 1985, she urged him to get in touch with Rudolf, saying how much he now needed the support of old friends.

It's a lonely job running a huge company . . . and when he has finished his long days in the theatre (no rests in the afternoon like he used to have) and he gets home, often at 8 o'clock or later, he doesn't want

---

* Rudolf was to have danced the Buddha in *Shadowplay*, but presumably because of Tudor's misgivings the idea was dropped. 'God knows what they are going to do with *Shadowplay* and Buddha's countenance of serenity if Rudolf does it with all his face contortions,' the choreographer told Maude. 'So, if I've always been disregarded by France, this will not be much worse.'

anything except to relax by the TV or play Bach on his harpsichord, and go to bed where he doesn't sleep well. As ever. Then of course, because what he still wants to do more than anything else in the world is to dance himself, he dashes off all over Europe for a couple of nights, either to Vienna, Venice, all over Italy, Berlin, and last week even 2 nights in Stratford on Avon. He lives on planes now, more than ever, and never seems to rest at all. Only a giant could stand the pressure, and he wonders why he is tired. At the moment he is also having – for 15 consecutive days – to go to the hospital for 3 hours every day to have some sort of vaccine, I think, put into his blood, and that sometimes means getting up at 6 or seven to go to the hospital in order to fit everything in. For instance, last Sunday he left the house at 7 a.m., went and had his session at the hospital, then caught a plane to Modena in Italy, where he did a matinee and evening perf with a small group from the Opéra, dancing himself in almost every ballet (Apollo, Wayfarer etc). Then another plane at 7 a.m. the next morning, back to hospital for next treatment, then straight back to the Opéra for rehearsal until about 8 o'clock again.

The treatment Rudolf was undergoing was transfusions of HPA23 (antimoniotungstate), a compound known to inhibit virus replication. In the 23 February 1985 issue of the Lancet, a letter to the editor appeared signed by nine of France's AIDS pioneers – Willy Rozenbaum and Luc Montagnier among them. It describes how four patients, three of whom had been diagnosed with AIDS in May 1984, had started HPA23 in July and were all alive a year later. The treatment had had no significant effect on their immunodeficiency but had nonetheless reduced LAV replication, and one patient showed no further deterioration in his previously rapidly progressive Kaposi's sarcoma. As this was the first demonstration of inhibition of the growth of LAV, the doctors had been encouraged to try HPA23 in eleven more patients.

Willy Rozenbaum had first heard about the drug in April 1983 and seized the chance of giving his AIDS patients HPA23, even though it could not be guaranteed to work. 'Sometimes faced with the moral distress of the patient and the fear of his entourage, we were carried away by anger, and for my part, I would have been ready to prescribe virtually any tentative treatment . . . People who are sick with SIDA truly have nothing to lose.' He arranged for Rudolf to come to La Pitié three times a week for slow infusions. Marie-Suzanne drove him there at seven in the morning and sat quietly by his hospital bed for the three hours the treatment took. Five months later the movie actor Rock Hudson flew to Paris to begin a course of HPA23, too (it was administered by Dominique Dormont, another signatory of the *Lancet* letter). After the fourth week, Hudson, who had stopped losing weight, was convinced that the drug had worked. 'I don't have AIDS,' he exclaimed elatedly. 'I've licked it!' Rudolf, however, was more circumspect. To Charles Jude, who knew he was having hospital treatment but not what it was for, Rudolf confided, 'If it works, I'm alive, if not . . .' And he shrugged.

Conserving energy for his work, Rudolf, as Maude observed, had become very reclusive. 'I'm not like I used to be – *wind machine*! I find that I can concentrate and read without this constant dialogue with the world outside.' Paris friends such as Jacques Loyau found him 'more tranquil and less amusing' since he had been running the Opéra. 'The rue Dauphine days were over.' There would always be a new boy around, and during this period it was Stephen Sherriff, a Royal Ballet dancer now working in the Netherlands, who began an affair with Rudolf during the making of *The Tempest* and often came to Paris by train to see him. Stephen never had any money, wore hippyish clothes and had long tousled hair. Rudolf called him the Gypsy, clearly appreciating his affectionate, uncomplicated nature. The sexual side of things was very minor, Stephen says, 'more like a relief for him', and although they sometimes went out to dinner, Rudolf preferred to spend evenings at home, trying to cook scrambled eggs. Mostly, though, he chose to be alone. 'With age you learn to live with yourself. You finally accept this marriage and you find your own company great.' His regular *confident de nuit* was now his Ruckers, the Stradivarius of harpsichords, which he had positioned overlooking the Seine. In another room an organ – 'the rival clavichord' – occupied one entire wall. 'I can play for hours in a row on one or the other instrument, according to my mood.' Invariably it was Bach in any form, the music more therapeutic to Rudolf than any medication. 'It makes me feel that life is all right, that I can go and do it.'

18 DANCING WITH
THE DEVIL

In the spring of 1985, while mounting a revival of his *Romeo and Juliet* at the Palais de Congrès, Rudolf came down with pneumonia. He was dancing the part of Mercutio and so troubled by an incessant cough that just before the point at which he mimes drinking from a goblet, he would stand near the wings so that Marie-Suzanne could fill the cup with tea or bouillon. 'And then I'd run around to another wing to fill it again.' Rudolf had suffered from problems with his lungs since childhood (and Michel Canesi had confirmed that this was not the HIV-related *pneumocystis carinii*), but even so he had convinced himself that his illness was fatal. 'You know I'm dying,' he said to Jimmy Douglas one night during dinner. 'It can't be possible,' protested Douglas, but he, too, suspected the worst.

Of the many ballet versions of *Romeo and Juliet*, only Rudolf's is so permeated by death and disease. Drawing on Boccaccio's Prologue to the *Decameron*, it begins with a tumbril of dead bodies pulled across the stage, all victims of the Black Death, which swept Italy at the time the story is set. We see Romeo's sudden shudder when the beggar to whom he has tossed a coin rolls over dead – an indication of the fear of contagion that is the direct cause of *Romeo and Juliet*'s tragic conclusion. 'The infectious pestilence' was real enough to Shakespeare himself, who as an infant escaped a major epidemic in Stratford-upon-Avon, and to Rudolf, three centuries later, it was again a chillingly contemporary issue. (Petrarch's words in a letter to a friend could just as well be from Edmund White's *Farewell Symphony*: 'There was a crowd of us, now we are almost alone . . . One minute someone hears that another has gone, the next he is following in his footsteps.') It was as if this *Romeo and Juliet* were one of Rudolf's 'premonition dreams', tauntingly playing out his own battle with mortality. Watching his Mercutio from the wings, Franck Raoul-Duval remembers the dancer's hoarse whisper as he passed by, 'I'm dying, I'm dying, I'm dying.'

Rumours about the ailing Rudolf had begun ricocheting around the world. There was talk among Royal Ballet dancers that he was so weak he needed a wheelchair waiting in the wings to transport him back to the dressing room. In New York, Richard Buckle, who was staying at the Dakota apartment, took it upon himself to inform Robert Tracy, 'who appears to know nothing', about Rudolf's pneumonia, which was now compounded by hepatitis. In a diary entry dated 15 May 1985, the critic recorded their subsequent exchange:

Robert: How's the morbid one?

RB: How's the sordid one?

Robert: I'm amazed that someone with your intelligence should have such a morbid side.

RB: I'm not morbid, just realistic, and I wanted to tell you –

Robert (yelling): I don't want to hear! I don't want to hear! Asshole! Asshole!

RB (yelling louder): Don't try to shout me down. I've just been told that Ballet Theatre is rife with rumours about Rudolf's illness. You'd better be prepared to deal with the press. The building may be surrounded.

Robert: Asshole! Asshole!

Hearing about this, Rudolf instructed Robert to 'throw [Buckle] out of the house', but there was no stopping the speculation. The *New York Times*'s Anna Kisselgoff asked Jean-Luc Choplin outright whether the pneumonia was caused by AIDS ('I said I didn't think it was'); and when Robert Gable, Rudolf's great New York fan, next saw the dancer he rushed over to enquire about his health. 'Rudolf said, "I'm OK, Bob." It was a wonderful denial, and it put me to rest. The implication was, "Tell the others there's nothing to worry about." I did. And we believed it.' But Rudolf's nightmare – the fear, in Roland Petit's words, 'of no longer dancing and of being sidelined if the ballet world learned that he had signed a pact with the devil' – threatened to become a reality. Anxious letters were arriving daily. 'I heard a terrible rumour about your health,' wrote John Lanchbery from Australia, and Antony Tudor, who had learned from Maude about Rudolf's 'miserable pneumonia', begged him to take care of himself. 'You have proven yourself irreplaceable in your dance career, and already with your job at the Paris Opéra you will have proved again that as Directeur, you are also irreplaceable . . . This may seem a dumb letter but too many people are of a like mind with me. We owe you too much.'

Erik's friend Arlette Castagnier had called him in Toronto to say that Rudolf had been spotted at an AIDS hospital. 'I must go to him!' cried Erik, but when he rang to announce his arrival in Paris, Rudolf sounded surprised, and asked whether it was because he wanted to see Tudor's *Lilac Garden*. 'Can you believe it?' Erik exclaimed to Arlette. 'I'm coming especially to see him and he tells me that!' But although he did not succeed in getting Rudolf to admit the truth, Erik, who had been 'heartbroken to watch what Rudolf was doing to his career', decided to use his friend's ill health as an opportunity to convince him to stop performing. 'I am sure your problem with your lungs could be solved with a long rest from the company and the dancing. I got very worried when I heard you were doing a season in London again dancing every night. I know how much being on the stage means to you and how little you seem to care about your life and now your health.'

Upset by the rumours, Margot had arrived in Paris without alerting Rudolf, so that he couldn't put up a brave front. After reassuring herself that everything was fine, that it was nothing more than a cold, she returned to Panama, telling Maude that Rudolf was right to go ahead with his scheduled performances of *Giselle*. 'I know just how he would feel. It's better to get back on the stage and keep going.' But as the old Shaker hymn goes, 'It's hard to dance with the Devil on your back,' and Rudolf was forced to cancel. As a special favour, Baryshnikov flew in to replace him, and, alarmed by Rudolf's deterioration, called Jeannette Etheredge as soon as he got back to New York. 'Misha told me, "He's really sick. If you're any kind of friend, you should pay attention."' So Jeannette joined Rudolf in Cleveland, where he was taking a group of Paris Opéra dancers on a short tour of the States. 'I kept looking for signs that he wasn't well, but he didn't seem very different to me. I'd heard about night sweats and AIDS, and looked at his sheets, but I thought, "Well he's always slept like that – all bundled up." He just looked a little thin and was coughing a lot, but then he had pneumonia.'

Rudolf had asked Maude if she would come to Paris and stay with him. 'He wanted me to be with him because he was feeling so terrible.' But he also wanted to break the news to her himself. She had been badly shocked by the rumours, telling Marie-Suzanne, 'It's impossible – it's only gossip!' But when Rudolf asked her calmly one day, 'Maude, you know what I have in my blood?' she just answered, 'Yes.' 'And he never mentioned it again.'

Rudolf was working at the time on a new ballet based on Henry James's *Washington Square*, and to fill Nigel's role in helping with the libretto had turned to the screenwriter Jean-Claude Carrière. An integral part of Peter Brook's Paris team, Carrière was becoming increasingly interested in the theatre, and had first encountered

Rudolf when the Bouffes du Nord Theatre opened. 'I saw him coming alone. He was the very first one to enter and buy a ticket – he was that kind of a man.' They had since become friends, and dined on several occasions at each other's homes. Rudolf had encouraged conversations about French writers, particularly Proust, which he admitted had been difficult for him to understand. 'Finally, he read it in Russian.' With *Washington Square* Rudolf asked Carrière to guide him in choosing important moments, even though he was bursting with ideas of his own – few of which had any relevance to the novel. 'One of the things that preoccupied him most was the notion of guilt; guilt towards whom you don't remember.' This would manifest itself in the way the heroine's father, Doctor Sloper (performed by Rudolf), appears to be punishing himself for the loss of his wife. It is an excuse for a tortured, Grahamesque solo, and another example of Rudolf wanting to explain what has taken place before the actual story begins.

While developing the ballet he also spent a lot of time with Charles Jude, whom he had chosen for the role of Morris Townshend, Catherine's fortune-hunting suitor. Although the dancer was known to be somewhat mercenary himself – 'Charles loves money – he has dollar signs for eyes' – it is unlikely that Rudolf was typecasting, as Jude says they both forgot the story while collaborating on the ballet. He remembers their complicity as they worked on a jazzy, Astaire-inspired sequence for Townshend and the Doctor, the two repeatedly exchanging places as they danced up and down a staircase. 'We were like a father and son – and finally the son becomes the father of the man.' Jude also maintains that Rudolf intended *Washington Square* to represent the two countries in which he spent the most time – his reclusive Paris life versus the social clamour and dollar-driven culture of New York. The result was like the creation of two different ballets: the intimate, genteel world of James's novel contrasted with phantasmagoric outdoor parade scenes of nineteenth-century Americana. And for this fantastic side, what Rudolf called 'the freedom and cacophony of the street', he chose the marching bands of Charles Ives: 'Ives's father was manager of a band and with son they would experiment: one orchestra marching towards square in one key; opposite would be another orchestra marching in another key and different rhythm. And they would clash. And [Ives] had that in his music.'

He asked the Ives specialist Michael Tilson Thomas to be musical director and make a selection of the composer's pieces. Rudolf's own idea was to use the Ives's chamber music for the interior scenes 'as if Dr Sloper were playing', but later claimed that Tilson Thomas objected to not conducting throughout. Moreover, when Rudolf took it upon himself to change the order of the numbers, 'he got very upset and walked out'. It is doubtful, however, whether even the atmospheric musical contrast Rudolf wanted could have made a success of *Washington Square*. Ives's style, as he himself admitted, is 'not at all Henry James', since its brassy populism is completely at odds with the psychological subtlety of the book, and the ballet itself is a bewildering mess. Ten minutes in, there is still no narrative, just one opportunity after another for Rudolf to dance, the audience given no clue as to the identity of the three different women he partners (dead wife, daughter, sister). His inspiration for the enigmatic emotional drama was Antony Tudor, whose work he had the chance to study while mounting the Opéra's homage. A master at telling a story or specifying character through gesture, Tudor achieves his effect by anchoring one's attention to the situation in hand, whereas Rudolf is constantly distracting the eye. And although the ensembles in the square's Fourth of July parade are artfully staged in contrapuntal rhythms and criss-crossing blocs, the mood taking on an atonal edge of hysteria, the crowd action is never constructively fused with the family drama. Croce's dismissal of Rudolf as 'a choreographer of staggering incompetence' is borne out in the interior scenes by weak love duets and a truly awful, leg-clutching 'comic' number – an exchange between Morris and the Aunt – to the melody of 'God Save the Queen'. And yet, the ballet has its redeeming moments. One arrestingly telling scene is the pas de deux, during which Morris courts Catherine on a sofa while, in the background, dancing to a different tempo, is the disturbed, fluttery presence of the Doctor and his sister. The way Catherine keeps recoiling from her suitor's touch in a slow, stylized contortion instantly reveals the character in the novel: a plain, gauche girl unable to cope with the role of romantic heroine. It is the kind of psychological imagery that came so easily to Tudor, and proves that there are isolated instances when Rudolf, too, was capable of making dance more eloquent than words.

For the Parisians, however, *Washington Square*, with its abstruse story and razzmatazz of cowboys, soldiers, wildcatters, pioneer women, black-faced minstrels, Ku Klux Klan figures and Statue of Liberty chorus girls was mystifying to an almost offensive degree. Few were familiar with the novel or the music, and only half the audience could see what was going on. Rudolf had planned the set to move with the action like a Steadycam, but had not managed to convey this to the designer, who constructed a cumbersome edifice depicting both the

Square and the house, whose wall was blocking many people's view. There was a near riot in the auditorium with boos and catcalls – 'like the first night of the *Rite of Spring*' – and Rudolf, who had created this ballet against all odds, was devastated by the response. He had been going every day to the hospital 'to have this stuff taken out of his lungs', and then working for seven-hour stretches. By the time it was all over he appeared to be in a kind of daze, and when Monica Mason, who had mounted MacMillan's *Song of the Earth* for the same programme, came onstage to say goodbye, he hardly registered that she was there. 'It had been years since I'd seen Rudolf, and I was really quite shocked by how thin and unwell he was. I remember wondering whether I'd ever see him again.'

But Rudolf was allowing himself no respite. In September and October, taking Maude and Marie-Suzanne with him, he travelled to China and Japan to stage his *Don Quixote*. He had grown fond of Dai Ailian, the director of Beijing's Central Ballet, a remarkable woman whom he called his 'Chinese mother'. Regarded as a National Living Treasure, Dai Ailian was almost single-handedly responsible for establishing China's ballet tradition, and adored Rudolf for his generosity towards her dancers. 'You are a good friend for what you have done for us,' she wrote in one of her many letters. 'You have a home in Beijing whenever you want to come.' But if Rudolf had agreed to mount and perform the ballet for a fraction of his usual fee, it was largely due to the rare opportunity to be onstage with a company that was glad to have him. It was the same with Japan's Matzuama Ballet, which, in turn, benefited hugely from its Nureyev association (it had been invited to join his Friends season at the London Coliseum in July). In addition to a stint at the Edinburgh Festival and a week of performances in Manchester, he had spent the summer touring a number of towns in Italy, in a season arranged by his masseur, Luigi Pignotti, who had recently become an impresario. Needless to say, Luigi's small-budget tours had upset Sandor Gorlinsky, who told Rudolf that this was not the kind of work a great star should be doing. 'But it was a time Rudolf would have gone anywhere,' says Tessa Kennedy. 'He just wanted to dance. Period.'

Rudolf's answer to what he called the Hiroshima Question – the question of when he was going to give up – was always the same: 'I'll stop dancing when people stop coming to see me.' For many of his fans and colleagues there were still 'incredible moments of what it used to be', the kind of 'incisive strokes' that Edwin Denby described on seeing the fading Tamara Toumanova perform. Despite the 'careless feet, limp wormy arms, brutally deformed phrasings', she had so much vitality 'that she made everyone else look as if they merely crept or scuttled about her'. The ballerina Marie-Christine Mouis felt much the same about Rudolf during a performance of *Raymonda*. 'These *beautiful* young dancers were coming forward to bow, but the only person you could see was Rudolf: the energy he gave off was phenomenal.' And yet instead of modulating his performance to compensate for his age and failing technique (as Baryshnikov was soon to do), Rudolf continued trying to execute all the bravura steps he had danced in his youth. 'He's incredibly honest in his endeavour not to fake things,' said Wayne Eagling. 'You never see Rudolf trying to fudge the difficult bits. The dishonest thing is within himself: he thinks he gets away with it.'

Rudolf, however, had no illusions about how he looked onstage. He would joke about his '*arabesque canapé*', referring to his horizontal, sagging back. Seeing Clara Saint after a gap of many years, he said, 'If you want to see *un vieux con* onstage, come and see me perform!' Dance was, as Violette Verdy realized, therapy he could not do without. 'With the sweat comes much more than just mineral salts: a great deal of anger comes out, a great deal of nonsense and negativity – you burn all that when you do a good barre. My guess is that he'll do a barre until he cannot walk any more.' And it was dance alone that could distract Rudolf from his condition. 'I think that he was frightened at first,' said Michel Canesi. 'And then afterwards, seeing that things were going well, that he could dance and choreograph, he forgot his illness a little bit.'

As such an intense schedule of performances made it impossible for Rudolf to continue HPA23 treatment at La Pitié-Salpêtrière, Canesi had volunteered to leave his patients with a replacement and go on the road with him. This meant that he could not only administer the daily injections but also keep an eye on falling platelet counts, which was the main side effect of the drug. There were those, Douce in particular, who questioned Canesi's competence in the field of AIDS, but at no point did Rudolf lose faith in his doctor. It was a time when all sorts of theories were emerging about possible cures, from injections of ozone to a blood-cleansing procedure known as plasmapheresis, but Rudolf ignored them. For him having Canesi by his side was a way of deflecting the issue. 'It was as if he was saying, "I'm handing this problem over to you. You deal with it because I have work to do."'

In November 1985 they both went on tour with the Nancy Ballet, starting off in Valencia and travelling to Florence and Germany. To the company, Michel was not Rudolf's doctor but a young dermatologist, probably a boyfriend, who clearly relished being part of a star's entourage. 'I never had sex with Rudolf, though there was a moment when it could have happened. I wasn't attracted to him, and anyway, I wanted to keep a certain distance.' It was an exhilarating experience nonetheless – 'like travelling with the Beatles' – and Canesi admits being grateful for the chance it gave him to escape from his Paris practice. 'Those were the years of horror. I was overwhelmed with AIDS patients in my office, and near to burnout. It was really dreadful; half of my patients were *séropositif*. They'd come and show me what they had on their skin, and I knew they had AIDS and were going to die in a few months. There was also the shame attached – bisexual men passing it on to their wives – and I found myself having to enter the most secret parts of peoples' lives.'

In France it was only in 1985 that people were becoming aware of the gravity of AIDS, and yet there was still no real sense of panic. This was the year the New York bathhouses were closed down by the city, but in Paris business at gay saunas appeared unchanged, and the *quais* – especially between the Pont Neuf and the Tuileries – remained as popular as ever for late-night cruising. Advertisements for condoms were banned, and doctors were divided about whether or not it was their duty to alert AIDS patients to the danger they could inflict on others. Willy Rozenbaum believed that demonizing 'this practice or that pleasure' meant destroying the confidence essential to the doctor–patient relationship; some gay members of the profession advocated caution, others considered this to be a new form of repression. Responding to an article written by the president of the Gay Association, which argued that there was no reason for homosexual men to change their behaviour, Michel Canesi published a counter-attack. 'I said that it was not natural for human beings to have sex with a dozen different partners in one day, but people began calling me "Cassandra" – the prophet of doom.'

Rudolf himself, according to Canesi, although very secretive about his sexual habits, was 'sometimes conscious of the dangers and sometimes absolutely not'. Confirming this, Stephen Sherriff remembers how it was Rudolf who would suggest they use condoms – 'though I'd have to go out and get them' – whereas Robert Tracy claims that there were a number of partners with whom Rudolf admitted having had unprotected sex. 'A whole bunch of people. All dead.' And while some were struck by Rudolf's attitude of 'total denial', others describe it more as an act of defiance. 'Rudolf wasn't a person to deny.' Certainly we know from biographer Otis Stuart's eyewitness account of Rudolf servicing 'a sylvan blond youth' that the dancer was still frequenting le Trap as late as the winter of '85. 'With one last swallow of his drink, [he] . . . mounts the stairs. First at a trickle, then en masse the entire room follows . . . among the most fervently attentive audiences of Nureyev's career.'

Towards the end of December, Sandor Gorlinsky told Rudolf about a letter he had received from a Nice solicitor saying that Rosa had arrived in his office without an appointment and rambled without stopping for nearly two hours. 'My own contribution may have lasted perhaps five minutes.' Clearly suffering from what seemed to be a state of paranoia, she spoke of espionage charges and surveillance by French police, which were making local shop owners 'friendly at one moment and hostile at another'. Finding it impossible to deal with Rudolf's sister, 'who believes that everyone has it in for her, is perse-cuting her and stealing her money', La Turbie's BNP bank had refused to give Rosa a chequebook, which only confirmed her belief that everyone in the village was conspiring against her: 'She is certain that a number of people are trying to poison her and therefore sleeps on the table in the kitchen because the ceiling is low and she is more able to wash and clean the various surfaces (including the ceiling) each day so as to dissipate the noxious substances . . . Other rooms are subject to draughts and she suspects that the poisoners use such draughts to introduce the substances into the house.'

Having learned the previous year that her brother was thinking of selling the villa at La Turbie, Rosa had become more and more disturbed, consulting the solicitor for the first time in November 1984 (and expecting Rudolf to pay the bill). She was refusing to move into the Monaco apartment and wanted to be appointed caretaker of Villa Arcadie: 'Her strongest wish is to take care of her brother's assets.' Clearly dictated by Rudolf, Gorlinsky's reply to Armand Schonfrucht & Co. shows more impatience than compassion. 'Mr Nureyev does not wish her to be concerned with protecting his property in France. He is perfectly capable of doing so . . . and he does not wish to have any interference from her . . . Also, Mr Nureyev has no intention of appointing her caretaker of the villa as the whole atmosphere is so poisonous for her at La Turbie.'

And yet Rudolf was worried enough to contact Canesi. 'He called me one day and said, "Michel, I want my sister to be in a psychiatric hospital. At once. She's crazy." I tried to explain to him that this was a rather Soviet attitude, that it is not easy in France to have someone sectioned, and he didn't bring the matter up again.' But the situation only compounded Rudolf's persistent sense of guilt. His defection had affected Rosa badly, preventing any chance of promotion in her teaching job, and the KGB's intimidation further fuelled her increasing anxiety. Banishment to the remote Villa Arcadie only made matters worse, and when Marika Besobrasova arrived there one day, she found Rosa 'washing, washing, washing herself'. Visitors were warned that Rudolf's sister kept a shotgun she was very likely to use, and Marie-Suzanne received a phone call from La Turbie's mayor complaining that Madame François was not allowing tradespeople to set foot on the property. Most troubling of all was the fact that Rosa was refusing to cooperate in the divorce with Pierre François, now understandably expecting to regain his freedom.[*]

'Bringing Rosa to the West was the one time in Rudolf's life that he really made the wrong decision,' says Franck Raoul-Duval, who had visited her a few years earlier in Leningrad and observed that she had a job that occupied her time, and friends of her own.

> Rudolf wanted her to come because of the link with his family and mother, but he was too caught up in his own life to see that it wouldn't work. Rosa hung on to him in a way he couldn't understand and could never accept. This is very tragic. You can't move a Soviet person who has lived in Soviet conditions all her life – what could she do in the West? When you uproot people who are used to a certain existence, they perish right away, or become resentful, or go mad.

Rudolf, however, was now on the brink of his own descent into hell. This had begun in March 1986 with what his colleagues still refer to as '*l'affaire Béjart*'. At his invitation Maurice Béjart had come to Paris to create a new work for the company, and during rehearsals (when Rudolf was away on tour), appeared to be preparing the ground for some kind of putsch. 'He was clearly getting as much information as he could about the situation with Rudolf,' says Jean-Luc Choplin. 'It was a time when there was a lot of criticism about his directorship, and also a lot of gossip about who was going to follow him. Béjart was finding

---

[*] In April 1986 Rosa agreed to take French nationality as a first step towards consenting to a divorce.

Rudolf photographed in Geneva with a camera-shy Clara Saint on tour with the de Cuevas Company in 1961.

Below left: Facing a blitzkrieg of flashbulbs at his post-defection press conference in Paris, June 1961.

Below right: Rudolf picking out a tune in London's Baron's Court studios during rehearsals for his debut solo, *Poème tragique*, 2 November 1961.

Above: Rudolf being coached in 1965 by Erik Bruhn, the love of his life and his only lodestar.

Below: Rudolf and Erik taking a class at the American Ballet Theatre school, June 1965.

The sixties pop star, photographed by Richard Avedon in New York, May 1967.

PHOTOGRAPH RICHARD AVEDON

PHOTOGRAPH RICHARD AVEDON

A private lesson with Valentina Pereyaslavec, one of the teachers Rudolf most admired, in an American Ballet Theatre school studio, New York, 5 May 1963.

PHOTOGRAPH RICHARD AVEDON

Posing on 6 May 1963 for Avedon, whom Rudolf regarded as
a kindred spirit with the same passion for art in all its forms.

PHOTOGRAPH RICHARD AVEDON

The famous legs that Rudolf dismissed as too short, New York, 29 May 1967.

Above: Rudolf working with Nigel Gosling on his autobiography in the drawing room of 27 Victoria Road.

Right: On the road during a tour of America in the late sixties.

In San Francisco with
his Russian-Armenian
adopted mother,
Armen Bali.

Wallace Potts and
Jeannette Etheredge
at the end of an evening
at Bali's, her mother's
restaurant.

On the set of
Valentino with
Leslie Caron – two
dancers 'talking
foot talk'.

Above, left to right: Monique van Vooren, Rudolf and
Maria Tallchief at the New York première of *Valentino*.

Below left: Rudolf and a radiant Douce François
at a party in Paris.

Below right: On vacation with interior designer Tessa
Kennedy, the close friend Rudolf tried to persuade
to mother his child. 'I'd had all these boys, so he
thought he'd be sure of having a son with me.'

On board Stavros Niarchos's yacht *Atlantis ll*
with their mutual friend Princess Firyal.

Below left: Island-hopping in Greece, Rudolf poses with his
Parisian friend and lover Franck Raoul-Duval.

Below right: In Turkey with Maude and Nigel Gosling. Rudolf watches
a local woman spinning wool as she walks – an idea he had
in mind for his production of *The Sleeping Beauty*.

The 1986 sailing trip around the south-western coast
of Turkey with Wallace, *far left,* Douce and Robert Tracy.

Clockwise from left: The 1987 Turkey group.
Stephen Sherriff, Yasemin Pirinccioglu, Jane Hermann,
Wallace, Douce and Rudolf.

Rudolf being led offstage by Charles Jude in a 1980s performance
of Béjart's *Songs of a Wayfarer*, a work that became as resonant
in his late career as *Giselle* had been in his youth.

PHOTOGRAPH RICHARD AVEDON

Kenneth Greve, the young Danish dancer with whom Rudolf was in love
during the late eighties. Richard Avedon photographed him for
the *New Yorker* in London on 3 December 1997.

Charles Jude and Elisabeth Platel in a pas de deux
from Rudolf's Paris Opéra production of *Swan Lake*.

Rudolf rehearsing the Paris Opéra's corps de ballet
in his production of *Don Quixote*, 1981.

The dining room at quai Voltaire, with Rudolf's kilim-covered Russian birchwood furniture and collection of academic nude paintings.

Preparing to conduct the Vienna Residenz Orchestra in September 1991 – a concert organized by his young Italian friend Alexandra della Porta Rodiani, who took this photograph.

The last holiday, October 1992: Rudolf on the terrace
of his house on St Bart's with his young Rottweiler, Solaria.

Ezio Frigerio's memorial marking Rudolf's grave at the Russian cemetery in
St Geneviève-des-Bois. In homage to the Tatar nomad, it represents a travelling
trunk covered with an astonishingly authentic, softly folding fringed kilim made
from bronze and glass mosaics in the Bashkiri colours of turquoise and coral.

out who would be on his side – trying to be friendly to me, to the general director – and I felt that he was ready to seize any opportunity to get the Paris Opéra.'

This was certainly not something Rudolf had been expecting. Relations between the two men had never been straightforward, but recently both had expressed a keen desire to collaborate again. Béjart had written to say that he was looking forward 'with joy' to working with Rudolf at the Opéra, and Rudolf had scheduled a Béjart soirée at the Palais Garnier 'in love and admiration'. But having proposed a version of Bartók's *The Miraculous Mandarin* with Rudolf in the lead (greeted by him as 'a miraculous Christmas present to me and the Opéra'), the choreographer had then changed his mind. Deciding instead on a comic homage to the Paris company – which he called *Arepo*, the word 'opera' spelled backwards – he did not create a part for Rudolf, and seemed to be using the opportunity of his absence to fan hostility against him. When Rudolf returned in time for the première, the tension in the air was palpable. 'We *knew* Béjart would try to do something,' Choplin recalls. 'We both smelled it, and decided to post ourselves *côté cour* [stage right] in the wings.'

The new ballet was enthusiastically applauded, and after the final curtain call the choreographer came onstage, silencing the audience to make an announcement. Taking the hands of two of the young dancers, Eric Vu An and Manuel Legris, he declared that he was nominating both as *étoiles*. There was a roar of approval in the auditorium, but the pair looked uncertain – as Elisabeth Platel put it, 'They felt in their hearts that it was wrong.' Only the director of dance, after first clearing the promotion with the general director, had the right to appoint an *étoile*. In the past, however, it had been something of a Béjart tradition 'to kind of consecrate' a major work at the Opéra by making *étoiles* of its leading dancers (as he had done with Jean-Pierre Bonnefous and Michael Denard). 'Béjart was a little bit in love with Eric, and he wanted to do something special for him,' Legris has said. 'He knew that Rudolf liked me as a dancer, so he figured perhaps if I make both *étoiles* . . .' Béjart himself now claims that he had tried without success to consult Rudolf before the performance, but at the interval had been told, 'Nureyev agrees, you can go ahead, you have the green light.' But although Rudolf appreciated Vu An's considerable talent, he had never considered him to be a classical star. And in the case of Legris (who, along with Laurent Hilaire, he was forming in his own image), Rudolf had no intention of letting any advancement be decided by anyone other than himself. Turning to look at their director for confirmation, the two dancers saw him waving his index finger slowly and implacably from side to side in an unmistakable gesture of no.*

Immediately an order was given for the curtain to be brought down, and Rudolf strode out onstage. '*Poisson d'avril!*' (April Fool!) he quipped coldly to the dancers, and then, turning to Béjart, unleashed his 'monstrous anger'. 'It was a very bad moment for the whole house,' recalls Platel. 'The company had been so happy, and one minute later everyone was crying.' A crisis meeting was called in the general director's office in order to prepare a press release: whatever the dancers had been led to believe, the administration had to take an institutional position. 'Maybe Béjart thought we would not dare undo his decision because it had been witnessed by the public,' says Choplin. 'But we did.'

Rudolf had threatened to walk out that night if he did not have the Opéra's full backing. 'They gave it to me.' EMBROUILLE À L'OPÉRA: 'BÉJART A TORT' ('Turmoil at the Opéra: "Béjart Is Wrong"') blazed the front-page headline of *Le Matin de Paris*. But on the lunchtime broadcast of TF1, two days after the première, the choreographer got his revenge. Whereas Rudolf, as Michel Canesi says, 'lacked the weapons to speak to the media in French', Béjart was a friend of the celebrated television journalist Yves Mourousy, who had given him this opportunity to answer back. With Zola-like intensity Béjart called Rudolf a liar, and accused him of bringing the Opéra to ruins by destabilizing Claude Bessy's school and France's '*grande danse traditionale*'. M Nureyev, he went on, had insulted Roland Petit and sidelined Patrick Dupond; he was a terrible choreographer, and as director was a 'phantom of the Opéra' because he was hardly ever there.

Seizing this image, the press pitted '*Mephisto contre le fantôme*', and Robert Denvers, a week away from the end of his teaching engagement at the Opéra, felt so caught between the two – 'both very close to my heart' – that he asked Rudolf to let him go. 'For me, this was a turning point in my perception of Béjart. He was always a cool person, the intellectual, and Rudolf more of the visceral one. Actually it was Béjart who lost his control and became aggressive and resentful

---

* Three months later, on the stage of the Metropolitan Opera in New York, Rudolf nominated Legris as an *étoile*. Eric Vu An, however, who never progressed beyond the secondary rank of *grand sujet*, decided to leave.

and really overstepped the boundaries of his role. Rudolf behaved incredibly well and with incredible dignity. He won that battle fair and square.'

It had all been extremely unpleasant and an affront, and yet this was not what had really shattered Rudolf over the previous few days. That month Erik Bruhn's doctor friend Lennart Pasborg had received a telephone call from the dancer saying that he was 'really sick'. Erik, now fifty-eight, had always been a heavy smoker, getting through at least three packs of cigarettes a day, and he had been coughing badly since the winter of '85. 'He'd asked me what he should do. "Get yourself X-rayed and give up smoking," I said. But he just laughed.' Now, more than a year later, Erik had discovered that he was in the final stages of lung cancer. Deciding to leave immediately for Toronto, Lennart went out to buy a supply of the alternative medicines that had helped to prolong his father's life. 'My father had cancer for some years and found mistletoe injections enormously effective. I told Erik, "He was helped – you can be helped too."' But although Lennart administered the medication, within half an hour of arriving at Erik's apartment, he could see that it was too late.

On 20 March Erik was admitted to Toronto General Hospital. The National Ballet's artistic administrator, Valerie Wilder, had contacted Rudolf through a mutual friend, urging him to come immediately, but he made it clear that the furore at the Opéra was going to delay him. 'Erik asked about his visit daily and was very distressed when it kept being put off,' she says. 'This was of great concern to me, too, because I was not sure if Rudolf would get to Toronto in time.' On Friday 28 March, two days after his trial by television, Rudolf went straight from the airport to the hospital, where he was met by Lennart and Erik's partner, Constantin Patsalas, who then left the room so that the two dancers could be alone.

Only recently the pair had been making idealistic plans for a future together, talking about starting a ballet academy in Spain, or building a house in Turkey. 'The idea . . . is beginning to sound very attractive to me,' Erik wrote on 5 July the previous year. 'I am not going to run a company forever . . . [and] it would be nice to retire to a beautiful place sometime.' But over the last few days Erik had significantly withdrawn into himself, and although still conscious, was so drowsy and confused that he barely acknowledged Rudolf's presence. 'We didn't have contact,' Rudolf told Charles Jude on his return. 'He's already dead for me. It was like something had been cut.' After staying only about a quarter of an hour, Rudolf went straight to the National Ballet's studios: he badly needed the catharis of class. 'He looked pretty shaken,' says Veronica Tennant. 'We didn't talk about why he was in Toronto. Though of course we all knew.'

The following day he went to the hospital again, where Constantin was in the room with Erik. 'Don't worry,' Rudolf heard him whispering. 'It will be wonderful up there. You'll find lots of friends.' 'Rudolf was shocked by that,' said Maude. 'It was the sort of thing he would never have said.' Erik, however, was now oblivious to anything and anyone. The morphine was making him hallucinate, and while Rudolf sat alone beside him, he began talking about putting on his makeup for *Moor's Pavane*. 'Erik was totally out of it,' he told his Toronto friend, the dancer Linda Maybarduk. 'Finally all I could do was get into bed and just hold him in my arms.'

Returning to Paris, Rudolf then left again almost immediately, taking a small group of Opéra dancers to perform with the Ballet du Louvre in the Seychelles. On the afternoon of 1 April Lennart called to say that Erik had just died. It had been 2.45 p.m. Toronto time. Rudolf took the news with little emotion, his voice soft but steady, and mentioned nothing to his dancers during dinner that night. Maude was there, too, and after everyone had gone to bed, they sat together on the balcony between their adjoining rooms. It was a balmy night, the air thick with the scent of tropical flowers, and as they rested their legs on the railing, looking up at the stars, Rudolf said simply, 'Erik died today.' Maude took his hand. 'Doesn't something like that make those attacks in the press seem trivial?' 'Yes, it does,' he replied. 'And that was all he said.'

Erik's last letter to Rudolf had been darkly prescient in tone. Written on 10 January, when he had no idea of his own fatal illness, it tells of the death the day before of Lucia Chase, the American Ballet Theatre's director, and that, two days earlier, of the National Ballet's young conductor in a car crash. 'Death,' wrote Erik, 'is very confusing and upsetting but something we must accept.' To Rudolf, however, this was heresy. He refused to allow himself to believe that he could die from AIDS. Not only was he convinced that a medicine would be discovered in time to help him – 'They cured syphilis,' he declared to Robert Tracy – but illness, like injury, was something he felt he could overcome, just as he had managed to overcome every other obstacle in his life. Remembering the time he was hospitalized in Leningrad for tearing a ligament in his leg, Rudolf said, 'A furious desire to defeat the injury was born in me, a determination not to let fate overwhelm me.' Erik, on the other hand, on learning that he had cancer, had showed no desire to fight but, as Lennart put it, 'went into his death process with all his psychic power'. 'He did leave us with astounding speed,' adds Valerie Wilder. 'He always said he would go quickly, and it is almost as if he willed himself to do just that.'

The difference between the two dancers extended even to the grave. In stark contrast to Rudolf's state funeral seven years later, Erik asked to be cremated without any service. On 20 April fewer than a dozen people, including his sister, lawyer, housekeeper, and a few close friends, gathered for half an hour in Mariebjerg Church cemetery in Lyngby, outside Copenhagen. They were there to honour this great dancer's final wish: to have his urn of ashes placed in the Unknowns' Grave.

Meanwhile, in Paris, the campaign to oust Rudolf as director continued, Roland Petit now aligning himself with Béjart. 'It was the same old story.' Choplin smiles. ' "*We* should run the Paris Opéra" – two frustrated choreographers trying to pretend.' In the 5 May edition of *Le Figaro*, a joint letter appeared outlining proposals to put France's national ballet 'back on the rails'. Although not mentioning Rudolf by name, it criticizes his retrospective approach to the repertory – describing the Petipa classics as 'works other companies have created long ago' – and derides the choice of a star dancer at the helm of a major institution. 'We demand the formation of a national enquiry to stop the star system of personalities unqualified to run a company.'

More than a decade later, in his short book *Temps liés avec Noureev*, Petit castigates himself for having allowed 'a renowned choreographer' to persuade him to co-sign 'this perfidious, tasteless message'. And yet, in an interview with Gerard Mannoni appearing two weeks before the *Figaro* piece, the choreographer had volunteered an unprovoked, anti-Rudolf diatribe of his own.

The Opéra Ballet does not have to wait for M. Noureev to know how to dance. We have no need of *ce monsieur*, neither at the level of the school, that is admirably run by Madame Bessy, nor at the level of the corps de ballet. I do not think that Maurice Béjart wishes to take on the Opéra de Paris. Neither do I, but we must be able to work there in all sympathy with an administration which is for us and the dancers . . . I will not go to the Opéra while M. Noureev and his administration are there . . . I do not want to depend on a director who slaps a professor, who insults a choreographer, says April Fool to another choreographer who has just made an announcement with which he had agreed before.

Petit admits in his memoir to having refused several attempts made by Igor Eisner, the minister of culture, to unite the two estranged friends. 'I was only waiting for a sign from the monster for the reconciliation for which I hoped.' And which he got. 'My dear Roland,' Rudolf had written in December 1985, 'Let's forget the past. The Opéra must restage your works or else commission new ones. Let's talk about this as soon as possible.' It was André Larquié who met the choreographer later that month, having been warned beforehand by Rudolf that they must commission only proven Petit successes, and 'avoid works like *Chat botté*'. Although an agreement could not be reached, the administration was confident that 'it was just a matter of time before Petit would come around' (three years to be precise: *Notre Dame de Paris* was revived in November 1988).

Nevertheless it was galling for Rudolf to be constantly aware that French ballet had turned against him. 'They don't like foreigners here, you know,' Lifar had warned Balanchine in 1928, and it was this sense of being '*le sale étranger*' that was making Rudolf's job increasingly unpleasant. 'We must not be suspected of chauvinism . . . [but] our tradition is a French tradition,' the *Figaro* letter had crowed, a view with which Claude Bessy, who fervently admired Béjart and disliked Rudolf, was in fierce accord. Responding to his client's threat to leave and withdraw all his ballets, Mario Bois wrote advising Rudolf on his legal and moral responsibilities, warning him to be prudent, as he might end up forfeiting a lot of money. But Jean-Luc Choplin remembers their director handing in his notice at least a dozen times. 'My secretary would be in tears as she was typing his letter of resignation, and Rudolf was so sensitive to Sophie's crying that he would rip out the paper and tear it up.' Finally, after turning to Jean-Claude Carrière to help him compose a reply to recent accusations,* Rudolf announced his intention to stay. 'Because cowardice and inconstancy are not part of my character, it would be inconceivable and totally

---

*Among the points he makes in a letter of self-defence to the dancers, Rudolf writes, 'Roland Petit pretends he withdrew his ballets from Opéra repertoire because "I had insulted him." Actually it was after a quarrel with Bernard Lefort in 1981 or 1982 – I was not there – that Petit withdrew his ballets . . . [And] how can one believe I "hate" the dancer Eric Vu An when I myself promoted him by sending him to Vienna Opera to perform Don Q?'

illogical and unfortunate for the whole Opéra Ballet if I were to renounce my duty.'

A major tour of the United States just days away was reason enough to hold on. Transatlantic success could transform the image of a company overnight, just as Sadler's Wells' triumphant New York debut had brought instant world fame to English ballet in 1949. In his previous role as administrator of Roland Petit's troupe, Jean-Luc Choplin had forged a strong link with the Director of Presentations at the Metropolitan Opera House, Jane Hermann. 'Because I was successful in persuading her to take the company with Rudolf and Makarova as guest stars, it was easy for me to sit down and negotiate a season for Paris Opéra.' The groundwork, however, had already been laid by Rudolf. Intuiting that beneath Hermann's tough-talking, abrasive façade was a middle-aged romantic, unashamedly susceptible to his appeal, he went out of his way to flirt with her, 'holding hands when we were walking . . . and sometimes crawling into my bed to look at television'. He took her on vacation, invited her to dinner and to the movies, and in response Jane expedited things for him. 'I'd cash his cheques, get him tickets, dispatch one of the Met's cleaning staff to the Dakota – I never said no.'

And it was Jane Hermann who would go to greater lengths than anyone else in the world to pay tribute to Rudolf's achievement. 'There was no artist I admired more,' she has said. As part of the Lincoln Center's 'France Salutes New York' festival she arranged a fund-raising gala to launch the Paris Opéra's season, the high point of which was Sylvie Guillem and Patrick Dupond provoking 'a near-hysterical standing ovation' with their explosive *Corsaire* duet. As it was a joint affair with Baryshnikov's American Ballet Theatre (the million-dollar proceeds to be shared by the two companies), there was a Franco-American slant to it all with 'La Marseillaise' and 'The Star-Spangled Banner' sung as an overture; Laurent Hilaire partnered ABT's Cynthia Harvey in the pas de deux from Lifar's *Suite en blanc*; and Rudolf and Baryshnikov hoofed onstage together in an Astaire-inspired number with Leslie Caron 'as the butter to bind them'. The critics' verdict was music to Rudolf's ears: 'This was very much the Paris Opéra Ballet's show,' declared Anna Kisselgoff; 'The French won hands down!' echoed Clive Barnes. For the first time since Baryshnikov's defection, Rudolf felt that he was outshining his young rival, convinced – and rightly so – that he was the more inspired leader.

Misha Baryshnikov and me – both of us loved and worshipped Kirov Ballet and both of us tried to reproduce or re-create Kirov Ballet in the West. He created his Kirov Ballet by repeating exactly the same choreography, the same mannerisms of the company; I created the *idea* of what Kirov should be – most beautiful line, most precise, most lyrical . . . I did not deny what was West . . . I didn't make them caricatures of the Kirov.

'Rudolf thought himself a choreographer and a post-Petipa improver, which Misha did not,' says the dance critic Robert Greskovic, pointing out how much closer Baryshnikov's productions are to the original Russian text, something Rudolf was the first to admit. 'I think Kirov and Moscow will just die if they saw Paris Opéra when they do *Sleeping Beauty* or *Swan Lake* or *Raymonda* or *Don Q.* They can't compare.' Rudolf had never shown any compunction about rechoreographing the classics to suit himself, although not everyone saw these innovations as improvements. His signature obsession with Bournonville *petite batterie* – what Joan Acocella calls 'Nureyev's goddamn *ronds de jambe* and those little steppy things' – made his choreography almost comically cluttered at times. Ghislaine Thesmar agrees. 'Nobody dares to clear the ballets out a bit, which is a pity.'

Of far greater value to the companies Rudolf influenced was his merging of native style with genuine Maryinsky schooling. In the sixties his Shades scene from *La Bayadère* had literally retrained the English ballerinas, bringing out a Russian classical side of themselves they hardly knew was there. 'This kind of dancing was new to the Royal Ballet, but they did not deliver a carbon copy of the Kirov production,' writes the British critic Zoë Anderson. 'They kept their own Ashtonian arabesques, their British *épaulement* . . . [It was] Petipa grandeur with a Royal Ballet accent.' To Elisabeth Platel, one of the great exemplars of French schooling (and what Edwin Denby might have called the company's 'central dynamo'), Rudolf's arrival was a whole new education. 'We learned . . . a pure classical style that he inherited from the Kirov . . . We were able to find his energy in ourselves, we found his severity and above all else, his respect for all of the teachers and partners that he knew at the Kirov.' To Thesmar, too, Rudolf had 'brought back the structure of classical ballet with such authority; put everything back in its place in a space of two or three years.' Not in Arlene Croce's opinion, however:

The real surprise was the impoverished classical style of the Opéra dancers. The bad things one had always known about them – the things that the Nureyev regime, with its illustrious new stars, was supposed to have changed – were right there on the stage: weak lower backs, unworked turnout, careless feet. Lots of pretty faces, to be sure, and charming manners. The Paris dancers are virtuosos of charm. But the legs have no force.

But these were early days – during which 'half the dancers were with Rudolf and half weren't'. Nor did he have the backing of Claude Bessy to instil his ideas in the students, and without a school, there can be no homogeneous, integral company style. Nevertheless, to Marie-Christine Mouis, who left the Paris Opéra Ballet in 1981, the standard of dancing was now unrecognizably high; and to Jerome Robbins, 'the company had moved under Rudolf from being not really first class to quite superb'.

During the Paris Opéra Ballet's 1948 New York debut, under Lifar, the repertory was viewed as 'woefully dated'.* And yet (as if wanting America to support his antipathy towards his predecessor's work), Rudolf had chosen to bring back Lifar's turgid *Les Mirages*. But whereas the only Petipa offering by 'Lifar's company' had been his Divertissements from *Sleeping Beauty*, Rudolf's intention was to showcase the French dancers' new mastery of the classics. In this he was only partly successful. Cut almost in half to fit the programme, *Raymonda* seemed to Croce not so much authentic Petipa as 'Nureyev trying to be creative', while his intrusively prominent, predatory Tutor in *Swan Lake* was not liked by anyone. It was the inclusion of *Washington Square*, however, the season's only contemporary offering, that proved Rudolf's biggest mistake. Knowing that it had been choreographed with an American tour in mind, Jane Hermann had considered it a risk worth taking.

I wanted the American public to see Rudolf as Dr Sloper because it's a part that has character and maturity. And I wanted them to see how this work filtered through his mind and became what it is: a view of America that could only be taken by someone like him. What

* An exception was *Palais de cristal*, a masterpiece in four movements to Bizet's *Symphony in C* (now the title of the ballet), which Balanchine created for the Paris Opéra in July 1947. Included by Rudolf on the New York tour, it caused a roar of approval from the audience.

everyone else would have done was a chamber ballet, but Rudolf's vision is so large and monumental that you begin to see a lot of deeper ramifications in James's novel.

To the critics the ballet was 'unforgettably awful', 'an ignominious assault', and only served to heighten Rudolf's shortcomings as a choreographer. And yet their final verdict of the Paris season was positive in the extreme: this had been one of the Met's most successful foreign engagements, 'a resounding transatlantic triumph', 'the sensation of the year'. Rudolf had not only worked a minor miracle by pulling together a world-class troupe in such a short period of time, but he had also reconquered New York. As he stood onstage for over twenty minutes acknowledging the cheering and bouquet hurling, he looked happier than he had in decades. Paris Opéra, Clive Barnes wrote, should start making plans for a follow-up tour, the message from America being, 'Come back soon!'

The rest of the summer was blissfully carefree. Rudolf had decided to rent a caïque and sail the southwest coast of Turkey, craving, he told Maude, 'Absolute peace – nothing but putting in at little deserted bays and bathing and reading and sleeping.' The trip had been arranged, as in previous years, by a young Turkish woman, Yasemin Pirinccioglu, who had become a friend. Having also won Douce's confidence, she would observe how Rudolf – 'the Sultan', as she called him – 'made these women go crazy', scolding him by saying, 'You just love this Byzantine intrigue!' 'Those powerful eyes,' he said laughingly. 'They see right through me.' For some time now Yasemin had been helping Rudolf look for a plot of land in the Fethiye region, which is much greener than most of Turkey's sun-scorched terrain. Having set his heart on a particular peninsula on the western side of Gemile Island, he had gone so far as to write to the president of Turkey, hoping to facilitate the purchase. Heavily forested, the land turned out to have no deeds, electricity or infrastructure, but Rudolf was determined to keep searching. As Yasemin recalls, 'He had this dream of building a house with a dome to put all his kilims.'

The collecting of antique kilims had become a serious passion, and Rudolf often headed straight from the airport to the bazaars. There is a ritual involved in rug buying, a kind of courtship, which Rudolf relished, beginning with the ceremonious pouring of apple tea or syrupy coffee. Friends remember how amused he would be by the way the initial etiquette of evasion and flirtation could often crescendo into desperate bargaining, with the merchant chasing after him in the street, shouting, 'A hundred dollars off! Two hundred dollars off!' Theirs is not always a reputable trade (*marchand de tapis* is a pejorative term in French), but these were people with whom Rudolf felt a natural kinship. As a Tatar he had in him the spirit of the nomadic Turk, whose most important piece of furniture was a rug. 'They would fold it up and take it with them.'

Picking out interesting pieces from among the crammed piles was an art in itself. It was easy enough to spot the kilims mass produced for the tourist market with their garish colours chemically dyed, their thick-pile wool of poor quality. But it took knowledge and skill to distinguish an authentic eighteenth-century prayer rug, say, from a convincing fake rewoven from old wool. Rudolf only ever wanted the muted shades produced by vegetable dyes, the primitiveness of some reminding him of the Bashkirian fabrics of his childhood. Creating dyes had once been a treasured craft. The old recipes combined roots, nuts, leaves, fruits, dried herbs and dead insects. Some recipes, such as the mixture for the pale sky tint called Birbul's blue, are as sensuously poetic as a passage from the Song of Songs: 'Take cinnabar, indigo and alum, grind and sift lighter than the light dust of the high hills.' These colours found their way into Rudolf's ballets. 'When he was choreographing *Romeo and Juliet* he was into reds, but with *Raymonda* it was different shades of rust,' recalls Tessa Kennedy, also an ardent collector. And just as inspiring were the patterns themselves, their spatial harmony and the fusing of tradition with the personal and spontaneous a parallel art to his own. 'Look!' he exclaimed to Yasemin. 'You see this design, how intricate it is? This is how I choreograph my ballets.'

After a few days of kilim buying, swimming and trekking up into hillside villages, Rudolf was a different person – 'free and happy because nobody knew him.' And that summer he had surrounded himself with the ideal circle of friends. As Maude was nervous about the sea and had declined to come in previous years, Rudolf had gone out of his way to renew links with Wallace. 'He knew that would make me feel safe. He'd say, "You'll come if Wallace comes, won't you?" And then to Wallace, "You'll come if Maude comes, won't you?"' With nothing much changed in Wallace's life (he was out of a job and painting houses while working on a screenplay), he decided that enough time had passed for him to consider a holiday with Rudolf. 'I no longer had any emotional entanglements, or felt intimidated, anxious or whatever.' Nor was he fazed by Robert Tracy's presence on the trip. 'There wasn't much happening between them; in fact, I probably got along better with Robert than Rudolf did.' Completing the party were Michel Canesi and Douce, who recorded much of the journey on video. Wearing nautical white, Maude rarely strays from Rudolf's side, while he, either swaddled in woollen layers and a turban, or totally naked except for a snorkel and mask, is seen to be in exceptionally high spirits. At one moment, taking charge of the camera, he directs a high-diving display; at another, holding a motorized float he exclaims, Wodehouse-style, 'It's the tops!' For the whole group this was a wonderful two weeks – 'The best summer of my life, bar none!' says Wallace – and for Rudolf, it was to be his last taste of real contentment.

His immediate task on returning to Paris was to choreograph a new ballet for the autumn season. In March 1985 he had written to Frederick Ashton to ask for his *Cinderella*, hoping that news of the Tudor homage might change his mind about working at the Opéra. 'The time has now come for the success of English choreographers in Paris . . . At last!' But with Ashton refusing to budge, Rudolf decided to do his own production, having already spotted a designer he admired. It was Petrika Ionesco's suggestion to set *Cinderella* in a film studio, and although Rudolf was unconvinced at first, he found the idea 'eating me up until I couldn't think to do it any other way'. There was undoubtedly an element of wish fulfilment in the prospect of being able to stop the clock, as Cinderella does when she signs a movie contract, 'thus assuring her immortality'. And it was the ballet's preoccupation with time that Rudolf was eager to explore. In addition to the traditional divertissements for the four seasons, he planned a clock dance, as well as the appearance of an allegorical 'Mae West kind of figure' who passes through the clock and emerges as an old crone.

   In the back of his mind as a model for the heroine was his niece Gouzel, who had ambitions to cast off her lowly origins by becoming a Hollywood star. (Jeannette Etheredge remembers her 'calling me up to ask if I knew Mickey Rooney. She said, "I'd like to be in his next movie."' Gouzel also contacted Rudolf's friend Gloria Venturi, announcing that she was 'coming to Roma to try to do a movie'.) There would be several other private jokes. *Cinderella*'s Prince Charming was a Valentino look-alike; the name of the movie producer (Rudolf's own role) was 'Pygmalion Diaghilev', a character who then turns into a composite of Sandor Gorlinsky and Groucho Marx – complete with cigar and joke Jewish nose. And although the ballet was a showcase not for him this time but for Sylvie Guillem, Rudolf could indulge his passion for old Hollywood movies by getting the ballerina to embody his icons by donning a derby and baggy pants as Charlie Chaplin, and paying homage to Fred Astaire by partnering a coat rack, as he did in *Royal Wedding*. ('If you want to make fast, flying footwork,' Rudolf told his dancers, 'you need to know Bournonville, Balanchine – and Astaire.')

With 'You want, you take!' as her motto, Sylvie could never be a convincingly downtrodden heroine, and even at the start is more Cyd Charisse than Cinderella, her high-fashion physique enhanced by designer Hanae Mori, a protégée of Coco Chanel. This was Rudolf giving the French the chic and novelty they loved, but in doing so he compromised what he had always described as his 'principal goal': the movement itself. The ballet is held together by its gimmicky concept rather than the choreography, which is dismally lacking in originality. 'These superb artists deserve better than this,' complained Gérard Mannoni in a vituperative review, but to René Sirvin the new ballet was 'a triumph – the word is not too strong'. Audiences were just as delighted and, going with the flow, Mannoni did a complete turn-around a week later, admitting that *Cinderella* 'still triumphs . . . It is the composition of a great artist.'

But it was as a dancer that Rudolf was still determined to triumph. At the beginning of the year, on a train to Venice, he had confided to Luigi that he was HIV positive, saying, 'I'm going to be very sick, but I want to dance as much as I can.' Understanding that this was Rudolf's way of 'distracting the mind from the tunnel of death', Luigi proceeded to make it happen, even towards the very end. Baryshnikov was also aware of Rudolf's need to keep dancing, and offered him two opportunities to appear with the American Ballet Theatre in *Giselle* – 'a ballet he could still do'. His 8 May '87 performance drew unexpectedly laudatory reviews, Dale Harris calling it his finest in New York for a decade. Reiterating what Rudolf himself believed, the critic remarked how much there was for young male stars to learn from watching the mature Nureyev, whose sense of commitment and motivation no one then performing with ABT seemed able to achieve. This Albrecht, 'burdened with guilt, grief and repentance', was Rudolf playing the man he had become, the moment at which he is compelled by the Wilis to dance himself to death, deriving its feverish power from his own desperation.

Over the next few months, there followed what Ghislaine Thesmar called 'a bulimia of performances'. Rudolf had recently signed up with

Andrew Grossman of Columbia Artist Management, Inc., purely, Wallace says, 'because Grossman could get him the gigs'. In addition there were a number of provincial tours with the London Festival Ballet, the Northern Ballet Theatre, the Ballet du Louvre and the Nancy Ballet (dismissed by art historian Roy Strong as a company of 'second-rate awfulness, pounding their way through a programme called *Homage to Diaghilev*'). Even the partisan John Percival was now urging Rudolf to give up roles such as *Le Spectre de la rose*, but with fewer and fewer engagements on offer, he was determined to seize any chance that came his way. Dancing, he believed, 'depends on demand and supply: no demand, no supply'.

And what inevitably ceased if he no longer danced was the supply of money, an obsession that became almost pathological in Rudolf's final years. 'When things get really bad I can live in Virginia and grow potatoes,' he told close friends, appearing genuinely to believe that he risked ending his life in the poverty in which he had begun it. 'Rudolf was terrified of going back to being poor again,' says Jeannette. 'There had always been a bit of that in him – it's why he never paid for anything – but it started getting much worse.' The conviction (planted by Margot) that Gorlinsky was cheating him out of money also began to obsess Rudolf. This, as Barry Weinstein confirms, was complete nonsense. 'Sandor was a heads-up guy. As an agent he was entitled to ten per cent, but he never took a nickel that didn't belong to him. He *loved* Rudolf, and had always taken special care of him. He had no children of his own, and I sensed some kind of paternal feeling there.' But in July 1987, when Rudolf learned that Gorlinsky, without consulting him, had sold the house in Fife Road, he was outraged: it didn't matter that he hadn't lived there in years. He felt it was not only a betrayal on Gorlinsky's part but a sign that things were starting to spiral out of his control.

In late July, Rudolf tried to repeat the Turkish holiday of the previous summer. Yasemin had arranged to charter the same boat, and the group gathered at Victoria Road on the eve of their departure included Jane Hermann; Douce; Wallace, who had flown in from Los Angeles with his brother, Tom; and Stephen Sherriff, a last-minute invited guest. The young dancer had driven Rudolf back from a taping of the *Dame Edna Experience* television show which had not gone well, his performance coming across as crudely scripted and unfunny. 'It was pretty clear that it was an endeavour he shouldn't have agreed to,' Wallace says. 'It was done purely for the money.' Compounding the palpable edginess in the house on this, the hottest night of the year, was the fact that Maude, who had recently broken her ankle, was insisting that she was not fit enough to travel. 'We'll carry you,' Rudolf pleaded, trying again and again to get her to change her mind. 'I could see how upset I was making him, but my doctor had told me that on no account was I to go.' At around two in the morning, the temperature still chokingly hot, Rudolf went downstairs to pack. Shortly afterwards a violent crash was heard, followed by the sound of breaking glass. Intending to take his portable keyboard and failing to fit it into the box, Rudolf had flung the instrument against the door, shattering several glass panes. It was, Maude said ruefully, the only time she had ever known Rudolf to be angry in their house.

The night of 'heat, chaos, temper' was a sign of things to come, as the trip proved tense and problematic from start to finish. Rudolf and Douce were not on speaking terms, and Rudolf was snarlingly unpleasant towards Wallace, resenting Tom's presence and refusing to participate in any vacation activities. 'Jane and I had a lot of fun, and Rudolf would get upset at that, but when we tried to include him, he just wasn't in the mood.' Having recently lost his mother and discovered that he, too, was HIV positive, Wallace found it hard to sustain his high spirits for long, a fact that only exacerbated Rudolf's bad humour.

When Stephen Sherriff felt trouble starting he would take himself off to the prow of the boat, sitting with his legs dangling in the sea. There was no longer any romantic interest between the two dancers; in fact, as if finally conceding to Yeats's view that it was only the young who belonged in each other's arms, Rudolf had helped to matchmake Stephen with the captain's hunky son. And instead of practising on board as he would have done in the past, Rudolf gave a barre to Stephen without joining in himself. He had been suffering from an injured knee, and after one long trek returned with it swollen to three times its size. 'He should never have gone scrambling up goat tracks,' Stephen remarks, 'but he'd been there with Maude and Nigel and was determined to see the same view again. He could hardly walk after that, and must have thought: I can't even get up a hill, so how am I ever going to dance?' Also feeling feverish, Rudolf began spending more and more time in his cabin, and when he reappeared was silent and withdrawn. 'He was sick – he knew he was sick,' says Wallace. 'It felt as if we were watching him implode.' The image he describes was that of a supernova, which after driving blast waves into the atmosphere collapses inwards. 'It was the death of a celestial star.'

A CIRCULAR CIRCLE.
COMPLETE

Dear Rudik,

A good friend of mine, an acupuncturist, was flying to Ufa to spend the summer with a colleague, and I asked him to visit your mother . . . Unfortunately, Evgenii Petrovich Kozhevnikov found your mother in a very bad way. She wasn't moving, and was all hunched up and unable to speak. Obviously she has had a stroke. EP was there with his colleague and they managed with the help of needles to rouse her a little . . . [and] your mother started to react to words. But EP returned very disturbed by what he had seen: he said your mother's life is waning. I don't know what to do about it. I think you will not be able to bring her to you: she would not survive the journey and I think she wouldn't want it. Come yourself? Problematic. Fortunately we have different times now and things are improving. Unfortunately there are fools and idiots who remain, but it's harder for them to act. So I can't advise you about it. I do think, though, that it would be a good idea to call that Ufa doctor, who is very well known in the city. First of all you will get first-hand information . . . and second, maybe you can arrange for medical help . . . Don't delay – in Evgenii Petrovich's words, there's not much time left.

This letter dated 9 October 1987 from Liuba Romankova (now Myasnikova) confirmed Rudolf's fears. He had not spoken to his mother for months and was having recurring anxiety dreams about her. (In one he saw her at the top of a flight of stairs, but he could not climb up to her because the stairs were made of bread.) There was a telephone in the Ufa apartment where Farida lived with her granddaughter Alfia and her family, but on the few occasions Rudolf had managed to get through, Alfia would promise to fetch Farida and then the line would go dead. Douce, who had travelled to St Petersburg in the spring of '86 to attend the exhibition 'Three Generations of Wyeths in American Art', spent an evening with the Romankovs also trying in vain to call. After Douce had gone back to Paris, Liuba persevered, and 'after the hundredth attempt' reached Alfia, who told her that Farida had been ill for a long time. 'The doctors could do nothing for her, and Alfia did not know where to turn.' Her own mother, Lilia (Rudolf's deaf-mute sister), was also bedridden, having recently been nearly paralysed in a hit-and-run accident, and in addition to 'shuttling between two helpless, silent women', Alfia was working as a bookkeeper and caring for her husband and four-year-old son. 'I have never seen such misery,' Evgenii Petrovich told Liuba on his return, urging her to contact Rudolf immediately to say that if it was impossible for him to come to Russia himself, he must at least arrange for his mother 'to die in decent circumstances'. But with all her letters having failed to reach the dancer in the past, Liuba thought it best to wait until October when she was away from St Petersburg working on an archaeological site in the then Russian province of Tadzhikiskaya (now Tajikistan). 'I'm hurrying to write to you from here in order to give this letter to Moscow people,' she added. 'They're flying back tomorrow, and can post it from there.'

Although every word in the letter rang true, Rudolf could not help suspecting a trap: the Soviets had used the excuse of his sick mother before. Taking Liuba's advice, he telephoned Phail, the Ufa acupuncturist ('causing a great scandal in the hospital where he worked'), who confirmed everything she had said, explaining that it was only by performing acupuncture to stimulate the cerebral cortex that they had been able to coax Farida into showing any sign of life. Jean-Luc Choplin remembers a tired, dishevelled-looking Rudolf coming into his office one morning and (not mentioning any letter), announcing, 'I dreamed last night that my mother is dying. I have to get to Ufa.' They started making calls.

Over the past two years times had begun to change in Russia. When Mikhail Gorbachev rose to power as general secretary in 1985 he made one of his priorities the release from internal exile of Nobel Peace Prize-winning dissident Andrei Sakharov, the nuclear physicist and human-rights advocate. Would Rudolf be considered important enough to receive a similar dispensation? In order to get his seven-year prison sentence revoked, authorization was required from the highest level, something Choplin claims hurriedly took place. 'My understanding was that Mitterrand did it – called Gorbachev directly.' The result was a Soviet visa valid for just thirty-six hours.

But for all the new openness (glasnost) in Russia, many members of the Politburo's old guard had survived, the KGB still retained its intimidating power, and the ending of the Cold War was three years away. Understandably Rudolf could see things only as they were when he left, fearing even as plans went ahead for the trip that he 'might end up in Siberia'. Wanting someone official to accompany him, he had telephoned the Cultural Ministry's Roch-Olivier Maître at home, stressing the urgency of the mission. He had also been in touch with Janine Ringuet, the impresario's assistant who had been responsible for first bringing him to the West, still regarding her, she felt, 'as some kind of symbolic link with Russia'. But with only a week to go before his departure, Rudolf could hardly contain his excitement. When Liuba returned to Leningrad, her mother told her that Rudik had already called three times to say that he would be arriving in Moscow the following Saturday and wanted her to meet him there. She had barely walked in the door when the telephone rang again. 'Well, Liubashka, about time! What do you think – is it too dangerous to come? . . . I've already telephoned Jackie, just in case, and asked her to sound the alarm if I'm not back in Paris after three days.'

Jackie was Jacqueline Onassis, who was concerned enough about Rudolf's safety to contact her brother-in-law on his behalf, and on 13 November Washington's Soviet ambassador, Yuri V. Dubinin, received the following letter from Senator Edward Kennedy:

> I am writing on behalf of my friend Rudolf Nureyev. Mr Nureyev is traveling to the Soviet Union from Paris on Saturday, November 14, for a two-day visit with his family. The purpose of his trip is to see his mother who is quite ill.
>
> I would be grateful if you would convey to Ambassador [Anatoly] Dobrynin and to Foreign Minister [Eduard] Shevardnadze my own personal concern that Mr Nureyev's trip go smoothly. It is a very sensitive time in relations between our two countries, and I think you would agree it would be important to avoid any incidents.

Arriving at Moscow's Sheremetyevo airport, a striking figure in a long herringbone overcoat, Missoni scarf and tam-o'-shanter, Rudolf was immediately surrounded by representatives of the world's press. Asked to comment on Gorbachev's new policies, he nimbly deflected the question by paraphrasing Joseph Brodsky: 'I believe Mr Brodsky said, "I would rather have him at the head of government than someone else."'[*] When he spotted Liuba in the crowd he called her over, saying with mock pomposity, 'Would you like to share my fame?' But

---

[*] He was less circumspect in later interviews: 'I think not only Russia but the whole world is fortunate to have Mr Gorbachev as the leader of this country. I think he deserves a Nobel Prize or something like that' (Dutch TV interview). And to Lynn Barber, Rudolf said, 'Unfortunately [Gorbachev] was not consistent all the way, but it was a great landmark. The Russians are not ready, they are completely uneducated, they cannot think for themselves.'

still nervous of being publicly linked to a defector, she dropped her glove in order to duck down and avoid being photographed. Rudolf, who with his two minders had been invited to the French Embassy, asked Liuba to join them, but that was out of the question, she said. 'For me to get permission to enter a foreign consulate would take six months!' Instead she suggested they go to the apartment of a close friend, who was waiting to receive them.

Tanya Petrova, an attractive widow, lived with her French-born mother and teenage daughter near the Leningrad railway station, in what Maître described as 'a cheap, tiny Muscovite apartment which barely had electricity and running water'. The elderly Elena Mikhailovna Nikiforova had been extremely agitated at receiving in her home not only the infamous dancer but two foreigners, and yet gave them a typically Russian welcome – a celebratory spread of soaked cowberries, salted mushrooms and blinis. While the French sat down to eat, entertained by sixteen-year-old Masha playing the guitar and singing folk songs, Liuba asked permission to go to another room with Rudolf 'to talk and talk and talk'.

> It was difficult at first. We had to find each other again. 'Twenty-eight years had passed – a whole life!' I told him. 'Not whole life,' he said. 'Maybe just the best part. See, I haven't changed that much – I don't have glasses, I still have all my teeth.' I told him he was crazy to be addressing me as '*vy*' [the Russian equivalent of the French formal *vous*], and he explained that in English there is only one word for 'you.' But I said, 'Let's behave as if nothing has happened, and go back to how things were in our youth.' He agreed, and after that all the barriers disappeared. I asked him about his life, about his feelings, about ballet, about his plans for the future (we both understood that his dance career was coming to an end). He asked me about our life, about my parents, about the new line of policy, about Kirov Ballet, and mutual friends. It was chaotic! We jumped from one subject to another, but in the end it was much too little time.

The three visitors were still expected at the French Embassy, where a dinner had been planned before their departure to Ufa. To Rudolf it was just a blur. 'He hardly said a word,' recalls Janine. 'For him this was such an event.'[*] As they were due to leave around midnight, he had

---

[*] And not only to Rudolf. Rostropovich, told by Luigi that Rudolf was on his way to Ufa, could not believe it. 'It's not possible,' he kept saying. 'No, no, no, no! Not possible' (Diane Solway, *Nureyev*).

assumed that a private plane had been arranged specially for him, but he discovered on arrival at Moscow's domestic airport that he was just one of a hundred other people booked on an Aeroflot flight. Sitting unrecognized at the back of the plane, 'squashed up with all the peasants with cases and cartons on their laps', Rudolf looked half stunned, clearly appalled by the conditions. Slowly, however, he began to open up, reminiscing to Janine about his life as a child. 'Everything was coming back. He told me for the first time how their father was never there, and how it was their mother who did everything for them. He said how strong she was – strong and clever – and I felt from the way he spoke of her that it had become a kind of idealization.' (Jackie Onassis had felt much the same watching Rudolf in *Swan Lake* at the moment when Siegfried kisses the Queen's hand – 'the homage, the duty, the respect he has for the idea of a mother'.)

After the lack of preferential treatment on the plane, Rudolf was pleased to see a photographer awaiting his arrival in Ufa. 'Good, good. Splendid,' he said when Viktor Vonog greeted him on the runway, announcing that he would be recording the whole trip. 'Is anybody meeting me?' 'Yes, your sister, nephews and niece.' In the Intourist lounge were Razida and her two sons, Viktor (twenty-five) and Yuri (eighteen), as well as Alfia, whom Rudolf had last seen hours after she was born. 'I remember you as so small and red,' he said teasingly, but to Alfia it was her uncle who 'looked very odd – so odd that everyone turned to stare'. As it was now almost five a.m. – the time in Ufa is two hours ahead of Moscow – everyone was too tired to start getting to know one another, and so they arranged to meet later that morning, Rudolf heading off with his two acquaintances to the Hotel Rossiya. (He must then have gone out again, because when Viktor arrived to pick him up as planned, the attendant on the floor said that he had not been back long and was still asleep.) At around eleven Viktor returned to drive Rudolf to the October Prospekt apartment, but when he asked to photograph the reunion with Farida, Rudolf snapped, 'With my mother, no!' instructing him to come back in forty minutes.

This was the moment Rudolf had been anticipating for years. 'There's so much I want to ask her,' he had told Linda Maybarduk, who remembers how 'he had always been curious to find out things like the time of his birth, and whether he was really born on a train'. He had no delusions, understanding that when finally they met, he and his mother would be different people to each other – 'We would have to relearn everything.' And now, of course, he knew about her desperate state of health. Yet nothing had prepared him for the shock of what he saw – the picture of poverty and misery that Evgenii Petrovich had described. 'The room was completely bare . . . just a worn ottoman covered with an oilcloth and a small night-table. An old woman was lying in a doubled-up position . . . She did not even open her eyes. Only the fact that she slowly moved her legs and fingers from time to time told you that she was alive.'

To this day Liuba regrets not having suggested to Rudolf that Phail go with him, since 'with acupuncture, maybe their contact could have been more fruitful'. As it was, Farida showed no reaction to Rudolf's presence. 'She didn't know me,' as he later told friends. Razida says that after he left she asked their mother if she realized who had been there. 'Yes. It was Rudik,' she murmured. But what shattered Rudolf was not so much that his mother had shown no sign of recognizing him but that he had not recognized *her*. 'She had become someone else,' he confided to Charles Jude, saying that it had been the same with Erik. 'Like something finish.' Once again Rudolf had arrived too late, and this time it was the Soviet government he could not forgive. They were 'masters of torture', he told Linda Maybarduk. 'They delivered last blow.'

Rudolf had stayed in the room less than ten minutes, and although he said nothing when he emerged, his relatives could see that he was badly shaken. 'That I know for sure,' says Alfia. 'But he managed to hide his emotions and act as if everything was normal.' The family was also putting on something of an act, doing their best to show Rudolf that they were doing well. 'They bought meat in the marketplace, made *pelmeni*, were happy to see him. But it was all just a "Potemkin village",'[*] remarked Evgenii Petrovich. 'Were Rudik to have arrived unannounced, he would have seen the real situation.' In fact, a large meal was the last thing Rudolf wanted but, to be polite, he ate the Russian bread he loved with butter and drank four glasses of tea. 'We all felt a bit awkward,' Razida remembers. 'It was hard to start a conversation because we didn't know what to say. We could see the difference between him and us.' Rudolf told them that it was difficult for him to speak Russian because he had to translate it to himself first into English and then back again. But aware how unapproachable he must seem, he did most of the talking, questioning his nephews with

* A reference to the story that Catherine the Great's favourite minister, Grigori Alexsandrovich Potemkin, strove to impress her during her tours of the Ukraine and Crimea by constructing elaborate façades of villages whose inhabitants were forced to dance and act as if they were happy.

genuine interest about what they did in Ufa. To Yuri's reply that he was learning German, Rudolf said, 'Hmm, that's good. Anything you do you must do well. If you work hard success will come.' And then he asked Razida, 'What would you like to do? Is there anything you would like to learn?' No, she was too old, she protested, and he smiled, as if to say, 'Well, so be it.'

Rudolf did not go back in again to see Farida, and when Viktor saw him approach the car, he noticed 'something in his face, some cloud of sadness'. They began a tour of the city, stopping off at the market, where Rudolf bought *babushki*'s woollen stockings, which he planned to wear in class as leg warmers. It was not the same Ufa he remembered, most of the wooden *isbi* having been replaced by modern apartment houses. 'I sort of regret that it goes modern,' he later remarked. 'Nice wide streets, the highest building is five storeys, so it's not too ugly, a lot of trees.' He wanted to go first to the opera house, and headed straight up to one of the studios, commenting on photographs of dancers he remembered. The director arrived, and Rudolf asked to be taken onstage, where he tried out a few steps, grimacing at the floorboards' lack of spring. 'Metal?' 'No, no,' replied the director, oblivious to the irony. 'The floor is oak.' 'Metal,' repeated Rudolf. As he was being led around he asked Viktor to call the information service for three or four numbers, one being that of Zaituna Nazretdinova, the ballerina who had danced in *Song of the Cranes* on the day the seven-year-old Rudik's fate was sealed. When neither she nor anyone else answered the telephone, he shrugged, 'Oh, well, what can we do then?' Victor suggested going to 37 Zentsova Street, which used to be the Nureyevs' home, but was now the site of a corrugated-iron garage. After asking to be photographed in front of a typical *isba* and in the yard of another ('very much reminiscent of Polenov's painting'), they went to the hill of Salavat, where he used to sit watching the trains beckoning him West. As the Muslim cemetery was nearby, Viktor suggested that Rudolf visit his father's grave and was shocked when he refused, asking instead to be driven to School number 2 on Sverdlova Street.

School number 2 had become Ufa's Choreographic Academy,[*] and its director, Alik Bikchurin (the Vaganova pupil Rudolf had once persuaded to introduce him to his Leningrad teachers), claims that the authorities had deliberately sent him two hundred kilometres away so that he wouldn't be there to welcome Rudolf. 'They wanted to give

* Now known as the Rudolf Nureyev Ballet School.

the impression that they were indifferent to his visit, that it was a stranger who was coming. In the theatre they gave everyone the day off.' At the Philharmonic Hall the musicians, who had been rehearsing, were sent home an hour before the star's arrival, and at the Nesterov Museum a surly woman guard followed Rudolf around, yelling with fury when she saw him take a photograph. Aware of the farcical turn his visit was taking, Rudolf was more than ready to leave when the time came to catch his flight.

At Moscow's Domodedovo airport the attitude was just as hostile. 'I began to be a little afraid,' says Janine, describing how customs officers had immediately confiscated the Bashkirian honey that Rudolf's family had given him. The reason, she discovered, was the Chernobyl nuclear disaster, after which certain produce (mushrooms, too) from even thousands of kilometres away was forbidden to be sold. 'You must explain that,' said Janine, noticing Rudolf getting angry. 'I'm not allowed to,' the official replied.* 'Well then, I shall.' Just as unpleasant was the squalor of the terminal with its stinking urinals and human detritus spread around on the floor, 'like Calcutta', murmured Rudolf. But he cheered up when he saw that standing waiting for him with Liuba was her brother, Leonid, the object of his youthful crush.

Although he was reluctant to discuss his time in Ufa during the hour-long journey into Moscow, sitting wedged between the Romankov twins in the embassy car, Rudolf soon relaxed into their old intimacy. He told them how much he had envied the tranquil cultural atmosphere of their home; how in listening to their conversations about painting, samizdat literature or the poets of the Russian Renaissance, he had been afraid to speak for fear of exposing his provincialism. He had not stopped trying to educate himself since then, he said. 'But everything I know has been grabbed here and there in bits. When I was doing a ballet I would read Shakespeare or Byron, but never with any real depth.' They went to the home of the young Bolshoi star Andris Liepa, whom Rudolf wanted to meet. The twenty-five-year-old dancer had a performance of *Giselle* that night but was so anxious to have enough time with Rudolf that he arrived still wearing full stage makeup. They drank a lot, talked a lot, and at last, in the company of these like-minded Russians, Rudolf felt that he had come home.

---

* It took the authorities eighteen days to admit the extent of the disaster that took place at the nuclear power station in the Ukraine in April 1986, and even then the accounts were heavily expurgated.

But if his family was left with the impression that 'he was estranged from Russia', that it 'hadn't made any impression on him', they were wrong. Back in Paris, he felt such nostalgia for Ufa that he announced to Janine, 'I want to buy one of those wooden houses – can you help me?' 'I was surprised, because I thought it was an awful provincial little town, but from that moment he wanted to keep his links with Ufa.' Rudolf had already re-created his own Bashkiria in Virginia, with its shuttered house and barns, streams, fields and silver birches, telling his relatives that he hoped they would all come and live there one day. There was also a painting he had long coveted, and was now determined to have. This was Romney's study of Alope with her baby son (Zeus's love child) at her breast, which was owned by Jimmy Douglas. So resonant was the painting's subject, not only the mother–son image but its story of a child cast into the wilderness under the protection of a god, that Rudolf persuaded Jimmy (who had bought it in the 1950s for a thousand pounds) to sell it to him for fifty thousand dollars. This was more than double its worth: in Christie's 1995 Nureyev auction, the Romney sold for twenty thousand dollars.

Rudolf would find himself increasingly drawn back to his homeland, but for now Paris was where he wanted to be, and his fifth season with the Opéra was proving to be the most stimulating of his tenure there. With Jacques Chirac's Conservative government in force since 1986, Marie-Suzanne's husband, Raymond Soubie, had been named the Opéra's president, and although not the close friend and ally André Larquié had been, he was firmly on Rudolf's side. He had lost his 'pillar', Claire Motte, who died of cancer in the summer of '86, but had appointed the superbly capable Patrice Bart as ballet master, a colleague who remained faithful to the end. Betty Anderton, who had proved unpopular with the dancers, had left ('she had a rather superior, colonial attitude that the French didn't take to'), and Rudolf had invited Pat Ruanne ('more of a trouper') to take over. Confident that he had a forceful new team in place, Rudolf began making big plans. The Bastille was soon to open, and his idea was that the Palais Garnier should be devoted entirely to dance, with Jean-Luc Choplin taking charge as its general director. 'The Dance must have its theatre,' they wrote in a manifesto outlining key points. 'It must be a centre of influence in Europe; of research; of information.' There would be an audiovisual department to record ballets for the archives and commissions to create dance for the camera, a centre of choreology to notate the repertory, a medical centre, a library, a museum, a dance journal and an annual festival of dance throughout France. 'We have to prepare today for the future. *Vive la danse!*'

Rudolf was also showing himself to be more accommodating when it came to respecting French tradition. In October 1986 Igor Eisner had written urging him to reconsider his attitude towards Serge Lifar. 'One can bring different historical judgements to the ballets of Lifar, but the fact is that he created a style and that his name will stay synonymous with a brilliant period in the history of the Paris Opéra. Certainly, one must look towards the future, but one must also respect past memories.' As if in direct response, Rudolf arranged a homage to Lifar in January 1988, juxtaposing it two months later with his most avant-garde programming to date (Maguy Marin's *Leçons de ténèbres,* William Forsythe's *In the middle somewhat elevated* and *Le Martyre de Saint Sébastien*, Robert Wilson's three-hour ballet for the new generation of stars, led by Sylvie Guillem). These contemporary works were also to be shown during the New York summer season, since Rudolf had achieved his ambition of returning annually to the Met as the Royal Ballet had done in the past.

In February, while holding a press conference in New York to announce his company's plans, he discovered that Wallace and Jeannette were in town, staying with millionaire Howard Gillman, who was hosting the launch party for the musical *Phantom of the Opera.* Rudolf had not been invited and having obtained a last-minute ticket for him, Jeannette was somewhat put out when he began procrastinating about whether or not he wanted to come. 'He sounded very sad, and said, "Call me at interval." So I did, and I told him the show was really great.' But in the end Rudolf couldn't be persuaded to join them, which upset Wallace, who presumed it was because of his jealousy of Gillman: 'Howard had this big thing on me – he was in love with me, I guess – and he was also part of Misha's clan. All this interlocked in Rudolf's mind, and the next day when we met I felt so much tension. He was saying things like "Who are you going to see more of?" wanting everything to revolve around him. I felt I'd had enough, and flew back to LA that day.'

Rudolf was still in an oddly sombre mood when his friend Natasha Harley took him to lunch at La Côte Basque. Trying to cheer him up, she suggested that they go antiquing, and called her office to send a car to take them downtown. 'With the driver following us, we walked, walked, walked. Then Rudolf said, "*Basta.* I'm going to go home."' Natasha had not been home long herself when she got a call from Gouzel to say that Farida had died. She immediately called Rudolf, who already knew. Jeannette was convinced 'he had got the phone call the previous day but hadn't volunteered anything'.

He had not even confided in Maude, 'but he guessed that was why I rang', she wrote to Wallace, who had been shocked to hear that Rudolf's idea of mourning was to go shopping. 'I can understand why,' she told him. 'It helped him not to have to think about something that he could do nothing about . . . it helped to blur the pain that I am sure he was feeling.' With Jeannette, too, Rudolf had wanted to go to the downtown antiques shops later that day, and when she dropped him off at the Dakota, said bluntly, 'We're going to Mrs Harley's for dinner tonight. And by the way, my mother died.' 'And then he slammed the door.'

When Hamet died, the only person Rudolf had wanted to be with was Paklusha, and Natasha Harley was Paklusha's New York equivalent, an adoring Russian earth mother, who had also been introduced to him by Margot. She; her Russian husband, André; and their two daughters, Tatiana and Tamara, had become another surrogate family, providing the Russian culture and background that were a source of constant pleasure to him. Both their parents had been patrons of Diaghilev, and André's mother, Ginrietta Hirschman, had been a famous beauty whose Paris house was a salon for artists, writers and musicians. Rudolf loved paging through the Hirschmans' guest book, which contained a poem by Balmont, bars of music by Prokofiev, a paean of praise to her by Stanislavsky and inscriptions by, among others, Robert de Montesquiou, Rachmaninoff, Chaliapin and Joyce.

Natasha's huge airy East Sixty-eighth Street apartment was itself a salon to visiting ballet companies (when Ashton saw her in London, he would exclaim, 'Ah, *New York*!') and it was she on whom Rudolf now depended to host his own dinner parties. One evening she cooked for Martha Graham and another for Lincoln Kirstein, 'a very tense occasion', when Rudolf had exploded because Kirstein was bringing caviar and Natasha had prepared the wrong kind of potatoes with which to serve it.[*] Natasha was a powerful figure in the cosmetics and perfume industry, but she could not have been more unassuming and sweet-natured; she seemed almost childlike, with her apple cheeks, uncoiffed hair and school sandals. 'When I think of her,' says Jamie

---

[*] Wanting to settle past scores, Rudolf confronted Kirstein by saying, 'Why did you hate me so much?' 'So many years had passed, but Rudolf felt he needed to know about that,' says Robert Tracy, who remembers how Kirstein, without attempting to reply, suddenly got up and left. The two never saw each other again.

Wyeth, 'I see her gazing up at Rudolf with those huge dark eyes. She would do *anything* for him.' 'From the very beginning Natasha was someone Rudolf could always trust,' adds Robert Tracy.

When Rudolf's niece Gouzel first arrived in the West it was Natasha whom Rudolf had asked to take her in. 'She came with her husband, and we made room for them, but it was pretty much a catastrophe. She was against everything American, and would strew the living room with her shoes, her underwear . . . She went to the country, but it was no better there.' Almost as if testing the limits of Natasha's loyalty, Rudolf called her one day to say he had a favour to ask: 'I've invited a friend to the farm for dinner and I can't be there on time. Could you please go?' With no hesitation she went food shopping in New York and, taking her assistant with her, caught an early evening flight to Virginia. Finding the house practically unfurnished, they had just hunted up a board and cloth with which to improvise a table when the bell rang. It was Jackie Onassis, smiling and informal in blue jeans. (She was publishing a children's book by Pushkin* and wanted Rudolf to write the introduction.)

On the night of 6 February 1988, when Natasha answered her doorbell, it was Baryshnikov she found standing on the steps, apologizing for being early. Rudolf followed some time afterwards with Jeannette, and while she and Natasha made dinner, the two dancers sat together, talking intently. At around midnight Andris Liepa and his young Bolshoi partner, Nina Ananiashvili, dropped in, invited by Rudolf, who clearly felt the need to surround himself with Russians. The ballerina, a dark, sophisticated Georgian beauty, was strikingly matched with the boyish, blond Liepa. They had come to America to make their debut with the New York City Ballet, realizing Rudolf's own dream of dancing the Balanchine repertory while still being free to return to Russia. (Liepa would be invited later that year by Baryshnikov to join ABT, becoming the first Soviet to win a contract abroad.) Natasha remembers how the couple themselves hardly said a word, but just sat rapt, listening to the advice and experiences of the two defectors. 'It was a lovely, lovely evening. Very late, very cosy, very personal.'

A month later the next ordeal facing Rudolf was his fiftieth birthday. Knowing that the best present anyone could give him was the opportunity to dance, Jeannette had cajoled Misha into offering him

* *The Golden Cockerel and Other Fairy Tales*, by Aleksandr Pushkin, illustrated by Boris Zvorykin (New York: Doubleday, 1989).

more performances of *Giselle* (the first of three was on 17 March, the night of his birthday), and in June, he finally made his own debut with the New York City Ballet. He had wanted to dance Apollo, but Peter Martins, who had succeeded Balanchine as director, told him that he was too old, and cast him in *Orpheus*, an old-fashioned mime role. Appearing in a ballet Arlene Croce has described as 'an ashen meditation permeated by the sweetish odour of death' was hardly a momentous celebration, and it was left to Jane Hermann to give Rudolf the homage he deserved. Rounding up almost every partner, peer and choreographer with whom he had worked in the West, she scheduled 'a bang-up gala' at the Met, launching the Paris Opéra's summer season.

To everyone's astonishment, Rudolf was appalled. 'He accused Jane of trying to force him off the stage,' says Wallace. 'He thought of this as a final tribute. The kind of thing people do when your career is over.' 'He *dreaded* it,' added Maude. ' "This is burying me," he said. He felt it was an imposition, that afterwards, everything would be finished.' On Sunday 26 June, the night before the gala, Rudolf was having dinner at the Café des Artistes with Maude, Wallace and Jane, when the conversation turned to English critics. Getting more and more upset, he suddenly jumped up, cursed everyone at the table and stormed out. 'I rushed after him, and Jane rushed after me,' says Wallace. 'It was so traumatic Maude developed shingles as a result.'

Having threatened not to appear at all, Rudolf, in the end, couldn't help being moved by his birthday gala. 'The evening was quite spectacular,' Linda Maybarduk recalls. 'Jane really outdid herself.' It was not so much the repertory that was memorable,* but what came afterwards. To close, the Parisians performed their famous defilé for the first time outside France, the entire company and students from the school advancing to centre stage according to their rank. There, lining up in an inverted V to await Rudolf's entrance, were the great and good of international dance: Lincoln Kirstein, Peter Martins, Peter Schaufuss, Rudi van Dantzig, Murray Louis, together with Rudolf's ballerinas – Margot, Maria Tallchief, Carla Fracci, Yvette Chauviré, Karen Kain, Cynthia Gregory, Violette Verdy, Yoko Morishita, Eva Evdokimova.†

* The programme, conducted by James Levine, included the new William Forsythe ballet *In the middle somewhat elevated* and *Songs of a Wayfarer*, with Jessye Norman as the soprano.
† Evdokimova became Rudolf's favourite partner in the latter stage of his career. Earning his high regard for her versatility (her multifaceted training combined the Royal Ballet, Bournonville and Vaganova styles), Evdokimova could adapt herself, as he did, to numerous companies and a diversity of repertory, spanning Petipa to Glen Tetley.

(Even Miss Piggy, whom Rudolf had once partnered on television's *The Muppet Show* was there.) As he took his solo bow, a huge banner emblazoned with 'Nureyev' unfurled from the ceiling, hundreds of balloons floated down, and gold and silver confetti rained on the stage. After leading his Opéra dancers forward he turned to his left, directly in line with Baryshnikov, who was waiting to embrace him, hugging him so exuberantly that he lifted Rudolf off his feet. He then continued down the line, greeting one person after the next, and only when he reached the end and turned around did he see Margot. 'This was what everyone was waiting for, and when he kissed her the room just exploded,' says Marilyn La Vine. 'It was exciting and gratifying to see Rudolf so appreciated. He looked *very*, *very*, *very* happy.'

Maude maintains, however, that Rudolf was happy only because it was all over, and that his ongoing black mood was so engulfing that it had even distanced the two of them. 'I certainly felt that my presence there didn't give Rudolf any help in his unhappiness,' she told Wallace. 'He has too much on his mind, too many things to resolve for his future, and the loss of closeness with Jane didn't help . . . She so hopes that Rudolf will come back to friendship again, but will leave it to him.' Others, Linda Maybarduk among them, felt that Rudolf had 'no right to be so ungrateful'; that Jane Hermann had, after all, planned the gala as a great celebration, not an 'obituary', to use his word.

To make it clear that there was no emblematic closure about his appearance in *Songs of a Wayfarer* (the image that evening of the older dancer being led offstage by Charles Jude had suggested to Linda that 'he would never leave the spotlight of his own free will'), Rudolf insisted on dancing the ballet at every subsequent performance, arranging to have 'By popular demand!' mendaciously blazed across the advertising hoardings, which further antagonized Jane Hermann. In addition to the Béjart piece, he was dancing in his productions of *Swan Lake* and *The Nutcracker* (the US première), causing Anna Kisselgoff to comment that he was no longer able to perform the easy steps, 'but perversely, carries off the difficult ones'. Clive Barnes added, 'Even so, enough is enough, especially in the cruel world of classical dance.'

At La Scala, however, where he had appeared earlier that year in *The Nutcracker* and *Giselle*, Rudolf knew that he could still get away with his classical roles. As critic Vittoria Ottolenghi remarks, 'Nobody in Italy would ever hiss him offstage. When you're a maestro, you're always a maestro.' Giorgio Cattarello agrees. An admirer from the beginning, he admits having 'treasured the good times; and justified and pardoned the worst'.

Vienna, too, was somewhere Rudolf '*always* had a job'. As a present to himself he had danced not Rothbart but the Prince at his fiftieth-birthday performance of *Swan Lake*, an occasion that his fan Traude Klockl remembers as being hard to watch. 'But Viennese audiences are very special: they go with an artist they love to the *end*. They're still faithful and they still cheer.' And in Vienna was a family that Rudolf had come to regard as his own. Wilhelm 'Papa' Hübner, his half-Russian wife, Lydia, and their children, Elizabeth and Waxy, had become Rudolf's Austrian Romankovs, although this was a friendship that had taken a long time to establish. In the sixties, when the critic Linda Zamponi had him to dinner, asking Lydia to made *pelmeni* for the occasion, Rudolf had refused to eat, suspecting that the dish was poisoned. And when, some five or six years later, Papa Hübner, who was president of the Vienna Philharmonic, invited Rudolf to a concert followed by a meal at their home, it had been difficult, Waxy says, 'to convince him that we were a normal family and were not leading him into a trap'. Their simple sitting room with its display cabinet of ornaments and profusion of framed photographs and books had much the same atmosphere as Tchaikovsky Street, and Rudolf soon dropped his guard. It is understandable why. A musician-guru father, Russian mother, nineteen-year-old medical student 'sitting there looking beautiful', with a sister who was an adoring Nureyev fan, comprised Rudolf's dream unit. Not only that, but the Hübners were to prove his salvation, steering him away from the stage and towards what he had always claimed was his primary passion. 'In the first place is music, which will remain with me to the end of my days; and then ballet, which someday will betray me.'

In January 1982 Rudolf had adopted Austrian citizenship, and yet he did not consider Vienna a place in which to live. What he had coveted for many years was somewhere by the sea – '*pied en l'eau*', as the French say – and, failing to secure his Turkish peninsula, had been looking at property in Hawaii. Not for long. 'Houses now cost $6, 7, 8 million and it's not that attractive,' he told Lynn Barber. In July 1988, hearing that Luchino Visconti's villa in Forio d'Ischia was on the market, Rudolf went to see it, only to find that it was 'not on the water [and] in the middle of hotels'. He had even begun to consider a three-masted schooner: 'Finally, I thought that only a boat in the middle of the sea might quiet my thirst for blue, for sun, for silence.' And then he was told that Léonide Massine's island was for sale.

Staying with Russian friends in Positano in the 1920s, Massine had looked out of his window and noticed an island several miles off the coast. Known as Li Galli, this was in fact an archipelago of three islands belonging to a local family, who used them only for quail-hunting in the spring. Visiting Gallo Lungo, the largest, and overcome by the beauty of the view across the sea towards the Gulf of Salerno, Massine struck a deal with the family, paying what today would be around ten thousand dollars. Locals called him 'the mad Russian who has bought a rocky island where only rabbits could live', warning that he would never get anything to grow. But he spent several months helping the workers to terrace the neglected vineyards, planting new vines to make his own wine ('tastes like a poison', Rudolf had been told), as well as cypress trees and southern pines. His industry impressed Rudolf. 'He built so many things at a time there was no technical help, and he built those enormous houses, very comfortable, and made irrigation and big cisterns for gathering rainwater.' The terraced garden with its fountain and scent of rosemary faced Capri, and the five-bedroom house had views of the Lattari Mountains. But what especially appealed to Rudolf was the eleventh-century Saracen tower on the northern end of the island in which the choreographer had built a ballet studio.

The price Massine's estate was asking for Li Galli was $2.4 million. 'We argued for a while – then I remembered the prices of Hawaii and decided it was a very good deal.' Gorlinsky, however, thought otherwise, and sternly counselled against the purchase. In retaliation, Rudolf asked his Chicago lawyer, Barry Weinstein, to fly to Switzerland to review the portfolio of his properties. 'He was irritated with his European advisers and said, "They're treating me like a baby." He wanted to know more about what was going on in his life financially.' On 14 September 1988 the deeds of Li Galli passed from Massine's name to Rudolf's, a lineage that in itself explains much of Li Galli's appeal. While interviewing Massine on Gallo Lungo in the summer of 1967 for a television programme on Diaghilev, John Drummond had felt the Russian spirit permeating the place. 'Voices were calling from the house in Russian, answered in French. I remembered Benois's family scrapbooks of the Crimea before the revolution; the sense of history and continuity and Russianness was overwhelming.'

Rudolf's sixth season at the Opéra was marred by the 'national catastrophe' of losing Sylvie Guillem. There had been warning signs for several months: the renewal of her contract was due, and she was not only demanding huge fees but a non-exclusive arrangement that would allow her to perform abroad. 'We had endless meetings,'

Jean-Luc Choplin says, 'but Rudolf saw that he could not break Paris
Opéra rules or single her out any more than he had already done. On
the New York tour she had been very difficult, making us feel that she
was no longer respecting the company. So we let her go.' The double
blow for Rudolf was learning that Sylvie would be joining the Royal
Ballet, a relationship he himself had initiated.* He had called angrily
at midnight, and yet Sylvie was certain that he 'deeply understood why
I had to go. I was like him – I felt I was losing my time.' Determined
to forge her own destiny, solipsistic and impossibly demanding, she
was indeed like Rudolf: she, too, would lay claim to '*le style anglais*',
iconoclastically change choreography and costumes on a whim, and
bring a contemporary relevance to nineteenth-century classical roles.
Recognizing this, Rudolf, who kept a photograph of Sylvie beside his
bed, freely admitted that he had never met any dancer who challenged
him to such a degree.

But no one, as Diaghilev announced after Nijinsky's defection, is
irreplaceable, and a new protégé, challenging in a completely different
way, would emerge in no time. One day, after a Stanley Williams class
in New York, Rudolf was approached by an astoundingly tall, astoundingly beautiful young Danish dancer whose name was Kenneth Greve.
Hoping to secure an American visa, he was in the process of collecting
influential signatures for a reference letter and asked Rudolf if he
would mind adding his. 'Well,' he replied, 'first I must see you dance.'
They stayed on together in the studio, Rudolf watching the nineteen-
year-old perform a series of bravura steps. There was something of his
young self in the boy's Slavic cheekbones, sensuous lips, and flying
mop, but there were traces of Erik, too. With his Apollonian proportions, blond hair and Danish schooling, Kenneth was the dancer they
might, had nature allowed, have created together – potentially the
perfect Nureyev–Bruhn progeny. 'I'll sign your paper. No problem,'
Rudolf grinned, taking things no further until a couple of months
later. They were both in a class Baryshnikov was teaching, and when it
was over, Rudolf went up to Kenneth. 'Listen,' he said, 'I need a big
boy for Paris Opéra, and I think you have talent.' To be certain, he
spent another hour and a half auditioning the dancer, commenting at
the end, 'You can do everything, but you need work.' ' Rudolf told me
that he realized what he was considering was provocative, but he
wanted to take me because of what he thought I could *become*.' Not

* By choosing her as his partner in *Giselle* – a January 1988 performance commemorating
his fiftieth birthday.

long afterwards Kenneth was woken by the telephone at around four in the morning: it was Rudolf calling from Paris to offer him a three-year contract as an *étoile*.

Before Kenneth started at the Opéra, even though he had never before performed a major role, Rudolf wanted him to appear as Siegfried in a Grand Palais season of the Nureyev *Swan Lake*. With only ten days to learn the ballet he was coached in turn by Rudolf, Pat Ruanne and Genia Poliakov, finding the pressure '*very*, *very* hard'. 'You have to get smart, my little peasant boy from Denmark,' Rudolf urged him. 'You have feeling – *use* your feeling: I want to make a dancer out of you.' Kenneth received virtually no help from his partner, Isabelle Guérin, who was 'not at all pleased to be dancing with this young inexperienced kid'. But he himself admits that he was 'one huge baby – one metre ninety-five tall. I'd been growing for ever, and was just starting to get control over my body.'

At quai Voltaire on 27 June, the eve of the performance, Mario Bois watched Rudolf, who was clearly besotted, sitting on the sofa at two in the morning with his hand on the teenager's knee. The picture it brought to mind – an ageing performer drawing inspiration from a young dancer – reminded Bois of Chaplin's *Limelight*, the film in which a beautiful ballerina helps a music-hall clown achieve a last moment of glory. But the situation's erotic undertow makes it closer to Ibsen's *The Master Builder*, where we see how the potency of youth can dazzle an artist into believing that he still retains his former creative powers. 'Imagine at my age being so blown over!' Rudolf remarked with no trace of remorse as, to him, this had become the only type of relationship that counted: the Diaghilev–Nijinsky dynamic of 'art and love indissolubly entwined'. And for the moment, it was gratifying to see that in performing the proselytising Tutor to Kenneth's Siegfried, his conception of *Swan Lake* had never been more resonant or true. 'Rudolf was always very direct about his attraction to me. He kept trying to convince me that I was gay and just didn't know it. He said, "Dream . . . use your imagination." "I can't," I told him. "I'm incapable. I'm sorry, I'm very flattered, but I love women – what can I do? I can only love you as a father and as a teacher."'

To the majority of Opéra dancers, however, the young Dane was 'Rudolf's little sexpot'; two of the boys had already tried to pick a fight with him, and during the performance, another had crouched, 'mooning' Kenneth from the wings. 'There was literally a guy there with his trousers off showing me his rear end.' But there was no point letting the hostility upset him: he needed all his concentration to get through the ballet. Having seen the ending for the first time during Charles Jude's performance the day before, Kenneth admits that he had walked into the fourth act not really knowing what to do. And yet to Jacques Loyau, who was in the audience that night, the dancer came across as 'Very beautiful, very good . . . Although the details weren't yet there.' Studying the videotape with Kenneth after the performance, Rudolf, he says, reached much the same conclusion. 'He's a careful prince. And you can see that he's pretty scared.'

The reason the other dancers were so furious, Loyau insists, was because the young intruder had been a success although this is a view with which even Rudolf's closest allies disagree. 'The *étoiles* felt he didn't have the technique,' says André Larquié, 'and I think their opposition was quite right. I was very surprised by this choice of Rudolf's, and, like the critics, thought: Why him?' 'Rudolf is mad,' wrote Mario Bois, describing how, when Elisabeth Platel refused to have Kenneth as a partner, Rudolf told the ballerina that he no longer wanted her dancing any of his ballets. Genia Poliakov was convinced that Rudolf 'knew he was wrong', but if this was so, he was still determined to hold out. He wanted to make a statement, he told Kenneth, saying, 'If *I* can't decide, who can?'

This was a period when Rudolf's authority was seriously being called into question. With the reelection of François Mitterrand in March 1988, Jack Lang had resumed his role as minister of culture, and in February 1989 he appointed Jean-Albert Cartier as administrator general of the Opéra. One of Cartier's first moves was to tell Choplin that he was no longer required. 'This was the beginning of the end. For both of us. Rudolf had never liked Cartier, he had no trust in his taste, and he could see that from now on he was going to be working under bureaucrats. He would continue as head of the company, but in this reduced, secondary role.' Rudolf remained optimistic, nevertheless, that he would be able to count on the support of the new president of the Opéra-Bastille, Pierre Bergé (chosen by Mitterrand after he had helped him to finance his campaign). One of his first friends in Paris, the lover and business partner of Yves Saint Laurent, as well as a confidant of Clara Saint, Bergé was no bureaucrat, but an impresario of culture and vision. 'When I was made head of the Opéra, Rudolf said, "All my problems will be solved,"' but Bergé told him, 'Rudi, you're wrong . . . Maybe this is the beginning of your problems.'

It was. Whereas most Opéra presidents had been figureheads, 'like chairmen of charity balls', Bergé, a diminutive man with huge self-regard, had creative ambitions of his own. In January 1989, 'tired of

being a businessman to someone else's artist', he fired Daniel Barenboim, the music and artistic director, prompting Pierre Boulez to
resign from the board in protest. The president, Boulez remarked, had
'delusions of grandeur . . . and no sense of the ridiculous'. Then one
of the wealthiest men in France and, given his intimacy with the president, one of the most powerful, Bergé had a dangerous reputation,
being seen by his enemies as foul tempered, controlling and vindic-
tive. In January, however, when Bergé alerted Rudolf to the fact that
his contract was coming to an end, he was also well aware of Rudolf's
achievements and had every intention of retaining him. But he was
determined, too, to keep Rudolf under control – and that meant
keeping him in Paris. 'He wanted me to stay not for six months but
twelve. I said, "Let's not even discuss it."' Jean-Luc Choplin believes
that if the Palais Garnier had become the 'temple of dance' they had
planned, Rudolf would have devoted himself entirely to the Paris
Opéra Ballet. 'He was very excited by the idea, and if those conditions
had been met, would have stopped everything else. For him, though,
the only way was full responsibility. Total artistic freedom.'

'What can I do now?' Rudolf complained to Charles Jude one day. 'I
can't just be in my office. I have to *do* something.' And that meant
dancing. With the Opéra restricting his number of performances, he was
now more intent than ever on finding opportunities elsewhere. While
on tour with the company in Copenhagen, Rudolf ran into the
choreographer Flemming Flindt, who was also staying at the Hôtel
d'Angleterre. They were getting into the lift when Flindt said, 'I saw
you in *Swan Lake* last night. It was *awful*.' 'Was it?' replied Rudolf, with
surprising meekness. 'Yes, it was,' insisted Flindt. 'You can't do it any
more. You're way too old.' 'So what we do?' 'Let's do something which
is right for your age and you will bring the house down.' 'What's
that?' 'Well, we could do Gogol's *Overcoat*.' Rudolf looked unconvinced. Akaky Akakyevich Bashmak, the impoverished clerk whose
worn, shapeless coat is an object of mockery to his fellow civil servants,
is 'a mere fly' of a man, unworthy of anyone's respect. 'You know
what his name is in Russian?' challenged Rudolf. '*Bashmak* means "doormat".'* Then glancing imperiously at himself in the lift's mirror, he
added, 'Do I *look* like doormat?' 'I didn't say that,' protested Flindt. 'I said
we have to do something. You can't carry on dancing *Swan Lake* – it's
ridiculous.' ' OK. When we do this?'

Flindt began trying to sell the idea of the ballet to different

---

* In fact the word means 'an old shoe'.

companies, but without success. 'I have access to stage in Firenze,' Rudolf told him. 'Poliakov is there – he will take it.' Commuting between Paris and Florence, having resumed his role of director of Maggio Musicale, Genia Poliakov was delighted by the idea. He had been begging his friend for years to give up virtuoso dancing and ease into more mature roles, and a ballet of Gogol's story was precisely the kind of literature-based repertory he had in mind. ('We spoke about *The Brothers Karamazov*, *King Lear* and *Richard III*, perhaps some Chekhov pieces.') Poliakov gave Flindt a number of expressionistic Soviet films to watch to help him create an authentic atmosphere of St Petersburg, and the result was a work that (in Alla Osipenko's words) is 'not simply a Russian ballet, it's distinctly about Russia'.*

It was also about Rudolf. The tale of Akaky Akakyevich's quest for a new overcoat has been interpreted as anything from an allegory of sexual and material temptation to the quest for ultimate meaning. With Rudolf in the role one could expect the coat to take on the significance of Prospero's cape, a symbol, perhaps, of youthful artistry (in Gogol's description, the clerk 'astonished by how animated he becomes when he wears his new coat'), but in the ballet the opposite occurs. This is an Akaky Akakyevich who feels liberated and fulfilled only without his fancy coat. During the party scene, when it is taken from him by a footman, the clerk begins to dance in imitation of the young Nureyev, performing almost step for step his signature *Swan Lake* solo, as well as coping with a number of technical hurdles. Rudolf had asked the choreographer if he could 'do [his] own stuff' and Flindt had readily agreed.

> Who cares? I thought. From a dramatic point of view, I wouldn't normally have stopped the action like that, and I certainly wouldn't have given that freedom to any other performer. But this was for *him*. It's

---

* Invited to Florence by French diplomat friends, Alla was reunited with Rudolf for the first time in twenty-eight years. They saw a lot of each other, and, before he left, Rudolf asked her to come to Paris with him. Having long given up dancing, the ballerina had fallen on bad times (her ticket to Europe was a present from Makarova), and Rudolf was determined to help by offering her work at the Opéra. 'We could celebrate the anniversary of 16 June and your birthday at the same time. Would you like to?' 'That's exactly how he said it, as if it were nothing at all. Just pure, simple, human benevolence.' Alla's time in Paris did not last long – she had warned Rudolf that she was 'a rotten teacher' – but, refusing to give up on her, he asked Marika to take her on for the summer season at her Monte Carlo academy. 'That experience turned out to be one of the most interesting chapters of my life. And never once did Rudik breathe a word that he was the one behind it.'

very simple: When you're making a vehicle for the greatest living star you're not going to start arguing. This is a man with too many complexes, a man who never really grew up. He wanted to show his audience that he could still do double *tours* to the left and to the right from fifth. And I wanted to make him happy.

Rudolf genuinely believed that he 'could still pull it off', but to the critic Judith Mackrell the visible effort this took was a deliberate manifestation of character. Reviewing the work when it was shown at the Edinburgh Festival, she persuasively argued that 'it is out of the ruin of Nureyev the dancer' that Rudolf had created his searingly expressive portrayal of Gogol's social misfit.

As a ballet *The Overcoat* is in fact unremarkable, a somewhat rambling succession of scenes from Akakyevich's life . . . With almost any artist in the leading role the whole work would probably sink into deserved oblivion. Yet as a vehicle for Nureyev *The Overcoat* is guaranteed a place in dance history, for it extracts from him a performance of unquestionable greatness – utterly unfaked in its characterisation . . . In his dusty trousers and flapping coat, making no effort to conceal his thinning hair, Nureyev allows himself to look much older than he really is . . . Painfully exposed, [he] thus reveals how hard these moves now come to him, allowing the shakiness of the pirouette, the fumbled finish of the *tours en l'air*, the gravity-bound jumps to convey the absurd and pitiful extremes of Akakyevich's aspirations and ineptitude . . . One of the revelations of this role is its demonstration that the classical vocabulary doesn't have to be a celebration of beauty and youth, that it can deal successfully with failure and age.

On 26 June 1989 Mario Bois notes in his diary: 'The Bergé/Nureyev tension is at its height.' It had been exacerbated by Rudolf signing a three-year contract to appear in the United States in a new version of the Rodgers and Hammerstein musical *The King and I*. 'Why?' Bergé asked Bois. '*Le fric*,' he explained, and Jamie Wyeth agrees: 'This was all about m-o-n-e-y.' The fee Rudolf had been offered was certainly large: a guaranteed annual income of more than a million dollars, with the amount increasing in the second and third years to $1,500,000 and $1,750,000. 'Are you really in need of that?' Hugues Gall asked. '*Desperately!*' Rudolf replied. 'I've got to be able to finance my island.' Jane Hermann and Sandor Gorlinsky were among those who '*begged* him not to do it', but Rudolf had convinced himself that, with the team he now had in place, he could run the Paris Opéra Ballet from America. Choplin remembers how he had often directed in the past by telephone – 'Thirty-minute conversations every day at two o'clock in the morning . . . Rudolf's sense of control did not allow him to become out of touch.' Pat Ruanne confirms this. 'When he was away we knew *exactly* where he was – it's not like he went off the map. He would leave his itinerary; he was always findable.'

Understandably, though, Bergé wanted his director in the house. Not only that, but as negotiations continued, Rudolf was showing what Mario Bois calls a 'near-suicidal' impulse. On one occasion he failed to turn up at a press conference ('I don't have a contract,' he told Bois, 'so why do you want me to come and "blahblah"?'); on another, he forbade Jean-Yves Lormeau to continue dancing the Prince in *The Sleeping Beauty*. 'Bergé was furious. He added another clause: the casting of Nureyev's ballets, apart from the première, would be decided by the Opéra. But it was unthinkable to Rudolf to be dispossessed of the artistic ownership of his own works.'

On 11 July Bergé wrote Rudolf a warning letter. It came, he insisted, not from the president but from 'a friend of twenty-five years who loves and admires you infinitely' and yet its tone was headmasterly and condescending:

> Everybody is willing to respect you, but for that you have to be respectable. Your various misbehaviours in language or gestures are simply not up to your standard . . . Now it is up to you: either you are ready to become this director of ballet I am talking about, or you believe that your past behaviour is correct . . . [If so] it would then be better to face courageously the situation, and find for yourself and the Opéra the best solution . . . Do not forget I am your friend, that I admire you and love you, and will continue to do so regardless of whatever may happen.

Rudolf was enraged, telling his real friends that he had received from Bergé 'a terribly rude letter' (as Margot described it), and was definitely going to leave. 'He might be happier without *them*,' she wrote to Maude, 'but they will never find anyone else who could do the half of what he has done.'

The breach that now existed between Rudolf and his young Opéra stars was revealed when Charles Jude alone joined that summer's Friends' tour of Mexico. But this was hardly surprising, as its main purpose was to give Kenneth Greve further opportunities to perform. Rudolf had cast him as the lead in Erik's version of *Flower Festival of Genzano* – 'a very hard version with even more beats' – as if wanting to conjure up images of the dancer he once worshipped. He often told Kenneth how much he reminded him of Erik. 'He'd say things like, "Your accent, when you said that sounded just like him"' – and they spent hours discussing Bournonville and Stanley Williams. 'It was the first time since Erik that Rudolf fell in love,' says Luigi. 'He was getting back to the beginning of his life. Like going full circle.'

But although Rudolf's foisting of Kenneth on the Paris Opéra Ballet is considered to be his only blatantly unprofessional move, it was not entirely the irrational *coup de foudre* it appeared. 'He saw in that Danish schooling all that he adored in Erik Bruhn. And he wanted to bring that to the boys at the Opéra,' says Elisabeth Platel, the ballerina whom Rudolf expected to benefit most from having this young colossus as a partner. ('He was always telling me I was a giant.') But although she could see that her director was following Balanchine's example in importing that other Apollonian Dane, Peter Martins, for Suzanne Farrell, Platel still maintains that his decision was misjudged. 'Kenneth was *beautiful*, but he was not ready. "Take him into the company," I told Rudolf. "Let him do one exam; one year in the corps de ballet; make him work with us."' Flemming Flindt agrees. 'If you know how the Paris Opéra Ballet runs, Rudolf was completely out of line and stupid. You can't take a nineteen-year-old foreigner and make him an *étoile*. Forget it. It's way off. If he'd taken Greve as a *sujet* for a couple of years, then *premier danseur* . . .' But Rudolf, as Platel now realizes, was fighting time. 'He was in a hurry. He thought he might not have one more year.'

On 15 September 1989 the Opéra dancers delivered a letter to the general administrator threatening to strike if Kenneth Greve danced that season. It was Elisabeth Platel, Rudolf believed, who had initiated it, 'and for the whole of that year he didn't say hello to me'. Distressed by the chaos he was causing, Kenneth begged Rudolf to back down. '"Just forget it," I told him. "I'll go someplace else," but Rudolf was implacable. "It's not to do with you, it's to do with me," he said. "They can't come and tell *me* how to run this company."'

Once again, he found himself imitating Diaghilev, a man whose power was so absolute that he could force the eighteen-year-old half-formed Léonide Massine on Michel Fokine, insisting that he dance the lead in Fokine's new ballet. It was at the Moscow opera that the impresario, still mourning the departure of Nijinsky, had spotted an extra of compelling presence and beauty, deciding that he should be the star in Fokine's new *La Légende de Joseph*. After his audition, Diaghilev took the boy directly to the Hermitage Museum, 'and from there presumably to bed. Massine's education had begun.' Kenneth himself remembers asking Rudolf once, 'Do you really think I can dance, or are you just after my ass?' 'He said, "Well, if I am, I can't get it."' With or without any return favours, Rudolf was determined to mould his protégé just as assiduously. He had begun showing him paintings in the Louvre, bought him books (*Madame Bovary*, *Hamlet*, Nabokov's *Lectures on Literature*) and taken him to Venice, the place Diaghilev had so adored. Later that summer, he brought Kenneth to Massine's island.

For two hours every day the pair worked together in the tower's studio, Rudolf exploding with anger if Kenneth complained of being tired.

> 'What's tired?' he'd say. 'You have to work *through* that.' But physically I couldn't handle what he was asking me to do. He might have perceived it as laziness, but at that point I didn't know how to find it in myself. I had to be pushed. He knew that when he stood there and forced me, I would do it. He tried to give me this drive, but it's one of the things I don't possess the way he does. This *total* concentration. As much as I want to have it, I don't. But the times we had alone in the studio were amazing. I infuriated him, but I also gave him a thrill. Because *when* he got me to do it, when I'd finally get my act together, his face would light up with this radiant smile. He was just in heaven! So it was a two-way thing: I was taking all these pearls from him, but I was also making him happy – giving him back a life of joy or joy of life, however you want to put it.

And Rudolf loved the fact that Kenneth was unusually practical, taking pleasure in repairing cars, houses, 'getting the stones between my hands'. 'You're so smart,' Rudolf would say. 'Fix it, fix it for me!' Wanting Margot's blessing – just as he had with Sylvie – Rudolf called her in Texas one day, standing on a rock to get a signal from his mobile phone (the island having no landline), saying, 'You *have* to speak to this boy!' And as the two dancers he loved most tried to make themselves heard on the crackly line, Rudolf hovered next to Kenneth, 'like an excited little kid'. 'I'm sure the Danish boy is good if Rudolf thinks so,' Margot wrote to Maude. 'But 6'8" must be basketball height. [It] will help him to defend himself among the Opéra dancers!' Maude, however, who was staying on Li Galli at the same time, was convinced that it was Kenneth from whom Rudolf needed protection. 'I was terribly afraid he would get hurt. He'd become much too fond of the boy.' When Kenneth asked her if he could go to the mainland to ring his girlfriend in New York, Maude persuaded him not to. 'I said it would be unkind. Too painful for Rudolf.' But when she told Rudolf of her concern, he tried to make light of it. 'Just let me enjoy having him around, Maude. He's so beautiful and so young.'

In New York, Robert Tracy was also disturbed by the dancer's hold on Rudolf. 'He was gaga about this boy. His new Erik.' Kenneth's birthday was on 11 August and, wanting to give him a party at the Dakota, Rudolf had asked Robert to draw up a list of guests. 'I was inviting a young crowd. Absolutely not. Rudolf wanted people there like Alwin Nikolais – basically, a lot of old queens.' Rudolf was irrationally jealous of Kenneth's best friend in New York, a young Greek man, and the night when Kenneth went to a party at his apartment, he had not been able to conceal his distress. 'When I came back that night he was *so* nice: he said, "I'm sorry, I realize I have to give you space." And I told him, "Rudolf, you're talking as if we were a couple. You know it's not like that."' Kenneth's relationship with his New York girlfriend was coming to an end as he had met someone else, but Rudolf did not want to hear about it. Instead, thinking perhaps of Rothbart destroying Siegfried's love for Odette by sexually blinding him with Odile, Rudolf, who had called in a hustler for himself one night, asked beguilingly, 'Do you want me to get someone for you?'

At no point, Kenneth says, did Rudolf ever mention the fact that he had AIDS. 'But he gave me so many hints. I remember him saying, "I don't know how much time I've got, and I want my island to be finished." And sometimes it seemed as if he was indirectly screaming to me, "I'm very sick. Be careful!"' One such occasion was when he saw Kenneth about to drink from his mineral water bottle, and snatched it away, snapping, 'We don't know. *Do* we?' He had reacted with the same concern during a rehearsal with Pat Ruanne. A dancer's hairpin had scratched his nose, and when Pat wiped it with her finger, exclaiming, 'Famous drop of blood!' Rudolf had immediately asked her to come to his dressing room. 'Wash your hands, please,' he said quietly. 'Then I knew.' 'Oh, Rudolf –' she began, but he cut her off. 'Don't talk. There's nothing more to say.' And yet there were times when he was astonishingly ignorant about the risk of contagion, suggesting to Charles Jude, for example, that they mix their sperm in a test tube in order to give his wife, Florence, a designer baby. 'He wanted to have a boy with my body and his head.' Rudolf even went so

far as consulting Michel Canesi about it. 'Would it be a good idea for
me to have babies?' he asked one day. 'Impossible,' Canesi replied.
'OK, forget it.'

For some months now Wallace had been sending Maude clippings
from American newspapers about the latest HIV treatments, 'hoping
that she would pass them on to Rudolf, that they would seep into his
consciousness and he'd take care of himself'. It was the antiviral drug
AZT that was being most talked about, and Rudolf asked Michel
Canesi to give it to him. With its side effects already known to be
severely debilitating (they included muscle-wasting disease and kidney
damage), Canesi, naturally, was reluctant to prescribe it. 'I was worried that it would affect Rudolf's dancing, but he was furious with me
and demanded to have it.' Having started the course, however, Rudolf
would stop taking the pills as soon as he felt significantly better. 'He
didn't seem to realize that this was something you had to do regularly,'
Wallace says. 'He hated taking any kind of drugs. He believed in sweating out toxins, whether they be from alcohol or disease.' Rudolf, who
was then living in the Dakota, was made wary, too, by Robert Tracy's
alarmist views about AIDS. Tracy was among those who believed that
the disease was a form of chemical warfare designed to destroy
minorities, and was incensed by the medical establishment's routine
distribution of AZT. 'It was banned in the fifties for being too toxic.'

Rudolf had come to New York to begin rehearsals on *The King and I*,
a role he had been tempted by ten years earlier – 'all dancers dream of
being on Broadway' – but had turned down, as he thought it would
impede his dancing. Having recently fitted an old pipe organ into a
wall of the Dakota apartment, he began having singing lessons at
home, voice coach Don Pippin giving him scales and arpeggios in an
attempt to 'redirect the croaking'. Yodelling, 'Ya, ya, ya, ya, ya, ya, *ya*,
ya' to the tune of 'Oh What a Beautiful Morning' would make Rudolf
crack up with laughter, but he felt, nonetheless, that Pippin 'somehow
did manufacture some semblance of singing'. Rudolf also consulted
with Baryshnikov, who was then appearing in a production of *Metamorphosis*, wanting to know 'how many weeks I rehearsed, how I learned
the text, what I feel from performance to performance'.

Pauline Kael, reviewing *Valentino,* had pointed out Rudolf's resemblance to Yul Brynner – the 'high cheekbones, his imperious sniff and
the set of his full mouth'. But although some famous mannerisms were
imposed (the spread-leg stance with hands on hips, for instance), it was
not Brynner he was attempting to impersonate, Rudolf insisted, but
the king of Siam. 'King is like me,' he told Linda Maybarduk. 'He loves

absolute power and control. He has burning desire to learn everything.' Since its choreography was by Jerome Robbins, Rudolf had assumed that the part would come easily to him – 'Dancing is very much related; both are dependent on the music. Music means phrasing' – but, in fact, he had badly underestimated the demands of musical comedy: his delivery of the lines was self-consciously arch, his singing inept enough to cause sniggers. 'Let's say he got through it,' says Robert Gable. 'But he wasn't good and he knew it.' Wallace agrees. 'He should have taken it more seriously. But he looked upon doing musicals as less than using all of his talents and resources, and he didn't get any satisfaction out of it.'

It was hardly surprising: Rudolf was a pedagogue of genius, not a 'dumb-footed' pupil. Rarely focused on the action onstage, he spent every free moment either on the telephone to the Opéra or coaching Kenneth Greve. 'We're going to make a two-metre blond Basilio of you,' he promised, having persuaded Poliakov to stage his version of *Don Quixote*. While *The King and I* was playing in Toronto, Rudolf asked Karen Kain to rehearse Kenneth, hoping that she would perform with him. 'He was angry with me when I said I couldn't go to Florence.' Finding her young partner capable but far too inexperienced, Karen was amazed to see Rudolf 'so smitten'. Linda Maybarduk felt the same.

> On the sofa in our house he was touching, pawing, kissing Kenneth – we'd never seen him being demonstrative like that. He was *totally* in love. And from the way the kid was responding, we assumed he must be gay; he was playing Rudolf like a fiddle. It made Bill, my husband, so angry that he took Kenneth aside at one point and said, 'Listen, either give this up or walk out.'

Like most dancers, Kenneth was unselfconsciously physical, thinking nothing of scrubbing Rudolf's back in the bath, or giving him scalp massages. 'But I could see how much it tortured him.' Finally Rudolf could take no more. They had been to the Russian circus with the Maybarduks, dining afterwards in the star's hotel room, where they stayed until around five in the morning. It was then, after Linda and Bill had left, that Rudolf came into Kenneth's bed 'and pounced'. Having been alerted the next day by Karen Kain to the fact that Kenneth had decided to leave, Linda called Rudolf to invite him to a family dinner. 'I don't know. I'm not much company,' he said, but allowed himself to be persuaded. 'And then who should arrive with Rudolf but Kenneth.

So we thought, Oh well, they must have patched things up.' At interval the next night, however, Rudolf called to ask if they would come and have dinner with him after the show. 'Because, this time, Kenneth really had walked.'

A month later, however, Kenneth was back on the road with Rudolf. Marie-Christine Mouis, who had left the Paris Opéra to join the Boston ballet, received a phone call from Rudolf saying, 'I'm coming to town with Kenneth Greve. Would you be able to partner him in *Don Q?*' He had always liked her Kitri, inviting her to perform the role in a number of Nureyev and Friends seasons, and now he saw that at five foot seven – an unusual height for a ballerina – she would make an ideal match for Kenneth. Remembering him as a student in Stanley Williams's classes and thinking at the time that he was talented, though not nearly ready, with some trepidation Marie-Christine agreed to help. But at their first rehearsal she hardly recognized Kenneth as the same dancer. 'I was blown away by what Rudolf had done; the work must have been *incredible*. The level of his technique was so high that I found myself wondering what that whole Paris Opéra Ballet fuss was about.' Personal relations between teacher and pupil, on the other hand, had deteriorated even further. There was a fight in their hotel room, one or the other having pushed over and broken the television set, and a second incident in which Marie-Christine was directly involved.

> We were trying out a lift backstage and missed it. And as we were both holding each other, laughing, I suddenly saw Rudolf come walking toward us very fast. Confronting Kenneth, he *slapped* him across the face, saying, 'How dare you!' I had no idea what was going on. 'No, no,' I told Rudolf. 'He's doing really well. He's a very good partner.' But Kenneth was very upset, and later he told me about what was happening. He said, 'I respect Rudolf, I owe him everything. But he wants more and I can't give it to him.'

Luigi then received a phone call from Rudolf. 'Why don't you come to Boston?' he said. 'I need you.' Discovering that he was needed as an intermediary, Luigi volunteered to take Kenneth to a restaurant and plead Rudolf's case. 'You know, don't you, that Rudolf is in love with you. He needs to dedicate his life to somebody, and he wants to help you.' Once again Kenneth explained that he could not give Rudolf 'something else', expecting the heterosexual Luigi to understand. And later, when they were in Florence together, he begged Luigi not to tell

Rudolf that his new girlfriend, who was also a dancer, was with him. 'But between Rudolf and me was *big* feeling. He was my brother. So I told Kenneth he had to stop playing games.' But this was no game. The dancer was soon to become Kenneth's wife and the mother of his first child.

When Nijinsky committed the unpardonable sin of getting married, Diaghilev vengefully punished him by firing him. Rudolf, by contrast, continued striving to create opportunities for his protégé. 'He took a passionate interest in making sure the boy was happy,' says Robert Denvers, then director of a company in Flanders.

It was the only time I saw Rudolf go head over heels about someone. He called me and said, 'Please take Kenneth, he's beautiful – he's this, he's that.' He was really pushy, and called me all the time. So, given Kenneth's facility and his looks, I took him into the company, only to find that he had absolutely no ambition. We had *Camelot* created on the boy, and on the day of the première he was shopping in the afternoon and came in with a camera. He was a *tourist*, not really serious about his career.

But Rudolf's faith in Kenneth has proved well founded. Having made his name as an international guest artist – winning great acclaim for his partnership with the Royal Ballet's superbly Amazonian Zenaida Yenowsky – he is today, at the age of thirty-nine, establishing himself as a choreographer and a coach. Like Rudolf, he was photographed dancing in the nude by Richard Avedon, who was overwhelmed by his physical beauty, describing him as 'a god, a Nordic god'. But if he has not attained the superstardom his mentor had in mind, it is, Kenneth maintains, because he chose to have 'more of a life'. (Married for a second time, he is now the father of three.) Rudolf always vowed he could detect an aura of domesticity around a dancer. 'It shows onstage. You watch and you can see, he or she has a family, children, a cottage in the country and goes there every Friday. Dancing can't be a job, like going to the office. It means everything.' And Kenneth admits that, without Rudolf there to force it out of him, he did not have that extra dimension, the ability to dedicate himself to the point where nothing else exists. 'Rudolf gave the possibility, the option, but I also wanted a family. And in the end I think I've taken the best from both worlds.'

In the autumn of '89, as *The King and I* tour headed west with no deal struck for a Broadway run, Rudolf made up for his disappointment by keeping abreast of the box-office takings. 'Almost every day he was checking how they were doing so that – God forbid – they couldn't be cheating him out of his percentage.' Friends dutifully travelled great distances to see the show. Rudolf's Vaganova room-mate Leo Ahonen drove with his dancer wife, Soili Arova, from Texas to Tampa. Grateful for any words of praise ('He *died* very well'), Rudolf asked Leo to tell Margot that he had enjoyed it, as someone had sent her bad reviews. Spending Halloween with the Wyeths while playing in Wilmington, Rudolf appeared in good spirits, though he was reprimanded by Phyllis when she spotted him doing ballet exercises instead of practising his scales. 'They were making a huge to-do about his singing.' Rudolf's co-star, Liz Robertson, did her best to help – 'She was wonderful with him' – but to no avail. The Wyeths found Rudolf's performance 'pretty painful to watch', as did Maude and Wallace, who also saw the show in Wilmington. 'He didn't ask us what we thought, and we didn't volunteer.'

Almost daily Rudolf telephoned Mario Bois to find out how the Opéra negotiations were going, 'hoping that he would get his way'. Maude was trying hard to persuade him to give up the show and return to Paris, telling him quite rightly that Pierre Bergé wouldn't be there much longer. With the Opéra-Bastille losing millions of dollars a year, it was obvious that a new president would be chosen as soon as the Right resumed power. Bergé was seen to be 'incompetent at the administrative level and still more on the artistic level', and the list of musical titans who had now withdrawn their support included not only Pierre Boulez but Herbert von Karajan, Zubin Mehta and Georg Solti. 'Rudolf,' said Maude, 'I think you should go back.' 'But he told me, "There can only be one artistic director. If I'm not in full charge I won't accept. Do you want me to go if I'll be unhappy?" Well, of course, I had to say no.'

Also finding his authority undermined, Baryshnikov had abruptly left the American Ballet Theatre in September. Jane Hermann had been named executive director and replaced Misha's lieutenant, Charles France, who had been sick and on a year's leave of absence. Naturally Rudolf expected to take over. 'My name was proposed everywhere . . . on everybody's lips.' When he realized that he was not after all being considered for the job, he began to rally support for himself in a self-defeatingly serpentine way, getting John Taras, for example, to advise the board to appoint Margot. 'He always thought he would like to direct a ballet company with her,' says Maude. 'Because she was a diplomat and he wasn't.' But as Rudolf well knew,

Margot was in no fit state to run a ballet company. Having been diagnosed with terminal cancer, she was receiving treatment for it in Houston, and since August had had two major operations.

'I fired Taras,' says Hermann, 'and then Rudolf got even nastier. Ultimately he thought that I owed it to him to give him ABT.' But not only did the board not want another Russian in charge, Rudolf, as Hermann says, had not considered how much harder it was to run a company in America, especially one with a five-and-a-half-million-dollar debt. 'There was *no money*. I certainly didn't want the job myself, but no good artistic director would have taken on a company under those conditions. It was just a big illusion on Rudolf's part. Plus the fact you don't bring in some AIDS-ridden guy.'

He had another idea. When once asked if he could imagine himself at the age of sixty running the Kirov, Rudolf had replied without hesitation, 'I can. This relation with the Kirov Ballet is something special. You can't extinguish it. Neither could Balanchine . . . I am sure that no dancer of the Bolshoi theatre can have similar ties, similar feelings. You are forged for your whole life.' He had already reestablished a link with the company's current director, Oleg Vinogradov, a Vaganova school contemporary, whom Rudolf had asked to mount his production of *Paquita* in Paris in 1988. And at the beginning of 1989, when he heard that Natalia Makarova had been invited to perform with the Kirov, he called Vinogradov saying that he would like to follow. 'So come and dance,' the director had offered, and they agreed to talk later about dates. Rudolf's trip took place just one week after the collapse of the Berlin Wall on 6 November, a sign, in his mind, that this was somehow all fated. 'I left USSR when the construction of the Berlin Wall had begun and returned when it was demolished – that's a symbol, isn't it?'

Arriving in Leningrad, wearing his signature Missoni shawl and tam-o'-shanter, Rudolf was accompanied by Douce, Luigi and Phyllis Wyeth, together with a number of international reporters and an American television crew. The first person to greet him was Tamara Zakrzhevskaya, who had been wondering, as she managed to slip past the uniformed guards, whether Rudolf would recognize her. 'Well, at least Tamara came,' he grinned, and as they embraced, a cluster of cushiony *babushki* in woollen hats surrounded him, pressing straggly carnations into his hands. These were his Leningrad fans of three decades before – the pretty, plump smiling girls whose passion for their 'Malchiska' was so intense that one had physically attacked Tamara out of jealousy. To Rudolf 'they looked like people who came out of the Gulag. Strange, worn, shabby old people, like in one of those science-fiction films . . . Depressing.' To the fans, however, despite the myths and rumours about his baroque lifestyle,* 'he was still our Rudik'.

Tamara remembers being surprised that no one from the Kirov Theatre had come to the airport, although, coincidentally, Vinogradov had arrived around the same time on another flight. 'He made a little bow to Rudolf, said a couple of words, and left.' The reason for the director's offhandedness, she suggests, were the feelings of envy and inferiority that went back to their student days, when Rudolf was invited into the Kirov as a soloist and Vinogradov went to Novosibirsk to join the corps de ballet. 'Rudolf was the star and he was a loser. Years fly by, Vinogradov is artistic director of the Kirov and Rudolf is asking him favours: all his youthful complexes came into play. These were not Yeltsin's times, and he was very afraid that Rudolf, being director of the Grand Opéra, might receive an invitation from our cultural department to lead the theatre.'

If this was Rudolf's ultimate aim, his immediate priority was less ambitious: 'He had one intention – to arrange for the Kirov to stage his *Cinderella*.' But as this was the ballet that had been Vinogradov's first major work as a choreographer, the director let it be known that 'There are many better versions than Rudolf's – *mine*, for example.' Rudolf was enraged. 'The fucker is refusing to let me do it,' he exploded to Tamara, telling her also how Vinogradov was trying to sabotage his visit. He had wanted to perform *The Overcoat*, but Vinogradov had insisted, 'It's *La Sylphide*, *Giselle* or nothing,' his motive, Rudolf felt, being to shame and 'bury' him. Although aware that the effect of a fifty-one-year-old Albrecht would be devastatingly anticlimactic to an audience who remembered the genius of the 'hooligan boy,' Rudolf had no option, and chose the Bournonville ballet. Vaganova, a pupil of Christian Johansson, had incorporated elements of Danish technique into her training (and *La Sylphide* had been performed by the Kirov since 1981), but, nevertheless Rudolf knew that everything he had learned from Erik and Stanley Williams would blow the dust off what many Russian dancers regarded as a museum piece.

To Rudolf the most visible signs of glasnost in Leningrad were the photographs of himself, Makarova and Baryshnikov now hanging

---

* 'In town you would hear anything,' said Tamara. 'Nureyev bought a Louis XVI palace and moved there with his lovers, opened a harem, and has a personal cameraman who is there to film all his love affairs' (Radik Kudoyarov, *The Myth of Rudolf*, documentary).

alongside ballet history's icons in the Vaganova museum. Followed by reporters and cameramen and stopping to sign autographs, the disgraced star made his grand comeback, his imperiousness giving way to genuine warmth when he spotted Natalia Dudinskaya, now a little old lady with a bad wig and smeared lipstick. '*Zdrazvitya*, Madame!' he beamed, hugging her hard. Later, visiting the hundred-year-old Anna Udeltsova and holding her trembling hand, Rudolf looked amused and touched by his teacher's delighted cries of '*Oi, oi, oi!*' reminding her how she would give him treats like cucumbers marinaded in honey and mushrooms. 'My greatest worry,' she said, 'was to find things to build up your strength because you worked so terribly hard. The others had to be pushed to work, but you I had to hold back.' (He told friends, though, that when she teased him about the 'dirty little Tatar boy' he had been, he felt slapped in the face – except expressed, Rudolf-style, in *mat* obscenities.)

At the theatre, with 'the same old *babushki* sitting in every exit,' he noticed how run-down everything was. 'Nothing had changed, and I found people there at the same level they had been thirty years ago.' But this was exactly what he planned to set right. When Makarova came to Leningrad she not only donated her costume and shoes to the museum, but charmed everyone at the theatre by distributing gifts and souvenirs. Rudolf 'brought nothing', although he saw his visit as far more enriching in dance terms: 'first take everything from there to the West, *then* take as much as possible back to Russia'.

Wearing yellow clogs and a dressing gown over several woollen layers, Rudolf made his way to the studio, where an elegantly dressed Ninel Kurgapkina was waiting to begin the first rehearsal. He still used the formal *vy* to her informal *ty*, and yet the authority of their roles had changed, and as Rudolf warmed up, performing Stanley Williams's multiple *battement tendu* exercises, Ninel leaned on the barre listening to him explain the basics of this unfamiliar method. When he turned to face the other side she weighed him up and down with a professional eye although for the most part she took the opportunity to reminisce, giggling as she remembered one particularly outrageous incident of his youthful arrogance. Across the studio, waiting to begin, Rudolf's Sylph, Zhanna Ayupova, sized him up in the mirror as he took off his cloth cap, his thinning hair plastered to his scalp with sweat. Stopping his solo midway, he collapsed on to a chair, but as the young ballerina began to dance, he instinctively rallied to instil a quality of port de bras that he noticed was missing.

In a subsequent rehearsal watched by Tamara, he stopped four times to stretch out, exhausted, on the floor. This was depressing enough, but she couldn't understand why, having brought his own 'luxury costume' to Russia, Rudolf insisted on trying on 'a whole pile of rotten old clothes' that he had found in one of the dressing rooms. 'I was sitting next to a critic who had never seen him dance and said, "What kind of *thing* is that? It can't be the great Nureyev."' 'No one wanted to take seriously the image that Nureyev presented of himself,' wrote Inna Sklarevskaya. 'We were left with the hope that some kind of magical transformation would occur at the next day's performance.' During the dress rehearsal, however, Rudolf felt something snap, and having arrived in Leningrad with an injured foot, now found himself with a torn calf muscle in the other leg. Instead of cancelling, he decided to 'show some style of the school of Margot Fonteyn . . . If you can stand, you can improvise something,' although Ninel remembers the degree to which he was vacillating about whether or not to perform. 'I can't give you advice,' she told him. 'You have to make that decision yourself.' Tamara, on the other hand, knowing that Rudolf had valued her frankness in the past, steeled herself to telephone him at his hotel and put him off.

'Rudik, are you feeling OK?' 'Yes. *Why?* I'm feeling wonderful.' 'Really? It seemed to me you were having problems with your foot.' 'My foot is absolutely fine.' 'Well, are you really going to appear onstage in those old costumes? They're a joke.' 'You don't like them? Well, you'll just have to survive that.' 'Rudik, you know I've survived a lot of things . . .' and then I hung up. We never talked again. I didn't know that he was ill – if I had, I'd never have called.

Gabriella Komleva had also spoken her mind. 'I said, "Why are you doing this? It's not what you should be showing yourself in."' 'You don't understand,' Rudolf told her vehemently. 'I've *got* to dance on this stage.' It was as if he believed that the Kirov stage had some miraculous power, a power that could return him to his former, prelapsarian state. 'That stage is sacred.' 'This was like a pilgrimage for my soul . . . It was a kind of purification.' (He felt so passionately that he had even taken a photograph of its bare boards, and the reason he had wanted to dance in worn-out costumes was simply because they were Kirov costumes.) 'All that time in the West I wanted to dance in Russia,' he confided to Ninel, and to a television journalist on his return he admitted that he had now achieved his dream. 'It's a circular kind of circle. Complete.'

Compared with Rudolf's recent form, his performance, recorded by CBS television, is surprisingly accomplished. Once again, despite his two injuries, he proved that he could still do double *tours* to both sides, and his grasp of Bournonville-style footwork was seen to be 'brilliant'. What has gone is the refinement he acquired in the West, his hunched shoulders and stiff, flapping arms oddly reminiscent of his student performance of *Corsaire*. But while the majority of fans caught only 'a hint here, and a stroke there' of the Rudik they remembered, Faina Rokhind, his great fan from the old days, saw much more. 'I still argue about it to this day. I was sitting in the second row and he danced *very* well, and in the image he was famous for. I was amazed by the scene with the witch – so much sincere anger and passion. I think the acting was absolutely fantastic. He really danced with a soul. It made me understand even more clearly why I love him so much.'

The contrast was too painful for Tamara. 'The audience was giving him an ovation for his return. And maybe for the changes in our country that had allowed him to come. But I wish we could have seen him dance something worthy of him, something that showed us another side.' Only too aware that the Leningrad audience was the most discerning in the world, Rudolf knew, of course, that he should never have danced. And yet the horror of what lay in store for him was reason enough to indulge 'a kind of caprice . . . for myself, nobody else'. Inscribing a photograph for Phyllis Wyeth of himself as James kissing the hand of Ayupova's Sylph, Rudolf wrote, 'To dear Philiss, this hideous moment in a few years will be the sweetest memory.'

Paris, 10 January 1990: 'Rudolf quits,' Mario Bois notes in his diary. 'Nine months of negotiations for nothing.' But it was not quite over yet. Pierre Bergé was proposing a role for Rudolf as principal choreographer, which would mean staging one new ballet a year and one revival. A meeting between the two was needed – 'Only if Nureyev comes to my office.' 'Only if Bergé comes to me' – but, as neither was prepared to give way, nothing could be finalized. Then Rudolf heard that his successor was Patrick Dupond, the audience-pleasing *étoile* whom he had been accused of overlooking. Since 1988 Dupond had been in charge of the Nancy ballet, nevertheless, as far as Rudolf was concerned his appointment at the Opéra was a travesty, threatening to undo everything he had achieved. 'He's a very nice boy. He's charming at the dinner. But he doesn't know classical dance.' Bergé, however, who had controversially engaged the less-known Myung-Whun Chung to replace Daniel Barenboim, wanted his ballet director to be just as tractable. 'Dupond would be his poodle.'

On 11 February the final performance of *The King and I* took place in San Francisco. The show was closing because of scathing reviews and minimal box-office takings. Anyone who had seen it recently, such as the American Ballet Theatre's assistant artistic director David Richardson, was not in the least surprised. 'I felt Rudolf wasn't respecting it. He was leaving his hotel at curtain time, and was just walking through it. It was a gruesome performance, and when we met afterwards at Jeannette's bar* I found a way to pass over it, *but he wanted to hear more.* It was painful the way he was looking for approval.' True to

---

* For the last decade, Jeannette had owned and run Tosca, the legendary bar at 242 Columbus whose jukebox to this day plays opera arias. Rudolf was always urging her to buy it, and in 1980 when its owner retired, she persuaded him to sell it to her, promising to keep things exactly as they were. Once the favourite hang-out of Beat Generation poets and, in Jeannette's words, 'people coming in glittering from the opera', Tosca, with its red leather banquettes and nicotine-stained walls, has retained its unique atmosphere and mix, although there is perhaps more of a movie crowd than before, with George Lucas, Francis Ford Coppola and Sean Penn among regulars who have also become friends of Jeannette.

character, Jane Hermann was more direct. 'I told him it was awful, which it was. He didn't even know his lines.' But this had only compounded Rudolf's hostility toward Jane, now the artistic director of ABT, a job he thought he should have had, and he still blamed her for his not getting it. 'She never had the guts to speak to me about the company.' They were in a restaurant when Rudolf, who had been drinking too much, started obscenely to berate her, an occasion she remembers as 'that ghastly night he made his "Jewish cunt" speech'. 'Gorlinsky warned me not to get too emotionally involved with Rudolf. "He's *ruthless*," Sandor said. And he was right. He ruins your life – but that's because I let him. I should have extricated myself, not put myself in harm's way. But I really *loved* Rudolf.'

It was the same night, Jane later discovered, that Rudolf had learned that the Hammerstein estate was withdrawing the rights to *The King and I*, but even so, she decided that this time he had gone too far. 'There was no one close to Rudolf who could say, *What* are you doing? To the one promoter who has given you most loyalty.' In fact Armen Bali had said exactly this when they were alone together later, reminding Rudolf, 'She knows the business and she adores you.' In the end, though, Armen took his side, saying, 'All of a sudden she turns against him because he called her names. This is the thing he couldn't understand; why people are so sensitive.'

And yet she herself had been hurt when, in San Francisco, Rudolf chose to stay not with her as usual but with Jeannette. 'My mother didn't know he was ill, so I told her it was because I had a VCR machine and he could watch his films at night. Before, he'd be naked in the bathtub, and she'd be scrubbing his back as they quoted Pushkin, but now he didn't want her to see him that way.' Changing the sheets one morning Jeannette noticed a lot of loose pills under the bed – 'He'd been throwing them there.' She called Michel Canesi, who begged her to make sure that he took them. 'So I would just stand there until he did. But it was hard for him to swallow this stuff. They were like horse pills.' (Gay activists would later suggest that it was 'in accord with a sound instinct' that Rudolf did not always take the prescribed doses. 'Like many tens of thousands of others,' wrote John Lauritsen, 'Nureyev was poisoned with AZT.')

To fill Rudolf's blank calendar Luigi had promised to take him 'around the world to dance', hastily setting up what would be billed as the 'Farewell Tour'. Rudolf's fan Bob Gable caught the show in Washington, where the dancers were performing 'in a small room, not even a theatre'. Despite the telegram that had arrived in 1986 from Béjart 'forbidding any and all performances by Nureyev', *Songs of a Wayfarer* was included on the programme, and so was *Apollo*, which the Balanchine estate had also vetoed. 'He was *terrible* in them both, and he even did *The Lesson* badly – old standard things that were just beyond him now. That was hard for me to take.' But Maude's line on hearing of the 'total disaster' of the tour was, 'Well then, don't go and see him.' She would point out that there were people who still derived pleasure from 'certain things Rudolf can do that nobody else can: the way he holds himself, and his intelligent approach to a role.' Marika Besobrasova had long given up seeing Rudolf onstage, and yet she, too, understood why he kept going. 'Getting old, you refine these *internal* feelings that are so much stronger than your body. Rudolf felt in spirit so strongly, so clearly, that he thought he was *that* being, and he did not see the image that we saw. *Now* I would go to watch him perform, but only with my spirit watching his spirit.'

Baryshnikov was also sympathetic. 'Definitely, for him, it was a death to be offstage. No matter how he was dancing. At least it was killing time, because he knew time was killing him.' Rudolf admitted this himself. 'When the lights are extinguished I die. But tomorrow, I will dance; tomorrow, I will be reborn.' The act of extreme exertion – the astonishing resilience that boxers call 'heart' – was in itself a kind of redemption. 'It is as if by way of the most strenuous exigencies of the physical self a boxer can – sometimes – transcend the merely physical,' writes Joyce Carol Oates. 'He can, if he is lucky, be absolved of his mortality.'

Rudolf was convinced that he had found a way of extending his longevity as a dancer. 'Practise in nice warm weather. Good climate. Not in winter; not up north. Then no problem.' To have sunshine all year round he signed the deeds on a seafront house on the tiny Caribbean island of St Barthélemy.* With dark wooden shutters, it was as simple as a Russian *dacha* – 'No paintings, no statues, no harpsichords' – and situated off the single-track coastal road that runs along the wild, southeastern side, a world away from the Parisian cafés, restaurants and designer boutiques of St-Jean and Gustavia Harbour. Rudolf had bought the house complete with everything in

---

* Rudolf, with his phobia of flying, could hardly have chosen a more harrowing destination than the St Barts airstrip, which is boxed in by hills on three sides, with the sea on the fourth. Reaching the island, the twenty-seater plane dips down, down, down to the water, steadies itself, and then makes a heart-stopping Big Dipper landing, skimming cars on the hill road, and screeching to a stop only feet from the sunbathers on the white sands.

it, from an ugly upright piano with termites in the wood, to the kind of plastic-cushioned cane-and-plywood furniture one finds in an English seaside bed and breakfast. Jackie Onassis, who went there for tea one day, was unimpressed. 'If Rudolf invites you to visit, say no,' she told a mutual acquaintance, but Rudolf would not have minded. 'My houses are all strange, isolated places that would not appeal to society people. They are not presentable.' His only major addition was a vast driftwood-grey deck jutting vertiginously over the rocks – a stage, in fact, its backdrop the shadowy outline of St Kitts and a changing panorama of sea and sky. Under the deck was a little grotto, and when he failed to get planning permission to turn it into a bed-room, Rudolf had a mattress-size platform built, intending to spend nights sleeping in the open, a few feet above the waves. (The next owner found candles in crevices of the rocks.) He had once compared his solitary houses to 'wolves' lairs', but never had he craved such a primitive existence. 'Like a wild animal – close to the essential.'

In April 1990, the moment the house was officially his, Rudolf went there with Douce, Charles Jude and Simon 'Blue' Robinson, a young English PA he had employed towards the end of *The King and I* tour. Tall, sporty and good-natured about rebuffing his boss's occasional advances, Blue had met Rudolf on St Barts six months earlier while working as a professional mate on a racing yacht. (His experience as a Boy Friday would be recorded in a sharply observed memoir, both amusing and poignant, entitled *A Year with Rudolf Nureyev*.) Padding around barefoot Rudolf allowed himself easy days, stretched out napping in the sun on a floral sheet, naked except for a woman's straw hat, or attempting to swim – 'always naked' – in the swirling surges of surf below the house. On the nearby nudist beach Rudolf would always have with him the water- and sand-proof Walkman that Blue had bought him. 'He wore a hat and the headphones and nothing else and listened to symphonies while he followed the score on sheet music that often blew away.' Mostly, though, he sat at the piano solemnly working his way through Bach. 'You can play him at any tempo and his music does not disintegrate no matter what speed and how badly you play.'

Trying to convince himself that he could do something else, 'to trick his mind into believing that he didn't have to be onstage all the time', Rudolf had begun seriously studying music. He claimed to have asked Herbert von Karajan how he managed to stay so energetic. 'My son,' the maestro replied, 'if you want to live long, you need to finish dancing and conduct.' And it was von Karajan's idea that he should start by teaching himself Bach's forty-eight Preludes and Fugues. With Leonard Bernstein (Rudolf's Dakota neighbour), and John Lanchbery both pledging their support, Rudolf was confident that it was not too late to switch to a career that would allow him to stay in the dance world, continue to earn big money and travel the world. What he lacked in technical schooling he believed he could make up for with his own charisma, qualities of leadership and ferocious determination. As he told Blue, 'I have decided to be conductor, so I *will* be conductor.'

In May 1990 the meeting with Bergé finally took place (on the neutral ground of Mario Bois's premises), and to seal his new arrangement with the Opéra, Rudolf announced that he would be mounting *La Bayadère*. There was no complete Minkus score available, but when he was in Russia, Rudolf had hunted out the original and, with Douce's help, had clandestine photocopies made, which she then smuggled through customs under her clothes. *La Bayadère* was, in Rudolf's view, Petipa's masterpiece – the one full-length Russian classic he had always wanted to bring to the West. 'Without [it] there would not have been *Swan Lake*.' And as the work of a Frenchman, with a libretto influenced by Théophile Gautier's *Sacountala*, it rightly belonged, as he said, to the patrimony of France. 'I have brought it back to its own country.' Not only that, but to Rudolf the ballet had become a parable of sorts, replaying his unhappy relationship with the Paris Opéra Ballet. 'A love story which ended badly. It's a betrayal. It's like *La Bayadère*.'

The Opéra, he told Elizabeth Kaye, could not decide the extent to which it wanted to maintain its link with him. 'They want my ballets, but they don't want me to be around . . . They want to do what Lifar did many years ago with Balanchine. He was pushed out. They did the same to Fokine. And before that, same with Jules Perrot.' But having felt bitter and unprized in Paris – 'Nobody's dying to delve into my baggage of knowledge' . . . [teaching is] 'dry bread and it's ingratitude' – during a brief spell of working with the Royal Ballet, he reverted to being what Monica Mason called 'the Rudolf of twenty years before. You could *feel* what the dancers felt for him. He was warm and loving; he talked to them, watched them. With us he was the most unselfish, giving person. He so believed in the art form that the more people he could convert to his passion, the better he felt.'

The occasion was a gala performance of *Romeo and Juliet*, whose purpose was to raise money for Margot. 'She'd really been living from hand to mouth,' said John Tooley who, in his role of general director, had helped the ballerina financially at various times during the eighties. 'She rang me one day to say that her medical insurance was about to be cut off, but when I suggested a benefit evening she was very resistant to the idea.' 'I *can't* accept it,' Margot told a close friend, finding it too demeaning. Tooley, by then retired from the Opera House, came up with a face-saving plan to donate the proceeds to a trust for young dancers, the interest from which would go to Margot. This she agreed to, although she still felt reluctant to attend the occasion itself. 'Rudolph [*sic*] seems to be trying to blackmail me to go to the 30th May gala!' she wrote from Panama to Maude. 'It is not going to be easy for me so I still haven't made up my mind. I pray that either way he will dance Mercutio.'

With Sylvie Guillem and the twenty-seven-year-old Jonathan Cope as the lovers, the company had planned to cast a young Mercutio, but not only had Rudolf taken it for granted that he would be dancing the role, Margot had declared 'it would be criminal not to'. (As Maria Tallchief once said, 'He was still her Romeo. Her Armand.' And Maude felt the same. 'They should have let him do Romeo.') In fact, though, Rudolf hated MacMillan's version of Mercutio, particularly the death scene – 'It just goes on and on, it's embarrassing' – and instead of going to a rehearsal, he had stayed in bed at Victoria Road.

To the gala audience that night, which included Princess Diana and Princess Margaret, it was entirely fitting that Rudolf should be performing for Margot, 'the dear friend of my soul', but few of the *cognoscenti* were able to look at the stage. 'It was heartbreaking,' said Monica Mason. 'Because of course it was a reminder of what happens to us.' From the wings Stephen Sherriff called out encouragement. 'I was trying to pump him up, saying, "*Go* for it, Rudolf!" But he knew how awful he was. He knew, he knew.'

Not wanting to see anyone after the performance, Rudolf was waiting at the stage door for a cab when Anya Sainsbury came to tell him that Margot was looking for him. 'She doesn't need me,' he mumbled, but Anya told him how distraught he was making her. 'I begged him to stay, and he did. But he was really upset about something.' It was not only his pitiful performance – his last appearance on the Royal Opera House stage – but the sight of Margot, whose glittering Saint Laurent gown did little to disguise how seriously ill and emaciated she had become. In Paris, when they last had seen each other at a quai Voltaire supper, she had been in radiant form, and, sitting by her side, Rudolf was clearly loving every second of their time together. 'He was being so gentle with her,' recalls Stephen Sherriff, 'like he was with Maude.' They had been reminiscing about the old days, and Stephen heard him say, 'You were the dance.' 'No,' said Margot, reaching for Rudolf's hand, '*we* were the dance.'

Now, however, unable to walk without a cane, Margot was so weak that at a dinner the night before Rudolf had been impelled to carry her on the stairs. And whereas they had always been there for each other in the past – 'Things that could not be faced alone, they could face together' – neither would confide in the other about their illnesses. 'You've got two twin souls there,' said Margot's close friend Ana Cristina Alvarado. 'For them it was almost degrading to talk about it.' Rudolf had been shocked when the *Observer*'s Lynn Barber asked during an interview whether the ballerina's death would be a great loss to him ('You don't *say* things like that,' he later protested to Maude). To Barber he replied, 'Why, why should we speak about it? She looks very well, the English doctors gave her not one week, but she went away, she had the operation, kept her chin up and checked up the cancer, and there she is.'

He longed to be able to spoil Margot – 'Oh, take her here, there' – but within weeks she was back in Houston having treatment, and all he could do was make arrangements for money to be transferred to help with the bill. Jeannette remembers the phone calls and the 'kids' funny backpack' that he wanted sent to Margot. Romantically alluding to their *Marguerite and Armand*, Rudolf tried to have camellias delivered to her room, but the closest the florist could get were butterfly orchids. Fighting his phobia of hospitals, he made several visits to Houston, though he never stayed long. 'He couldn't cope with seeing Margot like that. It would break his heart,' said Ana Cristina, vividly recalling the jocular act he put on when the ballerina was resisting having her leg amputated.

> Rudolf said, 'What's wrong with crutches? You lose one leg? You have another leg. Do as Doctor Benjamin says. You have to be well. This thing [never cancer] has to be removed. Losing a leg is not difficult. You hop.' Margot laughs and picks up the phone to doctor. 'Rudolf thinks it's a very good thing that I should have this operation. He thinks it's going to make me well.' Rudolf goes out. Starts crying like a baby in the corridor.

And he could not cope when Margot's mind started to wander. They were having a telephone conversation while he was on St Barts, but nothing was making sense. 'Rudolf just sat there, looking beaten down by sadness. "I can't . . . ," he said. "She's gone . . . I can't understand what she says or . . ."' Blue took the phone from his hand, and Rudolf walked away.

He was on tour in Chicago in February when a handwritten fax in broken English arrived at the Hilton from Douce. 'Dear Rudolf, Margot had gone to open the door of the paradis. I am deeply concerned about the sadness you must feel.' The ballerina had died on 21 February – the anniversary of their first *Giselle*. Spending the rest of the day in his room, not even contacting Charles Jude, who was waiting to have lunch with him as usual, Rudolf arrived at the theatre with barely enough time to get ready. After the performance Charles went to his dressing room. '"I heard about Margot. I'm very sorry." He just look at me. "*C'est la vie.*" He's ill and he know that it finish.'

Unlike Margot, who found great inner peace as the end approached, Rudolf was desperately afraid of death. At the Russian Orthodox funeral of Alexandre Kalioujny, a teacher he had come to love, Charles remembers the wide berth he gave the open coffin. 'I see him sweating. He didn't want to go past.' It was not Hamlet's fear of something after death – 'When you're dead, you're dead,' Rudolf believed. 'Finish! Full stop!' – but the thought of a force he could not control taking over his body. Hearing that Charles's father had died of cancer, Rudolf had wanted to know every detail of how it happened and how much he had suffered. And when he learned that Leonard Bernstein had died in the next-door apartment at the Dakota, Rudolf had immediately left the building. Not only was he fleeing from the proximity of the corpse, he also felt let down. Like von Karajan, Bernstein had promised, 'Conductors live a long, long time,' but now both maestros were dead.

In late February 1991, a bitter winter, Rudolf had sequestered himself in his overheated apartment, his croaked reply to Blue's cheery 'How are you?' never varying. 'Alive.' With Natasha Harley cooking, Robert Tracy often arranged for friends to come by, the idea being to convince Rudolf that nothing in his life had changed. (It had not been like that in Paris, where, as Jean-Luc Choplin recalled, 'Nobody had respect for him at that time. I remember how tough it was; how often I went to dinner with Rudolf alone because nobody else wanted to come. We'd be there, just the two of us, watching TV and eating something prepared by Manuel.') It was Robert's intention, Violette Verdy says, 'to keep him going through the bad times by continuing with the dinner parties so that Rudolf felt that it was still the same . . . his dancing and his popularity.' But his efforts went unappreciated by Rudolf, who complained that Robert was arranging dinners with people he did not want to see in order to enhance his own connections. The fact he was allowing 'that shit-boy' to live rent-free at the Dakota entitled him, he believed, to an unpaid social secretary, house sitter and amanuensis (Robert carried out any research he wanted, and had recently edited a collection of Nigel Gosling's art criticism, *Prowling the Pavements.* Again to little avail. 'He provided me with tiddly bits about life of Shakespeare,' Rudolf once acknowledged, with the stinging caveat, 'But he was bluffing most of the time.')

Phyllis Wyeth, one of the few members of the Nureyev circle who was fond of Robert, felt that he was 'badly used'. Natasha Harley agrees. 'I always felt that Robert was some kind of commodity for him – somebody who would take care of the apartment. Rudolf didn't want to pay for anybody. Not even a maid.' During the weeks they were living in the Dakota, Blue saw that Robert was growing noticeably edgy. 'When Rudolf left New York, Robert sometimes became so upset that I had to go out and leave him alone . . . He wanted to hear from Rudolf, and Rudolf wasn't interested in him any longer.' Wallace had sensed much the same. 'It seemed to me that their relationship had deteriorated even further. Rudolf at that point appeared to tolerate his presence, but that was about it. I'm pretty sure he would have been very happy if Robert had walked out of his life.' Asked by a mutual friend if he felt responsible for Robert, Rudolf replied, 'Not at all. We screwed fifteen years ago.' In fact he was now becoming so determined to have the Dakota apartment to himself that he had asked Tessa Kennedy to tell Robert to find somewhere else to live.

'Rudolf, it's not for me to do that.'

'Please, it's making me sick. I can't stand having him there any more. You can at least put the idea into his head.'

So I did, but Robert wouldn't go. And it got worse and worse, with Rudolf losing his temper all the time.

The reason for the urgency was that Rudolf had decided to settle permanently in New York, and by the spring of 1991 had begun bringing over many of his possessions from quai Voltaire. 'I guess I'll close that French chapter,' he announced, telling a journalist that twice he had been 'barking up the wrong tree' (meaning his choices of London and Paris). 'America has been the most generous and faithful, and they still come to see my performance.' First, though, resigned to the fact that 'the only thing left for me is to dance', Rudolf intended to put England's loyalty to the test one last time.

Managed by a small-time promoter, the twenty-one-day Farewell Tour worked its way south from Sunderland on 26 April, ending up on the coast in Brighton. The cover of the souvenir programme was a dazzlingly glamorous 1970s photograph of Rudolf, and with this image in mind, he would sit in front of his dressing-room mirror, silently watched by Luigi and Blue. 'I had such beautiful hair,' he said softly . . . After a long while, just staring and thinking, he'd pinch his cheeks. 'What d'you think, Shluigi? Should I have a cheek job? Couple of tucks?' Meanwhile, in the auditorium, ushers were giving women in the front orchestra seats a pink rose to throw onstage, but with the star appearing in *The Lesson* and *The Moor's Pavane* – 'walking dances', Blue called them – the final curtain went down on a sense of anticlimax. This was the nadir: Rudolf lumbering through the same tired repertory like a bottom-of-the-bill vaudeville act, and despite his vow never to dance to taped music was now performing to a disastrously faulty sound system. 'If you don't have an orchestra,' he had been told, 'you can have more money.' *The Times* reported 'cries of refund, refund'; the *Sunday Telegraph* claimed that touts were offering tickets at half price, and published a vengeful photograph of a snarling, geriatric Rudolf with a walking stick (omitting to mention that he was in the character of Dr Coppélius). 'Your newspapers are edited by Kitty Kelley. You are only interested in character assassination,' he told one journalist, adding, 'Maybe it's time to turn my back on England.' Maude remembered feeling physically hurt by the brutality of the reviews, but it was affecting Rudolf, too, and during a long car journey back to London he started to open up.

He said, 'Maude, why do I go on? I should *really* stop, shouldn't I . . .' 'Well, it's up to you, Rudolf. You've got plenty of other things you could do.' 'But it keeps me well.' Rudolf truly couldn't comprehend how he could live without doing a class every day and working every night. It distressed me terribly, of course. I tried not to go round with him when he was doing those tours because it made me so sad on his behalf.

Balanchine had predicted this. 'He'll end up badly, you'll see,' he told Cecil Beaton. 'He is too selfish and a dancer cannot afford to be selfish . . . He'll be like Pavlova.' But Balanchine was only half right, because, if there were young dancers to be helped, there was no one more generous than Rudolf. Blue describes him standing in the wings during a rehearsal in Edinburgh, shouting, '*Mooskva! Mooskva!*' at André Fedatov, who was performing *Le Corsaire.* Another dancer explained. Rudolf was implying, 'Go to Moscow! Distance! Travel! Stretch! Extend yourself!' as he was using this British tour to introduce and train potential young stars. 'Some came from Russia; it was a big break for them, and good money.' And despite commenting on the 'shit towns' in which they were appearing, Rudolf was not apologetic about his troupe performing in the provinces. '*Those* are the people to dance to. They came, brought family, enjoyed dance. Get out, do it. Show dance to people.' It was the kind of audience for whom Pavlova had danced across the globe, 'injecting' the thirteen-year-old Frederick Ashton with his passion when she appeared in his then home town of Lima, Peru. And it was a ballet performance in Ufa's opera house twenty-eight years later that had decided the fate of another enraptured young boy.

Rudolf's last appearance on a London stage was on 3 May at the Wembley Conference Centre. The ninety-three-year-old Ninette de Valois had made her way out to the suburb by public transport and she asked Maude to take her to Rudolf's dressing room. 'The moment she came in, he just lit up. They talked a while, and she said, "Rudolf, you're still great." She came back to the house afterwards and they talked and talked until two in the morning. Ninette could still see the quality in what he was doing.' But that was, in fact, not the case. Five years earlier de Valois had confided to a dance writer, 'Between you and me it's tragic, dear, I wish he'd stop.' This, as Rudolf knew, was an act of friendship; de Valois wanting to express gratitude for the past, and to say goodbye. 'He sent her flowers the next day.'

At the end of May, Rudolf made his debut in *Death in Venice,* a two-act ballet Flemming Flindt had created specially for him. Far from being the ailing, pathetic figure portrayed by Peter Pears in Britten's opera, or by Dirk Bogarde in Visconti's film, Rudolf's Aschenbach was more reminiscent of Jay Gatsby, svelte and agile in a white flannel suit with twenties cropped hair. 'Britten and Visconti were fixated about their own sexuality, but I didn't think of this as a homosexual story,' Flindt says. 'It was more about a journey to God.' To Rudolf it was a quest for lost youth, and although Flindt insists that his choice of Bach's Passacaglia – the music of *Jeune homme et la mort* – was not deliberate, it powerfully reinforces memories of the twenty-eight-year-old Nureyev. (At the start he even dances with the same props – a table and simple wooden chair.) He saw an image of his former self in Tadzio, the beautiful boy, just as he did in each of the academic nudes that hung on the walls of quai Voltaire. 'When you start to look,' says Luigi, who was more familiar than any lover with Nureyev's body, 'they all have something of Rudolf – his neck, his chest with no hair . . . Rudolf was totally in love with himself. And he wanted to make love to himself.' Coming at such a late stage of his career, this was an astonishing performance, Rudolf calling up hidden reserves of strength for feats of acrobatic partnering that would have taxed a healthy dancer half his age. It was, however, stamina he was reserving for nothing but the stage, and when Flindt offered him a second beer at a bar one night, Rudolf replied, 'I have to choose: either that or I lift the boy tomorrow.'[*]

Exhausted by the short run of *Death in Venice*, he went to Li Galli to recover, growing, in Blue's account, increasingly reclusive and misanthropic. At night the pair would sit watching television or videos of old Hollywood movies, mostly Fred Astaire's. 'One night we were watching a documentary about wildlife in the Florida swamps. Somebody tossed a dead sheep into the water. At once there was a frenzy of alligators feeding on it. "Ah!" Rudolf said. "Paris Opéra." ' If any tourists came too close to the island he was furious, immediately jumping on his Kawasaki jet ski and driving it maniacally towards the trespassing boat to chase it away. Once, when he saw a woman disembark and start strolling around, he lost all control. 'He ran down and cursed her and she cursed him back until he was in a frenzy,' recalled Blue, who was forced to come between them.

Rudolf was now even more money obsessed, convinced that he was being cheated out of television repeat fees, and sending off angry faxes to the head of the Royal Opera House, accusing 'Mr, Sir or Lord [Jeremy] Isaacs' of owing him £5,000 and claiming to be too poor to afford even a taxi to Covent Garden. Blue was struggling to cater for them both as Rudolf gave him so little money to buy provisions in Positano – 'yet Nureyev could have *bought* the grocer'. Benito, a local builder working on the property, was aware of Blue's difficulties, and provided an occasional cash handout, which he then absorbed into the construction costs. Benito's wife had taught Blue how to cook risotto, and this became the pair's sustenance, 'thirty days in a row'. Rudolf must have realized that imposing such a spartan existence on his young

---

[*] With Tadzio at his feet, Rudolf's Aschenbach dies onstage – a wish fulfilment of his own, and a continuation of the pattern of recent roles – Marco Spada, Mercutio, Dr Sloper and Akaky Akakyevich.

assistant was unfair, as he strolled up one day and asked, 'How long can you live here?' Blue, who was indeed starting to despair at finding himself on 'a rugged chunk of rock' as gaunt and isolated as Alcatraz, did not answer immediately. '*Foof! Too slow!*' exclaimed Rudolf, strolling away. Blue's slow-wittedness had earned him the nickname 'Death' – 'Here comes *death* . . .' his employer used to drawl, clearly aware of the irony of their situation. Rudolf had anyway decided that he could do without any human companionship, that music was all he needed to fill his life. 'This is preparation for my solitude . . . I will sit in front of my clavichord.' It was only Bach he played, not only because the music was more instructive to him than any other composer's, but because it provided the kind of spiritual peace others find in religion.

Now that music was assuming more and more importance in his life – 'a consolation in the moments where I felt myself injured' – Rudolf was grateful when an opportunity arose to learn to conduct. It was through the Hübner family that he had been introduced to the director of one of Vienna's leading music venues, the Palais Auersperg. Dr Franz Moser who, together with a young Austrian conductor, had met Rudolf at Victoria Road in May, was enthralled by the idea of launching the star in a new career, but needed reassurance that this was something within Rudolf's grasp. It would be simple enough to teach him how to use a baton – and even how to get an orchestra to play together and in tune – but to be merely competent he would have to transmit a huge amount of musical information, the gathering of which can be a lifetime's work. In his *New Yorker* article exploring the complexities of conducting, Justin Davidson marvels at the way this constant flow of minutiae – 'How quick or flexible the pulse should be, how biting a staccato, how distended a pause, how graceful a phrase, how heavy a march' – is channelled to a hundred players by one person with a stick. A maestro's art is, as Davidson says, 'a mysterious mechanism . . . a gestural form of communication' – but then so is dance. Rudolf, who had been seeking out different versions of scores and reading them for pleasure since his student days, was undaunted by the challenge, and after a five-hour grilling had managed to convince his two Austrian interlocutors that he was up to it.

The first lessons in baton technique took place in the Hübners' summerhouse situated in vineyards forty-five kilometres north of Vienna. The atmosphere had been made as informal as possible with a cellist and two violinists (one being Papa Hübner) playing Mozart as they sat round a large pine table cluttered with cups of tea. Rudolf, however, was decidedly tense. He knew that a maestro has to project authority and put his musicians at ease, but here the situation was reversed. The two young string players had been asked by Papa Hübner, 'Please, help him,' and their sceptical response of 'Hmmm, we will see' was matched by Rudolf's unease. 'They were professionals who knew he was a beginner,' remarked Blue, who observed it all. 'They would notice every mistake he made. Even worse, they would spot mistakes he didn't *know* he'd made.' But once Rudolf saw that he had gained the musicians' respect his confidence began to grow, and it was not long before Hübner had moved him to the Palais Auersperg so that he could work with a full orchestra.

Taking charge of a large group of performers waiting expectantly in a rehearsal room was something that came naturally to Rudolf. When he first mounted *La Bayadère* for the Royal Ballet in 1963 he had compared himself to 'a conductor in front of an orchestra', while his favourite method of choreographing – moving an ensemble of dancers in contrapuntal blocs – was very similar to that of a maestro bringing in the wind section, the brass and the strings. Papa Hübner had advised him not to look at the score, as it was important to develop a rapport with the players, keeping their attention through eye contact, but Rudolf was still feeling the need to prove himself, and replied that he had to show that he could read music. Watching these early rehearsals, Waxy Hübner could see that he was not really in control, though he had been aided considerably by the fact that this was a group of young people, all open-minded and intent on just doing their job. 'He wasn't superfast at coping, but this kept the musicians alert and so it was good because it was all very *alive*.'

Blue videotaped the sessions so that Rudolf could study his performance. There is no standard semaphore in conducting; every maestro develops his own personal dialect of face and body language – sometimes communicating just by lifting an eyebrow. 'What one conductor achieves with a minuscule vibration of a finger, another will accomplish with a sledgehammer swing of an arm,' writes Justin Davidson, who watched the way that Robert Spano's rapid series of gesticulations were instantly picked up by the musicians. 'He made as if to squeeze an orange (the message: "Give me a succulent tone"). He then mimed sliding a toy car down a ramp ("But don't drag; push right into the next beat"), whisking eggs ("Keep the sound vibrant"), and swatting a table tennis ball ("Give the phrase a sharp, light bounce").'

Rudolf, the world's most explosive dancer, was remarkably restrained on the podium. Waxy Hübner was reminded of the ageing Karl Böhm (one of the first conductors to encourage Rudolf), 'in that he was clear with the baton but did very little'. To La Scala's resident conductor, Michael Sassoon, little was not enough. 'Rudolf had a good ear – when the second trombone didn't come in, he would know. But he didn't speak the music language of the musicians. Transferring that to an orchestra needs professional signals.' Vienna ballet's director Gerhard Brunner thought that Rudolf should never have put himself in the spotlight so soon, but 'moved to Austria and not been seen or heard for a while to give him time to learn'. Time, though, was precisely what Rudolf did not have. He had told only Waxy, a doctor, his reason, and although the Hübner parents never spoke of Rudolf's condition, they, too, seemed aware of it. 'It would have been a different story if we knew he was going to have fifteen to twenty years to conduct,' Waxy says. 'My father would have worked with him for a year or two before he made his debut.'

The mixed programme of Haydn, Mozart, and Tchaikovsky took place at the Palais Auersperg on 25 June 1991. Video footage of the concert shows that Rudolf had already managed to establish an empathy with the Wiener Residenz players, particularly its first violinist Naomi Kazama, who encourages him with little smiles of complicity. 'It was an *attempt*,' Brunner concedes, and the braveness of the attempt was what continued to impress. Six months later, attending a performance of Rudolf conducting *The Nutcracker* in Poland, Elizabeth Kendall described a local music critic leaping to his feet at the end and shouting '*Molodetz!*' which in Russian means, 'Good for you, you did it!' Thierry Fouquet, on the other hand, says that he never really took Rudolf's conducting phase seriously. 'He was a good actor and could make himself *look* like a maestro in front of a nicely disposed orchestra. But any pianist or composer could have done the same thing.' Papa Hübner would have disagreed. When Maude asked whether Rudolf could have made a great conductor given another ten years, he replied, 'In far less time than that.' Yet this, as Rudolf admitted, was work he had 'made myself want'. When he conducted Stravinsky's *Apollo* five days after his debut, the score he followed was the one used when he danced the role in Vienna in 1967. On the opening page was written: 'To wait until Nureyev arrives in the middle of the stage and raises his arms.'

After the intense activity in Vienna, Rudolf went straight to Li Galli to recover, sleeping most of the time. Every morning at nine o'clock a tourist boat circled the islands, the female guide giving a running commentary, first in Italian, then in English, about their famous inhabitant. It made Gore Vidal, whose Ravello villa was another port of call, 'feel as if I were being forced to listen in on an extension telephone where I am being discussed', whereas Rudolf rather enjoyed waking up to an account of his glorious past. What most preoccupied him during those three weeks was the decoration of a room underneath the house, which he was having tiled from floor to ceiling. Staying the previous summer with Mario Bois in Seville, Rudolf had chosen the *azulejos* he wanted, insisting that they be delivered two weeks later to his house in Italy. Hearing that October was the earliest he could have them, he had protested, 'I have no time,' and returned himself soon afterwards with two vans to collect them. 'He wanted to die on Li Galli,' says Jeannette. 'Why do you think that room was all tiled?' Long and domed, it was Rudolf's mausoleum, dedicated to Farida, whose name was spelled out in Arabic motifs. When Carla Fracci visited the island, he showed her the room with pride, oblivious to her surprise at the primitive conditions he had chosen for himself. 'There was no bed, Rudolf was sleeping on a carpet on the floor. And he was living on potatoes – *basta!*'

This was a voluntary return to his Tatar peasant roots, a bizarre riches-to-rags regression, but the combination of self-indulgence with wilful miserliness was driving away the faithful Blue. In Vienna he had resented having to scrounge money from Franz Moser to pay off a masseur who had given Rudolf a hand job for five hundred dollars – half Blue's monthly salary. But the final straw was discovering that Benito had been shortchanged for his work on the island. '[Rudolf] had got what he wanted. He was indifferent to other people's needs. This was Nureyev at his worst: selfish and dishonest.' Asking for six weeks' leave to take a butlering course in London, Blue never saw Rudolf again.

After carrying out conducting engagements in Deauville, Vienna and Romania, Rudolf was suddenly struck by severe abdominal pains. On the advice of Waxy, who specialized in urology, he was admitted to a hospital in Vienna, where he underwent surgery for an obstructed kidney. The moment he awoke from the anaesthetic Rudolf had tried to get up and leave, but Lydia Hübner, being physically much stronger, managed to hold him down. Eight days later he had discharged himself and was back in Paris, where Mario Bois urged him to calm down and rest for a while in one of his houses. Rudolf's reply was now his catchphrase: 'I have no time.'

Telling Maude that he needed the money to pay for his 'enormous hospital bills', Rudolf had his mind set on spending a month dancing in

Australia. He was still in considerable pain and would have to perform with a catheter hidden inside his costume – 'the plumbing', as he called it. But when Charles Jude and Luigi told him that he could not possibly dance in such bad shape he refused to cancel the tour, agreeing only to a change in the programme. (*Songs of a Wayfarer*, which Béjart had once again begged him '*de ne plus interpréter*', was replaced with a shortened version of *Afternoon of a Faun*.) Undertaking the role of full-time nurse, Luigi put the ailing dancer to bed and took him to the bathroom, while Charles Jude had become Rudolf's real-life *Wayfarer* companion. 'In Paris I had my wife, my family, but on tour I was always with him. We stay in the same hotel, we eat together, we're together twenty-four hours. This is why he wanted so much to go. We didn't talk about his malady, and I tried to get him to evacuate all thoughts. But it was a good time for him – the sun, the swimming.'

Before the trip Maude had been convinced it was 'really the end of his dancing', but Rudolf's swan song was still to come. On 9 April 1991 he had received a letter from a Hungarian writer, Ildikó Kóródy, who was working on a libretto commissioned by the Hungarian State Opera for a three-act ballet based on the life of Christopher Columbus. He had been feeling that his work was 'not complete, not total', when the idea came to him to cast Rudolf as a central figure, 'the spirit of Cristoforo', who directs events from the first scene until the last. 'You have been sent to us by the Lord! . . . . Let's call you Angel.' Telling the opera administration, 'I have no time for this. I accept only a small part,' Rudolf arrived in Budapest in February 1992 to prepare his cameo role as the Columbus's guiding Angel in Gábor Keveházi's *Cristoforo*. Wearing a little woollen hat, his wizened monkey face and eyes now bearing the startled expression common to HIV victims in their final phase, Rudolf peered out above vast Loie Fuller-size wings, his feeble manipulation of the Angel-engulfing mantle evoking a mocking, evanescent memory of the young Nureyev's flying cape.

At a press conference before the première one of the first questions had been, 'Excuse me, Maestro, do you have AIDS?' Seemingly unfazed, Rudolf had replied, 'I'm very ill, but I don't have AIDS.' To the Hungarian National Ballet's director, however, he had already admitted that the rumours were true. Rudolf had clearly warmed to Roland Boker, an admiring, multilingual young man whom he had got to know while performing *Death in Venice* in Verona. 'He wanted to speak Russian with me,' says Boker, who discovered that Rudolf was spending most of the day in his hotel room watching Russian television. 'He liked to hear everything that was happening at home.' At two o'clock one morning he was woken by a phone call from Rudolf. 'He said, "Roland, please come to me. And bring yoghurt, please."* He couldn't sleep, and he didn't want to be alone.' Opening up to Boker in a way that he had not felt able to do with close friends, Rudolf claimed that he had been HIV positive for more than ten years. 'I had courage, and so I had no time for thinking about this. But now when I work only a little I feel very bad.'

To remedy this Rudolf had arranged to fly between his two performances of Cristoforo to Berlin, where he was making his debut as the wicked fairy Carabosse in The Sleeping Beauty. Pat Ruanne, who had mounted the production, remembers this as an extraordinarily highly charged performance. Looking like a crazed, overpainted English dowager, Rudolf 'broke all his own rules regarding subtlety of interpretation,' she said. 'But I know that he had a great time.' On 1 March he returned to Budapest, repeating his role as the Angel, and after that, there were no more engagements.

The conducting continued, however, taking Rudolf to Russia later in March. Learning from a radio broadcast that he wanted to go to Kazan in memory of his mother, the Kazan Opera's general director, Raufal Tziaynov, had invited him to conduct Romeo and Juliet there. Arriving on the overnight train from Moscow, Rudolf expressed surprise that there were no TV cameras or press there to meet him. 'But no one thought his appearance such an event,' says Tziaynov. Nor did the musicians, who grudgingly credited the foreign guest with 'knowing the right rhythm for the dancers', but very little else. 'He was dancing the music in his head, and only then putting it in movements of his hands,' remarked first violinist German Drushenitsky, and his colleague, violinist Natasha Novinova, agreed. Rudolf, she felt, knew the music only because he had danced to it, but was clearly unfamiliar with the instruments and separate sections of the orchestra.

The question is whether the conductor gives you his vision, and Nureyev did not. I can see that it was hard for him being at the top of the artistic world and having to go all the way to the bottom. But with his wealth, his fame, he could afford to do this as a hobby. It was just a caprice. If he'd been really cultured, he'd have seen that our instruments were terribly old and broken; he could at least have presented new ones

---

* The yoghurt was to help soothe the fungal sores in his mouth caused by the HIV-induced thrush infection candidiasis.

for the orchestra. It would have been a thousand times better than just conducting – it would have helped our culture.

Rudolf had been travelling through Eastern Europe with a bearded young Russian conductor, Vladimir Keradjeyav, who was there to help him rehearse the various orchestras. The Kazan musicians felt he was doing too much, and evidently so did Rudolf. 'He was often swearing at Volodya with *mat* words,' says Drushenitsky, remembering how Keradjeyav had taken offence and suddenly left. 'And I don't think he was ever paid.' This orchestra, as Novinova says, could play itself, but Rudolf seemed to feel that he was in charge. Overshadowed by Keradjeyav, he had been stony-faced and uncommunicative with the musicians, but now began to relax. 'He softened and became a totally different person,' Tziaynov recalls. 'I think he liked feeling that he was in a kind of family.' Kazan, with its frozen river, streets shored up with dirty snow and *isba*-style wooden houses, reminded Rudolf of an Eastern version of Ufa, and he made the most of his time there, drinking the Puligny-Montrachet he had brought from Paris, and provocatively asking Tziaynov, 'Do you have ass in Kazan?' He had summoned a masseuse to his hotel bed, but when a woman arrived, he muttered, 'No. Only man,' and pulled the blanket back over his head.

Rudolf had taken along his new assistant to Russia, an obliging young Australian by the name of Neil Boyd, and he also had Douce in tow. Having fallen out the previous summer, they had been reconciled at a Christmas party at the Rothschilds', Douce carrying out an elaborate charade *en travesti* designed to amuse and win back Rudolf. 'He didn't stick to people unless they did something for him,' says Leslie Caron. 'Douce was the greatest energizer; she had this quality of picking you up and supporting you.' She also had a video camera, and spent hours filming Rudolf on the podium and recording the high points of their journey. 'I hope you have this – don't look at me,' he snaps at one point in the footage, indicating a church wall entirely covered with golden icons. Then, accompanying Rudolf to a military *banya*, a laughing Douce films right inside the pine-panelled steam room, pointing her lens at fat naked officers, and following them as they plunged into an icy pool.

It was after this occasion that Rudolf caught pneumonia, his temperature soaring so high that the alarmed Raufal Tziaynov had tried to take him to a hospital. 'No. No hospital,' countered Rudolf, determined to press on with the next stage of the tour. This was in Leningrad, where he moved into Ninel Kurgapkina's apartment, surprising his old friend by how frugal his expectations were. 'He didn't want luxury of any kind. I asked him what he liked to eat and he said, "*Schi* [cabbage soup] and porridge – I love Russian food."' The forthright Ninel had immediately confronted Rudolf with 'I hear you've got AIDS,' but although he emphatically denied it, he collapsed soon after his arrival and had to be rushed to a hospital. No one at Leningrad's Military Medical Academy, the best clinic in the city, had known how to treat him as he refused to have a blood test. But almost immediately he checked himself out, and when Ninel called a doctor to her home, 'spat out the medicines he was given'. Needed at the theatre and worried about leaving Rudolf alone she asked Liuba to come round to the apartment. 'But he wouldn't stay there,' said Liuba. 'He insisted that I take him to see Jerry Robbins's ballet [*In the Night*] at the Kirov. I tried to stop him but it was useless.'

As Rudolf was determined to carry out his commitment to conduct *Schéhérazade* in Leningrad, Ninel had asked a concertmaster she knew to go through the music with him. In Yuri Gamaley's account, Rudolf, who began by opening his score at the wrong place, hardly knew what he was doing.

> He confessed that he was lost and asked me to play once again from the beginning, but slower . . . I started to show him where and which voices are most important. With my directions he marked those places and important entrances for instruments. Very soon I realized that Nureyev had no experience working with a score. I was teaching him like a beginner; stopping a lot and giving serious instructions. That way we groped to the end of the first part.

After two hours Ninel arrived to collect Rudolf, whispering to Gamaley that she would get in touch about paying for the lessons. He had not expected any money, 'perhaps a big bouquet of flowers, or a bottle of good brandy', but when Ninel saw him on a subsequent occasion, she opened her bag and took out four notes Rudolf had given her to pass on. 'Twenty-five roubles – less than one dollar. That was how the millionaire paid me.'

Rudolf was supposed to go on to conduct in Yalta, but as his fever was still raging, Douce went behind his back and cancelled the engagement. She had intended to take him straight back to Paris, but 17 March was his fifty-fourth birthday, and Rudolf did not want to disappoint Liuba, who had invited two dozen people for a sit-down dinner at Tchaikovsky Street. The gathering included Romankov relatives and their children; Kirov star Altinai Assylmuratova; Faina Rokhind, Rudolf's devoted fan; and Jerome Robbins, who felt so moved by the event that he stood up to make a speech. 'Everyone who speaks to you here seems to be part of your second family,' he told Rudolf. 'I'm not part of your family, but part of your *world* family, and I want to toast you and thank you for all you have done for the ballet in our country particularly. And I saw what you did in France, and saw your influence . . . I always have very much love for you.' Sitting at the head of the table beside his beloved Leonid, Rudolf was smiling, although he looked sicker than ever, his face leached of colour. Liuba's sister, Marina, a doctor, had warned her that he had AIDS, advising her to keep his plate and cutlery separate. But Rudolf hardly ate that night, and the next day, when Liuba took him to the airport, he seemed to have deteriorated even further. 'He was so weak, and frankly speaking, I thought this was the end.' As Rudolf was going through passport control, he turned towards Liuba and murmured, 'Light a candle for me.'

Rudolf's assistant, Neil, also thought that he was about to die, and when their plane made a stopover at Helsinki airport, arranged to move him into a private room. 'His clothes were drenched. I was drying them with a hairdryer, but in the end I bought an "I love Helsinki" T-shirt for him to wear.' On landing in Paris, Rudolf was taken straight to the Ambroise-Paré Clinic in Neuilly, where it was discovered that he had a cytomegalo virus infection of the heart, which had caused a litre of fluid to build up around it. The doctors were convinced that if he had stayed another day in Russia he would not have made it back. But when Rudolf was told they were going to operate he panicked, gabbling, 'No, no, I go out. I have a dinner.' Charles Jude, who was with him, begged him to come to his senses. 'OK, I stay,' he said gruffly, but he wanted the dancer to promise that he would still be there when he came out of the anaesthetic. The next day, hearing that Charles's wife and daughter were also at the hospital, Rudolf asked to see the five-year-old Joanna. 'They told me it wasn't a good idea to let her see him like that,' but feeling that Rudolf might draw strength and energy from the child, Charles brought Joanna to his bedside. 'He took her hand and I saw his eyes light up.' 'I'm alive, I'm alive!' Rudolf exclaimed.

It was soon after this that Jane Hermann arrived in Paris. She was in her hotel room one night when she got a call from Andrew Grossman. 'He had long given up finding gigs for Rudolf, but he told me, "I think you should go over if you want to see him again. He's refusing medication."' There had been no contact between the dancer and impresario since that terrible night in San Francisco, and Jane admits that there was no longer any affection on her side. Nevertheless, 'mainly out of tremendous sentiment', she went as quickly as she could to quai Voltaire. Rudolf welcomed her warmly, and they began to talk as if they had seen each other just the day before. Then Jane heard herself saying, 'You've got to behave yourself and take your medicine. Because I have a plan for you to conduct at the Met.' Rudolf did not believe her at first – in his current condition he could no more have stood on a podium for several hours than danced a full-length ballet – but Jane convinced him that this was a serious proposition. 'I was doing it for both of us. He was the most significant artist in my career, and it kind of shut the door for me. I knew it was the last time he'd ever do anything important in the US, and so I offered this last great chance to him in the hope that maybe, before he died, he would understand what a true friend is. He really did thank me tremendously.'

'Jane gave life back to Rudolf with that,' said Wallace. 'Knowing that he had the Met kept him going, because otherwise I think he would have just given up.' Back on his medication, and receiving infusions of ganciclovir into his heart every two hours, Rudolf was soon sitting up in bed wearing headphones and familiarizing himself with the score of *Romeo and Juliet*. He was to conduct the American Ballet Theatre orchestra with his protégés Sylvie Guillem and Laurent Hilaire dancing the lead roles, an epic feat that Michel Canesi was allowing only on condition that Rudolf employ a full-time nurse. Hearing that this would cost him four thousand dollars for the two weeks, however, Rudolf not only refused to pay for the nurse but when Canesi exploded in frustration, told the doctor that he would no longer be needing his services. Three days later, realizing what he would be jeopardizing, a penitent Rudolf called to apologize.

Canesi had been dreading telling Rudolf that the time had come to put his affairs in order, but in fact this turned out to be what he describes as 'one of those moments of great quietness, calm and friendship between us'. On 14 April Rudolf's American lawyer, Barry Weinstein, accompanied by attorney Jeannette Thurnherr from Liechtenstein, arrived at quai Voltaire to draw up a will. If the lawyers made a suggestion Rudolf didn't like, he said nothing but picked up a newspaper and held it over his face. His own wishes were very clear. 'While he provided for their well-being, he never wanted his family to have everything,' maintains Weinstein. 'He wanted them to work and educate themselves.' The only friend Rudolf singled out was Maude, unequivocally instructing Weinstein to establish an income for her. 'He didn't care about providing gifts or benefits for anyone else. I think he finally realized that Douce should not be left in the cold, but it was out of some guilt. It didn't come naturally.' Among other documents executed that day was one establishing the Rudolf Nureyev Dance Foundation, to which the dancer would bequeath all his personal effects and property located in America. In addition a Ballet Promotion Foundation (now known as the Rudolf Nureyev Foundation) would receive his European assets, both organizations undertaking to perpetuate Rudolf's name and legacy through financial support of individuals, organizations and events.

Arriving in New York on 21 April, sixteen days before the performance, Rudolf began working each morning with Charles Barker, the principal conductor of ABT, and a pianist. He was too frail to have more than a single rehearsal with the orchestra, but the musicians were already united in their esteem for him, and determined to do their best. 'They were helping out a legend,' says ABT's David Richardson. 'It was payback time.' On the night of the performance, 6 May 1992, Rudolf had to be assisted into his conductor's tails by Maude and Wallace, both of whom were convinced he would not make it through the evening. 'He didn't even have the strength to fasten the buttons, but *somehow* he got out there and did it.' He made some errors (the mandoline dancers began before the music and had to start again; the tempo of the last two acts was funereally slow), but Rudolf had never commanded more respect from an audience. 'It was thrilling,' Richardson recalls. 'Not perfect, but there was something so heroic about his determination to do it. I think everyone was excited to be at a performance which we knew was giving him a little more life.' In a note delivered to Rudolf backstage, Jackie Onassis had written, 'For dear Rudolf with all my love and admiration on your great opening night. Now the world has a new Maestro – and he is my favorite.'

It was a typical New York gala audience, its familiar society figures including Monique van Vooren, who had come to make peace with Rudolf. 'It was kind of wonderful,' recalled Wallace, 'because it was as if she hadn't missed a beat. She just got into Rudolf's car and they drove off together through the tunnel at Lincoln Center.' Back at the Dakota the post-performance party went on until 3.30 in the morning, with Rudolf swathed in scarves and 'all puffed up with pride'. 'Everybody was paying tribute to him and adoring him so much,' said Georgina Parkinson. 'Sylvie was sitting on the floor at his feet.' As far as Rudolf was concerned, though, this was not the 'farewell New York' performance Jane

Hermann had intended, but an opportunity to solicit further engage-ments. Being his 'own impresario' once again, he asked NYCB's director Peter Martins, 'When am I going to conduct for you?' and, during a dis-cussion with Frank Augustyn, he finalized a plan to conduct in Ottawa. 'I wanted Rudolf for a gala, and asked him what he charged. "Pay me whatever you can," he said, and when I suggested a fee, he laughed. "Well, that's a lot more than ABT gave me!"'

The next morning Rudolf went straight to his farm in Virginia for a few days to recuperate. Jeannette baked corn bread, Wallace barbe-cued, and Waxy Hübner arrived from Washington. 'You know what?' Rudolf confided to Waxy when they were alone. 'I just feel terribly tired.' 'I don't know if I was able to answer; probably I said nothing. But it was a moment when I thought that maybe he had stopped fight-ing a little bit. A *little bit*. And then it came back to him.'

After conducting a Rossini and Mozart programme in Vienna, Rudolf flew to San Francisco in mid-July to lead an orchestra of University of California students in selections from *Romeo and Juliet* and Beethoven's *Eroica* Symphony – a concert that, although he did not realize it at the time, would be his last. Accompanied by Jeannette and Armen, he went on to spend a couple of days in the Napa Valley home of Natalia Makarova, eating extremely well because the chef Jeremiah Tower and a restaurateur friend were also visiting. 'They went into the vegetable garden and picked things to make incredible salads,' says Jeannette, who also remembers being taken to see the little Russian chapel that Makarova had had built – 'the kind of thing White Russians had on their land before the Revolution.' Rudolf seemed greatly amused by this, quipping, 'It will take more than a chapel to save her soul!' But shocked by how sick he was, Makarova says that she 'couldn't be cross with him any more.' All the same a hint of the old combativeness surfaced when she challenged Rudolf to a game of chess. He won but was too tired to play another game, and so Jean-nette offered to teach him gin rummy. They were still playing long after everyone had retired. 'Natasha came down and said, "It's very late. You should get some sleep." But Rudolf didn't want to.' Early the next morning, Jeannette had not been long asleep, when she woke to see Rudolf standing at the foot of her bed. 'What's wrong?' 'It's cold in my room. Where's Armen?' 'He was looking for my mother so that she could warm him up. I couldn't remember which room she was in either – so he got into bed with me.'

*

Returning to Paris towards the end of July he began work on *La Bayadère*, which was due to be premièred in October. Set in fifth-century India, Petipa's ballet takes its name from the *bayadère*, or temple dancer, Nikiya, with whom Solor, a noble warrior, is in love. Like *Swan Lake*, *La Sylphide* and *Giselle*, it is another story of infidelity and broken promises; by agreeing to marry the Rajah's daughter, Gamzatti, the hero indirectly colludes in Nikiya's murder, which takes place during his betrothal ceremony. Still in her thrall, Solor conjures up Nikiya's spirit during an opium trance, a glorious hallucination in which she appears to have been multiplied thirty-two times by the corps de ballet. This is Act 3's Kingdom of the Shades scene (staged in Paris by Rudolf in 1974), a transcendent distillation of classical dance, and a total contrast to the melodrama and vivid spectacle that has preceded it. Act 1 of the original 1877 version was almost entirely pantomime, while Act 2, in which Solor makes his entrance on a full-scale elephant, called for 230 dancers and supernumeraries to fill the stage as black children, slaves, *bayadères*, armed guards, Brahmans, courtesans and hunters. Not surprisingly the full-length ballet remained unperformed outside Russia until 1980, when Makarova, making one act out of Petipa's first two, staged it for ABT. In Rudolf's view, however, her severe cuts were a mistake, removing much of *La Bayadère*'s colour and exuberance. 'Petipa had great esteem for folkloric dance, and I try to stay faithful to Petipa.'

To help him create '*une* Bayadère *Petipa, Kirov, vraie*', Rudolf brought Ninel Kurgapkina to Paris, although he still had every intention of adding more dancing for the men. This was to be expected, Ninel claiming that she 'was not there to authenticate the ballet, but just follow Rudolf's ideas'.* What was surprising, though, was his volte-face on the value of mime. Had he staged the ballet as he longed to in his twenties, he would almost certainly have disdained the traditional gesturing for 'I love you,' 'She's beautiful,' and so on, just as he had boycotted Margot's mime sequence as Odette in 1962. Working with him on the role of Solor, however, Charles Jude remembers Rudolf getting Ninel to demonstrate 'what they do in Russia', and then complying immediately

---

* As the part of Solor as created by Petipa for Gerdt consisted mostly of mimed passages and partnering, Chaboukiani had choreographed all his own variations. Given this precedent, Rudolf, despite Sergeyev's disapproval, introduced a *manège* of *doubles assemblés* into Solor's variation when he performed the role in 1958. In his full-length version for the Paris Opéra Ballet, still convinced that there was not enough opportunity in the ballet for male dancers, he added new variations for Solor's friends.

with, 'OK do that.' The reason, Charles believes, was because Rudolf no longer had the force to argue or make improvements, but there was also the fact that his ideas had changed. Since creating the role of Juliet and joining him at the Opéra as *répétiteuse*, Pat Ruanne noticed a profound difference in Rudolf's attitude. When she began to rehearse his *Swan Lake* he had warned her that the French dancers were very 'resistant' to mime, as resistant, in fact, as he himself had once been. But whereas in *Romeo and Juliet* he had wanted all the emotion to be expressed through movement, he had come to understand that mime is an essential part of the classical repertory, and was, Ruanne says, 'very precise in his directives to maintain its clarity and formality'.

The jealous confrontation between the two rivals for Solor's love is conveyed entirely in high melodrama ('It's a duo,' says Patrice Bart, comparing the ballerinas to a mezzo and soprano in a Verdi opera), and it was this scene that Rudolf considered so important that he wanted to tackle it first, while he still had the strength. Helping to stage the ballet, both Bart and Pat Ruanne had expected that Rudolf would want to augment the choreography in the early acts, but found that he was 'leaving things be'. Ruanne explains:

> I think he felt that the simplicity of the choreography was telling enough, and would prepare for the tour de force of the Kingdom of Shades . . . But I have no doubt that his failing health was also a factor. Many of the dances he intended to rework had to be left in their original format, as he was just too ill by that time. The things that he did change were for a few people, and therefore controllable and reasonably quick to do . . . I think the unpredictability of his strength was the main element. You can't totally restructure a big waltz in one rehearsal when you're not sure that you'll be up to it the following day.

Having commissioned Ezio Frigerio and his wife, Franca Squarciapino, to create what he called a '*Thousand and One Nights*' vision of the Orient, Rudolf had hoped to get the designer to reproduce *Bayadère*'s long-lost ending. Abandoned in Russia since 1919, Act 4 of the ballet, the wedding scene, not only provided a logical conclusion to the plot, but was also a thrilling *coup de théâtre*. Enraged by the marriage between Solor and Gamzetti, the gods exact revenge by causing the entire edifice of the temple to collapse, crushing everyone with the exception of the hero. Makarova's production had restored the final act with its destruction of the temple, but the music she used consisted more of John Lanchbery's pastiche than of Minkus's own score.

Rudolf, on the other hand, had at his disposal the pages copied and transcribed in Russia of the complete work. Kurgapkina remembers him asking Frigerio how much it would cost to stage a simulated earthquake. 'A million dollars,' replied the designer. 'Then skip it,' countered Rudolf – a disappointment that was, Pat Ruanne believes, a blessing in disguise. 'There was no longer a full reference to the original work to use as a guideline, and I think he realized that he simply would not have the strength to start a whole new act from scratch.' As it was, Kurgapkina found herself having to take on Rudolf's battles over the design. The scenery department had refused to make the elephant; Frigerio intended to do away with the famous ramp for the Shades' entrance – 'He can't have ever *seen Bayadère!*' – she exclaimed during a panicky call to Rudolf; and they were both equally worried that far too little room had been left for the dancers. 'Rudolf didn't like the Frigerio sets,' claims Charles Jude. '"This is shit," he said. But he didn't have the energy to fight.'

With rehearsals coming to an end because of the August holiday, Rudolf had arranged to go to Li Galli with Wallace, who had flown to Paris from LA with his two dogs. Rudolf had been to the hospital for a cardiogram, and the night before they were due to leave Michel Canesi called to say that the CMV infection had returned, and they should call off their trip. 'But Rudolf wanted to go to the island even if it meant he was going to die,' said Wallace. 'Which I think was what he felt would happen.' That same evening, Neil Boyd had given his notice, as he had been offered a job in Australia, and Wallace found himself in sole charge of a terminally ill man – the reality of which proved even more daunting than he had feared.

> We arrived to find the building work half finished because Rudolf hadn't paid the contractors. The electrical wiring was hanging out of the walls, and there were more wires, and tubes were running all over the place. There was mildew, so much mildew that you could watch paint falling off the ceiling. There was only enough fuel to run the generator for half of the day, there were amoebas in the water supply, and the temperature was 110 with humidity at 100 per cent. It was a nightmare. I lost ten pounds in that time, and I thought I was going to die there as well.

Their daily routine hardly varied. Rudolf would get up for the meals Wallace had prepared and then go back to bed. After dinner they sat watching television, as neither had the energy for conversation. 'But at least my dogs were there, and he enjoyed playing with them. They were the only thing that made him laugh.' Out of desperation Wallace began calling up people in Rudolf's address book whom he might invite over for a meal. A new boat had been delivered, a motor cruiser that Rudolf decided to call *Margot*, and together with a replacement assistant found by Maude (Barry Joule, who had been 'sort of a handyman' to Francis Bacon towards the end of his life), they went on various excursions. Rudolf was much cheered by a visit to Gore Vidal, letting 'his AIDS-wasted body collapse beside [Vidal's] pool' while drinking white wine and keeping his host amused with a fund of gossipy revelations. On another day they anchored the boat outside Zeffirelli's gates and hooted until a servant arrived. 'He disappeared and came back with an invitation to lunch.' Having long forgiven Rudolf, Zeffirelli was appalled and upset by the state his friend was in, telling Wallace that he would not make it to Christmas. Joule's photographs, on the other hand, show Rudolf in good spirits that day. Wearing jazzy shorts and a loose Missoni top, he sunbathes on a lounge bed, playing with the ear of Zeffirelli's terrier, and poses with the director, both dressed in identical blue-and-white-striped djellabas. One of these snaps, showing a gaunt Rudolf with his head turbaned in a towel, was given by Joule to Francis Bacon, who was so taken by the image that he 'stuck it on the wall of his chaotic studio'.[*]

After ten days Wallace flew back home thinking that he would rest up for a week, leave his dogs in LA, and return if necessary. By this time, however, Liuba and her husband, Slom, had arrived from Leningrad to take over. Refusing to think of himself as an invalid, Rudolf would not talk about his health, bringing an end to their anxious questions by saying, 'Don't you have any other topic to discuss?' On a night when they had all dined with Zeffirelli and were trying to locate their boat, Rudolf was swigging from a bottle as he weaved along the quay. 'It was like being with a Russian tramp,' remarks Liuba. 'He was drinking to block things out.' As they reached Li Galli the inlet was in darkness, the sea rough, and the wind blowing hard, and yet Rudolf, as weak as he was inebriated, refused to take Slom's hand to help him disembark. Jumping from the deck, he lost his balance and

---

* 'As the old master painted only from photographs, [Joule] thought, "Maybe, just maybe,"' but Bacon returned the snapshot a week before he died, saying, 'You have it back. I know I will never paint him.' In the artist's archive, however, there are early photographs of Rudolf that he 'Baconized' with daubs and swirls of paint.

would have fallen on the rocks if Slom had not 'caught him and thrown him through the air'. To Liuba he seemed more wilfully reckless by the day. 'We were walking on the path together when suddenly he said, "Instant death." "Rudolf, it isn't so easy," I told him. "One has to earn it."' A day or so later, he took his watercycle and asked her to come for a ride. 'He started driving with this mad velocity towards the rocks, and I thought, My goodness, he wants "instant death" and he's going to take me with him.' Rudolf stopped just in time, and yet Liuba is convinced that he was thinking of ways to kill himself. 'He wanted to die, he wanted to drown, he wanted a boat to go down.'

But it was not in Rudolf's nature to give up on life, any more than it was for Byron's Manfred, who could not find what it took to release himself from despair.

> I feel the impulse – yet I do not plunge;
> I see the peril – yet do not recede . . .
> There is a power upon me which withholds.
> And makes it my fatality to live . . .

'Life stirs my mind, it stirs my blood inside,' Rudolf once said, admitting the extent to which he was 'thrilled, excited by beautiful things – and maybe ugly things'. And however self-deluding it may seem, he was still making serious plans for his future. Shortly before Liuba left he asked her to look for a house for him to buy on the Neva Embankment, and he also asked her to help him get the position of director of the Maly Theatre, the city's second-largest opera house. 'Impossible,' she told him. 'The director is appointed by party committee.' Rudolf argued that, just as anywhere else in the world, it would be a question of networking. By extraordinary coincidence an opportunity presented itself the next day. While sailing in the Mediterranean, Anatoli Sobchak, St Petersburg's fiery radical mayor, stopped off at Li Galli.[*] A mutual friend, Vladimir Renne, had offered to take him to meet Rudolf, and, as Renne had anticipated, these two charismatic men took an instant liking to each other. Hearing Rudolf talk about his dream of starting his own ballet company in Russia, Sobchak offered his help. He could not fail to have been aware of

---

[*] Sobchak cemented his reputation in August 1991 when he faced down Leningrad's military commander and almost singlehandedly prevented Soviet troops from occupying the city in the short-lived coup. As changes reverberated in the wake of the failed coup of 1991, Leningraders voted overwhelmingly to rename their city St Petersburg.

the star's condition, and yet Liuba insists that the mayor meant what he said. Urged by Rudolf to follow up, she managed to speak to the mayor by telephone. 'Sobchak was very kind. He said to me that he didn't see any problem – Rudolf could use the stage of the Hermitage Theatre. He also talked about restoring an old theatre on Krestovsky Island.'

Soon after this, however, Rudolf's condition suddenly deteriorated. When Gloria Venturi called to arrange to come to see him, she heard his voice suddenly change after she had told him that it would not be for a few days. 'No. Please come tomorrow,' he said. 'Then I understood that it was very serious.' 'Glorinski', as he called her because of her Russian grandmother, was another of Rudolf's adoring women prepared to follow him across the globe. 'But not like poor Douce. If he asked me to come somewhere and I was busy, I could say no.' Extremely wealthy and well connected in her own right, she believes Rudolf liked the fact that she was not drawn to his celebrity. 'I didn't need his money, his famous friends. I was interested in him as a human being, and I could be very natural with him.' But knowing how she had always been willing to extend her own privileges to him – whether offering to send a car or hosting a dinner – Rudolf was now counting on Gloria 'to make things happen'. Arriving on the island, she found him in the care of Marika Besobrasova and the dance critic Vittoria Ottolenghi – both completely out of their depth.

> It was a disaster. The man was dying, and these people didn't know what to do. For lunch Vittoria had prepared a soup, and suddenly Rudolf got up and went back to his bedroom. They said, 'Follow him. Ask if he wants something.' So I knocked and went in. 'Please, Rudolf, come and eat. Or would you prefer to rest?' 'You know as well as I do . . . Soon I have one very long rest.' I started to cry. 'But it's *true*,' he said. Not gently, he was angry.

Gloria went out and immediately made a call to Sorrento, booking a helicopter to take Rudolf back to Paris the following morning. In her Nureyev book Valeria Crippa describes the dancer kissing the rocks of Li Galli as he left, 'knowing he would not return'. But Rudolf was not yet bidding his island goodbye. In a letter dated 14 September, two weeks later, Liuba tells him that she has found people through whom he can buy a Russian war helicopter. She also says that she knows someone willing to be a security guard. (The Italian ex-policeman Rudolf currently employed for six hundred dollars a month was demanding a four-hundred-dollar raise. Russian labour rates would obviously be a lot cheaper.)

Time was at a premium, nonetheless, and Rudolf was desperate to finish *La Bayadère*. There were less than six weeks before the première on 8 October – a performance he would also be conducting. Charles Jude was still with his family in the South of France when he got a call from Rudolf asking why he had not come back to Paris. 'Because rehearsals don't start until the eleventh,' he replied. Returning at the beginning of September, Charles went directly to quai Voltaire, where he was surprised to see a large black dog. 'What's this?' 'It's mine,' said Rudolf. 'You were not here. So I bought a dog.' Choosing a young Rottweiler from a dog pound near the Châtelet, Rudolf had decided on the name of *Bayadère*'s Solor, changing it to Solaria on discovering that he had mistaken the dog's sex. 'The masculine has become feminine – never mind.' Rudolf wanted the dog constantly with him but, clearly maltreated at some point, she would disappear in fear when called, skidding along the polished parquet. She was also not house-trained, and Maude, who was staying there at the time, remembers 'wading through puddles'. There was now a slight taint of squalor to the tsarist splendour of quai Voltaire, with burned-out candle stubs in the chandeliers, vases of dead flowers, and unwashed glasses and crockery littering the neoclassical tables. Commuting to and from Monte Carlo, Marika did her best, but was hugely relieved when Mario Bois offered the services of his maid. 'I'm capable of making food but I can't wash floors.' Ghislaine Thesmar remembers arriving one evening to see if she could help, and finding the glorious sunset over the Seine was barely visible through the dirty panes of glass. 'I asked Rudolf why he didn't get someone in to clean the windows, and he said, "I'm not going to pay for that – who needs clean windows to die."' But it was also the fact that Paris, the city that had rejected him, no longer held any romance.

Ninel Kurgapkina had moved into quai Voltaire for the duration of rehearsals and saw the effort it cost Rudolf to leave his bed each morning. 'It took as much as an hour sometimes, and then he would be drenched with sweat.' Knowing what *Bayadère* meant to him, the dancers, even those who had been against him, worked feverishly hard, wanting to make up for all the conflicts of the past. But Rudolf had not forgotten. In answer to Ninel's surprise that he had not cast Elisabeth Platel as Nikiya he said, 'She doesn't deserve it. She signed the letter.' Playing the vengeful Gamzatti to Isabelle Guérin's Nikiya, Platel admits to feeling slighted at first, though he believed this gave an added dimension to her performance. 'I was rather angry with him, and my interpretation may have come from that.' She, too, sensed the complete change in the company's attitude towards Rudolf. 'By the time of *Bayadère* we were *all* with him. Without Kenneth in the middle.' But it was during those three weeks that Rudolf's condition began to deteriorate with terrifying speed.

Getting up to demonstrate a movement he would fall to one side, and he could barely speak above a whisper. Too troubled by the change in his friend to contemplate performing, Charles Jude told Rudolf, 'I'm sorry. I can't do your *Bayadère*.' (Laurent Hilaire, who was a decade younger, was cast in his place – a decision Rudolf believed had 'hurt Charles'.)

Two or three days before the première Hélène Traïlene, the Opéra's programme adviser, received a call from Pierre Bergé's assistant asking her to inform M. Nureyev that he would not be conducting *Bayadère*. 'The president has engaged someone else.' Anticipating Rudolf's reaction, Hélène, in turn, called Michel Canesi. 'Bergé was scared of telling Rudolf himself. I was not scared, but if *I* was telling him it would be for artistic reasons, and the real reason was his health.' Remembering the number of times his patient had spurned his advice in the past, Canesi arrived at quai Voltaire in a state of trepidation.

'Are you sure you want to conduct the première?'

'Yes, *why*?'

'Because I think it's quite dangerous for you. Remember how tiring New York was? If you collapse, it would be a disaster for the dancers. I would advise you not to. We can watch from small loge at the side.' He became *furious*. 'Don't shit on my brain!' And then the phone rang – it was Carla Fracci from Rome – and I heard Rudolf say, 'I'm fine but my doctor doesn't want me to conduct so I'm just going to attend the première.' I could hear in his voice that he was quite relieved. He knew in his heart that he could never have done it.

At the 7 October general rehearsal Rudolf lay on a divan in the wings, with Maude, Douce and Gloria close by. As Isabelle Guérin left the stage at the end of an act Mario Bois watched her fall sobbing into Rudolf's arms. 'I will never forget that moment; his face of a sphinx, not moving, expressing nothing, staring into the distance.' There are several possible explanations. Although she was developing her Nikiya interpretation into something sublime, it was Guérin who had been less than cooperative during Kenneth's debut in *Swan Lake*. There was the fact Rudolf did not like extravagant displays of emotion – 'you weren't allowed to say goodbye'. And, finally, it was too late. 'At the Opéra I waited. If the dancers loved me they were not telling me so. And me, deep down, was saying to them: come and embrace me. Finally I bought a dog.'

On the night of the première itself, 8 October, Rudolf lay propped up by pillows in a box to the right of the stage. With him were Canesi, Luigi, Marika and Jeannette, the latter two asserting their position at the top of the hierarchy of seven women who had helped to prepare him for the occasion. In another box sat Ninel Kurgapkina with the choreographer Yuri Grigorovich[*] – Gamzatti and the Golden Idol in the 1959 Kirov performance in which Rudolf had danced Solor. This audience, as Platel said, 'was very special – it was his whole life'. It included Rosella Hightower, Violette Verdy, John Taras, Noëlla Pontois, Roland Petit, Ghislaine Thesmar, Pierre Lacotte, Anthony Dowell, Sylvie Guillem '*et tous les Rothschild de Paris*'. And at the first interval, as Rudolf stayed recumbent in his loge, many old friends and colleagues lined up to congratulate him and say goodbye. He was spotted by his New York fan Marilyn La Vine at the second interval slowly making his way down the corridor, supported by Marika on one side and Luigi on the other. 'I rushed up to him and he took my hands and leaned close to hear what I was saying. His hands were warm but his face was bluish. He was extraordinarily weak, but his eyes were alive and blazing. So, it was like seeing the essence of him peering out of a decaying form. I was staring death in the face and yet that powerful wild spirit was so strong in his eyes. You could see the separation of spirit and body.'

When it was time for the final curtain calls Canesi asked Rudolf if he was sure he wanted to go onstage. 'Yes, I must do it. But let's make it quick.' As Genia Poliakov once remarked, there could be no admission of weakness with Rudolf: 'Crippled or wrapped in bandages, he went onstage. It was the spirit before the body.' And now, supported on each side, the dying Nureyev shuffled on from the wings, his shawl and bonnet reminding Mario Bois of 'the imaginary Invalid, a dying Molière'. Not believing what they were seeing, the audience was silent for several seconds before the explosion of their ovation broke.

---

[*] On his brief trip to Russia in 1987 Rudolf had tried, through Liuba, to engineer a *rapprochement* with Grigorovich, who was then director of the Bolshoi, but time had been too short. Still believing that Grigorovich might prove useful, Rudolf had invited him to the Paris première of *La Bayadère*.

'We were attending a tragic miracle,' writes Bois. 'On this same stage where, thirty-one years earlier, an unknown young man had flung himself into his variations from *La Bayadère*, this evening the great Nureyev was giving us his *Bayadère* to say goodbye.' After the curtain had fallen, when Jack Lang hung a medal around his neck honouring him with the title of Commander of Arts and Letters, it seemed that only Rudolf was dry-eyed. Several onlookers, Luigi among them, observed the gesture with more than a little scorn. 'Everybody who was enemy of Rudolf – who push him out – now crowning him with laurels.' Sylvie Guillem felt the same. 'I think he was victorious in a way. He had this look in his eyes: "Now I've got you. Even if I'm dying, I've got you."' But there were no hard feelings on Rudolf's part that night. Asked by Michel Canesi, 'Are you happy?' he said, 'Yes. Very very happy.' Too exhausted to do more than put in an appearance at the post-performance dinner, Rudolf wanted Michel and Luigi to take him home. As they helped him make his way out, pulling him up by the elbows so that he could walk without sinking on bent knees, they were stopped by Bergé, who had arranged for him to be photographed by *Paris-Match*. 'No,' insisted Marika, anticipating the consequences, but Rudolf saw no reason why not: in his mind he was still Byron's Corsaire, his spirit 'burning but unbent'.

His *Bayadère* had been a personal triumph – the apotheosis of a thirty-year mission to bring Petipa's unknown classics to the West. Brilliantly paced, it contrasts silent-movie mime and rhapsodic love duets with formulaic divertissements of classroom steps interspersed with vibrant character dances, which have all the ensemble excitement of a Broadway musical. If the beginning of Act 1 lacks action, Scene 2 more than compensates, with Rudolf's new variations for Solor's friends – heralding a choreographic departure for him, with not a single frenetic *rond de jambe* in sight – and ending with the deadly confrontation between the two heroines. Act 2 provides an upsurge of glorious dancing, when Gamzatti, exchanging her sari and slippers for pointe shoes and a tutu, comes into her own as a virtuosic diva, her technical feats, alone and in tandem with Solor, as much fun to watch as the ethnic corps de ballet routines. Then there is the minimalist masterpiece of Act 3's Kingdom of the Shades – 'the essence, the heartbeat of ballet' – its academic severity crescendoing into a beatific climax of ineffable power and beauty.

To this day *La Bayadère* remains the company's showcase, the lush St Petersburg plastique of the women, the taut strides, electric presence and imperious port de bras of the men still bearing their former director's indelible mark. When first asked to produce his Shades act for the Opéra, Rudolf had been reluctant to let it go, telling Rolf Liebermann, 'When your dancers and your critics are ready for this ballet. It's not a ballet you get, it's a ballet you grow with. You probably need ten years. To do it the dancers have to be self-effacing, to breathe like one. This is indigenous with English dancers . . . While in Paris, like Moscow, it's individuality that counts . . . It doesn't quite work.' Ninel Kurgapkina agrees that it had been hard for her to instil Kirov style in the French. 'It's not in their schooling. They don't want to and they can't.' But as Rudolf realized, *La Bayadère* is a work to which dancers must aspire. It would take years for the principals to appreciate and master the mime scenes, for the corps de ballet 'to breathe like one'. As much time, in fact, as it would take French critics to come round to Petipa's pure classicism. The first reviews – even that of Rudolf's great champion René Sirvin – complained that the ballet lacked audacity and imagination, that a more contemporary approach was required.

Whatever Rudolf's reasons for contributing so little of his own to the choreography, the fact that his dancing career was over meant that he could see a production as a whole for the first time, and not just as another vehicle for himself. Violette Verdy had predicted this, remarking in 1986, 'I'm convinced that his greatest years as a choreographer are still ahead when he has totally removed himself as a performer. *Then*, we will see the full measure of his knowledge and creativity.' John Percival, however, was not alone in drawing attention to 'one big disappointment': namely, that Rudolf had been prevented from carrying out his wish to restore the missing last act. In the circumstances, though, this was surely meant to be. How apt that the ballet Rudolf regarded as a reflection of his turmoil with the Paris Opéra Ballet should end with an image of forgiveness and love rather than with an act of retribution. What comes to mind is the reconciliatory mood of Shakespeare late romances; the final denouement of *The Winter's Tale* not the tragedy we expect but resolving, like Rudolf's *Bayadère*, into tranquillity and renewed friendship.

The day after the performance Barry Weinstein went to quai Voltaire to discuss various issues, among them what he called Rudolf's 'resting place'. Scorning the euphemism, Rudolf snapped back, 'What do you mean? Do you mean *buried*?' 'Yes,' Weinstein said, 'the final place.' But this was not the moment. 'He felt immortal,' said Charles Jude, who had barely arrived when Rudolf insisted that he go immediately to the

Air France office to buy tickets to St Barts. When Grigorovich called to congratulate him on his success, Rudolf began talking excitedly about what he had in mind to do next. 'I want to sell myself,' he exclaimed. 'I want to stage my productions or to conduct something else.' He was just as euphoric when Liuba spoke to him. 'I asked how the evening had gone and he said, "Superb! I'm so happy." And then he wanted to know if I had talked to Sobchak, and told me to make sure that he hadn't forgotten his promise.' As far as Rudolf was concerned, he still had 'some free time left', and he intended to make use of every remaining hour. There were firm invitations for at least half a dozen conducting engagements: *Coppélia* later in the autumn for Roland Petit's company in Marseilles; *The Nutcracker* for the San Francisco Ballet; *Petrushka* for the Dutch National Ballet on New Year's Day 1993; *Don Quixote* for the Australian ballet's revival of his production in February '93; and *The Nutcracker* in March in Graz, where Rudolf's old friend from Vienna, Gerhard Brunner, was now director. 'No one knew if it would be a year or two years – or just a week.'

To Rudi van Dantzig, who also visited quai Voltaire the day after the première, it was completely absurd to be talking seriously about the future. He and Toer van Schayk had gone there intending to say goodbye, but instead found themselves listening to Rudolf outline his plans while at the same time 'looking for disbelief' in their eyes. 'We had to play along with that, and it was as if we were acting,' says Rudi. 'I felt such a hypocrite – a comedian, in a way – because it was so *double*.' In his Nureyev memoir a hauntingly vivid chapter titled 'A Million Love Songs Later'* describes the scene as it really was. An emaciated Rudolf lies in a darkened room as Marika and Jeannette come and go, 'listening, washing, feeding', and Douce screens the newspapers for any mention of *la maladie de notre temps* ('so only a couple of reviews land on Rudolf's bed'). Not wanting to tire him Rudi and Toer move into another room 'and have a hushed conversation with "the women"'. Resenting their 'greyish presence', however, Marika decided to speak her mind. 'These men were in the salon *pouring* with sadness, and I had to tell them, "Rudolf is sensitive to these things, so please cheer yourselves up." They had brought such deep misery, and Rudolf was feeling it through the walls.' Like James Redfield, author of the

---

* The title derives from a song, 'A million love songs later, here I am', which was being sung on television by a youth who, to van Dantzig, seemed to be addressing his hoarse, desperate lyrics directly to the dying star. 'The sound and the words and Rudolf's childish concentration tear me apart at that moment, so that I can hardly contain my emotion.'

Celestine books, Marika believed in 'the Importance of Uplifting Others'; that by completely focusing on a person you can become a channel for a higher spiritual energy, which originates 'from the divine source'. 'I sat seven hours one time with Rudolf holding my hand. It was not to hold *my* hand but it was the energy you could bring him. That was the main purpose of the presence. At that moment, you can say: "I'm with you *deeply* and wherever you go, I'll go. To sustain you."'

Jeannette also did everything she could to raise Rudolf's spirits, and when Lee Radziwill called to send her love, urged Lee to visit him herself. 'I went into the bedroom to tell him she was coming and watched him just perk up. He didn't want her to see him looking bad, so I helped make him a turban from a Ralph Lauren towel.' As Lee arrived, Rudolf was 'stretched out like Mme Recamier' on a divan in the drawing room. 'It was a brilliantly convincing act. Totally nineteenth century. His dignity and nobility were extraordinary. The dignity with which he died.' Jeannette also encouraged Rudolf to see Madonna, who had sent a vast bouquet of flowers with a note saying that she was staying at the Ritz in Paris and would be honoured to meet him. 'Who's Madonna?' he asked. Jeannette explained, and Rudolf said, 'OK, call and invite her to tea.' As the day Madonna suggested was the day they were leaving for St Barts, she asked if they could postpone their trip. At this point, though, nothing could have stopped Rudolf. Michel Canesi had tried hard enough: it was an exhausting journey, flying first to America, changing in Haiti, and again in St Martin, before getting the tiny island-hopping plane. Looking at his dying friend, Rudi van Dantzig was convinced he would never get there. 'It is a dream, a chimera.' But not to Rudolf. 'You just wait till you drop off the tree. Meanwhile you enjoy life to the full, deny nothing.'

Discovering that they were on a plane full of paparazzi and English tabloid journalists, Jeannette and Charles Jude pleaded with the Air France staff to be allowed to disembark with Rudolf and catch another flight. But the press caught up with them on the island, and one night a photographer attempted to break into the house. Hearing the noise, Jeannette ran out with a flashlight. 'It wasn't turned on, and this guy must have thought it was a gun because he got down on his knees with his hands up and begged me not to shoot.' With the *Paris-Match* photographs syndicated around the world, a rush of fan letters arrived; one, from Argentina, addressed only to 'Rudolf Nureyev Island, Saint Barthélemy, Antilles', another, from Amsterdam, offering eleventh-hour salvation.

Maybe I can help you . . . I'm Roman Catholic, and can send to you special water from Lourdes (H Virgin) and Heiloo (Netherlands, St Willibrord) and Dokkum (Friesland, St Bonifatius) . . . Oh you are so great . . . I enjoyed your dance with Dame Fonteyn in '68 especially your entrée Corsaire . . . If you don't object I send to you the special water and shall pray for you – the special prayer from St Bernardus Clairvaux.

There were calls throughout the day from friends, among them Misha Baryshnikov, who also owned a house on the island. 'Rudolf was worried that he would come over,' says Jeannette. 'He didn't want Misha seeing him like that.' But Baryshnikov was calling from New York, and they spoke for about twenty minutes. 'He was very very weak and then he said, "I have to go to Paris to take care of my *Nutcracker.*" We never talked about any illness . . . No, no, no, no, no.' When Frank Augustyn called about the Ottawa gala, Rudolf, anxious for him to see that it was now out of the question, suggested that he come to St Barts. 'I told him why it was hard for me to get away, and he said, "Well, if you plan to come – just don't be too late."' Frank put down the phone, and immediately booked a flight. 'Eighteen hours later I was there.' As Rudolf lay on a divan in the dining room alcove, with Frank sitting next to him on the floor, Solaria skulked away, still unwilling to stay close to her master. 'She's the only bitch I've never been able to get into bed with me,' quipped Rudolf, and, when discussing the music Frank wanted him to conduct, his wit was just as quick. Hearing that it was the second movement of Beethoven's *Eroica* Symphony, Rudolf said, without a second's hesitation, 'Ah, the funeral march.' And yet, however evident it was that the end was near, Frank, when leaving the next day, told Rudolf with genuine conviction that he would see him in March. 'I wasn't giving up hope.'

It was while he was on St Barts that Rudolf heard that Robert Tracy was suing him. Jeannette had taken the call from Barry Weinstein and passed the phone to Rudolf, who was lying in his usual place in the alcove. When she returned, the receiver was on his chest. 'You finished?' He nodded. 'So what was that about?' 'He wants to live in dignity.' 'Who?' 'You know who.' In April 1992, as Robert was witnessing the execution of the will, he noticed that no provision had been made for him, and Rudolf's friends began to suspect that he had the Dakota apartment in mind. As Barry Weinstein warned Gorlinsky: 'People have a sense of entitlement in this country.' Not only that, but there were rumours that Robert considered Rudolf responsible for

infecting him with the HIV virus. At Rudolf's request, Wallace agreed
to confront him, and later wrote an account of their conversation:

> Robert was evasive, saying only that he felt Rudolf owed him the capa-
> bilities of living the rest of his life in dignity. He said he didn't expect to
> get the Dakota . . . [but] only wanted a roof over his head – meaning,
> I guess, a decent apartment – and some money to get by on. I asked
> him how much he had in mind. Robert said that he felt a thousand
> dollars a month seemed reasonable . . . Robert denied that he was
> going around town telling people that Rudolf gave him AIDS, however,
> moments later, he interjected: 'But you know that it is possible consid-
> ering the kind of sex we had' . . . We talked for a good fifteen
> minutes. At times he was quite emotional. Digressing and making
> off-the-wall remarks about the governments of the world nefariously
> conspiring to keep HPA-23 off the market, Robert said people were
> unfairly siding with Rudolf and didn't want anything to do with him.

Hearing this, Rudolf made no comment. 'He knew that Robert had
already contacted Marvin Mitchelson, a lawyer who isn't renowned for
settling for the kind of small stakes Robert told me he wanted.' Feeling
that he 'had to be protected,' Robert hoped to get Wallace to join him
in a two-party suit, and called him a couple of times during the summer, ostensibly asking about Rudolf's health. 'During one of our phone
calls, Robert changed the subject unexpectedly and asked about my
financial standing . . . He said that he felt Rudolf should take care of
both of us. That he owed it to us after all we'd done for him . . . I told
him that Rudolf had already given me so much during my lifetime that
I expected no financial gift from him.' According to Armen, Rudolf
would sometimes despair at this element of self-abnegation in Wallace.
'He'd get angry that Wallace was not doing more for himself. He'd say,
"Look at Tracy – he gets everything out of me. Why doesn't Wallace do
the same?"'* And yet, there had been no lover whose loyalty Rudolf valued more. 'I should have stayed with him,' he told Tessa. 'Wallace was
the true one.'

Meanwhile, on the island Rudolf was testing to the limit the loyalty
of his two other close friends. 'The money I spent!' says Jeannette.
'You wouldn't believe the cost of Montrachet in the Caribbean.'
Adopting the role of volunteer 'AIDS Buddies', they shaved and show-
ered him, even getting into the stall themselves. 'I'd fetch Charles to

---

* In fact, a suit was never filed. The matter was settled after Rudolf's death.

help Rudolf on to a little table. I'd shampoo his hair, and then I'd give him the mitt, and point and say, "Your turn. Scrub it!" He'd scrub it.' On good days they bundled Rudolf in layers and went to the beach – 'Gustavia, the fancy one, which was empty because it was off season' – and Charles would support him under the water as if he were a child learning to swim. Michel Canesi had given them a box of medicines, but Rudolf was refusing to take anything, claiming that the pills made him nauseous. It was starting to get very difficult and frightening at times, especially when Rudolf fell into lapses during which he would not remember where he was or who they were. Charles grew increasingly anxious to take him back to Paris for treatment, but on their last day Rudolf did not want to leave. 'He knew it was finished. But we always have hope, and if I'd known that he had such a short time left, I'd have stayed with him on St Barts until the end.'

Jeannette went back to San Francisco, and Wallace flew to Paris. 'One of the reasons I was there was to make sure that a nurse was installed at quai Voltaire because Rudolf still didn't want one.' François 'Frank' Loussassa, a hefty young émigré from Guadeloupe, soon won Rudolf over, opening the curtains to let in the light and refusing to treat him like an invalid. But the women were always on hand, Marika making food 'that he could swallow, that he could eat with a certain appetite' – what Rudi van Dantzig referred to as 'some mashed substance' and she called '*des fruits de Monte Carlo*'. Douce had been barred from quai Voltaire at that time. 'Someone told him, "Douce must now be so rich with all the money she took from you." It was a fantasy, but he was trusting nobody, and suddenly the door was closed to me.' Ghislaine Thesmar went in relays with a few friends from the Opéra. 'We'd make a simple dinner of roast veal and a bit of rice, clean everything up, and leave him when he was starting to get tired. We just wanted to be helpful. To make a little atmosphere.' Natasha Harley spent a week in Paris cooking for Rudolf, and one night thought she would encourage him to eat in the dining room. 'There was a chandelier with candles. All gone. So I called my limo service, and said, "I don't need a car, just some candles in about two hours' time." It was a Sunday, and all the shops were closed, but a driver arrived with about a dozen – he'd taken them from a church!' With Ezio Frigerio's help they got Rudolf to the table, but instead of facing ahead, he turned towards an icon on the wall. 'He was staring at it for the longest time. And it was the only time I wondered if, maybe, he feels something. Something religious.' Or maybe something Russian. 'I think at the end he would have liked to be surrounded by the people who loved him – not for his talent and brilliant career,' says Liuba, 'but merely as the human being. As Rudik.'

Although wincing every time he swallowed, Rudolf never uttered a word of complaint. 'He seems to accept his being ill like an animal, resigned, without protest,' remarked Rudi van Dantzig. Nor did he ever talk about AIDS. 'By not discussing it, he did not have to recognize its existence,' Linda Maybarduk said. 'And if it didn't exist, he hoped to defy it – and death itself. There were times when we thought he just might succeed.' Rudolf talked to Natasha Harley that week about plans for the summer, about his farm in Virginia, which he wanted to turn into a ballet academy. 'There was a big stable and a lot of outbuildings, and his idea was to have different teachers come and teach a different method of ballet in each of those barns.' There were still things that soothed him – a good massage, a passage of music or a visit from Maude, but Maude did not come often these days, her sight and hearing having deteriorated badly. 'She was afraid she might fall,' says Marika, 'and I think she didn't want Rudolf to be too aware of how miserable she was.' Then, like a tornado, Jane Hermann arrived.

I was astounded – the home care was *appalling*. It was filthy. That hideous dog was crapping everywhere, there was no proper laundry coming in. I was petrified that Rudolf was going to get bedbugs, so I threw everything out. I had the washing machine fixed, I was washing floors and doors. *Why?* Because I wasn't going to stand by and see one of the greatest artists the world has ever known dying in such disgraceful conditions. I couldn't watch it, it was revolting. And I guess Rudolf knew it. He was going back to the peasant life – or maybe he liked the fact that people *served* him . . . All the people closest to him were subservient to him. When my daughter arrived and saw the setup, she got so furious that I was letting myself stay in this shithouse. She told me, 'Are you nuts? You gotta get out of there.' Rudolf couldn't stand up, he couldn't go on his own to the john . . . He was being taken care of by amateurs – but he wouldn't pay for first-class professional care. That guy was a nurse like I'm a nurse. He urgently needed medical care, and I was the one who called Canesi to have him taken to hospital.

She was not much more impressed by the care at Notre Dame du Perpétuel Secours, having arrived the next morning to find Rudolf still wearing his street clothes from the night before. 'I took him into the bathroom and washed his face.' By the time Maude got to the hospital a few days later, Rudolf's skeletal arms were trembling constantly, and he had bronchoscopy tubes down his throat. '"You're having a horrible time," I told him, and very quietly he said to me, "It's so humiliating."' He weighed so little that when Tessa Kennedy visited she was able to pick him up and carry him to the bathroom. 'As he caught sight of himself in the mirror over the basin this look of horror came into his face.' Other friends came and went: Jerome Robbins, who was rehearsing at the Opéra, looked in every day; Yasemin brought a Thermos of chicken soup 'the way we cook it in Turkey'; Waxy Hübner, whose eyes now fill with tears at the memory of Rudolf lying there in his little hat, was greeted with 'only a glimmer of recognition'; Douce was still under instructions to keep away, but would go to the hospital at six a.m. when there was a gap between the night and day nurses. 'She would sit there for two hours. I don't think Rudolf even knew.' André Larquié, who had been making plans for Rudolf's funeral, came into the room one day exclaiming, 'We've got a *plot*!' Rudolf had wanted to be buried on Li Galli, but as the islands were going to be sold, Larquié had offered him a more realistic alternative. 'I asked which he would prefer: Père-Lachaise or the Russian cemetery in Saint-Geneviève-des-Bois, which was about twenty-three kilometres from Paris. "Saint-Geneviève-des-Bois," Rudolf said. "But not next to Serge Lifar."' Now, however, like Gogol's Arkaky overhearing discussions of the choice of a pine or an oak coffin for his funeral, Rudolf flinched at the news of Larquié's success. 'He just didn't want to know,' says Tessa.

In mid-December Wallace got a call from Michel Canesi telling him that Rudolf might die at any moment. 'So I put my dogs in the kennel and got on the first plane to Paris. But Rudolf pulled out of that real high fever – 106 degrees – and went into another a few days later. Then he pulled out of that one, fevers any normal person would have died from. The body was wasted, but you could see it shaking, *fighting* to survive. I begged him, "Rudolf, give up. Please, please give up."'

By now Rosa had arrived from Monte Carlo, and immediately stepped in to take charge. When she found Marika in her brother's room 'they began screaming at each other like banshees', causing such a commotion that the hospital threatened to ban any visitors. When Rudolf, drifting in and out of consciousness, woke up, Wallace told him that his sister had arrived. 'It took him ten or fifteen seconds to understand what I said, and then he slowly got out, "I had a feeling she was here." And I said, "Well, do you want to see her?" He didn't answer. And then I said, "I can bring her up here for an hour each day." Then another ten or fifteen seconds passed before he was able to say, "Too much."'

But Rosa insisted on feeding Rudolf the greasy chicken broth she had brought, and refused to listen to the protests of Michel Canesi or anyone else. It was the family's prerogative, she believed, to keep vigil at the deathbed, and she tried hard to get rid of Rudolf's friends, taking Gloria's arm one day and saying, 'You must go away. My brother keeps your soul. If you don't leave, maybe you die too.' There was also a confrontation with Wallace at quai Voltaire, which ended with him picking her up and depositing her outside the apartment. 'I went back inside wiping the spit from my face. But the next day she had returned, holding out a stubbly chicken she wanted to singe on the gas flame. It was as if nothing had happened. I saw so much of Rudolf in Rosa – the temper that flares and subsides and is forgotten.' Marika, too, felt that 'the power of these Mongol people' gave her a deeper insight into Rudolf's character. 'That mixture of great power, great presence, and then some things that are absolutely out of our habits.'

A bodyguard had been hired to prevent unwelcome visitors from slipping into the room – 'the trustees were afraid of someone taking a photograph' – and Wallace, in particular, was concerned that Rudolf might be served with a legal suit by Robert Tracy's lawyers.

> We didn't want him being presented with some paper he didn't know he was signing, so Douce, Frank, and I would do shifts, with one of us sitting outside the room at this little fourth-grade desk with the bodyguard, Damien. He was half French/half Italian, very handsome and a lot of fun. We all got along, though Douce was looking so traumatized and unkempt – like a bag woman – and she was telling Rudolf off-the-wall things like, 'There's a sale on at Galeries Lafayette!'

On 23 December Charles Jude told Rudolf that he would not be able to see him on Christmas Day because he had a performance in Germany. 'Are you taking Joanna?' Rudolf wanted to know. 'Yes, of course,' said Charles. '*Bon Papa*,' murmured Rudolf. Liuba and her husband, Slom, then arrived from St Petersburg, only to be told by Michel Canesi that Rudolf would be unlikely to recognize them. When they went into his room, however, Liuba was sure that she heard Rudolf gasp. 'Michel told me that his reaction was merely a reflex one. But I don't think so, because the next day he asked Gloria, "Will Liuba come?" ' She read him the letter she had brought from her mother ('It told Rudik he must survive until the spring when we would bring him to Leningrad, and our doctors would save him'), and she spent most of her days in Paris sitting by Rudolf's bedside holding his hand. He was seldom conscious now, and on 27 December, when Charles returned from his trip, Rudolf had stopped speaking. 'Serrez-moi la main,' Charles urged, and three or four times felt his hand being squeezed. But a few days later Gloria was sure that she heard him murmur something. 'It sounded like "Moby-Dick", and I thought, What can this mean? And then I looked up at the television, and I saw Gregory Peck in a movie that was playing.' It was John Huston's 1956 Moby-Dick, and the two words of its title were the last Rudolf ever spoke. 'But still there were things he understood,' Gloria maintains. She was in his room telling Frank that she had to go to a meeting in London when she felt Rudolf tighten his grasp on her hand. 'I was so shocked, because I didn't think he had that kind of strength left. It was like a vice, and the nurse had to come and release it.'

'When it seemed that he had less than a month to live, he held on for two months,' said Michel Canesi. 'When we thought there was maybe only a week left, he lived on for two weeks . . . Finally, when we thought death was imminent that morning, Rudolf held on until the afternoon.' It was 3.45 on the afternoon of Wednesday, 6 January 1993 and shortly after this Gloria, who had left the hospital for London at 10.30 that morning, received a telephone call from Frank. He had also broken the news to Tessa. 'He had been with Rudolf, and told me that he was very peaceful and very calm.' Later that day, hearing an announcement on his car radio, Charles drove straight to the hospital. 'There were a lot of people milling about, but nobody was in the room. I asked a nurse, "What time did it happen?" "We don't know," she said. "Nobody was there."' A postmodern choice, then, of two alternative endings – both equally convincing. It is as fitting for Rudolf, a million love songs later, to have died in the company of a virtual stranger as it is for him to have died alone. 'He is, you know, with all his friends. He is absolutely alone.'

On 11 January, the eve of the funeral, the simple oak casket in which Rudolf lay dressed in his conducting tails and 'funny little hat', was brought to quai Voltaire from the hospital by his friends. It was placed on the long, low coffee table in the salon – 'the Coffin', as he had presciently called it, which was actually a trunk in which he stored his kilims, and which itself was covered with a length of antique fabric.*

---

* This macabre still life turns out to have been a prefiguration of the memorial Ezio Frigerio designed three years later to mark Rudolf's grave. In homage to the Tatar nomad, it represents a travelling trunk covered with an astonishingly authentic, softly folding, fringed kilim made from bronze and glass mosaics in the Bashkiri colours of turquoise and coral.

According to custom, the coffin lid was raised that night for the Russians to say their farewell, and when the family had gone to bed, Frank kept watch until the morning, 'reassuring him that he had not been abandoned'. As a violent storm broke over Paris, many of Rudolf's circle, spending the night next door at the Hotel Quai Voltaire, were kept awake by the thunder and rattling windows. 'Boy, was the room shaking!' recalls Linda Maybarduk, who was not alone in wondering whether this could be one final manifestation of Nureyev rage. 'It occurred to me that it had been caused by Rudolf gate-crashing once again . . . this time through the gates of heaven.'

A police motorcade escorted the convoy of family and friends from quai Voltaire to the Opéra – the route that he himself had taken every day as director. Posted along the Garnier's grand staircase was a guard of honor of '*petits rats*', the students from the school, and at ten a.m., six male dancers carried Rudolf's coffin slowly to the top. The civil ceremony took place in the rococo foyer, where the crowd of mourners – from French nobility, seasoned jet-setters and international ballet elite to his sisters, two small *babushki* in black wearing peasant headscarves – was a reminder of the dancer's global reach. Five friends read extracts from poems in five languages, a chamber orchestra played Tchaikovsky and Bach, including *Fugue no. 14*, with one of the most abrupt endings in music, and symbolic here of Rudolf's unfinished life. At a climactic point a medal was placed on a velvet cushion on the top step. It was the Order of the Légion d'honneur – the highest decoration the French can bestow. English newspapers covering the event reported that Nureyev had been 'brought home to lie for a moment among those who loved him best'; that 'the Opéra had been his fortress and those who prayed were his real family'; that Paris was 'his home, his real home – and here, too, he returned to die'. Those who knew him knew better. And as the funeral cortège finally arrived at the cemetery of Saint-Geneviève-des-Bois, this 'little piece of Russia' with its blue-onion-dome chapel, silver birches and elusively poetic atmosphere left no one in any doubt that Rudolf's life was ending where it had begun.

As he would have wished, the most moving tributes that day were those of the dancers: the sight of Charles Jude among the sextet carrying the coffin aloft to the accompaniment of Mahler's *Wayfarer* songs, 'Now, in death, as in the duet . . . leading Rudolf to his fate'; the eloquent lines sent by Baryshnikov (and read by Jack Lang), 'He had the charisma and the simplicity of a man of the earth and the untouchable arrogance of the gods'; the moment at Saint-Geneviève when

Paris Opéra ballerinas threw their pointe shoes into the open grave. But the greatest epitaph of all came two weeks later. There was, as Laurent Hilaire said, 'a kind of doomsday feeling' to the 29 January performance of *La Bayadère*, the sense 'of a cycle coming to an end'. The hypnotic repetition of the corps de ballet's long, slow, two-phrase entrance in Act 3 had become the dirgelike ritual of a Roman Catholic funeral procession, the queue of mourners inching its way through the streets – two steps forward, one step back. Its monotony and melancholy seemed to reinforce the Cleopatra-like lament, voiced by Ghislaine Thesmar, that after Rudolf's death there was nothing left remarkable in their world. 'There is no motivation. We realized after he went away how much we depended on his energy, and the whole thing didn't mean anything to many of us. So we just kept on doing our duty and keeping the values he would care for. But it was as if the sun had faded out.' There were many, however, who found consolation that evening, telling Laurent Hilaire when they saw him later, 'Oh God, we sensed him through you.' The dancer himself remembers feeling blessed at being able to transmit the qualities Rudolf had instilled. 'I left the stage overjoyed, and told myself, "What luck. We are always with him."' And ultimately, the final impression left by the Shades is transcendental. There is the sense, as Arlene Croce has written, of the annihilation of all time – 'No reason it could not go on forever. It's Elysian bliss and its setting is eternity.' And this eternity – a 'nirvana of pure dance' – was Rudolf's idea of heaven.

One year later, preparing an article to commemorate the first anniversary of Nureyev's death, the English writer and broadcaster Francine Stock went out to the suburb of Saint-Geneviève-des-Bois. Taking more than forty-five minutes by car and up to two hours by train and infrequent local bus, this can be a demanding pilgrimage. Jeannette gave up on one attempt at trying to find the cemetery with Wallace, and returned to Paris. 'It's *criminal* for Rudolf to be stuck out there. He should have been at Père-Lachaise.' With its ugly apartment blocks and dearth of any atmospheric cafés or restaurants, the town has little to redeem it, but the Orthodox cemetery is a world apart. Rudolf rightfully belongs to this gathering of Russia's elite, though he would no doubt consider Lifar's bombastic marble tomb farther down the gravel path too close for comfort. The day Francine Stock visited the grave, Frigerio's memorial had not yet been created, and there was something poignantly unimposing about the grey stone slab marking the place, the heap of flowers, 'some withered, some artificial, a few fresh', and the plastic frame someone had left with a faded photograph of Rudolf in mid-air. It was early afternoon as she left the cemetery gates, when suddenly, from nowhere, she heard a clatter of hooves on the road. 'A black horse without saddle or bridle cantered along the road . . . The horse was part Arab and beautiful, but in this context, suddenly unpredictable and dangerous. It was an extraordinary moment in a very ordinary, ordered town. Pure coincidence, of course.'

SOURCE NOTES

Unless sources are given, all interviews were conducted by the author. Where no note is cited for a Nureyev quotation it may be assumed that it comes from my own taped interviews with the dancer (for 'Nureyev Speaks!' published in British *Cosmopolitan* in May 1977 and 'Nureyev Dances On', published in *Vanity Fair* in July 1986). Quotations attributed to Nureyev, if not sourced, are from my own interviews with his friends and associates, or from material to which I have been given exclusive access. (This includes the 1997 interviews with Wallace Potts, Jeannette Etheredge and Maude Gosling conducted by Robert Gottlieb in preparation for the authorized Rudolf Nureyev biography.) Quotations from Margot Fonteyn, Frederick Ashton and Ninette de Valois, if not sourced, are from my own interviews (for the *Vanity Fair* article and for my Frederick Ashton biography, *Secret Muses*). To avoid overloading the text with names, many quotations are attributed below and are from my interviews with the persons named. Unless otherwise noted, Roman Gerasimov was the translator of all Russian interviews and written material.

Access to the Nureyev film archive – a virtually complete collection of the dancer's every known performance on film and video, compiled by Wallace Potts with the backing of the Rudolf Nureyev Foundation – is available through the Performing Arts Department of the New York Public Library (the online catalogue is available at www.catnyp.nypl. org.htm). Key works in the collection have also been placed at the Centre National de la Danse in Paris.

Press material on Nureyev was drawn largely from the Marilyn J. La Vine collection – an archive of fifty volumes of approximately five thousand reviews, interviews and articles – which is housed in the Music Division of the Library of Congress in Washington, DC. A complete chronology compiled by La Vine can be located on www.nureyev.org. This incorporates every Nureyev performance until 1963 (a full Russian chronology has never before been published in the West), followed by the first performance of every new role until 1992. It also cites all Nureyev productions, original ballets and his 1991–2 conducting schedule.

ABBREVIATIONS OF FREQUENTLY CITED SOURCES

Auto Rudolf Nureyev, *An Autobiography*

A Bl Alexander Bland

Blue Simon Robinson, *A Year with Rudolf Nureyev*

Bois Mario Bois, *Rudolf Noureev*

Cl B's N Clive Barnes, *Nureyev*

DD David Daniel's interviews for his unpublished book *Nureyev Observed* (an extract of conversations with

Alexander Minz, Paul Taylor and Merle Park was published in the August 1976 issue of *Christopher Street*. Daniel's interview with Violette Verdy was published in *Ballet Review* 5, no. 2, 1975–6)

D&D *Dance & Dancers*

DS Diane Solway, *Nureyev: His Life*

DT *Dancing Times*

EB Erik Bruhn

EB John Gruen, *Erik Bruhn*

*EB*trs Transcripts of interviews for *EB*

Eg B Transcript of RN interview, courtesy of Egon Bischoff

F&N Fonteyn & Nureyev: Ballet's Legendary Partnership, written and directed by Peter Batty; produced by Peter Batty Productions for Britain's Channel Four Television, 1985

FOY-MF *Margot Fonteyn*, produced and directed by Patricia Foy, an Antelope / Aurora production for Channel Four Television, 1989

FOY-RN From the documentary *Nureyev*, produced and directed by Patricia Foy, a London Weekend Television production, produced by Antelope Films, 1991

GB Transcript of interviews by Gerhard Brunner, 29 October 1980, 30 March 1982, 13 May 1982

I nb B Francis Mason, *I Remember Balanchine*

JP's *N* John Percival, *Nureyev*

LB Transcripts for 'The Lynn Barber Interview: A Dance to Defy Time', *Independent on Sunday*, 19 August 1990

MB/JA Transcript of interview with Joan Acocella for Mikhail Baryshnikov's article 'Memories of Nureyev', *Vogue*, March 1993

MF *Auto* Margot Fonteyn, *Autobiography*

MG Maude Gosling

MT Maria Tallchief: America's Prima Ballerina

NC@NYDL Nureyev Collection at Jerome Robbins Dance Division, New York Public Library at Lincoln Center

NdV Ninette de Valois

NG Nigel Gosling

NYDL New York Dance Library

NYT New York Times

PW Peter Watson, *Nureyev: A Biography*

RNA Rudolf Nureyev Archive

RN/EK Interviews for Elizabeth Kaye's *Esquire* article, 'Dancing in His Own Shadow', March 1991, sound recording, NC@NYDL

RN/NG Taped interviews for *Auto*

SAtrs Transcript of John Gruen interview for *EB*

SG 'Sylvie Guillem discusses Rudolf Nureyev' unedited footage, 2003, NC@NYDL

3 Yrs T. I. Zakrzhevskaya, L. P. Myasnikova, et al., *Rudolf Nureyev: Three Years in the Kirov Theatre*

Unz Transcripts for *Nureyev Unzipped*, produced and directed by Ross MacGibbon, a Landseer production for Channel Four Television, 1998

UTM Ufa Theatre Museum

---

1 · A VAGABOND SOUL

Rosa Kolesnikova's account of the train journey and life in the barracks of Alkino is drawn from my own interviews and from her handwritten notes, which were translated into English for this book by Ann Pasternak Slater.

4 'vagabond soul': LB.

5 'shaken out of the womb': FOY-RN.

5 'overjoyed, Father came': *Auto*.

6 'it came from inside': Tausia Sultanova.

7 'very good at attracting': Lieda Husainova.

7 'wanted to be different': Hamet to Razida Evgrafova.

7 'Studying was his passion': Hamza Ula.

9 'People liked him': Ibid.

10 'We were like priests': Igor Nikitin.

11 'She wanted us . . . My mother wished': GB.

12 'The peasants there': Ibid.

12 'narrow, frightening path': *Auto*.

13 'Six people and': GB.
13 'These days you don't': Amina Galiakbarova.
13 'When the family': Federat Musin.
13 'I remember those endless': *Auto.*
14 'Farida-*apa*': Amina Galiakbarova.
14 'Before the end': *Auto.*
15 'In great poverty': LB.
15 'I knew. That's it': GB.
15 'You ran in front': Igor Nikitin.
16 'communicating with': Local Party archive.
16 'He has a general': Ibid.
16 'a severe, very powerful': Ibid.
17 'wanting to find a pal . . . suddenly I saw': FOY-RN.
17 'very uncomfortable . . . From early years': Ibid.
18 '*almost* a real': Ibid.
19 'At school boys': Valentina Malofieva.
19 'Anna Ivanovna knew': Ibid.
19–20 'I don't remember him . . . There were days': Taisia Ilchininova interview, UTM.
20 'somehow different': Marat Saidashev memoir, ibid.
20 'terrible little radio': LB.
20 'He was a big authority': Valentina Malofieva.
20 'He was jumping': Konstantin Slovohotov.
21 'That to me was heaven': FOY-RN.
21 'At home she must': Alfat Valiev.
21 'What's the matter': Razida Evgrafova.
22 'He would come out': Federat Musin.
22 'She told me about': GB.
23 'This conception thrilled': *Auto.*
23 'little Tatar boy': FOY-RN.
23 'She forgave him': Galina Artemieva.
24 'He took it': Svetlana Shagieva.
24 'I am the wrong shape': To Philip Oakes, *Sunday Times*, 30 April 1972.
25 'That comes from': Svetlana Baisheva.
25 'wasn't only giving': Ilmira Goforova.
25 'Elena Konstantinovna set': Shamile Teregulov.
25 'a one-person orchestra': Ibid.
25 'She adored Rudolf': Pamira Suleimanova.
26 'You can't carry': LB.

26 'So that I could go . . . You can dance': Jerome Oremland.
26–7 'a little like a wolf pack . . . We were all for one': Federat Musin.
27 'When it got destroyed': Ibid.
27 'I remember those': Quoted in Jean-Claude Carrière, 'Le Cinéma de Rudolf Noureev', *Studio Magazine*, May 1987.
28 'This was the first': Solomon Volkov, *Conversations with Joseph Brodsky.*
28 'stepping on people's heads': Albert Aslanov.
28 'as wildly improvised': *Auto.*
28 'He had all the goodwill': To David Letterman, *Late Night with David Letterman*, NBC, 16 August 1989.
29 'It took me days': *Auto.*
29 'He could think of': Svetlana Baisheva.
29 'In newspapers': Galina Vishnevskaya, *Galina: A Russian Story.*
30 'Before, we had just': Eldus Habirov.
30 'He would come with . . . He would arrive . . . I criticize only': Pamira Suleimanova.
31 'Rudik sent his mother': Azalia Cuchimova.
31 'Never had I encountered': *Auto.*
31 'No one looked down': Magafura Saligaskarova.
32 'Later when I saw': Lina Smakova.
32 'If he didn't like': Svetlana Baisheva.
32 'At my age, given': *Auto.*
33 'Finally something came': To Lindsay Anderson, *Omnibus*, BBC-TV, 1974, NC@NYDL.
34 'That's it. I'm going': *Auto.*
34 'Calling you, beckoning you': FOY-RN.

2 · HOLLYWOOD STORY

35 'Do you know': Solomon Volkov, *St Petersburg: A Cultural History.*
35 'The architecture in Moscow': Eg B.
36 'Rudolf loved the atmosphere': Elena Zueva.
36–7 'Well, boy . . . He is a very talented': Eg B.

37 'He didn't say hello': Sergiu
     Stefanschi.

37 'They said, "Pushkin is there" ': Dutch
     TV footage, courtesy of Wallace
     Potts.

37 'Shelkov was slighting me': Ibid.

37 'an absolute Soviet product': Igor
     Stupnikov.

38 'She read in English' and subsequent
     quotations: Sergiu Stefanschi.

39 'more adventurously curious':
     Grigore Vintila.

39 'sold his soul': Igor Stupnikov.

39 'You had to be on a list . . . She was
     our goddess . . . Privately, never in
     front': Sergiu Stefanschi.

41 'You know, I am seventeen': Marina
     Vivien.

41 'two holy hours': Eg B.

41 'His colour would change': Igor
     Stupnikov.

41 'He was working in a great tradition':
     MB/JA.

41 'kind of irresistible': FOY-RN.

42 'because Shelkov repressed': Tamara
     Zakrzhevskaya.

42 'Maybe Lilen'ka': Liuba Myasnikova.

43 'Father didn't like to show': Razida
     Evgrafova interview, UTM.

43 'He played one piece': Albert Aslanov
     interview, ibid.

43 'He seemed like some kind of
     fanatic': Alexander Minz, quoted
     in DD.

43 'in Pushkin's class': Vadim Kiselev.

44 'Pushkin would set': Sergiu
     Stefanschi.

44 'a real torture': Marina Vasilieva.

45 'Director never forgave me': Eg B.

45 'Every day there was news':
     Alexander Minz, quoted in DD.

46 'Shelkov used to love': Ibid.

46 'I was intruder': To Lindsay Anderson,
     Omnibus, BBC-TV, NC@NYDL.

46 'with big jail keys': Leo Ahonen.

46 'When we played': Ibid.

46-7 'Sleep was more important . . . He
       didn't like': Sergiu Stefanschi.

47 'We didn't mind': Leo Ahonen.

47 'danced like crazy': Anatoly Nikiforov.

48 'The pictures are only acting': Ibid.

48 'To us it was': To Jean-Claude

Carrière, 'Le Cinéma de Rudolf
Noureev', Studio Magazine, May 1987.

48 'Maybe they put': Leo Ahonen.

49 'He was too busy': Sergiu Stefanschi.

49 'She used to sit': Ursula Collein.

50 'She was a serious Communist . . .
     such an extraordinary event':
     Bella Kurgina.

50 'I was astonished': Menia Martinez,
     DS.

51 'Conversation with': Liuba
     Myasnikova.

51 'You get a most weird': Walter Terry,
     15 April 1978, Oral History Project,
     NYDL.

51 'Western art': MB/JA.

52 'I could not lose a second': Eg B.

52 'You think I'm good': Roberta
     Lazzarini, quoted in Unz.

53 'Male dancing was very rough':
     Cl B's N.

53 'Before class, when': MB/JA.

54 'this one towards': Igor Stupnikov s.v.
     'Pushkin,' International Dictionary of
     Ballet.

54 'He used to say': Eg B.

54 'He changed so much': Anatoly
     Nikiforov.

55 'Bursting out of': T. M. Vecheslova,
     quoted in 3 Yrs.

55 'I thought, God': Vladimir Vasiliev,
     quoted in DS.

55 'It was a totally different': Ibid.

56 'In Moscow they did not': Solomon
     Volkov, Balanchine's Tchaikovsky.

56 'Moscow style – well': Alexandra
     Danilova, quoted in DD.

56 'At the Kirov, everything is best':
     Cl B's N.

57 'You will see': Elena Tchernichova,
     Ballet Review, Spring 1994.

57 'I hear you're going to': Auto.

57 'We had the Bronze Horseman':
     Tamara Zakrzhevskaya, quoted
     in PW.

58 'Sounds like Hollywood story': To
     Lindsay Anderson, Omnibus.

59 'It was an intoxicating . . . Our
     whole lives . . . Not for
     anything . . . He was too immersed':
     Liuba Myasnikova, 3 Yrs.

59 'We never knew': Alla Sizova

interview, translated by Geoff
Whitlock, *Unz.*

60 'This was the first time': Ibid.

60 'I said they were . . . I cried on the
pavement': To Lindsay Anderson,
Omnibus.

60 'Why are you making': *Auto.*

61 'Have you heard?': Ninel Kurgapkina,
quoted in *3 Yrs.*

61 'hated each other . . . just a *Yivreka*':
Source withheld.

62 'But Dudinskaya': Sergiu Stefanschi.

62 'In his duets': Valenia Chistyakova,
quoted in *3 Yrs.*

62 'an eruption of Vesuvius': Alexander
Minz, quoted in DD.

62 'It was not just Pushkin': RN/EK.

62 'This was the nineteenth-century':
Kaye, *Esquire*, March 1991.

62 'It was the first experience' Liuba
Myasnikova.

63 'although it was obviously' and other
Gorskaya descriptions: Liuba
Myasnikova, quoted in *3 Yrs.*

64 'Here, in the Pushkins'': Nikita
Dolgushin, quoted in ibid.

64 'That's what impressed': Liuba
Myasnikova.

3 · XENIA AND MENIA

66 'She was always running': Alla Bor.

66 'He was a very modest man': Dimitri
Filatov.

67 'She didn't want': Galina Baranchukova.

67 'Alexander Ivanovich worked':
Dimitri Filatov.

67 'wanted to hear': Liuba Myasnikova.

67 'Was Alexander Ivanovich': Ibid.

67 'It was very painful . . . she never
again': Galina Baranchukova.

67 'He was such an excitement': Liuba
Myasnikova.

68 'intelligent people': Alla Bor.

68 'When *I* leap': Lubov Filatova.

68 'She knew how': Dimitri Filatov.

68 'She fell totally in love': Liuba
Myasnikova.

69 'enormous sexual appetite': Chinko
Rafique.

69 'wanted to know': Menia Martinez.

69 'He loved Rudik as a son': Source
withheld.

69 'I want you to know': *Nureyev: From
Russia with Love*, BBC2 documentary
produced and directed by John
Bridcut, 2007.

69 'her husband correcting': Nikita
Dolgushin, quoted in *3 Yrs.*

69 'Hey, how can you not . . . Getting
your two turns': Nicolai Kovmir.

70 'overfed with her care . . . She tried
to create': Tamara Zakrzhevskaya.

70 'very against . . . He would
tell . . . like a lioness': Liuba
Myasnikova.

72 'as if he'd been sentenced . . . it
seemed to me': Tamara
Zakrzhevskaya, quoted in *3 Yrs.*

72 'Everything seemed to disturb him':
Vadim Kiselev.

72 'amazing quality of earthiness': Ibid.

72 'Don't mess!': Quoted in DS.

72 'He saw real professionalism': Vadim
Desnitsky.

73 'You didn't like it': Vladimir Katayev.

73 'the Salieris': Lynn Seymour, *DT,*
April 2000.

73 'life-long enemies . . . I didn't want':
Auto.

73 '*grilled*': FOY-RN.

74 'the gayest, most beautiful': Ibid.

74 'Not then': Ibid.

75 'I felt that': GB.

75 'young Cossack's curiosity . . . I see
you': Roland Petit, *Temps liés avec
Noureev.*

75 'I don't need that': Alla Sizova interview, translated by Geoff Whitlock.
Unz.

75 'Unique Phenomenon . . . Nu-re-
yev! . . . It was events': Ninel
Kurgapkina, quoted in *3 Yrs.*

76 'a lonely figure': *The Dictionary of Art.*

76 'I told my friend': *Auto.*

76 'Have you heard? . . . One day he's':
Alla Osipenko.

76 'We had never': Razida Evgrafova.

76 'We talked for a bit': Pamira
Sulamenova interview, UTM.

76 'He'd grown up so much': FOY-RN.

76–7 'feeble boy . . . Exercise and food!':
RN memoir, courtesy Alik Bikchurin.

77 'He told me that . . . I was really impressed': Aslanov interview, UTM.

77 'And that was my great mistake': Tamara Zakrzhevskaya.

78 'She got very jealous': Slava Santto.

78 'very unpleasant . . . This is not for your ears': Alla Sizova, quoted in Unz.

78 'not to pay attention': MB/JA.

78 'gave the impression': quoted in DS.

78 'It's not difficult': Ibid.

78 'In Russia he met': Dimitri Filatov.

79 'It was a real': *Inoplanetyane*, August 1993.

79 'Seriozha knew everything': Chinko Rafique.

79 'a choreographic Hermitage': Vadim Kiselev.

80 'Rudolf felt pity': Ibid.

81 'He was looking at him': Tamara Zakrzhevskaya.

81 'knew for sure': Faina Rokhind.

82 'like a god of wind': Olga Moiseyeva.

82 'She was a dear': Tamara Zakrzhevskaya, *3 Yrs.*

83 'Rudolf understood very early': Vadim Kiselev.

83 'genius with colour': Ibid.

83 'We never saw such impudence': Faina Rokhind.

83 'Naturally people would say . . . Everyone, let me tell you': Sergiu Stefanschi, quoted in DD.

83 'like a hooligan boy': Irina Kolpakova, translated by Yelena Demikovsky.

83 'a sparkling, beautiful': Sergiu Stefanschi, quoted in DD.

84 'as if he had awakened': Alla Osipenko.

85 'tenderness that breathed': Alla Shelest, translated by Geoff Whitlock, *Kultura*, 20 March 1993.

85 'behind a mask': Tamara Zakrzhevskaya, quoted in *3 Yrs.*

85 'This was possibly': Ibid.

85–6 'Soon a wonderful thing . . . Then suddenly': Sergiu Stefanschi, quoted in DD.

86 'If you are a poet': Translated by Alexander Storozhuk, quoted in *3 Yrs.*

86 'No sleep for you . . . What do you': Tamara Zakrzhevskaya, quoted in *3 Yrs.*

87 'She was completely obsessed': Source withheld.

87 'For the rest of her life': Slava Santto.

87 'odd ménage': Quoted in DS.

87 'But she didn't want': Source withheld.

87 'Everybody did it': Ibid.

88 'practically to rape': Ibid.

88 'Do you speak English?': LB.

88 'the athletics of': *New Yorker*, 7 August 2000.

88 'You could spot him': Igor Stupnikov.

89 'do it quickly': Ninel Kurgapkina, quoted in *3 Yrs.*

89 'Why should I?' he argued . . . terribly upset': Ibid.

89 'Replace me': Tchernichova interview, *Ballet Review*, Spring 1994.

90 'an indecent and improper': Bronislava Nijinska, *Early Memoirs*.

90 'After that night': Tchernichova interview, *Ballet Review*, Spring 1994.

90 'Why on earth . . . This is unforgivable': *3 Yrs.*

90 'went crazy . . . an exultant Rudik': *3 Yrs.*

90 'Lola began telling him' and subsequent quotations: Tamara Zakrzhevskaya, quoted in *3 Yrs.*

91 'whose name is sacred': Faina Rokhind.

91 'What are you saying': Natasha Zaltsman to ibid.

91 'unusual inner liveliness . . . It was not necessary': *Kultura*, 20 March 1993.

92 'They both knew': *Auto.*

93 'He played full out': Sergiu Stefanschi.

94 'sprang from Xenia . . . Don't use the primitive': Liuba Myasnikova, quoted in *3 Yrs.*

4 · BLOOD BROTHERS

96 'Rudolf got a lot': Vladimir Fedianin.

97 'My teacher say to me': RN/EK.

97 'I prepared whatever little': Ibid.

97 'I made that so clear': Quoted by Francis Mason, Nureyev Conference, St Petersburg, 13–15 March 1998.

98 'There were clowns': Ninel Kurgapkina.

98 'There is a teacher here': Ibid.

98 'I could go . . . This money . . . My friend said': RN/EK.

101 'That's Teja': Axel Mouwitz.

102 'Teja was always open': Source withheld.

102 'the art of male love': Chinko Rafique.

103 'It became a fixation': Tamara Zakrzhevskaya.

103 'a very free life': Source withheld.

103 'strange, closed': Leonid Romankov.

103 'Xenia Josifovna': Source withheld.

104 'It was a liaison': Chinko Rafique.

104 'Both of them enjoyed it': Quoted in DS.

104 'Alexander Ivanovich was': Source withheld.

104 'He'd say, Go': Chinko Rafique.

106 'Natalya Mihailovna': Margarita Alexeyeva.

106 'doesn't so much depart': G. Dobrovolskaya, quoted in 3 Yrs.

107 'I was agog . . . It came back': I nb B.

107 'They were literally': Nikita Dolgushin, quoted in 3 Yrs.

107 'I don't think that': Yuri Grigorovich interview, courtesy Nina Alovert.

108 'Rudik, where are you going': Tamara Zakrzhevskaya, quoted in 3 Yrs.

109 'a dissertation on': Igor Stupnikov, s.v. 'Legend of Love', International Dictionary of Ballet.

109 'The score is 2–0': Tamara Zakrzhevskaya, quoted in 3 Yrs.

110 'They were comrades': Vladimir Fedianin.

110 'washing away the classical': Ninel Kurgapkina.

110 'They felt that his energy': Boris Bregvadze.

110 'more freedom-loving': Unpublished memoir, courtesy of Faina Rokhind.

111 'It was as if he was born': Yuri Naidich.

111 'Petipa didn't want': RN/NG.

111 'We scarcely said': Kultura, 20 March 1993.

112 'He would have died': MB/JA.

112 'In Russia . . . I did not belong to myself': Eg B.

112 'the most beautiful ballet': I nb B.

113 'Whether as friend': RN/EK.

113 'prepared inside': Vadim Kiselev.

113 'They have quarrelled . . . There was only one': Slava Santto.

114 'I did not have the possibility': Quoted in Patrick Thevenon, Paris-Jour, 23 June 1961.

5 · SIX STEPS EXACTLY

Reports on RN's conduct at the Kirov were located in the Archive of the St Petersburg State Museum of Theatre and Musical Art. All accounts leading up to and including the defection came from the dancer's KGB file currently held in Moscow's Central Committee of the Communist Party of the Soviet Union, and Leningrad's Regional Committee of the CPSU. Further accounts of the defection were drawn from depositions made in preparation for RN's trial on 2 April 1962, and currently held in the Archive of Federal Security Service Headquarters in the St Petersburg region, which also houses all other material relating to the trial.

116 'dressed but not dressed': Pierre Lacotte.

117 'Without saying hello': RN/EK.

117 'He gave me chance': Ibid.

118 'coup de tonnerre': Figaro Littéraire, 27 May 1961.

118 'comme un figurant': Pierre Lacotte.

118 'like a perpetual party': Auto.

122 'façon féline': Olivier Merlin, Le Monde, 24 May 1961.

122 'Maybe his legs': MB/JA.

122 'C'était déjà': Merlin, Le Monde.

122 'He is taller': René Sirvin, 'Noureev choisit la liberté à Paris', Le roman vrai de la Vème République: La déchirure, 1961–1962, by Gilbert Guilleminault.

122 'the soaring angel': Bronislava Nijinska, Early Memories.

122 'He opened the eyes': Elle (US ed.), March 1993.

122 'In the back of the car': Auto.

123 'very spectacular': Herbert Grunwald.

124 'a little shocked': René Sirvin.

126 'l'époque Nijinski': Sirvin, Le roman vrai.

127 'We even went to': Sasha Shavrov.

127 'that he was suppressed': Source withheld.

127 'One day he came': RN/EK.

129 'blonde, like Marilyn': Clara Saint.

129 'That's the first time': Alla Osipenko, quoted in 3 Yrs.

129 'I went to Mary': Cl B's N.

129 'Finally he answered': Tamara Zakrzhevskaya, quoted in 3 Yrs.

129 'They devised plan': RN/EK.

130 'Whisked away': Ibid.

130 'all anti-intellectual': Valery Panov, To Dance.

130 'joined with those': Le Monde, 16 June 1961.

131 'Vitaly Dmitrievich': Alla Osipenko, quoted in 3 Yrs.

131 'He understood': Igor Stupnikov.

131 'Ask your mother' and subsequent Osipenko quotations: 3 Yrs.

132 'In the bus they gather': RN/EK.

132 'jeune, beau et blond': René Sirvin.

133 'Khrushchev wants to see you': FOY-RN.

133 'Corps de ballets have place': RN/EK.

133 'go white like enamel': Pierre Lacotte.

133 'Bad news' and subsequent Panov quotations: To Dance.

133 'No foreign travel': Auto.

134 'We all understood': Olga Moiseyeva.

134 'Go and get me . . . I say all right . . . Don't touch me': RN/EK.

135 'During our whole': Auto.

136 'So I decide': FOY-RN.

137 'six steps . . . No jumping': Ibid.

137 'They were pushing . . . Ah non!': Clara Saint.

137 'He literally fell down!': Janine Ringuet.

137 'He took a paper knife': Lacotte, Paris-Match, 21 January 1993.

137 'He was banging his head': DS.

137 'Osipenko said – she swore': RN/EK.

137 'screaming': FOY-RN.

139 'The room, they told me': Auto.

139 'For me this was already': Cl B's N.

139 'The systematic wearing down': To Neil Amdur, NYT, 14 July 1969.

139 'I was saving my life . . . If I'd gone back': Eg B.

139 'this would be utter . . . to learn, to see': Auto.

139 'No, we are not engaged': Daily Mail, 17 June 1961.

139 'It didn't appear': France-Soir, 17 June 1961.

141 'could be in charge': Panov, To Dance.

141 'I had already danced': RN/EK.

141 'I had travelled a lot': Marie Claire, October 1961.

141 'My friends were laughing': Ibid.

142 'DANCE TO': Daily Express, 17 June 1961.

142 'super-vedette': L'Aurore, 20 June 1961.

142 'I accept only three': FOY-RN.

143 'I didn't know the source': RN/EK.

143 'special action' and subsequent quotations: Christopher Andrew and Vasili Mitrokhin, The Mitrokhin Archive.

143 'This meant that I lived . . . hardly changed . . . exactly the way': Auto.

145 'Pushkin's sign of the cross': Rosella Hightower.

145 'I am far more worried': To Thevenon, Paris-Jour, 23 June 1961.

145 'each of these names': Tamara Zakrzhevskaya, quoted in 3 Yrs.

145–6 'Rudik's never understood . . . But I was no longer . . . Tamara, dear': Ibid.

146 'Mahmoudka': Ibid.

146 'Liubka, the Voice': 'Rudolf Nureyev: The Sixties and After', unpublished memoir by Liuba Myasnikova.

146 'Mikhail Gorbachev's advance': New Yorker, 18 January 1993.

146 'Molodetz': Ute Mitreuter.

147 'They didn't throw him out': Berdin Pavel.

147 'crazy, crazy, crazy': Pierre Lacotte.

147 'In Russia we are just not': To Franz Spelman, Show Business Illustrated, 31 October 1961.

147 'In Leningrad it was very': To Thevenon, Paris-Jour, 21 June 1961.

148 'which took her by surprise': *L'Aurore*, 24 and 25 June 1961.

148 '*Noureiev [sic] a pleuré*': *France-Soir*, 20 June 1961.

148 'not the most finished': *NYT*, 24 June 1961.

148 'He had conceived': *Ballet Review* 5, no. 2 (1975–6).

149 'The letter from Pushkin': *Auto*.

149 'the real Maryinsky Blue Bird': Ibid.

149 'The duet is a tender': *Neva*, no. 10, 1960, reprinted in *3 Yrs*.

149 '*À Moscou! Traître!*': *France-Soir*, 2 July 1961.

149 'softly moving . . . to show a bird': *Auto*.

149 'slipshod and improvised': Nina Alovert, *Smena*, 9 June 1960.

150 'Nureyev choosing freedom': From a poem by an anonymous Russian fan, RNA.

6 · MAKING LUCK

The account of Teja Kremke's interrogation by the Stasi is drawn from the deposition made available to the author by his daughter Jurico Siegmann. It was translated for this book by Uli Minoggio, who also translated interviews conducted in German.

151 'Even in winter': Clara Saint.

151–2 'He wasn't just using . . . Rudolf was still testing': Verdy, DD.

152 'its people, its freedom': To Jean Fayard, *Le Figaro Littéraire*, 15 July 1961.

152–3 'He had to choose . . . Wait until': Ute Kremke.

153 'Holden Caulfield vocabulary': *Evidence, 1944–1994 / Richard Avedon*, with essays by Jane Livingston and Adam Gopnik (New York: Whitney Museum of American Art, in association with Random House, 1994).

154 'occasions are performances': Ibid.

155 'the nervous edge': Avedon, *Observations*.

155 '*terrible et*': Cocteau, quoted in ibid.

156 'Everything was a drama': Ghislaine Thesmar.

156 'He was very spoiled': Jacqueline de Ribes.

157 'It was a combination': Douce François.

157 'Babylon of beauty': Jacques Mousseau, *Le Siècle de Paul-Louis Weiller, 1893–1993*.

157 'He wasn't friendly': Jacqueline de Ribes.

157 'like a prisoner': Douce François.

158 'outside civilization . . . In July': Ute Kremke.

158 'thinking, remembering . . . When we came': Tamara Zakrzhevskaya, quoted in *3 Yrs*.

158 'He blamed Sergeyev': Dimitri Filatov.

159 'He knew Rudik would understand': Nicolai Kovmir.

159 'If you miss him so much': Razida Evgrafova.

160 'I mean, what do they . . . Oh your country': FOY-RN.

160 'Sometimes you have to remind': *Nureyev*, Thames TV, 1981, NC@NYDL.

161 'Before I could catch my breath . . . Please, I have proposal': *MT*.

161 'He kept talking': Ibid.

162 'the most audacious': Edwin Denby, 'A Letter on NYC's Ballet', *Dance Writings*.

162 'Nothing impresses him': *Show Business Illustrated*, 31 October 1961.

163 'superindividualistic I': Faubion Bowers, *The New Scriabin: Enigma and Answers*.

163 'a real *Russkie malchik*': *MT*.

164 'Whatever it takes, he will go': Sally Ann Kriegsman, *Ballet Review*, Winter 1993.

164 'utterly forsaken': *MT*.

164 'very demanding': Glen Tetley.

164 'I simply couldn't handle it': *EB*.

165 'But of course': Ibid.

165 'Bruhn is cold . . . Yes, he's so cold': RN/EK (and cf. JP's *N*: 'Cool, yes – so cool that it burns').

165 'a certain style': *EB*.

166 'Of course, I could see': *EB*trs.

166 'But we're not in America': Ibid.

166 'Why do the Danish people': *EB*.

166 'the obvious lascivious': *My Theatre Life*.

166 'a dirty dancer': DS.
166 'different lives . . . It was certainly not': *D&D*, June 1962.
167 'Seeing Rudik move': *EB*.
167 'I am so sorry': *EB*trs.
167 'At beginning I came': RN/EK.
167 'rather sinister Mephistophelian': Glen Tetley, quoted in *EB*.
167 'We saw this wild-eyed': Glen Tetley.
168 'The men were becoming': *MT*.
168 'as a freak': *Show Business Illustrated*, 31 October 1961.
168 'It must have been horrible': *MT*.
169 'You must *svoooosch* . . . You are hugging': Gilbert Vernon.
169 'What [Volkova] had': RN/NG.
169 'That's wrong': *EB*trs.
169 'quite dull. Very dry': RN/NG.
169–70 'didn't have any desire . . . I did every day': Ibid.
170 'I want so much to go beyond': *EB*trs.
170 'When Erik dances': RN/NG.
171 'to the lasting shame': *Ballet Today*, December 1961.
171 'just sat up' and subsequent quotations: MG.
173 'I thought, well': *F&N*.

7 · JAZZ, LONDON

174 'I looked too scruffy': RN/EK.
175 'stonily unmoved . . . Her flashing smile': *D&D*, June 1961.
176 'I became aware': *Nureyev*, Thames TV, 1981, NC@NYDL.
176 'hunting and shooting': NG diaries.
177 'only ever be': MG.
177 'seemed to belong': David Astor, quoted in *Prowling the Pavements*.
178 'a Renaissance patron . . . everybody's spiritual . . . the last great': Anthony Sampson, *Observer Review*, 9 December 2001.
178 'But I'm not a journalist': MG.
179 'Tell me about Freud': To Joseph Houseal, *Ballet Review*, Spring 1994.
179 'nine-tenths': MF *Auto*.
179 'Jazz, London': RN to Viktor Rona, Hungarian Dance Archives, Budapest.

180 'How good is Brian Shaw': Colette Clark.
180 'just *beginning*': Stewart Grimshaw.
180 'dancers, choreographers': *DT*, November 1961.
181 '[Rudik] was staying with me . . . absolutely pale': *EB*trs.
181 'All Rudi did was eye me . . . Sex is sex': SAtrs.
182 'We didn't wait for him': Quoted in DS.
183 'The appearance of ease': August Bournonville, *August Bournonville*.
183 'The art of dancing': NG unpublished notes.
183 'That was the only time': SAtrs.
184 'In the very beginning': *EB*trs.
184 'These two people': *EB*.
184 'He combined the teacher': Ray Barra.
184 'It could be a car': Tamara Zakrzhevskaya.
185 'In the theatres': Stasi deposition.
186 'a totally reciprocal': Glen Tetley.
186 'It was like speaking': *EB*.
187 'That's how we began': Ibid.
187 'When you listen to Bach': *Dance Magazine*, May 1990.
187 'something *total*': *EB*trs.
187 'Not "I did it!"': RN/EK.
187 'Romantic kind of': To Cl B's *N*, *Monitor: Rudolf Nureyev*, BBC-TV, 1962, NC@NYDL.
188 'a whiplike quality': *Ballet Today*, December 1961.
189 '*n'importe quoi*': Ghislaine Thesmar.
190 'darting round': Cecil Beaton, *Self Portrait with Friends*.
190 'bounding passionately': Gosling draft (deleted by RN).
190 'Reeking of revolution': Bowers, *The New Scriabin*.
190 'very much akin to sex': *Dance Magazine*, May 1990.
191 'enormous sexual impulse . . . a kind of animalism': DD.
191 'so charged with things': DD.
191 'nervous, intense': MF *Auto*.
191 'palpitating with a lust': John Taras, Nureyev conference, St Petersburg, 13–15 March 1998.
191 'mixture of sobs': Cl B's *N*.
191 'rebellious, charismatic': Taras, Nureyev conference.

192 'The audience was for a moment': Beaton, *Self Portrait with Friends*.

192 'not so much what he danced': *F&N*.

192 'All I thought was': To Houseal, *Ballet Review*, Summer 1994.

192 'terrifying mob': *DT*, December 1961.

192 'hyena baying': Ibid.

192 'Where does that': *EB*trs.

192 'a nostalgic shadow': *D&D*, December 1961.

193 worst performance ever: MF *Auto*.

193 'Is story better not': Ibid.

193 'something almost perfect': Beaton, *Self Portrait with Friends*.

193 'in fits & starts': Letter to Violette Verdy.

194 'More About the Man': *Sunday Times*, 12 November 1961.

194 'an absolutely back number': FOY-MF.

194 'one-track tastes': Tito Arias letter, MF *Auto*.

198 'as if each existed': Elizabeth Kaye, *Esquire*, March 1991.

198 'But once the Dane': Rosella Hightower.

8 · A CELESTIAL ACCIDENT

204 'I cannot talk about her': *Life*, 27 November 1964.

206 'Xenia transferred all her desires': Source withheld.

207 'new revelation': Zizi Jeanmaire, quoted in DS.

207 'the kind of collective': 25 January 1962.

207 'peculiar, pinch-hit': Ibid.

207 'Everybody was only': Quoted in DS.

208 'It was strictly for the experiment': EB, quoted in *D&D*, June 1962.

208 'If you can arrange it': SAtrs.

209 'Opera singers partnered': Edward Villella, *Prodigal Son*.

209 'for some heavy duty': Barbara Horgan.

209 'I said, "Ah, Nureyev"': Quoted in DD.

210 'story of the body': To Walter Terry, *Theatre Arts*, July 1962.

210 'reach, get it': Suki Schorer, *On Balanchine Technique*.

210 'went gaga over': To Terry, *Theatre Arts*, July 1962.

210 'I love the Americans': Eg B.

210 'Everything tends to neglect': *Show Business Illustrated*, 31 October 1961.

211 '*self* out of the picture': Arlene Croce s.v. 'Balanchine', *International Encyclopedia of Dance*.

211 'I was still stuck': EB, *Beyond Technique*.

211 'Why relax?': Schorer, *On Balanchine Technique*.

211 'Braque, Pushkin': Bernard Taper, *Balanchine*.

211 'I loved *Pique Dame*': I nb B.

211 'Balanchine wanted linkage': Villella, *Prodigal Son*.

212 'each partaking of virtues': Croce, s.v. 'Balanchine', *International Encyclopedia of Dance*.

212 'put the 'Russe' legend': Ibid.

212 'You must not!': To Terry, *Theatre Arts*, July 1962.

212 'We were too busy': Maria Tallchief.

212 'both an expression': DS.

212 'frightful yellow': Richard Buckle, *Sunday Times*, 5 November 1961.

213 'Everyone was saying': Colette Clark.

213 'ruffled up': Vera Krasovskaya, *Nijinsky*.

213 'Ordinarily he would never': *MT*.

213 'movement where your': EB, *Beyond Technique*.

213 'This was not quite Danish': A Bl, *Observer of the Dance*.

214 'the Tate to the Royal': Jane Pritchard, s.v. 'Ballet Rambert', *International Dictionary of Ballet*.

214–15 'He stood in my dressing room . . . I am like dying': MF *Auto*.

215 'If he was on the stage': FOY-MF.

216 'This is a classical ballet': 18 February 1962.

216 'a fifty-fifty compromise': Unmarked clipping, 21 February 1962.

216 'He is completely engaged': *Sunday Times*, 18 February 1962.

216 'I study photographs': *Saturday Review*, 11 November 1978.

216 'one of the earliest': Cl B's N.

217 'I remember corps de ballet crying': Ibid.

217 'Never had I seen each step': MF *Auto*.
217 'Left arm is too back': Ibid.
217 'It did work and suddenly': Cl B's *N*.
217 '*the* Albrecht': EB, *Beyond Technique*.
217 'In a more mature state': Ibid.
218 'that kind of hypnotic': Glen Tetley, quoted in DS.
218 'I suddenly see': FOY-MF.
219 'In the West they use': Cl B's *N*.
219 'the stilted Maryinsky style': *D&D*, June 1961.
219 'a lonely little man . . . the supposed once upon': NdV, *Step by Step*.
220 'a revolution in dance': Unedited *Magic of Dance* footage, NC@NYDL.
220 'king of ballets': Eg B.
220 'I simply draw from the original': EB, *Beyond Technique*.
220 'I came to her, and I said': Cl B's *N*.
220 'Just you try': MF *Auto*.
221 'I just really emptied myself totally': RN/EK.
222 'riotous': MG.
222 'beautiful pansy-shaped': Patrick White in Michael Peppiatt's *Francis Bacon*.
222 'My dear, you simply must': NG, *Thicker than Water* (London: Longmans, 1938).
222 'one was tempted': Terence Kilmartin, quoted in introduction, A Bl, *Observer of the Dance*.
222 'could even talk': RN, quoted in introduction, ibid.
222 'Nigel was the only': To Houseal, *Ballet Review*, Spring 1994.
223 'Not even the queen': Unmarked clipping.
223 'moved as one body': Roberta Lazzarini, quoted in *F&N*.
223 'He came on stealthily': MG, *Ballet Review*, Spring 1994.
223 'This is Ulanova's style': A Bl, *Observer*, 25 February 1962.
223 'playboy': EB, *Beyond Technique*.
223 'complete cad': Konstantin Sergeyev, *Ballet Today*, August/September 1961.
224 'It is the James Dean': A Bl, *Observer*, 25 February 1962.
224 'The Giselle she gave': Cl B's *N*.
224 'the real thing, stark and raving': Cl B unmarked clipping.

224 'one sudden glance': Cl B, *D&D*, April 1962.
224 'I wonder if it was not': *DT*, March 1963.
224 'Here one would ultimately': Cl B, *The Times*, 22 February 1962.
224 'You couldn't believe . . . two ends': NdV, quoted in *F&N*.
225 'My husband called it a celestial accident': LB.
225 'practical, unmoonshiny qualities': Richard Buckle, *Adventures of a Ballet Critic*.
225 'Emotionally, technically': NdV, quoted in *F&N*.
225 'all hell broke loose': Unidentified voice, ibid.
225 'It has happened in opera': Cl B, *D&D*.
226 'It is more effective': Cl B's *N*.
226 'brilliantly, wonderfully': Cl B, *D&D*, April 1962.
226 'tending upwards': *DT*, March 1963.
226 'those sturdy': *Ballet Today*, June 1962.
226 'all lilies and languors': Andrew Porter, DS.
226 'all the things we are afraid of': EB, *Beyond Technique*.
227 'so-white, so-tight': unmarked clipping.
227 'What we were watching': *Secret Lives*, produced and directed by Madonna Benjamin, Channel Four Television, 1997.
227 'a strange attachment . . . desperately in love': MF *Auto*.
227 'I was running after him': RN/EK.

9 · THE BEATNIK AND
THE PRINCE

Unless otherwise cited, or extracted from his letters, Erik Bruhn quotations are drawn from John Gruen's interviews for *EB*. Quotations from Lincoln Kirstein's letters to Richard Buckle are from Buckle's unpublished memoir, 'Lincoln Kirstein: Ups and Downs of a Friendship over 44 years'.

228 the 'Dream Duo': *Time*, 2 March 1961.
228 'the success of the century': Tom

Fisher, letter to George Skibine, Ruth Page archive, NYDL.

228 *'Le tout New York'*: John Martin, *Ruth Page: An Intimate Biography.*

228 'an audible sigh': *DT*, April 1962.

228 'a veritable Niagara roar': Unmarked clipping.

229 'Mr Balanchine's ballets': April 1962.

229 'It wasn't his idea . . . a magician of theatre': RN/EK.

229 'It was a great fortune': Unedited *Magic of Dance* footage, NC@NYDL.

229 'Fokine discovered': Cl B's *N.*

230 'We were all striving': Villella, *Prodigal Son.*

230 'the accompaniment . . . only the second half': Solomon Volkov, *Balanchine's Tchaikovsky.*

230 'I wanted to learn . . . soaked . . . rubbed off': unedited *Magic of Dance* footage.

230 'something deeper': Croce s.v. 'Balanchine', *International Encyclopedia of Dance.*

230 'physical and metaphysical': Ibid.

230 'all night': Volkov, *Balanchine's Tchaikovsky.*

230 'kind of foreshortened': Arlene Croce, 'Makarova with Ballet Theatre', *Afterimages.*

231 'Ballet isn't a museum': Volkov, *Balanchine's Tchaikovsky.*

231 'not much more modern': To Terry, *Theatre Arts*, July 1962.

231 'a cold, distant, uncompromising': Ashton letter, courtesy of Dick Beard.

231 'true Petersburger': Volkov, *Balanchine's Tchaikovsky.*

232 'He said, "Rudka, let me"': Cl B's *N.*

232 'old chestnut': Ruth Page, *Page by Page.*

232 'Behind me were': Balanchine, to Leon Harris, *Esquire*, July 1968.

232 'Actually when you dance': Volkov, *Balanchine's Tchaikovsky.*

232 'But I like them dry': *I nb B.*

232 'It's not that he didn't': *New Yorker*, 22 July 2002.

233 '[Balanchine] does not compromise': DD.

233 'It takes teamwork': To Harris, *Esquire*, July 1968.

233 'small part of big machine': Ibid.

233 'that the leading role': Kirov souvenir booklet.

233 'total cooperation': Lincoln Kirstein, *Portrait of Mr. B.*

233 'insubordination, nonassimilation': To Harris, *Esquire.*

233–4 'nothing was described . . . Don't talk . . . No one was allowed': Villella, *Prodigal Son.*

234 'When you are tired': To Terry, *Theatre Arts*, July 1962.

235 'the higher mathematics': Villella, *Prodigal Son.*

235 'on circuit . . . too selfish': To Cecil Beaton, *The Parting Years.*

235 'People don't seem to': To Terry, *Theatre Arts*, July 1962.

235 'There was some kind of black . . . The rift, I think': *I nb B.*

235 'The thing misfired': *EB*trs.

236 'hustling, animating': Nicholas Jenkins, 'Profile', *New Yorker*, 13 April 1998.

236–7 'like Gulliver among . . . life's breviary . . . picturesque, romantic': Ibid.

237 'an advanced manifestation . . . It is a virus': *NYT*, 25 March 1962.

237 'Without your first notices': Lincoln Kirstein, 'Entries from an Early Diary', *Dance Perspectives*, 1973.

238 'to the point of unmannerliness': Martin, *Ruth Page.*

238 'shocking breach . . . the starry-eyed gullibility': *NYT*, 25 March 1962.

238 'as immediately and decisively': P. W. Manchester, unmarked clipping.

238 'About John Martin's': Tom Fisher, Page archive, NYDL.

238 'the two most fully': and subsequent Martin quotes about Russian ballet, *Dance Magazine*, September 1956.

239 'When you came with us': Kirstein, 'Early Diary'.

240 'a Beatnik and a Prince': Walter Terry, *New York Herald Tribune*, 10 June 1962.

240–41 'That became a bit tiring . . . He was very considerate . . . learn to like': *EB*trs.

240 'There was no sensation': A. H. Franks, *DT*, May 1962.

241 'anxious to efface himself': Ibid.

241 'It's Erik's fault': Sonia Arova, quoted in DS.

241 'You are two of the most': SAtrs.

241 'The Matinée that Made': *Dance News*, June 1955.

241 'It is a pleasure to see': *Dance News Annual*, 1953.

242 'Bruhn is too reserved': *DT*, May 1962.

242 'dimmed down': unsigned item, *D&D*, May 1962.

242 'inwardly rigid': 'Separate Worlds', *Afterimages*.

242 'I receive. I am no longer empty': To Terry, *Theatre Arts*, July 1962.

242 'Go there and *suck*': RN/EK.

242 'He was draining': SAtrs.

244 'cloak-and-dagger': MF *Auto*.

244 'It was so that she could': Alla Bor.

245 'I'm inviting you but': Tamara Zakrzhevskaya.

247 'When a dancer of genius': To Hubert Saal, *Newsweek*, 19 April 1965.

247 'a sort of permanent': A Bl, *Royal Ballet: First 50 Years*.

248 'When Reach was confronted': Kenneth Tynan, *Bull Fever*.

248 'artistry was almost of': Cl B's *N*.

248 'In France, the blouson': Tynan, *Bull Fever*.

248 '*le Beatle des toreros*': 27 June 2002.

248 'ballet's first pop star': DS.

248 'collective madness': Tynan, *Bull Fever*.

248 'mad old maids . . . squealing bobbysoxers': *Sunday Times*, 20 May 1962.

248 'By the age of twenty-five': Quoted in DD.

249 'The Prince was exceptional': Cl B's *N*.

249 'the Nureyev version': *DT*, August 1962.

250 'What he has not taken': January 1963.

250 'an Angry Young Man': *Ballet: Bias & Belief*.

250 'if the right breeze . . . this romantic spark': Buckle, *Adventures of a Ballet Critic*.

251 'the impact of the present': NdV, *Come Dance with Me*.

251 'It shows a great weakness': To A Bl, *Observer of the Dance*.

251 'a fighting point': Kathrine Sorley Walker, *Ninette de Valois*.

251 'Nureyev's alterations': To A Bl, *Observer of the Dance*.

251 'They really laughed together': MG.

252 'the moving thought': NdV, *Step by Step*.

252 'He didn't run away from Russia': NdV quoted in *F&N*.

252 'Essentially he remains': NdV, *Step by Step*.

252 'undoubtedly brought on': Gennady Albert, *Alexander Pushkin: Master Teacher of Dance*.

252 'Rudi demoralized him': To Stuart, *Perpetual Motion*.

252 'It broke us both up': MF *Auto*.

253 'Lack-lustre Lac': *D&D*, April 1962.

253 'elemental and exciting': Cl B, *Spectator*, 29 June 1962.

253 'with this young lion': FOY-MF.

253 'So – you are Great Ballerina': Keith Money, *Fonteyn & Nureyev*.

253 'without technique': Cl B's *N*.

253 'felt a bit': FOY-MF.

253 'She came onstage': RN/EK.

253 'inspired – egged on': FOY-MF.

253 'I've found the perfect': To Elena Nielson, *Dance Magazine*, September 1962.

253 'We become one body': FOY-MF.

254 'He could give an impeccable': *Esquire*, March 1991.

256 'He could explain Pavlova': Marika Besobrasova.

257 'A gruesome person': Source withheld.

259 'As long as he got a steak': Martin, *Ruth Page*.

259 'I grabbed it': Page, *Page by Page*.

260 'how very good': Sonia Arova letter to Ruth Page, 19 May 1962, Ruth Page archive, NYDL.

260 'fancied up . . . I don't think Fokine': Martin, *Ruth Page*.

260 'helped the illness . . . For the two . . . No, Rudi': SAtrs.

261 'Better to have stone': MF *Auto.*

10 · THE HORSE WHISPERER

262 'just pours': Quoted in DD.
262 'I had animal power . . . subtlety': RN, unmarked clipping.
262 'bang-on Nureyev territory': *D&D*, December 1962.
263 'brought her out . . . brought him up': NdV, quoted in Meredith Daneman, *Margot Fonteyn.*
263 'For him': Violette Verdy, quoted in ibid.
263 'like a great Moslem whore . . . scene of seduction': Verdy, quoted in DD.
263 *'Sexy* pants!' and subsequent quotes, Keith Money.
264 'It's as though we work': RN, quoted in *TV Times*, 17 December 1970.
264 'something quite special . . . It's odd': Ibid.
265 'burst headlong': MF *Auto.*
265 'the divine soul': Hans Christian Anderson s.v. 'Liszt', *New Grove Dictionary of Music.*
265 'He was transfigured': Marilyn La Vine.
265 'It may not have been': DD.
265 'Was sitting already': F&N.
265 'Margot throw herself': RN/EK.
266 'a symbol of duty': A Bl, *Observer*, 10 March 1963.
266 *'Totally* improvised . . . Nobody remembered not one': RN/EK.
267 'definitely agreed': Letter from Tom Fisher to Sonia Arova, Ruth Page archive, NYDL.
267 'I'd rather deal with ten': *Time*, 30 November 1962.
269 'You could feel the tension': SAtrs.
270 'It was not Balanchine': Quoted in DS.
273 'We were after': To in Margaret Willis, *Dance Magazine*, February 1994.
273 'pompous': Edwin Denby, 'Antigone . . .' *Dance Writings.*
273 'cold wave of disapproval': *DT*, March 1963.

273 'a new Nureyev, an English': *Sunday Times*, 10 February 1963.
273 'an expression of spirit': Daneman, *Margot Fonteyn.*
273 'a little symphony': *Dance Theatre Journal* 9, no. 2 (Autumn 1991).
274 'They seemed aware of each other': A Bl, *Observer*, undated clipping.
274 'He cannot be allowed': *Spectator*, 2 March 1962.
274 'Had I been younger': Quoted in DD.
274 'That's when you put up': Georgina Parkinson.
274 'bouts of whoring': Daneman, *Margot Fonteyn.*
274 'two distinct people': Keith Money.
275 'what you call "charisma"': To Harris, *Esquire*, July 1968.
275 'He hated the whole thing': Lynn Seymour.
275 'a mixture of romantic ardour': Cl B's *N.*
275 'kind of genius': RN/EK.
275 'You have extrasensory': Ibid.
275 'I start to observe': Ibid.
276 'I told him, "Rudi"': NdV quoted in DD.
276 the 'Fiery Russian': Undated, unattributed clipping.
277 'the most artificial': Peter Brook, *Observer*, 17 March 1963.
277 'ROYALS AND SUBJECTS': cable from Ashton to Tony Lizzul.
278 'They're all equal': Quoted in DD.
278 'unintentional star': James Monahan, *DT*, May 1963.
278 'A deep, almost mystical': A Bl *Observer*, undated clipping.
278 'Something of this emotional dimension': Unmarked clipping.
279 'No Nureyev, no Royal Ballet': NdV, quoted in Quoted in DD.
279 'play him slowly . . . In ballet as it': Montague Haltrecht, *The Quiet Showman.*
280 'new Nijinsky's . . . show-me': *Newsweek*, 6 May 1963.
280 'yes, screamed': Walter Terry, *New York Herald Tribune*, undated clipping.
280 'pounded': To Terry, audio interview, 25 April 1978, NYDL.

280 'old-fashioned and danceless': Allen Hughes, unpublished article, 'About the House', Royal Opera House archives.

280 'one of the miracles': 4 May 1963.

280 'slashing [Rudolf] to shreds': To Walter Terry, audio interview.

280 'While Nureyev could be an asset': Haltrecht, *The Quiet Showman*.

280 'front and centre': and subsequent Martin quotations, *Saturday Review*, 25 May 1963.

281 'black-and-blue pulp': *NYT Magazine,* 13 December 1981.

281 'fearful of the political repercussions': Harlow Robinson, *The Last Impresario*.

281 'a sort of eating-place . . . all that cultural jazz': Lord Longford, *Kennedy*.

281 'then brandy, then rum': Unmarked clipping.

282 'a very, very Waspy, uptight': Linda Maybarduk.

282 'give us a good kick': *Daily Mail*, 7 June 1963.

282 'very emotional': *Dance Magazine*, July 1963.

282 'wonderful, understanding policemen': David Palmer.

282 'I found the man affable': Undated clipping, *Studio* magazine.

282 'So . . . they think we are just': Cathleen Nesbitt, *A Little Love and Good Company*.

283 'We hugged and kissed . . . What are you doing here': Quoted in DS.

283 'full of exciting new schemes': 29 July 1963.

284 'more St Tropez': Page, *Page by Page*.

285 'A sort of celestial privilege . . . began also to look for': Vittoria Ottolenghi, *Rudolf Nureyev Confessioni*.

285 'Outside, mountains, sky': *Realities* 182, January 1966.

285 '*What* does he want': Martin, *Ruth Page*.

285 'decides one's worth': *Show Business Illustrated*, 31 October 1961.

285 'Charlik, Erik say you help': *Spectator*, 16 January 1993.

286 'not necessarily money earned': *Time*, 9 August 1968.

286 'Sometime I go there': To Saal, *Newsweek*, 19 April 1965.

288 Quotes on MF in Athens: Money, *Fonteyn & Nureyev*.

288 'You might get the beast': Ibid.

289 'Tonight I dance *Corsaire*': *Literary Review*, February 2003.

290 'the formerly love-sick girl . . . just fundamentally complete': MF *Auto*.

290 'very elusiveness': Daneman, *Margot Fonteyn*.

290 'desperately unhappy': Annette Page.

290 'competing with each other': Joan Thring.

291 'diminishing in perspective': MF *Auto*.

292 'take him out . . . I discovered': Tennessee Williams, quoted in DD.

292 'virtually impossible for any rational': A Bl, *The Nureyev Image*.

292 'But it just didn't go with me': *NYT*, 4 March 1979.

292 'the Michelangelo of him': Colum McCann, *Dancer*.

292 'too much blood': Peter Williams, *D&D*, December 1963.

293 'although very much in the hands': John Tooley.

293 'At the Kirov Theatre I was all eyes': Cl B's *N*.

294 'She's not what you would call a robust . . . pull up [your] socks': *Margot Fonteyn*, BBC Radio 3, produced by Jann Parry, transmitted 4 February 1992.

294 'Suddenly everything was *perfect*': RN/EK.

294 'He wanted it done like': DS.

294–5 'the beginning of . . . I'd never been taught': DD.

295 'plastique is what makes magic': RN/NG.

295 'All of the body must dance': Ibid.

295 'to force . . . They naturally take': RN/EK.

295 'good old British Cecchetti': Croce, 'How to Be Very, Very Popular', *Afterimages*.

295 'Kingpin at the time': Meredith Daneman.

296 'very floaty, romantic . . . male with a capital': Christopher Gable, quoted in DS.

296 'frighteningly exacting': Peter Williams, *D&D*, March 1964.

296 'made rather a hash . . . throw caution': Annette Page.

297 'the authentic frisson': DT, March 1964.

297 'to duck them seems rather': Cl B, D&D, March 1964.

297 'As Gable showed': Williams, D&D, March 1964.

297 'those double-double things': Gable, DS.

297 'always looked centred': Keith Money.

297 'He comes on to the stage': DD.

297 'If he were to fly away': A Bl, Fonteyn and Nureyev.

297 'chaste and flowing' and subsequent quotes: Croce, 'How to Be Very, Very Popular', Afterimages.

297 'a stern severity . . . He has given us': A Bl, Observer of the Dance.

299 'Forging as a dancer': Compilation cassette, courtesy of Landseer Films.

299 'Sometimes, like in Swan Lake': Ibid.

299 'Margot was Home': Daneman, Margot Fonteyn.

299 'There was no condescension . . . She ate everything': RN/EK.

299 'Go next door and find out': Quoted in DS.

299 'kissed properly': Source withheld.

299 'ninety per cent': Colette Clark.

300 'to make copy out of': Money, Fonteyn & Nureyev.

300 'Heavens, Tito' and subsequent quotes: Secret Lives, produced and directed by Madonna Benjamin, Channel Four Films, 1997.

300 'somehow become very feminine': Nadia Nerina, ibid.

301 'Perhaps I should have married': Blue.

301 'She can activate me': Constant Lambert to Anthony Powell, quoted in Daneman, Margot Fonteyn.

301 'That's all I need': Quoted by Joan Thring.

301–302 'listening to Mozart . . . I returned here': Daily Mirror, 12 December 1963.

302 'extremely physical': Joan Acocella, New Yorker, 6 January 2003.

302 'A love affair without scars . . . consummated on the stage': quoted in DS.

302 'too absorbed . . . He remains': Croce, 'Separate Worlds', Afterimages.

302–303 'Everybody knew who he was . . . I told him': EB.

303 'Soviet ballet is the best': RN/EK.

304 'Madam, there is your first': Omnibus on Dowell, 'All the Superlatives' BBC Television, 1976.

304 'How can there be conversation': To Saal, Newsweek, 19 April 1965.

304 'It was Dowell who went beyond': Alastair Macaulay, Times Literary Supplement, 9 May 2003.

305 'What happens to me': Ashton, quoted in DD.

305 'Fred got so rubbed up': William Chappell.

305 'never very comfortable': Georgina Parkinson.

305 'a very kinky modern': Ballet Today, May/June 1964.

306 'He did it by getting angry': MF Auto.

306 'She'd just walk up': Noel Pelly.

306 'heavenly place': MF Auto.

307 'Somehow, against the odds': Keith Money.

307 'We walked' and subsequent quotations: From Money, Fonteyn & Nureyev.

307 'looking anxious but': Joan Thring.

308 'her usual giggly self': Ibid.

309 'filleting out the trash': Money, Fonteyn & Nureyev.

309 'the star in an avowed': A Bl, Observer of the Dance.

309 'The whole enterprise now': Money, Fonteyn & Nureyev.

310 'It thudded into one': Ibid.

310 'He was fine': Coward, Diaries.

310 'What he did – which': Quoted in DD.

310 'No performance, no pay': MF Auto.

311 'Such was the irradiance': Trudy Goth, Ballet Today, October 1964.

311 'one of the great moments': Coward, Diaries.

311 'a tiny smile': Money, Fonteyn & Nureyev.

11 · SACRED V. PROFANE, EAST V. WEST

313 'tactics of obstruction' and subsequent quotes from police report: Andrea Amort, Nurejew und Wien.

314 'Already, I didn't trust': JP's N.

314 'A beautiful stone must have': DD.

314 'how to become truly . . . That's why I took': *Sunday Times*, 27 December 1964.

314 'Things can be old-fashioned': Ashton article on Petipa, 31 July 1967.

314 'a questionable business': Arlene Croce, *New York Review of Books*, 12 August 1999.

315 'nothing for Siegfried to do': *Sunday Times*, 27 December 1964.

315 'So there were': *D&D*, January 1972.

315 'sits on his ass': To Martin Bernheimer, *Los Angeles Times*, 4 September 1977.

315 'too radical a departure': *Sunday Times*, undated clipping.

315 'a free hand . . . not only in the original': Aurel Milloss letter to Egon Hilbert, 30 October 1964.

316 'other unpleasant things': *NYT*, 15 October 1964.

317 'He lost . . . This was tragic': To Cl B, *NYT*, 18 April 1965.

317 'the banal optimism . . . broken sighs': Vera Krasovskaya s.v. '*Swan Lake*', *International Dictionary of Dance*.

317 'they already have in them': Horst Koegler, *D&D*, undated clipping.

317 'a manic-depressive': Cl B, unmarked clipping.

317 'a spirit of love . . . both the pure love': EB, *Beyond Technique*.

317 'loyal and disloyal': *Time*, 16 April 1965.

317 'existential and artistic': *D&D*, July 1966.

318 'Suddenly he got excited': RN to James E. Neufeld, *Power to Rise*.

318 'a sort of Diaghilev': *D&D*, July 1966.

319 'alone without Nureyev': Neufeld, *Power to Rise*.

319 'The Ballet Called Siegfried': *DT*, December 1964.

319 'a belly flop position': *Dance Theatre Journal* 9, no. 2 (Autumn 1991).

320 'as a lawyer': *NYT*, 15 October 1964.

320 'Here in Central Europe': *Dance Magazine*, December 1964.

321 'Turgid Lake': *D&D*, December 1964.

321 'glean as much as he could': Lynn Seymour.

321 'a modern incarnation': Vittoria Ottolenghi s.v. 'Fracci', *International Encyclopedia of Dance.*

321 'the Magnani of dance actresses': Croce, 'The Royal Line', *Afterimages.*

322 'Feel! If the coat isn't worthy': Lynn Seymour with Paul Gardner, *Lynn: The Autobiography of Lynn Seymour.*

322 'We've become very very': Ibid.

322 'She is *fabulous*': Unedited footage, *Four Faces of Ballet*, Canadian Broadcasting Corporation, 1965, NC@NYDL.

322 'What you give to the public': Ibid.

322 'Every time you dance': JP's N.

322 'developed a bad knee': Betty Oliphant, *Miss O: My Life in Dance.*

322 'We all knew': Linda Maybarduk.

322 'What about Rudik?': Oliphant, *Miss O.*

322 'something like learning *Hamlet*': *Dance Magazine*, February 1965.

322-3 'half broken foot': *Four Faces* footage.

323 'a profoundly exciting': Neufeld, *Power to Rise.*

323 'mysteriously walking . . . an emergency good turn': *Dance Magazine*, February 1965.

323 'I tell you how it was': *Four Faces* footage.

323 'miraculously recovered': Betty Oliphant.

323 'the still undisputed master': *Dance Magazine*, February 1965.

323 'There was established': Ralph Hicklin, *Toronto Globe & Daily Mail*, 6 January 1965.

324 'the same liquid quality': Anthony Crickmay and Clement Crisp, *Lynn Seymour.*

324 'as if she had drawn them': Richard Austin, *Lynn Seymour: An Authorised Biography.*

324 'Kenneth was determined' and subsequent quotations: Seymour, *Lynn: The Autobiography.*

325 'Neither dancer fills a balletic': Undated clipping, *Vogue* (US ed.).

325 'succeeded by other . . . a decree': Haltrecht, *The Quiet Showman.*

326 but something that 'melts': Austin, *Lynn Seymour.*

326 'almost revolting': To Barbara
Newman, *Striking a Balance: Dancers
Talk About Dancing.*

326 'instinctively made adjustments':
Seymour, *Lynn: The Autobiography.*

326 'most refined': Cl B, *NYT*, 24 April
1965.

327 'double something or others': Gable,
quoted in DS.

327 'nice, normal fellow': Seymour, *Lynn:
The Autobiography.*

327 'so still you can almost hear': Marilyn
La Vine.

328 'darling, terrible children': Undated
clipping, *Vogue* (US ed.).

328 'company-wide': Annette Page.

329 'the symbols of the Royal': Cl B, *NYT*,
24 April 1965.

329 the 'New Nijinsky': *Newsweek*,
19 April 1965.

329 'effects that mark': *Time*, 19 April 1965.

330 'Each person not only united':
Claudia Roth Pierpont, 'After God',
New Yorker, 8 April 2002.

330 'archangel and satyr': Cecil Beaton,
*Beaton in the Sixties: More Unexpurgated
Diaries*, ed. Hugo Vickers.

330 'dowdy little Welsh mouse': Shelley
Winters, *Best of Times, Worst of Times.*

331 'a pert young girl . . . He can't
dance . . . where they could cuddle':
Dorothy Kilgallen, *New York
Journal-American*, 6 May 1965.

331 'a young kid . . . when the stars':
Andy Warhol and Pat Hackett, *Popism:
The Warhol Sixties.*

331 'dressed in black leather': Mary
Woronov, *Swimming Underground.*

331 'looking beautiful . . . She staggered
forward': Warhol and Hackett, *Popism.*

332 'the Sleeping Ballerina': Title of
Dolin's Spessivtseva book.

333 'jumping night place': Christopher
Gibbs, *Men in Vogue* (UK ed.),
15 September 1966.

333 'Everything went through her': Liuba
Myasnikova.

333 'What, better . . . Completely
different': Albert, *Alexander Pushkin.*

334 'give something a little extra':
Undated clipping, *D&D.*

334 'He don't like you come': DD.

334 'I'm sorry. We take from second':
Interview for *Unz.*

335 'He so inspire me . . . Because I don't
want': Valentina Pereyaslavec, DD.

335 'He is my touchstone . . . try never
to move in': Hector Zaraspe, DD.

335 'Everyone thought that': Daneman,
Margot Fonteyn.

335 'volte-face from prospective': Ibid.

340 'the outsider, the neurotic male':
Cl B, *NYT*, 27 June 1966.

340 'a tone poem of the subconscious':
Piers Pollitzer, *DT*, July 1966.

341 'because he loves nobody': Horst
Koegler, *D&D*, July 1966.

341 'divided up the music': JP's N.

341 'an indefinite visit': *Atlantic Monthly*,
March 1986.

341 'quite a lot . . . There is so much
there': *Show*, undated clipping.

342 'where the accents go': DD.

343 'A wonderful girl': Rosella
Hightower.

344–5 'not once, not twice, but': Nicholas
Dromgoole, unmarked clipping.

345 'friend, partner and master': *Ballet
News*, July 1981.

345 'most beautiful and magical':
Introduction, *Vivere è Danzare . . .
Danzare è Vivere.*

346 'When you know . . . It is my duty':
Quoted in Barbara Gail Rowes,
unmarked clipping.

346 'the *Parsifal* of ballet': *D&D*, January
1972.

346 'the peculiar Russian furs': *DT*,
November 1966.

346 'great gardens, a great empire': Ibid.

347 'mere breathing pauses': Gerhard
Brunner, *D&D*, January 1967.

348 'certainly more Nureyev': *DT*,
November 1966.

348 'sad dynasty to which': Brunner, *D&D*,
January 1967.

12 · WILD THING

351 'her own inimitable fantasies': *Vogue*
(UK ed.), 15 April 1971.

352 'would all but ruin': Russell Miller,
The House of Getty.

352 'chic avant d'être . . . You want it?':
Bois.

353 'the druggists': Beaton, *Beaton in the
Sixties.*

353 'They couldn't get off the floor': John
Hopkins, *The Tangier Diaries.*

353 'the daring one': Christopher Gibbs.

353 'He preferred to ignore bad things':
Wallace Potts.

353 'tripping regularly': Alice Rawsthorn,
Yves Saint Laurent: A Biography.

353 'two of the prettiest houses': Lee
Radziwill.

354 'like Nora in': Quoted in Diana
DuBois, *In Her Sister's Shadow.*

354 'The music, the painting': Ibid.

354 'faded Russian-y': *Vogue* (US. ed.),
July 1971.

354 'Eighty per cent Lila': Lee Radziwill.

355 'blaze of Turquerie': *Vogue* (US ed.),
December 1966.

355 'a fantasy girl': DuBois, *In Her Sister's
Shadow.*

355 'infinitely more beautiful': Beaton,
Beaton in the Sixties.

355 'After all, she's not just a socialite':
DuBois, *In Her Sister's Shadow.*

356 'in the way that you just *do*': Joan
Thring.

356 'from their body language': DuBois,
In Her Sister's Shadow.

356 'That Boy': Joan Thring.

357 'Maybe . . . it's that Margot has
gained . . . silly, but stronger': *Time,*
16 April 1965.

357 'was everywhere . . . the shock': *Unz.*

357 'Yes, Babilée created it': Denise Tual,
Le Temps Devoré.

358 'a sort of asexual fury': Gérard
Mannoni, *Roland Petit: un chorégraphe et
ses peintres.*

358 'The third day a sportscar': Tual, *Le
Temps.*

358 'that idea alone excited him': Denise
Tual.

359 'Enter the young girl': From scenario
reprinted in Ballet de l'Opéra de Paris
1992–93 season tribute to Roland
Petit.

359 'the style of Petipa': *Le Mystère Babilée,*
directed by Patrick Bensard, 2001,
Cinématheque de la Danse.

359 'like a wild boy': Cl B, ibid.

359 'angel-thug': Croce, 'Back to the
Forties', *Afterimages.*

359 'The eyes outlined in blue': Tual, *Le
Temps.*

360 'we get the perfume of him': Sally
Ann Kriegsman, *Ballet Review,* Winter
1993.

360 'Cocteau is no longer there': *Ballet
Review,* Summer 1994.

360 'She used to say': *Le Mystère Babilée.*

361 'did everything': Babilée, *Ballet
Review,* Summer 1994.

361 'The diamonds': Mannoni, *Roland
Petit.*

361 'I would tell him how photogenic':
Quoted in DS.

361 'the world of nightclubs': Walter
Terry, *Saturday Review,* 27 May
1967.

362 'un Swann "Pop"': Pierre Le-Tan,
Carnet des anneés Pop.

362 'Every paradise is found': *D&D,* April
1967.

362 'le même que celui': *Vogue* (French ed.),
February 1967.

362 'le joli moujik': Roland Petit, *Temps liés
avec Noureev.*

362 'the erogenous zone . . . The way
girls model': Jonathan Green, *All
Dressed Up.*

362 'body sculptures à deux': Unmarked
clipping.

363 'absolutely fantastic': Marianne
Faithfull, quoted in Philip Norman,
The Stones.

363 'two peculiarly gross': Tom Wolfe, *the
kandy-kolored tangerine-flake streamline
baby.*

363 'It was like seeing himself': Norman,
The Stones.

363 'a kind of dancing *creature*': DD.

363 'You must go back to Louis XIV':
Quoted in Norman, *The Stones.*

364 'hugely admired – possibly even
desired': Christopher Gibbs.

364 'He was always saying': Faithfull,
quoted in Norman, *The Stones.*

364 'which totally burned': RN/EK.

364 'Buy me a taxi': Blue.

364 *Dazzled* by Rudolf': Keith Baxter.

364 'Peter O'Toole and Nureyev': To Paul

Anstee, 13 February 1964, *Gielgud's Letters*.

364 'Picking up a smallish . . . Come on, munch . . . wanting to kiss us all': Siân Phillips, *Public Places: The Autobiography*.

364 'his real business': DD.

365 'When Russian student caps . . . natty "Nuri" way': To DS.

365 'He too began to experiment': Norman, *The Stones*.

365 'the fearful ritual': *Unz*.

365 'You couldn't get near': Robert Gable.

366 'the only one who could touch': Bonnie Prandato.

367 'He simply didn't have': Ibid.

367 'the first fraying threads': Croce, 'The Other Royal Ballet', *Afterimages*.

368 'quite the uninhibited': Winthrop Sargeant, *New Yorker*, 27 May 1967.

369 'hypersophisticated, hyperdramatic': Bob Colacello, *Holy Terror*.

369 'to be a movie star . . . just couldn't get . . . kind of aimless': Monique Van Vooren.

370 'Rudi had a hard time': To DS.

370 'his pale skin, his Slavic bones': Van Vooren, *Night Sanctuary*.

371 'scruffy and irksome . . . I can't take my eyes': Daneman, *Margot Fonteyn*.

372 'or any of the usual . . . For heaven's sake': MF *Auto*.

372 'but didn't look too happy': Unmarked clipping.

373 'THE END OF THE TRIP': Undated clipping.

374 'I felt they didn't know *how*': EB.

374 'It's like pouring water': Oliphant, *Miss O*.

374 'raging some days about fat': Per Arthur Segerström.

374 'We discovered that he was not': Anneli Alhanko.

374 '*had* to be rough': EB.

375 'dear little furry mice': A Bl, *Observer of the Dance*.

376 'dramatically in the true line . . . more like a kid': Undated clipping.

376 'she just fell into Rudolf's lap': Source withheld.

378 'which meant you *had* to go home': Gösta Svalberg.

378 'We had a tough time': Gerd Andersson.

378 'You have an excellent chance': Swedish TV compilation tape, courtesy of Gunilla Jensen.

379 'not great but very blond': Marit Gentele Gruson.

379 'depressingly unimaginative': *Ballet Today*, March/April 1968.

379 'He did some beautiful things': Quoted in DD.

379 'poultry going into a chicken coop': Peter Williams, *D&D*, April 1968.

381 'I have corps de ballet': Quoted in DS.

383 'Tatar physique': Le-Tan, *Carnet des années Pop*.

384 'I had to cut out all': To Joan Juliet Buck, *Vogue* (UK ed.), December 1978.

13 · TIME TO CRASH THE GATES

Unless otherwise noted, all quotations in this chapter by Rudi van Dantzig and Toer van Schayk (as well as those attributed to RN) are drawn either from my interviews or from excerpts in English of van Dantzig's memoir, *Het spoor van een komeet (Remembering Nureyev: The Trail of a Comet)*, translated by Katie de Haan, who generously gave me access to her then unpublished text.

386 'just about ideal': A Bl, *Observer*, 10 March 1968.

386 'the best *Nutcracker*': *Omnibus*, BBC-TV, 1993. NC@NYDL.

386 'worked on the principle': JP's *N*.

386 'an awful black plastic number': Derek Jarman, *Dancing Ledge*.

386 'a *little* ballet': *D&D*, April 1967.

387 'Frey's not even a star': MG.

387 'much obsessed': Unedited footage, 'Sir Fred: a Celebration', courtesy of Wallace Potts.

387 'a direct affront to': Horst Koegler, *D&D*, December 1968.

388 'If Covent Garden can't': *Nureyev*, Thames TV, 1981, NC@NYDL.

388 'everything everywhere': To Terry, *Theatre Arts*, July 1962.

388 'Idea was not just': Unedited 'Magic of Dance' footage, NC@NYDL.

388 'When I came to the West': To John Gruen, transcript for *NYT* article, 18 April 1974.

388 'his whole foot seeming to caress': *DT*, March 1966.

388 'It has taken a very long time': *D&D*, January 1972.

388 'no more than Puccini': *Realities* 182, January 1966.

388 'You have Isaac Stern, Richter': Unmarked clipping.

390 'does not depend on': Agnes de Mille, *Martha*.

390 'allows one to delve': Unedited 'Magic of Dance' footage.

390 'Martha did all the ballets': To Jane Perlez, *New York Post*, undated clipping.

390 'With these new movements': Eg B.

390 'large, magical aura': Arlene Croce, *New Yorker*, 11 November 1974.

390 'crash the gates': Gruen transcript.

390 'like a medieval fortress': *L'Avant-Scène: Rudolf Noureev* 1983/1985.

390 'He took the plunge': Murray Louis, *Inside Dance*.

390 'a sort of bastard': *D&D*, May 1966.

392 'I thought, "That's not" ': Unedited 'Magic of Dance' footage.

393 'The Soviet ballet': To Francine Stock, *Guardian Week-End*, 1 January 1994.

395 'to create a character': A Bl, *Observer*, undated clipping

396 'a pretty impressive': Peter Williams, *D&D*, February 1970.

396 'yawns of exasperation . . . Oh dear!': Peter Williams, *D&D*, May 1969.

396 'ugly . . . pullings across': Cecil Beaton, unpublished diaries, quoted in DS.

396 'Oh dear!': *DT*, May 1969.

396 'contemptible farrago': Cl B, *NYT*, undated clipping.

396 'except for that Royal Charter': Letter from Lincoln Kirstein to Richard Buckle, 12 April 1969.

396 'to run a national company': Quoted in DD.

396 'the finest classical stylist': Croce, 'The Royal Ballet in New York', *Afterimages*.

396 'discreetly become even more': Beaton, unpublished diaries, DS.

397 'There are times when': *NYT*, 1 May 1969.

397 'va-va-voom': DS.

397 'It was just a shell': Robert Hutchinson.

398 'the pansy men': Internet comment.

399 'partner in crime': Wallace Potts.

402 'daisy chains of fucking': Internet comment.

402 'a bit of a melting pot': Christopher Gibbs.

403 'Every time': Quoted in DS.

403 'Gargantuan throne': Beaton, *Beaton in the Sixties*.

403 'A vague host': Ibid.

404 'He'd asked her to do something': MG.

406 'It is like somebody who speaks': Van Dantzig, quoted in *Unz.*

408 'so similar to the performances': Mary Clarke, *DT*, undated clipping.

408 'the most wanton': Croce, 'The Royal Ballet in New York', *Afterimages*.

408–409 'zoomed right in . . . a bit like . . . purely because of': Gailene Stock.

409 'teacher, friend . . . What? When? . . . The only thing': Carolyn Soutar, *The Real Nureyev*.

411 '*Je t'attends*': Jean-Claude Brialy, *J'ai oublié de vous dire.*

411 'all kinds of hindering . . . as with Moira Shearer . . . I thought if you do': RN/EK.

411 'stars – everything' and subsequent quotations: Ibid.

412 'sort of half-assed': 12 February 1970.

413 'There was not enough money': Edward Albee.

417 'this big, beautiful' and subsequent Baryshnikov quotations: MB/JA.

419 'mental outrage and physical anguish': Seymour, *Lynn: The Autobiography.*

420 'I don't want the audience': Greg Lawrence, *Dance with Demons: The Life of Jerome Robbins.*

420 'Rudi – is Rudi': Deborah Jowitt, *Jerome Robbins: His Life, His Theatre, His Dance.*

421 'love & being & togetherness': Ibid.

421 'He conforms, but he is also': *DT*, December 1970.

421 'a feeling of the muscularity': *D&D*, December 1970.

421 'We're all still alive, we're all still on the earth': To Barbara Newman, *Antoinette Sibley.*

422 'punch & sharp & dramatically': Jowitt, *Jerome Robbins.*

422 'part of the company': RN/EK.

14 · CAMERA FRONT, CAMERA SIDE

423 'total-theatre concept': Marie-Françoise Christout s.v. 'Béjart', *International Encyclopedia of Dance.*

423 'the boys in their blue jeans': Croce, 'Folies Béjart', *Afterimages.*

423 'a genius – a marvellous': Paolo Bortoluzzi to John Gruen, *The Private World of Ballet.*

423 'the guru of classicism': Robert Denvers.

424 *'Agitation. Vide. Paresse.'*: Maurice Béjart, *La vie de qui? Mémoires 2.*

424 'that world of nonsense . . . Béjart fell in love with stars': Robert Denvers.

424 'an alien and diseased': Croce, 'Folies Béjart', *Afterimages.*

424 'as if Farrell had run off': *New Yorker*, 6 January 2003.

425 'no other star than Béjart': *Les Saisons de la Danse*, April 1985.

425 'if Nureyev will accept': *Dance Magazine*, January 1971.

426 '[Rudolf] understood that': Béjart, *La vie de qui?*

427 'Public carried on': To Lindsay Anderson, *Omnibus*, BBC-TV, 1974, NC@NYDL.

428 'He knew – he didn't need Rudolf': Menia Martinez.

428 'For the first time in my life': *L'Avant scène: Rudolf Noureev 1983/1985.*

428 'with a sort of drunkenness': *Les Saisons de la Danse*, April 1985.

430 'to not use all my ideas': Robert Gottlieb, *George Balanchine: The Ballet Maker.*

430 'Neoclassicism . . . exemplified by': Villella, *Prodigal Son.*

430 'Royal Ballet would not let me dance *Apollo*': *I nb B.*

430 '*dying* to do . . . Nureyev is *anything*': Quoted in DD.

431 'a wild, half-human youth . . . Etruscan . . . archaic': Arlene Croce, 'News from the Muses', *Going to the Dance.*

431 'He becomes god by the end': BBC compilation, courtesy of Wallace Potts.

431 'really extremely good in it': Quoted in DD.

431 'the perfect expression of the Apollonian': Croce, 'News from the Muses', *Going to the Dance.*

431 'the meaning of every moment': *I nb B.*

431 'All his elementary powers': *D&D*, February 1968.

431 'You know, I was in Soviet Union': Villella, *Prodigal Son.*

432 'Soccer Step . . . He was telling me': Ibid.

432 'strangely enough': Quoted in DD.

435 'baptism of fire': Nureyev, Thames TV, 1981, NC@NYDL.

435 'hours and hours just': Deanne Bergsma to Newman, *Striking a Balance.*

435 'the other face of Romanticism': *Observer*, 30 January 1972.

435 'a little bit B picture': Quoted in DD.

436 'a trojan worker . . . again and again': Richard Cragun.

436 'Without her, *Raymonda* is not': To John Gruen, for *NYT* article, 18 April 1974.

436 'three more than Petipa': Croce, 'Separate Worlds', *Afterimages.*

437 'to keep [him] out of the theatre': LB.

438 'go and choose brain': Eg B.

438 'Well, it's a remarkable thing': Quoted in DD.

438 'So, we became friends': Eg B.

438 'did realize that this guy': Quoted in DD.

438 'a major establishment': Croce, 'Taylor in Excelsis', *Going to the Dance.*

438 'Everything happens in rehearsals': Quoted in DD.

438 'ethereal, uplifted, open': Sally Banes, *Connoisseur*, March 1986.

438 'I knew it would be difficult': To Laura Bell, *Show* magazine, undated clipping.

438 'to switch over': Paul Taylor.

439 'The style no one could': Taylor quoted in DD.

439 'I hadn't realized how': To Bell, *Show*.

439 'He did not come as a': Quoted in DD.

439 'all that monkey business . . . I told him': John Gruen, *The Private World of Ballet*.

439 'a rapturous reception': Keith Money, s.v. 'Wall', *International Dictionary of Ballet*.

440 'I used to fly to Paris': Blue.

442 'dead against': Betty Oliphant.

442 'the parsley round the salmon': Betty Oliphant documentary, 'A Life in Dance', produced and directed by Gil Gauvreau, Canadian Broadcasting Corporation, 1999.

442 'What we hadn't expected': Veronica Tennant, script for 1993 CBS telecast of *The Sleeping Beauty*.

443 'as if a door was opening': Frank Augustyn.

444 '*Pillars* were being thrown away': Veronica Tennant.

444 'didn't get into my soup': Neufeld, *Power to Rise*.

444 'Try to find impulse': Linda Maybarduk, *The Dancer Who Flew*.

445 'She suggested you try for strength': Tennant CBS script.

445 'You have to give everything': Sergiu Stefanschi.

445 'Tell them to play the whole thing': Betty Oliphant.

445 'With Rudi, we came of age': Tennant CBS script.

446 'let his feelings come seething': Ann Barzel, Quoted in DS.

446 'The minute they get hold of you': To Philip Oakes, unmarked clipping.

446 'One day Rudolf say, "What camera" ': Quoted in DD.

447 'inoffensive stills photographer': Bryan Forbes, *A Divided Life*.

447 'to do for ballet what *Singing in the Rain*': Wallace Potts, Nureyev

conference, St Petersburg, 13–15 March 1998.

448 'real as real': Lucette Aldous.

448–9 'We had a director for a day . . . Provided you don't delude him': *A Little Bit of Don Quixote*, documentary on the making of the film, NC@NYDL.

15 · NEW BOY IN TOWN

453 'like a character out of Dickens': Wallace Potts.

453 'an all-party place': Terence Benton.

454 'That's what Rudolf got out of it': Ibid.

454 'ignorant of life': Benton, unpublished memoir, chapter 1, 'The First Defectors'.

455 'She took a taxi home': Lubov Filatova.

456 'I am Armen Bali': Outline of unpublished Armen Baliantz autobiography.

458 ' "Do like Margot – puff up" ': Karen Kain with Stephen Godfrey and Penelope Reed Doob, *Movement Never Lies: An Autobiography*.

458 'an unexpected blend': *Boston Globe*, 22 September 1972.

458 'The audience knew it was hubris': Ellen Forman, unmarked clipping.

459 'totally unmusical': John Gruen transcript for *NYT* article, 18 April 1974.

459 'a drama about freedom': Croce, 'Swans', *Afterimages*.

460 'decided to be Sleeping Beauty': Gruen transcript.

460 'announcing to the world': Ibid.

463 'almost masochistically': John Gruen, 'Three Nights with Nureyev, from the Nureyev Diaries', *Christopher Street* 223, March 1995.

465 '*la première* "one-man show" *de la danse*': André-Philippe Hersin, *Les Saisons de la Danse* 66 (Summer 1974).

466 'one of the last courtesans': Source withheld.

466 'Present at all the great moments': Hugues Gall.

468 'the greatest male dancer': Croce, 'Makarova's Miracle', *Afterimages*.

468 'a different ballet': MB/JA.

468 'his lodestar, a fantasy figure': Charles France.

469 'no spirit, no soul, no trembling': Eg B.

469 'Misha may well be': *EB*.

469 'Erik told me I WILL KILL HIM': Letter from Lincoln Kirstein to Richard Buckle, 21 May 1974.

469 'a perfect way to release': *EB*.

469 'each step one of them': Quoted in DS.

469–470 'amazed that a Russian . . . cold power . . . an incredible white': *EB*.

470 'So you're with Erik': Quoted in DS.

470 'He was dying to hear': Tessa Kennedy.

470 'A fortune-teller . . . Breakfast in London': Armen Baliantz autobiography outline.

473 'burst into screams . . . These are not spectacular ballets': *National Observer*, 25 January 1975.

473 'the ballet world's no. 1': 19 January 1975.

474 'I said to him, "Rudik" ': *EB*.

474 'egotistical vulgarity': Undated letter from NdV to NG.

474 'a senseless moneymaking' and subsequent NdV quotes: Ibid.

475 'the hysterical . . . to lick the whole map . . . He would never stay': To Houseal, *Ballet Review* (Summer 1994).

475 'the most aristocratic style': Quoted in DD.

475 'for Maude reads – and often amends': NG letter, 12 March 1975.

477 'a modest figure': Proof dated 6 November 1986, NG archives.

478 'instinctively sympathetic': Terence Kilmartin, *Observer of the Dance*.

478 'who excited me . . . to catch up . . . had to see more': RN, ibid.

478 'the complete alphabet': To John Gruen, sound recording, 3 November 1975, NYDL.

478 'Merce [Cunningham] and Paul': Robert Tracy, *Goddess*.

479 'the post-Freudian psyche': *New Yorker*, 9 May 2005.

479 'an incredible command': John Gruen, *After Dark*, April 1976.

479 'giant dildos': *New Yorker*, 19 and 26 February 2001.

479 'the cry from her vagina': De Mille, *Martha*.

479 'he did not like my dance': Martha Graham, *Blood Memory*.

479 'I'm not very good with words': Gruen, *After Dark*.

479 'brutality, even savagery': De Mille, *Martha*.

479 'That was that': Gruen, *After Dark*.

479 'enraptured selfishness': Walter Prude quoted in de Mille, *Martha*.

480 'a lucifer–he brought light': RN/EK.

480 'Rudolf is not a substitute': Undated clipping, *NYT*.

480 'to gibber-jabber . . . sounding like a monkey': Ibid.

480 'Martha had movement': Tracy, *Goddess*.

480 'because of her fourth . . . Go directly . . . Martha wouldn't let me': Ibid.

480 '*bourrées* on the knees': Joan Acocella, *New Yorker*, 9 May 2005.

480–81 'the life impulse . . . Arch the spine . . . much as the thong . . . a descent and lowering': De Mille, *Martha*.

481 'Be comfortable': Daneman, *Margot Fonteyn*.

481 'like silk': MF quoted in Graham, *Blood Memory*.

481 'not a shred of continuity': Acocella, *New Yorker*, 9 May 2005.

481 'This was not just a new period': Ibid.

482 'The element of camp . . . blown out like': Croce, 'Personal Appearance', *Afterimages*.

482 'a passable portrayal': Terry, *Saturday Review*, 7 February 1976.

482 'a publicity stunt with me': Tracy, *Goddess*.

483 'life was radically different': Edmund White, *The Burning Library*.

483 'venereal boiler-rooms': Martin Amis, *Visiting Mrs. Nabokov and Other Excursions*.

485 'So . . . it's always bandages': To Jane Perlez, *New York Post*, 19 July 1975.

486 'In those few minutes': Louis, *Inside Dance*.

486 'for male dancers': To Gruen, sound recording, 3 November 1975.

486 'We're comfortable': To Ellen Jacobs, unmarked clipping, 24 April 1978.

486-7 'to support Fonteyn . . . left dangling': *Dance News*, January 1976.

487 'Well, Royal Ballet doesn't hire': To Gruen, *NYT*, 18 April 1974.

487 '*Genuine* respect . . . The oneness': To Gruen, sound recording, 3 November 1975.

487 'After every performance': To Gruen, *NYT*, 18 April 1974.

487 'When my time comes': RN/EK.

487 'a work-in-progress': Terry, *Saturday Review*, 7 February 1976.

487 'fierceness of belief': Cl B's *N.*

487 'I don't claim to be an expert': To Hubert Saal, 22 December 1975.

488 'Even the preparation': Quoted in DD.

489 'beat the hell . . . that awful confrontation': *Time*, 27 January 1975.

489 'I had some very rough moments': To Carol Lawson, *NYT*, 9 May 1976.

489 'The old Nureyev magic': *NYT*, 22 April 1976.

489 'to quiet down': Lawson, *NYT*, 9 May 1976.

489 'I thought it would force me': Gruen, *After Dark*.

490 'He would hold': A Bl, *The Nureyev Valentino*.

490 'He will slither down the tree': *Newsweek*, 27 July 1964.

491 'The person is without doubt': 'Le Cinéma de Rudolf Noureev', *Studio Magazine*, May 1987.

491 'very keen on the girls': Leslie Caron.

492 'a very fascinating type . . . hard and empty': Gruen, *Christopher Street*.

492 'I hope you understand': Stuart, *Perpetual Motion*.

492 'Just because you play cunt in film': Leslie Caron.

492 'so mischievous, so game': Stuart, *Perpetual Motion*.

493 '*Kenrussellisé à mort*': *L'Express*, 12-18 September 1977.

493 'All my films are choreography': A Bl, *The Nureyev Valentino*.

493 'Most directors start from': Ibid.

493 'tantalizing': Croce, 'Nureyev as Nijinsky', *Going to the Dance*.

494 'There is no artistry': and subsequent quotations Pauline Kael, *When the Lights Go Down*.

495 'willing to be used for that': Quoted in Francis Steegmuller, *Cocteau*.

495 'the mother we all wanted to have': Quoted in *Tatler*, undated clipping.

496 'He speaks holiday': Quoted by Kenneth Tynan, Memorial Service Address.

496 'a slight anxiety . . . You don't see men dancing': *Time*, 27 January 1975.

497 'astounding . . . was there no room': van Dantzig, *Het spoor van een komeet*.

497 'I was bored . . . You move so well . . . I went the same': MB/JA.

498 'to create Russian ballet': RN/EK.

498 'where they book him': Gorlinsky to RN, 25 November 1974.

499 'the happiest of reconciliations': A Bl, *Observer of the Dance*.

499 'making even senior critics': Alastair Macaulay, *Times Literary Supplement*, 9 May 2003.

499 'We had all right vibrations': *Washington Star*, 3 April 1977.

499 'like two conspirators . . . I felt like a mother': Louis, *Inside Dance*.

16 · THIS THING OF DARKNESS

500 'Culture of the Night . . . supposedly a prim': Anthony Haden-Guest, *The Last Party*.

500 'Isn't it too bad that Proust': Clarke, *Capote*.

501 'best things': Ibid.

501 'I don't know if I was in heaven': Haden-Guest, *The Last Party*.

501 'You'd glance in': Wallace Potts.

501 'We were isolated': Edmund White, *Nocturnes for the King of Naples*.

502 'Stage is a cathedral': RN/EK.

502 'There's almost a fanatical religious': Quoted in DD.

502 'always white, always': unedited 'Magic of Dance' footage, courtesy of Wallace Potts.

502 'He's soaking in moonlight': Ibid.

502 'There was an innocence': Ninette de Valois, Step by Step.

503 'as if hungering': Cyril Beaumont, The Complete Book of Ballets.

504 'always some reciprocal': To Gruen, After Dark, April 1976.

505 'quite cold': Marie Rambert letter to Lincoln Kirstein, 30 August 1978.

505 'the next heir apparent': Robert Tracy.

506 'Rudolf, if you stay here': Quoted in Esquire, March 1991.

508 'be carried by': RN/NG.

508 'I have dream': To John Gruen, sound recording, 24 December 1975, NYDL.

509 'For people who knew the play': Patricia Ruanne, Dance Now, Spring 2002, 11, no. 1.

509 'is definitely not cups': To Richard Davies, Classical Music, 7 February 1977.

509 'had in common sex and violence': To Jacqueline Cartier, L'Avant Scène: Ballet/Danse: Romeo et Juliette, 1984.

510 'that was dark, anguished': Ibid.

512 'when good . . . very, very good': James Monahan, DT, July 1977.

512 'one extraordinary week': Alastair Macaulay, Times Literary Supplement, 9 May 2003.

512 'uneven and uneasy': Dance News, February 1978.

512 'suddenly brilliant': Ibid.

512 'triumphant': Ibid.

512 'less forced and separate': Dance News, December 1977.

512 'twilight zone . . . made a liar': Martin Bernheimer, LA Times, 8 September 1977.

512 'seemed forced': D&D, March 1978.

512 'roaring back': Bob Micklin, Newsday, 19 April 1978.

512–13 'at his most thrilling': Anna Kisselgoff, NYT, 19 April 1978.

513 'still perfectly capable': Micklin, Newsday, 19 April 1978.

513 'choreographed for him': Murray Louis.

513 'like having a ball of energy': RN, NYT, 9 April 1978.

513 'a feeble try at humour': Newsday, 19 April 1978.

514 'He often told me so': Nijinsky, The Diary of Vaslav Nijinsky.

515 'mind broke . . . because': Unmarked clipping.

515 'time to indulge': Saturday Review, 11 November 1978.

516 'in the atmosphere of Bakst': NYT, 4 March 1979.

516 'like a skin disease . . . There are two ways': Ibid.

517 'creaturely warmth . . . pose to pose': Croce, 'Nureyev as Nijinsky', Going to the Dance.

517 'expressive, hollowed-out': Hubert Saal, Newsweek, 19 March 1979.

517 'He is a truly terrible': Croce, 'Nureyev as Nijinsky', Going to the Dance.

517 'a gift from God': Patricia Neary, DS.

517 'entering the ideal future': Joan Acocella, Mikhail Baryshnikov in Black and White.

518 'Tell Rudolf if he wants . . . Nothing much . . . I'm not an optimist': To Moira Hodgson, NYT, 8 May 1979.

518 'no hype or hullabaloo': Cue, 30 March 1979.

518 'I think Balanchine was surprised': Stuart, Perpetual Motion.

519 'If anything happens to George': I nb B.

519 'Are you going to go home . . . He learns so slowly': Quoted in DS.

519 'All I can remember': Stuart, Perpetual Motion.

519 'one of those developments': Croce, 'Bourgeois and Blank', Going to the Dance.

520 'if he had any idea': Gelsey Kirkland with Greg Lawrence, Dancing on My Grave.

520 'My advice to you': Letter from Richard Buckle to RN, 18 June 1979.

520 'believe it or not': Letter from Richard Buckle to Lincoln Kirstein, 31 August 1979.

520 'You may think me manic': Letter from Richard Buckle to NG, 14 July 1979.

521 'the lackey who carried': Robert Tracy.

522 'there were going to be lots of boys': Guardian, 30 January 2003.

524 'Stavros was always competing': Rosemarie Kanzler, quoted in DS.

524 'this blond nothing . . . None of us could see': Tessa Kennedy.

525 'he was upset with Sandor': MG.

526 'Reading Byron non-stop': Saturday Review, 11 November 1978.

526 'a wild mountain colt . . . the feeling of belonging to no country . . . To seek abroad': Fiona MacCarthy, Byron: Life and Legend.

526 'a pompous bore': Saturday Review, undated clipping.

526 'All that torment': Guardian, 12 June 1972.

527 'most favourite': Saturday Review, undated clipping.

527 'It became my "Bible"': Guardian, 12 June 1972.

527 'the heavy-gay, pre-AIDS': Amis, Visiting Mrs. Nabokov and Other Excursions.

527 'What an antithetical mind' and subsequent quotations: Byron, Selected Letters and Journals, 6 December 1819.

528 'half dust, half deity': Manfred, Act 1, SC. 2, 1.40.

529 'Alas, alas': Anne Duvernoy, Danse, January 1980.

529 'Not only did the relentlessly': Dance News, February 1980.

530 'sort of his trademark': MB/JA.

530 'lesson in simplicity': Newsday, 8 April 1989.

530 'It's baffling to see him chunter': DT, August 1982.

530 'a few flashes of bravura': Chicago Tribune, undated clipping.

531 'the beginning, the middle': MacCarthy, Byron.

532 'a little devil, an adventuress': Leslie Caron.

532 'motivated by a kind of delirium': Source withheld.

533 'He would disappear in the function': Quoted in DS.

534 'soaring beyond or sinking': Byron, Lara, canto 1, xviii.

535 'There's always the betrayal': To Luke Jennings, Sunday Correspondent, 27 May 1990.

538 'an Ulsterman's predilection': Murland obituary, unmarked clipping.

538 'How else did a London banker': Source withheld.

538 'He would often arrive': Keith Money.

538 'Charles was like an overprotective': Gregory King.

539 'My doctor will send you': Stuart, Perpetual Motion.

539 'Speaking of bardashes': Flaubert to Louis Bouilhet, Cairo, 15 January 1850, Flaubert in Egypt.

540 'the lecherous, blood-stained . . . It was a means': Mario Praz, The Romantic Agony.

540 'Sex was very liberating': NYT Magazine, 13 December 1981.

540 'venereal souvenirs': Judith Thurman, New Yorker, 6 May 2002.

540 'niece of ballet artist': telex from American Embassy, Quito RNA.

541 'a magic abode': Tessa Kennedy.

541 'except bucket . . . new crew': To Barry Norman, Bryony Brind, Omnibus, BBC Television, 1982.

542 'an old man': Bruce Sansom.

542 'They were marvellous': Brind, Omnibus.

543 'the ecstasy of socialism . . . Culture, Beauty': Jane Kramer, New Yorker, 21 November 1994.

543 'une menace de veto . . . OK, Mitterrand agrees': André Larquié.

543 'Ritorna vincitor!': Quoted in DS.

545 'proudly eminent': Milton, Paradise Lost, book 1, l. 590., quoted in ibid.

545 'God has put his foot': To Michael Pye, Harper's & Queen, December 1982.

547 'unbelievable form . . . the best bedside clock': Tessa Kennedy.

548 'He would sit me quietly': LB.

549 'narrowly missing Franco': Christopher Hampton.

550 'Come along, pony!' Quoted in PW.

550 'It may be that no successful man': *Esquire*, March 1991.

550 'a devil, a born devil . . . a thing of darkness': Ibid.

550 'higher spirit, his better self': To Stoddart Martin, *Avant-Garde*, 1983.

550 'The tempest . . . is not something . . . Well, . . . I think': Ibid.

551 'Spare, intense' and subsequent quotations: Anne Barton, introduction to *New Penguin Shakespeare, The Tempest*, (London: Penguin, 1968).

551 'First I didn't want to touch': To Stoddart Martin, *Avant-Garde*, 1983.

552 'The whole thing is metaphor': Ibid.

552 'We switch in a flash': *Sunday Times*, 5 December 1982.

553 'his big fantasy': Wallace Potts.

553 'looking like Rudolf in a skirt': Tessa Kennedy.

554 'We talked Russian': *I nb B*.

555 'the little flashlights': *New York Post*, 9 May 1983.

555 'They were coming to look': Teddy Heywood.

17 · PYGMALION DIAGHILEV

557 'unable to explain': Kirkland with Lawrence, *Dancing on my Grave*.

557 'la sacro-sainte hierarchie': *Le Figaro* magazine, 10 November 1984.

558 'If you were good': *Raymonda* documentary, NC@NYDL.

558 'He *knew* the importance': SG.

558 'to *force-feed*': *NYT*, 9 April 1983.

558 'a Bournonville course': To Marcelle Michel, *Le Monde Aujourd'hui*, 9 and 10 June 1985.

558 'a fluster of waist wriggles': Denby, 'An Open Letter about the Paris Opera Ballet', *Dance Writings*.

558 'attack on all fronts': Stuart, *Perpetual Motion*.

558 'I thought if they all': Unpublished *Vanity Fair* article, RNA.

559 'Stanley was too private': Ghislaine Thesmar.

559 *garbo* . . . 'It's more like Grace': *Eugene Polyakov; Maître de ballet, Chorégraphe*, directed by Vladimir Kara, 2004, NC@NYDL.

560 'It's only when': *Le Monde Aujourd'hui*, 9 and 10 June 1985.

561 'Lifar was more than a star': *Dance Magazine*, October 1997.

561 'incontestably the star': *Sunday Times*, 18 June 1961.

561 'a diamond in the rough': *Dance Magazine*, October 1997.

561 'almost certainly – if unwittingly': 18 June 1961.

562 'choreographed entrance': To Robert Tracy, transcript of RN introduction to Aleksandr Pushkin, *The Golden Cockerel and Other Fairy Tales*.

562 'a glamorous deco god': Lynn Garafola, *Dance Magazine*, October 1997.

562 'I never do that again': To Robert Gottlieb.

562 'kitsch, and "everything" ': Patricia Ruanne.

562 'a curious anti-musical': Denby, 'An Open Letter', *Dance Writings*.

562 'not what Balanchine could be': To Francis Mason, *Ballet Review*, Autumn 1986.

563 'the Opéra cut itself off': *Le Monde Aujourd'hui*, 9 and 10 June 1985.

563 'everywhere . . . In rehearsal halls': Vidal, *Palimpsest*.

563 'not to be a new Lifar' and subsequent quotes: *Le Monde Aujourd'hui*, 9 and 10 June 1985.

563 'fifty-fifty classical and contemporary': Jean-Luc Choplin.

563 'second excruciating . . . to see the French cancan': De Mille, *Martha*.

564 'notre *Faust*': 19 November 1984, RNA.

564 'It does not seem that the French': *Le Monde Aujourd'hui*, 9 and 10 June 1985.

564 'because that's where it was invented': Ibid.

565 'The Parisian audience like what is outré': De Mille, *Martha*.

565 'that the British programmes': Marie-Françoise Christout, *Ballet Annual*, 1956.

565 'The French public want novelty': *Le Monde Aujourd'hui*, 9 and 10 June 1985.

565 'cringe': Denby, 'An Open Letter', *Dance Writings*.

565 'treated very unjustly': *L'Avant-Scène: Rudolf Noureev* 1983/1985.

565 'I don't even know': *Opéra de Paris* 11, 1 October 1983.

565 'We were *armed . . . everyone* in the company': *Raymonda*, documentary, NC@NYDL.

566 'I have finally found a nest': *Paris-Match*, 18 January 1985.

567 'next passion': Tessa Kennedy.

567 'They knew that after a performance': Marie-Suzanne Soubie.

567 'dancing for the furniture': Tessa Kennedy.

568 'I have only one dream': *Paris-Match*, undated clipping.

569 'It could belong only': *Vanity Fair*, January 1997.

570 'She expected complete loyalty': James Douglas.

570 'an instrument in the hands': typescript of Marie-Hélène de Rothschild article, RNA.

570 'Pinball machines. A garish': Stuart, *Perpetual Motion*.

571 '*la prétendue maladie*': Willy Rozenbaum, *La vie est une maladie sexuellement transmissible constamment mortelle*.

571 'Something's happened': Ibid.

571 'It would become famous': Luc Montagnier, *Virus: The Co-Discoverer of HIV Tracks Its Rampage and Charts the Future*.

572 '*le secret médical*': Rozenbaum, *La vie*.

572 'that strange state': Ibid.

572 'to make sure you're ok': Rock Hudson and Sara Davidson, *Rock Hudson, His Story*.

573 'If I tell people': To Rudi van Dantzig, *Unz*.

574 'The brigand chief's role': *DT*, June 1981.

574 '*gargouillades, ronds de jambe*': Olivier Merlin, *Paris-Match*, 21 January 1993.

574 'In the saraband': Francine Lancelot, *La Lettre de Rudolf journal des Adhérents du Cercle des Amis de Rudolf Noureev*, 13 (winter 2004–5: 'La Belle Danse').

574 'a great solitude': Ibid.

575 'I have been thrown': *Le Monde Aujourd'hui*, 9 and 10 June 1985.

575 '*Quand Noureev boxe*': *France-Soir*, 5 August 1984.

575 'Silva went up to him': Valentina Mironova.

576 'They do each isolated gesture . . . a certain respiration': *L'Avant-Scène: Rudolf Noureev* 1983/1985.

577 'like a tigress': Violette Verdy, to Francis Mason, *Ballet Review*, Autumn 1986.

577 'We just take from the school': Unmarked clipping.

577 'fully informed . . . This was not a popular idea': *I nb B*.

578 'I understand that you attach': 17 September 1985, RNF.

578 'That's how he really managed': Patrice Bart quoted in DS.

578 'I admit that those who know': GB.

578 'tragic approximation . . . What a shame': *Quotidien de Paris*, 22 December 1983.

579 'kind of indicator . . . For me and my body': GB.

579 'Rudolf said, "The whole story"': Charles Jude.

580 'an ersatz *Swan Lake*': Quoted in DS.

580 'minus six voices': *France-Soir*, 9 November 1984.

580 'like a guilty man': Marie-Suzanne Soubie.

581 'A school must not stay' and subsequent RN quotations: Open letter to the Paris Opéra dancers, RNA.

581 'un gentleman agreement': Unmarked clipping.

582 'felt cheated': 11 March 1985.

582 'He wanted to go towards': SG.

582–3 'go and repair . . . Nobody felt insulted': Ghislaine Thesmar.

583 'a lamb: very tender': Jacques Loyau.

583 'this bitterness Genia felt': *Eugene Polyakov*, film, NC@NYDL.

583 'a rare quality of *lightness*': Blue.

585 'this little girl': Dominique Frétard, *Invitation: Sylvie Guillem*.

585 'screaming at each other': Ghislaine Thesmar.

585 'I was too young': SG.

586 'I learned a way of being': Ibid.

586 'an untamed young animal': Ghislaine Thesmar.

586 'part Garbo, part gamine': Frétard, *Invitation*.

586 'That. . . . is my *raison d'être*': 18 January 1984.

586 'a rare lapse in his': Stuart, *Perpetual Motion*.

587 'You can see Rudolf onstage': *Unz*. 'somewhat unmusical': *D&D*, November 1954.

587 'Swedish gymnastic exercises . . . tennis shirts': *Ballet Today*, December 1954.

587 'Maybe not this year': Unedited footage for 'Sir Fred: A Celebration', BBC-TV, 1988, courtesy of Wallace Potts.

587 'I spurned this': To Anna Kisselgoff, *NYT*, 8 July 1986.

587 '*Please* go and see . . . With my little': SG.

587 'No going': Unedited footage, 'Sir Fred'.

587 'soft-pedalled': Letter from Antony Tudor to MG, 9 February 1983.

587 '[Rudolf] should know well': Ibid.

589 'Sometimes faced with': *La vie*.

590 'I don't have AIDS': Hudson and Davidson, *Rock Hudson: His Story*.

590 '*confident de nuit* . . . the rival clavichord . . . I can play for hours': Marie-Hélène de Rothschild article, RNA.

590 'It makes me feel that life': *NYT*, 14 June 1987.

18 · DANCING WITH THE DEVIL

591 'The infectious pestilence': Shakespeare, *Romeo and Juliet*, Act 5, Sc. 2, l. 10.

592 'of no longer dancing': Petit, *Temps liés*.

592 'miserable pneumonia . . . You have proven': 18 June 1985.

593 'heartbroken to watch': Arlette Castagnier.

594 'Charles loves money': Source withheld.

594 'Ives's father was manager' and subsequent quotations: RN/EK.

595 'a choreographer of staggering': Arlene Croce, 'Nureyev and Baryshnikov: Paris and New York', *Sight Lines*.

596 'like the first night': Monica Mason.

596 'to have this stuff': MG.

596 'incredible moments': Marilyn La Vine.

596 'incisive strokes . . . careless feet': Denby, 'An Open Letter', *Dance Writings*.

597 '*arabesque canapé*': Michael Slubicki e-mail to Alastair Macaulay.

597 'With the sweat comes': Violette Verdy.

598 'This practice or that pleasure': Willy Rozenbaum, *La vie*.

598 'Rudolf wasn't a person to deny': Linda Maybarduk.

599 'a sylvan blond . . . With one last swallow': Stuart, *Perpetual Motion*.

599 'My own contribution . . . She is certain': Letter from Armand Schönfrucht, 17 December 1985.

601 'with joy': 19 September 1985.

601 'in love and admiration . . . a miraculous Christmas present': 27 December 1984.

601 'to kind of consecrate': Robert Denvers.

601 'Béjart was a little bit in love': Quoted in DS.

601 'Nureyev agrees, you can go': Maurice Béjart, *La Vie de Qui?*

602 'monstrous anger': Ibid.

602 'EMBROUILLE A L'OPÉRA': *Le Matin de Paris*, undated clipping.

602 'phantom of the Opéra': Ibid.

602 '*Mephisto contre le fantôme*': *Événement du jeudi*, undated clipping.

604 'A furious desire to defeat': Mario Pasi typescript, RNA.

605 'The Opéra Ballet': *Le Quotidien de Paris*, no. 1994, 19 and 20 April 1986.

606 'avoid works like *Chat botté*': Letter to Larquié, 11 December 1985.

606 'They don't like foreigners': Bernard Taper, *Balanchine*.

607 'a near-hysterical': *NYT*, 10 July 1986.

607 'as the butter to bind': *NYT*, 9 July 1986.

607 'This was very much': *NYT*, 10 July 1986.

607 'The French won hands down!' *New York Post*, undated clipping.

608 'Misha Baryshnikov and me . . . I think Kirov and Moscow': RN/EK.

608 'Nureyev's goddamn *ronds de jambe*': MB/JA.

608 'This kind of dancing was new': Zöe Anderson, *The Royal Ballet*.

609 'The real surprise': Croce, 'Nureyev and Baryshnikov', *Sight Lines*.

609 'half the dancers were with Rudolf': Robert Tracy.

609 'woefully dated . . . Lifar's company': *Ballet Review*, summer 1993.

610 'unforgettably awful': Francis Mason, *Ballet Review*, Autumn 1986.

610 'an ignominious assault': Croce, 'Nureyev and Baryshnikov', *Sight Lines*.

610 'a resounding transatlantic': Cl B, *New York Post*, 21 July 1986.

610 'the sensation of the year': Anna Kisselgoff, *NYT*, 14 July 1986.

610 'Come back soon!': *New York Post*, 21 July 1986.

610 'Absolute peace – nothing but': 8 March 1985.

611 'They would fold it up': Yasemin Pirinccioglu.

611 'Take cinnabar': *New Yorker*, 6 March 2000.

611 'free and happy': Yasemin Pirinccioglu.

612 'eating me up until': *NYT*, 14 June 1987.

612 'thus assuring her immortality': Janice Berman, unmarked clipping.

612 'Mae West kind of figure': *NYT*, 14 June 1987.

613 'If you want to make fast': *Observer Review*, 28 June 1987.

613 'You want, you take': Dominique Frétard, *Invitation: Sylvie Guillem*.

613 'These superb artists': *Le Quotidien*, 27 October 1986.

613 'a triumph – the word': *Le Figaro*, 27 October 1986.

613 'burdened with guilt': Jack Anderson, *NYT*, 9 May 1987.

614 'second-rate awfulness': Roy Strong, entry for 13 July 1983, The *Roy Strong Diaries 1967–1987*.

614 'depends on demand': RN/EK.

615 'heat, chaos, temper': Wallace Potts.

19 · A CIRCULAR CIRCLE.
COMPLETE

617 'shuttling between two' and subsequent Evgenii Kozhevnikov quotations: From Liuba Myasnikova's unpublished memoir 'Rudolf Nureyev: The Sixties and After'.

617 'causing a great scandal': Liuba Myasnikova.

617–18 'might end up in Siberia': Roch-Olivier Maître, quoted in DS.

618 'Well, Liubashka, about time': Myasnikova memoir.

618 'I believe Mr Brodsky': *NYT*, 15 November 1987.

619 'a cheap, tiny Muscovite': Roch-Olivier Maître, quoted in DS.

620 'the homage, the duty': *NYT Magazine*, 13 December 1981.

620 'Good, good. Splendid' and subsequent Victor Vonog quotations and observations: From transcript of interview, courtesy UTM.

621 'masters of torture': Maybarduk, *The Dancer Who Flew*.

622 'I sort of regret that it': LB.

624 'he was estranged . . . hadn't made any impression': Razida Evgrafova.

624 'she had a rather superior . . . more of a trouper': Ghislaine Thesmar.

626 'but he guessed that was why': Letter from MG to Wallace Potts, 12 February 1988.

628 'an ashen meditation': Croce,

'Repertory Dead and Alive', *Going to the Dance*.

629 'I certainly felt that': 25 July 1988.

630 '*always* had a job': GB.

630 'In the first place is music': *Ballet Review*, Winter 1993.

630 'Houses now cost . . . not on the water': LB.

630 'Finally, I thought that only': Ottolenghi, *Rudolf Nureyev Confessioni*.

631 'the mad Russian': Léonide Massine, *My Life in Ballet*.

631 'tastes like a poison . . . He built so many things': LB.

631 'We argued for a while': LB.

631 'Voices were calling': John Drummond, *Speaking of Diaghilev*.

632 'deeply understood why': SG.

633 'art and love indissolubly': Arthur Gold and Robert Fizdale, *Misia: the Life of Misia Sert*.

634 'Rudolf is mad': Bois.

634 'knew he was wrong': DS.

634 'like chairmen of charity . . . tired of being . . . delusions of grandeur': Profile by Jane Kramer, *New Yorker*, 21 November 1994.

635 'He wanted me to stay': *San Francisco Chronicle*, 4 February 1990.

636 'We spoke about *The Brothers*': Quoted in DS.

636 'not simply a Russian ballet': *3 Yrs*.

637 'could still pull it off': RN/EK.

637 'it is out of the ruin': *Independent*, 31 August 1990.

638 'near-suicidal . . . I don't have a contract . . . Bergé was furious': Bois.

638 'a terribly rude . . . He might be happier': Letter from MF to MG, 27 August 1989.

640 'and from there presumably': Gold and Fizdale, *Misia*.

640 'I'm sure the Danish boy': Letter from MF to MG, 27 August 1989.

642 'all dancers dream': *Late Night with David Letterman*, NBC-TV, 16 August 1989.

642 'redirect the croaking': To Jennifer Dunning, *NYT*, 16 August 1989.

642 'somehow did manufacture': *Good Morning America*, ABC-TV, 4 October 1989.

642 'how many weeks I rehearsed': MB/JA.

642 'high cheekbones': Kael, *When the Lights Go Down*.

642 'King is like me': Maybarduk, *The Dancer Who Flew*.

643 'Dancing is very much related': *Dance Magazine*, May 1990.

643 'dumb-footed': *Late Night*, 16 August 1989.

643 'He was angry with me': Quoted in DS.

645 'It shows onstage': Unmarked clipping, 21 November 1979.

646 'Almost every day he was': David Richardson.

646 'incompetent at the': Kramer, *New Yorker*, 21 November 1994.

646 'My name was proposed': RN/EK.

647 'I can. This relation': GB.

647 'So come and dance': *Dance Magazine*, May 1989.

647 'I left USSR when': To René Sirvin, *Le Figaro*, 2–3 December 1989.

647 'they looked like people': *The Times Saturday Review*, 30 March 1991.

648 'he was still our Rudik': Faina Rokhind.

648 'He had one intention': Tamara Zakrzhevskaya.

648 'There are many better versions': Liuba Myasnikova.

649 'My greatest worry': To Sirvin, *Le Figaro*.

649 'the same old *babushki*': LB.

649 'brought nothing': Tamara Zakrzhevskaya.

650 'luxury costume . . . a whole pile': Ibid.

650 'No one wanted to take seriously': *Dance Magazine*, May 1990.

650 'show some style': To Luke Jennings, *Sunday Correspondent*, 27 May 1990.

650 'That stage is sacred': Ibid.

650 'This was like a pilgrimage': *San Francisco Chronicle*, 4 February 1990.

650 'It's a circular kind of circle': Dutch TV footage, courtesy of Wallace Potts.

651 'brilliant . . . a hint here': Inna Sklarevskaya, *Dance Magazine*, May 1990.

651 'a kind of caprice': LB.

20 · A FATALITY TO LIVE

652 'Only if Nureyev comes': Bois.

652 'He's a very nice boy': *Esquire*, March 1991.

652 'Dupond would be his poodle': Hélène Traïlene.

653 'in accord with . . . Like many tens': *New York Native*, 1 February 1993.

654 'forbidding any and all': Quoted by Andrew Grossman, 13 June 1986.

654 'He was *terrible* in them': Robert Gable.

654 'Definitely, for him, it was a death': Mikhail Baryshnikov quoted in *New Yorker*, 8 February 1993.

654 'When the lights are extinguished': *Opéra de Paris* 11, 1 October 1983.

654 'It is as if by way': Joyce Carol Oates, *On Boxing*.

654 'Practise in nice warm weather': RN/EK.

654 'No paintings, no statues': Blue.

655 'If Rudolf invites you': Querube Arias, quoted in DS.

655 'My houses are all strange': Quoted in DS.

655 'wolves' lairs': Blue.

655 'Like a wild animal': Katrine Feric.

655 'always naked . . . He wore a hat': Blue.

655 'You can play him at any tempo': LB.

655 'to trick his mind into': Wallace Potts.

655 'My son . . . if you want to live long': To Roland Boker.

656 'Without [it] there would not . . . I have brought it back . . . A love story which ended badly': *Événement du jeudi*, 8–14 October 1992.

656 'Nobody's dying to delve': RN/EK.

656 'dry bread and it's ingratitude': Eg B.

657 'I *can't* accept it': Daneman, *Margot Fonteyn*.

657 'He was still her Romeo': MT.

657 'It just goes on and on': Luke Jennings, *Sunday Correspondent*, 27 May 1990.

657 'the dear friend of my soul': *La Prensa*, 18 March 1987.

657 'It was heartbreaking': Quoted in DS.

658 'Things that could not be faced . . . You've got two twin souls': Quoted in Daneman, *Margot Fonteyn*.

658 'Oh, take her here, there': Jennings, *Sunday Correspondent*, 27 May 1990.

658 'He couldn't cope . . . Rudolf said, "What's wrong"': Daneman, *Margot Fonteyn*.

659 'Rudolf just sat there': Blue.

659 'When you're dead': *Mail on Sunday*, 3 July 1983.

659 'Conductors live a long, long time': Blue.

659 'to keep him going': Quoted in DS.

660 'that shit-boy': Blue.

660 'I guess I'll close . . . barking up the wrong . . . the only thing left for me': *Times Saturday Review*, 30 March 1991.

661 'I had such beautiful hair . . . If you don't have an orchestra': Blue.

661 'cries of refund, refund': *The Times*, 29 April 1991.

661 'Your newspapers are edited': The *Times*, 3 May 1991.

661 'He'll end up badly': To Cecil Beaton, *The Parting Years*.

664 'This is preparation for': *Evening Standard*, 19 April 1991.

664 'How quick or flexible': Justin Davidson, 'Measure for Measure', *New Yorker*, 21 August 2006.

665 'a conductor in front': Cl B.

666 'Rudolf had a good ear': RN conference, St Petersburg, 13–15 March 1998.

666 '*Molodetz!* . . . Good for you': *Elle* (US ed.), March 1993.

666 'made myself want': *San Francisco Examiner*, 12 July 1992.

666 'To wait until Nureyev arrives': *France-Soir*, undated clipping.

666–7 'feel as if I were being forced': Vidal, *Palimpsest*.

667 'I have no time': Bois.

668 '*de ne plus intérpreter*': Letter from Maurice Béjart to RN, 17 January 1991.

668 'really the end of his dancing': Letter from MG to Wallace Potts, 30 November 1991.

671 'He confessed that he was lost' and subsequent quotations: From Yuri Gamaley, *Mariinka and I*.

673 'one of those moments': Quoted in DS.

674 'all puffed up with pride': Georgina Parkinson.

675 'When am I going to conduct': Quoted in DS.

675 'It will take more than a chapel': Ibid.

676 'Petipa had great esteem': *Événement du jeudi*, 8–14 October 1992.

676 'une Bayadère Petipa, Kirov, vraie': Bois.

677 'It's a duo': *Bayadère* documentary, NC@NYDL.

677 '*Thousand and One Nights*': *Événement du jeudi*, 8–14 October 1992.

679 'his AIDS-wasted body': Vidal, *Palimpsest*.

679 'He disappeared and came back': Wallace Potts.

680 'I feel the impulse': *Manfred*, Act 1, Sc. 2.

680 'Life stirs my mind . . . thrilled, excited': *Dance Magazine*, May 1990.

682 'The masculine has become': *Événement du jeudi*, 8–14 October 1992.

683 'I was rather angry': *Bayadère* documentary.

683 'I will never forget': Bois.

684 'you weren't allowed': Linda Maybarduk.

684 'At the Opéra I waited': *Événement du jeudi*, 8–14 October 1992.

684 'was very special': *Bayadère* documentary.

684 '*et tous les Rothschilds*': René Sirvin, *Le Figaro*, 11 October 1992.

684 'Crippled or wrapped': Quoted in DS.

684 'the imaginary Invalid': Bois.

685 'I think he was victorious': *Guardian*, undated clipping.

685 'burning but unbent': Byron, *Le Corsaire*, canto 2, stanza 10.

685 'the essence, the heartbeat': Janice Berman, *New York Newsday*, 29 March 1993.

686 'When your dancers . . . breathe like one': To Joan Buck, unpublished *Vanity Fair* article, RNA.

686 'one big disappointment': *D&D*, January 1993.

687 'I want to sell myself': Article on Grigorovich in programme of the State Opera and Ballet Theatre of the Republic of Bashkortostan.

687 'some free time left': Van Dantzig excerpt from *Remembering Nureyev*, *D&D*, January 1994.

688 'the Importance of Uplifting': James Redfield, *The Celestine Vision*.

688 'You just wait till you drop': *The Times Saturday Review*, 30 March 1991.

689 'He was very very weak': MB/JA.

689 'Ah, the funeral march': Quoted in DS.

692 'By not discussing it': Maybarduk, *The Dancer Who Flew*.

693 'they began screaming': Wallace Potts.

694 'the power of these . . . That mixture': Quoted in DS.

694 'the trustees were afraid': Glora Venturi.

695 'When it seemed that': Quoted in DS.

695 'He is, you know, with all': Countess Giovanna Augusta, unmarked clipping.

695 'funny little hat': Gloria Venturi.

696 'reassuring him that': Quoted in DS.

696 'It occurred to me that': Maybarduk, *The Dancer Who Flew*.

696 'brought home to lie': Paul Webster, *Guardian*, 13 January 1993.

696 'the Opéra had been his fortress': Paul Callan, *Daily Express*, 12 January 1993.

696 'his home, his real home': Webster, *Guardian*, 13 January 1993.

696 'little piece of Russia': Hélène Traïlene.

696 'Now, in death, as in': Maybarduk, *The Dancer Who Flew*.

697 'a kind of doomsday . . . of a cycle': *Bayadère* documentary, NC@NYDL.

697 'Oh God, we sensed him . . . I left the stage': Ibid.

697 'No reason it could not . . . nirvana of': Croce, 'Markova's Miracle', *Afterimages*.

697–8 'some withered . . . A black horse': *Guardian Weekend*, 13 January 2002.

BIBLIOGRAPHY

BOOKS ON NUREYEV

Amort, Andrea. *Nurejew und Wien: Ein leidenschaftliches Verhältnis*. Vienna: Verlag Christian Brandstatter, 2003.

Barnes, Clive. *Nureyev*. New York: Helene Obolensky Enterprises, 1982.

Bland, Alexander. *The Nureyev Image*. London: Studio Vista, 1977.

———. *Fonteyn and Nureyev: The Story of a Partnership*. London: Orbis, 1979.

———. *The Nureyev Valentino: Portrait of a Film*. London: Studio Vista, 1977.

Bois, Mario. *Rudolf Noureev*. Paris: Éditions Plume, 1993.

Crippa, Valeria, and Ralph Fassey. *Nureyev*. New York: Rizzoli, 2003.

Dollfus, Ariane. *Noureev, l'insoumis*. Paris: Flammarion, 2007.

Farnsworth Art Museum. *Capturing Nureyev: James Wyeth Paints the Dancer*. Rockland, Maine: Farnsworth Art Museum, 2002.

Geitel, Klaus. *Der Tanzer Rudolf Nurejew*. West Berlin: Rembrandt, 1967.

Maybarduk, Linda. *The Dancer Who Flew: A Memoir of Rudolf Nureyev*. Toronto: Tundra Books, 1999.

McCann, Colum. *Dancer*. London: Weidenfeld & Nicolson, 2003.

Meyer-Stabley, Bertrand. *Noureev*. Paris: Payot, 2003.

Money, Keith. *Fonteyn & Nureyev: The Great Years*. London: Harvill, 1994.

Nureyev [photographs]. London: Phaidon Press, 1993.

Nureyev, Rudolf. *An Autobiography*. London: Hodder & Stoughton, 1962.

Opéra National de Paris. *Rudolf Noureev à Paris*. Paris: Éditions de La Martinière, 1993.

Ottolenghi, Vittoria. *Rudolf Nureyev Confessioni: Una conversazione lunga trent' anni*. Rome: Editoriale Pantheon, 1995.

Pasi, Mario, and Luigi Pignotti. *Nureyev: la sua arte la sua vita*. Milan: Sperling Kupfer Editori, 1993.

Percival, John. *Nureyev: Aspect of the Dancer*. rev. ed. London: Granada, 1979.

Petit, Roland. *Temps liés avec Noureev*. Paris: Grasset, 1998.

Robinson, Simon, with Derek Robinson. *A Year with Rudolf Nureyev*. London: Robert Hale, 1997.

Rodiani, Alexandre della Porta. *Rudolf Nureyev-Margot Fonteyn 'Marguerite & Armand'*. Milan: Arnaldo Mondadori Editore, 1995.

Rudolf Nureyev and the Royal Ballet. London: Oberon, 2005.

Solway, Diane. *Nureyev: His Life*. New York: William Morrow, 1998.

Soutar, Carolyn. *The Real Nureyev: An Intimate Memoir of Ballet's Greatest Hero*. Edinburgh: Mainstream Publishing, 2004.

Stuart, Otis. *Perpetual Motion: The Public and Private Lives of Rudolf Nureyev*. New York: Simon & Schuster, 1995.

Trombetta, Sergio. *Rudolf Nureyev*. Milan: Liber, 1993.

van Dantzig, Rudi. *Het spoor van een komeet* [Remembering Nureyev: The Trail of a Comet]. Zutphen, Netherlands: Gaillarde Pers, 1993.

Vollmer, Jurgen, and John Devere. *Nureyev in Paris: Le Jeune Homme et la mort.* New York: Modernismo Publications, 1975.

Watson, Peter. *Nureyev: A Biography.* London: Hodder & Stoughton, 1994.

Zakrzhevskaya, T. I., L. P. Myasnikova and A. G. Storozhuk, compilers. *Rudolf Nureyev: Three Years in the Kirov Theatre.* St Petersburg: Pushkinsky Fond, 1995.

FURTHER READING

Acocella, Joan. *Mikhail Baryshnikov in Black and White.* London: Bloomsbury, 2002.

Albert, Gennedy. *Alexander Pushkin: Master Teacher of Dance.* New York: The New York Public Library, 2001.

Amis, Martin. *Visiting Mrs. Nabokov and Other Excursions.* New York: Random House, 1995.

Anderson, Zoë. *The Royal Ballet: 75 Years.* London: Faber, 2006.

Andrew, Christopher, and Vasili Mitrokhin. *The Mitrokhin Archive: The KGB in Europe and the West.* London: Allen Lane, 1999.

Austin, Richard. *Lynn Seymour: An Authorised Biography.* Angus and Robertson, 1980.

Avedon, Richard. *Observations.* London: Weidenfeld & Nicolson, 1959.

Ballet Society Press. *Portrait of Mr. B: Photographs of George Balanchine.* Introduction by Lincoln Kirstein. New York: Viking, 1984.

Beaton, Cecil. *Beaton in the Sixties: More Unexpurgated Diaries.* Edited by Hugo Vickers. London: Weidenfeld & Nicolson, 2003.

————. *Self Portrait with Friends: The Selected Diaries of Cecil Beaton 1922–1974.* Edited by Richard Buckle. New York: Times Books, 1979.

————. *The Parting Years: Diaries 1963–74.* London, Weidenfeld & Nicolson, 1978.

Beaumont, Cyril. *The Complete Book of Ballets.* London: Putnam, 1949.

Béjart, Maurice. *La vie de qui? Mémoires,* vol. 2. Paris: Flammarion, 1996.

Bland, Alexander. *Observer of the Dance 1958–1982.* London: Dance Books, 1985.

————. *The Royal Ballet: First 50 Years.* London: Threshold Books, 1981.

Bournonville, August. *My Theatre Life.* London: A and C Black, 1979.

Bowers, Faubion. *The New Scriabin: Enigma and Answers.* New York: St. Martin's Press, 1973.

Brialy, Jean-Claude. *J'ai oublié de vous dire.* Paris: Pocket, 2005.

Bruhn, Erik. *Beyond Technique.* New York: Johnson Reprint Corp., 1973.

Buckle, Richard. *Buckle at the Ballet.* Dance Books, 1980.

————. *Adventures of a Ballet Critic.* London: Cresset Press, 1953.

Byron, Lord. *Selected Letters and Journals.* Edited by Leslie A. Marchand. London: John Murray, 1982.

Clarke, Gerald. *Capote: A Biography.* London: Hamish Hamilton, 1988.

Colacello, Bob. *Holy Terror: Andy Warhol Close Up.* New York: HarperCollins, 1990.

Conquest, Robert. *The Harvest of Sorrow: Soviet Collectivization and the Terror Famine.* London: Hutchinson, 1986.

Coward, Noël. *The Noël Coward Diaries.* Edited by Graham Payne and Sheridan Morley. London: Weidenfeld & Nicolson, 1982.

Crickmay, Anthony, and Clement Crisp. *Lynn Seymour.* London: Studio Vista, 1980.

Croce, Arlene. *Sight Lines.* New York: Knopf, 1987.

————. *Going to the Dance.* New York: Knopf, 1982.

————. *Afterimages.* New York: Knopf, 1977.

Daneman, Meredith. *Margot Fonteyn.* London: Viking, 2004.

Denby, Edwin. *Dance Writings.* Edited by Robert Cornfield and William Mackay. New York: Knopf, 1986.

de Mille, Agnes. *Martha: The Life and Work of Martha Graham.* New York: Vintage Books, 1992.

de Valois, Ninette. *Come Dance with Me*. London: World Publishing, 1957.
————. *Step by Step*. London: W. H. Allen, 1977.
Drummond, John. *Speaking of Diaghilev*. London: Faber, 1997.
DuBois, Diana. *In Her Sister's Shadow: The Bitter Legacy of Lee Radziwill*. New York: St. Martin's Press, 1997.
Flaubert, Gustave. *Flaubert in Egypt*. Translated and edited with an introduction by Francis Steegmuller. New York: Penguin Books, 1972.
Fonteyn, Margot. *Autobiography*. London: Hamish Hamilton, 1989.
Forbes, Bryan. *A Divided Life: Memoirs*. London: Heinemann, 1992.
Fracci, Carla. *Vivere è danzare . . . Danzare è vivere*. Rome: Gregoriana, 1976.
Frétard, Dominique. *Invitation: Sylvie Guillem*. London: Éditions Cercle d'Art/Oberon Books, 2005.
Gamaley, Yuri. *Mariinka and I*. St Petersburg: Papirus, 1999.
Garafola, Lynn. *Diaghilev's Ballets Russes*. New York: Oxford University Press, 1989.
Gielgud, John. *Gielgud's Letters*. Edited with an introduction by Richard Mangan. London: Weidenfeld & Nicolson, 2004.
Gold, Arthur, and Robert Fizdale. *Misia: The Life of Misia Sert*. New York: Knopf, 1980.
Gosling, Nigel. *Prowling the Pavements: Selected Art Writings, 1950–1980*. Edited by Robert Tracy. N.p.: A Lives Examined Book/Winchell Company, 1986.
————. *Leningrad*. London: Studio Vista, 1965.
Gottlieb, Robert. *George Balanchine: The Ballet Maker*. New York: HarperCollins, 2004.
Graham, Martha. *Blood Memory*. New York: Doubleday, 1991.
Green, Jonathan. *All Dressed Up: The Sixties and the Counter-Culture*. London: Pimlico, 1999.
Gruen, John. *Erik Bruhn: Danseur Noble*. New York: Viking Press, 1979.
————. *The Private World of Ballet*. New York: Penguin Books, 1976.
Guest, Ivor. *Le Ballet de l'Opéra de Paris*. Paris: Flammarion, 2001.
Guilleminault, Gilbert. *Le roman vrai de la Vème République: La déchirure 1961–1962*. Paris: Juilliard, 1980.
Hackett, Pat, ed. *The Andy Warhol Diaries*. New York: Warner Books, 1989.
Haden-Guest, Anthony. *The Last Party: Studio 54, Disco and the Culture of the Night*. New York: William Morrow, 1997.
Haltrecht, Montague. *The Quiet Showman: Sir David Webster and the Royal Opera*. London: Collins, 1975.
Heymann, C. David. *RFK: A Candid Biography of Robert F. Kennedy*. New York: Dutton, 1998.
Hopkins, John. *The Tangier Diaries 1962–1979*. London: Arcadia, 1997.
Hudson, Rock, and Sara Davidson. *Rock Hudson: His Story*. New York: William Morrow, 1986.
Jarman, Derek. *Dancing Ledge*. London: Quartet Books, 1984.
Jowitt, Deborah. *Jerome Robbins: His Life, His Theater, His Dance*. New York: Simon & Schuster, 2004.
Kael, Pauline. *When the Lights Go Down*. London: Boyers, 1980.
Kain, Karen, with Stephen Godfrey and Penelope Reed Doob. *Movement Never Lies: An Autobiography*. Toronto: McClelland and Stewart, 1994.
Karsavina, Tamara. *Theatre Street*. London: Dance Books, 1981.
Kirkland, Gelsey, with Greg Lawrence. *Dancing on My Grave*. London: Hamish Hamilton, 1986.
Kirstein, Lincoln. *For John Martin: Entries from an Early Diary*. New York: Dance Perspectives Foundation, 1973.
Krasovskaya, Vera. *Nijinsky*. New York: Schirmer Books, 1979.
Lawrence, Greg. *Dance with Demons: The Life of Jerome Robbins*. New York: G. P. Putnam, 2001.
Le-Tan, Pierre. *Carnet des anneés Pop*. Paris: Gallimard, 1997.

Liszt, Franz. *Selected Letters.* Translated and edited by Adrian Williams. Oxford: Clarendon Press, 1998.

Longford, Frank Pakenham, Earl of. *Kennedy.* London: Weidenfeld & Nicolson, 1976.

Louis, Murray. *Inside Dance.* New York: St. Martin's Press, 1980.

MacCarthy, Fiona. *Byron: Life and Legend.* London: Faber, 2003.

Mannoni, Gérard. *Roland Petit: un chorégraphe et ses peintres.* Paris: Hatier, 1990.

Mannoni, Gérard, and Pierre Jouhaud. *Les Étoiles de l'Opéra de Paris.* Paris: Éditions Sylvie Messinger et Théâtre National de l'Opéra de Paris, 1981.

Martin, John. *Ruth Page: An Intimate Biography.* New York: M. Dekker, 1977.

Mason, Francis. *I Remember Balanchine: Recollections of the Ballet Master by Those Who Knew Him.* New York: Doubleday, 1991.

Massine, Léonide. *My Life in Ballet.* London: Macmillan, 1968.

Miller, Russell. *The House of Getty.* London: Michael Joseph, 1985.

Money, Keith. *Fonteyn: The Making of a Legend.* London: Collins, 1973.

Montagnier, Luc. *Virus: The Co-Discoverer of HIV Tracks Its Rampage and Charts the Future.* New York: Norton, 2002.

Mousseau, Jacques. *Le Siècle de Paul-Louis Weiller 1893–1993.* Paris: Stock, 1998.

Nesbitt, Cathleen. *A Little Love and Good Company.* London: Faber, 1975.

Neufeld, James. *Power to Rise: The Story of the National Ballet of Canada.* Toronto: University of Toronto Press, 1996.

Newman, Barbara. *Antoinette Sibley: Reflections of a Ballerina.* London: Century Hutchinson, 1986.

————. *Striking a Balance: Dancers Talk About Dancing.* London: Elm Tree Books, 1982.

Nijinska, Bronislava. *Early Memoirs.* London: Faber, 1982.

Nijinsky, Vaslav. *The Diary of Vaslav Nijinsky.* Unexpurgated edition. Edited by Joan Acocella. New York: Farrar, Straus & Giroux, 1999.

Norman, Philip. *The Stones.* London: Elm Tree Books, 1984.

Oliphant, Betty. *Miss O: My Life in Dance.* Winnipeg, Canada: Turnstone Press, 1996.

Page, Ruth. *Page by Page.* Brooklyn, NY: Dance Horizons, 1978.

Panov, Valery, with George Feifer. *To Dance.* New York: Knopf, 1978.

Peppiatt, Michael. *Francis Bacon: Anatomy of an Enigma.* London: Weidenfeld & Nicolson, 1996.

Phillips, Siân. *Public Places: The Autobiography.* London: Hodder & Stoughton, 2001.

Poznansky, Alexander. *Tchaikovsky's Last Days.* Oxford: Clarendon Press, 1996.

Praz, Mario. *The Romantic Agony.* London: Oxford University Press, 1970.

Pushkin, Aleksandr. *The Golden Cockerel and Other Fairy Tales.* Translated by Jesse Wood; Introduction by Rudolf Nureyev. New York: Doubleday, 1989.

Rawsthorn, Alice. *Yves Saint Laurent: A Biography.* London: HarperCollins, 1996.

Redfield, James. *The Celestine Vision: Living the New Spiritual Awareness.* London: Bantam, 1997.

Robinson, Harlow. *The Last Impresario: The Life, Times, and Legacy of Sol Hurok.* New York: Penguin Books, 1994.

Schorer, Suki. *On Balanchine Technique.* New York: Knopf, 1999.

Seymour, Lynn, with Paul Gardner. *Lynn: The Autobiography of Lynn Seymour.* London: Granada Publishing, 1984.

Sorley Walker, Kathrine. *Ninette de Valois: Idealist Without Illusions.* London: Hamish Hamilton, 1987.

Steegmuller, Francis. *Cocteau: A Biography.* London: Constable and Co., 1986.

Strong, Roy. *The Roy Strong Diaries 1967–1987.* London: Weidenfeld & Nicolson, 1997.

Tallchief, Maria, with Larry Kaplan. *Maria Tallchief: America's Prima Ballerina.* New York: Henry Holt, 1997.

Taper, Bernard. *Balanchine: A Biography.* New York: Times Books, 1984.

Taranow, Gerda. *Sarah Bernhardt: The Art Within the Legend*. Princeton: Princeton University Press, 1972.

Taylor, Paul. *Private Domain*. New York: Knopf, 1987.

Tooley, John. *In House: Covent Garden, 50 Years of Opera and Ballet*. London: Faber, 1999.

Tracy, Robert. *Goddess: Martha Graham's Dancers Remember*. New York: Limelight Editions, 1997.

Tual, Denise. *Le Temps devoré*. Paris: Fayard, 1980.

Tynan, Kenneth. *Bull Fever*. 2nd ed. London: Longmans, 1966.

van Vooren, Monique. *Night Sanctuary*. New York: Summit Books, 1981.

Vaughan, David. *Frederick Ashton and His Ballets*. London: Adam and Charles Black, 1977.

Vickers, Hugo. *Cecil Beaton*. London: Weidenfeld & Nicolson, 1993.

Vidal, Gore. *Point to Point Navigation: A Memoir*. New York: Doubleday, 2006.

———. *Palimpsest: A Memoir*. New York: Random House, 1995.

Vishnevskaya, Galina. *Galina: A Russian Story*. Sevenoaks, Kent: Hodder & Stoughton, 1984.

Volkov, Solomon. *Conversations with Joseph Brodsky: A Poet's Journey Through the Twentieth Century*. Translated by Marian Schwartz. New York: The Free Press, 1998.

———. *St. Petersburg: A Cultural History*. New York: The Free Press, 1995.

———. *Balanchine's Tchaikovsky: Interviews with George Balanchine*. New York: Simon and Schuster, 1985.

Warhol, Andy, and Pat Hackett. *POPism: The Warhol '60s*. New York: Harvest Books, 1990.

White, Edmund. *The Farewell Symphony*. London: Chatto & Windus, 1997.

———. *The Burning Library: Writings on Art, Politics and Sexuality 1969–1993*. London: Chatto & Windus, 1994.

———. *Nocturnes for the King of Naples*. London: André Deutsch, 1979.

Wiley, Roland John. *Tchaikovsky's Ballets*. Oxford: Clarendon Press, 1985.

Winters, Shelley. *Best of Times, Worst of Times*. London: Muller, 1990.

Wishart, Michael. *High Diver*. London: Blond & Briggs, 1977.

Wolfe, Tom. *the kandy-kolored tangerine-flake streamline baby*. London: Picador, 1981.

Woronov, Mary. *Swimming Underground: My Years in the Warhol Factory*. London: Serpent's Tail, 2002.

Zeffirelli, Franco. *Zeffirelli: The Autobiography of Franco Zeffirelli*. London: Weidenfeld & Nicolson, 1986.

GENERAL REFERENCE

The Dictionary of Art. Edited by Jane Turner. New York: Grove, 1996.

International Dictionary of Ballet. Edited by Martha Bremser. London: St. James Press, 1993.

International Encyclopedia of Dance. 6 vols. New York: Oxford University Press, 1998.

New Grove Dictionary of Music. Edited by Stanley Sadie. London: Macmillan, 1980.

ILLUSTRATION CREDITS

Rudik as a toddler. Courtesy of the Rudolf Nureyev Foundation
Rudik's father. Courtesy of Alfia Rafikova
Hamet's photograph. Courtesy of Alfia Rafikova
A summer vacation. Courtesy of Inna Guskova, Ufa Theatre Museum
Summer vacation group shot. Courtesy of Inna Guskova, Ufa Theatre Museum
Rudik's innate elevation. Courtesy of Inna Guskova, Ufa Theatre Museum
Two of Rudik's mentors. Courtesy of Inna Guskova, Ufa Theatre Museum
Rudik with Ufa yard gang friend. Courtesy of Inna Guskova, Ufa Theatre Museum
Posing outside the Nureyevs' isba. Courtesy of Inna Guskova, Ufa Theatre Museum
Alexander Ivanovich Pushkin. Courtesy of Jutta Jellinek, © Teja Kremke
Alexander and Xenia Pushkin. Courtesy of Alla Bor and Lubov Filatova
Pushkins in their Rossi Street bed. Courtesy of Jutta Jellinek, © Teja Kremke
Marietta Frangopoulu. Courtesy of Egon Bischoff
Clowning in the Vaganova dormitory (all six images). Courtesy and © Leo Ahonen
Rehearsing with Alla Sizova. Courtesy of the Rudolf Nureyev Foundation
Portrait of Teja. Courtesy of Alla Bor and Lubov Filatova
Menia Martinez. Courtesy of Liuba Myasnikova
Dancing the solo from Le Corsaire. Courtesy of Inna Guskova
Tamara Zakrzhevskaya. Courtesy of Tamara Zakrzhevskaya
The Romankov family. Courtesy of Liuba Myasnikova
With Natalia Dudinskaya. Courtesy of Robert Greskovic
Soaring in *Gayane*. Courtesy of Maude Gosling
As Albrecht with Irina Kolpakova. Courtesy of Maude Gosling
With Alla Shelest. Courtesy of Maude Gosling
'Sit down on suitcase'. Courtesy of Faina Rokhind

Rudolf and Margot in Le Corsaire. © Leslie E. Spatt
Rehearsing Swan Lake. © Keith Money
Rudolf and Margot's 1962 Giselle. © Fox Photos; courtesy of Robert Greskovic
Rudolf and Margot in Swan Lake. © Agence de Presse Bernand; courtesy of Robert Greskovic
Rehearsing Marguerite and Armand. © Michael Peto
Kenneth MacMillan's Romeo and Juliet. © Keith Money
Roland Petit's Paradise Lost. © Keith Money
With Christopher Gable. © Donald Southern
In La Sylphide. Courtesy of the Rudolf Nureyev Foundation; © Zoë Dominic
The seduction scene in Le Jeune Homme et la mort. © Jürgen Vollmer
Rudolf surrounded by Claras. Courtesy of Robert Greskovic; © The Sunday Times

With Benjamin Feliksdal. © Hans van den Busken
In Balanchine's The Prodigal Son. Courtesy of the Rudolf Nureyev Foundation
The Sleeping Beauty with Karen Kain. Courtesy of Karen Kain
With Ann Jenner. Courtesy of Robert Gresovic; © Judy Cameron
With Jerome Robbins and cast. © Edward Griffiths; courtesy of Robert Greskovic
Discussing Scriabin's score with Frederick Ashton.© Michael Peto
Watching Kenneth MacMillan. © Keith Money
With Rudi van Dantzig in Amsterdam. © Bob van Dantzig
With Mikhail Baryshnikov and Paul Taylor. © Lois Greenfield
Rehearsing with Murray Louis. © Jack Vartoogian

With Clara Saint in Geneva. Courtesy of the Rudolf Nureyev Foundation
Facing a blitzkrieg of flashbulbs. © Serge Lido; courtesy of Robert Greskovic
Picking out a tune. Courtesy of the Rudolf Nureyev Foundation
Coached by Eric Bruhn. © Peter Ward
Rudolf and Erik in class.© Jack Mitchell
The sixties pop star. © 2007 The Richard Avedon Foundation. Courtesy The Richard
    Avedon Foundation
Private Lesson with Valentina Pereyaslavec. © 2007 The Richard Avedon Foundation.
    Courtesy The Richard Avedon Foundation
Posing for Avedon, 6 May 1963. © 2007 The Richard Avedon Foundation. Courtesy The
    Richard Avedon Foundation
The famous legs. © 2007 The Richard Avedon Foundation. Courtesy The Richard Avedon
    Foundation
Working with Nigel Gosling.© Michael Peto
On the road. Courtesy of the Rudolf Nureyev Dance Foundation
With Armen Bali. © Jeannette Etheredge
Wallace Potts and Jeannette Etheredge. Courtesy of Wallace Potts
With Leslie Caron. Courtesy of Leslie Caron
With Monique van Vooren and Maria Tallchief. © Louis Pérez; courtesy of Robert
    Greskovic
With Douce François. © Patrice Picot, Jour de France
With Tessa Kennedy. Courtesy of Tessa Kennedy
With Princess Firyal. © Tessa Kennedy
With Franck Raoul-Duval. © Tessa Kennedy
In Turkey with Maude and Nigel Gosling. © Tessa Kennedy
With Wallace, Douce, and Robert Tracy. © Tessa Kennedy
With Stephen Sherriff, Yasemin Pirinccioglu, Jane Herman, Wallace and Douce. Courtesy
    of the Rudolf Nureyev Dance Foundation
Being led offstage by Charles Jude. Courtesy of Charles Jude
Kenneth Greve. © 2007 The Richard Avedon Foundation. Courtesy The Richard Avedon
    Foundation
Charles Jude and Elisabeth Platel. Courtesy of the Rudolf Nureyev Dance Foundation
Rehearsing Don Quixote. © Francette Levieux
The dining room at quai Voltaire. © Douce François
Preparing to conduct.© Alexandra della Porta Rodigni
The last vacation. © Jeannette Etheredge
Ezio Frigerio's memorial. © Olivier Perrin

ACKNOWLEDGEMENTS

Without Europe's Rudolf Nureyev Foundation and America's Rudolf Nureyev Dance Foundation, this book could not have been written. Endorsing it as the authorized biography, the two Foundations underwrote my foreign research and gave me exclusive access to their archives of documents, photographs and films while, at the same time, entrusting me with complete editorial freedom. Few biographers can have been granted such generous and unqualified support. The respective chairmen, RNF's Sir John Tooley and RNDF's Barry Weinstein, have backed me every step of the way, whether funding a return trip to Ufa when I felt it necessary, or ungrudgingly extending their patronage when I missed my overoptimistic 2003 deadline (and the tie-in to the tenth anniversary of Rudolf's death). At the helm in RNF's Bath office, Alexandra Kelly guided me through the Foundation's extensive picture library and promptly replied to every query I sent her way; René Longini, handling financial affairs from Zurich, was unfailingly patient and accommodating; while the efficiency and helpfulness of RNDF's Linda Pilkington in Chicago have never wavered over a decade. I owe both RNF and RNDF more than I can say.

It was, however, the late Wallace Potts who set this whole project in motion. As attentive to the dancer's legacy as he was to the man himself, Wallace made it his mission to find a suitable biographer and, in the process, urged Rudolf's immediate coterie to reveal their stories to no one else. After consulting Knopf editor Robert Gottlieb (who got things going by tape-recording interviews with the key players), Wallace read my Frederick Ashton biography Secret Muses and decided that I was the one for the job. 'It's an affectionate portrait of Fred, but it's not a 'whitewash'. It's Fred with all his eccentricities and his good and bad qualities,' he wrote to Misha Baryshnikov and many others, urging each to be frank with me. From 1997, when I began my research, Wallace was always in the background, offering encouragement, making introductions, handing over his own deeply personal letters, and mailing dozens of videos of Rudolf's performances. By phone and fax – and later by e-mail – we were in touch several times a week. I relied not only on his sound feedback on the chapters I sent him, but also on his good sense and good humour about all manner of other things. His death in June 2006 brought the loss of my most prized source and a true friend. I am indebted to Wallace's brother, Tommy Potts, and his executor, Jack Larson, for allowing me to draw on Wallace's invaluable archive.

Next to Wallace, no one has been more dedicated to Rudolf's memory, or a fiercer champion in protecting and advancing it, than Jeannette Etheredge, also a Trustee of RNDF. My heartfelt thanks to her, and to the other members of Rudolf's adopted family: Jeannette's mother, Armen Bali; Tessa Kennedy; the late Douce François and the late Maude Gosling – my own acquaintance with whom has enabled me to see why it was that Rudolf so depended on these exceptionally loyal people. I never met Nigel Gosling, who died in 1982, and yet I feel I know him well – thanks to the superb archive of diaries, letters, audio tapes and notes that Maude unhesitatingly put my way. I owe an immeasurable amount to their son, Nicholas, for allowing me to quote from this material, and to their close friend Tristram Holland for her help and sharp insights. Special thanks, too, to Tessa, Jeannette and Douce for all the time they gave me, and for allowing me to use their own photographs in the book. Douce's brother, Pierre François, and her husband, the late Joe Freitas, were also immensely cooperative.

Among Russian sources, I owe the greatest debt to Liuba Myasnikova and Tamara Zakrzhevskaya. Where to begin to thank them for their enveloping St Petersburg hospitality, their memories and acute knowledge of the young Rudik, their letters and photographs, and for their unfailing patience in answering my questions year after year after year? Tamara's son Alexander 'Sasha' Storozhuk, a brilliant linguist, was always willing to act as translator; Liuba's twin brother, Leonid Romankov, played a key role in helping me piece together the Russian years. In addition I acknowledge with enormous gratitude the help I received from members of the Nureyev family: Rudolf's sister Razida Yevgrafova and his niece Alfia Rafikova gave up hours of their time, put me in contact with family members in far-flung places, and allowed me to use photographs from their albums. Rudolf's cousin Amina Galiakbarova was wonderfully kind and led me to discover much that was new about the enigmatic Hamet Nureyev's early years.

Then there are the others whose contribution to this book has been incalculable: Keith Money's instructive and eloquent e-mails about Rudolf's Royal Ballet years, together with his classic Fonteyn/Nureyev books, were my touchstone for writing about this period. I am deeply grateful for his knowledge, long-distance friendship and for the photographs he has allowed me to use. Katie de Haan's English translation of Rudi van Dantzig's memoir *Remembering Nureyev: The Trail of a Comet* (to be published by the University of Florida Press in 2008), provided me with a superbly immediate account of Rudolf's initiation into the alien world of modern dance, and I thank them both for so generously putting this at my disposal. Keith Baxter, the perfect interviewee with his novelistic instinct for telling traits of character, also let me have a vivid written account of his relationship with Rudolf. Without Ute Mitreuter and Chinko Rafique, the only Western friends in whom Rudolf confided about his 'first crush', Teja Kremke, I would never have unearthed the remarkable Cold War story (adapted by the BBC into a ninety-minute documentary, *Nureyev: From Russia with Love*). A first-hand witness, Ute was able to confirm Teja's role as a catalyst in Rudolf's defection, her husband, Teja's room-mate, Konstantin Russu, provided further proof of this dangerous liaison, while Chinko played a vital part in reconstructing the ambience surrounding Xenia and Alexander Pushkin. This trail then led to Jutta Jellinek, Teja's second wife, who showed me his invaluable 8mm footage of Rudolf in his last year in Leningrad, and generously allowed me to include Teja's photographs in my book. Ute Kremke, Teja's sister, found family letters and gave me a graphic picture of her brother's life in East Berlin. Teja's daughter Jurico and her husband, Stefan Siegmann, were instrumental in helping me narrate the sinister consequences of the friendship by passing on their copy of the Stasi's file. Jusuff Kremke, Teja's son, and Teja's first wife, Nuraini Niegbur, were also tremendously forthcoming.

In St Petersburg I acknowledge with particular gratitude the help of Faina Rokhind, who put at my disposal her extraordinary collection of photographs, cuttings and memorabilia, including the diaries of her friend the late Galina Palshina. For passing on their memories of the Pushkins, and for their warmth and friendship, I am indebted to Alla Bor and to Slava and Irina Santto. Thanks, too, to Dimitri and Lubov Filatov for their kind help, and for allowing me to use photographs from the Pushkins' album. In Ufa, Inna Guskova, then curator of the Theatre Museum, who knows more than anyone else about this early period of Rudolf's life, planned my itinerary, provided me with all the background I needed, and generously lent me a number of her own photographs. The dynamic and hospitable Galina Belskaya led me to Rosa Kolesnikova, whose untold reminiscences of 'the boy who was born on the train' gave me my opening to the book. My sincere thanks to them both.

Ten years ago, when I began my research, there appeared to be very few Nureyev papers in existence. Self-conscious about his faulty written English, Rudolf was renowned for never sending more than a postcard, and most of the letters he received were just fan mail. Pierre François, who took on the task of sorting through a mass of miscellaneous papers stored in his sister Douce's cave, found a few things of interest, but mostly contracts and bills. Tessa Kennedy, who helped to clear out the house in Fife Road, remembered Rudolf wanting all his letters, including those of Erik Bruhn, to be destroyed. There didn't seem much hope – and then came the breakthrough: a cache of love letters from Erik discovered by Maude Gosling in Rudolf's room in Victoria Road. More Erik letters came to light – as well as vital Russian correspondence from Teja, Xenia and the Nureyev family – among papers found in the Dakota apartment, now held in RNDF's Chicago office; and finally, as late as December 2004, a large tin trunk crammed with papers from quai Voltaire, previously stored in an out-of-town storage warehouse, was made available to me at Le Centre National de la Danse in Pantin, outside Paris. It's thanks to CND's archivist, the diligent, immensely cooperative Laurent Sebillotte, that I was able to raid this with ease, coming across some real treasures for the final chapters of my book. I am indebted to the Erik Bruhn Trust for permitting me to quote extensively from the Bruhn letters, and so enable me fully to narrate this pivotal relationship in Rudolf's life. My deepest thanks go to Valerie Wilder, and to her successors in charge of the Trust, Karen Kain and Kevin Garland, for their continuing support.

I have also been privileged to be able to quote from Lincoln Kirstein's correspondence, for which I owe special thanks to his executor, Nicholas Jenkins. Richard Buckle gave me access to the letters he received from Kirstein, as well as to his own unpublished Nureyev memoir, and I am grateful to his nephew and executor, Charles Graham, for permitting me to use this splendid material. Violette Verdy, one of the world's most eloquent ballerinas, not only gave me hours of her time, but also searched out lively letters sent to her by her ex-husband, Colin Clark, and his twin sister, Colette. My thanks go to the Clark siblings for letting me quote from this correspondence, and, above all, to Violette herself. Thanks, too, to Phyllis Wyeth for letting me draw on her diaries; to Joan Buck for kindly allowing me to quote from her unpublished *Vanity Fair* article on Rudolf's Paris Opéra appointment; to Lavinia Exham for permission to quote from Margot Fonteyn's letters; to Alex Stannus, executor of the estate of Ninette de Valois; to Maurice Béjart, Jiří Kylián, Jacob Rothschild and to a number of others kind enough to allow me to use material of which they hold the copyright: Thor Sutowski (Sonia Arova); Zoltan Dan (Viktor Rona); and Valerie Golovitser (Silva Lon).

One of the high points of working as London editor of the *New Yorker* in the late 90s was the chance it gave me to get to know Richard Avedon. Always interested in how my Nureyev project was progressing, Dick promised that when the time came he would choose for me a cover and a portfolio of his Nureyev photographs. He died before the book was complete, but Norma Stevens, the executive director of the Richard Avedon Foundation, made sure it happened and, for this, I will always be in her debt. There are further instances of exceptional generosity: from Arthur Elgort, who, with my dear friend Grace Coddington acting as go-between, took my photograph for the jacket; from Robert Greskovic, who opened up his collection of rare photographs of 'his nibs', and kept sending new jpegs almost until the day the book went to press. Leo Ahonen gave me the use of his unique Vaganova dormitory photographs; Robert Gable unstintingly provided me with New York clippings and photographs; and Alexandra della Porta Rodiani allowed me to choose from the outstanding pictures she took in the last years of Rudolf's life. My thanks to them all.

Then there are those who went out of their way to supply me with invaluable material: the ever-generous Michael Romain; René Sirvin; Helene Ciolkovitch and Joelle Galliot (co-editors of the superbly informative newsletter distributed by le Cercle des Amies de Rudolf Noureev); Egon Bischoff and Richard Cragun (both key dramatis personae in the story); the late David Daniel, John Gruen, Gregory King and Veronica Tennant. I drew extensively on transcripts of taped interviews that Elizabeth Kaye donated to the Nureyev Collection; and I am especially grateful to Gunilla Jensen for the compilation tape she sent me of Swedish television coverage of Nureyev.

For the hospitality I received in the process of my research, I must single out for thanks Jean Audy Rowland, who invited me to stay at her house on St Bart's, the evocative 'Maison

ACKNOWLEDGEMENTS

746

Noureev'; Soili Arvola and Leo Ahonen for help and generosity in Katy, Texas; Natasha Harley in New York and Long Island; the then British Ambassador Sir Andrew and Stephanie Wood in Moscow; Shamile Teregulov and his wife, Leonora, in Ufa; Zagida Tukmach in Asanova; Vittoria Ottolenghi in Rome; and Otmar and Elfgard Wintersteller in Vienna.

To my forthcoming and indefatigable prime sources I express the deepest gratitude: Frank Augustyn, Mikhail Baryshnikov, Maurice Béjart, Marika Besobrasova, Gerhard Brunner, Michel Canesi, Leslie Caron, Jean-Luc Choplin, Robert Denvers, Gilles Dufour, Thierry Fouquet, Carla Fracci, Hugues Gall, Nicole Gonzalez, Kenneth Greve, Jane Hermann, Barbara Horgan, Charles Jude, Karen Kain, Ninel Kurgapkina, Pierre Lacotte, André Larquié, Jacques Loyau, Heinz Mannigel, Menia Martinez, Linda Maybarduk, Axel Mowitz, Alla Osipenko, Lennart Pasborg, Luigi Pignotti, Yasemin Pirinccioglu, Elisabeth Platel, Lee Radziwill, Franck Raoul-Duval, Janine Ringuet, Patricia Ruanne and Frederic Jahn, Clara Saint, Toer van Schayk, Stephen Sherriff, Marie-Suzanne Soubie, Sergiu Stefanschi, Igor Stupnikov, Maria Tallchief, Ghislaine Thesmar, Joan Thring, Hélène Traïlene, the late Robert Tracy, Monique van Vooren, Jamie and Phyllis Wyeth.

I am also immensely grateful to: Anneli Ahanko, Natalia Akimova, Edward Albee, Gennedy Albert, Arthur Albrecht, Lucette Aldous, Margarita Alexeeva, Margarita Alfimova, Anneli Alhanko-Shoglund, Alicia Alonso, Nina Alovert, Andrea Amort, Elena Apakova, Galina Artemieva, Albert Aslanov, Claude Baignières, Svetlana Baisheva, Tania Bari, Julian Barnes, Patricia Barnes, Ray Barra, Galina Baranchukova, Edgar Battista, Dick Beard, Igor Belsky, Terence Benton, Pavel Berdin, Bill Beresford, Pierre Bergé, Deanne Bergsma, Claude Bessy, Clara Bikchova, Alik Bikchurin, David Bintley, Michael Birkmeyer, Jennie Bisset, Mario Bois, Roland Boker, Erica Bolton, Neil Boyd, Boris Bregvadze, John Bridcut, Lola Bubbosh, Claus von Bülow, Leo Carey, Jean-Claude Carrière, Arlette Castanier, Giorgio Cattarello, Yvette Chauviré, Sybil Christopher, Mary Clarke, Ursula Collein, Jennifer Rizzuto Congregane, Robert Conquest, Gilberte Cournande, David Cronin, Azalia Cuchimova, William Davidson, Vadim Desnitsky, Gerlinde Dill, Nikita Dolgushin, James Douglas, Anthony Dowell, German Drushenitsky, Irina Duddell, Natalia Dudinskaya, Wayne Eagling, Andrew Edmonson, Anne Enders, Vladimir Fedianin, Ralph Fiennes, Princess Firyal, Bryan Forbes, the late Charles France, Michelle Franco, Tim Garton-Ash, Roland Gawlik, the late Nico Georgiadis, Christopher Gibbs, Maina Gielgud, Ingrid Glindemann, Ilmira Goforova, Katia Gortchakoff, Alexander Grant, Beryl Grey, Stewart Grimshaw, Hubert Grunwald, Marit Gentele Gruson, Jean Guizerix, Eldus Habirov, Christopher Hampton, Robert Harris, Jonathan Haslam, Nicholas Haslam, Marcia Haydée-Schobert, Susan Hendl, Hans Werner Henze, Robert Hewison, Teddy Heywood, Rosella Hightower, Anna-Marie Holmes, Kate Horner, Jana Howlett, Elizabeth, Lydia and Waxy Hübner, Lieda Husainova, Robert Hutchinson, Ronald Hynd, Zizi Jeanmaire, Ellen Josefowitz, Barry Joule, Vladimir Kataev, Vadim Kiselev, Traude Klockl, Yuri Kobaladze, Irina Kolpakova, Gabriella Komleva, Nicolai Kovmir, Vera Krasovskaya, David Kuhn, Zsuzsa Kun, Bella Kurgina, Ilza Kurgusova, Edmund and Robert La Fosse, the late John Lanchbery, Nellie and Tony Liddell, Kerstin Lidström, Monique Loudières, Murray Louis, Richard McCabe, Valentina Malofeeva, Satu Marks, Monica Mason, Giuseppe 'Beppe' Menegatti, Billie du Mesnil, Valentina Mironova, Olga Moiseyeva, Gail Monahan, Marie-Christine Mouis, Axel Mowitz, Federat Musin, Madina Musina, Yuri Naidich, Zaituna Nazretdinova, Anatoly Nikiforov, Igor Nikitin, Natasha Novinova, Betty Oliphant, Jerome Oremland, Adèl Orosz, Annette Page, Anthony Page, the late David Palmer, Galina Palshina, Merle Park, Jacqueline Parker, Georgina Parkinson, Jann Parry, Elise Paschen, Noel Pelly, John Percival, Antony Petie, Claudia Roth Pierpoint, Geordano Ponticelli, Ray Powell, Bonnie Prandato, Jasper Rees, Gert Reinholm, Vladimir Renne, Viscountess Jacqueline de Ribes, David Richardson, the late Jerome Robbins, Allen Robertson, Maslime Sabitova, Anya Sainsbury, Bruce Sansom, Sandy Scott, David Scrase, Per-Arthur Segerström, Lynn Seymour, Svetlana Shagieva, Linda Shaughnessy, Sasha Shavrov, Michael Shipster, Antoinette Sibley, Nancy Sifton, Kirsten Simone, Alla Sizova, Majorie Skibine, Inna

Skidelskaya, Konstantin Slovohotov, Lina Smakova, Christina Sterner, Alexandra Stewart, Gailene Stock, Pamira Sulamanova, Gösta Svalberg, Paul Szilard, Marjorie Tallchief, Paul Taylor, the late Glen Tetley, Brigitta Thom, the late Esther Tonsgaard, Denise Tual, Raufal Tziaynov, Hamza Ula, Alfat Valeev, Marina Vasilieva, Gloria Venturi, Serge Vikulov, Grigore Vintila, Jean de Vuyst, Nina Vyroubova, David Wall, David Warner, Peter Watson, Anna-Marie Welch, Elizabeth White, Rosemary Winckley, Nicole Wisniak, Susse Wold, Peter Wright, Yuri Yevgrafov, Nina Zilenko and Elena Zueva.

In addition, I must express my debt to the following institutions: Ufa's Agricultural Institute, Local Party Archive and Nestorov Museum; Moscow's Central Committee of the Communist Party of the Soviet Union; the Archive of Federal Security Service Headquarters in the St Petersburg and Leningrad region; and the Archive of St Petersburg State Museum of Theatre and Musical Art. Special thanks go to Marina Vivien, ex-curator of the Vaganova Academy Museum; archivist Francesca Franchi and press officer Janine Limberg at the Royal Opera House; archivists Jane Pritchard at Ballet Rambert; Josseline la Bourius at Paris Opéra Ballet; and Eszter Szudy at the Hungarian Theatre Institute; librarians Janine Button of London's Condé Nast Publications and Elena Jack at the Royal Academy of Dance; and Madeline Nichols, Michelle Potter, Else Peck and Charles Perrier at the Dance Collection of New York's Public Library at Lincoln Center.

Throughout the decade it has taken to complete this project I have had the privilege of working with two people whom I came to regard as partners: Marilyn La Vine and Roman Gerasimov. One of Rudolf's most loyal New York fans, whose vocation it was to assemble a near-complete clipping archive (now housed in Washington's Library of Congress), Marilyn has played a crucial role in enriching my book. It's thanks to her that Rudolf's voice is so often present on the page, a result of being able to draw on thirty years of articles, which she tirelessly faxed to me. To my regret there was not enough space in the book to include her definitive chronology – another labour of love – but, with her consent, it has been posted on the official Nureyev website for the benefit of dance scholars world-wide. A perfectionist with an encyclopedic knowledge of Nureyev's career, Marilyn has been a sounding board as well as a heaven-sent collaborator: I thank her with all my heart. My Russian translator Roman Gerasimov was a nineteen-year-old star pupil of English professor Igor Stupnikov when he started to work with me. From day one he proved irreplaceable – whether opening the closed doors of classified archives or charming reluctant sources into telling their stories. A young man of culture, he is also irrepressibly entertaining and was the best possible travelling companion. Much of the new material in the early chapters was obtained through Roman's enterprise and perseverance. I must also thank my other Russian translators: Alex Bisset, Yelena Demikovsky, Ann Pasternak Slater and Geoff Whitlock; my German translators Uli Minoggio and Barbara Bischoff-Schnell; and Gedeon Diennes, who helped me with introductions and written material in Hungary.

To soulmates Peter Eyre and Selina Hastings (my lodestar biographer and unofficial editor), who read each chapter as I wrote it and responded with impeccable judgement and morale-boosting support, I send my warmest thanks. To my two critic friends who read the text at a late proof stage, I owe a huge debt: the hawk-eyed Godfather of dance scholarship, Clement Crisp, and the one and only Alastair Macaulay, whose spot-on suggestions were invaluable. Then I must thank Patrick O'Connor for my writing eyrie at the top of his Richmond house, and for two years of encouragement and stimulating companionship; Bob Gottlieb for lending me his rue Jacob apartment as my Paris base; Anniska's Gerry McGoldrick and Ilia Paliatseas for providing the Greek idyll where I (nearly) completed the book; and my own adopted family, Tina Brown, Harry, George and Izzy Evans, for ensuring that I always have a home in New York.

I count myself incredibly fortunate to have the dynamic Lynn Nesbit as my New York agent, as well as her fabulous young counterparts in London, Tif Loehnis and Rebecca Folland. How lucky, too, that the British rights were scooped up by Fig Tree's Juliet Annan, whose enthusiasm and forbearance I greatly appreciate, along with that of her splendid colleagues Jenny Lord, Sarah Hulbert, Rosie Gailer and Alex Elam. To Bela Cunha I owe special thanks for her scrupulous, eleventh-hour copy-editing. Finally, to my dream team at Pantheon: I express deep gratitude to Carol Janeway for handling my foreign rights; to Sue Llewellyn, for her dedication, wit and sensitive copy-editing of my text; to Andrew Dorko for his immense patience and *tour de force* of coordinating and overseeing the final copy-edit; to Ken Schneider and Robert Grover for their good-natured efficiency; and to Michiko Clark for her imaginative schedule of Nureyev events. I feel blessed to have been shared between two of the most eminent editors in New York: Bob Gottlieb and Shelley Wanger, for whose inspirational editorial guidance, fun and friendship I will for ever be in debt.

The Rudolf Nureyev Foundation (formerly Ballet Promotion Foundation) was founded in 1975 as a means of channelling funds for the encouragement and development of dance and dancers, and for transferring money to Rudolf's family in Russia. Registered in Liechtenstein, with a correspondence office in the United Kingdom, it is responsible for the investment and management of funds accruing to it. On Rudolf's death, RNF became responsible for paying legacies to the family and to a few close friends in accordance with his will, as well as observing other instructions related to the perpetuation of his memory and his dance credo. RNF encourages and funds East–West choreographer/dancer exchanges in Russia and Europe; awards annual scholarships in Rudolf's name at the principal ballet schools in the European cities with which he was closely associated. Ideally, candidates are Russian or Eastern European. The Royal Ballet's Ukrainian star Ivan Putrov was helped from 1996, while Ukrainian star-in-embryo Sergey Polunin, the Royal Ballet School's multiple award-winning student who is now a member of the company, received the Foundation's support from 2003. In addition, RNF helps finance the International Association for Dance Medicine and Science, and runs a medical website designed for dancers and doctors, established and overseen by Michel Canesi, in conjunction with a general Nureyev website, organized by Katia Gortchakoff. RNF licenses performances of Rudolf's productions, and promotes film screenings and exhibitions. It is developing a considerable Nureyev archive of photographs, letters and documents in its UK office in Bath (which can be made available to dance scholars by appointment).

Since it was established in 1992, the Rudolf Nureyev Dance Foundation has contributed more than four million dollars in grants to benefit dance in the United States. (In 2006 it won the Career Transitions for Dancers' Award for Outstanding Contributions to the World of Dance.) It provides a number of scholarship endowments, most notably in collaboration with the School of American Ballet, which since 1994 has granted the Rudolf Nureyev Dance Scholarship to thirty-one promising male dancers for advanced training. It has assisted various American dance companies to revive works in which Rudolf was associated: José Limón's *The Moor's Pavanne*; the Joffrey Ballet's revival of *L'Après midi d'un faune*; San Francisco Ballet's restaging of *Raymonda*; a full-season performance of *Aureole* by Paul Taylor Dance Company. In 1997 *Le Corsaire*, which had not previously been performed in the United States, was staged by Boston Ballet with RNDF's support, and filmed by WNET with RNDF as a primary sponsor, and is now in the permanent repertory of the American Ballet Theatre. RNDF helped finance the publication and distribution of English editions of two seminal books which throw light on Rudolf's Leningrad period – *Rudolf Nureyev: Three Years in the Kirov Theater* and Gennady Albert's analysis of Pushkin's classes, *Alexander Pushkin: Master Teacher of Dance*. In 2004 RNDF sponsored the exhibition at Lincoln Center mounted in homage to Margot Fonteyn and provided funds for the completion of the internationally acclaimed film *Ballets Russes*.

INDEX

He just wanted a decent book to read ...

Not too much to ask, is it? It was in 1935 when Allen Lane, Managing Director of Bodley Head Publishers, stood on a platform at Exeter railway station looking for something good to read on his journey back to London. His choice was limited to popular magazines and poor-quality paperbacks – the same choice faced every day by the vast majority of readers, few of whom could afford hardbacks. Lane's disappointment and subsequent anger at the range of books generally available led him to found a company – and change the world.

'We believed in the existence in this country of a vast reading public for intelligent books at a low price, and staked everything on it'
Sir Allen Lane, 1902–1970, founder of Penguin Books

The quality paperback had arrived – and not just in bookshops. Lane was adamant that his Penguins should appear in chain stores and tobacconists, and should cost no more than a packet of cigarettes.

Reading habits (and cigarette prices) have changed since 1935, but Penguin still believes in publishing the best books for everybody to enjoy. We still believe that good design costs no more than bad design, and we still believe that quality books published passionately and responsibly make the world a better place.

So wherever you see the little bird – whether it's on a piece of prize-winning literary fiction or a celebrity autobiography, political tour de force or historical masterpiece, a serial-killer thriller, reference book, world classic or a piece of pure escapism – you can bet that it represents the very best that the genre has to offer.

Whatever you like to read – trust Penguin.

read more
www.penguin.co.uk